Microsoft®
Visual C++®
MFC Library Reference, Part 1

Microsoft Press

PUBLISHED BY
Microsoft Press
A Division of Microsoft Corporation
One Microsoft Way
Redmond, Washington 98052-6399

Library of Congress Cataloging-in-Publication Data
   Microsoft Visual C++ MFC Library Reference / Microsoft Corporation.
       p.   cm.
   Includes index.
   ISBN 1-57231-518-0
   1. C++ (Computer program language)   2. Microsoft Visual C++.
   3. Microsoft foundation class library.   I. Microsoft Corporation.
   QA76.73.C153M535   1997
   005.26'8--dc21   97-2421
                                                              CIP

Printed and bound in the United States of America.

1 2 3 4 5 6 7 8 9   WCWC   2 1 0 9 8 7

Distributed to the book trade in Canada by Macmillan of Canada, a division of Canada Publishing Corporation.

A CIP catalogue record for this book is available from the British Library.

Microsoft Press books are available through booksellers and distributors worldwide. For further information about international editions, contact your local Microsoft Corporation office. Or contact Microsoft Press International directly at fax (206) 936-7329.

Macintosh and TrueType are registered trademarks of Apple Computer, Inc. FoxPro, Microsoft, Microsoft Press, MS, MS-DOS, Visual Basic, Visual C++, Win32, Windows, and Windows NT are registered trademarks of Microsoft Corporation. Other product and company names mentioned herein may be the trademarks of their respective owners.

Acquisitions Editor: Eric Stroo
Project Editor: Maureen Williams Zimmerman

Contents

Part 1

Index

Part 2

MFC Macros and Globals 2279

Introduction

The *Class Library Reference* covers the classes, global functions, global variables, and macros that make up the Microsoft® Foundation Class Library, version 4.21. The Class Hierarchy Chart online details the class relationships in the class library.

The Class Library Overview lists the classes in helpful categories. Use these lists to help locate a class that contains the functionality you are interested in. *Visual C++ Programmer's Guide* online explains how to use the class library to program for Microsoft Windows NT®, Microsoft Windows® 95, and other Win32® platforms. Practical examples and techniques are supplied in the tutorials in *Visual C++ Tutorials* online.

The remainder of the *Class Library Reference* consists of an alphabetical listing of the classes and an MFC Macros and Globals section that explains the global functions, global variables, and macros used with the class library.

The individual hierarchy charts included with each class are useful for locating base classes. The *Class Library Reference* usually does not describe inherited member functions, inherited operators, and overridden virtual member functions. For information on these functions, refer to the base classes depicted in the hierarchy diagrams.

In the alphabetical listing section, each class description includes a member summary by category, followed by alphabetical listings of member functions, overloaded operators, and data members.

Public and protected class members are documented only when they are normally used in application programs or derived classes. Occasionally, private members are listed because they override a public or protected member in the base class. See the class header files for a complete listing of class members.

Some C-language structures defined by Windows are so widely applicable that their descriptions have been reproduced completely in a section following the alphabetical reference.

Please note that the "See Also" sections refer to Win32 API functions by prefacing them with the scope resolution operator (::), for example, **::EqualRect**. More information on these functions can be found in the Win32 SDK documentation.

Class Library Overview

This overview categorizes and describes the classes in the Microsoft Foundation Class Library (MFC) version 4.21. The classes in MFC, taken together, constitute an "application framework"—the framework of an application written for the Windows API. Your programming task is to fill in the code that is specific to your application.

About the Microsoft Foundation Classes

The library's classes are presented here in the following categories:

- Root Class: **CObject**
- MFC Application Architecture Classes
  - Application and Thread Support Classes
  - Command Routing Classes
  - Document Classes
  - View Classes (Architecture)
  - Frame Window Classes (Architecture)
  - Document-Template Classes
- Window, Dialog, and Control Classes
  - Frame Window Classes (Windows)
  - View Classes (Windows)
  - Dialog Box Classes
  - Control Classes
  - Control Bar Classes
- Drawing and Printing Classes
  - Output (Device Context) Classes
  - Drawing Tool Classes
- Simple Data Type Classes
- Array, List, and Map Classes
  - Template Classes for Arrays, Lists, and Maps
  - Ready-to-Use Array Classes
  - Ready-to-Use List Classes
  - Ready-to-Use Map Classes

- File and Database Classes
  - File I/O Classes
  - DAO Classes
  - ODBC Classes
- Internet and Networking Classes
  - ISAPI Classes
  - Windows Sockets Classes
  - Win32 Internet Classes
- OLE Classes
  - OLE Container Classes
  - OLE Server Classes
  - OLE Drag-and-Drop and Data Transfer Classes
  - OLE Common Dialog Classes
  - OLE Automation Classes
  - OLE Control Classes
  - Active Document Classes
  - OLE-Related Classes
- Debugging and Exception Classes
  - Debugging Support Classes
  - Exception Classes

The section "General Class Design Philosophy" explains how the Microsoft Foundation Class Library was designed.

The framework is explained in detail in the *Visual C++ Programmer's Guide* online. (See "Using the Classes to Write Applications for Windows," for an overview.) Some of the classes listed above are general-purpose classes that can be used outside of the framework.and provide useful abstractions such as collections, exceptions, files, and strings.

To see the inheritance of a class, use the Class Hierarchy Chart online.

In addition to the classes listed in this overview, the Microsoft Foundation Class Library contains a number of global functions, global variables, and macros. There is an overview and detailed listing of these in the section "MFC Macros and Globals," which follows the alphabetical reference to the MFC classes.

General Class Design Philosophy

Microsoft Windows was designed long before the C++ language became popular. Because thousands of applications use the C-language Windows application programming interface (API), that interface will be maintained for the foreseeable future. Any C++ Windows interface must therefore be built on top of the procedural C-language API. This guarantees that C++ applications will be able to coexist with C applications.

The Microsoft Foundation Class Library is an object-oriented interface to Windows that meets the following design goals:

- Significant reduction in the effort to write an application for Windows.
- Execution speed comparable to that of the C-language API.
- Minimum code size overhead.
- Ability to call any Windows C function directly.
- Easier conversion of existing C applications to C++.
- Ability to leverage from the existing base of C-language Windows programming experience.
- Easier use of the Windows API with C++ than with C.
- Easier-to-use yet powerful abstractions of complicated features such as ActiveX, database support, printing, toolbars, and status bars.
- True Windows API for C++ that effectively uses C++ language features.

The Application Framework

The core of the Microsoft Foundation Class Library is an encapsulation of a large portion of the Windows API in C++ form. Library classes represent windows, dialog boxes, device contexts, common GDI objects such as brushes and pens, controls, and other standard Windows items. These classes provide a convenient C++ member function interface to the structures in Windows that they encapsulate. For more about using these classes, see "Window Object Topics" in the *Visual C++ Programmer's Guide* online.

But the Microsoft Foundation Class Library also supplies a layer of additional application functionality built on the C++ encapsulation of the Windows API. This layer is a working application framework for Windows that provides most of the common user interface expected of programs for Windows, including toolbars, status bars, printing, print preview, database support, and ActiveX support. "Using the Classes to Write Applications for Windows" in *Visual C++ Programmer's Guide* online explains the framework in detail, and *Visual C++ Tutorials* online provides the Scribble tutorial, which teaches application-framework programming.

Relationship to the C-Language API

The single characteristic that sets the Microsoft Foundation Class Library apart from other class libraries for Windows is the very close mapping to the Windows API written in the C language. Further, you can generally mix calls to the class library freely with direct calls to the Windows API. This direct access does not, however, imply that the classes are a complete replacement for that API. Developers must still occasionally make direct calls to some Windows functions—**SetCursor** and **GetSystemMetrics**, for example. A Windows function is wrapped by a class member function only when there is a clear advantage to doing so.

Because you sometimes need to make native Windows function calls, you should have access to the C-language Windows API documentation. This documentation is included with Microsoft Visual C++. Two useful books are *Advanced Windows*, by Jeffrey Richter, and *Programming Windows 95*, by Charles Petzold. Both are published by Microsoft Press®. Many of those books' examples can be easily converted to the Microsoft Foundation classes. For examples and additional information about programming with the Microsoft Foundation Class Library, see *Inside Visual C++* by David J. Kruglinski, also published by Microsoft Press.

Note For an overview of how the Microsoft Foundation Class Library framework operates, see "Using the Classes to Write Applications for Windows" in *Visual C++ Programmer's Guide* online. The overview material is no longer located in the *Class Library Reference*.

Class Summary by Category

The following is a brief summary of the classes in the Microsoft Foundation Class Library, divided by category to help you locate what you need. In some cases, a class is listed in more than one category. To see the inheritance of a class, use the Class Hierarchy Chart online.

Root Class: CObject

Most of the classes in the Microsoft Foundation Class Library are derived from a single base class at the root of the class hierarchy. **CObject** provides a number of useful capabilities to all classes derived from it, with very low overhead. For more information about **CObject** and its capabilities, see "CObject Class Topics" in *Visual C++ Programmer's Guide* online.

CObject The ultimate base class of most MFC classes. Supports serializing data and obtaining run-time information about a class.

CRuntimeClass Structure used to determine the exact class of an object at run time.

MFC Application Architecture Classes

Classes in this category contribute to the architecture of a framework application. They supply functionality common to most applications. You fill in the framework to add application-specific functionality. Typically, you do so by deriving new classes from the architecture classes, then adding new members and/or overriding existing member functions.

AppWizard generates several types of applications, all of which use the application framework in differing ways. SDI (single document interface) and MDI (multiple document interface) applications make full use of a part of the framework called document/view architecture. Other types of applications, such as dialog-based applications, form-based applications, and DLLs, use only some of document/view architecture features.

Document/view applications contain one or more sets of documents, views, and frame windows. A document-template object associates the classes for each document/view/frame set.

Although you do not have to use document/view architecture in your MFC application, there are a number of advantages to doing so. MFC's OLE container and server support is based on document/view architecture, as is support for printing and print preview.

All MFC applications have at least two objects: an application object derived from **CWinApp**, and some sort of main window object, derived (often indirectly) from **CWnd**. (Most often, the main window is derived from **CFrameWnd**, **CMDIFrameWnd**, or **CDialog**, all of which are derived from **CWnd**.)

Applications that use document/view architecture contain additional objects. The principal objects are as follows:

- An application object derived from class **CWinApp**, as mentioned before.
- One or more document class objects derived from class **CDocument**. Document class objects are responsible for the internal representation of the data manipulated in the view. They may be associated with a data file.
- One or more view objects derived from class **CView**. Each view is a window that is attached to a document and associated with a frame window. Views display and manipulate the data contained in a document class object.

Document/view applications also contain frame windows (derived from **CFrameWnd**) and document templates (derived from **CDocTemplate**).

Application and Thread Support Classes

Each application has one and only one application object; this object coordinates other objects in the running program and is derived from **CWinApp**.

The Microsoft Foundation Class Library supports multiple threads of execution within an application. All applications must have at least one thread; the thread used by your **CWinApp** object is this "primary" thread.

CWinThread encapsulates a portion of the operating system's threading capabilities. To make using multiple threads easier, MFC also provides synchronization object classes to provide a C++ interface to Win32 synchronization objects.

Application and Thread Classes

CWinApp   Encapsulates the code to initialize, run, and terminate the application. You will derive your application object from this class.

CWinThread   The base class for all threads. Use directly, or derive a class from **CWinThread** if your thread performs user-interface functions. **CWinApp** is derived from **CWinThread**.

ISAPI Application Classes

CHttpFilter   Filters selected HTTP requests sent to an ISAPI server.

CHttpServer   Extends the functionality of an ISAPI server by processing client requests.

Synchronization Object Classes

CSyncObject   Base class of the synchronization object classes.

CCriticalSection   A synchronization class that allows only one thread within a single process to access an object.

CSemaphore   A synchronization class that allows between one and a specified maximum number of simultaneous accesses to an object.

CMutex   A synchronization class that allows only one thread within any number of processes to access an object.

CEvent   A synchronization class that notifies an application when an event has occurred.

CSingleLock   Used in member functions of thread-safe classes to lock on one synchronization object.

CMultiLock   Used in member functions of thread-safe classes to lock on one or more synchronization objects from an array of synchronization objects.

Related Classes

CCommandLineInfo   Parses the command line with which your program was started.

CWaitCursor   Puts a wait cursor on the screen. Used during lengthy operations.

CDockState   Handles persistent storage of docking state data for control bars.

CRecentFileList   Maintains the most recently used (MRU) file list.

Command Routing Classes

As the user interacts with the application by choosing menus or control-bar buttons with the mouse, the application sends messages from the affected user-interface object to an appropriate command-target object. Command-target classes derived from **CCmdTarget** include **CWinApp**, **CWnd**, **CDocTemplate**, **CDocument**, **CView**, and the classes derived from them. The framework supports automatic command routing so that commands can be handled by the most appropriate object currently active in the application.

An object of class **CCmdUI** is passed to your command targets' update command UI (**ON_UPDATE_COMMAND_UI**) handlers to allow you to update the state of the user interface for a particular command (for instance, to check or remove the check from menu items). You call member functions of the **CCmdUI** object to update the state of the UI object. This process is the same whether the UI object associated with a particular command is a menu item or a button or both.

CCmdTarget   Serves as the base class for all classes of objects that can receive and respond to messages.

CCmdUI   Provides a programmatic interface for updating user-interface objects such as menu items or control-bar buttons. The command target object enables, disables, checks, and/or clears the user-interface object via this object.

Document Classes

Document class objects, created by document-template objects, manage the application's data. You will derive a class for your documents from one of these classes.

Document class objects interact with view objects. View objects represent the client area of a window, display a document's data, and allow users to interact with it. Documents and views are created by a document-template object.

CDocument   The base class for application-specific documents. Derive your document class(es) from **CDocument**.

COleDocument   Used for compound document implementation, as well as basic container support. Serves as a container for classes derived from **CDocItem**. This class can be used as the base class for container documents and is the base class for **COleServerDoc**.

COleLinkingDoc   A class derived from **COleDocument** that provides the infrastructure for linking. You should derive the document classes for your container applications from this class instead of from **COleDocument** if you want them to support links to embedded objects.

CRichEditDoc   Maintains the list of OLE client items that are in the rich edit control. Used with **CRichEditView** and **CRichEditCntrItem**.

COleServerDoc   Used as the base class for server-application document classes. **COleServerDoc** objects provide the bulk of server support through interactions with **COleServerItem** objects. Visual editing capability is provided using the class library's document/view architecture.

Related Classes

Document class objects can be persistent¾in other words, they can write their state to a storage medium and read it back. MFC provides the **CArchive** class to facilitate transferring the document's data to a storage medium.

CArchive   Cooperates with a **CFile** object to implement persistent storage for objects through serialization (see **CObject::Serialize**).

Documents can also contain OLE objects. **CDocItem** is the base class of the server and client items.

CDocItem   Abstract base class of **COleClientItem** and **COleServerItem**. Objects of classes derived from **CDocItem** represent parts of documents.

View Classes (Architecture)

CView and its derived classes are child windows that represent the client area of a frame window. Views show data and accept input for a document.

A view class is associated with a document class and a frame window class using a document-template object.

CView   The base class for application-specific views of a document's data. Views display data and accept user input to edit or select the data. Derive your view class(es) from **CView**.

CScrollView   The base class for views with scrolling capabilities. Derive your view class from **CScrollView** for automatic scrolling.

Form and Record Views

Form views are also scrolling views. They are based on a dialog box template.

Record views are derived from form views. In addition to the dialog box template, they also have a connection to a database.

CFormView   A scroll view whose layout is defined in a dialog box template. Derive a class from **CFormView** to implement a user interface based on a dialog box template.

CDaoRecordView   Provides a form view directly connected to a Data Access Object (DAO) recordset object. Like all form views, a **CDaoRecordView** is based on a dialog box template.

CRecordView   Provides a form view directly connected to an Open Database Connectivity (ODBC) recordset object. Like all form views, a **CRecordView** is based on a dialog box template.

Control Views

Control views display a control as their view.

CCtrlView   The base class for all views associated with Windows controls. The views based on controls are described below.

CEditView   A view that contains a Windows standard edit control (see **CEdit**). Edit controls support text-editing, searching, replacing, and scrolling capabilities.

CRichEditView   A view that contains a Windows rich edit control (see **CRichEditCtrl**). In addition to the capabilities of an edit control, rich edit controls support fonts, colors, paragraph formatting, and embedded OLE objects.

CListView   A view that contains a Windows list control (see **CListCtrl**). A list control displays icons and strings in a manner similar to the right-hand pane of the Windows 95 Explorer.

CTreeView   A view that contains a Windows tree control (see **CTreeCtrl**). A tree control displays icons and strings arranged in a hierarchy in a manner similar to the left-hand pane of the Windows 95 Explorer.

Frame Window Classes (Architecture)

In document/view architecture, frame windows are windows that contain a view window. They also support having control bars attached to them.

In multiple document interface (MDI) applications, the main window is derived from **CMDIFrameWnd**. It indirectly contains the documents' frames, which are **CMDIChildWnd** objects. The **CMDIChildWnd** objects, in turn, contain the documents' views.

In single document interface (SDI) applications, the main window, derived from **CFrameWnd**, contains the view of the current document.

CFrameWnd   The base class for an SDI application's main frame window. Also the base class for all other frame window classes.

CMDIFrameWnd   The base class for an MDI application's main frame window.

CMDIChildWnd   The base class for an MDI application's document frame windows.

COleIPFrameWnd   Provides the frame window for a view when a server document is being edited in place.

Document-Template Classes

Document-template objects coordinate the creation of document, view, and frame window objects when a new document and/or view is created.

CDocTemplate The base class for document templates. You will never use this class directly; instead, you'll use one of the other document-template classes derived from this class.

CMultiDocTemplate A template for documents in the multiple document interface (MDI). MDI applications can have multiple documents open at a time.

CSingleDocTemplate A template for documents in the single document interface (SDI). SDI applications have only one document open at a time.

Related Class

CCreateContext A structure passed by a document template to window-creation functions to coordinate the creation of document, view, and frame-window objects.

Window, Dialog, and Control Classes

Class **CWnd** and its derived classes encapsulate an **HWND**, a handle to a Windows window. **CWnd** can be used by itself or as a base for deriving new classes. The derived classes supplied by the class library represent various kinds of windows.

CWnd The base class for all windows. You can use one of the classes derived from **CWnd** or derive your own classes directly from it.

Frame Window Classes (Windows)

Frame windows are windows that frame an application or a part of an application. Frame windows usually contain other windows, such as views, tool bars, and status bars. In the case of **CMDIFrameWnd**, they may contain **CMDIChildWnd** objects indirectly.

CFrameWnd The base class for an SDI application's main frame window. Also the base class for all other frame window classes.

CMDIFrameWnd The base class for an MDI application's main frame window.

CMDIChildWnd The base class for an MDI application's document frame windows.

CMiniFrameWnd A half-height frame window typically seen around floating toolbars.

COleIPFrameWnd Provides the frame window for a view when a server document is being edited in place.

Related Class

Class **CMenu** provides an interface through which to access your application's menus. It is useful for manipulating menus dynamically at run time; for example, when adding or deleting menu items according to context. Although menus are most often used with frame windows, they can also be used with dialog boxes and other nonchild windows.

CMenu Encapsulates an **HMENU** handle to the application's menu bar and pop-up menus.

View Classes (Windows)

CView and its derived classes are child windows that represent the client area of a frame window. Views show data and accept input for a document.

A view class is associated with a document class and a frame window class using a document-template object.

CView The base class for application-specific views of a document's data. Views display data and accept user input to edit or select the data. Derive your view class(es) from **CView**.

CScrollView The base class for views with scrolling capabilities. Derive your view class from **CScrollView** for automatic scrolling.

Form and Record Views

Form views are also scrolling views. They are based on a dialog box template.

Record views are derived from form views. In addition to the dialog box template, they also have a connection to a database.

CFormView A scroll view whose layout is defined in a dialog box template. Derive a class from **CFormView** to implement a user interface based on a dialog box template.

CDaoRecordView Provides a form view directly connected to a Data Access Object (DAO) recordset object. Like all form views, a **CDaoRecordView** is based on a dialog box template.

CRecordView Provides a form view directly connected to an Open Database Connectivity (ODBC) recordset object. Like all form views, a **CRecordView** is based on a dialog box template.

Control Views

Control views display a control as their view.

CCtrlView The base class for all views associated with Windows controls. The views based on controls are described below.

CEditView   A view that contains a Windows standard edit control (see **CEdit**). Edit controls support text-editing, searching, replacing, and scrolling capabilities.

CRichEditView   A view that contains a Windows rich edit control (see **CRichEditCtrl**). In addition to the capabilities of an edit control, rich edit controls support fonts, colors, paragraph formatting, and embedded OLE objects.

CListView   A view that contains a Windows list control (see **CListCtrl**). A list control displays a collection of items, each consisting of an icon and a label, in a manner similar to the right-hand pane of the Windows 95 Explorer.

CTreeView   A view that contains a Windows tree control (see **CTreeCtrl**). A tree control displays a hierarchical list of icons and labels arranged in a manner similar to the left-hand pane of the Windows 95 Explorer.

Related Classes

CSplitterWnd allows you to have multiple views within a single frame window. **CPrintDialog** and **CPrintInfo** support the print and print preview ability of views. **CRichEditDoc** and **CRichEditCntrItem** are used with **CRichEditView** to implement OLE container capabilities.

CSplitterWnd   A window that the user can split into multiple panes. These panes can be resizable by the user or fixed size.

CPrintDialog   Provides a standard dialog box for printing a file.

CPrintInfo   A structure containing information about a print or print preview job. Used by **CView**'s printing architecture.

CRichEditDoc   Maintains the list of OLE client items that are in a **CRichEditView**.

CRichEditCntrItem   Provides client-side access to an OLE item stored in a **CRichEditView**.

Dialog Box Classes

Class **CDialog** and its derived classes encapsulate dialog-box functionality. Since a dialog box is a special kind of window, **CDialog** is derived from **CWnd**. Derive your dialog classes from **CDialog** or use one of the common dialog classes for standard dialog boxes, such as opening or saving a file, printing, selecting a font or color, initiating a search-and-replace operation, or performing various OLE-related operations.

CDialog   The base class for all dialog boxes—both modal and modeless.

CDataExchange   Supplies data exchange and validation information for dialog boxes.

Common Dialogs

These dialog box classes encapsulate the Windows common dialog boxes. They provide easy-to-use implementations of complicated dialog boxes.

CCommonDialog   This is the base class for all common dialog boxes.

CFileDialog   Provides a standard dialog box for opening or saving a file.

CColorDialog   Provides a standard dialog box for selecting a color.

CFontDialog   Provides a standard dialog box for selecting a font.

CFindReplaceDialog   Provides a standard dialog box for a search-and-replace operation.

CPrintDialog   Provides a standard dialog box for printing a file.

CPageSetupDialog   Encapsulates the services provided by the Windows common Page Setup dialog box with additional support for setting and modifying print margins.

OLE Common Dialogs

OLE adds several common dialog boxes to Windows. These classes encapsulate the OLE common dialog boxes.

COleDialog   Used by the framework to contain common implementations for all OLE dialog boxes. All dialog box classes in the user-interface category are derived from this base class. **COleDialog** cannot be used directly.

COleInsertDialog   Displays the Insert Object dialog box, the standard user interface for inserting new OLE linked or embedded items.

COlePasteSpecialDialog   Displays the Paste Special dialog box, the standard user interface for implementing the Edit Paste Special command.

COleLinksDialog   Displays the Edit Links dialog box, the standard user interface for modifying information about linked items.

COleChangeIconDialog   Displays the Change Icon dialog box, the standard user interface for changing the icon associated with an OLE embedded or linked item.

COleConvertDialog   Displays the Convert dialog box, the standard user interface for converting OLE items from one type to another.

COlePropertiesDialog   Encapsulates the Windows common OLE Properties dialog box. Common OLE Properties dialog boxes provide an easy way to display and modify the properties of an OLE document item in a manner consistent with Windows standards.

COleUpdateDialog   Displays the Update dialog box, the standard user interface for updating all links in a document. The dialog box contains a progress indicator to indicate how close the update procedure is to completion.

COleChangeSourceDialog   Displays the Change Source dialog box, the standard user interface for changing the destination or source of a link.

COleBusyDialog   Displays the Server Busy and Server Not Responding dialog boxes, the standard user interface for handling calls to busy applications. Usually displayed automatically by the **COleMessageFilter** implementation.

Property Sheet Classes

The property sheet classes allow your applications to use property sheets, also known as "tabbed dialogs." Property sheets are an efficient way to organize a large number of controls in a single dialog box.

CPropertyPage   Provides the individual pages within a property sheet. Derive a class from **CPropertyPage** for each page to be added to your property sheet.

CPropertySheet   Provides the frame for multiple property pages. Derive your property sheet class from **CPropertySheet** to implement your property sheets quickly.

COlePropertyPage   Displays the properties of an OLE control in a graphical interface, similar to a dialog box.

Related Classes

These classes are not dialog boxes per se, but they use dialog box templates and have much of the behavior of dialog boxes.

CDialogBar   A control bar that is based on a dialog box template.

CFormView   A scroll view whose layout is defined in a dialog box template. Derive a class from **CFormView** to implement a user interface based on a dialog box template.

CDaoRecordView   Provides a form view directly connected to a Data Access Object (DAO) recordset object. Like all form views, a **CDaoRecordView** is based on a dialog box template.

CRecordView   Provides a form view directly connected to an Open Database Connectivity (ODBC) recordset object. Like all form views, a **CRecordView** is based on a dialog box template.

CPrintInfo   A structure containing information about a print or print preview job. Used by the printing architecture of **CView**.

Control Classes

Control classes encapsulate a wide variety of standard Windows controls ranging from static text controls to tree controls. In addition, MFC provides some new controls, including buttons with bitmaps and control bars.

The controls whose class names end in "**Ctrl**" are new in Windows 95 and Windows NT version 3.51.

Static Display Controls

CStatic   A static-display window. Static controls are used to label, box, or separate other controls in a dialog box or window. They may also display graphical images rather than text or a box.

Text Controls

CEdit   An editable-text control window. Edit controls are used to accept textual input from the user.

CRichEditCtrl   A control in which the user can enter and edit text. Unlike the control encapsulated in **CEdit**, a rich edit control supports character and paragraph formatting and OLE objects.

Controls Which Represent Numbers

CSliderCtrl   A control containing a slider, which the user moves to select a value or set of values.

CSpinButtonCtrl   A pair of arrow buttons the user can click to increment or decrement a value.

CProgressCtrl   Displays a rectangle that is gradually filled from left to right to indicate the progress of an operation.

CScrollBar   A scroll-bar control window. The class provides the functionality of a scroll bar, for use as a control in a dialog box or window, through which the user can specify a position within a range.

Buttons

CButton   A button control window. The class provides a programmatic interface for a pushbutton, check box, or radio button in a dialog box or window.

CBitmapButton   A button with a bitmap rather than a text caption.

Lists

CListBox   A list-box control window. A list box displays a list of items that the user can view and select.

CDragListBox   Provides the functionality of a Windows list box; allows the user to move list box items, such as filenames and string literals, within the list box. List boxes with this capability are useful for an item list in an order other than alphabetical, such as include pathnames or files in a project.

CComboBox   A combo-box control window. A combo box consists of an edit control plus a list box.

CCheckListBox   Displays a list of items with check boxes, which the user can check or clear, next to each item.

CListCtrl   Displays a collection of items, each consisting of an icon and a label, in a manner similar to the right-hand pane of the Windows 95 Explorer.

CTreeCtrl   Displays a hierarchical list of icons and labels arranged in a manner similar to the left-hand pane of the Windows 95 Explorer.

Toolbars and Status Bars

CToolBarCtrl   Provides the functionality of the Windows toolbar common control. Most MFC programs use **CToolBar** instead of this class.

CStatusBarCtrl   A horizontal window, usually divided into panes, in which an application can display status information. Most MFC programs use **CStatusBar** instead of this class.

Miscellaneous Controls

CAnimateCtrl   Displays a simple video clip.

CToolTipCtrl   A small pop-up window that displays a single line of text describing the purpose of a tool in an application.

CHeaderCtrl   Displays titles or labels for columns.

CTabCtrl   A control with tabs on which the user can click, analogous to the dividers in a notebook.

CHotKeyCtrl   Enables the user to create a "hot key" combination, which the user can press to perform an action quickly.

Related Classes

CImageList   Provides the functionality of the Windows image list. Image lists are used with list controls and tree controls. They can also be used to store and archive a set of same-sized bitmaps.

CCtrlView   The base class for all views associated with Windows controls. The views based on controls are described below.

CEditView   A view that contains a Windows standard edit control.

CRichEditView   A view that contains a Windows rich edit control.

CListView   A view that contains a Windows list control.

CTreeView   A view that contains a Windows tree control.

Control Bar Classes

Control bars are attached to a frame window. They contain buttons, status panes, or a dialog template. Free-floating control bars, also called tool palettes, are implemented by attaching them to a **CMiniFrameWnd** object.

Framework Control Bars

These control bars are an integral part of the MFC framework. They are easier to use and more powerful than the Windows control bars because they're integrated with the framework. Most MFC applications use these control bars rather than the Windows control bars.

CControlBar   The base class for MFC control bars listed in this section. A control bar is a window aligned to the edge of a frame window. The control bar contains either **HWND**-based child controls or controls not based on an **HWND**, such as toolbar buttons.

CToolBar   Toolbar control windows that contain bitmap command buttons not based on an **HWND**. Most MFC applications use this class rather than **CToolBarCtrl**.

CStatusBar   The base class for status-bar control windows. Most MFC applications use this class rather than **CStatusBarCtrl**.

CDialogBar   A control bar that is based on a dialog box template.

Windows Control Bars

These control bars are thin wrappers for the corresponding Windows controls. Since they're not integrated with the framework, they're harder to use than the control bars listed above. Most MFC applications use the control bars listed above.

CStatusBarCtrl   A horizontal window, usually divided into panes, in which an application can display status information.

CToolBarCtrl   Provides the functionality of the Windows toolbar common control.

Related Classes

CToolTipCtrl   A small pop-up window that displays a single line of text describing the purpose of a tool in an application.

CDockState   Handles persistent storage of docking state data for control bars.

Drawing and Printing Classes

In Windows, all graphical output is drawn on a virtual drawing area called a device context (or DC). MFC provides classes to encapsulate the various types of DCs, as well as encapsulations for Windows drawing tools such as bitmaps, brushes, palettes, and pens.

Output (Device Context) Classes

These classes encapsulate the different types of device contexts available in Windows.

Most of the following classes encapsulate a handle to a Windows device context. A device context is a Windows object that contains information about the drawing attributes of a device such as a display or a printer. All drawing calls are made through a device-context object. Additional classes derived from **CDC** encapsulate specialized device-context functionality, including support for Windows metafiles.

CDC   The base class for device contexts. Used directly for accessing the whole display and for accessing nondisplay contexts such as printers.

CPaintDC   A display context used in **OnPaint** member functions of windows. Automatically calls **BeginPaint** on construction and **EndPaint** on destruction.

CClientDC   A display context for client areas of windows. Used, for example, to draw in an immediate response to mouse events.

CWindowDC   A display context for entire windows, including both the client and nonclient areas.

CMetaFileDC   A device context for Windows metafiles. A Windows metafile contains a sequence of graphics device interface (GDI) commands that can be replayed to create an image. Calls made to the member functions of a **CMetaFileDC** are recorded in a metafile.

Related Classes

CPoint   Holds coordinate (x, y) pairs.

CSize   Holds distance, relative positions, or paired values.

CRect   Holds coordinates of rectangular areas.

CRgn   Encapsulates a GDI region for manipulating an elliptical, polygonal, or irregular area within a window. Used in conjunction with the clipping member functions in class **CDC**.

CRectTracker   Displays and handles the user interface for resizing and moving rectangular objects.

CColorDialog   Provides a standard dialog box for selecting a color.

CFontDialog   Provides a standard dialog box for selecting a font.

CPrintDialog   Provides a standard dialog box for printing a file.

Drawing Tool Classes

These classes encapsulate drawing tools that are used to draw on a device context.

CGdiObject   The base class for GDI drawing tools.

CBrush   Encapsulates a GDI brush that can be selected as the current brush in a device context. Brushes are used for filling interiors of objects being drawn.

CPen   Encapsulates a GDI pen that can be selected as the current pen in a device context. Pens are used for drawing the border lines of objects.

CFont   Encapsulates a GDI font that can be selected as the current font in a device context.

CBitmap   Encapsulates a GDI bitmap, providing an interface for manipulating bitmaps.

CPalette   Encapsulates a GDI color palette for use as an interface between the application and a color output device such as a display.

CRectTracker   Displays and handles the user interface for resizing and moving rectangular objects.

Simple Data Type Classes

The following classes encapsulate drawing coordinates, character strings, and time and date information, allowing convenient use of C++ syntax. These objects are used widely as parameters to the member functions of Windows classes in the class library. Because **CPoint**, **CSize**, and **CRect** correspond to the **POINT**, **SIZE**, and **RECT** structures, respectively, in the Win32 SDK, you can use objects of these C++ classes wherever you can use these C-language structures. The classes provide useful interfaces through their member functions. **CString** provides very flexible dynamic character strings. **CTime**, **COleDateTime**, **CTimeSpan**, and **COleTimeSpan** represent time and date values. For more information about these classes, see the article "Date and Time" in *Visual C++ Programmer's Guide* online.

The classes that begin with "**COle**" are encapsulations of data types provided by OLE. These data types can be used in Windows programs regardless of whether other OLE features are used.

CString   Holds character strings.

CTime   Holds absolute time and date values.

COleDateTime   Wrapper for the OLE automation type **DATE**. Represents date and time values.

CTimeSpan   Holds relative time and date values.

COleDateTimeSpan   Holds relative **COleDateTime** values, such as the difference between two **COleDateTime** values.

CPoint   Holds coordinate (x, y) pairs.

CSize   Holds distance, relative positions, or paired values.

CRect   Holds coordinates of rectangular areas.

CImageList   Provides the functionality of the Windows image list. Image lists are used with list controls and tree controls. They can also be used to store and archive a set of same-sized bitmaps.

COleVariant   Wrapper for the OLE automation type **VARIANT**. Data in **VARIANT**s can be stored in many formats.

COleCurrency   Wrapper for the OLE automation type **CURRENCY**, a fixed-point arithmetic type, with 15 digits before the decimal point and 4 digits after.

Array, List, and Map Classes

For handling aggregates of data, the class library provides a group of collection classes—arrays, lists, and "maps"—that can hold a variety of object and predefined types. The collections are dynamically sized. These classes can be used in any program, whether written for Windows or not. However, they are most useful for implementing the data structures that define your document classes in the application framework. You can readily derive specialized collection classes from these, or you can create them based on the template classes. For more information about these approaches, see the article "Collections" in *Visual C++ Programmer's Guide* online and "Template Classes for Arrays, Lists, and Maps" in this overview for a list of the template collection classes.

Arrays are one-dimensional data structures that are stored contiguously in memory. They support very fast random access since the memory address of any given element can be calculated by multiplying the index of the element by the size of an element and adding the result to the base address of the array. But arrays are very expensive if you have to insert elements into the array, since the entire array past the element inserted has to be moved to make room for the element to be inserted. Arrays can grow and shrink as necessary.

Lists are similar to arrays but are stored very differently. Each element in a list also includes a pointer to the previous and next elements, making it a doubly-linked list. It's very fast to add or delete items because doing so only involves changing a few pointers. However, searching a list can be expensive since all searches need to start at one of the list's ends.

Maps relate a key value to a data value. For instance, the key of a map could be a string and the data a pointer into a list. You would ask the map to give you the pointer associated with a particular string. Map lookups are fast because maps use hash tables for key lookups. Adding and deleting items is also fast. Maps are often used with other data structures as auxiliary indices. MFC uses a special kind of map called a "message map" to map Windows messages to a pointer to the handler function for that message.

Template Classes for Arrays, Lists, and Maps

These collection classes are templates whose parameters determine the types of the objects stored in the aggregates. The **CArray**, **CMap**, and **CList** classes use global helper functions that must usually be customized. For more information about these helper functions, see Collection Class Helpers in the "Macros and Globals" section. The typed pointer classes are "wrappers" for other classes in the class library. By using these wrappers, you enlist the compiler's type-checking to help you avoid errors. For more information on using these classes, see the article "Collections" in *Visual C++ Programmer's Guide* online.

These classes provide templates you can use to create arrays, lists, and maps using any type you like.

CArray   Template class for making arrays of arbitrary types.

CList   Template class for making lists of arbitrary types.

CMap   Template class for making maps with arbitrary key and value types.

CTypedPtrArray   Template class for type-safe arrays of pointers.

CTypedPtrList   Template class for type-safe lists of pointers.

CTypedPtrMap   Template class for type-safe maps with pointers.

Ready-to-Use Array Classes

CByteArray   Stores elements of type **BYTE** in an array.

CDWordArray   Stores elements of type **DWORD** in an array.

CObArray   Stores pointers to objects of class **CObject** or to objects of classes derived from **CObject** in an array.

CPtrArray   Stores pointers to **void** (generic pointers) in an array.

CUIntArray   Stores elements of type **UINT** in an array.

CWordArray   Stores elements of type **WORD** in an array.

CStringArray   Stores **CString** objects in an array.

Ready-to-Use List Classes

CObList   Stores pointers to objects of class **CObject** or to objects of classes derived from **CObject** in a linked list.

CPtrList   Stores pointers to **void** (generic pointers) in a linked list.

CStringList   Stores **CString** objects in a linked list.

Ready-to-Use Map Classes

CMapPtrToPtr   Uses **void** pointers as keys for finding other **void** pointers.

CMapPtrToWord   Uses **void** pointers as keys for finding data of type **WORD**.

CMapStringToOb   Uses **CString** objects as keys for finding **CObject** pointers.

CMapStringToPtr   Uses **CString** objects as keys for finding **void** pointers.

CMapStringToString   Uses **CString** objects as keys for finding other **CString** objects.

CMapWordToOb Uses data of type **WORD** to find **CObject** pointers.

CMapWordToPtr Uses data of type **WORD** to find **void** pointers.

File and Database Classes

These classes allow you to store information to a database or a disk file. There are two sets of database classes—DAO and ODBC—which provide similar functionality. The DAO group is implemented using the Data Access Object, while the ODBC group is implemented using Open Database Connectivity. There are also a set of classes for manipulating standard files, ActiveX streams, and HTML streams.

The following categories of classes support data persistence.

- File I/O Classes
- DAO Classes
- ODBC Classes

File I/O Classes

These classes provide an interface to traditional disk files, in-memory files, ActiveX streams, and Windows sockets. All of the classes derived from **CFile** can be used with a **CArchive** object to perform serialization.

Use the following classes, particularly **CArchive** and **CFile**, if you write your own input/output processing. Normally you don't need to derive from these classes. If you use the application framework, the default implementations of the Open and Save commands on the File menu will handle file I/O (using class **CArchive**), as long as you override your document's **Serialize** function to supply details about how a document "serializes" its contents. For more information about the file classes and serialization, see the article "Files in MFC" and the article "Serialization (Object Persistence)" in *Visual C++ Programmer's Guide* online.

CFile Provides a file interface to binary disk files.

CStdioFile Provides a **CFile** interface to buffered stream disk files, usually in text mode.

CMemFile Provides a **CFile** interface to in-memory files.

CSharedFile Provides a **CFile** interface to shared in-memory files.

COleStreamFile Uses the COM **IStream** interface to provide **CFile** access to compound files.

CSocketFile Provides a **CFile** interface to a Windows Socket.

Related Classes

CArchive Cooperates with a **CFile** object to implement persistent storage for objects through serialization (see **CObject::Serialize**).

CArchiveException An archive exception.

CFileException A file-oriented exception.

CFileDialog Provides a standard dialog box for opening or saving a file.

CHtmlStream Handles caching HTML output. Functionally similar to **CMemFile**.

CRecentFileList Maintains the most recently used (MRU) file list.

DAO Classes

These classes work with the other application framework classes to give easy access to DAO (Data Access Object) databases, which use the same database engine as Microsoft Visual Basic® and Microsoft Access. The DAO classes can also access a wide variety of databases for which Open Database Connectivity (ODBC) drivers are available.

Programs that use DAO databases will have at least a **CDaoDatabase** object and a **CDaoRecordset** object.

CDaoWorkspace Manages a named, password-protected database session from login to logoff. Most programs use the default workspace.

CDaoDatabase A connection to a database through which you can operate on the data.

CDaoRecordset Represents a set of records selected from a data source.

CDaoRecordView A view that displays database records in controls.

CDaoQueryDef Represents a query definition, usually one saved in a database.

CDaoTableDef Represents the stored definition of a base table or an attached table.

CDaoException Represents an exception condition arising from the DAO classes.

CDaoFieldExchange Supports the DAO record field exchange (DFX) routines used by the DAO database classes. You will normally not directly use this class.

Related Classes

CLongBinary Encapsulates a handle to storage for a binary large object (or BLOB), such as a bitmap. **CLongBinary** objects are used to manage large data objects stored in database tables.

COleCurrency Wrapper for the OLE automation type **CURRENCY**, a fixed-point arithmetic type, with 15 digits before the decimal point and 4 digits after.

COleDateTime Wrapper for the OLE automation type **DATE**. Represents date and time values.

COleVariant Wrapper for the OLE automation type **VARIANT**. Data in **VARIANT**s can be stored in many formats.

ODBC Classes

These classes work with the other application framework classes to give easy access to a wide variety of databases for which Open Database Connectivity (ODBC) drivers are available.

Programs that use ODBC databases will have at least a **CDatabase** object and a **CRecordset** object.

CDatabase Encapsulates a connection to a data source, through which you can operate on the data source.

CRecordset Encapsulates a set of records selected from a data source. Recordsets enable scrolling from record to record, updating records (adding, editing, and deleting records), qualifying the selection with a filter, sorting the selection, and parameterizing the selection with information obtained or calculated at run time.

CRecordView Provides a form view directly connected to a recordset object. The dialog data exchange (DDX) mechanism exchanges data between the recordset and the controls of the record view. Like all form views, a record view is based on a dialog template resource. Record views also support moving from record to record in the recordset, updating records, and closing the associated recordset when the record view closes.

CDBException An exception resulting from failures in data access processing. This class serves the same purpose as other exception classes in the exception-handling mechanism of the class library.

CFieldExchange Supplies context information to support record field exchange (RFX), which exchanges data between the field data members and parameter data members of a recordset object and the corresponding table columns on the data source. Analogous to class **CDataExchange**, which is used similarly for dialog data exchange (DDX).

Related Classes

CLongBinary Encapsulates a handle to storage for a binary large object (or BLOB), such as a bitmap. **CLongBinary** objects are used to manage large data objects stored in database tables.

CDBVariant Allows you to store a value without worrying about the value's data type. **CDBVariant** tracks the data type of the current value, which is stored in a union.

Internet and Networking Classes

These classes allow you to exchange information with another computer using ISAPI or a Windows Socket. There are also a set of classes for creating ISAPI extension DLLs and a set of classes for manipulating Windows Sockets.

The following categories of classes support connectivity.

- ISAPI Classes
- Windows Sockets Classes
- Win32 Internet Classes

ISAPI Classes

ISAPI describes an interface for Internet servers. An example of an ISAPI server is Windows NT Server running Microsoft Internet Information Server (IIS).

HTTP filters handle server requests. They can be used to handle the following types of applications:

- Custom authentication schemes
- Data compression
- Encryption
- Logging

Filter Classes

CHttpFilter   Filters selected HTTP requests sent to an ISAPI server.

CHttpFilterContext   Manages the context for an HTTP filter. This is a helper class to handle multiple, concurrent requests of a **CHttpFilter** object.

Server Classes

ISAPI server extensions process server requests, including Common Gateway Interface (CGI).

CHttpServer   Extends the functionality of an ISAPI server by processing client requests.

CHttpServerContext   Manages the context for an ISAPI server extension. This is a helper class to handle multiple, concurrent requests of a **CHttpServer** object.

Related Classes

CHtmlStream   Handles caching HTML output. Functionally similar to **CMemFile**.

Windows Sockets Classes

Windows Sockets provide a network protocol-independent way to communicate between two computers. These sockets can be synchronous (your program waits until the communication is done) or asynchronous (your program continues running while the communication is going on).

CAsyncSocket   Encapsulates the Windows Sockets API in a thin wrapper.

CSocket   Higher-level abstraction derived from **CAsyncSocket**. It operates synchronously.

CSocketFile   Provides a **CFile** interface to a Windows Socket.

Win32 Internet Classes

MFC wraps the Win32 Internet (WinInet) and ActiveX technology to make Internet programming easier.

CInternetSession   Creates and initializes one Internet session or several simultaneous Internet sessions and, if necessary, describes the connection to a proxy server.

CInternetConnection   Manages your connection to an Internet server.

CInternetFile   This class and its derived classes allow access to files on remote systems that use Internet protocols.

CHttpConnection   Manages your connection to an HTTP server.

CHttpFile   Provides the functionality to find and read files on an HTTP server.

CGopherFile   Provides the functionality to find and read files on a gopher server.

CFtpConnection   Manages your connection to an FTP server.

CGopherConnection   Manages your connection to a gopher server.

CFileFind   Performs local and Internet file searches.

CFtpFileFind   Aids in Internet file searches of FTP servers.

CGopherFileFind   Aids in Internet file searches of gopher servers.

CGopherLocator   Gets a gopher "locator" from a gopher server, determines the locator's type, and makes the locator available to **CGopherFileFind**.

CInternetException   Represents an exception condition related to an Internet operation.

OLE Classes

The OLE classes work with the other application framework classes to provide easy access to the ActiveX API, giving your programs an easy way to provide the power of ActiveX to your users. Using ActiveX, you can:

- Create compound documents, which allow users to create and edit documents containing data created by multiple applications, including text, graphics, spreadsheets, sound, or other types of data.
- Create OLE objects that can be embedded in compound documents.
- Use OLE drag and drop to copy data between applications.
- Use Automation to control one program with another.
- Create ActiveX controls and ActiveX control containers (formerly called OLE controls and OLE control containers, respectively).

The following categories of classes support ActiveX:

- OLE Container Classes
- OLE Server Classes
- OLE Drag-and-Drop and Data Transfer Classes
- OLE Common Dialog Classes
- OLE Automation Classes
- OLE Control Classes
- Active Document Classes
- OLE-Related Classes

To see the inheritance of a class, use the Class Hierarchy Chart online.

OLE Container Classes

These classes are used by container applications. Both **COleLinkingDoc** and **COleDocument** manage collections of **COleClientItem** objects. Rather than deriving your document class from **CDocument**, you'll derive it from **COleLinkingDoc** or **COleDocument**, depending on whether or not you want support for links to objects embedded in your document.

Use a **COleClientItem** object to represent each OLE item in your document that is embedded from another document or is a link to another document.

COleDocument Used for compound document implementation, as well as basic container support. Serves as a container for classes derived from **CDocItem**. This class can be used as the base class for container documents and is the base class for **COleServerDoc**.

COleLinkingDoc A class derived from **COleDocument** that provides the infrastructure for linking. You should derive the document classes for your container applications from this class instead of from **COleDocument** if you want them to support links to embedded objects.

CRichEditDoc Maintains the list of OLE client items that are in the rich edit control. Used with **CRichEditView** and **CRichEditCntrItem**.

CDocItem Abstract base class of **COleClientItem** and **COleServerItem**. Objects of classes derived from **CDocItem** represent parts of documents.

COleClientItem A client item class that represents the client's side of the connection to an embedded or linked OLE item. Derive your client items from this class.

CRichEditCntrItem Provides client-side access to an OLE item stored in a rich edit control when used with **CRichEditView** and **CRichEditDoc**.

COleException An exception resulting from a failure in OLE processing. This class is used by both containers and servers.

OLE Server Classes

These classes are used by server applications. Server documents are derived from **COleServerDoc** rather than **CDocument**. Note that since **COleServerDoc** is derived from **COleLinkingDoc**, server documents can also be containers that support linking.

The **COleServerItem** class represents a document or portion of a document that can be embedded in another document or linked to.

COleIPFrameWnd and **COleResizeBar** support in-place editing while the object is in a container, and **COleTemplateServer** supports creation of document/view pairs so OLE objects from other applications can be edited.

COleServerDoc Used as the base class for server-application document classes. **COleServerDoc** objects provide the bulk of server support through interactions with **COleServerItem** objects. Visual editing capability is provided using the class library's document/view architecture.

CDocItem Abstract base class of **COleClientItem** and **COleServerItem**. Objects of classes derived from **CDocItem** represent parts of documents.

COleServerItem Used to represent the OLE interface to **COleServerDoc** items. There is usually one **COleServerDoc** object, which represents the embedded part of a document. In servers that support links to parts of documents, there can be many **COleServerItem** objects, each of which represents a link to a portion of the document.

COleIPFrameWnd Provides the frame window for a view when a server document is being edited in place.

COleResizeBar Provides the standard user interface for in-place resizing. Objects of this class are always used in conjunction with **COleIPFrameWnd** objects.

COleTemplateServer Used to create documents using the framework's document/view architecture. A **COleTemplateServer** object delegates most of its work to an associated **CDocTemplate** object.

COleException An exception resulting from a failure in OLE processing. This class is used by both containers and servers.

OLE Drag-and-Drop and Data Transfer Classes

These classes are used in OLE data transfers. They allow data to be transferred between applications by using the Clipboard or through drag and drop.

COleDropSource Controls the drag-and-drop operation from start to finish. This class determines when the drag operation starts and when it ends. It also displays cursor feedback during the drag-and-drop operation.

COleDataSource Used when an application provides data for a data transfer. **COleDataSource** could be viewed as an object-oriented Clipboard object.

COleDropTarget Represents the target of a drag-and-drop operation. A **COleDropTarget** object corresponds to a window on screen. It determines whether to accept any data dropped onto it and implements the actual drop operation.

COleDataObject Used as the receiver side to **COleDataSource**. **COleDataObject** objects provide access to the data stored by a **COleDataSource** object.

OLE Common Dialog Classes

These classes handle common OLE tasks by implementing a number of standard OLE dialog boxes. They also provide a consistent user interface for OLE functionality.

COleDialog Used by the framework to contain common implementations for all OLE dialog boxes. All dialog box classes in the user-interface category are derived from this base class. **COleDialog** cannot be used directly.

COleInsertDialog Displays the Insert Object dialog box, the standard user interface for inserting new OLE linked or embedded items.

COlePasteSpecialDialog Displays the Paste Special dialog box, the standard user interface for implementing the Edit Paste Special command.

COleLinksDialog Displays the Edit Links dialog box, the standard user interface for modifying information about linked items.

COleChangeIconDialog Displays the Change Icon dialog box, the standard user interface for changing the icon associated with an OLE embedded or linked item.

COleConvertDialog Displays the Convert dialog box, the standard user interface for converting OLE items from one type to another.

COlePropertiesDialog Encapsulates the Windows common OLE Properties dialog box. Common OLE Properties dialog boxes provide an easy way to display and modify the properties of an OLE document item in a manner consistent with Windows standards.

COleUpdateDialog Displays the Update dialog box, the standard user interface for updating all links in a document. The dialog box contains a progress indicator to indicate how close the update procedure is to completion.

COleChangeSourceDialog Displays the Change Source dialog box, the standard user interface for changing the destination or source of a link.

COleBusyDialog Displays the Server Busy and Server Not Responding dialog boxes, the standard user interface for handling calls to busy applications. Usually displayed automatically by the **COleMessageFilter** implementation.

OLE Automation Classes

These classes support automation clients (applications that control other applications). Automation servers (applications that can be controlled by other applications) are supported through dispatch maps.

COleDispatchDriver Used to call automation servers from your automation client. ClassWizard uses this class to create type-safe classes for automation servers that provide a type library.

COleDispatchException An exception resulting from an error during OLE automation. Automation exceptions are thrown by automation servers and caught by automation clients.

OLE Control Classes

These are the primary classes you'll use when writing OLE controls. The **COleControlModule** class in an OLE control module is like the **CWinApp** class in an application. Each module implements one or more OLE controls; these controls are represented by **COleControl** objects. These controls communicate with their containers using **CConnectionPoint** objects.

The **CPictureHolder** and **CFontHolder** classes encapsulate COM interfaces for pictures and fonts, while the **COlePropertyPage** and **CPropExchange** classes help you implement property pages and property persistence for your control.

COleControlModule Replaces the **CWinApp** class for your OLE control module. Derive from the **COleControlModule** class to develop an OLE control module object. It provides member functions for initializing your OLE control's module.

COleControl Derive from the **COleControl** class to develop an OLE control. Derived from **CWnd**, this class inherits all the functionality of a Windows window object plus additional OLE-specific functionality, such as event firing and the ability to support methods and properties.

CConnectionPoint The **CConnectionPoint** class defines a special type of interface used to communicate with other OLE objects, called a "connection point." A connection point implements an outgoing interface that is able to initiate actions on other objects, such as firing events and change notifications.

CPictureHolder Encapsulates the functionality of a Windows picture object and the **IPicture** COM interface; used to implement the custom Picture property of an OLE control.

CFontHolder Encapsulates the functionality of a Windows font object and the **IFont** COM interface; used to implement the stock Font property of an OLE control.

COlePropertyPage Displays the properties of an OLE control in a graphical interface, similar to a dialog box.

CPropExchange Supports the implementation of property persistence for your OLE controls. Analogous to **CDataExchange** for dialog boxes.

CMonikerFile Takes a moniker, or a string representation that it can make into a moniker, and binds it synchronously to the stream for which the moniker is a name.

CAsyncMonikerFile Works similarly to **CMonikerFile**; however, it binds the moniker asynchronously to the stream for which the moniker is a name.

CDataPathProperty Implements an OLE control property that can be loaded asynchronously.

CCachedDataPathProperty Implements an OLE control property transferred asynchronously and cached in a memory file.

COleCmdUI Allows an ActiveX document to receive commands that originate in its container's user interface (such as FileNew, Open, Print, and so on), and allows a container to receive commands that originate in the ActiveX document's user interface.

COleSafeArray Works with arrays of arbitrary type and dimension.

Active Document Classes

Active documents can be displayed either in the entire client window of a Web browser, such as Internet Explorer 3.0, or in an ActiveX container—such as the Microsoft Office Binder—that supports ActiveX documents.

CDocObjectServer   Maps the ActiveX document interfaces, and initializes and activates an ActiveX document object.

CDocObjectServerItem   Implements OLE server verbs specifically for ActiveX document servers.

OLE-Related Classes

These classes provide a number of different services, ranging from exceptions to file input and output.

COleObjectFactory   Used to create items when requested from other containers. This class serves as the base class for more specific types of factories, including **COleTemplateServer**.

COleMessageFilter   Used to manage concurrency with OLE Lightweight Remote Procedure Calls (LRPC).

COleStreamFile   Uses the COM **IStream** interface to provide **CFile** access to compound files. This class (derived from **CFile**) enables MFC serialization to use OLE structured storage.

CRectTracker   Used to allow moving, resizing, and reorientation of in-place items.

Debugging and Exception Classes

These classes provide support for debugging dynamic memory allocation and for passing exception information from the function where the exception is thrown to the function where it's caught.

Use classes **CDumpContext** and **CMemoryState** during development to assist with debugging, as described in "MFC Debugging Support." Use **CRuntimeClass** to determine the class of any object at run time, as described in the article "CObject Class: Accessing Run-Time Class Information." Both articles are in *Visual C++ Programmer's Guide* online. The framework uses **CRuntimeClass** to create objects of a particular class dynamically.

Debugging Support Classes

MFC provides the following classes to help you debug dynamic memory allocation problems.

CDumpContext   Provides a destination for diagnostic dumps.

CMemoryState   Structure that provides snapshots of memory use. Also used to compare earlier and later memory snapshots.

Exception Classes

The class library provides an exception-handling mechanism based on class **CException**. The application framework uses exceptions in its code; you can also use them in yours. For more information, see the article "Exceptions" in *Visual C++ Programmer's Guide* online. You can derive your own exception types from **CException**.

MFC provides an exception class from which you can derive your own exception as well as exception classes for all of the exceptions it supports.

CException   The base class for exceptions.

CArchiveException   An archive exception.

CDaoException   An exception resulting from a failure in a DAO database operation.

CDBException   An exception resulting from a failure in ODBC database processing.

CFileException   A file-oriented exception.

CMemoryException   An out-of-memory exception.

CNotSupportedException   An exception resulting from using an unsupported feature.

COleException   An exception resulting from a failure in OLE processing. This class is used by both containers and servers.

COleDispatchException   An exception resulting from an error during automation. Automation exceptions are thrown by automation servers and caught by automation clients.

CResourceException   An exception resulting from a failure to load a Windows resource.

CUserException   An exception used to stop a user-initiated operation. Typically the user has been notified of the problem before this exception is thrown.

CAnimateCtrl

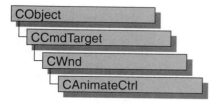

The **CAnimateCtrl** class provides the functionality of the Windows common animation control. This control (and therefore the **CAnimateCtrl** class) is available only to programs running under Windows 95 and Windows NT version 3.51 and later.

An animation control is a rectangular window that displays a clip in AVI (Audio Video Interleaved) format—the standard Windows video/audio format. An AVI clip is a series of bitmap frames, like a movie.

Animation controls can play only simple AVI clips. Specifically, the clips to be played by an animation control must meet the following requirements:

- There must be exactly one video stream and it must have at least one frame.

- There can be at most two streams in the file (typically the other stream, if present, is an audio stream, although the animation control ignores audio information).

- The clip must either be uncompressed or compressed with RLE8 compression.

- No palette changes are allowed in the video stream.

You can add the AVI clip to your application as an AVI resource, or it can accompany your application as a separate AVI file.

Since your thread continues executing while the AVI clip is displayed, one common use for an animation control is to indicate system activity during a lengthy operation. For example, the Find dialog box of the Windows 95 Explorer displays a moving magnifying glass as the system searches for a file.

If you create a **CAnimateCtrl** object within a dialog box or from a dialog resource using the dialog editor, it will be automatically destroyed when the user closes the dialog box.

If you create a **CAnimateCtrl** object within a window, you may need to destroy it. If you create the **CAnimateCtrl** object on the stack, it is destroyed automatically. If you create the **CAnimateCtrl** object on the heap by using the **new** function, you must call **delete** on the object to destroy it. If you derive a new class from **CAnimateCtrl** and allocate any memory in that class, override the **CAnimateCtrl** destructor to dispose of the allocations.

For more information on using **CAnimateCtrl**, see Technical Note 60 online.

#include <afxcmn.h>

See Also: Animation Control Styles in **CAnimateCtrl::Create**, **ON_CONTROL**

CAnimateCtrl Class Members

Construction

CAnimateCtrl	Constructs a **CAnimateCtrl** object.

Initialization

Create	Creates an animation control and attaches it to a **CAnimateCtrl** object.

Operations

Open	Opens an AVI clip from a file or resource and displays the first frame.
Play	Plays the AVI clip without sound.
Seek	Displays a selected single frame of the AVI clip.
Stop	Stops playing the AVI clip.
Close	Closes the AVI clip that was previously opened.

Member Functions
CAnimateCtrl::CAnimateCtrl

CAnimateCtrl( );

Remarks

Constructs a **CAnimateCtrl** object. You must call the **Create** member function before you can perform any other operations on the object you create.

See Also: **CAnimateCtrl::Create**

CAnimateCtrl::Close

BOOL Close( );

Return Value

Nonzero if successful; otherwise zero.

Remarks

Use the **Close** member function to close the AVI clip that was previously opened in the animation control (if any) and remove it from memory.

See Also: **CAnimateCtrl::Open**

CAnimateCtrl::Create

BOOL Create(DWORD *dwStyle*, **const RECT&** *rect*, **CWnd*** *pParentWnd*,
↪ **UINT** *nID* **);**

Return Value

Nonzero if successful; otherwise zero.

Parameters

dwStyle   Specifies the animation control's style. Apply any combination of the
window and animation control styles described under Remarks to the control.

rect   Specifies the animation control's position and size. It can be either a **CRect**
object or a **RECT** structure.

pParentWnd   Specifies the animation control's parent window, usually a **CDialog**.
It must not be **NULL.**

nID   Specifies the animation control's ID.

Remarks

You construct a **CAnimateCtrl** in two steps. First call the constructor, then call
Create, which creates the animation control and attaches it to the **CAnimateCtrl**
object.

Apply the following window styles to an animation control.

- **WS_CHILD**   Always
- **WS_VISIBLE**   Usually
- **WS_DISABLED**   Rarely

In addition to the window styles listed above, you may want to apply one or more of
the following animation control styles to an animation control:

- **ACS_CENTER**   Centers the AVI clip in the animation control's window and
leaves the animation control's size and position unchanged when the AVI clip is
opened. If this style is not specified, the control will be resized when the AVI clip
is opened to the size of the images in the AVI clip.

- **ACS_TRANSPARENT**   Causes the AVI clip to be drawn using a transparent
background rather than the background color specified in the AVI clip.

- **ACS_AUTOPLAY**   Causes the AVI clip to start playing as soon as it is opened.
When the clip is done playing, it will automatically be repeated.

See Also: CAnimateCtrl::CAnimateCtrl, CAnimateCtrl::Open,
CAnimateCtrl::Play, CAnimateCtrl::Seek

CAnimateCtrl::Open

BOOL Open(LPCTSTR *lpszFileName* **);**
BOOL Open(UINT *nID* **);**

Return Value

Nonzero if successful; otherwise zero.

Parameters

lpszFileName   A **CString** object or a pointer to a null-terminated string that contains either the name of the AVI file or the name of an AVI resource. If this parameter is **NULL**, the system closes the AVI clip that was previously opened for the animation control, if any.

nID   The AVI resource identifier. If this parameter is **NULL**, the system closes the AVI clip that was previously opened for the animation control, if any.

Remarks

Call this function to open an AVI clip and display its first frame.

If the animation control has the **ACS_AUTOPLAY** style, the animation control will automatically start playing the clip immediately after it opens it. It will continue to play the clip in the background while your thread continues executing. When the clip is done playing, it will automatically be repeated.

If the animation control has the **ACS_CENTER** style, the AVI clip will be centered in the control and the size of the control will not change. If the animation control does not have the **ACS_CENTER** style, the control will be resized when the AVI clip is opened to the size of the images in the AVI clip. The position of the top left corner of the control will not change, only the size of the control.

If the animation control has the **ACS_TRANSPARENT** style, the first frame will be drawn using a transparent background rather than the background color specified in the animation clip.

See Also: CAnimateCtrl::Close, CAnimateCtrl::Create

CAnimateCtrl::Play

BOOL Play(UINT *nFrom*, **UINT** *nTo*, **UINT** *nRep* **);**

Return Value

Nonzero if successful; otherwise zero.

Parameters

nFrom   Zero-based index of the frame where playing begins. Value must be less than 65,536. A value of 0 means begin with the first frame in the AVI clip.

nTo Zero-based index of the frame where playing ends. Value must be less than 65,536. A value of −1 means end with the last frame in the AVI clip.

nRep Number of times to replay the AVI clip. A value of −1 means replay the file indefinitely.

Remarks

Call this function to play an AVI clip in an animation control. The animation control will play the clip in the background while your thread continues executing. If the animation control has **ACS_TRANSPARENT** style, the AVI clip will be played using a transparent background rather than the background color specified in the animation clip.

See Also: **CAnimateCtrl::Open, CAnimateCtrl::Stop, CAnimateCtrl::Seek, CAnimateCtrl::Create**

CAnimateCtrl::Seek

BOOL Seek(UINT *nTo* **);**

Return Value

Nonzero if successful; otherwise zero.

Parameters

nTo Zero-based index of the frame to display. Value must be less than 65,536. A value of 0 means display the first frame in the AVI clip. A value of −1 means display the last frame in the AVI clip.

Remarks

Call this function to statically display a single frame of your AVI clip. If the animation control has **ACS_TRANSPARENT** style, the AVI clip will be drawn using a transparent background rather than the background color specified in the animation clip.

See Also: **CAnimateCtrl::Open, CAnimateCtrl::Play, CAnimateCtrl::Create**

CAnimateCtrl::Stop

BOOL Stop( );

Return Value

Nonzero if successful; otherwise zero.

Remarks

Call this function to stop playing an AVI clip in an animation control.

See Also: **CAnimateCtrl::Play**

CArchive

CArchive does not have a base class.

The **CArchive** class allows you to save a complex network of objects in a permanent binary form (usually disk storage) that persists after those objects are deleted. Later you can load the objects from persistent storage, reconstituting them in memory. This process of making data persistent is called "serialization."

You can think of an archive object as a kind of binary stream. Like an input/output stream, an archive is associated with a file and permits the buffered writing and reading of data to and from storage. An input/output stream processes sequences of ASCII characters, but an archive processes binary object data in an efficient, nonredundant format.

You must create a **CFile** object before you can create a **CArchive** object. In addition, you must ensure that the archive's load/store status is compatible with the file's open mode. You are limited to one active archive per file.

When you construct a **CArchive** object, you attach it to an object of class **CFile** (or a derived class) that represents an open file. You also specify whether the archive will be used for loading or storing. A **CArchive** object can process not only primitive types but also objects of **CObject**-derived classes designed for serialization. A serializable class usually has a **Serialize** member function, and it usually uses the **DECLARE_SERIAL** and **IMPLEMENT_SERIAL** macros, as described under class **CObject**.

The overloaded extraction (**>>**) and insertion (**<<**) operators are convenient archive programming interfaces that support both primitive types and **CObject**-derived classes.

CArchive also supports programming with the MFC Windows Sockets classes **CSocket** and **CSocketFile**. The **IsBufferEmpty** member function supports that usage.

For more information on **CArchive**, see the articles "Serialization (Object Persistence)" and "Windows Sockets: Using Sockets with Archives" in *Visual C++ Programmer's Guide* online.

#include <afx.h>

See Also: CFile, CObject, CSocket, CSocketFile

CArchive Class Members

Data Members

m_pDocument	Points to the **CDocument** object being serialized.

Construction

CArchive	Creates a **CArchive** object.
Abort	Closes an archive without throwing an exception.
Close	Flushes unwritten data and disconnects from the **CFile**.

Basic Input/Output

Flush	Flushes unwritten data from the archive buffer.
operator >>	Loads objects and primitive types from the archive.
operator <<	Stores objects and primitive types to the archive.
Read	Reads raw bytes.
Write	Writes raw bytes.
WriteString	Writes a single line of text.
ReadString	Reads a single line of text.

Status

GetFile	Gets the **CFile** object pointer for this archive.
GetObjectSchema	Called from the **Serialize** function to determine the version of the object that is being deserialized.
SetObjectSchema	Sets the object schema stored in the archive object.
IsLoading	Determines whether the archive is loading.
IsStoring	Determines whether the archive is storing.
IsBufferEmpty	Determines whether the buffer has been emptied during a Windows Sockets receive process.

Object Input/Output

ReadObject	Calls an object's **Serialize** function for loading.
WriteObject	Calls an object's **Serialize** function for storing.
MapObject	Places objects in the map that are not serialized to the file, but that are available for subobjects to reference.
SetStoreParams	Sets the hash table size and the block size of the map used to identify unique objects during the serialization process.
SetLoadParams	Sets the size to which the load array grows. Must be called before any object is loaded or before **MapObject** or **ReadObject** is called.
ReadClass	Reads a class reference previously stored with **WriteClass**.
WriteClass	Writes a reference to the **CRuntimeClass** to the **CArchive**.
SerializeClass	Reads or writes the class reference to the **CArchive** object depending on the direction of the **CArchive**.

Member Functions
CArchive::Abort

void Abort ( );

Remarks

Call this function to close the archive without throwing an exception. The **CArchive** destructor will normally call **Close**, which will flush any data that has not been saved to the associated **CFile** object. This can cause exceptions.

When catching these exceptions, it is a good idea to use **Abort**, so that destructing the **CArchive** object doesn't cause further exceptions. When handling exceptions, **CArchive::Abort** will not throw an exception on failures because, unlike **CArchive::Close**, **Abort** ignores failures.

If you used **new** to allocate the **CArchive** object on the heap, then you must delete it after closing the file.

See Also: **CArchive::Close, CFile::Close**

CArchive::CArchive

CArchive(CFile* *pFile*, **UINT** *nMode*, **int** *nBufSize* **= 4096, void*** *lpBuf* **= NULL);**
throw(CMemoryException, CArchiveException, CFileException);

Parameters

pFile   A pointer to the **CFile** object that is the ultimate source or destination of the persistent data.

nMode   A flag that specifies whether objects will be loaded from or stored to the archive. The *nMode* parameter must have one of the following values:

- **CArchive::load**   Loads data from the archive. Requires only **CFile** read permission.

- **CArchive::store**   Saves data to the archive. Requires **CFile** write permission.

- **CArchive::bNoFlushOnDelete**   Prevents the archive from automatically calling **Flush** when the archive destructor is called. If you set this flag, you are responsible for explicitly calling **Close** before the destructor is called. If you do not, your data will be corrupted.

nBufSize   An integer that specifies the size of the internal file buffer, in bytes. Note that the default buffer size is 4096 bytes. If you routinely archive large objects, you will improve performance if you use a larger buffer size that is a multiple of the file buffer size.

lpBuf An optional pointer to a user-supplied buffer of size *nBufSize*. If you do not specify this parameter, the archive allocates a buffer from the local heap and frees it when the object is destroyed. The archive does not free a user-supplied buffer.

Remarks

Constructs a **CArchive** object and specifies whether it will be used for loading or storing objects. You cannot change this specification after you have created the archive.

You may not use **CFile** operations to alter the state of the file until you have closed the archive. Any such operation will damage the integrity of the archive. You may access the position of the file pointer at any time during serialization by obtaining the archive's file object from the **GetFile** member function and then using the **CFile::GetPosition** function. You should call **CArchive::Flush** before obtaining the position of the file pointer.

Example

```
extern char* pFileName;
CFile f;
char buf[512];
if( !f.Open( pFileName, CFile::modeCreate | CFile::modeWrite ) ) {
   #ifdef _DEBUG
      afxDump << "Unable to open file" << "\n";
      exit( 1 );
   #endif
}
CArchive ar( &f, CArchive::store, 512, buf );
```

See Also: **CArchive::Close**, **CArchive::Flush**, **CFile::Close**

CArchive::Close

void Close( );
> **throw(CArchiveException, CFileException);**

Remarks

Flushes any data remaining in the buffer, closes the archive, and disconnects the archive from the file. No further operations on the archive are permitted. After you close an archive, you can create another archive for the same file or you can close the file.

The member function **Close** ensures that all data is transferred from the archive to the file, and it makes the archive unavailable. To complete the transfer from the file to the storage medium, you must first use **CFile::Close** and then destroy the **CFile** object.

See Also: **CArchive::Flush**, **CArchive::Abort**

CArchive::Flush

void Flush( );
    throw(CFileException);

Remarks

Forces any data remaining in the archive buffer to be written to the file.

The member function **Flush** ensures that all data is transferred from the archive to the file. You must call **CFile::Close** to complete the transfer from the file to the storage medium.

See Also: **CArchive::Close, CFile::Flush, CFile::Close**

CArchive::GetFile

CFile* GetFile( ) const;

Return Value

A constant pointer to the **CFile** object in use.

Remarks

Gets the **CFile** object pointer for this archive. You must flush the archive before using **GetFile**.

Example

```
extern CArchive ar;
const CFile* fp = ar.GetFile();
```

See Also: **CArchive::Flush**

CArchive::GetObjectSchema

UINT GetObjectSchema( ); ·

Return Value

During deserialization, the version of the object being read.

Remarks

Call this function from the **Serialize** function to determine the version of the object that is currently being deserialized. Calling this function is only valid when the **CArchive** object is being loaded (**CArchive::IsLoading** returns nonzero). It should be the first call in the **Serialize** function and called only once. A return value of (**UINT**)–1 indicates that the version number is unknown).

A **CObject**-derived class may use **VERSIONABLE_SCHEMA** combined (using bitwise **OR**) with the schema version itself (in the **IMPLEMENT_SERIAL** macro) to create a "versionable object," that is, an object whose **Serialize** member function can read multiple versions. The default framework functionality (without **VERSIONABLE_SCHEMA**) is to throw an exception when the version is mismatched.

Example

```
IMPLEMENT_SERIAL(CMyObject, CObject, VERSIONABLE_SCHEMA|1)

void CMyObject::Serialize(CArchive& ar)
{
    if (ar.IsLoading())
    {
        int nVersion = ar.GetObjectSchema();

        switch(nVersion)
        {
        case 0:
            // read in previous version of
            // this object
            break;
        case 1:
            // read in current version of
            // this object
            break;
        default:
            // report unknown version of
            // this object
            break;
        }
    }
    else
    {
        // Normal storing code goes here
    }
}
```

See Also: **CObject::Serialize, CObject::IsSerializable, IMPLEMENT_SERIAL, DECLARE_SERIAL, CArchive::IsLoading**

CArchive::IsBufferEmpty

BOOL IsBufferEmpty( ) const;

Return Value

Nonzero if the archive's buffer is empty; otherwise 0.

Remarks

Call this member function to determine whether the archive object's internal buffer is empty. This function is supplied to support programming with the MFC Windows Sockets class **CSocketFile**. You do not need to use it for an archive associated with a **CFile** object.

The reason for using **IsBufferEmpty** with an archive associated with a **CSocketFile** object is that the archive's buffer might contain more than one message or record. After receiving one message, you should use **IsBufferEmpty** to control a loop that continues receiving data until the buffer is empty. For more information, see the **Receive** member function of class **CAsyncSocket** and the MFC Advanced Concepts sample CHATSRVR, which shows how to use **IsBufferEmpty**.

For more information, see the article "Windows Sockets: Using Sockets with Archives" in *Visual C++ Programmer's Guide* online.

See Also: **CSocketFile**, **CAsyncSocket::Receive**

CArchive::IsLoading

BOOL IsLoading( ) const;

Return Value
Nonzero if the archive is currently being used for loading; otherwise 0.

Remarks
Determines whether the archive is loading data. This member function is called by the **Serialize** functions of the archived classes.

Example
```
int i;
extern CArchive ar;
if( ar.IsLoading() )
  ar >> i;
else
  ar << i;
```

See Also: **CArchive::IsStoring**

CArchive::IsStoring

BOOL IsStoring( ) const;

Return Value
Nonzero if the archive is currently being used for storing; otherwise 0.

Remarks
Determines whether the archive is storing data. This member function is called by the **Serialize** functions of the archived classes.

If the **IsStoring** status of an archive is nonzero, then its **IsLoading** status is 0, and vice versa.

Example

```
int i;
extern CArchive ar;
if( ar.IsStoring() )
  ar << i;
else
  ar >> i;
```

See Also: **CArchive::IsLoading**

CArchive::MapObject

void MapObject(const CObject* *pOb* **);**

Parameters

pOb   A constant pointer to the object being stored.

Remarks

Call this member function to place objects in the map that are not really serialized to the file, but that are available for subobjects to reference. For example, you might not serialize a document, but you would serialize the items that are part of the document. By calling **MapObject**, you allow those items, or subobjects, to reference the document. Also, serialized subitems can serialize their **m_pDocument** back pointer.

You can call **MapObject** when you store to and load from the **CArchive** object. **MapObject** adds the specified object to the internal data structures maintained by the **CArchive** object during serialization and deserialization, but unlike **ReadObject** and **WriteObject,** it does not call serialize on the object.

Example

```
// MyDoc.h
// Document should have DECLARE_SERIAL and IMPLEMENT_SERIAL

class CMyDocument : public CDocument
{
    CObList m_listOfSubItems;
    ...
    DECLARE_SERIAL(CMyDocument)
};

// MyDoc.cpp
...
IMPLEMENT_SERIAL(CMyDocument, CObject, 1)
...
void CMyDocument::Serialize(CArchive& ar)
{
```

```
        if (ar.IsStoring())
        {
            // TODO: add storing code here
        }
        else
        {
            // TODO: add loading code here
        }

        ar.MapObject(this);
        //serialize the subitems in the document;
        //they will be able to serialize their m_pDoc
        //back pointer
        m_listOfSubItems.Serialize(ar);

    }


    //SubItem.h
    class CSubItem : public CObject
    {
    public:
        CSubItem(CMyDocument * pDoc)
            { m_pDoc = pDoc; }

        // back pointer to owning document
        CMyDocument* m_pDoc;
        WORD m_i; // other item data

        virtual void Serialize(CArchive& ar);
    };

    //SubItem.cpp
    void CSubItem::Serialize(CArchive& ar)
    {
        if (ar.IsStoring())
        {
            // will serialize a reference
            //to the "mapped" document pointer
            ar << m_pDoc;
            ar << m_i;
        }
        else
        {
            // will load a reference to
            //the "mapped" document pointer
            ar >> m_pDoc;
            ar >> m_i;
        }
    }
```

See Also: CArchive::ReadObject, CArchive::WriteObject

CArchive::Read

UINT Read(void* *lpBuf,* **UINT** *nMax* **);**
   throw(CFileException);

Return Value

An unsigned integer containing the number of bytes actually read. If the return value is less than the number requested, the end of file has been reached. No exception is thrown on the end-of-file condition.

Parameters

lpBuf   A pointer to a user-supplied buffer that is to receive the data read from the archive.

nMax   An unsigned integer specifying the number of bytes to be read from the archive.

Remarks

Reads a specified number of bytes from the archive. The archive does not interpret the bytes.

You can use the **Read** member function within your **Serialize** function for reading ordinary structures that are contained in your objects.

Example

```
extern CArchive ar;
char pb[100];
UINT nr = ar.Read( pb, 100 );
```

CArchive::ReadClass

CRuntimeClass* ReadClass(const CRuntimeClass* *pClassRefRequested* **= NULL,**
  ↪ **UINT*** *pSchema* **= NULL, DWORD*** *obTag* **= NULL);**
   throw CArchiveException;
   throw CNotSupportedException;

Return Value

A pointer to the **CRuntimeClass** structure.

Parameters

pClassRefRequested   A pointer to the **CRuntimeClass** structure that corresponds to the class reference requested. Can be **NULL**.

pSchema   A pointer to a schema of the run-time class previously stored.

obTag   A number that refers to an object's unique tag. Used internally by the implementation of **ReadObject**. Exposed for advanced programming only; *obTag* normally should be **NULL**.

Remarks

Call this member function to read a reference to a class previously stored with **WriteClass**.

If *pClassRefRequested* is not **NULL**, **ReadClass** verifies that the archived class information is compatible with your runtime class. If it is not compatible, **ReadClass** will throw a **CArchiveException**.

Your runtime class must use **DECLARE_SERIAL** and **IMPLEMENT_SERIAL**; otherwise, **ReadClass** will throw a **CNotSupportedException**.

If *pSchema* is **NULL**, the schema of the stored class can be retrieved by calling **CArchive::GetObjectSchema**; otherwise, **pSchema* will contain the schema of the run-time class that was previously stored.

You can use **SerializeClass** instead of **ReadClass**, which handles both reading and writing of the class reference.

See Also: CArchive::WriteClass, CArchive::GetObjectSchema, CArchive::SetObjectSchema, CArchiveException, CNotSupportedException, CArchive::SerializeClass

---

CArchive::ReadObject

CObject* ReadObject(const CRuntimeClass* *pClass* **);**
  throw(CFileException, CArchiveException, CMemoryException);

Return Value

A **CObject** pointer that must be safely cast to the correct derived class by using **CObject::IsKindOf**.

Parameters

pClass A constant pointer to the **CRuntimeClass** structure that corresponds to the object you expect to read.

Remarks

Reads object data from the archive and constructs an object of the appropriate type.

This function is normally called by the **CArchive** extraction (**>>**) operator overloaded for a **CObject** pointer. **ReadObject**, in turn, calls the **Serialize** function of the archived class.

If you supply a nonzero *pClass* parameter, which is obtained by the **RUNTIME_CLASS** macro, then the function verifies the run-time class of the archived object. This assumes you have used the **IMPLEMENT_SERIAL** macro in the implementation of the class.

See Also: CArchive::WriteObject, CObject::IsKindOf

CArchive::ReadString

Bool ReadString(CString& *rString* **);**
LPTSTR ReadString(LPTSTR *lpsz*, **UINT** *nMax* **);**
   throw(CArchiveException);

Return Value

In the version that returns **Bool**, **TRUE** if successful; **FALSE** otherwise.

In the version that returns an **LPTSTR**, a pointer to the buffer containing the text data; **NULL** if end-of-file was reached.

Parameters

rString A reference to a **CString** that will contain the resultant string after it is read from the file associated with the CArchive object.

lpsz Specifies a pointer to a user-supplied buffer that will receive a null-terminated text string.

nMax Specifies the maximum number of characters to read. Should be one less than the size of the *lpsz* buffer.

Remarks

Call this member function to read text data into a buffer from the file associated with the **CArchive** object. In the version of the member function with the *nMax* parameter, the buffer will hold up to a limit of *nMax*-1 characters. Reading is stopped by a carriage return-linefeed pair. Trailing newline characters are always removed. A null character ('\0') is appended in either case.

CArchive::Read is also available for text-mode input, but it does not terminate on a carriage return-linefeed pair.

See Also: **CArchive::Read**, **CArchive::Write**, **CArchive::WriteString**, **CArchiveException**

CArchive::SerializeClass

void SerializeClass(const CRuntimeClass* *pRuntimeClass* **);**

Parameters

pRuntimeClass A pointer to a run-time class object for the base class.

Remarks

Call this member function when you want to store and load the version information of a base class. **SerializeClass** reads or writes the reference to a class to the **CArchive** object, depending on the direction of the **CArchive**. Use **SerializeClass** in place of **ReadClass** and **WriteClass** as a convenient way to serialize base-class objects; **SerializeClass** requires less code and fewer parameters.

Like **ReadClass**, **SerializeClass** verifies that the archived class information is compatible with your runtime class. If it is not compatible, **SerializeClass** will throw a **CArchiveException**.

Your runtime class must use **DECLARE_SERIAL** and **IMPLEMENT_SERIAL**; otherwise, **SerializeClass** will throw a **CNotSupportedException**.

Use the **RUNTIME_CLASS** macro to retrieve the value for the *pRuntimeClass* parameter. The base class must have used the **IMPLEMENT_SERIAL** macro.

Example

```
class CBaseClass : public CObject { ... };
class CDerivedClass : public CBaseClass { ... };
void CDerivedClass::Serialize(CArchive& ar)
{
    if (ar.IsStoring())
    {
        //normal code for storing contents
        //of this object
    }
    else
    {
        //normal code for reading contents
        //of this object
    }

    //allow the base class to serialize along
    //with its version information
    ar.SerializeClass(RUNTIME_CLASS(CBaseClass));
    CBaseClass::Serialize(ar);
}
```

See Also: CArchive::ReadClass, CArchive::WriteClass, CArchive::GetObjectSchema, CArchive::SetObjectSchema, CArchiveException, CNotSupportedException

---

CArchive::SetLoadParams

void SetLoadParams(UINT *nGrowBy* **= 1024);**

Parameters

nGrowBy   The minimum number of element slots to allocate if a size increase is necessary.

Remarks

Call **SetLoadParams** when you are going to read a large number of **CObject**-derived objects from an archive. **CArchive** uses a load array to resolve references to objects stored in the archive. **SetLoadParams** allows you to set the size to which the load array grows.

You must not call **SetLoadParams** after any object is loaded, or after **MapObject** or **ReadObject** is called.

Example

```
class CMyLargeDocument : public CDocument { ... };
void CMyLargeDocument::Serialize(CArchive& ar)
{
    if (ar.IsStoring())
        ar.SetStoreParams();  // use large defaults
    else
        ar.SetLoadParams();

    if (ar.IsStoring())
    {
        // code for storing CMyLargeDocument
    }
    else
    {
        // code for loading CMyLargeDocument
    }
}
```

See Also: **CArchive::SetStoreParams**

CArchive::SetObjectSchema

void SetObjectSchema(UINT *nSchema* **);**

Parameters

nSchema   Specifies the object's schema.

Remarks

Call this member function to set the object schema stored in the archive object to *nSchema*. The next call to **GetObjectSchema** will return the value stored in *nSchema*.

Use **SetObjectSchema** for advanced versioning; for example, when you want to force a particular version to be read in a **Serialize** function of a derived class.

See Also: **CArchive::GetObjectSchema**

CArchive::SetStoreParams

void SetStoreParams(UINT *nHashSize* **= 2053, UINT** *nBlockSize* **= 128);**

Parameters

nHashSize   The size of the hash table for interface pointer maps. Should be a prime number.

nBlockSize   Specifies the memory-allocation granularity for extending the parameters. Should be a power of 2 for the best performance.

Remarks

Use **SetStoreParams** when storing a large number of **CObject**-derived objects in an archive.

SetStoreParams allows you to set the hash table size and the block size of the map used to identify unique objects during the serialization process.

You must not call **SetStoreParams** after any objects are stored, or after **MapObject** or **WriteObject** is called.

Example

```
class CMyLargeDocument : public CDocument { ... };
void CMyLargeDocument::Serialize(CArchive& ar)
{
    if (ar.IsStoring())
        ar.SetStoreParams();   // use large defaults
    else
        ar.SetLoadParams();

    if (ar.IsStoring())
    {
        // code for storing CMyLargeDocument
    }
    else
    {
        // code for loading CMyLargeDocument
    }
}
```

See Also: **CArchive::SetLoadParams**

CArchive::Write

void Write(const void* *lpBuf*, **UINT** *nMax* **);**
    throw(CFileException);

Parameters

lpBuf A pointer to a user-supplied buffer that contains the data to be written to the archive.

nMax An integer that specifies the number of bytes to be written to the archive.

Remarks

Writes a specified number of bytes to the archive. The archive does not format the bytes.

You can use the **Write** member function within your **Serialize** function to write ordinary structures that are contained in your objects.

Example

```
extern CArchive ar;
char pb[100];
ar.Write( pb, 100 );
```

See Also: **CArchive::Read**

CArchive::WriteClass

void WriteClass(const CRuntimeClass* *pClassRef* **);**

Parameters

> *pClassRef* A pointer to the **CRuntimeClass** structure that corresponds to the class reference requested.

Remarks

> Use **WriteClass** to store the version and class information of a base class during serialization of the derived class. **WriteClass** writes a reference to the **CRuntimeClass** for the base class to the **CArchive**. Use **CArchive::ReadClass** to retrieve the reference.
>
> **WriteClass** verifies that the archived class information is compatible with your runtime class. If it is not compatible, **WriteClass** will throw a **CArchiveException**.
>
> Your runtime class must use **DECLARE_SERIAL** and **IMPLEMENT_SERIAL**; otherwise, **WriteClass** will throw a **CNotSupportedException**.
>
> You can use **SerializeClass** instead of **WriteClass**, which handles both reading and writing of the class reference.
>
> **See Also:** CArchive::ReadClass, CArchive::GetObjectSchema, CArchive::SetObjectSchema, CArchive::SerializeClass, CArchiveException, CNotSupportedException.

CArchive::WriteObject

void WriteObject(const CObject* *pOb* **);**
    throw(CFileException, CArchiveException);

Parameters

> *pOb* A constant pointer to the object being stored.

Remarks

> Stores the specified **CObject** to the archive.
>
> This function is normally called by the **CArchive** insertion (<<) operator overloaded for **CObject**. **WriteObject**, in turn, calls the **Serialize** function of the archived class.
>
> You must use the **IMPLEMENT_SERIAL** macro to enable archiving. **WriteObject** writes the ASCII class name to the archive. This class name is validated later during the load process. A special encoding scheme prevents unnecessary duplication of the class name for multiple objects of the class. This scheme also prevents redundant storage of objects that are targets of more than one pointer.

The exact object encoding method (including the presence of the ASCII class name) is an implementation detail and could change in future versions of the library.

Note . Finish creating, deleting, and updating all your objects before you begin to archive them. Your archive will be corrupted if you mix archiving with object modification.

See Also: **CArchive::ReadObject**

CArchive::WriteString

void WriteString(LPCTSTR *lpsz* **);**
  throw(CFileException);

Parameters

lpsz   Specifies a pointer to a buffer containing a null-terminated text string.

Remarks

Use this member function to write data from a buffer to the file associated with the **CArchive** object. The terminating null character ('\0') is not written to the file; nor is a newline automatically written.

WriteString throws an exception in response to several conditions, including the disk-full condition.

Write is also available, but rather than terminating on a null character, it writes the requested number of bytes to the file.

See Also: **CArchive::Write**, **CArchive::Read**, **CArchive::ReadString**, **CFileException**

Operators
CArchive::operator <<

friend CArchive& operator <<(CArchive& *ar*, **const CObject*** *pOb* **);**
  throw(CArchiveException, CFileException);
CArchive& operator <<(BYTE *by* **);**
  throw(CArchiveException, CFileException);
CArchive& operator <<(WORD *w* **);**
  throw(CArchiveException, CFileException);
CArchive& operator <<(int *i* **);**
  throw(CArchiveException, CFileException);
CArchive& operator <<(LONG *l* **);**
  throw(CArchiveException, CFileException);

CArchive& operator <<(DWORD *dw* **);**
   throw(CArchiveException, CFileException);
CArchive& operator <<(float *f* **);**
   throw(CArchiveException, CFileException);
CArchive& operator <<(double *d* **);**
   throw(CArchiveException, CFileException);

Return Value

A **CArchive** reference that enables multiple extraction operators on a single line.

Remarks

Stores the indicated object or primitive type to the archive.

If you used the **IMPLEMENT_SERIAL** macro in your class implementation, then the insertion operator overloaded for **CObject** calls the protected **WriteObject**. This function, in turn, calls the **Serialize** function of the class.

Example

```
long l;
int i;
extern CArchive ar;
if( ar.IsStoring() )
  ar << l << i;
```

See Also: **CArchive::WriteObject**, **CObject::Serialize**

CArchive::operator >>

friend CArchive& operator >>(CArchive& *ar*, **CObject *&** *pOb* **);**
   throw(CArchiveException, CFileException, CMemoryException);
friend CArchive& operator >>(CArchive& *ar*, **const CObject *&** *pOb* **);**
   throw(CArchiveException, CFileException, CMemoryException);
CArchive& operator >>(BYTE& *by* **);**
   throw(CArchiveException, CFileException);
CArchive& operator >>(WORD& *w* **);**
   throw(CArchiveException, CFileException);
CArchive& operator >>(int& *i* **);**
   throw(CArchiveException, CFileException);
CArchive& operator >>(LONG& *l* **);**
   throw(CArchiveException, CFileException);
CArchive& operator >>(DWORD& *dw* **);**
   throw(CArchiveException, CFileException);
CArchive& operator >>(float& *f* **);**
   throw(CArchiveException, CFileException);
CArchive& operator >>(double& *d* **);**
   throw(CArchiveException, CFileException);

Return Value

A **CArchive** reference that enables multiple insertion operators on a single line.

Remarks

Loads the indicated object or primitive type from the archive.

If you used the **IMPLEMENT_SERIAL** macro in your class implementation, then the extraction operators overloaded for **CObject** call the protected **ReadObject** function (with a nonzero run-time class pointer). This function, in turn, calls the **Serialize** function of the class.

Example

```
int i;
extern CArchive ar;
if( ar.IsLoading() )
  ar >> i;
```

See Also: **CArchive::ReadObject, CObject::Serialize**

Data Members
CArchive::m_pDocument

Remarks

Set to **NULL** by default, this pointer to a **CDocument** can be set to anything the user of the **CArchive** instance wants. A common usage of this pointer is to convey additional information about the serialization process to all objects being serialized. This is achieved by initializing the pointer with the document (a **CDocument**-derived class) that is being serialized, in such a way that objects within the document can access the document if necessary. This pointer is also used by **COleClientItem** objects during serialization.

The framework sets **m_pDocument** to the document being serialized when a user issues a File Open or Save command. If you serialize an Object Linking and Embedding (OLE) container document for reasons other than File Open or Save, you must explicitly set **m_pDocument**. For example, you would do this when serializing a container document to the Clipboard.

See Also: **CDocument, COleClientItem**

CArchiveException

A **CArchiveException** object represents a serialization exception condition. The **CArchiveException** class includes a public data member that indicates the cause of the exception.

CArchiveException objects are constructed and thrown inside **CArchive** member functions. You can access these objects within the scope of a **CATCH** expression. The cause code is independent of the operating system. For more information about exception processing, see the article "Exceptions" in *Visual C++ Programmer's Guide* online.

#include <afx.h>

See Also: **CArchive**, **AfxThrowArchiveException**, Exception Processing

CArchiveException Class Members

Data Members

m_cause	Indicates the exception cause.

Construction

CArchiveException	Constructs a **CArchiveException** object.

Member Functions
CArchiveException::CArchiveException

CArchiveException(int *cause* **= CArchiveException::none);**

Parameters

    cause An enumerated type variable that indicates the reason for the exception. For a list of the enumerators, see the **m_cause** data member.

Remarks

Constructs a **CArchiveException** object, storing the value of *cause* in the object. You can create a **CArchiveException** object on the heap and throw it yourself or let the global function **AfxThrowArchiveException** handle it for you.

Do not use this constructor directly; instead, call the global function **AfxThrowArchiveException**.

Data Members

CArchiveException::m_cause

Remarks

Specifies the cause of the exception. This data member is a public variable of type **int**. Its values are defined by a **CArchiveException** enumerated type. The enumerators and their meanings are as follows:

- **CArchiveException::none**   No error occurred.
- **CArchiveException::generic**   Unspecified error.
- **CArchiveException::readOnly**   Tried to write into an archive opened for loading.
- **CArchiveException::endOfFile**   Reached end of file while reading an object.
- **CArchiveException::writeOnly**   Tried to read from an archive opened for storing.
- **CArchiveException::badIndex**   Invalid file format.
- **CArchiveException::badClass**   Tried to read an object into an object of the wrong type.
- **CArchiveException::badSchema**   Tried to read an object with a different version of the class.

Note   These **CArchiveException** cause enumerators are distinct from the **CFileException** cause enumerators.

CArray

template< class *TYPE***, class** *ARG_TYPE* **> class CArray : public CObject**

Parameters

TYPE   Template parameter specifying the type of objects stored in the array. TYPE is a parameter that is returned by **CArray**.

ARG_TYPE   Template parameter specifying the argument type used to access objects stored in the array. Often a reference to *TYPE*. ARG_TYPE is a parameter that is passed to **CArray**.

Remarks

The **CArray** class supports arrays that are similar to C arrays, but can dynamically shrink and grow as necessary.

Array indexes always start at position 0. You can decide whether to fix the upper bound or allow the array to expand when you add elements past the current bound. Memory is allocated contiguously to the upper bound, even if some elements are null.

As with a C array, the access time for a **CArray** indexed element is constant and is independent of the array size.

Tip Before using an array, use **SetSize** to establish its size and allocate memory for it. If you do not use **SetSize**, adding elements to your array causes it to be frequently reallocated and copied. Frequent reallocation and copying are inefficient and can fragment memory.

If you need a dump of individual elements in an array, you must set the depth of the **CDumpContext** object to 1 or greater.

Certain member functions of this class call global helper functions that must be customized for most uses of the **CArray** class. See the topic "Collection Class Helpers" in the MFC Macros and Globals section.

When elements are removed from a **CArray** object, the helper function **DestructElements** is called. When elements are added, the helper function **ConstructElements** is called.

Array class derivation is similar to list derivation.

For more information on using **CArray**, see the article "Collections" in *Visual C++ Programmer's Guide* online.

#include <afxtempl.h>

See Also: **CObArray, DestructElements, ConstructElements**, "Collection Class Helpers"

CArray Class Members

Construction

CArray	Constructs an empty array.

Attributes

GetSize	Gets the number of elements in this array.
GetUpperBound	Returns the largest valid index.
SetSize	Sets the number of elements to be contained in this array.

Operations

FreeExtra	Frees all unused memory above the current upper bound.
RemoveAll	Removes all the elements from this array.

Element Access

GetAt	Returns the value at a given index.
SetAt	Sets the value for a given index; array not allowed to grow.
ElementAt	Returns a temporary reference to the element pointer within the array.
GetData	Allows access to elements in the array. Can be **NULL**.

Growing the Array

SetAtGrow	Sets the value for a given index; grows the array if necessary.
Add	Adds an element to the end of the array; grows the array if necessary.
Append	Appends another array to the array; grows the array if necessary
Copy	Copies another array to the array; grows the array if necessary.

Insertion/Removal

InsertAt	Inserts an element (or all the elements in another array) at a specified index.
RemoveAt	Removes an element at a specific index.

Operators

operator []	Sets or gets the element at the specified index.

Member Functions

CArray::Add

int Add(*ARG_TYPE newElement* **);**
    throw(CMemoryException);

Return Value

The index of the added element.

Parameters

ARG_TYPE   Template parameter specifying the type of arguments referencing elements in this array.

newElement   The element to be added to this array.

Remarks

Adds a new element to the end of an array, growing the array by 1. If **SetSize** has been used with an *nGrowBy* value greater than 1, then extra memory may be allocated. However, the upper bound will increase by only 1.

Example

```
// example for CArray::Add
CArray<CPoint,CPoint> ptArray;

CPoint pt(10,20);
ptArray.Add(pt);               // Element 0
ptArray.Add(CPoint(30,40));  // Element 1
```

See Also: **CArray::SetAt**, **CArray::SetAtGrow**, **CArray::InsertAt**, **CArray::operator []**

CArray::Append

int Append(const CArray& *src* **);**

Return Value

The index of the first appended element.

Parameters

src   Source of the elements to be appended to an array.

Remarks

Call this member function to add the contents of one array to the end of another. The arrays must be of the same type.

If necessary, **Append** may allocate extra memory to accommodate the elements appended to the array.

See Also: **CArray::Copy**

CArray::CArray

CArray( );

Remarks

Constructs an empty array. The array grows one element at a time.

See Also: CObArray::CObArray

CArray::Copy

void Copy(const CArray& *src* **);**

Parameters

src   Source of the elements to be copied to an array.

Remarks

Use this member function to copy the elements of one array to another.

Call this member function to overwrite the elements of one array with the elements of another array.

Copy does not free memory; however, if necessary, **Copy** may allocate extra memory to accommodate the elements copied to the array.

See Also: CArray::Append

CArray::ElementAt

*TYPE***& ElementAt(int** *nIndex* **);**

Return Value

A reference to an array element.

Parameters

TYPE   Template parameter specifying the type of elements in the array.

nIndex   An integer index that is greater than or equal to 0 and less than or equal to the value returned by **GetUpperBound**.

Remarks

Returns a temporary reference to the specified element within the array. It is used to implement the left-side assignment operator for arrays.

See Also: CArray::operator []

CArray::FreeExtra

void FreeExtra( );

Remarks

Frees any extra memory that was allocated while the array was grown. This function has no effect on the size or upper bound of the array.

CArray::GetAt

TYPE **GetAt(int** *nIndex* **) const;**

Return Value

The array element currently at this index.

Parameters

TYPE   Template parameter specifying the type of the array elements.

nIndex   An integer index that is greater than or equal to 0 and less than or equal to the value returned by **GetUpperBound**.

Remarks

Returns the array element at the specified index.

Note   Passing a negative value or a value greater than the value returned by **GetUpperBound** will result in a failed assertion.

See Also: CArray::SetAt, CArray::operator [], ConstructElements

---

CArray::GetData

const *TYPE** **GetData( ) const;**
TYPE* **GetData( );**

Return Value

A pointer to an array element.

Parameters

TYPE   Template parameter specifying the type of the array elements.

Remarks

Use this member function to gain direct access to the elements in an array. If no elements are available, **GetData** returns a null value.

While direct access to the elements of an array can help you work more quickly, use caution when calling **GetData**; any errors you make directly affect the elements of your array.

See Also: CArray::GetAt, CArray::SetAt, CArray::ElementAt

CArray::GetSize

int GetSize( ) const;

Remarks

Returns the size of the array. Since indexes are zero-based, the size is 1 greater than the largest index.

See Also: **CArray::GetUpperBound, CArray::SetSize**

CArray::GetUpperBound

int GetUpperBound( ) const;

Remarks

Returns the current upper bound of this array. Because array indexes are zero-based, this function returns a value 1 less than **GetSize**.

The condition **GetUpperBound( ) = −1** indicates that the array contains no elements.

See Also: **CArray::GetSize, CArray::SetSize**

CArray::InsertAt

void InsertAt(int *nIndex***, ARG_TYPE** *newElement***, int** *nCount* **= 1);**
    throw(CMemoryException);
void InsertAt(int *nStartIndex***, CArray*** *pNewArray* **);**
    throw(CMemoryException);

Parameters

nIndex An integer index that may be greater than the value returned by **GetUpperBound**.

ARG_TYPE Template parameter specifying the type of elements in this array.

newElement The element to be placed in this array.

nCount The number of times this element should be inserted (defaults to 1).

nStartIndex An integer index that may be greater than the value returned by **GetUpperBound**.

pNewArray Another array that contains elements to be added to this array.

Remarks

The first version of **InsertAt** inserts one element (or multiple copies of an element) at a specified index in an array. In the process, it shifts up (by incrementing the index) the existing element at this index, and it shifts up all the elements above it.

The second version inserts all the elements from another **CArray** collection, starting at the *nStartIndex* position.

The **SetAt** function, in contrast, replaces one specified array element and does not shift any elements.

Example

```
// example for CArray::InsertAt

CArray<CPoint,CPoint> ptArray;

ptArray.Add(CPoint(10,20));// Element 0
ptArray.Add(CPoint(30,40));// Element 1 (will become element 2)
ptArray.InsertAt(1, CPoint(50,60));   // New element 1
```

See Also: GetUpperBound, **CArray::SetAt**, **CArray::RemoveAt**

CArray::RemoveAll

void RemoveAll( );

Remarks

Removes all the elements from this array. If the array is already empty, the function still works.

CArray::RemoveAt

void RemoveAt(int *nIndex,* **int** *nCount* **= 1);**

Parameters

nIndex   An integer index that is greater than or equal to 0 and less than or equal to the value returned by **GetUpperBound**.

nCount   The number of elements to remove.

Remarks

Removes one or more elements starting at a specified index in an array. In the process, it shifts down all the elements above the removed element(s). It decrements the upper bound of the array but does not free memory.

If you try to remove more elements than are contained in the array above the removal point, then the Debug version of the library asserts.

See Also: CArray::SetAt, **CArray::SetAtGrow**, **CArray::InsertAt**

CArray::SetAt

void SetAt(int *nIndex***,** *ARG_TYPE newElement* **);**

Parameters

nIndex   An integer index that is greater than or equal to 0 and less than or equal to the value returned by **GetUpperBound**.

ARG_TYPE   Template parameter specifying the type of arguments used for referencing array elements.

newElement   The new element value to be stored at the specified position.

Remarks

Sets the array element at the specified index. **SetAt** will not cause the array to grow. Use **SetAtGrow** if you want the array to grow automatically.

You must ensure that your index value represents a valid position in the array. If it is out of bounds, then the Debug version of the library asserts.

See Also: CArray::GetAt, CArray::SetAtGrow, CArray::ElementAt, CArray::operator []

CArray::SetAtGrow

void SetAtGrow(int *nIndex***,** *ARG_TYPE newElement* **);**
  throw(CMemoryException);

Parameters

nIndex   An integer index that is greater than or equal to 0.

ARG_TYPE   Template parameter specifying the type of elements in the array.

newElement   The element to be added to this array. A **NULL** value is allowed.

Remarks

Sets the array element at the specified index. The array grows automatically if necessary (that is, the upper bound is adjusted to accommodate the new element).

Example

```
// example for CArray::SetAtGrow
CArray<CPoint,CPoint> ptArray;

ptArray.Add(CPoint(10,20));// Element 0
ptArray.Add(CPoint(30,40));// Element 1
                   // Element 2 deliberately skipped
ptArray.SetAtGrow(3, CPoint(50,60)); // Element 3
```

See Also: CArray::GetAt, CArray::SetAt, CArray::ElementAt, CArray::operator []

CArray::SetSize

void SetSize(int *nNewSize***, int** *nGrowBy* **= –1);**
   throw(CMemoryException);

Parameters

nNewSize The new array size (number of elements). Must be greater than or equal to 0.

nGrowBy The minimum number of element slots to allocate if a size increase is necessary.

Remarks

Establishes the size of an empty or existing array; allocates memory if necessary.

If the new size is smaller than the old size, then the array is truncated and all unused memory is released.

Use this function to set the size of your array before you begin using the array. If you do not use **SetSize**, adding elements to your array causes it to be frequently reallocated and copied. Frequent reallocation and copying are inefficient and can fragment memory.

The *nGrowBy* parameter affects internal memory allocation while the array is growing. Its use never affects the array size as reported by **GetSize** and **GetUpperBound**. If the default value is used, MFC allocates memory in a way calculated to avoid memory fragmentation and optimize efficiency for most cases.

See Also: **CArray::GetUpperBound, CArray::GetSize**

Operators

CArray::operator [ ]

*TYPE***& operator [](int** *nIndex* **);**
TYPE **operator [](int** *nIndex* **) const;**

Parameters

TYPE Template parameter specifying the type of elements in this array.

nIndex Index of the element to be accessed.

Remarks

These subscript operators are a convenient substitute for the **SetAt** and **GetAt** functions.

The first operator, called for arrays that are not **const**, may be used on either the right (r-value) or the left (l-value) of an assignment statement. The second, called for **const** arrays, may be used only on the right.

The Debug version of the library asserts if the subscript (either on the left or right side of an assignment statement) is out of bounds.

See Also: CArray::GetAt, CArray::SetAt, CArray::ElementAt

CAsyncMonikerFile

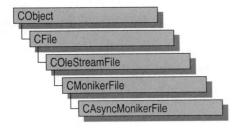

CAsyncMonikerFile provides functionality for the use of asynchronous monikers in ActiveX controls (formerly OLE controls). Derived from **CMonikerFile**, which in turn is derived from **COleStreamFile**, **CAsyncMonikerFile** uses the IMoniker interface to access any data stream asynchronously, including loading files asynchronously from a URL. The files can be datapath properties of ActiveX controls.

Asynchronous monikers are used primarily in Internet-enabled applications and ActiveX controls to provide a responsive user-interface during file transfers. A prime example of this is the use of **CDataPathProperty** to provide asynchronous properties for ActiveX controls. The **CDataPathProperty** object will repeatedly get a callback to indicate availability of new data during a lengthy property exchange process.

For more information about how to use asynchronous monikers and ActiveX controls in Internet applications, see the following articles in *Visual C++ Programmer's Guide* online:

- Internet First Steps: Asynchronous Monikers
- Internet First Steps: ActiveX Controls

#include <afxole.h>

See Also: **CMonikerFile**, **CDataPathProperty**, Asynchronous Versus Synchronous Monikers in the *OLE Programmer's Reference* in the Win32 SDK

CAsyncMonikerFile Class Members

Construction

CAsyncMonikerFile	Constructs a **CAsyncMonikerFile** object.

Operations

GetBinding	Retrieves a pointer to the asynchronous transfer binding.
GetFormatEtc	Retrieves the format of the data in the stream.

Overridables

Close	Closes and releases all resources.
CreateBindStatusCallback	Creates a COM object that implements **IBindStatusCallback**.
GetBindInfo	Called by the OLE system library to request information on the type of bind to be created.
GetPriority	Called by the OLE system library to get the priority of the binding.
OnDataAvailable	Called to provide data as it becomes available to the client during asynchronous bind operations.
OnLowResource	Called when resources are low.
OnProgress	Called to indicate progress on the data downloading process.
OnStartBinding	Called when binding is starting up.
OnStopBinding	Called when asynchronous transfer is stopped.
Open	Opens a file asynchronously.

Member Functions
CAsyncMonikerFile::CAsyncMonikerFile

CAsyncMonikerFile( );

Remarks

Constructs a **CAsyncMonikerFile** object. It does not create the **IBindHost** interface. **IBindHost** is used only if you provide it in the **Open** member function.

For a description of the **IBindHost** interface, see the *ActiveX SDK*.

See Also: **CDataPathProperty**, **CAsyncMonikerFile::Open**

CAsyncMonikerFile::Close

virtual void Close( );

Remarks

Call this function to close and release all resources. Can be called on unopened or already closed files.

See Also: **CAsyncMonikerFile::Open**

CAsyncMonikerFile::CreateBindStatusCallback

virtual IUnknown* CreateBindStatusCallback(IUnknown* *pUnkControlling* **);**

Return Value

If *pUnkControlling* is not **NULL**, the function returns a pointer to the inner **IUnknown** on a new COM object supporting **IBindStatusCallback**. If *pUnkControlling* is **NULL**, the function returns a pointer to an **IUnknown** on a new COM object supporting **IBindStatusCallback**.

Parameters

pUnkControlling   A pointer to the controlling unknown (the outer **IUnknown**) or **NULL** if aggregation is not being used.

Remarks

CAsyncMonikerFile requires a COM object that implements **IBindStatusCallback**. MFC implements such an object, and it is aggregatable. You can override **CreateBindStatusCallback** to return your own COM object. Your COM object can aggregate MFC's implementation by calling **CAsyncMonikerFile::CreateBindStatusCallback** with the controlling unknown of your COM object.

Alternately, your COM object can delegate to MFC's implementation by calling **CAsyncMonikerFile::CreateBindStatusCallback(NULL)**.

CAsyncMonikerFile::Open calls **CreateBindStatusCallback(NULL)**.

For details about the asynchronous binding, see "How Asynchronous Binding and Storage Work" in the *OLE Programmer's Reference* in the Win32 SDK . For a discussion of aggregation, see "Aggregation" in the *OLE Programmer's Reference* in the Win32 SDK.

CAsyncMonikerFile::GetBindInfo

virtual DWORD GetBindInfo( ) const;

Return Value

Retrieves the settings for **IBindStatusCallBack**. For a description of the **IBindStatusCallback** interface, see the *ActiveX SDK*.

Remarks

Called from the client of an asynchronous moniker to tell the asynchronous moniker how it wants to bind. The default implementation sets the binding to be asynchronous, to use a storage medium (a stream), and to use the data-push model. Override this function if you want to change the behavior of the binding.

One reason for doing this would be to bind using the data-pull model instead of the data-push model. In a data-pull model, the client drives the bind operation, and the moniker only provides data to the client when it is read. In a data-push model, the moniker drives the asynchronous bind operation and continuously notifies the client whenever new data is available.

CAsyncMonikerFile::GetBinding

IBinding* GetBinding( ) const;

Return Value

A pointer to the **IBinding** interface provided when asynchronous transfer begins. Returns **NULL** if for any reason the transfer cannot be made asynchronously.

Remarks

Call this function to retrieve a pointer to the asynchronous transfer binding. This allows you to control the data transfer process through the **IBinding** interface, for example, with **IBinding::Abort**, **IBinding::Pause**, and **IBinding::Resume**.

For a description of the **IBinding** interface, see the *ActiveX SDK*.

CAsyncMonikerFile::GetFormatEtc

FORMATETC* GetFormatEtc( ) const;

Return Value

A pointer to the Windows structure **FORMATETC** for the currently opened stream. Returns **NULL** if the moniker has not been bound, if it is not asynchronous, or if the asynchronous operation has not begun.

Remarks

Call this function to retrieve the format of the data in the stream.

CAsyncMonikerFile::GetPriority

virtual long GetPriority( ) const;

Return Value

The priority at which the asynchronous transfer will take place. One of the standard thread priority flags: **THREAD_PRIORITY_ABOVE_NORMAL**, **THREAD_PRIORITY_BELOW_NORMAL**, **THREAD_PRIORITY_HIGHEST**, **THREAD_PRIORITY_IDLE**, **THREAD_PRIORITY_LOWEST**, **THREAD_PRIORITY_NORMAL**, and **THREAD_PRIORITY_TIME_CRITICAL**. See the Windows function **SetThreadPriority** for a description of these values.

Remarks

Called from the client of an asynchronous moniker as the binding process starts to receive the priority given to the thread for the binding operation. **GetPriority** should not be called directly. **THREAD_PRIORITY_NORMAL** is returned by the default implementation.

CAsyncMonikerFile::OnDataAvailable

virtual void OnDataAvailable(DWORD *dwsize*, **DWORD** *bscfFlag* **);**

Parameters

dwsize   The cumulative amount (in bytes) of data available since the beginning of the binding. Can be zero, indicating that the amount of data is not relevant to the operation, or that no specific amount became available.

bscfFlag   A **BSCF** enumeration value. Can be one or more of the following values:

- **BSCF_FIRSTDATANOTIFICATION**   Identifies the first call to **OnDataAvailable** for a given bind operation.

- **BSCF_INTERMEDIATEDATANOTIFICATION**   Identifies an intermediary call to **OnDataAvailable** for a bind operation.

- **BSCF_LASTDATANOTIFICATION**   Identifies the last call to **OnDataAvailable** for a bind operation.

Remarks

An asynchronous moniker calls **OnDataAvailable** to provide data to the client as it becomes available, during asynchronous bind operations. The default implementation of this function does nothing. See the following example for a sample implementation.

Example

```
// refer to CDataPathProperty.
void CAsyncMyTextProperty::OnDataAvailable(CFile* pfile,
↪ DWORD dwSize, DWORD grfBSCF)
{
    if ((grfBSCF & BSCF_FIRSTDATANOTIFICATION) != 0)
    {
        m_dwReadBefore = 0;
        m_strText.Empty();
    }

    DWORD dwArriving = dwSize - m_dwReadBefore;

    if (dwArriving > 0)
    {
        int nLen = m_strText.GetLength();
        ASSERT(nLen == m_dwReadBefore);
        LPTSTR psz = m_strText.GetBuffer(nLen + dwArriving);
        pFile->Read(psz + nLen, dwArriving);
        m_strText.ReleaseBuffer(nLen + dwArriving);
        m_dwReadBefore = dwSize;
        GetControl()->Invalidate();
    }
}
```

See Also: CDataPathProperty

CAsyncMonikerFile::OnLowResource

virtual void OnLowResource( );

Remarks

Called by the moniker when resources are low. The default implementation calls
`GetBinding( )-> Abort( )`.

CAsyncMonikerFile::OnProgress

virtual void OnProgress(ULONG *ulProgress*, **ULONG** *ulProgressMax*,
↪ **ULONG** *ulStatusCode*, **LPCTSTR** *szStatusText*);

Parameters

ulProgress Indicates the current progress of the bind operation relative to the
expected maximum indicated in *ulProgressMax*.

ulProgressMax Indicates the expected maximum value of *ulProgress* for the duration
of calls to **OnProgress** for this operation.

ulStatusCode Provides additional information regarding the progress of the bind
operation. Valid values are taken from the **BINDSTATUS** enumeration. See
Remarks for possible values.

szStatusText Information about the current progress, depending on the value of
ulStatusCode. See Remarks for possible values.

Remarks

Called by the moniker repeatedly to indicate the current progress of this bind
operation, typically at reasonable intervals during a lengthy operation.

Possible values for *ulStatusCode* (and the *szStatusText* for each value) are:

BINDSTATUS_FINDINGRESOURCE The bind operation is finding the resource
that holds the object or storage being bound to. The *szStatusText* provides the
display name of the resource being searched for (for example,
"www.microsoft.com").

BINDSTATUS_CONNECTING The bind operation is connecting to the resource
that holds the object or storage being bound to. The *szStatusText* provides the
display name of the resource being connected to (for example, an IP address).

BINDSTATUS_SENDINGREQUEST The bind operation is requesting the object
or storage being bound to. The *szStatusText* provides the display name of the object
(for example, a file name).

BINDSTATUS_REDIRECTING The bind operation has been redirected to a
different data location. The *szStatusText* provides the display name of the new data
location.

BINDSTATUS_USINGCACHEDCOPY   The bind operation is retrieving the requested object or storage from a cached copy. The *szStatusText* is **NULL**.

BINDSTATUS_BEGINDOWNLOADDATA   The bind operation has begun receiving the object or storage being bound to. The *szStatusText* provides the display name of the data location.

BINDSTATUS_DOWNLOADINGDATA   The bind operation continues to receive the object or storage being bound to. The *szStatusText* provides the display name of the data location.

BINDSTATUS_ENDDOWNLOADDATA   The bind operation has finished receiving the object or storage being bound to. The *szStatusText* provides the display name of the data location.

BINDSTATUS_CLASSIDAVAILABLE   An instance of the object being bound to is just about to be created. The *szStatusText* provides the CLSID of the new object in string format, allowing the client an opportunity to cancel the bind operation, if desired.

CAsyncMonikerFile::OnStartBinding

virtual void OnStartBinding( );

Remarks

Override this function in your derived classes to perform actions when binding is starting up. This function is called back by the moniker. The default implementation does nothing.

See Also: CAsyncMonikerFile::OnStopBinding

CAsyncMonikerFile::OnStopBinding

virtual void OnStopBinding(HRESULT *hresult*, LPCTSTR *szError*);

Parameters

hresult   An **HRESULT** that is the error or warning value.

szErrort   A character string describing the error.

Remarks

Called by the moniker at the end of the bind operation. Override this function to perform actions when the transfer is stopped. By default, the function releases **IBinding**.

For a description of the **IBinding** interface, see the *ActiveX SDK*.

See Also: CAsyncMonikerFile::OnStartBinding

CAsyncMonikerFile::Open

virtual BOOL Open(LPCTSTR *lpszURL*, **CFileException*** *pError* = **NULL**);
virtual BOOL Open(IMoniker* *pMoniker*, **CFileException*** *pError* = **NULL**);
virtual BOOL Open(LPCTSTR *lpszURL*, **IBindHost*** *pBindHost*,
  ↳ **CFileException*** *pError* = **NULL**);
virtual BOOL Open(IMoniker* *pMoniker*, **IBindHost*** *pBindHost*,
  ↳ **CFileException*** *pError* = **NULL**);
virtual BOOL Open(LPCTSTR *lpszURL*, **IServiceProvider*** *pServiceProvider*,
  ↳ **CFileException*** *pError* = **NULL**);
virtual BOOL Open(IMoniker* *pMoniker*, **IServiceProvider*** *pServiceProvider*,
  ↳ **CFileException*** *pError* = **NULL**);
virtual BOOL Open(LPCTSTR *lpszURL*, **IUnknown*** *pUnknown*,
  ↳ **CFileException*** *pError* = **NULL**);
virtual BOOL Open(IMoniker* *pMoniker*, **IUnknown*** *pUnknown*,
  ↳ **CFileException*** *pError* = **NULL**);

Return Value

Nonzero if the file is opened successfully; otherwise 0.

Parameters

lpszURL   A pointer to file to be opened asynchronously. The file can be any valid URL or filename.

pError   A pointer to the file exceptions. In the event of an error, it will be set to the cause.

pMoniker   A pointer to the asynchronous moniker interface **IMoniker**, a precise moniker that is the combination of the document's own moniker, which you can retrieve with **IOleClientSite::GetMoniker(** *OLEWHICHMK_CONTAINER*), and a moniker created from the path name. The control can use this moniker to bind, but this is not the moniker the control should save.

pBindHost   A pointer to the **IBindHost** interface that will be used to create the moniker from a potentially relative pathname. If the bind host is invalid or does not provide a moniker, the call defaults to **Open(** *lpszFileName*, *pError*). For a description of the **IBindHost** interface, see the *ActiveX SDK*.

pServiceProvider   A pointer to the **IServiceProvider** interface. If the service provider is invalid or fails to provide the service for **IBindHost**, the call defaults to **Open(** *lpszFileName*, *pError*).

pUnknown   A pointer to the **IUnknown** interface. If **IServiceProvider** is found, the function queries for **IBindHost**. If the service provider is invalid or fails to provide the service for **IBindHost**, the call defaults to **Open(** *lpszFileName*, *pError*).

Remarks

Call this member function to open a file asynchronously. This call initiates the binding process.

You can use a URL or a filename for the *lpszURL* parameter. For example:

```
CMyAsyncMonFile mamf;
mamf.Open(_T("http://www.microsoft.com"));
```

—or—

```
CMyAsyncMonFile mamf;
mamf.Open(_T("file:c:\mydata.dat"));
```

See Also: CAsyncMonikerFile::CAsyncMonikerFile

CAsyncSocket

A **CAsyncSocket** object represents a Windows Socket—an endpoint of network communication. Class **CAsyncSocket** encapsulates the Windows Sockets API, providing an object-oriented abstraction for programmers who want to use Windows Sockets in conjunction with MFC.

This class is based on the assumption that you understand network communications. You are responsible for handling blocking, byte-order differences, and conversions between Unicode and multibyte character set (MBCS) strings. If you want a more convenient interface that manages these issues for you, see class **CSocket**.

To use a **CAsyncSocket** object, call its constructor, then call the **Create** function to create the underlying socket handle (type **SOCKET**), except on accepted sockets. For a server socket call the **Listen** member function, and for a client socket call the **Connect** member function. The server socket should call the **Accept** function upon receiving a connection request. Use the remaining **CAsyncSocket** functions to carry out communications between sockets. Upon completion, destroy the **CAsyncSocket** object if it was created on the heap; the destructor automatically calls the **Close** function. The **SOCKET** data type is described in the article "Windows Sockets: Background" in *Visual C++ Programmer's Guide* online.

For more information, see "Windows Sockets: Using Class CAsyncSocket" and related articles in *Visual C++ Programmer's Guide* online, as well as "Overview of Windows Sockets 2" and "Windows Sockets Programming Considerations" in the Win32 SDK documentation.

#include <afxsock.h>

See Also: **CSocket, CSocketFile**

CAsyncSocket Class Members

Construction

CAsyncSocket	Constructs a **CAsyncSocket** object.
Create	Creates a socket.

Attributes

Attach	Attaches a socket handle to a **CAsyncSocket** object.
Detach	Detaches a socket handle from a **CAsyncSocket** object.
FromHandle	Returns a pointer to a **CAsyncSocket** object, given a socket handle.
GetLastError	Gets the error status for the last operation that failed.
GetPeerName	Gets the address of the peer socket to which the socket is connected.
GetSockName	Gets the local name for a socket.
GetSockOpt	Retrieves a socket option.
SetSockOpt	Sets a socket option.

Operations

Accept	Accepts a connection on the socket.
AsyncSelect	Requests event notification for the socket.
Bind	Associates a local address with the socket.
Close	Closes the socket.
Connect	Establishes a connection to a peer socket.
IOCtl	Controls the mode of the socket.
Listen	Establishes a socket to listen for incoming connection requests.
Receive	Receives data from the socket.
ReceiveFrom	Receives a datagram and stores the source address.
Send	Sends data to a connected socket.
SendTo	Sends data to a specific destination.
ShutDown	Disables **Send** and/or **Receive** calls on the socket.

Overridable Notification Functions

OnAccept	Notifies a listening socket that it can accept pending connection requests by calling **Accept**.
OnClose	Notifies a socket that the socket connected to it has closed.
OnConnect	Notifies a connecting socket that the connection attempt is complete, whether successfully or in error.
OnOutOfBandData	Notifies a receiving socket that there is out-of-band data to be read on the socket, usually an urgent message.
OnReceive	Notifies a listening socket that there is data to be retrieved by calling **Receive**.
OnSend	Notifies a socket that it can send data by calling **Send**.

Data Members

m_hSocket	Indicates the **SOCKET** handle attached to this **CAsyncSocket** object.

Member Functions

CAsyncSocket::Accept

virtual BOOL Accept(CAsyncSocket& *rConnectedSocket*,
↳ **SOCKADDR*** *lpSockAddr* **= NULL, int*** *lpSockAddrLen* **= NULL);**

Return Value

Nonzero if the function is successful; otherwise 0, and a specific error code can be retrieved by calling **GetLastError**. The following errors apply to this member function:

- **WSANOTINITIALISED** A successful **AfxSocketInit** must occur before using this API.

- **WSAENETDOWN** The Windows Sockets implementation detected that the network subsystem failed.

- **WSAEFAULT** The *lpSockAddrLen* argument is too small (less than the size of a **SOCKADDR** structure).

- **WSAEINPROGRESS** A blocking Windows Sockets call is in progress.

- **WSAEINVAL** **Listen** was not invoked prior to accept.

- **WSAEMFILE** The queue is empty upon entry to accept and there are no descriptors available.

- **WSAENOBUFS** No buffer space is available.

- **WSAENOTSOCK** The descriptor is not a socket.

- **WSAEOPNOTSUPP** The referenced socket is not a type that supports connection-oriented service.

- **WSAEWOULDBLOCK** The socket is marked as nonblocking and no connections are present to be accepted.

Parameters

rConnectedSocket A reference identifying a new socket that is available for connection.

lpSockAddr A pointer to a **SOCKADDR** structure that receives the address of the connecting socket, as known on the network. The exact format of the *lpSockAddr* argument is determined by the address family established when the socket was created. If *lpSockAddr* and/or *lpSockAddrLen* are equal to **NULL**, then no information about the remote address of the accepted socket is returned.

lpSockAddrLen A pointer to the length of the address in *lpSockAddr* in bytes. The *lpSockAddrLen* is a value-result parameter: it should initially contain the amount of space pointed to by *lpSockAddr*; on return it will contain the actual length (in bytes) of the address returned.

Remarks

Call this member function to accept a connection on a socket. This routine extracts the first connection in the queue of pending connections, creates a new socket with the same properties as this socket, and attaches it to *rConnectedSocket*. If no pending connections are present on the queue, **Accept** returns zero and **GetLastError** returns an error. The accepted socket (*rConnectedSocket)* cannot be used to accept more connections. The original socket remains open and listening.

The argument *lpSockAddr* is a result parameter that is filled in with the address of the connecting socket, as known to the communications layer. **Accept** is used with connection-based socket types such as **SOCK_STREAM**.

See Also: **CAsyncSocket::Bind**, **CAsyncSocket::Connect**, **CAsyncSocket::Listen**, **CAsyncSocket::Create**, **::WSAAsyncSelect**

CAsyncSocket::AsyncSelect

BOOL AsyncSelect(long *lEvent* **= FD_READ | FD_WRITE | FD_OOB |**
↪ FD_ACCEPT | FD_CONNECT | FD_CLOSE);

Return Value

Nonzero if the function is successful; otherwise 0, and a specific error code can be retrieved by calling **GetLastError**. The following errors apply to this member function:

- **WSANOTINITIALISED**   A successful **AfxSocketInit** must occur before using this API.

- **WSAENETDOWN**   The Windows Sockets implementation detected that the network subsystem failed.

- **WSAEINVAL**   Indicates that one of the specified parameters was invalid.

- **WSAEINPROGRESS**   A blocking Windows Sockets operation is in progress.

Parameters

lEvent   A bitmask which specifies a combination of network events in which the application is interested.

- **FD_READ**   Want to receive notification of readiness for reading.

- **FD_WRITE**   Want to receive notification when data is available to be read.

- **FD_OOB**   Want to receive notification of the arrival of out-of-band data.

- **FD_ACCEPT**   Want to receive notification of incoming connections.

- **FD_CONNECT**   Want to receive notification of connection results.

- **FD_CLOSE**   Want to receive notification when a socket has been closed by a peer.

Remarks

Call this member function to request event notification for a socket. This function is used to specify which MFC callback notification functions will be called for the socket. **AsyncSelect** automatically sets this socket to nonblocking mode. For more information, see the article "Windows Sockets: Socket Notifications" in *Visual C++ Programmer's Guide* online and "Overview of Windows Sockets 2" and "Windows Sockets Programming Considerations" in the Win32 SDK documentation.

See Also: **CAsyncSocket::GetLastError**, **::WSAAsyncSelect**

CAsyncSocket::Attach

BOOL Attach(SOCKET *hSocket*, **long** *lEvent* = **FD_READ** | **FD_WRITE** |
↳ **FD_OOB** | **FD_ACCEPT** | **FD_CONNECT** | **FD_CLOSE**);

Return Value

Nonzero if the function is successful.

Parameters

hSocket   Contains a handle to a socket.

lEvent   A bitmask which specifies a combination of network events in which the application is interested.

- **FD_READ**   Want to receive notification of readiness for reading.

- **FD_WRITE**   Want to receive notification when data is available to be read.

- **FD_OOB**   Want to receive notification of the arrival of out-of-band data.

- **FD_ACCEPT**   Want to receive notification of incoming connections.

- **FD_CONNECT**   Want to receive notification of connection results.

- **FD_CLOSE**   Want to receive notification when a socket has been closed by a peer.

Remarks

Call this member function to attach the *hSocket* handle to an **CAsyncSocket** object. The **SOCKET** handle is stored in the object's **m_hSocket** data member.

See Also: **CAsyncSocket::Detach**

CAsyncSocket::Bind

BOOL Bind(UINT *nSocketPort*, **LPCTSTR** *lpszSocketAddress* = **NULL**);
BOOL Bind (const SOCKADDR* *lpSockAddr*, **int** *nSockAddrLen*);

Return Value

Nonzero if the function is successful; otherwise 0, and a specific error code can be retrieved by calling **GetLastError**. The following errors apply to this member function:

- **WSANOTINITIALISED**   A successful **AfxSocketInit** must occur before using this API.

- **WSAENETDOWN**   The Windows Sockets implementation detected that the network subsystem failed.

- **WSAEADDRINUSE**   The specified address is already in use. (See the **SO_REUSEADDR** socket option under **SetSockOpt**.)

- **WSAEFAULT**   The *nSockAddrLen* argument is too small (less than the size of a **SOCKADDR** structure).

- **WSAEINPROGRESS**   A blocking Windows Sockets call is in progress.

- **WSAEAFNOSUPPORT**   The specified address family is not supported by this port.

- **WSAEINVAL**   The socket is already bound to an address.

- **WSAENOBUFS**   Not enough buffers available, too many connections.

- **WSAENOTSOCK**   The descriptor is not a socket.

Parameters

nSocketPort   The port identifying the socket application.

lpszSocketAddress   The network address, a dotted number such as "128.56.22.8".

lpSockAddr   A pointer to a **SOCKADDR** structure that contains the address to assign to this socket.

nSockAddrLen   The length of the address in *lpSockAddr* in bytes.

Remarks

Call this member function to associate a local address with the socket. This routine is used on an unconnected datagram or stream socket, before subsequent **Connect** or **Listen** calls. Before it can accept connection requests, a listening server socket must select a port number and make it known to Windows Sockets by calling **Bind**. **Bind** establishes the local association (host address/port number) of the socket by assigning a local name to an unnamed socket.

See Also: **CAsyncSocket::Connect**, **CAsyncSocket::Listen**, **CAsyncSocket::GetSockName**, **CAsyncSocket::SetSockOpt**, **CAsyncSocket::Create**

CAsyncSocket::CAsyncSocket

CAsyncSocket( );

Remarks

Constructs a blank socket object. After constructing the object, you must call its **Create** member function to create the **SOCKET** data structure and bind its address.

(On the server side of a Windows Sockets communication, when the listening socket creates a socket to use in the **Accept** call, you do not call **Create** for that socket.)

See Also: CAsyncSocket::Create

CAsyncSocket::Close

virtual void Close( );

Remarks

This function closes the socket. More precisely, it releases the socket descriptor, so that further references to it will fail with the error **WSAENOTSOCK**. If this is the last reference to the underlying socket, the associated naming information and queued data are discarded. The socket object's destructor calls **Close** for you.

For **CAsyncSocket**, but not for **CSocket**, the semantics of **Close** are affected by the socket options **SO_LINGER** and **SO_DONTLINGER**. For further information, see member function **GetSockOpt** and "Overview of Windows Sockets 2" and "Windows Sockets Programming Considerations" in the Win32 SDK documentation.

See Also: CAsyncSocket::Accept, CAsyncSocket::CAsyncSocket, CAsyncSocket::IOCtl, CAsyncSocket::GetSockOpt, CAsyncSocket::SetSockOpt, CAsyncSocket::AsyncSelect

CAsyncSocket::Connect

BOOL Connect(LPCTSTR *lpszHostAddress***, UINT** *nHostPort* **);**
BOOL Connect(const SOCKADDR* *lpSockAddr***, int** *nSockAddrLen* **);**

Return Value

Nonzero if the function is successful; otherwise 0, and a specific error code can be retrieved by calling **GetLastError**. If this indicates an error code of **WSAEWOULDBLOCK**, and your application is using the overridable callbacks, your application will receive an **OnConnect** message when the connect operation is complete. The following errors apply to this member function:

- **WSANOTINITIALISED** A successful **AfxSocketInit** must occur before using this API.
- **WSAENETDOWN** The Windows Sockets implementation detected that the network subsystem failed.
- **WSAEADDRINUSE** The specified address is already in use.
- **WSAEINPROGRESS** A blocking Windows Sockets call is in progress.
- **WSAEADDRNOTAVAIL** The specified address is not available from the local machine.

- **WSAEAFNOSUPPORT**   Addresses in the specified family cannot be used with this socket.
- **WSAECONNREFUSED**   The attempt to connect was rejected.
- **WSAEDESTADDRREQ**   A destination address is required.
- **WSAEFAULT**   The *nSockAddrLen* argument is incorrect.
- **WSAEINVAL**   The socket is not already bound to an address.
- **WSAEISCONN**   The socket is already connected.
- **WSAEMFILE**   No more file descriptors are available.
- **WSAENETUNREACH**   The network cannot be reached from this host at this time.
- **WSAENOBUFS**   No buffer space is available. The socket cannot be connected.
- **WSAENOTSOCK**   The descriptor is not a socket.
- **WSAETIMEDOUT**   Attempt to connect timed out without establishing a connection.
- **WSAEWOULDBLOCK**   The socket is marked as nonblocking and the connection cannot be completed immediately.

Parameters

lpszHostAddress   The network address of the socket to which this object is connected: a machine name such as "ftp.microsoft.com", or a dotted number such as "128.56.22.8".

nHostPort   The port identifying the socket application.

lpSockAddr   A pointer to a **SOCKADDR** structure that contains the address of the connected socket.

nSockAddrLen   The length of the address in *lpSockAddr* in bytes.

Remarks

Call this member function to establish a connection to an unconnected stream or datagram socket. If the socket is unbound, unique values are assigned to the local association by the system, and the socket is marked as bound. Note that if the address field of the name structure is all zeroes, **Connect** will return zero. To get extended error information, call the **GetLastError** member function.

For stream sockets (type **SOCK_STREAM**), an active connection is initiated to the foreign host. When the socket call completes successfully, the socket is ready to send/receive data.

For a datagram socket (type **SOCK_DGRAM**), a default destination is set, which will be used on subsequent **Send** and **Receive** calls.

See Also: **CAsyncSocket::Accept**, **CAsyncSocket::Bind**, **CAsyncSocket::GetSockName**, **CAsyncSocket::Create**, **CAsyncSocket::AsyncSelect**

CAsyncSocket::Create

BOOL Create(UINT *nSocketPort* **= 0, int** *nSocketType* **= SOCK_STREAM,**
↪ **long** *lEvent* **= FD_READ | FD_WRITE | FD_OOB | FD_ACCEPT |**
↪ **FD_CONNECT | FD_CLOSE, LPCTSTR** *lpszSocketAddress* **= NULL);**

Return Value

Nonzero if the function is successful; otherwise 0, and a specific error code can be retrieved by calling **GetLastError**. The following errors apply to this member function:

- **WSANOTINITIALISED** A successful **AfxSocketInit** must occur before using this API.

- **WSAENETDOWN** The Windows Sockets implementation detected that the network subsystem failed.

- **WSAEAFNOSUPPORT** The specified address family is not supported.

- **WSAEINPROGRESS** A blocking Windows Sockets operation is in progress.

- **WSAEMFILE** No more file descriptors are available.

- **WSAENOBUFS** No buffer space is available. The socket cannot be created.

- **WSAEPROTONOSUPPORT** The specified port is not supported.

- **WSAEPROTOTYPE** The specified port is the wrong type for this socket.

- **WSAESOCKTNOSUPPORT** The specified socket type is not supported in this address family.

Parameters

nSocketPort A well-known port to be used with the socket, or 0 if you want Windows Sockets to select a port.

nSocketType **SOCK_STREAM** or **SOCK_DGRAM**.

lEvent A bitmask which specifies a combination of network events in which the application is interested.

- **FD_READ** Want to receive notification of readiness for reading.

- **FD_WRITE** Want to receive notification of readiness for writing.

- **FD_OOB** Want to receive notification of the arrival of out-of-band data.

- **FD_ACCEPT** Want to receive notification of incoming connections.

- **FD_CONNECT** Want to receive notification of completed connection.

- **FD_CLOSE** Want to receive notification of socket closure.

lpszSockAddress A pointer to a string containing the network address of the connected socket, a dotted number such as "128.56.22.8".

Remarks

Call the **Create** member function after constructing a socket object to create the Windows socket and attach it. **Create** then calls **Bind** to bind the socket to the specified address. The following socket types are supported:

- **SOCK_STREAM**   Provides sequenced, reliable, full-duplex, connection-based byte streams. Uses the Transmission Control Protocol (TCP) for the Internet address family.

- **SOCK_DGRAM**   Supports datagrams, which are connectionless, unreliable packets of a fixed (typically small) maximum length. Uses the User Datagram Protocol (UDP) for the Internet address family.

  Note   The **Accept** member function takes a reference to a new, empty **CSocket** object as its parameter. You must construct this object before you call **Accept**. Keep in mind that if this socket object goes out of scope, the connection closes. Do not call **Create** for this new socket object.

For more information about stream and datagram sockets, see the articles "Windows Sockets: Background" and "Windows Sockets: Ports and Socket Addresses" in *Visual C++ Programmer's Guide* online and "Overview of Windows Sockets 2" and "Windows Sockets Programming Considerations" in the Win32 SDK documentation.

See Also: **CAsyncSocket::Accept**, **CAsyncSocket::Bind**, **CAsyncSocket::Connect**, **CAsyncSocket::GetSockName**, **CAsyncSocket::IOCtl**, **CAsyncSocket::Listen**, **CAsyncSocket::Receive**, **CAsyncSocket::Send**, **CAsyncSocket::ShutDown**

CAsyncSocket::Detach

SOCKET Detach( );

Remarks

Call this member function to detach the **SOCKET** handle in the **m_hSocket** data member from the **CAsyncSocket** object and set **m_hSocket** to **NULL**.

See Also: **CAsyncSocket::Attach**

CAsyncSocket::FromHandle

static CAsyncSocket* PASCAL FromHandle(SOCKET *hSocket* **);**

Return Value

A pointer to an **CAsyncSocket** object, or **NULL** if there is no **CAsyncSocket** object attached to *hSocket*.

Parameters

hSocket   Contains a handle to a socket.

Remarks

Returns a pointer to a **CAsyncSocket** object. When given a **SOCKET** handle, if a **CAsyncSocket** object is not attached to the handle, the member function returns **NULL**.

See Also: **CSocket::FromHandle, CAsyncSocket::Attach, CAsyncSocket::Detach**

CAsyncSocket::GetLastError

static int GetLastError( );

Return Value

The return value indicates the error code for the last Windows Sockets API routine performed by this thread.

Remarks

Call this member function to get the error status for the last operation that failed. When a particular member function indicates that an error has occurred, **GetLastError** should be called to retrieve the appropriate error code. See the individual member function descriptions for a list of applicable error codes.

For more information about the error codes, see "Overview of Windows Sockets 2" and "Windows Sockets Programming Considerations" in the Win32 SDK documentation.

See Also: **::WSASetLastError**

CAsyncSocket::GetPeerName

BOOL GetPeerName(CString& *rPeerAddress*, **UINT&** *rPeerPort* **);**
BOOL GetPeerName(SOCKADDR* *lpSockAddr*, **int*** *lpSockAddrLen* **);**

Return Value

Nonzero if the function is successful; otherwise 0, and a specific error code can be retrieved by calling **GetLastError**. The following errors apply to this member function:

- **WSANOTINITIALISED** A successful **AfxSocketInit** must occur before using this API.

- **WSAENETDOWN** The Windows Sockets implementation detected that the network subsystem failed.

- **WSAEFAULT** The *lpSockAddrLen* argument is not large enough.

- **WSAEINPROGRESS** A blocking Windows Sockets call is in progress.

- **WSAENOTCONN** The socket is not connected.

- **WSAENOTSOCK** The descriptor is not a socket.

Parameters

rPeerAddress   Reference to a **CString** object that receives a dotted number IP address.

rPeerPort   Reference to a **UINT** that stores a port.

lpSockAddr   A pointer to the **SOCKADDR** structure that receives the name of the peer socket.

lpSockAddrLen   A pointer to the length of the address in *lpSockAddr* in bytes. On return, the *lpSockAddrLen* argument contains the actual size of *lpSockAddr* returned in bytes.

Remarks

Call this member function to get the address of the peer socket to which this socket is connected.

See Also: **CAsyncSocket::Bind**, **CAsyncSocket::Connect**, **CAsyncSocket::Create**, **CAsyncSocket::GetSockName**

CAsyncSocket::GetSockName

BOOL GetSockName(CString& *rSocketAddress***, UINT&** *rSocketPort* **);**
BOOL GetSockName(SOCKADDR* *lpSockAddr***, int*** *lpSockAddrLen* **);**

Return Value

Nonzero if the function is successful; otherwise 0, and a specific error code can be retrieved by calling **GetLastError**. The following errors apply to this member function:

- **WSANOTINITIALISED**   A successful **AfxSocketInit** must occur before using this API.

- **WSAENETDOWN**   The Windows Sockets implementation detected that the network subsystem failed.

- **WSAEFAULT**   The *lpSockAddrLen* argument is not large enough.

- **WSAEINPROGRESS**   A blocking Windows Sockets operation is in progress.

- **WSAENOTSOCK**   The descriptor is not a socket.

- **WSAEINVAL**   The socket has not been bound to an address with **Bind**.

Parameters

rSocketAddress   Reference to a **CString** object that receives a dotted number IP address.

rSocketPort   Reference to a **UINT** that stores a port.

lpSockAddr   A pointer to a **SOCKADDR** structure that receives the address of the socket.

lpSockAddrLen   A pointer to the length of the address in *lpSockAddr* in bytes.

Remarks

Call this member function to get the local name for a socket. This call is especially useful when a **Connect** call has been made without doing a **Bind** first; this call provides the only means by which you can determine the local association which has been set by the system. For more information, see "Overview of Windows Sockets 2" and "Windows Sockets Programming Considerations" in the Win32 SDK documentation.

See Also: **CAsyncSocket::Bind, CAsyncSocket::Create, CAsyncSocket::GetPeerName**

CAsyncSocket::GetSockOpt

BOOL GetSockOpt(int *nOptionName*, **void*** *lpOptionValue*, **int*** *lpOptionLen*, ⮡ **int** *nLevel* = **SOL_SOCKET**);

Return Value

Nonzero if the function is successful; otherwise 0, and a specific error code can be retrieved by calling **GetLastError**. If an option was never set with **SetSockOpt**, then **GetSockOpt** returns the default value for the option. The following errors apply to this member function:

- **WSANOTINITIALISED** A successful **AfxSocketInit** must occur before using this API.

- **WSAENETDOWN** The Windows Sockets implementation detected that the network subsystem failed.

- **WSAEFAULT** The *lpOptionLen* argument was invalid.

- **WSAEINPROGRESS** A blocking Windows Sockets operation is in progress.

- **WSAENOPROTOOPT** The option is unknown or unsupported. In particular, **SO_BROADCAST** is not supported on sockets of type **SOCK_STREAM**, while **SO_ACCEPTCONN, SO_DONTLINGER, SO_KEEPALIVE, SO_LINGER,** and **SO_OOBINLINE** are not supported on sockets of type **SOCK_DGRAM**.

- **WSAENOTSOCK** The descriptor is not a socket.

Parameters

nOptionName The socket option for which the value is to be retrieved.

lpOptionValue A pointer to the buffer in which the value for the requested option is to be returned. The value associated with the selected option is returned in the buffer *lpOptionValue*. The integer pointed to by *lpOptionLen* should originally contain the size of this buffer in bytes; and on return, it will be set to the size of the value returned. For **SO_LINGER**, this will be the size of a **LINGER** structure; for all other options it will be the size of a **BOOL** or an **int**, depending on the option. See the list of options and their sizes in the Remarks section.

lpOptionLen A pointer to the size of the *lpOptionValue* buffer in bytes.

nLevel   The level at which the option is defined; the only supported levels are **SOL_SOCKET** and **IPPROTO_TCP**.

Remarks

Call this member function to retrieve a socket option. **GetSockOpt** retrieves the current value for a socket option associated with a socket of any type, in any state, and stores the result in *lpOptionValue*. Options affect socket operations, such as the routing of packets, out-of-band data transfer, and so on.

The following options are supported for **GetSockOpt**. The Type identifies the type of data addressed by *lpOptionValue*. The **TCP_NODELAY** option uses level **IPPROTO_TCP**; all other options use level **SOL_SOCKET**.

Value	Type	Meaning
SO_ACCEPTCONN	BOOL	Socket is listening.
SO_BROADCAST	BOOL	Socket is configured for the transmission of broadcast messages.
SO_DEBUG	BOOL	Debugging is enabled.
SO_DONTLINGER	BOOL	If true, the **SO_LINGER** option is disabled.
SO_DONTROUTE	BOOL	Routing is disabled.
SO_ERROR	int	Retrieve error status and clear.
SO_KEEPALIVE	BOOL	Keep-alives are being sent.
SO_LINGER	struct LINGER	Returns the current linger options.
SO_OOBINLINE	BOOL	Out-of-band data is being received in the normal data stream.
SO_RCVBUF	int	Buffer size for receives.
SO_REUSEADDR	BOOL	The socket can be bound to an address which is already in use.
SO_SNDBUF	int	Buffer size for sends.
SO_TYPE	int	The type of the socket (for example, **SOCK_STREAM**).
TCP_NODELAY	BOOL	Disables the Nagle algorithm for send coalescing.

Berkeley Software Distribution (BSD) options not supported for **GetSockOpt** are:

Value	Type	Meaning
SO_RCVLOWAT	int	Receive low water mark.
SO_RCVTIMEO	int	Receive timeout.
SO_SNDLOWAT	int	Send low water mark.
SO_SNDTIMEO	int	Send timeout.
IP_OPTIONS		Get options in IP header.
TCP_MAXSEG	int	Get TCP maximum segment size.

Calling **GetSockOpt** with an unsupported option will result in an error code of **WSAENOPROTOOPT** being returned from **GetLastError**.

See Also: **CAsyncSocket::SetSockOpt**

CAsyncSocket::IOCtl

BOOL IOCtl(long *lCommand*, **DWORD*** *lpArgument* **);**

Return Value

Nonzero if the function is successful; otherwise 0, and a specific error code can be retrieved by calling **GetLastError**. The following errors apply to this member function:

- **WSANOTINITIALISED** A successful **AfxSocketInit** must occur before using this API.

- **WSAENETDOWN** The Windows Sockets implementation detected that the network subsystem failed.

- **WSAEINVAL** *lCommand* is not a valid command, or *lpArgument* is not an acceptable parameter for *lCommand*, or the command is not applicable to the type of socket supplied.

- **WSAEINPROGRESS** A blocking Windows Sockets operation is in progress.

- **WSAENOTSOCK** The descriptor is not a socket.

Parameters

lCommand The command to perform on the socket.

lpArgument A pointer to a parameter for *lCommand*.

Remarks

Call this member function to control the mode of a socket. This routine can be used on any socket in any state. It is used to get or retrieve operating parameters associated with the socket, independent of the protocol and communications subsystem. The following commands are supported:

- **FIONBIO** Enable or disable nonblocking mode on the socket. The *lpArgument* parameter points at a **DWORD**, which is nonzero if nonblocking mode is to be enabled and zero if it is to be disabled. If **AsyncSelect** has been issued on a socket, then any attempt to use **IOCtl** to set the socket back to blocking mode will fail with **WSAEINVAL**. To set the socket back to blocking mode and prevent the **WSAEINVAL** error, an application must first disable **AsyncSelect** by calling **AsyncSelect** with the *lEvent* parameter equal to 0, then call **IOCtl**.

- **FIONREAD** Determine the maximum number of bytes that can be read with one **Receive** call from this socket. The *lpArgument* parameter points at a **DWORD** in which **IOCtl** stores the result. If this socket is of type **SOCK_STREAM**, **FIONREAD** returns the total amount of data which can be read in a single

Receive; this is normally the same as the total amount of data queued on the socket. If this socket is of type **SOCK_DGRAM**, **FIONREAD** returns the size of the first datagram queued on the socket.

- **SIOCATMARK** Determine whether all out-of-band data has been read. This applies only to a socket of type **SOCK_STREAM** which has been configured for in-line reception of any out-of-band data (**SO_OOBINLINE**). If no out-of-band data is waiting to be read, the operation returns nonzero. Otherwise it returns 0, and the next **Receive** or **ReceiveFrom** performed on the socket will retrieve some or all of the data preceding the "mark"; the application should use the **SIOCATMARK** operation to determine whether any data remains. If there is any normal data preceding the "urgent" (out-of-band) data, it will be received in order. (Note that a **Receive** or **ReceiveFrom** will never mix out-of-band and normal data in the same call.) The *lpArgument* parameter points at a **DWORD** in which **IOCtl** stores the result.

This function is a subset of **ioctl()** as used in Berkeley sockets. In particular, there is no command which is equivalent to **FIOASYNC**, while **SIOCATMARK** is the only socket-level command which is supported.

See Also: **CAsyncSocket::AsyncSelect, CAsyncSocket::Create, CAsyncSocket::GetSockOpt, CAsyncSocket::SetSockOpt**

CAsyncSocket::Listen

BOOL Listen(int *nConnectionBacklog* **= 5);**

Return Value

Nonzero if the function is successful; otherwise 0, and a specific error code can be retrieved by calling **GetLastError**. The following errors apply to this member function:

- **WSANOTINITIALISED** A successful **AfxSocketInit** must occur before using this API.
- **WSAENETDOWN** The Windows Sockets implementation detected that the network subsystem failed.
- **WSAEADDRINUSE** An attempt has been made to listen on an address in use.
- **WSAEINPROGRESS** A blocking Windows Sockets operation is in progress.
- **WSAEINVAL** The socket has not been bound with **Bind** or is already connected.
- **WSAEISCONN** The socket is already connected.
- **WSAEMFILE** No more file descriptors are available.
- **WSAENOBUFS** No buffer space is available.
- **WSAENOTSOCK** The descriptor is not a socket.
- **WSAEOPNOTSUPP** The referenced socket is not of a type that supports the **Listen** operation.

Parameters

nConnectionBacklog   The maximum length to which the queue of pending connections can grow. Valid range is from 1 to 5.

Remarks

Call this member function to listen for incoming connection requests. To accept connections, the socket is first created with **Create**, a backlog for incoming connections is specified with **Listen**, and then the connections are accepted with **Accept**. **Listen** applies only to sockets that support connections, that is, those of type **SOCK_STREAM**. This socket is put into "passive" mode where incoming connections are acknowledged and queued pending acceptance by the process.

This function is typically used by servers (or any application that wants to accept connections) that could have more than one connection request at a time: if a connection request arrives with the queue full, the client will receive an error with an indication of **WSAECONNREFUSED**.

Listen attempts to continue to function rationally when there are no available ports (descriptors). It will accept connections until the queue is emptied. If ports become available, a later call to **Listen** or **Accept** will refill the queue to the current or most recent "backlog," if possible, and resume listening for incoming connections.

See Also: CAsyncSocket::Accept, CAsyncSocket::Connect, CAsyncSocket::Create

---

CAsyncSocket::OnAccept

virtual void OnAccept(int *nErrorCode* **);**

Parameters

nErrorCode   The most recent error on a socket. The following error codes applies to the **OnAccept** member function:

- **0**   The function executed successfully.

- **WSAENETDOWN**   The Windows Sockets implementation detected that the network subsystem failed.

Remarks

Called by the framework to notify a listening socket that it can accept pending connection requests by calling the **Accept** member function. For more information, see the article "Windows Sockets: Socket Notifications" in *Visual C++ Programmer's Guide* online.

See Also: CAsyncSocket::Accept, CAsyncSocket::GetLastError, CAsyncSocket::OnClose, CAsyncSocket::OnConnect, CAsyncSocket::OnOutOfBandData, CAsyncSocket::OnReceive, CAsyncSocket::OnSend

CAsyncSocket::OnClose

virtual void OnClose(int *nErrorCode* **);**

Parameters

> *nErrorCode* The most recent error on a socket. The following error codes apply to the **OnClose** member function:
>
> - **0** The function executed successfully.
> - **WSAENETDOWN** The Windows Sockets implementation detected that the network subsystem failed.
> - **WSAECONNRESET** The connection was reset by the remote side.
> - **WSAECONNABORTED** The connection was aborted due to timeout or other failure.

Remarks

> Called by the framework to notify this socket that the connected socket is closed by its process. For more information, see the article "Windows Sockets: Socket Notifications" in *Visual C++ Programmer's Guide* online.
>
> **See Also:** **CAsyncSocket::Close, CAsyncSocket::GetLastError, CAsyncSocket::OnAccept, CAsyncSocket::OnConnect, CAsyncSocket::OnOutOfBandData, CAsyncSocket::OnReceive, CAsyncSocket::OnSend**

CAsyncSocket::OnConnect

virtual void OnConnect(int *nErrorCode* **);**

Parameters

> *nErrorCode* The most recent error on a socket. The following error codes apply to the **OnConnect** member function:
>
> - **0** The function executed successfully.
> - **WSAEADDRINUSE** The specified address is already in use.
> - **WSAEADDRNOTAVAIL** The specified address is not available from the local machine.
> - **WSAEAFNOSUPPORT** Addresses in the specified family cannot be used with this socket.
> - **WSAECONNREFUSED** The attempt to connect was forcefully rejected.
> - **WSAEDESTADDRREQ** A destination address is required.
> - **WSAEFAULT** The *lpSockAddrLen* argument is incorrect.
> - **WSAEINVAL** The socket is already bound to an address.

- **WSAEISCONN**   The socket is already connected.

- **WSAEMFILE**   No more file descriptors are available.

- **WSAENETUNREACH**   The network cannot be reached from this host at this time.

- **WSAENOBUFS**   No buffer space is available. The socket cannot be connected.

- **WSAENOTCONN**   The socket is not connected.

- **WSAENOTSOCK**   The descriptor is a file, not a socket.

- **WSAETIMEDOUT**   The attempt to connect timed out without establishing a connection.

Remarks

Called by the framework to notify this connecting socket that its connection attempt is completed, whether successfully or in error.

Important   In **CSocket**, the **OnSend** and **OnConnect** notification functions are never called.

To send data, you simply call **Send**, which won't return until all the data has been sent. The use of the notification to complete this task is an MFC implementation detail for **CSocket**. For connections, you simply call **Connect**, which will return when the connection is completed (either successfully or in error). How connection notifications are handled is also an MFC implementation detail.

For more information, see the article "Windows Sockets: Socket Notifications" in *Visual C++ Programmer's Guide* online.

See Also: **CAsyncSocket::Connect, CAsyncSocket::GetLastError, CAsyncSocket::OnAccept, CAsyncSocket::OnClose, CAsyncSocket::OnOutOfBandData, CAsyncSocket::OnReceive, CAsyncSocket::OnSend**

CAsyncSocket::OnOutOfBandData

virtual void OnOutOfBandData(int *nErrorCode* **);**

Parameters

nErrorCode   The most recent error on a socket. The following error codes apply to the **OnOutOfBandData** member function:

- **0**   The function executed successfully.

- **WSAENETDOWN**   The Windows Sockets implementation detected that the network subsystem failed.

Remarks

Called by the framework to notify the receiving socket that the sending socket has out-of-band data to send. Out-of-band data is a logically independent channel that is associated with each pair of connected sockets of type **SOCK_STREAM**. The channel is generally used to send urgent data.

MFC supports out-of-band data, but users of class **CAsyncSocket** are discouraged from using it. The easier way is to create a second socket for passing such data. For more information about out-of-band data, see the article "Windows Sockets: Socket Notifications" in *Visual C++ Programmer's Guide* online and "Overview of Windows Sockets 2" and "Windows Sockets Programming Considerations" in the Win32 SDK documentation.

See Also: **CAsyncSocket::GetLastError, CAsyncSocket::OnAccept, CAsyncSocket::OnClose, CAsyncSocket::OnConnect, CAsyncSocket::OnReceive, CAsyncSocket::OnSend**

CAsyncSocket::OnReceive

virtual void OnReceive(int *nErrorCode* **);**

Parameters

nErrorCode   The most recent error on a socket. The following error codes apply to the **OnReceive** member function:

- **0**   The function executed successfully.

- **WSAENETDOWN**   The Windows Sockets implementation detected that the network subsystem failed.

Remarks

Called by the framework to notify this socket that there is data in the buffer that can be retrieved by calling the **Receive** member function. For more information, see the article "Windows Sockets: Socket Notifications" in *Visual C++ Programmer's Guide* online.

See Also: **CAsyncSocket::GetLastError, CAsyncSocket::OnAccept, CAsyncSocket::OnClose, CAsyncSocket::OnConnect, CAsyncSocket::OnOutOfBandData, CAsyncSocket::OnSend, CAsyncSocket::Receive**

CAsyncSocket::OnSend

virtual void OnSend(int *nErrorCode* **);**

Parameters

nErrorCode   The most recent error on a socket. The following error codes apply to the **OnSend** member function:

- **0**   The function executed successfully.

- **WSAENETDOWN**   The Windows Sockets implementation detected that the network subsystem failed.

Remarks

Called by the framework to notify the socket that it can now send data by calling the **Send** member function.

Important In **CSocket**, the **OnSend** and **OnConnect** notification functions are never called.

To send data, you simply call **Send**, which won't return until all the data has been sent. The use of the notification to complete this task is an MFC implementation detail for **CSocket**. For connections, you simply call **Connect**, which will return when the connection is completed (either successfully or in error). How connection notifications are handled is also an MFC implementation detail.

For more information, see the article "Windows Sockets: Socket Notifications" in *Visual C++ Programmer's Guide* online.

See Also: **CAsyncSocket::GetLastError, CAsyncSocket::OnAccept, CAsyncSocket::OnClose, CAsyncSocket::OnConnect, CAsyncSocket::OnOutOfBandData, CAsyncSocket::OnReceive, CAsyncSocket::Send**

CAsyncSocket::Receive

virtual int Receive(void* *lpBuf***, int** *nBufLen***, int** *nFlags* **= 0);**

Return Value

If no error occurs, **Receive** returns the number of bytes received. If the connection has been closed, it returns 0. Otherwise, a value of **SOCKET_ERROR** is returned, and a specific error code can be retrieved by calling **GetLastError**. The following errors apply to this member function:

- **WSANOTINITIALISED** A successful **AfxSocketInit** must occur before using this API.

- **WSAENETDOWN** The Windows Sockets implementation detected that the network subsystem failed.

- **WSAENOTCONN** The socket is not connected.

- **WSAEINPROGRESS** A blocking Windows Sockets operation is in progress.

- **WSAENOTSOCK** The descriptor is not a socket.

- **WSAEOPNOTSUPP** **MSG_OOB** was specified, but the socket is not of type **SOCK_STREAM**.

- **WSAESHUTDOWN** The socket has been shut down; it is not possible to call **Receive** on a socket after **ShutDown** has been invoked with *nHow* set to 0 or 2.

- **WSAEWOULDBLOCK** The socket is marked as nonblocking and the **Receive** operation would block.

- **WSAEMSGSIZE** The datagram was too large to fit into the specified buffer and was truncated.

- **WSAEINVAL** The socket has not been bound with **Bind**.

- **WSAECONNABORTED** The virtual circuit was aborted due to timeout or other failure.

- **WSAECONNRESET** The virtual circuit was reset by the remote side.

Parameters

lpBuf A buffer for the incoming data.

nBufLen The length of *lpBuf* in bytes.

nFlags Specifies the way in which the call is made. The semantics of this function are determined by the socket options and the *nFlags* parameter. The latter is constructed by combining any of the following values with the C++ **OR** operator:

- **MSG_PEEK** Peek at the incoming data. The data is copied into the buffer but is not removed from the input queue.

- **MSG_OOB** Process out-of-band data (see "Windows Sockets Programming Considerations" in the Win32 SDK documentation for a discussion of this topic).

Remarks

Call this member function to receive data from a socket. This function is used for connected stream or datagram sockets and is used to read incoming data.

For sockets of type **SOCK_STREAM**, as much information as is currently available up to the size of the buffer supplied is returned. If the socket has been configured for in-line reception of out-of-band data (socket option **SO_OOBINLINE**) and out-of-band data is unread, only out-of-band data will be returned. The application can use the **IOCtl SIOCATMARK** option or **OnOutOfBandData** to determine whether any more out-of-band data remains to be read.

For datagram sockets, data is extracted from the first enqueued datagram, up to the size of the buffer supplied. If the datagram is larger than the buffer supplied, the buffer is filled with the first part of the datagram, the excess data is lost, and **Receive** returns a value of **SOCKET_ERROR** with the error code set to **WSAEMSGSIZE**. If no incoming data is available at the socket, a value of **SOCKET_ERROR** is returned with the error code set to **WSAEWOULDBLOCK**. The **OnReceive** callback function can be used to determine when more data arrives.

If the socket is of type **SOCK_STREAM** and the remote side has shut down the connection gracefully, a **Receive** will complete immediately with 0 bytes received. If the connection has been reset, a **Receive** will fail with the error **WSAECONNRESET**.

See Also: CAsyncSocket::AsyncSelect, CAsyncSocket::Create, CAsyncSocket::ReceiveFrom, CAsyncSocket::Send

CAsyncSocket::ReceiveFrom

int ReceiveFrom(void* *lpBuf*, **int** *nBufLen*, **CString&** *rSocketAddress*,
 ↳ **UINT&** *rSocketPort*, **int** *nFlags* = **0**);
int ReceiveFrom(void* *lpBuf*, **int** *nBufLen*, **SOCKADDR*** *lpSockAddr*,
 ↳ **int*** *lpSockAddrLen*, **int** *nFlags* = **0**);

Return Value

If no error occurs, **ReceiveFrom** returns the number of bytes received. If the connection has been closed, it returns 0. Otherwise, a value of **SOCKET_ERROR** is returned, and a specific error code can be retrieved by calling **GetLastError**. The following errors apply to this member function:

- **WSANOTINITIALISED**   A successful **AfxSocketInit** must occur before using this API.
- **WSAENETDOWN**   The Windows Sockets implementation detected that the network subsystem failed.
- **WSAEFAULT**   The *lpSockAddrLen* argument was invalid: the *lpSockAddr* buffer was too small to accommodate the peer address.
- **WSAEINPROGRESS**   A blocking Windows Sockets operation is in progress.
- **WSAEINVAL**   The socket has not been bound with **Bind**.
- **WSAENOTCONN**   The socket is not connected (**SOCK_STREAM** only).
- **WSAENOTSOCK**   The descriptor is not a socket.
- **WSAEOPNOTSUPP**   **MSG_OOB** was specified, but the socket is not of type **SOCK_STREAM**.
- **WSAESHUTDOWN**   The socket has been shut down; it is not possible to call **ReceiveFrom** on a socket after **ShutDown** has been invoked with *nHow* set to 0 or 2.
- **WSAEWOULDBLOCK**   The socket is marked as nonblocking and the **ReceiveFrom** operation would block.
- **WSAEMSGSIZE**   The datagram was too large to fit into the specified buffer and was truncated.
- **WSAECONNABORTED**   The virtual circuit was aborted due to timeout or other failure.
- **WSAECONNRESET**   The virtual circuit was reset by the remote side.

Parameters

lpBuf   A buffer for the incoming data.

nBufLen   The length of *lpBuf* in bytes.

rSocketAddress   Reference to a **CString** object that receives a dotted number IP address.

rSocketPort   Reference to a **UINT** that stores a port.

lpSockAddr   A pointer to a **SOCKADDR** structure that holds the source address upon return.

lpSockAddrLen   A pointer to the length of the source address in *lpSockAddr* in bytes.

nFlags   Specifies the way in which the call is made. The semantics of this function are determined by the socket options and the *nFlags* parameter. The latter is constructed by combining any of the following values with the C++ **OR** operator:

- **MSG_PEEK**   Peek at the incoming data. The data is copied into the buffer but is not removed from the input queue.

- **MSG_OOB**   Process out-of-band data (see "Windows Sockets Programming Considerations" in the Win32 SDK documentation for a discussion of this topic).

Remarks

Call this member function to receive a datagram and store the source address in the **SOCKADDR** structure or in *rSocketAddress*. This function is used to read incoming data on a (possibly connected) socket and capture the address from which the data was sent.

For sockets of type **SOCK_STREAM**, as much information as is currently available up to the size of the buffer supplied is returned. If the socket has been configured for in-line reception of out-of-band data (socket option **SO_OOBINLINE**) and out-of-band data is unread, only out-of-band data will be returned. The application can use the **IOCtl SIOCATMARK** option or **OnOutOfBandData** to determine whether any more out-of-band data remains to be read. The *lpSockAddr* and *lpSockAddrLen* parameters are ignored for **SOCK_STREAM** sockets.

For datagram sockets, data is extracted from the first enqueued datagram, up to the size of the buffer supplied. If the datagram is larger than the buffer supplied, the buffer is filled with the first part of the message, the excess data is lost, and **ReceiveFrom** returns a value of **SOCKET_ERROR** with the error code set to **WSAEMSGSIZE**.

If *lpSockAddr* is nonzero, and the socket is of type **SOCK_DGRAM**, the network address of the socket which sent the data is copied to the corresponding **SOCKADDR** structure. The value pointed to by *lpSockAddrLen* is initialized to the size of this structure, and is modified on return to indicate the actual size of the address stored there. If no incoming data is available at the socket, the **ReceiveFrom** call waits for data to arrive unless the socket is nonblocking. In this case, a value of **SOCKET_ERROR** is returned with the error code set to **WSAEWOULDBLOCK**. The **OnReceive** callback can be used to determine when more data arrives.

If the socket is of type **SOCK_STREAM** and the remote side has shut down the connection gracefully, a **ReceiveFrom** will complete immediately with 0 bytes received.

See Also: CAsyncSocket::AsyncSelect, CAsyncSocket::Create, CAsyncSocket::Receive, CAsyncSocket::Send

CAsyncSocket::Send

virtual int Send(const void* *lpBuf*, **int** *nBufLen*, **int** *nFlags* **= 0);**

Return Value

If no error occurs, **Send** returns the total number of characters sent. (Note that this can be less than the number indicated by *nBufLen*.) Otherwise, a value of **SOCKET_ERROR** is returned, and a specific error code can be retrieved by calling **GetLastError**. The following errors apply to this member function:

- **WSANOTINITIALISED**   A successful **AfxSocketInit** must occur before using this API.

- **WSAENETDOWN**   The Windows Sockets implementation detected that the network subsystem failed.

- **WSAEACCES**   The requested address is a broadcast address, but the appropriate flag was not set.

- **WSAEINPROGRESS**   A blocking Windows Sockets operation is in progress.

- **WSAEFAULT**   The *lpBuf* argument is not in a valid part of the user address space.

- **WSAENETRESET**   The connection must be reset because the Windows Sockets implementation dropped it.

- **WSAENOBUFS**   The Windows Sockets implementation reports a buffer deadlock.

- **WSAENOTCONN**   The socket is not connected.

- **WSAENOTSOCK**   The descriptor is not a socket.

- **WSAEOPNOTSUPP**   **MSG_OOB** was specified, but the socket is not of type **SOCK_STREAM**.

- **WSAESHUTDOWN**   The socket has been shut down; it is not possible to call **Send** on a socket after **ShutDown** has been invoked with *nHow* set to 1 or 2.

- **WSAEWOULDBLOCK**   The socket is marked as nonblocking and the requested operation would block.

- **WSAEMSGSIZE**   The socket is of type **SOCK_DGRAM**, and the datagram is larger than the maximum supported by the Windows Sockets implementation.

- **WSAEINVAL**   The socket has not been bound with **Bind**.

- **WSAECONNABORTED**   The virtual circuit was aborted due to timeout or other failure.

- **WSAECONNRESET**   The virtual circuit was reset by the remote side.

Parameters

lpBuf   A buffer containing the data to be transmitted.

nBufLen   The length of the data in *lpBuf* in bytes.

nFlags   Specifies the way in which the call is made. The semantics of this function are determined by the socket options and the *nFlags* parameter. The latter is constructed by combining any of the following values with the C++ **OR** operator:

- **MSG_DONTROUTE**   Specifies that the data should not be subject to routing. A Windows Sockets supplier can choose to ignore this flag; see also the discussion of the **SO_DONTROUTE** option in "Windows Sockets Programming Considerations" in the Win32 SDK documentation.

- **MSG_OOB**   Send out-of-band data (**SOCK_STREAM** only).

Remarks

Call this member function to send data on a connected socket. **Send** is used to write outgoing data on connected stream or datagram sockets. For datagram sockets, care must be taken not to exceed the maximum IP packet size of the underlying subnets, which is given by the **iMaxUdpDg** element in the **WSADATA** structure returned by **AfxSocketInit**. If the data is too long to pass atomically through the underlying protocol, the error **WSAEMSGSIZE** is returned via **GetLastError**, and no data is transmitted.

Note that for a datagram socket the successful completion of a **Send** does not indicate that the data was successfully delivered.

On **CAsyncSocket** objects of type **SOCK_STREAM**, the number of bytes written can be between 1 and the requested length, depending on buffer availability on both the local and foreign hosts.

See Also: **CAsyncSocket::Create**, **CAsyncSocket::Receive**, **CAsyncSocket::ReceiveFrom**, **CAsyncSocket::SendTo**

CAsyncSocket::SendTo

int SendTo(const void* *lpBuf*, **int** *nBufLen*, **UINT** *nHostPort*,
↪ **LPCTSTR** *lpszHostAddress* = **NULL**, **int** *nFlags* = **0**);
int SendTo(const void* *lpBuf*, **int** *nBufLen*, **const SOCKADDR*** *lpSockAddr*,
↪ **int** *nSockAddrLen*, **int** *nFlags* = **0**);

Return Value

If no error occurs, **SendTo** returns the total number of characters sent. (Note that this can be less than the number indicated by *nBufLen*.) Otherwise, a value of **SOCKET_ERROR** is returned, and a specific error code can be retrieved by calling **GetLastError**. The following errors apply to this member function:

- **WSANOTINITIALISED** A successful **AfxSocketInit** must occur before using this API.

- **WSAENETDOWN** The Windows Sockets implementation detected that the network subsystem failed.

- **WSAEACCES** The requested address is a broadcast address, but the appropriate flag was not set.

- **WSAEINPROGRESS** A blocking Windows Sockets operation is in progress.

- **WSAEFAULT** The *lpBuf* or *lpSockAddr* parameters are not part of the user address space, or the *lpSockAddr* argument is too small (less than the size of a **SOCKADDR** structure).

- **WSAENETRESET** The connection must be reset because the Windows Sockets implementation dropped it.

- **WSAENOBUFS** The Windows Sockets implementation reports a buffer deadlock.

- **WSAENOTCONN** The socket is not connected (**SOCK_STREAM** only).

- **WSAENOTSOCK** The descriptor is not a socket.

- **WSAEOPNOTSUPP** **MSG_OOB** was specified, but the socket is not of type **SOCK_STREAM**.

- **WSAESHUTDOWN** The socket has been shut down; it is not possible to call **SendTo** on a socket after **ShutDown** has been invoked with *nHow* set to 1 or 2.

- **WSAEWOULDBLOCK** The socket is marked as nonblocking and the requested operation would block.

- **WSAEMSGSIZE** The socket is of type **SOCK_DGRAM**, and the datagram is larger than the maximum supported by the Windows Sockets implementation.

- **WSAECONNABORTED** The virtual circuit was aborted due to timeout or other failure.

- **WSAECONNRESET** The virtual circuit was reset by the remote side.

- **WSAEADDRNOTAVAIL** The specified address is not available from the local machine.

- **WSAEAFNOSUPPORT** Addresses in the specified family cannot be used with this socket.

- **WSAEDESTADDRREQ** A destination address is required.

- **WSAENETUNREACH** The network cannot be reached from this host at this time.

Parameters

lpBuf A buffer containing the data to be transmitted.

nBufLen The length of the data in *lpBuf* in bytes.

nHostPort   The port identifying the socket application.

lpszHostAddress   The network address of the socket to which this object is connected: a machine name such as "ftp.microsoft.com," or a dotted number such as "128.56.22.8".

nFlags   Specifies the way in which the call is made. The semantics of this function are determined by the socket options and the *nFlags* parameter. The latter is constructed by combining any of the following values with the C++ **OR** operator:

- **MSG_DONTROUTE**   Specifies that the data should not be subject to routing. A Windows Sockets supplier can choose to ignore this flag; see also the discussion of the **SO_DONTROUTE** option in "Windows Sockets Programming Considerations" in the Win32 SDK documentation.

- **MSG_OOB**   Send out-of-band data (**SOCK_STREAM** only).

lpSockAddr   A pointer to a **SOCKADDR** structure that contains the address of the target socket.

nSockAddrLen   The length of the address in *lpSockAddr* in bytes.

Remarks

Call this member function to send data to a specific destination. **SendTo** is used on datagram or stream sockets and is used to write outgoing data on a socket. For datagram sockets, care must be taken not to exceed the maximum IP packet size of the underlying subnets, which is given by the **iMaxUdpDg** element in the **WSADATA** structure filled out by **AfxSocketInit**. If the data is too long to pass atomically through the underlying protocol, the error **WSAEMSGSIZE** is returned, and no data is transmitted.

Note that the successful completion of a **SendTo** does not indicate that the data was successfully delivered.

SendTo is only used on a **SOCK_DGRAM** socket to send a datagram to a specific socket identified by the *lpSockAddr* parameter.

To send a broadcast (on a **SOCK_DGRAM** only), the address in the *lpSockAddr* parameter should be constructed using the special IP address **INADDR_BROADCAST** (defined in the Windows Sockets header file WINSOCK.H) together with the intended port number. Or, if the *lpszHostAddress* parameter is **NULL**, the socket is configured for broadcast. It is generally inadvisable for a broadcast datagram to exceed the size at which fragmentation can occur, which implies that the data portion of the datagram (excluding headers) should not exceed 512 bytes.

See Also: **CAsyncSocket::Create, CAsyncSocket::Receive, CAsyncSocket::ReceiveFrom, CAsyncSocket::Send**

CAsyncSocket::SetSockOpt

BOOL SetSockOpt(int *nOptionName*, **const void*** *lpOptionValue*, **int** *nOptionLen*,
↪ **int** *nLevel* = **SOL_SOCKET**);

Return Value

Nonzero if the function is successful; otherwise 0, and a specific error code can be retrieved by calling **GetLastError**. The following errors apply to this member function:

- **WSANOTINITIALISED**   A successful **AfxSocketInit** must occur before using this API.

- **WSAENETDOWN**   The Windows Sockets implementation detected that the network subsystem failed.

- **WSAEFAULT**   *lpOptionValue* is not in a valid part of the process address space.

- **WSAEINPROGRESS**   A blocking Windows Sockets operation is in progress.

- **WSAEINVAL**   *nLevel* is not valid, or the information in *lpOptionValue* is not valid.

- **WSAENETRESET**   Connection has timed out when **SO_KEEPALIVE** is set.

- **WSAENOPROTOOPT**   The option is unknown or unsupported. In particular, **SO_BROADCAST** is not supported on sockets of type **SOCK_STREAM**, while **SO_DONTLINGER**, **SO_KEEPALIVE**, **SO_LINGER**, and **SO_OOBINLINE** are not supported on sockets of type **SOCK_DGRAM**.

- **WSAENOTCONN**   Connection has been reset when **SO_KEEPALIVE** is set.

- **WSAENOTSOCK**   The descriptor is not a socket.

Parameters

nOptionName   The socket option for which the value is to be set.

lpOptionValue   A pointer to the buffer in which the value for the requested option is supplied.

nOptionLen   The size of the *lpOptionValue* buffer in bytes.

nLevel   The level at which the option is defined; the only supported levels are **SOL_SOCKET** and **IPPROTO_TCP**.

Remarks

Call this member function to set a socket option. **SetSockOpt** sets the current value for a socket option associated with a socket of any type, in any state. Although options can exist at multiple protocol levels, this specification only defines options that exist at the uppermost "socket" level. Options affect socket operations, such as whether expedited data is received in the normal data stream, whether broadcast messages can be sent on the socket, and so on.

There are two types of socket options: Boolean options that enable or disable a feature or behavior, and options which require an integer value or structure. To enable a Boolean option, *lpOptionValue* points to a nonzero integer. To disable the option *lpOptionValue* points to an integer equal to zero. *nOptionLen* should be equal to **sizeof(BOOL)** for Boolean options. For other options, *lpOptionValue* points to the integer or structure that contains the desired value for the option, and *nOptionLen* is the length of the integer or structure.

SO_LINGER controls the action taken when unsent data is queued on a socket and the **Close** function is called to close the socket. For more information, see "Windows Sockets Programming Considerations" in the Win32 SDK documentation.

By default, a socket cannot be bound (see **Bind**) to a local address which is already in use. On occasion, however, it may be desirable to "reuse" an address in this way. Since every connection is uniquely identified by the combination of local and remote addresses, there is no problem with having two sockets bound to the same local address as long as the remote addresses are different.

To inform the Windows Sockets implementation that a **Bind** call on a socket should not be disallowed because the desired address is already in use by another socket, the application should set the **SO_REUSEADDR** socket option for the socket before issuing the **Bind** call. Note that the option is interpreted only at the time of the **Bind** call: it is therefore unnecessary (but harmless) to set the option on a socket which is not to be bound to an existing address, and setting or resetting the option after the **Bind** call has no effect on this or any other socket.

An application can request that the Windows Sockets implementation enable the use of "keep-alive" packets on Transmission Control Protocol (TCP) connections by turning on the **SO_KEEPALIVE** socket option. (For information about "keep-alive" packets, see "Windows Sockets Programming Considerations" in the Win32 SDK documentation.) A Windows Sockets implementation need not support the use of keep-alives: if it does, the precise semantics are implementation-specific but should conform to section 4.2.3.6 of RFC 1122: "Requirements for Internet Hosts— Communication Layers." If a connection is dropped as the result of "keep-alives" the error code **WSAENETRESET** is returned to any calls in progress on the socket, and any subsequent calls will fail with **WSAENOTCONN**.

The **TCP_NODELAY** option disables the Nagle algorithm. The Nagle algorithm is used to reduce the number of small packets sent by a host by buffering unacknowledged send data until a full-size packet can be sent. However, for some applications this algorithm can impede performance, and **TCP_NODELAY** can be used to turn it off. Application writers should not set **TCP_NODELAY** unless the impact of doing so is well-understood and desired, since setting **TCP_NODELAY** can have a significant negative impact on network performance. **TCP_NODELAY** is the only supported socket option which uses level **IPPROTO_TCP**; all other options use level **SOL_SOCKET**.

Some implementations of Windows Sockets supply output debug information if the **SO_DEBUG** option is set by an application.

The following options are supported for **SetSockOpt**. The Type identifies the type of data addressed by *lpOptionValue*.

Value	Type	Meaning
SO_BROADCAST	**BOOL**	Allow transmission of broadcast messages on the socket.
SO_DEBUG	**BOOL**	Record debugging information.
SO_DONTLINGER	**BOOL**	Don't block **Close** waiting for unsent data to be sent. Setting this option is equivalent to setting **SO_LINGER** with **l_onoff** set to zero.
SO_DONTROUTE	**BOOL**	Don't route: send directly to interface.
SO_KEEPALIVE	**BOOL**	Send keep-alives.
SO_LINGER	**struct LINGER**	Linger on **Close** if unsent data is present.
SO_OOBINLINE	**BOOL**	Receive out-of-band data in the normal data stream.
SO_RCVBUF	**int**	Specify buffer size for receives.
SO_REUSEADDR	**BOOL**	Allow the socket to be bound to an address which is already in use. (See **Bind**.)
SO_SNDBUF	**int**	Specify buffer size for sends.
TCP_NODELAY	**BOOL**	Disables the Nagle algorithm for send coalescing.

Berkeley Software Distribution (BSD) options not supported for **SetSockOpt** are:

Value	Type	Meaning
SO_ACCEPTCONN	**BOOL**	Socket is listening
SO_ERROR	**int**	Get error status and clear.
SO_RCVLOWAT	**int**	Receive low water mark.
SO_RCVTIMEO	**int**	Receive timeout
SO_SNDLOWAT	**int**	Send low water mark.
SO_SNDTIMEO	**int**	Send timeout.
SO_TYPE	**int**	Type of the socket.
IP_OPTIONS		Set options field in IP header.

See Also: **CAsyncSocket::AsyncSelect, CAsyncSocket::Bind, CAsyncSocket::Create, CAsyncSocket::GetSockOpt, CAsyncSocket::IOCtl**

CAsyncSocket::ShutDown

BOOL ShutDown(int *nHow* **= sends);**

Return Value

Nonzero if the function is successful; otherwise 0, and a specific error code can be retrieved by calling **GetLastError**. The following errors apply to this member function:

- **WSANOTINITIALISED**   A successful **AfxSocketInit** must occur before using this API.

- **WSAENETDOWN**   The Windows Sockets implementation detected that the network subsystem failed.

- **WSAEINVAL**   *nHow* is not valid.

- **WSAEINPROGRESS**   A blocking Windows Sockets operation is in progress.

- **WSAENOTCONN**   The socket is not connected (**SOCK_STREAM** only).

- **WSAENOTSOCK**   The descriptor is not a socket.

Parameters

nHow   A flag that describes what types of operation will no longer be allowed, using the following enumerated values:

- **receives = 0**

- **sends = 1**

- **both = 2**

Remarks

Call this member function to disable sends and/or receives on the socket. **ShutDown** is used on all types of sockets to disable reception, transmission, or both. If *nHow* is 0, subsequent receives on the socket will be disallowed. This has no effect on the lower protocol layers.

For Transmission Control Protocol (TCP), the TCP window is not changed and incoming data will be accepted (but not acknowledged) until the window is exhausted. For User Datagram Protocol (UDP), incoming datagrams are accepted and queued. In no case will an ICMP error packet be generated. If *nHow* is 1, subsequent sends are disallowed. For TCP sockets, a FIN will be sent. Setting *nHow* to 2 disables both sends and receives as described above.

Note that **ShutDown** does not close the socket, and resources attached to the socket will not be freed until **Close** is called. An application should not rely on being able to reuse a socket after it has been shut down. In particular, a Windows Sockets implementation is not required to support the use of **Connect** on such a socket.

See Also: **CAsyncSocket::Connect, CAsyncSocket::Create**

Data Members

CAsyncSocket::m_hSocket

Remarks

Contains the **SOCKET** handle for the socket encapsulated by this **CAsyncSocket** object.

CBitmap

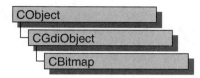

The **CBitmap** class encapsulates a Windows graphics device interface (GDI) bitmap and provides member functions to manipulate the bitmap. To use a **CBitmap** object, construct the object, attach a bitmap handle to it with one of the initialization member functions, and then call the object's member functions.

For more information on using graphic objects like **CBitmap**, see "Graphic Objects" in *Visual C++ Programmer's Guide* online.

#include <afxwin.h>

CBitmap Class Members

Construction

CBitmap	Constructs a **CBitmap** object.

Initialization

LoadBitmap	Initializes the object by loading a named bitmap resource from the application's executable file and attaching the bitmap to the object.
LoadOEMBitmap	Initializes the object by loading a predefined Windows bitmap and attaching the bitmap to the object.
LoadMappedBitmap	Loads a bitmap and maps colors to current system colors.
CreateBitmap	Initializes the object with a device-dependent memory bitmap that has a specified width, height, and bit pattern.
CreateBitmapIndirect	Initializes the object with a bitmap with the width, height, and bit pattern (if one is specified) given in a **BITMAP** structure.
CreateCompatibleBitmap	Initializes the object with a bitmap so that it is compatible with a specified device.
CreateDiscardableBitmap	Initializes the object with a discardable bitmap that is compatible with a specified device.

Attributes

GetBitmap	Fills a **BITMAP** structure with information about the bitmap.
operator HBITMAP	Returns the Windows handle attached to the **CBitmap** object.

Operations

FromHandle	Returns a pointer to a **CBitmap** object when given a handle to a Windows **HBITMAP** bitmap.
SetBitmapBits	Sets the bits of a bitmap to the specified bit values.
GetBitmapBits	Copies the bits of the specified bitmap into the specified buffer.
SetBitmapDimension	Assigns a width and height to a bitmap in 0.1-millimeter units.
GetBitmapDimension	Returns the width and height of the bitmap. The height and width are assumed to have been set previously by the **SetBitmapDimension** member function.

Member Functions

CBitmap::CBitmap

CBitmap( );

Remarks

Constructs a **CBitmap** object. The resulting object must be initialized with one of the initialization member functions.

See Also: CBitmap::LoadBitmap, CBitmap::LoadOEMBitmap, CBitmap::CreateBitmap, CBitmap::CreateBitmapIndirect, CBitmap::CreateCompatibleBitmap, CBitmap::CreateDiscardableBitmap

CBitmap::CreateBitmap

BOOL CreateBitmap(int *nWidth*, **int** *nHeight*, **UINT** *nPlanes*, **UINT** *nBitcount*,
↪ **const void*** *lpBits* **);**

Return Value

Nonzero if successful; otherwise 0.

Parameters

nWidth   Specifies the width (in pixels) of the bitmap.

nHeight   Specifies the height (in pixels) of the bitmap.

nPlanes   Specifies the number of color planes in the bitmap.

nBitcount   Specifies the number of color bits per display pixel.

lpBits   Points to a short-integer array that contains the initial bitmap bit values. If it is **NULL**, the new bitmap is left uninitialized.

Remarks

Initializes a device-dependent memory bitmap that has the specified width, height, and bit pattern.

For a color bitmap, either the *nPlanes* or *nBitcount* parameter should be set to 1. If both of these parameters are set to 1, **CreateBitmap** creates a monochrome bitmap.

Although a bitmap cannot be directly selected for a display device, it can be selected as the current bitmap for a "memory device context" by using **CDC::SelectObject** and copied to any compatible device context by using the **CDC::BitBlt** function.

When you finish with the **CBitmap** object created by the **CreateBitmap** function, first select the bitmap out of the device context, then delete the **CBitmap** object.

For more information, see the description of the **bmBits** field in the **BITMAP** structure. The **BITMAP** structure is described under the **CBitmap::CreateBitmapIndirect** member function.

See Also: CDC::SelectObject, CGdiObject::DeleteObject, CDC::BitBlt, ::CreateBitmap

---

CBitmap::CreateBitmapIndirect

BOOL CreateBitmapIndirect(LPBITMAP *lpBitmap* **);**

Return Value
Nonzero if successful; otherwise 0.

Parameters
lpBitmap   Points to a **BITMAP** structure that contains information about the bitmap.

Remarks
Initializes a bitmap that has the width, height, and bit pattern (if one is specified) given in the structure pointed to by *lpBitmap*. Although a bitmap cannot be directly selected for a display device, it can be selected as the current bitmap for a memory device context by using **CDC::SelectObject** and copied to any compatible device context by using the **CDC::BitBlt** or **CDC::StretchBlt** function. (The **CDC::PatBlt** function can copy the bitmap for the current brush directly to the display device context.)

If the **BITMAP** structure pointed to by the *lpBitmap* parameter has been filled in by using the **GetObject** function, the bits of the bitmap are not specified and the bitmap is uninitialized. To initialize the bitmap, an application can use a function such as **CDC::BitBlt** or **::SetDIBits** to copy the bits from the bitmap identified by the first parameter of **CGdiObject::GetObject** to the bitmap created by **CreateBitmapIndirect**.

When you finish with the **CBitmap** object created with **CreateBitmapIndirect** function, first select the bitmap out of the device context, then delete the **CBitmap** object.

See Also: CDC::SelectObject, CDC::BitBlt, CGdiObject::DeleteObject, CGdiObject::GetObject, ::CreateBitmapIndirect

CBitmap::CreateCompatibleBitmap

BOOL CreateCompatibleBitmap(CDC* *pDC***, int** *nWidth***, int** *nHeight* **);**

Return Value

Nonzero if successful; otherwise 0.

Parameters

pDC   Specifies the device context.

nWidth   Specifies the width (in pixels) of the bitmap.

nHeight   Specifies the height (in pixels) of the bitmap.

Remarks

Initializes a bitmap that is compatible with the device specified by *pDC*. The bitmap has the same number of color planes or the same bits-per-pixel format as the specified device context. It can be selected as the current bitmap for any memory device that is compatible with the one specified by *pDC*.

If *pDC* is a memory device context, the bitmap returned has the same format as the currently selected bitmap in that device context. A "memory device context" is a block of memory that represents a display surface. It can be used to prepare images in memory before copying them to the actual display surface of the compatible device.

When a memory device context is created, GDI automatically selects a monochrome stock bitmap for it.

Since a color memory device context can have either color or monochrome bitmaps selected, the format of the bitmap returned by the **CreateCompatibleBitmap** function is not always the same; however, the format of a compatible bitmap for a nonmemory device context is always in the format of the device.

When you finish with the **CBitmap** object created with the **CreateCompatibleBitmap** function, first select the bitmap out of the device context, then delete the **CBitmap** object.

See Also: ::CreateCompatibleBitmap, CGdiObject::DeleteObject

CBitmap::CreateDiscardableBitmap

BOOL CreateDiscardableBitmap(CDC* *pDC***, int** *nWidth***, int** *nHeight* **);**

Return Value

Nonzero if successful; otherwise 0.

Parameters

pDC   Specifies a device context.

nWidth   Specifies the width (in bits) of the bitmap.

nHeight   Specifies the height (in bits) of the bitmap.

Remarks

Initializes a discardable bitmap that is compatible with the device context identified by *pDC*. The bitmap has the same number of color planes or the same bits-per-pixel format as the specified device context. An application can select this bitmap as the current bitmap for a memory device that is compatible with the one specified by *pDC*.

Windows can discard a bitmap created by this function only if an application has not selected it into a display context. If Windows discards the bitmap when it is not selected and the application later attempts to select it, the **CDC::SelectObject** function will return **NULL**.

When you finish with the **CBitmap** object created with the **CreateDiscardableBitmap** function, first select the bitmap out of the device context, then delete the **CBitmap** object.

See Also: **::CreateDiscardableBitmap**, **CGdiObject::DeleteObject**

CBitmap::FromHandle

static CBitmap* PASCAL FromHandle(HBITMAP *hBitmap*);

Return Value

A pointer to a **CBitmap** object if successful; otherwise **NULL**.

Parameters

hBitmap   Specifies a Windows GDI bitmap.

Remarks

Returns a pointer to a **CBitmap** object when given a handle to a Windows GDI bitmap. If a **CBitmap** object is not already attached to the handle, a temporary **CBitmap** object is created and attached. This temporary **CBitmap** object is valid only until the next time the application has idle time in its event loop, at which time all temporary graphic objects are deleted. Another way of saying this is that the temporary object is only valid during the processing of one window message.

CBitmap::GetBitmap

int GetBitmap(BITMAP* *pBitMap*);

Return Value

Nonzero if successful; otherwise 0.

Parameters

pBitMap   Pointer to a **BITMAP** structure. Must not be **NULL**.

Remarks

Call this member function to retrieve information about a **CBitmap** object. This information is returned in the **BITMAP** structure referred to by *pBitmap*.

See Also: BITMAP

CBitmap::GetBitmapBits

DWORD GetBitmapBits(DWORD *dwCount*, **LPVOID** *lpBits*) **const;**

Return Value

The actual number of bytes in the bitmap, or 0 if there is an error.

Parameters

dwCount Specifies the number of bytes to be copied.

lpBits Points to the buffer that is to receive the bitmap. The bitmap is an array of bytes. The bitmap byte array conforms to a structure where horizontal scan lines are multiples of 16 bits.

Remarks

Copies the bit pattern of the **CBitmap** object into the buffer that is pointed to by *lpBits*. The *dwCount* parameter specifies the number of bytes to be copied to the buffer. Use **CGdiObject::GetObject** to determine the correct *dwCount* value for the given bitmap.

See Also: CGdiObject::GetObject, ::GetBitmapBits

CBitmap::GetBitmapDimension

CSize GetBitmapDimension( ) const;

Return Value

The width and height of the bitmap, measured in 0.1-millimeter units. The height is in the **cy** member of the **CSize** object, and the width is in the **cx** member. If the bitmap width and height have not been set by using **SetBitmapDimension**, the return value is 0.

Remarks

Returns the width and height of the bitmap. The height and width are assumed to have been set previously by using the **SetBitmapDimension** member function.

See Also: CBitmap::SetBitmapDimension

CBitmap::LoadBitmap

BOOL LoadBitmap(LPCTSTR *lpszResourceName* **);**
BOOL LoadBitmap(UINT *nIDResource* **);**

Return Value

Nonzero if successful; otherwise 0.

Parameters

lpszResourceName   Points to a null-terminated string that contains the name of
the bitmap resource.

nIDResource   Specifies the resource ID number of the bitmap resource.

Remarks

Loads the bitmap resource named by *lpszResourceName* or identified by the ID
number in *nIDResource* from the application's executable file. The loaded bitmap is
attached to the **CBitmap** object.

If the bitmap identified by *lpszResourceName* does not exist or if there is insufficient
memory to load the bitmap, the function returns 0.

An application must call the **CGdiObject::DeleteObject** function to delete any
bitmap loaded by the **LoadBitmap** function.

The following bitmaps were added to Windows versions 3.1 and later:

OBM_UPARRROWI
OBM_DNARROWI
OBM_RGARROWI
OBM_LFARROWI

These bitmaps are not found in device drivers for Windows versions 3.0 and earlier.
For a complete list of bitmaps and a display of their appearance, see the *Win32
Programmer's Reference*.

**See Also: CBitmap::LoadOEMBitmap, ::LoadBitmap,
CGdiObject::DeleteObject**

CBitmap::LoadMappedBitmap

BOOL LoadMappedBitmap(UINT *nIDBitmap*, **UINT** *nFlags* **= 0,**
↪ **LPCOLORMAP** *lpColorMap* **= NULL, int** *nMapSize* **= 0);**

Return Value

Nonzero if successful; otherwise 0.

Parameters

nIDBitmap   The ID of the bitmap resource.

nFlags   A flag for a bitmap. Can be zero or **CMB_MASKED**.

    lpColorMap   A pointer to a **COLORMAP** structure that contains the color information needed to map the bitmaps. If this parameter is **NULL**, the function uses the default color map.

    nMapSize   The number of color maps pointed to by *lpColorMap*.

Remarks

Call this member function to load a bitmap and map the colors to the current system colors. By default, **LoadMappedBitmap** will map colors commonly used in button glyphs.

For information about creating a mapped bitmap, see the Windows function **::CreateMappedBitmap** and the **COLORMAP** structure in the *Win32 Programmer's Reference*.

See Also: **::LoadBitmap**, **::CreateMappedBitmap**

CBitmap::LoadOEMBitmap

    BOOL LoadOEMBitmap(UINT *nIDBitmap* **);**

Return Value

Nonzero if successful; otherwise 0.

Parameters

    nIDBitmap   ID number of the predefined Windows bitmap. The possible values are listed below from WINDOWS.H:

OBM_BTNCORNERS	**OBM_OLD_RESTORE**
OBM_BTSIZE	**OBM_OLD_RGARROW**
OBM_CHECK	**OBM_OLD_UPARROW**
OBM_CHECKBOXES	**OBM_OLD_ZOOM**
OBM_CLOSE	**OBM_REDUCE**
OBM_COMBO	**OBM_REDUCED**
OBM_DNARROW	**OBM_RESTORE**
OBM_DNARROWD	**OBM_RESTORED**
OBM_DNARROWI	**OBM_RGARROW**
OBM_LFARROW	**OBM_RGARROWD**
OBM_LFARROWD	**OBM_RGARROWI**
OBM_LFARROWI	**OBM_SIZE**
OBM_MNARROW	**OBM_UPARROW**
OBM_OLD_CLOSE	**OBM_UPARROWD**
OBM_OLD_DNARROW	**OBM_UPARROW**
OBM_OLD_LFARROW	**OBM_ZOOM**
OBM_OLD_REDUCE	**OBM_ZOOMD**

Remarks

Loads a predefined bitmap used by Windows.

Bitmap names that begin with **OBM_OLD** represent bitmaps used by Windows versions prior to 3.0.

Note that the constant **OEMRESOURCE** must be defined before including WINDOWS.H in order to use any of the **OBM_** constants.

See Also: **CBitmap::LoadBitmap**, **::LoadBitmap**

CBitmap::operator HBITMAP

operator HBITMAP( ) const;

Return Value

If successful, a handle to the Windows GDI object represented by the **CBitmap** object; otherwise **NULL**.

Remarks

Use this operator to get the attached Windows GDI handle of the **CBitmap** object. This operator is a casting operator, which supports direct use of an **HBITMAP** object.

For more information about using graphic objects, see "Graphic Objects" in the *Win32 Programmer's Reference*.

CBitmap::SetBitmapBits

DWORD SetBitmapBits(DWORD *dwCount*, **const void*** *lpBits* **);**

Return Value

The number of bytes used in setting the bitmap bits; 0 if the function fails.

Parameters

dwCount   Specifies the number of bytes pointed to by *lpBits*.

lpBits   Points to the **BYTE** array that contains the bit values to be copied to the **CBitmap** object.

Remarks

Sets the bits of a bitmap to the bit values given by *lpBits*.

See Also: **::SetBitmapBits**

CBitmap::SetBitmapDimension

CSize SetBitmapDimension(int *nWidth***, int** *nHeight* **);**

Return Value

The previous bitmap dimensions. Height is in the **cy** member variable of the **CSize** object, and width is in the **cx** member variable.

Parameters

nWidth   Specifies the width of the bitmap (in 0.1-millimeter units).

nHeight   Specifies the height of the bitmap (in 0.1-millimeter units).

Remarks

Assigns a width and height to a bitmap in 0.1-millimeter units. The GDI does not use these values except to return them when an application calls the **GetBitmapDimension** member function.

See Also: CBitmap::GetBitmapDimension

CBitmapButton

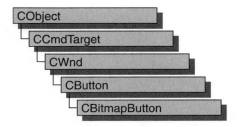

CObject
CCmdTarget
CWnd
CButton
CBitmapButton

Use the **CBitmapButton** class to create pushbutton controls labeled with bitmapped images instead of text. **CBitmapButton** objects contain up to four bitmaps, which contain images for the different states a button can assume: up (or normal), down (or selected), focused, and disabled. Only the first bitmap is required; the others are optional.

Bitmap-button images include the border around the image as well as the image itself. The border typically plays a part in showing the state of the button. For example, the bitmap for the focused state usually is like the one for the up state but with a dashed rectangle inset from the border or a thick solid line at the border. The bitmap for the disabled state usually resembles the one for the up state but has lower contrast (like a dimmed or grayed menu selection).

These bitmaps can be of any size, but all are treated as if they were the same size as the bitmap for the up state.

Various applications demand different combinations of bitmap images:

Up	Down	Focused	Disabled	Application
×				Bitmap
×	×			Button without **WS_TABSTOP** style
×	×	×	×	Dialog button with all states
×	×	×		Dialog button with **WS_TABSTOP** style

When creating a bitmap-button control, set the **BS_OWNERDRAW** style to specify that the button is owner-drawn. This causes Windows to send the **WM_MEASUREITEM** and **WM_DRAWITEM** messages for the button; the framework handles these messages and manages the appearance of the button for you.

To create a bitmap-button control in a window's client area, follow these steps:

1. Create one to four bitmap images for the button.

2. Construct the **CBitmapButton** object.

3. Call the **Create** function to create the Windows button control and attach it to the **CBitmapButton** object.

4. Call the **LoadBitmaps** member function to load the bitmap resources after the bitmap button is constructed.

To include a bitmap-button control in a dialog box, follow these steps:

1. Create one to four bitmap images for the button.

2. Create a dialog template with an owner-draw button positioned where you want the bitmap button. The size of the button in the template does not matter.

3. Set the button's caption to a value such as "MYIMAGE" and define a symbol for the button such as IDC_MYIMAGE.

4. In your application's resource script, give each of the images created for the button an ID constructed by appending one of the letters "U," "D," "F," or "X" (for up, down, focused, and disabled) to the string used for the button caption in step 3. For the button caption "MYIMAGE," for example, the IDs would be "MYIMAGEU," "MYIMAGED," "MYIMAGEF," and "MYIMAGEX." You **must** specify the ID of your bitmaps within double quotes. Otherwise the resource editor will assign an integer to the resource and MFC will fail when loading the image.

5. In your application's dialog class (derived from **CDialog**), add a **CBitmapButton** member object.

6. In the **CDialog** object's **OnInitDialog** routine, call the **CBitmapButton** object's **AutoLoad** function, using as parameters the button's control ID and the **CDialog** object's **this** pointer.

If you want to handle Windows notification messages, such as **BN_CLICKED**, sent by a bitmap-button control to its parent (usually a class derived from **CDialog**), add to the **CDialog**-derived object a message-map entry and message-handler member function for each message. The notifications sent by a **CBitmapButton** object are the same as those sent by a **CButton** object.

The class **CToolBar** takes a different approach to bitmap buttons.

For more information on **CBitmapButton**, see "Control Topics" in *Visual C++ Programmer's Guide* online.

#include <afxext.h>

CBitmapButton Class Members

Construction

CBitmapButton	Constructs a **CBitmapButton** object.
LoadBitmaps	Initializes the object by loading one or more named bitmap resources from the application's resource file and attaching the bitmaps to the object.
AutoLoad	Associates a button in a dialog box with an object of the **CBitmapButton** class, loads the bitmap(s) by name, and sizes the button to fit the bitmap.

Operations

SizeToContent	Sizes the button to accommodate the bitmap.

Member Functions
CBitmapButton::AutoLoad

BOOL AutoLoad(UINT *nID*, **CWnd*** *pParent* **);**

Return Value

Nonzero if successful; otherwise 0.

Parameters

nID   The button's control ID.

pParent   Pointer to the object that owns the button.

Remarks

Associates a button in a dialog box with an object of the **CBitmapButton** class, loads the bitmap(s) by name, and sizes the button to fit the bitmap.

Use the **AutoLoad** function to initialize an owner-draw button in a dialog box as a bitmap button. Instructions for using this function are in the remarks for the **CBitmapButton** class.

See Also: **CBitmapButton::LoadBitmaps, CBitmapButton::SizeToContent**

CBitmapButton::CBitmapButton

CBitmapButton( );

Remarks

Creates a **CBitmapButton** object.

After creating the C++ **CBitmapButton** object, call **CButton::Create** to create the Windows button control and attach it to the **CBitmapButton** object.

See Also: **CBitmapButton::LoadBitmaps, CBitmapButton::AutoLoad, CBitmapButton::SizeToContent, CButton::Create**

CBitmapButton::LoadBitmaps

BOOL LoadBitmaps(LPCTSTR *lpszBitmapResource*, **LPCTSTR**
↳ *lpszBitmapResourceSel* = **NULL, LPCTSTR** *lpszBitmapResourceFocus* = **NULL,**
↳ **LPCTSTR** *lpszBitmapResourceDisabled* = **NULL);**

BOOL LoadBitmaps(UINT *nIDBitmapResource*, **UINT** *nIDBitmapResourceSel* **= 0,**
↪ **UINT** *nIDBitmapResourceFocus* **= 0, UINT** *nIDBitmapResourceDisabled* **= 0);**

Return Value

Nonzero if successful; otherwise 0.

Parameters

lpszBitmapResource   Points to the null-terminated string that contains the name of the bitmap for a bitmap button's normal or "up" state. Required.

lpszBitmapResourceSel   Points to the null-terminated string that contains the name of the bitmap for a bitmap button's selected or "down" state. May be **NULL**.

lpszBitmapResourceFocus   Points to the null-terminated string that contains the name of the bitmap for a bitmap button's focused state. May be **NULL**.

lpszBitmapResourceDisabled   Points to the null-terminated string that contains the name of the bitmap for a bitmap button's disabled state. May be **NULL**.

nIDBitmapResource   Specifies the resource ID number of the bitmap resource for a bitmap button's normal or "up" state. Required.

nIDBitmapResourceSel   Specifies the resource ID number of the bitmap resource for a bitmap button's selected or "down" state. May be 0.

nIDBitmapResourceFocus   Specifies the resource ID number of the bitmap resource for a bitmap button's focused state. May be 0.

nIDBitmapResourceDisabled   Specifies the resource ID number of the bitmap resource for a bitmap button's disabled state. May be 0.

Remarks

Use this function when you want to load bitmap images identified by their resource names or ID numbers, or when you cannot use the **AutoLoad** function because, for example, you are creating a bitmap button that is not part of a dialog box.

See Also: CBitmapButton::AutoLoad, CBitmapButton::SizeToContent, CButton::Create, CBitmap::LoadBitmap

---

CBitmapButton::SizeToContent

void SizeToContent( );

Remarks

Call this function to resize a bitmap button to the size of the bitmap.

See Also: CBitmapButton::LoadBitmaps, CBitmapButton::AutoLoad

CBrush

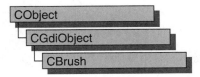

The **CBrush** class encapsulates a Windows graphics device interface (GDI) brush. To use a **CBrush** object, construct a **CBrush** object and pass it to any **CDC** member function that requires a brush.

Brushes can be solid, hatched, or patterned.

For more information on **CBrush**, see "Graphic Objects" in *Visual C++ Programmer's Guide* online.

#include <afxwin.h>

See Also: CBitmap, **CDC**

CBrush Class Members

Construction

CBrush	Constructs a **CBrush** object.

Initialization

CreateSolidBrush	Initializes a brush with the specified solid color.
CreateHatchBrush	Initializes a brush with the specified hatched pattern and color.
CreateBrushIndirect	Initializes a brush with the style, color, and pattern specified in a **LOGBRUSH** structure.
CreatePatternBrush	Initializes a brush with a pattern specified by a bitmap.
CreateDIBPatternBrush	Initializes a brush with a pattern specified by a device-independent bitmap (DIB).
CreateSysColorBrush	Creates a brush that is the default system color.

Operations

FromHandle	Returns a pointer to a **CBrush** object when given a handle to a Windows **HBRUSH** object.

Attributes

GetLogBrush	Gets a **LOGBRUSH** structure.
operator HBRUSH	Returns the Windows handle attached to the **CBrush** object.

Member Functions
CBrush::CBrush

CBrush( );
CBrush(COLORREF *crColor* **);**
   throw(CResourceException);
CBrush(int *nIndex*, **COLORREF** *crColor* **);**
   throw(CResourceException);
CBrush(CBitmap* *pBitmap* **);**
   throw(CResourceException);

Parameters

crColor Specifies the foreground color of the brush as an RGB color. If the brush is hatched, this parameter specifies the color of the hatching.

nIndex Specifies the hatch style of the brush. It can be any one of the following values:

- **HS_BDIAGONAL** Downward hatch (left to right) at 45 degrees

- **HS_CROSS** Horizontal and vertical crosshatch

- **HS_DIAGCROSS** Crosshatch at 45 degrees

- **HS_FDIAGONAL** Upward hatch (left to right) at 45 degrees

- **HS_HORIZONTAL** Horizontal hatch

- **HS_VERTICAL** Vertical hatch

pBitmap Points to a **CBitmap** object that specifies a bitmap with which the brush paints.

Remarks

Has four overloaded constructors. The constructor with no arguments constructs an uninitialized **CBrush** object that must be initialized before it can be used.

If you use the constructor with no arguments, you must initialize the resulting **CBrush** object with **CreateSolidBrush**, **CreateHatchBrush**, **CreateBrushIndirect**, **CreatePatternBrush**, or **CreateDIBPatternBrush**. If you use one of the constructors that takes arguments, then no further initialization is necessary. The constructors with arguments can throw an exception if errors are encountered, while the constructor with no arguments will always succeed.

The constructor with a single **COLORREF** parameter constructs a solid brush with the specified color. The color specifies an RGB value and can be constructed with the **RGB** macro in WINDOWS.H.

The constructor with two parameters constructs a hatch brush. The *nIndex* parameter specifies the index of a hatched pattern. The *crColor* parameter specifies the color.

The constructor with a **CBitmap** parameter constructs a patterned brush. The parameter identifies a bitmap. The bitmap is assumed to have been created by using **CBitmap::CreateBitmap**, **CBitmap::CreateBitmapIndirect**, **CBitmap::LoadBitmap**, or **CBitmap::CreateCompatibleBitmap**. The minimum size for a bitmap to be used in a fill pattern is 8 pixels by 8 pixels.

See Also: **CBrush::CreateSolidBrush, CBrush::CreateHatchBrush, CBrush::CreateBrushIndirect, CBrush::CreatePatternBrush, CBrush::CreateDIBPatternBrush, CGdiObject::CreateStockObject**

CBrush::CreateBrushIndirect

BOOL CreateBrushIndirect(const LOGBRUSH* *lpLogBrush* **);**

Return Value

Nonzero if the function is successful; otherwise 0.

Parameters

lpLogBrush   Points to a **LOGBRUSH** structure that contains information about the brush.

Remarks

Initializes a brush with a style, color, and pattern specified in a **LOGBRUSH** structure. The brush can subsequently be selected as the current brush for any device context.

A brush created using a monochrome (1 plane, 1 bit per pixel) bitmap is drawn using the current text and background colors. Pixels represented by a bit set to 0 will be drawn with the current text color. Pixels represented by a bit set to 1 will be drawn with the current background color.

See Also: **CBrush::CreateDIBPatternBrush, CBrush::CreatePatternBrush, CBrush::CreateSolidBrush, CBrush::CreateHatchBrush, CGdiObject::CreateStockObject, CGdiObject::DeleteObject, ::CreateBrushIndirect**

CBrush::CreateDIBPatternBrush

BOOL CreateDIBPatternBrush(HGLOBAL *hPackedDIB***, UINT** *nUsage* **);**
BOOL CreateDIBPatternBrush(const void* *lpPackedDIB***, UINT** *nUsage* **);**

Return Value

Nonzero if successful; otherwise 0.

Parameters

hPackedDIB   Identifies a global-memory object containing a packed device-independent bitmap (DIB).

nUsage   Specifies whether the **bmiColors[]** fields of the **BITMAPINFO** data structure (a part of the "packed DIB") contain explicit RGB values or indices into the currently realized logical palette. The parameter must be one of the following values:

- **DIB_PAL_COLORS**   The color table consists of an array of 16-bit indexes.

- **DIB_RGB_COLORS**   The color table contains literal RGB values.

The following value is available only in the second version of this member function:

- **DIB_PAL_INDICES**   No color table is provided. The bitmap itself contains indices into the logical palette of the device context into which the brush is to be selected.

lpPackedDIB   Points to a packed DIB consisting of a **BITMAPINFO** structure immediately followed by an array of bytes defining the pixels of the bitmap.

Remarks

Initializes a brush with the pattern specified by a device-independent bitmap (DIB). The brush can subsequently be selected for any device context that supports raster operations.

The two versions differ in the way you handle the DIB:

- In the first version, to obtain a handle to the DIB you call the Windows **::GlobalAlloc** function to allocate a block of global memory and then fill the memory with the packed DIB.

- In the second version, it is not necessary to call **::GlobalAlloc** to allocate memory for the packed DIB.

A packed DIB consists of a **BITMAPINFO** data structure immediately followed by the array of bytes that defines the pixels of the bitmap. Bitmaps used as fill patterns should be 8 pixels by 8 pixels. If the bitmap is larger, Windows creates a fill pattern using only the bits corresponding to the first 8 rows and 8 columns of pixels in the upper-left corner of the bitmap.

When an application selects a two-color DIB pattern brush into a monochrome device context, Windows ignores the colors specified in the DIB and instead displays the pattern brush using the current text and background colors of the device context. Pixels mapped to the first color (at offset 0 in the DIB color table) of the DIB are displayed using the text color. Pixels mapped to the second color (at offset 1 in the color table) are displayed using the background color.

For information about using the following Windows functions, see the *Win32 SDK Programmer's Reference*:

- **::CreateDIBPatternBrush** (This function is provided only for compatibility with applications written for versions of Windows earlier than 3.0; use the **::CreateDIBPatternBrushPt** function.)

- **::CreateDIBPatternBrushPt** (This function should be used for Win32-based applications.)

- **::GlobalAlloc**

See Also: **CBrush::CreatePatternBrush**, **CBrush::CreateBrushIndirect**, **CBrush::CreateSolidBrush**, **CBrush::CreateHatchBrush**, **CGdiObject::CreateStockObject**, **CDC::SelectObject**, **CGdiObject::DeleteObject**, **CDC::GetBrushOrg**, **CDC::SetBrushOrg**

CBrush::CreateHatchBrush

BOOL CreateHatchBrush(int *nIndex*, COLORREF *crColor*);

Return Value

Nonzero if successful; otherwise 0.

Parameters

nIndex Specifies the hatch style of the brush. It can be any one of the following values:

- **HS_BDIAGONAL** Downward hatch (left to right) at 45 degrees

- **HS_CROSS** Horizontal and vertical crosshatch

- **HS_DIAGCROSS** Crosshatch at 45 degrees

- **HS_FDIAGONAL** Upward hatch (left to right) at 45 degrees

- **HS_HORIZONTAL** Horizontal hatch

- **HS_VERTICAL** Vertical hatch

crColor Specifies the foreground color of the brush as an RGB color (the color of the hatches). See **COLORREF** in the Win32 SDK documentation for more information.

Remarks

Initializes a brush with the specified hatched pattern and color. The brush can subsequently be selected as the current brush for any device context.

See Also: **CBrush::CreateBrushIndirect**, **CBrush::CreateDIBPatternBrush**, **CBrush::CreatePatternBrush**, **CBrush::CreateSolidBrush**, **CGdiObject::CreateStockObject**, **::CreateHatchBrush**

CBrush::CreatePatternBrush

BOOL CreatePatternBrush(CBitmap* *pBitmap* **);**

Return Value

Nonzero if successful; otherwise 0.

Parameters

pBitmap   Identifies a bitmap.

Remarks

Initializes a brush with a pattern specified by a bitmap. The brush can subsequently be selected for any device context that supports raster operations. The bitmap identified by *pBitmap* is typically initialized by using the **CBitmap::CreateBitmap**, **CBitmap::CreateBitmapIndirect**, **CBitmap::LoadBitmap**, or **CBitmap::CreateCompatibleBitmap** function.

Bitmaps used as fill patterns should be 8 pixels by 8 pixels. If the bitmap is larger, Windows will only use the bits corresponding to the first 8 rows and columns of pixels in the upper-left corner of the bitmap.

A pattern brush can be deleted without affecting the associated bitmap. This means the bitmap can be used to create any number of pattern brushes.

A brush created using a monochrome bitmap (1 color plane, 1 bit per pixel) is drawn using the current text and background colors. Pixels represented by a bit set to 0 are drawn with the current text color. Pixels represented by a bit set to 1 are drawn with the current background color.

For information about using **::CreatePatternBrush**, a Windows function, see the *Win32 SDK Programmer's Reference*.

See Also: **CBitmap, CBrush::CreateBrushIndirect, CBrush::CreateDIBPatternBrush, CBrush::CreateHatchBrush, CBrush::CreateSolidBrush, CGdiObject::CreateStockObject**

CBrush::CreateSolidBrush

BOOL CreateSolidBrush(COLORREF *crColor* **);**

Return Value

Nonzero if successful; otherwise 0.

Parameters

crColor   A **COLORREF** structure that specifies the color of the brush. The color specifies an RGB value and can be constructed with the **RGB** macro in WINDOWS.H.

Remarks

Initializes a brush with a specified solid color. The brush can subsequently be selected as the current brush for any device context.

When an application has finished using the brush created by **CreateSolidBrush**, it should select the brush out of the device context.

See Also: **CBrush::CreateBrushIndirect, CBrush::CreateDIBPatternBrush, CBrush::CreateHatchBrush, CBrush::CreatePatternBrush, ::CreateSolidBrush, CGdiObject::DeleteObject**

CBrush::CreateSysColorBrush

BOOL CreateSysColorBrush(int *nIndex*);

Return Value

Nonzero if successful; otherwise 0.

Parameters

nIndex Specifies the hatch style of the brush. It can be any one of the following values:

- **HS_BDIAGONAL** Downward hatch (left to right) at 45 degrees
- **HS_CROSS** Horizontal and vertical crosshatch
- **HS_DIAGCROSS** Crosshatch at 45 degrees
- **HS_FDIAGONAL** Upward hatch (left to right) at 45 degrees
- **HS_HORIZONTAL** Horizontal hatch
- **HS_VERTICAL** Vertical hatch

Remarks

Initializes a brush color. The brush can subsequently be selected as the current brush for any device context.

When an application has finished using the brush created by **CreateSysColorBrush**, it should select the brush out of the device context.

See Also: **CBrush::CreateBrushIndirect, CBrush::CreateDIBPatternBrush, CBrush::CreateHatchBrush, CBrush::CreatePatternBrush, ::CreateSolidBrush, CBrush::CreateSolidBrush, ::GetSysColorBrush, CGdiObject::DeleteObject**

CBrush::FromHandle

static CBrush* PASCAL FromHandle(HBRUSH *hBrush* **);**

Return Value

A pointer to a **CBrush** object if successful; otherwise **NULL**.

Parameters

hBrush   **HANDLE** to a Windows GDI brush.

Remarks

Returns a pointer to a **CBrush** object when given a handle to a Windows **HBRUSH** object. If a **CBrush** object is not already attached to the handle, a temporary **CBrush** object is created and attached. This temporary **CBrush** object is valid only until the next time the application has idle time in its event loop. At this time, all temporary graphic objects are deleted. In other words, the temporary object is valid only during the processing of one window message.

For more information about using graphic objects, see "Graphic Objects" in the *Win32 SDK Programmer's Reference.*

CBrush::GetLogBrush

int GetLogBrush(LOGBRUSH* *pLogBrush* **);**

Return Value

If the function succeeds, and *pLogBrush* is a valid pointer, the return value is the number of bytes stored into the buffer.

If the function succeeds, and *pLogBrush* is **NULL**, the return value is the number of bytes required to hold the information the function would store into the buffer.

If the function fails, the return value is 0.

Parameters

pLogBrush   Points to a **LOGBRUSH** structure that contains information about the brush.

Remarks

Call this member function to retrieve the **LOGBRUSH** structure. The **LOGBRUSH** structure defines the style, color, and pattern of a brush.

For example, call **GetLogBrush** to match the particular color or pattern of a bitmap.

Example

```
LOGBRUSH logbrush;
brushExisting.GetLogBrush( &logbrush );
CBrush brushOther( logbrush.lbColor);
```

See Also: LOGBRUSH, ::GetObject

CBrush::operator HBRUSH

operator HBRUSH( ) const;

Return Value

If successful, a handle to the Windows GDI object represented by the **CBrush** object; otherwise **NULL**.

Remarks

Use this operator to get the attached Windows GDI handle of the **CBrush** object. This operator is a casting operator, which supports direct use of an **HBRUSH** object.

For more information about using graphic objects, see "Graphic Objects" in the *Win32 SDK Programmer's Reference*.

CButton

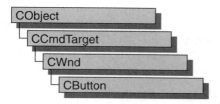

The **CButton** class provides the functionality of Windows button controls. A button control is a small, rectangular child window that can be clicked on and off. Buttons can be used alone or in groups and can either be labeled or appear without text. A button typically changes appearance when the user clicks it.

Typical buttons are the check box, radio button, and pushbutton. A **CButton** object can become any of these, according to the button style specified at its initialization by the **Create** member function.

In addition, the **CBitmapButton** class derived from **CButton** supports creation of button controls labeled with bitmap images instead of text. A **CBitmapButton** can have separate bitmaps for a button's up, down, focused, and disabled states.

You can create a button control either from a dialog template or directly in your code. In both cases, first call the constructor **CButton** to construct the **CButton** object; then call the **Create** member function to create the Windows button control and attach it to the **CButton** object.

Construction can be a one-step process in a class derived from **CButton**. Write a constructor for the derived class and call **Create** from within the constructor.

If you want to handle Windows notification messages sent by a button control to its parent (usually a class derived from **CDialog**), add a message-map entry and message-handler member function to the parent class for each message.

Each message-map entry takes the following form:

ON_ Notification(*id*, *memberFxn*)

where *id* specifies the child window ID of the control sending the notification and *memberFxn* is the name of the parent member function you have written to handle the notification.

The parent's function prototype is as follows:

afx_msg void *memberFxn*( );

Potential message-map entries are as follows:

Map entry	Sent to parent when...
ON_BN_CLICKED	The user clicks a button.
ON_BN_DOUBLECLICKED	The user double-clicks a button.

If you create a **CButton** object from a dialog resource, the **CButton** object is automatically destroyed when the user closes the dialog box.

If you create a **CButton** object within a window, you may need to destroy it. If you create the **CButton** object on the heap by using the **new** function, you must call **delete** on the object to destroy it when the user closes the Windows button control. If you create the **CButton** object on the stack, or it is embedded in the parent dialog object, it is destroyed automatically.

#include <afxwin.h>

See Also: **CWnd**, **CComboBox**, **CEdit**, **CListBox**, **CScrollBar**, **CStatic**, **CBitmapButton**, **CDialog**

CButton Class Members

Construction

CButton	Constructs a **CButton** object.

Initialization

Create	Creates the Windows button control and attaches it to the **CButton** object.

Operations

GetState	Retrieves the check state, highlight state, and focus state of a button control.
SetState	Sets the highlighting state of a button control.
GetCheck	Retrieves the check state of a button control.
SetCheck	Sets the check state of a button control.
GetButtonStyle	Retrieves information about the button control style.
SetButtonStyle	Changes the style of a button.
GetIcon	Retrieves the handle of the icon previously set with **SetIcon**.
SetIcon	Specifies an icon to be displayed on the button.
GetBitmap	Retrieves the handle of the bitmap previously set with **SetBitmap**.
SetBitmap	Specifies a bitmap to be displayed on the button.
GetCursor	Retrieves the handle of the cursor image previously set with **SetCursor**.
SetCursor	Specifies a cursor image to be displayed on the button.

Overridables

DrawItem	Override to draw an owner-drawn **CButton** object.

Member Functions
CButton::CButton

CButton( );

Remarks

Constructs a **CButton** object.

See Also: **CButton::Create**

CButton::Create

BOOL Create(LPCTSTR *lpszCaption*, **DWORD** *dwStyle*,
➛ **const RECT&** *rect*, **CWnd*** *pParentWnd*, **UINT** *nID*);

Return Value

Nonzero if successful; otherwise 0.

Parameters

lpszCaption   Specifies the button control's text.

dwStyle   Specifies the button control's style. Apply any combination of button styles to the button.

rect   Specifies the button control's size and position. It can be either a **CRect** object or a **RECT** structure.

pParentWnd   Specifies the button control's parent window, usually a **CDialog**. It must not be **NULL**.

nID   Specifies the button control's ID.

Remarks

You construct a **CButton** object in two steps. First call the constructor, then call **Create**, which creates the Windows button control and attaches it to the **CButton** object.

If the **WS_VISIBLE** style is given, Windows sends the button control all the messages required to activate and show the button.

Apply the following window styles to a button control:

- **WS_CHILD**   Always
- **WS_VISIBLE**   Usually
- **WS_DISABLED**   Rarely

- **WS_GROUP**   To group controls
- **WS_TABSTOP**   To include the button in the tabbing order

See Also: CButton::CButton

CButton::DrawItem

virtual void DrawItem(LPDRAWITEMSTRUCT *lpDrawItemStruct* **);**

Parameters

lpDrawItemStruct   A long pointer to a **DRAWITEMSTRUCT** structure. The structure contains information about the item to be drawn and the type of drawing required.

Remarks

Called by the framework when a visual aspect of an owner-drawn button has changed. An owner-drawn button has the **BS_OWNERDRAW** style set. Override this member function to implement drawing for an owner-drawn **CButton** object. The application should restore all graphics device interface (GDI) objects selected for the display context supplied in *lpDrawItemStruct* before the member function terminates.

Also see the **BS_** style values.

See Also: CButton::SetButtonStyle, WM_DRAWITEM

CButton::GetBitmap

HBITMAP GetBitmap( ) const;

Return Value

A handle to a bitmap. **NULL** if no bitmap is previously specified.

Remarks

Call this member function to get the handle of a bitmap, previously set with **SetBitmap**, that is associated with a button.

See Also: CButton::SetBitmap, CBitmapButton::LoadBitmaps, "Bitmaps" online

---

CButton::GetButtonStyle

UINT GetButtonStyle( ) const;

Return Value

Returns the button styles for this **CButton** object.

Remarks

This function returns only the **BS_** style values, not any of the other window styles.

CButton::GetCheck

int GetCheck( ) const;

Return Value

The return value from a button control created with the **BS_AUTOCHECKBOX**, **BS_AUTORADIOBUTTON**, **BS_AUTO3STATE**, **BS_CHECKBOX**, **BS_RADIOBUTTON**, or **BS_3STATE** style is one of the following values:

Value	Meaning
0	Button state is unchecked.
1	Button state is checked.
2	Button state is indeterminate (applies only if the button has the **BS_3STATE** or **BS_AUTO3STATE** style).

If the button has any other style, the return value is 0.

Remarks

Retrieves the check state of a radio button or check box.

See Also: **CButton::GetState, CButton::SetState, CButton::SetCheck, BM_GETCHECK**

CButton::GetCursor

HCURSOR GetCursor( );

Return Value

A handle to a cursor image. **NULL** if no cursor is previously specified.

Remarks

Call this member function to get the handle of a cursor, previously set with **SetCursor**, that is associated with a button.

See Also: **CButton::SetCursor, CBitmapButton::LoadBitmaps**, "Bitmaps" online

---

CButton::GetIcon

HICON GetIcon( ) const;

Return Value

A handle to an icon. **NULL** if no icon is previously specified.

Remarks

Call this member function to get the handle of an icon, previously set with **SetIcon**, that is associated with a button.

See Also: **CButton::SetIcon, CBitmapButton::LoadBitmaps**, "Bitmaps" online

CButton::GetState

UINT GetState( ) const;

Return Value

Specifies the current state of the button control. You can use the following masks against the return value to extract information about the state:

Mask	Meaning
0x0003	Specifies the check state (radio buttons and check boxes only). A 0 indicates the button is unchecked. A 1 indicates the button is checked. A radio button is checked when it contains a bullet (•). A check box is checked when it contains an **X**. A 2 indicates the check state is indeterminate (three-state check boxes only). The state of a three-state check box is indeterminate when it contains a halftone pattern.
0x0004	Specifies the highlight state. A nonzero value indicates that the button is highlighted. A button is highlighted when the user clicks and holds the left mouse button. The highlighting is removed when the user releases the mouse button.
0x0008	Specifies the focus state. A nonzero value indicates that the button has the focus.

Remarks

Retrieves the state of a radio button or check box.

See Also: CButton::GetCheck, CButton::SetCheck, CButton::SetState, BM_GETSTATE

CButton::SetBitmap

HBITMAP SetBitmap(HBITMAP *hBitmap* **);**

Return Value

The handle of a bitmap previously associated with the button.

Parameters

hBitmap   The handle of a bitmap.

Remarks

Call this member function to associate a new bitmap with the button.

The bitmap will be automatically placed on the face of the button, centered by default. If the bitmap is too large for the button, it will be clipped on either side. You can choose other alignment options, including the following:

- **BS_TOP**
- **BS_LEFT**
- **BS_RIGHT**

- **BS_CENTER**
- **BS_BOTTOM**
- **BS_VCENTER**

Unlike **CBitmapButton**, which uses four bitmaps per button, **SetBitmap** uses only one bitmap per the button. When the button is pressed, the bitmap appears to shift down and to the right.

See Also: **CButton::GetBitmap**, **CBitmapButton**, **CBitmapButton::LoadBitmaps**, "Bitmaps" online

CButton::SetButtonStyle

> **void SetButtonStyle(UINT** *nStyle*, **BOOL** *bRedraw* = **TRUE**);

Parameters

nStyle   Specifies the button style.

bRedraw   Specifies whether the button is to be redrawn. A nonzero value redraws the button. A 0 value does not redraw the button. The button is redrawn by default.

Remarks

Changes the style of a button.

Use the **GetButtonStyle** member function to retrieve the button style. The low-order word of the complete button style is the button-specific style.

CButton::SetCheck

> **void SetCheck(int** *nCheck*);

Parameters

nCheck   Specifies the check state. This parameter can be one of the following:

Value	Meaning
0	Set the button state to unchecked.
1	Set the button state to checked.
2	Set the button state to indeterminate. This value can be used only if the button has the **BS_3STATE** or **BS_AUTO3STATE** style.

Remarks

Sets or resets the check state of a radio button or check box. This member function has no effect on a pushbutton.

See Also: **CButton::GetCheck**, **CButton::GetState**, **CButton::SetState**, **BM_SETCHECK**

CButton::SetCursor

HCURSOR SetCursor(HCURSOR *hCursor* **);**

Return Value

The handle of a cursor previously associated with the button.

Parameters

hCursor The handle of a cursor.

Remarks

Call this member function to associate a new cursor with the button.

The cursor will be automatically placed on the face of the button, centered by default. If the cursor is too large for the button, it will be clipped on either side. You can choose other alignment options, including the following:

- **BS_TOP**
- **BS_LEFT**
- **BS_RIGHT**
- **BS_CENTER**
- **BS_BOTTOM**
- **BS_VCENTER**

Unlike **CBitmapButton**, which uses four bitmaps per button, **SetCursor** uses only one cursor per the button. When the button is pressed, the cursor appears to shift down and to the right.

See Also: **CButton::GetCursor**, **CBitmapButton::LoadBitmaps**, "Bitmaps" online

---

CButton::SetIcon

HICON SetIcon(HICON *hIcon* **);**

Return Value

The handle of an icon previously associated with the button.

Parameters

hIcon The handle of an icon.

Remarks

Call this member function to associate a new icon with the button.

The icon will be automatically placed on the face of the button, centered by default. If the icon is too large for the button, it will be clipped on either side. You can choose other alignment options, including the following:

- **BS_TOP**
- **BS_LEFT**
- **BS_RIGHT**
- **BS_CENTER**
- **BS_BOTTOM**
- **BS_VCENTER**

Unlike **CBitmapButton**, which uses four bitmaps per button, **SetIcon** uses only one icon per the button. When the button is pressed, the icon appears to shift down and to the right.

See Also: **CButton::GetIcon**, **CBitmapButton::LoadBitmaps**, "Bitmaps" online

---

CButton::SetState

void SetState(BOOL *bHighlight* **);**

Parameters

bHighlight   Specifies whether the button is to be highlighted. A nonzero value highlights the button; a 0 value removes any highlighting.

Remarks

Sets the highlighting state of a button control.

Highlighting affects the exterior of a button control. It has no effect on the check state of a radio button or check box.

A button control is automatically highlighted when the user clicks and holds the left mouse button. The highlighting is removed when the user releases the mouse button.

See Also: **CButton::GetState**, **CButton::SetCheck**, **CButton::GetCheck**, **BM_SETSTATE**

CByteArray

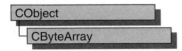

The **CByteArray** class supports dynamic arrays of bytes.

The member functions of **CByteArray** are similar to the member functions of class **CObArray**. Because of this similarity, you can use the **CObArray** reference documentation for member function specifics. Wherever you see a **CObject** pointer as a function parameter or return value, substitute a **BYTE**.

```
CObject* CObArray::GetAt( int <nIndex> ) const;
```

for example, translates to

```
BYTE CByteArray::GetAt( int <nIndex> ) const;
```

CByteArray incorporates the **IMPLEMENT_SERIAL** macro to support serialization and dumping of its elements. If an array of bytes is stored to an archive, either with the overloaded insertion (<<) operator or with the **Serialize** member function, each element is, in turn, serialized.

Note Before using an array, use **SetSize** to establish its size and allocate memory for it. If you do not use **SetSize**, adding elements to your array causes it to be frequently reallocated and copied. Frequent reallocation and copying are inefficient and can fragment memory.

If you need debug output from individual elements in the array, you must set the depth of the **CDumpContext** object to 1 or greater.

For more information on using **CByteArray**, see the article "Collections" in *Visual C++ Programmer's Guide* online.

#include <afxcoll.h>

See Also: CObArray

CByteArray Class Members

Construction

CByteArray	Constructs an empty array for bytes.

Bounds

GetSize	Gets the number of elements in this array.
GetUpperBound	Returns the largest valid index.
SetSize	Sets the number of elements to be contained in this array.

Operations

FreeExtra	Frees all unused memory above the current upper bound.
RemoveAll	Removes all the elements from this array.

Element Access

GetAt	Returns the value at a given index.
SetAt	Sets the value for a given index; array not allowed to grow.
ElementAt	Returns a temporary reference to the byte within the array.
GetData	Allows access to elements in the array. Can be **NULL**.

Growing the Array

SetAtGrow	Sets the value for a given index; grows the array if necessary.
Add	Adds an element to the end of the array; grows the array if necessary.
Append	Appends another array to the array; grows the array if necessary.
Copy	Copies another array to the array; grows the array if necessary.

Insertion/Removal

InsertAt	Inserts an element (or all the elements in another array) at a specified index.
RemoveAt	Removes an element at a specific index.

Operators

operator []	Sets or gets the element at the specified index.

CCachedDataPathProperty

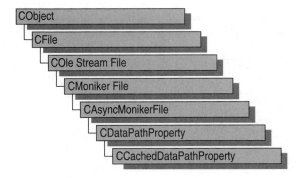

CObject
CFile
COle Stream File
CMoniker File
CAsyncMonikerFile
CDataPathProperty
CCachedDataPathProperty

Class **CCachedDataPathProperty** implements an OLE control property transferred asynchronously and cached in a memory file. A memory file is stored in RAM rather than on disk and is useful for fast temporary transfers.

Along with **CAysncMonikerFile** and **CDataPathProperty**, **CCachedDataPathProperty** provides functionality for the use of asynchronous monikers in OLE controls. With **CCachedDataPathProperty** objects, you to transfer data asynchronously from a URL or file source and store it in a memory file via the **m_Cache** public variable. All the data is stored in the memory file, and there is no need to override **OnDataAvailable** unless you want to watch for notifications and respond. For example, if you are transferring a large .GIF file and want to notify your control that more data has arrived and it should redraw itself, override **OnDataAvailable** to make the notification.

The class **CCachedDataPathProperty** is derived from **CDataPathProperty**.

For more information about how to use asynchronous monikers and ActiveX controls in Internet applications, see the following topics in *Visual C++ Programmer's Guide* online:

- Internet First Steps: ActiveX Controls
- Internet First Steps: Asynchronous Monikers

#include <afxctl.h>

See Also: **CDataPathProperty**

CCachedDataPathProperty Class Members

Data Members

m_Cache **CMemFile** object in which to cache data.

Data Members

CCachedDataPathProperty::m_Cache

CMemFile m_Cache;

Remarks

Contains the class name of the memory file into which data is cached. A memory file is stored in RAM rather than on disk.

See Also: **CDataPathProperty**

CCheckListBox

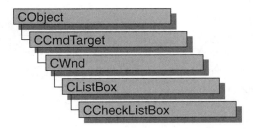

The **CCheckListBox** class provides the functionality of a Windows checklist box. A "checklist box" displays a list of items, such as filenames. Each item in the list has a check box next to it that the user can check or clear.

CCheckListBox is only for owner-drawn controls because the list contains more than text strings. At its simplest, a checklist box contains text strings and check boxes, but you do not need to have text at all. For example, you could have a list of small bitmaps with a check box next to each item.

To create your own checklist box, you must derive your own class from **CCheckListBox**. To derive your own class, write a constructor for the derived class, then call **Create**.

If your checklist box is a default checklist box (a list of strings with the default-sized checkboxes to the left of each), you can use the default **CCheckListBox::DrawItem** to draw the checklist box. Otherwise, you must override the **CListBox::CompareItem** function and the **CCheckListBox::DrawItem** and **CCheckListBox::MeasureItem** functions.

You can create a checklist box either from a dialog template or directly in your code.

#include <afxwin.h>

See Also: **CListBox**

CCheckListBox Class Members

Construction

CCheckListBox	Constructs a **CCheckListBox** object.
Create	Creates the Windows checklist box and attaches it to the **CCheckListBox** object.

Attributes

SetCheckStyle	Sets the style of the control's check boxes.
GetCheckStyle	Gets the style of the control's check boxes.
SetCheck	Sets the state of an item's check box.
GetCheck	Gets the state of an item's check box.
Enable	Enables or disables a checklist box item.
IsEnabled	Determines whether an item is enabled.
OnGetCheckPosition	Called by the framework to get the position of an item's check box.

Overridables

DrawItem	Called by the framework when a visual aspect of an owner-draw list box changes.
MeasureItem	Called by the framework when a list box with an owner-draw style is created.

Member Functions

CCheckListBox::CCheckListBox

CCheckListBox( );

Remarks

Constructs a **CCheckListBox** object.

You construct a **CCheckListBox** object in two steps. First define a class derived from **CCheckListBox**, then call **Create**, which initializes the Windows checklist box and attaches it to the **CCheckListBox** object. For example:

```
class CMyCheckListBox : public CCheckListBox
{
    DECLARE_DYNAMIC(CMyCheckListBox)

// Constructors
public:
    CMyCheckListBox();
    BOOL Create(DWORD dwStyle, const RECT& rect, CWnd* pParentWnd,
    ↳ UINT nID);
...
```

See Also: **CCheckListBox::Create**

CCheckListBox::Create

BOOL Create(DWORD *dwStyle*, **const RECT&** *rect*, **CWnd*** *pParentWnd*, **UINT** *nID* **);**

Return Value

Nonzero if successful; otherwise 0.

Parameters

dwStyle   Specifies the style of the checklist box. The style must be either
LBS_OWNERDRAWFIXED (all items in the list are the same height) or
LBS_OWNERDRAWVARIABLE (items in the list are of varying heights).
This style can be combined with other list-box styles.

rect   Specifies the checklist-box size and position. Can be either a **CRect** object or
a **RECT** structure.

pParentWnd   Specifies the checklist box's parent window (usually a **CDialog** object).
It must not be **NULL**.

nID   Specifies the checklist box's control ID.

Remarks

You construct a **CCheckListBox** object in two steps. First define a class derived from
CCheckListBox, then call **Create**, which initializes the Windows checklist box and
attaches it to the **CCheckListBox**. See **CCheckListBox::CCheckListBox** for a
sample.

When **Create** executes, Windows sends the **WM_NCCREATE, WM_CREATE,**
WM_NCCALCSIZE, and **WM_GETMINMAXINFO** messages to the
checklist-box control.

These messages are handled by default by the **OnNcCreate, OnCreate,**
OnNcCalcSize, and **OnGetMinMaxInfo** member functions in the **CWnd** base class.
To extend the default message handling, add a message map to the your derived class
and override the preceding message-handler member functions. Override **OnCreate,**
for example, to perform needed initialization for a new class.

Apply the following window styles to a checklist-box control:

- **WS_CHILD**   Always
- **WS_VISIBLE**   Usually
- **WS_DISABLED**   Rarely
- **WS_VSCROLL**   To add a vertical scroll bar
- **WS_HSCROLL**   To add a horizontal scroll bar
- **WS_GROUP**   To group controls
- **WS_TABSTOP**   To allow tabbing to this control

See Also: **CCheckListBox::CCheckListBox**

CCheckListBox::DrawItem

virtual void DrawItem(LPDRAWITEMSTRUCT *lpDrawItemStruct* **);**

Parameters

lpDrawItemStruct A long pointer to a **DRAWITEMSTRUCT** structure that contains information about the type of drawing required.

Remarks

Called by the framework when a visual aspect of an owner-drawn checklist box changes. The **itemAction** and **itemState** members of the **DRAWITEMSTRUCT** structure define the drawing action that is to be performed.

By default, this function draws a default checkbox list, consisting of a list of strings each with a default-sized checkbox to the left. The checkbox list size is the one specified in **Create**.

Override this member function to implement drawing of owner-draw checklist boxes that are not the default, such as checklist boxes with lists that aren't strings, with variable-height items, or with checkboxes that aren't on the left. The application should restore all graphics device interface (GDI) objects selected for the display context supplied in *lpDrawItemStruct* before the termination of this member function.

If checklist box items are not all the same height, the checklist box style (specified in **Create**) must be **LBS_OWNERVARIABLE**, and you must override the **MeasureItem** function.

See Also: CCheckListBox::Create, CCheckListBox::MeasureItem

CCheckListBox::Enable

void Enable(int *nIndex***, BOOL** *bEnabled* **= TRUE);**

Parameters

nIndex Index of the checklist box item to be enabled.

bEnabled Specifies whether the item is enabled or disabled.

Remarks

Call this function to enable or disable a checklist box item.

See Also: CCheckListBox::IsEnabled

CCheckListBox::GetCheck

int GetCheck(int *nIndex* **);**

Return Value

Zero if the item is not checked, 1 if it is checked, and 2 if it is indeterminate.

Parameters

    nIndex   Index of the item whose check status is to be retrieved.

Remarks

    Call this function to determine the check state of an item.

    See Also: **CCheckListBox::OnGetCheckPosition, CCheckListBox::SetCheck, CCheckListBox::SetCheckStyle, CCheckListBox::GetCheckStyle**

CCheckListBox::GetCheckStyle

    UINT GetCheckStyle( );

Return Value

    The style of the control's check boxes.

Remarks

    Call this function to get the checklist box's style. For information on possible styles, see **SetCheckStyle**.

    See Also: **CCheckListBox::OnGetCheckPosition, CCheckListBox::SetCheck, CCheckListBox::SetCheckStyle, CCheckListBox::GetCheck**

CCheckListBox::IsEnabled

    BOOL IsEnabled(int *nIndex*);

Return Value

    Nonzero if the item is enabled; otherwise 0.

Parameters

    nIndex   Index of the item.

Remarks

    Call this function to determine whether an item is enabled.

    See Also: **CCheckListBox::Enable**

CCheckListBox::MeasureItem

    virtual void MeasureItem(LPMEASUREITEMSTRUCT *lpMeasureItemStruct*);

Parameters

    lpMeasureItemStruct   A long pointer to a **MEASUREITEMSTRUCT** structure.

Remarks

    Called by the framework when a checklist box with anon-default style is created.

By default, this member function does nothing. Override this member function and fill in the **MEASUREITEMSTRUCT** structure to inform Windows of the dimensions of checklist-box items. If the checklist box is created with the **LBS_OWNERDRAWVARIABLE** style, the framework calls this member function for each item in the list box. Otherwise, this member is called only once.

See Also: CCheckListBox::Create, CCheckListBox::DrawItem

CCheckListBox::OnGetCheckPosition

virtual CRect OnGetCheckPosition(CRect *rectItem***, CRect** *rectCheckBox* **);**

Return Value

The position and size of an item's check box.

Parameters

rectItem   The position and size of the list item.

rectCheckBox   The default position and size of an item's check box.

Remarks

The framework calls this function to get the position and size of the check box in an item.

The default implementation only returns the default position and size of the check box (*rectCheckBox*). By default, a check box is aligned in the upper-left corner of an item and is the standard check box size. There may be cases where you want the check boxes on the right, or want a larger or smaller check box. In these cases, override **OnGetCheckPosition** to change the check box position and size within the item.

For example, the following function overrides the default and puts the check box on the right of the item, makes it the same height as the item (minus a pixel offset at the top and bottom), and makes it the standard check box width:

```
CRect CMyCheckListBox::OnGetCheckPosition(CRect rectItem,
↪ CRect rectCheckBox)
{
    CRect rectMyCheckBox;
    rectMyCheckBox.top = rectItem.top -1;
    rectMyCheckBox.bottom = rectItem.bottom -1;
    rectMyCheckBox.right = rectItem.right -1;
    rectMyCheckBox.left = rectItem.right -1 - rectCheckBox.Width();
    return rectMyCheckBox;
}
```

See Also: CCheckListBox::SetCheck, CCheckListBox::SetCheckStyle, CCheckListBox::GetCheck, CCheckListBox::GetCheckStyle

CCheckListBox::SetCheck

void SetCheck(int *nIndex*, **int** *nCheck* **);**

Parameters

nIndex   Index of the item whose check box is to be set.

nCheck   State of the check box: 0 for clear, 1 for checked, and 2 for indeterminate.

Remarks

Call this function to set the check box of the item specified by *nIndex*.

**See Also: CCheckListBox::SetCheckStyle, CCheckListBox::GetCheck,
CCheckListBox::GetCheckStyle**

CCheckListBox::SetCheckStyle

void SetCheckStyle(UINT *nStyle* **);**

Parameters

nStyle   Determines the style of check boxes in the checklist box.

Remarks

Call this function to set the style of check boxes in the checklist box. Valid styles are:

- **BS_CHECKBOX**
- **BS_AUTOCHECKBOX**
- **BS_AUTO3STATE**
- **BS_3STATE**

For information on these styles, see "Button Styles."

**See Also: CCheckListBox::SetCheck, CCheckListBox::GetCheck,
CCheckListBox::GetCheckStyle**

CClientDC

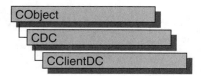

The **CClientDC** class is derived from **CDC** and takes care of calling the Windows functions **GetDC** at construction time and **ReleaseDC** at destruction time. This means that the device context associated with a **CClientDC** object is the client area of a window.

For more information on **CClientDC**, see "Device Contexts" in *Visual C++ Programmer's Guide* online.

#include <afxwin.h>

See Also: CDC

CClientDC Class Members

Construction

CClientDC	Constructs a **CClientDC** object connected to the **CWnd**.

Data Members

m_hWnd	The **HWND** of the window for which this **CClientDC** is valid.

Member Functions
CClientDC::CClientDC

CClientDC(CWnd* *pWnd* **);**
    throw(CResourceException);

Parameters

pWnd   The window whose client area the device context object will access.

Remarks

Constructs a **CClientDC** object that accesses the client area of the **CWnd** pointed to by *pWnd*. The constructor calls the Windows function **GetDC**.

An exception (of type **CResourceException**) is thrown if the Windows **GetDC** call fails. A device context may not be available if Windows has already allocated all of its available device contexts. Your application competes for the five common display contexts available at any given time under Windows.

Data Members
CClientDC::m_hWnd

Remarks

The **HWND** of the **CWnd** pointer used to construct the **CClientDC** object. **m_hWnd** is a protected variable.

CCmdTarget

CCmdTarget is the base class for the Microsoft Foundation Class Library message-map architecture. A message map routes commands or messages to the member functions you write to handle them. (A command is a message from a menu item, command button, or accelerator key.)

Key framework classes derived from **CCmdTarget** include **CView**, **CWinApp**, **CDocument**, **CWnd**, and **CFrameWnd**. If you intend for a new class to handle messages, derive the class from one of these **CCmdTarget**-derived classes. You will rarely derive a class from **CCmdTarget** directly.

For an overview of command targets and **OnCmdMsg** routing, see "Command Targets," "Command Routing," and "Mapping Messages" in *Visual C++ Programmer's Guide* online.

CCmdTarget includes member functions that handle the display of an hourglass cursor. Display the hourglass cursor when you expect a command to take a noticeable time interval to execute.

Dispatch maps, similar to message maps, are used to expose OLE automation **IDispatch** functionality. By exposing this interface, other applications (such as Visual Basic) can call into your application. For more information on the **IDispatch** interfaces, see "Creating the IDispatch Interface" and "Dispatch Interface and API Functions" in the *Win32 SDK OLE Programmer's Reference*.

#include <afxwin.h>

See Also: **CCmdUI**, **CDocument**, **CDocTemplate**, **CWinApp**, **CWnd**, **CView**, **CFrameWnd**, **COleDispatchDriver**

CCmdTarget Class Members

Attributes

FromIDispatch	Returns a pointer to the **CCmdTarget** object associated with the **IDispatch** pointer.
GetIDispatch	Returns a pointer to the **IDispatch** object associated with the **CCmdTarget** object.
IsResultExpected	Returns nonzero if an automation function should return a value.

Operations

BeginWaitCursor	Displays the cursor as an hourglass cursor.
EnableAutomation	Allows OLE automation for the **CCmdTarget** object.
EndWaitCursor	Returns to the previous cursor.
RestoreWaitCursor	Restores the hourglass cursor.

Overridables

OnCmdMsg	Routes and dispatches command messages.
OnFinalRelease	Cleans up after the last OLE reference is released.

Member Functions
CCmdTarget::BeginWaitCursor

void BeginWaitCursor( );

Remarks

Call this function to display the cursor as an hourglass when you expect a command to take a noticeable time interval to execute. The framework calls this function to show the user that it is busy, such as when a **CDocument** object loads or saves itself to a file.

The actions of **BeginWaitCursor** are not always effective outside of a single message handler as other actions, such as **OnSetCursor** handling, could change the cursor.

Call **EndWaitCursor** to restore the previous cursor.

Example

```
// The following example illustrates the most common case
// of displaying the hourglass cursor during some lengthy
// processing of a command handler implemented in some
// CCmdTarget-derived class, such as a document or view.

void CMyView::OnSomeCommand()
{
    BeginWaitCursor(); // display the hourglass cursor

    // do some lengthy processing

    EndWaitCursor(); // remove the hourglass cursor
}

// The next example illustrates RestoreWaitCursor.
void CMyView::OnSomeCommand()
{
```

```
        BeginWaitCursor(); // display the hourglass cursor

        // do some lengthy processing

        // The dialog box will normally change the cursor to
        // the standard arrow cursor, and leave the cursor in
        // as the standard arrow cursor when the dialog box is
        // closed.
        CMyDialog dlg;
        dlg.DoModal();

        // It is necessary to call RestoreWaitCursor here in order
        // to change the cursor back to the hourglass cursor.
        RestoreWaitCursor();

        // do some more lengthy processing

        EndWaitCursor(); // remove the hourglass cursor
    }


// In the above example, the dialog was clearly invoked between
// the pair of calls to BeginWaitCursor and EndWaitCursor.
// Sometimes it may not be clear whether the dialog is invoked
// in between a pair of calls to BeginWaitCursor and EndWaitCursor.
// It is permissable to call RestoreWaitCursor, even if
// BeginWaitCursor was not previously called.  This case is
// illustrated below, where CMyView::AnotherFunction does not
// need to know whether it was called in the context of an
// hourglass cursor.
void CMyView::AnotherFunction()
{
    // some processing ...

    CMyDialog dlg;
    dlg.DoModal();
    RestoreWaitCursor();

    // some more processing ...
}


// If the dialog is invoked from a member function of
// some non-CCmdTarget, then you can call CWinApp::DoWaitCursor
// with a 0 parameter value to restore the hourglass cursor.
void CMyObject::AnotherFunction()
{
    CMyDialog dlg;
    dlg.DoModal();
    AfxGetApp()->DoWaitCursor(0); // same as CCmdTarget::RestoreWaitCursor
}
```

**See Also: CWaitCursor, CCmdTarget::EndWaitCursor,
CCmdTarget::RestoreWaitCursor, CWinApp::DoWaitCursor**

CCmdTarget::EnableAutomation

void EnableAutomation( );

Remarks

Call this function to enable OLE automation for an object. This function is typically called from the constructor of your object and should only be called if a dispatch map has been declared for the class. For more information on automation see the articles "Automation Clients" and "Automation Servers" in *Visual C++ Programmer's Guide* online.

See Also: DECLARE_DISPATCH_MAP, DECLARE_OLECREATE

CCmdTarget::EndWaitCursor

void EndWaitCursor( );

Remarks

Call this function after you have called the **BeginWaitCursor** member function to return from the hourglass cursor to the previous cursor. The framework also calls this member function after it has called the hourglass cursor.

Example

```
// The following example illustrates the most common case
// of displaying the hourglass cursor during some lengthy
// processing of a command handler implemented in some
// CCmdTarget-derived class, such as a document or view.

void CMyView::OnSomeCommand()
{
    BeginWaitCursor(); // display the hourglass cursor

    // do some lengthy processing

    EndWaitCursor(); // remove the hourglass cursor
}

// The next example illustrates RestoreWaitCursor.
void CMyView::OnSomeCommand()
{
    BeginWaitCursor(); // display the hourglass cursor

    // do some lengthy processing

    // The dialog box will normally change the cursor to
    // the standard arrow cursor, and leave the cursor in
    // as the standard arrow cursor when the dialog box is
    // closed.
    CMyDialog dlg;
    dlg.DoModal();
```

```
        // It is necessary to call RestoreWaitCursor here in order
        // to change the cursor back to the hourglass cursor.
        RestoreWaitCursor();

        // do some more lengthy processing

        EndWaitCursor(); // remove the hourglass cursor
    }

    // In the above example, the dialog was clearly invoked between
    // the pair of calls to BeginWaitCursor and EndWaitCursor.
    // Sometimes it may not be clear whether the dialog is invoked
    // in between a pair of calls to BeginWaitCursor and EndWaitCursor.
    // It is permissable to call RestoreWaitCursor, even if
    // BeginWaitCursor was not previously called.  This case is
    // illustrated below, where CMyView::AnotherFunction does not
    // need to know whether it was called in the context of an
    // hourglass cursor.
    void CMyView::AnotherFunction()
    {
        // some processing ...

        CMyDialog dlg;
        dlg.DoModal();
        RestoreWaitCursor();

        // some more processing ...
    }

    // If the dialog is invoked from a member function of
    // some non-CCmdTarget, then you can call CWinApp::DoWaitCursor
    // with a 0 parameter value to restore the hourglass cursor.
    void CMyObject::AnotherFunction()
    {
        CMyDialog dlg;
        dlg.DoModal();
        AfxGetApp()->DoWaitCursor(0); // same as CCmdTarget::RestoreWaitCursor
    }
```

See Also: **CWaitCursor, CCmdTarget::BeginWaitCursor, CCmdTarget::RestoreWaitCursor, CWinApp::DoWaitCursor**

CCmdTarget::FromIDispatch

static CCmdTarget* FromIDispatch(LPDISPATCH *lpDispatch* **);**

Return Value

A pointer to the **CCmdTarget** object associated with *lpDispatch*. This function returns **NULL** if the **IDispatch** object is not recognized as a Microsoft Foundation Class **IDispatch** object.

Parameters

lpDispatch   A pointer to an **IDispatch** object.

Remarks

Call this function to map an **IDispatch** pointer, received from automation member functions of a class, into the **CCmdTarget** object that implements the interfaces of the **IDispatch** object.

The result of this function is the inverse of a call to the member function **GetIDispatch**.

See Also: **CCmdTarget::GetIDispatch, COleDispatchDriver**

CCmdTarget::GetIDispatch

LPDISPATCH GetIDispatch(BOOL *bAddRef* **);**

Return Value

The **IDispatch** pointer associated with the object.

Parameters

bAddRef Specifies whether to increment the reference count for the object.

Remarks

Call this member function to retrieve the **IDispatch** pointer from an automation method that either returns an **IDispatch** pointer or takes an **IDispatch** pointer by reference.

For objects that call **EnableAutomation** in their constructors, making them automation enabled, this function returns a pointer to the Foundation Class implementation of **IDispatch** that is used by clients who communicate via the **IDispatch** interface. Calling this function automatically adds a reference to the pointer, so it is not necessary to make a call to **IUnknown::AddRef**.

See Also: **CCmdTarget::EnableAutomation, COleDispatchDriver, IUnknown::Release**

CCmdTarget::IsResultExpected

BOOL IsResultExpected( );

Return Value

Nonzero if an automation function should return a value; otherwise 0.

Remarks

Use **IsResultExpected** to ascertain whether a client expects a return value from its call to an automation function. The OLE interface supplies information to MFC about whether the client is using or ignoring the result of a function call, and MFC in turn uses this information to determine the result of a call to **IsResultExpected**. If production of a return value is time- or resource-intensive, you can increase efficiency by calling this function before computing the return value.

This function returns 0 only once so that you will get valid return values from other automation functions if you call them from the automation function that the client has called.

IsResultExpected returns a nonzero value if called when an automation function call is not in progress.

See Also: **CCmdTarget::GetIDispatch**, **CCmdTarget::EnableAutomation**

CCmdTarget::OnCmdMsg

virtual **BOOL OnCmdMsg**(**UINT** *nID*, **int** *nCode*, **void*** *pExtra*,
  ➞ **AFX_CMDHANDLERINFO*** *pHandlerInfo*);

Return Value

Nonzero if the message is handled; otherwise 0.

Parameters

nID   Contains the command ID.

nCode   Identifies the command notification code.

pExtra   Used according to the value of *nCode*.

pHandlerInfo   If not **NULL**, **OnCmdMsg** fills in the **pTarget** and **pmf** members of the *pHandlerInfo* structure instead of dispatching the command. Typically, this parameter should be **NULL**.

Remarks

Called by the framework to route and dispatch command messages and to handle the update of command user-interface objects. This is the main implementation routine of the framework command architecture.

At run time, **OnCmdMsg** dispatches a command to other objects or handles the command itself by calling the root class **CCmdTarget::OnCmdMsg**, which does the actual message-map lookup. For a complete description of the default command routing, see "Message Handling and Mapping Topics" in *Visual C++ Programmer's Guide* online.

On rare occasions, you may want to override this member function to extend the framework's standard command routing. Refer to Technical Note 21 online for advanced details of the command-routing architecture.

Example

```
// This example illustrates extending the framework's standard command
// route from the view to objects managed by the view.  This example
// is from an object-oriented drawing application, similar to the
// DRAWCLI sample application, which draws and edits "shapes".

BOOL CMyView::OnCmdMsg(UINT nID, int nCode, void* pExtra,
    AFX_CMDHANDLERINFO* pHandlerInfo)
{
```

```
// Extend the framework's command route from the view to
// the application-specific CMyShape that is currently selected
// in the view. m_pActiveShape is NULL if no shape object
// is currently selected in the view.
if ((m_pActiveShape != NULL)
    && m_pActiveShape->OnCmdMsg(nID, nCode, pExtra, pHandlerInfo))
    return TRUE;

// If the object(s) in the extended command route don't handle
// the command, then let the base class OnCmdMsg handle it.
return CView::OnCmdMsg(nID, nCode, pExtra, pHandlerInfo);
}

// The command handler for ID_SHAPE_COLOR (menu command to change
// the color of the currently selected shape) was added to
// the message map of CMyShape (note, not CMyView) using ClassWizard.

// The menu item will be automatically enabled or disabled, depending
// on whether a CMyShape is currently selected in the view, that is,
// depending on whether CMyView::m_pActiveView is NULL.  It is not
// necessary to implement an ON_UPDATE_COMMAND_UI handler to enable
// or disable the menu item.

BEGIN_MESSAGE_MAP(CMyShape, CCmdTarget)
    //{{AFX_MSG_MAP(CMyShape)
    ON_COMMAND(ID_SHAPE_COLOR, OnShapeColor)
    //}}AFX_MSG_MAP
END_MESSAGE_MAP()
```

See Also: CCmdUI

CCmdTarget::OnFinalRelease

virtual void OnFinalRelease( );

Remarks

Called by the framework when the last OLE reference to or from the object is released. Override this function to provide special handling for this situation. The default implementation deletes the object.

See Also: COleServerItem

CCmdTarget::RestoreWaitCursor

void RestoreWaitCursor( );

Remarks

Call this function to restore the appropriate hourglass cursor after the system cursor has changed (for example, after a message box has opened and then closed while in the middle of a lengthy operation).

Example

```
// The following example illustrates the most common case
// of displaying the hourglass cursor during some lengthy
// processing of a command handler implemented in some
// CCmdTarget-derived class, such as a document or view.

void CMyView::OnSomeCommand()
{
    BeginWaitCursor(); // display the hourglass cursor

    // do some lengthy processing

    EndWaitCursor(); // remove the hourglass cursor
}

// The next example illustrates RestoreWaitCursor.
void CMyView::OnSomeCommand()
{
    BeginWaitCursor(); // display the hourglass cursor

    // do some lengthy processing

    // The dialog box will normally change the cursor to
    // the standard arrow cursor, and leave the cursor in
    // as the standard arrow cursor when the dialog box is
    // closed.
    CMyDialog dlg;
    dlg.DoModal();

    // It is necessary to call RestoreWaitCursor here in order
    // to change the cursor back to the hourglass cursor.
    RestoreWaitCursor();

    // do some more lengthy processing

    EndWaitCursor(); // remove the hourglass cursor
}

// In the above example, the dialog was clearly invoked between
// the pair of calls to BeginWaitCursor and EndWaitCursor.
// Sometimes it may not be clear whether the dialog is invoked
// in between a pair of calls to BeginWaitCursor and EndWaitCursor.
// It is permissable to call RestoreWaitCursor, even if
// BeginWaitCursor was not previously called.  This case is
// illustrated below, where CMyView::AnotherFunction does not
// need to know whether it was called in the context of an
// hourglass cursor.
void CMyView::AnotherFunction()
{
    // some processing ...
```

```
   CMyDialog dlg;
   dlg.DoModal();
   RestoreWaitCursor();

   // some more processing ...
}

// If the dialog is invoked from a member function of
// some non-CCmdTarget, then you can call CWinApp::DoWaitCursor
// with a 0 parameter value to restore the hourglass cursor.
void CMyObject::AnotherFunction()
{
   CMyDialog dlg;
   dlg.DoModal();
   AfxGetApp()->DoWaitCursor(0); // same as CCmdTarget::RestoreWaitCursor
}
```

See Also: CWaitCursor, **CCmdTarget::EndWaitCursor**,
CCmdTarget::BeginWaitCursor, **CWinApp::DoWaitCursor**

CCmdUI

CCmdUI does not have a base class.

The **CCmdUI** class is used only within an **ON_UPDATE_COMMAND_UI** handler in a **CCmdTarget**-derived class.

When a user of your application pulls down a menu, each menu item needs to know whether it should be displayed as enabled or disabled. The target of a menu command provides this information by implementing an **ON_UPDATE_COMMAND_UI** handler. Use ClassWizard to browse the command user-interface objects in your application and create a message-map entry and function prototype for each handler.

When the menu is pulled down, the framework searches for and calls each **ON_UPDATE_COMMAND_UI** handler, each handler calls **CCmdUI** member functions such as **Enable** and **Check**, and the framework then appropriately displays each menu item.

A menu item can be replaced with a control-bar button or other command user-interface object without changing the code within the **ON_UPDATE_COMMAND_UI** handler.

The following table summarizes the effect **CCmdUI**'s member functions have on various command user-interface items.

User-Interface Item	Enable	SetCheck	SetRadio	SetText
Menu item	Enables or disables	Checks (×) or unchecks	Checks using dot (•)	Sets item text
Toolbar button	Enables or disables	Selects, unselects, or indeterminate	Same as **SetCheck**	(Not applicable)
Status-bar pane	Makes text visible or invisible	Sets pop-out or normal border	Same as **SetCheck**	Sets pane text
Normal button in **CDialogBar**	Enables or disables	Checks or unchecks check box	Same as **SetCheck**	Sets button text
Normal control in **CDialogBar**	Enables or disables	(Not applicable)	(Not applicable)	Sets window text

For more on the use of this class, see "Constructing the User Interface" in *Visual C++ Tutorials* online and "How to Update User-Interface Objects" in *Visual C++ Programmer's Guide* online.

#include <afxwin.h>

See Also: **CCmdTarget**

CCmdUI Class Members

Data Members

m_nID	The ID of the user-interface object.
m_nIndex	The index of the user-interface object.
m_pMenu	Points to the menu represented by the **CCmdUI** object.
m_pSubMenu	Points to the contained sub-menu represented by the **CCmdUI** object.
m_pOther	Points to the window object that sent the notification.

Operations

Enable	Enables or disables the user-interface item for this command.
SetCheck	Sets the check state of the user-interface item for this command.
SetRadio	Like the **SetCheck** member function, but operates on radio groups.
SetText	Sets the text for the user-interface item for this command.
ContinueRouting	Tells the command-routing mechanism to continue routing the current message down the chain of handlers.

Member Functions

CCmdUI::ContinueRouting

void ContinueRouting( );

Remarks

Call this member function to tell the command-routing mechanism to continue routing the current message down the chain of handlers.

This is an advanced member function that should be used in conjunction with an **ON_COMMAND_EX** handler that returns **FALSE**. For more information, see Technical Note 21 online.

CCmdUI::Enable

virtual void Enable(BOOL *bOn* **= TRUE);**

Parameters

bOn   **TRUE** to enable the item, **FALSE** to disable it.

Remarks

Call this member function to enable or disable the user-interface item for this command.

See Also: **CCmdUI::SetCheck**

CCmdUI::SetCheck

virtual void SetCheck(int *nCheck* **= 1);**

Parameters

nCheck   Specifies the check state to set. If 0, unchecks; if 1, checks; and if 2, sets indeterminate.

Remarks

Call this member function to set the user-interface item for this command to the appropriate check state. This member function works for menu items and toolbar buttons. The indeterminate state applies only to toolbar buttons.

See Also: CCmdUI::SetRadio

CCmdUI::SetRadio

virtual void SetRadio(BOOL *bOn* **= TRUE);**

Parameters

bOn   **TRUE** to enable the item; otherwise **FALSE**.

Remarks

Call this member function to set the user-interface item for this command to the appropriate check state. This member function operates like **SetCheck**, except that it operates on user-interface items acting as part of a radio group. Unchecking the other items in the group is not automatic unless the items themselves maintain the radio-group behavior.

See Also: CCmdUI::SetCheck

CCmdUI::SetText

virtual void SetText(LPCTSTR *lpszText* **);**

Parameters

lpszText   A pointer to a text string.

Remarks

Call this member function to set the text of the user-interface item for this command.

See Also: CCmdUI::Enable

Data Members
CCmdUI::m_nID

Remarks

The ID of the menu item, toolbar button, or other user-interface object represented by the **CCmdUI** object.

CCmdUI::m_nIndex

Remarks

The index of the menu item, toolbar button, or other user-interface object represented by the **CCmdUI** object.

CCmdUI::m_pMenu

Remarks

Pointer (of **CMenu** type) to the menu represented by the **CCmdUI** object. **NULL** if the item is not a menu.

See Also: **CMenu**

CCmdUI::m_pSubMenu

Remarks

Pointer (of **CMenu** type) to the contained sub-menu represented by the **CCmdUI** object. **NULL** if the item is not a menu. If the sub menu is a pop-up, **m_nID** contains the ID of the first item in the pop-up menu. For more information, see Technical Note 21 online.

See Also: **CMenu**

CCmdUI::m_pOther

Remarks

Pointer (of type **CWnd**) to the window object, such as a tool or status bar, that sent the notification. **NULL** if the item is a menu or a non-**CWnd** object.

See Also: **CWnd**

CColorDialog

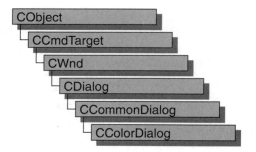

CObject
CCmdTarget
CWnd
CDialog
CCommonDialog
CColorDialog

The **CColorDialog** class allows you to incorporate a color-selection dialog box into your application. A **CColorDialog** object is a dialog box with a list of colors that are defined for the display system. The user can select or create a particular color from the list, which is then reported back to the application when the dialog box exits.

To construct a **CColorDialog** object, use the provided constructor or derive a new class and use your own custom constructor.

Once the dialog box has been constructed, you can set or modify any values in the m_cc structure to initialize the values of the dialog box's controls. The **m_cc** structure is of type **CHOOSECOLOR**.

After initializing the dialog box's controls, call the **DoModal** member function to display the dialog box and allow the user to select a color. **DoModal** returns the user's selection of either the dialog box's OK (**IDOK**) or Cancel (**IDCANCEL**) button.

If **DoModal** returns **IDOK**, you can use one of **CColorDialog**'s member functions to retrieve the information input by the user.

You can use the Windows **CommDlgExtendedError** function to determine whether an error occurred during initialization of the dialog box and to learn more about the error.

CColorDialog relies on the COMMDLG.DLL file that ships with Windows versions 3.1 and later.

To customize the dialog box, derive a class from **CColorDialog**, provide a custom dialog template, and add a message map to process the notification messages from the extended controls. Any unprocessed messages should be passed to the base class.

Customizing the hook function is not required.

Note On some installations the **CColorDialog** object will not display with a gray background if you have used the framework to make other **CDialog** objects gray.

For more information on using **CColorDialog**, see "Common Dialog Classes" in *Visual C++ Programmer's Guide* online.

#include <afxdlgs.h>

CColorDialog Class Members

Data Members

m_cc	A structure used to customize the settings of the dialog box.

Construction

CColorDialog	Constructs a **CColorDialog** object.

Operations

DoModal	Displays a color dialog box and allows the user to make a selection.
GetColor	Returns a **COLORREF** structure containing the values of the selected color.
GetSavedCustomColors	Retrieves custom colors created by the user.
SetCurrentColor	Forces the current color selection to the specified color.

Overridables

OnColorOK	Override to validate the color entered into the dialog box.

Member Functions

CColorDialog::CColorDialog

CColorDialog(COLORREF *clrInit* **= 0, DWORD** *dwFlags* **= 0,**
   ↳ **CWnd*** *pParentWnd* **= NULL);**

Parameters

clrInit The default color selection. If no value is specified, the default is RGB(0,0,0) (black).

dwFlags A set of flags that customize the function and appearance of the dialog box. For more information, see the **CHOOSECOLOR** structure in the Win32 SDK documentation.

pParentWnd A pointer to the dialog box's parent or owner window.

Remarks

Constructs a **CColorDialog** object.

See Also: **CDialog::DoModal**

CColorDialog::DoModal

virtual int DoModal( );

Return Value

IDOK or **IDCANCEL** if the function is successful; otherwise 0. **IDOK** and **IDCANCEL** are constants that indicate whether the user selected the OK or Cancel button.

If **IDCANCEL** is returned, you can call the Windows **CommDlgExtendedError** function to determine whether an error occurred.

Remarks

Call this function to display the Windows common color dialog box and allow the user to select a color.

If you want to initialize the various color dialog-box options by setting members of the **m_cc** structure, you should do this before calling **DoModal** but after the dialog-box object is constructed.

After calling **DoModal**, you can call other member functions to retrieve the settings or information input by the user into the dialog box.

See Also: **CDialog::DoModal**, **CColorDialog::CColorDialog**

CColorDialog::GetColor

COLORREF GetColor( ) const;

Return Value

A **COLORREF** value that contains the RGB information for the color selected in the color dialog box.

Remarks

Call this function after calling **DoModal** to retrieve the information about the color the user selected.

See Also: **CColorDialog::SetCurrentColor**

CColorDialog::GetSavedCustomColors

static COLORREF * GetSavedCustomColors( );

Return Value

A pointer to an array of 16 RGB color values that stores custom colors created by the user.

Remarks

CColorDialog objects permit the user, in addition to choosing colors, to define up to 16 custom colors. The **GetSavedCustomColors** member function provides access to these colors. These colors can be retrieved after **DoModal** returns **IDOK**.

Each of the 16 RGB values in the returned array is initialized to RGB(255,255,255) (white). The custom colors chosen by the user are saved only between dialog box invocations within the application. If you wish to save these colors between invocations of the application, you must save them in some other manner, such as in an initialization (.INI) file.

See Also: CColorDialog::GetColor

CColorDialog::OnColorOK

virtual BOOL OnColorOK( );

Return Value

Nonzero if the dialog box should not be dismissed; otherwise 0 to accept the color that was entered.

Remarks

Override this function only if you want to provide custom validation of the color entered into the dialog box. This function allows you to reject a color entered by a user into a common color dialog box for any application-specific reason. Normally, you do not need to use this function because the framework provides default validation of colors and displays a message box if an invalid color is entered.

Use the **GetColor** member function to get the RGB value of the color.

If 0 is returned, the dialog box will remain displayed in order for the user to enter another filename.

CColorDialog::SetCurrentColor

void SetCurrentColor(COLORREF *clr* **);**

Parameters

clr An RGB color value.

Remarks

Call this function after calling **DoModal** to force the current color selection to the color value specified in *clr*. This function is called from within a message handler or **OnColorOK**. The dialog box will automatically update the user's selection based on the value of the *clr* parameter.

See Also: **CColorDialog::GetColor, CColorDialog::OnColorOK**

Data Members

CColorDialog::m_cc

CHOOSECOLOR m_cc;

Remarks

A structure of type **CHOOSECOLOR**, whose members store the characteristics and values of the dialog box. After constructing a **CColorDialog** object, you can use **m_cc** to set various aspects of the dialog box before calling the **DoModal** member function.

CComboBox

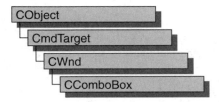

The **CComboBox** class provides the functionality of a Windows combo box.

A combo box consists of a list box combined with either a static control or edit control. The list-box portion of the control may be displayed at all times or may only drop down when the user selects the drop-down arrow next to the control.

The currently selected item (if any) in the list box is displayed in the static or edit control. In addition, if the combo box has the drop-down list style, the user can type the initial character of one of the items in the list, and the list box, if visible, will highlight the next item with that initial character.

The following table compares the three combo-box styles.

Style	When is list box visible?	Static or edit control?
Simple	Always	Edit
Drop-down	When dropped down	Edit
Drop-down list	When dropped down	Static

You can create a **CComboBox** object from either a dialog template or directly in your code. In both cases, first call the constructor **CComboBox** to construct the **CComboBox** object; then call the **Create** member function to create the control and attach it to the **CComboBox** object.

If you want to handle Windows notification messages sent by a combo box to its parent (usually a class derived from **CDialog**), add a message-map entry and message-handler member function to the parent class for each message.

Each message-map entry takes the following form:

ON_ Notification(*id*, *memberFxn*)

where *id* specifies the child-window ID of the combo-box control sending the notification and *memberFxn* is the name of the parent member function you have written to handle the notification.

The parent's function prototype is as follows:

afx_msg void *memberFxn*( );

The order in which certain notifications will be sent cannot be predicted. In particular, a **CBN_SELCHANGE** notification may occur either before or after a **CBN_CLOSEUP** notification.

Potential message-map entries are the following:

- **ON_CBN_CLOSEUP**   (Windows 3.1 and later.) The list box of a combo box has closed. This notification message is not sent for a combo box that has the **CBS_SIMPLE** style.

- **ON_CBN_DBLCLK**   The user double-clicks a string in the list box of a combo box. This notification message is only sent for a combo box with the **CBS_SIMPLE** style. For a combo box with the **CBS_DROPDOWN** or **CBS_DROPDOWNLIST** style, a double-click cannot occur because a single click hides the list box.

- **ON_CBN_DROPDOWN**   The list box of a combo box is about to drop down (be made visible). This notification message can occur only for a combo box with the **CBS_DROPDOWN** or **CBS_DROPDOWNLIST** style.

- **ON_CBN_EDITCHANGE**   The user has taken an action that may have altered the text in the edit-control portion of a combo box. Unlike the **CBN_EDITUPDATE** message, this message is sent after Windows updates the screen. It is not sent if the combo box has the **CBS_DROPDOWNLIST** style.

- **ON_CBN_EDITUPDATE**   The edit-control portion of a combo box is about to display altered text. This notification message is sent after the control has formatted the text but before it displays the text. It is not sent if the combo box has the **CBS_DROPDOWNLIST** style.

- **ON_CBN_ERRSPACE**   The combo box cannot allocate enough memory to meet a specific request.

- **ON_CBN_SELENDCANCEL**   (Windows 3.1 and later.) Indicates the user's selection should be canceled. The user clicks an item and then clicks another window or control to hide the list box of a combo box. This notification message is sent before the **CBN_CLOSEUP** notification message to indicate that the user's selection should be ignored. The **CBN_SELENDCANCEL** or **CBN_SELENDOK** notification message is sent even if the **CBN_CLOSEUP** notification message is not sent (as in the case of a combo box with the **CBS_SIMPLE** style).

- **ON_CBN_SELENDOK**   The user selects an item and then either presses the ENTER key or clicks the DOWN ARROW key to hide the list box of a combo box. This notification message is sent before the **CBN_CLOSEUP** message to indicate that the user's selection should be considered valid. The **CBN_SELENDCANCEL** or **CBN_SELENDOK** notification message is sent even if the **CBN_CLOSEUP** notification message is not sent (as in the case of a combo box with the **CBS_SIMPLE** style).

- **ON_CBN_KILLFOCUS**   The combo box is losing the input focus.

- **ON_CBN_SELCHANGE**   The selection in the list box of a combo box is about to be changed as a result of the user either clicking in the list box or changing the selection by using the arrow keys. When processing this message, the text in the edit control of the combo box can only be retrieved via **GetLBText** or another similar function. **GetWindowText** cannot be used.

- **ON_CBN_SETFOCUS**   The combo box receives the input focus.

If you create a **CComboBox** object within a dialog box (through a dialog resource), the **CComboBox** object is automatically destroyed when the user closes the dialog box.

If you embed a **CComboBox** object within another window object, you do not need to destroy it. If you create the **CComboBox** object on the stack, it is destroyed automatically. If you create the **CComboBox** object on the heap by using the **new** function, you must call **delete** on the object to destroy it when the Windows combo box is destroyed.

#include <afxwin.h>

See Also: **CWnd, CButton, CEdit, CListBox, CScrollBar, CStatic, CDialog**

CComboBox Class Members

Construction

CComboBox	Constructs a **CComboBox** object.

Initialization

Create	Creates the combo box and attaches it to the **CComboBox** object.
InitStorage	Preallocates blocks of memory for items and strings in the list-box portion of the combo box.

General Operations

GetCount	Retrieves the number of items in the list box of a combo box.
GetCurSel	Retrieves the index of the currently selected item, if any, in the list box of a combo box.
SetCurSel	Selects a string in the list box of a combo box.
GetEditSel	Gets the starting and ending character positions of the current selection in the edit control of a combo box.
SetEditSel	Selects characters in the edit control of a combo box.
SetItemData	Sets the 32-bit value associated with the specified item in a combo box.
SetItemDataPtr	Sets the 32-bit value associated with the specified item in a combo box to the specified pointer (**void***).

(continued)

General Operations *(continued)*

GetItemData	Retrieves the application-supplied 32-bit value associated with the specified combo-box item.
GetItemDataPtr	Retrieves the application-supplied 32-bit value associated with the specified combo-box item as a pointer (**void***).
GetTopIndex	Returns the index of the first visible item in the list-box portion of the combo box.
SetTopIndex	Tells the list-box portion of the combo box to display the item with the specified index at the top.
SetHorizontalExtent	Sets the width in pixels that the list-box portion of the combo box can be scrolled horizontally.
GetHorizontalExtent	Returns the width in pixels that the list-box portion of the combo box can be scrolled horizontally.
SetDroppedWidth	Sets the minimum allowable width for the drop-down list-box portion of a combo box.
GetDroppedWidth	Retrieves the minimum allowable width for the drop-down list-box portion of a combo box.
Clear	Deletes (clears) the current selection (if any) in the edit control.
Copy	Copies the current selection (if any) onto the Clipboard in **CF_TEXT** format.
Cut	Deletes (cuts) the current selection, if any, in the edit control and copies the deleted text onto the Clipboard in **CF_TEXT** format.
Paste	Inserts the data from the Clipboard into the edit control at the current cursor position. Data is inserted only if the Clipboard contains data in **CF_TEXT** format.
LimitText	Limits the length of the text that the user can enter into the edit control of a combo box.
SetItemHeight	Sets the height of list items in a combo box or the height of the edit-control (or static-text) portion of a combo box.
GetItemHeight	Retrieves the height of list items in a combo box.
GetLBText	Gets a string from the list box of a combo box.
GetLBTextLen	Gets the length of a string in the list box of a combo box.
ShowDropDown	Shows or hides the list box of a combo box that has the **CBS_DROPDOWN** or **CBS_DROPDOWNLIST** style.
GetDroppedControlRect	Retrieves the screen coordinates of the visible (dropped-down) list box of a drop-down combo box.
GetDroppedState	Determines whether the list box of a drop-down combo box is visible (dropped down).
SetExtendedUI	Selects either the default user interface or the extended user interface for a combo box that has the **CBS_DROPDOWN** or **CBS_DROPDOWNLIST** style.
GetExtendedUI	Determines whether a combo box has the default user interface or the extended user interface.

General Operations *(continued)*

GetLocale	Retrieves the locale identifier for a combo box.
SetLocale	Sets the locale identifier for a combo box.

String Operations

AddString	Adds a string to the end of the list in the list box of a combo box or at the sorted position for list boxes with the **CBS_SORT** style.
DeleteString	Deletes a string from the list box of a combo box.
InsertString	Inserts a string into the list box of a combo box.
ResetContent	Removes all items from the list box and edit control of a combo box.
Dir	Adds a list of filenames to the list box of a combo box.
FindString	Finds the first string that contains the specified prefix in the list box of a combo box.
FindStringExact	Finds the first list-box string (in a combo box) that matches the specified string.
SelectString	Searches for a string in the list box of a combo box and, if the string is found, selects the string in the list box and copies the string to the edit control.

Overridables

DrawItem	Called by the framework when a visual aspect of an owner-draw combo box changes.
MeasureItem	Called by the framework to determine combo box dimensions when an owner-draw combo box is created.
CompareItem	Called by the framework to determine the relative position of a new list item in a sorted owner-draw combo box.
DeleteItem	Called by the framework when a list item is deleted from an owner-draw combo box.

Member Functions
CComboBox::AddString

int AddString(LPCTSTR *lpszString* **);**

Return Value
If the return value is greater than or equal to 0, it is the zero-based index to the string in the list box. The return value is **CB_ERR** if an error occurs; the return value is **CB_ERRSPACE** if insufficient space is available to store the new string.

Parameters
lpszString   Points to the null-terminated string that is to be added.

CCombo Box::CCombo Box

Remarks

Adds a string to the list box of a combo box. If the list box was not created with the **CBS_SORT** style, the string is added to the end of the list. Otherwise, the string is inserted into the list, and the list is sorted.

To insert a string into a specific location within the list, use the **InsertString** member function.

See Also: **CComboBox::InsertString**, **CComboBox::DeleteString**, **CB_ADDSTRING**

CComboBox::CComboBox

CComboBox( );

Remarks

Constructs a **CComboBox** object.

See Also: **CComboBox::Create**

CComboBox::Clear

void Clear( );

Remarks

Deletes (clears) the current selection, if any, in the edit control of the combo box.

To delete the current selection and place the deleted contents onto the Clipboard, use the **Cut** member function.

See Also: **CComboBox::Copy**, **CComboBox::Cut**, **CComboBox::Paste**, **WM_CLEAR**

CComboBox::CompareItem

virtual int CompareItem(LPCOMPAREITEMSTRUCT *lpCompareItemStruct* **);**

Return Value

Indicates the relative position of the two items described in the **COMPAREITEMSTRUCT** structure. It can be any of the following values:

Value	Meaning
−1	Item 1 sorts before item 2.
0	Item 1 and item 2 sort the same.
1	Item 1 sorts after item 2.

See **CWnd::OnCompareItem** for a description of **COMPAREITEMSTRUCT**.

Parameters

   lpCompareItemStruct   A long pointer to a **COMPAREITEMSTRUCT** structure.

Remarks

   Called by the framework to determine the relative position of a new item in the
   list-box portion of a sorted owner-draw combo box. By default, this member function
   does nothing. If you create an owner-draw combo box with the **LBS_SORT** style, you
   must override this member function to assist the framework in sorting new items
   added to the list box.

   See Also: **WM_COMPAREITEM, CComboBox::DrawItem,**
   CComboBox::MeasureItem, CComboBox::DeleteItem

CComboBox::Copy

   void Copy( );

Remarks

   Copies the current selection, if any, in the edit control of the combo box onto the
   Clipboard in **CF_TEXT** format.

   See Also: **CComboBox::Clear, CComboBox::Cut, CComboBox::Paste,**
   WM_COPY

CComboBox::Create

   BOOL Create(DWORD *dwStyle*, **const RECT&** *rect*, **CWnd*** *pParentWnd*, **UINT** *nID* **);**

Return Value

   Nonzero if successful; otherwise 0.

Parameters

   dwStyle   Specifies the style of the combo box. Apply any combination of combo-box
      styles to the box.

   rect   Points to the position and size of the combo box. Can be a **RECT** structure or a
      CRect object.

   pParentWnd   Specifies the combo box's parent window (usually a **CDialog**). It must
      not be **NULL**.

   nID   Specifies the combo box's control ID.

Remarks

   You construct a **CComboBox** object in two steps. First call the constructor, then call
   Create, which creates the Windows combo box and attaches it to the **CComboBox**
   object.

When **Create** executes, Windows sends the **WM_NCCREATE**, **WM_CREATE**, **WM_NCCALCSIZE**, and **WM_GETMINMAXINFO** messages to the combo box.

These messages are handled by default by the **OnNcCreate**, **OnCreate**, **OnNcCalcSize**, and **OnGetMinMaxInfo** member functions in the **CWnd** base class. To extend the default message handling, derive a class from **CComboBox**, add a message map to the new class, and override the preceding message-handler member functions. Override **OnCreate**, for example, to perform needed initialization for a new class.

Apply the following window styles to a combo-box control. :

- **WS_CHILD**   Always
- **WS_VISIBLE**   Usually
- **WS_DISABLED**   Rarely
- **WS_VSCROLL**   To add vertical scrolling for the list box in the combo box
- **WS_HSCROLL**   To add horizontal scrolling for the list box in the combo box
- **WS_GROUP**   To group controls
- **WS_TABSTOP**   To include the combo box in the tabbing order

See Also: **CComboBox::CComboBox**, "Combo-Box Styles"

CComboBox::Cut

void Cut( );

Remarks

Deletes (cuts) the current selection, if any, in the combo-box edit control and copies the deleted text onto the Clipboard in **CF_TEXT** format.

To delete the current selection without placing the deleted text onto the Clipboard, call the **Clear** member function.

See Also: **CComboBox::Clear**, **CComboBox::Copy**, **CComboBox::Paste**, **WM_CUT**

CComboBox::DeleteItem

virtual void DeleteItem(LPDELETEITEMSTRUCT *lpDeleteItemStruct* **);**

Parameters

lpDeleteItemStruct   A long pointer to a Windows **DELETEITEMSTRUCT** structure that contains information about the deleted item. See **CWnd::OnDeleteItem** for a description of this structure.

Remarks

Called by the framework when the user deletes an item from an owner-draw **CComboBox** object or destroys the combo box. The default implementation of this function does nothing. Override this function to redraw the combo box as needed.

See Also: **CComboBox::CompareItem**, **CComboBox::DrawItem**, **CComboBox::MeasureItem**, **WM_DELETEITEM**

CComboBox::DeleteString

int DeleteString(UINT *nIndex* **);**

Return Value

If the return value is greater than or equal to 0, then it is a count of the strings remaining in the list. The return value is **CB_ERR** if *nIndex* specifies an index greater then the number of items in the list.

Parameters

nIndex   Specifies the index to the string that is to be deleted.

Remarks

Deletes a string in the list box of a combo box.

See Also: **CComboBox::InsertString**, **CComboBox::AddString**, **CB_DELETESTRING**

CComboBox::Dir

int Dir(UINT *attr*, **LPCTSTR** *lpszWildCard* **);**

Return Value

If the return value is greater than or equal to 0, it is the zero-based index of the last filename added to the list. The return value is **CB_ERR** if an error occurs; the return value is **CB_ERRSPACE** if insufficient space is available to store the new strings.

Parameters

attr   Can be any combination of the **enum** values described in **CFile::GetStatus** or any combination of the following values:

- **DDL_READWRITE**   File can be read from or written to.
- **DDL_READONLY**   File can be read from but not written to.
- **DDL_HIDDEN**   File is hidden and does not appear in a directory listing.
- **DDL_SYSTEM**   File is a system file.
- **DDL_DIRECTORY**   The name specified by *lpszWildCard* specifies a directory.

- **DDL_ARCHIVE**   File has been archived.

- **DDL_DRIVES**   Include all drives that match the name specified by *lpszWildCard*.

- **DDL_EXCLUSIVE**   Exclusive flag. If the exclusive flag is set, only files of the specified type are listed. Otherwise, files of the specified type are listed in addition to "normal" files.

lpszWildCard   Points to a file-specification string. The string can contain wildcards (for example, *.*).

Remarks

Adds a list of filenames and/or drives to the list box of a combo box.

See Also: CWnd::DlgDirList, CB_DIR, CFile::GetStatus

CComboBox::DrawItem

virtual void DrawItem(LPDRAWITEMSTRUCT *lpDrawItemStruct* **);**

Parameters

lpDrawItemStruct   A pointer to a **DRAWITEMSTRUCT** structure that contains information about the type of drawing required.

Remarks

Called by the framework when a visual aspect of an owner-draw combo box changes. The **itemAction** member of the **DRAWITEMSTRUCT** structure defines the drawing action that is to be performed. See **CWnd::OnDrawItem** for a description of this structure.

By default, this member function does nothing. Override this member function to implement drawing for an owner-draw **CComboBox** object. Before this member function terminates, the application should restore all graphics device interface (GDI) objects selected for the display context supplied in *lpDrawItemStruct*.

See Also: CComboBox::CompareItem, WM_DRAWITEM, CComboBox::MeasureItem, CComboBox::DeleteItem

---

CComboBox::FindString

int FindString(int *nStartAfter*, **LPCTSTR** *lpszString* **) const;**

Return Value

If the return value is greater than or equal to 0, it is the zero-based index of the matching item. It is **CB_ERR** if the search was unsuccessful.

Parameters

nStartAfter   Contains the zero-based index of the item before the first item to be searched. When the search reaches the bottom of the list box, it continues from the top of the list box back to the item specified by *nStartAfter*. If –1, the entire list box is searched from the beginning.

lpszString   Points to the null-terminated string that contains the prefix to search for. The search is case independent, so this string can contain any combination of uppercase and lowercase letters.

Remarks

Finds, but doesn't select, the first string that contains the specified prefix in the list box of a combo box.

See Also: CComboBox::SelectString, **CComboBox::SetCurSel**, **CB_FINDSTRING**

CComboBox::FindStringExact

int FindStringExact(int *nIndexStart***, LPCTSTR** *lpszFind* **) const;**

Return Value

The zero-based index of the matching item, or **CB_ERR** if the search was unsuccessful.

Parameters

nIndexStart   Specifies the zero-based index of the item before the first item to be searched. When the search reaches the bottom of the list box, it continues from the top of the list box back to the item specified by *nIndexStart*. If *nIndexStart* is –1, the entire list box is searched from the beginning.

lpszFind   Points to the null-terminated string to search for. This string can contain a complete filename, including the extension. The search is not case sensitive, so this string can contain any combination of uppercase and lowercase letters.

Remarks

Call the **FindStringExact** member function to find the first list-box string (in a combo box) that matches the string specified in *lpszFind*.

If the combo box was created with an owner-draw style but without the **CBS_HASSTRINGS** style, **FindStringExact** attempts to match the doubleword value against the value of *lpszFind*.

See Also: CComboBox::FindString, CB_FINDSTRINGEXACT

CComboBox::GetCount

int GetCount( ) const;

Return Value

The number of items. The returned count is one greater than the index value of the last item (the index is zero-based). It is **CB_ERR** if an error occurs.

Remarks

Call this member function to retrieve the number of items in the list-box portion of a combo box.

See Also: CB_GETCOUNT

CComboBox::GetCurSel

int GetCurSel( ) const;

Return Value

The zero-based index of the currently selected item in the list box of a combo box, or **CB_ERR** if no item is selected.

Remarks

Call this member function to determine which item in the combo box is selected. **GetCurSel** returns an index into the list.

See Also: CComboBox::SetCurSel, CB_GETCURSEL

CComboBox::GetDroppedControlRect

void GetDroppedControlRect(LPRECT *lprect* **) const;**

Parameters

lprect   Points to the **RECT** structure that is to receive the coordinates.

Remarks

Call the **GetDroppedControlRect** member function to retrieve the screen coordinates of the visible (dropped-down) list box of a drop-down combo box.

See Also: CB_GETDROPPEDCONTROLRECT

CComboBox::GetDroppedState

BOOL GetDroppedState( ) const;

Return Value

Nonzero if the list box is visible; otherwise 0.

Remarks

Call the **GetDroppedState** member function to determine whether the list box of a drop-down combo box is visible (dropped down).

See Also: **CB_SHOWDROPDOWN**, **CB_GETDROPPEDSTATE**

CComboBox::GetDroppedWidth

int GetDroppedWidth( ) const;

Return Value

If successful, the minimum allowable width, in pixels; otherwise, **CB_ERR**.

Remarks

Call this function to retrieve the minimum allowable width, in pixels, of the list box of a combo box. This function only applies to combo boxes with the **CBS_DROPDOWN** or **CBS_DROPDOWNLIST** style.

By default, the minimum allowable width of the drop-down list box is 0. The minimum allowable width can be set by calling **SetDroppedWidth**. When the l ist-box portion of the combo box is displayed, its width is the larger of the minimum allowable width or the combo box width.

See Also: **CComboBox::SetDroppedWidth**, **CB_GETDROPPEDWIDTH**

CComboBox::GetEditSel

DWORD GetEditSel( ) const;

Return Value

A 32-bit value that contains the starting position in the low-order word and the position of the first nonselected character after the end of the selection in the high-order word. If this function is used on a combo box without an edit control, **CB_ERR** is returned.

Remarks

Gets the starting and ending character positions of the current selection in the edit control of a combo box.

See Also: **CComboBox::SetEditSel**, **CB_GETEDITSEL**

CComboBox::GetExtendedUI

BOOL GetExtendedUI( ) const;

Return Value

Nonzero if the combo box has the extended user interface; otherwise 0.

Remarks

Call the **GetExtendedUI** member function to determine whether a combo box has the default user interface or the extended user interface. The extended user interface can be identified in the following ways:

- Clicking the static control displays the list box only for combo boxes with the **CBS_DROPDOWNLIST** style.

- Pressing the DOWN ARROW key displays the list box (F4 is disabled).

Scrolling in the static control is disabled when the item list is not visible (arrow keys are disabled).

See Also: **CComboBox::SetExtendedUI, CB_GETEXTENDEDUI**

CComboBox::GetHorizontalExtent

UINT GetHorizontalExtent( ) const;

Return Value

The scrollable width of the list-box portion of the combo box, in pixels.

Remarks

Retrieves from the combo box the width in pixels by which the list-box portion of the combo box can be scrolled horizontally. This is applicable only if the list-box portion of the combo box has a horizontal scroll bar.

See Also: **CListBox::SetHorizontalExtent, CB_GETHORIZONTALEXTENT**

CComboBox::GetItemData

DWORD GetItemData(int *nIndex*) const;

Return Value

The 32-bit value associated with the item, or **CB_ERR** if an error occurs.

Parameters

nIndex Contains the zero-based index of an item in the combo box's list box.

Remarks

Retrieves the application-supplied 32-bit value associated with the specified combo-box item. The 32-bit value can be set with the *dwItemData* parameter of a **SetItemData** member function call. Use the **GetItemDataPtr** member function if the 32-bit value to be retrieved is a pointer (**void***).

See Also: **CComboBox::SetItemData, CComboBox::GetItemDataPtr, CComboBox::SetItemDataPtr, CB_GETITEMDATA**

CComboBox::GetItemDataPtr

void* GetItemDataPtr(int *nIndex* **) const;**

Return Value

Retrieves a pointer, or –1 if an error occurs.

Parameters

nIndex   Contains the zero-based index of an item in the combo box's list box.

Remarks

Retrieves the application-supplied 32-bit value associated with the specified combo-box item as a pointer (**void***).

See Also: CComboBox::SetItemDataPtr, CComboBox::GetItemData, CComboBox::SetItemData, CB_GETITEMDATA

CComboBox::GetItemHeight

int GetItemHeight(int *nIndex* **) const;**

Return Value

The height, in pixels, of the specified item in a combo box. The return value is **CB_ERR** if an error occurs.

Parameters

nIndex   Specifies the component of the combo box whose height is to be retrieved.
If the *nIndex* parameter is –1, the height of the edit-control (or static-text) portion of the combo box is retrieved. If the combo box has the **CBS_OWNERDRAWVARIABLE** style, *nIndex* specifies the zero-based index of the list item whose height is to be retrieved. Otherwise, *nIndex* should be set to 0.

Remarks

Call the **GetItemHeight** member function to retrieve the height of list items in a combo box.

See Also: CComboBox::SetItemHeight, WM_MEASUREITEM, CB_GETITEMHEIGHT

CComboBox::GetLBText

int GetLBText(int *nIndex***, LPTSTR** *lpszText* **) const;**
void GetLBText(int *nIndex***, CString&** *rString* **) const;**

Return Value

The length (in bytes) of the string, excluding the terminating null character. If *nIndex* does not specify a valid index, the return value is **CB_ERR**.

Parameters

nIndex   Contains the zero-based index of the list-box string to be copied.

lpszText   Points to a buffer that is to receive the string. The buffer must have sufficient space for the string and a terminating null character.

rString   A reference to a **CString**.

Remarks

Gets a string from the list box of a combo box. The second form of this member function fills a **CString** object with the item's text.

See Also: **CComboBox::GetLBTextLen, CB_GETLBTEXT**

CComboBox::GetLBTextLen

int GetLBTextLen(int *nIndex*) const;

Return Value

The length of the string in bytes, excluding the terminating null character. If *nIndex* does not specify a valid index, the return value is **CB_ERR**.

Parameters

nIndex   Contains the zero-based index of the list-box string.

Remarks

Gets the length of a string in the list box of a combo box.

See Also: **CComboBox::GetLBText, CB_GETLBTEXTLEN**

CComboBox::GetLocale

LCID GetLocale( ) const;

Return Value

The locale identifier (LCID) value for the strings in the combo box.

Remarks

Retrieves the locale used by the combo box. The locale is used, for example, to determine the sort order of the strings in a sorted combo box.

See Also: **CComboBox::SetLocale, ::GetStringTypeW, ::GetSystemDefaultLCID, ::GetUserDefaultLCID**

CComboBox::GetTopIndex

int GetTopIndex( ) const;

Return Value

The zero-based index of the first visible item in the list-box portion of the combo box if successful, **CB_ERR** otherwise.

Remarks

Retrieves the zero-based index of the first visible item in the list-box portion of the combo box. Initially, item 0 is at the top of the list box, but if the list box is scrolled, another item may be at the top.

See Also: **CComboBox::SetTopIndex, CB_GETTOPINDEX**

CComboBox::InitStorage

int InitStorage(int *nItems*, UINT *nBytes*);

Return Value

If successful, the maximum number of items that the list-box portion of the combo box can store before a memory reallocation is needed, otherwise **CB_ERR**, meaning not enough memory is available.

Parameters

nItems Specifies the number of items to add.

nBytes Specifies the amount of memory, in bytes, to allocate for item strings.

Remarks

Allocates memory for storing list box items in the list-box portion of the combo box. Call this function before adding a large number of items to the list-box portion of the **CComboBox**.

Windows 95 only: The *wParam* parameter is limited to 16-bit values. This means list boxes cannot contain more than 32,767 items. Although the number of items is restricted, the total size of the items in a list box is limited only by available memory.

This function helps speed up the initialization of list boxes that have a large number of items (more than 100). It preallocates the specified amount of memory so that subsequent **AddString**, **InsertString**, and **Dir** functions take the shortest possible time. You can use estimates for the parameters. If you overestimate, some extra memory is allocated; if you underestimate, the normal allocation is used for items that exceed the preallocated amount.

See Also: **CComboBox::CComboBox, CComboBox::Create, CComboBox::ResetContent, CB_INITSTORAGE**

CComboBox::InsertString

int InsertString(int *nIndex***, LPCTSTR** *lpszString* **);**

Return Value

The zero-based index of the position at which the string was inserted. The return value is **CB_ERR** if an error occurs. The return value is **CB_ERRSPACE** if insufficient space is available to store the new string.

Parameters

nIndex   Contains the zero-based index to the position in the list box that will receive the string. If this parameter is –1, the string is added to the end of the list.

lpszString   Points to the null-terminated string that is to be inserted.

Remarks

Inserts a string into the list box of a combo box. Unlike the **AddString** member function, the **InsertString** member function does not cause a list with the **CBS_SORT** style to be sorted.

See Also: CComboBox::AddString, CComboBox::DeleteString, CComboBox::ResetContent, CB_INSERTSTRING

CComboBox::LimitText

BOOL LimitText(int *nMaxChars* **);**

Return Value

Nonzero if successful. If called for a combo box with the style **CBS_DROPDOWNLIST** or for a combo box without an edit control, the return value is **CB_ERR**.

Parameters

nMaxChars   Specifies the length (in bytes) of the text that the user can enter. If this parameter is 0, the text length is set to 65,535 bytes.

Remarks

Limits the length in bytes of the text that the user can enter into the edit control of a combo box.

If the combo box does not have the style **CBS_AUTOHSCROLL**, setting the text limit to be larger than the size of the edit control will have no effect.

LimitText only limits the text the user can enter. It has no effect on any text already in the edit control when the message is sent, nor does it affect the length of the text copied to the edit control when a string in the list box is selected.

See Also: CB_LIMITTEXT

CComboBox::MeasureItem

virtual void MeasureItem(LPMEASUREITEMSTRUCT *lpMeasureItemStruct* **);**

Parameters

lpMeasureItemStruct   A long pointer to a **MEASUREITEMSTRUCT** structure.

Remarks

Called by the framework when a combo box with an owner-draw style is created.

By default, this member function does nothing. Override this member function and fill in the **MEASUREITEMSTRUCT** structure to inform Windows of the dimensions of the list box in the combo box. If the combo box is created with the **CBS_OWNERDRAWVARIABLE** style, the framework calls this member function for each item in the list box. Otherwise, this member is called only once.

Using the **CBS_OWNERDRAWFIXED** style in an owner-draw combo box created with the **SubclassDlgItem** member function of **CWnd** involves further programming considerations. See the discussion in Technical Note 14 online.

See **CWnd::OnMeasureItem** for a description of the **MEASUREITEMSTRUCT** structure.

See Also: **CComboBox::CompareItem**, **CComboBox::DrawItem**, **WM_MEASUREITEM**, **CComboBox::DeleteItem**

CComboBox::Paste

void Paste( );

Remarks

Inserts the data from the Clipboard into the edit control of the combo box at the current cursor position. Data is inserted only if the Clipboard contains data in **CF_TEXT** format.

See Also: **CComboBox::Clear**, **CComboBox::Copy**, **CComboBox::Cut**, **WM_PASTE**

CComboBox::ResetContent

void ResetContent( );

Remarks

Removes all items from the list box and edit control of a combo box.

See Also: **CB_RESETCONTENT**

CComboBox::SelectString

int SelectString(int *nStartAfter***, LPCTSTR** *lpszString* **);**

Return Value

The zero-based index of the selected item if the string was found. If the search was unsuccessful, the return value is **CB_ERR** and the current selection is not changed.

Parameters

nStartAfter   Contains the zero-based index of the item before the first item to be searched. When the search reaches the bottom of the list box, it continues from the top of the list box back to the item specified by *nStartAfter*. If −1, the entire list box is searched from the beginning.

lpszString   Points to the null-terminated string that contains the prefix to search for. The search is case independent, so this string can contain any combination of uppercase and lowercase letters.

Remarks

Searches for a string in the list box of a combo box, and if the string is found, selects the string in the list box and copies it to the edit control.

A string is selected only if its initial characters (from the starting point) match the characters in the prefix string.

Note that the **SelectString** and **FindString** member functions both find a string, but the **SelectString** member function also selects the string.

See Also: CComboBox::FindString, CB_SELECTSTRING

CComboBox::SetCurSel

int SetCurSel(int *nSelect* **);**

Return Value

The zero-based index of the item selected if the message is successful. The return value is **CB_ERR** if *nSelect* is greater than the number of items in the list or if *nSelect* is set to −1, which clears the selection.

Parameters

nSelect   Specifies the zero-based index of the string to select. If −1, any current selection in the list box is removed and the edit control is cleared.

Remarks

Selects a string in the list box of a combo box. If necessary, the list box scrolls the string into view (if the list box is visible). The text in the edit control of the combo box is changed to reflect the new selection. Any previous selection in the list box is removed.

See Also: **CComboBox::GetCurSel, CB_SETCURSEL**

CComboBox::SetDroppedWidth

int SetDroppedWidth(UINT *nWidth* **);**

Return Value

If successful, the new width of the list box, otherwise **CB_ERR**.

Parameters

nWidth   The minimum allowable width of the list-box portion of the combo box, in pixels.

Remarks

Call this function to set the minimum allowable width, in pixels, of the list box of a combo box. This function only applies to combo boxes with the **CBS_DROPDOWN** or **CBS_DROPDOWNLIST** style.

By default, the minimum allowable width of the drop-down list box is 0. When the list-box portion of the combo box is displayed, its width is the larger of the minimum allowable width or the combo box width.

See Also: **CComboBox::GetDroppedWidth, CB_SETDROPPEDWIDTH**

CComboBox::SetEditSel

BOOL SetEditSel(int *nStartChar***, int** *nEndChar* **);**

Return Value

Nonzero if the member function is successful; otherwise 0. It is **CB_ERR** if **CComboBox** has the **CBS_DROPDOWNLIST** style or does not have a list box.

Parameters

nStartChar   Specifies the starting position. If the starting position is set to –1, then any existing selection is removed.

nEndChar   Specifies the ending position. If the ending position is set to –1, then all text from the starting position to the last character in the edit control is selected.

Remarks

Selects characters in the edit control of a combo box.

The positions are zero-based. To select the first character of the edit control, you specify a starting position of 0. The ending position is for the character just after the last character to select. For example, to select the first four characters of the edit control, you would use a starting position of 0 and an ending position of 4.

See Also: **CComboBox::GetEditSel, CB_SETEDITSEL**

CComboBox::SetExtendedUI

int SetExtendedUI(BOOL *bExtended* = **TRUE**);

Return Value

CB_OKAY if the operation is successful, or CB_ERR if an error occurs.

Parameters

bExtended   Specifies whether the combo box should use the extended user interface or the default user interface. A value of **TRUE** selects the extended user interface; a value of **FALSE** selects the standard user interface.

Remarks

Call the **SetExtendedUI** member function to select either the default user interface or the extended user interface for a combo box that has the **CBS_DROPDOWN** or **CBS_DROPDOWNLIST** style.

The extended user interface can be identified in the following ways:

- Clicking the static control displays the list box only for combo boxes with the **CBS_DROPDOWNLIST** style.
- Pressing the DOWN ARROW key displays the list box (F4 is disabled).

Scrolling in the static control is disabled when the item list is not visible (the arrow keys are disabled).

See Also: **CComboBox::GetExtendedUI, CB_SETEXTENDEDUI**

CComboBox::SetHorizontalExtent

void SetHorizontalExtent(UINT *nExtent*);

Parameters

nExtent   Specifies the number of pixels by which the list-box portion of the combo box can be scrolled horizontally.

Remarks

Sets the width, in pixels, by which the list-box portion of the combo box can be scrolled horizontally. If the width of the list box is smaller than this value, the horizontal scroll bar will horizontally scroll items in the list box. If the width of the list box is equal to or greater than this value, the horizontal scroll bar is hidden or, if the combo box has the **CBS_DISABLENOSCROLL** style, disabled.

See Also: **CComboBox::GetHorizontalExtent, CB_SETHORIZONTALEXTENT**

CComboBox::SetItemData

int SetItemData(int *nIndex*, **DWORD** *dwItemData* **);**

Return Value

CB_ERR if an error occurs.

Parameters

nIndex   Contains a zero-based index to the item to set.

dwItemData   Contains the new value to associate with the item.

Remarks

Sets the 32-bit value associated with the specified item in a combo box. Use the **SetItemDataPtr** member function if the 32-bit item is to be a pointer.

See Also: **CComboBox::GetItemData, CComboBox::GetItemDataPtr, CComboBox::SetItemDataPtr, CB_SETITEMDATA, CComboBox::AddString, CComboBox::InsertString**

CComboBox::SetItemDataPtr

int SetItemDataPtr(int *nIndex*, **void*** *pData* **);**

Return Value

CB_ERR if an error occurs.

Parameters

nIndex   Contains a zero-based index to the item.

pData   Contains the pointer to associate with the item.

Remarks

Sets the 32-bit value associated with the specified item in a combo box to be the specified pointer (**void***). This pointer remains valid for the life of the combo box, even though the item's relative position within the combo box might change as items are added or removed. Hence, the item's index within the box can change, but the pointer remains reliable.

See Also: **CComboBox::GetItemData, CComboBox::GetItemDataPtr, CComboBox::SetItemData, CB_SETITEMDATA, CComboBox::AddString, CComboBox::InsertString**

CComboBox::SetItemHeight

> int **SetItemHeight**(int *nIndex*, UINT *cyItemHeight*);

Return Value

CB_ERR if the index or height is invalid; otherwise 0.

Parameters

nIndex   Specifies whether the height of list items or the height of the edit-control (or static-text) portion of the combo box is set.

If the combo box has the **CBS_OWNERDRAWVARIABLE** style, *nIndex* specifies the zero-based index of the list item whose height is to be set; otherwise, *nIndex* must be 0 and the height of all list items will be set.

If *nIndex* is –1, the height of the edit-control or static-text portion of the combo box is to be set.

cyItemHeight   Specifies the height, in pixels, of the combo-box component identified by *nIndex*.

Remarks

Call the **SetItemHeight** member function to set the height of list items in a combo box or the height of the edit-control (or static-text) portion of a combo box.

The height of the edit-control (or static-text) portion of the combo box is set independently of the height of the list items. An application must ensure that the height of the edit-control (or static-text) portion is not smaller than the height of a particular list-box item.

See Also: CComboBox::GetItemHeight, WM_MEASUREITEM, CB_SETITEMHEIGHT

CComboBox::SetLocale

> LCID **SetLocale**(LCID *nNewLocale*);

Return Value

The previous locale identifier (LCID) value for this combo box.

Parameters

nNewLocale   The new locale identifier (LCID) value to set for the combo box.

Remarks

Sets the locale identifier for this combo box. If **SetLocale** is not called, the default locale is obtained from the system. This system default locale can be modified by using Control Panel's Regional (or International) application.

See Also: CComboBox::GetLocale

CComboBox::SetTopIndex

int SetTopIndex(int *nIndex* **);**

Return Value

Zero if successful, or **LB_ERR** if an error occurs.

Parameters

nIndex   Specifies the zero-based index of the list-box item.

Remarks

Ensures that a particular item is visible in the list-box portion of the combo box.

The system scrolls the list box until either the item specified by *nIndex* appears at the top of the list box or the maximum scroll range has been reached.

See Also: **CComboBox::GetTopIndex**, **CB_SETTOPINDEX**

CComboBox::ShowDropDown

void ShowDropDown(BOOL *bShowIt* **= TRUE);**

Parameters

bShowIt   Specifies whether the drop-down list box is to be shown or hidden. A value of **TRUE** shows the list box. A value of **FALSE** hides the list box.

Remarks

Shows or hides the list box of a combo box that has the **CBS_DROPDOWN** or **CBS_DROPDOWNLIST** style. By default, a combo box of this style will show the list box.

This member function has no effect on a combo box created with the **CBS_SIMPLE** style.

See Also: **CB_SHOWDROPDOWN**

CCommandLineInfo

CCommandLineInfo does not have a base class.

The **CCommandLineInfo** class aids in parsing the command line at application startup.

An MFC application will typically create a local instance of this class in the **InitInstance** function of its application object. This object is then passed to **CWinApp::ParseCommandLine**, which repeatedly calls **ParseParam** to fill the **CCommandLineInfo** object. The **CCommandLineInfo** object is then passed to **CWinApp::ProcessShellCommand** to handle the command-line arguments and flags.

You can use this object to encapsulate the following command-line options and parameters:

Command-line argument	Command executed
app	New file.
app filename	Open file.
app **/p** filename	Print file to default printer.
app **/pt** filename printer driver port	Print file to the specified printer.
app **/dde**	Start up and await DDE command.
app **/Automation**	Start up as an OLE automation server.
app **/Embedding**	Start up to edit an embedded OLE item.

Derive a new class from **CCommandLineInfo** to handle other flags and parameter values. Override **ParseParam** to handle the new flags.

#include <afxwin.h>

See Also: **CWinApp::ParseCommandLine**, **CWinApp::ProcessShellCommand**

CCommandLineInfo Class Members

Construction

CommandLineInfo	Constructs a default **CCommandLineInfo** object.

Operations

ParseParam	Override this callback to parse individual parameters.

Data Members

m_bShowSplash	Indicates if a splash screen should be shown.
m_bRunEmbedded	Indicates the command-line **/Embedding** option was found.
m_bRunAutomated	Indicates the command-line **/Automation** option was found.
m_nShellCommand	Indicates the shell command to be processed.
m_strFileName	Indicates the filename to be opened or printed; empty if the shell command is New or DDE.
m_strPrinterName	Indicates the printer name if the shell command is Print To; otherwise empty.
m_strDriverName	Indicates the driver name if the shell command is Print To; otherwise empty.
m_strPortName	Indicates the port name if the shell command is Print To; otherwise empty.

Member Functions

CCommandLineInfo::CCommandLineInfo

CCommandLineInfo( );

Remarks

This constructor creates a **CCommandLineInfo** object with default values. The default is to show the splash screen (**m_bShowSplash = TRUE**) and to execute the New command on the File menu (**m_nShellCommand = NewFile**).

The application framework calls **ParseParam** to fill data members of this object.

See Also: **CCommandLineInfo::ParseParam**

CCommandLineInfo::ParseParam

virtual void ParseParam(LPCTSTR *lpszParam***, BOOL** *bFlag***, BOOL** *bLast* **);**

Parameters

lpszParam   The parameter or flag.

bFlag   Indicates whether *lpszParam* is a parameter or a flag.

bLast   Indicates if this is the last parameter or flag on the command line.

Remarks

The framework calls this function to parse/interpret individual parameters from the command line. **CWinApp::ParseCommandLine** calls **ParseParam** once for each parameter or flag on the command line, passing the argument to *lpszParam*. If the first character of the parameter is a '-' or a '/', then it is removed and *bFlag* is set to **TRUE**. When parsing the final parameter, *bLast* is set to **TRUE**.

The default implementation of this function recognizes the following flags: **/p**, **/pt**, **/dde**, **/Automation**, and **/Embedding**, as shown in the following table:

Command-line argument	Command executed
app	New file.
app filename	Open file.
app **/p** filename	Print file to default printer.
app **/pt** filename printer driver port	Print file to the specified printer.
app **/dde**	Start up and await DDE command.
app **/Automation**	Start up as an OLE automation server.
app **/Embedding**	Start up to edit an embedded OLE item.

This information is stored in **m_bRunAutomated**, **m_bRunEmbedded**, and **m_nShellCommand**. Flags are marked by either a forward-slash '/' or hyphen '-'.

The default implementation puts the first non-flag parameter into **m_strFileName**. In the case of the **/pt** flag, the default implementation puts the second, third, and fourth non-flag parameters into **m_strPrinterName**, **m_strDriverName**, and **m_strPortName**, respectively.

The default implementation also sets **m_bShowSplash** to **TRUE** only in the case of a new file. In the case of a new file, the user has taken action involving the application itself. In any other case, including opening existing files using the shell, the user action involves the file directly. In a document-centric standpoint, the splash screen does not need to announce the application starting up.

Override this function in your derived class to handle other flag and parameter values.

See Also: **CWinApp::ParseCommandLine**

Data Members
CCommandLineInfo::m_bRunAutomated

Remarks

Indicates that the **/Automation** flag was found on the command line. If **TRUE**, this means start up as an OLE automation server.

See Also: **CCommandLineInfo::ParseParam**, **CWinApp::ProcessShellCommand**

CCommandLineInfo::m_bRunEmbedded

Remarks

Indicates that the **/Embedding** flag was found on the command line. If **TRUE**, this means start up for editing an embedded OLE item.

See Also: **CCommandLineInfo::m_bShowSplash**,
CWinApp::ProcessShellCommand

CCommandLineInfo::m_bShowSplash

Remarks

Indicates that the splash screen should be displayed. If **TRUE**, this means the splash screen for this application should be displayed during startup. The default implementation of **ParseParam** sets this data member to **TRUE** if **m_nShellCommand** is equal to **CCommandLineInfo::FileNew**.

See Also: **CCommandLineInfo::m_bRunAutomated**,
CCommandLineInfo::m_bRunEmbedded,
CCommandLineInfo::m_nShellCommand, **CCommandLineInfo::ParseParam**,
CWinApp::ProcessShellCommand

CCommandLineInfo::m_nShellCommand

Remarks

Indicates the shell command for this instance of the application.

The type for this data member is the following enumerated type, which is defined within the **CCommandLineInfo** class.

```
enum{
    FileNew,
    FileOpen,
    FilePrint,
    FilePrintTo,
    FileDDE,
    FileNothing = -1
};
```

For a brief description of these values, see the following list.

- **CCommandLineInfo::FileNew**   Indicates that no filename was found on the command line.

- **CCommandLineInfo::FileOpen**   Indicates that a filename was found on the command line and that none of the following flags were found on the command line: **/p**, **/pt**, **/dde**.

- **CCommandLineInfo::FilePrint**   Indicates that the **/p** flag was found on the command line.

- **CCommandLineInfo::FilePrintTo**   Indicates that the **/pt** flag was found on the command line.

- **CCommandLineInfo::FileDDE**   Indicates that the **/dde** flag was found on the command line.

- **CCommandLineInfo::FileNothing**   Turns off the display of a new MDI child window on startup. By design, AppWizard generated MDI applications display a new child window on startup. To turn off this feature, an application can use **CCommandLineInfo::FileNothing** as the shell command when calling **ProcessShellCommand**. **ProcessShellCommand** is called by the **InitInstance( )** of all **CWinApp** derived classes.

Example

```
BOOL CMyWinApp::InitInstance()
{
...
// Parse command line for standard shell commands, DDE, file open
   CCommandLineInfo cmdInfo;
   ParseCommandLine(cmdInfo);
// DON'T display a new MDI child window during startup!!!
   cmdInfo.m_nShellCommand = CCommandLineInfo::FileNothing;
// Dispatch commands specified on the command line
   if (!ProcessShellCommand(cmdInfo))
       return FALSE;
...
};
```

See Also: **CCommandLineInfo::m_strFileName,
CCommandLineInfo::m_strPrinterName,
CCommandLineInfo::m_strDriverName,
CCommandLineInfo::m_strPortName, CWinApp::ProcessShellCommand**

CCommandLineInfo::m_strFileName

Remarks

Stores the value of the first non-flag parameter on the command line. This parameter is typically the name of the file to open.

See Also: **CCommandLineInfo::m_strPrinterName,
CCommandLineInfo::m_strDriverName,
CCommandLineInfo::m_strPortName, CWinApp::ProcessShellCommand**

CCommandLineInfo::m_strDriverName

Remarks

Stores the value of the third non-flag parameter on the command line. This parameter is typically the name of the printer driver for a Print To shell command. The default implementation of **ParseParam** sets this data member only if the **/pt** flag was found on the command line.

See Also: **CCommandLineInfo::m_strFileName,
CCommandLineInfo::m_strPrinterName,
CCommandLineInfo::m_strPortName, CWinApp::ProcessShellCommand**

CCommandLineInfo::m_strPortName

Remarks

Stores the value of the fourth non-flag parameter on the command line. This parameter is typically the name of the printer port for a Print To shell command. The default implementation of **ParseParam** sets this data member only if the **/pt** flag was found on the command line.

See Also: **CCommandLineInfo::m_strFileName,
CCommandLineInfo::m_strPrinterName,
CCommandLineInfo::m_strDriverName, CWinApp::ProcessShellCommand**

CCommandLineInfo::m_strPrinterName

Remarks

Stores the value of the second non-flag parameter on the command line. This parameter is typically the name of the printer for a Print To shell command. The default implementation of **ParseParam** sets this data member only if the **/pt** flag was found on the command line.

See Also: **CCommandLineInfo::m_strFileName,
CCommandLineInfo::m_strDriverName,
CCommandLineInfo::m_strPortName, CWinApp::ProcessShellCommand**

CCommonDialog

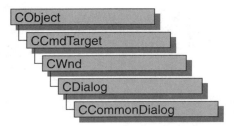

CCommonDialog is the base class for classes that encapsulate functionality of the Windows common dialogs:

- **CFileDialog**
- **CFontDialog**
- **CColorDialog**
- **CPageSetupDialog**
- **CPrintDialog**
- **CFindReplaceDialog**
- **COleDialog**

#include <afxdlgs.h>

See Also: **CFileDialog**, **CFontDialog**, **CColorDialog**, **CPageSetupDialog**, **CPrintDialog**, **CFindReplaceDialog**, **COleDialog**

CCommonDialog Class Members

Construction

CCommonDialog	Constructs a **CCommonDialog** object.

Member Functions
CCommonDialog::CCommonDialog

CCommonDialog(CWnd* *pParentWnd* **);**

Parameters

pParentWnd   Points to the parent or owner window object (of type **CWnd**) to which the dialog object belongs. If it is **NULL**, the dialog object's parent window is set to the main application window.

Remarks

Constructs a **CCommonDialog** object. See **CDialog::CDialog** for complete information.

See Also: **CDialog::CDialog**

CConnectionPoint

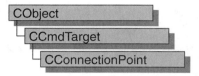

The **CConnectionPoint** class defines a special type of interface used to communicate with other OLE objects, called a "connection point." Unlike normal OLE interfaces, which are used to implement and expose the functionality of an OLE control, a connection point implements an outgoing interface that is able to initiate actions on other objects, such as firing events and change notifications.

A connection consists of two parts: the object calling the interface, called the "source," and the object implementing the interface, called the "sink." By exposing a connection point, a source allows sinks to establish connections to itself. Through the connection point mechanism, a source object obtains a pointer to the sink's implementation of a set of member functions. For example, to fire an event implemented by the sink, the source can call the appropriate method of the sink's implementation.

By default, a **COleControl**-derived class implements two connection points: one for events and one for property change notifications. These connections are used, respectively, for event firing and for notifying a sink (for example, the control's container) when a property value has changed. Support is also provided for OLE controls to implement additional connection points. For each additional connection point implemented in your control class, you must declare a "connection part" that implements the connection point. If you implement one or more connection points, you also need to declare a single "connection map" in your control class.

The following example demonstrates a simple connection map and one connection point for the Sample OLE control, consisting of two fragments of code: the first portion declares the connection map and point; the second implements this map and point. The first fragment is inserted into the declaration of the control class, under the **protected** section:

```
// Connection point for ISample interface
BEGIN_CONNECTION_PART(CSampleCtrl, SampleConnPt)
   CONNECTION_IID(IID_ISampleSink)
END_CONNECTION_PART(SampleConnPt)

DECLARE_CONNECTION_MAP()
```

The **BEGIN_CONNECTION_PART** and **END_CONNECTION_PART** macros declare an embedded class, XSampleConnPt (derived from **CConnectionPoint**) that implements this particular connection point. If you want to override any **CConnectionPoint** member functions, or add member functions of your own, declare them between these two macros. For example, the **CONNECTION_IID** macro overrides the **CConnectionPoint::GetIID** member function when placed between these two macros.

The second code fragment is inserted into the implementation file (.CPP) of your control class. This code implements the connection map, which includes the additional connection point, SampleConnPt:

```
BEGIN_CONNECTION_MAP(CSampleCtrl, COleControl)
    CONNECTION_PART(CSampleCtrl, IID_ISampleSink, SampleConnPt)
END_CONNECTION_MAP()
```

Once these code fragments have been inserted, the Sample OLE control exposes a connection point for the **ISampleSink** interface.

Typically, connection points support "multicasting"; the ability to broadcast to multiple sinks connected to the same interface. The following code fragment demonstrates how to accomplish multicasting by iterating through each sink on a connection point:

```
void CSampleCtrl::CallSinkFunc()
{
    const CPtrArray* pConnections = m_xSampleConnPt.GetConnections();
    ASSERT(pConnections != NULL);

    int cConnections = pConnections->GetSize();
    ISampleSink* pSampleSink;
    for (int i = 0; i < cConnections; i++)
    {
        pSampleSink = (ISampleSink*)(pConnections->GetAt(i));
        ASSERT(pSampleSink != NULL);
        pSampleSink->SinkFunc();
    }
}
```

This example retrieves the current set of connections on the SampleConnPt connection point with a call to CConnectionPoint::GetConnections. It then iterates through the connections and calls ISampleSink::SinkFunc on every active connection.

For more information on using **CConnectionPoint**, see the article "Connection Points" in *Visual C++ Programmer's Guide* online.

#include <afxctl.h>

CConnectionPoint Class Members

Operations

GetConnections	Retrieves all connection points in a connection map.

Overridables

GetContainer	Retrieves the container of the control that owns the connection map.
GetIID	Retrieves the interface ID of a connection point.
GetMaxConnections	Retrieves the maximum number of connection points supported by a control.
OnAdvise	Called by the framework when establishing or breaking connections.

Member Functions

CConnectionPoint::GetConnections

const CPtrArray* GetConnections( );

Return Value

A pointer to an array of active connections (sinks). Each pointer in this array can be safely converted to a pointer to the sink interface using a cast operator.

Remarks

Call this function to retrieve all active connections for a connection point.

See Also: CConnectionPoint::GetMaxConnections

CConnectionPoint::GetContainer

virtual LPCONNECTIONPOINTCONTAINER GetContainer( ) = 0;

Return Value

If successful, a pointer to the container; otherwise **NULL**.

Remarks

Called by the framework to retrieve the **IConnectionPointContainer** for the connection point. This function is typically implemented by the **BEGIN_CONNECTION_PART** macro.

See Also: BEGIN_CONNECTION_PART

CConnectionPoint::GetIID

virtual REFIID GetIID( ) = 0;

Return Value

A reference to the connection point's interface ID.

Remarks

Called by the framework to retrieve the interface ID of a connection point.

Override this function to return the interface ID for this connection point.

See Also: CONNECTION_IID

CConnectionPoint::GetMaxConnections

virtual int GetMaxConnections( );

Return Value

The maximum number of connections supported by the control, or –1 if no limit.

Remarks

Called by the framework to retrieve the maximum number of connections supported by the connection point. The default implementation returns –1, indicating no limit.

Override this function if you want to limit the number of sinks that can connect to your control.

See Also: CConnectionPoint::GetConnections

CConnectionPoint::OnAdvise

virtual void OnAdvise(BOOL *bAdvise*);

Parameters

bAdvise **TRUE**, if a connection is being established; otherwise **FALSE**.

Remarks

Called by the framework when a connection is being established or broken. The default implementation does nothing.

Override this function if you want notification when sinks connect to or disconnect from your connection point.

CControlBar

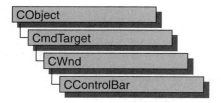

CControlBar is the base class for the control-bar classes **CStatusBar**, **CToolBar**, **CDialogBar**, and **COleResizeBar**. A control bar is a window that is usually aligned to the left or right of a frame window. It may contain child items that are either **HWND**-based controls, which are Windows windows that generate and respond to Windows messages, or non-**HWND**-based items, which are not windows and are managed by application code or framework code. List boxes and edit controls are examples of **HWND**-based controls; status-bar panes and bitmap buttons are examples of non-**HWND**-based controls.

Control-bar windows are usually child windows of a parent frame window and are usually siblings to the client view or MDI client of the frame window. A **CControlBar** object uses information about the parent window's client rectangle to position itself. It then informs the parent window as to how much space remains unallocated in the parent window's client area.

For more information on **CControlBar**, see the article "Control Bar Topics" in *Visual C++ Programmer's Guide* online and Technical Note 31 online, "Control Bars."

#include <afxext.h>

See Also: **CToolBar**, **CDialogBar**, **CStatusBar**

CControlBar Class Members

Data Members

m_bAutoDelete	If nonzero, the **CControlBar** object is deleted when the Windows control bar is destroyed.

Attributes

GetBarStyle	Retrieves the control bar style settings.
SetBarStyle	Modifies the control bar style settings.
GetCount	Returns the number of non-**HWND** elements in the control bar.
GetDockingFrame	Returns a pointer to the frame to which a control bar is docked.

Attributes *(continued)*

GetDockingFrame	Returns a pointer to the frame to which a control bar is docked.
IsFloating	Returns a nonzero value if the control bar in question is a floating control bar.
CalcFixedLayout	Returns the size of the control bar as a **CSize** object.
CalcDynamicLayout	Returns the size of a dynamic control bar as a **CSize** object.

Overridables

OnUpdateCmdUI	Calls the Command UI handlers.

Operations

EnableDocking	Allows a control bar to be docked or floating.

Member Functions

CControlBar::CalcDynamicLayout

virtual CSize CalcDynamicLayout(int *nLength***, DWORD** *dwMode* **);**

Return Value

The control bar size, in pixels, of a **CSize** object.

Parameters

nLength The requested dimension of the control bar, either horizontal or vertical, depending on *dwMode*.

dwMode The following predefined flags are used to determine the height and width of the dynamc control bar. Use the bitwise-OR (|) operator to combine the flags.

Layout mode flags	What it means
LM_STRETCH	Indicates whether the control bar should be stretched to the size of the frame. Set if the bar is not a docking bar (not available for docking). Not set when the bar is docked or floating (available for docking). If set, **LM_STRETCH** ignores *nLength* and returns dimensions based on the **LM_HORZ** state. **LM_STRETCH** works similarly to the the *bStretch* parameter used in **CalcFixedLayout**; see that member function for more information about the relationship between stretching and orientation.
LM_HORZ	Indicates that the bar is horizontally or vertically oriented. Set if the bar is horizontally oriented, and if it is vertically oriented, it is not set. **LM_HORZ** works similarly to the the *bHorz* parameter used in **CalcFixedLayout**; see that member function for more information about the relationship between stretching and orientation.

(continued)

(continued)

Layout mode flags	What it means
LM_MRUWIDTH	Most Recently Used Dynamic Width. Ignores *nLength* parameter and uses the remembered most recently used width.
LM_HORZDOCK	Horizontal Docked Dimensions. Ignores *nLength* parameter and returns the dynamic size with the largest width.
LM_VERTDOCK	Vertical Docked Dimensions. Ignores *nLength* parameter and returns the dynamic size with the largest height.
LM_LENGTHY	Set if *nLength* indicates height (Y-direction) instead of width.
LM_COMMIT	Resets **LM_MRUWIDTH** to current width of floating control bar.

Remarks

The framework calls this member function to calculate the dimensions of a dynamic toolbar.

Override this member function to provide your own dynamic layout in classes you derive from **CControlBar**. MFC classes derived from **CControlBar**, such as **CToolbar**, override this member function and provide their own implementation.

See Also: **CControlBar::CalcFixedLayout, CToolbar**

CControlBar::CalcFixedLayout

virtual CSize CalcFixedLayout(BOOL *bStretch***, BOOL** *bHorz* **);**

Return Value

The control bar size, in pixels, of a **CSize** object.

Parameters

bStretch Indicates whether the bar should be stretched to the size of the frame. The *bStretch* parameter is nonzero when the bar is not a docking bar (not available for docking) and is 0 when it is docked or floating (available for docking).

bHorz Indicates that the bar is horizontally or vertically oriented. The *bHorz* parameter is nonzero if the bar is horizontally oriented and is 0 if it is vertically oriented.

Remarks

Call this member function to calculate the horizontal size of a control bar.

Control bars such as toolbars can stretch horizontally or vertically to accommodate the buttons contained in the control bar.

If *bStretch* is **TRUE**, stretch the dimension along the orientation provided by *bHorz*. In other words, if *bHorz* is **FALSE**, the control bar is stretched vertically. If *bStretch* is **FALSE**, no stretch occurs. The following table shows the possible permutations, and resulting control-bar styles, of *bStretch* and *bHorz*.

bStretch	bHorz	Stretching	Orientation	Docking/Not docking
TRUE	TRUE	Horizontal stretching	Horizontally oriented	Not docking
TRUE	FALSE	Vertical stretching	Vertically oriented	Not docking
FALSE	TRUE	No stretching available	Horizontally oriented	Docking
FALSE	FALSE	No stretching available	Vertically oriented	Docking

See Also: **CControlBar::CalcDynamicLayout**

CControlBar::EnableDocking

void EnableDocking(DWORD *dwStyle* **);**

Parameters

dwStyle   Specifies whether the control bar supports docking and the sides of its parent window to which the control bar can be docked, if supported. Can be one or more of the following:

- **CBRS_ALIGN_TOP**   Allows docking at the top of the client area.
- **CBRS_ALIGN_BOTTOM**   Allows docking at the bottom of the client area.
- **CBRS_ALIGN_LEFT**   Allows docking on the left side of the client area.
- **CBRS_ALIGN_RIGHT**   Allows docking on the right side of the client area.
- **CBRS_ALIGN_ANY**   Allows docking on any side of the client area.
- **CBRS_FLOAT_MULTI**   Allows multiple control bars to be floated in a single mini-frame window.

If 0 (that is, indicating no flags), the control bar will not dock.

Remarks

Call this function to enable a control bar to be docked. The sides specified must match one of the sides enabled for docking in the destination frame window, or the control bar cannot be docked to that frame window.

See Also: **CFrameWnd::EnableDocking, CFrameWnd::DockControlBar, CFrameWnd::FloatControlBar, CControlBar::SetBarStyle**

CControlBar::GetBarStyle

DWORD GetBarStyle( );

Return Value

The current **CBRS_** (control bar styles) settings for the control bar. See **CControlBar::SetBarStyle** for the complete list of available styles.

Remarks

Call this function to determine which **CBRS_** (control bar styles) settings are currently set for the control bar. Does not handle **WS_** (window style) styles.

See Also: **CControlBar::SetBarStyle**

CControlBar::GetCount

int GetCount( ) const;

Return Value

The number of non-**HWND** items on the **CControlBar** object. This function returns 0 for a **CDialogBar** object.

Remarks

Returns the number of non-**HWND** items on the **CControlBar** object. The type of the item depends on the derived object: panes for **CStatusBar** objects, and buttons and separators for **CToolBar** objects.

See Also: **CToolBar::SetButtons, CStatusBar::SetIndicators, CStatusBar, CToolBar, CDialogBar**

CControlBar::GetDockingFrame

CFrameWnd* GetDockingFrame( ) const;

Return Value

A pointer to a frame window if successful; otherwise **NULL**.

Remarks

Call this member function to obtain a pointer to the current frame window to which your control bar is docked.

For more information about dockable control bars, see **CControlBar::EnableDocking** and **CFrameWnd::DockControlBar**.

See Also: **CControlBar::EnableDocking, CFrameWnd::DockControlBar**

CControlBar::IsFloating

BOOL IsFloating( ) const;

Return Value

Nonzero if the control bar is floating; otherwise 0.

Remarks

Call this member function to determine whether the control bar is floating or docked.

To change the state of a control bar from docked to floating, call **CFrameWnd::FloatControlBar**.

See Also: **CFrameWnd::FloatControlBar**

CControlBar::OnUpdateCmdUI

virtual void OnUpdateCmdUI(CFrameWnd* *pTarget*,
↳ **BOOL** *bDisableIfNoHndler* **) = 0;**

Parameters

pTarget   Points to the main frame window of the application. This pointer is used for routing update messages.

bDisableIfNoHndler   Flag that indicates whether a control that has no update handler should be automatically displayed as disabled.

Remarks

This member function is called by the framework to update the status of the toolbar or status bar.

To update an individual button or pane, use the **ON_UPDATE_COMMAND_UI** macro in your message map to set an update handler appropriately. See **ON_UPDATE_COMMAND_UI** for more information about using this macro.

OnUpdateCmdUI is called by the framework when the application is idle. The frame window to be updated must be a child window, at least indirectly, of a visible frame window. **OnUpdateCmdUI** is an advanced overridable.

See Also: **ON_UPDATE_COMMAND_UI**, Technical Note 31 online: "Control Bars"

CControlBar::SetBarStyle

void SetBarStyle(DWORD *dwStyle* **);**

Parameters

dwStyle The desired styles for the control bar. Can be one or more of the following:

- **CBRS_ALIGN_TOP** Allows the control bar to be docked to the top of the client area of a frame window.

- **CBRS_ALIGN_BOTTOM** Allows the control bar to be docked to the bottom of the client area of a frame window.

- **CBRS_ALIGN_LEFT** Allows the control bar to be docked to the left side of the client area of a frame window.

- **CBRS_ALIGN_RIGHT** Allows the control bar to be docked to the right side of the client area of a frame window.

- **CBRS_ALIGN_ANY** Allows the control bar to be docked to any side of the client area of a frame window.

- **CBRS_BORDER_TOP** Causes a border to be drawn on the top edge of the control bar when it would be visible.

- **CBRS_BORDER_BOTTOM** Causes a border to be drawn on the bottom edge of the control bar when it would be visible.

- **CBRS_BORDER_LEFT** Causes a border to be drawn on the left edge of the control bar when it would be visible.

- **CBRS_BORDER_RIGHT** Causes a border to be drawn on the right edge of the control bar when it would be visible.

- **CBRS_FLOAT_MULTI** Allows multiple control bars to be floated in a single mini-frame window.

- **CBRS_TOOLTIPS** Causes tool tips to be displayed for the control bar.

- **CBRS_FLYBY** Causes message text to be updated at the same time as tool tips.

Remarks

Call this function to set the desired **CBRS_** styles for the control bar. Does not affect the **WS_** (window style) settings.

See Also: **CControlBar::GetBarStyle**

Data Members

CControlBar::m_bAutoDelete

Remarks

m_bAutoDelete is a public variable of type **BOOL**. If it is nonzero when the Windows control-bar object is destroyed, the **CControlBar** object is deleted.

A control-bar object is usually embedded in a frame-window object. In this case, **m_bAutoDelete** is 0 because the embedded control-bar object is destroyed when the frame window is destroyed.

Set this variable to a nonzero value if you allocate a **CControlBar** object on the heap and you do not plan to call **delete**.

See Also: **CWnd::DestroyWindow**

CCreateContext

CCreateContext does not have a base class.

The framework uses the **CCreateContext** structure when it creates the frame windows and views associated with a document. When creating a window, the values in this structure provide information used to connect the components that make up a document and the view of its data. You will only need to use **CCreateContext** if you are overriding parts of the creation process.

A **CCreateContext** structure contains pointers to the document, the frame window, the view, and the document template. It also contains a pointer to a **CRuntimeClass** that identifies the type of view to create. The run-time class information and the current document pointer are used to create a new view dynamically. The following table suggests how and when each **CCreateContext** member might be used:

Member	What it is for
m_pNewViewClass	**CRuntimeClass** of the new view to create.
m_pCurrentDoc	The existing document to be associated with the new view.
m_pNewDocTemplate	The document template associated with the creation of a new MDI frame window.
m_pLastView	The original view upon which additional views are modeled, as in the creation of a splitter window's views or the creation of a second view on a document.
m_pCurrentFrame	The frame window upon which additional frame windows are modeled, as in the creation of a second frame window on a document.

When a document template creates a document and its associated components, it validates the information stored in the **CCreateContext** structure. For example, a view should not be created for a nonexistent document.

Note All of the pointers in **CCreateContext** are optional and can be **NULL** if unspecified or unknown.

CCreateContext is used by the member functions listed under "See Also." Consult the descriptions of these functions for specific information if you plan to override them.

Here are a few general guidelines:

- When passed as an argument for window creation, as in **CWnd::Create**, **CFrameWnd::Create**, and **CFrameWnd::LoadFrame**, the create context specifies what the new window should be connected to. For most windows, the entire structure is optional and a **NULL** pointer can be passed.

- For overridable member functions, such as **CFrameWnd::OnCreateClient**, the **CCreateContext** argument is optional.

- For member functions involved in view creation, you must provide enough information to create the view. For example, for the first view in a splitter window, you must supply the view class information and the current document.

In general, if you use the framework defaults, you can ignore **CCreateContext**. If you attempt more advanced modifications, the Microsoft Foundation Class Library source code or the sample programs, such as VIEWEX, will guide you. If you do forget a required parameter, a framework assertion will tell you what you forgot.

For more information on **CCreateContext**, see the MFC sample VIEWEX.

#include <afxext.h>

See Also: **CFrameWnd::Create**, **CFrameWnd::LoadFrame**, **CFrameWnd::OnCreateClient**, **CSplitterWnd::Create**, **CSplitterWnd::CreateView**, **CWnd::Create**

CCriticalSection

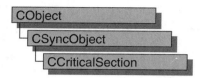

An object of class **CCriticalSection** represents a "critical section"— a synchronization object that allows one thread at a time to access a resource or section of code. Critical sections are useful when only one thread at a time can be allowed to modify data or some other controlled resource. For example, adding nodes to a linked list is a process that should only be allowed by one thread at a time. By using a **CCriticalSection** object to control the linked list, only one thread at a time can gain access to the list.

Critical sections are used instead of mutexes when speed is critical and the resource will not be used across process boundaries. For more information on using mutexes in MFC, see **CMutex**.

To use a **CCriticalSection** object, construct the **CCriticalSection** object when it is needed. You can then access the critical section when the constructor returns. Call **Unlock** when you are done accessing the critical section.

To access a resource controlled by a **CCriticalSection** object in this manner, first create a variable of either type **CSingleLock** or type **CMultiLock** in your resource's access member function. Then call the lock object's **Lock** member function (for example, **CSingleLock::Lock**). At this point, your thread will either gain access to the resource, wait for the resource to be released and gain access, or wait for the resource to be released and time out, failing to gain access to the resource. In any case, your resource has been accessed in a thread-safe manner. To release the resource, use the lock object's **Unlock** member function (for example, **CSingleLock::Unlock**), or allow the lock object to fall out of scope.

Alternatively, you can create a **CCriticalSection** object stand-alone, and access it explicitly before attempting to access the controlled resource. This method, while clearer to someone reading your source code, is more prone to error as you must remember to lock and unlock the critical section before and after access.

For more information on using **CCriticalSection** objects, see the article "Multithreading: How to Use the Synchronization Classes" in *Visual C++ Programmer's Guide* online.

#include <afxmt.h>

See Also: **CMutex**

CCriticalSection Class Members

Construction

CCriticalSection	Constructs a **CCriticalSection** object.

Methods

Unlock	Releases the **CCriticalSection** object.
Lock	Use to gain access to the **CCriticalSection** object.

Member Functions
CCriticalSection::CCriticalSection

CCriticalSection( );

Remarks

Constructs a **CCriticalSection** object. To access or release a **CCriticalSection** object, create a **CMultiLock** or **CSingleLock** object and call its **Lock** and **Unlock** member functions. If the **CCriticalSection** object is being used stand-alone, call its **Unlock** member function to release it.

CCriticalSection::Lock

BOOL Lock( );
BOOL Lock(DWORD *dwTimeout* **);**

Return Value

Nonzero if the function was successful; otherwise 0.

Parameters

dwTimeout   **Lock** ignores this parameter value.

Remarks

Call this member function to gain access to the critical section object. **Lock** is a blocking call that will not return until the critical section object is signaled (becomes available).

If timed waits are necessary, you can use a **CMutex** object instead of a **CCriticalSection** object.

See Also: **CSingleLock::Lock**, **CMultiLock::Lock**

CCriticalSection::Unlock

virtual BOOL Unlock( );

Return Value

Nonzero if the **CCriticalSection** object was owned by the thread and the release was successful; otherwise 0.

Remarks

Releases the **CCriticalSection** object for use by another thread. If the **CCriticalSection** is being used stand-alone, **Unlock** must be called immediately after completing use of the resource controlled by the critical section. If a **CSingleLock** or **CMultiLock** object is being used, **CCriticalSection::Unlock** will be called by the lock object's **Unlock** member function.

CCtrlView

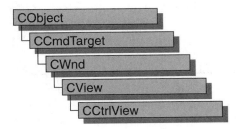

The class **CCtrlView** and its derivatives, **CEditView**, **CListView**, **CTreeView**, and **CRichEditView**, adapt the document-view architecture to the new common controls supported by Windows 95 and Windows NT versions 3.51 and later. For more information on the document-view architecture, see "Document/View Architecture Topics" in *Visual C++ Programmer's Guide* online.

#include <afxwin.h>

See Also: **CTreeView**, **CListView**, **CRichEditView**

CCtrlView Class Members

Construction

CCtrlView	Constructs a **CCtrlView** object.

Data Members

m_strClass	Contains the Windows class name for the view class.
m_dwDefaultStyle	Contains the default style for the view class.

Member Functions
CCtrlView::CCtrlView

> **CCtrlView(LPCTSTR** *lpszClass*, **DWORD** *dwStyle* **);**

Parameters

lpszClass Windows class name of the view class.

dwStyle Style of the view class.

Remarks

Constructs a **CCtrlView** object. The framework calls the constructor when a new frame window is created or a window is split. Override **CView::OnInitialUpdate** to initialize the view after the document is attached. Call **CWnd::Create** or **CWnd::CreateEx** to create the Windows object.

See Also: **CWnd::PreCreateWindow**

Data Members

CCtrlView::m_dwDefaultStyle

DWORD m_dwDefaultStyle;

Remarks

Contains the default style for the view class. This style is applied when a window is created.

See Also: **CCtrlView::m_strClass**

CCtrlView::m_strClass

CString m_strClass;

Remarks

Contains the Windows class name for the view class.

See Also: **CCtrlView::m_dwDefaultStyle**

CDaoDatabase

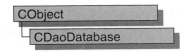

A **CDaoDatabase** object represents a connection to a database through which you can operate on the data. For information about the database formats supported, see the **GetName** member function. You can have one or more **CDaoDatabase** objects active at a time in a given "workspace," represented by a **CDaoWorkspace** object. The workspace maintains a collection of open database objects, called the Databases collection.

Note The MFC DAO database classes are distinct from the MFC database classes based on ODBC. All DAO database class names have the "CDao" prefix. Class **CDaoDatabase** supplies an interface similar to that of the ODBC class **CDatabase**. The main difference is that **CDatabase** accesses the DBMS through Open Database Connectivity (ODBC) and an ODBC driver for that DBMS. **CDaoDatabase** accesses data through a Data Access Object (DAO) based on the Microsoft Jet database engine. In general, the MFC classes based on DAO are more capable than the MFC classes based on ODBC; the DAO-based classes can access data, including through ODBC drivers, via their own database engine. The DAO-based classes also support Data Definition Language (DDL) operations, such as adding tables via the classes, without having to call DAO directly.

Usage

You can create database objects implicitly, when you create recordset objects. But you can also create database objects explicitly. To use an existing database explicitly with **CDaoDatabase**, do either of the following:

- Construct a **CDaoDatabase** object, passing a pointer to an open **CDaoWorkspace** object.

- Or construct a **CDaoDatabase** object without specifying the workspace (MFC creates a temporary workspace object).

To create a new Microsoft Jet (.MDB) database, construct a **CDaoDatabase** object and call its **Create** member function. Do *not* call **Open** after **Create**.

To open an existing database, construct a **CDaoDatabase** object and call its **Open** member function.

Any of these techniques appends the DAO database object to the workspace's Databases collection and opens a connection to the data. When you then construct **CDaoRecordset**, **CDaoTableDef**, or **CDaoQueryDef** objects for operating on the connected database, pass the constructors for these objects a pointer to your **CDaoDatabase** object. When you finish using the connection, call the **Close** member function and destroy the **CDaoDatabase** object. **Close** closes any recordsets you have not closed previously.

Transactions

Database transaction processing is supplied at the workspace level — see the **BeginTrans**, **CommitTrans**, and **Rollback** member functions of class **CDaoWorkspace**. For more information, see the article "DAO Workspace: Managing Transactions" in *Visual C++ Programmer's Guide* online.

ODBC Connections

The recommended way to work with ODBC data sources is to attach external tables to a Microsoft Jet (.MDB) database. For more information, see the article "DAO External: Working with External Data Sources" in *Visual C++ Programmer's Guide* online.

Collections

Each database maintains its own collections of tabledef, querydef, recordset, and relation objects. Class **CDaoDatabase** supplies member functions for manipulating these objects.

Note   The objects are stored in DAO, not in the MFC database object. MFC supplies classes for tabledef, querydef, and recordset objects but not for relation objects.

For more information about **CDaoDatabase**, see the article "DAO Database" in *Visual C++ Programmer's Guide* online.

#include <afxdao.h>

See Also: **CDaoWorkspace, CDaoRecordset, CDaoTableDef, CDaoQueryDef, CDatabase, CDaoException**

CDaoDatabase Class Members

Data Members

m_pWorkspace	A pointer to the **CDaoWorkspace** object that contains the database and defines its transaction space.
m_pDAODatabase	A pointer to the underlying DAO database object.

Construction

CDaoDatabase	Constructs a **CDaoDatabase** object. Call **Open** to connect the object to a database.

Attributes

CanTransact	Returns nonzero if the database supports transactions.
CanUpdate	Returns nonzero if the **CDaoDatabase** object is updatable (not read-only).

Attributes *(continued)*

GetConnect	Returns the connect string used to connect the **CDaoDatabase** object to a database. Used for ODBC.
GetName	Returns the name of the database currently in use.
GetQueryTimeout	Returns the number of seconds after which database query operations will time out. Affects all subsequent open, add new, update, and edit operations and other operations on ODBC data sources (only) such as **Execute** calls.
GetRecordsAffected	Returns the number of records affected by the last update, edit, or add operation or by a call to **Execute**.
GetVersion	Returns the version of the database engine associated with the database.
IsOpen	Returns nonzero if the **CDaoDatabase** object is currently connected to a database.
SetQueryTimeout	Sets the number of seconds after which database query operations (on ODBC data sources only) will time out. Affects all subsequent open, add new, update, and delete operations.

Operations

Close	Closes the database connection.
Create	Creates the underlying DAO database object and initializes the **CDaoDatabase** object.
CreateRelation	Defines a new relation among the tables in the database.
DeleteQueryDef	Deletes a querydef object saved in the database's QueryDefs collection.
DeleteRelation	Deletes an existing relation between tables in the database.
DeleteTableDef	Deletes the definition of a table in the database. This deletes the actual table and all of its data.
Execute	Executes an action query. Calling **Execute** for a query that returns results throws an exception.
GetQueryDefCount	Returns the number of queries defined for the database.
GetQueryDefInfo	Returns information about a specified query defined in the database.
GetRelationCount	Returns the number of relations defined between tables in the database.
GetRelationInfo	Returns information about a specified relation defined between tables in the database.
GetTableDefCount	Returns the number of tables defined in the database.
GetTableDefInfo	Returns information about a specified table in the database.
Open	Establishes a connection to a database.

Member Functions

CDaoDatabase::CanTransact

> **BOOL CanTransact( );**
> **throw(CDaoException, CMemoryException);**

Return Value

Nonzero if the database supports transactions; otherwise 0.

Remarks

Call this member function to determine whether the database allows transactions. Transactions are managed in the database's workspace. For information about transactions, see the article "DAO Workspace: Managing Transactions" in *Visual C++ Programmer's Guide* online.

See Also: **CDaoWorkspace::BeginTrans**, **CDaoWorkspace::CommitTrans**, **CDaoWorkspace::Rollback**

CDaoDatabase::CanUpdate

> **BOOL CanUpdate( );**
> **throw(CDaoException, CMemoryException);**

Return Value

Nonzero if the **CDaoDatabase** object allows updates; otherwise 0, indicating either that you passed **TRUE** in *bReadOnly* when you opened the **CDaoDatabase** object or that the database itself is read-only. See the **Open** member function.

Remarks

Call this member function to determine whether the **CDaoDatabase** object allows updates. For information about database updatability, see the article "DAO Recordset: Recordset Operations" in *Visual C++ Programmer's Guide* online and see the topic "Updatable Property" in DAO Help.

CDaoDatabase::CDaoDatabase

> **CDaoDatabase(CDaoWorkspace*** *pWorkspace* **= NULL);**

Parameters

pWorkspace   A pointer to the **CDaoWorkspace** object that will contain the new database object. If you accept the default value of **NULL**, the constructor creates a temporary **CDaoWorkspace** object that uses the default DAO workspace. You can get a pointer to the workspace object via the **m_pWorkspace** data member.

Remarks

Constructs a **CDaoDatabase** object. After constructing the object, if you are creating a new Microsoft Jet (.MDB) database, call the object's **Create** member function. If you are, instead, opening an existing database, call the object's **Open** member function.

When you finish with the object, you should call its **Close** member function and then destroy the **CDaoDatabase** object.

You might find it convenient to embed the **CDaoDatabase** object in your document class.

Note A **CDaoDatabase** object is also created implicitly if you open a **CDaoRecordset** object without passing a pointer to an existing **CDaoDatabase** object. This database object is closed when you close the recordset object.

For information about workspaces, see the article "DAO Workspace." For information about using **CDaoDatabase** objects, see the article "DAO Database." These articles are in *Visual C++ Programmer's Guide* online.

CDaoDatabase::Close

virtual void Close( );

Remarks

Call this member function to disconnect from a database and close any open recordsets, tabledefs, and querydefs associated with the database. It is good practice to close these objects yourself before you call this member function. Closing a **CDaoDatabase** object removes it from the Databases collection in the associated workspace. Because **Close** does not destroy the **CDaoDatabase** object, you can reuse the object by opening the same database or a different database.

Caution Call the **Update** member function (if there are pending edits) and the **Close** member function on all open recordset objects before you close a database. If you exit a function that declares **CDaoRecordset** or **CDaoDatabase** objects on the stack, the database is closed, any unsaved changes are lost, all pending transactions are rolled back, and any pending edits to your data are lost.

Caution If you try to close a database object while any recordset objects are open, or if you try to close a workspace object while any database objects belonging to that specific workspace are open, those recordset objects will be closed and any pending updates or edits will be rolled back. If you try to close a workspace object while any database objects belonging to it are open, the operation closes all database objects belonging to that specific workspace object, which may result in unclosed recordset objects being closed. If you do not close your database object, MFC reports an assertion failure in debug builds.

If the database object is defined outside the scope of a function, and you exit the function without closing it, the database object will remain open until explicitly closed or the module in which it is defined is out of scope.

For more information about **CDaoDatabase** objects, see the article "DAO Database" in *Visual C++ Programmer's Guide* online. For related information, see the topic "Close Method" in DAO Help.

See Also: **CDaoDatabase::Open, CDaoRecordset::Close, CDaoWorkspace::Close, CDaoQueryDef::Close, CDaoTableDef::Close**

CDaoDatabase::Create

virtual void Create(LPCTSTR *lpszName***, LPCTSTR** *lpszLocale* **= dbLangGeneral,
↪ int** *dwOptions* **= 0);
throw(CDaoException, CMemoryException);**

Parameters

lpszName   A string expression that is the name of the database file that you are creating. It can be the full path and filename, such as "C:\\MYDB.MDB". You must supply a name. If you do not supply a filename extension, .MDB is appended. If your network supports the uniform naming convention (UNC), you can also specify a network path, such as "\\\\MYSERVER\\MYSHARE\\MYDIR\\MYDB". Only Microsoft Jet (.MDB) database files can be created using this member function. (Double backslashes are required in string literals because "\" is the C++ escape character.)

lpszLocale   A string expression used to specify collating order for creating the database. The default value is **dbLangGeneral**. Possible values are:

- **dbLangGeneral**   English, German, French, Portuguese, Italian, and Modern Spanish

- **dbLangArabic**   Arabic

- **dbLangCyrillic**   Russian

- **dbLangCzech**   Czech

- **dbLangDutch**   Dutch

- **dbLangGreek**   Greek

- **dbLangHebrew**   Hebrew

- **dbLangHungarian**   Hungarian

- **dbLangIcelandic**   Icelandic

- **dbLangNordic**   Nordic languages (Microsoft Jet database engine version 1.0 only)

- **dbLangNorwdan**   Norwegian and Danish

- **dbLangPolish**   Polish

- **dbLangSpanish**   Traditional Spanish

- **dbLangSwedfin**   Swedish and Finnish

- **dbLangTurkish**   Turkish

dwOptions   An integer that indicates one or more options. Possible values are:

- **dbEncrypt**   Create an encrypted database.

- **dbVersion10**   Create a database with Microsoft Jet database version 1.0.

- **dbVersion11**   Create a database with Microsoft Jet database version 1.1.

- **dbVersion20**   Create a database with Microsoft Jet database version 2.0.

- **dbVersion30**   Create a database with Microsoft Jet database version 3.0.

If you omit the encryption constant, an unencrypted database is created. You can specify only one version constant. If you omit a version constant, a database that uses the Microsoft Jet database version 3.0 is created.

Caution   If a database is not encrypted, it is possible, even if you implement user/password security, to directly read the binary disk file that constitutes the database.

Remarks

To create a new Microsoft Jet (.MDB) database, call this member function after you construct a **CDaoDatabase** object. **Create** creates the database file and the underlying DAO database object and initializes the C++ object. The object is appended to the associated workspace's Databases collection. The database object is in an open state; do not call **Open** after **Create**.

Note   With **Create**, you can create only Microsoft Jet (.MDB) databases. You cannot create ISAM databases or ODBC databases.

For information about databases, see the article "DAO Database" in *Visual C++ Programmer's Guide* online. For related information, see the topic "CreateDatabase Method" in DAO Help.

See Also: **CDaoDatabase::CDaoDatabase**

CDaoDatabase::CreateRelation

> **void CreateRelation(LPCTSTR** *lpszName***, LPCTSTR** *lpszTable***,**
> ➥ **LPCTSTR** *lpszForeignTable***, long** *lAttributes***, LPCTSTR** *lpszField***,**
> ➥ **LPCTSTR** *lpszForeignField* **);**
> **throw(CDaoException, CMemoryException);**
> **void CreateRelation(CDaoRelationInfo&** *relinfo* **);**
> **throw(CDaoException, CMemoryException);**

Parameters

lpszName   The unique name of the relation object. The name must start with a letter and can contain a maximum of 40 characters. It can include numbers and underscore characters but cannot include punctuation or spaces.

lpszTable   The name of the primary table in the relation. If the table does not exist, MFC throws an exception of type **CDaoException**.

lpszForeignTable   The name of the foreign table in the relation. If the table does not exist, MFC throws an exception of type **CDaoException**.

lAttributes   A long value that contains information about the relationship type. You can use this value to enforce referential integrity, among other things. You can use the bitwise-OR operator (|) to combine any of the following values (as long as the combination makes sense):

- **dbRelationUnique**   Relationship is one-to-one.

- **dbRelationDontEnforce**   Relationship is not enforced (no referential integrity).

- **dbRelationInherited**   Relationship exists in a noncurrent database that contains the two attached tables.

- **dbRelationUpdateCascade**   Updates will cascade (for more on cascades, see Remarks).

- **dbRelationDeleteCascade**   Deletions will cascade.

lpszField   A pointer to a null-terminated string containing the name of a field in the primary table (named by *lpszTable*).

lpszForeignField   A pointer to a null-terminated string containing the name of a field in the foreign table (named by *lpszForeignTable*).

relinfo   A reference to a **CDaoRelationInfo** object that contains information about the relation you want to create.

Remarks

Call this member function to establish a relation between one or more fields in a primary table in the database and one or more fields in a foreign table (another table in the database). The relationship cannot involve a query or an attached table from an external database.

Use the first version of the function when the relation involves one field in each of the two tables. Use the second version when the relation involves multiple fields. The maximum number of fields in a relation is 14.

This action creates an underlying DAO relation object, but this is an MFC implementation detail since MFC's encapsulation of relation objects is contained within class **CDaoDatabase**. MFC does not supply a class for relations.

If you set the relation object's attributes to activate cascade operations, the database engine automatically updates or deletes records in one or more other tables when changes are made to related primary key tables.

For example, suppose you establish a cascade delete relationship between a Customers table and an Orders table. When you delete records from the Customers table, records in the Orders table related to that customer are also deleted. In addition, if you establish cascade delete relationships between the Orders table and other tables, records from those tables are automatically deleted when you delete records from the Customers table.

For related information, see the topic "CreateRelation Method" in DAO Help.

See Also: CDaoDatabase::DeleteRelation

CDaoDatabase::DeleteQueryDef

void DeleteQueryDef(LPCTSTR *lpszName* **);**
   throw(CDaoException, CMemoryException);

Parameters
lpszName   The name of the saved query to delete.

Remarks
Call this member function to delete the specified querydef¾saved query¾from the **CDaoDatabase** object's QueryDefs collection. Afterwards, that query is no longer defined in the database.

For information about creating querydef objects, see class **CDaoQueryDef**. A querydef object becomes associated with a particular **CDaoDatabase** object when you construct the **CDaoQueryDef** object, passing it a pointer to the database object.

For information about querydefs, see the article "DAO QueryDef" in *Visual C++ Programmer's Guide* online. For related information, see the topic "Delete Method" in DAO Help.

See Also: CDaoQueryDef::Create, CDaoDatabase::CreateRelation, CDaoTableDef::Create

CDaoDatabase::DeleteRelation

void DeleteRelation(LPCTSTR *lpszName* **);**
   throw(CDaoException, CMemoryException);

Parameters
lpszName   The name of the relation to delete.

Remarks

Call this member function to delete an existing relation from the database object's Relations collection. Afterwards, the relation no longer exists.

For related information, see the topic "Delete Method" in DAO Help.

See Also: **CDaoDatabase::CreateRelation**, **CDaoTableDef::Create**, **CDaoQueryDef::Create**

CDaoDatabase::DeleteTableDef

void DeleteTableDef(LPCTSTR *lpszName* **);**
   throw(CDaoException, CMemoryException);

Parameters

lpszName   The name of the tabledef to delete.

Remarks

Call this member function to delete the specified table and all of its data from the **CDaoDatabase** object's TableDefs collection. Afterwards, that table is no longer defined in the database.

Warning   Be very careful not to delete system tables.

For information about creating tabledef objects, see class **CDaoTableDef**. A tabledef object becomes associated with a particular **CDaoDatabase** object when you construct the **CDaoTableDef** object, passing it a pointer to the database object.

For information about tabledefs, see the article "DAO TableDef" in *Visual C++ Programmer's Guide* online. For related information, see the topic "Delete Method" in DAO Help.

See Also: **CDaoTableDef::Create**, **CDaoQueryDef::Create**, **CDaoDatabase::CreateRelation**

CDaoDatabase::Execute

void Execute(LPCTSTR *lpszSQL***, int** *nOptions* **= 0);**
   throw(CDaoException, CMemoryException);

Parameters

lpszSQL   Pointer to a null-terminated string containing a valid SQL command to execute.

nOptions   An integer that specifies options relating to the integrity of the query. You can use the bitwise-OR operator (|) to combine any of the following constants (provided the combination makes sense—for example, you would not combine **dbInconsistent** with **dbConsistent**):

- **dbDenyWrite**   Deny write permission to other users.

- **dbInconsistent**   (Default) Inconsistent updates.

- **dbConsistent**   Consistent updates.

- **dbSQLPassThrough**   SQL pass-through. Causes the SQL statement to be passed to an ODBC data source for processing.

- **dbFailOnError**   Roll back updates if an error occurs.

- **dbSeeChanges**   Generate a run-time error if another user is changing data you are editing.

Note If both **dbInconsistent** and **dbConsistent** are included or if neither is included, the result is the default. For an explanation of these constants, see the topic "Execute Method" in DAO Help.

Remarks

Call this member function to run an action query or execute an SQL statement on the database. **Execute** works only for action queries or SQL pass-through queries that do not return results. It does not work for select queries, which return records.

For a definition and information about action queries, see the topics "Action Query" and "Execute Method" in DAO Help.

Tip Given a syntactically correct SQL statement and proper permissions, the **Execute** member function will not fail even if not a single row can be modified or deleted. Therefore, always use the **dbFailOnError** option when using the **Execute** member function to run an update or delete query. This option causes MFC to throw an exception of type **CDaoException** and rolls back all successful changes if any of the records affected are locked and cannot be updated or deleted. Note that you can always call **GetRecordsAffected** to see how many records were affected.

Call the **GetRecordsAffected** member function of the database object to determine the number of records affected by the most recent **Execute** call. For example, **GetRecordsAffected** returns information about the number of records deleted, updated, or inserted when executing an action query. The count returned will not reflect changes in related tables when cascade updates or deletes are in effect.

Execute does not return a recordset. Using **Execute** on a query that selects records causes MFC to throw an exception of type **CDaoException**. (There is no **ExecuteSQL** member function analogous to **CDatabase::ExecuteSQL**.)

For more information about using the **Execute** member function, see the article "DAO Querydef: Using Querydefs" in *Visual C++ Programmer's Guide* online.

CDaoDatabase::GetConnect

CString GetConnect( );
throw(CDaoException, CMemoryException);

Return Value

The connect string if **Open** has been called successfully on an ODBC data source; otherwise, an empty string. For a Microsoft Jet (.MDB) database, the string is always empty unless you set it for use with the **dbSQLPassThrough** option used with the **Execute** member function or used in opening a recordset.

Remarks

Call this member function to retrieve the connect string used to connect the **CDaoDatabase** object to an ODBC or ISAM database. The string provides information about the source of an open database or a database used in a pass-through query. The connect string is composed of a database type specifier and zero or more parameters separated by semicolons. For additional information about connect strings in DAO, see the topic "Connect Property" in DAO Help.

Important Using the MFC DAO classes to connect to a data source via ODBC is less efficient than connecting via an attached table. For more information, see the article "DAO External: Working with External Data Sources" in *Visual C++ Programmer's Guide* online.

Note The connect string is used to pass additional information to ODBC and certain ISAM drivers as needed. It is not used for .MDB databases. For Microsoft Jet database base tables, the connect string is an empty string ("") except when you use it for an SQL pass-through query as described under Return Value above.

See the **Open** member function for a description of how the connect string is created. Once the connect string has been set in the **Open** call, you can later use it to check the setting to determine the type, path, user ID, Password, or ODBC data source of the database.

For connect string syntax, see the topic "Connect Property" in DAO Help.

CDaoDatabase::GetName

CString GetName( );
throw(CDaoException, CMemoryException);

Return Value

The full path and filename for the database if successful; otherwise, an empty **CString**.

Remarks

Call this member function to retrieve the name of the currently open database, which is the name of an existing database file or registered ODBC data source name. If your network supports the uniform naming convention (UNC), you can also specify a network path, such as "\\\\MYSERVER\\MYSHARE\\MYDIR\\MYDB.MDB". (Double backslashes are required in string literals because "\" is the C++ escape character.)

You might, for example, want to display this name in a heading. If an error occurs while retrieving the name, MFC throws an exception of type **CDaoException**.

Important For better performance when accessing external databases, it is recommended that you attach external database tables to a Microsoft Jet engine database (.MDB) rather than connecting directly to the data source.

The database type is indicated by the file or directory that the path points to, as follows:

Pathname points to..	Database type
.MDB file	Microsoft Jet database (Microsoft Access)
.DDF file	Btrieve® database
Directory containing .DBF file(s)	dBASE® database
Directory containing .XLS file	Microsoft Excel database
Directory containing .DBF files(s)	Microsoft FoxPro® database
Directory containing .PDX file(s)	Paradox® database
Directory containing appropriately formatted text database files	Text format database

For ODBC databases, such as Microsoft SQL Server and Oracle®, the database's connect string identifies a data source name (DSN) registered by ODBC.

For more about attaching external tables, see the article "DAO External: Attaching External Tables" in *Visual C++ Programmer's Guide* online.

See Also: **CDatabase::Open**, **CDatabase::GetConnect**

CDaoDatabase::GetQueryDefCount

short GetQueryDefCount( );
   throw(CDaoException, CMemoryException);

Return Value

The number of queries defined in the database.

Remarks

Call this member function to retrieve the number of queries defined in the database's QueryDefs collection. **GetQueryDefCount** is useful if you need to loop through all querydefs in the QueryDefs collection. To obtain information about a given query in the collection, see **GetQueryDefInfo**.

For information about queries and querydef objects, see the articles "DAO Queries" and "DAO QueryDef." Both articles are in *Visual C++ Programmer's Guide* online.

CDaoDatabase::GetQueryDefInfo

void GetQueryDefInfo(int *nIndex***, CDaoQueryDefInfo&** *querydefinfo***,**
  ↳ **DWORD** *dwInfoOptions* **= AFX_DAO_PRIMARY_INFO);**
  throw(CDaoException, CMemoryException);
void GetQueryDefInfo(LPCTSTR *lpszName***, CDaoQueryDefInfo&** *querydefinfo***,**
  ↳ **DWORD** *dwInfoOptions* **= AFX_DAO_PRIMARY_INFO);**
  throw(CDaoException, CMemoryException);

Parameters

nIndex The index of the predefined query in the database's QueryDefs collection, for lookup by index.

querydefinfo A reference to a **CDaoQueryDefInfo** object that returns the information requested.

dwInfoOptions Options that specify which information about the recordset to retrieve. The available options are listed here along with what they cause the function to return about the recordset:

- **AFX_DAO_PRIMARY_INFO** (Default) Name, Type

- **AFX_DAO_SECONDARY_INFO** Primary information plus: Date Created, Date of Last Update, Returns Records, Updatable

- **AFX_DAO_ALL_INFO** Primary and secondary information plus: SQL, Connect, ODBCTimeout

lpszName A string containing the name of a query defined in the database, for lookup by name.

Remarks

Call this member function to obtain various kinds of information about a query defined in the database. Two versions of the function are supplied so you can select a query either by index in the database's QueryDefs collection or by the name of the query.

For a description of the information returned in *querydefinfo*, see the **CDaoQueryDefInfo** structure. This structure has members that correspond to the items of information listed above in the description of *dwInfoOptions*. If you request one level of information, you get any prior levels of information as well.

For information about queries and querydef objects, see the articles "DAO Queries" and "DAO QueryDef." Both articles are in *Visual C++ Programmer's Guide* online.

See Also: **CDaoDatabase::GetQueryDefCount**

CDaoDatabase::GetQueryTimeout

short GetQueryTimeout( );
    throw(CDaoException, CMemoryException);

Return Value

A short integer containing the timeout value in seconds.

Remarks

Call this member function to retrieve the current number of seconds to allow before subsequent operations on the connected database are timed out. An operation might time out due to network access problems, excessive query processing time, and so on. While the setting is in effect, it affects all open, add new, update, and delete operations on any recordsets associated with this **CDaoDatabase** object. You can change the current timeout setting by calling **SetQueryTimeout**. Changing the query timeout value for a recordset after opening does not change the value for the recordset. For example, subsequent **Move** operations do not use the new value. The default value is initially set when the database engine is initialized.

The default value for query timeouts is taken from the Windows registry. If there is no registry setting, the default is 60 seconds. Not all databases support the ability to set a query timeout value. If you set a query timeout value of 0, no timeout occurs; and communication with the database may hang. This behavior may be useful during development. If the call fails, MFC throws an exception of type **CDaoException**.

For more information about database objects, see the article "DAO Database" in *Visual C++ Programmer's Guide* online. For related information, see the topic "QueryTimeout Property" in DAO Help.

See Also: **CDaoWorkspace::SetLoginTimeout**

CDaoDatabase::GetRecordsAffected

long GetRecordsAffected( );
    throw(CDaoException, CMemoryException);

Return Value

A long integer containing the number of records affected.

Remarks

Call this member function to determine the number of records affected by the most recent call of the **Execute** member function. The value returned includes the number of records deleted, updated, or inserted by an action query run with **Execute**. The count returned will not reflect changes in related tables when cascade updates or deletes are in effect.

For more information about database objects, see the article "DAO Database" in *Visual C++ Programmer's Guide* online. For related information, see the topic "RecordsAffected Property" in DAO Help.

CDaoDatabase::GetRelationCount

short GetRelationCount( );
 throw(CDaoException, CMemoryException);

Return Value

The number of relations defined between tables in the database.

Remarks

Call this member function to obtain the number of relations defined between tables in the database. **GetRelationCount** is useful if you need to loop through all defined relations in the database's Relations collection. To obtain information about a given relation in the collection, see **GetRelationInfo**.

To illustrate the concept of a relation, consider a Suppliers table and a Products table, which might have a one-to-many relationship. In this relationship, one supplier can supply more than one product. Other relations are one-to-one and many-to-many.

For more information about database objects, see the article "DAO Database" in *Visual C++ Programmer's Guide* online.

CDaoDatabase::GetRelationInfo

void GetRelationInfo(int *nIndex***, CDaoRelationInfo&** *relinfo***,**
 ↪ **DWORD** *dwInfoOptions* **= AFX_DAO_PRIMARY_INFO);**
 throw(CDaoException, CMemoryException);
void GetRelationInfo(LPCTSTR *lpszName***, CDaoRelationInfo&** *relinfo***,**
 ↪ **DWORD** *dwInfoOptions* **= AFX_DAO_PRIMARY_INFO);**
 throw(CDaoException, CMemoryException);

Parameters

nIndex The index of the relation object in the database's Relations collection, for lookup by index.

relinfo A reference to a **CDaoRelationInfo** object that returns the information requested.

dwInfoOptions Options that specify which information about the relation to retrieve. The available options are listed here along with what they cause the function to return about the relation:

- **AFX_DAO_PRIMARY_INFO** (Default) Name, Table, Foreign Table

- **AFX_DAO_SECONDARY_INFO** Attributes, Field Information

The Field Information is a **CDaoRelationFieldInfo** object containing the fields from the primary table involved in the relation.

lpszName A string containing the name of the relation object, for lookup by name.

Remarks

Call this member function to obtain information about a specified relation in the database's Relations collection. Two versions of this function provide access either by index or by name. For a description of the information returned in *relinfo*, see the **CDaoRelationInfo** structure. This structure has members that correspond to the items of information listed above in the description of *dwInfoOptions*. If you request information at one level, you also get information at any prior levels as well.

Note If you set the relation object's attributes to activate cascade operations (**dbRelationUpdateCascades** or **dbRelationDeleteCascades**), the Microsoft Jet database engine automatically updates or deletes records in one or more other tables when changes are made to related primary key tables. For example, suppose you establish a cascade delete relationship between a Customers table and an Orders table. When you delete records from the Customers table, records in the Orders table related to that customer are also deleted. In addition, if you establish cascade delete relationships between the Orders table and other tables, records from those tables are automatically deleted when you delete records from the Customers table.

For more information about database objects, see the article "DAO Database" in *Visual C++ Programmer's Guide* online.

See Also: **CDaoDatabase::GetRelationCount**

CDaoDatabase::GetTableDefCount

    short GetTableDefCount( );
        throw(CDaoException, CMemoryException);

Return Value

The number of tabledefs defined in the database.

Remarks

Call this member function to retrieve the number of tables defined in the database. **GetTableDefCount** is useful if you need to loop through all tabledefs in the database's TableDefs collection. To obtain information about a given table in the collection, see **GetTableDefInfo**.

For more information about tables and tabledef objects, see the article "DAO TableDef" in *Visual C++ Programmer's Guide* online.

CDaoDatabase::GetTableDefInfo

void GetTableDefInfo(int *nIndex,* **CDaoTableDefInfo&** *tabledefinfo,*
↪ **DWORD** *dwInfoOptions* = **AFX_DAO_PRIMARY_INFO);**
throw(CDaoException, CMemoryException);
void GetTableDefInfo(LPCTSTR *lpszName,* **CDaoTableDefInfo&** *tabledefinfo,*
↪ **DWORD** *dwInfoOptions* = **AFX_DAO_PRIMARY_INFO);**
throw(CDaoException, CMemoryException);

Parameters

nIndex   The index of the tabledef object in the database's TableDefs collection, for lookup by index.

tabledefinfo   A reference to a **CDaoTableDefInfo** object that returns the information requested.

dwInfoOptions   Options that specify which information about the table to retrieve. The available options are listed here along with what they cause the function to return about the relation:

- **AFX_DAO_PRIMARY_INFO**   (Default) Name, Updatable, Attributes

- **AFX_DAO_SECONDARY_INFO**   Primary information plus: Date Created, Date Last Updated, Source Table Name, Connect

- **AFX_DAO_ALL_INFO**   Primary and secondary information plus: Validation Rule, Validation Text, Record Count

lpszName   The name of the tabledef object, for lookup by name.

Remarks

Call this member function to obtain various kinds of information about a table defined in the database. Two versions of the function are supplied so you can select a table either by index in the database's TableDefs collection or by the name of the table.

For a description of the information returned in *tabledefinfo*, see the **CDaoTableDefInfo** structure. This structure has members that correspond to the items of information listed above in the description of *dwInfoOptions*. If you request information at one level, you get information for any prior levels as well.

Warning   The **AFX_DAO_ALL_INFO** option provides information that can be slow to obtain. In this case, counting the records in the table could be very time consuming if there are many records.

For more information about tables and tabledef objects, see the article "DAO TableDef" in *Visual C++ Programmer's Guide* online.

See Also: **CDaoDatabase::GetTableDefCount**

CDaoDatabase::GetVersion

CString GetVersion( );
    throw(CDaoException, CMemoryException);

Return Value

A **CString** that indicates the version of the database file associated with the object.

Remarks

Call this member function to determine the version of the Microsoft Jet database file. The value returned represents the version number in the form "major.minor"; for example, "3.0". The product version number (for example, 3.0) consists of the version number (3), a period, and the release number (0). The versions to date are 1.0, 1.1, 2.0, and 3.0.

For more information about database objects, see the article "DAO Database" in *Visual C++ Programmer's Guide* online. For related information, see the topic "Version Property" in DAO Help.

CDaoDatabase::IsOpen

BOOL IsOpen( ) const;

Return Value

Nonzero if the **CDaoDatabase** object is currently open; otherwise 0.

Remarks

Call this member function to determine whether the **CDaoDatabase** object is currently open on a database.

For more information about database objects, see the article "DAO Database" in *Visual C++ Programmer's Guide* online.

See Also: CDatabase::Open

CDaoDatabase::Open

virtual void Open(LPCTSTR *lpszName***, BOOL** *bExclusive* **= FALSE,**
   ↳ **BOOL** *bReadOnly* **= FALSE, LPCTSTR** *lpszConnect* **= _T(""));**
    throw(CDaoException, CMemoryException);

Parameters

lpszName   A string expression that is the name of an existing Microsoft Jet (.MDB) database file. If the filename has an extension, it is required. If your network supports the uniform naming convention (UNC), you can also specify a network path, such as "\\\\MYSERVER\\MYSHARE\\MYDIR\\MYDB.MDB". (Double backslashes are required in string literals because "\" is the C++ escape character.)

Some considerations apply when using *lpszName*. If it:

- Refers to a database that is already open for exclusive access by another user, MFC throws an exception of type **CDaoException**. Trap that exception to let your user know that the database is unavailable.

- Is an empty string ("") and *lpszConnect* is "ODBC;", a dialog box listing all registered ODBC data source names is displayed so the user can select a database. You should avoid direct connections to ODBC data sources; use an attached table instead. For information, see the article "DAO External: Working with External Data Sources" in *Visual C++ Programmer's Guide* online.

- Otherwise does not refer to an existing database or valid ODBC data source name, MFC throws an exception of type **CDaoException**.

Note For details about DAO error codes, see the DAOERR.H file. For related information, see the topic "Trappable Data Access Errors" in DAO Help.

bExclusive A Boolean value that is **TRUE** if the database is to be opened for exclusive (nonshared) access and **FALSE** if the database is to be opened for shared access. If you omit this argument, the database is opened for shared access.

bReadOnly A Boolean value that is **TRUE** if the database is to be opened for read-only access and **FALSE** if the database is to be opened for read/write access. If you omit this argument, the database is opened for read/write access. All dependent recordsets inherit this attribute.

lpszConnect A string expression used for opening the database. This string constitutes the ODBC connect arguments. You must supply the exclusive and read-only arguments to supply a source string. For syntax, see the topic "Connect Property" in DAO Help. If the database is a Microsoft Jet database (.MDB), this string is empty (""). The syntax for the default value — **_T**("") — provides portability for Unicode as well as ANSI builds of your application.

Remarks

You must call this member function to initialize a newly constructed **CDaoDatabase** object that represents an existing database. **Open** associates the database with the underlying DAO object. You cannot use the database object to construct recordset, tabledef, or querydef objects until it is initialized. **Open** appends the database object to the associated workspace's Databases collection.

Use the parameters as follows:

- If you are opening a Microsoft Jet (.MDB) database, use the *lpszName* parameter and pass an empty string for the *lpszConnect* parameter or pass a password string of the form ";PWD=password" if the database is password-protected (.MDB databases only).

- If you are opening an ODBC data source, pass a valid ODBC connect string in *lpszConnect* and an empty string in *lpszName*.

For related information, see the topic "OpenDatabase Method" in DAO Help.

Important For better performance when accessing external databases, including ISAM databases and ODBC data sources, it is recommended that you attach external database tables to a Microsoft Jet engine database (.MDB) rather than connecting directly to the data source.

It is possible for a connection attempt to time out if, for example, the DBMS host is unavailable. If the connection attempt fails, **Open** throws an exception of type **CDaoException**.

The remaining remarks apply only to ODBC databases:

If the database is an ODBC database and the parameters in your **Open** call do not contain enough information to make the connection, the ODBC driver opens a dialog box to obtain the necessary information from the user. When you call **Open**, your connect string, *lpszConnect*, is stored privately and is available by calling the **GetConnect** member function.

If you wish, you can open your own dialog box before you call **Open** to get information from the user, such as a password, then add that information to the connect string you pass to **Open**. Or you might want to save the connect string you pass (perhaps in the Windows registry) so you can reuse it the next time your application calls **Open** on a **CDaoDatabase** object.

You can also use the connect string for multiple levels of login authorization (each for a different **CDaoDatabase** object) or to convey other database-specific information.

For related information about connect strings, see the topic "Connect Property" in DAO Help.

See Also: **CDatabase::CDatabase, CDatabase::Close**

CDaoDatabase::SetQueryTimeout

void SetQueryTimeout(short *nSeconds*);
    throw(CDaoException, CMemoryException);

Parameters

nSeconds The number of seconds to allow before a query attempt times out.

Remarks

Call this member function to override the default number of seconds to allow before subsequent operations on the connected database time out. An operation might time out due to network access problems, excessive query processing time, and so on. Call **SetQueryTimeout** prior to opening your recordset or prior to calling the recordset's **AddNew**, **Update**, or **Delete** member functions if you want to change the query timeout value. The setting affects all subsequent **Open**, **AddNew**, **Update**, and **Delete** calls to any recordsets associated with this **CDaoDatabase** object. Changing the query timeout value for a recordset after opening does not change the value for the recordset. For example, subsequent **Move** operations do not use the new value.

The default value for query timeouts is 60 seconds. Not all databases support the ability to set a query timeout value. If you set a query timeout value of 0, no timeout occurs; the communication with the database may hang. This behavior may be useful during development.

For related information, see the topic "QueryTimeout Property" in DAO Help.

See Also: **CDaoWorkspace::SetLoginTimeout**

Data Members
CDaoDatabase::m_pDAODatabase

Remarks

Contains a pointer to the OLE interface for the DAO database object underlying the **CDaoDatabase** object. Use this pointer if you need to access the DAO interface directly.

For more information about DAO databases, see the article "DAO Database" in *Visual C++ Programmer's Guide* online. For information about calling DAO directly, see Technical Note 54 online.

CDaoDatabase::m_pWorkspace

Remarks

Contains a pointer to the **CDaoWorkspace** object that contains the database object. Use this pointer if you need to access the workspace directly—for example, to obtain pointers to other database objects in the workspace's Databases collection.

For more information about workspaces, see the article "DAO Workspace" in *Visual C++ Programmer's Guide* online.

CDaoException

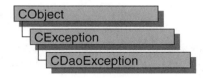

CObject
CException
CDaoException

A **CDaoException** object represents an exception condition arising from the MFC database classes based on data access objects (DAO). The class includes public data members you can use to determine the cause of the exception. **CDaoException** objects are constructed and thrown by member functions of the DAO database classes.

Note The DAO database classes are distinct from the MFC database classes based on Open Database Connectivity (ODBC). All DAO database class names have the "CDao" prefix. You can still access ODBC data sources with the DAO classes. In general, the MFC classes based on DAO are more capable than the MFC classes based on ODBC; the DAO-based classes can access data, including through ODBC drivers, via their own database engine. The DAO-based classes also support Data Definition Language (DDL) operations, such as adding tables via the classes, without having to call DAO directly. For information on exceptions thrown by the ODBC classes, see **CDBException**.

You can access exception objects within the scope of a **CATCH** expression. You can also throw **CDaoException** objects from your own code with the **AfxThrowDaoException** global function.

In MFC, all DAO errors are expressed as exceptions, of type **CDaoException**. When you catch an exception of this type, you can use **CDaoException** member functions to retrieve information from any DAO error objects stored in the database engine's Errors collection. As each error occurs, one or more error objects are placed in the Errors collection. (Normally the collection contains only one error object; if you are using an ODBC data source, you are more likely to get multiple error objects.) When another DAO operation generates an error, the Errors collection is cleared, and the new error object is placed in the Errors collection. DAO operations that do not generate an error have no effect on the Errors collection.

For DAO error codes, see the file DAOERR.H. For related information, see the topic "Trappable Data Access Errors" in DAO Help.

For more information about exception handling in general, or about **CDaoException** objects, see the articles "Exceptions" and "Exceptions: Database Exceptions" in *Visual C++ Programmer's Guide* online. The second article contains example code that illustrates exception handling in DAO.

#include <afxdao.h>

See Also: CException

CDaoException Class Members

Data Members

m_scode	The **SCODE** value associated with the error.
m_nAfxDaoError	Contains an extended error code for any error in the MFC DAO classes.
m_pErrorInfo	A pointer to a **CDaoErrorInfo** object that contains information about one DAO error object.

Construction

CDaoException	Constructs a **CDaoException** object.

Operations

GetErrorCount	Returns the number of errors in the database engine's Errors collection.
GetErrorInfo	Returns error information about a particular error object in the Errors collection.

Member Functions

CDaoException::CDaoException

CDaoException( );

Remarks

Constructs a **CDaoException** object. Ordinarily, the framework creates exception objects when its code throws an exception. You seldom need to construct an exception object explicitly. If you want to throw a **CDaoException** from your own code, call the global function **AfxThrowDaoException**.

However, you might want to explicitly create an exception object if you are making direct calls to DAO via the DAO interface pointers that MFC classes encapsulate. In that case, you might need to retrieve error information from DAO. Suppose an error occurs in DAO when you call a DAO method via, say, the DAODatabases interface to a workspace's Databases collection. To retrieve the DAO error information:

1. Construct a **CDaoException** object.

2. Call the exception object's **GetErrorCount** member function to determine how many error objects are in the database engine's Errors collection. (Normally only one, unless you are using an ODBC data source.)

3. Call the exception object's **GetErrorInfo** member function to retrieve one specific error object at a time, by index in the collection, via the exception object. Think of the exception object as a proxy for one DAO error object.

4. Examine the current **CDaoErrorInfo** structure that **GetErrorInfo** returns in the **m_pErrorInfo** data member. Its members provide information on the DAO error.

5. In the case of an ODBC data source, repeat steps 3 and 4 as needed, for more error objects.

6. If you constructed the exception object on the heap, delete it with the **delete** operator when you finish.

For more information about handling errors in the MFC DAO classes, see the article "Exceptions: Database Exceptions" in *Visual C++ Programmer's Guide* online.

CDaoException::GetErrorCount

short GetErrorCount( );

Return Value

The number of DAO error objects in the database engine's Errors collection.

Remarks

Call this member function to retrieve the number of DAO error objects in the database engine's Errors collection. This information is useful for looping through the Errors collection to retrieve each of the one or more DAO error objects in the collection. To retrieve an error object by index or by DAO error number, call the **GetErrorInfo** member function.

Note Normally there is only one error object in the Errors collection. If you are working with an ODBC data source, however, there could be more than one.

CDaoException::GetErrorInfo

void GetErrorInfo(int *nIndex*);

Parameters

nIndex   The index of the error information in the database engine's Errors collection, for lookup by index.

Remarks

Call this member function to obtain the following kinds of information about the exception:

- Error Code
- Source
- Description
- Help File
- Help Context

GetErrorInfo stores the information in the exception object's **m_pErrorInfo** data member. For a brief description of the information returned, see **m_pErrorInfo**. If you catch an exception of type **CDaoException** thrown by MFC, the **m_pErrorInfo** member will already be filled in. If you choose to call DAO directly, you must call the exception object's **GetErrorInfo** member function yourself to fill **m_pErrorInfo**. For a more detailed description, see the **CDaoErrorInfo** structure.

For information about DAO exceptions, and example code, see the article "Exceptions: Database Exceptions." For more about getting information from DAO object collections, see the article "DAO Collections: Obtaining Information About DAO Objects. Both articles are in *Visual C++ Programmer's Guide* online.

See Also: **CDaoException::GetErrorCount**

Data Members
CDaoException::m_nAfxDaoError

Remarks

Contains an MFC extended error code. This code is supplied in cases where a specific component of the MFC DAO classes has erred.

Possible values are:

- **NO_AFX_DAO_ERROR** The most recent operation did not result in an MFC extended error. However, the operation could have produced other errors from DAO or OLE, so you should check **m_pErrorInfo** and possibly **m_scode**.

- **AFX_DAO_ERROR_ENGINE_INITIALIZATION** MFC could not initialize the Microsoft Jet database engine. OLE might have failed to initialize, or it might have been impossible to create an instance of the DAO database engine object. These problems usually suggest a bad installation of either DAO or OLE.

- **AFX_DAO_ERROR_DFX_BIND** An address used in a DAO record field exchange (DFX) function call does not exist or is invalid (the address was not used to bind data). You might have passed a bad address in a DFX call, or the address might have become invalid between DFX operations.

- **AFX_DAO_ERROR_OBJECT_NOT_OPEN** You attempted to open a recordset based on a querydef or a tabledef object that was not in an open state.

For more information about DFX, see the article "DAO Record Field Exchange (DFX)" in *Visual C++ Programmer's Guide* online.

See Also: **CDaoException::GetErrorCount**, **CDaoException::GetErrorInfo**

CDaoException::m_pErrorInfo

Remarks

Contains a pointer to a **CDaoErrorInfo** structure that provides information on the DAO error object that you last retrieved by calling **GetErrorInfo**. This object contains the following information:

CDaoErrorInfo member	Information	Meaning
m_lErrorCode	Error Code	The DAO error code
m_strSource	Source	The name of the object or application that originally generated the error
m_strDescription	Description	A descriptive string associated with the error
m_strHelpFile	Help File	A path to a Windows Help file in which the user can get information about the problem
m_lHelpContext	Help Context	The context ID for a topic in the DAO Help file

For full details about the information contained in the **CDaoErrorInfo** object, see the **CDaoErrorInfo** structure.

See Also: **CDaoException::m_scode, CDaoException::m_nAfxDaoError**

CDaoException::m_scode

Remarks

Contains a value of type **SCODE** that describes the error. This is an OLE code. You will seldom need to use this value because, in almost all cases, more specific MFC or DAO error information is available in the other **CDaoException** data members.

For information about **SCODE**, see the topic "Structure of OLE Error Codes" in the Win32 SDK, *OLE Programmer's Reference, Volume 1*. The **SCODE** data type maps to the **HRESULT** data type.

See Also: **CDaoException::m_pErrorInfo, CDaoException::m_nAfxDaoError**

CDaoFieldExchange

CDaoFieldExchange does not have a base class.

The **CDaoFieldExchange** class supports the DAO record field exchange (DFX) routines used by the DAO database classes. Use this class if you are writing data exchange routines for custom data types; otherwise, you will not directly use this class. DFX exchanges data between the field data members of your **CDaoRecordset** object and the corresponding fields of the current record on the data source. DFX manages the exchange in both directions, from the data source and to the data source. See Technical Note 53 online for information about writing custom DFX routines.

Note The DAO database classes are distinct from the MFC database classes based on Open Database Connectivity (ODBC). All DAO database class names have the "CDao" prefix. You can still access ODBC data sources with the DAO classes. In general, the MFC classes based on DAO are more capable than the MFC classes based on ODBC. The DAO-based classes can access data, including through ODBC drivers, via their own database engine. They also support Data Definition Language (DDL) operations, such as adding tables via the classes instead of having to call DAO yourself.

Note DAO record field exchange (DFX) is very similar to record field exchange (RFX) in the ODBC-based MFC database classes (**CDatabase**, **CRecordset**). If you understand RFX, you will find it easy to use DFX.

A **CDaoFieldExchange** object provides the context information needed for DAO record field exchange to take place. **CDaoFieldExchange** objects support a number of operations, including binding parameters and field data members and setting various flags on the fields of the current record. DFX operations are performed on recordset-class data members of types defined by the **enum FieldType** in **CDaoFieldExchange**. Possible **FieldType** values are:

- **CDaoFieldExchange::outputColumn** for field data members.
- **CDaoFieldExchange::param** for parameter data members.

The **IsValidOperation** member function is provided for writing your own custom DFX routines. You will use **SetFieldType** frequently in your **CDaoRecordset::DoFieldExchange** functions. For details about the DFX global functions, see "Record Field Exchange Functions." For information about writing custom DFX routines for your own data types, see Technical Note 53 online.

For information about DFX, see the article "DAO Record Field Exchange (DFX)" in *Visual C++ Programmer's Guide* online.

#include <afxdao.h>

See Also: **CDaoRecordset**

CDaoFieldExchange Class Members

Data Members

m_nOperation	The DFX operation being performed by the current call to the recordset's **DoFieldExchange** member function.
m_prs	A pointer to the recordset on which DFX operations are being performed.

Member Functions

IsValidOperation	Returns nonzero if the current operation is appropriate for the type of field being updated.
SetFieldType	Specifies the type of recordset data member — column or parameter—represented by all subsequent calls to DFX functions until the next call to **SetFieldType**.

Member Functions

CDaoFieldExchange::IsValidOperation

BOOL IsValidOperation( );

Return Value

Nonzero if the current operation is appropriate for the type of field being updated.

Remarks

If you write your own DFX function, call **IsValidOperation** at the beginning of your function to determine whether the current operation can be performed on a particular field data member type (a **CDaoFieldExchange::outputColumn** or a **CDaoFieldExchange::param**). Some of the operations performed by the DFX mechanism apply only to one of the possible field types. Follow the model of the existing DFX functions.

For more information about DFX, see the article "DAO Record Field Exchange (DFX)" in *Visual C++ Programmer's Guide* online. For additional information on writing custom DFX routines, see Technical Note 53 online.

See Also: CDaoFieldExchange::SetFieldType

CDaoFieldExchange::SetFieldType

void SetFieldType(UINT *nFieldType* **);**

Parameters

nFieldType   A value of the **enum FieldType**, declared in **CDaoFieldExchange**, which can be either of the following:

- **CDaoFieldExchange::outputColumn**

- **CDaoFieldExchange::param**

Remarks

Call **SetFieldType** in your **CDaoRecordset** class's **DoFieldExchange** override. Normally, ClassWizard writes this call for you. If you write your own function and are using the wizard to write your **DoFieldExchange** function, add calls to your own function outside the field map. If you do not use the wizard, there will not be a field map. The call precedes calls to DFX functions, one for each field data member of your class, and identifies the field type as **CDaoFieldExchange::outputColumn**.

If you parameterize your recordset class, you should add DFX calls for all parameter data members (outside the field map) and precede these calls with a call to **SetFieldType**. Pass the value **CDaoFieldExchange::param**. (You can, instead, use a **CDaoQueryDef** and set its parameter values.)

In general, each group of DFX function calls associated with field data members or parameter data members must be preceded by a call to **SetFieldType**. The *nFieldType* parameter of each **SetFieldType** call identifies the type of the data members represented by the DFX function calls that follow the **SetFieldType** call.

For more information about DFX, see the article "DAO Record Field Exchange (DFX)" in *Visual C++ Programmer's Guide* online.

See Also: **CDaoFieldExchange::IsValidOperation**, **CDaoRecordset::DoFieldExchange**

Data Members
CDaoFieldExchange::m_nOperation

Remarks

Identifies the operation to be performed on the **CDaoRecordset** object associated with the field exchange object. The **CDaoFieldExchange** object supplies the context for a number of different DFX operations on the recordset.

Note The **PSEUDO NULL** value described under the MarkForAddNew and SetFieldNull operations below is a value used to mark fields Null. The DAO record field exchange mechanism (DFX) uses this value to determine which fields have been explicitly marked Null. **PSEUDO NULL** is not required for **COleDateTime** and **COleCurrency** fields.

For more information about DFX and these operations, see the article "DAO Record Field Exchange (DFX)" in *Visual C++ Programmer's Guide* online.

Possible values of **m_nOperation** are:

Operation	Description
AddToParameterList	Builds the **PARAMETERS** clause of the SQL statement.
AddToSelectList	Builds the **SELECT** clause of the SQL statement.
BindField	Binds a field in the database to a memory location in your application.
BindParam	Sets parameter values for the recordset's query.
Fixup	Sets the Null status for a field.
AllocCache	Allocates the cache used to check for "dirty" fields in the recordset.
StoreField	Saves the current record to the cache.
LoadField	Restores the cached data member variables in the recordset.
FreeCache	Frees the cache used to check for "dirty" fields in the recordset.
SetFieldNull	Sets a field's status to Null and value to **PSEUDO NULL**.
MarkForAddNew	Marks fields "dirty" if not **PSEUDO NULL**.
MarkForEdit	Marks fields "dirty" if they do not match the cache.
SetDirtyField	Sets field values marked as "dirty."
DumpField	Dumps a field's contents (debug only).
MaxDFXOperation	Used for input checking.

See Also: **CDaoFieldExchange::IsValidOperation, CDaoFieldExchange::m_prs, CDaoRecordset::DoFieldExchange**

CDaoFieldExchange::m_prs

Remarks

Contains a pointer to the **CDaoRecordset** object associated with the **CDaoFieldExchange** object.

For more information about DFX, see the article "DAO Record Field Exchange (DFX)" in *Visual C++ Programmer's Guide* online.

See Also: **CDaoFieldExchange::m_nOperation, CDaoRecordset**

CDaoQueryDef

A **CDaoQueryDef** object represents a query definition, or "querydef," usually one saved in a database. A querydef is a data access object that contains the SQL statement that describes a query, and its properties, such as "Date Created" and "ODBC Timeout." You can also create temporary querydef objects without saving them, but it is convenient—and much more efficient—to save commonly reused queries in a database. A **CDaoDatabase** object maintains a collection, called the QueryDefs collection, that contains its saved querydefs.

Note The DAO database classes are distinct from the MFC database classes based on Open Database Connectivity (ODBC). All DAO database class names have the "CDao" prefix. You can still access ODBC data sources with the DAO classes. In general, the MFC classes based on DAO are more capable than the MFC classes based on ODBC; the DAO-based classes can access data, including through ODBC drivers, via their own database engine. The DAO-based classes also support Data Definition Language (DDL) operations, such as adding tables via the classes, without having to call DAO directly.

Usage

Use querydef objects either to work with an existing saved query or to create a new saved query or temporary query:

1. In all cases, first construct a **CDaoQueryDef** object, supplying a pointer to the **CDaoDatabase** object to which the query belongs.

2. Then do the following, depending on what you want:

   - To use an existing saved query, call the querydef object's **Open** member function, supplying the name of the saved query.

   - To create a new saved query, call the querydef object's **Create** member function, supplying the name of the query. Then call **Append** to save the query by appending it to the database's QueryDefs collection. **Create** puts the querydef into an open state, so after calling **Create** you do not call **Open**.

   - To create a temporary querydef, call **Create**. Pass an empty string for the query name. Do not call **Append**.

When you finish using a querydef object, call its **Close** member function; then destroy the querydef object.

Tip The easiest way to create saved queries is to create them and store them in your database using Microsoft Access. Then you can open and use them in your MFC code.

Purposes

You can use a querydef object for any of the following purposes:

- To create a **CDaoRecordset** object
- To call the object's **Execute** member function to directly execute an action query or an SQL pass-through query

You can use a querydef object for any type of query, including select, action, crosstab, delete, update, append, make-table, data definition, SQL pass-through, union, and bulk queries. The query's type is determined by the content of the SQL statement that you supply. For information about query types, see the **Execute** and **GetType** member functions. Recordsets are commonly used for row-returning queries, usually those using the **SELECT ... FROM** keywords. **Execute** is most commonly used for bulk operations. For more information, see **Execute** and **CDaoRecordset**.

Querydefs and Recordsets

To use a querydef object to create a **CDaoRecordset** object, you typically create or open a querydef as described above. Then construct a recordset object, passing a pointer to your querydef object when you call **CDaoRecordset::Open**. The querydef you pass must be in an open state. For more information, see class **CDaoRecordset**.

You cannot use a querydef to create a recordset (the most common use for a querydef) unless it is in an open state. Put the querydef into an open state by calling either **Open** or **Create**.

External Databases

Querydef objects are the preferred way to use the native SQL dialect of an external database engine. For example, you can create a Transact SQL query (as used on Microsoft SQL Server) and store it in a querydef object. When you need to use a SQL query not based on the Microsoft Jet database engine, you must provide a connect string that points to the external data source. Queries with valid connect strings bypass the database engine and pass the query directly to the external database server for processing.

Tip The preferred way to work with ODBC tables is to attach them to a Microsoft Jet (.MDB) database. For more information, see the article "DAO External: Working with External Data Sources" in *Visual C++ Programmer's Guide* online.

For more information about querydefs, see the article "DAO Querydef" in *Visual C++ Programmer's Guide* online. For related information, see the topics "QueryDef Object," "QueryDefs Collection," and "Accessing External Databases with DAO" in DAO Help.

#include <afxdao.h>

See Also: **CDaoRecordset, CDaoDatabase, CDaoTableDef, CDaoException**

CDaoQueryDef Class Members

Data Members

m_pDatabase	A pointer to the **CDaoDatabase** object with which the querydef is associated. The querydef might be saved in the database or not.
m_pDAOQueryDef	A pointer to the OLE interface for the underlying DAO querydef object.

Construction

CDaoQueryDef	Constructs a **CDaoQueryDef** object. Next call **Open** or **Create**, depending on your needs.
Create	Creates the underlying DAO querydef object. Use the querydef as a temporary query, or call **Append** to save it in the database.
Append	Appends the querydef to the database's QueryDefs collection as a saved query.
Open	Opens an existing querydef stored in the database's QueryDefs collection.
Close	Closes the querydef object. Destroy the C++ object when you finish with it.

Attributes

CanUpdate	Returns nonzero if the query can update the database.
GetConnect	Returns the connect string associated with the querydef. The connect string identifies the data source. (For SQL pass-through queries only; otherwise an empty string.)
GetDateCreated	Returns the date the saved query was created.
GetDateLastUpdated	Returns the date the saved query was last updated.
GetName	Returns the name of the querydef.
GetODBCTimeout	Returns the timeout value used by ODBC (for an ODBC query) when the querydef is executed. This determines how long to allow for the query's action to complete.
GetRecordsAffected	Returns the number of records affected by an action query.
GetReturnsRecords	Returns nonzero if the query defined by the querydef returns records.
GetSQL	Returns the SQL string that specifies the query defined by the querydef.
GetType	Returns the query type: delete, update, append, make-table, and so on.
IsOpen	Returns nonzero if the querydef is open and can be executed.
SetConnect	Sets the connect string for an SQL pass-through query on an ODBC data source.
SetName	Sets the name of the saved query, replacing the name in use when the querydef was created.

Attributes *(continued)*

SetODBCTimeout	Sets the timeout value used by ODBC (for an ODBC query) when the querydef is executed.
SetReturnsRecords	Specifies whether the querydef returns records. Setting this attribute to **TRUE** is only valid for SQL pass-through queries.
SetSQL	Sets the SQL string that specifies the query defined by the querydef.

Operations

Execute	Executes the query defined by the querydef object.
GetFieldCount	Returns the number of fields defined by the querydef.
GetFieldInfo	Returns information about a specified field defined in the query.
GetParameterCount	Returns the number of parameters defined for the query.
GetParameterInfo	Returns information about a specified parameter to the query.
GetParamValue	Returns the value of a specified parameter to the query.
SetParamValue	Sets the value of a specified parameter to the query.

Member Functions
CDaoQueryDef::Append

> **virtual void Append( );**
> **throw(CDaoException, CMemoryException);**

Remarks

Call this member function after you call **Create** to create a new querydef object. **Append** saves the querydef in the database by appending the object to the database's QueryDefs collection. You can use the querydef as a temporary object without appending it, but if you want it to persist, you must call **Append**.

If you attempt to append a temporary querydef object, MFC throws an exception of type **CDaoException**.

For information about querydefs, see the article "DAO Querydef" in *Visual C++ Programmer's Guide* online.

CDaoQueryDef::CanUpdate

> **BOOL CanUpdate( );**
> **throw(CDaoException, CMemoryException);**

Return Value

Nonzero if you are permitted to modify the querydef; otherwise 0.

Remarks

Call this member function to determine whether you can modify the querydef—such as changing its name or SQL string. You can modify the querydef if:

- It is not based on a database that is open read-only.

- You have update permissions for the database.

    This depends on whether you have implemented security features. MFC does not provide support for security; you must implement it yourself by calling DAO directly or by using Microsoft Access. See the topic "Permissions Property" in DAO Help.

For information about querydefs, see the article "DAO Querydef" in *Visual C++ Programmer's Guide* online.

CDaoQueryDef::CDaoQueryDef

CDaoQueryDef(CDaoDatabase* *pDatabase* **);**

Parameters

pDatabase   A pointer to an open **CDaoDatabase** object.

Remarks

Constructs a **CDaoQueryDef** object. The object can represent an existing querydef stored in the database's QueryDefs collection, a new query to be stored in the collection, or a temporary query, not to be stored. Your next step depends on the type of querydef:

- If the object represents an existing querydef, call the object's **Open** member function to initialize it.

- If the object represents a new querydef to be saved, call the object's **Create** member function. This adds the object to the database's QueryDefs collection. Then call **CDaoQueryDef** member functions to set the object's attributes. Finally, call **Append**.

- If the object represents a temporary querydef (not to be saved in the database), call **Create**, passing an empty string for the query's name. After calling **Create**, initialize the querydef by directly setting its attributes. Do not call **Append**.

To set the attributes of the querydef, you can use the **SetName**, **SetSQL**, **SetConnect**, **SetODBCTimeout**, and **SetReturnsRecords** member functions.

When you finish with the querydef object, call its **Close** member function. If you have a pointer to the querydef, use the **delete** operator to destroy the C++ object.

For information about querydefs, see the article "DAO Querydef" in *Visual C++ Programmer's Guide* online.

See Also: CDaoQueryDef::GetConnect, CDaoQueryDef::GetDateCreated, CDaoQueryDef::GetDateLastUpdated, CDaoQueryDef::GetName, CDaoQueryDef::GetODBCTimeout, CDaoQueryDef::GetReturnsRecords, CDaoQueryDef::GetSQL

CDaoQueryDef::Close

virtual void Close( );

Remarks

Call this member function when you finish using the querydef object. Closing the querydef releases the underlying DAO object but does not destroy the saved DAO querydef object or the C++ **CDaoQueryDef** object. This is not the same as **CDaoDatabase::DeleteQueryDef**, which deletes the querydef from the database's QueryDefs collection in DAO (if not a temporary querydef).

For information about querydefs, see the article "DAO Querydef" in *Visual C++ Programmer's Guide* online.

See Also: CDaoQueryDef::Open, CDaoQueryDef::Create, CDaoQueryDef::CDaoQueryDef

CDaoQueryDef::Create

virtual void Create(LPCTSTR *lpszName* **= NULL, LPCTSTR** *lpszSQL* **= NULL);**
  throw(CDaoException, CMemoryException);

Parameters

lpszName   The unique name of the query saved in the database. For details about the string, see the topic "CreateQueryDef Method" in DAO Help. If you accept the default value, an empty string, a temporary querydef is created. Such a query is not saved in the QueryDefs collection.

lpszSQL   The SQL string that defines the query. If you accept the default value of **NULL**, you must later call **SetSQL** to set the string. Until then, the query is undefined. You can, however, use the undefined query to open a recordset; see Remarks for details. The SQL statement must be defined before you can append the querydef to the QueryDefs collection.

Remarks

Call this member function to create a new saved query or a new temporary query. If you pass a name in *lpszName*, you can then call **Append** to save the querydef in the database's QueryDefs collection. Otherwise, the object is a temporary querydef and is not saved. In either case, the querydef is in an open state, and you can either use it to create a **CDaoRecordset** object or call the querydef's **Execute** member function.

If you do not supply an SQL statement in *lpszSQL*, you cannot run the query with **Execute** but you can use it to create a recordset. In that case, MFC uses the recordset's default SQL statement.

For information about querydefs, see the article "DAO Querydef" in *Visual C++ Programmer's Guide* online.

See Also: **CDaoQueryDef::Open, CDaoQueryDef::CDaoQueryDef, CDaoRecordset::GetSQL**

CDaoQueryDef::Execute

virtual void Execute(int *nOptions* = **dbFailOnError);**
   throw(CDaoException, CMemoryException);

Parameters

nOptions   An integer that determines the characteristics of the query. For related information, see the topic "Execute Method" in DAO Help. You can use the bitwise-OR operator (I) to combine the following constants for this argument:

- **dbDenyWrite**   Deny write permission to other users.

- **dbInconsistent**   Inconsistent updates.

- **dbConsistent**   Consistent updates.

- **dbSQLPassThrough**   SQL pass-through. Causes the SQL statement to be passed to an ODBC database for processing.

- **dbFailOnError**   Default value. Roll back updates if an error occurs and report the error to the user.

- **dbSeeChanges**   Generate a run-time error if another user is changing data you are editing.

Note   For an explanation of the terms "inconsistent" and "consistent," see the topic "Execute Method" in DAO Help.

Remarks

Call this member function to run the query defined by the querydef object. Querydef objects used for execution in this manner can only represent one of the following query types:

- Action queries
- SQL pass-through queries

Execute does not work for queries that return records, such as select queries. **Execute** is commonly used for bulk operation queries, such as **UPDATE**, **INSERT**, or **SELECT INTO**, or for data definition language (DDL) operations.

For an explanation of action queries and SQL pass-through queries, see the article "DAO Querydef: Action Queries and SQL Pass-Through Queries" in *Visual C++ Programmer's Guide* online.

Tip The preferred way to work with ODBC data sources is to attach tables to a Microsoft Jet (.MDB) database. For more information, see the topic "Accessing External Databases with DAO" in DAO Help and the article "DAO External: Working with External Data Sources" in *Visual C++ Programmer's Guide* online.

Call the **GetRecordsAffected** member function of the querydef object to determine the number of records affected by the most recent **Execute** call. For example, **GetRecordsAffected** returns information about the number of records deleted, updated, or inserted when executing an action query. The count returned will not reflect changes in related tables when cascade updates or deletes are in effect.

If you include both **dbInconsistent** and **dbConsistent** or if you include neither, the result is the default, **dbInconsistent**.

Execute does not return a recordset. Using **Execute** on a query that selects records causes MFC to throw an exception of type **CDaoException**.

For more information about using the **Execute** member function for querydef objects, see the article "DAO Querydef: Using Querydefs" in *Visual C++ Programmer's Guide* online.

CDaoQueryDef::GetConnect

CString GetConnect( );
    throw(CDaoException, CMemoryException);

Return Value

A **CString** containing the connect string for the querydef.

Remarks

Call this member function to get the connect string associated with the querydef's data source. This function is used only with ODBC data sources and certain ISAM drivers. It is not used with Microsoft Jet (.MDB) databases; in this case, **GetConnect** returns an empty string. For more information, see **SetConnect**.

Tip The preferred way to work with ODBC tables is to attach them to an .MDB database. For more information, see the topic "Accessing External Databases with DAO" in DAO Help and the article "DAO External: Working with External Data Sources" in *Visual C++ Programmer's Guide* online.

For information about connect strings, see the topic "Connect Property" in DAO Help. For information about querydefs, see the article "DAO Querydef" in *Visual C++ Programmer's Guide* online.

CDaoQueryDef::GetDateCreated

COleDateTime GetDateCreated( );
  throw(CDaoException, CMemoryException);

Return Value

A **COleDateTime** object containing the date and time the querydef was created.

Remarks

Call this member function to get the date the querydef object was created.

For information about querydefs, see the article "DAO Querydef" in *Visual C++ Programmer's Guide* online. For related information, see the topic "DateCreated, LastUpdated Properties" in DAO Help.

See Also: **CDaoQueryDef::GetDateLastUpdated**

CDaoQueryDef::GetDateLastUpdated

COleDateTime GetDateLastUpdated( );
  throw(CDaoException, CMemoryException);

Return Value

A **COleDateTime** object containing the date and time the querydef was last updated.

Remarks

Call this member function to get the date the querydef object was last updated—when any of its properties were changed, such as its name, its SQL string, or its connect string.

For information about querydefs, see the article "DAO Querydef" in *Visual C++ Programmer's Guide* online. For related information, see the topic "DateCreated, LastUpdated Properties" in DAO Help.

See Also: **CDaoQueryDef::GetDateCreated**

CDaoQueryDef::GetFieldCount

short GetFieldCount( );
  throw(CDaoException, CMemoryException);

Return Value

The number of fields defined in the query.

Remarks

Call this member function to retrieve the number of fields in the query. **GetFieldCount** is useful for looping through all fields in the querydef. For that purpose, use **GetFieldCount** in conjunction with **GetFieldInfo**.

For information about obtaining information about querydef fields, see the article "DAO Collections: Obtaining Information About DAO Objects" in *Visual C++ Programmer's Guide* online.

CDaoQueryDef::GetFieldInfo

void GetFieldInfo(int *nIndex*, **CDaoFieldInfo&** *fieldinfo*,
↳ **DWORD** *dwInfoOptions* = **AFX_DAO_PRIMARY_INFO**);
throw(CDaoException, CMemoryException);
void GetFieldInfo(LPCTSTR *lpszName*, **CDaoFieldInfo&** *fieldinfo*,
↳ **DWORD** *dwInfoOptions* = **AFX_DAO_PRIMARY_INFO**);
throw(CDaoException, CMemoryException);

Parameters

nIndex   The zero-based index of the desired field in the querydef's Fields collection, for lookup by index.

fieldinfo   A reference to a **CDaoFieldInfo** object that returns the information requested.

dwInfoOptions   Options that specify which information about the field to retrieve. The available options are listed here along with what they cause the function to return:

- **AFX_DAO_PRIMARY_INFO**   (Default) Name, Type, Size, Attributes

- **AFX_DAO_SECONDARY_INFO**   Primary information plus: Ordinal Position, Required, Allow Zero Length, Source Field, Foreign Name, Source Table, Collating Order

- **AFX_DAO_ALL_INFO**   Primary and secondary information plus: Default Value, Validation Text, Validation Rule

lpszName   A string containing the name of the desired field, for lookup by name. You can use a **CString**.

Remarks

Call this member function to obtain various kinds of information about a field defined in the querydef. For a description of the information returned in *fieldinfo*, see the **CDaoFieldInfo** structure. This structure has members that correspond to the descriptive information under *dwInfoOptions* above. If you request one level of information, you get any prior levels of information as well.

For more information about obtaining field information, see the article "DAO Collections: Obtaining Information About DAO Objects" in *Visual C++ Programmer's Guide* online.

See Also: CDaoQueryDef::GetFieldCount

CDaoQueryDef::GetName

CString GetName( );
    throw(CDaoException, CMemoryException);

Return Value

The name of the query.

Remarks

Call this member function to retrieve the name of the query represented by the querydef. Querydef names are unique user-defined names. For more information about querydef names, see the topic "Name Property" in DAO Help.

For information about querydefs, see the article "DAO Querydef" in *Visual C++ Programmer's Guide* online.

See Also: **CDaoQueryDef::SetName, CDaoQueryDef::GetSQL, CDaoQueryDef::GetReturnsRecords, CDaoQueryDef::GetODBCTimeout**

CDaoQueryDef::GetODBCTimeout

short GetODBCTimeout( );
    throw(CDaoException, CMemoryException);

Return Value

The number of seconds before a query times out.

Remarks

Call this member function to retrieve the current time limit before a query to an ODBC data source times out. For information about this time limit, see the topic "ODBCTimeout Property" in DAO Help.

Tip The preferred way to work with ODBC tables is to attach them to a Microsoft Jet (.MDB) database. For more information, see the topic "Accessing External Databases with DAO" in DAO Help and the article "DAO External: Working with External Data Sources" in *Visual C++ Programmer's Guide* online.

For information about querydefs, see the article "DAO Querydef" in *Visual C++ Programmer's Guide* online.

See Also: **CDaoQueryDef::SetODBCTimeout, CDaoQueryDef::GetName, CDaoQueryDef::GetSQL, CDaoQueryDef::GetReturnsRecords**

CDaoQueryDef::GetParameterCount

short GetParameterCount( );
    throw(CDaoException, CMemoryException);

Return Value

The number of parameters defined in the query.

Remarks

Call this member function to retrieve the number of parameters in the saved query. **GetParameterCount** is useful for looping through all parameters in the querydef. For that purpose, use **GetParameterCount** in conjunction with **GetParameterInfo**.

For information about parameterizing queries, see the article "DAO Queries: Filtering and Parameterizing Queries" in *Visual C++ Programmer's Guide* online. For related information, see the topics "Parameter Object," "Parameters Collection," and "PARAMETERS Declaration (SQL)" in DAO Help.

See Also: **CDaoQueryDef::GetParamValue, CDaoQueryDef::SetParamValue**

CDaoQueryDef::GetParameterInfo

void GetParameterInfo(int *nIndex***, CDaoParameterInfo&** *paraminfo***,**
↪ **DWORD** *dwInfoOptions* **= AFX_DAO_PRIMARY_INFO);**
throw(CDaoException, CMemoryException);
void GetParameterInfo(LPCTSTR *lpszName***, CDaoParameterInfo&** *paraminfo***,**
↪ **DWORD** *dwInfoOptions* **= AFX_DAO_PRIMARY_INFO);**
throw(CDaoException, CMemoryException);

Parameters

nIndex   The zero-based index of the desired parameter in the querydef's Parameters collection, for lookup by index.

paraminfo   A reference to a **CDaoParameterInfo** object that returns the information requested.

dwInfoOptions   Options that specify which information about the parameter to retrieve. The available option is listed here along with what it causes the function to return:

- **AFX_DAO_PRIMARY_INFO**   (Default) Name, Type

lpszName   A string containing the name of the desired parameter, for lookup by name. You can use a **CString**.

Remarks

Call this member function to obtain information about a parameter defined in the querydef. For a description of the information returned in *paraminfo*, see the **CDaoParameterInfo** structure. This structure has members that correspond to the descriptive information under *dwInfoOptions* above.

For more information about obtaining parameter information, see the article "DAO Collections: Obtaining Information About DAO Objects." For more information about parameterizing queries, see the article "DAO Queries: Filtering and Parameterizing

Queries." Both articles are in *Visual C++ Programmer's Guide* online. For related information, see the topic "PARAMETERS Declaration (SQL)" in DAO Help.

See Also: **CDaoQueryDef::GetParameterCount**

CDaoQueryDef::GetParamValue

COleVariant GetParamValue(LPCTSTR *lpszName* **);**
    throw(CDaoException, CMemoryException);
COleVariant GetParamValue(int *nIndex* **);**
    throw(CDaoException, CMemoryException);

Return Value

An object of class **COleVariant** that contains the parameter's value.

Parameters

lpszName   The name of the parameter whose value you want, for lookup by name.

nIndex   The zero-based index of the parameter in the querydef's Parameters collection, for lookup by index. You can obtain this value with calls to **GetParameterCount** and **GetParameterInfo**.

Remarks

Call this member function to retrieve the current value of the specified parameter stored in the querydef's Parameters collection. You can access the parameter either by name or by its ordinal position in the collection.

For examples and more information about parameterizing queries, see the article "DAO Queries: Filtering and Parameterizing Queries" in *Visual C++ Programmer's Guide* online. For related information, see the topic "PARAMETERS Declaration (SQL)" in DAO Help.

See Also: **CDaoQueryDef::SetParamValue**

CDaoQueryDef::GetRecordsAffected

long GetRecordsAffected( );
    throw(CDaoException, CMemoryException);

Return Value

The number of records affected.

Remarks

Call this member function to determine how many records were affected by the last call of **Execute**. The count returned will not reflect changes in related tables when cascade updates or deletes are in effect.

For information about querydefs, see the article "DAO Querydef" in *Visual C++ Programmer's Guide* online. For related information see the topic "RecordsAffected Property" in DAO Help.

CDaoQueryDef::GetReturnsRecords

BOOL GetReturnsRecords( );
throw(CDaoException, CMemoryException);

Return Value

Nonzero if the querydef is based on a query that returns records; otherwise 0.

Remarks

Call this member function to determine whether the querydef is based on a query that returns records. This member function is only used for SQL pass-through queries. For more information about SQL queries, see the **Execute** member function. For more information about working with SQL pass-through queries, see the **SetReturnsRecords** member function.

For information about querydefs, see the article "DAO Querydef" in *Visual C++ Programmer's Guide* online. For related information, see the topic "ReturnsRecords Property" in DAO Help.

See Also: CDaoQueryDef::GetName, CDaoQueryDef::GetSQL, CDaoQueryDef::GetODBCTimeout

CDaoQueryDef::GetSQL

CString GetSQL( );
throw(CDaoException, CMemoryException);

Return Value

The SQL statement that defines the query on which the querydef is based.

Remarks

Call this member function to retrieve the SQL statement that defines the query on which the querydef is based. You will then probably parse the string for keywords, table names, and so on.

For information about querydefs, see the article "DAO Querydef" in *Visual C++ Programmer's Guide* online. For related information, see the topics "SQL Property," "Comparison of Microsoft Jet Database Engine SQL and ANSI SQL," and "Querying a Database with SQL in Code" in DAO Help.

See Also: CDaoQueryDef::SetSQL, CDaoQueryDef::GetName, CDaoQueryDef::GetReturnsRecords, CDaoQueryDef::GetODBCTimeout

CDaoQueryDef::GetType

> **short GetType( );**
> **throw(CDaoException, CMemoryException);**

Return Value

The type of the query defined by the querydef. For values, see Remarks.

Remarks

Call this member function to determine the query type of the querydef. The query type is set by what you specify in the querydef's SQL string when you create the querydef or call an existing querydef's **SetSQL** member function. The query type returned by this function can be one of the following values:

- **dbQSelect**   Select
- **dbQAction**   Action
- **dbQCrosstab**   Crosstab
- **dbQDelete**   Delete
- **dbQUpdate**   Update
- **dbQAppend**   Append
- **dbQMakeTable**   Make-table
- **dbQDDL**   Data-definition
- **dbQSQLPassThrough**   Pass-through
- **dbQSetOperation**   Union
- **dbQSPTBulk**   Used with **dbQSQLPassThrough** to specify a query that does not return records.

Note   To create an SQL pass-through query, don't set the **dbSQLPassThrough** constant. This is set automatically by the Microsoft Jet database engine when you create a querydef object and set the connect string.

For information about SQL strings, see **GetSQL**. For information about query types, see **Execute**.

CDaoQueryDef::IsOpen

> **BOOL IsOpen( ) const;**

Return Value

Nonzero if the **CDaoQueryDef** object is currently open; otherwise 0.

Remarks

Call this member function to determine whether the **CDaoQueryDef** object is currently open. A querydef must be in an open state before you use it to call

Execute or to create a **CDaoRecordset** object. To put a querydef into an open state call either **Create** (for a new querydef) or **Open** (for an existing querydef).

For information about querydefs, see the article "DAO Querydef" in *Visual C++ Programmer's Guide* online.

CDaoQueryDef::Open

virtual void Open(LPCTSTR *lpszName* **= NULL);**
   throw(CDaoException, CMemoryException);

Parameters

lpszName A string that contains the name of the saved querydef to open. You can use a **CString**.

Remarks

Call this member function to open a querydef previously saved in the database's QueryDefs collection. Once the querydef is open, you can call its **Execute** member function or use the querydef to create a **CDaoRecordset** object.

For information about querydefs, see the article "DAO Querydef" in *Visual C++ Programmer's Guide* online.

See Also: **CDaoQueryDef::IsOpen, CDaoQueryDef::Close, CDaoQueryDef::SetName, CDaoQueryDef::Create**

CDaoQueryDef::SetConnect

void SetConnect(LPCTSTR *lpszConnect* **);**
   throw(CDaoException, CMemoryException);

Parameters

lpszConnect A string that contains a connect string for the associated **CDaoDatabase** object.

Remarks

Call this member function to set the querydef object's connect string. The connect string is used to pass additional information to ODBC and certain ISAM drivers as needed. It is not used for Microsoft Jet (.MDB) databases.

Tip The preferred way to work with ODBC tables is to attach them to an .MDB database. For more information, see the topic "Accessing External Databases with DAO" in DAO Help and the article "DAO External: Working with External Data Sources" in *Visual C++ Programmer's Guide* online.

Before executing a querydef that represents an SQL pass-through query to an ODBC data source, set the connect string with **SetConnect** and call **SetReturnsRecords** to specify whether the query returns records.

For more information about the connect string's structure and examples of connect string components, see the topic "Connect Property" in DAO Help. For information about querydefs, see the article "DAO Querydef" in *Visual C++ Programmer's Guide* online.

CDaoQueryDef::SetName

void SetName(LPCTSTR *lpszName* **);**
    throw(CDaoException, CMemoryException);

Parameters

lpszName   A string that contains the new name for a nontemporary query in the associated **CDaoDatabase** object.

Remarks

Call this member function if you want to change the name of a querydef that is not temporary. Querydef names are unique, user-defined names. You can call **SetName** before the querydef object is appended to the QueryDefs collection.

For information about querydefs, see the article "DAO Querydef" in *Visual C++ Programmer's Guide* online. For more information about the querydef name, see the topic "Name Property" in DAO Help.

See Also: **CDaoQueryDef::GetName, CDaoQueryDef::SetSQL, CDaoQueryDef::SetConnect, CDaoQueryDef::SetODBCTimeout, CDaoQueryDef::SetReturnsRecords**

CDaoQueryDef::SetODBCTimeout

void SetODBCTimeout(short *nODBCTimeout* **);**
    throw(CDaoException, CMemoryException);

Parameters

nODBCTimeout   The number of seconds before a query times out.

Remarks

Call this member function to set the time limit before a query to an ODBC data source times out.

Tip The preferred way to work with ODBC tables is to attach them to a Microsoft Jet (.MDB) database. For more information, see the topic "Accessing External Databases with DAO" in DAO Help and the article "DAO External: Working with External Data Sources" in *Visual C++ Programmer's Guide* online.

This member function lets you override the default number of seconds before subsequent operations on the connected data source "time out." An operation might time out due to network access problems, excessive query processing time, and so on. Call **SetODBCTimeout** prior to executing a query with this querydef if you want to change the query timeout value. (As ODBC reuses connections, the timeout value is the same for all clients on the same connection.)

The default value for query timeouts is 60 seconds.

For information about querydefs, see the article "DAO Querydef" in *Visual C++ Programmer's Guide* online. For related information, see the topic "ODBCTimeout Property" in DAO Help.

See Also: **CDaoQueryDef::GetODBCTimeout**, **CDaoQueryDef::SetName**, **CDaoQueryDef::SetSQL**, **CDaoQueryDef::SetConnect**, **CDaoQueryDef::SetReturnsRecords**

CDaoQueryDef::SetParamValue

void SetParamValue(LPCTSTR *lpszName*, **const COleVariant&** *varValue* **);**
  throw(CDaoException, CMemoryException);
void SetParamValue(int *nOrdinal*, **const COleVariant&** *varValue* **);**
  throw(CDaoException, CMemoryException);

Parameters

lpszName   The name of the parameter whose value you want to set.

varValue   The value to set; see Remarks.

nOrdinal   The ordinal position of the parameter in the querydef's Parameters collection. You can obtain this value with calls to **GetParameterCount** and **GetParameterInfo**.

Remarks

Call this member function to set the value of a parameter in the querydef at run time. The parameter must already have been established as part of the querydef's SQL string. You can access the parameter either by name or by its ordinal position in the collection.

Specify the value to set as a **COleVariant** object. For information about setting the desired value and type in your **COleVariant** object, see class **COleVariant**.

For examples and more information about parameterizing queries, see the article "DAO Queries: Filtering and Parameterizing Queries" in *Visual C++ Programmer's Guide* online. For related information, see the topic "PARAMETERS Declaration (SQL)" in DAO Help.

See Also: **CDaoQueryDef::GetParamValue**

CDaoQueryDef::SetReturnsRecords

void SetReturnsRecords(BOOL *bReturnsRecords* **);**
    throw(CDaoException, CMemoryException);

Parameters

bReturnsRecords Pass **TRUE** if the query on an external database returns records; otherwise, **FALSE**.

Remarks

Call this member function as part of the process of setting up an SQL pass-through query to an external database. In such a case, you must create the querydef and set its properties using other **CDaoQueryDef** member functions. For a description of external databases, see **SetConnect**.

For information about querydefs, see the article "DAO Querydef." For information about external data sources, see the article "DAO External: Working with External Data Sources." Both articles are in *Visual C++ Programmer's Guide* online. For related information, see the topic "ReturnsRecords Property" in DAO Help.

See Also: **CDaoQueryDef::GetReturnsRecords, CDaoQueryDef::SetName, CDaoQueryDef::SetSQL, CDaoQueryDef::SetConnect, CDaoQueryDef::SetODBCTimeout**

CDaoQueryDef::SetSQL

void SetSQL(LPCTSTR *lpszSQL* **);**
    throw(CDaoException, CMemoryException);

Parameters

lpszSQL A string containing a complete SQL statement, suitable for execution. The syntax of this string depends on the DBMS that your query targets. For a discussion of syntax used in the Microsoft Jet database engine, see the topic "Building SQL Statements in Code" in DAO Help.

Remarks

Call this member function to set the SQL statement that the querydef executes. A typical use of **SetSQL** is setting up a querydef object for use in an SQL pass-through query. (For the syntax of SQL pass-through queries on your target DBMS, see the documentation for your DBMS.)

For information about querydefs, see the article "DAO Querydef" in *Visual C++ Programmer's Guide* online. For more information about SQL, see the topics "SQL Property," "Microsoft Jet Database Engine SQL Data Types," and "Querying a Database with SQL in Code" in DAO Help.

See Also: **CDaoQueryDef::GetSQL**, **CDaoQueryDef::SetName**, **CDaoQueryDef::SetConnect**, **CDaoQueryDef::SetODBCTimeout**, **CDaoQueryDef::SetReturnsRecords**

Data Members

CDaoQueryDef::m_pDatabase

Remarks

Contains a pointer to the **CDaoDatabase** object associated with the querydef object. Use this pointer if you need to access the database directly—for example, to obtain pointers to other querydef or recordset objects in the database's collections.

For information about querydefs, see the article "DAO Querydef" in *Visual C++ Programmer's Guide* online.

CDaoQueryDef::m_pDAOQueryDef

Remarks

Contains a pointer to the OLE interface for the underlying DAO querydef object. This pointer is provided for completeness and consistency with the other classes. However, because MFC rather fully encapsulates DAO querydefs, you are unlikely to need it. If you do use it, do so cautiously—in particular, do not change the value of the pointer unless you know what you are doing.

For information about querydefs, see the article "DAO Querydef" in *Visual C++ Programmer's Guide* online.

CDaoRecordset

A **CDaoRecordset** object represents a set of records selected from a data source. Known as "recordsets," **CDaoRecordset** objects are available in the following three forms:

- Table-type recordsets represent a base table that you can use to examine, add, change, or delete records from a single database table.

- Dynaset-type recordsets are the result of a query that can have updatable records. These recordsets are a set of records that you can use to examine, add, change, or delete records from an underlying database table or tables. Dynaset-type recordsets can contain fields from one or more tables in a database.

- Snapshot-type recordsets are a static copy of a set of records that you can use to find data or generate reports. These recordsets can contain fields from one or more tables in a database but cannot be updated.

Each form of recordset represents a set of records fixed at the time the recordset is opened. When you scroll to a record in a table-type recordset or a dynaset-type recordset, it reflects changes made to the record after the recordset is opened, either by other users or by other recordsets in your application. (A snapshot-type recordset cannot be updated.) You can use **CDaoRecordset** directly or derive an application-specific recordset class from **CDaoRecordset**. You can then:

- Scroll through the records.

- Set an index and quickly look for records using **Seek** (table-type recordsets only).

- Find records based on a string comparison: "<", "<=", "=", ">=", or ">" (dynaset-type and snapshot-type recordsets).

- Update the records and specify a locking mode (except snapshot-type recordsets).

- Filter the recordset to constrain which records it selects from those available on the data source.

- Sort the recordset.

- Parameterize the recordset to customize its selection with information not known until run time.

Class **CDaoRecordset** supplies an interface similar to that of class **CRecordset**. The main difference is that class **CDaoRecordset** accesses data through a Data Access Object (DAO) based on OLE. Class **CRecordset** accesses the DBMS through Open Database Connectivity (ODBC) and an ODBC driver for that DBMS.

Note The DAO database classes are distinct from the MFC database classes based on Open Database Connectivity (ODBC). All DAO database class names have the "CDao" prefix. You can still access ODBC data sources with the DAO classes; the DAO classes generally offer superior capabilities because they are specific to the Microsoft Jet database engine.

You can either use **CDaoRecordset** directly or derive a class from **CDaoRecordset**. To use a recordset class in either case, open a database and construct a recordset object, passing the constructor a pointer to your **CDaoDatabase** object. You can also construct a **CDaoRecordset** object and let MFC create a temporary **CDaoDatabase** object for you. Then call the recordset's **Open** member function, specifying whether the object is a table-type recordset, a dynaset-type recordset, or a snapshot-type recordset. Calling **Open** selects data from the database and retrieves the first record.

Use the object's member functions and data members to scroll through the records and operate on them. The operations available depend on whether the object is a table-type recordset, a dynaset-type recordset, or a snapshot-type recordset, and whether it is updatable or read-only—this depends on the capability of the database or Open Database Connectivity (ODBC) data source. To refresh records that may have been changed or added since the **Open** call, call the object's **Requery** member function. Call the object's **Close** member function and destroy the object when you finish with it.

CDaoRecordset uses DAO record field exchange (DFX) to support reading and updating of record fields through type-safe C++ members of your **CDaoRecordset** or **CDaoRecordset**-derived class. You can also implement dynamic binding of columns in a database without using the DFX mechanism using **GetFieldValue** and **SetFieldValue**.

For more information about recordsets, see the article "DAO: Recordset Architecture" in *Visual C++ Programmer's Guide* online. For related information, see the topic "Recordset Object" in DAO Help.

#include <afxdao.h>

See Also: CDaoTableDef, CDaoWorkspace, CDaoDatabase, CDaoQueryDef

CDaoRecordset Class Members

Data Members

m_bCheckCacheForDirtyFields	Contains a flag indicating whether fields are automatically marked as changed.
m_pDAORecordset	A pointer to the DAO interface underlying the recordset object.
m_nFields	Contains the number of field data members in the recordset class and the number of columns selected by the recordset from the data source.

(continued)

Data Members *(continued)*

m_nParams	Contains the number of parameter data members in the recordset class — the number of parameters passed with the recordset's query
m_pDatabase	Source database for this result set. Contains a pointer to a **CDaoDatabase** object.
m_strFilter	Contains a string used to construct an SQL **WHERE** statement.
m_strSort	Contains a string used to construct an SQL **ORDER BY** statement.

Construction

CDaoRecordset	Constructs a **CDaoRecordset** object.
Close	Closes the recordset.
Open	Creates a new recordset from a table, dynaset, or snapshot.

Attributes

CanAppend	Returns nonzero if new records can be added to the recordset via the **AddNew** member function.
CanBookmark	Returns nonzero if the recordset supports bookmarks.
CanRestart	Returns nonzero if **Requery** can be called to run the recordset's query again.
CanScroll	Returns nonzero if you can scroll through the records.
CanTransact	Returns nonzero if the data source supports transactions.
CanUpdate	Returns nonzero if the recordset can be updated (you can add, update, or delete records).
GetCurrentIndex	Returns a **CString** containing the name of the index most recently used on an indexed, table-type **CDaoRecordset**.
GetDateCreated	Returns the date and time the base table underlying a **CDaoRecordset** object was created
GetDateLastUpdated	Returns the date and time of the most recent change made to the design of a base table underlying a **CDaoRecordset** object.
GetEditMode	Returns a value that indicates the state of editing for the current record.
GetLastModifiedBookmark	Used to determine the most recently added or updated record.
GetName	Returns a **CString** containing the name of the recordset.
GetParamValue	Retrieves the current value of the specified parameter stored in the underlying DAOParameter object.

Attributes *(continued)*

GetRecordCount	Returns the number of records accessed in a recordset object.
GetSQL	Gets the SQL string used to select records for the recordset.
GetType	Called to determine the type of a recordset: table-type, dynaset-type, or snapshot-type.
GetValidationRule	Returns a **CString** containing the value that validates data as it is entered into a field.
GetValidationText	Retrieves the text that is displayed when a validation rule is not satisfied.
IsBOF	Returns nonzero if the recordset has been positioned before the first record. There is no current record.
IsDeleted	Returns nonzero if the recordset is positioned on a deleted record.
IsEOF	Returns nonzero if the recordset has been positioned after the last record. There is no current record.
IsFieldDirty	Returns nonzero if the specified field in the current record has been changed.
IsFieldNull	Returns nonzero if the specified field in the current record is Null (having no value).
IsFieldNullable	Returns nonzero if the specified field in the current record can be set to Null (having no value).
IsOpen	Returns nonzero if **Open** has been called previously.
SetCurrentIndex	Called to set an index on a table-type recordset.
SetParamValue	Sets the current value of the specified parameter stored in the underlying DAOParameter object
SetParamValueNull	Sets the current value of the specified parameter to Null (having no value).

Recordset Update Operations

AddNew	Prepares for adding a new record. Call **Update** to complete the addition.
CancelUpdate	Cancels any pending updates due to an **Edit** or **AddNew** operation.
Delete	Deletes the current record from the recordset. You must explicitly scroll to another record after the deletion.
Edit	Prepares for changes to the current record. Call **Update** to complete the edit.
Update	Completes an **AddNew** or **Edit** operation by saving the new or edited data on the data source.

Recordset Navigation Operations

Find	Locates the first, next, previous, or last location of a particular string in a dynaset-type recordset that satisfies the specified criteria and makes that record the current record.
FindFirst	Locates the first record in a dynaset-type or snapshot-type recordset that satisfies the specified criteria and makes that record the current record.
FindLast	Locates the last record in a dynaset-type or snapshot-type recordset that satisfies the specified criteria and makes that record the current record.
FindNext	Locates the next record in a dynaset-type or snapshot-type recordset that satisfies the specified criteria and makes that record the current record.
FindPrev	Locates the previous record in a dynaset-type or snapshot-type recordset that satisfies the specified criteria and makes that record the current record.
GetAbsolutePosition	Returns the record number of a recordset object's current record.
GetBookmark	Returns a value that represents the bookmark on a record.
GetPercentPosition	Returns the position of the current record as a percentage of the total number of records.
Move	Positions the recordset to a specified number of records from the current record in either direction.
MoveFirst	Positions the current record on the first record in the recordset.
MoveLast	Positions the current record on the last record in the recordset.
MoveNext	Positions the current record on the next record in the recordset.
MovePrev	Positions the current record on the previous record in the recordset.
Seek	Locates the record in an indexed table-type recordset object that satisfies the specified criteria for the current index and makes that record the current record.
SetAbsolutePosition	Sets the record number of a recordset object's current record.
SetBookmark	Positions the recordset on a record containing the specified bookmark.
SetPercentPosition	Sets the position of the current record to a location corresponding to a percentage of the total number of records in a recordset.

Other Recordset Operations

FillCache	Fills all or a part of a local cache for a recordset object that contains data from an ODBC data source.
GetCacheSize	Returns a value that specifies the number of records in a dynaset-type recordset containing data to be locally cached from an ODBC data source.
GetCacheStart	Returns a value that specifies the bookmark of the first record in the recordset to be cached.
GetFieldCount	Returns a value that represents the number of fields in a recordset.
GetFieldInfo	Returns specific kinds of information about the fields in the recordset.
GetFieldValue	Returns the value of a field in a recordset.
GetIndexCount	Retrieves the number of indexes in a table underlying a recordset.
GetIndexInfo	Returns various kinds of information about an index.
GetLockingMode	Returns a value that indicates the type of locking that is in effect during editing.
Requery	Runs the recordset's query again to refresh the selected records.
SetCacheSize	Sets a value that specifies the number of records in a dynaset-type recordset containing data to be locally cached from an ODBC data source.
SetCacheStart	Sets a value that specifies the bookmark of the first record in the recordset to be cached.
SetFieldDirty	Marks the specified field in the current record as changed.
SetFieldNull	Sets the value of the specified field in the current record to Null (having no value).
SetFieldValue	Sets the value of a field in a recordset.
SetFieldValueNull	Sets the value of a field in a recordset to Null. (having no value).
SetLockingMode	Sets a value that indicates the type of locking to put into effect during editing.

Overridables

DoFieldExchange	Called to exchange data (in both directions) between the field data members of the recordset and the corresponding record on the data source. Implements DAO record field exchange (DFX).
GetDefaultDBName	Returns the name of the default data source.
GetDefaultSQL	Called to get the default SQL string to execute.

Member Functions
CDaoRecordset::AddNew

virtual void AddNew( );
    throw(CDaoException, CMemoryException);

Remarks

Call this member function to add a new record to a table-type or dynaset-type recordset. The record's fields are initially Null. (In database terminology, Null means "having no value" and is not the same as **NULL** in C++.) To complete the operation, you must call the **Update** member function. **Update** saves your changes to the data source.

Caution If you edit a record and then scroll to another record without calling **Update**, your changes are lost without warning.

If you add a record to a dynaset-type recordset by calling **AddNew**, the record is visible in the recordset and included in the underlying table where it becomes visible to any new **CDaoRecordset** objects.

The position of the new record depends on the type of recordset:

- In a dynaset-type recordset, records are inserted at the end of the recordset, regardless of any sorting or ordering rules that may have been in effect when the recordset was opened.

- In a table-type recordset for which an index has been specified, records are returned in their proper place in the sort order. If no index has been specified, new records are returned at the end of the recordset.

The record that was current before you used **AddNew** remains current. If you want to make the new record current and the recordset supports bookmarks, call **SetBookmark** to the bookmark identified by the LastModified property setting of the underlying DAO recordset object. Doing so is useful for determining the value for counter (auto-increment) fields in an added record. For more information, see **GetLastModifiedBookmark**.

If the database supports transactions, you can make your **AddNew** call part of a transaction. For more information about transactions, see class **CDaoWorkspace**. Note that you should call **CDaoWorkspace::BeginTrans** before calling **AddNew**.

It is illegal to call **AddNew** for a recordset whose **Open** member function has not been called. A **CDaoException** is thrown if you call **AddNew** for a recordset that cannot be appended. You can determine whether the recordset is updatable by calling **CanAppend**.

The framework marks changed field data members to ensure they will be written to the record on the data source by the DAO record field exchange (DFX) mechanism. Changing the value of a field generally sets the field dirty automatically, so you will seldom need to call **SetFieldDirty** yourself, but you might sometimes want to ensure that columns will be explicitly updated or inserted regardless of what value is in the field data member. The DFX mechanism also employs the use of **PSEUDO NULL**. For more information, see **CDaoFieldExchange::m_nOperation**.

If the double-buffering mechanism is not being used, then changing the value of the field does not automatically set the field as dirty. In this case, it will be necessary to explicity set the field dirty. The flag contained in **m_bCheckCacheForDirtyFields** controls this automatic field checking.

Note If records are double-buffered (that is, automatic field checking is enabled), calling **CancelUpdate** will restore the member variables to the values they had before **AddNew** or **Edit** was called.

For more information about updating records, see the article "DAO Recordset: Recordset Operations" in *Visual C++ Programmer's Guide* online. For related information, see the topics "AddNew Method," "CancelUpdate Method," "LastModified Property," and "EditMode Property" in DAO Help.

See Also: CDaoRecordset::CanUpdate, CDaoRecordset::CancelUpdate, CDaoRecordset::Delete, CDaoRecordset::Edit, CDaoRecordset::Update, CDaoRecordset::CanTransact

CDaoRecordset::CanAppend

BOOL CanAppend( ) const;

Return Value

Nonzero if the recordset allows adding new records; otherwise 0. **CanAppend** will return 0 if you opened the recordset as read-only.

Remarks

Call this member function to determine whether the previously opened recordset allows you to add new records by calling the **AddNew** member function.

For more information about updating records, see the article "DAO Recordset: Recordset Operations" in *Visual C++ Programmer's Guide* online. For related information, see the topic "Append Method" in DAO Help.

See Also: CDaoRecordset::CanBookmark, CDaoRecordset::CanRestart, CDaoRecordset::CanScroll, CDaoRecordset::CanTransact, CDaoRecordset::CanUpdate

CDaoRecordset::CanBookmark

BOOL CanBookmark( ) const;
   throw(CDaoException, CMemoryException);

Return Value

Nonzero if the recordset supports bookmarks, otherwise 0.

Remarks

Call this member function to determine whether the previously opened recordset allows you to individually mark records using bookmarks. If you are using recordsets based entirely on Microsoft Jet database engine tables, bookmarks can be used except on snapshot-type recordsets flagged as forward-only scrolling recordsets. Other database products (external ODBC data sources) may not support bookmarks.

For more information about recordset navigation, see the article "DAO Recordset: Recordset Navigation" in *Visual C++ Programmer's Guide* online. For related information, see the topic "Bookmarkable Property" in DAO Help.

See Also: **CDaoRecordset::CanAppend**, **CDaoRecordset::CanRestart**, **CDaoRecordset::CanScroll**, **CDaoRecordset::CanTransact**, **CDaoRecordset::CanUpdate**

CDaoRecordset::CancelUpdate

virtual void CancelUpdate( );
   throw(CDaoException, CMemoryException);

Remarks

The **CancelUpdate** member function cancels any pending updates due to an **Edit** or **AddNew** operation. For example, if an application calls the **Edit** or **AddNew** member function and has not called **Update**, **CancelUpdate** cancels any changes made after **Edit** or **AddNew** was called.

Note If records are double-buffered (that is, automatic field checking is enabled), calling **CancelUpdate** will restore the member variables to the values they had before **AddNew** or **Edit** was called.

If there is no **Edit** or **AddNew** operation pending, **CancelUpdate** causes MFC to throw an exception. Call the **GetEditMode** member function to determine if there is a pending operation that can be canceled.

For more information about updating data, see the article "DAO Recordset: Recordset Operations" in *Visual C++ Programmer's Guide* online. For related information, see the topic "CancelUpdate Method" in DAO Help.

See Also: **CDaoRecordset::AddNew**, **CDaoRecordset::Delete**, **CDaoRecordset::Edit**, **CDaoRecordset::Update**, **CDaoRecordset::CanTransact**

CDaoRecordset::CanRestart

BOOL CanRestart( );
    throw(CDaoException, CMemoryException);

Return Value

Nonzero if **Requery** can be called to run the recordset's query again, otherwise 0.

Remarks

Call this member function to determine whether the recordset allows restarting its query (to refresh its records) by calling the **Requery** member function. Table-type recordsets do not support **Requery**.

If **Requery** is not supported, call **Close** then **Open** to refresh the data. You can call **Requery** to update a recordset object's underlying parameter query after the parameter values have been changed.

For more information about working with DAO objects, see the article "DAO: Creating, Opening, and Closing DAO Objects" in *Visual C++ Programmer's Guide* online. For related information, see the topic "Restartable Property" in DAO Help.

See Also: **CDaoRecordset::CanAppend, CDaoRecordset::CanBookmark, CDaoRecordset::CanScroll, CDaoRecordset::CanTransact, CDaoRecordset::CanUpdate**

CDaoRecordset::CanScroll

BOOL CanScroll( ) const;

Return Value

Nonzero if you can scroll through the records, otherwise 0.

Remarks

Call this member function to determine whether the recordset allows scrolling. If you call **Open** with **dbForwardOnly**, the recordset can only scroll forward.

For more information about navigating through recordsets, see the article "DAO Recordset: Recordset Navigation" in *Visual C++ Programmer's Guide* online. For related information, see the topic "Positioning the Current Record Pointer with DAO" in DAO Help.

See Also: **CDaoRecordset::CanAppend, CDaoRecordset::CanBookmark, CDaoRecordset::CanRestart, CDaoRecordset::CanTransact, CDaoRecordset::CanUpdate, CDaoRecordset::Open**

CDaoRecordset::CanTransact

BOOL CanTransact( ) const;
    throw(CDaoException, CMemoryException);

Return Value

Nonzero if the underlying data source supports transactions, otherwise 0.

Remarks

Call this member function to determine whether the recordset allows transactions.

For more information about updating data, see the article "DAO Recordset: Recordset Operations" in *Visual C++ Programmer's Guide* online. For related information, see the topic "Transactions Property" in DAO Help.

See Also: **CDaoRecordset::AddNew, CDaoRecordset::CanAppend, CDaoRecordset::CancelUpdate, CDaoRecordset::CanScroll, CDaoRecordset::CanRestart, CDaoRecordset::CanUpdate, CDaoRecordset::Delete, CDaoRecordset::Edit, CDaoRecordset::Update**

CDaoRecordset::CanUpdate

BOOL CanUpdate( ) const;
    throw(CDaoException, CMemoryException);

Return Value

Nonzero if the recordset can be updated (add, update, and delete records), otherwise 0.

Remarks

Call this member function to determine whether the recordset can be updated. A recordset might be read-only if the underlying data source is read-only or if you specified **dbReadOnly** for *nOptions* when you called **Open** for the recordset.

For more information about updating data, see the article "DAO Recordset: Recordset Operations" in *Visual C++ Programmer's Guide* online. For related information, see the topics "AddNew Method," "Edit Method," "Delete Method," "Update Method," and "Updatable Property" in DAO Help.

See Also: **CDaoRecordset::CanAppend, CDaoRecordset::CanBookmark, CDaoRecordset::CanScroll, CDaoRecordset::CanRestart, CDaoRecordset::CanTransact**

CDaoRecordset::CDaoRecordset

CDaoRecordset(CDaoDatabase* *pDatabase* **= NULL);**

Parameters

pDatabase Contains a pointer to a **CDaoDatabase** object or the value **NULL**. If not **NULL** and the **CDaoDatabase** object's **Open** member function has not been called to connect it to the data source, the recordset attempts to open it for you during its own **Open** call. If you pass **NULL**, a **CDaoDatabase** object is constructed and connected for you using the data source information you specified if you derived your recordset class from **CDaoRecordset**.

Remarks

Constructs a **CDaoRecordset** object. You can either use **CDaoRecordset** directly or derive an application-specific class from **CDaoRecordset**. You can use ClassWizard to derive your recordset classes.

Note If you derive a **CDaoRecordset** class, your derived class must supply its own constructor. In the constructor of your derived class, call the constructor **CDaoRecordset::CDaoRecordset**, passing the appropriate parameters along to it.

Pass **NULL** to your recordset constructor to have a **CDaoDatabase** object constructed and connected for you automatically. This is a useful shortcut that does not require you to construct and connect a **CDaoDatabase** object prior to constructing your recordset. If the **CDaoDatabase** object is not open, a **CDaoWorkspace** object will also be created for you that uses the default workspace. For more information, see **CDaoDatabase::CDaoDatabase**.

For more information about constructing recordsets, see the article "DAO: Creating, Opening, and Closing DAO Objects" in *Visual C++ Programmer's Guide* online.

See Also: **CDaoRecordset::GetDefaultDBName**, **CDaoRecordset::GetDefaultSQL**, **CDaoRecordset::GetDateCreated**, **CDaoRecordset::GetDateLastUpdated**

CDaoRecordset::Close

virtual void Close( );
    throw(CDaoException);

Remarks

Closing a **CDaoRecordset** object removes it from the collection of open recordsets in the associated database. Because **Close** does not destroy the **CDaoRecordset** object, you can reuse the object by calling **Open** on the same data source or a different data source.

All pending **AddNew** or **Edit** statements are canceled, and all pending transactions are rolled back. If you want to preserve pending additions or edits, call **Update** before you call **Close** for each recordset.

You can call **Open** again after calling **Close**. This lets you reuse the recordset object. A better alternative is to call **Requery**, if possible.

For more information about working with recordsets, see the article "DAO: Creating, Opening, and Closing DAO Objects" in *Visual C++ Programmer's Guide* online. For related information, see the topic "Close Method" in DAO Help.

See Also: **CDaoRecordset::Open**, **CDaoRecordset::CDaoRecordset**

CDaoRecordset::Delete

virtual void Delete( );
    throw(CDaoException, CMemoryException);

Remarks

Call this member function to delete the current record in an open dynaset-type or table-type recordset object. After a successful deletion, the recordset's field data members are set to a Null value, and you must explicitly call one of the recordset navigation member functions (**Move**, **Seek**, **SetBookmark**, and so on) in order to move off the deleted record. When you delete records from a recordset, there must be a current record in the recordset before you call **Delete**; otherwise, MFC throws an exception.

Delete removes the current record and makes it inaccessible. Although you cannot edit or use the deleted record, it remains current. Once you move to another record, however, you cannot make the deleted record current again.

Caution   The recordset must be updatable and there must be a valid record current in the recordset when you call **Delete**. For example, if you delete a record but do not scroll to a new record before you call **Delete** again, **Delete** throws a **CDaoException**.

You can undelete a record if you use transactions and you call the **CDaoWorkspace::Rollback** member function. If the base table is the primary table in a cascade delete relationship, deleting the current record may also delete one or more records in a foreign table. For more information, see the definition "cascade delete" in DAO Help.

Unlike **AddNew** and **Edit**, a call to **Delete** is not followed by a call to **Update**.

For more information about updating data, see the article "DAO Recordset: Recordset Operations" in *Visual C++ Programmer's Guide* online. For related information, see the topics "AddNew Method," "Edit Method," "Delete Method," "Update Method," and "Updatable Property" in DAO Help.

See Also: **CDaoRecordset::AddNew**, **CDaoRecordset::CancelUpdate**, **CDaoRecordset::Edit**, **CDaoRecordset::Update**, **CDaoRecordset::CanTransact**

CDaoRecordset::DoFieldExchange

virtual void DoFieldExchange(CDaoFieldExchange* *pFX* **);**

Parameters

> *pFX* Contains a pointer to a **CDaoFieldExchange** object. The framework will already have set up this object to specify a context for the field exchange operation.

Remarks

> The framework calls this member function to automatically exchange data between the field data members of your recordset object and the corresponding columns of the current record on the data source. It also binds your parameter data members, if any, to parameter placeholders in the SQL statement string for the recordset's selection. The exchange of field data, called DAO record field exchange (DFX), works in both directions: from the recordset object's field data members to the fields of the record on the data source, and from the record on the data source to the recordset object. If you are binding columns dynamically, you are not required to implement **DoFieldExchange**.

> The only action you must normally take to implement **DoFieldExchange** for your derived recordset class is to create the class with ClassWizard and specify the names and data types of the field data members. You might also add code to what ClassWizard writes to specify parameter data members. If all fields are to be bound dynamically, this function will be inactive unless you specify parameter data members. For more information, see the article "DAO Recordset: Binding Records Dynamically" in *Visual C++ Programmer's Guide* online.

> When you declare your derived recordset class with ClassWizard, the wizard writes an override of **DoFieldExchange** for you, which resembles the following example:

```
void CCustSet::DoFieldExchange(CDaoFieldExchange* pFX)
{
    //{{AFX_FIELD_MAP(CCustSet)
    pFX->SetFieldType(CDaoFieldExchange::outputColumn);
    DFX_Text(pFX, "Name", m_strName);
    DFX_Short(pFX, "Age", m_wAge);
    //}}AFX_FIELD_MAP
}
```

> For more information about record field exchange, see the article "DAO Record Field Exchange (DFX)" in *Visual C++ Programmer's Guide* online.

> **See Also:** **CDaoException**

CDaoRecordset::Edit

virtual void Edit( );
    throw(CDaoException, CMemoryException);

Remarks

Call this member function to allow changes to the current record.

Once you call the **Edit** member function, changes made to the current record's fields are copied to the copy buffer. After you make the desired changes to the record, call **Update** to save your changes. **Edit** saves the values of the recordset's data members. If you call **Edit**, make changes, then call **Edit** again, the record's values are restored to what they were before the first **Edit** call.

Caution If you edit a record and then perform any operation that moves to another record without first calling **Update**, your changes are lost without warning. In addition, if you close the recordset or the parent database, your edited record is discarded without warning.

In some cases, you may want to update a column by making it Null (containing no data). To do so, call **SetFieldNull** with a parameter of **TRUE** to mark the field Null; this also causes the column to be updated. If you want a field to be written to the data source even though its value has not changed, call **SetFieldDirty** with a parameter of **TRUE**. This works even if the field had the value Null.

The framework marks changed field data members to ensure they will be written to the record on the data source by the DAO record field exchange (DFX) mechanism. Changing the value of a field generally sets the field dirty automatically, so you will seldom need to call **SetFieldDirty** yourself, but you might sometimes want to ensure that columns will be explicitly updated or inserted regardless of what value is in the field data member. The DFX mechanism also employs the use of **PSEUDO NULL**. For more information, see **CDaoFieldExchange::m_nOperation**.

If the double-buffering mechanism is not being used, then changing the value of the field does not automatically set the field as dirty. In this case, it will be necessary to explicity set the field dirty. The flag contained in **m_bCheckCacheForDirtyFields** controls this automatic field checking.

When the recordset object is pessimistically locked in a multiuser environment, the record remains locked from the time **Edit** is used until the updating is complete. If the recordset is optimistically locked, the record is locked and compared with the pre-edited record just before it is updated in the database. If the record has changed since you called **Edit**, the **Update** operation fails and MFC throws an exception. You can change the locking mode with **SetLockingMode**.

Note Optimistic locking is always used on external database formats, such as ODBC and installable ISAM.

The current record remains current after you call **Edit**. To call **Edit**, there must be a current record. If there is no current record or if the recordset does not refer to an open table-type or dynaset-type recordset object, an exception occurs. Calling **Edit** causes a **CDaoException** to be thrown under the following conditions:

- There is no current record.
- The database or recordset is read-only.
- No fields in the record are updatable.
- The database or recordset was opened for exclusive use by another user.
- Another user has locked the page containing your record.

If the data source supports transactions, you can make the **Edit** call part of a transaction. Note that you should call **CDaoWorkspace::BeginTrans** before calling **Edit** and after the recordset has been opened. Also note that calling **CDaoWorkspace::CommitTrans** is not a substitute for calling **Update** to complete the **Edit** operation. For more information about transactions, see class **CDaoWorkspace**.

For more information about updating data, see the article "DAO Recordset: Recordset Operations" in *Visual C++ Programmer's Guide* online. For related information, see the topics "AddNew Method," "Edit Method," "Delete Method," "Update Method," and "Updatable Property" in DAO Help.

See Also: **CDaoRecordset::AddNew**, **CDaoRecordset::CancelUpdate**, **CDaoRecordset::CanTransact**, **CDaoRecordset::Delete**, **CDaoRecordset::Update**

CDaoRecordset::FillCache

void FillCache(long* *pSize* **= NULL, COleVariant*** *pBookmark* **= NULL);**
   throw(CDaoException, CMemoryException);

Parameters

pSize   Specifies the number of rows to fill in the cache. If you omit this parameter, the value is determined by the CacheSize property setting of the underlying DAO object.

pBookmark   A **COleVariant** specifying a bookmark. The cache is filled starting from the record indicated by this bookmark. If you omit this parameter, the cache is filled starting from the record indicated by the CacheStart property of the underlying DAO object.

Remarks

Call this member function to cache a specified number of records from the recordset. Caching improves the performance of an application that retrieves, or fetches, data from a remote server. A cache is space in local memory that holds the data most recently fetched from the server on the assumption that the data will probably be requested again while the application is running. When data is requested, the Microsoft Jet database engine checks the cache for the data first rather than fetching it from the server, which takes more time. Using data caching on non-ODBC data sources has no effect as the data is not saved in the cache.

Rather than waiting for the cache to be filled with records as they are fetched, you can explicitly fill the cache at any time by calling the **FillCache** member function. This is a faster way to fill the cache because **FillCache** fetches several records at once instead of one at a time. For example, while each screenful of records is being displayed, you can have your application call **FillCache** to fetch the next screenful of records.

Any ODBC database accessed with recordset objects can have a local cache. To create the cache, open a recordset object from the remote data source, and then call the **SetCacheSize** and **SetCacheStart** member functions of the recordset. If *lSize* and *lBookmark* create a range that is partly or wholly outside the range specified by **SetCacheSize** and **SetCacheStart**, the portion of the recordset outside this range is ignored and is not loaded into the cache. If **FillCache** requests more records than remain in the remote data source, only the remaining records are fetched, and no exception is thrown.

Records fetched from the cache do not reflect changes made concurrently to the source data by other users.

FillCache fetches only records not already cached. To force an update of all the cached data, call the **SetCacheSize** member function with an *lSize* parameter equal to 0, call **SetCacheSize** again with the *lSize* parameter equal to the size of the cache you originally requested, and then call **FillCache**.

For more information about caching records, see the article "DAO External: Improving Performance with External Data Sources" in *Visual C++ Programmer's Guide* online. For related information, see the topic "FillCache Method" in DAO Help.

See Also: **CDaoRecordset::GetCacheSize, CDaoRecordset::GetCacheStart, CDaoRecordset::SetCacheSize, CDaoRecordset::SetCacheStart**

CDaoRecordset::Find

virtual BOOL Find(long *lFindType*, **LPCTSTR** *lpszFilter* **);**
    throw(CDaoException, CMemoryException);

Return Value

Nonzero if matching records are found, otherwise 0.

Parameters

lFindType   A value indicating the type of Find operation desired. The possible values are:

- **AFX_DAO_NEXT**   Find the next location of a matching string.

- **AFX_DAO_PREV** Find the previous location of a matching string.

- **AFX_DAO_FIRST** Find the first location of a matching string.

- **AFX_DAO_LAST** Find the last location of a matching string.

lpszFilter A string expression (like the **WHERE** clause in an SQL statement without the word **WHERE**) used to locate the record. For example:

```
Find(AFX_DAO_FIRST, "colRecID = 7")
Find(AFX_DAO_NEXT, "customerName = 'Jones'")
```

Remarks

Call this member function to locate a particular string in a dynaset- or snapshot-type recordset using a comparison operator. You can find the first, next, previous, or last instance of the string. **Find** is a virtual function, so you can override it and add your own implementation. The **FindFirst**, **FindLast**, **FindNext**, and **FindPrev** member functions call the **Find** member function, so you can use **Find** to control the behavior of all Find operations.

To locate a record in a table-type recordset, call the **Seek** member function.

Tip The smaller the set of records you have, the more effective **Find** will be. In general, and especially with ODBC data, it is better to create a new query that retrieves just the records you want.

For more information about finding records, see the article "DAO Recordset: Recordset Navigation" in *Visual C++ Programmer's Guide* online. For related information, see the topic "FindFirst, FindLast, FindNext, FindPrevious Methods" in DAO Help.

See Also: **CDaoRecordset::FindFirst**, **CDaoRecordset::FindLast**, **CDaoRecordset::FindNext**, **CDaoRecordset::FindPrev**

CDaoRecordset::FindFirst

BOOL FindFirst(LPCTSTR *lpszFilter* **);**
  throw(CDaoException, CMemoryException);

Return Value

Nonzero if matching records are found, otherwise 0.

Parameters

lpszFilter A string expression (like the **WHERE** clause in an SQL statement without the word **WHERE**) used to locate the record.

Remarks

Call this member function to find the first record that matches a specified condition. The **FindFirst** member function begins its search from the beginning of the recordset and searches to the end of the recordset.

If you want to include all the records in your search (not just those that meet a specific condition) use one of the Move operations to move from record to record. To locate a record in a table-type recordset, call the **Seek** member function.

If a record matching the criteria is not located, the current record pointer is undetermined, and **FindFirst** returns zero. If the recordset contains more than one record that satisfies the criteria, **FindFirst** locates the first occurrence, **FindNext** locates the next occurrence, and so on.

Caution If you edit the current record, be sure to save the changes by calling the **Update** member function before you move to another record. If you move to another record without updating, your changes are lost without warning.

The **Find** member functions search from the location and in the direction specified in the following table:

Find operations	Begin	Search direction
FindFirst	Beginning of recordset	End of recordset
FindLast	End of recordset	Beginning of recordset
FindNext	Current record	End of recordset
FindPrevious	Current record	Beginning of recordset

Important When you call **FindLast**, the Microsoft Jet database engine fully populates your recordset before beginning the search, if this has not already been done. The first search may take longer than subsequent searches.

Using one of the Find operations is not the same as calling **MoveFirst** or **MoveNext**, however, which simply makes the first or next record current without specifying a condition. You can follow a Find operation with a Move operation.

Keep the following in mind when using the Find operations:

- If **Find** returns nonzero, the current record is not defined. In this case, you must position the current record pointer back to a valid record.

- You cannot use a Find operation with a forward-only scrolling snapshot-type recordset.

- You should use the U.S. date format (month-day-year) when you search for fields containing dates, even if you are not using the U.S. version of the Microsoft Jet database engine; otherwise, matching records may not be found.

- When working with ODBC databases and large dynasets, you may discover that using the Find operations is slow, especially when working with large recordsets. You can improve performance by using SQL queries with customized **ORDER BY** or **WHERE** clauses, parameter queries, or **CDaoQuerydef** objects that retrieve specific indexed records.

For more information about finding records, see the article "DAO Recordset: Recordset Navigation" in *Visual C++ Programmer's Guide* online. For related information, see the topic "FindFirst, FindLast, FindNext, FindPrevious Methods" in DAO Help.

See Also: CDaoRecordset::Find, **CDaoRecordset::FindLast**, **CDaoRecordset::FindNext**, **CDaoRecordset::FindPrev**

CDaoRecordset::FindLast

BOOL FindLast(LPCTSTR *lpszFilter* **);**
   throw(CDaoException, CMemoryException);

Return Value

Nonzero if matching records are found, otherwise 0.

Parameters

lpszFilter   A string expression (like the **WHERE** clause in an SQL statement without the word **WHERE**) used to locate the record.

Remarks

Call this member function to find the last record that matches a specified condition. The **FindLast** member function begins its search at the end of the recordset and searches backward towards the beginning of the recordset.

If you want to include all the records in your search (not just those that meet a specific condition) use one of the Move operations to move from record to record. To locate a record in a table-type recordset, call the **Seek** member function.

If a record matching the criteria is not located, the current record pointer is undetermined, and **FindLast** returns zero. If the recordset contains more than one record that satisfies the criteria, **FindFirst** locates the first occurrence, **FindNext** locates the next occurrence after the first occurrence, and so on.

Caution   If you edit the current record, be sure you save the changes by calling the **Update** member function before you move to another record. If you move to another record without updating, your changes are lost without warning.

Using one of the Find operations is not the same as calling **MoveFirst** or **MoveNext**, however, which simply makes the first or next record current without specifying a condition. You can follow a Find operation with a Move operation.

Keep the following in mind when using the Find operations:

- If **Find** returns nonzero, the current record is not defined. In this case, you must position the current record pointer back to a valid record.

- You cannot use a Find operation with a forward-only scrolling snapshot-type recordset.

- You should use the U.S. date format (month-day-year) when you search for fields containing dates, even if you are not using the U.S. version of the Microsoft Jet database engine; otherwise, matching records may not be found.

- When working with ODBC databases and large dynasets, you may discover that using the Find operations is slow, especially when working with large recordsets. You can improve performance by using SQL queries with customized **ORDER BY** or **WHERE** clauses, parameter queries, or **CDaoQuerydef** objects that retrieve specific indexed records.

For more information about finding records, see the article "DAO Recordset: Recordset Navigation" in *Visual C++ Programmer's Guide* online. For related information, see the topic "FindFirst, FindLast, FindNext, FindPrevious Methods" in DAO Help.

See Also: **CDaoRecordset::Find**, **CDaoRecordset::FindFirst**, **CDaoRecordset::FindNext**, **CDaoRecordset::FindPrev**

CDaoRecordset::FindNext

> **BOOL FindNext(LPCTSTR** *lpszFilter* **);**
> **throw(CDaoException, CMemoryException);**

Return Value

Nonzero if matching records are found, otherwise 0.

Parameters

lpszFilter   A string expression (like the **WHERE** clause in an SQL statement without the word **WHERE**) used to locate the record.

Remarks

Call this member function to find the next record that matches a specified condition. The **FindNext** member function begins its search at the current record and searches to the end of the recordset.

If you want to include all the records in your search (not just those that meet a specific condition) use one of the Move operations to move from record to record. To locate a record in a table-type recordset, call the **Seek** member function.

If a record matching the criteria is not located, the current record pointer is undetermined, and **FindNext** returns zero. If the recordset contains more than one record that satisfies the criteria, **FindFirst** locates the first occurrence, **FindNext** locates the next occurrence, and so on.

Caution If you edit the current record, be sure you save the changes by calling the **Update** member function before you move to another record. If you move to another record without updating, your changes are lost without warning.

Using one of the Find operations is not the same as calling **MoveFirst** or **MoveNext**, however, which simply makes the first or next record current without specifying a condition. You can follow a Find operation with a Move operation.

Keep the following in mind when using the Find operations:

- If **Find** returns nonzero, the current record is not defined. In this case, you must position the current record pointer back to a valid record.

- You cannot use a Find operation with a forward-only scrolling snapshot-type recordset.

- You should use the U.S. date format (month-day-year) when you search for fields containing dates, even if you are not using the U.S. version of the Microsoft Jet database engine; otherwise, matching records may not be found.

- When working with ODBC databases and large dynasets, you may discover that using the Find operations is slow, especially when working with large recordsets. You can improve performance by using SQL queries with customized **ORDER BY** or **WHERE** clauses, parameter queries, or **CDaoQuerydef** objects that retrieve specific indexed records.

For more information about finding records, see the article "DAO Recordset: Recordset Navigation" in *Visual C++ Programmer's Guide* online. For related information, see the topic "FindFirst, FindLast, FindNext, FindPrevious Methods" in DAO Help.

See Also: **CDaoRecordset::Find**, **CDaoRecordset::FindFirst**, **CDaoRecordset::FindLast**, **CDaoRecordset::FindPrev**

CDaoRecordset::FindPrev

BOOL FindPrev(LPCTSTR *lpszFilter* **);**
    throw(CDaoException, CMemoryException);

Return Value

Nonzero if matching records are found, otherwise 0.

Parameters

lpszFilter A string expression (like the **WHERE** clause in an SQL statement without the word **WHERE**) used to locate the record.

Remarks

Call this member function to find the previous record that matches a specified condition. The **FindPrev** member function begins its search at the current record and searches backward towards the beginning of the recordset.

If you want to include all the records in your search (not just those that meet a specific condition) use one of the Move operations to move from record to record. To locate a record in a table-type recordset, call the **Seek** member function.

If a record matching the criteria is not located, the current record pointer is undetermined, and **FindPrev** returns zero. If the recordset contains more than one record that satisfies the criteria, **FindFirst** locates the first occurrence, **FindNext** locates the next occurrence, and so on.

Caution If you edit the current record, be sure you save the changes by calling the **Update** member function before you move to another record. If you move to another record without updating, your changes are lost without warning.

Using one of the Find operations is not the same as calling **MoveFirst** or **MoveNext**, however, which simply makes the first or next record current without specifying a condition. You can follow a Find operation with a Move operation.

Keep the following in mind when using the Find operations:

- If **Find** returns nonzero, the current record is not defined. In this case, you must position the current record pointer back to a valid record.

- You cannot use a Find operation with a forward-only scrolling snapshot-type recordset.

- You should use the U.S. date format (month-day-year) when you search for fields containing dates, even if you are not using the U.S. version of the Microsoft Jet database engine; otherwise, matching records may not be found.

- When working with ODBC databases and large dynasets, you may discover that using the Find operations is slow, especially when working with large recordsets. You can improve performance by using SQL queries with customized **ORDER BY** or **WHERE** clauses, parameter queries, or **CDaoQuerydef** objects that retrieve specific indexed records.

For more information about finding records, see the article "DAO Recordset: Recordset Navigation" in *Visual C++ Programmer's Guide* online. For related information, see the topic "FindFirst, FindLast, FindNext, FindPrevious Methods" in DAO Help.

See Also: **CDaoRecordset::Find, CDaoRecordset::FindFirst, CDaoRecordset::FindLast, CDaoRecordset::FindNext**

CDaoRecordset::GetAbsolutePosition

long GetAbsolutePosition( );
throw(CDaoException, CMemoryException);

Return Value

An integer from 0 to the number of records in the recordset. Corresponds to the ordinal position of the current record in the recordset.

Remarks

Returns the record number of a recordset object's current record. The AbsolutePosition property value of the underlying DAO object is zero-based; a setting of 0 refers to the first record in the recordset. You can determine the number of populated records in the recordset by calling **GetRecordCount**. Calling **GetRecordCount** may take some time because it must access all records to determine the count.

If there is no current record, as when there are no records in the recordset, -1 is returned. If the current record is deleted, the AbsolutePosition property value is not defined, and MFC throws an exception if it is referenced. For dynaset-type recordsets, new records are added to the end of the sequence.

Note This property is not intended to be used as a surrogate record number. Bookmarks are still the recommended way of retaining and returning to a given position and are the only way to position the current record across all types of recordset objects. In particular, the position of a given record changes when record(s) preceding it are deleted. There is also no assurance that a given record will have the same absolute position if the recordset is re-created again because the order of individual records within a recordset is not guaranteed unless it is created with an SQL statement using an **ORDER BY** clause.

Note This member function is valid only for dynaset-type and snapshot-type recordsets.

For more information about finding records, see the article "DAO Recordset: Recordset Navigation" in *Visual C++ Programmer's Guide* online. For related information, see the topic "AbsolutePosition Property" in DAO Help.

See Also: CDaoRecordset::SetAbsolutePosition

CDaoRecordset::GetBookmark

COleVariant GetBookmark( );
throw(CDaoException, CMemoryException);

Return Value

Returns a value representing the bookmark on the current record.

Remarks

Call this member function to obtain the bookmark value in a particular record. When a recordset object is created or opened, each of its records already has a unique bookmark if it supports them. Call **CanBookmark** to determine whether a recordset supports bookmarks.

You can save the bookmark for the current record by assigning the value of the bookmark to a **COleVariant** object. To quickly return to that record at any time after moving to a different record, call **SetBookmark** with a parameter corresponding to the value of that **COleVariant** object.

For more information about finding records, see the article "DAO Recordset: Recordset Navigation" in *Visual C++ Programmer's Guide* online. For related information, see the topic "Bookmark Property" in DAO Help.

See Also: **CDaoRecordset::SetBookmark**, **CDaoRecordset::CanBookmark**

CDaoRecordset::GetCacheSize

long GetCacheSize( );
   throw(CDaoException, CMemoryException);

Return Value

A value that specifies the number of records in a dynaset-type recordset containing data to be locally cached from an ODBC data source.

Remarks

Call this member function to obtain the number of records cached. Data caching improves the performance of an application that retrieves data from a remote server through dynaset-type recordset objects. A cache is a space in local memory that holds the data most recently retrieved from the server in the event that the data will be requested again while the application is running. When data is requested, the Microsoft Jet database engine checks the cache for the requested data first rather than retrieving it from the server, which takes more time. Data that does not come from an ODBC data source is not saved in the cache.

Any ODBC data source, such as an attached table, can have a local cache.

For more information about caching records, see the article "DAO External: Improving Performance with External Data Sources" in *Visual C++ Programmer's Guide* online. For related information, see the topic "CacheSize, CacheStart Properties" in DAO Help.

See Also: **CDaoRecordset::FillCache**, **CDaoRecordset::GetCacheStart**, **CDaoRecordset::SetCacheSize**, **CDaoRecordset::SetCacheStart**

CDaoRecordset::GetCacheStart

COleVariant GetCacheStart( );
 throw(CDaoException, CMemoryException);

Return Value

A **COleVariant** that specifies the bookmark of the first record in the recordset to be cached.

Remarks

Call this member function to obtain the bookmark value of the first record in the recordset to be cached. The Microsoft Jet database engine requests records within the cache range from the cache, and it requests records outside the cache range from the server.

Note Records retrieved from the cache do not reflect changes made concurrently to the source data by other users.

For more information about caching records, see the article "DAO External: Improving Performance with External Data Sources" in *Visual C++ Programmer's Guide* online. For related information, see the topic "CacheSize, CacheStart Properties" in DAO Help.

See Also: **CDaoRecordset::FillCache, CDaoRecordset::GetCacheSize, CDaoRecordset::SetCacheSize, CDaoRecordset::SetCacheStart**

CDaoRecordset::GetCurrentIndex

CString GetCurrentIndex( );
 throw(CDaoException, CMemoryException);

Return Value

A **CString** containing the name of the index currently in use with a table-type recordset. Returns an empty string if no index has been set.

Remarks

Call this member function to determine the index currently in use in an indexed table-type **CDaoRecordset** object. This index is the basis for ordering records in a table-type recordset, and is used by the **Seek** member function to locate records.

A **CDaoRecordset** object can have more than one index but can use only one index at a time (although a **CDaoTableDef** object may have several indexes defined on it).

For more information about finding records, see the article "DAO Recordset: Recordset Navigation" in *Visual C++ Programmer's Guide* online. For related information, see the topic "Index Object" and the definition "current index" in DAO Help.

See Also: **CDaoRecordset::SetCurrentIndex**

CDaoRecordset::GetDateCreated

COleDateTime GetDateCreated( );
   throw(CDaoException, CMemoryException);

Return Value

A **COleDateTime** object containing the date and time the base table was
created.

Remarks

Call this member function to retrieve the date and time a base table was created.
Date and time settings are derived from the computer on which the base table
was created.

For more information about creating recordsets, see the article "DAO: Creating,
Opening, and Closing DAO Objects" in *Visual C++ Programmer's Guide* online.
For related information, see the topic "DateCreated, LastUpdated Properties" in
DAO Help.

See Also: CDaoRecordset::GetDateLastUpdated

CDaoRecordset::GetDateLastUpdated

COleDateTime GetDateLastUpdated( );
   throw(CDaoException, CMemoryException);

Return Value

A **COleDateTime** object containing the date and time the base table structure
(schema) was last updated.

Remarks

Call this member function to retrieve the date and time the schema was last
updated. Date and time settings are derived from the computer on which the base
table structure (schema) was last updated.

For more information about creating recordsets, see the article "DAO: Creating,
Opening, and Closing DAO Objects" in *Visual C++ Programmer's Guide* online.
For related information, see the topic "DateCreated, LastUpdated Properties" in
DAO Help.

See Also: CDaoRecordset::GetDateCreated

CDaoRecordset::GetDefaultDBName

virtual CString GetDefaultDBName( );

Return Value

A **CString** that contains the path and name of the database from which this recordset is derived.

Remarks

Call this member function to determine the name of the database for this recordset. If a recordset is created without a pointer to a **CDaoDatabase**, then this path is used by the recordset to open the default database. By default, this function returns an empty string. When ClassWizard derives a new recordset from **CDaoRecordset**, it will create this function for you.

The following example illustrates the use of the double backslash (\\) in the string, as is required for the string to be interpreted correctly.

```
CString CMyRecordset::GetDefaultDBName(void)
{
    return _T("c:\\mydir\\datasrc.mdb");
}
```

For more information about connecting to databases, see the article "DAO: Creating, Opening, and Closing DAO Objects" in *Visual C++ Programmer's Guide* online.

See Also: **CDaoRecordset::GetDefaultSQL, CDaoRecordset::GetName, CDaoRecordset::GetSQL, CDaoRecordset::GetType**

CDaoRecordset::GetDefaultSQL

virtual CString GetDefaultSQL( );

Return Value

A **CString** that contains the default SQL statement.

Remarks

The framework calls this member function to get the default SQL statement on which the recordset is based. This might be a table name or an SQL **SELECT** statement.

You indirectly define the default SQL statement by declaring your recordset class with ClassWizard, and ClassWizard performs this task for you.

If you pass a null SQL string to **Open**, then this function is called to determine the table name or SQL for your recordset.

For more information about connecting to databases, see the article "DAO: Creating, Opening, and Closing DAO Objects" in *Visual C++ Programmer's Guide* online.

See Also: **CDaoRecordset::GetDefaultDBName**, **CDaoRecordset::GetName**, **CDaoRecordset::GetSQL**, **CDaoRecordset::GetType**

CDaoRecordset::GetEditMode

short GetEditMode( );
    throw(CDaoException, CMemoryException);

Return Value

Returns a value that indicates the state of editing for the current record.

Remarks

Call this member function to determine the state of editing, which is one of the following values:

Value	Description
dbEditNone	No editing operation is in progress.
dbEditInProgress	**Edit** has been called.
dbEditAdd	**AddNew** has been called.

For more information about updating data, see the article "DAO Recordset: Recordset Operations" in *Visual C++ Programmer's Guide* online. For related information, see the topic "EditMode Property" in DAO Help.

CDaoRecordset::GetFieldCount

short GetFieldCount( );
    throw(CDaoException, CMemoryException);

Return Value

The number of fields in the recordset.

Remarks

Call this member function to retrieve the number of fields (columns) defined in the recordset.

For more information about creating recordsets, see the article "DAO Recordset: Creating Recordsets" in *Visual C++ Programmer's Guide* online. For related information, see the topic "Count Property" in DAO Help.

See Also: **CDaoRecordset::GetFieldInfo**, **CDaoRecordset::GetFieldValue**, **CDaoRecordset::GetIndexCount**, **CDaoRecordset::GetIndexInfo**

CDaoRecordset::GetFieldInfo

void GetFieldInfo(int *nIndex,* **CDaoFieldInfo&** *fieldinfo,*
↳ **DWORD** *dwInfoOptions* **= AFX_DAO_PRIMARY_INFO);**
throw(CDaoException, CMemoryException);
void GetFieldInfo(LPCTSTR *lpszName,* **CDaoFieldInfo&** *fieldinfo,*
↳ **DWORD** *dwInfoOptions* **= AFX_DAO_PRIMARY_INFO);**
throw(CDaoException, CMemoryException);

Parameters

nIndex   The zero-based index of the predefined field in the recordset's Fields collection, for lookup by index.

fieldinfo   A reference to a **CDaoFieldInfo** structure.

dwInfoOptions   Options that specify which information about the recordset to retrieve. The available options are listed here along with what they cause the function to return. For best performance, retrieve only the level of information you need:

- **AFX_DAO_PRIMARY_INFO**   (Default) Name, Type, Size, Attributes

- **AFX_DAO_SECONDARY_INFO**   Primary information, plus: Ordinal Position, Required, Allow Zero Length, Collating Order, Foreign Name, Source Field, Source Table

- **AFX_DAO_ALL_INFO**   Primary and secondary information, plus: Default Value, Validation Rule, Validation Text

lpszName   The name of the field.

Remarks

Call this member function to obtain information about the fields in a recordset. One version of the function lets you look up a field by index. The other version lets you look up a field by name.

For a description of the information returned, see the **CDaoFieldInfo** structure. This structure has members that correspond to the items of information listed above in the description of *dwInfoOptions*. When you request information at one level, you get information for any prior levels as well.

For more information about creating recordsets, see the article "DAO Recordset: Creating Recordsets" in *Visual C++ Programmer's Guide* online. For related information, see the topic "Attributes Property" in DAO Help.

See Also: **CDaoRecordset::GetFieldCount, CDaoRecordset::GetFieldValue, CDaoRecordset::GetIndexCount, CDaoRecordset::GetIndexInfo**

CDaoRecordset::GetFieldValue

virtual void GetFieldValue(LPCTSTR *lpszName***, COleVariant&** *varValue* **);**
    throw(CDaoException, CMemoryException);
virtual void GetFieldValue(int *nIndex***, COleVariant&** *varValue* **);**
    throw(CDaoException, CMemoryException);
virtual COleVariant GetFieldValue(LPCTSTR *lpszName* **);**
    throw(CDaoException, CMemoryException);
virtual COleVariant GetFieldValue(int *nIndex* **);**
    throw(CDaoException, CMemoryException);

Return Value

The two versions of **GetFieldValue** that return a value return a **COleVariant** object that contains the value of a field.

Parameters

lpszName   A pointer to a string that contains the name of a field.

varValue   A reference to a **COleVariant** object that will store the value of a field.

nIndex   A zero-based index of the field in the recordset's Fields collection, for lookup by index.

Remarks

Call this member function to retrieve data in a recordset. You can look up a field by name or by ordinal position.

Note It is more efficient to call one of the versions of this member function that takes a **COleVariant** object reference as a parameter, rather than calling a version that returns a **COleVariant** object.

Use **GetFieldValue** and **SetFieldValue** to dynamically bind fields at run time rather than statically binding columns using the **DoFieldExchange** mechanism.

GetFieldValue and the **DoFieldExchange** mechanism can be combined to improve performance. For example, use **GetFieldValue** to retrieve a value that you need only on demand, and assign that call to a "More Information" button in the interface.

For more information about binding fields dynamically, see the article "DAO Recordset: Binding Records Dynamically" in *Visual C++ Programmer's Guide* online. For related information, see the topics "Field Object" and "Value Property" in DAO Help.

See Also: **CDaoRecordset::SetFieldValue**

CDaoRecordset::GetIndexCount

short GetIndexCount( );
  throw(CDaoException, CMemoryException);

Return Value

The number of indexes in the table-type recordset.

Remarks

Call this member function to determine the number of indexes available on the table-type recordset. **GetIndexCount** is useful for looping through all indexes in the recordset. For that purpose, use **GetIndexCount** in conjunction with **GetIndexInfo**. If you call this member function on dynaset-type or snapshot-type recordsets, MFC throws an exception.

For more information about creating recordsets, see the article "DAO Recordset: Creating Recordsets" in *Visual C++ Programmer's Guide* online. For related information, see the topic "Attributes Property" in DAO Help.

See Also: CDaoRecordset::GetFieldCount, CDaoRecordset::GetFieldInfo, CDaoRecordset::GetIndexInfo

---

CDaoRecordset::GetIndexInfo

void GetIndexInfo(int *nIndex***, CDaoIndexInfo&** *indexinfo***,**
  ↳ DWORD *dwInfoOptions* **= AFX_DAO_PRIMARY_INFO);**
  throw(CDaoException, CMemoryException);
void GetIndexInfo(LPCTSTR *lpszName***, CDaoIndexInfo&** *indexinfo***,**
  ↳ DWORD *dwInfoOptions* **= AFX_DAO_PRIMARY_INFO);**
  throw(CDaoException, CMemoryException);

Parameters

nIndex   The zero-based index in the table's Indexes collection, for lookup by numerical position.

indexinfo   A reference to a **CDaoIndexInfo** structure.

dwInfoOptions   Options that specify which information about the index to retrieve. The available options are listed here along with what they cause the function to return. For best performance, retrieve only the level of information you need:

- **AFX_DAO_PRIMARY_INFO**   (Default) Name, Field Info, Fields

- **AFX_DAO_SECONDARY_INFO**   Primary information, plus: Primary, Unique, Clustered, IgnoreNulls, Required, Foreign

- **AFX_DAO_ALL_INFO**   Primary and secondary information, plus: Distinct Count

lpszName   A pointer to the name of the index object, for lookup by name.

Remarks

Call this member function to obtain various kinds of information about an index defined in the base table underlying a recordset. One version of the function lets you look up a index by its position in the collection. The other version lets you look up an index by name.

For a description of the information returned, see the **CDaoIndexInfo** structure. This structure has members that correspond to the items of information listed above in the description of *dwInfoOptions*. When you request information at one level, you get information for any prior levels as well.

For more information about creating recordsets, see the article "DAO Recordset: Creating Recordsets" in *Visual C++ Programmer's Guide* online. For related information, see the topic "Attributes Property" in DAO Help.

See Also: **CDaoRecordset::GetFieldCount, CDaoRecordset::GetFieldInfo, CDaoRecordset::GetIndexCount, CDaoRecordset::GetLastModifiedBookmark**

CDaoRecordset::GetLastModifiedBookmark

COleVariant GetLastModifiedBookmark( );
 throw(CDaoException, CMemoryException);

Return Value

A **COleVariant** containing a bookmark that indicates the most recently added or changed record.

Remarks

Call this member function to retrieve the bookmark of the most recently added or updated record. When a recordset object is created or opened, each of its records already has a unique bookmark if it supports them. Call **GetBookmark** to determine if the recordset supports bookmarks. If the recordset does not support bookmarks, a **CDaoException** is thrown.

When you add a record, it appears at the end of the recordset, and is not the current record. To make the new record current, call **GetLastModifiedBookmark** and then call **SetBookmark** to return to the newly added record.

For more information about navigating in recordsets, see the article "DAO Recordset: Recordset Navigation" in *Visual C++ Programmer's Guide* online. For related information, see the topic "LastModified Property" in DAO Help.

See Also: **CDaoRecordset::GetBookmark, CDaoRecordset::SetBookmark**

CDaoRecordset::GetLockingMode

BOOL GetLockingMode( );
throw(CDaoException, CMemoryException);

Return Value

Nonzero if the type of locking is pessimistic, otherwise 0 for optimistic record locking.

Remarks

Call this member function to determine the type of locking in effect for the recordset. When pessimistic locking is in effect, the data page containing the record you are editing is locked as soon as you call the **Edit** member function. The page is unlocked when you call the **Update** or **Close** member function or any of the Move or Find operations.

When optimistic locking is in effect, the data page containing the record is locked only while the record is being updated with the **Update** member function.

When working with ODBC data sources, the locking mode is always optimistic.

For more information about updating data, see the article "DAO Recordset: Recordset Operations" in *Visual C++ Programmer's Guide* online. For related information, see the topics "LockEdits Property" and "Locking Behavior in Multiuser Applications" in DAO Help.

See Also: **CDaoRecordset::SetLockingMode**

CDaoRecordset::GetName

CString GetName( );
throw(CDaoException, CMemoryException);

Return Value

A **CString** containing the name of the recordset.

Remarks

Call this member function to retrieve the name of the recordset. The name of the recordset must start with a letter and can contain a maximum of 40 characters. It can include numbers and underscore characters but can't include punctuation or spaces.

For more information about creating recordsets, see the article "DAO Recordset: Creating Recordsets" in *Visual C++ Programmer's Guide* online. For related information, see the topic "Name Property" in DAO Help.

See Also: **CDaoRecordset::GetDefaultDBName,**
CDaoRecordset::GetDefaultSQL, CDaoRecordset::GetSQL,
CDaoRecordset::GetType

CDaoRecordset::GetParamValue

virtual COleVariant GetParamValue(int *nIndex* **);**
    throw(CDaoException, CMemoryException);
virtual COleVariant GetParamValue(LPCTSTR *lpszName* **);**
    throw(CDaoException, CMemoryException);

Return Value

An object of class **COleVariant** that contains the parameter's value.

Parameters

nIndex   The numerical position of the parameter in the underlying DAOParameter object.

lpszName   The name of the parameter whose value you want.

Remarks

Call this member function to retrieve the current value of the specified parameter stored in the underlying DAOParameter object. You can access the parameter either by name or by its numerical position in the collection.

For more information about parameters, see the article "DAO Queries: Filtering and Parameterizing Queries" in *Visual C++ Programmer's Guide* online. For related information, see the topic "Parameter Object" in DAO Help.

See Also: **CDaoRecordset::SetParamValue, CDaoRecordset::m_nParams**

CDaoRecordset::GetPercentPosition

float GetPercentPosition( );
    throw(CDaoException, CMemoryException);

Return Value

A number between 0 and 100 that indicates the approximate location of the current record in the recordset object based on a percentage of the records in the recordset.

Remarks

When working with a dynaset-type or snapshot-type recordset, if you call **GetPercentPosition** before fully populating the recordset, the amount of movement is relative to the number of records accessed as indicated by calling **GetRecordCount**. You can move to the last record by calling **MoveLast** to complete the population of all recordsets, but this may take a significant amount of time.

You can call **GetPercentPosition** on all three types of recordset objects, including tables without indexes. However, you cannot call **GetPercentPosition** on forward-only scrolling snapshots, or on a recordset opened from a pass-through query against an external database. If there is no current record, or he current record has been deleted, a **CDaoException** is thrown.

For more information about navigating in recordsets, see the article "DAO Recordset: Recordset Navigation" in *Visual C++ Programmer's Guide* online. For related information, see the topic "PercentPosition Property" in DAO Help.

See Also: **CDaoRecordset::SetPercentPosition**

CDaoRecordset::GetRecordCount

long GetRecordCount( );
   throw(CDaoException, CMemoryException);

Return Value

Returns the number of records in a recordset.

Remarks

Call this member function to find out how many records in a recordset have been accessed. **GetRecordCount** does not indicate how many records are contained in a dynaset-type or snapshot-type recordset until all records have been accessed. This member function call may take a significant amount of time to complete.

Once the last record has been accessed, the return value indicates the total number of undeleted records in the recordset. To force the last record to be accessed, call the **MoveLast** or **FindLast** member function for the recordset. You can also use a SQL Count to determine the approximate number of records your query will return.

As your application deletes records in a dynaset-type recordset, the return value of **GetRecordCount** decreases. However, records deleted by other users are not reflected by **GetRecordCount** until the current record is positioned to a deleted record. If you execute a transaction that affects the record count and subsequently roll back the transaction, **GetRecordCount** will not reflect the actual number of remaining records.

The value of **GetRecordCount** from a snapshot-type recordset is not affected by changes in the underlying tables.

The value of **GetRecordCount** from a table-type recordset reflects the approximate number of records in the table and is affected immediately as table records are added and deleted.

A recordset with no records returns a value of 0. When working with attached tables or ODBC databases, **GetRecordCount** always returns−1. Calling the **Requery** member function on a recordset resets the value of **GetRecordCount** just as if the query were re-executed.

For more information about navigating in recordsets, see the article "DAO Recordset: Recordset Navigation" in *Visual C++ Programmer's Guide* online. For related information, see the topic "RecordCount Property" in DAO Help.

See Also: **CDaoRecordset::GetFieldCount, CDaoRecordset::GetFieldInfo, CDaoRecordset::GetIndexCount, CDaoRecordset::GetIndexInfo**

CDaoRecordset::GetSQL

CString GetSQL( ) const;

Return Value

A **CString** that contains the SQL statement.

Remarks

Call this member function to get the SQL statement that was used to select the recordset's records when it was opened. This will generally be an SQL **SELECT** statement.

The string returned by **GetSQL** is typically different from any string you may have passed to the recordset in the *lpszSQL* parameter to the **Open** member function. This is because the recordset constructs a full SQL statement based on what you passed to **Open**, what you specified with ClassWizard, and what you may have specified in the **m_strFilter** and **m_strSort** data members.

Important Call this member function only after calling **Open**.

For more information about creating recordsets, see the article "DAO Recordset: Creating Recordsets" in *Visual C++ Programmer's Guide* online. For related information, see the topic "SQL Property" in DAO Help.

See Also: **CDaoRecordset::GetDefaultSQL, CDaoRecordset::GetDefaultDBName, CDaoRecordset::GetName, CDaoRecordset::GetType**

CDaoRecordset::GetType

short GetType( );
    throw(CDaoException, CMemoryException);

Return Value

One of the following values that indicates the type of a recordset:

- **dbOpenTable**   Table-type recordset
- **dbOpenDynaset**   Dynaset-type recordset
- **dbOpenSnapshot**   Snapshot-type recordset

Remarks

Call this member function after opening the recordset to determine the type of the recordset object.

For more information about creating recordsets, see the article "DAO Recordset: Creating Recordsets" in *Visual C++ Programmer's Guide* online. For related information, see the topic "Type Property" in DAO Help.

See Also: **CDaoRecordset::GetDefaultDBName,
CDaoRecordset::GetDefaultSQL, CDaoRecordset::GetName,
CDaoRecordset::GetSQL**

CDaoRecordset::GetValidationRule

**CString GetValidationRule( );
    throw(CDaoException, CMemoryException);**

Return Value

A **CString** object containing a value that validates the data in a record as it is changed or added to a table.

Remarks

Call this member function to determine the rule used to validate data. This rule is text-based, and is applied each time the underlying table is changed. If the data is not legal, MFC throws an exception. The returned error message is the text of the ValidationText property of the underlying field object, if specified, or the text of the expression specified by the ValidationRule property of the underlying field object. You can call **GetValidationText** to obtain the text of the error message.

For example, a field in a record that requires the day of the month might have a validation rule such as "DAY BETWEEN 1 AND 31."

For more information about creating recordsets, see the article "DAO Recordset: Creating Recordsets" in *Visual C++ Programmer's Guide* online. For related information, see the topic "ValidationRule Property" in DAO Help.

See Also: **CDaoRecordset::GetValidationText**

CDaoRecordset::GetValidationText

**CString GetValidationText( );
    throw(CDaoException, CMemoryException);**

Return Value

A **CString** object containing the text of the message that is displayed if the value of a field does not satisfy the validation rule of the underlying field object.

Remarks

Call this member function to retrieve the text of the ValidationText property of the underlying field object.

For more information about creating recordsets, see the article "DAO Recordset: Creating Recordsets" in *Visual C++ Programmer's Guide* online. For related information, see the topic "ValidationText Property" in DAO Help.

See Also: CDaoRecordset::GetValidationRule

CDaoRecordset::IsBOF

BOOL IsBOF( ) const;
   throw(CDaoException, CMemoryException);

Return Value

Nonzero if the recordset contains no records or if you have scrolled backward before the first record; otherwise 0.

Remarks

Call this member function before you scroll from record to record to learn whether you have gone before the first record of the recordset. You can also call **IsBOF** along with **IsEOF** to determine whether the recordset contains any records or is empty. Immediately after you call **Open**, if the recordset contains no records, **IsBOF** returns nonzero. When you open a recordset that has at least one record, the first record is the current record and **IsBOF** returns 0.

If the first record is the current record and you call **MovePrev**, **IsBOF** will subsequently return nonzero. If **IsBOF** returns nonzero and you call **MovePrev**, an exception is thrown. If **IsBOF** returns nonzero, the current record is undefined, and any action that requires a current record will result in an exception.

Effect of specific methods on **IsBOF** and **IsEOF** settings:

- Calling **Open** internally makes the first record in the recordset the current record by calling **MoveFirst**. Therefore, calling **Open** on an empty set of records causes **IsBOF** and **IsEOF** to return nonzero. (See the following table for the behavior of a failed **MoveFirst** or **MoveLast** call.)

- All Move operations that successfully locate a record cause both **IsBOF** and **IsEOF** to return 0.

- An **AddNew** call followed by an **Update** call that successfully inserts a new record will cause **IsBOF** to return 0, but only if **IsEOF** is already nonzero. The state of **IsEOF** will always remain unchanged. As defined by the Microsoft Jet database engine, the current record pointer of an empty recordset is at the end of a file, so any new record is inserted after the current record.

- Any **Delete** call, even if it removes the only remaining record from a recordset, will not change the value of **IsBOF** or **IsEOF**.

This table shows which Move operations are allowed with different combinations of **IsBOF/IsEOF**.

	MoveFirst, MoveLast	MovePrev, Move < 0	Move 0	MoveNext, Move > 0
IsBOF=nonzero, **IsEOF**=0	Allowed	Exception	Exception	Allowed
IsBOF=0, **IsEOF**=nonzero	Allowed	Allowed	Exception	Exception
Both nonzero	Exception	Exception	Exception	Exception
Both 0	Allowed	Allowed	Allowed	Allowed

Allowing a Move operation does not mean that the operation will successfully locate a record. It merely indicates that an attempt to perform the specified Move operation is allowed and will not generate an exception. The value of the **IsBOF** and **IsEOF** member functions may change as a result of the attempted move.

The effect of Move operations that do not locate a record on the value of **IsBOF** and **IsEOF** settings is shown in the following table.

	IsBOF	IsEOF
MoveFirst, MoveLast	Nonzero	Nonzero
Move 0	No change	No change
MovePrev, Move < 0	Nonzero	No change
MoveNext, Move > 0	No change	Nonzero

For more information about navigating in recordsets, see the article "DAO Recordset: Recordset Navigation" in *Visual C++ Programmer's Guide* online. For related information, see the topic "BOF, EOF Properties" in DAO Help.

See Also: CDaoRecordset::IsEOF

CDaoRecordset::IsDeleted

BOOL IsDeleted( ) const;

Return Value

Nonzero if the recordset is positioned on a deleted record; otherwise 0.

Remarks

Call this member function to determine whether the current record has been deleted. If you scroll to a record and **IsDeleted** returns **TRUE** (nonzero), then you must scroll to another record before you can perform any other recordset operations.

Note   You don't need to check the deleted status for records in a snapshot or table-type recordset. Because records cannot be deleted from a snapshot, there is no need to call **IsDeleted**. For table-type recordsets, deleted records are actually removed from the recordset. Once a record has been deleted, either by you, another user, or in another recordset, you cannot scroll back to that record. Therefore, there is no need to call **IsDeleted**.

When you delete a record from a dynaset, it is removed from the recordset and you cannot scroll back to that record. However, if a record in a dynaset is deleted either by another user or in another recordset based on the same table, **IsDeleted** will return **TRUE** when you later scroll to that record.

For more information about navigating in recordsets, see the article "DAO Recordset: Recordset Navigation" in *Visual C++ Programmer's Guide* online. For related information, see the topics "Delete Method," "LastModified Property," and "EditMode Property" in DAO Help.

See Also: **CDaoRecordset::Delete, CDaoRecordset::IsBOF, CDaoRecordset::IsEOF**

CDaoRecordset::IsEOF

BOOL IsEOF( ) const;
  throw(CDaoException, CMemoryException);

Return Value

Nonzero if the recordset contains no records or if you have scrolled beyond the last record; otherwise 0.

Remarks

Call this member function as you scroll from record to record to learn whether you have gone beyond the last record of the recordset. You can also call **IsEOF** to determine whether the recordset contains any records or is empty. Immediately after you call **Open**, if the recordset contains no records, **IsEOF** returns nonzero. When you open a recordset that has at least one record, the first record is the current record and **IsEOF** returns 0.

If the last record is the current record when you call **MoveNext**, **IsEOF** will subsequently return nonzero. If **IsEOF** returns nonzero and you call **MoveNext**, an exception is thrown. If **IsEOF** returns nonzero, the current record is undefined, and any action that requires a current record will result in an exception.

Effect of specific methods on **IsBOF** and **IsEOF** settings:

- Calling **Open** internally makes the first record in the recordset the current record by calling **MoveFirst**. Therefore, calling **Open** on an empty set of records causes **IsBOF** and **IsEOF** to return nonzero. (See the following table for the behavior of a failed **MoveFirst** call.)

- All Move operations that successfully locate a record cause both **IsBOF** and **IsEOF** to return 0.

- An **AddNew** call followed by an **Update** call that successfully inserts a new record will cause **IsBOF** to return 0, but only if **IsEOF** is already nonzero. The state of **IsEOF** will always remain unchanged. As defined by the Microsoft Jet database engine, the current record pointer of an empty recordset is at the end of a file, so any new record is inserted after the current record.

- Any **Delete** call, even if it removes the only remaining record from a recordset, will not change the value of **IsBOF** or **IsEOF**.

This table shows which Move operations are allowed with different combinations of **IsBOF/IsEOF**.

	MoveFirst, MoveLast	MovePrev, Move < 0	Move 0	MoveNext, Move > 0
IsBOF=nonzero, **IsEOF**=0	Allowed	Exception	Exception	Allowed
IsBOF=0, **IsEOF**=nonzero	Allowed	Allowed	Exception	Exception
Both nonzero	Exception	Exception	Exception	Exception
Both 0	Allowed	Allowed	Allowed	Allowed

Allowing a Move operation does not mean that the operation will successfully locate a record. It merely indicates that an attempt to perform the specified Move operation is allowed and will not generate an exception. The value of the **IsBOF** and **IsEOF** member functions may change as a result of the attempted Move.

The effect of Move operations that do not locate a record on the value of **IsBOF** and **IsEOF** settings is shown in the following table.

	IsBOF	IsEOF
MoveFirst, **MoveLast**	Nonzero	Nonzero
Move 0	No change	No change
MovePrev, **Move** < 0	Nonzero	No change
MoveNext, **Move** > 0	No change	Nonzero

For more information about navigating in recordsets, see the article "DAO Recordset: Recordset Navigation" in *Visual C++ Programmer's Guide* online. For related information, see the topic "BOF, EOF Properties" in DAO Help.

See Also: **CDaoRecordset::IsBOF**

CDaoRecordset::IsFieldDirty

BOOL IsFieldDirty(void* *pv* **) const;**
    throw(CDaoException, CMemoryException);

Return Value

Nonzero if the specified field data member is flagged as dirty; otherwise 0.

Parameters

pv A pointer to the field data member whose status you want to check, or **NULL** to determine if any of the fields are dirty.

Remarks

Call this member function to determine whether the specified field data member of a dynaset has been flagged as "dirty" (changed). The data in all dirty field data members will be transferred to the record on the data source when the current record is updated by a call to the **Update** member function of **CDaoRecordset** (following a call to **Edit** or **AddNew**). With this knowledge, you can take further steps, such as unflagging the field data member to mark the column so it will not be written to the data source. For more information on the dirty flag, see the article "DAO Recordset: Caching Multiple Records" in *Visual C++ Programmer's Guide* online.

IsFieldDirty is implemented through **DoFieldExchange**.

For more information about record field exchange, see the article "DAO Record Field Exchange (DFX)" in *Visual C++ Programmer's Guide* online.

See Also: **CDaoRecordset::IsFieldNull, CDaoRecordset::IsFieldNullable**

CDaoRecordset::IsFieldNull

BOOL IsFieldNull(void* *pv* **);**
  throw(CDaoException, CMemoryException);

Return Value

Nonzero if the specified field data member is flagged as Null; otherwise 0.

Parameters

pv A pointer to the field data member whose status you want to check, or **NULL** to determine if any of the fields are Null.

Remarks

Call this member function to determine whether the specified field data member of a recordset has been flagged as Null. (In database terminology, Null means "having no value" and is not the same as **NULL** in C++.) If a field data member is flagged as Null, it is interpreted as a column of the current record for which there is no value.

Note In certain situations, using **IsFieldNull** can be inefficient, as the following code example illustrates:

```
COleVariant varValue;

// this code is inefficient because data
// must be retrieved for both IsFieldNull
// and GetFieldValue
if ( !rs.IsFieldNull( nField ) )
    rs.GetFieldValue( nField, varValue );

// this code is more efficient
rs.GetFieldValue( nField, varValue );
if ( varValue.vt == VT_NULL )
    // do something
```

See Also: **CDaoRecordset::IsFieldDirty, CDaoRecordset::IsFieldNullable**

CDaoRecordset::IsFieldNullable

BOOL IsFieldNullable(void* *pv* **);**
    throw(CDaoException, CMemoryException);

Return Value

Nonzero if the specified field data member can be made Null; otherwise 0.

Parameters

pv A pointer to the field data member whose status you want to check, or **NULL** to determine if any of the fields are Null.

Remarks

Call this member function to determine whether the specified field data member is "nullable" (can be set to a Null value; C++ **NULL** is not the same as Null, which, in database terminology, means "having no value").

A field that cannot be Null must have a value. If you attempt to set such a field to Null when adding or updating a record, the data source rejects the addition or update, and **Update** will throw an exception. The exception occurs when you call **Update**, not when you call **SetFieldNull**.

See Also: **CDaoRecordset::IsFieldDirty, CDaoRecordset::IsFieldNull**

CDaoRecordset::IsOpen

BOOL IsOpen( ) const;

Return Value

Nonzero if the recordset object's **Open** or **Requery** member function has previously been called and the recordset has not been closed; otherwise 0.

Remarks

Call this member function to determine if the recordset is open.

For more information about creating recordsets, see the article "DAO Recordset: Creating Recordsets" in *Visual C++ Programmer's Guide* online.

See Also: **CDaoRecordset::Open, CDaoRecordset::Close**

CDaoRecordset::Move

virtual void Move(long *lRows* **);**
    throw(CDaoException, CMemoryException);

Parameters

lRows The number of records to move forward or backward. Positive values move forward, toward the end of the recordset. Negative values move backward, toward the beginning.

Remarks

Call this member function to position the recordset *lRows* records from the current record. You can move forward or backward. `Move( 1 )` is equivalent to **MoveNext**, and `Move( - 1 )` is equivalent to **MovePrev**.

Caution Calling any of the **Move** functions throws an exception if the recordset has no records. In general, call both **IsBOF** and **IsEOF** before a Move operation to determine whether the recordset has any records. After you call **Open** or **Requery**, call either **IsBOF** or **IsEOF**.

If you have scrolled past the beginning or end of the recordset (**IsBOF** or **IsEOF** returns nonzero), a call to **Move** throws a **CDaoException**.

If you call any of the **Move** functions while the current record is being updated or added, the updates are lost without warning.

When you call **Move** on a forward-only scrolling snapshot, the *lRows* parameter must be a positive integer and bookmarks are not allowed, so you can move forward only.

To make the first, last, next, or previous record in a recordset the current record, call the **MoveFirst**, **MoveLast**, **MoveNext**, or **MovePrev** member function.

For more information about finding records, see the article "DAO Recordset: Recordset Navigation" in *Visual C++ Programmer's Guide* online. For related information, see the topics "Move Method" and "MoveFirst, MoveLast, MoveNext, MovePrevious Methods" in DAO Help.

See Also: **CDaoRecordset::MoveFirst, CDaoRecordset::MoveLast, CDaoRecordset::MoveNext, CDaoRecordset::MovePrev**

CDaoRecordset::MoveFirst

void MoveFirst( );
    throw(CDaoException, CMemoryException);

Remarks

Call this member function to make the first record in the recordset (if any) the current record. You do not have to call **MoveFirst** immediately after you open the recordset. At that time, the first record (if any) is automatically the current record.

Caution Calling any of the **Move** functions throws an exception if the recordset has no records. In general, call both **IsBOF** and **IsEOF** before a Move operation to determine whether the recordset has any records. After you call **Open** or **Requery**, call either **IsBOF** or **IsEOF**.

If you call any of the **Move** functions while the current record is being updated or added, the updates are lost without warning.

Use the **Move** functions to move from record to record without applying a condition. Use the Find operations to locate records in a dynaset-type or snapshot-type recordset object that satisfy a certain condition. To locate a record in a table-type recordset object, call **Seek**.

If the recordset refers to a table-type recordset, movement follows the table's current index. You can set the current index by using the Index property of the underlying DAO object. If you do not set the current index, the order of returned records is undefined.

If you call **MoveLast** on a recordset object based on an SQL query or querydef, the query is forced to completion and the recordset object is fully populated.

You cannot call the **MoveFirst** or **MovePrev** member function with a forward-only scrolling snapshot.

To move the position of the current record in a recordset object a specific number of records forward or backward, call **Move**.

For more information about finding records, see the article "DAO Recordset: Recordset Navigation" in *Visual C++ Programmer's Guide* online. For related information, see the topics "Move Method" and "MoveFirst, MoveLast, MoveNext, MovePrevious Methods" in DAO Help.

See Also: **CDaoRecordset::Move, CDaoRecordset::MoveLast, CDaoRecordset::MoveNext, CDaoRecordset::MovePrev**

CDaoRecordset::MoveLast

> **void MoveLast( );**
> **throw(CDaoException, CMemoryException);**

Remarks

Call this member function to make the last record (if any) in the recordset the current record.

Caution Calling any of the **Move** functions throws an exception if the recordset has no records. In general, call both **IsBOF** and **IsEOF** before a Move operation to determine whether the recordset has any records. After you call **Open** or **Requery**, call either **IsBOF** or **IsEOF**.

If you call any of the **Move** functions while the current record is being updated or added, the updates are lost without warning.

Use the **Move** functions to move from record to record without applying a condition. Use the Find operations to locate records in a dynaset-type or snapshot-type recordset object that satisfy a certain condition. To locate a record in a table-type recordset object, call **Seek**.

If the recordset refers to a table-type recordset, movement follows the table's current index. You can set the current index by using the Index property of the underlying

DAO object. If you do not set the current index, the order of returned records is undefined.

If you call **MoveLast** on a recordset object based on an SQL query or querydef, the query is forced to completion and the recordset object is fully populated.

To move the position of the current record in a recordset object a specific number of records forward or backward, call **Move**.

For more information about finding records, see the article "DAO Recordset: Recordset Navigation" in *Visual C++ Programmer's Guide* online. For related information, see the topics "Move Method" and "MoveFirst, MoveLast, MoveNext, MovePrevious Methods" in DAO Help.

See Also: **CDaoRecordset::Move, CDaoRecordset::MoveFirst, CDaoRecordset::MoveNext, CDaoRecordset::MovePrev**

CDaoRecordset::MoveNext

void MoveNext( );
    throw(CDaoException, CMemoryException);

Remarks

Call this member function to make the next record in the recordset the current record. It is recommended that you call **IsBOF** before you attempt to move to the previous record. A call to **MovePrev** will throw a **CDaoException** if **IsBOF** returns nonzero, indicating either that you have already scrolled before the first record or that no records were selected by the recordset.

Caution   Calling any of the **Move** functions throws an exception if the recordset has no records. In general, call both **IsBOF** and **IsEOF** before a Move operation to determine whether the recordset has any records. After you call **Open** or **Requery**, call either **IsBOF** or **IsEOF**.

If you call any of the **Move** functions while the current record is being updated or added, the updates are lost without warning.

Use the **Move** functions to move from record to record without applying a condition. Use the Find operations to locate records in a dynaset-type or snapshot-type recordset object that satisfy a certain condition. To locate a record in a table-type recordset object, call **Seek**.

If the recordset refers to a table-type recordset, movement follows the table's current index. You can set the current index by using the Index property of the underlying DAO object. If you do not set the current index, the order of returned records is undefined.

To move the position of the current record in a recordset object a specific number of records forward or backward, call **Move**.

For more information about finding records, see the article "DAO Recordset: Recordset Navigation" in *Visual C++ Programmer's Guide* online. For related information, see the topics "Move Method" and "MoveFirst, MoveLast, MoveNext, MovePrevious Methods" in DAO Help.

See Also: **CDaoRecordset::Move**, **CDaoRecordset::MoveFirst**, **CDaoRecordset::MoveLast**, **CDaoRecordset::MovePrev**

CDaoRecordset::MovePrev

void MovePrev( );
    throw(CDaoException, CMemoryException);

Remarks

Call this member function to make the previous record in the recordset the current record.

It is recommended that you call **IsBOF** before you attempt to move to the previous record. A call to **MovePrev** will throw a **CDaoException** if **IsBOF** returns nonzero, indicating either that you have already scrolled before the first record or that no records were selected by the recordset.

Caution   Calling any of the **Move** functions throws an exception if the recordset has no records. In general, call both **IsBOF** and **IsEOF** before a Move operation to determine whether the recordset has any records. After you call **Open** or **Requery**, call either **IsBOF** or **IsEOF**.

If you call any of the **Move** functions while the current record is being updated or added, the updates are lost without warning.

Use the **Move** functions to move from record to record without applying a condition. Use the Find operations to locate records in a dynaset-type or snapshot-type recordset object that satisfy a certain condition. To locate a record in a table-type recordset object, call **Seek**.

If the recordset refers to a table-type recordset, movement follows the table's current index. You can set the current index by using the Index property of the underlying DAO object. If you do not set the current index, the order of returned records is undefined.

You cannot call the **MoveFirst** or **MovePrev** member function with a forward-only scrolling snapshot.

To move the position of the current record in a recordset object a specific number of records forward or backward, call **Move**.

For more information about finding records, see the article "DAO Recordset: Recordset Navigation" in *Visual C++ Programmer's Guide* online. For related information, see the topics "Move Method" and "MoveFirst, MoveLast, MoveNext, MovePrevious Methods" in DAO Help.

See Also: **CDaoRecordset::Move**, **CDaoRecordset::MoveFirst**, **CDaoRecordset::MoveLast**, **CDaoRecordset::MoveNext**

CDaoRecordset::Open

virtual void Open(int *nOpenType* **= AFX_DAO_USE_DEFAULT_TYPE,**
   ↪ **LPCTSTR** *lpszSQL* **= NULL, int** *nOptions* **= 0);**
   throw(CDaoException, CMemoryException);
virtual void Open(CDaoTableDef* *pTableDef*, **int** *nOpenType* **= dbOpenTable,**
   ↪ **int** *nOptions* **= 0);**
   throw(CDaoException, CMemoryException);
virtual void Open(CDaoQueryDef* *pQueryDef*, **int** *nOpenType* **= dbOpenDynaset,**
   ↪ **int** *nOptions* **= 0);**
   throw(CDaoException, CMemoryException);

Parameters

nOpenType   One of the following values:

- **dbOpenDynaset**   A dynaset-type recordset with bidirectional scrolling. This is the default.

- **dbOpenTable**   A table-type recordset with bidirectional scrolling.

- **dbOpenSnapshot**   A snapshot-type recordset with bidirectional scrolling.

lpszSQL   A string pointer containing one of the following:

- A **NULL** pointer.

- The name of one or more tabledefs and/or querydefs (comma-separated).

- An SQL **SELECT** statement (optionally with an SQL **WHERE** or **ORDER BY** clause).

- A pass-through query.

nOptions   One or more of the options listed below. The default value is 0. Possible values are as follows:

- **dbAppendOnly**   You can only append new records (dynaset-type recordset only). This option means literally that records may only be appended. The MFC ODBC database classes have an append-only option that allows records to be retrieved and appended.

- **dbForwardOnly**   The recordset is a forward-only scrolling snapshot.

- **dbSeeChanges**   Generate an exception if another user is changing data you are editing.

- **dbDenyWrite**   Other users cannot modify or add records.

- **dbDenyRead**   Other users cannot view records (table-type recordset only).

- **dbReadOnly**   You can only view records; other users can modify them.

- **dbInconsistent**   Inconsistent updates are allowed (dynaset-type recordset only).

- **dbConsistent**   Only consistent updates are allowed (dynaset-type recordset only).

Note   The constants **dbConsistent** and **dbInconsistent** are mutually exclusive. You can use one or the other, but not both in a given instance of **Open**.

pTableDef   A pointer to a **CDaoTableDef** object. This version is valid only for table-type recordsets. When using this option, the **CDaoDatabase** pointer used to construct the **CDaoRecordset** is not used; rather, the database in which the tabledef resides is used.

pQueryDef   A pointer to a **CDaoQueryDef** object. This version is valid only for dynaset-type and snapshot-type recordsets. When using this option, the **CDaoDatabase** pointer used to construct the **CDaoRecordset** is not used; rather, the database in which the querydef resides is used.

Remarks

You must call this member function to retrieve the records for the recordset. Before calling **Open**, you must construct the recordset object. There are several ways to do this:

- When you construct the recordset object, pass a pointer to a **CDaoDatabase** object that is already open.

- When you construct the recordset object, pass a pointer to a **CDaoDatabase** object that is not open. The recordset opens a **CDaoDatabase** object, but will not close it when the recordset object closes.

- When you construct the recordset object, pass a **NULL** pointer. The recordset object calls **GetDefaultDBName** to get the name of the Microsoft Access .MDB file to open. The recordset then opens a **CDaoDatabase** object and keeps it open as long as the recordset is open. When you call **Close** on the recordset, the **CDaoDatabase** object is also closed.

Note   When the recordset opens the **CDaoDatabase** object, it opens the data source with nonexclusive access.

For the version of **Open** that uses the *lpszSQL* parameter, once the recordset is open you can retrieve records in one of several ways. The first option is to have DFX functions in your **DoFieldExchange**. The second option is to use dynamic binding by calling the **GetFieldValue** member function. These options can be implemented separately or in combination. If they are combined, you will have to pass in the SQL statement yourself on the call to **Open**. For more information about dynamic binding, see the article "DAO Recordset: Binding Records Dynamically" in *Visual C++ Programmer's Guide* online.

When you use the second version of **Open** where you pass in a **CDaoTableDef** object, the resulting columns will be available for you to bind via **DoFieldExchange** and the DFX mechanism, and/or bind dynamically via **GetFieldValue**.

Note You can only call **Open** using a **CDaoTableDef** object for table-type recordsets.

When you use the third version of **Open** where you pass in a **CDaoQueryDef** object, that query will be executed, and the resulting columns will be available for you to bind via **DoFieldExchange** and the DFX mechanism, and/or bind dynamically via **GetFieldValue**.

Note You can only call **Open** using a **CDaoQueryDef** object for dynaset-type and snapshot-type recordsets.

For the first version of **Open** that uses the *lpszSQL* parameter, records are selected based on criteria shown in the following table.

Value of the *lpszSQL* parameter	Records selected are determined by	Example
NULL	The string returned by **GetDefaultSQL**.	
A comma-separated list of one or more tabledefs and/or querydef names.	All columns represented in the **DoFieldExchange**.	`"Customer"`
SELECT column-list **FROM** table-list	The specified columns from the specified tabledef(s) and/or querydef(s).	`"SELECT CustId, CustName FROM Customer"`

The usual procedure is to pass **NULL** to **Open**; in that case, **Open** calls **GetDefaultSQL**, an overridable member function that ClassWizard generates when creating a **CDaoRecordset**-derived class. This value gives the tabledef(s) and/or querydef name(s) you specified in ClassWizard. You can instead specify other information in the *lpszSQL* parameter.

Whatever you pass, **Open** constructs a final SQL string for the query (the string may have SQL **WHERE** and **ORDER BY** clauses appended to the *lpszSQL* string you passed) and then executes the query. You can examine the constructed string by calling **GetSQL** after calling **Open**.

The field data members of your recordset class are bound to the columns of the data selected. If any records are returned, the first record becomes the current record.

If you want to set options for the recordset, such as a filter or sort, set **m_strSort** or **m_strFilter** after you construct the recordset object but before you call **Open**. If you want to refresh the records in the recordset after the recordset is already open, call **Requery**.

If you call **Open** on a dynaset-type or snapshot-type recordset, or if the data source refers to an SQL statement or a tabledef that represents an attached table, you cannot use **dbOpenTable** for the type argument; if you do, MFC throws an exception. To determine whether a tabledef object represents an attached table, create a **CDaoTableDef** object and call its **GetConnect** member function.

Use the **dbSeeChanges** flag if you wish to trap changes made by another user or another program on your machine when you are editing or deleting the same record. For example, if two users start editing the same record, the first user to call the **Update** member function succeeds. When **Update** is called by the second user, a **CDaoException** is thrown. Similarly, if the second user tries to call **Delete** to delete the record, and it has already been changed by the first user, a **CDaoException** occurs.

Typically, if the user gets this **CDaoException** while updating, your code should refresh the contents of the fields and retrieve the newly modified values. If the exception occurs in the process of deleting, your code could display the new record data to the user and a message indicating that the data has recently changed. At this point, your code can request a confirmation that the user still wants to delete the record.

Tip Use the forward-only scrolling option (**dbForwardOnly**) to improve performance when your application makes a single pass through a recordset opened from an ODBC data source.

For more information about opening recordsets, see the articles "DAO Recordset: Creating Recordsets" and "DAO: Creating, Opening, and Closing DAO Objects" in *Visual C++ Programmer's Guide* online. For related information, see the topic "OpenRecordset Method" in DAO Help.

See Also: **CDaoRecordset::Close**, **CDaoRecordset::CDaoRecordset**

CDaoRecordset::Requery

virtual void Requery( );
    throw(CDaoException, CMemoryException);

Remarks

Call this member function to rebuild (refresh) a recordset. If any records are returned, the first record becomes the current record.

In order for the recordset to reflect the additions and deletions that you or other users are making to the data source, you must rebuild the recordset by calling **Requery**. If the recordset is a dynaset, it automatically reflects updates that you or other users make to its existing records (but not additions). If the recordset is a snapshot, you must call **Requery** to reflect edits by other users as well as additions and deletions.

For either a dynaset or a snapshot, call **Requery** any time you want to rebuild the recordset using parameter values. Set the new filter or sort by setting **m_strFilter** and **m_strSort** before calling **Requery**. Set new parameters by assigning new values to parameter data members before calling **Requery**.

If the attempt to rebuild the recordset fails, the recordset is closed. Before you call **Requery**, you can determine whether the recordset can be requeried by calling the **CanRestart** member function. **CanRestart** does not guarantee that **Requery** will succeed.

Caution Call **Requery** only after you have called **Open**.

You can't call **Requery** on a dynaset-type or snapshot-type recordset if calling **CanRestart** returns 0, nor can you use it on a table-type recordset.

If both **IsBOF** and **IsEOF** return nonzero after you call **Requery**, the query didn't return any records and the recordset will contain no data.

For more information about updating data, see the article "DAO Recordset: Recordset Operations" in *Visual C++ Programmer's Guide* online. For related information, see the topic "Requery Method" in DAO Help.

See Also: **CDaoRecordset::CanRestart**

CDaoRecordset::Seek

BOOL Seek(LPCTSTR *lpszComparison*, **COleVariant*** *pKey1*,
  ↪ **COleVariant*** *pKey2* = **NULL, COleVariant*** *pKey3* = **NULL**);
  throw(CDaoException, CMemoryException);
BOOL Seek (LPCTSTR *lpszComparison*, **COleVariant*** *pKeyArray*, **WORD** *nKeys*);
  throw(CDaoException, CMemoryException);

Return Value

Nonzero if matching records are found, otherwise 0.

Parameters

lpszComparison One of the following string expressions: "<", "<=", "=", ">=", or ">".

pKey1 A pointer to a **COleVariant** whose value corresponds to the first field in the index. Required.

pKey2 A pointer to a **COleVariant** whose value corresponds to the second field in the index, if any. Defaults to **NULL**.

pKey3 A pointer to a **COleVariant** whose value corresponds to the third field in the index, if any. Defaults to **NULL**.

pKeyArray A pointer to an array of variants. The array size corresponds to the number of fields in the index.

nKeys   An integer corresponding to the size of the array, which is the number of fields in the index.

Note   Do not specify wildcards in the keys. Wildcards will cause **Seek** to return no matching records.

Remarks

Call this member function to locate the record in an indexed table-type recordset object that satisfies the specified criteria for the current index and make that record the current record. Use the second (array) version of **Seek** to handle indexes of four fields or more.

Seek enables high-performance index searching on table-type recordsets. You must set the current index by calling **SetCurrentIndex** before calling **Seek**. If the index identifies a nonunique key field or fields, **Seek** locates the first record that satisfies the criteria. If you do not set an index, an exception is thrown.

Note that if you are not creating a UNICODE recordset, the **COleVariant** objects must be explicitly declared ANSI. This can be done by using the **COleVariant::COleVariant(** *lpszSrc*, *vtSrc* **)** form of constructor with *vtSrc* set to **VT_BSTRT** (ANSI) or by using the **COleVariant** function **SetString(** *lpszSrc*, *vtSrc* **)** with *vtSrc* set to **VT_BSTRT**.

When you call **Seek**, you pass one or more key values and a comparison operator ("<", "<=", "=", ">=", or ">"). **Seek** searches through the specified key fields and locates the first record that satisfies the criteria specified by *lpszComparison* and *pKey1*. Once found, **Seek** returns nonzero, and makes that record current. If **Seek** fails to locate a match, **Seek** returns zero, and the current record is undefined. When using DAO directly, you must explicitly check the NoMatch property.

If *lpszComparison* is "=", ">=", or ">", **Seek** starts at the beginning of the index. If *lpszComparison* is "<" or "<=", **Seek** starts at the end of the index and searches backward unless there are duplicate index entries at the end. In this case, **Seek** starts at an arbitrary entry among the duplicate index entries at the end of the index.

There does not have to be a current record when you use **Seek**.

To locate a record in a dynaset-type or snapshot-type recordset that satisfies a specific condition, use the Find operations. To include all records, not just those that satisfy a specific condition, use the Move operations to move from record to record.

You cannot call **Seek** on an attached table of any type because attached tables must be opened as dynaset-type or snapshot-type recordsets. However, if you call **CDaoDatabase::Open** to directly open an installable ISAM database, you can call **Seek** on tables in that database, although the performance may be slow.

For more information about finding records, see the article "DAO Recordset: Recordset Navigation" in *Visual C++ Programmer's Guide* online. For related information, see the topic "Seek Method" in DAO Help.

See Also: **CDaoRecordset::FindFirst**, **CDaoRecordset::FindLast**, **CDaoRecordset::FindNext**, **CDaoRecordset::FindPrev**, **CDaoRecordset::Move**, **CDaoRecordset::MoveFirst**, **CDaoRecordset::MoveLast**, **CDaoRecordset::MoveNext**, **CDaoRecordset::MovePrev**, **COleVariant::COleVariant**, **COleVariant::SetString**

CDaoRecordset::SetAbsolutePosition

void SetAbsolutePosition(long *lPosition* **);**
 throw(CDaoException, CMemoryException);

Parameters

 lPosition   Corresponds to the ordinal position of the current record in the recordset.

Remarks

 Sets the relative record number of a recordset object's current record. Calling **SetAbsolutePosition** enables you to position the current record pointer to a specific record based on its ordinal position in a dynaset-type or snapshot-type recordset. You can also determine the current record number by calling **GetAbsolutePosition**.

 Note   This member function is valid only for dynaset-type and snapshot-type recordsets.

 The AbsolutePosition property value of the underlying DAO object is zero-based; a setting of 0 refers to the first record in the recordset. Setting a value greater than the number of populated records causes MFC to throw an exception. You can determine the number of populated records in the recordset by calling the **GetRecordCount** member function.

 If the current record is deleted, the AbsolutePosition property value is not defined, and MFC throws an exception if it is referenced. New records are added to the end of the sequence.

 Note   This property is not intended to be used as a surrogate record number. Bookmarks are still the recommended way of retaining and returning to a given position and are the only way to position the current record across all types of recordset objects that support bookmarks. In particular, the position of a given record changes when record(s) preceding it are deleted. There is also no assurance that a given record will have the same absolute position if the recordset is re-created again because the order of individual records within a recordset is not guaranteed unless it is created with an SQL statement using an **ORDER BY** clause.

 For more information about finding records, see the article "DAO Recordset: Recordset Navigation" in *Visual C++ Programmer's Guide* online. For related information, see the topic "AbsolutePosition Property" in DAO Help.

 See Also: **CDaoRecordset::GetAbsolutePosition**

CDaoRecordset::SetBookmark

void SetBookmark(COleVariant *varBookmark* **);**
    throw(CDaoException, CMemoryException);

Parameters

    varBookmark   A **COleVariant** object containing the bookmark value for a specific
    record.

Remarks

    Call this member function to position the recordset on the record containing the
    specified bookmark. When a recordset object is created or opened, each of its records
    already has a unique bookmark. You can retrieve the bookmark for the current record
    by calling **GetBookmark** and saving the value to a **COleVariant** object. You can
    later return to that record by calling **SetBookmark** using the saved bookmark value.

    Note that if you are not creating a UNICODE recordset, the **COleVariant** object
    must be explicitly declared ANSI. This can be done by using the
    COleVariant::COleVariant(*lpszSrc*, *vtSrc* **)** form of constructor with *vtSrc* set
    to **VT_BSTRT** (ANSI) or by using the **COleVariant** function
    SetString(*lpszSrc*, *vtSrc* **)** with *vtSrc* set to **VT_BSTRT**.

    For more information about finding records, see the article "DAO Recordset:
    Recordset Navigation" in *Visual C++ Programmer's Guide* online. For related
    information, see the topics "Bookmark Property" and "Bookmarkable Property"
    in DAO Help.

    See Also: **CDaoRecordset::GetBookmark**

CDaoRecordset::SetCacheSize

void SetCacheSize(long *lSize* **);**
    throw(CDaoException, CMemoryException);

Parameters

    lSize   Specifies the number of records. A typical value is 100. A setting of 0 turns
    off caching. The setting must be between 5 and 1200 records. The cache may use
    a considerable amount of memory.

Remarks

    Call this member function to set the number of records to be cached. A cache is a
    space in local memory that holds the data most recently retrieved from the server
    in the event that the data will be requested again while the application is running.
    Data caching improves the performance of an application that retrieves data from a
    remote server through dynaset-type recordset objects. When data is requested, the

Microsoft Jet database engine checks the cache for the requested data first rather than retrieving it from the server, which takes more time. Data that does not come from an ODBC data source is not saved in the cache.

Any ODBC data source, such as an attached table, can have a local cache. To create the cache, open a recordset object from the remote data source, call the **SetCacheSize** and **SetCacheStart** member functions, and then call the **FillCache** member function or step through the records by using one of the Move operations. The *lSize* parameter of the **SetCacheSize** member function can be based on the number of records your application can work with at one time. For example, if you are using a recordset as the source of the data to be displayed on screen, you could pass the **SetCacheSize** *lSize* parameter as 20 to display 20 records at one time.

For more information about finding records, see the article "DAO Recordset: Recordset Navigation" in *Visual C++ Programmer's Guide* online. For related information, see the topic "CacheSize, CacheStart Properties" in DAO Help.

See Also: **CDaoRecordset::FillCache**, **CDaoRecordset::GetCacheSize**, **CDaoRecordset::GetCacheStart**, **CDaoRecordset::SetCacheStart**

CDaoRecordset::SetCacheStart

void SetCacheStart(COleVariant *varBookmark* **);**
    throw(CDaoException, CMemoryException);

Parameters

varBookmark   A **COleVariant** that specifies the bookmark of the first record in the recordset to be cached.

Remarks

Call this member function to specify the bookmark of the first record in the recordset to be cached. You can use the bookmark value of any record for the *varBookmark* parameter of the **SetCacheStart** member function. Make the record you want to start the cache with the current record, establish a bookmark for that record using **SetBookmark**, and pass the bookmark value as the parameter for the **SetCacheStart** member function.

The Microsoft Jet database engine requests records within the cache range from the cache, and it requests records outside the cache range from the server.

Records retrieved from the cache do not reflect changes made concurrently to the source data by other users.

To force an update of all the cached data, pass the *lSize* parameter of **SetCacheSize** as 0, call **SetCacheSize** again with the size of the cache you originally requested, and then call the **FillCache** member function.

Note that if you are not creating a UNICODE recordset, the **COleVariant** object must be explicitly declared ANSI. This can be done by using the **COleVariant::COleVariant(** *lpszSrc*, *vtSrc* **)** form of constructor with *vtSrc* set to **VT_BSTRT** (ANSI) or by using the **COleVariant** function **SetString(** *lpszSrc*, *vtSrc* **)** with *vtSrc* set to **VT_BSTRT**.

For more information about finding records, see the article "DAO Recordset: Recordset Navigation" in *Visual C++ Programmer's Guide* online. For related information, see the topic "CacheSize, CacheStart Properties" in DAO Help.

See Also: **CDaoRecordset::FillCache**, **CDaoRecordset::GetCacheSize**, **CDaoRecordset::GetCacheStart**, **CDaoRecordset::SetCacheSize**

CDaoRecordset::SetCurrentIndex

void SetCurrentIndex(LPCTSTR *lpszIndex* **);**
    throw(CDaoException, CMemoryException);

Parameters

lpszIndex   A pointer containing the name of the index to be set.

Remarks

Call this member function to set an index on a table-type recordset. Records in base tables are not stored in any particular order. Setting an index changes the order of records returned from the database, but it does not affect the order in which the records are stored. The specified index must already be defined. If you try to use an index object that does not exist, or if the index is not set when you call **Seek**, MFC throws an exception.

You can create a new index for the table by calling **CDaoTableDef::CreateIndex** and appending the new index to the Indexes collection of the underlying tabledef by calling **CDaoTableDef::Append**, and then reopening the recordset.

Records returned from a table-type recordset can be ordered only by the indexes defined for the underlying tabledef. To sort records in some other order, you can open a dynaset-type or snapshot-type recordset using an SQL **ORDER BY** clause stored in **CDaoRecordset::m_strSort**.

For more information about finding records, see the article "DAO Recordset: Recordset Navigation" in *Visual C++ Programmer's Guide* online. For related information, see the topic "Index Object" and the definition "current index" in DAO Help.

See Also: **CDaoRecordset::GetCurrentIndex**

CDaoRecordset::SetFieldDirty

void SetFieldDirty(void* *pv*, **BOOL** *bDirty* = **TRUE);**
    throw(CDaoException, CMemoryException);

Parameters

pv   Contains the address of a field data member in the recordset or **NULL**. If **NULL**, all field data members in the recordset are flagged. (C++ **NULL** is not the same as Null in database terminology, which means "having no value.")

bDirty   **TRUE** if the field data member is to be flagged as "dirty" (changed). Otherwise **FALSE** if the field data member is to be flagged as "clean" (unchanged).

Remarks

Call this member function to flag a field data member of the recordset as changed or as unchanged. Marking fields as unchanged ensures the field is not updated.

The framework marks changed field data members to ensure they will be written to the record on the data source by the DAO record field exchange (DFX) mechanism. Changing the value of a field generally sets the field dirty automatically, so you will seldom need to call **SetFieldDirty** yourself, but you might sometimes want to ensure that columns will be explicitly updated or inserted regardless of what value is in the field data member. The DFX mechanism also employs the use of **PSEUDO NULL**. For more information, see **CDaoFieldExchange::m_nOperation**.

If the double-buffering mechanism is not being used, then changing the value of the field does not automatically set the field as dirty. In this case, it will be necessary to explicity set the field as dirty. The flag contained in **m_bCheckCacheForDirtyFields** controls this automatic field checking.

Important Call this member function only after you have called **Edit** or **AddNew**.

Using **NULL** for the first argument of the function will apply the function to all **outputColumns**, not **params** in **CDaoFieldExchange**. For instance, the call

```
SetFieldDirty( NULL );
```

will set only **outputColumns** to **NULL**. The value of **param** will be unaffected.

To work on a **param**, you must supply the actual address of the individual **param** you want to work on, such as:

```
SetFieldDirty( &m_strParam );
```

This means you cannot set all **params NULL**, as you can with **outputColumns**.

SetFieldDirty is implemented through **DoFieldExchange**.

For more information about record field exchange, see the articles "DAO Record Field Exchange (DFX)" and "DAO Recordset: Binding Records Dynamically" in *Visual C++ Programmer's Guide* online.

See Also: **CDaoRecordset::SetFieldNull**, **CDaoRecordset::SetFieldValue**

CDaoRecordset::SetFieldNull

void SetFieldNull(void* *pv*, **BOOL** *bNull* = **TRUE**);
    throw(CDaoException, CMemoryException);

Parameters

pv Contains the address of a field data member in the recordset or **NULL**. If **NULL**, all field data members in the recordset are flagged. (C++ **NULL** is not the same as Null in database terminology, which means "having no value.")

bNull Nonzero if the field data member is to be flagged as having no value (Null). Otherwise 0 if the field data member is to be flagged as non-Null.

Remarks

Call this member function to flag a field data member of the recordset as Null (specifically having no value) or as non-Null. The first version of **SetFieldNull** is used for fields bound in the **DoFieldExchange** mechanism. If you choose to bind your fields dynamically, you must use either the second or third version of this member function. You can mix the calls as necessary.

When you add a new record to a recordset, all field data members are initially set to a Null value and flagged as "dirty" (changed). When you retrieve a record from a data source, its columns either already have values or are Null. If it is not appropriate to make a field Null, a **CDaoException** is thrown.

If you are using the double-buffering mechanism, for example, if you specifically wish to designate a field of the current record as not having a value, call **SetFieldNull** with *bNull* set to **TRUE** to flag it as Null. If a field was previously marked Null and you now want to give it a value, simply set its new value. You do not have to remove the Null flag with **SetFieldNull**. To determine whether the field is allowed to be Null, call **IsFieldNullable**.

If you are not using the double-buffering mechanism, then changing the value of the field does not automatically set the field as dirty and non-Null. You must specifically set the fields dirty and non-Null. The flag contained in **m_bCheckCacheForDirtyFields** controls this automatic field checking.

The DFX mechanism employs the use of **PSEUDO NULL**. For more information, see **CDaoFieldExchange::m_nOperation**.

Important Call this member function only after you have called **Edit** or **AddNew**.

Using **NULL** for the first argument of the function will apply the function only to **outputColumns**, not **params** in **CDaoFieldExchange**. For instance, the call

```
SetFieldNull( NULL );
```

will set only **outputColumns** to **NULL**. The value of **param** will be unaffected.

For more information about record field exchange, see the articles "DAO Record Field Exchange (DFX)" and "DAO Recordset: Binding Records Dynamically" in *Visual C++ Programmer's Guide* online.

See Also: CDaoRecordset::SetParamValue

CDaoRecordset::SetFieldValue

void SetFieldValue(LPCTSTR *lpszName*, **const COleVariant&** *varValue* **);**
  throw(CDaoException, CMemoryException);
void SetFieldValue(int *nOrdinal*, **const COleVariant&** *varValue* **);**
  throw(CDaoException, CMemoryException);
void SetFieldValue(LPCTSTR *lpszName*, **LPCTSTR** *lpszValue* **);**
void SetFieldValue(int *nOrdinal*, **LPCTSTR** *lpszValue* **);**

Parameters

lpszName   A pointer to a string containing the name of a field.

varValue   A reference to a **COleVariant** object containing the value of the field's contents.

nOrdinal   An integer that represents the ordinal position of the field in the recordset's Fields collection (zero-based).

lpszValue   A pointer to a string containing the value of the field's contents.

Remarks

Call this member function to set the value of a field, either by ordinal position or by changing the value of the string. Use **SetFieldValue** and **GetFieldValue** to dynamically bind fields at run time rather than statically binding columns using the **DoFieldExchange** mechanism.

Note that if you are not creating a UNICODE recordset, you must either use a form of **SetFieldValue** that does not contain a **COleVariant** parameter (one of the last two syntax forms), or the **COleVariant** object must be explicitly declared ANSI. This can be done by using the **COleVariant::COleVariant(** *lpszSrc*, *vtSrc* **)** form of constructor with *vtSrc* set to **VT_BSTRT** (ANSI) or by using the **COleVariant** function **SetString(** *lpszSrc*, *vtSrc* **)** with *vtSrc* set to **VT_BSTRT**.

For more information about record field exchange, see the articles "DAO Record Field Exchange (DFX)" and "DAO Recordset: Binding Records Dynamically" in *Visual C++ Programmer's Guide* online. For related information, see the topics "Field Object" and "Value Property" in DAO Help.

See Also: CDaoRecordset::GetFieldValue, CDaoRecordset::m_nParams, CDaoRecordset::SetFieldValueNull, COleVariant::COleVariant, COleVariant::SetString

CDaoRecordset::SetFieldValueNull

void SetFieldValueNull(short *nIndex* **);**
    throw(CDaoException, CMemoryException);
void SetFieldValueNull(LPCTSTR *lpszName* **);**
    throw(CDaoException, CMemoryException);

Parameters

nIndex   The index of the field in the recordset, for lookup by zero-based index.

lpszName   The name of the field in the recordset, for lookup by name.

Remarks

Call this member function to set the field to a Null value. C++ **NULL** is not the same as Null, which, in database terminology, means "having no value."

For more information about record field exchange, see the articles "DAO Record Field Exchange (DFX)" and "DAO Recordset: Binding Records Dynamically" in *Visual C++ Programmer's Guide* online. For related information, see the topics "Field Object" and "Value Property" in DAO Help.

See Also: CDaoRecordset::SetFieldValue

CDaoRecordset::SetLockingMode

void SetLockingMode(BOOL *bPessimistic* **);**
    throw(CDaoException, CMemoryException);

Parameters

bPessimistic   A flag that indicates the type of locking.

Remarks

Call this member function to set the type of locking for the recordset. When pessimistic locking is in effect, the 2K page containing the record you are editing is locked as soon as you call the **Edit** member function. The page is unlocked when you call the **Update** or **Close** member function or any of the Move or Find operations.

When optimistic locking is in effect, the 2K page containing the record is locked only while the record is being updated with the **Update** member function.

If a page is locked, no other user can edit records on the same page. If you call **SetLockingMode** and pass a nonzero value and another user already has the page locked, an exception is thrown when you call **Edit**. Other users can read data from locked pages.

If you call **SetLockingMode** with a zero value and later call **Update** while the page is locked by another user, an exception occurs. To see the changes made to your record by another user (and lose your changes), call the **SetBookmark** member function with the bookmark value of the current record.

When working with ODBC data sources, the locking mode is always optimistic.

For more information about updating data, see the article "DAO Recordset: Recordset Operations" in *Visual C++ Programmer's Guide* online. For related information, see the topics "LockEdits Property," "EditMode Property," and "Locking Behavior in Multiuser Applications" in DAO Help.

See Also: **CDaoRecordset::GetLockingMode**

CDaoRecordset::SetParamValue

virtual void SetParamValue(int *nIndex*, **const COleVariant&** *var* **);**
    throw(CDaoException, CMemoryException);
virtual void SetParamValue(LPCTSTR *lpszName*, **const COleVariant&** *var* **);**
    throw(CDaoException, CMemoryException);

Parameters

nIndex The numerical position of the parameter in the querydef's Parameters collection.

var The value to set; see Remarks.

lpszName The name of the parameter whose value you want to set.

Remarks

Call this member function to set the value of a parameter in the recordset at run time. The parameter must already have been established as part of the recordset's SQL string. You can access the parameter either by name or by its index position in the collection.

Specify the value to set as a **COleVariant** object. For information about setting the desired value and type in your **COleVariant** object, see class **COleVariant**. Note that if you are not creating a UNICODE recordset, the **COleVariant** object must be explicitly declared ANSI. This can be done by using the **COleVariant::COleVariant** (*lpszSrc*, *vtSrc*) form of constructor with *vtSrc* set to **VT_BSTRT** (ANSI) or by using the **COleVariant** function **SetString**(*lpszSrc*, *vtSrc*) with *vtSrc* set to **VT_BSTRT**.

For more information about updating data, see the article "DAO Recordset: Recordset Operations" in *Visual C++ Programmer's Guide* online. For related information, see the topic "Parameter Object" in DAO Help.

See Also: **CDaoRecordset::GetParamValue, CDaoRecordset::m_nParams, CDaoRecordset::SetParamValueNull**

CDaoRecordset::SetParamValueNull

void SetParamValueNull(short *nIndex* **);**
   throw(CDaoException, CMemoryException);
void SetParamValueNull(LPCTSTR *lpszName* **);**
   throw(CDaoException, CMemoryException);

Parameters

nIndex   The index of the field in the recordset, for lookup by zero-based index.

lpszName   The name of the field in the recordset, for lookup by name.

Remarks

Call this member function to set the parameter to a Null value. C++ **NULL** is not the same as Null, which, in database terminology, means "having no value."

For more information about updating data, see the article "DAO Recordset: Recordset Operations" in *Visual C++ Programmer's Guide* online. For related information, see the topic "Parameter Object" in DAO Help.

CDaoRecordset::SetPercentPosition

void SetPercentPosition(float *fPosition* **);**
   throw(CDaoException, CMemoryException);

Parameters

fPosition   A number between 0 and 100.

Remarks

Call this member function to set a value that changes the approximate location of the current record in the recordset object based on a percentage of the records in the recordset.

When working with a dynaset-type or snapshot-type recordset, first populate the recordset by moving to the last record before you call **SetPercentPosition**. If you call **SetPercentPosition** before fully populating the recordset, the amount of movement is relative to the number of records accessed as indicated by the value of **GetRecordCount**. You can move to the last record by calling **MoveLast**.

Once you call **SetPercentPosition**, the record at the approximate position corresponding to that value becomes current.

Note Calling **SetPercentPosition** to move the current record to a specific record in a recordset is not recommended. Call the **SetBookmark** member function instead.

For more information about navigating in recordsets, see the article "DAO Recordset: Recordset Navigation" in *Visual C++ Programmer's Guide* online. For related information, see the topic "PercentPosition Property" in DAO Help.

See Also: **CDaoRecordset::GetPercentPosition**

CDaoRecordset::Update

virtual void Update( );
    throw(CDaoException, CMemoryException);

Remarks

Call this member function after a call to the **AddNew** or **Edit** member function. This call is required to complete the **AddNew** or **Edit** operation.

Both **AddNew** and **Edit** prepare an edit buffer in which the added or edited data is placed for saving to the data source. **Update** saves the data. Only those fields marked or detected as changed are updated.

If the data source supports transactions, you can make the **Update** call (and its corresponding **AddNew** or **Edit** call) part of a transaction. For more information about transactions, see the article "DAO Workspace: Managing Transactions" in *Visual C++ Programmer's Guide* online.

Caution   If you call **Update** without first calling either **AddNew** or **Edit**, **Update** throws a **CDaoException**. If you call **AddNew** or **Edit**, you must call **Update** before you call **MoveNext** or close either the recordset or the data source connection. Otherwise, your changes are lost without notification.

When the recordset object is pessimistically locked in a multiuser environment, the record remains locked from the time **Edit** is used until the updating is complete. If the recordset is optimistically locked, the record is locked and compared with the pre-edited record just before it is updated in the database. If the record has changed since you called **Edit**, the **Update** operation fails and MFC throws an exception. You can change the locking mode with **SetLockingMode**.

Note   Optimistic locking is always used on external database formats, such as ODBC and installable ISAM.

For more information about updating data, see the article "DAO Recordset: Recordset Operations" in *Visual C++ Programmer's Guide* online. For related information, see the topics "AddNew Method," "CancelUpdate Method," "Delete Method," "LastModified Property," "Update Method," and "EditMode Property" in DAO Help.

See Also: **CDaoRecordset::AddNew, CDaoRecordset::CancelUpdate, CDaoRecordset::Delete, CDaoRecordset::Edit, CDaoRecordset::CanTransact**

Data Members
CDaoRecordset::m_bCheckCacheForDirtyFields

Remarks

Contains a flag indicating whether cached fields are automatically marked as dirty (changed) and Null. The flag defaults to **TRUE**. The setting in this data member controls the entire double-buffering mechanism. If you set the flag to **TRUE**, you can turn off the caching on a field-by-field basis using the DFX mechanism. If you set the flag to **FALSE**, you must call **SetFieldDirty** and **SetFieldNull** yourself.

Set this data member before calling **Open**. This mechanism is primarily for ease-of-use. Performance may be slower because of the double-buffering of fields as changes are made.

For more information about binding records dynamically, see the article "DAO Recordset: Binding Records Dynamically" in *Visual C++ Programmer's Guide* online.

See Also: **CDaoRecordset::SetFieldNull**, **CDaoRecordset::IsFieldNull**, **CDaoRecordset::IsFieldDirty**, **CDaoRecordset::SetFieldDirty**

CDaoRecordset::m_nFields

Remarks

Contains the number of field data members in the recordset class and the number of columns selected by the recordset from the data source. The constructor for the recordset class must initialize **m_nFields** with the correct number of statically bound fields. ClassWizard writes this initialization for you when you use it to declare your recordset class. You can also write it manually.

The framework uses this number to manage interaction between the field data members and the corresponding columns of the current record on the data source.

Note   This number must correspond to the number of output columns registered in **DoFieldExchange** after a call to **SetFieldType** with the parameter **CDaoFieldExchange::outputColumn**.

You can bind columns dynamically by way of **CDaoRecordset::GetFieldValue** and **CDaoRecordset::SetFieldValue**, as explained in the article "DAO Recordset: Binding Records Dynamically." If you do so, you do not need to increment the count in **m_nFields** to reflect the number of DFX function calls in your **DoFieldExchange** member function.

For more information, see the article "DAO Record Field Exchange (DFX)" in *Visual C++ Programmer's Guide* online.

See Also: CDaoRecordset::SetFieldValue, CDaoRecordset::GetFieldValue

CDaoRecordset::m_nParams

Remarks

Contains the number of parameter data members in the recordset class — the number of parameters passed with the recordset's query. If your recordset class has any parameter data members, the constructor for the class must initialize **m_nParams** with the correct number. The value of **m_nParams** defaults to 0. If you add parameter data members — which you must do manually — you must also manually add an initialization in the class constructor to reflect the number of parameters (which must be at least as large as the number of '?' placeholders in your **m_strFilter** or **m_strSort** string).

The framework uses this number when it parameterizes the recordset's query.

Important   This number must correspond to the number of "params" registered in **DoFieldExchange** after a call to **SetFieldType** with the parameter **CFieldExchange::param**.

For more information about selecting records, see the article "DAO Queries: Filtering and Parameterizing Queries" in *Visual C++ Programmer's Guide* online. For related information, see the topic "Parameter Object" in DAO Help.

CDaoRecordset::m_pDAORecordset

Remarks

Contains a pointer to the OLE interface for the DAO recordset object underlying the **CDaoRecordset** object. Use this pointer if you need to access the DAO interface directly.

For more information about accessing underlying DAO objects, see the article "DAO Collections: Obtaining Information About DAO Objects" in *Visual C++ Programmer's Guide* online. For related information, see the topic "Recordset Object" in DAO Help.

See Also: CDaoRecordset::m_pDatabase

CDaoRecordset::m_pDatabase

Remarks

Contains a pointer to the **CDaoDatabase** object through which the recordset is connected to a data source. This variable is set in two ways. Typically, you pass a pointer to an already open **CDaoDatabase** object when you construct the recordset object. If you pass **NULL** instead, **CDaoRecordset** creates a **CDaoDatabase** object for you and opens it. In either case, **CDaoRecordset** stores the pointer in this variable.

Normally you will not directly need to use the pointer stored in **m_pDatabase**. If you write your own extensions to **CDaoRecordset**, however, you might need to use the pointer. For example, you might need the pointer if you throw your own **CDaoException**(s).

For more information about accessing underlying DAO objects, see the article "DAO Collections: Obtaining Information About DAO Objects" in *Visual C++ Programmer's Guide* online. For related information, see the topic "Database Object" in DAO Help.

See Also: **CDaoRecordset::m_pDAORecordset**

CDaoRecordset::m_strFilter

Remarks

Contains a string that is used to construct the **WHERE** clause of an SQL statement. It does not include the reserved word **WHERE** to filter the recordset. The use of this data member is not applicable to table-type recordsets. The use of **m_strFilter** has no effect when opening a recordset using a **CDaoQueryDef** pointer.

Use the U.S. date format (month-day-year) when you filter fields containing dates, even if you are not using the U.S. version of the Microsoft Jet database engine; otherwise, the data may not be filtered as you expect.

For more information about selecting records, see the article "DAO Queries: Filtering and Parameterizing Queries" in *Visual C++ Programmer's Guide* online. For related information, see the topic "Filter Property" in DAO Help.

See Also: **CDaoRecordset::m_strSort**

CDaoRecordset::m_strSort

Remarks

Contains a string containing the **ORDER BY** clause of an SQL statement without the reserved words **ORDER BY**. You can sort on dynaset- and snapshot-type recordset objects.

You cannot sort table-type recordset objects. To determine the sort order of a table-type recordset, call **SetCurrentIndex**.

The use of **m_strSort** has no effect when opening a recordset using a **CDaoQueryDef** pointer.

For more information about selecting records, see the article "DAO Queries: Filtering and Parameterizing Queries" in *Visual C++ Programmer's Guide* online. For related information, see the topic "Sort Property" in DAO Help.

See Also: **CDaoRecordset::m_strFilter**

CDaoRecordView

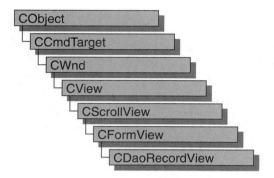

A **CDaoRecordView** object is a view that displays database records in controls. The view is a form view directly connected to a **CDaoRecordset** object. The view is created from a dialog template resource and displays the fields of the **CDaoRecordset** object in the dialog template's controls. The **CDaoRecordView** object uses dialog data exchange (DDX) and DAO record field exchange (DFX) to automate the movement of data between the controls on the form and the fields of the recordset. **CDaoRecordView** also supplies a default implementation for moving to the first, next, previous, or last record and an interface for updating the record currently in view.

Note The DAO database classes are distinct from the MFC database classes based on Open Database Connectivity (ODBC). All DAO database class names have the "CDao" prefix. You can still access ODBC data sources with the DAO classes; the DAO classes generally offer superior capabilities because they use the Microsoft Jet database engine.

The most common way to create your record view is with AppWizard. AppWizard creates both the record view class and its associated recordset class as part of your skeleton starter application.

If you simply need a single form, the AppWizard approach is easier. ClassWizard lets you decide to use a record view later in the development process. If you don't create the record view class with AppWizard, you can create it later with ClassWizard. Using ClassWizard to create a record view and a recordset separately and then connect them is the most flexible approach because it gives you more control in naming the recordset class and its .H/.CPP files. This approach also lets you have multiple record views on the same recordset class.

To make it easy for end-users to move from record to record in the record view, AppWizard creates menu (and optionally toolbar) resources for moving to the first, next, previous, or last record. If you create a record view class with ClassWizard, you need to create these resources yourself with the menu and bitmap editors. For more information about these resources, see "Overview: Creating a Program That Supports a Database" and "ClassWizard: Creating a Database Form."

For information about the default implementation for moving from record to record, see **IsOnFirstRecord** and **IsOnLastRecord** and the article "Record Views: Using a Record View," which applies to both **CRecordView** and **CDaoRecordView**.

CDaoRecordView keeps track of the user's position in the recordset so that the record view can update the user interface. When the user moves to either end of the recordset, the record view disables user interface objects—such as menu items or toolbar buttons—for moving further in the same direction.

For more information about declaring and using your record view and recordset classes, see "Designing and Creating a Record View" in the article "Record Views." For more information about how record views work and how to use them, see the article "Record Views: Using a Record View." All the articles mentioned above apply to both **CRecordView** and **CDaoRecordView** and are found in *Visual C++ Programmer's Guide* online.

#include <afxdao.h>

See Also: CDaoRecordset, CDaoTableDef, CDaoQueryDef, CDaoDatabase, CDaoWorkspace, CFormView

CDaoRecordView Class Members

Construction

CDaoRecordView	Constructs a **CDaoRecordView** object.

Attributes

OnGetRecordset	Returns a pointer to an object of a class derived from **CDaoRecordset**. ClassWizard overrides this function for you and creates the recordset if necessary.
IsOnLastRecord	Returns nonzero if the current record is the last record in the associated recordset.
IsOnFirstRecord	Returns nonzero if the current record is the first record in the associated recordset.

Operations

OnMove	If the current record has changed, updates it on the data source, then moves to the specified record (next, previous, first, or last).

Member Functions
CDaoRecordView::CDaoRecordView

CDaoRecordView(LPCSTR *lpszTemplateName*);
CDaoRecordView(UINT *nIDTemplate*);

Parameters

lpszTemplateName   Contains a null-terminated string that is the name of a dialog template resource.

nIDTemplate   Contains the ID number of a dialog template resource.

Remarks

When you create an object of a type derived from **CDaoRecordView**, call either form of the constructor to initialize the view object and identify the dialog resource on which the view is based. You can either identify the resource by name (pass a string as the argument to the constructor) or by its ID (pass an unsigned integer as the argument). Using a resource ID is recommended.

Note   Your derived class must supply its own constructor. In the constructor of your derived class, call the constructor **CDaoRecordView::CDaoRecordView** with the resource name or ID as an argument.

CDaoRecordView::OnInitialUpdate calls **CWnd::UpdateData**, which calls **CWnd::DoDataExchange**. This initial call to **DoDataExchange** connects **CDaoRecordView** controls (indirectly) to **CDaoRecordset** field data members created by ClassWizard. These data members cannot be used until after you call the base class **CFormView::OnInitialUpdate** member function.

Note   If you use ClassWizard, the wizard defines an **enum** value CDaoRecordView::IDD and specifies it in the member initialization list for the constructor where you see IDD_MYFORM.

```
CMyRecordView::CMyRecordView()

    : CDaoRecordView( IDD_MYFORM )
{
    //{{AFX_DATA_INIT( CMyRecordView )
        // NOTE: the ClassWizard will add member initialization here
    //}}AFX_DATA_INIT
    // Other construction code, such as data initialization
}
```

See Also: **CWnd::UpdateData**, **CWnd::DoDataExchange**

CDaoRecordView::IsOnFirstRecord

BOOL IsOnFirstRecord( );

Return Value

Nonzero if the current record is the first record in the recordset; otherwise 0.

Remarks

Call this member function to determine whether the current record is the first record in the recordset object associated with this record view. This function is useful for writing your own implementations of the default command update handlers written by ClassWizard.

If the user moves to the first record, the framework disables any user interface objects (for example, menu items or toolbar buttons) you have for moving to the first or the previous record.

See Also: **CDaoRecordView::IsOnLastRecord**

CDaoRecordView::IsOnLastRecord

BOOL IsOnLastRecord( );

Return Value

Nonzero if the current record is the last record in the recordset; otherwise 0.

Remarks

Call this member function to determine whether the current record is the last record in the recordset object associated with this record view. This function is useful for writing your own implementations of the default command update handlers that ClassWizard writes to support a user interface for moving from record to record.

Caution The result of this function is reliable except that the view may not be able to detect the end of the recordset until the user has moved past it. The user might have to move beyond the last record before the record view can tell that it must disable any user interface objects for moving to the next or last record. If the user moves past the last record and then moves back to the last record (or before it), the record view can track the user's position in the recordset and disable user interface objects correctly.

See Also: **CDaoRecordView::IsOnFirstRecord**

CDaoRecordView::OnGetRecordset

virtual CDaoRecordset* OnGetRecordset( ) = 0;

Return Value

A pointer to a **CDaoRecordset**-derived object if the object was successfully created; otherwise a **NULL** pointer.

Remarks

Returns a pointer to the **CDaoRecordset**-derived object associated with the record view. You must override this member function to construct or obtain a recordset object and return a pointer to it. If you declare your record view class with ClassWizard, the wizard writes a default override for you. ClassWizard's default implementation returns the recordset pointer stored in the record view if one exists. If not, it constructs a recordset object of the type you specified with ClassWizard and calls its **Open** member function to open the table or run the query, and then returns a pointer to the object.

For more information and examples, see the article "Record Views: Using a Record View" in *Visual C++ Programmer's Guide* online.

See Also: **CDaoRecordset**, **CDaoRecordset::Open**

CDaoRecordView::OnMove

virtual BOOL OnMove(UINT *nIDMoveCommand*);

Return Value

Nonzero if the move was successful; otherwise 0 if the move request was denied.

Parameters

nIDMoveCommand One of the following standard command ID values:

- **ID_RECORD_FIRST** Move to the first record in the recordset.
- **ID_RECORD_LAST** Move to the last record in the recordset.
- **ID_RECORD_NEXT** Move to the next record in the recordset.
- **ID_RECORD_PREV** Move to the previous record in the recordset.

Remarks

Call this member function to move to a different record in the recordset and display its fields in the controls of the record view. The default implementation calls the appropriate Move member function of the **CDaoRecordset** object associated with the record view.

By default, **OnMove** updates the current record on the data source if the user has changed it in the record view.

AppWizard creates a menu resource with First Record, Last Record, Next Record, and Previous Record menu items. If you select the Initial Toolbar option, AppWizard also creates a toolbar with buttons corresponding to these commands.

If you move past the last record in the recordset, the record view continues to display the last record. If you move backward past the first record, the record view continues to display the first record.

Caution Calling **OnMove** throws an exception if the recordset has no records. Call the appropriate user interface update handler function—**OnUpdateRecordFirst**, **OnUpdateRecordLast**, **OnUpdateRecordNext**, or **OnUpdateRecordPrev**—before the corresponding move operation to determine whether the recordset has any records. For information about the update handlers, see "Overview: Creating a Program That Supports a Database" in *Visual C++ Programmer's Guide* online.

See Also: **CDaoRecordset::Move**

CDaoTableDef

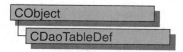

A **CDaoTableDef** object represents the stored definition of a base table or an attached table. Each DAO database object maintains a collection, called TableDefs, that contains all saved DAO tabledef objects.

You manipulate a table definition using a **CDaoTableDef** object. For example, you can:

- Examine the field and index structure of any local, attached, or external table in a database.

- Call the **SetConnect** and **SetSourceTableName** member functions for attached tables, and use the **RefreshLink** member function to update connections to attached tables.

- Call the **CanUpdate** member function to determine if you can edit field definitions in the table.

- Get or set validation conditions using the **GetValidationRule** and **SetValidationRule**, and the **GetValidationText** and **SetValidationText** member functions.

- Use the **Open** member function to create a table-, dynaset-, or snapshot-type **CDaoRecordset** object.

Note The DAO database classes are distinct from the MFC database classes based on Open Database Connectivity (ODBC). All DAO database class names have the "CDao" prefix. You can still access ODBC data sources with the DAO classes; the DAO classes generally offer superior capabilities because they are specific to the Microsoft Jet database engine.

Use tabledef objects either to work with an existing table or to create a new table:

1. In all cases, first construct a **CDaoTableDef** object, supplying the a pointer to a **CDaoDatabase** object to which the table belongs.

2. Then do the following, depending on what you want:

   - To use an existing saved table, call the tabledef object's **Open** member function, supplying the name of the saved table.

   - To create a new table, call the tabledef object's **Create** member function, supplying the name of the table. Call **CreateField** and **CreateIndex** to add fields and indexes to the table.

- Call **Append** to save the table by appending it to the database's TableDefs collection. **Create** puts the tabledef into an open state, so after calling **Create** you do not call **Open**.

Tip The easiest way to create saved tables is to create them and store them in your database using Microsoft Access. Then you can open and use them in your MFC code.

To use the tabledef object you have opened or created, create and open a **CDaoRecordset** object, specifying the name of the tabledef with a **dbOpenTable** value in the *nOpenType* parameter.

To use a tabledef object to create a **CDaoRecordset** object, you typically create or open a tabledef as described above, then construct a recordset object, passing a pointer to your tabledef object when you call **CDaoRecordset::Open**. The tabledef you pass must be in an open state. For more information, see class **CDaoRecordset**.

When you finish using a tabledef object, call its **Close** member function; then destroy the tabledef object.

For more information on tabledefs, see the articles "DAO Tabledef" and "DAO Tabledef: Using Tabledefs" in *Visual C++ Programmer's Guide* online.

#include <afxdao.h>

See Also: **CDaoDatabase**, **CDaoRecordset**

CDaoTableDef Class Members

Data Members

m_pDatabase	Source database for this table.
m_pDAOTableDef	A pointer to the DAO interface underlying the tabledef object.

Construction

Append	Adds a new table to the database.
CdaoTableDef	Constructs a **CDaoTableDef** object.
Close	Closes an open tabledef.
Create	Creates a table which can be added to the database using **Append**.
Open	Opens an existing tabledef stored in the database's TableDef's collection.

Attributes

CanUpdate	Returns nonzero if the table can be updated (you can modify the definition of fields or the table properties).
GetAttributes	Returns a value that indicates one or more characteristics of a **CDaoTableDef** object.

(continued)

Attributes *(continued)*

GetConnect	Returns a value that provides information about the source of a table.
GetDateCreated	Returns the date and time the base table underlying a **CDaoTableDef** object was created.
GetDateLastUpdated	Returns the date and time of the most recent change made to the design of the base table.
GetFieldCount	Returns a value that represents the number of fields in the table.
GetFieldInfo	Returns specific kinds of information about the fields in the table.
GetIndexCount	Returns the number of indexes for the table.
GetIndexInfo	Returns specific kinds of information about the indexes for the table.
GetName	Returns the user-defined name of the table.
GetRecordCount	Returns the number of records in the table.
GetSourceTableName	Returns a value that specifies the name of the attached table in the source database.
GetValidationRule	Returns a value that validates the data in a field as it is changed or added to a table.
GetValidationText	Returns a value that specifies the text of the message that your application displays if the value of a Field object does not satisfy the specified validation rule.
IsOpen	Returns nonzero if the table is open.
SetAttributes	Sets a value that indicates one or more characteristics of a **CDaoTableDef** object.
SetConnect	Sets a value that provides information about the source of a table.
SetName	Sets the name of the table.
SetSourceTableName	Sets a value that specifies the name of an attached table in the source database.
SetValidationRule	Sets a value that validates the data in a field as it is changed or added to a table.
SetValidationText	Sets a value that specifies the text of the message that your application displays if the value of a Field object does not satisfy the specified validation rule.

Operations

CreateField	Called to create a field for a table.
CreateIndex	Called to create an index for a table.
DeleteField	Called to delete a field from a table.
DeleteIndex	Called to delete an index from a table.
RefreshLink	Updates the connection information for an attached table.

Member Functions

CDaoTableDef::Append

virtual void Append( );
    throw(CDaoException, CMemoryException);

Remarks

Call this member function after you call **Create** to create a new tabledef object to save the tabledef in the database. The function appends the object to the database's TableDefs collection. You can use the tabledef as a temporary object while defining it by not appending it, but if you want to save and use it, you must call **Append**.

Note   If you attempt to append an unnamed tabledef (containing a null or empty string), MFC throws an exception.

For more information on tabledefs, see the articles "DAO Tabledef" and "DAO Tabledef: Using Tabledefs" in *Visual C++ Programmer's Guide* online. For related information, see the topic "Append Method" in DAO Help.

See Also: **CDaoTableDef::Create**

CDaoTableDef::CanUpdate

BOOL CanUpdate( );
    throw(CDaoException, CMemoryException);

Return Value

Nonzero if the table structure (schema) can be modified (add or delete fields and indexes), otherwise 0.

Remarks

Call this member function to determine whether the definition of the table underlying a **CDaoTableDef** object can be changed.

By default, a newly created table underlying a **CDaoTableDef** object can be updated, and an attached table underlying a **CDaoTableDef** object cannot be updated. A **CDaoTableDef** object may be updatable, even if the resulting recordset is not updatable.

For more information on tabledefs, see the articles "DAO Tabledef" and "DAO Tabledef: Using Tabledefs" in *Visual C++ Programmer's Guide* online. For related information, see the topic "Updatable Property" in DAO Help.

See Also: **CDaoTableDef::GetDateLastUpdated**

CDaoTableDef::CDaoTableDef

CDaoTableDef(CDaoDatabase* *pDatabase* **);**

Parameters

pDatabase   A pointer to a **CDaoDatabase** object.

Remarks

Constructs a **CDaoTableDef** object. After constructing the object, you must call the **Create** or **Open** member function. When you finish with the object, you must call its **Close** member function and destroy the **CDaoTableDef** object.

For more information on tabledefs, see the articles "DAO Tabledef" and "DAO Tabledef: Using Tabledefs" in *Visual C++ Programmer's Guide* online.

See Also: **CDaoTableDef::Open, CDaoTableDef::Close, CDaoTableDef::Create, CDaoDatabase**

CDaoTableDef::Close

virtual void Close( );
  throw(CDaoException, CMemoryException);

Remarks

Call this member function to close and release the tabledef object. Usually after calling **Close**, you delete the tabledef object if it was allocated with **new**.

You can call **Open** again after calling **Close**. This lets you reuse the tabledef object.

For more information on tabledefs, see the articles "DAO Tabledef" and "DAO Tabledef: Using Tabledefs" in *Visual C++ Programmer's Guide* online. For related information, see the topic "Close Method" in DAO Help.

See Also: **CDaoTableDef::Open, CDaoTableDef::Create**

CDaoTableDef::Create

virtual void Create(LPCTSTR *lpszName*, **long** *lAttributes* = **0,**
  ↪ **LPCTSTR** *lpszSrcTable* = **NULL, LPCTSTR** *lpszConnect* = **NULL);**
  throw(CDaoException, CMemoryException);

Parameters

lpszName   A pointer to a string containing the name of the table.

lAttributes   A value corresponding to characteristics of the table represented by the tabledef object. You can use the bitwise-OR to combine any of the following constants:

Constant	Description
dbAttachExclusive	For databases that use the Microsoft Jet database engine, indicates the table is an attached table opened for exclusive use.
dbAttachSavePWD	For databases that use the Microsoft Jet database engine, indicates that the user ID and password for the attached table are saved with the connection information.
dbSystemObject	Indicates the table is a system table provided by the Microsoft Jet database engine.
dbHiddenObject	Indicates the table is a hidden table provided by the Microsoft Jet database engine.

lpszSrcTable   A pointer to a string containing the source table name. By default this value is initialized as **NULL**.

lpszConnect   A pointer to a string containing the default connect string. By default this value is initialized as **NULL**.

Remarks

Call this member function to create a new saved table. Once you have named the tabledef, you can then call **Append** to save the tabledef in the database's TableDefs collection. After calling **Append**, the tabledef is in an open state, and you can use it to create a **CDaoRecordset** object.

For more information on tabledefs, see the articles "DAO Tabledef" and "DAO Tabledef: Using Tabledefs" in *Visual C++ Programmer's Guide* online. For related information, see the topic "CreateTableDef Method" in DAO Help.

See Also: CDaoTableDef::Open, CDaoTableDef::Close, CDaoRecordset

CDaoTableDef::CreateField

void CreateField(LPCTSTR *lpszName,* **short** *nType,* **long** *lSize,* **long** *lAttributes* = **0**);
    throw(CDaoException, CMemoryException);**
void CreateField(CDaoFieldInfo& *fieldinfo*);
    throw(CDaoException, CMemoryException);**

Parameters

lpszName   A pointer to a string expression specifying the name of this field.

nType   A value indicating the data type of the field. The setting can be one of these values:

Type	Size (bytes)	Description
dbBoolean	1 byte	BOOL
dbByte	1	BYTE
dbInteger	2	int

(continued)

(continued)

Type	Size (bytes)	Description
dbLong	4	long
dbCurrency	8	Currency (**COleCurrency**)
dbSingle	4	float
dbDouble	8	double
dbDate	8	Date/Time (**COleDateTime**)
dbText	1–255	Text (**CString**)
dbLongBinary	0	Long Binary (OLE Object), **CLongBinary** or **CByteArray**
dbMemo	0	Memo (**CString**)

lSize   A value that indicates the maximum size, in bytes, of a field that contains text, or the fixed size of a field that contains text or numeric values. The *lSize* parameter is ignored for all but text fields.

lAttributes   A value corresponding to characteristics of the field and that can be combined using a bitwise-OR.

Constant	Description
dbFixedField	The field size is fixed (default for Numeric fields).
dbVariableField	The field size is variable (Text fields only).
dbAutoIncrField	The field value for new records is automatically incremented to a unique long integer that cannot be changed. Only supported for Microsoft Jet database tables.
dbUpdatableField	The field value can be changed.
dbDescending	The field is sorted in descending (Z–A or 100–0) order (applies only to a Field object in a Fields collection of an Index object). If you omit this constant, the field is sorted in ascending (A–Z or 0–100) order (default).

fieldinfo   A reference to a **CDaoFieldInfo** structure.

Remarks

Call this member function to add a field to the table. A **DAOField** (OLE) object is created and appended to the Fields collection of the **DAOTableDef** (OLE) object. Besides its use for examining object properties, you can also use **CDaoFieldInfo** to construct an input parameter for creating new fields in a tabledef. The first version of **CreateField** is simpler to use, but if you want finer control, you can use the second version of **CreateField**, which takes a **CDaoFieldInfo** parameter.

If you use the version of **CreateField** that takes a **CDaoFieldInfo** parameter, you must carefully set each of the following members of the **CDaoFieldInfo** structure:

- **m_strName**
- **m_nType**

- **m_lSize**
- **m_lAttributes**
- **m_bAllowZeroLength**

The remaining members of **CDaoFieldInfo** should be set to **0**, **FALSE**, or an empty string, as appropriate for the member, or a **CDaoException** may occur.

For more information on tabledefs, see the articles "DAO Tabledef" and "DAO Tabledef: Using Tabledefs" in *Visual C++ Programmer's Guide* online. For related information, see the topic "CreateField Method" in DAO Help.

See Also: **CDaoTableDef::DeleteField**, **CDaoTableDef::CreateIndex**, **CDaoTableDef::DeleteIndex**

CDaoTableDef::CreateIndex

void CreateIndex(CDaoIndexInfo& *indexinfo* **);**
  throw(CDaoException, CMemoryException);

Parameters

indexinfo   A reference to a **CDaoIndexInfo** structure.

Remarks

Call this function to add an index to a table. Indexes specify the order of records accessed from database tables and whether or not duplicate records are accepted. Indexes also provide efficient access to data.

You do not have to create indexes for tables, but in large, unindexed tables, accessing a specific record or creating a recordset can take a long time. On the other hand, creating too many indexes slows down update, append, and delete operations as all indexes are automatically updated. Consider these factors as you decide which indexes to create.

The following members of the **CDaoIndexInfo** structure must be set:

- **m_strName**   A name must be supplied.
- **m_pFieldInfos**   Must point to an array of **CDaoIndexFieldInfo** structures.
- **m_nFields**   Must specify the number of fields in the array of **CDaoFieldInfo** structures.

The remaining members will be ignored if set to **FALSE**. In addition, the **m_lDistinctCount** member is ignored during creation of the index.

For more information on tabledefs, see the articles "DAO Tabledef" and "DAO Tabledef: Using Tabledefs" in *Visual C++ Programmer's Guide* online. For related information, see the topic "CreateIndex Method" in DAO Help.

See Also: **CDaoTableDef::DeleteIndex**, **CDaoTableDef::CreateField**, **CDaoTableDef::DeleteField**, **CDaoIndexInfo**

CDaoTableDef::DeleteField

void DeleteField(LPCTSTR *lpszName* **);**
    throw(CDaoException, CMemoryException);
void DeleteField(int *nIndex* **);**
    throw(CDaoException, CMemoryException);

Parameters

lpszName   A pointer to a string expression that is the name of an existing field.

nIndex   The index of the field in the table's zero-based Fields collection, for lookup by index.

Remarks

Call this member function to remove a field and make it inaccessible. You can use this member function on a new object that has not been appended to the database or when **CanUpdate** returns nonzero.

For more information on tabledefs, see the articles "DAO Tabledef" and "DAO Tabledef: Using Tabledefs" in *Visual C++ Programmer's Guide* online. For related information, see the topic "Delete Method" in DAO Help.

See Also: **CDaoTableDef::CreateField**, **CDaoTableDef::CreateIndex**, **CDaoTableDef::DeleteIndex**

CDaoTableDef::DeleteIndex

void DeleteIndex(LPCTSTR *lpszName* **);**
    throw(CDaoException, CMemoryException);
void DeleteIndex(int *nIndex* **);**
    throw(CDaoException, CMemoryException);

Parameters

lpszName   A pointer to a string expression that is the name of an existing index.

nIndex   The array index of the index object in the database's zero-based TableDefs collection, for lookup by index.

Remarks

Call this member function to delete an index in an underlying table. You can use this member function on a new object that hasn't been appended to the database or when **CanUpdate** returns nonzero.

For more information on tabledefs, see the articles "DAO Tabledef" and "DAO Tabledef: Using Tabledefs" in *Visual C++ Programmer's Guide* online. For related information, see the topic "Delete Method" in DAO Help.

See Also: **CDaoTableDef::CreateIndex, CDaoTableDef::CreateField, CDaoTableDef::DeleteField**

CDaoTableDef::GetAttributes

long GetAttributes( );
> **throw(CDaoException, CMemoryException);**

Return Value

Returns a value that indicates one or more characteristics of a **CDaoTableDef** object.

Remarks

For a **CDaoTableDef** object, the return value specifies characteristics of the table represented by the **CDaoTableDef** object and can be a sum of these constants:

Constant	Description
dbAttachExclusive	For databases that use the Microsoft Jet database engine, indicates the table is an attached table opened for exclusive use.
dbAttachSavePWD	For databases that use the Microsoft Jet database engine, indicates that the user ID and password for the attached table are saved with the connection information.
dbSystemObject	Indicates the table is a system table provided by the Microsoft Jet database engine.
dbHiddenObject	Indicates the table is a hidden table provided by the Microsoft Jet database engine.
dbAttachedTable	Indicates the table is an attached table from a non-ODBC database, such as a Paradox database.
dbAttachedODBC	Indicates the table is an attached table from an ODBC database, such as Microsoft SQL Server.

A system table is a table created by the Microsoft Jet database engine to contain various internal information.

A hidden table is a table created for temporary use by the Microsoft Jet database engine.

For more information on tabledefs, see the articles "DAO Tabledef" and "DAO Tabledef: Using Tabledefs" in *Visual C++ Programmer's Guide* online. For related information, see the topic "Attributes Property" in DAO Help.

See Also: **CDaoTableDef::SetAttributes**

CDaoTableDef::GetConnect

CString GetConnect( );
throw(CDaoException, CMemoryException);

Return Value

A **CString** object containing the path and database type for the table.

Remarks

Call this member function to obtain the connect string for a data source. For a **CDaoTableDef** object that represents an attached table, the **CString** object consists of one or two parts (a database type specifier and a path to the database).

The path as shown in the table below is the full path for the directory containing the database files and must be preceded by the identifier "DATABASE=". In some cases (as with Microsoft Jet, Btrieve, and Microsoft Excel databases), a specific filename is included in the database path argument.

The following table shows possible database types and their corresponding database specifiers and paths:

Database type	Specifier	Path
Database using the Jet database engine	";"	"drive:\path\filename.MDB"
dBASE III	"dBASE III;"	"drive:\path"
dBASE IV	"dBASE IV;"	"drive:\path"
Paradox 3.x	"Paradox 3.x;"	"drive:\path"
Paradox 4.x	"Paradox 4.x;"	"drive:\path"
Btrieve	"Btrieve;"	"drive:\path\filename.DDF"
FoxPro 2.0	"FoxPro 2.0;"	"drive:\path"
FoxPro 2.5	"FoxPro 2.5;"	"drive:\path"
FoxPro 2.6	"FoxPro 2.6;"	"drive:\path"
Excel 3.0	"Excel 3.0;"	"drive:\path\filename.XLS"
Excel 4.0	"Excel 4.0;"	"drive:\path\filename.XLS"
Excel 5.0	"Excel 5.0;"	"drive:\path\filename.XLS"
Text	"Text;"	"drive:\path"
ODBC	"ODBC; DATABASE=*defaultdatabase*; UID=*user*;PWD=*password*; DSN=*datasourcename*; LOGINTIMEOUT=*seconds*" (This may not be a complete connection string for all servers; it is just an example. It is very important not to have spaces between the parameters.)	None

For Microsoft Jet database base tables, the specifier is a empty string ("").

If a password is required but not provided, the ODBC driver displays a login dialog box the first time a table is accessed and again if the connection is closed and reopened. If an attached table has the **dbAttachSavePWD** attribute, the login prompt will not appear when the table is reopened.

For more information on tabledefs, see the articles "DAO Tabledef" and "DAO Tabledef: Using Tabledefs" in *Visual C++ Programmer's Guide* online. For related information, see the topic "Connect Property" in DAO Help.

See Also: **CDaoTableDef::SetConnect**

CDaoTableDef::GetDateCreated

COleDateTime GetDateCreated( );
    throw(CDaoException, CMemoryException);

Return Value

A value containing the date and time of the creation of the table underlying the **CDaoTableDef** object.

Remarks

Call this function to determine the date and time the table underlying the **CDaoTableDef** object was created.

The date and time settings are derived from the computer on which the base table was created or last updated. In a multiuser environment, users should get these settings directly from the file server to avoid discrepancies; that is, all clients should use a "standard" time source—perhaps from one server.

For more information on tabledefs, see the articles "DAO Tabledef" and "DAO Tabledef: Using Tabledefs" in *Visual C++ Programmer's Guide* online. For related information, see the topic "DateCreated, LastUpdated Properties" in DAO Help.

See Also: **CDaoTableDef::GetLastDateUpdated**

CDaoTableDef::GetDateLastUpdated

COleDateTime GetDateLastUpdated( );
    throw(CDaoException, CMemoryException);

Return Value

A value that contains the date and time the table underlying the **CDaoTableDef** object was last updated.

Remarks

Call this function to determine the date and time the table underlying the **CDaoTableDef** object was last updated.

The date and time settings are derived from the computer on which the base table was created or last updated. In a multiuser environment, users should get these settings directly from the file server to avoid discrepancies; that is, all clients should use a "standard" time source—perhaps from one server.

For more information on tabledefs, see the articles "DAO Tabledef" and "DAO Tabledef: Using Tabledefs" in *Visual C++ Programmer's Guide* online. For related information, see the topic "DateCreated, LastUpdated Properties" in DAO Help.

See Also: **CDaoTableDef::GetDateCreated**

CDaoTableDef::GetFieldCount

short GetFieldCount( );
throw(CDaoException, CMemoryException);

Return Value

The number of fields in the table.

Remarks

Call this member function to retrieve the number of fields defined in the table. If its value is 0, there are no objects in the collection.

For more information on tabledefs, see the articles "DAO Tabledef" and "DAO Tabledef: Using Tabledefs" in *Visual C++ Programmer's Guide* online. For related information, see the topic "Count Property" in DAO Help.

See Also: **CDaoTableDef::GetFieldInfo**, **CDaoTableDef::GetIndexInfo**, **CDaoTableDef::GetIndexCount**

CDaoTableDef::GetFieldInfo

void GetFieldInfo(int *nIndex*, **CDaoFieldInfo&** *fieldinfo*,
 ➥ **DWORD** *dwInfoOptions* = **AFX_DAO_PRIMARY_INFO**);
 throw(CDaoException, CMemoryException);
void GetFieldInfo(LPCTSTR *lpszName*, **CDaoFieldInfo&** *fieldinfo*,
 ➥ **DWORD** *dwInfoOptions* = **AFX_DAO_PRIMARY_INFO**);
 throw(CDaoException, CMemoryException);

Parameters

nIndex The index of the field object in the table's zero-based Fields collection, for lookup by index.

fieldinfo A reference to a **CDaoFieldInfo** structure.

dwInfoOptions   Options that specify which information about the field to retrieve. The available options are listed here along with what they cause the function to return:

- **AFX_DAO_PRIMARY_INFO**   (Default) Name, Type, Size, Attributes. Use this option for fastest performance.

- **AFX_DAO_SECONDARY_INFO**   Primary information, plus: Ordinal Position, Required, Allow Zero Length, Collating Order, Foreign Name, Source Field, Source Table

- **AFX_DAO_ALL_INFO**   Primary and secondary information, plus: Validation Rule, Validation Text, Default Value

lpszName   A pointer to the name of the field object, for lookup by name. The name is a string with up to 64 characters that uniquely names the field.

Remarks

Call this member function to obtain various kinds of information about a field defined in the tabledef. One version of the function lets you look up a field by index. The other version lets you look up a field by name.

For a description of the information returned, see the **CDaoFieldInfo** structure. This structure has members that correspond to the items of information listed above in the description of *dwInfoOptions*. When you request information at one level, you get information for any prior levels as well.

For more information on tabledefs, see the articles "DAO Tabledef" and "DAO Tabledef: Using Tabledefs" in *Visual C++ Programmer's Guide* online. For related information, see the topic "Attributes Property" in DAO Help.

See Also: CDaoTableDef::GetIndexInfo, CDaoTableDef::GetIndexCount, CDaoTableDef::GetFieldCount

---

CDaoTableDef::GetIndexCount

short GetIndexCount( );
    throw(CDaoException, CMemoryException);

Return Value

The number of indexes for the table.

Remarks

Call this member function to obtain the number of indexes for a table. If its value is 0, there are no indexes in the collection.

For more information on tabledefs, see the articles "DAO Tabledef" and "DAO Tabledef: Using Tabledefs" in *Visual C++ Programmer's Guide* online. For related information, see the topic "Count Property" in DAO Help.

See Also: **CDaoTableDef::GetIndexInfo, CDaoTableDef::GetFieldInfo, CDaoTableDef::GetFieldCount**

CDaoTableDef::GetIndexInfo

void GetIndexInfo(int *nIndex***, CDaoIndexInfo&** *indexinfo***,**
   ↳ **DWORD** *dwInfoOptions* **= AFX_DAO_PRIMARY_INFO);**
   throw(CDaoException, CMemoryException);
void GetIndexInfo(LPCTSTR *lpszName***, CDaoIndexInfo&** *indexinfo***,**
   ↳ **DWORD** *dwInfoOptions* **= AFX_DAO_PRIMARY_INFO);**
   throw(CDaoException, CMemoryException);

Parameters

nIndex   The numeric index of the Index object in the table's zero-based Indexes collection, for lookup by its position in the collection.

indexinfo   A reference to a **CDaoIndexInfo** structure.

dwInfoOptions   Options that specify which information about the index to retrieve. The available options are listed here along with what they cause the function to return:

- **AFX_DAO_PRIMARY_INFO**   Name, Field Info, Fields. Use this option for fastest performance.

- **AFX_DAO_SECONDARY_INFO**   Primary information, plus: Primary, Unique, Clustered, Ignore Nulls, Required, Foreign

- **AFX_DAO_ALL_INFO**   Primary and secondary information, plus: Distinct Count

lpszName   A pointer to the name of the index object, for lookup by name.

Remarks

Call this member function to obtain various kinds of information about an index defined in the tabledef. One version of the function lets you look up an index by its position in the collection. The other version lets you look up an index by name.

For a description of the information returned, see the **CDaoIndexInfo** structure. This structure has members that correspond to the items of information listed above in the description of *dwInfoOptions*. When you request information at one level, you get information for any prior levels as well.

For more information on tabledefs, see the articles "DAO Tabledef" and "DAO Tabledef: Using Tabledefs" in *Visual C++ Programmer's Guide* online. For related information, see the topic "Attributes Property" in DAO Help.

See Also: **CDaoTableDef::GetFieldInfo, CDaoTableDef::GetIndexCount, CDaoTableDef::GetFieldCount**

CDaoTableDef::GetName

CString GetName( );
    throw(CDaoException, CMemoryException);

Return Value

A user-defined name for a table.

Remarks

Call this member function to obtain the user-defined name of the underlying table. This name starts with a letter and can contain a maximum of 64 characters. It can include numbers and underscore characters but cannot include punctuation or spaces.

For more information on tabledefs, see the articles "DAO Tabledef" and "DAO Tabledef: Using Tabledefs" in *Visual C++ Programmer's Guide* online. For related information, see the topic "Name Property" in DAO Help.

See Also: **CDaoTableDef::SetName, CDaoTableDef::GetConnect, CDaoTableDef::SetConnect**

CDaoTableDef::GetRecordCount

long GetRecordCount( );
    throw(CDaoException, CMemoryException);

Return Value

The number of records accessed in a tabledef object.

Remarks

Call this member function to find out how many records are in a **CDaoTableDef** object.

Calling **GetRecordCount** for a table-type **CDaoTableDef** object reflects the approximate number of records in the table and is affected immediately as table records are added and deleted. Rolled back transactions will appear as part of the record count until you call **CDaoWorkSpace::CompactDatabase**. A **CDaoTableDef** object with no records has a record count property setting of 0. When working with attached tables or ODBC databases, **GetRecordCount** always returns −1.

For more information on tabledefs, see the articles "DAO Tabledef" and "DAO Tabledef: Using Tabledefs" in *Visual C++ Programmer's Guide* online. For related information, see the topic "RecordCount Property" in DAO Help.

See Also: **CDaoTableDef::GetSourceTableName, CDaoTableDef::SetSourceTableName**

CDaoTableDef::GetSourceTableName

CString GetSourceTableName( );
    throw(CDaoException, CMemoryException);

Return Value

A **CString** object that specifies the source name of an attached table, or an empty string if a native data table.

Remarks

Call this member function to retrieve the name of an attached table in a source database. An attached table is a table in another database linked to a Microsoft Jet database. Data for attached tables remains in the external database, where it can be manipulated by other applications.

For more information on tabledefs, see the articles "DAO Tabledef" and "DAO Tabledef: Using Tabledefs" in *Visual C++ Programmer's Guide* online. For related information, see the topic "SourceTableName Property" in DAO Help.

See Also: **CDaoTableDef::GetRecordCount**, **CDaoTableDef::SetSourceTableName**

CDaoTableDef::GetValidationRule

CString GetValidationRule( );
    throw(CDaoException, CMemoryException);

Return Value

A **CString** object that validates the data in a field as it is changed or added to a table.

Remarks

Call this member function to retrieve the validation rule for a tabledef. Validation rules are used in connection with update operations. If a tabledef contains a validation rule, updates to that tabledef must match predetermined criteria before the data is changed. If the change does not match the criteria, an exception containing the value of **GetValidationText** is thrown. For a **CDaoTableDef** object, this **CString** is read-only for an attached table and read/write for a base table.

For more information on tabledefs, see the articles "DAO Tabledef" and "DAO Tabledef: Using Tabledefs" in *Visual C++ Programmer's Guide* online. For related information, see the topic "ValidationRule Property" in DAO Help.

See Also: **CDaoTableDef::SetValidationRule**, **CDaoTableDef::GetValidationText**, **CDaoTableDef::SetValidationText**

CDaoTableDef::GetValidationText

CString GetValidationText( );
    throw(CDaoException, CMemoryException);

Return Value

A **CString** object that specifies the text displayed if the user enters data that does not match the validation rule.

Remarks

Call this function to retrieve the string to display when a user enters data that does not match the validation rule. For a **CDaoTableDef** object, this **CString** is read-only for an attached table and read/write for a base table.

For more information on tabledefs, see the articles "DAO Tabledef" and "DAO Tabledef: Using Tabledefs" in *Visual C++ Programmer's Guide* online. For related information, see the topic "ValidationText Property" in DAO Help.

See Also: **CDaoTableDef::SetValidationRule, CDaoTableDef::SetValidationText, CDaoTableDef::GetValidationRule**

CDaoTableDef::IsOpen

BOOL IsOpen( ) const;
    throw(CDaoException, CMemoryException);

Return Value

Nonzero if the **CDaoTableDef** object is open; otherwise 0.

Remarks

Call this member function to determine whether the **CDaoTableDef** object is currently open.

For more information on tabledefs, see the articles "DAO Tabledef" and "DAO Tabledef: Using Tabledefs" in *Visual C++ Programmer's Guide* online.

See Also: **CDaoTableDef::Open**

CDaoTableDef::Open

virtual void Open(LPCTSTR *lpszName* **);**
    throw(CDaoException, CMemoryException);

Parameters

lpszName   A pointer to a string that specifies a table name.

Remarks

Call this member function to open a tabledef previously saved in the database's TableDef's collection.

For more information on tabledefs, see the articles "DAO Tabledef" and "DAO Tabledef: Using Tabledefs" in *Visual C++ Programmer's Guide* online.

See Also: **CDaoTableDef::IsOpen, CDaoTableDef::Create, CDaoTableDef::Close**

CDaoTableDef::RefreshLink

> **void RefreshLink( );**
> **throw(CDaoException, CMemoryException);**

Remarks

Call this member function to update the connection information for an attached table. You change the connection information for an attached table by calling **SetConnect** on the corresponding **CDaoTableDef** object and then using the **RefreshLink** member function to update the information. When you call **RefreshLink**, the attached table's properties are not changed.

To force the modified connect information to take effect, all open **CDaoRecordset** objects based on this tabledef must be closed.

For more information on tabledefs, see the articles "DAO Tabledef" and "DAO Tabledef: Using Tabledefs" in *Visual C++ Programmer's Guide* online. For related information, see the topic "RefreshLink Method" in DAO Help.

See Also: **CDaoTableDef::SetConnect**

CDaoTableDef::SetAttributes

> **void SetAttributes(long *lAttributes*);**
> **throw(CDaoException, CMemoryException);**

Parameters

lAttributes   Characteristics of the table represented by the **CDaoTableDef** object and can be a sum of these constants:

Constant	Description
dbAttachExclusive	For databases that use the Microsoft Jet database engine, indicates the table is an attached table opened for exclusive use.
dbAttachSavePWD	For databases that use the Microsoft Jet database engine, indicates that the user ID and password for the attached table are saved with the connection information.

(continued)

Constant	Description
dbSystemObject	Indicates the table is a system table provided by the Microsoft Jet database engine.
dbHiddenObject	Indicates the table is a hidden table provided by the Microsoft Jet database engine.

Remarks

When setting multiple attributes, you can combine them by summing the appropriate constants using the bitwise-OR operator. Setting **dbAttachExclusive** on a nonattached table produces an exception. Combining the following values also produce an exception:

- **dbAttachExclusive | dbAttachedODBC**
- **dbAttachSavePWD | dbAttachedTable**

For more information on tabledefs, see the articles "DAO Tabledef" and "DAO Tabledef: Using Tabledefs" in *Visual C++ Programmer's Guide* online. For related information, see the topic "Attributes Property" in DAO Help.

See Also: CDaoTableDef::SetConnect

CDaoTableDef::SetConnect

void SetConnect(LPCTSTR *lpszConnect* **);**
　　throw(CDaoException, CMemoryException);

Parameters

lpszConnect　A pointer to a string expression that specifies additional parameters to pass to ODBC or installable ISAM drivers.

Remarks

For a **CDaoTableDef** object that represents an attached table, the string object consists of one or two parts (a database type specifier and a path to the database).

The path as shown in the table below is the full path for the directory containing the database files and must be preceded by the identifier "DATABASE=". In some cases (as with Microsoft Jet, Btrieve, and Microsoft Excel databases), a specific filename is included in the database path argument.

Note　Do not include whitespace around the equal sign in path statements of the form "DATABASE=drive:\\path". This will result in an exception being thrown and the connection failing.

The following table shows possible database types and their corresponding database specifiers and paths:

Database type	Specifier	Path
Database using the Jet database engine	";"	"drive:\\path\\filename.MDB"
dBASE III	"dBASE III;"	"drive:\\path"
dBASE IV	"dBASE IV;"	"drive:\\path"
Paradox 3.x	"Paradox 3.x;"	"drive:\\path"
Paradox 4.x	"Paradox 4.x;"	"drive:\\path"
Btrieve	"Btrieve;"	"drive:\\path\\filename.DDF"
FoxPro 2.0	"FoxPro 2.0;"	"drive:\\path"
FoxPro 2.5	"FoxPro 2.5;"	"drive:\\path"
FoxPro 2.6	"FoxPro 2.6;"	"drive:\\path"
Excel 3.0	"Excel 3.0;"	"drive:\\path\\filename.XLS"
Excel 4.0	"Excel 4.0;"	"drive:\\path\\filename.XLS"
Excel 5.0	"Excel 5.0;"	"drive:\\path\\filename.XLS"
Text	"Text;"	"drive:\\path"
ODBC	"ODBC; DATABASE=*defaultdatabase*; UID=*user*;PWD=*password*; DSN=*datasourcename;* LOGINTIMEOUT=*seconds*" (This may not be a complete connection string for all servers; it is just an example. It is very important not to have spaces between the parameters.)	None

For Microsoft Jet database base tables, the specifier is an empty string ("").

You must use a double backslash (\\) in the connect strings. If you have modified the properties of an existing connection using **SetConnect**, you must subsequently call **RefreshLink**. If you are initializing the connection properties using **SetConnect**, you need not call **RefreshLink**, but should you choose to do so, first append the tabledef.

If a password is required but not provided, the ODBC driver displays a login dialog box the first time a table is accessed and again if the connection is closed and reopened.

You can set the connect string for a **CDaoTableDef** object by providing a source argument to the **Create** member function. You can check the setting to determine the type, path, user ID, password, or ODBC data source of the database. For more information, see the documentation for the specific driver.

For more information on tabledefs, see the articles "DAO Tabledef" and "DAO Tabledef: Using Tabledefs" in *Visual C++ Programmer's Guide* online. For related information, see the topic "Connect Property" in DAO Help.

See Also: **CDaoTableDef::RefreshLink**, **CDaoTableDef::SetAttributes**

CDaoTableDef::SetName

void SetName(LPCTSTR *lpszName* **);**
    throw(CDaoException, CMemoryException);

Parameters

lpszName   A pointer to a string expression that specifies a name for a table.

Remarks

Call this member function to set a user-defined name for a table. The name must start with a letter and can contain a maximum of 64 characters. It can include numbers and underscore characters but cannot include punctuation or spaces.

For more information on tabledefs, see the articles "DAO Tabledef" and "DAO Tabledef: Using Tabledefs" in *Visual C++ Programmer's Guide* online. For related information, see the topic "Name Property" in DAO Help.

See Also: **CDaoTableDef::RefreshLink**, **CDaoTableDef::SetConnect**

CDaoTableDef::SetSourceTableName

void SetSourceTableName(LPCTSTR *lpszSrcTableName* **);**
    throw(CDaoException, CMemoryException);

Parameters

lpszSrcTableName   A pointer to a string expression that specifies a table name in the external database. For a base table, the setting is an empty string ("").

Remarks

Call this member function to specify the name of an attached table or the name of the base table on which the **CDaoTableDef** object is based, as it exists in the original source of the data. You must then call **RefreshLink**. This property setting is empty for a base table and read/write for an attached table or an object not appended to a collection.

For more information on tabledefs, see the articles "DAO Tabledef" and "DAO Tabledef: Using Tabledefs" in *Visual C++ Programmer's Guide* online. For related information, see the topic "SourceTableName Property" in DAO Help.

See Also: **CDaoTableDef::RefreshLink**, **CDaoTableDef::GetSourceTableName**

CDaoTableDef::SetValidationRule

void SetValidationRule(LPCTSTR *lpszValidationRule* **);**
   throw(CDaoException, CMemoryException);

Parameters

lpszValidationRule   A pointer to a string expression that validates an operation.

Remarks

Call this member function to set a validation rule for a tabledef. Validation rules are used in connection with update operations. If a tabledef contains a validation rule, updates to that tabledef must match predetermined criteria before the data is changed. If the change does not match the criteria, an exception containing the text of **GetValidationText** is displayed.

Validation is supported only for databases that use the Microsoft Jet database engine. The expression cannot refer to user-defined functions, domain aggregate functions, SQL aggregate functions, or queries. A validation rule for a **CDaoTableDef** object can refer to multiple fields in that object.

For example, for fields named `hire_date` and `termination_date`, a validation rule might be:

```
CString strRule = _T("termination_date>hire_date");
MyRs.SetValidationRule(strRule);
```

For more information on tabledefs, see the articles "DAO Tabledef" and "DAO Tabledef: Using Tabledefs" in *Visual C++ Programmer's Guide* online. For related information, see the topic "ValidationRule Property" in DAO Help.

See Also: CDaoTableDef::GetValidationText, CDaoTableDef::SetValidationText, CDaoTableDef::GetValidationRule

---

CDaoTableDef::SetValidationText

void SetValidationText(LPCTSTR *lpszValidationText* **);**
   throw(CDaoException, CMemoryException);

Parameters

lpszValidationText   A pointer to a string expression that specifies the text displayed if entered data is invalid.

Remarks

Call this member function to set the exception text of a validation rule for a **CDaoTableDef** object with an underlying base table supported by the Microsoft Jet database engine. You cannot set the validation text of an attached table.

For more information on tabledefs, see the articles "DAO Tabledef" and "DAO Tabledef: Using Tabledefs" in *Visual C++ Programmer's Guide* online. For related information, see the topic "ValidationText Property" in DAO Help.

See Also: **CDaoTableDef::SetValidationRule, CDaoTableDef::GetValidationText, CDaoTableDef::GetValidationRule**

Data Members
CDaoTableDef::m_pDatabase

Remarks

Contains a pointer to the **CDaoDatabase** object for this table.

For more information on accessing underlying DAO objects, see the article "DAO Collections: Obtaining Information About DAO Objects" in *Visual C++ Programmer's Guide* online.

See Also: **CDaoTableDef::m_pDAOTableDef**

CDaoTableDef::m_pDAOTableDef

Remarks

Contains a pointer to the OLE interface for the DAO tabledef object underlying the **CDaoTableDef** object. Use this pointer if you need to access the DAO interface directly.

For more information on accessing underlying DAO objects, see the article "DAO Collections: Obtaining Information About DAO Objects" in *Visual C++ Programmer's Guide* online.

See Also: **CDaoTableDef::m_pDatabase**

CDaoWorkspace

A **CDaoWorkspace** object manages a named, password-protected database session from login to logoff, by a single user. In most cases, you will not need multiple workspaces, and you will not need to create explicit workspace objects; when you open database and recordset objects, they use DAO's default workspace. However, if needed, you can run multiple sessions at a time by creating additional workspace objects. Each workspace object can contain multiple open database objects in its own Databases collection. In MFC, a workspace is primarily a transaction manager, specifying a set of open databases all in the same "transaction space."

Note The DAO database classes are distinct from the MFC database classes based on Open Database Connectivity (ODBC). All DAO database class names have a "CDao" prefix. In general, the MFC classes based on DAO are more capable than the MFC classes based on ODBC. The DAO-based classes access data through the Microsoft Jet database engine, including ODBC drivers. They also support Data Definition Language (DDL) operations, such as creating databases and adding tables and fields via the classes, without having to call DAO directly.

Capabilities

Class **CDaoWorkspace** provides the following:

- Explicit access, if needed, to a default workspace, created by initializing the database engine. Usually you use DAO's default workspace implicitly by creating database and recordset objects.

- A transaction space in which transactions apply to all databases open in the workspace. You can create additional workspaces to manage separate transaction spaces.

- An interface to many properties of the underlying Microsoft Jet database engine (see the static member functions). Opening or creating a workspace, or calling a static member function before open or create, initializes the database engine.

- Access to the database engine's Workspaces collection, which stores all active workspaces that have been appended to it. You can also create and work with workspaces without appending them to the collection.

Security

MFC does not implement the Users and Groups collections in DAO, which are used for security control. If you need those aspects of DAO, you must program them yourself via direct calls to DAO interfaces. For information, see Technical Note 54 online.

Usage

You can use class **CDaoWorkspace** to:

- Explicitly open the default workspace.

  Usually your use of the default workspace is implicit — when you open new **CDaoDatabase** or **CDaoRecordset** objects. But you might need to access it explicitly—for example, to access database engine properties or the Workspaces collection. See "Implicit Use of the Default Workspace" below.

- Create new workspaces. Call **Append** if you want to add them to the Workspaces collection.

- Open an existing workspace in the Workspaces collection.

Creating a new workspace that does not already exist in the Workspaces collection is described under the **Create** member function. Workspace objects do not persist in any way between database engine sessions. If your application links MFC statically, ending the application uninitializes the database engine. If your application links with MFC dynamically, the database engine is uninitialized when the MFC DLL is unloaded.

Feature Only in Professional and Enterprise Editions   Static linking to MFC is supported only in Visual C++ Professional and Enterprise Editions. For more information, see "Visual C++ Editions" online.

Explicitly opening the default workspace, or opening an existing workspace in the Workspaces collection, is described under the **Open** member function.

End a workspace session by closing the workspace with the **Close** member function. **Close** closes any databases you have not closed previously, rolling back any uncommitted transactions.

Transactions

DAO manages transactions at the workspace level; hence, transactions on a workspace with multiple open databases apply to all of the databases. For example, if two databases have uncommitted updates and you call **CommitTrans**, all of the updates are committed. If you want to limit transactions to a single database, you need a separate workspace object for it.

Implicit Use of the Default Workspace

MFC uses DAO's default workspace implicitly under the following circumstances:

- If you create a new **CDaoDatabase** object but do not do so through an existing **CDaoWorkspace** object, MFC creates a temporary workspace object for you, which corresponds to DAO's default workspace. If you do so for multiple databases, all of the database objects are associated with the default workspace. You can access a database's workspace through a **CDaoDatabase** data member.

- Similarly, if you create a **CDaoRecordset** object without supplying a pointer to a **CDaoDatabase** object, MFC creates a temporary database object and, by extension, a temporary workspace object. You can access a recordset's database, and indirectly its workspace, through a **CDaoRecordset** data member.

Other Operations

Other database operations are also provided, such as repairing a corrupted database or compacting a database.

For more about **CDaoWorkspace**, see the article "DAO Workspace." For information about calling DAO directly and about DAO security, see Technical Note 54 online. For more about working with ODBC data sources through DAO, see the article "DAO External: Working with External Data Sources." For information about the database engine, see the article "DAO Workspace: The Database Engine." All articles are in *Visual C++ Programmer's Guide* online. The MFC Database sample DAOVIEW illustrates using **CDaoWorkspace**.

#include <afxdao.h>

See Also: **CDaoDatabase, CDaoRecordset, CDaoTableDef, CDaoQueryDef, CDaoException**

CDaoWorkspace Class Members

Data Members

m_pDAOWorkspace	Points to the underlying DAO workspace object.

Construction

CDaoWorkspace	Constructs a workspace object. Afterwards, call **Create** or **Open**.

Attributes

GetIsolateODBCTrans	Returns a value that indicates whether multiple transactions that involve the same ODBC data source are isolated via forced multiple connections to the data source.
GetName	Returns the user-defined name for the workspace object.
GetUserName	Returns the user name specified when the workspace was created. This is the name of the workspace owner.
IsOpen	Returns nonzero if the workspace is open.
SetIsolateODBCTrans	Specifies whether multiple transactions that involve the same ODBC data source are isolated by forcing multiple connections to the data source.

Operations

Append	Appends a newly created workspace to the database engine's Workspaces collection.
BeginTrans	Begins a new transaction, which applies to all databases open in the workspace.
Close	Closes the workspace and all of the objects it contains. Pending transactions are rolled back.
CommitTrans	Completes the current transaction and saves the changes.
CompactDatabase	Compacts (or duplicates) a database.
Create	Creates a new DAO workspace object.
GetDatabaseCount	Returns the number of DAO database objects in the workspace's Databases collection.
GetDatabaseInfo	Returns information about a specified DAO database defined in the workspace's Databases collection.
GetWorkspaceCount	Returns the number of DAO workspace objects in the database engine's Workspaces collection.
GetWorkspaceInfo	Returns information about a specified DAO workspace defined in the database engine's Workspaces collection.
Open	Explicitly opens a workspace object associated with DAO's default workspace.
RepairDatabase	Attempts to repair a damaged database.
Rollback	Ends the current transaction and does not save the changes.
Idle	Allows the database engine to perform background tasks.

Database Engine Properties

GetVersion	Returns a string that contains the version of the database engine associated with the workspace.
GetIniPath	Returns the location of the Microsoft Jet database engine's initialization settings in the Windows registry.
GetLoginTimeout	Returns the number of seconds before an error occurs when the user attempts to log in to an ODBC database.
SetDefaultPassword	Sets the password that the database engine uses when a workspace object is created without a specific password.
SetDefaultUser	Sets the user name that the database engine uses when a workspace object is created without a specific user name.
SetIniPath	Sets the location of the Microsoft Jet database engine's initialization settings in the Windows registry.
SetLoginTimeout	Sets the number of seconds before an error occurs when the user attempts to log in to an ODBC data source.

Member Functions

CDaoWorkspace::Append

void Append( );
   throw(CDaoException, CMemoryException);

Remarks

Call this member function after you call **Create**. **Append** appends a newly created workspace object to the database engine's Workspaces collection. Workspaces do not persist between database engine sessions; they are stored only in memory, not on disk. You do not have to append a workspace; if you do not, you can still use it.

An appended workspace remains in the Workspaces collection, in an active, open state, until you call its **Close** member function.

For more information about workspaces, see the article "DAO Workspace." For more information about the database engine, see the article "DAO Workspace: The Database Engine." Both articles are in *Visual C++ Programmer's Guide* online. For related information, see the topic "Append Method" in DAO Help.

CDaoWorkspace::BeginTrans

void BeginTrans( );
   throw(CDaoException, CMemoryException);

Remarks

Call this member function to initiate a transaction. After you call **BeginTrans**, updates you make to your data or database structure take effect when you commit the transaction. Because the workspace defines a single transaction space, the transaction applies to all open databases in the workspace. There are two ways to complete the transaction:

- Call the **CommitTrans** member function to commit the transaction and save changes to the data source.

- Or call the **Rollback** member function to cancel the transaction.

Closing the workspace object or a database object while a transaction is pending rolls back all pending transactions.

If you need to isolate transactions on one ODBC data source from those on another ODBC data source, see the **SetIsolateODBCTrans** member function.

For information about transactions, see the article "DAO Workspace: Managing Transactions." For more information about workspaces, see the article "DAO Workspace." Both articles are in *Visual C++ Programmer's Guide* online.

See Also: **CDaoWorkspace::GetIsolateODBCTrans**,
CDaoWorkspace::CommitTrans, **CDaoWorkspace::Rollback**

CDaoWorkspace::CDaoWorkspace

CDaoWorkspace( );

Remarks

Constructs a **CDaoWorkspace** object. After constructing the C++ object, you have
two options:

- Call the object's **Open** member function to open the default workspace or to open
  an existing object in the Workspaces collection.

- Or call the object's **Create** member function to create a new DAO workspace
  object. This explicitly starts a new workspace session, which you can refer to via
  the **CDaoWorkspace** object. After calling **Create**, you can call **Append** if you
  want to add the workspace to the database engine's Workspaces collection.

See the class overview for **CDaoWorkspace** for information about when you need to
explicitly create a **CDaoWorkspace** object. Usually, you use workspaces created
implicitly when you open a **CDaoDatabase** object without specifying a workspace or
when you open a **CDaoRecordset** object without specifying a database object. MFC
DAO objects created in this way use DAO's default workspace, which is created once
and reused.

To release a workspace and its contained objects, call the workspace object's **Close**
member function.

For more information about workspaces, see the article "DAO Workspace." For more
information about implicit workspace creation, see the article "DAO: Accessing
Implicit MFC DAO Objects." Both articles are in *Visual C++ Programmer's Guide*
online.

CDaoWorkspace::Close

virtual void Close( );
    throw(CDaoException, CMemoryException);

Remarks

Call this member function to close the workspace object. Closing an open workspace
object releases the underlying DAO object and, if the workspace is a member of the
Workspaces collection, removes it from the collection. Calling **Close** is good
programming practice.

Caution Closing a workspace object closes any open databases in the workspace. This results in any recordsets open in the databases being closed as well, and any pending edits or updates are rolled back. For related information, see the **CDaoDatabase::Close**, **CDaoRecordset::Close**, **CDaoTableDef::Close**, and **CDaoQueryDef::Close** member functions.

Workspace objects are not permanent; they only exist while references to them exist. This means that when the database engine session ends, the workspace and its Databases collection do not persist. You must re-create them for the next session by opening your workspace and database(s) again.

For more information about workspaces, see the article "DAO Workspace" in *Visual C++ Programmer's Guide* online. For related information, see the topic "Close Method" in DAO Help.

See Also: **CDaoWorkspace::Open**

CDaoWorkspace::CommitTrans

void CommitTrans( );
    throw(CDaoException, CMemoryException);

Remarks

Call this member function to commit a transaction—save a group of edits and updates to one or more databases in the workspace. A transaction consists of a series of changes to the database's data or its structure, beginning with a call to **BeginTrans**. When you complete the transaction, either commit it or roll it back (cancel the changes) with **Rollback**. By default, without transactions, updates to records are committed immediately. Calling **BeginTrans** causes commitment of updates to be delayed until you call **CommitTrans**.

Caution Within one workspace, transactions are always global to the workspace and are not limited to only one database or recordset. If you perform operations on more than one database or recordset within a workspace transaction, **CommitTrans** commits all pending updates, and **Rollback** restores all operations on those databases and recordsets.

When you close a database or workspace with pending transactions, the transactions are all rolled back.

Note This is not a two-phase commit mechanism. If one update fails to commit, others still will commit.

For more information about workspaces, see the article "DAO Workspace." For more about transactions, including information about separate transaction spaces, see the article "DAO Workspace: Managing Transactions." Both articles are in *Visual C++ Programmer's Guide* online.

CDaoWorkspace::CompactDatabase

static void PASCAL CompactDatabase(LPCTSTR *lpszSrcName,*
→ **LPCTSTR** *lpszDestName,* **LPCTSTR** *lpszLocale* **= dbLangGeneral, int** *nOptions* **= 0);**
throw(CDaoException, CMemoryException);
static void PASCAL CompactDatabase(LPCTSTR *lpszSrcName,*
→ **LPCTSTR** *lpszDestName,* **LPCTSTR** *lpszLocale,* **int** *nOptions,*
→ **LPCTSTR** *lpszPassword* **);**
throw(CDaoException, CMemoryException);

Parameters

lpszSrcName The name of an existing, closed database. It can be a full path and filename, such as "C:\\MYDB.MDB". If the filename has an extension, you must specify it. If your network supports the uniform naming convention (UNC), you can also specify a network path, such as "\\\\MYSERVER\\MYSHARE\\MYDIR\\MYDB.MDB". (Double backslashes are required in the path strings because "\" is the C++ escape character.)

lpszDestName The full path of the compacted database that you are creating. You can also specify a network path as with *lpszSrcName*. You cannot use the *lpszDestName* argument to specify the same database file as *lpszSrcName*.

lpszPassword A password, used when you want to compact a password-protected database. Note that if you use the version of **CompactDatabase** that takes a password, you must supply all parameters.

lpszLocale A string expression used to specify collating order for creating *lpszDestName*. If you omit this argument by accepting the default value of **dbLangGeneral** (see below), the locale of the new database is the same as that of the old database. Possible values are:

- **dbLangGeneral** English, German, French, Portuguese, Italian, and Modern Spanish

- **dbLangArabic** Arabic

- **dbLangCyrillic** Russian

- **dbLangCzech** Czech

- **dbLangDutch** Dutch

- **dbLangGreek** Greek

- **dbLangHebrew** Hebrew

- **dbLangHungarian** Hungarian

- **dbLangIcelandic** Icelandic

- **dbLangNordic** Nordic languages (Microsoft Jet database engine version 1.0 only)

- **dbLangNorwdan** Norwegian and Danish
- **dbLangPolish** Polish
- **dbLangSpanish** Traditional Spanish
- **dbLangSwedfin** Swedish and Finnish
- **dbLangTurkish** Turkish

nOptions Indicates one or more options for the target database, *lpszDestName*. If you omit this argument by accepting the default value, the *lpszDestName* will have the same encryption and the same version as *lpszSrcName*. You can combine the **dbEncrypt** or **dbDecrypt** option with one of the version options using the bitwise-OR operator. Possible values, which specify a database format, not a database engine version, are:

- **dbEncrypt** Encrypt the database while compacting.
- **dbDecrypt** Decrypt the database while compacting.
- **dbVersion10** Create a database that uses the Microsoft Jet database engine version 1.0 while compacting.
- **dbVersion11** Create a database that uses the Microsoft Jet database engine version 1.1 while compacting.
- **dbVersion20** Create a database that uses the Microsoft Jet database engine version 2.0 while compacting.
- **dbVersion30** Create a database that uses the Microsoft Jet database engine version 3.0 while compacting.

You can use **dbEncrypt** or **dbDecrypt** in the options argument to specify whether to encrypt or to decrypt the database as it is compacted. If you omit an encryption constant or if you include both **dbDecrypt** and **dbEncrypt**, *lpszDestName* will have the same encryption as *lpszSrcName*. You can use one of the version constants in the options argument to specify the version of the data format for the compacted database. This constant affects only the version of the data format of *lpszDestName*. You can specify only one version constant. If you omit a version constant, *lpszDestName* will have the same version as *lpszSrcName*. You can compact *lpszDestName* only to a version that is the same or later than that of *lpszSrcName*.

Caution If a database is not encrypted, it is possible, even if you implement user/password security, to directly read the binary disk file that constitutes the database.

Remarks

Call this member function to compact a specified Microsoft Jet (.MDB) database. As you change data in a database, the database file can become fragmented and use more disk space than necessary. Periodically, you should compact your database to defragment the database file. The compacted database is usually smaller. You can also choose to change the collating order, the encryption, or the version of the data format while you copy and compact the database.

Warning   The **CompactDatabase** member function will not correctly convert a complete Microsoft Access database from one version to another. Only the data format is converted. Microsoft Access-defined objects, such as forms and reports, are not converted. However, the data is correctly converted.

Tip   You can also use **CompactDatabase** to copy a database file.

For more information about workspaces, see the article "DAO Workspace" in *Visual C++ Programmer's Guide* online. For more information about compacting databases, see the topic "CompactDatabase Method" in DAO Help.

See Also: CDaoWorkspace::RepairDatabase

CDaoWorkspace::Create

> **virtual void Create(LPCTSTR** *lpszName*, **LPCTSTR** *lpszUserName*,
> ↪ **LPCTSTR** *lpszPassword* **);**
> **throw(CDaoException, CMemoryException);**

Parameters

lpszName   A string with up to 14 characters that uniquely names the new workspace object. You must supply a name. For related information, see the topic "Name Property" in DAO Help.

lpszUserName   The user name of the workspace's owner. For requirements, see the *lpszDefaultUser* parameter to the **SetDefaultUser** member function. For related information, see the topic "UserName Property" in DAO Help.

lpszPassword   The password for the new workspace object. A password can be up to 14 characters long and can contain any character except ASCII 0 (null). Passwords are case-sensitive. For related information, see the topic "Password Property" in DAO Help.

Remarks

Call this member function to create a new DAO workspace object and associate it with the MFC **CDaoWorkspace** object. The overall creation process is:

1. Construct a **CDaoWorkspace** object.

2. Call the object's **Create** member function to create the underlying DAO workspace. You must specify a workspace name.

3. Optionally call **Append** if you want to add the workspace to the database engine's Workspaces collection. You can work with the workspace without appending it.

After the **Create** call, the workspace object is in an open state, ready for use. You do not call **Open** after **Create**. You do not call **Create** if the workspace already exists in the Workspaces collection. **Create** initializes the database engine if it has not already been initialized for your application.

For more information about workspaces, see the article "DAO Workspace" in *Visual C++ Programmer's Guide* online.

See Also: **CDaoWorkspace::CDaoWorkspace**, **CDaoWorkspace::Close**, **CDaoWorkspace::Open**

CDaoWorkspace::GetDatabaseCount

short GetDatabaseCount( );
    throw(CDaoException, CMemoryException);

Return Value

The number of open databases in the workspace.

Remarks

Call this member function to retrieve the number of DAO database objects in the workspace's Databases collection — the number of open databases in the workspace. **GetDatabaseCount** is useful if you need to loop through all defined databases in the workspace's Databases collection. To obtain information about a given database in the collection, see **GetDatabaseInfo**. Typical usage is to call **GetDatabaseCount** for the number of open databases, then use that number as a loop index for repeated calls to **GetDatabaseInfo**.

For more information about obtaining database information, see the article "DAO Collections: Obtaining Information About DAO Objects" in *Visual C++ Programmer's Guide* online.

CDaoWorkspace::GetDatabaseInfo

void GetDatabaseInfo(int *nIndex***, CDaoDatabaseInfo&** *dbinfo***,**
    ↪ DWORD *dwInfoOptions* **= AFX_DAO_PRIMARY_INFO);**
    throw(CDaoException, CMemoryException);
void GetDatabaseInfo(LPCTSTR *lpszName***, CDaoDatabaseInfo&** *dbinfo***,**
    ↪ DWORD *dwInfoOptions* **= AFX_DAO_PRIMARY_INFO);**
    throw(CDaoException, CMemoryException);

Parameters

nIndex   The zero-based index of the database object in the workspace's Databases collection, for lookup by index.

dbinfo   A reference to a **CDaoDatabaseInfo** object that returns the information requested.

dwInfoOptions   Options that specify which information about the database to retrieve. The available options are listed here along with what they cause the function to return:

- **AFX_DAO_PRIMARY_INFO**   (Default) Name, Updatable, Transactions
- **AFX_DAO_SECONDARY_INFO**   Primary information plus: Version, Collating Order, Query Timeout
- **AFX_DAO_ALL_INFO**   Primary and secondary information plus: Connect

lpszName   The name of the database object, for lookup by name. The name is a string with up to 14 characters that uniquely names the new workspace object.

Remarks

Call this member function to obtain various kinds of information about a database open in the workspace. One version of the function lets you look up a database by index. The other version lets you look up a database by name.

For a description of the information returned in *dbinfo*, see the **CDaoDatabaseInfo** structure. This structure has members that correspond to the items of information listed above in the description of *dwInfoOptions*. When you request information at one level, you get information for any prior levels as well.

For more information about obtaining database information, see the article "DAO Collections: Obtaining Information About DAO Objects" in *Visual C++ Programmer's Guide* online.

See Also: **CDaoWorkspace::GetDatabaseCount**

CDaoWorkspace::GetIniPath

static CString PASCAL GetIniPath( );
    throw(CDaoException, CMemoryException);

Return Value

A **CString** containing the registry location.

Remarks

Call this member function to obtain the location of the Microsoft Jet database engine's initialization settings in the Windows registry. You can use the location to obtain information about settings for the database engine. The information returned is actually the name of a registry subkey.

For more information about the database engine, see the article "DAO Workspace: The Database Engine" in *Visual C++ Programmer's Guide* online. For related information, see the topics "IniPath Property" and "Customizing Windows Registry Settings for Data Access" in DAO Help.

See Also: **CDaoWorkspace::SetIniPath, CDaoWorkspace::GetVersion**

CDaoWorkspace::GetIsolateODBCTrans

BOOL GetIsolateODBCTrans( );
throw(CDaoException, CMemoryException);

Return Value

Nonzero if ODBC transactions are isolated; otherwise 0.

Remarks

Call this member function to get the current value of the DAO IsolateODBCTrans property for the workspace. In some situations, you might need to have multiple simultaneous transactions pending on the same ODBC database. To do this, you need to open a separate workspace for each transaction. Keep in mind that although each workspace can have its own ODBC connection to the database, this slows system performance. Because transaction isolation is not normally required, ODBC connections from multiple workspace objects opened by the same user are shared by default.

Some ODBC servers, such as Microsoft SQL Server, do not allow simultaneous transactions on a single connection. If you need to have more than one transaction at a time pending against such a database, set the IsolateODBCTrans property to **TRUE** on each workspace as soon as you open it. This forces a separate ODBC connection for each workspace.

For more information about workspaces, see the article "DAO Workspace." For more information about working with ODBC data sources through DAO, see the article "DAO External: Working with External Data Sources." Both articles are in *Visual C++ Programmer's Guide* online. For related information, see the topic "IsolateODBCTrans Property" in DAO Help.

See Also: **CDaoWorkspace::SetIsolateODBCTrans**

CDaoWorkspace::GetLoginTimeout

static short PASCAL GetLoginTimeout( );
throw(CDaoException, CMemoryException);

Return Value

The number of seconds before an error occurs when you attempt to log in to an ODBC database.

Remarks

Call this member function to get the current value of the DAO LoginTimeout property for the workspace. This value represents the number of seconds before an error occurs when you attempt to log in to an ODBC database. The default LoginTimeout setting is 20 seconds. When LoginTimeout is set to 0, no timeout occurs and the communication with the data source might hang.

When you are attempting to log in to an ODBC database, such as Microsoft SQL Server, the connection may fail as a result of network errors or because the server is not running. Rather than waiting for the default 20 seconds to connect, you can specify how long the database engine waits before it produces an error. Logging in to the server happens implicitly as part of a number of different events, such as running a query on an external server database.

For more information about workspaces, see the article "DAO Workspace." For more information about working with ODBC data sources through DAO, see the article "DAO External: Working with External Data Sources." Both articles are in *Visual C++ Programmer's Guide* online. For related information, see the topic "LoginTimeout Property" in DAO Help.

See Also: CDaoWorkspace::SetLoginTimeout

CDaoWorkspace::GetName

CString GetName( );
   throw(CDaoException, CMemoryException);

Return Value

A **CString** containing the user-defined name of the DAO workspace object.

Remarks

Call this member function to get the user-defined name of the DAO workspace object underlying the **CDaoWorkspace** object. The name is useful for accessing the DAO workspace object in the database engine's Workspaces collection by name.

For more information about workspaces, see the article "DAO Workspace" in *Visual C++ Programmer's Guide* online. For related information, see the topic "Name Property" in DAO Help.

CDaoWorkspace::GetUserName

CString GetUserName( );
   throw(CDaoException, CMemoryException);

Return Value

A **CString** that represents the owner of the workspace object.

Remarks

Call this member function to obtain the name of the owner of the workspace.

To get or set the permissions for the workspace owner, call DAO directly to check the Permissions property setting; this determines what permissions that user has. To work with permissions, you need a SYSTEM.MDA file.

For more information about workspaces, see the article "DAO Workspace." For information about calling DAO directly, see Technical Note 54 online. For related information, see the topic "UserName Property" in DAO Help.

See Also: CDaoWorkspace::SetDefaultUser

CDaoWorkspace::GetVersion

static CString PASCAL GetVersion( );
 throw(CDaoException, CMemoryException);

Return Value

A **CString** that indicates the version of the database engine associated with the object.

Remarks

Call this member function to determine the version of the Microsoft Jet database engine in use. The value returned represents the version number in the form "major.minor"; for example, "3.0". The product version number (for example, 3.0) consists of the version number (3), a period, and the release number (0).

For more information about obtaining workspace information, see the article "DAO Collections: Obtaining Information About DAO Objects" in *Visual C++ Programmer's Guide* online. For related information, see the topic "Version Property" in DAO Help.

See Also: CDaoDatabase::GetVersion

CDaoWorkspace::GetWorkspaceCount

short GetWorkspaceCount( );
 throw(CDaoException, CMemoryException);

Return Value

The number of open workspaces in the Workspaces collection.

Remarks

Call this member function to retrieve the number of DAO workspace objects in the database engine's Workspaces collection. This count does not include any open workspaces not appended to the collection. **GetWorkspaceCount** is useful if you need to loop through all defined workspaces in the Workspaces collection. To obtain information about a given workspace in the collection, see **GetWorkspaceInfo**. Typical usage is to call **GetWorkspaceCount** for the number of open workspaces, then use that number as a loop index for repeated calls to **GetWorkspaceInfo**.

For more information about obtaining workspace information, see the article "DAO Collections: Obtaining Information About DAO Objects" in *Visual C++ Programmer's Guide* online.

CDaoWorkspace::GetWorkspaceInfo

void GetWorkspaceInfo(int *nIndex*, **CDaoWorkspaceInfo&** *wkspcinfo*
↳ **DWORD** *dwInfoOptions* = **AFX_DAO_PRIMARY_INFO**);
throw(CDaoException, CMemoryException);
void GetWorkspaceInfo(LPCTSTR *lpszName*, **CDaoWorkspaceInfo&** *wkspcinfo*
↳ **DWORD** *dwInfoOptions* = **AFX_DAO_PRIMARY_INFO**);
throw(CDaoException, CMemoryException);

Parameters

nIndex   The zero-based index of the database object in the Workspaces collection, for lookup by index.

wkspcinfo   A reference to a **CDaoWorkspaceInfo** object that returns the information requested.

dwInfoOptions   Options that specify which information about the workspace to retrieve. The available options are listed here along with what they cause the function to return:

- **AFX_DAO_PRIMARY_INFO**   (Default) Name
- **AFX_DAO_SECONDARY_INFO**   Primary information plus: User Name
- **AFX_DAO_ALL_INFO**   Primary and secondary information plus: Isolate ODBCTrans

lpszName   The name of the workspace object, for lookup by name. The name is a string with up to 14 characters that uniquely names the new workspace object.

Remarks

Call this member function to obtain various kinds of information about a workspace open in the session. For a description of the information returned in *wkspcinfo*, see the **CDaoWorkspaceInfo** structure. This structure has members that correspond to the items of information listed above in the description of *dwInfoOptions*. When you request information at one level, you get information for prior levels as well.

For more information about obtaining workspace information, see the article "DAO Collections: Obtaining Information About DAO Objects" in *Visual C++ Programmer's Guide* online.

See Also: **CDaoWorkspace::GetWorkspaceCount**

CDaoWorkspace::Idle

static void PASCAL Idle(int *nAction* = **dbFreeLocks**);
throw(CDaoException, CMemoryException);

Parameters

nAction   An action to take during the idle processing. Currently the only valid action is **dbFreeLocks**.

Remarks

Call **Idle** to provide the database engine with the opportunity to perform background tasks that may not be up-to-date because of intense data processing. This is often true in multiuser, multitasking environments in which there is not enough background processing time to keep all records in a recordset current.

Important Calling **Idle** is not necessary with databases created with version 3.0 of the Microsoft Jet database engine. Use **Idle** only for databases created with earlier versions.

Usually, read locks are removed and data in local dynaset-type recordset objects is updated only when no other actions (including mouse movements) are occurring. If you periodically call **Idle**, you provide the database engine with time to catch up on background processing tasks by releasing unneeded read locks. Specifying the **dbFreeLocks** constant as an argument delays processing until all read locks are released.

This member function is not needed in single-user environments unless multiple instances of an application are running. The **Idle** member function may increase performance in a multiuser environment because it forces the database engine to flush data to disk, releasing locks on memory. You can also release read locks by making operations part of a transaction.

For more information about workspaces, see the article "DAO Workspace" in *Visual C++ Programmer's Guide* online. For related information, see the topic "Idle Method" in DAO Help.

CDaoWorkspace::IsOpen

BOOL IsOpen( ) const;

Return Value

Nonzero if the workspace object is open; otherwise 0.

Remarks

Call this member function to determine whether the **CDaoWorkspace** object is open—that is, whether the MFC object has been initialized by a call to **Open** or a call to **Create**. You can call any of the member functions of a workspace that is in an open state.

For more information about workspaces, see the article "DAO Workspace" in *Visual C++ Programmer's Guide* online.

CDaoWorkspace::Open

virtual void Open(LPCTSTR *lpszName* **= NULL);**
  throw(CDaoException, CMemoryException);

Parameters

> *lpszName* The name of the DAO workspace object to open—a string with up to 14 characters that uniquely names the workspace. Accept the default value **NULL** to explicitly open the default workspace. For naming requirements, see the *lpszName* parameter for **Create**. For related information, see the topic "Name Property" in DAO Help.

Remarks

> After constructing a **CDaoWorkspace** object, call this member function to do one of the following:
>
> - Explicitly open the default workspace. Pass **NULL** for *lpszName*.
>
> - Open an existing **CDaoWorkspace** object, a member of the Workspaces collection, by name. Pass a valid name for an existing workspace object.
>
> **Open** puts the workspace object into an open state and also initializes the database engine if it has not already been initialized for your application.
>
> Although many **CDaoWorkspace** member functions can only be called after the workspace has been opened, the following member functions, which operate on the database engine, are available after construction of the C++ object but before a call to **Open**:

Create	**GetVersion**	**SetDefaultUser**
GetIniPath	**Idle**	**SetIniPath**
GetLoginTimeout	**SetDefaultPassword**	**SetLoginTimeout**

> For more information about workspaces, see the article "DAO Workspace" in *Visual C++ Programmer's Guide* online.
>
> **See Also:** **CDaoWorkspace::IsOpen, CDaoWorkspace::CDaoWorkspace, CDaoWorkspace::Create, CDaoWorkspace::Close**

CDaoWorkspace::RepairDatabase

static void PASCAL RepairDatabase(LPCTSTR *lpszName* **);**
  throw(CDaoException, CMemoryException);

Parameters

> *lpszName* The path and filename for an existing Microsoft Jet engine database file. If you omit the path, only the current directory is searched. If your system supports the uniform naming convention (UNC), you can also specify a network path, such

as: "\\\\MYSERVER\\MYSHARE\\MYDIR\\MYDB.MDB". (Double backslashes are required in the path string because "\" is the C++ escape character.)

Remarks

Call this member function if you need to attempt to repair a corrupted database that accesses the Microsoft Jet database engine. You must close the database specified by *lpszName* before you repair it. In a multiuser environment, other users cannot have *lpszName* open while you are repairing it. If *lpszName* is not closed or is not available for exclusive use, an error occurs.

This member function attempts to repair a database that was marked as possibly corrupt by an incomplete write operation. This can occur if an application using the Microsoft Jet database engine is closed unexpectedly because of a power outage or computer hardware problem. If you complete the operation and call the **Close** member function or you quit the application in a usual way, the database will not be marked as possibly corrupt.

Note   After repairing a database, it is also a good idea to compact it using the **CompactDatabase** member function to defragment the file and to recover disk space.

For more information about workspaces, see the article "DAO Workspace" in *Visual C++ Programmer's Guide* online. For more information about repairing databases, see the topic "RepairDatabase Method" in DAO Help.

CDaoWorkspace::Rollback

void Rollback( );
    throw(CDaoException, CMemoryException);

Remarks

Call this member function to end the current transaction and restore all databases in the workspace to their condition before the transaction was begun.

Caution   Within one workspace object, transactions are always global to the workspace and are not limited to only one database or recordset. If you perform operations on more than one database or recordset within a workspace transaction, **Rollback** restores all operations on all of those databases and recordsets.

If you close a workspace object without saving or rolling back any pending transactions, the transactions are automatically rolled back. If you call **CommitTrans** or **Rollback** without first calling **BeginTrans**, an error occurs.

Note   When you begin a transaction, the database engine records its operations in a file kept in the directory specified by the TEMP environment variable on the workstation. If the transaction log file exhausts the available storage on your TEMP drive, the database engine will cause MFC to throw a **CDaoException** (DAO error 2004). At this point, if you call **CommitTrans**, an indeterminate number of operations are committed but the remaining uncompleted operations are lost, and the operation has to be restarted. Calling **Rollback** releases the transaction log and rolls back all operations in the transaction.

For more information about workspaces, see the article "DAO Workspace." For more about transactions, see the article "DAO Workspace: Managing Transactions." Both articles are in *Visual C++ Programmer's Guide* online.

See Also: CDaoRecordset

CDaoWorkspace::SetDefaultPassword

static void PASCAL SetDefaultPassword(LPCTSTR *lpszPassword* **);**
    throw(CDaoException, CMemoryException);

Parameters

lpszPassword   The default password. A password can be up to 14 characters long and can contain any character except ASCII 0 (null). Passwords are case-sensitive.

Remarks

Call this member function to set the default password that the database engine uses when a workspace object is created without a specific password. The default password that you set applies to new workspaces you create after the call. When you create subsequent workspaces, you do not need to specify a password in the **Create** call.

To use this member function:

1. Construct a **CDaoWorkspace** object but do not call **Create**.
2. Call **SetDefaultPassword** and, if you like, **SetDefaultUser**.
3. Call **Create** for this workspace object or subsequent ones, without specifying a password.

By default, the DefaultUser property is set to "admin" and the DefaultPassword property is set to an empty string ("").

For more information about workspaces, see the article "DAO Workspace" in *Visual C++ Programmer's Guide* online. For more about security, see the topic "Permissions Property" in DAO Help. For related information, see the topics "DefaultPassword Property" and "DefaultUser Property" in DAO Help.

CDaoWorkspace::SetDefaultUser

static void PASCAL SetDefaultUser(LPCTSTR *lpszDefaultUser* **);**
    throw(CDaoException, CMemoryException);

Parameters

lpszDefaultUser   The default user name. A user name can be 1–20 characters long and include alphabetic characters, accented characters, numbers, spaces, and symbols

except for: " (quotation marks), / (forward slash), \ (backslash), [ ] (brackets), :
(colon), | (pipe), < (less-than sign), > (greater-than sign), + (plus sign), = (equal sign),
; (semicolon), , (comma), ? (question mark), * (asterisk), leading spaces, and control
characters (ASCII 00 to ASCII 31). For related information, see the topic "UserName
Property" in DAO Help.

Remarks

Call this member function to set the default user name that the database engine uses
when a workspace object is created without a specific user name. The default user
name that you set applies to new workspaces you create after the call. When you
create subsequent workspaces, you do not need to specify a user name in the **Create**
call.

To use this member function:

1. Construct a **CDaoWorkspace** object but do not call **Create**.

2. Call **SetDefaultUser** and, if you like, **SetDefaultPassword**.

3. Call **Create** for this workspace object or subsequent ones, without specifying a
   user name.

By default, the DefaultUser property is set to "admin" and the DefaultPassword
property is set to an empty string ("").

For more information about workspaces, see the article "DAO Workspace" in
Visual C++ Programmer's Guide online. For related information, see the topics
"DefaultUser Property" and "DefaultPassword Property" in DAO Help.

CDaoWorkspace::SetIniPath

static void PASCAL SetIniPath(LPCTSTR *lpszRegistrySubkey* **);**
throw(CDaoException, CMemoryException);

Parameters

lpszRegistrySubkey   A string containing the name of a Windows registry subkey for
the location of Microsoft Jet database engine settings or parameters needed for
installable ISAM databases.

Remarks

Call this member function to specify the location of Windows registry settings for the
Microsoft Jet database engine. Call **SetIniPath** only if you need to specify special
settings. For more information, see the topic "IniPath Property" in DAO Help.

Important Call **SetIniPath** during application installation, not when the application runs. **SetIniPath** must be called before you open any workspaces, databases, or recordsets; otherwise, MFC throws an exception.

You can use this mechanism to configure the database engine with user-provided registry settings. The scope of this attribute is limited to your application and cannot be changed without restarting your application.

For more information about workspaces, see the article "DAO Workspace" in *Visual C++ Programmer's Guide* online.

CDaoWorkspace::SetIsolateODBCTrans

void SetIsolateODBCTrans(BOOL *bIsolateODBCTrans* **);**
    throw(CDaoException, CMemoryException);

Parameters

bIsolateODBCTrans   Pass **TRUE** if you want to begin isolating ODBC transactions. Pass **FALSE** if you want to stop isolating ODBC transactions.

Remarks

Call this member function to set the value of the DAO IsolateODBCTrans property for the workspace. In some situations, you might need to have multiple simultaneous transactions pending on the same ODBC database. To do this, you need to open a separate workspace for each transaction. Although each workspace can have its own ODBC connection to the database, this slows system performance. Because transaction isolation is not normally required, ODBC connections from multiple workspace objects opened by the same user are shared by default.

Some ODBC servers, such as Microsoft SQL Server, do not allow simultaneous transactions on a single connection. If you need to have more than one transaction at a time pending against such a database, set the IsolateODBCTrans property to **TRUE** on each workspace as soon as you open it. This forces a separate ODBC connection for each workspace.

For more information about workspaces, see the article "DAO Workspace." For more about transactions, see the article "DAO Workspace: Managing Transactions." For more about working with ODBC data sources through DAO, see the article "DAO External: Working with External Data Sources." All articles are in *Visual C++ Programmer's Guide* online.

See Also: **CDaoWorkspace::GetIsolateODBCTrans**

CDaoWorkspace::SetLoginTimeout

static void PASCAL SetLoginTimeout(short *nSeconds*);
throw(CDaoException, CMemoryException);

Parameters

nSeconds   The number of seconds before an error occurs when you attempt to log in to an ODBC database.

Remarks

Call this member function to set the value of the DAO LoginTimeout property for the workspace. This value represents the number of seconds before an error occurs when you attempt to log in to an ODBC database. The default LoginTimeout setting is 20 seconds. When LoginTimeout is set to 0, no timeout occurs and the communication with the data source might hang.

When you are attempting to log in to an ODBC database, such as Microsoft SQL Server, the connection may fail as a result of network errors or because the server is not running. Rather than waiting for the default 20 seconds to connect, you can specify how long the database engine waits before it produces an error. Logging on to the server happens implicitly as part of a number of different events, such as running a query on an external server database. The timeout value is determined by the current setting of the LoginTimeout property.

For more information about workspaces, see the article "DAO Workspace." For more information about working with ODBC data sources through DAO, see the article "DAO External: Working with External Data Sources." Both articles are in *Visual C++ Programmer's Guide* online. For related information, see the topic "LoginTimeout Property" in DAO Help.

See Also: CDaoWorkspace::GetLoginTimeout

Data Members

CDaoWorkspace::m_pDAOWorkspace

Remarks

A pointer to the underlying DAO workspace object. Use this data member if you need direct access to the underlying DAO object. You can call the DAO object's interfaces through this pointer.

For information about accessing DAO objects directly, see Technical Note 54 online.

CDatabase

A **CDatabase** object represents a connection to a data source, through which you can operate on the data source. A data source is a specific instance of data hosted by some database management system (DBMS). Examples include Microsoft SQL Server, Microsoft Access, Borland® dBASE®, and xBASE. You can have one or more **CDatabase** objects active at a time in your application.

Note If you are working with the Data Access Objects (DAO) classes rather than the Open Database Connectivity (ODBC) classes, use class **CDaoDatabase** instead. For more information, see the articles "Database Topics (General)" and "DAO and MFC." Both articles are in *Visual C++ Programmer's Guide* online.

To use **CDatabase**, construct a **CDatabase** object and call its **OpenEx** member function. This opens a connection. When you then construct **CRecordset** objects for operating on the connected data source, pass the recordset constructor a pointer to your **CDatabase** object. When you finish using the connection, call the **Close** member function and destroy the **CDatabase** object. **Close** closes any recordsets you have not closed previously.

For more information about **CDatabase**, see the articles "Data Source (ODBC)" and "Database Topics (General)" in *Visual C++ Programmer's Guide* online.

#include <afxdb.h>

See Also: **CRecordset**

CDatabase Class Members

Data Members

m_hdbc	Open Database Connectivity (ODBC) connection handle to a data source. Type **HDBC**.

Construction

CDatabase	Constructs a **CDatabase** object. You must initialize the object by calling **OpenEx** or **Open**.
Open	Establishes a connection to a data source (through an ODBC driver).
OpenEx	Establishes a connection to a data source (through an ODBC driver).
Close	Closes the data source connection.

Database Attributes

GetConnect	Returns the ODBC connect string used to connect the **CDatabase** object to a data source.
IsOpen	Returns nonzero if the **CDatabase** object is currently connected to a data source.
GetDatabaseName	Returns the name of the database currently in use.
CanUpdate	Returns nonzero if the **CDatabase** object is updatable (not read-only).
CanTransact	Returns nonzero if the data source supports transactions.
SetLoginTimeout	Sets the number of seconds after which a data source connection attempt will time out.
SetQueryTimeout	Sets the number of seconds after which database query operations will time out. Affects all subsequent recordset **Open**, **AddNew**, **Edit**, and **Delete** calls.
GetBookmarkPersistence	Identifies the operations through which bookmarks persist on recordset objects.
GetCursorCommitBehavior	Identifies the effect of committing a transaction on an open recordset object.
GetCursorRollbackBehavior	Identifies the effect of rolling back a transaction on an open recordset object.

Database Operations

BeginTrans	Starts a "transaction"—a series of reversible calls to the **AddNew**, **Edit**, **Delete**, and **Update** member functions of class **CRecordset**—on the connected data source. The data source must support transactions for **BeginTrans** to have any effect.
CommitTrans	Completes a transaction begun by **BeginTrans**. Commands in the transaction that alter the data source are carried out.
Rollback	Reverses changes made during the current transaction. The data source returns to its previous state, as defined at the **BeginTrans** call, unaltered.
Cancel	Cancels an asynchronous operation or a process from a second thread.
ExecuteSQL	Executes an SQL statement. No data records are returned.

Database Overridables

OnSetOptions	Called by the framework to set standard connection options. The default implementation sets the query timeout value. You can establish these options ahead of time by calling **SetQueryTimeout**.

Member Functions
CDatabase::BeginTrans

BOOL BeginTrans( );

Return Value

Nonzero if the call was successful and changes are committed only manually; otherwise 0.

Remarks

Call this member function to begin a transaction with the connected data source. A transaction consists of one or more calls to the **AddNew**, **Edit**, **Delete**, and **Update** member functions of a **CRecordset** object. Before beginning a transaction, the **CDatabase** object must already have been connected to the data source by calling its **OpenEx** or **Open** member function. To end the transaction, call **CommitTrans** to accept all changes to the data source (and carry them out) or call **Rollback** to abort the entire transaction. Call **BeginTrans** after you open any recordsets involved in the transaction and as close to the actual update operations as possible.

Caution   Depending on your ODBC driver, opening a recordset before calling **BeginTrans** may cause problems when calling **Rollback**. You should check the specific driver you are using. For example, when using the Microsoft Access driver included in the Microsoft ODBC Desktop Driver Pack 3.0, you must account for the Jet database engine's requirement that you should not begin a transaction on any database that has an open cursor. In the MFC database classes, an open cursor means an open **CRecordset** object. For more information, see Technical Note 68 online.

BeginTrans may also lock data records on the server, depending on the requested concurrency and the capabilities of the data source. For information about locking data, see the article "Recordset: Locking Records (ODBC)" in *Visual C++ Programmer's Guide* online.

User-defined transactions are explained in the article "Transaction (ODBC)" in *Visual C++ Programmer's Guide* online.

BeginTrans establishes the state to which the sequence of transactions can be rolled back (reversed). To establish a new state for rollbacks, commit any current transaction, then call **BeginTrans** again.

Warning   Calling **BeginTrans** again without calling **CommitTrans** or **Rollback** is an error.

Call the **CanTransact** member function to determine whether your driver supports transactions for a given database. You should also call **GetCursorCommitBehavior** and **GetCursorRollbackBehavior** to determine the support for cursor preservation.

For more information about transactions, see the article "Transaction (ODBC)" in *Visual C++ Programmer's Guide* online.

Example

See the article "Transaction: Performing a Transaction in a Recordset (ODBC)" in *Visual C++ Programmer's Guide* online.

See Also: **CDatabase::CommitTrans, CDatabase::Rollback, CRecordset::CanTransact**

CDatabase::Cancel

void Cancel( );

Remarks

Call this member function to request that the data source cancel either an asynchronous operation in progress or a process from a second thread. Note that the MFC ODBC classes no longer use asynchronous processing; to perform an aychronous operation, you must directly call the ODBC API function **SQLSetConnectOption**. For more information, see the topic "Executing Functions Asynchronously" in the *ODBC SDK Programmer's Guide* online.

CDatabase::CanTransact

BOOL CanTransact( ) const;

Return Value

Nonzero if recordsets using this **CDatabase** object allow transactions; otherwise 0.

Remarks

Call this member function to determine whether the database allows transactions. For information about transactions, see the article "Transaction (ODBC)" in *Visual C++ Programmer's Guide* online.

See Also: **CDatabase::BeginTrans, CDatabase::CommitTrans, CDatabase::Rollback**

CDatabase::CanUpdate

BOOL CanUpdate( ) const;

Return Value

Nonzero if the **CDatabase** object allows updates; otherwise 0, indicating either that you passed **TRUE** in *bReadOnly* when you opened the **CDatabase** object or that the data source itself is read-only. The data source is read-only if a call to the ODBC API function **::SQLGetInfo** for **SQL_DATASOURCE_READ_ONLY** returns "y".

Remarks

Call this member function to determine whether the **CDatabase** object allows updates. Not all drivers support updates.

CDatabase::CDatabase

CDatabase( );

Remarks

Constructs a **CDatabase** object. After constructing the object, you must call its **OpenEx** or **Open** member function to establish a connection to a specified data source.

You may find it convenient to embed the **CDatabase** object in your document class.

Example

```
// This example illustrates using CDatabase
// in a CDocument-derived class.

class CMyDocument : public CDocument
{
public:
    // Declare a CDatabase embedded in the document
    CDatabase m_dbCust;
    // ...
};

// ...

// Initialize when needed
CDatabase* CMyDocument::GetDatabase( )
{
    // Connect the object to a data source
    if( !m_dbCust.IsOpen( ) &&
        !m_dbCust.OpenEx( NULL ) )
        return NULL;

    return &m_dbCust;
}
```

See Also: **CDatabase::OpenEx**, **CDatabase::Open**

CDatabase::Close

virtual void Close( );

Remarks

Call this member function if you want to disconnect from a data source. You must close any recordsets associated with the **CDatabase** object before you call this member function. Because **Close** does not destroy the **CDatabase** object, you can reuse the object by opening a new connection to the same data source or a different data source.

All pending **AddNew** or **Edit** statements of recordsets using the database are canceled, and all pending transactions are rolled back. Any recordsets dependent on the **CDatabase** object are left in an undefined state.

Example

```
// Close the current connection
m_dbCust.Close( );

// Perhaps connect the object to a
// different data source
m_dbCust.OpenEx("DSN=MYDATASOURCE;UID=JOES");
```

See Also: **CDatabase::OpenEx, CDatabase::Open**

CDatabase::CommitTrans

BOOL CommitTrans( );

Return Value

Nonzero if the updates were successfully committed; otherwise 0. If **CommitTrans** fails, the state of the data source is undefined. You must check the data to determine its state.

Remarks

Call this member function upon completing transactions. A transaction consists of a series of calls to the **AddNew**, **Edit**, **Delete**, and **Update** member functions of a **CRecordset** object that began with a call to the **BeginTrans** member function. **CommitTrans** commits the transaction. By default, updates are committed immediately; calling **BeginTrans** causes commitment of updates to be delayed until **CommitTrans** is called.

Until you call **CommitTrans** to end a transaction, you can call the **Rollback** member function to abort the transaction and leave the data source in its original state. To begin a new transaction, call **BeginTrans** again.

For more information about transactions, see the article "Transaction (ODBC)" in *Visual C++ Programmer's Guide* online.

Example

See the article "Transaction: Performing a Transaction in a Recordset (ODBC)" in *Visual C++ Programmer's Guide* online.

See Also: **CDatabase::BeginTrans, CDatabase::Rollback**

CDatabase::ExecuteSQL

void ExecuteSQL(LPCSTR *lpszSQL* **); throw(CDBException);**

Parameters

lpszSQL   Pointer to a null-terminated string containing a valid SQL command to
execute. You can pass a **CString**.

Remarks

Call this member function when you need to execute an SQL command directly.
Create the command as a null-terminated string. **ExecuteSQL** does not return data
records. If you want to operate on records, use a recordset object instead.

Most of your commands for a data source are issued through recordset objects, which
support commands for selecting data, inserting new records, deleting records, and
editing records. However, not all ODBC functionality is directly supported by the
database classes, so you may at times need to make a direct SQL call with
ExecuteSQL.

Example

```
CString strCmd = "UPDATE Taxes SET Federal = 36%";

TRY
{
    m_dbCust.ExecuteSQL( strCmd );
}

CATCH(CDBException, e)
{
    // The error code is in e->m_nRetCode
}

END_CATCH
```

See Also: CDatabase::SetLoginTimeout, CRecordset

CDatabase::GetBookmarkPersistence

DWORD GetBookmarkPersistence( ) const;

Return Value

A bitmask that identifies the operations through which bookmarks persist on a
recordset object. For details, see Remarks.

Remarks

Call this member function to determine the persistence of bookmarks on a recordset
object after certain operations. For example, if you call **CRecordset::GetBookmark**
and then call **CRecordset::Requery**, the bookmark obtained from **GetBookmark**

may no longer be valid. You should call **GetBookmarkPersistence** before calling **CRecordset::SetBookmark**.

The following table lists the bitmask values that can be combined for the return value of **GetBookmarkPersistence**.

Bitmask value	Bookmark persistence
SQL_BP_CLOSE	Bookmarks are valid after a **Requery** operation.
SQL_BP_DELETE	The bookmark for a row is valid after a **Delete** operation on that row.
SQL_BP_DROP	Bookmarks are valid after a **Close** operation.
SQL_BP_SCROLL	Bookmarks are valid after any **Move** operation. This simply identifies if bookmarks are supported on the recordset, as returned by **CRecordset::CanBookmark**.
SQL_BP_TRANSACTION	Bookmarks are valid after a transaction is committed or rolled back.
SQL_BP_UPDATE	The bookmark for a row is valid after an **Update** operation on that row.
SQL_BP_OTHER_HSTMT	Bookmarks associated with one recordset object are valid on a second recordset.

For more information about this return value, see the ODBC API function **SQLGetInfo** in the *ODBC SDK Programmer's Reference*. For more information about bookmarks, see the article "Recordset: Bookmarks and Absolute Positions (ODBC)" in *Visual C++ Programmer's Guide* online.

See Also: **CRecordset**, **CRecordset::CanBookmark**, **CRecordset::GetBookmark**, **CRecordset::SetBookmark**

CDatabase::GetConnect

const CString& GetConnect( ) const;

Return Value

A **const** reference to a **CString** containing the connect string if **OpenEx** or **Open** has been called; otherwise, an empty string.

Remarks

Call this member function to retrieve the connect string used during the call to **OpenEx** or **Open** that connected the **CDatabase** object to a data source.

See **CDatabase::Open** for a description of how the connect string is created.

See Also: **CDatabase::OpenEx**, **CDatabase::Open**

CDatabase::GetCursorCommitBehavior

int GetCursorCommitBehavior( ) const;

Return Value

A value indicating the effect of transactions on open recordset objects. For details, see Remarks.

Remarks

Call this member function to determine how a **CommitTrans** operation affects cursors on open recordset objects.

The following table lists the possible return values for **GetCursorCommitBehavior** and the corresponding effect on the open recordset.

Return value	Effect on CRecordset objects
SQL_CB_CLOSE	Call **CRecordset::Requery** immediately following the transaction commit.
SQL_CB_DELETE	Call **CRecordset::Close** immediately following the transaction commit.
SQL_CB_PRESERVE	Proceed normally with **CRecordset** operations.

For more information about this return value, see the ODBC API function **SQLGetInfo** in the *ODBC SDK Programmer's Reference*. For more information about transactions, see the article "Transaction (ODBC)" in *Visual C++ Programmer's Guide* online.

See Also: **CDatabase::GetCursorRollbackBehavior, CDatabase::CanTransact, CDatabase::BeginTrans, CDatabase::CommitTrans, CDatabase::Rollback, CRecordset**

CDatabase::GetCursorRollbackBehavior

int GetCursorRollbackBehavior( ) const;

Return Value

A value indicating the effect of transactions on open recordset objects. For details, see Remarks.

Remarks

Call this member function to determine how a **Rollback** operation affects cursors on open recordset objects.

The following table lists the possible return values for **GetCursorRollbackBehavior** and the corresponding effect on the open recordset.

Return value	Effect on CRecordset objects
SQL_CB_CLOSE	Call **CRecordset::Requery** immediately following the transaction rollback.
SQL_CB_DELETE	Call **CRecordset::Close** immediately following the transaction rollback.
SQL_CB_PRESERVE	Proceed normally with **CRecordset** operations.

For more information about this return value, see the ODBC API function **SQLGetInfo** in the *ODBC SDK Programmer's Reference*. For more information about transactions, see the article "Transaction (ODBC)" in *Visual C++ Programmer's Guide* online.

See Also: **CDatabase::GetCursorCommitBehavior, CDatabase::CanTransact, CDatabase::BeginTrans, CDatabase::CommitTrans, CDatabase::Rollback, CRecordset**

CDatabase::GetDatabaseName

CString GetDatabaseName( ) const;

Return Value

A **CString** containing the database name if successful; otherwise, an empty **CString**.

Remarks

Call this member function to retrieve the name of the currently connected database (provided that the data source defines a named object called "database"). This is not the same as the data source name (DSN) specified in the **OpenEx** or **Open** call. What **GetDatabaseName** returns depends on ODBC. In general, a database is a collection of tables. If this entity has a name, **GetDatabaseName** returns it.

You might, for example, want to display this name in a heading. If an error occurs while retrieving the name from ODBC, **GetDatabaseName** returns an empty **Cstring**.

See Also: **CDatabase::OpenEx, CDatabase::Open, CDatabase::GetConnect**

CDatabase::IsOpen

BOOL IsOpen( ) const;

Return Value

Nonzero if the **CDatabase** object is currently connected; otherwise 0.

Remarks

Call this member function to determine whether the **CDatabase** object is currently connected to a data source.

See Also: **CDatabase::OpenEx, CDatabase::Open**

CDatabase::OnSetOptions

>**virtual void OnSetOptions(HSTMT** *hstmt* **);**

Parameters

>*hstmt*   The ODBC statement handle for which options are being set.

Remarks

>The framework calls this member function when directly executing an SQL statement with the **ExecuteSQL** member function. **CRecordset::OnSetOptions** also calls this member function.

>**OnSetOptions** sets the login timeout value. If there have been previous calls to the **SetQueryTimeout** and member function, **OnSetOptions** reflects the current values; otherwise, it sets default values.

>**Note**   Prior to MFC 4.2, **OnSetOptions** also set the processing mode to either snychronous or asynchronous. Beginning with MFC 4.2, all operations are synchronous. To perform an asynchronous operation, you must make a direct call to the ODBC API function **SQLSetPos**.

>You do not need to override **OnSetOptions** to change the timeout value. Instead, to customize the query timeout value, call **SetQueryTimeout** before creating a recordset; **OnSetOptions** will use the new value. The values set apply to subsequent operations on all recordsets or direct SQL calls.

>Override **OnSetOptions** if you want to set additional options. Your override should call the base class **OnSetOptions** either before or after you call the ODBC API function **::SQLSetStmtOption**. Follow the method illustrated in the framework's default implementation of **OnSetOptions**.

>**See Also:**   **CDatabase::ExecuteSQL, CDatabase::SetQueryTimeout, CRecordset::OnSetOptions**

CDatabase::Open

>**virtual BOOL Open(LPCTSTR** *lpszDSN*, **BOOL** *bExclusive* = **FALSE,**
> ↳ **BOOL** *bReadOnly* = **FALSE, LPCTSTR** *lpszConnect* = **"ODBC;",**
> ↳ **BOOL** *bUseCursorLib* = **TRUE);**
> **throw(CDBException, CMemoryException);**

Return Value

>Nonzero if the connection is successfully made; otherwise 0 if the user chooses Cancel when presented a dialog box asking for more connection information. In all other cases, the framework throws an exception.

Parameters

>*lpszDSN*   Specifies a data source name—a name registered with ODBC through the ODBC Administrator program. If a DSN value is specified in *lpszConnect* (in the

form "DSN=<data-source>"), it must not be specified again in *lpszDSN*. In this case, *lpszDSN* should be **NULL**. Otherwise, you can pass **NULL** if you want to present the user with a Data Source dialog box in which the user can select a data source. For further information, see Remarks.

bExclusive Not supported in this version of the class library. Currently, an assertion fails if this parameter is **TRUE**. The data source is always opened as shared (not exclusive).

bReadOnly **TRUE** if you intend the connection to be read-only and to prohibit updates to the data source. All dependent recordsets inherit this attribute. The default value is **FALSE**.

lpszConnect Specifies a connect string. The connect string concatenates information, possibly including a data source name, a user ID valid on the data source, a user authentication string (password, if the data source requires one), and other information. The whole connect string must be prefixed by the string "ODBC;" (uppercase or lowercase). The "ODBC;" string is used to indicate that the connection is to an ODBC data source; this is for upward compatibility when future versions of the class library might support non-ODBC data sources.

bUseCursorLib **TRUE** if you want the ODBC Cursor Library DLL to be loaded. The cursor library masks some functionality of the underlying ODBC driver, effectively preventing the use of dynasets (if the driver supports them). The only cursors supported if the cursor library is loaded are static snapshots and forward-only cursors. The default value is **TRUE**. If you plan to create a recordset object directly from **CRecordset** without deriving from it, you should not load the cursor library.

Remarks

Call this member function to initialize a newly constructed **CDatabase** object. Your database object must be initialized before you can use it to construct a recordset object.

Note Calling the **OpenEx** member function is the preferred way to connect to a data source and initialize your database object.

If the parameters in your **Open** call do not contain enough information to make the connection, the ODBC driver opens a dialog box to obtain the necessary information from the user. When you call **Open**, your connect string, *lpszConnect*, is stored privately in the **CDatabase** object and is available by calling the **GetConnect** member function.

If you wish, you can open your own dialog box before you call **Open** to get information from the user, such as a password, then add that information to the connect string you pass to **Open**. Or you might want to save the connect string you pass so you can reuse it the next time your application calls **Open** on a **CDatabase** object.

You can also use the connect string for multiple levels of login authorization (each for a different **CDatabase** object) or to convey other data source-specific information. For more information about connect strings, see Chapter 5 in the *ODBC SDK Programmer's Reference*.

It is possible for a connection attempt to time out if, for example, the DBMS host is unavailable. If the connection attempt fails, **Open** throws a **CDBException**.

Example

```
// Embed a CDatabase object
// in your document class
CDatabase m_dbCust( );

// Connect the object to a
// data source (no password)
// the ODBC connection dialog box
// will always remain hidden
m_dbCust.Open( _T( "MYDATASOURCE" ), FALSE,
               FALSE, _T( "ODBC;UID=JOES" ) ),

// ...Or, query the user for all
// connection information
m_dbCust.Open( NULL );
```

See Also: **CDatabase::OpenEx**, **CDatabase::CDatabase**, **CDatabase::Close**, **CDBException**, **CRecordset::Open**

CDatabase::OpenEx

virtual BOOL OpenEx(LPCTSTR *lpszConnectString*,
↳ **DWORD** *dwOptions* **= 0**);throw(CDBException, CMemoryException);

Return Value

Nonzero if the connection is successfully made; otherwise 0 if the user chooses Cancel when presented a dialog box asking for more connection information. In all other cases, the framework throws an exception.

Parameters

lpszConnectString   Specifies an ODBC connect string. This includes the data source name as well as other optional information, such as a user ID and password. For example, "DSN=SQLServer_Source;UID=SA;PWD=abc123" is a possible connect string. Note that if you pass **NULL** for *lpszConnectString*, a Data Source dialog box will prompt the user to select a data source.

dwOptions   A bitmask which specifies a combination of the following values. The default value is 0, meaning that the database will be opened as shared with write access, the ODBC Cursor Library DLL will not be loaded, and the ODBC connection dialog box will display only if there is not enough information to make the connection.

- **CDatabase::openExclusive** Not supported in this version of the class library. A data source is always opened as shared (not exclusive). Currently, an assertion fails if you specify this option.

- **CDatabase::openReadOnly** Open the data source as read-only.

- **CDatabase::useCursorLib** Load the ODBC Cursor Library DLL. The cursor library masks some functionality of the underlying ODBC driver, effectively preventing the use of dynasets (if the driver supports them). The only cursors supported if the cursor library is loaded are static snapshots and forward-only cursors. If you plan to create a recordset object directly from **CRecordset** without deriving from it, you should not load the cursor library.

- **CDatabase::noOdbcDialog** Do not display the ODBC connection dialog box, regardless of whether enough connection information is supplied.

- **CDatabase::forceOdbcDialog** Always display the ODBC connection dialog box.

Remarks

Call this member function to initialize a newly constructed **CDatabase** object. Your database object must be initialized before you can use it to construct a recordset object.

If the *lpszConnectString* parameter in your **OpenEx** call does not contain enough information to make the connection, the ODBC driver opens a dialog box to obtain the necessary information from the user, provided you have not set **CDatabase::noOdbcDialog** or **CDatabase::forceOdbcDialog** in the *dwOptions* parameter. When you call **OpenEx**, your connect string, *lpszConnectString*, is stored privately in the **CDatabase** object and is available by calling the **GetConnect** member function.

If you wish, you can open your own dialog box before you call **OpenEx** to get information from the user, such as a password, and then add that information to the connect string you pass to **OpenEx**. Or you might want to save the connect string you pass so you can reuse it the next time your application calls **OpenEx** on a **CDatabase** object.

You can also use the connect string for multiple levels of login authorization (each for a different **CDatabase** object) or to convey other data source-specific information. For more information about connect strings, see Chapter 5 in the *ODBC SDK Programmer's Reference*.

It is possible for a connection attempt to time out if, for example, the DBMS host is unavailable. If the connection attempt fails, **OpenEx** throws a **CDBException**.

Example

```
// Embed a CDatabase object
// in your document class
CDatabase m_dbCust( );

// Connect the object to a
// read-only data source where
// the ODBC connection dialog box
// will always remain hidden
m_dbCust.OpenEx( _T( "DSN=MYDATASOURCE;UID=JOES" ),
                 CDatabase::openReadOnly |
                 CDatabase::noOdbcDialog ) );
```

See Also: CDatabase::Open, CDatabase::CDatabase, CDatabase::Close, CDBException, CRecordset::Open

---

CDatabase::Rollback

BOOL Rollback( );

Return Value

Nonzero if the transaction was successfully reversed; otherwise 0. If a **Rollback** call fails, the data source and transaction states are undefined. If **Rollback** returns 0, you must check the data source to determine its state.

Remarks

Call this member function to reverse the changes made during a transaction. All **CRecordset AddNew**, **Edit**, **Delete**, and **Update** calls executed since the last **BeginTrans** are rolled back to the state that existed at the time of that call.

After a call to **Rollback**, the transaction is over, and you must call **BeginTrans** again for another transaction. The record that was current before you called **BeginTrans** becomes the current record again after **Rollback**.

After a rollback, the record that was current before the rollback remains current. For details about the state of the recordset and the data source after a rollback, see the article "Transaction (ODBC)" in *Visual C++ Programmer's Guide* online.

Example

See the article "Transaction: Performing a Transaction in a Recordset (ODBC)" in *Visual C++ Programmer's Guide* online.

See Also: CDatabase::BeginTrans, CDatabase::CommitTrans

CDatabase::SetLoginTimeout

void SetLoginTimeout(DWORD *dwSeconds* **);**

Parameters

> *dwSeconds*   The number of seconds to allow before a connection attempt times out.

Remarks

> Call this member function—before you call **OpenEx** or **Open**—to override the default number of seconds allowed before an attempted data source connection times out. A connection attempt might time out if, for example, the DBMS is not available. Call **SetLoginTimeout** after you construct the uninitialized **CDatabase** object but before you call **OpenEx** or **Open**.
>
> The default value for login timeouts is 15 seconds. Not all data sources support the ability to specify a login timeout value. If the data source does not support timeout, you get trace output but not an exception. A value of 0 means "infinite."

> **See Also:**   **CDatabase::OnSetOptions**, **CDatabase::SetQueryTimeout**

CDatabase::SetQueryTimeout

void SetQueryTimeout(DWORD *dwSeconds* **);**

Parameters

> *dwSeconds*   The number of seconds to allow before a query attempt times out.

Remarks

> Call this member function to override the default number of seconds to allow before subsequent operations on the connected data source time out. An operation might time out due to network access problems, excessive query processing time, and so on. Call **SetQueryTimeout** prior to opening your recordset or prior to calling the recordset's **AddNew**, **Update** or **Delete** member functions if you want to change the query timeout value. The setting affects all subsequent **Open**, **AddNew**, **Update**, and **Delete** calls to any recordsets associated with this **CDatabase** object. Changing the query timeout value for a recordset after opening does not change the value for the recordset. For example, subsequent **Move** operations do not use the new value.
>
> The default value for query timeouts is 15 seconds. Not all data sources support the ability to set a query timeout value. If you set a query timeout value of 0, no timeout occurs; the communication with the data source may hang. This behavior may be useful during development. If the data source does not support timeout, you get trace output but not an exception.

> **See Also:**   **CDatabase::SetLoginTimeout**

Data Members

CDatabase::m_hdbc

Remarks

Contains a public handle to an ODBC data source connection—a "connection handle." Normally, you will have no need to access this member variable directly. Instead, the framework allocates the handle when you call **OpenEx** or **Open**. The framework deallocates the handle when you call the **delete** operator on the **CDatabase** object. Note that the **Close** member function does not deallocate the handle.

Under some circumstances, however, you may need to use the handle directly. For example, if you need to call ODBC API functions directly rather than through class **CDatabase**, you may need a connection handle to pass as a parameter. See the code example below.

Example

```
// Using m_hdbc for a direct ODBC API call.
// m_db is the CDatabase object; m_hdbc is
// its HDBC member variable
nRetcode = ::SQLGetInfo( m_db.m_hdbc,
                         SQL_ODBC_SQL_CONFORMANCE,
                         &nValue,
                         sizeof( nValue ),
                         &cbValue );
```

See Also: **CDatabase::OpenEx**, **CDatabase::Open**, **CDatabase::Close**

CDataExchange

CDataExchange does not have a base class.

The **CDataExchange** class supports the dialog data exchange (DDX) and dialog data validation (DDV) routines used by the Microsoft Foundation classes. Use this class if you are writing data exchange routines for custom data types or controls, or if you are writing your own data validation routines. For more information on writing your own DDX and DDV routines, see Technical Note 26 online. For an overview of DDX and DDV, see "Dialog Data Exchange" and "Validation and Dialog Box Topics" in *Visual C++ Programmer's Guide* online.

A **CDataExchange** object provides the context information needed for DDX and DDV to take place. The flag **m_bSaveAndValidate** is **FALSE** when DDX is used to fill the initial values of dialog controls from data members. The flag **m_bSaveAndValidate** is **TRUE** when DDX is used to set the current values of dialog controls into data members and when DDV is used to validate the data values. If the DDV validation fails, the DDV procedure will display a message box explaining the input error. The DDV procedure will then call **Fail** to reset the focus to the offending control and throw an exception to stop the validation process.

#include <afxwin.h>

See Also: **CWnd::DoDataExchange**, **CWnd::UpdateData**

CDataExchange Class Members

Data Members

m_bSaveAndValidate	Flag for the direction of DDX and DDV.
m_pDlgWnd	The dialog box or window where the data exchange takes place.

Operations

PrepareCtrl	Prepares the specified control for data exchange or validation. Use for nonedit controls.
PrepareEditCtrl	Prepares the specified edit control for data exchange or validation.
Fail	Called when validation fails. Resets focus to the previous control and throws an exception.

Member Functions

CDataExchange::Fail

void Fail( );
  throw(CUserException);

Remarks

The framework calls this member function when a dialog data validation (DDV) operation fails. **Fail** restores the focus and selection to the control whose validation failed (if there is a control to restore). **Fail** then throws an exception of type **CUserException** to stop the validation process. The exception causes a message box explaining the error to be displayed. After DDV validation fails, the user can reenter data in the offending control.

Implementors of custom DDV routines can call **Fail** from their routines when a validation fails.

For more information on writing your own DDX and DDV routines, see Technical Note 26 online. For an overview of DDX and DDV, see "Dialog Data Exchange" and "Validation and Dialog Box Topics" in *Visual C++ Programmer's Guide* online.

See Also: **CDataExchange::PrepareCtrl**, **CDataExchange::PrepareEditCtrl**

CDataExchange::PrepareCtrl

HWND PrepareCtrl(int *nIDC*);
  throw(CNotSupportedException);

Return Value

The **HWND** of the control being prepared for DDX or DDV.

Parameters

nIDC   The ID of the control to be prepared for DDX or DDV.

Remarks

The framework calls this member function to prepare the specified control for dialog data exchange (DDX) and validation (DDV). Use **PrepareEditCtrl** instead for edit controls; use this member function for all other controls.

Preparation consists of storing the control's **HWND** in the **CDataExchange** class. The framework uses this handle to restore the focus to the previously focused control in the event of a DDX or DDV failure.

Implementors of custom DDX or DDV routines should call **PrepareCtrl** for all non-edit controls for which they are exchanging data via DDX or validating data via DDV.

For more information on writing your own DDX and DDV routines, see Technical Note 26 online. For an overview of DDX and DDV, see "Dialog Data Exchange" and "Validation and Dialog Box Topics" in *Visual C++ Programmer's Guide* online.

See Also: CDataExchange::Fail

CDataExchange::PrepareEditCtrl

> **HWND PrepareEditCtrl(int *nIDC*);**
>   **throw(CNotSupportedException);**

Return Value

The **HWND** of the edit control being prepared for DDX or DDV.

Parameters

nIDC   The ID of the edit control to be prepared for DDX or DDV.

Remarks

The framework calls this member function to prepare the specified edit control for dialog data exchange (DDX) and validation (DDV). Use **PrepareCtrl** instead for all non-edit controls.

Preparation consists of two things. First, **PrepareEditCtrl** stores the control's **HWND** in the **CDataExchange** class. The framework uses this handle to restore the focus to the previously focused control in the event of a DDX or DDV failure. Second, **PrepareEditCtrl** sets a flag in the **CDataExchange** class to indicate that the control whose data is being exchanged or validated is an edit control.

Implementors of custom DDX or DDV routines should call **PrepareEditCtrl** for all edit controls for which they are exchanging data via DDX or validating data via DDV.

For more information on writing your own DDX and DDV routines, see Technical Note 26 online. For an overview of DDX and DDV, see "Dialog Data Exchange" and "Validation and Dialog Box Topics" in *Visual C++ Programmer's Guide* online.

See Also: CDataExchange::Fail

Data Members
CDataExchange::m_bSaveAndValidate

Remarks

This flag indicates the direction of a dialog data exchange (DDX) operation. The flag is nonzero if the **CDataExchange** object is being used to move data from the dialog controls to dialog-class data members after the user edits the controls. The flag is zero if the object is being used to initialize dialog controls from dialog-class data members.

The flag is also nonzero during dialog data validation (DDV).

For more information on writing your own DDX and DDV routines, see Technical Note 26 online. For an overview of DDX and DDV, see "Dialog Data Exchange" and "Validation and Dialog Box Topics" in *Visual C++ Programmer's Guide* online.

CDataExchange::m_pDlgWnd

Remarks

Contains a pointer to the **CWnd** object for which dialog data exchange (DDX) or validation (DDV) is taking place. This object is usually a **CDialog** object. Implementors of custom DDX or DDV routines can use this pointer to obtain access to the dialog window that contains the controls they are operating on.

For more information on writing your own DDX and DDV routines, see Technical Note 26 online. For an overview of DDX and DDV, see "Dialog Data Exchange" and "Validation and Dialog Box Topics" in *Visual C++ Programmer's Guide* online.

CDataPathProperty

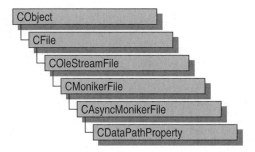

Class **CDataPathProperty** implements an OLE control property that can be loaded asynchronously. Asynchronous properties are loaded after synchronous initiation.

The class **CDataPathProperty** is derived from **CAysncMonikerFile**. To implement asynchronous properties in your OLE controls, derive a class from **CDataPathProperty**, and override **OnDataAvailable**.

For more information about how to use asynchronous monikers and ActiveX controls in Internet applications, see the following articles in *Visual C++ Programmer's Guide* online:

- "Internet First Steps: ActiveX Controls"
- "Internet First Steps: Asynchronous Monikers"

#include <afxctl.h>

See Also: CAsyncMonikerFile

CDataPathProperty Class Members

Construction

CDataPathProperty	Constructs a **CDataPathProperty** object.

Operations

GetControl	Retrieves the asynchronous OLE control associated with the **CDataPathProperty** object.
GetPath	Retrieves the pathname of the property.
Open	Initiates loading of the asynchronous property for the associated ActiveX (OLE) control.
ResetData	Calls **CAsyncMonikerFile::OnDataAvailable** to notify the container that the control properties have changed.
SetControl	Sets the asynchronous ActiveX (OLE) control associated with the property.
SetPath	Sets the pathname of the property.

Member Functions

CDataPathProperty::CDataPathProperty

CDataPathProperty(COleControl* *pControl* **);**
CDataPathProperty(LPCTSTR *lpszPath*, **COleControl*** *pControl* **);**

Parameters

pControl   A pointer to the OLE control object to be associated with this
CDataPathProperty object.

lpszPath   The path, which may be absolute or relative, used to create an
asynchronous moniker that references the actual absolute location of the
property. **CDataPathProperty** uses URLs, not filenames. If you want a
CDataPathProperty object for a file, prepend file:// to the path.

Remarks

Constructs a **CDataPathProperty** object. The **COleControl** object pointed to by
pControl is used by **Open** and retrieved by derived classes. If *pControl* is **NULL**,
the control used with **Open** should be set with **SetControl**. If *lpszPath* is **NULL**,
you can pass in the path through **Open** or set it with **SetPath**.

See Also: CDataPathProperty::Open, CDataPathProperty::SetControl

---

CDataPathProperty::GetControl

COleControl* GetControl( );

Return Value

Returns a pointer to the OLE control associated with the **CDataPathProperty** object.
NULL if not control is associated.

Remarks

Call this member function to retrieve the **COleControl** object associated with the
CDataPathProperty object.

See Also: CDataPathProperty::SetControl

CDataPathProperty::GetPath

CString GetPath( ) const;

Return Value

Returns the pathname to the property itself. Can be empty if no path has been
specified.

Remarks

Call this member function to retrieve the path, set when the **CDataPathProperty** object was constructed, or specified in **Open**, or specified in a previous call to the **SetPath** member function.

See Also: **CDataPathProperty::SetPath, CDataPathProperty::Open, CDataPathProperty::CDataPathProperty**

CDataPathProperty::Open

virtual BOOL Open(COleControl* *pControl***, CFileException*** *pError* **= NULL);**
virtual BOOL Open(LPCTSTR *lpszPath***, COleControl*** *pControl***,**
  ↪ **CFileException*** *pError* **= NULL);**
virtual BOOL Open(LPCTSTR *lpszPath***, CFileException*** *pError* **= NULL);**
virtual BOOL Open(CFileException* *pError* **= NULL);**

Return Value

Nonzero if successful; otherwise 0.

Parameters

pControl   A pointer to the OLE control object to be associated with this **CDataPathProperty** object.

pError   A pointer to a file exception. In the event of an error, will be set to the cause.

lpszPath   The path, which may be absolute or relative, used to create an asynchronous moniker that references the actual absolute location of the property. **CDataPathProperty** uses URLs, not filenames. If you want a **CDataPathProperty** object for a file, prepend file:// to the path.

Remarks

Call this member function to initiate loading of the asynchronous property for the associated control. The function attempts to obtain the **IBindHost** interface from the control.

Before calling **Open** without a path, the value for the property's path must be set. This can be done when the object is constructed, or by calling the **SetPath** member function.

Before calling **Open** without a control, an ActiveX control (formerly known as an OLE control) can be associated with the object. This can be done when the object is constructed, or by calling **SetControl**.

All overloads of **CAsyncMonikerFile::Open** are also available from **CDataPathProperty**.

See Also: **CDataPathProperty::SetControl, CDataPathProperty::CDataPathProperty, CAsyncMonikerFile::Open**

CDataPathProperty::ResetData

virtual void ResetData( );

Remarks

Call this function to get **CAsyncMonikerFile::OnDataAvailable** to notify the container that the control properties have changed, and all the information loaded asynchronously is no longer useful. Opening should be restarted. Derived classes can override this function for different defaults.

See Also: CAsyncMonikerFile::OnDataAvailable, CDataPathProperty::Open

CDataPathProperty::SetControl

void SetControl(COleControl* *pControl*);

Parameters

pControl A pointer to the asynchronous OLE control to be associated with the property.

Remarks

Call this member function to associate an asynchronous OLE control with the **CDataPathProperty** object.

See Also: CDataPathProperty::GetControl, CDataPathProperty::SetPath, CDataPathProperty::CDataPathProperty

CDataPathProperty::SetPath

void SetPath(LPCTSTR *lpszPath*);

Parameters

lpszPath A path, which may be absolute or relative, to the property being loaded asynchronously. **CDataPathProperty** uses URLs, not filenames. If you want a **CDataPathProperty** object for a file, prepend file:// to the path.

Remarks

Call this member function to set the pathname of the property.

See Also: CDataPathProperty::GetPath, CDataPathProperty::SetControl, CDataPathProperty::CDataPathProperty

CDBException

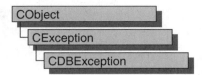

CObject
  CException
    CDBException

A **CDBException** object represents an exception condition arising from the database classes. The class includes two public data members you can use to determine the cause of the exception or to display a text message describing the exception. **CDBException** objects are constructed and thrown by member functions of the database classes.

Note This class is one of MFC's Open Database Connectivity (ODBC) classes. If you are instead using the newer Data Access Objects (DAO) classes, use **CDaoException** instead. All DAO class names have "CDao" as a prefix. For more information, see the articles "DatabaseTopics (General)" and "DAO and MFC" in *Visual C++ Programmer's Guide* online.

Exceptions are cases of abnormal execution involving conditions outside the program's control, such as data source or network I/O errors. Errors that you might expect to see in the normal course of executing your program are usually not considered exceptions.

You can access these objects within the scope of a **CATCH** expression. You can also throw **CDBException** objects from your own code with the **AfxThrowDBException** global function.

For more information about exception handling in general, or about **CDBException** objects, see the articles "Exceptions" and "Exceptions: Database Exceptions" in *Visual C++ Programmer's Guide* online.

#include <afxdb.h>

See Also: **CDatabase, CRecordset, CFieldExchange, AfxThrowDBException, CRecordset::Update, CRecordset::Delete, CException**

CDBException Class Members

Data Members

m_nRetCode	Contains an Open Database Connectivity (ODBC) return code, of type **RETCODE**.
m_strError	Contains a string that describes the error in alphanumeric terms.
m_strStateNativeOrigin	Contains a string describing the error in terms of the error codes returned by ODBC.

Data Members

CDBException::m_nRetCode

Remarks

Contains an ODBC error code of type **RETCODE** returned by an ODBC application programming interface (API) function. This type includes SQL-prefixed codes defined by ODBC and AFX_SQL-prefixed codes defined by the database classes. For a **CDBException**, this member will contain one of the following values:

- **AFX_SQL_ERROR_API_CONFORMANCE**   The driver for a **CDatabase::OpenEx** or **CDatabase::Open** call does not conform to required ODBC API Conformance level 1 (**SQL_OAC_LEVEL1**).

- **AFX_SQL_ERROR_CONNECT_FAIL**   Connection to the data source failed. You passed a **NULL CDatabase** pointer to your recordset constructor and the subsequent attempt to create a connection based on **GetDefaultConnect** failed.

- **AFX_SQL_ERROR_DATA_TRUNCATED**   You requested more data than you have provided storage for. For information on increasing the provided data storage for **CString** or **CByteArray** data types, see the *nMaxLength* argument for **RFX_Text** and **RFX_Binary** under "Macros and Globals."

- **AFX_SQL_ERROR_DYNASET_NOT_SUPPORTED**   A call to **CRecordset::Open** requesting a dynaset failed. Dynasets are not supported by the driver.

- **AFX_SQL_ERROR_EMPTY_COLUMN_LIST**   You attempted to open a table (or what you gave could not be identified as a procedure call or **SELECT** statement) but there are no columns identified in record field exchange (RFX) function calls in your **DoFieldExchange** override.

- **AFX_SQL_ERROR_FIELD_SCHEMA_MISMATCH**   The type of an RFX function in your **DoFieldExchange** override is not compatible with the column data type in the recordset.

- **AFX_SQL_ERROR_ILLEGAL_MODE**   You called **CRecordset::Update** without previously calling **CRecordset::AddNew** or **CRecordset::Edit**.

- **AFX_SQL_ERROR_LOCK_MODE_NOT_SUPPORTED**   Your request to lock records for update could not be fulfilled because your ODBC driver does not support locking.

- **AFX_SQL_ERROR_MULTIPLE_ROWS_AFFECTED**   You called **CRecordset::Update** or **Delete** for a table with no unique key and changed multiple records.

- **AFX_SQL_ERROR_NO_CURRENT_RECORD** You attempted to edit or delete a previously deleted record. You must scroll to a new current record after a deletion.

- **AFX_SQL_ERROR_NO_POSITIONED_UPDATES** Your request for a dynaset could not be fulfilled because your ODBC driver does not support positioned updates.

- **AFX_SQL_ERROR_NO_ROWS_AFFECTED** You called **CRecordset::Update** or **Delete**, but when the operation began the record could no longer be found.

- **AFX_SQL_ERROR_ODBC_LOAD_FAILED** An attempt to load the ODBC.DLL failed; Windows could not find or could not load this DLL. This error is fatal.

- **AFX_SQL_ERROR_ODBC_V2_REQUIRED** Your request for a dynaset could not be fulfilled because a Level 2-compliant ODBC driver is required.

- **AFX_SQL_ERROR_RECORDSET_FORWARD_ONLY** An attempt to scroll did not succeed because the data source does not support backward scrolling.

- **AFX_SQL_ERROR_SNAPSHOT_NOT_SUPPORTED** A call to **CRecordset::Open** requesting a snapshot failed. Snapshots are not supported by the driver. (This should only occur when the ODBC cursor library—ODBCCURS.DLL—is not present.)

- **AFX_SQL_ERROR_SQL_CONFORMANCE** The driver for a **CDatabase::OpenEx** or **CDatabase::Open** call does not conform to the required ODBC SQL Conformance level of "Minimum" (**SQL_OSC_MINIMUM**).

- **AFX_SQL_ERROR_SQL_NO_TOTAL** The ODBC driver was unable to specify the total size of a **CLongBinary** data value. The operation probably failed because a global memory block could not be preallocated.

- **AFX_SQL_ERROR_RECORDSET_READONLY** You attempted to update a read-only recordset, or the data source is read-only. No update operations can be performed with the recordset or the **CDatabase** object it is associated with.

- **SQL_ERROR** Function failed. The error message returned by **::SQLError** is stored in the **m_strError** data member.

- **SQL_INVALID_HANDLE** Function failed due to an invalid environment handle, connection handle, or statement handle. This indicates a programming error. No additional information is available from **::SQLError**.

The SQL-prefixed codes are defined by ODBC. The AFX-prefixed codes are defined in AFXDB.H, found in MFC\INCLUDE.

See Also: CDatabase, CLongBinary, CRecordset

CDBException::m_strError

Remarks

Contains a string describing the error that caused the exception. The string describes the error in alphanumeric terms. For more detailed information and an example, see **m_strStateNativeOrigin**.

See Also: **CDBException::m_strStateNativeOrigin**

CDBException::m_strStateNativeOrigin

Remarks

Contains a string describing the error that caused the exception. The string is of the form "State:%s,Native:%ld,Origin:%s", where the format codes, in order, are replaced by values that describe:

- The **SQLSTATE**, a null-terminated string containing a five-character error code returned in the *szSqlState* parameter of the **::SQLError** function. **SQLSTATE** values are listed in Appendix A, "ODBC Error Codes," in the *ODBC SDK Programmer's Reference*. Example: "S0022".

- The native error code, specific to the data source, returned in the *pfNativeError* parameter of the **::SQLError** function. Example: 207.

- The error message text returned in the *szErrorMsg* parameter of the **::SQLError** function. This message consists of several bracketed names. As an error is passed from its source to the user, each ODBC component (data source, driver, Driver Manager) appends its own name. This information helps to pinpoint the origin of the error. Example: [Microsoft][ODBC SQL Server Driver][SQL Server]

The framework interprets the error string and puts its components into **m_strStateNativeOrigin**; if **m_strStateNativeOrigin** contains information for more than one error, the errors are separated by newlines. The framework puts the alphanumeric error text into **m_strError**.

For additional information about the codes used to make up this string, see the **::SQLError** function in the *ODBC SDK Programmer's Reference*.

Example

From ODBC: "State:S0022,Native:207,Origin:[Microsoft][ODBC SQL Server Driver][SQL Server] Invalid column name 'ColName'"

In **m_strStateNativeOrigin**: "State:S0022,Native:207,Origin:[Microsoft][ODBC SQL Server Driver][SQL Server]"

In **m_strError**: "Invalid column name 'ColName'"

See Also: **CDBException::m_strError**

CDBVariant

CDBVariant does not have a base class.

A **CDBVariant** object represents a variant data type for the MFC ODBC classes. **CDBVariant** is similar to **COleVariant**; however, **CDBVariant** does not use OLE. **CDBVariant** allows you to store a value without worrying about the value's data type. **CDBVariant** tracks the data type of the current value, which is stored in a union.

Class **CRecordset** utilizes **CDBVariant** objects in three member functions: **GetFieldValue**, **GetBookmark**, and **SetBookmark**. For example, **GetFieldValue** allows you to dynamically fetch data in a column. Because the data type of the column may not be known at run time, **GetFieldValue** uses a **CDBVariant** object to store the column's data.

#include <afxdb.h>

See Also: CRecordset, CRecordset::GetFieldValue, CRecordset::GetBookmark, CRecordset::SetBookmark

CDBVariant Class Members

Data Members

m_dwType	Contains the data type of the currently stored value. Type **DWORD**.
m_boolVal	Contains a value of type **BOOL**.
m_chVal	Contains a value of type **unsigned char**.
m_iVal	Contains a value of type **short**.
m_lVal	Contains a value of type **long**.
m_fltVal	Contains a value of type **float**.
m_dblVal	Contains a value of type **double**.
m_pdate	Contains a pointer to an object of type **TIMESTAMP_STRUCT**.
m_pstring	Contains a pointer to an object of type **CString**.
m_pbinary	Contains a pointer to an object of type **CLongBinary**.

Construction

CDBVariant	Constructs a **CDBVariant** object.

Operations

Clear	Clears the **CDBVariant** object.

Member Functions
CDBVariant::CDBVariant

CDBVariant( );

Creates a NULL **CDBVariant** object. Sets the **m_dwType** data member to **DBVT_NULL**.

See Also: CDBVariant::m_dwType

CDBVariant::Clear

void Clear( );

Call this member function to clear the **CDBVariant** object. If the value of the **m_dwType** data member is **DBVT_DATE**, **DBVT_STRING**, or **DBVT_BINARY**, **Clear** frees the memory associated with the union pointer member. **Clear** sets **m_dwType** to **DBVT_NULL**.

The **CDBVariant** destructor calls **Clear**.

See Also: CDBVariant::m_dwType

Data Members
CDBVariant::m_boolVal

Stores a value of type **BOOL**. The **m_boolVal** data member belongs to a union. Before accessing **m_boolVal**, first check the value of **CDBVariant::m_dwType**. If **m_dwType** is set to **DBVT_BOOL**, then **m_boolVal** will contain a valid value; otherwise, accessing **m_boolVal** will produce unreliable results.

See Also: CDBVariant::m_dwType

CDBVariant::m_chVal

Remarks

Stores a value of type **unsigned char**. The **m_chVal** data member belongs to a union. Before accessing **m_chVal**, first check the value of **CDBVariant::m_dwType**. If **m_dwType** is set to **DBVT_UCHAR**, then **m_chVal** contains a valid value; otherwise, accessing **m_chVal** will produce unreliable results.

See Also: **CDBVariant::m_dwType**

CDBVariant::m_dblVal

Remarks

Stores a value of type **double**. The **m_dblVal** data member belongs to a union. Before accessing **m_dblVal**, first check the value of **CDBVariant::m_dwType**. If **m_dwType** is set to **DBVT_DOUBLE**, then **m_dblVal** contains a valid value; otherwise, accessing **m_dblVal** will produce unreliable results.

See Also: **CDBVariant::m_dwType**

CDBVariant::m_dwType

Remarks

This data member contains the data type for the value that is currently stored in the **CDBVariant** object's union data member. Before accessing this union, you must check the value of **m_dwType** in order to determine which union data member to access. The following table lists the possible values for **m_dwType** and the corresponding union data member.

m_dwType	Union data member
DBVT_NULL	No union member is valid for access.
DBVT_BOOL	**m_boolVal**
DBVT_UCHAR	**m_chVal**
DBVT_SHORT	**m_iVal**
DBVT_LONG	**m_lVal**
DBVT_SINGLE	**m_fltVal**
DBVT_DOUBLE	**m_dblVal**
DBVT_DATE	**m_pdate**
DBVT_STRING	**m_pstring**
DBVT_BINARY	**m_pbinary**

CDBVariant::m_fltVal

Remarks

Stores a value of type **float**. The **m_fltVal** data member belongs to a union. Before accessing **m_fltVal**, first check the value of **CDBVariant::m_dwType**. If **m_dwType** is set to **DBVT_SINGLE**, then **m_fltVal** contains a valid value; otherwise, accessing **m_fltVal** will produce unreliable results.

See Also: **CDBVariant::m_dwType**

CDBVariant::m_iVal

Remarks

Stores a value of type **short**. The **m_iVal** data member belongs to a union. Before accessing **m_iVal**, first check the value of **CDBVariant::m_dwType**. If **m_dwType** is set to **DBVT_SHORT**, then **m_iVal** contains a valid value; otherwise, accessing **m_iVal** will produce unreliable results.

See Also: **CDBVariant::m_dwType**

CDBVariant::m_lVal

Remarks

Stores a value of type **long**. The **m_lVal** data member belongs to a union. Before accessing **m_lVal**, first check the value of **CDBVariant::m_dwType**. If **m_dwType** is set to **DBVT_LONG**, then **m_lVal** contains a valid value; otherwise, accessing **m_lVal** will produce unreliable results.

See Also: **CDBVariant::m_dwType**

CDBVariant::m_pbinary

Remarks

Stores a pointer to an object of type **CLongBinary**. The **m_pbinary** data member belongs to a union. Before accessing **m_pbinary**, first check the value of **CDBVariant::m_dwType**. If **m_dwType** is set to **DBVT_BINARY**, then **m_pbinary** contains a valid pointer; otherwise, accessing **m_pbinary** will produce unreliable results.

See Also: **CDBVariant::m_dwType**

CDBVariant::m_pdate

Remarks

Stores a pointer to an object of type **TIMESTAMP_STRUCT**. The **m_pdate** data member belongs to a union. Before accessing **m_pdate**, first check the value of **CDBVariant::m_dwType**. If **m_dwType** is set to **DBVT_DATE**, then **m_pdate** contains a valid pointer; otherwise, accessing **m_pdate** will produce unreliable results.

For more information about the **TIMESTAMP_STRUCT** data type, see the topic "C Data Types" in Appendix D of the *ODBC SDK Programmer's Reference*.

See Also: **CDBVariant::m_dwType**

CDBVariant::m_pstring

Remarks

Stores a pointer to an object of type **CString**. The **m_pstring** data member belongs to a union. Before accessing **m_pstring**, first check the value of **CDBVariant::m_dwType**. If **m_dwType** is set to **DBVT_STRING**, then **m_pstring** contains a valid pointer; otherwise, accessing **m_pstring** will produce unreliable results.

See Also: **CDBVariant::m_dwType**

CDC

The **CDC** class defines a class of device-context objects. The **CDC** object provides member functions for working with a device context, such as a display or printer, as well as members for working with a display context associated with the client area of a window.

Do all drawing through the member functions of a **CDC** object. The class provides member functions for device-context operations, working with drawing tools, type-safe graphics device interface (GDI) object selection, and working with colors and palettes. It also provides member functions for getting and setting drawing attributes, mapping, working with the viewport, working with the window extent, converting coordinates, working with regions, clipping, drawing lines, and drawing simple shapes, ellipses, and polygons. Member functions are also provided for drawing text, working with fonts, using printer escapes, scrolling, and playing metafiles.

To use a **CDC** object, construct it, and then call its member functions that parallel Windows functions that use device contexts.

Note   Under Windows 95, all screen coordinates are limited to 16 bits. Therefore, an **int** passed to a **CDC** member function must lie in the range –32768 to 32767.

For specific uses, the Microsoft Foundation Class Library provides several classes derived from **CDC**. **CPaintDC** encapsulates calls to **BeginPaint** and **EndPaint**. **CClientDC** manages a display context associated with a window's client area. **CWindowDC** manages a display context associated with an entire window, including its frame and controls. **CMetaFileDC** associates a device context with a metafile.

CDC contains two device contexts, **m_hDC** and **m_hAttribDC**, which, on creation of a **CDC** object, refer to the same device. **CDC** directs all output GDI calls to **m_hDC** and most attribute GDI calls to **m_hAttribDC**. (An example of an attribute call is **GetTextColor**, while **SetTextColor** is an output call.)

For example, the framework uses these two device contexts to implement a **CMetaFileDC** object that will send output to a metafile while reading attributes from a physical device. Print preview is implemented in the framework in a similar fashion. You can also use the two device contexts in a similar way in your application-specific code.

There are times when you may need text-metric information from both the **m_hDC** and **m_hAttribDC** device contexts. The following pairs of functions provide this capability:

Uses m_hAttribDC	Uses m_hDC
GetTextExtent	**GetOutputTextExtent**
GetTabbedTextExtent	**GetOutputTabbedTextExtent**
GetTextMetrics	**GetOutputTextMetrics**
GetCharWidth	**GetOutputCharWidth**

For more information on **CDC**, see "Device Contexts" in *Visual C++ Programmer's Guide* online.

#include <afxwin.h>

See Also: **CPaintDC**, **CWindowDC**, **CClientDC**, **CMetaFileDC**

CDC Class Members

Data Members

m_hDC	The output-device context used by this **CDC** object.
m_hAttribDC	The attribute-device context used by this **CDC** object.

Construction

CDC	Constructs a **CDC** object.

Initialization

CreateDC	Creates a device context for a specific device.
CreateIC	Creates an information context for a specific device. This provides a fast way to get information about the device without creating a device context.
CreateCompatibleDC	Creates a memory-device context that is compatible with another device context. You can use it to prepare images in memory.
DeleteDC	Deletes the Windows device context associated with this **CDC** object.
FromHandle	Returns a pointer to a **CDC** object when given a handle to a device context. If a **CDC** object is not attached to the handle, a temporary **CDC** object is created and attached.
DeleteTempMap	Called by the **CWinApp** idle-time handler to delete any temporary **CDC** object created by **FromHandle**. Also detaches the device context.
Attach	Attaches a Windows device context to this **CDC** object.
Detach	Detaches the Windows device context from this **CDC** object.
SetAttribDC	Sets **m_hAttribDC**, the attribute device context.
SetOutputDC	Sets **m_hDC**, the output device context.

(continued)

Initialization *(continued)*

ReleaseAttribDC	Releases **m_hAttribDC**, the attribute device context.
ReleaseOutputDC	Releases **m_hDC**, the output device context.
GetCurrentBitmap	Returns a pointer to the currently selected **CBitmap** object.
GetCurrentBrush	Returns a pointer to the currently selected **CBrush** object.
GetCurrentFont	Returns a pointer to the currently selected **CFont** object.
GetCurrentPalette	Returns a pointer to the currently selected **CPalette** object.
GetCurrentPen	Returns a pointer to the currently selected **CPen** object.
GetWindow	Returns the window associated with the display device context.

Device-Context Functions

GetSafeHdc	Returns **m_hDC**, the output device context.
SaveDC	Saves the current state of the device context.
RestoreDC	Restores the device context to a previous state saved with **SaveDC**.
ResetDC	Updates the **m_hAttribDC** device context.
GetDeviceCaps	Retrieves a specified kind of device-specific information about a given display device's capabilities.
IsPrinting	Determines whether the device context is being used for printing.

Drawing-Tool Functions

GetBrushOrg	Retrieves the origin of the current brush.
SetBrushOrg	Specifies the origin for the next brush selected into a device context.
EnumObjects	Enumerates the pens and brushes available in a device context.

Type-Safe Selection Helpers

SelectObject	Selects a GDI drawing object such as a pen.
SelectStockObject	Selects one of the predefined stock pens, brushes, or fonts provided by Windows.

Color and Color Palette Functions

GetNearestColor	Retrieves the closest logical color to a specified logical color that the given device can represent.
SelectPalette	Selects the logical palette.
RealizePalette	Maps palette entries in the current logical palette to the system palette.
UpdateColors	Updates the client area of the device context by matching the current colors in the client area to the system palette on a pixel-by-pixel basis.
GetHalftoneBrush	Retrieves a halftone brush.

Drawing-Attribute Functions

GetBkColor	Retrieves the current background color.
SetBkColor	Sets the current background color.
GetBkMode	Retrieves the background mode.
SetBkMode	Sets the background mode.
GetPolyFillMode	Retrieves the current polygon-filling mode.
SetPolyFillMode	Sets the polygon-filling mode.
GetROP2	Retrieves the current drawing mode.
SetROP2	Sets the current drawing mode.
GetStretchBltMode	Retrieves the current bitmap-stretching mode.
SetStretchBltMode	Sets the bitmap-stretching mode.
GetTextColor	Retrieves the current text color.
SetTextColor	Sets the text color.
GetColorAdjustment	Retrieves the color adjustment values for the device context.
SetColorAdjustment	Sets the color adjustment values for the device context using the specified values.

Mapping Functions

GetMapMode	Retrieves the current mapping mode.
SetMapMode	Sets the current mapping mode.
GetViewportOrg	Retrieves the x- and y-coordinates of the viewport origin.
SetViewportOrg	Sets the viewport origin.
OffsetViewportOrg	Modifies the viewport origin relative to the coordinates of the current viewport origin.
GetViewportExt	Retrieves the x- and y-extents of the viewport.
SetViewportExt	Sets the x- and y-extents of the viewport.
ScaleViewportExt	Modifies the viewport extent relative to the current values.
GetWindowOrg	Retrieves the x- and y-coordinates of the origin of the associated window.
SetWindowOrg	Sets the window origin of the device context.
OffsetWindowOrg	Modifies the window origin relative to the coordinates of the current window origin.
GetWindowExt	Retrieves the x- and y-extents of the associated window.
SetWindowExt	Sets the x- and y-extents of the associated window.
ScaleWindowExt	Modifies the window extents relative to the current values.

Coordinate Functions

DPtoHIMETRIC	Converts device units into **HIMETRIC** units.
DPtoLP	Converts device units into logical units.
HIMETRICtoDP	Converts **HIMETRIC** units into device units.

(continued)

Coordinate Functions *(continued)*

HIMETRICtoLP	Converts **HIMETRIC** units into logical units.
LPtoDP	Converts logical units into device units.
LPtoHIMETRIC	Converts logical units into **HIMETRIC** units.

Region Functions

FillRgn	Fills a specific region with the specified brush.
FrameRgn	Draws a border around a specific region using a brush.
InvertRgn	Inverts the colors in a region.
PaintRgn	Fills a region with the selected brush.

Clipping Functions

SetBoundsRect	Controls the accumulation of bounding-rectangle information for the specified device context.
GetBoundsRect	Returns the current accumulated bounding rectangle for the specified device context.
GetClipBox	Retrieves the dimensions of the tightest bounding rectangle around the current clipping boundary.
SelectClipRgn	Combines the given region with the current clipping region by using the specified mode.
ExcludeClipRect	Creates a new clipping region that consists of the existing clipping region minus the specified rectangle.
ExcludeUpdateRgn	Prevents drawing within invalid areas of a window by excluding an updated region in the window from a clipping region.
IntersectClipRect	Creates a new clipping region by forming the intersection of the current region and a rectangle.
OffsetClipRgn	Moves the clipping region of the given device.
PtVisible	Specifies whether the given point is within the clipping region.
RectVisible	Determines whether any part of the given rectangle lies within the clipping region.

Line-Output Functions

GetCurrentPosition	Retrieves the current position of the pen (in logical coordinates).
MoveTo	Moves the current position.
LineTo	Draws a line from the current position up to, but not including, a point.
Arc	Draws an elliptical arc.
ArcTo	Draws an elliptical arc. This function is similar to **Arc**, except that the current position is updated.
AngleArc	Draws a line segment and an arc, and moves the current position to the ending point of the arc.
GetArcDirection	Returns the current arc direction for the device context.
SetArcDirection	Sets the drawing direction to be used for arc and rectangle functions.

Line-Output Functions *(continued)*

PolyDraw	Draws a set of line segments and Bézier splines. This function updates the current position.
Polyline	Draws a set of line segments connecting the specified points.
PolyPolyline	Draws multiple series of connected line segments. The current position is neither used nor updated by this function.
PolylineTo	Draws one or more straight lines and moves the current position to the ending point of the last line.
PolyBezier	Draws one or more Bézier splines. The current position is neither used nor updated.
PolyBezierTo	Draws one or more Bézier splines, and moves the current position to the ending point of the last Bézier spline.

Simple Drawing Functions

FillRect	Fills a given rectangle by using a specific brush.
FrameRect	Draws a border around a rectangle.
InvertRect	Inverts the contents of a rectangle.
DrawIcon	Draws an icon.
DrawDragRect	Erases and redraws a rectangle as it is dragged.
FillSolidRect	Fills a rectangle with a solid color.
Draw3dRect	Draws a three-dimensional rectangle.
DrawEdge	Draws the edges of a rectangle.
DrawFrameControl	Draw a frame control.
DrawState	Displays an image and applies a visual effect to indicate a state.

Ellipse and Polygon Functions

Chord	Draws a chord (a closed figure bounded by the intersection of an ellipse and a line segment).
DrawFocusRect	Draws a rectangle in the style used to indicate focus.
Ellipse	Draws an ellipse.
Pie	Draws a pie-shaped wedge.
Polygon	Draws a polygon consisting of two or more points (vertices) connected by lines.
PolyPolygon	Creates two or more polygons that are filled using the current polygon-filling mode. The polygons may be disjoint or they may overlap.
Polyline	Draws a polygon consisting of a set of line segments connecting specified points.
Rectangle	Draws a rectangle using the current pen and fills it using the current brush.
RoundRect	Draws a rectangle with rounded corners using the current pen and filled using the current brush.

Bitmap Functions

PatBlt	Creates a bit pattern.
BitBlt	Copies a bitmap from a specified device context.
StretchBlt	Moves a bitmap from a source rectangle and device into a destination rectangle, stretching or compressing the bitmap if necessary to fit the dimensions of the destination rectangle.
GetPixel	Retrieves the RGB color value of the pixel at the specified point.
SetPixel	Sets the pixel at the specified point to the closest approximation of the specified color.
SetPixelV	Sets the pixel at the specified coordinates to the closest approximation of the specified color. **SetPixelV** is faster than **SetPixel** because it does not need to return the color value of the point actually painted.
FloodFill	Fills an area with the current brush.
ExtFloodFill	Fills an area with the current brush. Provides more flexibility than the **FloodFill** member function.
MaskBlt	Combines the color data for the source and destination bitmaps using the given mask and raster operation.
PlgBlt	Performs a bit-block transfer of the bits of color data from the specified rectangle in the source device context to the specified parallelogram in the given device context.

Text Functions

TextOut	Writes a character string at a specified location using the currently selected font.
ExtTextOut	Writes a character string within a rectangular region using the currently selected font.
TabbedTextOut	Writes a character string at a specified location, expanding tabs to the values specified in an array of tab-stop positions.
DrawText	Draws formatted text in the specified rectangle.
GetTextExtent	Computes the width and height of a line of text on the attribute device context using the current font to determine the dimensions.
GetOutputTextExtent	Computes the width and height of a line of text on the output device context using the current font to determine the dimensions.
GetTabbedTextExtent	Computes the width and height of a character string on the attribute device context.
GetOutputTabbedTextExtent	Computes the width and height of a character string on the output device context.
GrayString	Draws dimmed (grayed) text at the given location.
GetTextAlign	Retrieves the text-alignment flags.
SetTextAlign	Sets the text-alignment flags.
GetTextFace	Copies the typeface name of the current font into a buffer as a null-terminated string.

Text Functions *(continued)*

GetTextMetrics	Retrieves the metrics for the current font from the attribute device context.
GetOutputTextMetrics	Retrieves the metrics for the current font from the output device context.
SetTextJustification	Adds space to the break characters in a string.
GetTextCharacterExtra	Retrieves the current setting for the amount of intercharacter spacing.
SetTextCharacterExtra	Sets the amount of intercharacter spacing.

Font Functions

GetFontData	Retrieves font metric information from a scalable font file. The information to retrieve is identified by specifying an offset into the font file and the length of the information to return.
GetKerningPairs	Retrieves the character kerning pairs for the font that is currently selected in the specified device context.
GetOutlineTextMetrics	Retrieves font metric information for TrueType fonts.
GetGlyphOutline	Retrieves the outline curve or bitmap for an outline character in the current font.
GetCharABCWidths	Retrieves the widths, in logical units, of consecutive characters in a given range from the current font.
GetCharWidth	Retrieves the fractional widths of consecutive characters in a given range from the current font.
GetOutputCharWidth	Retrieves the widths of individual characters in a consecutive group of characters from the current font using the output device context.
SetMapperFlags	Alters the algorithm that the font mapper uses when it maps logical fonts to physical fonts.
GetAspectRatioFilter	Retrieves the setting for the current aspect-ratio filter.

Printer Escape Functions

QueryAbort	Calls the **AbortProc** callback function for a printing application and queries whether the printing should be terminated.
Escape	Allows applications to access facilities that are not directly available from a particular device through GDI. Also allows access to Windows escape functions. Escape calls made by an application are translated and sent to the device driver.
DrawEscape	Accesses drawing capabilities of a video display that are not directly available through the graphics device interface (GDI).
StartDoc	Informs the device driver that a new print job is starting.
StartPage	Informs the device driver that a new page is starting.
EndPage	Informs the device driver that a page is ending.

(continued)

Printer Escape Functions *(continued)*

SetAbortProc	Sets a programmer-supplied callback function that Windows calls if a print job must be aborted.
AbortDoc	Terminates the current print job, erasing everything the application has written to the device since the last call of the **StartDoc** member function.
EndDoc	Ends a print job started by the **StartDoc** member function.

Scrolling Functions

ScrollDC	Scrolls a rectangle of bits horizontally and vertically.

Metafile Functions

PlayMetaFile	Plays the contents of the specified metafile on the given device. The enhanced version of **PlayMetaFile** displays the picture stored in the given enhanced-format metafile. The metafile can be played any number of times.
AddMetaFileComment	Copies the comment from a buffer into a specified enhanced-format metafile.

Path Functions

AbortPath	Closes and discards any paths in the device context.
BeginPath	Opens a path bracket in the device context.
CloseFigure	Closes an open figure in a path.
EndPath	Closes a path bracket and selects the path defined by the bracket into the device context.
FillPath	Closes any open figures in the current path and fills the path's interior by using the current brush and polygon-filling mode.
FlattenPath	Transforms any curves in the path selected into the current device context, and turns each curve into a sequence of lines.
GetMiterLimit	Returns the miter limit for the device context.
GetPath	Retrieves the coordinates defining the endpoints of lines and the control points of curves found in the path that is selected into the device context.
SelectClipPath	Selects the current path as a clipping region for the device context, combining the new region with any existing clipping region by using the specified mode.
SetMiterLimit	Sets the limit for the length of miter joins for the device context.
StrokeAndFillPath	Closes any open figures in a path, strikes the outline of the path by using the current pen, and fills its interior by using the current brush.
StrokePath	Renders the specified path by using the current pen.
WidenPath	Redefines the current path as the area that would be painted if the path were stroked using the pen currently selected into the device context.

Member Functions
CDC::AbortDoc

int AbortDoc( );

A value greater than or equal to 0 if successful, or a negative value if an error has occurred. The following list shows common error values and their meanings:

- **SP_ERROR**   General error.
- **SP_OUTOFDISK**   Not enough disk space is currently available for spooling, and no more space will become available.
- **SP_OUTOFMEMORY**   Not enough memory is available for spooling.
- **SP_USERABORT**   User terminated the job through the Print Manager.

Terminates the current print job and erases everything the application has written to the device since the last call to the **StartDoc** member function.

This member function replaces the **ABORTDOC** printer escape.

AbortDoc should be used to terminate the following:

- Printing operations that do not specify an abort function using **SetAbortProc**.
- Printing operations that have not yet reached their first **NEWFRAME** or **NEXTBAND** escape call.

If an application encounters a printing error or a canceled print operation, it must not attempt to terminate the operation by using either the **EndDoc** or **AbortDoc** member functions of class **CDC**. GDI automatically terminates the operation before returning the error value.

If the application displays a dialog box to allow the user to cancel the print operation, it must call **AbortDoc** before destroying the dialog box.

If Print Manager was used to start the print job, calling **AbortDoc** erases the entire spool job—the printer receives nothing. If Print Manager was not used to start the print job, the data may have been sent to the printer before **AbortDoc** was called. In this case, the printer driver would have reset the printer (when possible) and closed the print job.

See Also: **CDC::StartDoc, CDC::EndDoc, CDC::SetAbortProc**

CDC::AbortPath

BOOL AbortPath( )

Return Value

Nonzero if the function is successful; otherwise 0.

Remarks

Closes and discards any paths in the device context. If there is an open path bracket in the device context, the path bracket is closed and the path is discarded. If there is a closed path in the device context, the path is discarded.

See Also: CDC::BeginPath, CDC::EndPath

CDC::AddMetaFileComment

BOOL AddMetaFileComment(UINT *nDataSize***, const BYTE*** *pCommentData* **);**

Return Value

Nonzero if the function is successful; otherwise 0.

Parameters

nDataSize   Specifies the length of the comment buffer, in bytes.

pCommentData   Points to the buffer that contains the comment.

Remarks

Copies the comment from a buffer into a specified enhanced-format metafile. A comment may include any private information—for example, the source of the picture and the date it was created. A comment should begin with an application signature, followed by the data. Comments should not contain position-specific data. Position-specific data specifies the location of a record, and it should not be included because one metafile may be embedded within another metafile. This function can only be used with enhanced metafiles.

See Also: CMetaFileDC::CreateEnhanced, ::GdiComment

CDC::AngleArc

BOOL AngleArc(int *x***, int** *y***, int** *nRadius***, float** *fStartAngle***, float** *fSweepAngle* **);**

Return Value

Nonzero if successful; otherwise 0.

Parameters

x   Specifies the logical x-coordinate of the center of the circle.

y   Specifies the logical y-coordinate of the center of the circle.

nRadius Specifies the radius of the circle in logical units. This value must be positive.

fStartAngle Specifies the starting angle in degrees relative to the x-axis.

fSweepAngle Specifies the sweep angle in degrees relative to the starting angle.

Remarks

Draws a line segment and an arc. The line segment is drawn from the current position to the beginning of the arc. The arc is drawn along the perimeter of a circle with the given radius and center. The length of the arc is defined by the given start and sweep angles.

AngleArc moves the current position to the ending point of the arc. The arc drawn by this function may appear to be elliptical, depending on the current transformation and mapping mode. Before drawing the arc, this function draws the line segment from the current position to the beginning of the arc. The arc is drawn by constructing an imaginary circle with the specified radius around the specified center point. The starting point of the arc is determined by measuring counterclockwise from the x-axis of the circle by the number of degrees in the start angle. The ending point is similarly located by measuring counterclockwise from the starting point by the number of degrees in the sweep angle.

If the sweep angle is greater than 360 degrees the arc is swept multiple times. This function draws lines by using the current pen. The figure is not filled.

See Also: **CDC::Arc, CDC::ArcTo, CDC::MoveTo, ::AngleArc**

CDC::Arc

BOOL Arc(int *x1*, **int** *y1*, **int** *x2*, **int** *y2*, **int** *x3*, **int** *y3*, **int** *x4*, **int** *y4* **);**
BOOL Arc(LPCRECT *lpRect*, **POINT** *ptStart*, **POINT** *ptEnd* **);**

Return Value

Nonzero if the function is successful; otherwise 0.

Parameters

x1 Specifies the x-coordinate of the upper-left corner of the bounding rectangle (in logical units).

y1 Specifies the y-coordinate of the upper-left corner of the bounding rectangle (in logical units).

x2 Specifies the x-coordinate of the lower-right corner of the bounding rectangle (in logical units).

y2 Specifies the y-coordinate of the lower-right corner of the bounding rectangle (in logical units).

x3 Specifies the x-coordinate of the point that defines the arc's starting point (in logical units). This point does not have to lie exactly on the arc.

y3 Specifies the y-coordinate of the point that defines the arc's starting point (in logical units). This point does not have to lie exactly on the arc.

x4 Specifies the x-coordinate of the point that defines the arc's endpoint (in logical units). This point does not have to lie exactly on the arc.

y4 Specifies the y-coordinate of the point that defines the arc's endpoint (in logical units). This point does not have to lie exactly on the arc.

lpRect Specifies the bounding rectangle (in logical units). You can pass either an **LPRECT** or a **CRect** object for this parameter.

ptStart Specifies the x- and y-coordinates of the point that defines the arc's starting point (in logical units). This point does not have to lie exactly on the arc. You can pass either a **POINT** structure or a **CPoint** object for this parameter.

ptEnd Specifies the x- and y-coordinates of the point that defines the arc's ending point (in logical units). This point does not have to lie exactly on the arc. You can pass either a **POINT** structure or a **CPoint** object for this parameter.

Remarks

Draws an elliptical arc. The arc drawn by using the function is a segment of the ellipse defined by the specified bounding rectangle.

The actual starting point of the arc is the point at which a ray drawn from the center of the bounding rectangle through the specified starting point intersects the ellipse. The actual ending point of the arc is the point at which a ray drawn from the center of the bounding rectangle through the specified ending point intersects the ellipse. The arc is drawn in a counterclockwise direction. Since an arc is not a closed figure, it is not filled. Both the width and height of the rectangle must be greater than 2 units and less than 32,767 units.

See Also: **CDC::Chord**, **::Arc**, **POINT**, **RECT**

CDC::ArcTo

BOOL ArcTo(int *x1*, **int** *y1*, **int** *x2*, **int** *y2*, **int** *x3*, **int** *y3*, **int** *x4*, **int** *y4* **);**
BOOL ArcTo(LPCRECT *lpRect*, **POINT** *ptStart*, **POINT** *ptEnd* **);**

Return Value

Nonzero if the function is successful; otherwise 0.

Parameters

x1 Specifies the x-coordinate of the upper-left corner of the bounding rectangle (in logical units).

y1 Specifies the y-coordinate of the upper-left corner of the bounding rectangle (in logical units).

x2 Specifies the x-coordinate of the lower-right corner of the bounding rectangle (in logical units).

y2 Specifies the y-coordinate of the lower-right corner of the bounding rectangle (in logical units).

x3 Specifies the x-coordinate of the point that defines the arc's starting point (in logical units). This point does not have to lie exactly on the arc.

y3 Specifies the y-coordinate of the point that defines the arc's starting point (in logical units). This point does not have to lie exactly on the arc.

x4 Specifies the x-coordinate of the point that defines the arc's endpoint (in logical units). This point does not have to lie exactly on the arc.

y4 Specifies the y-coordinate of the point that defines the arc's endpoint (in logical units). This point does not have to lie exactly on the arc.

lpRect Specifies the bounding rectangle (in logical units). You can pass either a pointer to a **RECT** data structure or a **CRect** object for this parameter.

ptStart Specifies the x- and y-coordinates of the point that defines the arc's starting point (in logical units). This point does not have to lie exactly on the arc. You can pass either a **POINT** data structure or a **CPoint** object for this parameter.

ptEnd Specifies the x- and y-coordinates of the point that defines the arc's ending point (in logical units). This point does not have to lie exactly on the arc. You can pass either a **POINT** data structure or a **CPoint** object for this parameter.

Remarks

Draws an elliptical arc. This function is similar to **CDC::Arc**, except that the current position is updated. The points $(x1,y1)$ and $(x2,y2)$ specify the bounding rectangle. An ellipse formed by the given bounding rectangle defines the curve of the arc. The arc extends counterclockwise (the default arc direction) from the point where it intersects the radial line from the center of the bounding rectangle to $(x3,y3)$. The arc ends where it intersects the radial line from the center of the bounding rectangle to $(x4,y4)$. If the starting point and ending point are the same, a complete ellipse is drawn.

A line is drawn from the current position to the starting point of the arc. If no error occurs, the current position is set to the ending point of the arc. The arc is drawn using the current pen; it is not filled.

See Also: **CDC::AngleArc, CDC::Arc, CDC::SetArcDirection, ::ArcTo**

CDC::Attach

BOOL Attach(HDC *hDC* **);**

Return Value

Nonzero if the function is successful; otherwise 0.

Parameters

hDC A Windows device context.

Remarks

Use this member function to attach an *hDC* to the **CDC** object. The *hDC* is stored in both **m_hDC**, the output device context, and in **m_hAttribDC**, the attribute device context.

See Also: **CDC::Detach, CDC::m_hDC, CDC::m_hAttribDC**

CDC::BeginPath

BOOL BeginPath( );

Return Value

Nonzero if the function is successful; otherwise 0.

Remarks

Opens a path bracket in the device context. After a path bracket is open, an application can begin calling GDI drawing functions to define the points that lie in the path. An application can close an open path bracket by calling the **EndPath** member function. When an application calls **BeginPath**, any previous paths are discarded.

The following drawing functions define points in a path:

AngleArc	**PolyBezierTo**
Arc	**PolyDraw**
ArcTo	**Polygon**
Chord	**Polyline**
CloseFigure	**PolylineTo**
Ellipse	**PolyPolygon**
ExtTextOut	**PolyPolyline**
LineTo	**Rectangle**
MoveToEx	**RoundRec**
Pie	**TextOut**
PolyBezier	

See Also: **CDC::EndPath, CDC::FillPath, CRgn::CreateFromPath, CDC::SelectClipPath, CDC::StrokeAndFillPath, CDC::StrokePath, CDC::WidenPath, ::BeginPath**

CDC::BitBlt

BOOL BitBlt(int *x*, **int** *y*, **int** *nWidth*, **int** *nHeight*, **CDC*** *pSrcDC*, **int** *xSrc*, **int** *ySrc*,
↳ **DWORD** *dwRop* **);**

Return Value

Nonzero if the function is successful; otherwise 0.

Parameters

x Specifies the logical x-coordinate of the upper-left corner of the destination rectangle.

y Specifies the logical y-coordinate of the upper-left corner of the destination rectangle.

nWidth Specifies the width (in logical units) of the destination rectangle and source bitmap.

nHeight Specifies the height (in logical units) of the destination rectangle and source bitmap.

pSrcDC Pointer to a **CDC** object that identifies the device context from which the bitmap will be copied. It must be **NULL** if *dwRop* specifies a raster operation that does not include a source.

xSrc Specifies the logical x-coordinate of the upper-left corner of the source bitmap.

ySrc Specifies the logical y-coordinate of the upper-left corner of the source bitmap.

dwRop Specifies the raster operation to be performed. Raster-operation codes define how the GDI combines colors in output operations that involve a current brush, a possible source bitmap, and a destination bitmap. The following lists raster-operation codes for *dwRop* and their descriptions:

- **BLACKNESS** Turns all output black.

- **DSTINVERT** Inverts the destination bitmap.

- **MERGECOPY** Combines the pattern and the source bitmap using the Boolean AND operator.

- **MERGEPAINT** Combines the inverted source bitmap with the destination bitmap using the Boolean OR operator.

- **NOTSRCCOPY** Copies the inverted source bitmap to the destination.

- **NOTSRCERASE** Inverts the result of combining the destination and source bitmaps using the Boolean OR operator.

- **PATCOPY** Copies the pattern to the destination bitmap.

- **PATINVERT** Combines the destination bitmap with the pattern using the Boolean XOR operator.

- **PATPAINT** Combines the inverted source bitmap with the pattern using the Boolean OR operator. Combines the result of this operation with the destination bitmap using the Boolean OR operator.

- **SRCAND** Combines pixels of the destination and source bitmaps using the Boolean AND operator.

- **SRCCOPY** Copies the source bitmap to the destination bitmap.

- **SRCERASE** Inverts the desination bitmap and combines the result with the source bitmap using the Boolean AND operator.

- **SRCINVERT** Combines pixels of the destination and source bitmaps using the Boolean XOR operator.

- **SRCPAINT** Combines pixels of the destination and source bitmaps using the Boolean OR operator.

- **WHITENESS** Turns all output white.

For a complete list of raster-operation codes, see "About Raster Operation Codes" in the Appendices section of the *Win32 SDK Programmer's Reference*.

Remarks

Copies a bitmap from the source device context to this current device context.

The application can align the windows or client areas on byte boundaries to ensure that the **BitBlt** operations occur on byte-aligned rectangles. (Set the **CS_BYTEALIGNWINDOW** or **CS_BYTEALIGNCLIENT** flags when you register the window classes.)

BitBlt operations on byte-aligned rectangles are considerably faster than **BitBlt** operations on rectangles that are not byte aligned. If you want to specify class styles such as byte-alignment for your own device context, you will have to register a window class rather than relying on the Microsoft Foundation classes to do it for you. Use the global function **AfxRegisterWndClass**.

GDI transforms *nWidth* and *nHeight*, once by using the destination device context, and once by using the source device context. If the resulting extents do not match, GDI uses the Windows **StretchBlt** function to compress or stretch the source bitmap as necessary.

If destination, source, and pattern bitmaps do not have the same color format, the **BitBlt** function converts the source and pattern bitmaps to match the destination. The foreground and background colors of the destination bitmap are used in the conversion.

When the **BitBlt** function converts a monochrome bitmap to color, it sets white bits (1) to the background color and black bits (0) to the foreground color. The foreground and background colors of the destination device context are used. To convert color to monochrome, **BitBlt** sets pixels that match the background color to white and sets all other pixels to black. **BitBlt** uses the foreground and background colors of the color device context to convert from color to monochrome.

Note that not all device contexts support **BitBlt**. To check whether a given device context does support **BitBlt**, use the **GetDeviceCaps** member function and specify the **RASTERCAPS** index.

See Also: **CDC::GetDeviceCaps**, **CDC::PatBlt**, **CDC::SetTextColor**, **CDC::StretchBlt**, **::StretchDIBits**, **::BitBlt**

CDC::CDC

CDC( );

Remarks

Constructs a **CDC** object.

See Also: **CDC::CreateDC**, **CDC::CreateIC**, **CDC::CreateCompatibleDC**

CDC::Chord

BOOL Chord(int *x1*, **int** *y1*, **int** *x2*, **int** *y2*, **int** *x3*, **int** *y3*, **int** *x4*, **int** *y4* **);**
BOOL Chord(LPCRECT *lpRect*, **POINT** *ptStart*, **POINT** *ptEnd* **);**

Return Value

Nonzero if the function is successful; otherwise 0.

Parameters

x1　Specifies the x-coordinate of the upper-left corner of the chord's bounding rectangle (in logical units).

y1　Specifies the y-coordinate of the upper-left corner of the chord's bounding rectangle (in logical units).

x2　Specifies the x-coordinate of the lower-right corner of the chord's bounding rectangle (in logical units).

y2　Specifies the y-coordinate of the lower-right corner of the chord's bounding rectangle (in logical units).

x3　Specifies the x-coordinate of the point that defines the chord's starting point (in logical units).

y3　Specifies the y-coordinate of the point that defines the chord's starting point (in logical units).

x4　Specifies the x-coordinate of the point that defines the chord's endpoint (in logical units).

y4 Specifies the y-coordinate of the point that defines the chord's endpoint (in logical units).

lpRect Specifies the bounding rectangle (in logical units). You can pass either a **LPRECT** or a **CRect** object for this parameter.

ptStart Specifies the x- and y-coordinates of the point that defines the chord's starting point (in logical units). This point does not have to lie exactly on the chord. You can pass either a **POINT** structure or a **CPoint** object for this parameter.

ptEnd Specifies the x- and y-coordinates of the point that defines the chord's ending point (in logical units). This point does not have to lie exactly on the chord. You can pass either a **POINT** structure or a **CPoint** object for this parameter.

Remarks

Draws a chord (a closed figure bounded by the intersection of an ellipse and a line segment). The $(x1, y1)$ and $(x2, y2)$ parameters specify the upper-left and lower-right corners, respectively, of a rectangle bounding the ellipse that is part of the chord. The $(x3, y3)$ and $(x4, y4)$ parameters specify the endpoints of a line that intersects the ellipse. The chord is drawn by using the selected pen and filled by using the selected brush.

The figure drawn by the **Chord** function extends up to, but does not include the right and bottom coordinates. This means that the height of the figure is $y2 - y1$ and the width of the figure is $x2 - x1$.

See Also: **CDC::Arc, ::Chord, POINT**

CDC::CloseFigure

BOOL CloseFigure( );

Return Value

Nonzero if the function is successful; otherwise 0.

Remarks

Closes an open figure in a path. The function closes the figure by drawing a line from the current position to the first point of the figure (usually, the point specified by the most recent call to the **MoveTo** member function) and connects the lines by using the line join style. If a figure is closed by using the **LineTo** member function instead of **CloseFigure**, end caps are used to create the corner instead of a join. **CloseFigure** should only be called if there is an open path bracket in the device context.

A figure in a path is open unless it is explicitly closed by using this function. (A figure can be open even if the current point and the starting point of the figure are the same.) Any line or curve added to the path after **CloseFigure** starts a new figure.

See Also: **CDC::BeginPath, CDC::EndPath, CDC::MoveTo, ::CloseFigure**

CDC::CreateCompatibleDC

virtual BOOL CreateCompatibleDC(CDC* *pDC* **);**

Return Value

Nonzero if the function is successful; otherwise 0.

Parameters

pDC   A pointer to a device context. If *pDC* is **NULL**, the function creates a memory device context that is compatible with the system display.

Remarks

Creates a memory device context that is compatible with the device specified by *pDC*. A memory device context is a block of memory that represents a display surface. It can be used to prepare images in memory before copying them to the actual device surface of the compatible device.

When a memory device context is created, GDI automatically selects a 1-by-1 monochrome stock bitmap for it. GDI output functions can be used with a memory device context only if a bitmap has been created and selected into that context.

This function can only be used to create compatible device contexts for devices that support raster operations. See the **CDC::BitBlt** member function for information regarding bit-block transfers between device contexts. To determine whether a device context supports raster operations, see the **RC_BITBLT** raster capability in the member function **CDC::GetDeviceCaps**.

See Also: **CDC::CDC, CDC::GetDeviceCaps, ::CreateCompatibleDC, CDC::BitBlt, CDC::CreateDC, CDC::CreateIC, CDC::DeleteDC**

CDC::CreateDC

virtual BOOL CreateDC(LPCTSTR *lpszDriverName*, **LPCTSTR** *lpszDeviceName*,
↪ **LPCTSTR** *lpszOutput*, **const void*** *lpInitData* **);**

Return Value

Nonzero if the function is successful; otherwise 0.

Parameters

lpszDriverName   Points to a null-terminated string that specifies the filename (without extension) of the device driver (for example, "EPSON"). You can also pass a **CString** object for this parameter.

lpszDeviceName   Points to a null-terminated string that specifies the name of the specific device to be supported (for example, "EPSON FX-80"). The *lpszDeviceName* parameter is used if the module supports more than one device. You can also pass a **CString** object for this parameter.

> *lpszOutput*   Points to a null-terminated string that specifies the file or device name for the physical output medium (file or output port). You can also pass a **CString** object for this parameter.
>
> *lpInitData*   Points to a **DEVMODE** structure containing device-specific initialization data for the device driver. The Windows **DocumentProperties** function retrieves this structure filled in for a given device. The *lpInitData* parameter must be **NULL** if the device driver is to use the default initialization (if any) specified by the user through the Control Panel.

Remarks

Creates a device context for the specified device.

The PRINT.H header file is required if the **DEVMODE** structure is used.

Device names follow these conventions: an ending colon (:) is recommended, but optional. Windows strips the terminating colon so that a device name ending with a colon is mapped to the same port as the same name without a colon. The driver and port names must not contain leading or trailing spaces. GDI output functions cannot be used with information contexts.

See Also: **::DocumentProperties**, **::CreateDC**, **CDC::DeleteDC**, **CDC::CreateIC**

CDC::CreateIC

> **virtual BOOL CreateIC(LPCTSTR** *lpszDriverName***, LPCTSTR** *lpszDeviceName***,**
> ↳ **LPCTSTR** *lpszOutput***, const void*** *lpInitData* **);**

Return Value

Nonzero if successful; otherwise 0.

Parameters

> *lpszDriverName*   Points to a null-terminated string that specifies the filename (without extension) of the device driver (for example, "EPSON"). You can pass a **CString** object for this parameter.
>
> *lpszDeviceName*   Points to a null-terminated string that specifies the name of the specific device to be supported (for example, "EPSON FX-80"). The *lpszDeviceName* parameter is used if the module supports more than one device. You can pass a **CString** object for this parameter.
>
> *lpszOutput*   Points to a null-terminated string that specifies the file or device name for the physical output medium (file or port). You can pass a **CString** object for this parameter.
>
> *lpInitData*   Points to device-specific initialization data for the device driver. The *lpInitData* parameter must be **NULL** if the device driver is to use the default initialization (if any) specified by the user through the Control Panel. See **CreateDC** for the data format for device-specific initialization.

Remarks

Creates an information context for the specified device. The information context provides a fast way to get information about the device without creating a device context.

Device names follow these conventions: an ending colon (:) is recommended, but optional. Windows strips the terminating colon so that a device name ending with a colon is mapped to the same port as the same name without a colon. The driver and port names must not contain leading or trailing spaces. GDI output functions cannot be used with information contexts.

See Also: **CDC::CreateDC**, **::CreateIC**, **CDC::DeleteDC**

CDC::DeleteDC

virtual BOOL DeleteDC( );

Return Value

Nonzero if the function completed successfully; otherwise 0.

Remarks

In general, do not call this function; the destructor will do it for you. The **DeleteDC** member function deletes the Windows device contexts that are associated with **m_hDC** in the current **CDC** object. If this **CDC** object is the last active device context for a given device, the device is notified and all storage and system resources used by the device are released.

An application should not call **DeleteDC** if objects have been selected into the device context. Objects must first be selected out of the device context before it it is deleted.

An application must not delete a device context whose handle was obtained by calling **CWnd::GetDC**. Instead, it must call **CWnd::ReleaseDC** to free the device context. The **CClientDC** and **CWindowDC** classes are provided to wrap this functionality.

The **DeleteDC** function is generally used to delete device contexts created with **CreateDC**, **CreateIC**, or **CreateCompatibleDC**.

See Also: **CDC::CDC**, **::DeleteDC**, **CDC::CreateDC**, **CDC::CreateIC**, **CDC::CreateCompatibleDC**, **CWnd::GetDC**, **CWnd::ReleaseDC**

CDC::DeleteTempMap

static void PASCAL DeleteTempMap( );

Remarks

Called automatically by the **CWinApp** idle-time handler, **DeleteTempMap** deletes any temporary **CDC** objects created by **FromHandle**, but does not destroy the device context handles (**hDCs**) temporarily associated with the **CDC** objects.

See Also: **CDC::Detach**, **CDC::FromHandle**, **CWinApp::OnIdle**

CDC::Detach

HDC Detach( );

Return Value

A Windows device context.

Remarks

Call this function to detach **m_hDC** (the output device context) from the **CDC** object and set both **m_hDC** and **m_hAttribDC** to **NULL**.

See Also: **CDC::Attach, CDC::m_hDC, CDC::m_hAttribDC**

CDC::DPtoHIMETRIC

void DPtoHIMETRIC(LPSIZE *lpSize* **) const;**

Parameters

lpSize Points to a **SIZE** structure or **CSize** object.

Remarks

Use this function when you give **HIMETRIC** sizes to OLE, converting pixels to **HIMETRIC**.

If the mapping mode of the device context object is **MM_LOENGLISH**, **MM_HIENGLISH**, **MM_LOMETRIC**, or **MM_HIMETRIC**, then the conversion is based on the number of pixels in the physical inch. If the mapping mode is one of the other non-constrained modes (e.g., **MM_TEXT**), then the conversion is based on the number of pixels in the logical inch.

See Also: **CDC::DPtoLP, CDC::LPtoDP, CDC::HIMETRICtoLP, CDC::HIMETRICtoDP, CDC::LPtoHIMETRIC**

CDC::DPtoLP

void DPtoLP(LPPOINT *lpPoints***, int** *nCount* **= 1) const;**
void DPtoLP(LPRECT *lpRect* **) const;**
void DPtoLP(LPSIZE *lpSize* **) const;**

Parameters

lpPoints Points to an array of **POINT** structures or **CPoint** objects.

nCount The number of points in the array.

lpRect Points to a **RECT** structure or **CRect** object. This parameter is used for the simple case of converting one rectangle from device points to logical points.

lpSize Points to a **SIZE** structure or **CSize** object.

Remarks

Converts device units into logical units. The function maps the coordinates of each point, or dimension of a size, from the device coordinate system into GDI's logical coordinate system. The conversion depends on the current mapping mode and the settings of the origins and extents for the device's window and viewport.

See Also: **CDC::LPtoDP**, **CDC::HIMETRICtoDP**, **::DPtoLP**, **POINT**, **RECT**, **CDC::GetWindowExt**, **CDC::GetWindowOrg**

CDC::Draw3dRect

void Draw3dRect(LPCRECT *lpRect*, **COLORREF** *clrTopLeft*,
↪ **COLORREF** *clrBottomRight* **);**
void Draw3dRect(int *x*, **int** *y*, **int** *cx*, **int** *cy*, **COLORREF** *clrTopLeft*,
↪ **COLORREF** *clrBottomRight* **);**

Parameters

lpRect Specifies the bounding rectangle (in logical units). You can pass either a pointer to a **RECT** structure or a **CRect** object for this parameter.

clrTopLeft Specifies the color of the top and left sides of the three-dimensional rectangle.

clrBottomRight Specifies the color of the bottom and right sides of the three-dimensional rectangle.

x Specifies the logical x-coordinate of the upper-left corner of the three-dimensional rectangle.

y Specifies the logical y-coordinate of the upper-left corner of the three-dimensional rectangle.

cx Specifies the width of the three-dimensional rectangle.

cy Specifies the height of the three-dimensional rectangle.

Remarks

Call this member function to draw a three-dimensional rectangle. The rectangle will be drawn with the top and left sides in the color specified by *clrTopLeft* and the bottom and right sides in the color specified by *clrBottomRight*.

See Also: **RECT**, **CRect**

CDC::DrawDragRect

void DrawDragRect(LPCRECT *lpRect*, **SIZE** *size*, **LPCRECT** *lpRectLast*,
↪ **SIZE** *sizeLast*, **CBrush*** *pBrush* = **NULL**, **CBrush*** *pBrushLast* = **NULL** **);**

Parameters

lpRect Points to a **RECT** structure or a **CRect** object that specifies the logical coordinates of a rectangle — in this case, the end position of the rectangle being redrawn.

size   Specifies the displacement from the top-left corner of the outer border to the top-left corner of the inner border (that is, the thickness of the border) of a rectangle.

lpRectLast   Points to a **RECT** structure or a **CRect** object that specifies the logical coordinates of the position of a rectangle — in this case, the original position of the rectangle being redrawn.

sizeLast   Specifies the displacement from the top-left corner of the outer border to the top-left corner of the inner border (that is, the thickness of the border) of the original rectangle being redrawn.

pBrush   Pointer to a brush object. Set to **NULL** to use the default halftone brush.

pBrushLast   Pointer to the last brush object used. Set to **NULL** to use the default halftone brush.

Remarks

Call this member function repeatedly to redraw a drag rectangle. Call it in a loop as you sample mouse position, in order to give visual feedback. When you call **DrawDragRect**, the previous rectangle is erased and a new one is drawn. For example, as the user drags a rectangle across the screen, **DrawDragRect** will erase the original rectangle and redraw a new one in its new position. By default, **DrawDragRect** draws the rectangle by using a halftone brush to eliminate flicker and to create the appearance of a smoothly moving rectangle.

The first time you call **DrawDragRect**, the *lpRectLast* parameter should be **NULL**.

See Also: RECT, CRect, CDC::GetHalftoneBrush

CDC::DrawEdge

BOOL DrawEdge(LPRECT *lpRect*, **UINT** *nEdge*, **UINT** *nFlags* **);**

Return Value

Nonzero if successful; otherwise 0.

Parameters

lpRect   A pointer to a **RECT** structure that contains the logical coordinates of the rectangle.

nEdge   Specifies the type of inner and outer edge to draw. This parameter must be a combination of one inner-border flag and one outer-border flag. See the Remarks section for a table of the parameter's types.

nFlags   The flags that specify the type of border to be drawn. See the Remarks section for a table of the parameter's values:

Remarks

Call this member function to draw the edges of a rectangle of the specified type and style.

The inner and outer border flags are as follows:

- Inner-border flags
  - **BDR_RAISEDINNER** Raised inner edge.
  - **BDR_SUNKENINNER** Sunken inner edge.
- Outer-border flags
  - **BDR_RAISEDOUTER** Raised outer edge.
  - **BDR_SUNKENOUTER** Sunken outer edge.

The *nEdge* parameter must be a combination of one inner and one outer border flag. The *nEdge* parameter can specify one of the following flags:

- **EDGE_BUMP** Combination of **BDR_RAISEDOUTER** and **BDR_SUNKENINNER**.
- **EDGE_ETCHED** Combination of **BDR_SUNKENOUTER** and **BDR_RAISEDINNER**.
- **EDGE_RAISED** Combination of **BDR_RAISEDOUTER** and **BDR_RAISEDINNER**.
- **EDGE_SUNKEN** Combination of **BDR_SUNKENOUTER** and **BDR_SUNKENINNER**.

The *nFlags* parameter types are as follows:

- **BF_RECT** Entire border rectangle.
- **BF_LEFT** Left side of border rectangle.
- **BF_BOTTOM** Bottom of border rectangle.
- **BF_RIGHT** Right side of border rectangle.
- **BF_TOP** Top of border rectangle.
- **BF_TOPLEFT** Top and left side of border rectangle.
- **BF_TOPRIGHT** Top and right side of border rectangle.
- **BF_BOTTOMLEFT** Bottom and left side of border rectangle.
- **BF_BOTTOMRIGHT** Bottom and right side of border rectangle.

For diagonal lines, the **BF_RECT** flags specify the end point of the vector bounded by the rectangle parameter.

- **BF_DIAGONAL_ENDBOTTOMLEFT** Diagonal border. The end point is the bottom-left corner of the rectangle; the origin is top-right corner.
- **BF_DIAGONAL_ENDBOTTOMRIGHT** Diagonal border. The end point is the bottom-right corner of the rectangle; the origin is top-left corner.
- **BF_DIAGONAL_ENDTOPLEFT** Diagonal border. The end point is the top-left corner of the rectangle; the origin is bottom-right corner.
- **BF_DIAGONAL_ENDTOPRIGHT** Diagonal border. The end point is the top-right corner of the rectangle; the origin is bottom-left corner.

For more information about the Windows API **DrawEdge**, see **::DrawEdge** in the *Win32 SDK Programmer's Reference*.

See Also: ::DrawEdge

CDC::DrawEscape

int DrawEscape(int *nEscape***, int** *nInputSize***, LPCSTR** *lpszInputData* **);**

Return Value

Specifies the outcome of the function. Greater than zero if successful, except for the **QUERYESCSUPPORT** draw escape, which checks for implementation only; or zero if the escape is not implemented; or less than zero if an error occurred.

Parameters

nEscape Specifies the escape function to be performed.

nInputSize Specifies the number of bytes of data pointed to by the *lpszInputData* parameter.

lpszInputData Points to the input structure required for the specified escape.

Remarks

Accesses drawing capabilities of a video display that are not directly available through the graphics device interface (GDI). When an application calls **DrawEscape**, the data identified by *nInputSize* and *lpszInputData* is passed directly to the specified display driver.

See Also: CDC::Escape, ::DrawEscape

CDC::DrawFocusRect

void DrawFocusRect(LPCRECT *lpRect* **);**

Parameters

lpRect Points to a **RECT** structure or a **CRect** object that specifies the logical coordinates of the rectangle to be drawn.

Remarks

Draws a rectangle in the style used to indicate that the rectangle has the focus.

Since this is a Boolean XOR function, calling this function a second time with the same rectangle removes the rectangle from the display. The rectangle drawn by this function cannot be scrolled. To scroll an area containing a rectangle drawn by this function, first call **DrawFocusRect** to remove the rectangle from the display, then scroll the area, and then call **DrawFocusRect** again to draw the rectangle in the new position.

See Also: CDC::FrameRect, ::DrawFocusRect, RECT

CDC::DrawFrameControl

BOOL DrawFrameControl(LPRECT *lpRect***, UINT** *nType***, UINT** *nState* **);**

Return Value

Nonzero if successful; otherwise 0.

Parameters

lpRect   A pointer to a **RECT** structure that contains the logical coordinates of the rectangle.

nType   Specifies the type of frame control to draw. This parameter can be one of the following values:

- **DFC_BUTTON**   Standard button
- **DFC_CAPTION**   Title bar
- **DFC_MENU**   Menu
- **DFC_SCROLL**   Scroll bar

nState   Specifies the initial state of the frame control. See the Remarks section for a table of the parameter's values.

Remarks

Call this member function to draw a frame control of the specified type and style.

Use the *nState* value **DFCS_ADJUSTRECT** to adjust the bounding rectangle to exclude the surrounding edge of the push button. One or more of the following values can be used to set the state of the control to be drawn:

- **DFCS_CHECKED**   Button is checked.
- **DFCS_FLAT**   Button has a flat border.
- **DFCS_INACTIVE**   Button is inactive (grayed).
- **DFCS_MONO**   Button has a monochrome border.
- **DFCS_PUSHED**   Button is pushed.

In several cases, *nState* depends on the *nType* parameter. The following list shows the relationship between the four *nType* values and *nState*:

- **DFC_BUTTON**
  - **DFCS_BUTTON3STATE**   Three-state button
  - **DFCS_BUTTONCHECK**   Check box
  - **DFCS_BUTTONPUSH**   Push button
  - **DFCS_BUTTONRADIO**   Radio button
  - **DFCS_BUTTONRADIOIMAGE**   Image for radio button (nonsquare needs image)

- **DFCS_BUTTONRADIOMASK** Mask for radio button (nonsquare needs mask)
- **DFC_CAPTION**
  - **DFCS_CAPTIONCLOSE** Close button
  - **DFCS_CAPTIONHELP** Help button
  - **DFCS_CAPTIONMAX** Maximize button
  - **DFCS_CAPTIONMIN** Minimize button
  - **DFCS_CAPTIONRESTORE** Restore button
- **DFC_MENU**
  - **DFCS_MENUARROW** Submenu arrow
  - **DFCS_MENUBULLET** Bullet
  - **DFCS_MENUCHECK** Check mark
- **DFC_SCROLL**
  - **DFCS_SCROLLCOMBOBOX** Combo box scroll bar
  - **DFCS_SCROLLDOWN** Down arrow of scroll bar
  - **DFCS_SCROLLLEFT** Left arrow of scroll bar
  - **DFCS_SCROLLRIGHT** Right arrow of scroll bar
  - **DFCS_SCROLLSIZEGRIP** Size grip in bottom-right corner of window
  - **DFCS_SCROLLUP** Up arrow of scroll bar

For more information about the Windows API **DrawFrameControl**, see **::DrawFrameControl** in the *Win32 SDK Programmer's Reference*.

See Also: **::DrawFrameControl**

CDC::DrawIcon

BOOL DrawIcon(int *x*, **int** *y*, **HICON** *hIcon* **);**
BOOL DrawIcon(POINT *point*, **HICON** *hIcon* **);**

Return Value

Nonzero if the function completed successfully; otherwise 0.

Parameters

x Specifies the logical x-coordinate of the upper-left corner of the icon.

y Specifies the logical y-coordinate of the upper-left corner of the icon.

hIcon Identifies the handle of the icon to be drawn.

point Specifies the logical x- and y-coordinates of the upper-left corner of the icon. You can pass a **POINT** structure or a **CPoint** object for this parameter.

Remarks

Draws an icon on the device represented by the current **CDC** object. The function places the icon's upper-left corner at the location specified by *x* and *y*. The location is subject to the current mapping mode of the device context.

The icon resource must have been previously loaded by using the functions **CWinApp::LoadIcon**, **CWinApp::LoadStandardIcon**, or **CWinApp::LoadOEMIcon**. The **MM_TEXT** mapping mode must be selected prior to using this function.

See Also: **CWinApp::LoadIcon**, **CWinApp::LoadStandardIcon**, **CWinApp::LoadOEMIcon**, **CDC::GetMapMode**, **CDC::SetMapMode**, **::DrawIcon**, **POINT**

CDC::DrawState

BOOL DrawState(CPoint *pt*, **CSize** *size*, **HBITMAP** *hBitmap*, **UINT** *nFlags*,
  ↳ **HBRUSH** *hBrush* = **NULL**);
BOOL DrawState(CPoint *pt*, **CSize** *size*, **CBitmap*** *pBitmap*, **UINT** *nFlags*,
  ↳ **CBrush*** *pBrush* = **NULL**);
BOOL DrawState(CPoint *pt*, **CSize** *size*, **HICON** *hIcon*, **UINT** *nFlags*,
  ↳ **HBRUSH** *hBrush* = **NULL**);
BOOL DrawState(CPoint *pt*, **CSize** *size*, **HICON** *hIcon*, **UINT** *nFlags*,
  ↳ **CBrush*** *pBrush* = **NULL**);
BOOL DrawState(CPoint *pt*, **CSize** *size*, **LPCTSTR** *lpszText*, **UINT** *nFlags*,
  ↳ **BOOL** *bPrefixText* = **TRUE**, **int** *nTextLen* = **0**, **HBRUSH** *hBrush* = **NULL**);
BOOL DrawState(CPoint *pt*, **CSize** *size*, **LPCTSTR** *lpszText*, **UINT** *nFlags*,
  ↳ **BOOL** *bPrefixText* = **TRUE**, **int** *nTextLen* = **0**, **CBrush*** *pBrush* = **NULL**);
BOOL DrawState(CPoint *pt*, **CSize** *size*, **DRAWSTATEPROC** *lpDrawProc*,
  ↳ **LPARAM** *lData*, **UINT** *nFlags*, **HBRUSH** *hBrush* = **NULL**);
BOOL DrawState(CPoint *pt*, **CSize** *size*, **DRAWSTATEPROC** *lpDrawProc*,
  ↳ **LPARAM** *lData*, **UINT** *nFlags*, **CBrush*** *pBrush* = **NULL**);

Return Value

Nonzero if successful; otherwise 0.

Parameters

pt   Specifies the location of the image.

size   Specifies the size of the image.

hBitmap   A handle to a bitmap.

nFlags   Flags that specify the image type and state. See the Remarks section for the possible *nFlags* types and states.

hBrush   A handle to a brush.

pBitmap   A pointer to a Cbitmap object.

pBrush   A pointer to a Cbrush object.

hIcon   A handle to an icon.

lpszText   A pointer to text.

bPrefixText   Text that may contain an accelerator mnemonic. The *lData* parameter specifies the address of the string, and the *nTextLen* parameter specifies the length. If *nTextLen* is 0, the string is assumed to be null-terminated.

nTextLen   Length of the text string pointed to by *lpszText*. If *nTextLen* is 0, the string is assumed to be null-terminated.

lpDrawProc   A pointer to a callback function used to render an image. This parameter is required if the image type in *nFlags* is **DST_COMPLEX**. It is optional and can be **NULL** if the image type is **DST_TEXT**. For all other image types, this parameter is ignored. For more information about the callback function, see the **::DrawStateProc** function in the *Win32 SDK Programmer's Reference*.

lData   Specifies information about the image. The meaning of this parameter depends on the image type.

Remarks

Call this member function to display an image and apply a visual effect to indicate a state, such as a disabled or default state.

The parameter *nFlag* type can be set to one of the following values:

- **DST_BITMAP**   The image is a bitmap. The low-order word of the *lData* parameter is the bitmap handle.

- **DST_COMPLEX**   The image is application defined. To render the image, **DrawState** calls the callback function specified by the *lpDrawProc* parameter.

- **DST_ICON**   The image is an icon. The low-order word of *lData* is the icon handle.

- **DST_PREFIXTEXT**   The image is text that may contain an accelerator mnemonic. **DrawState** interprets the ampersand (&) prefix character as a directive to underscore the character that follows. The *lData* parameter specifies the address of the string.

- **DST_TEXT**   The image is text. The *lData* parameter specifies the address of the string.

The parameter *nFlag* state can be one of following values:

- **DSS_NORMAL**   Draws the image without any modification.

- **DSS_UNION**   Dithers the image.

- **DSS_DISABLED**   Embosses the image.

- **DSS_DEFAULT**   Makes the image bold.

- **DSS_MONO**   Draws the image using the brush specified by the *hBrush* or *pBrush* parameter.

Note For all *nFlag* states except **DSS_NORMAL**, the image is converted to monochrome before the visual effect is applied.

For more information about the Windows API **DrawState**, see **::DrawState** in the *Win32 SDK Programmer's Reference*.

See Also: **::DrawState**, **::DrawStateProc**

CDC::DrawText

virtual int DrawText(LPCTSTR *lpszString*, **int** *nCount*, **LPRECT** *lpRect*, ↪ **UINT** *nFormat* **);**
int DrawText(const CString& *str*, **LPRECT** *lpRect*, **UINT** *nFormat* **);**

Return Value

The height of the text if the function is successful.

Parameters

lpszString Points to the string to be drawn. If *nCount* is –1, the string must be null-terminated.

nCount Specifies the number of chars in the string. If *nCount* is –1, then *lpszString* is assumed to be a long pointer to a null-terminated string and **DrawText** computes the character count automatically.

lpRect Points to a **RECT** structure or **CRect** object that contains the rectangle (in logical coordinates) in which the text is to be formatted.

str A **CString** object that contains the specified characters to be drawn.

nFormat Specifies the method of formatting the text. It can be any combination of the following values (combine using the bitwise OR operator):

- **DT_BOTTOM** Specifies bottom-justified text. This value must be combined with **DT_SINGLELINE**.

- **DT_CALCRECT** Determines the width and height of the rectangle. If there are multiple lines of text, **DrawText** will use the width of the rectangle pointed to by *lpRect* and extend the base of the rectangle to bound the last line of text. If there is only one line of text, **DrawText** will modify the right side of the rectangle so that it bounds the last character in the line. In either case, **DrawText** returns the height of the formatted text, but does not draw the text.

- **DT_CENTER** Centers text horizontally.

- **DT_EXPANDTABS** Expands tab characters. The default number of characters per tab is eight.

- **DT_EXTERNALLEADING** Includes the font's external leading in the line height. Normally, external leading is not included in the height of a line of text.

- **DT_LEFT** Aligns text flush-left.

- **DT_NOCLIP** Draws without clipping. **DrawText** is somewhat faster when **DT_NOCLIP** is used.

- **DT_NOPREFIX** Turns off processing of prefix characters. Normally, **DrawText** interprets the ampersand (**&**) mnemonic-prefix character as a directive to underscore the character that follows, and the two-ampersand (**&&**) mnemonic-prefix characters as a directive to print a single ampersand. By specifying **DT_NOPREFIX**, this processing is turned off.

- **DT_RIGHT** Aligns text flush-right.

- **DT_SINGLELINE** Specifies single line only. Carriage returns and linefeeds do not break the line.

- **DT_TABSTOP** Sets tab stops. The high-order byte of *nFormat* is the number of characters for each tab. The default number of characters per tab is eight.

- **DT_TOP** Specifies top-justified text (single line only).

- **DT_VCENTER** Specifies vertically centered text (single line only).

- **DT_WORDBREAK** Specifies word-breaking. Lines are automatically broken between words if a word would extend past the edge of the rectangle specified by *lpRect*. A carriage return–linefeed sequence will also break the line.

Note The values **DT_CALCRECT**, **DT_EXTERNALLEADING**, **DT_INTERNAL**, **DT_NOCLIP**, and **DT_NOPREFIX** cannot be used with the **DT_TABSTOP** value.

Remarks

Call this member function to format text in the given rectangle. It formats text by expanding tabs into appropriate spaces, aligning text to the left, right, or center of the given rectangle, and breaking text into lines that fit within the given rectangle. The type of formatting is specified by *nFormat*.

This member function uses the device context's selected font, text color, and background color to draw the text. Unless the **DT_NOCLIP** format is used, **DrawText** clips the text so that the text does not appear outside the given rectangle. All formatting is assumed to have multiple lines unless the **DT_SINGLELINE** format is given.

If the selected font is too large for the specified rectangle, the **DrawText** member function does not attempt to substitute a smaller font.

If the **DT_CALCRECT** flag is specified, the rectangle specified by *lpRect* will be updated to reflect the width and height needed to draw the text.

If the **TA_UPDATECP** text-alignment flag has been set (see **CDC::SetTextAlign**), **DrawText** will display text starting at the current position, rather than at the left of the given rectangle. **DrawText** will not wrap text when the **TA_UPDATECP** flag has been set (that is, the **DT_WORDBREAK** flag will have no effect).

The text color may be set by **CDC::SetTextColor**.

See Also: CDC::SetTextColor, CDC::ExtTextOut, CDC::TabbedTextOut, CDC::TextOut, ::DrawText, RECT, CDC::SetTextAlign

CDC::Ellipse

BOOL Ellipse(int *x1***, int** *y1***, int** *x2***, int** *y2* **);**
BOOL Ellipse(LPCRECT *lpRect* **);**

Return Value

Nonzero if the function is successful; otherwise 0.

Parameters

x1   Specifies the logical x-coordinate of the upper-left corner of the ellipse's bounding rectangle.

y1   Specifies the logical y-coordinate of the upper-left corner of the ellipse's bounding rectangle.

x2   Specifies the logical x-coordinate of the lower-right corner of the ellipse's bounding rectangle.

y2   Specifies the logical y-coordinate of the lower-right corner of the ellipse's bounding rectangle.

lpRect   Specifies the ellipse's bounding rectangle. You can also pass a **CRect** object for this parameter.

Remarks

Draws an ellipse. The center of the ellipse is the center of the bounding rectangle specified by *x1*, *y1*, *x2*, and *y2*, or *lpRect*. The ellipse is drawn with the current pen, and its interior is filled with the current brush.

The figure drawn by this function extends up to, but does not include, the right and bottom coordinates. This means that the height of the figure is $y2 - y1$ and the width of the figure is $x2 - x1$.

If either the width or the height of the bounding rectangle is 0, no ellipse is drawn.

See Also: CDC::Arc, CDC::Chord, ::Ellipse

CDC::EndDoc

int EndDoc( );

Return Value

Greater than or equal to 0 if the function is successful, or a negative value if an error occurred. The following list shows common error values:

- **SP_ERROR**   General error.

- **SP_OUTOFDISK**   Not enough disk space is currently available for spooling, and no more space will become available.

- **SP_OUTOFMEMORY**   Not enough memory is available for spooling.

- **SP_USERABORT**   User ended the job through the Print Manager.

Remarks

Ends a print job started by a call to the **StartDoc** member function. This member function replaces the **ENDDOC** printer escape, and should be called immediately after finishing a successful print job.

If an application encounters a printing error or a canceled print operation, it must not attempt to terminate the operation by using either **EndDoc** or **AbortDoc**. GDI automatically terminates the operation before returning the error value.

This function should not be used inside metafiles.

See Also: **CDC::AbortDoc**, **CDC::Escape**, **CDC::StartDoc**

CDC::EndPage

int EndPage( );

Return Value

Greater than or equal to 0 if successful; otherwise it is an error value, which can be one of the following:

- **SP_ERROR**   General error.

- **SP_APPABORT**   Job was ended because the application's abort function returned 0.

- **SP_USERABORT**   User ended the job through Print Manager.

- **SP_OUTOFDISK**   Not enough disk space is currently available for spooling, and no more space will become available.

- **SP_OUTOFMEMORY**   Not enough memory is available for spooling.

Remarks

Informs the device that the application has finished writing to a page. This member function is typically used to direct the device driver to advance to a new page.

This member function replaces the **NEWFRAME** printer escape. Unlike **NEWFRAME**, this function is always called after printing a page.

See Also: **CDC::StartPage**, **CDC::StartDoc**, **CDC::Escape**

CDC::EndPath

BOOL EndPath( );

Return Value

Nonzero if the function is successful; otherwise 0.

Remarks

Closes a path bracket and selects the path defined by the bracket into the device context.

See Also: CDC::BeginPath

CDC::EnumObjects

int EnumObjects(int *nObjectType***, int (CALLBACK EXPORT*** *lpfn* **)**
↳ **(LPVOID, LPARAM), LPARAM** *lpData* **);**

Return Value

Specifies the last value returned by the callback function. Its meaning is user-defined.

Parameters

nObjectType   Specifies the object type. It can have the values **OBJ_BRUSH** or **OBJ_PEN**.

lpfn   Is the procedure-instance address of the application-supplied callback function. See the "Remarks" section below.

lpData   Points to the application-supplied data. The data is passed to the callback function along with the object information.

Remarks

Enumerates the pens and brushes available in a device context. For each object of a given type, the callback function that you pass is called with the information for that object. The system calls the callback function until there are no more objects or the callback function returns 0.

Note that new features of Microsoft Visual C++ let you use an ordinary function as the function passed to **EnumObjects**. The address passed to **EnumObjects** is a pointer to a function exported with **EXPORT** and with the Pascal calling convention. In protect-mode applications, you do not have to create this function with the Windows **MakeProcInstance** function or free the function after use with the **FreeProcInstance** Windows function.

You also do not have to export the function name in an **EXPORTS** statement in your application's module-definition file. You can instead use the **EXPORT** function modifier, as in

int CALLBACK EXPORT AFunction(**LPSTR, LPSTR**);

to cause the compiler to emit the proper export record for export by name without aliasing. This works for most needs. For some special cases, such as exporting a function by ordinal or aliasing the export, you still need to use an **EXPORTS** statement in a module-definition file.

For compiling Microsoft Foundation programs, you will normally use the /GA and /GEs compiler options. The /Gw compiler option is not used with the Microsoft Foundation classes. (If you do use the Windows function **MakeProcInstance**, you will need to explicitly cast the returned function pointer from **FARPROC** to the type needed in this API.) Callback registration interfaces are now type-safe (you must pass in a function pointer that points to the right kind of function for the specific callback).

Also note that all callback functions must trap Microsoft Foundation exceptions before returning to Windows, since exceptions cannot be thrown across callback boundaries. For more information about exceptions, see the article "Exceptions" in *Visual C++ Programmer's Guide* online.

See Also: **::EnumObjects**

CDC::Escape

virtual int Escape(int *nEscape*, **int** *nCount*, **LPCSTR** *lpszInData*,
  ↪ **LPVOID** *lpOutData*);
int ExtEscape(int *nEscape*, **int** *nInputSize*, **LPCSTR** *lpszInputData*,
  ↪ **int** *nOutputSize*, **LPSTR** *lpszOutputData*);

Return Value

Positive if the function is successful, except for the **QUERYESCSUPPORT** escape, which only checks for implementation. Zero is returned if the escape is not implemented, and a negative value is returned if an error occurred. The following are common error values:

- **SP_ERROR**   General error.

- **SP_OUTOFDISK**   Not enough disk space is currently available for spooling, and no more space will become available.

- **SP_OUTOFMEMORY**   Not enough memory is available for spooling.

- **SP_USERABORT**   User ended the job through the Print Manager.

Parameters

nEscape   Specifies the escape function to be performed.

For a complete list of escape functions, see the information on printer escapes in the Windows Software Development Kit documentation.

nCount   Specifies the number of bytes of data pointed to by *lpszInData*.

lpszInData   Points to the input data structure required for this escape.

lpOutData   Points to the structure that is to receive output from this escape. The *lpOutData* parameter is **NULL** if no data is returned.

nInputSize   Specifies the number of bytes of data pointed to by the *lpszInputData* parameter.

lpszInputData   Points to the input structure required for the specified escape.

nOutputSize   Specifies the number of bytes of data pointed to by the *lpszOutputData* parameter.

lpszOutputData   Points to the structure that receives output from this escape. This parameter should be **NULL** if no data is returned.

Remarks

Allows applications to access facilities of a particular device that are not directly available through GDI. Use the first version of **Escape** to pass a driver-defined escape value to a device. Use the second version of **Escape** to pass one of the escape values defined by Windows to a device. Escape calls made by an application are translated and sent to the device driver.

The *nEscape* parameter specifies the escape function to be performed. For possible values, see the information on printer escapes in the Windows SDK documentation.

See Also: **CDC::StartDoc, CDC::StartPage, CDC::EndPage, CDC::SetAbortProc, CDC::AbortDoc, CDC::EndDoc, CDC::GetDeviceCaps, ::ExtEscape, ::Escape**

CDC::ExcludeClipRect

virtual int ExcludeClipRect(int *x1*, **int** *y1*, **int** *x2*, **int** *y2* **);**
virtual int ExcludeClipRect(LPCRECT *lpRect* **);**

Return Value

Specifies the new clipping region's type. It can be any of the following values:

- **COMPLEXREGION**   The region has overlapping borders.
- **ERROR**   No region was created.
- **NULLREGION**   The region is empty.
- **SIMPLEREGION**   The region has no overlapping borders.

Parameters

x1 Specifies the logical x-coordinate of the upper-left corner of the rectangle.

y1 Specifies the logical y-coordinate of the upper-left corner of the rectangle.

x2 Specifies the logical x-coordinate of the lower-right corner of the rectangle.

y2 Specifies the logical y-coordinate of the lower-right corner of the rectangle.

lpRect Specifies the rectangle. Can also be a **CRect** object.

Remarks

Creates a new clipping region that consists of the existing clipping region minus the specified rectangle.

The width of the rectangle, specified by the absolute value of $x2 - x1$, must not exceed 32,767 units. This limit applies to the height of the rectangle as well.

See Also: CDC::ExcludeUpdateRgn, ::ExcludeClipRect

CDC::ExcludeUpdateRgn

int ExcludeUpdateRgn(CWnd* *pWnd* **);**

Return Value

The type of excluded region. It can be any one of the following values:

- **COMPLEXREGION** The region has overlapping borders.
- **ERROR** No region was created.
- **NULLREGION** The region is empty.
- **SIMPLEREGION** The region has no overlapping borders.

Parameters

pWnd Points to the window object whose window is being updated.

Remarks

Prevents drawing within invalid areas of a window by excluding an updated region in the window from the clipping region associated with the **CDC** object.

See Also: CDC::ExcludeClipRect, ::ExcludeUpdateRgn

CDC::ExtFloodFill

BOOL ExtFloodFill(int *x*, **int** *y*, **COLORREF** *crColor*, **UINT** *nFillType* **);**

Return Value

Nonzero if the function is successful; otherwise 0 if the filling could not be completed, if the given point has the boundary color specified by *crColor* (if **FLOODFILLBORDER** was requested), if the given point does not have the color specified by *crColor* (if **FLOODFILLSURFACE** was requested), or if the point is outside the clipping region.

Parameters

x Specifies the logical x-coordinate of the point where filling begins.

y Specifies the logical y-coordinate of the point where filling begins.

crColor Specifies the color of the boundary or of the area to be filled. The interpretation of *crColor* depends on the value of *nFillType*.

nFillType Specifies the type of flood fill to be performed. It must be either of the following values:

- **FLOODFILLBORDER** The fill area is bounded by the color specified by *crColor*. This style is identical to the filling performed by **FloodFill**.

- **FLOODFILLSURFACE** The fill area is defined by the color specified by *crColor*. Filling continues outward in all directions as long as the color is encountered. This style is useful for filling areas with multicolored boundaries.

Remarks

Fills an area of the display surface with the current brush. This member function offers more flexibility than **FloodFill** because you can specify a fill type in *nFillType*.

If *nFillType* is set to **FLOODFILLBORDER**, the area is assumed to be completely bounded by the color specified by *crColor*. The function begins at the point specified by *x* and *y* and fills in all directions to the color boundary.

If *nFillType* is set to **FLOODFILLSURFACE**, the function begins at the point specified by *x* and *y* and continues in all directions, filling all adjacent areas containing the color specified by *crColor*.

Only memory-device contexts and devices that support raster-display technology support **ExtFloodFill**. For more information, see the **GetDeviceCaps** member function.

See Also: **CDC::FloodFill, CDC::GetDeviceCaps, ::ExtFloodFill**

CDC::ExtTextOut

> **virtual BOOL ExtTextOut(int** *x*, **int** *y*, **UINT** *nOptions*, **LPCRECT** *lpRect*,
>   → **LPCTSTR** *lpszString*, **UINT** *nCount*, **LPINT** *lpDxWidths* **);**
> **BOOL ExtTextOut(int** *x*, **int** *y*, **UINT** *nOptions*, **LPCRECT** *lpRect*,
>   → **const CString&** *str*, **LPINT** *lpDxWidths* **);**

Return Value

Nonzero if the function is successful; otherwise 0.

Parameters

x   Specifies the logical x-coordinate of the character cell for the first character in the specified string.

y   Specifies the logical y-coordinate of the top of the character cell for the first character in the specified string.

nOptions   Specifies the rectangle type. This parameter can be one, both, or neither of the following values:

- **ETO_CLIPPED**   Specifies that text is clipped to the rectangle.

- **ETO_OPAQUE**   Specifies that the current background color fills the rectangle. (You can set and query the current background color with the **SetBkColor** and **GetBkColor** member functions.)

lpRect   Points to a **RECT** structure that determines the dimensions of the rectangle. This parameter can be **NULL**. You can also pass a **CRect** object for this parameter.

lpszString   Points to the specified character string to be drawn. You can also pass a **CString** object for this parameter.

nCount   Specifies the number of characters in the string.

lpDxWidths   Points to an array of values that indicate the distance between origins of adjacent character cells. For instance, *lpDxWidths*[*i*] logical units will separate the origins of character cell *i* and character cell *i* + 1. If *lpDxWidths* is **NULL**, **ExtTextOut** uses the default spacing between characters.

str   A **CString** object that contains the specified characters to be drawn.

Remarks

Call this member function to write a character string within a rectangular region using the currently selected font. The rectangular region can be opaque (filled with the current background color), and it can be a clipping region.

If *nOptions* is 0 and *lpRect* is **NULL**, the function writes text to the device context without using a rectangular region. By default, the current position is not used or updated by the function. If an application needs to update the current position when it calls **ExtTextOut**, the application can call the **CDC** member function **SetTextAlign** with *nFlags* set to **TA_UPDATECP**. When this flag is set, Windows ignores *x* and *y* on subsequent calls to **ExtTextOut** and uses the current position instead. When an application uses **TA_UPDATECP** to update the current position, **ExtTextOut** sets the current position either to the end of the previous line of text or to the position specified by the last element of the array pointed to by *lpDxWidths*, whichever is greater.

See Also: **CDC::SetTextAlign, CDC::TabbedTextOut, CDC::TextOut, CDC::GetBkColor, CDC::SetBkColor, CDC::SetTextColor, ::ExtTextOut, RECT**

CDC::FillPath

BOOL FillPath( );

Return Value

Nonzero if the function is successful; otherwise 0.

Remarks

Closes any open figures in the current path and fills the path's interior by using the current brush and polygon-filling mode. After its interior is filled, the path is discarded from the device context.

See Also: **CDC::BeginPath, CDC::SetPolyFillMode, CDC::StrokeAndFillPath, CDC::StrokePath, ::FillPath**

CDC::FillRect

void FillRect(LPCRECT *lpRect*, **CBrush*** *pBrush* **);**

Parameters

lpRect   Points to a **RECT** structure that contains the logical coordinates of the rectangle to be filled. You can also pass a **CRect** object for this parameter.

pBrush   Identifies the brush used to fill the rectangle.

Remarks

Call this member function to fill a given rectangle using the specified brush. The function fills the complete rectangle, including the left and top borders, but it does not fill the right and bottom borders.

The brush needs to either be created using the **CBrush** member functions **CreateHatchBrush, CreatePatternBrush**, and **CreateSolidBrush**, or retrieved by the **::GetStockObject** Windows function.

When filling the specified rectangle, **FillRect** does not include the rectangle's right and bottom sides. GDI fills a rectangle up to, but does not include, the right column and bottom row, regardless of the current mapping mode. **FillRect** compares the values of the **top**, **bottom**, **left**, and **right** members of the specified rectangle. If **bottom** is less than or equal to **top**, or if **right** is less than or equal to **left**, the rectangle is not drawn.

FillRect is similar to **CDC::FillSolidRect**; however, **FillRect** takes a brush and therefore can be used to fill a rectangle with a solid color, a dithered color, hatched brushes, or a pattern. **FillSolidRect** uses only solid colors (indicated by a **COLORREF** parameter). **FillRect** usually is slower than **FillSolidRect**.

See Also: **CBrush::CreateHatchBrush, CBrush::CreatePatternBrush, CBrush::CreateSolidBrush, ::FillRect, ::GetStockObject, RECT, CBrush, CDC::FillSolidRect**

CDC::FillRgn

BOOL FillRgn(CRgn* *pRgn*, **CBrush*** *pBrush* **);**

Return Value

Nonzero if the function is successful; otherwise 0.

Parameters

pRgn   A pointer to the region to be filled. The coordinates for the given region are specified in device units.

pBrush   Identifies the brush to be used to fill the region.

Remarks

Fills the region specified by *pRgn* with the brush specified by *pBrush*.

The brush must either be created using the **CBrush** member functions **CreateHatchBrush**, **CreatePatternBrush**, **CreateSolidBrush**, or be retrieved by **GetStockObject**.

See Also: **CDC::PaintRgn**, **CDC::FillRect**, **CBrush**, **CRgn**, **::FillRgn**

CDC::FillSolidRect

void FillSolidRect(LPCRECT *lpRect*, **COLORREF** *clr* **);**
void FillSolidRect(int *x*, **int** *y*, **int** *cx*, **int** *cy*, **COLORREF** *clr* **);**

Parameters

lpRect   Specifies the bounding rectangle (in logical units). You can pass either a pointer to a **RECT** data structure or a **CRect** object for this parameter.

clr   Specifies the color to to be used to fill the rectangle.

x   Specifies the logical x-coordinate of the upper-left corner of the rectangle.

y   Specifies the logical y-coordinate of the upper-left corner of the destination rectangle.

cx   Specifies the width of the rectangle.

cy   Specifies the height of the rectangle.

Remarks

Call this member function to fill the given rectangle with the specified solid color.

FillSolidRect is very similar to **CDC::FillRect**; however, **FillSolidRect** uses only solid colors (indicated by the **COLORREF** parameter), while **FillRect** takes a brush and therefore can be used to fill a rectangle with a solid color, a dithered color, hatched brushes, or a pattern. **FillSolidRect** usually is faster than **FillRect**.

Note When you call **FillSolidRect**, the background color, which was previously set using **SetBkColor**, is set to the color indicated by *clr*.

See Also: **RECT**, **CRect**, **CDC::FillRect**

CDC::FlattenPath

BOOL FlattenPath( );

Return Value

Nonzero if the function is successful; otherwise 0.

Remarks

Transforms any curves in the path selected into the current device context, and turns each curve into a sequence of lines.

See Also: **CDC::WidenPath**

CDC::FloodFill

BOOL FloodFill(int *x*, int *y*, COLORREF *crColor*);

Return Value

Nonzero if the function is successful; otherwise 0 is returned if the filling could not be completed, the given point has the boundary color specified by *crColor*, or the point is outside the clipping region.

Parameters

x Specifies the logical x-coordinate of the point where filling begins.

y Specifies the logical y-coordinate of the point where filling begins.

crColor Specifies the color of the boundary.

Remarks

Fills an area of the display surface with the current brush. The area is assumed to be bounded as specified by *crColor*. The **FloodFill** function begins at the point specified by *x* and *y* and continues in all directions to the color boundary.

Only memory-device contexts and devices that support raster-display technology support the **FloodFill** member function. For information about **RC_BITBLT** capability, see the **GetDeviceCaps** member function.

The **ExtFloodFill** function provides similar capability but greater flexibility.

See Also: **CDC::ExtFloodFill**, **CDC::GetDeviceCaps**, **::FloodFill**

CDC::FrameRect

void FrameRect(LPCRECT *lpRect*, **CBrush*** *pBrush* **);**

Parameters

lpRect   Points to a **RECT** structure or **CRect** object that contains the logical coordinates of the upper-left and lower-right corners of the rectangle. You can also pass a **CRect** object for this parameter.

pBrush   Identifies the brush to be used for framing the rectangle.

Remarks

Draws a border around the rectangle specified by *lpRect*. The function uses the given brush to draw the border. The width and height of the border is always 1 logical unit.

If the rectangle's **bottom** coordinate is less than or equal to **top**, or if **right** is less than or equal to **left**, the rectangle is not drawn.

The border drawn by **FrameRect** is in the same position as a border drawn by the **Rectangle** member function using the same coordinates (if **Rectangle** uses a pen that is 1 logical unit wide). The interior of the rectangle is not filled by **FrameRect**.

See Also: CBrush, ::FrameRect, CDC::Rectangle, CDC::FrameRgn, RECT

CDC::FrameRgn

BOOL FrameRgn(CRgn* *pRgn*, **CBrush*** *pBrush*, **int** *nWidth*, **int** *nHeight* **);**

Return Value

Nonzero if the function is successful; otherwise 0.

Parameters

pRgn   Points to the **CRgn** object that identifies the region to be enclosed in a border. The coordinates for the given region are specified in device units.

pBrush   Points to the **CBrush** object that identifies the brush to be used to draw the border.

nWidth   Specifies the width of the border in vertical brush strokes in device units.

nHeight   Specifies the height of the border in horizontal brush strokes in device units.

Remarks

Draws a border around the region specified by *pRgn* using the brush specified by *pBrush*.

See Also: CDC::Rectangle, CDC::FrameRect, CBrush, CRgn, ::FrameRgn

CDC::FromHandle

static CDC* PASCAL FromHandle(HDC *hDC* **);**

Return Value

The pointer may be temporary and should not be stored beyond immediate use.

Parameters

hDC   Contains a handle to a Windows device context.

Remarks

Returns a pointer to a **CDC** object when given a handle to a device context. If a **CDC** object is not attached to the handle, a temporary **CDC** object is created and attached.

See Also: CDC::DeleteTempMap

CDC::GetArcDirection

int GetArcDirection( ) const;

Return Value

Specifies the current arc direction, if successful. Following are the valid return values:

- **AD_COUNTERCLOCKWISE**   Arcs and rectangles drawn counterclockwise.
- **AD_CLOCKWISE**   Arcs and rectangles drawn clockwise.

If an error occurs, the return value is zero.

Remarks

Returns the current arc direction for the device context. Arc and rectangle functions use the arc direction.

See Also: CDC::SetArcDirection, ::GetArcDirection

CDC::GetAspectRatioFilter

CSize GetAspectRatioFilter( ) const;

Return Value

A **CSize** object representing the aspect ratio used by the current aspect ratio filter.

Remarks

Retrieves the setting for the current aspect-ratio filter. The aspect ratio is the ratio formed by a device's pixel width and height. Information about a device's aspect ratio is used in the creation, selection, and display of fonts. Windows provides a special filter, the aspect-ratio filter, to select fonts designed for a particular aspect ratio from all of the available fonts. The filter uses the aspect ratio specified by the **SetMapperFlags** member function.

See Also: **CDC::SetMapperFlags, CSize**

CDC::GetBkColor

COLORREF GetBkColor( ) const;

Return Value

An RGB color value.

Remarks

Returns the current background color. If the background mode is **OPAQUE**, the system uses the background color to fill the gaps in styled lines, the gaps between hatched lines in brushes, and the background in character cells. The system also uses the background color when converting bitmaps between color and monochrome device contexts.

See Also: **CDC::GetBkMode, CDC::SetBkColor, CDC::SetBkMode, ::GetBkColor**

CDC::GetBkMode

int GetBkMode( ) const;

Return Value

The current background mode, which can be **OPAQUE**, **TRANSPARENT**, or **TRANSPARENT1**.

Remarks

Returns the background mode. The background mode defines whether the system removes existing background colors on the drawing surface before drawing text, hatched brushes, or any pen style that is not a solid line.

See Also: **CDC::GetBkColor, CDC::SetBkColor, CDC::SetBkMode, ::GetBkMode**

CDC::GetBoundsRect

UINT GetBoundsRect(LPRECT *lpRectBounds***, UINT** *flags* **);**

Return Value

Specifies the current state of the bounding rectangle if the function is successful. It can be a combination of the following values:

- **DCB_ACCUMULATE**   Bounding rectangle accumulation is occurring.
- **DCB_RESET**   Bounding rectangle is empty.

- **DCB_SET**   Bounding rectangle is not empty.
- **DCB_ENABLE**   Bounding accumulation is on.
- **DCB_DISABLE**   Bounding accumulation is off.

Parameters

lpRectBounds   Points to a buffer that will receive the current bounding rectangle. The rectangle is returned in logical coordinates.

flags   Specifies whether the bounding rectangle is to be cleared after it is returned. This parameter can be either of the following values:

- **DCB_RESET**   Forces the bounding rectangle to be cleared after it is returned.
- **DCB_WINDOWMGR**   Queries the Windows bounding rectangle instead of the application's.

Remarks

Returns the current accumulated bounding rectangle for the specified device context.

See Also: **CDC::SetBoundsRect**, **::GetBoundsRect**

CDC::GetBrushOrg

CPoint GetBrushOrg( ) const;

Return Value

The current origin of the brush (in device units) as a **CPoint** object.

Remarks

Retrieves the origin (in device units) of the brush currently selected for the device context.

The initial brush origin is at (0,0) of the client area. The return value specifies this point in device units relative to the origin of the desktop window.

See Also: **CDC::SetBrushOrg**, **CPoint**

CDC::GetCharABCWidths

BOOL GetCharABCWidths(UINT *nFirstChar***, UINT** *nLastChar***,**
  ↳ **LPABC** *lpabc* **) const;**
BOOL GetCharABCWidths(UINT *nFirstChar***, UINT** *nLastChar***,**
  ↳ **LPABCFLOAT** *lpABCF* **) const;**

Return Value

Nonzero if the function is successful; otherwise 0.

Parameters

nFirstChar Specifies the first character in the range of characters from the current font for which character widths are returned.

nLastChar Specifies the last character in the range of characters from the current font for which character widths are returned.

lpabc Points to an array of **ABC** structures that receive the character widths when the function returns. This array must contain at least as many **ABC** structures as there are characters in the range specified by the *nFirstChar* and *nLastChar* parameters.

lpABCF Points to an application-supplied buffer with an array of **ABCFLOAT** structures to receive the character widths when the function returns. The widths returned by this function are in the IEEE floating-point format.

Remarks

Retrieves the widths of consecutive characters in a specified range from the current TrueType font. The widths are returned in logical units. This function succeeds only with TrueType fonts.

The TrueType rasterizer provides "ABC" character spacing after a specific point size has been selected. "A" spacing is the distance that is added to the current position before placing the glyph. "B" spacing is the width of the black part of the glyph. "C" spacing is added to the current position to account for the white space to the right of the glyph. The total advanced width is given by A + B + C.

When the **GetCharABCWidths** member function retrieves negative "A" or "C" widths for a character, that character includes underhangs or overhangs.

To convert the ABC widths to font design units, an application should create a font whose height (as specified in the **lfHeight** member of the **LOGFONT** structure) is equal to the value stored in the **ntmSizeEM** member of the **NEWTEXTMETRIC** structure. (The value of the **ntmSizeEM** member can be retrieved by calling the **EnumFontFamilies** Windows function.)

The ABC widths of the default character are used for characters that are outside the range of the currently selected font.

To retrieve the widths of characters in non-TrueType fonts, applications should use the **GetCharWidth** member function.

See Also: ::**EnumFontFamilies**, **CDC::GetCharWidth**, ::**GetCharABCWidths**, ::**GetCharABCWidthsFloat**, ::**GetCharWidthFloat**

CDC::GetCharWidth

BOOL GetCharWidth(UINT *nFirstChar*, **UINT** *nLastChar*, **LPINT** *lpBuffer*) **const;**
BOOL GetCharWidth(UINT *nFirstChar*, **UINT** *nLastChar*, **float*** *lpFloatBuffer*) **const;**

Return Value

Nonzero if the function is successful; otherwise 0.

Parameters

nFirstChar   Specifies the first character in a consecutive group of characters in the current font.

nLastChar   Specifies the last character in a consecutive group of characters in the current font.

lpBuffer   Points to a buffer that will receive the width values for a consecutive group of characters in the current font.

lpFloatBuffer   Points to a buffer to receive the character widths. The returned widths are in the 32-bit IEEE floating-point format. (The widths are measured along the base line of the characters.)

Remarks

Retrieves the widths of individual characters in a consecutive group of characters from the current font, using **m_hAttribDC**, the input device context. For example, if *nFirstChar* identifies the letter 'a' and *nLastChar* identifies the letter 'z', the function retrieves the widths of all lowercase characters.

The function stores the values in the buffer pointed to by *lpBuffer*. This buffer must be large enough to hold all of the widths. That is, there must be at least 26 entries in the example given.

If a character in the consecutive group of characters does not exist in a particular font, it will be assigned the width value of the default character.

See Also: **CDC::GetOutputCharWidth, CDC::m_hAttribDC, CDC::m_hDC, CDC::GetCharABCWidths, ::GetCharWidth, ::GetCharABCWidths, ::GetCharABCWidthsFloat, ::GetCharWidthFloat**

CDC::GetClipBox

virtual int GetClipBox(LPRECT *lpRect* **) const;**

Return Value

The clipping region's type. It can be any of the following values:

- **COMPLEXREGION**   Clipping region has overlapping borders.
- **ERROR**   Device context is not valid.
- **NULLREGION**   Clipping region is empty.
- **SIMPLEREGION**   Clipping region has no overlapping borders.

Parameters

lpRect   Points to the **RECT** structure or **CRect** object that is to receive the rectangle dimensions.

Remarks

Retrieves the dimensions of the tightest bounding rectangle around the current clipping boundary. The dimensions are copied to the buffer pointed to by *lpRect*.

See Also: **CDC::SelectClipRgn**, **::GetClipBox**, **RECT**

CDC::GetColorAdjustment

BOOL GetColorAdjustment(LPCOLORADJUSTMENT *lpColorAdjust* **) const;**

Return Value

Nonzero if the function is successful; otherwise 0.

Parameters

lpColorAdjust   Points to a **COLORADJUSTMENT** data structure to receive the color adjustment values.

Remarks

Retrieves the color adjustment values for the device context.

See Also: **CDC::SetColorAdjustment**

CDC::GetCurrentBitmap

CBitmap* GetCurrentBitmap( ) const;

Return Value

Pointer to a **CBitmap** object, if successful; otherwise **NULL**.

Remarks

Returns a pointer to the currently selected **CBitmap** object. This member function may return temporary objects.

See Also: **CDC::SelectObject**, **::GetCurrentObject**

CDC::GetCurrentBrush

CBrush* GetCurrentBrush( ) const;

Return Value

Pointer to a **CBrush** object, if successful; otherwise **NULL**.

Remarks

Returns a pointer to the currently selected **CBrush** object. This member function may return temporary objects.

See Also: **CDC::SelectObject**, **::GetCurrentObject**

CDC::GetCurrentFont

CFont* GetCurrentFont( ) const;

Return Value

Pointer to a **CFont** object, if successful; otherwise **NULL**.

Remarks

Returns a pointer to the currently selected **CFont** object. This member function may return temporary objects.

See Also: **CDC::SelectObject**, **::GetCurrentObject**

CDC::GetCurrentPalette

CPalette* GetCurrentPalette( ) const;

Return Value

Pointer to a **CPalette** object, if successful; otherwise **NULL**.

Remarks

Returns a pointer to the currently selected **CPalette** object. This member function may return temporary objects.

See Also: **CDC::SelectObject**, **::GetCurrentObject**

CDC::GetCurrentPen

CPen* GetCurrentPen( ) const;

Return Value

Pointer to a **CPen** object, if successful; otherwise **NULL**.

Remarks

Returns a pointer to the currently selected **CPen** object. This member function may return temporary objects.

See Also: **CDC::SelectObject**, **::GetCurrentObject**

CDC::GetCurrentPosition

CPoint GetCurrentPosition( ) const;

Return Value

The current position as a **CPoint** object.

Remarks

Retrieves the current position (in logical coordinates). The current position can be set with the **MoveTo** member function.

See Also: **CDC::MoveTo, CPoint**

CDC::GetDeviceCaps

int GetDeviceCaps(int *nIndex* **) const;**

Return Value

The value of the requested capability if the function is successful.

Parameters

nIndex Specifies the type of information to return. It can be any one of the following values:

- **DRIVERVERSION** Version number; for example, 0x100 for 1.0.
- **TECHNOLOGY** Device technology. It can be any one of the following:

Value	Meaning
DT_PLOTTER	Vector plotter
DT_RASDISPLAY	Raster display
DT_RASPRINTER	Raster printer
DT_RASCAMERA	Raster camera
DT_CHARSTREAM	Character stream
DT_METAFILE	Metafile
DT_DISPFILE	Display file

- **HORZSIZE** Width of the physical display (in millimeters).
- **VERTSIZE** Height of the physical display (in millimeters).
- **HORZRES** Width of the display (in pixels).
- **VERTRES** Height of the display (in raster lines).
- **LOGPIXELSX** Number of pixels per logical inch along the display width.
- **LOGPIXELSY** Number of pixels per logical inch along the display height.
- **BITSPIXEL** Number of adjacent color bits for each pixel.
- **PLANES** Number of color planes.
- **NUMBRUSHES** Number of device-specific brushes.
- **NUMPENS** Number of device-specific pens.
- **NUMFONTS** Number of device-specific fonts.
- **NUMCOLORS** Number of entries in the device's color table.
- **ASPECTX** Relative width of a device pixel as used for line drawing.
- **ASPECTY** Relative height of a device pixel as used for line drawing.

- **ASPECTXY**   Diagonal width of the device pixel as used for line drawing.
- **PDEVICESIZE**   Size of the **PDEVICE** internal data structure.
- **CLIPCAPS**   Clipping capabilities of the device. It can be one of the following:

Value	Meaning
CP_NONE	Output is not clipped.
CP_RECTANGLE	Output is clipped to rectangles.
CP_REGION	Output is clipped to regions.

- **SIZEPALETTE**   Number of entries in the system palette. This index is valid only if the device driver sets the **RC_PALETTE** bit in the **RASTERCAPS** index.
- **NUMRESERVED**   Number of reserved entries in the system palette. This index is valid only if the device driver sets the **RC_PALETTE** bit in the **RASTERCAPS** index.
- **COLORRES**   Actual color resolution of the device in bits per pixel. This index is valid only if the device driver sets the **RC_PALETTE** bit in the **RASTERCAPS** index.
- **RASTERCAPS**   Value that indicates the raster capabilities of the device. It can be a combination of the following:

Value	Meaning
RC_BANDING	Requires banding support.
RC_BIGFONT	Supports fonts larger than 64K.
RC_BITBLT	Capable of transferring bitmaps.
RC_BITMAP64	Supports bitmaps larger than 64K.
RC_DEVBITS	Supports device bitmaps.
RC_DI_BITMAP	Capable of supporting the **SetDIBits** and **GetDIBits** Windows functions.
RC_DIBTODEV	Capable of supporting the **SetDIBitsToDevice** Windows function.
RC_FLOODFILL	Capable of performing flood fills.
RC_GDI20_OUTPUT	Capable of supporting Windows version 2.0 features.
RC_GDI20_STATE	Includes a state block in the device context.
RC_NONE	Supports no raster operations.
RC_OP_DX_OUTPUT	Supports dev opaque and DX array.
RC_PALETTE	Specifies a palette-based device.
RC_SAVEBITMAP	Capable of saving bitmaps locally.
RC_SCALING	Capable of scaling.
RC_STRETCHBLT	Capable of performing the **StretchBlt** member function.
RC_STRETCHDIB	Capable of performing the **StretchDIBits** Windows function.

- **CURVECAPS** The curve capabilities of the device. It can be a combination of the following:

Value	Meaning
CC_NONE	Supports curves.
CC_CIRCLES	Supports circles.
CC_PIE	Supports pie wedges.
CC_CHORD	Supports chords.
CC_ELLIPSES	Supports ellipses.
CC_WIDE	Supports wide borders.
CC_STYLED	Supports styled borders.
CC_WIDESTYLED	Supports wide, styled borders.
CC_INTERIORS	Supports interiors.
CC_ROUNDRECT	Supports rectangles with rounded corners.

- **LINECAPS** Line capabilities the device supports. It can be a combination of the following:

Value	Meaning
LC_NONE	Supports no lines.
LC_POLYLINE	Supports polylines.
LC_MARKER	Supports markers.
LC_POLYMARKER	Supports polymarkers.
LC_WIDE	Supports wide lines.
LC_STYLED	Supports styled lines.
LC_WIDESTYLED	Supports wide, styled lines.
LC_INTERIORS	Supports interiors.

- **POLYGONALCAPS** Polygonal capabilities the device supports. It can be a combination of the following:

Value	Meaning
PC_NONE	Supports no polygons.
PC_POLYGON	Supports alternate fill polygons.
PC_RECTANGLE	Supports rectangles.
PC_WINDPOLYGON	Supports winding number fill polygons.
PC_SCANLINE	Supports scan lines.
PC_WIDE	Supports wide borders.
PC_STYLED	Supports styled borders.
PC_WIDESTYLED	Supports wide, styled borders.
PC_INTERIORS	Supports interiors.

- **TEXTCAPS** Text capabilities the device supports. It can be a combination of the following:

Value	Meaning
TC_OP_CHARACTER	Supports character output precision, which indicates the device can place device fonts at any pixel location. This is required for any device with device fonts.
TC_OP_STROKE	Supports stroke output precision, which indicates the device can omit any stroke of a device font.
TC_CP_STROKE	Supports stroke clip precision, which indicates the device can clip device fonts to a pixel boundary.
TC_CR_90	Supports 90-degree character rotation, which indicates the device can rotate characters only 90 degrees at a time.
TC_CR_ANY	Supports character rotation at any degree, which indicates the device can rotate device fonts through any angle.
TC_SF_X_YINDEP	Supports scaling independent of x and y directions, which indicates the device can scale device fonts separately in x and y directions.
TC_SA_DOUBLE	Supports doubled characters for scaling, which indicates the device can double the size of device fonts.
TC_SA_INTEGER	Supports integer multiples for scaling, which indicates the device can scale the size of device fonts in any integer multiple.
TC_SA_CONTIN	Supports any multiples for exact scaling, which indicates the device can scale device fonts by any amount but still preserve the x and y ratios.
TC_EA_DOUBLE	Supports double-weight characters, which indicates the device can make device fonts bold. If this bit is not set for printer drivers, GDI attempts to create bold device fonts by printing them twice.
TC_IA_ABLE	Supports italics, which indicates the device can make device fonts italic. If this bit is not set, GDI assumes italics are not available.
TC_UA_ABLE	Supports underlining, which indicates the device can underline device fonts. If this bit is not set, GDI creates underlines for device fonts.
TC_SO_ABLE	Supports strikeouts, which indicates the device can strikeout device fonts. If this bit is not set, GDI creates strikeouts for device fonts.
TC_RA_ABLE	Supports raster fonts, which indicates that GDI should enumerate any raster or TrueType fonts available for this device in response to a call to the **EnumFonts** or **EnumFontFamilies** Windows functions. If this bit is not set, GDI-supplied raster or TrueType fonts are not enumerated when these functions are called.

(continued)

(continued)

Value	Meaning
TC_VA_ABLE	Supports vector fonts, which indicates that GDI should enumerate any vector fonts available for this device in response to a call to the **EnumFonts** or **EnumFontFamilies** Windows functions. This is significant for vector devices only (that is, for plotters). Display drivers (which must be able to use raster fonts) and raster printer drivers always enumerate vector fonts, because GDI rasterizes vector fonts before sending them to the driver.
TC_RESERVED	Reserved; must be 0.

Remarks

Retrieves a wide range of device-specific information about the display device.

See Also: ::GetDeviceCaps

CDC::GetFontData

DWORD GetFontData(DWORD *dwTable*, **DWORD** *dwOffset*, **LPVOID** *lpData*, ➥ **DWORD** *cbData*) **const;**

Return Value

Specifies the number of bytes returned in the buffer pointed to by *lpData* if the function is successful; otherwise –1.

Parameters

dwTable   Specifies the name of the metric table to be returned. This parameter can be one of the metric tables documented in the TrueType Font Files specification published by Microsoft Corporation. If this parameter is 0, the information is retrieved starting at the beginning of the font file.

dwOffset   Specifies the offset from the beginning of the table at which to begin retrieving information. If this parameter is 0, the information is retrieved starting at the beginning of the table specified by the *dwTable* parameter. If this value is greater than or equal to the size of the table, **GetFontData** returns 0.

lpData   Points to a buffer that will receive the font information. If this value is **NULL**, the function returns the size of the buffer required for the font data specified in the *dwTable* parameter.

cbData   Specifies the length, in bytes, of the information to be retrieved. If this parameter is 0, **GetFontData** returns the size of the data specified in the *dwTable* parameter.

Remarks

Retrieves font-metric information from a scalable font file. The information to retrieve is identified by specifying an offset into the font file and the length of the information to return.

An application can sometimes use the **GetFontData** member function to save a TrueType font with a document. To do this, the application determines whether the font can be embedded and then retrieves the entire font file, specifying 0 for the *dwTable*, *dwOffset*, and *cbData* parameters.

Applications can determine whether a font can be embedded by checking the **otmfsType** member of the **OUTLINETEXTMETRIC** structure. If bit 1 of **otmfsType** is set, embedding is not permitted for the font. If bit 1 is clear, the font can be embedded. If bit 2 is set, the embedding is read only.

If an application attempts to use this function to retrieve information for a non-TrueType font, the **GetFontData** member function returns –1.

See Also: **CDC::GetOutlineTextMetrics**, **::GetFontData**, **OUTLINETEXTMETRIC**

CDC::GetGlyphOutline

> **DWORD GetGlyphOutline(UINT** *nChar*, **UINT** *nFormat*, **LPGLYPHMETRICS** *lpgm*,
> ↪ **DWORD** *cbBuffer*, **LPVOID** *lpBuffer*, **const MAT2 FAR*** *lpmat2* **) const;**

Return Value

The size, in bytes, of the buffer required for the retrieved information if *cbBuffer* is 0 or *lpBuffer* is **NULL**. Otherwise, it is a positive value if the function is successful, or –1 if there is an error.

Parameters

nChar Specifies the character for which information is to be returned.

nFormat Specifies the format in which the function is to return information. It can be one of the following values, or 0:

Value	Meaning
GGO_BITMAP	Returns the glyph bitmap. When the function returns, the buffer pointed to by *lpBuffer* contains a 1-bit-per-pixel bitmap whose rows start on doubleword boundaries.
GGO_NATIVE	Returns the curve data points in the rasterizer's native format, using device units. When this value is specified, any transformation specified in *lpmat2* is ignored.

When the value of *nFormat* is 0, the function fills in a **GLYPHMETRICS** structure but does not return glyph-outline data.

lpgm   Points to a **GLYPHMETRICS** structure that describes the placement of the glyph in the character cell.

cbBuffer   Specifies the size of the buffer into which the function copies information about the outline character. If this value is 0 and the *nFormat* parameter is either the **GGO_BITMAP** or **GGO_NATIVE** values, the function returns the required size of the buffer.

lpBuffer   Points to a buffer into which the function copies information about the outline character. If *nFormat* specifies the **GGO_NATIVE** value, the information is copied in the form of **TTPOLYGONHEADER** and **TTPOLYCURVE** structures. If this value is **NULL** and *nFormat* is either the **GGO_BITMAP** or **GGO_NATIVE** value, the function returns the required size of the buffer.

lpmat2   Points to a **MAT2** structure that contains a transformation matrix for the character. This parameter cannot be **NULL**, even when the **GGO_NATIVE** value is specified for *nFormat*.

Remarks

Retrieves the outline curve or bitmap for an outline character in the current font.

An application can rotate characters retrieved in bitmap format by specifying a 2-by-2 transformation matrix in the structure pointed to by *lpmat2*.

A glyph outline is returned as a series of contours. Each contour is defined by a **TTPOLYGONHEADER** structure followed by as many **TTPOLYCURVE** structures as are required to describe it. All points are returned as **POINTFX** structures and represent absolute positions, not relative moves. The starting point given by the **pfxStart** member of the **TTPOLYGONHEADER** structure is the point at which the outline for a contour begins. The **TTPOLYCURVE** structures that follow can be either polyline records or spline records. Polyline records are a series of points; lines drawn between the points describe the outline of the character. Spline records represent the quadratic curves used by TrueType (that is, quadratic b-splines).

See Also: CDC::GetOutlineTextMetrics, ::GetGlyphOutline, GLYPHMETRICS, TTPOLYGONHEADER, TTPOLYCURVE

CDC::GetHalftoneBrush

static CBrush* PASCAL GetHalftoneBrush( );

Return Value

A pointer to a **CBrush** object if successful; otherwise **NULL**.

Remarks

Call this member function to retrieve a halftone brush. A halftone brush shows pixels that are alternately foreground and background colors to create a dithered pattern. The following is an example of a dithered pattern created by a halftone brush.

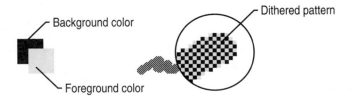

Background color

Dithered pattern

Foreground color

See Also: CBrush

CDC::GetKerningPairs

int GetKerningPairs(int *nPairs*, **LPKERNINGPAIR** *lpkrnpair*) **const;**

Return Value

Specifies the number of kerning pairs retrieved or the total number of kerning pairs in the font, if the function is successful. Zero is returned if the function fails or there are no kerning pairs for the font.

Parameters

nPairs   Specifies the number of **KERNINGPAIR** structures pointed to by *lpkrnpair*. The function will not copy more kerning pairs than specified by *nPairs*.

lpkrnpair   Points to an array of **KERNINGPAIR** structures that receive the kerning pairs when the function returns. This array must contain at least as many structures as specified by *nPairs*. If this parameter is **NULL**, the function returns the total number of kerning pairs for the font.

Remarks

Retrieves the character kerning pairs for the font that is currently selected in the specified device context.

See Also: ::GetKerningPairs, KERNINGPAIR

CDC::GetMapMode

int GetMapMode( ) const;

Return Value

The mapping mode.

Remarks

Retrieves the current mapping mode.

See the **SetMapMode** member function for a description of the mapping modes.

See Also: CDC::SetMapMode, ::GetMapMode

CDC::GetMiterLimit

float GetMiterLimit( ) const;

Return Value

Nonzero if the function is successful; otherwise 0.

Remarks

Returns the miter limit for the device context. The miter limit is used when drawing geometric lines that have miter joins.

See Also: **CDC::SetMiterLimit, ::GetMiterLimit**

CDC::GetNearestColor

COLORREF GetNearestColor(COLORREF *crColor* **) const;**

Return Value

An RGB (red, green, blue) color value that defines the solid color closest to the *crColor* value that the device can represent.

Parameters

crColor   Specifies the color to be matched.

Remarks

Returns the solid color that best matches a specified logical color. The given device must be able to represent this color.

See Also: **::GetNearestColor, CPalette::GetNearestPaletteIndex**

CDC::GetOutlineTextMetrics

UINT CDC::GetOutlineTextMetrics(UINT *cbData*,
↪ **LPOUTLINETEXTMETRIC** *lpotm* **) const;**

Return Value

Nonzero if the function is successful; otherwise 0.

Parameters

lpotm   Points to an array of **OUTLINETEXTMETRIC** structures. If this parameter is **NULL**, the function returns the size of the buffer required for the retrieved metric data.

cbData   Specifies the size, in bytes, of the buffer to which information is returned.

lpotm   Points to an **OUTLINETEXTMETRIC** structure. If this parameter is **NULL**, the function returns the size of the buffer required for the retrieved metric information.

Remarks

Retrieves metric information for TrueType fonts.

The **OUTLINETEXTMETRIC** structure contains most of the font metric information provided with the TrueType format, including a **TEXTMETRIC** structure. The last four members of the **OUTLINETEXTMETRIC** structure are pointers to strings. Applications should allocate space for these strings in addition to the space required for the other members. Because there is no system-imposed limit to the size of the strings, the simplest method for allocating memory is to retrieve the required size by specifying **NULL** for *lpotm* in the first call to the **GetOutlineTextMetrics** function.

See Also: **::GetTextMetrics**, **::GetOutlineTextMetrics**, **CDC::GetTextMetrics**

CDC::GetOutputCharWidth

BOOL GetOutputCharWidth(UINT *nFirstChar*, **UINT** *nLastChar*,
↪ **LPINT** *lpBuffer* **) const;**

Return Value

Nonzero if the function is successful; otherwise 0.

Parameters

nFirstChar   Specifies the first character in a consecutive group of characters in the current font.

nLastChar   Specifies the last character in a consecutive group of characters in the current font.

lpBuffer   Points to a buffer that will receive the width values for a consecutive group of characters in the current font.

Remarks

Uses the output device context, **m_hDC**, and retrieves the widths of individual characters in a consecutive group of characters from the current font. For example, if *nFirstChar* identifies the letter 'a' and *nLastChar* identifies the letter 'z', the function retrieves the widths of all lowercase characters.

The function stores the values in the buffer pointed to by *lpBuffer*. This buffer must be large enough to hold all of the widths; that is, there must be at least 26 entries in the example given.

If a character in the consecutive group of characters does not exist in a particular font, it will be assigned the width value of the default character.

See Also: **CDC::GetCharWidth**, **CDC::m_hAttribDC**, **CDC::m_hDC**, **::GetCharWidth**

CDC::GetOutputTabbedTextExtent

CSize GetOutputTabbedTextExtent(LPCTSTR *lpszString*, **int** *nCount*,
↪ **int** *nTabPositions*, **LPINT***lpnTabStopPositions* **) const;**
CSize GetOutputTabbedTextExtent(const CString& *str*, **int** *nTabPositions*,
↪ **LPINT** *lpnTabStopPositions* **) const;**

Return Value

The dimensions of the string (in logical units) in a **CSize** object.

Parameters

lpszString   Points to a character string to be measured. You can also pass a **CString**
object for this parameter.

nCount   Specifies the number of characters in the string. If *nCount* is –1, the length is
calculated.

nTabPositions   Specifies the number of tab-stop positions in the array pointed to by
lpnTabStopPositions.

lpnTabStopPositions   Points to an array of integers containing the tab-stop positions
in logical units. The tab stops must be sorted in increasing order; the smallest
x-value should be the first item in the array. Back tabs are not allowed.

str   A **CString** object that contains the specified characters to be measured.

Remarks

Call this member function to compute the width and height of a character string using
m_hDC, the output device context. If the string contains one or more tab characters,
the width of the string is based upon the tab stops specified by *lpnTabStopPositions*.
The function uses the currently selected font to compute the dimensions of the string.

The current clipping region does not offset the width and height returned by the
GetOutputTabbedTextExtent function.

Since some devices do not place characters in regular cell arrays (that is, they kern the
characters), the sum of the extents of the characters in a string may not be equal to the
extent of the string.

If *nTabPositions* is 0 and *lpnTabStopPositions* is **NULL**, tabs are expanded to eight
average character widths. If *nTabPositions* is 1, the tab stops will be separated by the
distance specified by the first value in the array to which *lpnTabStopPositions* points.
If *lpnTabStopPositions* points to more than a single value, a tab stop is set for each
value in the array, up to the number specified by *nTabPositions*.

See Also: **CDC::GetTextExtent, CDC::m_hAttribDC, CDC::m_hDC,
CDC::GetTabbedTextExtent, CDC::GetOutputTextExtent,
CDC::TabbedTextOut, ::GetTabbedTextExtent, Csize**

CDC::GetOutputTextExtent

CSize GetOutputTextExtent(LPCTSTR *lpszString***, int** *nCount* **) const;**
CSize GetOutputTextExtent(const CString& *str* **) const;**

Return Value

The dimensions of the string (in logical units) returned in a **CSize** object.

Parameters

lpszString   Points to a string of characters. You can also pass a **CString** object for this parameter.

nCount   Specifies the number of characters in the string. If *nCount* is –1, the length is calculated.

str   A **CString** object that contains the specified characters to be measured.

Remarks

Call this member function to use the output device context, **m_hDC**, and compute the width and height of a line of text, using the current font.

The current clipping region does not affect the width and height returned by **GetOutputTextExtent**.

Since some devices do not place characters in regular cell arrays (that is, they carry out kerning), the sum of the extents of the characters in a string may not be equal to the extent of the string.

See Also: CDC::GetTabbedTextExtent, CDC::GetOutputTabbedTextExtent, CDC::m_hAttribDC, CDC::m_hDC, CDC::GetTextExtent, CDC::SetTextJustification, CSize

---

CDC::GetOutputTextMetrics

BOOL GetOutputTextMetrics(LPTEXTMETRIC *lpMetrics* **) const;**

Return Value

Nonzero if the function is successful; otherwise 0.

Parameters

lpMetrics   Points to the **TEXTMETRIC** structure that receives the metrics.

Remarks

Retrieves the metrics for the current font using **m_hDC**, the output device context.

See Also: CDC::GetTextAlign, CDC::m_hAttribDC, CDC::m_hDC, CDC::GetTextMetrics, CDC::GetTextExtent, CDC::GetTextFace, CDC::SetTextJustification, ::GetTextMetrics

CDC::GetPath

int GetPath(LPPOINT *lpPoints***, LPBYTE** *lpTypes***, int** *nCount* **) const;**

Return Value

If the *nCount* parameter is nonzero, the number of points enumerated. If *nCount* is 0, the total number of points in the path (and **GetPath** writes nothing to the buffers). If *nCount* is nonzero and is less than the number of points in the path, the return value is −1.

Parameters

lpPoints   Points to an array of **POINT** data structures or **CPoint** objects where the line endpoints and curve control points are placed.

lpTypes   Points to an array of bytes where the vertex types are placed. Values are one of the following:

- **PT_MOVETO**   Specifies that the corresponding point in *lpPoints* starts a disjoint figure.

- **PT_LINETO**   Specifies that the previous point and the corresponding point in *lpPoints* are the endpoints of a line.

- **PT_BEZIERTO**   Specifies that the corresponding point in *lpPoints* is a control point or ending point for a Bézier curve.

PT_BEZIERTO types always occur in sets of three. The point in the path immediately preceding them defines the starting point for the Bézier curve. The first two **PT_BEZIERTO** points are the control points, and the third **PT_BEZIERTO** point is the end point (if hard-coded).

A **PT_LINETO** or **PT_BEZIERTO** type may be combined with the following flag (by using the bitwise operator **OR**) to indicate that the corresponding point is the last point in a figure and that the figure should be closed:

- **PT_CLOSEFIGURE**   Specifies that the figure is automatically closed after the corresponding line or curve is drawn. The figure is closed by drawing a line from the line or curve endpoint to the point corresponding to the last **PT_MOVETO**.

nCount   Specifies the total number of **POINT** data structures that may be placed in the *lpPoints* array. This value must be the same as the number of bytes that may be placed in the *lpTypes* array.

Remarks

Retrieves the coordinates defining the endpoints of lines and the control points of curves found in the path that is selected into the device context. The device context must contain a closed path. The points of the path are returned in logical coordinates. Points are stored in the path in device coordinates, so **GetPath** changes the points from device coordinates to logical coordinates by using the inverse of the current transformation. The **FlattenPath** member function may be called before **GetPath**, to convert all curves in the path into line segments.

See Also: **CDC::FlattenPath, CDC::PolyDraw, CDC::WidenPath**

CDC::GetPixel

COLORREF GetPixel(int *x*, int *y*) const;
COLORREF GetPixel(POINT *point*) const;

Return Value

For either version of the function, an RGB color value for the color of the given point. It is −1 if the coordinates do not specify a point in the clipping region.

Parameters

x   Specifies the logical x-coordinate of the point to be examined.

y   Specifies the logical y-coordinate of the point to be examined.

point   Specifies the logical x- and y-coordinates of the point to be examined.

Remarks

Retrieves the RGB color value of the pixel at the point specified by *x* and *y*. The point must be in the clipping region. If the point is not in the clipping region, the function has no effect and returns −1.

Not all devices support the **GetPixel** function. For more information, see the **RC_BITBLT** raster capability under the **GetDeviceCaps** member function.

The **GetPixel** member function has two forms. The first takes two coordinate values; the second takes either a **POINT** structure or a **CPoint** object.

See Also: **CDC::GetDeviceCaps, CDC::SetPixel, ::GetPixel, POINT, CPoint**

CDC::GetPolyFillMode

int GetPolyFillMode( ) const;

Return Value

The current polygon-filled mode, **ALTERNATE** or **WINDING**, if the function is successful.

Remarks

Retrieves the current polygon-filling mode.

See the **SetPolyFillMode** member function for a description of the polygon-filling modes.

See Also: **CDC::SetPolyFillMode, ::GetPolyFillMode**

CDC::GetROP2

int GetROP2( ) const;

Return Value

The drawing mode. For a list of the drawing mode values, see the **SetROP2** member function.

Remarks

Retrieves the current drawing mode. The drawing mode specifies how the colors of the pen and the interior of filled objects are combined with the color already on the display surface.

See Also: **CDC::GetDeviceCaps, CDC::SetROP2, ::GetROP2**

CDC::GetSafeHdc

HDC GetSafeHdc( ) const;

Return Value

A device context handle.

Remarks

Call this member function to get **m_hDC**, the output device context. This member function also works with null pointers.

CDC::GetStretchBltMode

int GetStretchBltMode( ) const;

Return Value

The return value specifies the current bitmap-stretching mode— **STRETCH_ANDSCANS**, **STRETCH_DELETESCANS**, or **STRETCH_ORSCANS**—if the function is successful.

Remarks

Retrieves the current bitmap-stretching mode. The bitmap-stretching mode defines how information is removed from bitmaps that are stretched or compressed by the **StretchBlt** member function.

The **STRETCH_ANDSCANS** and **STRETCH_ORSCANS** modes are typically used to preserve foreground pixels in monochrome bitmaps. The **STRETCH_DELETESCANS** mode is typically used to preserve color in color bitmaps.

See Also: **CDC::StretchBlt, CDC::SetStretchBltMode, ::GetStretchBltMode**

CDC::GetTabbedTextExtent

CSize GetTabbedTextExtent(LPCTSTR *lpszString*, **int** *nCount*, **int** *nTabPositions*,
    ↪ **LPINT** *lpnTabStopPositions*) **const;**
CSize GetTabbedTextExtent(const CString& *str*, **int** *nTabPositions*,
    ↪ **LPINT** *lpnTabStopPositions*) **const;**

Return Value

The dimensions of the string (in logical units) in a **CSize** object.

Parameters

lpszString   Points to a character string. You can also pass a **CString** object for this
parameter.

nCount   Specifies the number of characters in the string. If *nCount* is –1, the length is
calculated.

nTabPositions   Specifies the number of tab-stop positions in the array pointed to by
lpnTabStopPositions.

lpnTabStopPositions   Points to an array of integers containing the tab-stop positions
in logical units. The tab stops must be sorted in increasing order; the smallest
x-value should be the first item in the array. Back tabs are not allowed.

str   A **CString** object that contains the specified characters to be drawn.

Remarks

Call this member function to compute the width and height of a character string using
m_hAttribDC, the attribute device context. If the string contains one or more tab
characters, the width of the string is based upon the tab stops specified by
lpnTabStopPositions. The function uses the currently selected font to compute the
dimensions of the string.

The current clipping region does not offset the width and height returned by the
GetTabbedTextExtent function.

Since some devices do not place characters in regular cell arrays (that is, they kern the
characters), the sum of the extents of the characters in a string may not be equal to the
extent of the string.

If *nTabPositions* is 0 and *lpnTabStopPositions* is **NULL**, tabs are expanded to eight
times the average character width. If *nTabPositions* is 1, the tab stops will be
separated by the distance specified by the first value in the array to which
lpnTabStopPositions points. If *lpnTabStopPositions* points to more than a single value,
a tab stop is set for each value in the array, up to the number specified by
nTabPositions.

See Also: **CDC::GetTextExtent, CDC::GetOutputTabbedTextExtent,
CDC::GetOutputTextExtent, CDC::TabbedTextOut, ::GetTabbedTextExtent,
CSize**

CDC::GetTextAlign

UINT GetTextAlign( ) const;

Return Value

The status of the text-alignment flags. The return value is one or more of the following values:

- **TA_BASELINE**   Specifies alignment of the x-axis and the baseline of the chosen font within the bounding rectangle.
- **TA_BOTTOM**   Specifies alignment of the x-axis and the bottom of the bounding rectangle.
- **TA_CENTER**   Specifies alignment of the y-axis and the center of the bounding rectangle.
- **TA_LEFT**   Specifies alignment of the y-axis and the left side of the bounding rectangle.
- **TA_NOUPDATECP**   Specifies that the current position is not updated.
- **TA_RIGHT**   Specifies alignment of the y-axis and the right side of the bounding rectangle.
- **TA_TOP**   Specifies alignment of the x-axis and the top of the bounding rectangle.
- **TA_UPDATECP**   Specifies that the current position is updated.

Remarks

Retrieves the status of the text-alignment flags for the device context.

The text-alignment flags determine how the **TextOut** and **ExtTextOut** member functions align a string of text in relation to the string's starting point. The text-alignment flags are not necessarily single-bit flags and may be equal to 0. To test whether a flag is set, an application should follow these steps:

1. Apply the bitwise OR operator to the flag and its related flags, grouped as follows:
   - **TA_LEFT**, **TA_CENTER**, and **TA_RIGHT**
   - **TA_BASELINE**, **TA_BOTTOM**, and **TA_TOP**
   - **TA_NOUPDATECP** and **TA_UPDATECP**
2. Apply the bitwise-AND operator to the result and the return value of **GetTextAlign**.
3. Test for the equality of this result and the flag.

See Also: **CDC::ExtTextOut, CDC::SetTextAlign, CDC::TextOut, ::GetTextAlign**

CDC::GetTextCharacterExtra

int GetTextCharacterExtra( ) const;

Return Value

The amount of the intercharacter spacing.

Remarks

Retrieves the current setting for the amount of intercharacter spacing. GDI adds this spacing to each character, including break characters, when it writes a line of text to the device context.

The default value for the amount of intercharacter spacing is 0.

See Also: **CDC::SetTextCharacterExtra, ::GetTextCharacterExtra**

CDC::GetTextColor

COLORREF GetTextColor( ) const;

Return Value

The current text color as an RGB color value.

Remarks

Retrieves the current text color. The text color is the foreground color of characters drawn by using the GDI text-output member functions **TextOut**, **ExtTextOut**, and **TabbedTextOut**.

See Also: **CDC::GetBkColor, CDC::GetBkMode, CDC::SetBkMode, CDC::SetTextColor, ::GetTextColor**

CDC::GetTextExtent

CSize GetTextExtent(LPCTSTR *lpszString*, **int** *nCount* **) const;**
CSize GetTextExtent(const CString& *str* **) const;**

Return Value

The dimensions of the string (in logical units) in a **CSize** object.

Parameters

lpszString Points to a string of characters. You can also pass a **CString** object for this parameter.

nCount Specifies the number of characters in the string.

str A **CString** object that contains the specified characters.

Remarks

Call this member function to compute the width and height of a line of text using the current font to determine the dimensions. The information is retrieved from **m_hAttribDC**, the attribute device context.

The current clipping region does not affect the width and height returned by **GetTextExtent**.

Since some devices do not place characters in regular cell arrays (that is, they carry out kerning), the sum of the extents of the characters in a string may not be equal to the extent of the string.

See Also: **CDC::GetTabbedTextExtent, CDC::m_hAttribDC, CDC::m_hDC, CDC::GetOutputTextExtent, CDC::SetTextJustification, CSize**

CDC::GetTextFace

int GetTextFace(int *nCount***, LPTSTR** *lpszFacename* **) const;**
int GetTextFace(CString& *rString* **) const;**

Return Value

The number of bytes copied to the buffer, not including the terminating null character. It is 0 if an error occurs.

Parameters

nCount   Specifies the size of the buffer (in bytes). If the typeface name is longer than the number of bytes specified by this parameter, the name is truncated.

lpszFacename   Points to the buffer for the typeface name.

rString   A reference to a **CString** object.

Remarks

Call this member function to copy the typeface name of the current font into a buffer. The typeface name is copied as a null-terminated string.

See Also: **CDC::GetTextMetrics, CDC::SetTextAlign, CDC::TextOut, ::GetTextFace**

CDC::GetTextMetrics

BOOL GetTextMetrics(LPTEXTMETRIC *lpMetrics* **) const;**

Return Value

Nonzero if the function is successful; otherwise 0.

Parameters

lpMetrics   Points to the **TEXTMETRIC** structure that receives the metrics.

Remarks

Retrieves the metrics for the current font using the attribute device context.

See Also: **CDC::GetTextAlign, CDC::m_hAttribDC, CDC::m_hDC, CDC::GetOutputTextMetrics, CDC::GetTextExtent, CDC::GetTextFace, CDC::SetTextJustification, ::GetTextMetrics**

CDC::GetViewportExt

CSize GetViewportExt( ) const;

Return Value

The x- and y-extents (in device units) as a **CSize** object.

Remarks

Retrieves the x- and y-extents of the device context's viewport.

See Also: **CDC::SetViewportExt, CSize, CDC::SetWindowExt**

CDC::GetViewportOrg

CPoint GetViewportOrg( ) const;

Return Value

The origin of the viewport (in device coordinates) as a **CPoint** object.

Remarks

Retrieves the x- and y-coordinates of the origin of the viewport associated with the device context.

See Also: **CDC::GetWindowOrg, CPoint, CDC::SetViewportOrg**

CDC::GetWindow

CWnd* GetWindow( ) const;

Return Value

Pointer to a **CWnd** object if successful; otherwise **NULL**.

Remarks

Returns the window associated with the display device context. This is an advanced function. For example, this member function may not return the view window when printing or in print preview. It always returns the window associated with output. Output functions that use the given DC draw into this window.

See Also: **CWnd::GetDC, CWnd::GetWindowDC, ::GetWindow**

CDC::GetWindowExt

CSize GetWindowExt( ) const;

Return Value

The x- and y-extents (in logical units) as a **CSize** object.

Remarks

Retrieves the x- and y-extents of the window associated with the device context.

See Also: **CDC::SetWindowExt, CSize, CDC::GetViewportExt**

CDC::GetWindowOrg

CPoint GetWindowOrg( ) const;

Return Value

The origin of the window (in logical coordinates) as a **CPoint** object.

Remarks

Retrieves the x- and y-coordinates of the origin of the window associated with the device context.

See Also: **CDC::GetViewportOrg, CDC::SetWindowOrg, CPoint**

CDC::GrayString

virtual BOOL GrayString(CBrush* *pBrush***,**
↳ **BOOL (CALLBACK EXPORT*** *lpfnOutput* **) (HDC, LPARAM, int),**
↳ **LPARAM** *lpData***, int** *nCount***, int** *x***, int** *y***, int** *nWidth***, int** *nHeight* **);**

Return Value

Nonzero if the string is drawn, or 0 if either the **TextOut** function or the application-supplied output function returned 0, or if there was insufficient memory to create a memory bitmap for dimming.

Parameters

pBrush   Identifies the brush to be used for dimming (graying).

lpfnOutput   Specifies the procedure-instance address of the application-supplied callback function that will draw the string. For more information, see the description of the Windows **OutputFunc** callback function. If this parameter is **NULL**, the system uses the Windows **TextOut** function to draw the string, and *lpData* is assumed to be a long pointer to the character string to be output.

lpData   Specifies a far pointer to data to be passed to the output function. If *lpfnOutput* is **NULL**, *lpData* must be a long pointer to the string to be output.

nCount   Specifies the number of characters to be output. If this parameter is 0, **GrayString** calculates the length of the string (assuming that *lpData* is a pointer to the string). If *nCount* is –1 and the function pointed to by *lpfnOutput* returns 0, the image is shown but not dimmed.

x Specifies the logical x-coordinate of the starting position of the rectangle that encloses the string.

y Specifies the logical y-coordinate of the starting position of the rectangle that encloses the string.

nWidth Specifies the width (in logical units) of the rectangle that encloses the string. If *nWidth* is 0, **GrayString** calculates the width of the area, assuming *lpData* is a pointer to the string.

nHeight Specifies the height (in logical units) of the rectangle that encloses the string. If *nHeight* is 0, **GrayString** calculates the height of the area, assuming *lpData* is a pointer to the string.

Remarks

Draws dimmed (gray) text at the given location by writing the text in a memory bitmap, dimming the bitmap, and then copying the bitmap to the display. The function dims the text regardless of the selected brush and background. The **GrayString** member function uses the currently selected font. The **MM_TEXT** mapping mode must be selected before using this function.

An application can draw dimmed (grayed) strings on devices that support a solid gray color without calling the **GrayString** member function. The system color **COLOR_GRAYTEXT** is the solid-gray system color used to draw disabled text. The application can call the **GetSysColor** Windows function to retrieve the color value of **COLOR_GRAYTEXT**. If the color is other than 0 (black), the application can call the **SetTextColor** member function to set the text color to the color value and then draw the string directly. If the retrieved color is black, the application must call **GrayString** to dim (gray) the text.

If *lpfnOutput* is **NULL**, GDI uses the Windows **TextOut** function, and *lpData* is assumed to be a far pointer to the character to be output. If the characters to be output cannot be handled by the **TextOut** member function (for example, the string is stored as a bitmap), the application must supply its own output function.

Also note that all callback functions must trap Microsoft Foundation exceptions before returning to Windows, since exceptions cannot be thrown across callback boundaries. For more information about exceptions, see the article "Exceptions" in *Visual C++ Programmer's Guide* online.

The callback function passed to **GrayString** must use the Pascal calling convention, must be exported with **__export**, and must be declared **FAR**.

When the framework is in preview mode, a call to the **GrayString** member function is translated to a **TextOut** call, and the callback function is not called.

See Also: ::GetSysColor, CDC::SetTextColor, CDC::TextOut, ::GrayString

CDC::HIMETRICtoDP

> **void HIMETRICtoDP(LPSIZE** *lpSize* **) const;**

Parameters

lpSize   Points to a **SIZE** structure or **CSize** object.

Remarks

Use this function when you convert **HIMETRIC** sizes from OLE to pixels.

If the mapping mode of the device context object is **MM_LOENGLISH,**
MM_HIENGLISH, MM_LOMETRIC or **MM_HIMETRIC**, then the conversion
is based on the number of pixels in the physical inch. If the mapping mode is one of
the other non-constrained modes (e.g., **MM_TEXT**), then the conversion is based on
the number of pixels in the logical inch.

See Also: **CDC::LPtoDP, CDC::HIMETRICtoLP**

CDC::HIMETRICtoLP

> **void HIMETRICtoLP(LPSIZE** *lpSize* **) const;**

Parameters

lpSize   Points to a **SIZE** structure or **CSize** object.

Remarks

Call this function to convert **HIMETRIC** units into logical units. Use this function
when you get **HIMETRIC** sizes from OLE and wish to convert them to your
application's natural mapping mode.

The conversion is accomplished by first converting the **HIMETRIC** units into pixels
and then converting these units into logical units using the device context's current
mapping units. Note that the extents of the device's window and viewport will affect
the result.

See Also: **CDC::HIMETRICtoDP, CDC::DPtoLP**

CDC::IntersectClipRect

> **virtual int IntersectClipRect(int** *x1***, int** *y1***, int** *x2***, int** *y2* **);**
> **virtual int IntersectClipRect(LPCRECT** *lpRect* **);**

Return Value

The new clipping region's type. It can be any one of the following values:

- **COMPLEXREGION**   New clipping region has overlapping borders.
- **ERROR**   Device context is not valid.
- **NULLREGION**   New clipping region is empty.

- **SIMPLEREGION** New clipping region has no overlapping borders.

Parameters

x1 Specifies the logical x-coordinate of the upper-left corner of the rectangle.

y1 Specifies the logical y-coordinate of the upper-left corner of the rectangle.

x2 Specifies the logical x-coordinate of the lower-right corner of the rectangle.

y2 Specifies the logical y-coordinate of the lower-right corner of the rectangle.

lpRect Specifies the rectangle. You can pass either a **CRect** object or a pointer to a **RECT** structure for this parameter.

Remarks

Creates a new clipping region by forming the intersection of the current region and the rectangle specified by *x1*, *y1*, *x2*, and *y2*. GDI clips all subsequent output to fit within the new boundary. The width and height must not exceed 32,767.

See Also: **::IntersectClipRect**, **CRect**, **RECT**

CDC::InvertRect

void InvertRect(LPCRECT *lpRect* **);**

Parameters

lpRect Points to a **RECT** that contains the logical coordinates of the rectangle to be inverted. You can also pass a **CRect** object for this parameter.

Remarks

Inverts the contents of the given rectangle. Inversion is a logical NOT operation and flips the bits of each pixel. On monochrome displays, the function makes white pixels black and black pixels white. On color displays, the inversion depends on how colors are generated for the display. Calling **InvertRect** twice with the same rectangle restores the display to its previous colors.

If the rectangle is empty, nothing is drawn.

See Also: **CDC::FillRect**, **::InvertRect**, **CRect**, **RECT**

CDC::InvertRgn

BOOL InvertRgn(CRgn* *pRgn* **);**

Return Value

Nonzero if the function is successful; otherwise 0.

Parameters

pRgn Identifies the region to be inverted. The coordinates for the region are specified in device units.

Remarks

Inverts the colors in the region specified by *pRgn*. On monochrome displays, the function makes white pixels black and black pixels white. On color displays, the inversion depends on how the colors are generated for the display.

See Also: CDC::FillRgn, CDC::PaintRgn, CRgn, ::InvertRgn

CDC::IsPrinting

BOOL IsPrinting( ) const;

Return Value

Nonzero if the **CDC** object is a printer DC; otherwise 0.

CDC::LineTo

BOOL LineTo(int *x*, int *y*);
BOOL LineTo(POINT *point*);

Return Value

Nonzero if the line is drawn; otherwise 0.

Parameters

x   Specifies the logical x-coordinate of the endpoint for the line.

y   Specifies the logical y-coordinate of the endpoint for the line.

point   Specifies the endpoint for the line. You can pass either a **POINT** structure or a **CPoint** object for this parameter.

Remarks

Draws a line from the current position up to, but not including, the point specified by *x* and *y* (or *point*). The line is drawn with the selected pen. The current position is set to *x,y* or to *point*.

See Also: CDC::MoveTo, CDC::GetCurrentPosition, ::LineTo, CPoint, POINT

CDC::LPtoDP

void LPtoDP(LPPOINT *lpPoints*, int *nCount* = 1) const;
void LPtoDP(LPRECT *lpRect*) const;
void LPtoDP(LPSIZE *lpSize*) const;

Parameters

lpPoints   Points to an array of points. Each point in the array is a **POINT** structure or a **CPoint** object.

nCount   The number of points in the array.

lpRect   Points to a **RECT** structure or a **CRect** object. This parameter is used for the common case of mapping a rectangle from logical to device units.

lpSize   Points to a **SIZE** structure or a **CSize** object.

Remarks

Converts logical units into device units. The function maps the coordinates of each point, or dimensions of a size, from GDI's logical coordinate system into a device coordinate system. The conversion depends on the current mapping mode and the settings of the origins and extents of the device's window and viewport.

The x- and y-coordinates of points are 2-byte signed integers in the range –32,768 through 32,767. In cases where the mapping mode would result in values larger than these limits, the system sets the values to –32,768 and 32,767, respectively.

See Also: **CDC::DPtoLP**, **CDC::HIMETRICtoLP**, **::LPtoDP**, **CDC::GetWindowOrg**, **CDC::GetWindowExt**

CDC::LPtoHIMETRIC

void LPToHIMETRIC(LPSIZE *lpSize* **) const;**

Parameters

lpSize   Points to a **SIZE** structure or a **CSize** object.

Remarks

Call this function to convert logical units into **HIMETRIC** units. Use this function when you give **HIMETRIC** sizes to OLE, converting from your application's natural mapping mode. Note that the extents of the device's window and viewport will affect the result.

The conversion is accomplished by first converting the logical units into pixels using the device context's current mapping units and then converting these units into **HIMETRIC** units.

See Also: **CDC::HIMETRICtoLP**, **CDC::LPtoDP**, **CDC::DPtoHIMETRIC**

CDC::MaskBlt

BOOL MaskBlt(int *x*, **int** *y*, **int** *nWidth*, **int** *nHeight*, **CDC*** *pSrcDC*, **int** *xSrc*, **int** *ySrc*,
↪ **CBitmap&** *maskBitmap*, **int** *xMask*, **int** *yMask*, **DWORD** *dwRop* **);**

Return Value

Nonzero if the function is successful; otherwise 0.

Parameters

x   Specifies the logical x-coordinate of the upper-left corner of the destination rectangle.

y   Specifies the logical y-coordinate of the upper-left corner of the destination rectangle.

nWidth   Specifies the width, in logical units, of the destination rectangle and source bitmap.

nHeight   Specifies the height, in logical units, of the destination rectangle and source bitmap.

pSrcDC   Identifies the device context from which the bitmap is to be copied. It must be zero if the *dwRop* parameter specifies a raster operation that does not include a source.

xSrc   Specifies the logical x-coordinate of the upper-left corner of the source bitmap.

ySrc   Specifies the logical y-coordinate of the upper-left corner of the source bitmap.

maskBitmap   Identifies the monochrome mask bitmap combined with the color bitmap in the source device context.

xMask   Specifies the horizontal pixel offset for the mask bitmap specified by the *maskBitmap* parameter.

yMask   Specifies the vertical pixel offset for the mask bitmap specified by the *maskBitmap* parameter.

dwRop   Specifies both foreground and background ternary raster operation codes, which the function uses to control the combination of source and destination data. The background raster operation code is stored in the high byte of the high word of this value; the foreground raster operation code is stored in the low byte of the high word of this value; the low word of this value is ignored, and should be zero. The macro **MAKEROP4** creates such combinations of foreground and background raster operation codes. See the Remarks section for a discussion of foreground and background in the context of this function. See the **BitBlt** member function for a list of common raster operation codes.

Remarks

Combines the color data for the source and destination bitmaps using the given mask and raster operation. A value of 1 in the mask specified by *maskBitmap* indicates that the foreground raster operation code specified by *dwRop* should be applied at that location. A value of 0 in the mask indicates that the background raster operation code specified by *dwRop* should be applied at that location. If the raster operations require a source, the mask rectangle must cover the source rectangle. If it does not, the function will fail. If the raster operations do not require a source, the mask rectangle must cover the destination rectangle. If it does not, the function will fail.

If a rotation or shear transformation is in effect for the source device context when this function is called, an error occurs. However, other types of transformations are allowed.

If the color formats of the source, pattern, and destination bitmaps differ, this function converts the pattern or source format, or both, to match the destination format. If the mask bitmap is not a monochrome bitmap, an error occurs. When an enhanced metafile is being recorded, an error occurs (and the function returns 0) if the source device context identifies an enhanced-metafile device context. Not all devices support **MaskBlt**. An application should call **GetDeviceCaps** to determine whether a device supports this function. If no mask bitmap is supplied, this function behaves exactly like **BitBlt**, using the foreground raster operation code. The pixel offsets in the mask bitmap map to the point (0,0) in the source device context's bitmap. This is useful for cases in which a mask bitmap contains a set of masks; an application can easily apply any one of them to a mask-blitting task by adjusting the pixel offsets and rectangle sizes sent to **MaskBlt**.

See Also: **CDC::BitBlt, CDC::GetDeviceCaps, CDC::PlgBlt, CDC::StretchBlt, ::MaskBlt**

CDC::MoveTo

CPoint MoveTo(int *x*, **int** *y* **);**
CPoint MoveTo(POINT *point* **);**

Return Value

The x- and y-coordinates of the previous position as a **CPoint** object.

Parameters

x   Specifies the logical x-coordinate of the new position.

y   Specifies the logical y-coordinate of the new position.

point   Specifies the new position. You can pass either a **POINT** structure or a **CPoint** object for this parameter.

Remarks

Moves the current position to the point specified by *x* and *y* (or by *point*).

See Also: **CDC::GetCurrentPosition, CDC::LineTo, CPoint, POINT**

CDC::OffsetClipRgn

virtual int OffsetClipRgn(int *x*, **int** *y* **);**
virtual int OffsetClipRgn(SIZE *size* **);**

Return Value

The new region's type. It can be any one of the following values:

- **COMPLEXREGION**   Clipping region has overlapping borders.
- **ERROR**   Device context is not valid.
- **NULLREGION**   Clipping region is empty.
- **SIMPLEREGION**   Clipping region has no overlapping borders.

Parameters

x   Specifies the number of logical units to move left or right.

y   Specifies the number of logical units to move up or down.

size   Specifies the amount to offset.

Remarks

Moves the clipping region of the device context by the specified offsets. The function moves the region *x* units along the x-axis and *y* units along the y-axis.

See Also: CDC::SelectClipRgn, ::OffsetClipRgn

CDC::OffsetViewportOrg

virtual CPoint OffsetViewportOrg(int *nWidth*, **int** *nHeight* **);**

Return Value

The previous viewport origin (in device coordinates) as a **CPoint** object.

Parameters

nWidth   Specifies the number of device units to add to the current origin's x-coordinate.

nHeight   Specifies the number of device units to add to the current origin's y-coordinate.

Remarks

Modifies the coordinates of the viewport origin relative to the coordinates of the current viewport origin.

See Also: CDC::GetViewportOrg, CDC::OffsetWindowOrg, CDC::SetViewportOrg, CPoint

---

CDC::OffsetWindowOrg

CPoint OffsetWindowOrg(int *nWidth*, **int** *nHeight* **);**

Return Value

The previous window origin (in logical coordinates) as a **CPoint** object.

Parameters

nWidth   Specifies the number of logical units to add to the current origin's x-coordinate.

nHeight   Specifies the number of logical units to add to the current origin's y-coordinate.

Remarks

Modifies the coordinates of the window origin relative to the coordinates of the current window origin.

CDC::PaintRgn

BOOL PaintRgn(CRgn* *pRgn* **);**

Return Value

Nonzero if the function is successful; otherwise 0.

Parameters

pRgn   Identifies the region to be filled. The coordinates for the given region are
specified in device units.

Remarks

Fills the region specified by *pRgn* using the current brush.

See Also: **CBrush**, **CDC::SelectObject**, **CDC::FillRgn**, **::PaintRgn**, **CRgn**

CDC::PatBlt

BOOL PatBlt(int *x*, **int** *y*, **int** *nWidth*, **int** *nHeight*, **DWORD** *dwRop* **);**

Return Value

Nonzero if the function is successful; otherwise 0.

Parameters

x   Specifies the logical x-coordinate of the upper-left corner of the rectangle that is to
receive the pattern.

y   Specifies the logical y-coordinate of the upper-left corner of the rectangle that is to
receive the pattern.

nWidth   Specifies the width (in logical units) of the rectangle that is to receive the
pattern.

nHeight   Specifies the height (in logical units) of the rectangle that is to receive the
pattern.

dwRop   Specifies the raster-operation code. Raster-operation codes (ROPs) define
how GDI combines colors in output operations that involve a current brush, a
possible source bitmap, and a destination bitmap. This parameter can be one of the
following values:

- **PATCOPY**   Copies pattern to destination bitmap.

- **PATINVERT**   Combines destination bitmap with pattern using the Boolean
XOR operator.

- **DSTINVERT**   Inverts the destination bitmap.

- **BLACKNESS** Turns all output black.

- **WHITENESS** Turns all output white.

Remarks

Creates a bit pattern on the device. The pattern is a combination of the selected brush and the pattern already on the device. The raster-operation code specified by *dwRop* defines how the patterns are to be combined. The raster operations listed for this function are a limited subset of the full 256 ternary raster-operation codes; in particular, a raster-operation code that refers to a source cannot be used.

Not all device contexts support the **PatBlt** function. To determine whether a device context supports **PatBlt**, call the **GetDeviceCaps** member function with the **RASTERCAPS** index and check the return value for the **RC_BITBLT** flag.

See Also: **CDC::GetDeviceCaps, ::PatBlt**

CDC::Pie

BOOL Pie(int *x1*, **int** *y1*, **int** *x2*, **int** *y2*, **int** *x3*, **int** *y3*, **int** *x4*, **int** *y4* **);**
BOOL Pie(LPCRECT *lpRect*, **POINT** *ptStart*, **POINT** *ptEnd* **);**

Return Value

Nonzero if the function is successful; otherwise 0.

Parameters

x1   Specifies the x-coordinate of the upper-left corner of the bounding rectangle (in logical units).

y1   Specifies the y-coordinate of the upper-left corner of the bounding rectangle (in logical units).

x2   Specifies the x-coordinate of the lower-right corner of the bounding rectangle (in logical units).

y2   Specifies the y-coordinate of the lower-right corner of the bounding rectangle (in logical units).

x3   Specifies the x-coordinate of the arc's starting point (in logical units). This point does not have to lie exactly on the arc.

y3   Specifies the y-coordinate of the arc's starting point (in logical units). This point does not have to lie exactly on the arc.

x4   Specifies the x-coordinate of the arc's endpoint (in logical units). This point does not have to lie exactly on the arc.

y4   Specifies the y-coordinate of the arc's endpoint (in logical units). This point does not have to lie exactly on the arc.

lpRect   Specifies the bounding rectangle. You can pass either a **CRect** object or a pointer to a **RECT** structure for this parameter.

ptStart Specifies the starting point of the arc. This point does not have to lie exactly on the arc. You can pass either a **POINT** structure or a **CPoint** object for this parameter.

ptEnd Specifies the endpoint of the arc. This point does not have to lie exactly on the arc. You can pass either a **POINT** structure or a **CPoint** object for this parameter.

Remarks

Draws a pie-shaped wedge by drawing an elliptical arc whose center and two endpoints are joined by lines. The center of the arc is the center of the bounding rectangle specified by *x1*, *y1*, *x2*, and *y2* (or by *lpRect*). The starting and ending points of the arc are specified by *x3*, *y3*, *x4*, and *y4* (or by *ptStart* and *ptEnd*).

The arc is drawn with the selected pen, moving in a counterclockwise direction. Two additional lines are drawn from each endpoint to the arc's center. The pie-shaped area is filled with the current brush. If *x3* equals *x4* and *y3* equals *y4*, the result is an ellipse with a single line from the center of the ellipse to the point (*x3*, *y3*) or (*x4*, *y4*).

The figure drawn by this function extends up to but does not include the right and bottom coordinates. This means that the height of the figure is *y2* – *y1* and the width of the figure is *x2* – *x1*. Both the width and the height of the bounding rectangle must be greater than 2 units and less than 32,767 units.

See Also: **CDC::Chord**, **::Pie**, **RECT**, **POINT**, **CRect**, **CPoint**

CDC::PlayMetaFile

BOOL PlayMetaFile(HMETAFILE *hMF* **);**
BOOL PlayMetaFile(HENHMETAFILE *hEnhMetaFile*, **LPCRECT** *lpBounds* **);**

Return Value

Nonzero if the function is successful; otherwise 0.

Parameters

hMF Identifies the metafile to be played.

hEnhMetaFile Identifies the enhanced metafile.

lpBounds Points to a **RECT** structure or a **CRect** object that contains the coordinates of the bounding rectangle used to display the picture. The coordinates are specified in logical units.

Remarks

Plays the contents of the specified metafile on the device context. The metafile can be played any number of times.

The second version of **PlayMetaFile** displays the picture stored in the given enhanced-format metafile. When an application calls the second version of **PlayMetaFile**, Windows uses the picture frame in the enhanced-metafile header to map the picture onto the rectangle pointed to by the *lpBounds* parameter. (This picture may be sheared or rotated by setting the world transform in the output device before calling **PlayMetaFile**.) Points along the edges of the rectangle are included in the picture. An enhanced-metafile picture can be clipped by defining the clipping region in the output device before playing the enhanced metafile.

If an enhanced metafile contains an optional palette, an application can achieve consistent colors by setting up a color palette on the output device before calling the second version of **PlayMetaFile**. To retrieve the optional palette, use the **::GetEnhMetaFilePaletteEntries** function. An enhanced metafile can be embedded in a newly created enhanced metafile by calling the second version of **PlayMetaFile** and playing the source enhanced metafile into the device context for the new enhanced metafile.

The states of the output device context are preserved by this function. Any object created but not deleted in the enhanced metafile is deleted by this function. To stop this function, an application can call the **::CancelDC** function from another thread to terminate the operation. In this case, the function returns zero.

See Also: **::CancelDC**, **::GetEnhMetaFileHeader**, **::GetEnhMetaFilePaletteEntries**, **::SetWorldTransform**, **::PlayMetaFile**, **::PlayEnhMetaFile**, **::PlayMetaFile**

CDC::PlgBlt

BOOL PlgBlt(POINT *lpPoint*, **CDC*** *pSrcDC*, **int** *xSrc*, **int** *ySrc*, **int** *nWidth*, ⮡ **int** *nHeight*, **CBitmap&** *maskBitmap*, **int** *xMask*, **int** *yMask* **);**

Return Value

Nonzero if the function is successful; otherwise 0.

Parameters

lpPoint   Points to an array of three points in logical space that identifies three corners of the destination parallelogram. The upper-left corner of the source rectangle is mapped to the first point in this array, the upper-right corner to the second point in this array, and the lower-left corner to the third point. The lower-right corner of the source rectangle is mapped to the implicit fourth point in the parallelogram.

pSrcDC   Identifies the source device context.

xSrc   Specifies the x-coordinate, in logical units, of the upper-left corner of the source rectangle.

ySrc   Specifies the y-coordinate, in logical units, of the upper-left corner of the source rectangle.

nWidth   Specifies the width, in logical units, of the source rectangle.

nHeight   Specifies the height, in logical units, of the source rectangle.

maskBitmap   Identifies an optional monochrome bitmap that is used to mask the colors of the source rectangle.

xMask   Specifies the x-coordinate of the upper-left corner of the monochrome bitmap.

yMask   Specifies the y-coordinate of the upper-left corner of the monochrome bitmap.

Remarks

Performs a bit-block transfer of the bits of color data from the specified rectangle in the source device context to the specified parallelogram in the given device context. If the given bitmask handle identifies a valid monochrome bitmap, the function uses this bitmap to mask the bits of color data from the source rectangle.

The fourth vertex of the parallelogram (D) is defined by treating the first three points (A, B, and C) as vectors and computing D = B + C - A.

If the bitmask exists, a value of 1 in the mask indicates that the source pixel color should be copied to the destination. A value of 0 in the mask indicates that the destination pixel color is not to be changed.

If the mask rectangle is smaller than the source and destination rectangles, the function replicates the mask pattern.

Scaling, translation, and reflection transformations are allowed in the source device context; however, rotation and shear transformations are not. If the mask bitmap is not a monochrome bitmap, an error occurs. The stretching mode for the destination device context is used to determine how to stretch or compress the pixels, if that is necessary. When an enhanced metafile is being recorded, an error occurs if the source device context identifies an enhanced-metafile device context.

The destination coordinates are transformed according to the destination device context; the source coordinates are transformed according to the source device context. If the source transformation has a rotation or shear, an error is returned. If the destination and source rectangles do not have the same color format, **PlgBlt** converts the source rectangle to match the destination rectangle. Not all devices support **PlgBlt**. For more information, see the description of the **RC_BITBLT** raster capability in the **CDC::GetDeviceCaps** member function.

If the source and destination device contexts represent incompatible devices, **PlgBlt** returns an error.

See Also: **CDC::BitBlt, CDC::GetDeviceCaps, CDC::MaskBlt, CDC::StretchBlt, ::SetStretchBltMode , ::PlgBlt**

CDC::PolyBezier

BOOL PolyBezier(const POINT* *lpPoints***, int** *nCount* **);**

Return Value

Nonzero if the function is successful; otherwise 0.

Parameters

lpPoints Points to an array of **POINT** data structures that contain the endpoints and control points of the spline(s).

nCount Specifies the number of points in the *lpPoints* array. This value must be one more than three times the number of splines to be drawn, because each Bézier spline requires two control points and an endpoint, and the initial spline requires an additional starting point.

Remarks

Draws one or more Bézier splines. This function draws cubic Bézier splines by using the endpoints and control points specified by the *lpPoints* parameter. The first spline is drawn from the first point to the fourth point by using the second and third points as control points. Each subsequent spline in the sequence needs exactly three more points: the end point of the previous spline is used as the starting point, the next two points in the sequence are control points, and the third is the end point.

The current position is neither used nor updated by the **PolyBezier** function. The figure is not filled. This function draws lines by using the current pen.

See Also: CDC::PolyBezierTo, ::PolyBezier

CDC::PolyBezierTo

BOOL PolyBezierTo(const POINT* *lpPoints***, int** *nCount* **);**

Return Value

Nonzero if the function is successful; otherwise 0.

Parameters

lpPoints Points to an array of **POINT** data structures that contains the endpoints and control points.

nCount Specifies the number of points in the *lpPoints* array. This value must be three times the number of splines to be drawn, because each Bézier spline requires two control points and an end point.

Remarks

Draws one or more Bézier splines. This function draws cubic Bézier splines by using the control points specified by the *lpPoints* parameter. The first spline is drawn from the current position to the third point by using the first two points as control points. For each subsequent spline, the function needs exactly three more points, and uses the end point of the previous spline as the starting point for the next. **PolyBezierTo** moves the current position to the end point of the last Bézier spline. The figure is not filled. This function draws lines by using the current pen.

See Also: CDC::MoveTo, CDC::PolyBezier, ::PolyBezierTo

CDC::PolyDraw

BOOL PolyDraw(const POINT* *lpPoints***, const BYTE*** *lpTypes***, int** *nCount* **);**

Return Value

Nonzero if the function is successful; otherwise 0.

Parameters

lpPoints   Points to an array of **POINT** data structures that contains the endpoints for each line segment and the endpoints and control points for each Bézier spline.

lpTypes   Points to an array that specifies how each point in the *lpPoints* array is used. Values can be one of the following:

- **PT_MOVETO**   Specifies that this point starts a disjoint figure. This point becomes the new current position.

- **PT_LINETO**   Specifies that a line is to be drawn from the current position to this point, which then becomes the new current position.

- **PT_BEZIERTO**   Specifies that this point is a control point or ending point for a Bézier spline.

  PT_BEZIERTO types always occur in sets of three. The current position defines the starting point for the Bézier spline. The first two **PT_BEZIERTO** points are the control points, and the third **PT_BEZIERTO** point is the ending point. The ending point becomes the new current position. If there are not three consecutive **PT_BEZIERTO** points, an error results.

  A **PT_LINETO** or **PT_BEZIERTO** type can be combined with the following constant by using the bitwise operator OR to indicate that the corresponding point is the last point in a figure and the figure is closed:

- **PT_CLOSEFIGURE**   Specifies that the figure is automatically closed after the **PT_LINETO** or **PT_BEZIERTO** type for this point is done. A line is drawn from this point to the most recent **PT_MOVETO** or **MoveTo** point.

  This flag is combined with the **PT_LINETO** type for a line, or with the **PT_BEZIERTO** type of ending point for a Bézier spline, by using the bitwise **OR** operator. The current position is set to the ending point of the closing line.

nCount   Specifies the total number of points in the *lpPoints* array, the same as the number of bytes in the *lpTypes* array.

Remarks

Draws a set of line segments and Bézier splines. This function can be used to draw disjoint figures in place of consecutive calls to **CDC::MoveTo**, **CDC::LineTo**, and **CDC::PolyBezierTo** member functions. The lines and splines are drawn using the current pen, and figures are not filled. If there is an active path started by calling the **CDC::BeginPath** member function, **PolyDraw** adds to the path. The points contained in the *lpPoints* array and in *lpTypes* indicate whether each point is part of a **CDC::MoveTo**, a **CDC::LineTo**, or a **CDC::BezierTo** operation. It is also possible to close figures. This function updates the current position.

See Also: **CDC::BeginPath**, **CDC::EndPath**, **CDC::LineTo**, **CDC::MoveTo**, **CDC::PolyBezierTo**, **CDC::PolyLine**, **::PolyDraw**

CDC::Polygon

> **BOOL Polygon(LPPOINT** *lpPoints*, **int** *nCount*);

Return Value

Nonzero if the function is successful; otherwise 0.

Parameters

lpPoints Points to an array of points that specifies the vertices of the polygon. Each point in the array is a **POINT** structure or a **CPoint** object.

nCount Specifies the number of vertices in the array.

Remarks

Draws a polygon consisting of two or more points (vertices) connected by lines, using the current pen. The system closes the polygon automatically, if necessary, by drawing a line from the last vertex to the first.

The current polygon-filling mode can be retrieved or set by using the **GetPolyFillMode** and **SetPolyFillMode** member functions.

See Also: **CDC::GetPolyFillMode**, **CDC::Polyline**, **CDC::PolyPolygon**, **CDC::SetPolyFillMode**, **CPoint**, **::Polygon**

CDC::Polyline

> **BOOL Polyline(LPPOINT** *lpPoints*, **int** *nCount*);

Return Value

Nonzero if the function is successful; otherwise 0.

Parameters

lpPoints Points to an array of **POINT** structures or **CPoint** objects to be connected.

nCount Specifies the number of points in the array. This value must be at least 2.

Remarks

Draws a set of line segments connecting the points specified by *lpPoints*. The lines are drawn from the first point through subsequent points using the current pen. Unlike the **LineTo** member function, the **Polyline** function neither uses nor updates the current position.

For more information, see **::PolyLine** in the *Win32 SDK Programmer's Reference*.

See Also: **CDC::LineTo**, **CDC::Polygon**, **POINT**, **CPoint**

CDC::PolylineTo

BOOL PolylineTo(const POINT* *lpPoints*, **int** *nCount* **);**

Return Value

Nonzero if the function is successful; otherwise 0.

Parameters

lpPoints   Points to an array of **POINT** data structures that contains the vertices of the line.

nCount   Specifies the number of points in the array.

Remarks

Draws one or more straight lines. A line is drawn from the current position to the first point specified by the *lpPoints* parameter by using the current pen. For each additional line, the function draws from the ending point of the previous line to the next point specified by *lpPoints*. **PolylineTo** moves the current position to the ending point of the last line. If the line segments drawn by this function form a closed figure, the figure is not filled.

See Also: **CDC::LineTo**, **CDC::Polyline**, **CDC::MoveTo**, **::PolylineTo**

CDC::PolyPolygon

BOOL PolyPolygon(LPPOINT *lpPoints*, **LPINT** *lpPolyCounts*, **int** *nCount* **);**

Return Value

Nonzero if the function is successful; otherwise 0.

Parameters

lpPoints   Points to an array of **POINT** structures or **CPoint** objects that define the vertices of the polygons.

lpPolyCounts   Points to an array of integers, each of which specifies the number of points in one of the polygons in the *lpPoints* array.

nCount   The number of entries in the *lpPolyCounts* array. This number specifies the number of polygons to be drawn. This value must be at least 2.

Remarks

Creates two or more polygons that are filled using the current polygon-filling mode. The polygons may be disjoint or overlapping.

Each polygon specified in a call to the **PolyPolygon** function must be closed. Unlike polygons created by the **Polygon** member function, the polygons created by **PolyPolygon** are not closed automatically.

The function creates two or more polygons. To create a single polygon, an application should use the **Polygon** member function.

The current polygon-filling mode can be retrieved or set by using the **GetPolyFillMode** and **SetPolyFillMode** member functions.

See Also: **CDC::GetPolyFillMode**, **CDC::Polygon**, **CDC::Polyline**, **CDC::SetPolyFillMode**, **::PolyPolygon**, **POINT**, **CPoint**

CDC::PolyPolyline

BOOL PolyPolyline(const POINT* *lpPoints*, **const DWORD*** *lpPolyPoints*, ↪ **int** *nCount* **);**

Return Value

Nonzero if the function is successful; otherwise 0.

Parameters

lpPoints   Points to an array of structures that contains the vertices of the polylines. The polylines are specified consecutively.

lpPolyPoints   Points to an array of variables specifying the number of points in the *lpPoints* array for the corresponding polygon. Each entry must be greater than or equal to 2.

nCount   Specifies the total number of counts in the *lpPolyPoints* array.

Remarks

Draws multiple series of connected line segments. The line segments are drawn by using the current pen. The figures formed by the segments are not filled. The current position is neither used nor updated by this function.

See Also: **CDC::Polyline**, **CDC::PolylineTo**, **::PolyPolyline**

CDC::PtVisible

virtual BOOL PtVisible(int *x*, **int** *y* **) const;**
virtual BOOL PtVisible(POINT *point* **) const;**

Return Value

Nonzero if the specified point is within the clipping region; otherwise 0.

Parameters

x   Specifies the logical x-coordinate of the point.

y   Specifies the logical y-coordinate of the point.

point   Specifies the point to check in logical coordinates. You can pass either a **POINT** structure or a **CPoint** object for this parameter.

Remarks

Determines whether the given point is within the clipping region of the device context.

See Also: CDC::RectVisible, CDC::SelectClipRgn, CPoint, ::PtVisible, POINT

CDC::QueryAbort

BOOL QueryAbort( ) const;

Return Value

The return value is nonzero if printing should continue or if there is no abort procedure. It is 0 if the print job should be terminated. The return value is supplied by the abort function.

Remarks

Calls the abort function installed by the **SetAbortProc** member function for a printing application and queries whether the printing should be terminated.

See Also: CDC::SetAbortProc

CDC::RealizePalette

UINT RealizePalette( );

Return Value

Indicates how many entries in the logical palette were mapped to different entries in the system palette. This represents the number of entries that this function remapped to accommodate changes in the system palette since the logical palette was last realized.

Remarks

Maps entries from the current logical palette to the system palette.

A logical color palette acts as a buffer between color-intensive applications and the system, allowing an application to use as many colors as needed without interfering with its own displayed colors or with colors displayed by other windows.

When a window has the input focus and calls **RealizePalette**, Windows ensures that the window will display all the requested colors, up to the maximum number simultaneously available on the screen. Windows also displays colors not found in the window's palette by matching them to available colors.

In addition, Windows matches the colors requested by inactive windows that call the function as closely as possible to the available colors. This significantly reduces undesirable changes in the colors displayed in inactive windows.

See Also: CDC::SelectPalette, CPalette, ::RealizePalette

CDC::Rectangle

BOOL Rectangle(int *x1*, **int** *y1*, **int** *x2*, **int** *y2* **);**
BOOL Rectangle(LPCRECT *lpRect* **);**

Return Value

Nonzero if the function is successful; otherwise 0.

Parameters

x1   Specifies the x-coordinate of the upper-left corner of the rectangle (in logical units).

y1   Specifies the y-coordinate of the upper-left corner of the rectangle (in logical units).

x2   Specifies the x-coordinate of the lower-right corner of the rectangle (in logical units).

y2   Specifies the y-coordinate of the lower-right corner of the rectangle (in logical units).

lpRect   Specifies the rectangle in logical units. You can pass either a **CRect** object or a pointer to a **RECT** structure for this parameter.

Remarks

Draws a rectangle using the current pen. The interior of the rectangle is filled using the current brush.

The rectangle extends up to, but does not include, the right and bottom coordinates. This means that the height of the rectangle is $y2 - y1$ and the width of the rectangle is $x2 - x1$. Both the width and the height of a rectangle must be greater than 2 units and less than 32,767 units.

See Also: **::Rectangle, CDC::PolyLine, CDC::RoundRect, RECT, CRect**

CDC::RectVisible

virtual BOOL RectVisible(LPCRECT *lpRect* **) const;**

Return Value

Nonzero if any portion of the given rectangle lies within the clipping region; otherwise 0.

Parameters

lpRect   Points to a **RECT** structure or a **CRect** object that contains the logical coordinates of the specified rectangle.

Remarks

Determines whether any part of the given rectangle lies within the clipping region of the display context.

See Also: **CDC::PtVisible, CDC::SelectClipRgn, CRect, ::RectVisible, RECT**

CDC::ReleaseAttribDC

virtual void ReleaseAttribDC( );

Remarks

Call this member function to set **m_hAttribDC** to **NULL**. This does not cause a **Detach** to occur. Only the output device context is attached to the **CDC** object, and only it can be detached.

See Also: **CDC::SetOutputDC, CDC::SetAttribDC, CDC::ReleaseOutputDC, CDC::m_hAttribDC**

CDC::ReleaseOutputDC

virtual void ReleaseOutputDC( );

Remarks

Call this member function to set the **m_hDC** member to **NULL**. This member function cannot be called when the output device context is attached to the **CDC** object. Use the **Detach** member function to detach the output device context.

See Also: **CDC::SetAttribDC, CDC::SetOutputDC, CDC::ReleaseAttribDC, CDC::m_hDC**

CDC::ResetDC

BOOL ResetDC(const DEVMODE* *lpDevMode* **);**

Return Value

Nonzero if the function is successful; otherwise 0.

Parameters

lpDevMode   A pointer to a Windows **DEVMODE** structure.

Remarks

Call this member function to update the device context wrapped by the **CDC** object. The device context is updated from the information specified in the Windows **DEVMODE** structure. This member function only resets the attribute device context.

An application will typically use the **ResetDC** member function when a window processes a **WM_DEVMODECHANGE** message. You can also use this member function to change the paper orientation or paper bins while printing a document.

You cannot use this member function to change the driver name, device name, or output port. When the user changes the port connection or device name, you must delete the original device context and create a new device context with the new information.

Before you call this member function, you must ensure that all objects (other than stock objects) that had been selected into the device context have been selected out.

See Also: **CDC::m_hAttribDC**, **::ResetDC**, **WM_DEVMODECHANGE**, **DEVMODE**

CDC::RestoreDC

virtual BOOL RestoreDC(int *nSavedDC* **);**

Return Value

Nonzero if the specified context was restored; otherwise 0.

Parameters

nSavedDC   Specifies the device context to be restored. It can be a value returned by a previous **SaveDC** function call. If *nSavedDC* is –1, the most recently saved device context is restored.

Remarks

Restores the device context to the previous state identified by *nSavedDC*. **RestoreDC** restores the device context by popping state information off a stack created by earlier calls to the **SaveDC** member function.

The stack can contain the state information for several device contexts. If the context specified by *nSavedDC* is not at the top of the stack, **RestoreDC** deletes all state information between the device context specified by *nSavedDC* and the top of the stack. The deleted information is lost.

See Also: **CDC::SaveDC**, **::RestoreDC**

CDC::RoundRect

BOOL RoundRect(int *x1*, **int** *y1*, **int** *x2*, **int** *y2*, **int** *x3*, **int** *y3* **);**
BOOL RoundRect(LPCRECT *lpRect*, **POINT** *point* **);**

Return Value

Nonzero if the function is successful; otherwise 0.

Parameters

x1   Specifies the x-coordinate of the upper-left corner of the rectangle (in logical units).

y1   Specifies the y-coordinate of the upper-left corner of the rectangle (in logical units).

x2   Specifies the x-coordinate of the lower-right corner of the rectangle (in logical units).

y2   Specifies the y-coordinate of the lower-right corner of the rectangle (in logical units).

x3   Specifies the width of the ellipse used to draw the rounded corners (in logical units).

y3   Specifies the height of the ellipse used to draw the rounded corners (in logical units).

lpRect Specifies the bounding rectangle in logical units. You can pass either a **CRect** object or a pointer to a **RECT** structure for this parameter.

point The x-coordinate of *point* specifies the width of the ellipse to draw the rounded corners (in logical units). The y-coordinate of *point* specifies the height of the ellipse to draw the rounded corners (in logical units). You can pass either a **POINT** structure or a **CPoint** object for this parameter.

Remarks

Draws a rectangle with rounded corners using the current pen. The interior of the rectangle is filled using the current brush.

The figure this function draws extends up to but does not include the right and bottom coordinates. This means that the height of the figure is $y2 - y1$ and the width of the figure is $x2 - x1$. Both the height and the width of the bounding rectangle must be greater than 2 units and less than 32,767 units.

See Also: CDC::Rectangle, **::RoundRect**, **CRect**, **RECT**, **POINT**, **CPoint**

CDC::SaveDC

virtual int SaveDC( );

Return Value

An integer identifying the saved device context. It is 0 if an error occurs. This return value can be used to restore the device context by calling **RestoreDC**.

Remarks

Saves the current state of the device context by copying state information (such as clipping region, selected objects, and mapping mode) to a context stack maintained by Windows. The saved device context can later be restored by using **RestoreDC**.

SaveDC can be used any number of times to save any number of device-context states.

See Also: CDC::RestoreDC, **::SaveDC**

CDC::ScaleViewportExt

virtual CSize ScaleViewportExt(int *xNum*, **int** *xDenom*, **int** *yNum*, **int** *yDenom* **);**

Return Value

The previous viewport extents (in device units) as a **CSize** object.

Parameters

xNum Specifies the amount by which to multiply the current x-extent.

xDenom Specifies the amount by which to divide the result of multiplying the current x-extent by the value of the *xNum* parameter.

yNum Specifies the amount by which to multiply the current y-extent.

yDenom Specifies the amount by which to divide the result of multiplying the current y-extent by the value of the *yNum* parameter.

Remarks

Modifies the viewport extents relative to the current values. The formulas are written as follows:

```
xNewVE = ( xOldVE * xNum ) / xDenom
yNewVE = ( yOldVE * yNum ) / yDenom
```

The new viewport extents are calculated by multiplying the current extents by the given numerator and then dividing by the given denominator.

See Also: CDC::GetViewportExt, CSize

CDC::ScaleWindowExt

virtual CSize ScaleWindowExt(int *xNum*, **int** *xDenom*, **int** *yNum*, **int** *yDenom* **);**

Return Value

The previous window extents (in logical units) as a **CSize** object.

Parameters

xNum Specifies the amount by which to multiply the current x-extent.

xDenom Specifies the amount by which to divide the result of multiplying the current x-extent by the value of the *xNum* parameter.

yNum Specifies the amount by which to multiply the current y-extent.

yDenom Specifies the amount by which to divide the result of multiplying the current y-extent by the value of the *yNum* parameter.

Remarks

Modifies the window extents relative to the current values. The formulas are written as follows:

```
xNewWE = ( xOldWE * xNum ) / xDenom
yNewWE = ( yOldWE * yNum ) / yDenom
```

The new window extents are calculated by multiplying the current extents by the given numerator and then dividing by the given denominator.

See Also: CDC::GetWindowExt, CSize

CDC::ScrollDC

BOOL ScrollDC(int *dx*, **int** *dy*, **LPCRECT** *lpRectScroll*, **LPCRECT** *lpRectClip*,
↪ **CRgn*** *pRgnUpdate*, **LPRECT** *lpRectUpdate* **);**

Return Value

Nonzero if scrolling is executed; otherwise 0.

Parameters

dx   Specifies the number of horizontal scroll units.

dy   Specifies the number of vertical scroll units.

lpRectScroll   Points to the **RECT** structure or **CRect** object that contains the coordinates of the scrolling rectangle.

lpRectClip   Points to the **RECT** structure or **CRect** object that contains the coordinates of the clipping rectangle. When this rectangle is smaller than the original one pointed to by *lpRectScroll*, scrolling occurs only in the smaller rectangle.

pRgnUpdate   Identifies the region uncovered by the scrolling process. The **ScrollDC** function defines this region; it is not necessarily a rectangle.

lpRectUpdate   Points to the **RECT** structure or **CRect** object that receives the coordinates of the rectangle that bounds the scrolling update region. This is the largest rectangular area that requires repainting. The values in the structure or object when the function returns are in client coordinates, regardless of the mapping mode for the given device context.

Remarks

Scrolls a rectangle of bits horizontally and vertically.

If *lpRectUpdate* is **NULL**, Windows does not compute the update rectangle. If both *pRgnUpdate* and *lpRectUpdate* are **NULL**, Windows does not compute the update region. If *pRgnUpdate* is not **NULL**, Windows assumes that it contains a valid pointer to the region uncovered by the scrolling process (defined by the **ScrollDC** member function). The update region returned in *lpRectUpdate* can be passed to **CWnd::InvalidateRgn** if required.

An application should use the **ScrollWindow** member function of class **CWnd** when it is necessary to scroll the entire client area of a window. Otherwise, it should use **ScrollDC**.

See Also: **CWnd::InvalidateRgn, CWnd::ScrollWindow, ::ScrollDC, CRgn, RECT, CRect**

CDC::SelectClipPath

BOOL SelectClipPath(int *nMode* **);**

Return Value

Nonzero if the function is successful; otherwise 0.

Parameters

nMode   Specifies the way to use the path. The following values are allowed:

- **RGN_AND**   The new clipping region includes the intersection (overlapping areas) of the current clipping region and the current path.

- **RGN_COPY** The new clipping region is the current path.

- **RGN_DIFF** The new clipping region includes the areas of the current clipping region, and those of the current path are excluded.

- **RGN_OR** The new clipping region includes the union (combined areas) of the current clipping region and the current path.

- **RGN_XOR** The new clipping region includes the union of the current clipping region and the current path, but without the overlapping areas.

Remarks

Selects the current path as a clipping region for the device context, combining the new region with any existing clipping region by using the specified mode. The device context identified must contain a closed path.

See Also: CDC::BeginPath, CDC::EndPath

CDC::SelectClipRgn

virtual int SelectClipRgn(CRgn* *pRgn* **);**
int SelectClipRgn(CRgn* *pRgn***, int** *nMode* **);**

Return Value

The region's type. It can be any of the following values:

- **COMPLEXREGION** New clipping region has overlapping borders.

- **ERROR** Device context or region is not valid.

- **NULLREGION** New clipping region is empty.

- **SIMPLEREGION** New clipping region has no overlapping borders.

Parameters

pRgn   Identifies the region to be selected.

- For the first version of this function, if this value is **NULL**, the entire client area is selected and output is still clipped to the window.

- For the second version of this function, this handle can be **NULL** only when the **RGN_COPY** mode is specified.

nMode   Specifies the operation to be performed. It must be one of the following values:

- **RGN_AND** The new clipping region combines the overlapping areas of the current clipping region and the region identified by *pRgn*.

- **RGN_COPY** The new clipping region is a copy of the region identified by *pRgn*. This is functionality is identical to the first version of **SelectClipRgn**. If the region identified by *pRgn* is **NULL**, the new clipping region becomes the default clipping region (a null region).

- **RGN_DIFF** The new clipping region combines the areas of the current clipping region with those areas excluded from the region identified by *pRgn*.

- **RGN_OR** The new clipping region combines the current clipping region and the region identified by *pRgn*.

- **RGN_XOR** The new clipping region combines the current clipping region and the region identified by *pRgn* but excludes any overlapping areas.

Remarks

Selects the given region as the current clipping region for the device context. Only a copy of the selected region is used. The region itself can be selected for any number of other device contexts, or it can be deleted.

The function assumes that the coordinates for the given region are specified in device units. Some printer devices support text output at a higher resolution than graphics output in order to retain the precision needed to express text metrics. These devices report device units at the higher resolution, that is, in text units. These devices then scale coordinates for graphics so that several reported device units map to only 1 graphic unit. You should always call the **SelectClipRgn** function using text units.

Applications that must take the scaling of graphics objects in the GDI can use the **GETSCALINGFACTOR** printer escape to determine the scaling factor. This scaling factor affects clipping. If a region is used to clip graphics, GDI divides the coordinates by the scaling factor. If the region is used to clip text, GDI makes no scaling adjustment. A scaling factor of 1 causes the coordinates to be divided by 2; a scaling factor of 2 causes the coordinates to be divided by 4; and so on.

See Also: **CDC::GetClipBox**, **CDC::Escape**, **CRgn::SelectClipRgn**

CDC::SelectObject

CPen* SelectObject(CPen* *pPen* **);**
CBrush* SelectObject(CBrush* *pBrush* **);**
virtual CFont* SelectObject(CFont* *pFont* **);**
CBitmap* SelectObject(CBitmap* *pBitmap* **);**
int SelectObject(CRgn* *pRgn* **);**

Return Value

A pointer to the object being replaced. This is a pointer to an object of one of the classes derived from **CGdiObject**, such as **CPen**, depending on which version of the function is used. The return value is **NULL** if there is an error. This function may return a pointer to a temporary object. This temporary object is only valid during the processing of one Windows message. For more information, see **CGdiObject::FromHandle**.

The version of the member function that takes a region parameter performs the same task as the **SelectClipRgn** member function. Its return value can be any of the following:

- **COMPLEXREGION** New clipping region has overlapping borders.
- **ERROR** Device context or region is not valid.
- **NULLREGION** New clipping region is empty.
- **SIMPLEREGION** New clipping region has no overlapping borders.

Parameters

pPen A pointer to a **CPen** object to be selected.

pBrush A pointer to a **CBrush** object to be selected.

pFont A pointer to a **CFont** object to be selected.

pBitmap A pointer to a **CBitmap** object to be selected.

pRgn A pointer to a **CRgn** object to be selected.

Remarks

Selects an object into the device context. Class **CDC** provides five versions specialized for particular kinds of GDI objects, including pens, brushes, fonts, bitmaps, and regions. The newly selected object replaces the previous object of the same type. For example, if *pObject* of the general version of **SelectObject** points to a **CPen** object, the function replaces the current pen with the pen specified by *pObject*.

An application can select a bitmap into memory device contexts only and into only one memory device context at a time. The format of the bitmap must either be monochrome or compatible with the device context; if it is not, **SelectObject** returns an error.

For Windows 3.1 and later, the **SelectObject** function returns the same value whether it is used in a metafile or not. Under previous versions of Windows, **SelectObject** returned a nonzero value for success and 0 for failure when it was used in a metafile.

See Also: **CGdiObject::DeleteObject**, **CGdiObject::FromHandle**, **CDC::SelectClipRgn**, **CDC::SelectPalette**, **::SelectObject**

CDC::SelectPalette

CPalette* SelectPalette(CPalette* *pPalette***, BOOL** *bForceBackground* **);**

Return Value

A pointer to a **CPalette** object identifying the logical palette replaced by the palette specified by *pPalette*. It is **NULL** if there is an error.

Parameters

pPalette Identifies the logical palette to be selected. This palette must already have been created with the **CPalette** member function **CreatePalette**.

bForceBackground   Specifies whether the logical palette is forced to be a background palette. If *bForceBackground* is nonzero, the selected palette is always a background palette, regardless of whether the window has the input focus. If *bForceBackground* is 0 and the device context is attached to a window, the logical palette is a foreground palette when the window has the input focus.

Remarks

Selects the logical palette that is specified by *pPalette* as the selected palette object of the device context. The new palette becomes the palette object used by GDI to control colors displayed in the device context and replaces the previous palette.

An application can select a logical palette into more than one device context. However, changes to a logical palette will affect all device contexts for which it is selected. If an application selects a palette into more than one device context, the device contexts must all belong to the same physical device.

See Also: CDC::RealizePalette, **CPalette**, **::SelectPalette**

CDC::SelectStockObject

virtual CGdiObject* SelectStockObject(int *nIndex*);

Return Value

A pointer to the **CGdiObject** object that was replaced if the function is successful. The actual object pointed to is a **CPen**, **CBrush**, or **CFont** object. If the call is unsuccessful, the return value is **NULL**.

Parameters

nIndex   Specifies the kind of stock object desired. It can be one of the following values:

- **BLACK_BRUSH**   Black brush.
- **DKGRAY_BRUSH**   Dark gray brush.
- **GRAY_BRUSH**   Gray brush.
- **HOLLOW_BRUSH**   Hollow brush.
- **LTGRAY_BRUSH**   Light gray brush.
- **NULL_BRUSH**   Null brush.
- **WHITE_BRUSH**   White brush.
- **BLACK_PEN**   Black pen.
- **NULL_PEN**   Null pen.
- **WHITE_PEN**   White pen.
- **ANSI_FIXED_FONT**   ANSI fixed system font.

- **ANSI_VAR_FONT**   ANSI variable system font.

- **DEVICE_DEFAULT_FONT**   Device-dependent font.

- **OEM_FIXED_FONT**   OEM-dependent fixed font.

- **SYSTEM_FONT**   The system font. By default, Windows uses the system font to draw menus, dialog-box controls, and other text. In Windows versions 3.0 and later, the system font is proportional width; earlier versions of Windows use a fixed-width system font.

- **SYSTEM_FIXED_FONT**   The fixed-width system font used in Windows prior to version 3.0. This object is available for compatibility with earlier versions of Windows.

- **DEFAULT_PALETTE**   Default color palette. This palette consists of the 20 static colors in the system palette.

Remarks

Selects a **CGdiObject** object that corresponds to one of the predefined stock pens, brushes, or fonts.

See Also: **CGdiObject::GetObject**

CDC::SetAbortProc

int SetAbortProc(BOOL (CALLBACK EXPORT* *lpfn* **)(HDC, int));**

Return Value

Specifies the outcome of the **SetAbortProc** function. Some of the following values are more probable than others, but all are possible.

- **SP_ERROR**   General error.

- **SP_OUTOFDISK**   Not enough disk space is currently available for spooling, and no more space will become available.

- **SP_OUTOFMEMORY**   Not enough memory is available for spooling.

- **SP_USERABORT**   User ended the job through the Print Manager.

Parameters

lpfn   A pointer to the abort function to install as the abort procedure. For more about the callback function, see "Callback Function for CDC::SetAbortProc."

Remarks

Installs the abort procedure for the print job.

If an application is to allow the print job to be canceled during spooling, it must set the abort function before the print job is started with the **StartDoc** member function. The Print Manager calls the abort function during spooling to allow the application to cancel the print job or to process out-of-disk-space conditions. If no abort function is set, the print job will fail if there is not enough disk space for spooling.

Note that the features of Microsoft Visual C++ simplify the creation of the callback function passed to **SetAbortProc**. The address passed to the **EnumObjects** member function is a pointer to a function exported with **__export** and with the Pascal calling convention. In protect-mode applications, you do not have to create this function with the Windows **MakeProcInstance** function or free the function after use with the Windows function **FreeProcInstance**.

You also do not have to export the function name in an **EXPORTS** statement in your application's module-definition file. You can instead use the **EXPORT** function modifier, as in

BOOL CALLBACK EXPORT AFunction(**HDC, int**);

to cause the compiler to emit the proper export record for export by name without aliasing. This works for most needs. For some special cases, such as exporting a function by ordinal or aliasing the export, you still need to use an **EXPORTS** statement in a module-definition file.

For compiling Microsoft Foundation programs, you'll normally use the /GA and /GEs compiler options. The /Gw compiler option is not used with the Microsoft Foundation classes. (If you do use the Windows function **MakeProcInstance**, you will need to explicitly cast the returned function pointer from **FARPROC** to the type needed by this member function.) Callback registration interfaces are now type-safe (you must pass in a function pointer that points to the right kind of function for the specific callback).

Also note that all callback functions must trap Microsoft Foundation exceptions before returning to Windows, since exceptions cannot be thrown across callback boundaries. For more information about exceptions, see the article "Exceptions" in *Visual C++ Programmer's Guide* online.

CDC::SetArcDirection

int SetArcDirection(int *nArcDirection*);

Return Value

Specifies the old arc direction, if successful; otherwise 0.

Parameters

nArcDirection   Specifies the new arc direction. This parameter can be either of the following values:

- **AD_COUNTERCLOCKWISE**   Figures drawn counterclockwise.

- **AD_CLOCKWISE**   Figures drawn clockwise.

Remarks

Sets the drawing direction to be used for arc and rectangle functions. The default direction is counterclockwise. The **SetArcDirection** function specifies the direction in which the following functions draw:

Arc	**Pie**
ArcTo	**Rectangle**
Chord	**RoundRect**
Ellipse	

See Also: **CDC::GetArcDirection**, **::SetArcDirection**

CDC::SetAttribDC

virtual void SetAttribDC(HDC *hDC* **);**

Parameters

hDC   A Windows device context.

Remarks

Call this function to set the attribute device context, **m_hAttribDC**. This member function does not attach the device context to the **CDC** object. Only the output device context is attached to a **CDC** object.

See Also: **CDC::SetOutputDC**, **CDC::ReleaseAttribDC**, **CDC::ReleaseOutputDC**

CDC::SetBkColor

virtual COLORREF SetBkColor(COLORREF *crColor* **);**

Return Value

The previous background color as an RGB color value. If an error occurs, the return value is 0x80000000.

Parameters

crColor   Specifies the new background color.

Remarks

Sets the current background color to the specified color. If the background mode is **OPAQUE**, the system uses the background color to fill the gaps in styled lines, the gaps between hatched lines in brushes, and the background in character cells. The system also uses the background color when converting bitmaps between color and monochrome device contexts.

If the device cannot display the specified color, the system sets the background color to the nearest physical color.

See Also: **CDC::BitBlt**, **CDC::GetBkColor**, **CDC::GetBkMode**, **CDC::SetBkMode**, **CDC::StretchBlt**, **::SetBkColor**

CDC::SetBkMode

int SetBkMode(int *nBkMode* **);**

Return Value

The previous background mode.

Parameters

nBkMode Specifies the mode to be set. This parameter can be either of the following values:

- **OPAQUE** Background is filled with the current background color before the text, hatched brush, or pen is drawn. This is the default background mode.

- **TRANSPARENT** Background is not changed before drawing.

Remarks

Sets the background mode. The background mode defines whether the system removes existing background colors on the drawing surface before drawing text, hatched brushes, or any pen style that is not a solid line.

See Also: **CDC::GetBkColor**, **CDC::GetBkMode**, **CDC::SetBkColor**, **::SetBkMode**

CDC::SetBoundsRect

UINT SetBoundsRect(LPCRECT *lpRectBounds*, **UINT** *flags* **);**

Return Value

The current state of the bounding rectangle, if the function is successful. Like *flags*, the return value can be a combination of **DCB_** values:

- **DCB_ACCUMULATE** The bounding rectangle is not empty. This value will always be set.

- **DCB_DISABLE** Bounds accumulation is off.

- **DCB_ENABLE** Bounds accumulation is on.

Parameters

lpRectBounds Points to a **RECT** structure or **CRect** object that is used to set the bounding rectangle. Rectangle dimensions are given in logical coordinates. This parameter can be **NULL**.

flags Specifies how the new rectangle will be combined with the accumulated rectangle. This parameter can be a combination of the following values:

- **DCB_ACCUMULATE** Add the rectangle specified by *lpRectBounds* to the bounding rectangle (using a rectangle-union operation).

- **DCB_DISABLE** Turn off bounds accumulation.

- **DCB_ENABLE** Turn on bounds accumulation. (The default setting for bounds accumulation is disabled.)

Remarks

Controls the accumulation of bounding-rectangle information for the specified device context.

Windows can maintain a bounding rectangle for all drawing operations. This rectangle can be queried and reset by the application. The drawing bounds are useful for invalidating bitmap caches.

See Also: **CDC::GetBoundsRect**, **::SetBoundsRect**, **RECT**, **CRect**

CDC::SetBrushOrg

CPoint SetBrushOrg(int *x*, int *y*);
CPoint SetBrushOrg(POINT *point*);

Return Value

The previous origin of the brush in device units.

Parameters

x Specifies the x-coordinate (in device units) of the new origin. This value must be in the range 0–7.

y Specifies the y-coordinate (in device units) of the new origin. This value must be in the range 0–7.

point Specifies the x- and y-coordinates of the new origin. Each value must be in the range 0–7. You can pass either a **POINT** structure or a **CPoint** object for this parameter.

Remarks

Specifies the origin that GDI will assign to the next brush that the application selects into the device context.

The default coordinates for the brush origin are (0, 0). To alter the origin of a brush, call the **UnrealizeObject** function for the **CBrush** object, call **SetBrushOrg**, and then call the **SelectObject** member function to select the brush into the device context.

Do not use **SetBrushOrg** with stock **CBrush** objects.

See Also: **CBrush**, **CDC::GetBrushOrg**, **CDC::SelectObject**, **CGdiObject::UnrealizeObject**, **POINT**, **CPoint**

CDC::SetColorAdjustment

BOOL SetColorAdjustment(const COLORADJUSTMENT* *lpColorAdjust* **);**

Return Value

Nonzero if successful; otherwise 0.

Parameters

lpColorAdjust   Points to a **COLORADJUSTMENT** data structure containing the color adjustment values.

Remarks

Sets the color adjustment values for the device context using the specified values. The color adjustment values are used to adjust the input color of the source bitmap for calls to the **CDC::StretchBlt** member function when **HALFTONE** mode is set.

See Also: CDC::SetStretchBltMode, CDC::StretchBlt, ::StretchDIBits

---

CDC::SetMapMode

virtual int SetMapMode(int *nMapMode* **);**

Return Value

The previous mapping mode.

Parameters

nMapMode   Specifies the new mapping mode. It can be any one of the following values:

- **MM_ANISOTROPIC**   Logical units are converted to arbitrary units with arbitrarily scaled axes. Setting the mapping mode to **MM_ANISOTROPIC** does not change the current window or viewport settings. To change the units, orientation, and scaling, call the **SetWindowExt** and **SetViewportExt** member functions.

- **MM_HIENGLISH**   Each logical unit is converted to 0.001 inch. Positive x is to the right; positive y is up.

- **MM_HIMETRIC**   Each logical unit is converted to 0.01 millimeter. Positive x is to the right; positive y is up.

- **MM_ISOTROPIC**   Logical units are converted to arbitrary units with equally scaled axes; that is, 1 unit along the x-axis is equal to 1 unit along the y-axis. Use the **SetWindowExt** and **SetViewportExt** member functions to specify the desired units and the orientation of the axes. GDI makes adjustments as necessary to ensure that the x and y units remain the same size.

- **MM_LOENGLISH**   Each logical unit is converted to 0.01 inch. Positive x is to the right; positive y is up.

- **MM_LOMETRIC**   Each logical unit is converted to 0.1 millimeter. Positive x is to the right; positive y is up.

- **MM_TEXT**   Each logical unit is converted to 1 device pixel. Positive x is to the right; positive y is down.

- **MM_TWIPS**   Each logical unit is converted to 1/20 of a point. (Because a point is 1/72 inch, a twip is 1/1440 inch.) Positive x is to the right; positive y is up.

Remarks

Sets the mapping mode. The mapping mode defines the unit of measure used to convert logical units to device units; it also defines the orientation of the device's x- and y-axes. GDI uses the mapping mode to convert logical coordinates into the appropriate device coordinates. The **MM_TEXT** mode allows applications to work in device pixels, where 1 unit is equal to 1 pixel. The physical size of a pixel varies from device to device.

The **MM_HIENGLISH, MM_HIMETRIC, MM_LOENGLISH, MM_LOMETRIC,** and **MM_TWIPS** modes are useful for applications that must draw in physically meaningful units (such as inches or millimeters). The **MM_ISOTROPIC** mode ensures a 1:1 aspect ratio, which is useful when it is important to preserve the exact shape of an image. The **MM_ANISOTROPIC** mode allows the x- and y-coordinates to be adjusted independently.

See Also: **CDC::SetViewportExt, CDC::SetWindowExt, ::SetMapMode**

CDC::SetMapperFlags

DWORD SetMapperFlags(DWORD *dwFlag* **);**

Return Value

The previous value of the font-mapper flag.

Parameters

dwFlag   Specifies whether the font mapper attempts to match a font's aspect height and width to the device. When this value is **ASPECT_FILTERING**, the mapper selects only fonts whose x-aspect and y-aspect exactly match those of the specified device.

Remarks

Changes the method used by the font mapper when it converts a logical font to a physical font. An application can use **SetMapperFlags** to cause the font mapper to attempt to choose only a physical font that exactly matches the aspect ratio of the specified device.

An application that uses only raster fonts can use the **SetMapperFlags** function to ensure that the font selected by the font mapper is attractive and readable on the specified device. Applications that use scalable (TrueType) fonts typically do not use **SetMapperFlags**.

If no physical font has an aspect ratio that matches the specification in the logical font, GDI chooses a new aspect ratio and selects a font that matches this new aspect ratio.

See Also: **::SetMapperFlags**

CDC::SetMiterLimit

BOOL SetMiterLimit(float *fMiterLimit* **);**

Return Value

Nonzero if the function is successful; otherwise 0.

Parameters

fMiterLimit   Specifies the new miter limit for the device context.

Remarks

Sets the limit for the length of miter joins for the device context. The miter length is defined as the distance from the intersection of the line walls on the inside of the join to the intersection of the line walls on the outside of the join. The miter limit is the maximum allowed ratio of the miter length to the line width. The default miter limit is 10.0.

See Also: **CDC::GetMiterLimit**, **::SetMiterLimit**

CDC::SetOutputDC

virtual void SetOutputDC(HDC *hDC* **);**

Parameters

hDC   A Windows device context.

Remarks

Call this member function to set the output device context, **m_hDC**. This member function can only be called when a device context has not been attached to the **CDC** object. This member function sets **m_hDC** but does not attach the device context to the **CDC** object.

See Also: **CDC::SetAttribDC**, **CDC::ReleaseAttribDC**, **CDC::ReleaseOutputDC**, **CDC::m_hDC**

CDC::SetPixel

COLORREF SetPixel(int *x*, **int** *y*, **COLORREF** *crColor* **);**
COLORREF SetPixel(POINT *point*, **COLORREF** *crColor* **);**

Return Value

An RGB value for the color that the point is actually painted. This value can be different from that specified by *crColor* if an approximation of that color is used.

If the function fails (if the point is outside the clipping region), the return value is −1.

Parameters

x   Specifies the logical x-coordinate of the point to be set.

y   Specifies the logical y-coordinate of the point to be set.

crColor   Specifies the color used to paint the point.

point   Specifies the logical x- and y-coordinates of the point to be set. You can pass either a **POINT** structure or a **CPoint** object for this parameter.

Remarks

Sets the pixel at the point specified to the closest approximation of the color specified by *crColor*. The point must be in the clipping region. If the point is not in the clipping region, the function does nothing.

Not all devices support the **SetPixel** function. To determine whether a device supports **SetPixel**, call the **GetDeviceCaps** member function with the **RASTERCAPS** index and check the return value for the **RC_BITBLT** flag.

See Also: **CDC::GetDeviceCaps, CDC::GetPixel, ::SetPixel, POINT, CPoint**

CDC::SetPixelV

BOOL SetPixelV(int *x***, int** *y***, COLORREF** *crColor***)**;
BOOL SetPixelV(POINT *point***, COLORREF** *crColor* **)**;

Return Value

Nonzero if the function is successful; otherwise 0.

Parameters

x   Specifies the x-coordinate, in logical units, of the point to be set.

y   Specifies the y-coordinate, in logical units, of the point to be set.

crColor   Specifies the color to be used to paint the point.

point   Specifies the logical x- and y-coordinates of the point to be set. You can pass either a **POINT** data structure or a **CPoint** object for this parameter.

Remarks

Sets the pixel at the specified coordinates to the closest approximation of the specified color. The point must be in both the clipping region and the visible part of the device surface. Not all devices support the member function. For more information, see the **RC_BITBLT** capability in the **CDC::GetDeviceCaps** member function. **SetPixelV** is faster than **SetPixel** because it does not need to return the color value of the point actually painted.

See Also: **CDC::GetDeviceCaps, CDC::SetPixel, ::SetPixelV**

CDC::SetPolyFillMode

int **SetPolyFillMode**(int *nPolyFillMode*);

Return Value

The previous filling mode, if successful; otherwise 0.

Parameters

nPolyFillMode   Specifies the new filling mode. This value may be either
ALTERNATE or **WINDING**. The default mode set in Windows is
ALTERNATE.

Remarks

Sets the polygon-filling mode.

When the polygon-filling mode is **ALTERNATE**, the system fills the area between
odd-numbered and even-numbered polygon sides on each scan line. That is, the
system fills the area between the first and second side, between the third and fourth
side, and so on. This mode is the default.

When the polygon-filling mode is **WINDING**, the system uses the direction in which
a figure was drawn to determine whether to fill an area. Each line segment in a
polygon is drawn in either a clockwise or a counterclockwise direction. Whenever an
imaginary line drawn from an enclosed area to the outside of a figure passes through a
clockwise line segment, a count is incremented. When the line passes through a
counterclockwise line segment, the count is decremented. The area is filled if the
count is nonzero when the line reaches the outside of the figure.

See Also: **CDC::GetPolyFillMode**, **CDC::PolyPolygon**, **::SetPolyFillMode**

CDC::SetROP2

int **SetROP2**(int *nDrawMode*);

Return Value

The previous drawing mode.

It can be any of the values given in the Windows SDK documentation.

Parameters

nDrawMode   Specifies the new drawing mode. It can be any of the following values:

- **R2_BLACK**   Pixel is always black.

- **R2_WHITE**   Pixel is always white.

- **R2_NOP**   Pixel remains unchanged.

- **R2_NOT**   Pixel is the inverse of the screen color.

- **R2_COPYPEN**   Pixel is the pen color.

- **R2_NOTCOPYPEN**   Pixel is the inverse of the pen color.

- **R2_MERGEPENNOT**   Pixel is a combination of the pen color and the inverse of the screen color (final pixel = (NOT screen pixel) OR pen).

- **R2_MASKPENNOT**   Pixel is a combination of the colors common to both the pen and the inverse of the screen (final pixel = (NOT screen pixel) AND pen).

- **R2_MERGENOTPEN**   Pixel is a combination of the screen color and the inverse of the pen color (final pixel = (NOT pen) OR screen pixel).

- **R2_MASKNOTPEN**   Pixel is a combination of the colors common to both the screen and the inverse of the pen (final pixel = (NOT pen) AND screen pixel).

- **R2_MERGEPEN**   Pixel is a combination of the pen color and the screen color (final pixel = pen OR screen pixel).

- **R2_NOTMERGEPEN**   Pixel is the inverse of the **R2_MERGEPEN** color (final pixel = NOT(pen OR screen pixel)).

- **R2_MASKPEN**   Pixel is a combination of the colors common to both the pen and the screen (final pixel = pen AND screen pixel).

- **R2_NOTMASKPEN**   Pixel is the inverse of the **R2_MASKPEN** color (final pixel = NOT(pen AND screen pixel)).

- **R2_XORPEN**   Pixel is a combination of the colors that are in the pen or in the screen, but not in both (final pixel = pen XOR screen pixel).

- **R2_NOTXORPEN**   Pixel is the inverse of the **R2_XORPEN** color (final pixel = NOT(pen XOR screen pixel)).

Remarks

Sets the current drawing mode. The drawing mode specifies how the colors of the pen and the interior of filled objects are combined with the color already on the display surface.

The drawing mode is for raster devices only; it does not apply to vector devices. Drawing modes are binary raster-operation codes representing all possible Boolean combinations of two variables, using the binary operators AND, OR, and XOR (exclusive OR), and the unary operation NOT.

See Also: **CDC::GetDeviceCaps, CDC::GetROP2, ::SetROP2**

CDC::SetStretchBltMode

int SetStretchBltMode(int *nStretchMode* **);**

Return Value

The previous stretching mode. It can be **STRETCH_ANDSCANS**, **STRETCH_DELETESCANS**, or **STRETCH_ORSCANS**.

Parameters

nStretchMode   Specifies the stretching mode. It can be any of the following values:

Value	Description
BLACKONWHITE	Performs a Boolean AND operation using the color values for the eliminated and existing pixels. If the bitmap is a monochrome bitmap, this mode preserves black pixels at the expense of white pixels.
COLORONCOLOR	Deletes the pixels. This mode deletes all eliminated lines of pixels without trying to preserve their information.
HALFTONE	Maps pixels from the source rectangle into blocks of pixels in the destination rectangle. The average color over the destination block of pixels approximates the color of the source pixels.
	After setting the **HALFTONE** stretching mode, an application must call the Win32 function **::SetBrushOrgEx** to set the brush origin. If it fails to do so, brush misalignment occurs.
STRETCH_ANDSCANS	**Windows 95**: Same as **BLACKONWHITE**
STRETCH_DELETESCANS	**Windows 95**: Same as **COLORONCOLOR**
STRETCH_HALFTONE	**Windows 95**: Same as **HALFTONE**.
STRETCH_ORSCANS	**Windows 95**: Same as **WHITEONBLACK**
WHITEONBLACK	Performs a Boolean OR operation using the color values for the eliminated and existing pixels. If the bitmap is a monochrome bitmap, this mode preserves white pixels at the expense of black pixels.

Remarks

Sets the bitmap-stretching mode for the **StretchBlt** member function. The bitmap-stretching mode defines how information is removed from bitmaps that are compressed by using the function.

The **BLACKONWHITE** (**STRETCH_ANDSCANS**) and **WHITEONBLACK** (**STRETCH_ORSCANS**) modes are typically used to preserve foreground pixels in monochrome bitmaps. The **COLORONCOLOR** (**STRETCH_DELETESCANS**) mode is typically used to preserve color in color bitmaps.

The **HALFTONE** mode requires more processing of the source image than the other three modes; it is slower than the others, but produces higher quality images. Also note that **SetBrushOrgEx** must be called after setting the **HALFTONE** mode to avoid brush misalignment.

Additional stretching modes might also be available depending on the capabilities of the device driver.

See Also: **CDC::GetStretchBltMode**, **CDC::StretchBlt**, **::SetStretchBltMode**

CDC::SetTextAlign

UINT SetTextAlign(UINT *nFlags* **);**

Return Value

The previous text-alignment setting, if successful. The low-order byte contains the horizontal setting and the high-order byte contains the vertical setting; otherwise 0.

Parameters

nFlags   Specifies text-alignment flags. The flags specify the relationship between a point and a rectangle that bounds the text. The point can be either the current position or coordinates specified by a text-output function. The rectangle that bounds the text is defined by the adjacent character cells in the text string. The *nFlags* parameter can be one or more flags from the following three categories. Choose only one flag from each category. The first category affects text alignment in the x-direction:

- **TA_CENTER**   Aligns the point with the horizontal center of the bounding rectangle.

- **TA_LEFT**   Aligns the point with the left side of the bounding rectangle. This is the default setting.

- **TA_RIGHT**   Aligns the point with the right side of the bounding rectangle.

The second category affects text alignment in the y-direction:

- **TA_BASELINE**   Aligns the point with the base line of the chosen font.

- **TA_BOTTOM**   Aligns the point with the bottom of the bounding rectangle.

- **TA_TOP**   Aligns the point with the top of the bounding rectangle. This is the default setting.

The third category determines whether the current position is updated when text is written:

- **TA_NOUPDATECP**   Does not update the current position after each call to a text-output function. This is the default setting.

- **TA_UPDATECP**   Updates the current x-position after each call to a text-output function. The new position is at the right side of the bounding rectangle for the text. When this flag is set, the coordinates specified in calls to the **TextOut** member function are ignored.

Remarks

Sets the text-alignment flags.

The **TextOut** and **ExtTextOut** member functions use these flags when positioning a string of text on a display or device. The flags specify the relationship between a specific point and a rectangle that bounds the text. The coordinates of this point are passed as parameters to the **TextOut** member function. The rectangle that bounds the text is formed by the adjacent character cells in the text string.

See Also: CDC::ExtTextOut, CDC::GetTextAlign, CDC::TabbedTextOut, CDC::TextOut, ::SetTextAlign

CDC::SetTextCharacterExtra

int SetTextCharacterExtra(int *nCharExtra* **);**

Return Value

The amount of the previous intercharacter spacing.

Parameters

nCharExtra   Specifies the amount of extra space (in logical units) to be added to each character. If the current mapping mode is not **MM_TEXT**, *nCharExtra* is transformed and rounded to the nearest pixel.

Remarks

Sets the amount of intercharacter spacing. GDI adds this spacing to each character, including break characters, when it writes a line of text to the device context. The default value for the amount of intercharacter spacing is 0.

See Also: CDC::GetTextCharacterExtra, ::SetTextCharacterExtra

CDC::SetTextColor

virtual COLORREF SetTextColor(COLORREF *crColor* **);**

Return Value

An RGB value for the previous text color.

Parameters

crColor   Specifies the color of the text as an RGB color value.

Remarks

Sets the text color to the specified color. The system will use this text color when writing text to this device context and also when converting bitmaps between color and monochrome device contexts.

If the device cannot represent the specified color, the system sets the text color to the nearest physical color. The background color for a character is specified by the **SetBkColor** and **SetBkMode** member functions.

See Also: CDC::GetTextColor, CDC::BitBlt, CDC::SetBkColor, CDC::SetBkMode, ::SetTextColor

CDC::SetTextJustification

int **SetTextJustification**(int *nBreakExtra*, int *nBreakCount*);

Return Value

One if the function is successful; otherwise 0.

Parameters

nBreakExtra   Specifies the total extra space to be added to the line of text (in logical units). If the current mapping mode is not **MM_TEXT**, the value given by this parameter is converted to the current mapping mode and rounded to the nearest device unit.

nBreakCount   Specifies the number of break characters in the line.

Remarks

Adds space to the break characters in a string. An application can use the **GetTextMetrics** member functions to retrieve a font's break character.

After the **SetTextJustification** member function is called, a call to a text-output function (such as **TextOut**) distributes the specified extra space evenly among the specified number of break characters. The break character is usually the space character (ASCII 32), but may be defined by a font as some other character.

The member function **GetTextExtent** is typically used with **SetTextJustification**. **GetTextExtent** computes the width of a given line before alignment. An application can determine how much space to specify in the *nBreakExtra* parameter by subtracting the value returned by **GetTextExtent** from the width of the string after alignment.

The **SetTextJustification** function can be used to align a line that contains multiple runs in different fonts. In this case, the line must be created piecemeal by aligning and writing each run separately.

Because rounding errors can occur during alignment, the system keeps a running error term that defines the current error. When aligning a line that contains multiple runs, **GetTextExtent** automatically uses this error term when it computes the extent of the next run. This allows the text-output function to blend the error into the new run.

After each line has been aligned, this error term must be cleared to prevent it from being incorporated into the next line. The term can be cleared by calling **SetTextJustification** with *nBreakExtra* set to 0.

See Also: **CDC::GetMapMode, CDC::GetTextExtent, CDC::GetTextMetrics, CDC::SetMapMode, CDC::TextOut, ::SetTextJustification**

CDC::SetViewportExt

virtual CSize SetViewportExt(int *cx***, int** *cy* **);**
virtual CSize SetViewportExt(SIZE *size* **);**

Return Value

The previous extents of the viewport as a **CSize** object. When an error occurs, the x- and y-coordinates of the returned **CSize** object are both set to 0.

Parameters

cx   Specifies the x-extent of the viewport (in device units).

cy   Specifies the y-extent of the viewport (in device units).

size   Specifies the x- and y-extents of the viewport (in device units).

Remarks

Sets the x- and y-extents of the viewport of the device context. The viewport, along with the device-context window, defines how GDI maps points in the logical coordinate system to points in the coordinate system of the actual device. In other words, they define how GDI converts logical coordinates into device coordinates.

When the following mapping modes are set, calls to **SetWindowExt** and **SetViewportExt** are ignored:

MM_HIENGLISH	**MM_LOMETRIC**
MM_HIMETRIC	**MM_TEXT**
MM_LOENGLISH	**MM_TWIPS**

When **MM_ISOTROPIC** mode is set, an application must call the **SetWindowExt** member function before it calls **SetViewportExt**.

See Also: **CDC::SetWindowExt**, **CSize**, **CDC::GetViewportExt**

CDC::SetViewportOrg

virtual CPoint SetViewportOrg(int *x***, int** *y* **);**
virtual CPoint SetViewportOrg(POINT *point* **);**

Return Value

The previous origin of the viewport (in device coordinates) as a **CPoint** object.

Parameters

x   Specifies the x-coordinate (in device units) of the origin of the viewport. The value must be within the range of the device coordinate system.

y   Specifies the y-coordinate (in device units) of the origin of the viewport. The value must be within the range of the device coordinate system.

point   Specifies the origin of the viewport. The values must be within the range of the device coordinate system. You can pass either a **POINT** structure or a **CPoint** object for this parameter.

Remarks

Sets the viewport origin of the device context. The viewport, along with the device-context window, defines how GDI maps points in the logical coordinate system to points in the coordinate system of the actual device. In other words, they define how GDI converts logical coordinates into device coordinates.

The viewport origin marks the point in the device coordinate system to which GDI maps the window origin, a point in the logical coordinate system specified by the **SetWindowOrg** member function. GDI maps all other points by following the same process required to map the window origin to the viewport origin. For example, all points in a circle around the point at the window origin will be in a circle around the point at the viewport origin. Similarly, all points in a line that passes through the window origin will be in a line that passes through the viewport origin.

See Also: CDC::SetWindowOrg, CPoint, POINT, CDC::GetViewportOrg

CDC::SetWindowExt

virtual CSize SetWindowExt(int *cx*, **int** *cy* **);**
virtual CSize SetWindowExt(SIZE *size* **);**

Return Value

The previous extents of the window (in logical units) as a **CSize** object. If an error occurs, the x- and y-coordinates of the returned **CSize** object are both set to 0.

Parameters

cx   Specifies the x-extent (in logical units) of the window.

cy   Specifies the y-extent (in logical units) of the window.

size   Specifies the x- and y-extents (in logical units) of the window.

Remarks

Sets the x- and y-extents of the window associated with the device context. The window, along with the device-context viewport, defines how GDI maps points in the logical coordinate system to points in the device coordinate system.

When the following mapping modes are set, calls to **SetWindowExt** and **SetViewportExt** functions are ignored:

- **MM_HIENGLISH**
- **MM_HIMETRIC**
- **MM_LOENGLISH**
- **MM_LOMETRIC**

- **MM_TEXT**
- **MM_TWIPS**

When **MM_ISOTROPIC** mode is set, an application must call the **SetWindowExt** member function before calling **SetViewportExt**.

See Also: **CDC::GetWindowExt, CDC::SetViewportExt, CSize**

CDC::SetWindowOrg

CPoint SetWindowOrg(int *x*, **int** *y* **);**
CPoint SetWindowOrg(POINT *point* **);**

Return Value

The previous origin of the window as a **CPoint** object.

Parameters

x   Specifies the logical x-coordinate of the new origin of the window.

y   Specifies the logical y-coordinate of the new origin of the window.

point   Specifies the logical coordinates of the new origin of the window. You can pass either a **POINT** structure or a **CPoint** object for this parameter.

Remarks

Sets the window origin of the device context. The window, along with the device-context viewport, defines how GDI maps points in the logical coordinate system to points in the device coordinate system.

The window origin marks the point in the logical coordinate system from which GDI maps the viewport origin, a point in the device coordinate system specified by the **SetWindowOrg** function. GDI maps all other points by following the same process required to map the window origin to the viewport origin. For example, all points in a circle around the point at the window origin will be in a circle around the point at the viewport origin. Similarly, all points in a line that passes through the window origin will be in a line that passes through the viewport origin.

See Also: **CPoint, POINT, CDC::GetWindowOrg**

CDC::StartDoc

int StartDoc(LPDOCINFO *lpDocInfo* **);**

Return Value

The value –1 if there is an error such as insufficient memory or an invalid port specification occurs; otherwise a positive value.

Parameters

lpDocInfo   Points to a **DOCINFO** structure containing the name of the document file and the name of the output file.

Remarks

Informs the device driver that a new print job is starting and that all subsequent **StartPage** and **EndPage** calls should be spooled under the same job until an **EndDoc** call occurs. This ensures that documents longer than one page will not be interspersed with other jobs.

For Windows versions 3.1 and later, this function replaces the **STARTDOC** printer escape. Using this function ensures that documents containing more than one page are not interspersed with other print jobs.

StartDoc should not be used inside metafiles.

See Also: **CDC::Escape, CDC::EndDoc, CDC::AbortDoc**

CDC::StartPage

int StartPage( );

Remarks

Call this member function to prepare the printer driver to receive data. **StartPage** supersedes the **NEWFRAME** and **BANDINFO** escapes.

For an overview of the sequence of printing calls, see the **StartDoc** member function.

The system disables the **ResetDC** member function between calls to **StartPage** and **EndPage**.

See Also: **CDC::Escape, CDC::EndPage**

CDC::StretchBlt

BOOL StretchBlt(int *x***, int** *y***, int** *nWidth***, int** *nHeight***, CDC*** *pSrcDC***, int** *xSrc***,**
  ↪ **int** *ySrc***, int** *nSrcWidth***, int** *nSrcHeight***, DWORD** *dwRop* **);**

Return Value

Nonzero if the bitmap is drawn; otherwise 0.

Parameters

x   Specifies the x-coordinate (in logical units) of the upper-left corner of the destination rectangle.

y   Specifies the y-coordinate (in logical units) of the upper-left corner of the destination rectangle.

nWidth   Specifies the width (in logical units) of the destination rectangle.

nHeight   Specifies the height (in logical units) of the destination rectangle.

pSrcDC   Specifies the source device context.

xSrc   Specifies the x-coordinate (in logical units) of the upper-left corner of the source rectangle.

ySrc   Specifies the x-coordinate (in logical units) of the upper-left corner of the source rectangle.

nSrcWidth   Specifies the width (in logical units) of the source rectangle.

nSrcHeight   Specifies the height (in logical units) of the source rectangle.

dwRop   Specifies the raster operation to be performed. Raster operation codes define how GDI combines colors in output operations that involve a current brush, a possible source bitmap, and a destination bitmap. This parameter may be one of the following values:

- **BLACKNESS**   Turns all output black.
- **DSTINVERT**   Inverts the destination bitmap.
- **MERGECOPY**   Combines the pattern and the source bitmap using the Boolean AND operator.
- **MERGEPAINT**   Combines the inverted source bitmap with the destination bitmap using the Boolean OR operator.
- **NOTSRCCOPY**   Copies the inverted source bitmap to the destination.
- **NOTSRCERASE**   Inverts the result of combining the destination and source bitmaps using the Boolean OR operator.
- **PATCOPY**   Copies the pattern to the destination bitmap.
- **PATINVERT**   Combines the destination bitmap with the pattern using the Boolean XOR operator.
- **PATPAINT**   Combines the inverted source bitmap with the pattern using the Boolean OR operator. Combines the result of this operation with the destination bitmap using the Boolean OR operator.
- **SRCAND**   Combines pixels of the destination and source bitmaps using the Boolean AND operator.
- **SRCCOPY**   Copies the source bitmap to the destination bitmap.
- **SRCERASE**   Inverts the destination bitmap and combines the result with the source bitmap using the Boolean AND operator.
- **SRCINVERT**   Combines pixels of the destination and source bitmaps using the Boolean XOR operator.
- **SRCPAINT**   Combines pixels of the destination and source bitmaps using the Boolean OR operator.
- **WHITENESS**   Turns all output white.

Remarks

Copies a bitmap from a source rectangle into a destination rectangle, stretching or compressing the bitmap if necessary to fit the dimensions of the destination rectangle. The function uses the stretching mode of the destination device context (set by **SetStretchBltMode**) to determine how to stretch or compress the bitmap.

The **StretchBlt** function moves the bitmap from the source device given by *pSrcDC* to the destination device represented by the device-context object whose member function is being called. The *xSrc*, *ySrc*, *nSrcWidth*, and *nSrcHeight* parameters define the upper-left corner and dimensions of the source rectangle. The *x*, *y*, *nWidth*, and *nHeight* parameters give the upper-left corner and dimensions of the destination rectangle. The raster operation specified by *dwRop* defines how the source bitmap and the bits already on the destination device are combined.

The **StretchBlt** function creates a mirror image of a bitmap if the signs of the *nSrcWidth* and *nWidth* or *nSrcHeight* and *nHeight* parameters differ. If *nSrcWidth* and *nWidth* have different signs, the function creates a mirror image of the bitmap along the x-axis. If *nSrcHeight* and *nHeight* have different signs, the function creates a mirror image of the bitmap along the y-axis.

The **StretchBlt** function stretches or compresses the source bitmap in memory and then copies the result to the destination. If a pattern is to be merged with the result, it is not merged until the stretched source bitmap is copied to the destination. If a brush is used, it is the selected brush in the destination device context. The destination coordinates are transformed according to the destination device context; the source coordinates are transformed according to the source device context.

If the destination, source, and pattern bitmaps do not have the same color format, **StretchBlt** converts the source and pattern bitmaps to match the destination bitmaps. The foreground and background colors of the destination device context are used in the conversion.

If **StretchBlt** must convert a monochrome bitmap to color, it sets white bits (1) to the background color and black bits (0) to the foreground color. To convert color to monochrome, it sets pixels that match the background color to white (1) and sets all other pixels to black (0). The foreground and background colors of the device context with color are used.

Not all devices support the **StretchBlt** function. To determine whether a device supports **StretchBlt**, call the **GetDeviceCaps** member function with the **RASTERCAPS** index and check the return value for the **RC_STRETCHBLT** flag.

See Also: **CDC::BitBlt, CDC::GetDeviceCaps, CDC::SetStretchBltMode, ::StretchBlt**

CDC::StrokeAndFillPath

BOOL StrokeAndFillPath( );

Return Value

Nonzero if the function is successful; otherwise 0.

Remarks

Closes any open figures in a path, strokes the outline of the path by using the current pen, and fills its interior by using the current brush. The device context must contain a closed path. The **StrokeAndFillPath** member function has the same effect as closing all the open figures in the path, and stroking and filling the path separately, except that the filled region will not overlap the stroked region even if the pen is wide.

See Also: CDC::BeginPath, CDC::FillPath, CDC::SetPolyFillMode, CDC::StrokePath, ::StrokeAndFillPath

---

CDC::StrokePath

BOOL StrokePath( );

Return Value

Nonzero if the function is successful; otherwise 0.

Remarks

Renders the specified path by using the current pen. The device context must contain a closed path.

See Also: CDC::BeginPath, CDC::EndPath, ::StrokePath

CDC::TabbedTextOut

virtual CSize TabbedTextOut(int *x*, **int** *y*, **LPCTSTR** *lpszString*, **int** *nCount*,
↪ **int** *nTabPositions*, **LPINT** *lpnTabStopPositions*, **int** *nTabOrigin* **);**
CSize TabbedTextOut(int *x*, **int** *y*, **const CString&** *str*, **int** *nTabPositions*,
↪ **LPINT** *lpnTabStopPositions*, **int** *nTabOrigin* **);**

Return Value

The dimensions of the string (in logical units) as a **CSize** object.

Parameters

x Specifies the logical x-coordinate of the starting point of the string.

y Specifies the logical y-coordinate of the starting point of the string.

lpszString Points to the character string to draw. You can pass either a pointer to an array of characters or a **CString** object for this parameter.

nCount   Specifies the number of characters in the string. If *nCount* is –1, the length is calculated.

nTabPositions   Specifies the number of values in the array of tab-stop positions.

lpnTabStopPositions   Points to an array containing the tab-stop positions (in logical units). The tab stops must be sorted in increasing order; the smallest x-value should be the first item in the array.

nTabOrigin   Specifies the x-coordinate of the starting position from which tabs are expanded (in logical units).

str   A **CString** object that contains the specified characters.

Remarks

Call this member function to write a character string at the specified location, expanding tabs to the values specified in the array of tab-stop positions. Text is written in the currently selected font. If *nTabPositions* is 0 and *lpnTabStopPositions* is **NULL**, tabs are expanded to eight times the average character width.

If *nTabPositions* is 1, the tab stops are separated by the distance specified by the first value in the *lpnTabStopPositions* array. If the *lpnTabStopPositions* array contains more than one value, a tab stop is set for each value in the array, up to the number specified by *nTabPositions*. The *nTabOrigin* parameter allows an application to call the **TabbedTextOut** function several times for a single line. If the application calls the function more than once with the *nTabOrigin* set to the same value each time, the function expands all tabs relative to the position specified by *nTabOrigin*.

By default, the current position is not used or updated by the function. If an application needs to update the current position when it calls the function, the application can call the **SetTextAlign** member function with *nFlags* set to **TA_UPDATECP**. When this flag is set, Windows ignores the *x* and *y* parameters on subsequent calls to **TabbedTextOut**, using the current position instead.

See Also: **CDC::GetTabbedTextExtent**, **CDC::SetTextAlign**, **CDC::TextOut**, **CDC::SetTextColor**, **::TabbedTextOut**, **CSize**

CDC::TextOut

virtual BOOL TextOut(int *x***, int** *y***, LPCTSTR** *lpszString***, int** *nCount* **);**
BOOL TextOut(int *x***, int** *y***, const CString&** *str* **);**

Return Value

Nonzero if the function is successful; otherwise 0.

Parameters

x   Specifies the logical x-coordinate of the starting point of the text.

y   Specifies the logical y-coordinate of the starting point of the text.

lpszString   Points to the character string to be drawn.

nCount Specifies the number of bytes in the string.

str A **CString** object that contains the characters to be drawn.

Remarks

Writes a character string at the specified location using the currently selected font.

Character origins are at the upper-left corner of the character cell. By default, the current position is not used or updated by the function.

If an application needs to update the current position when it calls **TextOut**, the application can call the **SetTextAlign** member function with *nFlags* set to **TA_UPDATECP**. When this flag is set, Windows ignores the *x* and *y* parameters on subsequent calls to **TextOut**, using the current position instead.

See Also: **CDC::ExtTextOut, CDC::GetTextExtent, CDC::SetTextAlign, CDC::SetTextColor, CDC::TabbedTextOut, ::TextOut**

CDC::UpdateColors

void UpdateColors( );

Remarks

Updates the client area of the device context by matching the current colors in the client area to the system palette on a pixel-by-pixel basis. An inactive window with a realized logical palette may call **UpdateColors** as an alternative to redrawing its client area when the system palette changes.

For more information about using color palettes, see **::UpdateColors** in the *Win32 SDK Programmer's Reference*.

The **UpdateColors** member function typically updates a client area faster than redrawing the area. However, because the function performs the color translation based on the color of each pixel before the system palette changed, each call to this function results in the loss of some color accuracy.

See Also: **CDC::RealizePalette, CPalette, ::UpdateColors**

CDC::WidenPath

BOOL WidenPath( );

Return Value

Nonzero if the function is successful; otherwise 0.

Remarks

Redefines the current path as the area that would be painted if the path were stroked using the pen currently selected into the device context. This function is successful only if the current pen is a geometric pen created by the second version of **CreatePen** member function, or if the pen is created with the first version of **CreatePen** and has a width, in device units, of greater than 1. The device context must contain a closed path. Any Bézier curves in the path are converted to sequences of straight lines approximating the widened curves. As such, no Bézier curves remain in the path after **WidenPath** is called.

See Also: **CDC::BeginPath, CDC::EndPath, CDC::SetMiterLimit, ::WidenPath**

Data Members
CDC::m_hAttribDC

Remarks

The attribute device context for this **CDC** object. By default, this device context is equal to **m_hDC**. In general, **CDC** GDI calls that request information from the device context are directed to **m_hAttribDC**. See the **CDC** class description for more on the use of these two device contexts.

See Also: **CDC::m_hDC, CDC::SetAttribDC, CDC::ReleaseAttribDC**

CDC::m_hDC

Remarks

The output device context for this **CDC** object. By default, **m_hDC** is equal to **m_hAttribDC**, the other device context wrapped by **CDC**. In general, **CDC** GDI calls that create output go to the **m_hDC** device context. You can initialize **m_hDC** and **m_hAttribDC** to point to different devices. See the **CDC** class description for more on the use of these two device contexts.

See Also: **CDC::m_hAttribDC, CDC::SetOutputDC, CDC::ReleaseOutputDC**

CDialog

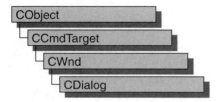

The **CDialog** class is the base class used for displaying dialog boxes on the screen. Dialog boxes are of two types: modal and modeless. A modal dialog box must be closed by the user before the application continues. A modeless dialog box allows the user to display the dialog box and return to another task without canceling or removing the dialog box.

A **CDialog** object is a combination of a dialog template and a **CDialog**-derived class. Use the dialog editor to create the dialog template and store it in a resource, then use ClassWizard to create a class derived from **CDialog**.

A dialog box, like any other window, receives messages from Windows. In a dialog box, you are particularly interested in handling notification messages from the dialog box's controls since that is how the user interacts with your dialog box. ClassWizard browses through the potential messages generated by each control in your dialog box, and you can select which messages you wish to handle. ClassWizard then adds the appropriate message-map entries and message-handler member functions to the new class for you. You only need to write application-specific code in the handler member functions.

If you prefer, you can always write message-map entries and member functions yourself instead of using ClassWizard.

In all but the most trivial dialog box, you add member variables to your derived dialog class to store data entered in the dialog box's controls by the user or to display data for the user. ClassWizard browses through those controls in your dialog box that can be mapped to data and prompts you to create a member variable for each control. At the same time, you choose a variable type and permissible range of values for each variable. ClassWizard adds the member variables to your derived dialog class.

ClassWizard then writes a data map to automatically handle the exchange of data between the member variables and the dialog box's controls. The data map provides functions that initialize the controls in the dialog box with the proper values, retrieve the data, and validate the data.

To create a modal dialog box, construct an object on the stack using the constructor for your derived dialog class and then call **DoModal** to create the dialog window and its controls. If you wish to create a modeless dialog, call **Create** in the constructor of your dialog class.

You can also create a template in memory by using a **DLGTEMPLATE** data structure as described in the Win32 SDK documentation. After you construct a **CDialog** object, call **CreateIndirect** to create a modeless dialog box, or call **InitModalIndirect** and **DoModal** to create a modal dialog box.

ClassWizard writes the exchange and validation data map in an override of **CWnd::DoDataExchange** that ClassWizard adds to your new dialog class. See the **DoDataExchange** member function in **CWnd** for more on the exchange and validation functionality.

Both the programmer and the framework call **DoDataExchange** indirectly through a call to **CWnd::UpdateData**.

The framework calls **UpdateData** when the user clicks the OK button to close a modal dialog box. (The data is not retrieved if the Cancel button is clicked.) The default implementation of **OnInitDialog** also calls **UpdateData** to set the initial values of the controls. You typically override **OnInitDialog** to further initialize controls. **OnInitDialog** is called after all the dialog controls are created and just before the dialog box is displayed.

You can call **CWnd::UpdateData** at any time during the execution of a modal or modeless dialog box.

If you develop a dialog box by hand, you add the necessary member variables to the derived dialog-box class yourself, and you add member functions to set or get these values.

For more on ClassWizard, see "Using ClassWizard" in the *Visual C++ Programmer's Guide* online.

Call **CWinApp::SetDialogBkColor** to set the background color for dialog boxes in your application.

A modal dialog box closes automatically when the user presses the OK or Cancel buttons or when your code calls the **EndDialog** member function.

When you implement a modeless dialog box, always override the **OnCancel** member function and call **DestroyWindow** from within it. Don't call the base class **CDialog::OnCancel**, because it calls **EndDialog**, which will make the dialog box invisible but will not destroy it. You should also override **PostNcDestroy** for modeless dialog boxes in order to delete **this**, since modeless dialog boxes are usually allocated with **new**. Modal dialog boxes are usually constructed on the frame and do not need **PostNcDestroy** cleanup.

For more information on **CDialog**, see the article "Dialog Box Topics" in *Visual C++ Programmer's Guide* online.

#include <afxwin.h>

CDialog Class Members

Construction

CDialog	Constructs a **CDialog** object.

Initialization

Create	Initializes the **CDialog** object. Creates a modeless dialog box and attaches it to the **CDialog** object.
CreateIndirect	Creates a modeless dialog box from a dialog-box template in memory (not resource-based).
InitModalIndirect	Creates a modal dialog box from a dialog-box template in memory (not resource-based). The parameters are stored until the function **DoModal** is called.

Operations

DoModal	Calls a modal dialog box and returns when done.
MapDialogRect	Converts the dialog-box units of a rectangle to screen units.
NextDlgCtrl	Moves the focus to the next dialog-box control in the dialog box.
PrevDlgCtrl	Moves the focus to the previous dialog-box control in the dialog box.
GotoDlgCtrl	Moves the focus to a specified dialog-box control in the dialog box.
SetDefID	Changes the default pushbutton control for a dialog box to a specified pushbutton.
GetDefID	Gets the ID of the default pushbutton control for a dialog box.
SetHelpID	Sets a context-sensitive help ID for the dialog box.
EndDialog	Closes a modal dialog box.

Overridables

OnInitDialog	Override to augment dialog-box initialization.
OnSetFont	Override to specify the font that a dialog-box control is to use when it draws text.
OnOK	Override to perform the OK button action in a modal dialog box. The default closes the dialog box and **DoModal** returns **IDOK**.
OnCancel	Override to perform the Cancel button or ESC key action. The default closes the dialog box and **DoModal** returns **IDCANCEL**.

Member Functions

CDialog::CDialog

> **CDialog(LPCTSTR** *lpszTemplateName*, **CWnd*** *pParentWnd* = **NULL**);
> **CDialog(UINT** *nIDTemplate*, **CWnd*** *pParentWnd* = **NULL**);
> **CDialog( );**

Parameters

> *lpszTemplateName*   Contains a null-terminated string that is the name of a dialog-box template resource.
>
> *nIDTemplate*   Contains the ID number of a dialog-box template resource.
>
> *pParentWnd*   Points to the parent or owner window object (of type **CWnd**) to which the dialog object belongs. If it is **NULL**, the dialog object's parent window is set to the main application window.

Remarks

> To construct a resource-based modal dialog box, call either public form of the constructor. One form of the constructor provides access to the dialog resource by template name. The other constructor provides access by template ID number, usually with an **IDD_** prefix (for example, IDD_DIALOG1).
>
> To construct a modal dialog box from a template in memory, first invoke the parameterless, protected constructor and then call **InitModalIndirect**.
>
> After you construct a modal dialog box with one of the above methods, call **DoModal**.
>
> To construct a modeless dialog box, use the protected form of the **CDialog** constructor. The constructor is protected because you must derive your own dialog-box class to implement a modeless dialog box. Construction of a modeless dialog box is a two-step process. First call the constructor; then call the **Create** member function to create a resource-based dialog box, or call **CreateIndirect** to create the dialog box from a template in memory.
>
> **See Also:**   **CDialog::Create**, **CWnd::DestroyWindow**, **CDialog::InitModalIndirect**, **CDialog::DoModal**, **::CreateDialog**

CDialog::Create

> **BOOL Create(LPCTSTR** *lpszTemplateName*, **CWnd*** *pParentWnd* = **NULL**);
> **BOOL Create(UINT** *nIDTemplate*, **CWnd*** *pParentWnd* = **NULL**);

Return Value

> Both forms return nonzero if dialog-box creation and initialization were successful; otherwise 0.

Parameters

lpszTemplateName   Contains a null-terminated string that is the name of a dialog-box template resource.

pParentWnd   Points to the parent window object (of type **CWnd**) to which the dialog object belongs. If it is **NULL**, the dialog object's parent window is set to the main application window.

nIDTemplate   Contains the ID number of a dialog-box template resource.

Remarks

Call **Create** to create a modeless dialog box using a dialog-box template from a resource. You can put the call to **Create** inside the constructor or call it after the constructor is invoked.

Two forms of the **Create** member function are provided for access to the dialog-box template resource by either template name or template ID number (for example, IDD_DIALOG1).

For either form, pass a pointer to the parent window object. If *pParentWnd* is **NULL**, the dialog box will be created with its parent or owner window set to the main application window.

The **Create** member function returns immediately after it creates the dialog box.

Use the **WS_VISIBLE** style in the dialog-box template if the dialog box should appear when the parent window is created. Otherwise, you must call **ShowWindow**. For further dialog-box styles and their application, see the **DLGTEMPLATE** structure in the Win32 SDK documentation and "Window Styles" in the *Class Library Reference*.

Use the **CWnd::DestroyWindow** function to destroy a dialog box created by the **Create** function.

See Also: **CDialog::CDialog**, **CWnd::DestroyWindow**, **CDialog::InitModalIndirect**, **CDialog::DoModal**, **::CreateDialog**

CDialog::CreateIndirect

BOOL CreateIndirect(LPCDLGTEMPLATE *lpDialogTemplate*,
↪ **CWnd*** *pParentWnd* = **NULL**);
BOOL CreateIndirect(HGLOBAL *hDialogTemplate*, **CWnd*** *pParentWnd* = **NULL**);

Return Value

Nonzero if the dialog box was created and initialized successfully; otherwise 0.

Parameters

lpDialogTemplate   Points to memory that contains a dialog-box template used to create the dialog box. This template is in the form of a **DLGTEMPLATE** structure and control information. For more information on this structure, see the Win32 SDK documentation.

pParentWnd   Points to the dialog object's parent window object (of type **CWnd**). If it is **NULL,** the dialog object's parent window is set to the main application window.

hDialogTemplate   Contains a handle to global memory containing a dialog-box template. This template is in the form of a **DLGTEMPLATE** structure and data for each control in the dialog box.

Remarks

Call this member function to create a modeless dialog box from a dialog-box template in memory.

The **CreateIndirect** member function returns immediately after it creates the dialog box.

Use the **WS_VISIBLE** style in the dialog-box template if the dialog box should appear when the parent window is created. Otherwise, you must call **ShowWindow** to cause it to appear. For more information on how you can specify other dialog-box styles in the template, see the **DLGTEMPLATE** structure in the Win32 SDK documentation.

Use the **CWnd::DestroyWindow** function to destroy a dialog box created by the **CreateIndirect** function.

See Also: **CDialog::CDialog, CWnd::DestroyWindow, CDialog::Create, ::CreateDialogIndirect**

CDialog::DoModal

virtual int DoModal( );

Return Value

An **int** value that specifies the value of the *nResult* parameter that was passed to the **CDialog::EndDialog** member function, which is used to close the dialog box. The return value is –1 if the function could not create the dialog box, or **IDABORT** if some other error occurred.

Remarks

Call this member function to invoke the modal dialog box and return the dialog-box result when done. This member function handles all interaction with the user while the dialog box is active. This is what makes the dialog box modal; that is, the user cannot interact with other windows until the dialog box is closed.

If the user clicks one of the pushbuttons in the dialog box, such as OK or Cancel, a message-handler member function, such as **OnOK** or **OnCancel**, is called to attempt to close the dialog box. The default **OnOK** member function will validate and update the dialog-box data and close the dialog box with result **IDOK,** and the default **OnCancel** member function will close the dialog box with result **IDCANCEL** without validating or updating the dialog-box data. You can override these message-handler functions to alter their behavior.

Note **PreTranslateMessage** is now called for modal dialog box message processing.

See Also: **::DialogBox**, **CWnd::IsDialogMessage**

CDialog::EndDialog

void EndDialog(int *nResult* **);**

Parameters

    nResult   Contains the value to be returned from the dialog box to the caller of **DoModal**.

Remarks

    Call this member function to terminate a modal dialog box. This member function returns *nResult* as the return value of **DoModal**. You must use the **EndDialog** function to complete processing whenever a modal dialog box is created.

    You can call **EndDialog** at any time, even in **OnInitDialog**, in which case you should close the dialog box before it is shown or before the input focus is set.

    EndDialog does not close the dialog box immediately. Instead, it sets a flag that directs the dialog box to close as soon as the current message handler returns.

    See Also: **CDialog::DoModal**, **CDialog::OnOK**, **CDialog::OnCancel**

CDialog::GetDefID

DWORD GetDefID( ) const;

Return Value

    A 32-bit value (**DWORD**). If the default pushbutton has an ID value, the high-order word contains **DC_HASDEFID** and the low-order word contains the ID value. If the default pushbutton does not have an ID value, the return value is 0.

Remarks

    Call the **GetDefID** member function to get the ID of the default pushbutton control for a dialog box. This is usually an OK button.

    See Also: **CDialog::SetDefID**, **DM_GETDEFID**

CDialog::GotoDlgCtrl

void GotoDlgCtrl(CWnd* *pWndCtrl* **);**

Parameters

pWndCtrl   Identifies the window (control) that is to receive the focus.

Remarks

Moves the focus to the specified control in the dialog box.

To get a pointer to the control (child window) to pass as *pWndCtrl*, call the **CWnd::GetDlgItem** member function, which returns a pointer to a **CWnd** object.

See Also: **CWnd::GetDlgItem**, **CDialog::PrevDlgCtrl**, **CDialog::NextDlgCtrl**

CDialog::InitModalIndirect

BOOL InitModalIndirect(LPCDLGTEMPLATE *lpDialogTemplate*,
 ↪ **CWnd*** *pParentWnd* = **NULL**);
BOOL InitModalIndirect(HGLOBAL *hDialogTemplate*,
 ↪ **CWnd*** *pParentWnd* = **NULL**);

Return Value

Nonzero if the dialog object was created and initialized successfully; otherwise 0.

Parameters

lpDialogTemplate   Points to memory that contains a dialog-box template used to create the dialog box. This template is in the form of a **DLGTEMPLATE** structure and control information. For more information on this structure, see the Win32 SDK documentation.

hDialogTemplate   Contains a handle to global memory containing a dialog-box template. This template is in the form of a **DLGTEMPLATE** structure and data for each control in the dialog box.

pParentWnd   Points to the parent or owner window object (of type **CWnd**) to which the dialog object belongs. If it is **NULL**, the dialog object's parent window is set to the main application window.

Remarks

Call this member function to initialize a modal dialog object using a dialog-box template that you construct in memory.

To create a modal dialog box indirectly, first allocate a global block of memory and fill it with the dialog box template. Then call the empty **CDialog** constructor to construct the dialog-box object. Next, call **InitModalIndirect** to store your handle to the in-memory dialog-box template. The Windows dialog box is created and displayed later, when the **DoModal** member function is called.

See Also: **::DialogBoxIndirect**, **CDialog::DoModal**, **CWnd::DestroyWindow**, **CDialog::Cdialog**

CDialog::MapDialogRect

void MapDialogRect(LPRECT *lpRect* **) const;**

Parameters

lpRect   Points to a **RECT** structure or **CRect** object that contains the dialog-box coordinates to be converted.

Remarks

Call to convert the dialog-box units of a rectangle to screen units. Dialog-box units are stated in terms of the current dialog-box base unit derived from the average width and height of characters in the font used for dialog-box text. One horizontal unit is one-fourth of the dialog-box base-width unit, and one vertical unit is one-eighth of the dialog-box base height unit.

The **GetDialogBaseUnits** Windows function returns size information for the system font, but you can specify a different font for each dialog box if you use the **DS_SETFONT** style in the resource-definition file. The **MapDialogRect** Windows function uses the appropriate font for this dialog box.

The **MapDialogRect** member function replaces the dialog-box units in *lpRect* with screen units (pixels) so that the rectangle can be used to create a dialog box or position a control within a box.

See Also: **::GetDialogBaseUnits**, **::MapDialogRect**, **WM_SETFONT**

CDialog::NextDlgCtrl

void NextDlgCtrl( ) const;

Remarks

Moves the focus to the next control in the dialog box. If the focus is at the last control in the dialog box, it moves to the first control.

See Also: **CDialog::PrevDlgCtrl**, **CDialog::GotoDlgCtrl**

CDialog::OnCancel

virtual void OnCancel( );

Remarks

The framework calls this member function when the user clicks the Cancel button or presses the ESC key in a modal or modeless dialog box.

Override this member function to perform Cancel button action. The default simply terminates a modal dialog box by calling **EndDialog** and causing **DoModal** to return **IDCANCEL**.

If you implement the Cancel button in a modeless dialog box, you must override the **OnCancel** member function and call **DestroyWindow** from within it. Don't call the base-class member function, because it calls **EndDialog**, which will make the dialog box invisible but not destroy it.

See Also: CDialog::OnOK, **CDialog::EndDialog**

CDialog::OnInitDialog

virtual BOOL OnInitDialog( );

Return Value

Specifies whether the application has set the input focus to one of the controls in the dialog box. If **OnInitDialog** returns nonzero, Windows sets the input focus to the first control in the dialog box. The application can return 0 only if it has explicitly set the input focus to one of the controls in the dialog box.

Remarks

This member function is called in response to the **WM_INITDIALOG** message. This message is sent to the dialog box during the **Create**, **CreateIndirect**, or **DoModal** calls, which occur immediately before the dialog box is displayed.

Override this member function if you need to perform special processing when the dialog box is initialized. In the overridden version, first call the base class **OnInitDialog** but disregard its return value. You will normally return **TRUE** from your overridden member function.

Windows calls the **OnInitDialog** function via the standard global dialog-box procedure common to all Microsoft Foundation Class Library dialog boxes, rather than through your message map, so you do not need a message-map entry for this member function.

See Also: CDialog::Create, **CDialog::CreateIndirect**, **WM_INITDIALOG**

CDialog::OnOK

virtual void OnOK( );

Remarks

Called when the user clicks the OK button (the button with an ID of **IDOK**).

Override this member function to perform the OK button action. If the dialog box includes automatic data validation and exchange, the default implementation of this member function validates the dialog-box data and updates the appropriate variables in your application.

If you implement the OK button in a modeless dialog box, you must override the **OnOK** member function and call **DestroyWindow** from within it. Don't call the base-class member function, because it calls **EndDialog**, which makes the dialog box invisible but does not destroy it.

See Also: **CDialog::OnCancel**, **CDialog::EndDialog**

CDialog::OnSetFont

virtual void OnSetFont(CFont* *pFont* **);**

Parameters

pFont Specifies a pointer to the font. Used as the default font for all controls in this dialog box.

Remarks

Specifies the font a dialog-box control will use when drawing text. The dialog-box control will use the specified font as the default for all dialog-box controls.

The dialog editor typically sets the dialog-box font as part of the dialog-box template resource.

See Also: **WM_SETFONT**, **CWnd::SetFont**

CDialog::PrevDlgCtrl

void PrevDlgCtrl( ) const;

Remarks

Sets the focus to the previous control in the dialog box. If the focus is at the first control in the dialog box, it moves to the last control in the box.

See Also: **CDialog::NextDlgCtrl**, **CDialog::GotoDlgCtrl**

CDialog::SetDefID

void SetDefID(UINT *nID* **);**

Parameters

nID Specifies the ID of the pushbutton control that will become the default.

Remarks

Changes the default pushbutton control for a dialog box.

See Also: **CDialog::GetDefID**

CDialog::SetHelpID

void SetHelpID(UINT *nIDR* **);**

Parameters

> *nIDR*   Specifies the context-sensitive help ID.

Remarks

> Sets a context-sensitive help ID for the dialog box.

CDialogBar

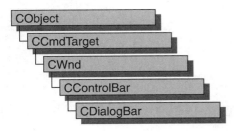

The **CDialogBar** class provides the functionality of a Windows modeless dialog box in a control bar. A dialog bar resembles a dialog box in that it contains standard Windows controls that the user can tab between. Another similarity is that you create a dialog template to represent the dialog bar.

Creating and using a dialog bar is similar to creating and using a **CFormView** object. First, use the dialog editor (described in the *Developer Studio User's Guide* online) to define a dialog template with the style **WS_CHILD** and no other style. The template must not have the style **WS_VISIBLE**. In your application code, call the constructor to construct the **CDialogBar** object, then call **Create** to create the dialog-bar window and attach it to the **CDialogBar** object.

For more information on **CDialogBar**, see the article "Dialog Bar Topics" in *Visual C++ Programmer's Guide* online and Technical Note 31 online, "Control Bars."

#include <afxext.h>

See Also: **CFormView**, **CControlBar**

CDialogBar Class Members

Construction

CDialogBar	Constructs a **CDialogBar** object.
Create	Creates a Windows dialog bar and attaches it to the **CDialogBar** object.

Member Functions
CDialogBar::CDialogBar

CDialogBar( );

Remarks

Constructs a **CDialogBar** object.

See Also: CControlBar

CDialogBar::Create

BOOL Create(CWnd* *pParentWnd*, **LPCTSTR** *lpszTemplateName*,
↳ **UINT** *nStyle*, **UINT** *nID* **);**
BOOL Create(CWnd* *pParentWnd*, **UINT** *nIDTemplate*, **UINT** *nStyle*, **UINT** *nID* **);**

Return Value

Nonzero if successful; otherwise 0.

Parameters

pParentWnd   A pointer to the parent **CWnd** object.

lpszTemplateName   A pointer to the name of the **CDialogBar** object's dialog-box resource template.

nStyle   The alignment style of the dialog bar. The following styles are supported:

- **CBRS_TOP**   Control bar is at the top of the frame window.

- **CBRS_BOTTOM**   Control bar is at the bottom of the frame window.

- **CBRS_NOALIGN**   Control bar is not repositioned when the parent is resized.

- **CBRS_LEFT**   Control bar is at the left of the frame window.

- **CBRS_RIGHT**   Control bar is at the right of the frame window.

nID   The control ID of the dialog bar.

nIDTemplate   The resource ID of the **CDialogBar** object's dialog-box template.

Remarks

Loads the dialog-box resource template specified by *lpszTemplateName* or *nIDTemplate*, creates the dialog-bar window, sets its style, and associates it with the **CDialogBar** object.

If you specify the **CBRS_TOP** or **CBRS_BOTTOM** alignment style, the dialog bar's width is that of the frame window and its height is that of the resource specified by *nIDTemplate*. If you specify the **CBRS_LEFT** or **CBRS_RIGHT** alignment style, the dialog bar's height is that of the frame window and its width is that of the resource specified by *nIDTemplate*.

See Also: CDialogBar::CDialogBar

CDocItem

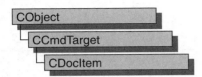

CDocItem is the base class for document items, which are components of a document's data. **CDocItem** objects are used to represent OLE items in both client and server documents.

For more information, see the article "Containers: Implementing a Container" in *Visual C++ Programmer's Guide* online.

#include <afxole.h>

See Also: **COleDocument, COleServerItem, COleClientItem**

CDocItem Class Members

Operations

GetDocument	Returns the document that contains the item.

Overridables

IsBlank	Determines whether the item contains any information.

Member Functions
CDocItem::IsBlank

virtual BOOL IsBlank( ) const;

Return Value

Nonzero if the item contains no information; otherwise 0.

Remarks

Called by the framework when default serialization occurs.

By default, **CDocItem** objects are not blank. **COleClientItem** objects are sometimes blank because they derive directly from **CDocItem**. However, **COleServerItem** objects are always blank. By default, OLE applications containing **COleClientItem** objects that have no x or y extent are serialized. This is done by returning **TRUE** from an override of **IsBlank** when the item has no x or y extent.

Override this function if you want to implement other actions during serialization.

See Also: **CObject::Serialize**

CDocItem::GetDocument

CDocument* GetDocument( ) const;

Return Value

A pointer to the document that contains the item; **NULL**, if the item is not part of a document.

Remarks

Call this function to get the document that contains the item.

This function is overridden in the derived classes **COleClientItem** and **COleServerItem**, returning a pointer to either a **COleDocument**, a **COleLinkingDoc**, or a **COleServerDoc** object.

See Also: **COleDocument, COleLinkingDoc, COleServerDoc, COleClientItem, COleServerItem**

CDockState

CObject
  └ CDockState

CDockState is a serialized **CObject** class that loads, unloads, or clears the state of one or more docking control bars in persistent memory (a file). The dock state includes the size and position of the bar and whether or not it is docked. When retrieving the stored dock state, **CDockState** checks the bar's position and, if the bar is not visible with the current screen settings, **CDockState** scales the bar's position so that it is visible. The main purpose of **CDockState** is to hold the entire state of a number of control bars and to allow that state to be saved and loaded either to the registry, the application's .INI file, or in binary form as part of a **CArchive** object's contents.

The bar can be any dockable control bar, including a toolbar, status bar, or dialog bar. **CDockState** objects are written and read to or from a file via a **CArchive** object.

CFrameWnd::GetDockState retrieves the state information of all the frame window's **CControlBar** objects and puts it into the **CDockState** object. You can then write the contents of the **CDockState** object to storage with **Serialize** or **CDockState::SaveState**. If you later want to restore the state of the control bars in the frame window, you can load the state with **Serialize** or **CDockState::LoadState**, then use **CFrameWnd::SetDockState** to apply the saved state to the frame window's control bars.

For more information on docking control bars, see the articles "Control Bar Topics," "Toolbars: Docking and Floating," and "Frame Window Topics" in *Visual C++ Programmer's Guide* online.

#include <afxadv.h>

CDockState Class Members

Data Members

m_arrBarInfo	Array of pointers to the stored dock state information with one entry for each control bar.

Construction

CDockState	Constructs a **CDockState** object.

Operations

Clear	Clears the dock state information.
GetVersion	Retrieves the version number of the stored bar state.

(continued)

Operations	*(continued)*
LoadState	Retrieves state information from the registry or .INI file.
SaveState	Saves state information to the registry or INI file.

Member Functions

CDockState::CDockState

CDockState( );

Remarks

Constructs a **CDockState** object.

See Also: **CDockState::Clear**, **CDockState::GetVersion**, **CDockState::LoadState**, **CDockState::SaveState**, **CFrameWnd::GetDockState**, **CFrameWnd::SetDockState**

CDockState::Clear

void Clear( );

Remarks

Call this function to clear all docking information stored in the **CDockState** object. This includes not only whether the bar is docked or not, but the bar's size and position and whether or not it is visible.

See Also: **CDockState::LoadState**, **CDockState::SaveState**, **CDockState::GetVersion**, **CFrameWnd::GetDockState**, **CFrameWnd::SetDockState**

CDockState::GetVersion

DWORD GetVersion( );

Return Value

1 if the stored bar information is older than current bar state; 2 if the stored bar information is the same as the current bar state.

Remarks

Call this function to retrieve the version number of the stored bar state. Version support enables a revised bar to add new persistent properties and still be able to detect and load the persistent state created by an earlier version of the bar.

See Also: **CDockState::LoadState**, **CDockState::SaveState**, **CDockState::Clear**, **CFrameWnd::GetDockState**, **CFrameWnd::SetDockState**

CDockState::LoadState

void LoadState(LPCTSTR *lpszProfileName* **);**

Parameters

lpszProfileName   Points to a null-terminated string that specifies the name of a
section in the initialization file or a key in the Windows registry where state
information is stored.

Remarks

Call this function to retrieve state information from the registry or .INI file. The
profile name is the section of the application's .INI file or the registry that contains the
bars' state information. You can save control bar state information to the registry or
.INI file with **SaveState**.

See Also: **CDockState::SaveState, CDockState::GetVersion, CDockState::Clear,
CFrameWnd::GetDockState, CFrameWnd::SetDockState**

CDockState::SaveState

void SaveState(LPCTSTR *lpszProfileName* **);**

Parameters

lpszProfileName   Points to a null-terminated string that specifies the name of a
section in the initialization file or a key in the Windows registry where state
information is stored.

Remarks

Call this function to save the state information to the registry or .INI file. The profile
name is the section of the application's .INI file or the registry that contains the
control bar's state information. **SaveState** also saves the current screen size. You can
retrieve control bar information from the registry or .INI file with **LoadState**.

See Also: **CDockState::LoadState, CDockState::GetVersion, CDockState::Clear,
CFrameWnd::GetDockState, CFrameWnd::SetDockState**

Data Members

CDockState::m_arrBarInfo

Remarks

A **CPtrArray** object that is an array of pointers to the stored control bar information
for each control bar that has saved state information in the **CDockState** object.

See Also: **CDockState::LoadState, CDockState::SaveState, CDockState::Clear,
CFrameWnd::GetDockState, CFrameWnd::SetDockState**

CDocObjectServer

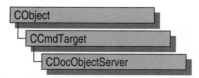

Class **CDocObjectServer** implements the additional OLE interfaces needed to make a normal **COleDocument** server into a full DocObject server: **IOleDocument**, **IOleDocumentView**, **IOleCommandTarget**, and **IPrint**. **CDocObjectServer** is derived from **CCmdTarget** and works closely with **COleServerDoc** to expose the interfaces.

A DocObject server document can contain **CDocObjectServerItem** objects, which represent the server interface to DocObject items.

To customize your DocObject server, derive your own class from **CDocObjectServer** and override its view setup functions, **OnActivateView**, **OnApplyViewState**, and **OnSaveViewState**. You will need to provide a new instance of your class in response to framework calls.

For further information on DocObjects, see **CDocObjectServerItem** and **COleCmdUI** in the *MFC Class Library Reference*. Also see "Internet First Steps: ActiveX Documents" and "ActiveX Documents" in *Visual C++ Programmer's Guide* online.

#include <afxdocobj.h>

See Also: **CDocObjectServerItem**

CDocObjectServer Class Members

Constructors

CDocObjectServer	Constructs a **CDocObjectServer** object.

Operations

ActivateDocObject	Activates the document object server, but does not show it.

Overrideables

OnActivateView	Displays the DocObject view.
OnApplyViewState	Restores the state of the DocObject view.
OnSaveViewState	Saves the state of the DocObject view.

Member Functions

CDocObjectServer::ActivateDocObject

void ActivateDocObject( );

Remarks

Call this function to activate (but not show) the document object server. **ActivateDocObject** calls **IOleDocumentSite**'s **ActivateMe** method, but does not show the view because it waits for specific instructions on how to set up and display the view, given in the call to **CDocObjectServer::OnActivateView**.

Together, **ActivateDocObject** and **OnActivateView** activate and display the DocObject view. DocObject activation differs from other kinds of OLE in-place activation. DocObject activation bypasses displaying in-place hatch borders and object adornments (such as sizing handles), ignores object extent functions, and draws scroll bars within the view rectangle as opposed to drawing them outside that rectangle (as in normal in-place activation).

See Also: **CDocObjectServerItem**

CDocObjectServer::CDocObjectServer

CDocObjectServer(COleServerDoc* *pOwner*,
  ↪ **LPOLEDOCUMENTSITE *pDocSite* = NULL);**

Parameters

pOwner A pointer to the client site document that is the client for the DocObject server.

pDocSite A pointer to the **IOleDocumentSite** interface implemented by the container.

Remarks

Constructs and initializes a **CDocObjectServer** object.

When a DocObject is active, the client site OLE interface (**IOleDocumentSite**) is what allows the DocObject server to communicate with its client (the container). When a DocObject server is activated, it first checks that the container implements the **IOleDocumentSite** interface. If so, **COleServerDoc::GetDocObjectServer** is called to see if the container supports DocObjects. By default, **GetDocObjectServer** returns **NULL**. You must override **COleServerDoc::GetDocObjectServer** to construct a new **CDocObjectServer** object or a derived object of your own, with pointers to the **COleServerDoc** container and its **IOleDocumentSite** interface as arguments to the constructor.

See Also: **CDocObjectServerItem**, **COleServerDoc::GetDocObjectServer**

CDocObjectServer::OnActivateView

virtual HRESULT OnActivateView( );

Return Value

Returns an error or warning value. By default, returns **NOERROR** if successful; otherwise, **E_FAIL**.

Remarks

Call this function to display the DocObject view. This function creates an in-place frame window, draws scrollbars within the view, sets up the menus the server shares with its container, adds frame controls, sets the active object, then finally shows the in-place frame window and sets the focus.

See Also: CDocObjectServer::OnApplyViewState

CDocObjectServer::OnApplyViewState

virtual void OnApplyViewState(CArchive& *ar* **);**

Parameters

ar   A **CArchive** object from which to serialize the view state.

Remarks

Override this function to restore the state of the DocObject view.

This function is called when the view is being displayed for the first time after its instantiation. **OnApplyViewState** instructs a view to reinitialize itself according to the data in the **CArchive** object previously saved with **OnSaveViewState**. The view must validate the data in the **CArchive** object because the container does not attempt to interpret the view state data in any way.

You can use **OnSaveViewState** to store persistent information specific to your view's state. If you override **OnSaveViewState** to store information, you will want to override **OnApplyViewState** to read that information and apply it to your view when it is newly activated.

See Also: CDocObjectServer::OnSaveViewState

CDocObjectServer::OnSaveViewState

virtual void OnSaveViewState(CArchive& *ar* **);**

Parameters

ar   A **CArchive** object to which the view state is serialized.

Remarks

Override this function to save extra state information about your DocObject view.

Your state might include properties like the view type, zoom factor, insertion and selection point, and so on. The container typically calls this function before deactivating the view. The saved state can later be restored through **OnApplyViewState**.

You can use **OnSaveViewState** to store persistent information specific to your view's state. If you override **OnSaveViewState** to store information, you will want to override **OnApplyViewState** to read that information and apply it to your view when it is newly activated.

See Also: **CDocObjectServer::OnApplyViewState**

CDocObjectServerItem

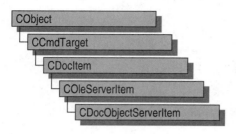

Class **CDocObjectServerItem**, derived from **COleServerItem**, implements OLE server verbs specifically for DocObject servers.

CDocObjectServerItem defines overridable member functions: **OnHide**, **OnOpen**, and **OnShow**.

To use **CDocObjectServerItem**, assure that the **OnGetEmbeddedItem** override in your **COleServerDoc**-derived class returns a new **CDocObjectServerItem** object. If you need to change any functionality in your item, you can create a new instance of your own **CDocObjectServerItem**-derived class.

For further information on DocObjects, see **CDocObjectServer** and **COleCmdUI** in the *MFC Class Library Reference*. Also see "Internet First Steps: ActiveX Documents" and "ActiveX Documents" in *Visual C++ Programmer's Guide* online.

#include <afxdocobj.h>

See Also: **CDocObjectServer**

CDocObjectServerItem Class Members

Constructors

CDocObjectServerItem	Constructs a **CDocObjectServerItem** object.

Overridables

OnHide	Throws an exception if the framework tries to hide a DocObject item.
OnOpen	Called by the framework to make the DocObject item in-place active. If the item is not a DocObject, calls **COleServerItem::OnOpen**.
OnShow	Called by the framework to make the DocObject item in-place active. If the item is not a DocObject, calls **COleServerItem::OnShow**.

Member Functions
CDocObjectServerItem::CDocObjectServerItem

CDocObjectServerItem(COleServerDoc* *pServerDoc*, **BOOL** *bAutoDelete* **);**

Parameters

>*pServerDoc*   A pointer to the document that will contain the new DocObject item.

>*bAutoDelete*   Indicates whether the object can be deleted when a link to it is released. Set the argument to **FALSE** if the **CDocObjectServerItem** object is an integral part of your document's data. Set it to **TRUE** if the object is a secondary structure used to identify a range in your document's data that can be deleted by the framework.

Remarks

>Constructs a **CDocObjectServerItem** object.

>**See Also: CDocObjectServer**

CDocObjectServerItem::OnHide

virtual void OnHide( );

Remarks

>Called by the framework to hide the item. The default implementation throws an exception if the item is a DocObject. You cannot hide an active DocObject item because it takes the whole view. You must deactivate the DocObject item to make it disappear. If the item is not a DocObject, the default implementation calls **COleServerItem::OnHide**.

>**See Also: CDocObjectServerItem::OnOpen**, **CDocObjectServerItem::OnShow**

CDocObjectServerItem::OnOpen

virtual void OnOpen( );

Remarks

>Called by the framework to instruct the server application to make the DocObject item in-place active. If the item is not a DocObject, the default implementation calls **COleServerItem::OnOpen**. Override this function if you want to perform special processing when opening a DocObject item.

>**See Also: CDocObjectServerItem::OnHide**, **CDocObjectServerItem::OnShow**

CDocObjectServerItem::OnShow

virtual void OnShow( );

Called by the framework to instruct the server application to make the DocObject item in-place active. If the item is not a DocObject, the default implementation calls **COleServerItem::OnShow**. Override this function if you want to perform special processing when opening a DocObject item.

See Also: **CDocObjectServerItem::OnHide**, **CDocObjectServerItem::OnOpen**

CDocTemplate

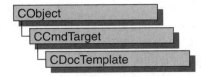

CObject

CCmdTarget

CDocTemplate

CDocTemplate is an abstract base class that defines the basic functionality for document templates. You usually create one or more document templates in the implementation of your application's **InitInstance** function. A document template defines the relationships among three types of classes:

- A document class, which you derive from **CDocument**.
- A view class, which displays data from the document class listed above. You can derive this class from **CView**, **CScrollView**, **CFormView**, or **CEditView**. (You can also use **CEditView** directly.)
- A frame window class, which contains the view. For a single document interface (SDI) application, you derive this class from **CFrameWnd**. For a multiple document interface (MDI) application, you derive this class from **CMDIChildWnd**. If you don't need to customize the behavior of the frame window, you can use **CFrameWnd** or **CMDIChildWnd** directly without deriving your own class.

Your application has one document template for each type of document that it supports. For example, if your application supports both spreadsheets and text documents, the application has two document template objects. Each document template is responsible for creating and managing all the documents of its type.

The document template stores pointers to the **CRuntimeClass** objects for the document, view, and frame window classes. These **CRuntimeClass** objects are specified when constructing a document template.

The document template contains the ID of the resources used with the document type (such as menu, icon, or accelerator table resources). The document template also has strings containing additional information about its document type. These include the name of the document type (for example, "Worksheet") and the file extension (for example, ".xls"). Optionally, it can contain other strings used by the application's user interface, the Windows File Manager, and Object Linking and Embedding (OLE) support.

If your application is an OLE container and/or server, the document template also defines the ID of the menu used during in-place activation. If your application is an OLE server, the document template defines the ID of the toolbar and menu used during in-place activation. You specify these additional OLE resources by calling **SetContainerInfo** and **SetServerInfo**.

Because **CDocTemplate** is an abstract class, you cannot use the class directly. A typical application uses one of the two **CDocTemplate**-derived classes provided by the Microsoft Foundation Class Library: **CSingleDocTemplate**, which implements SDI, and **CMultiDocTemplate**, which implements MDI. See those classes for more information on using document templates.

If your application requires a user-interface paradigm that is fundamentally different from SDI or MDI, you can derive your own class from **CDocTemplate**.

For more information on **CDocTemplate**, see "Document Templates and the Document/View Creation Process" in *Visual C++ Programmer's Guide* online.

include# <afxwin.h>

See Also: **CSingleDocTemplate, CMultiDocTemplate, CDocument, CView, CScrollView, CEditView, CFormView, CFrameWnd, CMDIChildWnd**

CDocTemplate Class Members

Constructors

CDocTemplate	Constructs a **CDocTemplate** object.

Attributes

SetContainerInfo	Determines the resources for OLE containers when editing an in-place OLE item.
SetServerInfo	Determines the resources and classes when the server document is embedded or edited in-place.
GetFirstDocPosition	Retrieves the position of the first document associated with this template.
GetNextDoc	Retrieves a document and the position of the next one.
LoadTemplate	Loads the resources for a given **CDocTemplate** or derived class.

Operations

AddDocument	Adds a document to a template.
RemoveDocument	Removes a document from a template.
GetDocString	Retrieves a string associated with the document type.
CreateOleFrame	Creates an OLE-enabled frame window.

Overridables

MatchDocType	Determines the degree of confidence in the match between a document type and this template.
CreateNewDocument	Creates a new document.
CreateNewFrame	Creates a new frame window containing a document and view.
InitialUpdateFrame	Initializes the frame window, and optionally makes it visible.

Overridables *(continued)*

SaveAllModified	Saves all documents associated with this template which have been modified.
CloseAllDocuments	Closes all documents associated with this template.
OpenDocumentFile	Opens a file specified by a pathname.
SetDefaultTitle	Displays the default title in the document window's title bar.

Member Functions

CDocTemplate::AddDocument

virtual void AddDocument(CDocument* *pDoc* **);**

Parameters

pDoc   A pointer to the document to be added.

Remarks

Use this function to add a document to a template. The derived classes **CMultiDocTemplate** and **CSingleDocTemplate** override this function. If you derive your own document-template class from **CDocTemplate**, your derived class must override this function.

See Also: **CDocTemplate::RemoveDocument, CMultiDocTemplate, CSingleDocTemplate**

CDocTemplate::CDocTemplate

CDocTemplate (UINT *nIDResource*, **CRuntimeClass*** *pDocClass*,
↪ **CRuntimeClass*** *pFrameClass*, **CRuntimeClass*** *pViewClass* **);**

Parameters

nIDResource   Specifies the ID of the resources used with the document type. This may include menu, icon, accelerator table, and string resources.

The string resource consists of up to seven substrings separated by the '\n' character (the '\n' character is needed as a place holder if a substring is not included; however, trailing '\n' characters are not necessary); these substrings describe the document type. For information on the substrings, see **GetDocString**. This string resource is found in the application's resource file. For example:

```
// MYCALC.RC
STRINGTABLE PRELOAD DISCARDABLE
BEGIN
  IDR_SHEETTYPE "\nSheet\nWorksheet\nWorksheets
↪ (*.myc)\n.myc\n MyCalcSheet\nMyCalc Worksheet"
END
```

Note that the string begins with a '\n' character; this is because the first substring is not used for MDI applications and so is not included. You can edit this string using the string editor; the entire string appears as a single entry in the String Editor, not as seven separate entries.

For more information about these resource types, see the *Developer Studio User's Guide* online.

pDocClass   Points to the **CRuntimeClass** object of the document class. This class is a **CDocument**-derived class you define to represent your documents.

pFrameClass   Points to the **CRuntimeClass** object of the frame window class. This class can be a **CFrameWnd**-derived class, or it can be **CFrameWnd** itself if you want default behavior for your main frame window.

pViewClass   Points to the **CRuntimeClass** object of the view class. This class is a **CView**-derived class you define to display your documents.

Remarks

Use this member function to construct a **CDocTemplate** object. Dynamically allocate a **CDocTemplate** object and pass it to **CWinApp::AddDocTemplate** from the `InitInstance` member function of your application class.

See Also: **CDocTemplate::GetDocString**, **CWinApp::AddDocTemplate**, **CWinApp::InitInstance**, **CRuntimeClass**

CDocTemplate::CloseAllDocuments

virtual void CloseAllDocuments(BOOL *bEndSession* **);**

Parameters

bEndSession   Specifies whether or not the session is being ended. It is **TRUE** if the session is being ended; otherwise **FALSE**.

Remarks

Call this member function to close all open documents. This member function is typically used as part of the File Exit command. The default implementation of this function calls the **CDocument::DeleteContents** member function to delete the document's data and then closes the frame windows for all the views attached to the document.

Override this function if you want to require the user to perform special cleanup processing before the document is closed. For example, if the document represents a record in a database, you may want to override this function to close the database.

See Also: **CDocTemplate::OpenDocumentFile**, **CDocTemplate::SaveAllModified**

CDocTemplate::CreateNewDocument

virtual CDocument* CreateNewDocument( );

Return Value

A pointer to the newly created document, or **NULL** if an error occurs.

Remarks

Call this member function to create a new document of the type associated with this document template.

See Also: **CDocTemplate::CreateNewFrame**

CDocTemplate::CreateNewFrame

virtual CFrameWnd* CreateNewFrame(CDocument* *pDoc***, CFrameWnd*** *pOther* **);**

Return Value

A pointer to the newly created frame window, or **NULL** if an error occurs.

Parameters

pDoc   The document to which the new frame window should refer. Can be **NULL**.

pOther   The frame window on which the new frame window is to be based. Can be **NULL**.

Remarks

CreateNewFrame uses the **CRuntimeClass** objects passed to the constructor to create a new frame window with a view and document attached. If the *pDoc* parameter is **NULL**, the framework outputs a TRACE message.

The *pOther* parameter is used to implement the Window New command. It provides a frame window on which to model the new frame window. The new frame window is usually created invisible. Call this function to create frame windows outside the standard framework implementation of File New and File Open.

See Also: **CCreateContext, CFrameWnd::LoadFrame, CDocTemplate::InitialUpdateFrame**

CDocTemplate::CreateOleFrame

CFrameWnd* CreateOleFrame(CWnd* *pParentWnd***, CDocument*** *pDoc***,**
↳ BOOL *bCreateView* **);**

Return Value

A pointer to a frame window if successful; otherwise **NULL**.

Parameters

pParentWnd   A pointer to the frame's parent window.

pDoc   A pointer to the document to which the new OLE frame window should refer.

bCreateView   Determines whether a view is created along with the frame.

Remarks

Creates an OLE frame window. If *bCreateView* is zero, an empty frame is created.

See Also: **CDocTemplate::CreateNewFrame, COleDocument, COleIPFrameWnd**

CDocTemplate::GetDocString

virtual BOOL GetDocString(CString& *rString***, enum DocStringIndex** *index* **) const;**

Return Value

Nonzero if the specified substring was found; otherwise 0.

Parameters

rString   A reference to a **CString** object that will contain the string when the function returns.

index   An index of the substring being retrieved from the string that describes the document type. This parameter can have one of the following values:

- **CDocTemplate::windowTitle**   Name that appears in the application window's title bar (for example, "Microsoft Excel"). Present only in the document template for SDI applications.

- **CDocTemplate::docName**   Root for the default document name (for example, "Sheet"). This root, plus a number, is used for the default name of a new document of this type whenever the user chooses the New command from the File menu (for example, "Sheet1" or "Sheet2"). If not specified, "Untitled" is used as the default.

- **CDocTemplate::fileNewName**   Name of this document type. If the application supports more than one type of document, this string is displayed in the File New dialog box (for example, "Worksheet"). If not specified, the document type is inaccessible using the File New command.

- **CDocTemplate::filterName**   Description of the document type and a wildcard filter matching documents of this type. This string is displayed in the List Files Of Type drop-down list in the File Open dialog box (for example, "Worksheets (*.xls)"). If not specified, the document type is inaccessible using the File Open command.

- **CDocTemplate::filterExt**   Extension for documents of this type (for example, ".xls"). If not specified, the document type is inaccessible using the File Open command.

- **CDocTemplate::regFileTypeId**   Identifier for the document type to be stored in the registration database maintained by Windows. This string is for internal use only (for example, "ExcelWorksheet"). If not specified, the document type cannot be registered with the Windows File Manager.

- **CDocTemplate::regFileTypeName**   Name of the document type to be stored in the registration database. This string may be displayed in dialog boxes of applications that access the registration database (for example, "Microsoft Excel Worksheet").

Remarks

Call this function to retrieve a specific substring describing the document type. The string containing these substrings is stored in the document template and is derived from a string in the resource file for the application. The framework calls this function to get the strings it needs for the application's user interface. If you have specified a filename extension for your application's documents, the framework also calls this function when adding an entry to the Windows registration database; this allows documents to be opened from the Windows File Manager.

Call this function only if you are deriving your own class from **CDocTemplate**.

See Also: **CMultiDocTemplate::CMultiDocTemplate**, **CSingleDocTemplate::CSingleDocTemplate**, **CWinApp::RegisterShellFileTypes**

CDocTemplate::GetFirstDocPosition

virtual POSITION GetFirstDocPosition( ) const = 0;

Return Value

A **POSITION** value that can be used to iterate through the list of documents associated with this document template; or **NULL** if the list is empty.

Remarks

Use this function to get the position of the first document in the list of documents associated with this template. Use the **POSITION** value as an argument to **CDocTemplate::GetNextDoc** to iterate through the list of documents associated with the template.

CSingleDocTemplate and **CMultiDocTemplate** both override this pure virtual function. Any class you derive from **CDocTemplate** must also override this function.

See Also: **CDocTemplate::GetNextDoc**, **CSingleDocTemplate**, **CMultiDocTemplate**

CDocTemplate::GetNextDoc

virtual CDocument* GetNextDoc(POSITION& *rPos* **) const = 0;**

Return Value

A pointer to the next document in the list of documents associated with this template.

Parameters

rPos　A reference to a **POSITION** value returned by a previous call to **GetFirstDocPosition** or **GetNextDoc**.

Remarks

Retrieves the list element identified by *rPos*, then sets r*rPos* to the **POSITION** value of the next entry in the list. If the retrieved element is the last in the list, then the new value of *rPos* is set to **NULL**.

You can use **GetNextDoc** in a forward iteration loop if you establish the initial position with a call to **GetFirstDocPosition**.

You must ensure that your **POSITION** value represents a valid position in the list. If it is invalid, then the Debug version of the Microsoft Foundation Class Library asserts.

See Also:　**CDocTemplate::GetFirstDocPosition**

CDocTemplate::InitialUpdateFrame

virtual void InitialUpdateFrame(CFrameWnd* *pFrame***, CDocument*** *pDoc***,**
↳ **BOOL** *bMakeVisible* **= TRUE);**

Parameters

pFrame　The frame window that needs the initial update.

pDoc　The document to which the frame is associated. Can be **NULL**.

bMakeVisible　Indicates whether the frame should become visible and active.

Remarks

Call **IntitialUpdateFrame** after creating a new frame with **CreateNewFrame**. Calling this function causes the views in that frame window to receive their **OnInitialUpdate** calls. Also, if there was not previously an active view, the primary view of the frame window is made active; the primary view is a view with a child ID of **AFX_IDW_PANE_FIRST**. Finally, the frame window is made visible if *bMakeVisible* is non-zero. If *bMakeVisible* is zero, the current focus and visible state of the frame window will remain unchanged.

It is not necessary to call this function when using the framework's implementation of File New and File Open.

See Also: **CView::OnInititalUpdate**, **CFrameWnd::SetActiveView**,
CDocTemplate::CreateNewFrame

CDocTempate::LoadTemplate

virtual void LoadTemplate( );

Remarks

This member function is called by the framework to load the resources for a given
CDocTemplate or derived class. Normally it is called during construction, except
when the template is being constructed globally. In that case, the call to
LoadTemplate is delayed until **CWinApp::AddDocTemplate** is called.

See Also: **CWinApp::AddDocTemplate**

CDocTemplate::MatchDocType

virtual Confidence MatchDocType(LPCTSTR *lpszPathName***,**
↪ **CDocument*&** *rpDocMatch* **);**
virtual Confidence MatchDocType(LPCTSTR *lpszPathName***,**
↪ **DWORD** *dwFileType***, CDocument*&** *rpDocMatch* **);**

Return Value

A value from the **Confidence** enumeration, which is defined as follows:

```
enum Confidence
{
      noAttempt,
      maybeAttemptForeign,
      maybeAttemptNative,
      yesAttemptForeign,
      yesAttemptNative,
      yesAlreadyOpen
};
```

Parameters

lpszPathName   Pathname of the file whose type is to be determined.

rpDocMatch   Pointer to a document that is assigned the matching document, if the
file specified by *lpszPathName* is already open.

dwFileType   The type of the document (Macintosh® only).

Remarks

Use this function to determine the type of document template to use for opening a file.
If your application supports multiple file types, for example, you can use this function
to determine which of the available document templates is appropriate for a given file
by calling **MatchDocType** for each template in turn, and choosing a template
according to the confidence value returned.

If the file specified by *lpszPathName* is already open, this function returns **CDocTemplate::yesAlreadyOpen** and copies the file's **Cdocument** object into the object at *rpDocMatch*.

If the file is not open but the extension in *lpszPathName* matches the extension specified by **CDocTemplate::filterExt** (or the Macintosh file type matches), this function returns **CDocTemplate::yesAttemptNative** and sets *rpDocMatch* to **NULL**. For more information on **CDocTemplate::filterExt**, see **CDocTemplate::GetDocString**.

If neither case is true, the function returns **CDocTemplate::yesAttemptForeign**.

The default implementation does not return **CDocTemplate::maybeAttemptForeign** or **CDocTemplate::maybeAttemptNative**. Override this function to implement type-matching logic appropriate to your application, perhaps using these two values from the **Confidence** enumeration.

See Also: **CDocTemplate::GetDocString**

CDocTemplate::OpenDocumentFile

virtual CDocument* OpenDocumentFile(LPCTSTR *lpszPathName*,
↪ **BOOL** *bMakeVisible* = **TRUE**) = 0;

Return Value

A pointer to the document whose file is named by *lpszPathName*; **NULL** if unsuccessful.

Parameters

lpszPathName Pointer to the pathname of the file containing the document to be opened.

bMakeVisible Determines whether the window containing the document is to be made visible.

Remarks

Opens the file whose pathname is specified by *lpzsPathName*. If *lpszPathName* is **NULL**, a new file, containing a document of the type associated with this template, is created.

See Also: **CDocTemplate::CloseAllDocuments**

CDocTemplate::RemoveDocument

virtual void RemoveDocument(CDocument* *pDoc*);

Parameters

pDoc Pointer to the document to be removed.

Remarks

Removes the document pointed to by *pDoc* from the list of documents associated with this template. The derived classes **CMultiDocTemplate** and **CSingleDocTemplate** override this function. If you derive your own document-template class from **CDocTemplate**, your derived class must override this function.

See Also: **CDocTemplate::AddDocument**, **CMultiDocTemplate**, **CSingleDocTemplate**

CDocTemplate::SaveAllModified

virtual BOOL SaveAllModified( );

Return Value

Non-zero if successful; otherwise 0.

Remarks

Saves all documents that have been modified.

See Also: **CDocTemplate::OpenDocumentFile**, **CDocTemplate::CloseAllDocuments**

CDocTemplate::SetContainerInfo

void SetContainerInfo(UINT *nIDOleInPlaceContainer* **);**

Parameters

nIDOleInPlaceContainer   The ID of the resources used when an embedded object is activated.

Remarks

Call this function to set the resources to be used when an OLE 2 object is in-place activated. These resources may include menus and accelerator tables. This function is usually called in the **CWinApp::InitInstance** function of your application.

The menu associated with *nIDOleInPlaceContainer* contains separators that allow the menu of the activated in-place item to merge with the menu of the container application. For more information about merging server and container menus, see the article "Menus and Resources (OLE)" in *Visual C++ Programmer's Guide* online.

See Also: **CDocTemplate::SetServerInfo**, **CWinApp::InitInstance**, **CMultiDocTemplate::CMultiDocTemplate**

CDocTemplate::SetDefaultTitle

virtual void SetDefaultTitle(CDocument* *pDocument* **) = 0;**

Parameters

pDocument   Pointer to the document whose title is to be set.

Remarks

Call this function to load the document's default title and display it in the document's title bar. For information on the default title, see the description of **CDocTemplate::docName** in **CDocTemplate::GetDocString**.

See Also: CDocTemplate::GetDocString

CDocTemplate::SetServerInfo

void SetServerInfo(UINT *nIDOleEmbedding*, **UINT** *nIDOleInPlaceServer* **= 0,**
➥ **CRuntimeClass*** *pOleFrameClass* **= NULL,**
➥ **CRuntimeClass*** *pOleViewClass* **= NULL);**

Parameters

nIDOleEmbedding   The ID of the resources used when an embedded object is opened in a separate window.

nIDOleInPlaceServer   The ID of the resources used when an embedded object is activated in-place.

pOleFrameClass   Pointer to a **CRuntimeClass** structure containing class information for the frame window object created when in-place activation occurs.

pOleViewClass   Pointer to a **CRuntimeClass** structure containing class information for the view object created when in-place activation occurs.

Remarks

Call this member function to identify resources that will be used by the server application when the user requests activation of an embedded object. These resources consist of menus and accelerator tables. This function is usually called in the **InitInstance** of your application.

The menu associated with *nIDOleInPlaceServer* contains separators that allow the server menu to merge with the menu of the container. For more information about merging server and container menus, see the article "Menus and Resources (OLE)" in *Visual C++ Programmer's Guide* online.

**See Also: CMultiDocTemplate::CMultiDocTemplate,
CDocTemplate::SetContainerInfo, CWinApp::InitInstance**

CDocument

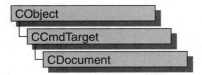

The **CDocument** class provides the basic functionality for user-defined document classes. A document represents the unit of data that the user typically opens with the File Open command and saves with the File Save command.

CDocument supports standard operations such as creating a document, loading it, and saving it. The framework manipulates documents using the interface defined by **CDocument**.

An application can support more than one type of document; for example, an application might support both spreadsheets and text documents. Each type of document has an associated document template; the document template specifies what resources (for example, menu, icon, or accelerator table) are used for that type of document. Each document contains a pointer to its associated **CDocTemplate** object.

Users interact with a document through the **CView** object(s) associated with it. A view renders an image of the document in a frame window and interprets user input as operations on the document. A document can have multiple views associated with it. When the user opens a window on a document, the framework creates a view and attaches it to the document. The document template specifies what type of view and frame window are used to display each type of document.

Documents are part of the framework's standard command routing and consequently receive commands from standard user-interface components (such as the File Save menu item). A document receives commands forwarded by the active view. If the document doesn't handle a given command, it forwards the command to the document template that manages it.

When a document's data is modified, each of its views must reflect those modifications. **CDocument** provides the **UpdateAllViews** member function for you to notify the views of such changes, so the views can repaint themselves as necessary. The framework also prompts the user to save a modified file before closing it.

To implement documents in a typical application, you must do the following:

- Derive a class from **CDocument** for each type of document.
- Add member variables to store each document's data.

- Implement member functions for reading and modifying the document's data. The document's views are the most important users of these member functions.

- Override the **CObject::Serialize** member function in your document class to write and read the document's data to and from disk.

CDocument supports sending your document via mail if mail support (MAPI) is present. See the articles "MAPI Topics" and "MAPI Support in MFC" in *Visual C++ Programmer's Guide* online.

For more information on **CDocument**, see "Serialization (Object Persistence)," "Document/View Architecture Topics," and "Document/View Creation" in *Visual C++ Programmer's Guide* online.

#include <afxwin.h>

See Also: CCmdTarget, CView, CDocTemplate

CDocument Class Members

Construction

CDocument	Constructs a **CDocument** object.

Operations

AddView	Attaches a view to the document.
GetDocTemplate	Returns a pointer to the document template that describes the type of the document.
GetFirstViewPosition	Returns the position of the first in the list of views; used to begin iteration.
GetNextView	Iterates through the list of views associated with the document.
GetPathName	Returns the path of the document's data file.
GetTitle	Returns the document's title.
IsModified	Indicates whether the document has been modified since it was last saved.
RemoveView	Detaches a view from the document.
SetModifiedFlag	Sets a flag indicating that you have modified the document since it was last saved.
SetPathName	Sets the path of the data file used by the document.
SetTitle	Sets the document's title.
UpdateAllViews	Notifies all views that document has been modified.

Overridables

CanCloseFrame	Advanced overridable; called before closing a frame window viewing this document.
DeleteContents	Called to perform cleanup of the document.
OnChangedViewList	Called after a view is added to or removed from the document.
OnCloseDocument	Called to close the document.
OnNewDocument	Called to create a new document.
OnOpenDocument	Called to open an existing document.
OnSaveDocument	Called to save the document to disk.
ReportSaveLoadException	Advanced overridable; called when an open or save operation cannot be completed because of an exception.
GetFile	Returns a pointer to the desired **CFile** object.
ReleaseFile	Releases a file to make it available for use by other applications.
SaveModified	Advanced overridable; called to ask the user whether the document should be saved.
PreCloseFrame	Called before the frame window is closed.

Mail Functions

OnFileSendMail	Sends a mail message with the document attached.
OnUpdateFileSendMail	Enables the Send Mail command if mail support is present.

Member Functions

CDocument::AddView

void AddView(CView* *pView* **);**

Parameters

pView   Points to the view being added.

Remarks

Call this function to attach a view to the document. This function adds the specified view to the list of views associated with the document; the function also sets the view's document pointer to this document. The framework calls this function when attaching a newly created view object to a document; this occurs in response to a File New, File Open, or New Window command or when a splitter window is split.

Call this function only if you are manually creating and attaching a view. Typically you will let the framework connect documents and views by defining a **CDocTemplate** object to associate a document class, view class, and frame window class.

Example

```
// The following example toggles two views in an SDI (single document
// interface) frame window. A design decision must be made as to
// whether to leave the inactive view connected to the document,
// such that the inactive view continues to receive OnUpdate
// notifications from the document. It is usually desirable to
// keep the inactive view continuously in sync with the document, even
// though it is inactive. However, doing so incurs a performance cost,
// as well as the programming cost of implementing OnUpdate hints.
// It may be less expensive, in terms of performance and/or programming,
// to re-sync the inactive view with the document only with it is
// reactivated. This example illustrates this latter approach, by
// reconnecting the newly active view and disconnecting the newly
// inactive view, via calls to CDocument::AddView and RemoveView.

BOOL CMainFrame::OnViewChange(UINT nCmdID)
{
 CView* pViewAdd;
 CView* pViewRemove;
 CDocument* pDoc = GetActiveDocument();
 UINT nCmdID;

 nCmdID = LOWORD(GetCurrentMessage()->wParam);

 if((nCmdID == ID_VIEW_VIEW1) && (m_currentView == 1))
   return;
 if((nCmdID == ID_VIEW_VIEW2) && (m_currentView == 2))
   return;

 if (nCmdID == ID_VIEW_VIEW2)
 {
  if (m_pView2 == NULL)
  {
   m_pView1 = GetActiveView();
   m_pView2 = new CMyView2;

//Note that if OnSize has been overridden in CMyView2
//and GetDocument() is used in this override it can
//cause assertions and, if the assertions are ignored,
//cause access violation.

   m_pView2->Create(NULL, NULL, AFX_WS_DEFAULT_VIEW,
   rectDefault, this, AFX_IDW_PANE_FIRST + 1, NULL);
  }
  pViewAdd = m_pView2;
  pViewRemove = m_pView1;
  m_currentView= 2;
 }
 else
 {
  pViewAdd = m_pView1;
  pViewRemove = m_pView2;
  m_currentView= 1;
 }
```

```
// Set the child i.d. of the active view to AFX_IDW_PANE_FIRST,
// so that CFrameWnd::RecalcLayout will allocate to this
// "first pane" that portion of  the frame window's client area
// not allocated to control  bars.  Set the child i.d. of the
// other view to anything other than AFX_IDW_PANE_FIRST; this
// examples switches the child id's of the two views.

 int nSwitchChildID = pViewAdd->GetDlgCtrlID();
 pViewAdd->SetDlgCtrlID(AFX_IDW_PANE_FIRST);
 pViewRemove->SetDlgCtrlID(nSwitchChildID);

 // Show the newly active view and hide the inactive view.

 pViewAdd->ShowWindow(SW_SHOW);
 pViewRemove->ShowWindow(SW_HIDE);

 // Connect the newly active view to the document, and
 // disconnect the inactive view.
 pDoc->AddView(pViewAdd);
 pDoc->RemoveView(pViewRemove);

 SetActiveView(pViewAdd);
 RecalcLayout();
}
```

**See Also: CDocTemplate, CDocument::GetFirstViewPosition,
CDocument::GetNextView, CDocument::RemoveView,
CView::GetDocument**

CDocument::CanCloseFrame

virtual BOOL CanCloseFrame(CFrameWnd* *pFrame*);

Return Value

Nonzero if it is safe to close the frame window; otherwise 0.

Parameters

pFrame   Points to the frame window of a view attached to the document.

Remarks

Called by the framework before a frame window displaying the document is closed.
The default implementation checks if there are other frame windows displaying the
document. If the specified frame window is the last one that displays the document,
the function prompts the user to save the document if it has been modified. Override
this function if you want to perform special processing when a frame window is
closed. This is an advanced overridable.

See Also: CDocument::SaveModified

CDocument::CDocument

CDocument( );

Remarks

Constructs a **CDocument** object. The framework handles document creation for you. Override the **OnNewDocument** member function to perform initialization on a per-document basis; this is particularly important in single document interface (SDI) applications.

See Also: **CDocument::OnNewDocument**, **CDocument::OnOpenDocument**

CDocument::DeleteContents

virtual void DeleteContents( );

Remarks

Called by the framework to delete the document's data without destroying the **CDocument** object itself. It is called just before the document is to be destroyed. It is also called to ensure that a document is empty before it is reused. This is particularly important for an SDI application, which uses only one document; the document is reused whenever the user creates or opens another document. Call this function to implement an "Edit Clear All" or similar command that deletes all of the document's data. The default implementation of this function does nothing. Override this function to delete the data in your document.

Example

```
// This example is the handler for an Edit Clear All command.

void CMyDoc::OnEditClearAll()
{
    DeleteContents();
    UpdateAllViews(NULL);
}

void CMyDoc::DeleteContents()
{
    // Re-initialize document data here.

}
```

See Also: **CDocument::OnCloseDocument**, **CDocument::OnNewDocument**, **CDocument::OnOpenDocument**

CDocument::GetDocTemplate

CDocTemplate* GetDocTemplate( ) const;

Return Value

A pointer to the document template for this document type, or **NULL** if the document is not managed by a document template.

Remarks

Call this function to get a pointer to the document template for this document type.

Example

```
// This example accesses the doc template object to construct
// a default document name such as SHEET.XLS, where "sheet"
// is the base document name and ".xls" is the file extension
// for the document type.
CString strDefaultDocName, strBaseName, strExt;
CDocTemplate* pDocTemplate = GetDocTemplate();
if (!pDocTemplate->GetDocString(strBaseName, CDocTemplate::docName)
    || !pDocTemplate->GetDocString(strExt, CDocTemplate::filterExt))
{
    AfxThrowUserException(); // These doc template strings will
        // be available if you created the application using AppWizard
        // and specified the file extension as an option for
        // the document class produced by AppWizard.
}
strDefaultDocName = strBaseName + strExt;
```

See Also: CDocTemplate

CDocument::GetFile

virtual CFile* GetFile(LPCTSTR *lpszFileName*, **UINT** *nOpenFlags*,
↳ **CFileException*** *pError* **);**

Return Value

A pointer to a **CFile** object.

Parameters

lpszFileName   A string that is the path to the desired file. The path may be relative or absolute.

pError   A pointer to an existing file-exception object that indicates the completion status of the operation.

nOpenFlags   Sharing and access mode. Specifies the action to take when opening the file. You can combine options listed in the CFile constructor **CFile::CFile** by using the bitwise OR (|) operator. One access permission and one share option are required; the **modeCreate** and **modeNoInherit** modes are optional.

Remarks

Call this member function to get a pointer to a **CFile** object.

See Also: CDocTemplate

CDocument::GetFirstViewPosition

virtual POSITION GetFirstViewPosition( ) const;

Return Value

A **POSITION** value that can be used for iteration with the **GetNextView** member function.

Remarks

Call this function to get the position of the first view in the list of views associated with the document.

Example

```
//To get the first view in the list of views:

POSITION pos = GetFirstViewPosition();
CView* pFirstView = GetNextView( pos );
// This example uses CDocument::GetFirstViewPosition
// and GetNextView to repaint each view.
void CMyDoc::OnRepaintAllViews()
{
    POSITION pos = GetFirstViewPosition();
    while (pos != NULL)
    {
        CView* pView = GetNextView(pos);
pView->UpdateWindow();
    }
}

// An easier way to accomplish the same result is to call
// UpdateAllViews(NULL);
```

See Also: CDocument::GetNextView

CDocument::GetNextView

virtual CView* GetNextView(POSITION& *rPosition* **) const;**

Return Value

A pointer to the view identified by *rPosition*.

Parameters

rPosition   A reference to a **POSITION** value returned by a previous call to the **GetNextView** or **GetFirstViewPosition** member functions. This value must not be **NULL**.

Remarks

Call this function to iterate through all of the document's views. The function returns the view identified by *rPosition* and then sets *rPosition* to the **POSITION** value of the next view in the list. If the retrieved view is the last in the list, then *rPosition* is set to **NULL**.

Example

```
// This example uses CDocument::GetFirstViewPosition
// and GetNextView to repaint each view.
void CMyDoc::OnRepaintAllViews()
{
    POSITION pos = GetFirstViewPosition();
    while (pos != NULL)
    {
        CView* pView = GetNextView(pos);
        pView->UpdateWindow();
    }
}

// An easier way to accomplish the same result is to call
// UpdateAllViews(NULL);
```

See Also: **CDocument::AddView, CDocument::GetFirstViewPosition, CDocument::RemoveView, CDocument::UpdateAllViews**

CDocument::GetPathName

const CString& GetPathName( ) const;

Return Value

The document's fully qualified path. This string is empty if the document has not been saved or does not have a disk file associated with it.

Remarks

Call this function to get the fully qualified path of the document's disk file.

See Also: **CDocument::SetPathName**

CDocument::GetTitle

const CString& GetTitle( ) const;

Return Value

The document's title.

Remarks

Call this function to get the document's title, which is usually derived from the document's filename.

See Also: **CDocument::SetTitle**

CDocument::IsModified

BOOL IsModified( );

Return Value

Nonzero if the document has been modified since it was last saved; otherwise 0.

Remarks

Call this function to determine whether the document has been modified since it was last saved.

See Also: **CDocument::SetModifiedFlag**, **CDocument::SaveModified**

CDocument::OnChangedViewList

virtual void OnChangedViewList( );

Remarks

Called by the framework after a view is added to or removed from the document. The default implementation of this function checks whether the last view is being removed and, if so, deletes the document. Override this function if you want to perform special processing when the framework adds or removes a view. For example, if you want a document to remain open even when there are no views attached to it, override this function.

See Also: **CDocument::AddView**, **CDocument::RemoveView**

CDocument::OnCloseDocument

virtual void OnCloseDocument( );

Remarks

Called by the framework when the document is closed, typically as part of the File Close command. The default implementation of this function calls the **DeleteContents** member function to delete the document's data and then closes the frame windows for all the views attached to the document.

Override this function if you want to perform special cleanup processing when the framework closes a document. For example, if the document represents a record in a database, you may want to override this function to close the database. You should call the base class version of this function from your override.

See Also: **CDocument::DeleteContents**, **CDocument::OnNewDocument**, **CDocument::OnOpenDocument**

CDocument::OnFileSendMail

void OnFileSendMail( );

Remarks

Sends a message via the resident mail host (if any) with the document as an attachment. **OnFileSendMail** calls **OnSaveDocument** to serialize (save) untitled and modified documents to a temporary file, which is then sent via electronic mail. If the document has not been modified, a temporary file is not needed; the original is sent. **OnFileSendMail** loads MAPI32.DLL if it has not already been loaded.

A special implementation of **OnFileSendMail** for **COleDocument** handles compound files correctly.

CDocument supports sending your document via mail if mail support (MAPI) is present. See the articles "MAPI Topics" and "MAPI Support in MFC" in *Visual C++ Programmer's Guide* online.

See Also: CDocument::OnUpdateFileSendMail, COleDocument::OnFileSendMail, CDocument::OnSaveDocument

---

CDocument::OnNewDocument

virtual BOOL OnNewDocument( );

Return Value

Nonzero if the document was successfully initialized; otherwise 0.

Remarks

Called by the framework as part of the File New command. The default implementation of this function calls the **DeleteContents** member function to ensure that the document is empty and then marks the new document as clean. Override this function to initialize the data structure for a new document. You should call the base class version of this function from your override.

If the user chooses the File New command in an SDI application, the framework uses this function to reinitialize the existing document, rather than creating a new one. If the user chooses File New in a multiple document interface (MDI) application, the framework creates a new document each time and then calls this function to initialize it. You must place your initialization code in this function instead of in the constructor for the File New command to be effective in SDI applications.

Example

```
// The following examples illustrate alternative methods of
// initializing a document object.

// Method 1: In an MDI application, the simplest place to do
// initialization is in the document constructor.  The framework
// always creates a new document object for File New or File Open.

CMyDoc::CMyDoc()
{
    // Do initialization of MDI document here.
    // ...
}

// Method 2: In an SDI or MDI application, do all initialization
// in an override of OnNewDocument, if you are certain that
// the initialization is effectively saved upon File Save
// and fully restored upon File Open, via serialization.

BOOL CMyDoc::OnNewDocument()
{
    if (!CDocument::OnNewDocument())
      return FALSE;

    // Do initialization of new document here.

    return TRUE;
}

// Method 3: If the initialization of your document is not
// effectively saved and restored by serialization (during File Save
// and File Open), then implement the initialization in single
// function (named InitMyDocument in this example).  Call the
// shared initialization function from overrides of both
// OnNewDocument and OnOpenDocument.

BOOL CMyDoc::OnNewDocument()
{
    if (!CDocument::OnNewDocument())
      return FALSE;

    InitMyDocument(); // call your shared initialization function

    // If your new document object requires additional initialization
    // not necessary when the document is deserialized via File Open,
    // then perform that additional initialization here.

    return TRUE;
}
```

**See Also: CDocument::CDocument, CDocument::DeleteContents,
CDocument::OnCloseDocument, CDocument::OnOpenDocument,
CDocument::OnSaveDocument**

CDocument::OnOpenDocument

virtual BOOL OnOpenDocument(LPCTSTR *lpszPathName* **);**

Return Value

Nonzero if the document was successfully loaded; otherwise 0.

Parameters

lpszPathName   Points to the path of the document to be opened.

Remarks

Called by the framework as part of the File Open command. The default implementation of this function opens the specified file, calls the **DeleteContents** member function to ensure that the document is empty, calls **CObject::Serialize** to read the file's contents, and then marks the document as clean. Override this function if you want to use something other than the archive mechanism or the file mechanism. For example, you might write an application where documents represent records in a database rather than separate files.

If the user chooses the File Open command in an SDI application, the framework uses this function to reinitialize the existing **CDocument** object, rather than creating a new one. If the user chooses File Open in an MDI application, the framework constructs a new **CDocument** object each time and then calls this function to initialize it. You must place your initialization code in this function instead of in the constructor for the File Open command to be effective in SDI applications.

Example

```
// The following examples illustrate alternative methods of
// initializing a document object.

// Method 1: In an MDI application, the simplest place to do
// initialization is in the document constructor.  The framework
// always creates a new document object for File New or File Open.

CMyDoc::CMyDoc()
{
    // Do initialization of MDI document here.
    // ...
}

// Method 2: In an SDI or MDI application, do all initialization
// in an override of OnNewDocument, if you are certain that
// the initialization is effectively saved upon File Save
// and fully restored upon File Open, via serialization.

BOOL CMyDoc::OnNewDocument()
{
    if (!CDocument::OnNewDocument())
        return FALSE;
```

```
    // Do initialization of new document here.

    return TRUE;
}


// Method 3: If the initialization of your document is not
// effectively saved and restored by serialization (during File Save
// and File Open), then implement the initialization in single
// function (named InitMyDocument in this example).  Call the
// shared initialization function from overrides of both
// OnNewDocument and OnOpenDocument.

BOOL CMyDoc::OnNewDocument()
{
    if (!CDocument::OnNewDocument())
        return FALSE;

    InitMyDocument(); // call your shared initialization function

    // If your new document object requires additional initialization
    // not necessary when the document is deserialized via File Open,
    // then perform that additional initialization here.

    return TRUE;
}
```

See Also: **CDocument::DeleteContents, CDocument::OnCloseDocument, CDocument::OnNewDocument, CDocument::OnSaveDocument, CDocument::ReportSaveLoadException, CObject::Serialize**

CDocument::OnSaveDocument

virtual BOOL OnSaveDocument(LPCTSTR *lpszPathName* **);**

Return Value

Nonzero if the document was successfully saved; otherwise 0.

Parameters

lpszPathName   Points to the fully qualified path to which the file should be saved.

Remarks

Called by the framework as part of the File Save or File Save As command. The default implementation of this function opens the specified file, calls **CObject::Serialize** to write the document's data to the file, and then marks the document as clean. Override this function if you want to perform special processing when the framework saves a document. For example, you might write an application where documents represent records in a database rather than separate files.

See Also: **CDocument::OnCloseDocument, CDocument::OnNewDocument, CDocument::OnOpenDocument, CDocument::ReportSaveLoadException, CObject::Serialize**

CDocument::OnUpdateFileSendMail

void OnUpdateFileSendMail(CCmdUI* *pCmdUI* **);**

Parameters

pCmdUI   A pointer to the **CCmdUI** object associated with the
ID_FILE_SEND_MAIL command.

Remarks

Enables the **ID_FILE_SEND_MAIL** command if mail support (MAPI) is present.
Otherwise the function removes the **ID_FILE_SEND_MAIL** command from the
menu, including separators above or below the menu item as appropriate. MAPI is
enabled if MAPI32.DLL is present in the path and, in the [Mail] section of the
WIN.INI file, MAPI=1. Most applications put this command on the File menu.

CDocument supports sending your document via mail if mail support (MAPI) is
present. See the articles "MAPI Topics" and "MAPI Support in MFC" in *Visual C++
Programmer's Guide* online.

See Also: CDocument::OnFileSendMail

CDocument::PreCloseFrame

virtual void PreCloseFrame(CFrameWnd* *pFrame* **);**

Parameters

pFrame   Pointer to the **CFrameWnd** that holds the associated **CDocument** object.

Remarks

This member function is called by the framework before the frame window is
destroyed. It can be overridden to provide custom cleanup, but be sure to call the
base class as well.

The default of **PreCloseFrame** does nothing in **CDocument**. The
CDocument-derived classes **COleDocument** and **CRichEditDoc** use this member
function.

CDocument::ReleaseFile

virtual void ReleaseFile(CFile* *pFile*, **BOOL** *bAbort* **);**

Parameters

pFile   A pointer to the CFile object to be released.

bAbort   Specifies whether the file is to be released by using either **CFile::Close** or
CFile::Abort. **FALSE** if the file is to be released using **CFile::Close**; **TRUE** if the
file is to be released using **CFile::Abort**.

Remarks

This member function is called by the framework to release a file, making it available for use by other applications. If *bAbort* is **TRUE**, **ReleaseFile** calls **CFile::Abort**, and the file is released. **CFile::Abort** will not throw an exception.

If *bAbort* is **FALSE**, **ReleaseFile** calls **CFile::Close** and the file is released.

Override this member function to require an action by the user before the file is released.

See Also: **CDocTemplate**, **CFile::Close**, **CFile::Abort**

CDocument::RemoveView

> **void RemoveView(CView*** *pView* **);**

Parameters

pView   Points to the view being removed.

Remarks

Call this function to detach a view from a document. This function removes the specified view from the list of views associated with the document; it also sets the view's document pointer to **NULL**. This function is called by the framework when a frame window is closed or a pane of a splitter window is closed.

Call this function only if you are manually detaching a view. Typically you will let the framework detach documents and views by defining a **CDocTemplate** object to associate a document class, view class, and frame window class.

See the example at **AddView** for a sample implementation.

See Also: **CDocument::AddView**, **CDocument::GetFirstViewPosition**, **CDocument::GetNextView**

CDocument::ReportSaveLoadException

> **virtual void ReportSaveLoadException(LPCTSTR** *lpszPathName*, **CException*** *e*,
> ↪ **BOOL** *bSaving*, **UINT** *nIDPDefault* **);**

Parameters

lpszPathName   Points to name of document that was being saved or loaded.

e   Points to the exception that was thrown. May be **NULL**.

bSaving   Flag indicating what operation was in progress; nonzero if the document was being saved, 0 if the document was being loaded.

nIDPDefault   Identifier of the error message to be displayed if the function does not specify a more specific one.

Remarks

Called if an exception is thrown (typically a **CFileException** or **CArchiveException**) while saving or loading the document. The default implementation examines the exception object and looks for an error message that specifically describes the cause. If a specific message is not found or if *e* is **NULL**, the general message specified by the *nIDPDefault* parameter is used. The function then displays a message box containing the error message. Override this function if you want to provide additional, customized failure messages. This is an advanced overridable.

See Also: **CDocument::OnOpenDocument, CDocument::OnSaveDocument, CFileException, CArchiveException**

CDocument::SaveModified

virtual BOOL SaveModified( );

Return Value

Nonzero if it is safe to continue and close the document; 0 if the document should not be closed.

Remarks

Called by the framework before a modified document is to be closed. The default implementation of this function displays a message box asking the user whether to save the changes to the document, if any have been made. Override this function if your program requires a different prompting procedure. This is an advanced overridable.

See Also: **CDocument::CanCloseFrame, CDocument::IsModified, CDocument::OnNewDocument, CDocument::OnOpenDocument, CDocument::OnSaveDocument**

CDocument::SetModifiedFlag

void SetModifiedFlag(BOOL *bModified* = **TRUE);**

Parameters

bModified   Flag indicating whether the document has been modified.

Remarks

Call this function after you have made any modifications to the document. By calling this function consistently, you ensure that the framework prompts the user to save changes before closing a document. Typically you should use the default value of **TRUE** for the *bModified* parameter. To mark a document as clean (unmodified), call this function with a value of **FALSE**.

See Also: **CDocument::IsModified, CDocument::SaveModified**

CDocument::SetPathName

virtual void SetPathName(LPCTSTR *lpszPathName*, **BOOL** *bAddToMRU* = **TRUE**);

Parameters

lpszPathName   Points to the string to be used as the path for the document.

bAddToMRU   Determines whether the filename is added to the most recently used (MRU) file list. If **TRUE,** the filename is added; if **FALSE**, it is not added.

Remarks

Call this function to specify the fully qualified path of the document's disk file. Depending on the value of *bAddToMRU* the path is added, or not added, to the MRU list maintained by the application. Note that some documents are not associated with a disk file. Call this function only if you are overriding the default implementation for opening and saving files used by the framework.

See Also: CDocument::GetPathName, CWinApp::AddToRecentFileList

CDocument::SetTitle

virtual void SetTitle(LPCTSTR *lpszTitle* **);**

Parameters

lpszTitle   Points to the string to be used as the document's title.

Remarks

Call this function to specify the document's title (the string displayed in the title bar of a frame window). Calling this function updates the titles of all frame windows that display the document.

See Also: CDocument::GetTitle

CDocument::UpdateAllViews

void UpdateAllViews(CView* *pSender*, **LPARAM** *lHint* = **0L, CObject*** *pHint* = **NULL**);

Parameters

pSender   Points to the view that modified the document, or **NULL** if all views are to be updated.

lHint   Contains information about the modification.

pHint   Points to an object storing information about the modification.

Remarks

Call this function after the document has been modified. You should call this function after you call the **SetModifiedFlag** member function. This function informs each view attached to the document, except for the view specified by *pSender*, that the document has been modified. You typically call this function from your view class after the user has changed the document through a view.

This function calls the **CView::OnUpdate** member function for each of the document's views except the sending view, passing *pHint* and *lHint*. Use these parameters to pass information to the views about the modifications made to the document. You can encode information using *lHint* and/or you can define a **CObject**-derived class to store information about the modifications and pass an object of that class using *pHint*. Override the **CView::OnUpdate** member function in your **CView**-derived class to optimize the updating of the view's display based on the information passed.

See Also: **CDocument::SetModifiedFlag, CDocument::GetFirstViewPosition, CDocument::GetNextView, CView::OnUpdate**

CDragListBox

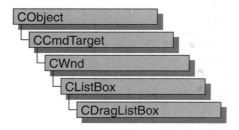

In addition to providing the functionality of a Windows list box, the **CDragListBox** class allows the user to move list box items, such as filenames, within the list box. List boxes with this capability allow users to order the items in a list in whatever manner is most useful to them. By default, the list box will move the item to the new location in the list. However, **CDragListBox** objects can be customized to copy items instead of moving them.

The list box control associated with the **CDragListBox** class must not have the **LBS_SORT** or the **LBS_MULTIPLESELECT** style. For a description of list box styles, see "List-Box Styles."

To use a drag list box in an existing dialog box of your application, add a list box control to your dialog template using the dialog editor and then assign a member variable (of Category `Control` and Variable Type `CDragListBox`) corresponding to the list box control in your dialog template.

For more information on assigning controls to member variables, see "Shortcut for Defining Member Variables for Dialog Controls" in the *Visual C++ Programmer's Guide* online.

#include <afxcmn.h>

See Also: CListBox

CDragListBox Class Members

Attributes

ItemFromPt	Returns the coordinates of the item being dragged.

Construction

CDragListBox	Constructs a **CDragListBox** object.

Operations	
DrawInsert	Draws the insertion guide of the drag list box.

Overridables	
BeginDrag	Called by the framework when a drag operation starts.
CancelDrag	Called by the framework when a drag operation has been canceled.
Dragging	Called by the framework during a drag operation.
Dropped	Called by the framework after the item has been dropped.

Member Functions

CDragListBox::BeginDrag

> **virtual BOOL BeginDrag(CPoint** *pt* **);**

Return Value

Nonzero if dragging is allowed, otherwise 0.

Parameters

pt   A **CPoint** object that contains the coordinates of the item being dragged.

Remarks

Called by the framework when an event occurs that could begin a drag operation, such as pressing the left mouse button. Override this function if you want to control what happens when a drag operation begins. The default implementation captures the mouse and stays in drag mode until the user clicks the left or right mouse button or presses ESC, at which time the drag operation is canceled.

See Also: CDragListBox::CancelDrag, CDragListBox::Dragging

CDragListBox::CancelDrag

> **virtual void CancelDrag(CPoint** *pt* **);**

Parameters

pt   A **CPoint** object that contains the coordinates of the item being dragged.

Remarks

Called by the framework when a drag operation has been canceled. Override this function to handle any special processing for your list box control.

See Also: CDragListBox::BeginDrag, CDragListBox::Dragging

CDragListBox::CDragListBox

CDragListBox( );

Remarks

Constructs a **CDragListBox** object.

See Also: CListBox::Create

CDragListBox::Dragging

virtual UINT Dragging(CPoint *pt* **);**

Return Value

The resource ID of the cursor to be displayed. The following values are possible:

- **DL_COPYCURSOR**   Indicates that the item will be copied.
- **DL_MOVECURSOR**   Indicates that the item will be moved.
- **DL_STOPCURSOR**   Indicates that the current drop target is not acceptable.

Parameters

pt   A **CPoint** object that contains the x and y screen coordinates of the cursor.

Remarks

Called by the framework when a list box item is being dragged within the **CDragListBox** object. The default behavior returns **DL_MOVECURSOR**. Override this function if you want to provide additional functionality.

See Also: CDragListBox::BeginDrag, **CDragListBox::CancelDrag**

CDragListBox::DrawInsert

virtual void DrawInsert(int *nItem* **);**

Parameters

nItem   Zero-based index of the insertion point.

Remarks

Called by the framework to draw the insertion guide before the item with the indicated index. A value of -1 clears the insertion guide. Override this function to modify the appearance or behavior of the insertion guide.

CDragListBox::Dropped

virtual void Dropped(int *nSrcIndex***, CPoint** *pt* **);**

Parameters

nSrcIndex   Specifies the zero-based index of the dropped string.

pt   A **CPoint** object that contains the coordinates of the drop site.

Remarks

Called by the framework when an item is dropped within a **CDragListBox** object.
The default behavior copies the list box item and its data to the new location and then
deletes the original item. Override this function to customize the default behavior,
such as enabling copies of list box items to be dragged to other locations within
the list.

See Also: CDragListBox::BeginDrag

CDragListBox::ItemFromPt

int ItemFromPt(CPoint *pt***, BOOL** *bAutoScroll* **= TRUE);**

Return Value

Zero-based index of the drag list box item.

Parameters

pt   A **CPoint** object containing the coordinates of a point within the list box.

bAutoScroll   Nonzero if scrolling is allowed, otherwise 0.

Remarks

Call this function to retrieve the zero-based index of the list box item located at *pt*.

CDumpContext

CDumpContext does not have a base class.

The **CDumpContext** class supports stream-oriented diagnostic output in the form of human-readable text. You can use **afxDump**, a predeclared **CDumpContext** object, for most of your dumping. The **afxDump** object is available only in the Debug version of the Microsoft Foundation Class Library.

Several of the memory diagnostic functions use **afxDump** for their output.

Under the Windows environment, the output from the predefined **afxDump** object, conceptually similar to the **cerr** stream, is routed to the debugger via the Windows function **OutputDebugString**.

The **CDumpContext** class has an overloaded insertion (**<<**) operator for **CObject** pointers that dumps the object's data. If you need a custom dump format for a derived object, override **CObject::Dump**. Most Microsoft Foundation classes implement an overridden **Dump** member function.

Classes that are not derived from **CObject**, such as **CString**, **CTime**, and **CTimeSpan**, have their own overloaded **CDumpContext** insertion operators, as do often-used structures such as **CFileStatus**, **CPoint**, and **CRect**.

If you use the **IMPLEMENT_DYNAMIC** or **IMPLEMENT_SERIAL** macro in the implementation of your class, then **CObject::Dump** will print the name of your **CObject**-derived class. Otherwise, it will print CObject.

The **CDumpContext** class is available with both the Debug and Release versions of the library, but the **Dump** member function is defined only in the Debug version. Use **#ifdef _DEBUG** / **#endif** statements to bracket your diagnostic code, including your custom **Dump** member functions.

Before you create your own **CDumpContext** object, you must create a **CFile** object that serves as the dump destination.

For more information on **CDumpContext**, see "MFC Debugging Support" in *Visual C++ Programmer's Guide* online.

#define _DEBUG

#include <afx.h>

See Also: CFile, CObject

CDumpContext Class Members

Construction

CDumpContext	Constructs a **CDumpContext** object.

Basic Input/Output

Flush	Flushes any data in the dump context buffer.
operator <<	Inserts variables and objects into the dump context.
HexDump	Dumps bytes in hexadecimal format.

Status

GetDepth	Gets an integer corresponding to the depth of the dump.
SetDepth	Sets the depth of the dump.

Member Functions

CDumpContext::CDumpContext

CDumpContext(CFile* *pFile*);
    throw(CMemoryException, CFileException);

Parameters

pFile   A pointer to the **CFile** object that is the dump destination.

Remarks

Constructs an object of class **CDumpContext**. The **afxDump** object is constructed automatically.

Do not write to the underlying **CFile** while the dump context is active; otherwise, you will interfere with the dump. Under the Windows environment, the output is routed to the debugger via the Windows function **OutputDebugString**.

Example

```
//example for CDumpContext::CDumpContext
CFile f;
if( !f.Open("dump.txt", CFile::modeCreate | CFile::modeWrite ) ) {
   afxDump << "Unable to open file" << "\n";
   exit( 1 );
}
CDumpContext dc( &f );
```

CDumpContext::Flush

void Flush( );
   throw(CFileException);

Remarks

Forces any data remaining in buffers to be written to the file attached to the dump context.

Example

```
//example for CDumpContext::Flush
afxDump.Flush();
```

CDumpContext::GetDepth

int GetDepth( ) const;

Return Value

The depth of the dump as set by **SetDepth**.

Remarks

Determines whether a deep or shallow dump is in process.

Example

See the example for **SetDepth**.

See Also: CDumpContext::SetDepth

CDumpContext::HexDump

void HexDump(LPCTSTR *lpszLine*, **BYTE*** *pby*, **int** *nBytes*, **int** *nWidth* **);**
   throw(CFileException);

Parameters

lpszLine   A string to output at the start of a new line.

pby   A pointer to a buffer containing the bytes to dump.

nBytes   The number of bytes to dump.

nWidth   Maximum number of bytes dumped per line (not the width of the output line).

Remarks

Dumps an array of bytes formatted as hexadecimal numbers.

Example

```
//example for CDumpContext::HexDump
char test[] = "This is a test of CDumpContext::HexDump\n";
afxDump.HexDump(".", (BYTE*) test, sizeof test, 20 );
```

The output from this program is:

```
. 54 68 69 73 20 69 73 20 61 20 74 65 73 74 20 6F 66 20 43 44
. 75 6D 70 43 6F 6E 74 65 78 74 3A 3A 48 65 78 44 75 6D 70 0A
. 00
```

CDumpContext::SetDepth

void SetDepth(int *nNewDepth* **);**

Parameters

nNewDepth   The new depth value.

Remarks

Sets the depth for the dump. If you are dumping a primitive type or simple **CObject** that contains no pointers to other objects, then a value of 0 is sufficient. A value greater than 0 specifies a deep dump where all objects are dumped recursively. For example, a deep dump of a collection will dump all elements of the collection. You may use other specific depth values in your derived classes.

Note   Circular references are not detected in deep dumps and can result in infinite loops.

Example

```
//example for CDumpContext::SetDepth
afxDump.SetDepth( 1 );  // Specifies deep dump
ASSERT( afxDump.GetDepth() == 1 );
```

See Also: CObject::Dump

Operators
CDumpContext::operator <<

CDumpContext& operator <<(const CObject* *pOb* **);**
   throw(CFileException);
CDumpContext& operator <<(const CObject& *ob* **);**
   throw(CFileException);
CDumpContext& operator <<(LPCTSTR *lpsz* **);**
   throw(CFileException);
CDumpContext& operator <<(const void* *lp* **);**
   throw(CFileException);
CDumpContext& operator <<(BYTE *by* **);**
   throw(CFileException);
CDumpContext& operator <<(WORD *w* **);**
   throw(CFileException);

CDumpContext& operator <<(DWORD *dw* **);**
    throw(CFileException);
CDumpContext& operator <<(int *n* **);**
    throw(CFileException);
CDumpContext& operator <<(double *d* **);**
    throw(CFileException);
CDumpContext& operator <<(float *f* **);**
    throw(CFileException);
CDumpContext& operator <<(LONG *l* **);**
    throw(CFileException);
CDumpContext& operator <<(UINT *u* **);**
    throw(CFileException);
CDumpContext& operator <<(LPCWSTR *lpsz* **);**
    throw(CFileException);
CDumpContext& operator <<(LPCSTR *lpsz* **);**
    throw(CFileException);

Return Value

A **CDumpContext** reference. Using the return value, you can write multiple insertions on a single line of source code.

Remarks

Outputs the specified data to the dump context.

The insertion operator is overloaded for **CObject** pointers as well as for most primitive types. A pointer to character results in a dump of string contents; a pointer to **void** results in a hexadecimal dump of the address only.

If you use the **IMPLEMENT_DYNAMIC** or **IMPLEMENT_SERIAL** macro in the implementation of your class, then the insertion operator, through **CObject::Dump**, will print the name of your **CObject**-derived class. Otherwise, it will print CObject. If you override the **Dump** function of the class, then you can provide a more meaningful output of the object's contents instead of a hexadecimal dump.

Example

```
//example for CDumpContext::operator <<
extern CObList li;
CString s = "test";
int i = 7;
long lo = 1000000000L;
afxDump << "list=" << &li << "string="
        << s << "int=" << i << "long=" << lo << "\n";
```

CDWordArray

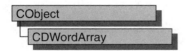

The **CDWordArray** class supports arrays of 32-bit doublewords.

The member functions of **CDWordArray** are similar to the member functions of class **CObArray**. Because of this similarity, you can use the **CObArray** reference documentation for member function specifics. Wherever you see a **CObject** pointer as a function parameter or return value, substitute a **DWORD**.

```
CObject* CObArray::GetAt( int <nIndex> ) const;
```

for example, translates to

```
DWORD CDWordArray::GetAt( int <nIndex> ) const;
```

CDWordArray incorporates the **IMPLEMENT_SERIAL** macro to support serialization and dumping of its elements. If an array of doublewords is stored to an archive, either with the overloaded insertion (**<<**) operator or with the **Serialize** member function, each element is, in turn, serialized.

Note Before using an array, use **SetSize** to establish its size and allocate memory for it. If you do not use **SetSize**, adding elements to your array causes it to be frequently reallocated and copied. Frequent reallocation and copying are inefficient and can fragment memory.

If you need debug output from individual elements in the array, you must set the depth of the **CDumpContext** object to 1 or greater.

For more information on using **CDWordArray**, see the article "Collections" in *Visual C++ Programmer's Guide* online.

#include <afxcoll.h>

See Also: **CObArray**

CDWordArray Class Members

Construction

CDWordArray	Constructs an empty array for doublewords.

Bounds

GetSize	Gets the number of elements in this array.
GetUpperBound	Returns the largest valid index.
SetSize	Sets the number of elements to be contained in this array.

Operations

FreeExtra	Frees all unused memory above the current upper bound.
RemoveAll	Removes all the elements from this array.

Element Access

GetAt	Returns the value at a given index.
SetAt	Sets the value for a given index; array not allowed to grow.
ElementAt	Returns a temporary reference to the doubleword within the array.
GetData	Allows access to elements in the array. Can be **NULL**.

Growing the Array

SetAtGrow	Sets the value for a given index; grows the array if necessary.
Add	Adds an element to the end of the array; grows the array if necessary.
Append	Appends another array to the array; grows the array if necessary.
Copy	Copies another array to the array; grows the array if necessary.

Insertion/Removal

InsertAt	Inserts an element (or all the elements in another array) at a specified index.
RemoveAt	Removes an element at a specific index.

Operators

operator []	Sets or gets the element at the specified index.

CEdit

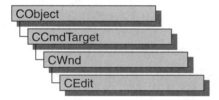

The **CEdit** class provides the functionality of a Windows edit control. An edit control is a rectangular child window in which the user can enter text.

You can create an edit control either from a dialog template or directly in your code. In both cases, first call the constructor **CEdit** to construct the **CEdit** object, then call the **Create** member function to create the Windows edit control and attach it to the **CEdit** object.

Construction can be a one-step process in a class derived from **CEdit**. Write a constructor for the derived class and call **Create** from within the constructor.

CEdit inherits significant functionality from **CWnd**. To set and retrieve text from a **CEdit** object, use the **CWnd** member functions **SetWindowText** and **GetWindowText**, which set or get the entire contents of an edit control, even if it is a multiline control. Also, if an edit control is multiline, get and set part of the control's text by calling the **CEdit** member functions **GetLine**, **SetSel**, **GetSel**, and **ReplaceSel**.

If you want to handle Windows notification messages sent by an edit control to its parent (usually a class derived from **CDialog**), add a message-map entry and message-handler member function to the parent class for each message.

Each message-map entry takes the following form:

ON_Notification(*id, memberFxn*)

where *id* specifies the child window ID of the edit control sending the notification, and *memberFxn* is the name of the parent member function you have written to handle the notification.

The parent's function prototype is as follows:

afx_msg void memberFxn( );

Following is a list of potential message-map entries and a description of the cases in which they would be sent to the parent:

- **ON_EN_CHANGE**   The user has taken an action that may have altered text in an edit control. Unlike the **EN_UPDATE** notification message, this notification message is sent after Windows updates the display.

- **ON_EN_ERRSPACE**   The edit control cannot allocate enough memory to meet a specific request.

- **ON_EN_HSCROLL**   The user clicks an edit control's horizontal scroll bar. The parent window is notified before the screen is updated.

- **ON_EN_KILLFOCUS**   The edit control loses the input focus.

- **ON_EN_MAXTEXT**   The current insertion has exceeded the specified number of characters for the edit control and has been truncated. Also sent when an edit control does not have the **ES_AUTOHSCROLL** style and the number of characters to be inserted would exceed the width of the edit control. Also sent when an edit control does not have the **ES_AUTOVSCROLL** style and the total number of lines resulting from a text insertion would exceed the height of the edit control.

- **ON_EN_SETFOCUS**   Sent when an edit control receives the input focus.

- **ON_EN_UPDATE**   The edit control is about to display altered text. Sent after the control has formatted the text but before it screens the text so that the window size can be altered, if necessary.

- **ON_EN_VSCROLL**   The user clicks an edit control's vertical scroll bar. The parent window is notified before the screen is updated.

If you create a **CEdit** object within a dialog box, the **CEdit** object is automatically destroyed when the user closes the dialog box.

If you create a **CEdit** object from a dialog resource using the dialog editor, the **CEdit** object is automatically destroyed when the user closes the dialog box.

If you create a **CEdit** object within a window, you may also need to destroy it. If you create the **CEdit** object on the stack, it is destroyed automatically. If you create the **CEdit** object on the heap by using the **new** function, you must call **delete** on the object to destroy it when the user terminates the Windows edit control. If you allocate any memory in the **CEdit** object, override the **CEdit** destructor to dispose of the allocations.

For more information on **CEdit**, see "Control Topics" in *Visual C++ Programmer's Guide* online.

#include <afxwin.h>

See Also: CWnd, CButton, CComboBox, CListBox, CScrollBar, CStatic, CDialog

CEdit Class Members

Construction

CEdit	Constructs a **CEdit** control object.
Create	Creates the Windows edit control and attaches it to the **CEdit** object.

General Operations

Note For single-line edit controls, use **CWnd::GetWindowText**

GetSel	Gets the starting and ending character positions of the current selection in an edit control.
ReplaceSel	Replaces the current selection in an edit control with the specified text.
SetSel	Selects a range of characters in an edit control.
Clear	Deletes (clears) the current selection (if any) in the edit control.
Copy	Copies the current selection (if any) in the edit control to the Clipboard in **CF_TEXT** format.
Cut	Deletes (cuts) the current selection (if any) in the edit control and copies the deleted text to the Clipboard in **CF_TEXT** format.
Paste	Inserts the data from the Clipboard into the edit control at the current cursor position. Data is inserted only if the Clipboard contains data in **CF_TEXT** format.
Undo	Reverses the last edit-control operation.
CanUndo	Determines whether an edit-control operation can be undone.
EmptyUndoBuffer	Resets (clears) the undo flag of an edit control.
GetModify	Determines whether the contents of an edit control have been modified.
SetModify	Sets or clears the modification flag for an edit control.
SetReadOnly	Sets the read-only state of an edit control.
GetPasswordChar	Retrieves the password character displayed in an edit control when the user enters text.
SetPasswordChar	Sets or removes a password character displayed in an edit control when the user enters text.
GetFirstVisibleLine	Determines the topmost visible line in an edit control.
LineLength	Retrieves the length of a line in an edit control.
LineScroll	Scrolls the text of a multiple-line edit control.
LineFromChar	Retrieves the line number of the line that contains the specified character index.
GetRect	Gets the formatting rectangle of an edit control.
LimitText	Limits the length of the text that the user may enter into an edit control.

Multiple-Line Operations

GetLineCount	Retrieves the number of lines in a multiple-line edit control.
GetLine	Retrieves a line of text from an edit control.
LineIndex	Retrieves the character index of a line within a multiple-line edit control.
FmtLines	Sets the inclusion of soft line-break characters on or off within a multiple-line edit control.
SetTabStops	Sets the tab stops in a multiple-line edit control.
SetRect	Sets the formatting rectangle of a multiple-line edit control and updates the control.
SetRectNP	Sets the formatting rectangle of a multiple-line edit control without redrawing the control window.
GetHandle	Retrieves a handle to the memory currently allocated for a multiple-line edit control.
SetHandle	Sets the handle to the local memory that will be used by a multiple-line edit control.

Windows 95 Operations

GetMargins	Gets the left and right margins for this **CEdit**.
SetMargins	Sets the left and right margins for this **CEdit**.
GetLimitText	Gets the maximum amount of text this **CEdit** can contain.
SetLimitText	Sets the maximum amount of text this **CEdit** can contain.
CharFromPos	Retrieves the line and character indices for the character closest to a specified position.
PosFromChar	Retrieves the coordinates of the upper-left corner of a specified character index.

Member Functions

CEdit::CanUndo

BOOL CanUndo( ) const;

Return Value

Nonzero if the last edit operation can be undone by a call to the **Undo** member function; 0 if it cannot be undone.

Remarks

Call this function to determine if the last edit operation can be undone.

For more information, see **EM_CANUNDO** in the Win32 documentation.

See Also: CEdit::Undo, CEdit::EmptyUndoBuffer

CEdit::CEdit

CEdit( );

Remarks

Constructs a **CEdit** object. Use **Create** to construct the Windows edit control.

See Also: **CEdit::Create**

CEdit::CharFromPos

int CharFromPos(CPoint *pt*) const;

Return Value

The character index in the low-order **WORD**, and the line index in the high-order **WORD**.

Parameters

pt The coordinates of a point in the client area of this **CEdit** object.

Remarks

Call this function to retrieve the zero-based line and character indices of the character nearest the specified point in this **CEdit** control

Note This member function is available only in Windows 95.

For more information, see **EM_CHARFROMPOS** in the Win32 documentation.

See Also: **CEdit::PosFromChar**

CEdit::Clear

void Clear( );

Remarks

Call this function to delete (clear) the current selection (if any) in the edit control.

The deletion performed by **Clear** can be undone by calling the **Undo** member function.

To delete the current selection and place the deleted contents into the Clipboard, call the **Cut** member function.

For more information, see **WM_CLEAR** in the Win32 documentation.

See Also: **CEdit::Undo, CEdit::Copy, CEdit::Cut, CEdit::Paste**

CEdit::Copy

void Copy( );

Remarks

Call this function to coy the current selection (if any) in the edit control to the Clipboard in **CF_TEXT** format.

For more information, see **WM_COPY** in the Win32 documentation.

See Also: **CEdit::Clear**, **CEdit::Cut**, **CEdit::Paste**

CEdit::Create

BOOL Create(DWORD *dwStyle***, const RECT&** *rect***, CWnd*** *pParentWnd***, UINT** *nID* **);**

Return Value

Nonzero if initialization is successful; otherwise 0.

Parameters

dwStyle   Specifies the edit control's style. Apply any combination of edit styles to the control.

rect   Specifies the edit control's size and position. Can be a **CRect** object or **RECT** structure.

pParentWnd   Specifies the edit control's parent window (usually a **CDialog**). It must not be **NULL**.

nID   Specifies the edit control's ID.

Remarks

You construct a **CEdit** object in two steps. First, call the **CEdit** constructor, then call **Create**, which creates the Windows edit control and attaches it to the **CEdit** object.

When **Create** executes, Windows sends the **WM_NCCREATE**, **WM_NCCALCSIZE**, **WM_CREATE**, and **WM_GETMINMAXINFO** messages to the edit control.

These messages are handled by default by the **OnNcCreate**, **OnNcCalcSize**, **OnCreate**, and **OnGetMinMaxInfo** member functions in the **CWnd** base class. To extend the default message handling, derive a class from **CEdit**, add a message map to the new class, and override the above message-handler member functions. Override **OnCreate**, for example, to perform needed initialization for the new class.

Apply the following window styles to an edit control.

- **WS_CHILD**   Always
- **WS_VISIBLE**   Usually
- **WS_DISABLED**   Rarely

- **WS_GROUP** To group controls
- **WS_TABSTOP** To include edit control in the tabbing order

See Also: CEdit::CEdit

CEdit::Cut

void Cut( );

Remarks

Call this function to delete (cut) the current selection (if any) in the edit control and copy the deleted text to the Clipboard in **CF_TEXT** format.

The deletion performed by **Cut** can be undone by calling the **Undo** member function.

To delete the current selection without placing the deleted text into the Clipboard, call the **Clear** member function.

For more information, see **WM_CUT** in the Win32 documentation.

See Also: CEdit::Undo, CEdit::Clear, CEdit::Copy, CEdit::Paste

CEdit::EmptyUndoBuffer

void EmptyUndoBuffer( );

Remarks

Call this function to reset (clear) the undo flag of an edit control. The edit control will now be unable to undo the last operation. The undo flag is set whenever an operation within the edit control can be undone.

The undo flag is automatically cleared whenever the **SetWindowText** or **SetHandle** **CWnd** member functions are called.

For more information, see **EM_EMPTYUNDOBUFFER** in the Win32 documentation.

See Also: CEdit::CanUndo, CEdit::SetHandle, CEdit::Undo, CWnd::SetWindowText

CEdit::FmtLines

BOOL FmtLines(BOOL *bAddEOL* **);**

Return Value

Nonzero if any formatting occurs; otherwise 0.

Parameters

> *bAddEOL*   Specifies whether soft line-break characters are to be inserted. A value of **TRUE** inserts the characters; a value of **FALSE** removes them.

Remarks

> Call this function to set the inclusion of soft line-break characters on or off within a multiple-line edit control. A soft line break consists of two carriage returns and a linefeed inserted at the end of a line that is broken because of word wrapping. A hard line break consists of one carriage return and a linefeed. Lines that end with a hard line break are not affected by **FmtLines**.
>
> Windows will only respond if the **CEdit** object is a multiple-line edit control.
>
> **FmtLines** only affects the buffer returned by **GetHandle** and the text returned by **WM_GETTEXT**. It has no impact on the display of the text within the edit control.
>
> For more information, see **EM_FMTLINES** in the Win32 documentation.
>
> **See Also:**   **CEdit::GetHandle**, **CWnd::GetWindowText**

CEdit::GetFirstVisibleLine

> **int GetFirstVisibleLine( ) const;**

Return Value

> The zero-based index of the topmost visible line. For single-line edit controls, the return value is 0.

Remarks

> Call this function to determine the topmost visible line in an edit control.
>
> For more information, see **EM_GETFIRSTVISIBLELINE** in the Win32 documentation.
>
> **See Also:**   **CEdit::GetLine**

CEdit::GetHandle

> **HLOCAL GetHandle( ) const;**

Return Value

> A local memory handle that identifies the buffer holding the contents of the edit control. If an error occurs, such as sending the message to a single-line edit control, the return value is 0.

Remarks

> Call this function to retrieve a handle to the memory currently allocated for a multiple-line edit control. The handle is a local memory handle and may be used by any of the **Local** Windows memory functions that take a local memory handle as a parameter.

GetHandle is processed only by multiple-line edit controls.

Call **GetHandle** for a multiple-line edit control in a dialog box only if the dialog box was created with the **DS_LOCALEDIT** style flag set. If the **DS_LOCALEDIT** style is not set, you will still get a nonzero return value, but you will not be able to use the returned value.

For more information, see **EM_GETHANDLE** in the Win32 documentation.

See Also: **CEdit::SetHandle**

CEdit::GetLimitText

UINT GetLimitText( ) const;

Return Value

The current text limit, in bytes, for this **CEdit** object.

Remarks

Call this member function to get the text limit for this **CEdit** object. The text limit is the maximum amount of text, in bytes, that the edit control can accept.

Note This member function is available only in Windows 95.

For more information, see **EM_GETLIMITTEXT** in the Win32 documentation.

See Also: **CEdit::SetLimitText**, **CEdit::LimitText**

CEdit::GetLine

int GetLine(int *nIndex*, **LPTSTR** *lpszBuffer* **) const;**
int GetLine(int *nIndex*, **LPTSTR** *lpszBuffer*, **int** *nMaxLength* **) const;**

Return Value

The number of bytes actually copied. The return value is 0 if the line number specified by *nIndex* is greater then the number of lines in the edit control.

Parameters

nIndex   Specifies the line number to retrieve from a multiple-line edit control. Line numbers are zero-based; a value of 0 specifies the first line. This parameter is ignored by a single-line edit control.

lpszBuffer   Points to the buffer that receives a copy of the line. The first word of the buffer must specify the maximum number of bytes that can be copied to the buffer.

nMaxLength   Specifies the maximum number of bytes that can be copied to the buffer. **GetLine** places this value in the first word of *lpszBuffer* before making the call to Windows.

Remarks

Call this function to retrieve a line of text from an edit control and places it in *lpszBuffer*. This call is not processed for a single-line edit control.

The copied line does not contain a null-termination character.

For more information, see **EM_GETLINE** in the Win32 documentation.

See Also: CEdit::LineLength, CWnd::GetWindowText

CEdit::GetLineCount

int GetLineCount( ) const;

Return Value

An integer containing the number of lines in the multiple-line edit control. If no text has been entered into the edit control, the return value is 1.

Remarks

Call this function to retrieve the number of lines in a multiple-line edit control.

GetLineCount is only processed by multiple-line edit controls.

For more information, see **EM_GETLINECOUNT** in the Win32 documentation.

CEdit::GetMargins

DWORD GetMargins( ) const;

Return Value

The width of the left margin in the low-order **WORD** and the width of the right margin in the high-order **WORD**.

Remarks

Call this member function to retrieve the left and right margins of this edit control. Margins are measured in pixels.

Note   This member function is available only in Windows 95.

For more information, see **EM_GETMARGINS** in the Win32 documentation.

See Also: CEdit::SetMargins

CEdit::GetModify

BOOL GetModify( ) const;

Return Value

Nonzero if the edit-control contents have been modified; 0 if they have remained unchanged.

Remarks

Call this function to determine whether the contents of an edit control have been modified.

Windows maintains an internal flag indicating whether the contents of the edit control have been changed. This flag is cleared when the edit control is first created and may also be cleared by calling the **SetModify** member function.

For more information, see **EM_GETMODIFY** in the Win32 documentation.

See Also: CEdit::SetModify

CEdit::GetPasswordChar

TCHAR GetPasswordChar( ) const;

Return Value

Specifies the character to be displayed in place of the character typed by the user. The return value is **NULL** if no password character exists.

Remarks

Call this function to retrieve the password character displayed in an edit control when the user enters text.

If the edit control is created with the **ES_PASSWORD** style, the default password character is set to an asterisk (*).

For more information, see **EM_GETPASSWORDCHAR** in the Win32 documentation.

See Also: CEdit::SetPasswordChar

CEdit::GetRect

void GetRect(LPRECT *lpRect* **) const;**

Parameters

lpRect   Points to the **RECT** structure that receives the formatting rectangle.

Remarks

Call this function to get the formatting rectangle of an edit control. The formatting rectangle is the limiting rectangle of the text, which is independent of the size of the edit-control window.

The formatting rectangle of a multiple-line edit control can be modified by the **SetRect** and **SetRectNP** member functions.

For more information, see **EM_GETRECT** in the Win32 documentation.

See Also: CEdit::SetRect, CEdit::SetRectNP

CEdit::GetSel

DWORD GetSel( ) const;
void GetSel(int& *nStartChar***, int&** *nEndChar* **) const;**

Return Value

The version that returns a **DWORD** returns a value that contains the starting position in the low-order word and the position of the first nonselected character after the end of the selection in the high-order word.

Parameters

nStartChar   Reference to an integer that will receive the position of the first character in the current selection.

nEndChar   Reference to an integer that will receive the position of the first nonselected character past the end of the current selection.

Remarks

Call this function to get the starting and ending character positions of the current selection (if any) in an edit control, using either the return value or the parameters.

For more information, see **EM_GETSEL** in the Win32 documentation.

See Also: CEdit::SetSel

CEdit::LimitText

void LimitText(int *nChars* **= 0);**

Parameters

nChars   Specifies the length (in bytes) of the text that the user can enter. If this parameter is 0, the text length is set to **UINT_MAX** bytes. This is the default behavior.

Remarks

Call this function to limit the length of the text that the user may enter into an edit control.

Changing the text limit restricts only the text the user can enter. It has no effect on any text already in the edit control, nor does it affect the length of the text copied to the edit control by the **SetWindowText** member function in **CWnd**. If an application uses the **SetWindowText** function to place more text into an edit control than is specified in the call to **LimitText**, the user can delete any of the text within the edit control. However, the text limit will prevent the user from replacing the existing text with new text, unless deleting the current selection causes the text to fall below the text limit.

Note   In Win32 (Windows NT and Windows 95), **SetLimitText** replaces this function.

For more information, see **EM_LIMITTEXT** in the Win32 documentation.

See Also: CWnd::SetWindowText, CEdit::GetLimitText, CEdit::SetLimitText

CEdit::LineFromChar

int LineFromChar(int *nIndex* **= –1) const;**

Return Value

The zero-based line number of the line containing the character index specified by *nIndex*. If *nIndex* is –1, the number of the line that contains the first character of the selection is returned. If there is no selection, the current line number is returned.

Parameters

nIndex Contains the zero-based index value for the desired character in the text of the edit control, or contains –1. If *nIndex* is –1, it specifies the current line, that is, the line that contains the caret.

Remarks

Call this function to retrieve the line number of the line that contains the specified character index. A character index is the number of characters from the beginning of the edit control.

This member function is only used by multiple-line edit controls.

For more information, see **EM_LINEFROMCHAR** in the Win32 documentation.

See Also: CEdit::LineIndex

CEdit::LineIndex

int LineIndex(int *nLine* **= –1) const;**

Return Value

The character index of the line specified in *nLine* or –1 if the specified line number is greater then the number of lines in the edit control.

Parameters

nLine Contains the index value for the desired line in the text of the edit control, or contains –1. If *nLine* is –1, it specifies the current line, that is, the line that contains the caret.

Remarks

Call this function to retrieve the character index of a line within a multiple-line edit control. The character index is the number of characters from the beginning of the edit control to the specified line.

This member function is only processed by multiple-line edit controls.

For more information, see **EM_LINEINDEX** in the Win32 documentation.

See Also: CEdit::LineFromChar

CEdit::LineLength

int LineLength(int *nLine* **= –1) const;**

Return Value

When **LineLength** is called for a multiple-line edit control, the return value is the length (in bytes) of the line specified by *nLine*. When **LineLength** is called for a single-line edit control, the return value is the length (in bytes) of the text in the edit control.

Parameters

nLine Specifies the character index of a character in the line whose length is to be retrieved. If this parameter is –1, the length of the current line (the line that contains the caret) is returned, not including the length of any selected text within the line. When **LineLength** is called for a single-line edit control, this parameter is ignored.

Remarks

Call this function to retrieve the length of a line in an edit control.

Use the **LineIndex** member function to retrieve a character index for a given line number within a multiple-line edit control.

For more information, see **EM_LINELENGTH** in the Win32 documentation.

See Also: CEdit::LineIndex

CEdit::LineScroll

void LineScroll(int *nLines*, **int** *nChars* **= 0);**

Parameters

nLines Specifies the number of lines to scroll vertically.

nChars Specifies the number of character positions to scroll horizontally. This value is ignored if the edit control has either the **ES_RIGHT** or **ES_CENTER** style.

Remarks

Call this function to scroll the text of a multiple-line edit control.

This member function is processed only by multiple-line edit controls.

The edit control does not scroll vertically past the last line of text in the edit control. If the current line plus the number of lines specified by *nLines* exceeds the total number of lines in the edit control, the value is adjusted so that the last line of the edit control is scrolled to the top of the edit-control window.

LineScroll can be used to scroll horizontally past the last character of any line.

For more information, see **EM_LINESCROLL** in the Win32 documentation.

See Also: **CEdit::LineIndex**

CEdit::Paste

> **void Paste( );**

Remarks

> Call this function to insert the data from the Clipboard into the **CEdit** at the insertion point. Data is inserted only if the Clipboard contains data in **CF_TEXT** format.
>
> For more information, see **WM_PASTE** in the Win32 documentation.
>
> **See Also:**   **CEdit::Clear**, **CEdit::Copy**, **CEdit::Cut**

CEdit::PosFromChar

> **CPoint PosFromChar(UINT** *nChar* **) const;**

Return Value

> The coordinates of the top-left corner of the character specified by *nChar*.

Parameters

> *nChar*   The zero-based index of the specified character.

Remarks

> Call this function to get the position (top-left corner) of a given character within this **CEdit** object. The character is specified by giving its zero-based index value. If *nChar* is greater than the index of the last character in this **CEdit** object, the return value specifies the coordinates of the character position just past the last character in this **CEdit** object.
>
> **Note**   This member function is available only in Windows 95.
>
> For more information, see **EM_POSFROMCHAR** in the Win32 documentation.
>
> **See Also:**   **CEdit::CharFromPos**

CEdit::ReplaceSel

> **void ReplaceSel(LPCTSTR** *lpszNewText*, **BOOL** *bCanUndo* **= FALSE);**

Parameters

> *lpszNewText*   Points to a null-terminated string containing the replacement text.
>
> *bCanUndo*   To specify that this function can be undone, set the value of this parameter to **TRUE** . The default value is **FALSE**.

Remarks

Call this function to replace the current selection in an edit control with the text specified by *lpszNewText*.

Replaces only a portion of the text in an edit control. If you want to replace all of the text, use the **CWnd::SetWindowText** member function.

If there is no current selection, the replacement text is inserted at the current cursor location.

For more information, see **EM_REPLACESEL** in the Win32 documentation.

See Also: CWnd::SetWindowText

CEdit::SetHandle

void SetHandle(HLOCAL *hBuffer* **);**

Parameters

hBuffer   Contains a handle to the local memory. This handle must have been created by a previous call to the **LocalAlloc** Windows function using the **LMEM_MOVEABLE** flag. The memory is assumed to contain a null-terminated string. If this is not the case, the first byte of the allocated memory should be set to 0.

Remarks

Call this function to set the handle to the local memory that will be used by a multiple-line edit control. The edit control will then use this buffer to store the currently displayed text instead of allocating its own buffer.

This member function is processed only by multiple-line edit controls.

Before an application sets a new memory handle, it should use the **GetHandle** member function to get the handle to the current memory buffer and free that memory using the **LocalFree** Windows function.

SetHandle clears the undo buffer (the **CanUndo** member function then returns 0) and the internal modification flag (the **GetModify** member function then returns 0). The edit-control window is redrawn.

You can use this member function in a multiple-line edit control in a dialog box only if you have created the dialog box with the **DS_LOCALEDIT** style flag set.

For more information, see **EM_SETHANDLE**, **LocalAlloc**, and **LocalFree** in the Win32 documentation.

See Also: CEdit::CanUndo, CEdit::GetHandle, CEdit::GetModify

CEdit::SetLimitText

void SetLimitText(UINT *nMax* **);**

Parameters

    nMax   The new text limit, in bytes.

Remarks

Call this member function to set the text limit for this **CEdit** object. The text limit is the maximum amount of text, in bytes, that the edit control can accept.

Changing the text limit restricts only the text the user can enter. It has no effect on any text already in the edit control, nor does it affect the length of the text copied to the edit control by the **SetWindowText** member function in **CWnd**. If an application uses the **SetWindowText** function to place more text into an edit control than is specified in the call to **LimitText**, the user can delete any of the text within the edit control. However, the text limit will prevent the user from replacing the existing text with new text, unless deleting the current selection causes the text to fall below the text limit.

This function replaces **LimitText** in Win32.

For more information, see **EM_SETLIMITTEXT** in the Win32 documentation.

See Also: **CEdit::GetLimitText, CEdit::LimitText**

CEdit::SetMargins

void SetMargins(UINT *nLeft*, **UINT** *nRight* **);**

Parameters

    nLeft   The width of the new left margin, in pixels.

    nRight   The width of the new right margin, in pixels.

Remarks

Call this member function to set the left and right margins of this edit control.

Note   This member function is available only in Windows 95.

For more information, see **EM_SETMARGINS** in the Win32 documentation.

See Also: **CEdit::GetMargins**

CEdit::SetModify

void SetModify(BOOL *bModified* = **TRUE);**

Parameters

bModified   A value of **TRUE** indicates that the text has been modified, and a value of **FALSE** indicates it is unmodified. By default, the modified flag is set.

Remarks

Call this function to set or clear the modified flag for an edit control. The modified flag indicates whether or not the text within the edit control has been modified. It is automatically set whenever the user changes the text. Its value may be retrieved with the **GetModify** member function.

For more information, see **EM_SETMODIFY** in the Win32 documentation.

See Also: **CEdit::GetModify**

CEdit::SetPasswordChar

void SetPasswordChar(TCHAR *ch* **);**

Parameters

ch   Specifies the character to be displayed in place of the character typed by the user. If *ch* is 0, the actual characters typed by the user are displayed.

Remarks

Call this function to set or remove a password character displayed in an edit control when the user types text. When a password character is set, that character is displayed for each character the user types.

This member function has no effect on a multiple-line edit control.

When the **SetPasswordChar** member function is called, **CEdit** will redraw all visible characters using the character specified by *ch*.

If the edit control is created with the **ES_PASSWORD** style, the default password character is set to an asterisk (*). This style is removed if **SetPasswordChar** is called with *ch* set to 0.

For more information, see **EM_SETPASSWORDCHAR** in the Win32 documentation.

See Also: **CEdit::GetPasswordChar**

CEdit::SetReadOnly

BOOL SetReadOnly(BOOL *bReadOnly* = **TRUE);**

Return Value

Nonzero if the operation is successful, or 0 if an error occurs.

Parameters

bReadOnly   Specifies whether to set or remove the read-only state of the edit control. A value of **TRUE** sets the state to read-only; a value of **FALSE** sets the state to read/write.

Remarks

Calls this function to set the read-only state of an edit control.

The current setting can be found by testing the **ES_READONLY** flag in the return value of **CWnd::GetStyle**.

For more information, see **EM_SETREADONLY** in the Win32 documentation.

See Also: **CWnd::GetStyle**

CEdit::SetRect

> **void SetRect(LPCRECT** *lpRect* **);**

Parameters

lpRect   Points to the **RECT** structure or **CRect** object that specifies the new dimensions of the formatting rectangle.

Remarks

Call this function to set the dimensions of a rectangle using the specified coordinates. This member is processed only by multiple-line edit controls.

Use **SetRect** to set the formatting rectangle of a multiple-line edit control. The formatting rectangle is the limiting rectangle of the text, which is independent of the size of the edit-control window. When the edit control is first created, the formatting rectangle is the same as the client area of the edit-control window. By using the **SetRect** member function, an application can make the formatting rectangle larger or smaller than the edit-control window.

If the edit control has no scroll bar, text will be clipped, not wrapped, if the formatting rectangle is made larger than the window. If the edit control contains a border, the formatting rectangle is reduced by the size of the border. If you adjust the rectangle returned by the **GetRect** member function, you must remove the size of the border before you pass the rectangle to **SetRect**.

When **SetRect** is called, the edit control's text is also reformatted and redisplayed.

For more information, see **EM_SETRECT** in the Win32 documentation.

See Also: **CRect::CRect**, **CRect::CopyRect**, **CRect::operator =**, **CRect::SetRectEmpty**, **CEdit::GetRect**, **CEdit::SetRectNP**

CEdit::SetRectNP

void SetRectNP(LPCRECT *lpRect* **);**

Parameters

lpRect   Points to a **RECT** structure or **CRect** object that specifies the new dimensions of the rectangle.

Remarks

Call this function to set the formatting rectangle of a multiple-line edit control. The formatting rectangle is the limiting rectangle of the text, which is independent of the size of the edit-control window.

SetRectNP is identical to the **SetRect** member function except that the edit-control window is not redrawn.

When the edit control is first created, the formatting rectangle is the same as the client area of the edit-control window. By calling the **SetRectNP** member function, an application can make the formatting rectangle larger or smaller than the edit-control window.

If the edit control has no scroll bar, text will be clipped, not wrapped, if the formatting rectangle is made larger than the window.

This member is processed only by multiple-line edit controls.

For more information, see **EM_SETRECTNP** in the Win32 documentation.

See Also: **CRect::CRect**, **CRect::CopyRect**, **CRect::operator =**, **CRect::SetRectEmpty**, **CEdit::GetRect**, **CEdit::SetRect**

CEdit::SetSel

void SetSel(DWORD *dwSelection*, **BOOL** *bNoScroll* = **FALSE**);
void SetSel(int *nStartChar*, **int** *nEndChar*, **BOOL** *bNoScroll* = **FALSE**);

Parameters

dwSelection   Specifies the starting position in the low-order word and the ending position in the high-order word. If the low-order word is 0 and the high-order word is –1, all the text in the edit control is selected. If the low-order word is –1, any current selection is removed.

bNoScroll   Indicates whether the caret should be scrolled into view. If **FALSE**, the caret is scrolled into view. If **TRUE**, the caret is not scrolled into view.

nStartChar   Specifies the starting position. If *nStartChar* is 0 and *nEndChar* is –1, all the text in the edit control is selected. If *nStartChar* is –1, any current selection is removed.

nEndChar   Specifies the ending position.

Remarks

Call this function to select a range of characters in an edit control.

For more information, see **EM_SETSEL** in the Win32 documentation.

See Also: **CEdit::GetSel, CEdit::ReplaceSel**

CEdit::SetTabStops

void SetTabStops( );
BOOL SetTabStops(const int& *cxEachStop* **);**
BOOL SetTabStops(int *nTabStops*, **LPINT** *rgTabStops* **);**

Return Value

Nonzero if the tabs were set; otherwise 0.

Parameters

cxEachStop   Specifies that tab stops are to be set at every *cxEachStop* dialog units.

nTabStops   Specifies the number of tab stops contained in *rgTabStops*. This number must be greater than 1.

rgTabStops   Points to an array of unsigned integers specifying the tab stops in dialog units. A dialog unit is a horizontal or vertical distance. One horizontal dialog unit is equal to one-fourth of the current dialog base width unit, and 1 vertical dialog unit is equal to one-eighth of the current dialog base height unit. The dialog base units are computed based on the height and width of the current system font. The **GetDialogBaseUnits** Windows function returns the current dialog base units in pixels.

Remarks

Call this function to set the tab stops in a multiple-line edit control. When text is copied to a multiple-line edit control, any tab character in the text will cause space to be generated up to the next tab stop.

To set tab stops to the default size of 32 dialog units, call the parameterless version of this member function. To set tab stops to a size other than 32, call the version with the *cxEachStop* parameter. To set tab stops to an array of sizes, use the version with two parameters.

This member function is only processed by multiple-line edit controls.

SetTabStops does not automatically redraw the edit window. If you change the tab stops for text already in the edit control, call **CWnd::InvalidateRect** to redraw the edit window.

For more information, see **EM_SETTABSTOPS** and **GetDialogBaseUnits** in the Win32 documentation.

See Also: **CWnd::InvalidateRect**

CEdit::Undo

BOOL Undo( );

Return Value

For a single-line edit control, the return value is always nonzero. For a multiple-line edit control, the return value is nonzero if the undo operation is successful, or 0 if the undo operation fails.

Remarks

Call this function to undo the last edit-control operation.

An undo operation can also be undone. For example, you can restore deleted text with the first call to **Undo**. As long as there is no intervening edit operation, you can remove the text again with a second call to **Undo**.

For more information, see **EM_UNDO** in the Win32 documentation.

See Also: CEdit::CanUndo

CEditView

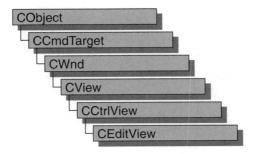

A **CEditView** object is a view that, like the **CEdit** class, provides the functionality of a Windows edit control and can be used to implement simple text-editor functionality. The **CEditView** class provides the following additional functions:

- Printing
- Find and replace

Because class **CEditView** is a derivative of class **CView**, objects of class **CEditView** can be used with documents and document templates.

Each **CEditView** control's text is kept in its own global memory object. Your application can have any number of **CEditView** objects.

Create objects of type **CEditView** if you want an edit window with the added functionality listed above, or if you want simple text-editor functionality. A **CEditView** object can occupy the entire client area of a window. Derive your own classes from **CEditView** to add or modify the basic functionality, or to declare classes that can be added to a document template.

The default implementation of class **CEditView** handles the following commands: **ID_EDIT_SELECT_ALL**, **ID_EDIT_FIND**, **ID_EDIT_REPLACE**, **ID_EDIT_REPEAT**, and **ID_FILE_PRINT**.

Objects of type **CEditView** (or of types derived from **CEditView**) have the following limitations:

- **CEditView** does not implement true WYSIWYG (what you see is what you get) editing. Where there is a choice between readability on the screen and matching printed output, **CEditView** opts for screen readability.
- **CEditView** can display text in only a single font. No special character formatting is supported. See class **CRichEditView** for greater capabilities.
- The amount of text a **CEditView** can contain is limited. The limits are the same as for the **CEdit** control.

For more information on **CEditView**, see "Derived View Classes" in *Visual C++ Programmer's Guide* online.

#include <afxext.h>

See Also: **CEdit**, **CDocument**, **CDocTemplate**, **CCtrlView**, **CRichEditView**

CEditView Class Members

Data Members

dwStyleDefault	Default style for objects of type **CEditView.**

Construction

CEditView	Constructs an object of type **CEditView**.

Attributes

GetEditCtrl	Provides access to the **CEdit** portion of a **CEditView** object (the Windows edit control).
GetPrinterFont	Retrieves the current printer font.
GetSelectedText	Retrieves the current text selection.
LockBuffer	Locks the buffer.
UnlockBuffer	Unlocks the buffer.
GetBufferLength	Obtains the length of the character buffer.
SetPrinterFont	Sets a new printer font.
SetTabStops	Sets tab stops for both screen display and printing.

Operations

FindText	Searches for a string within the text.
PrintInsideRect	Renders text inside a given rectangle.
SerializeRaw	Serializes a **CEditView** object to disk as raw text.

Overridables

OnFindNext	Finds next occurrence of a text string.
OnReplaceAll	Replaces all occurrences of a given string with a new string.
OnReplaceSel	Replaces current selection.
OnTextNotFound	Called when a find operation fails to match any further text.

Member Functions

CEditView::CEditView

CEditView( );

Remarks

Constructs an object of type **CEditView**. After constructing the object, you must call the **CWnd::Create** function before the edit control is used. If you derive a class from **CEditView** and add it to the template using **CWinApp::AddDocTemplate**, the framework calls both this constructor and the **Create** function.

See Also: **CWnd::Create, CWinApp::AddDocTemplate**

CEditView::FindText

BOOL FindText(LPCTSTR *lpszFind***, BOOL** *bNext* **= TRUE, BOOL** *bCase* **= TRUE);**

Return Value

Nonzero if the search text is found; otherwise 0.

Parameters

lpszFind   The text to be found.

bNext   Specifies the direction of the search. If **TRUE**, the search direction is toward the end of the buffer. If **FALSE**, the search direction is toward the beginning of the buffer.

bCase   Specifies whether the search is case sensitive. If **TRUE**, the search is case sensitive. If **FALSE**, the search is not case sensitive.

Remarks

Call the **FindText** function to search the **CEditView** object's text buffer. This function searches the text in the buffer for the text specified by *lpszFind*, starting at the current selection, in the direction specified by *bNext*, and with case sensitivity specified by *bCase*. If the text is found, it sets the selection to the found text and returns a nonzero value. If the text is not found, the function returns 0.

You normally do not need to call the **FindText** function unless you override **OnFindNext**, which calls **FindText**.

See Also: **CEditView::OnFindNext, CEditView::OnReplaceAll, CEditView::OnReplaceSel, CEditView::OnTextNotFound**

CEditView::GetBufferLength

UINT GetBufferLength( ) const;

Return Value

The length of the string in the buffer.

Remarks

Call this member function to obtain the number of characters currently in the edit control's buffer, not including the null terminator.

See Also: CEditView::LockBuffer, CEditView::UnlockBuffer

CEditView::GetEditCtrl

CEdit& GetEditCtrl( ) const;

Return Value

A reference to a **CEdit** object.

Remarks

Call **GetEditCtrl** to get a reference to the edit control used by the edit view. This control is of type **CEdit**, so you can manipulate the Windows edit control directly using the **CEdit** member functions.

Warning   Using the **CEdit** object can change the state of the underlying Windows edit control. For example, you should not change the tab settings using the **CEdit::SetTabStops** function because **CEditView** caches these settings for use both in the edit control and in printing. Instead, use **CEditView::SetTabStops**.

See Also: CEdit, CEditView::SetTabStops

CEditView::GetPrinterFont

CFont* GetPrinterFont( ) const;

Return Value

A pointer to a **CFont** object that specifies the current printer font; **NULL** if the printer font has not been set. The pointer may be temporary and should not be stored for later use.

Remarks

Call **GetPrinterFont** to get a pointer to a **CFont** object that describes the current printer font. If the printer font has not been set, the default printing behavior of the **CEditView** class is to print using the same font used for display.

Use this function to determine the current printer font. If it is not the desired printer font, use **CEditView::SetPrinterFont** to change it.

See Also: **CEditView::SetPrinterFont**

CEditView::GetSelectedText

void GetSelectedText(CString& *strResult* **) const;**

Parameters

strResult   A reference to the **CString** object that is to receive the selected text.

Remarks

Call **GetSelectedText** to copy the selected text into a **CString** object, up to the end of the selection or the character preceding the first carriage-return character in the selection.

See Also: **CEditView::OnReplaceSel**

CEditView::LockBuffer

LPCTSTR LockBuffer( ) const;

Return Value

A pointer to the edit control's buffer.

Remarks

Call this member function to obtain a pointer to the buffer. The buffer should not be modified.

See Also: **CEditView::UnlockBuffer, CEditView::GetBufferLength**

CEditView::OnFindNext

virtual void OnFindNext(LPCTSRT *lpszFind***, BOOL** *bNext***, BOOL** *bCase* **);**

Parameters

lpszFind   The text to be found.

bNext   Specifies the direction of the search. If **TRUE**, the search direction is toward the end of the buffer. If **FALSE**, the search direction is toward the beginning of the buffer.

bCase   Specifies whether the search is case sensitive. If **TRUE**, the search is case sensitive. If **FALSE**, the search is not case sensitive.

Remarks

Searches the text in the buffer for the text specified by *lpszFind*, in the direction specified by *bNext*, with case sensitivity specified by *bCase*. The search starts at the beginning of the current selection and is accomplished through a call to **FindText**. In the default implementation, **OnFindNext** calls **OnTextNotFound** if the text is not found.

Override **OnFindNext** to change the way a **CEditView**-derived object searches text. **CEditView** calls **OnFindNext** when the user chooses the Find Next button in the standard Find dialog box.

See Also: **CEditView::OnTextNotFound, CEditView::FindText, CEditView::OnReplaceAll, CEditView::OnReplaceSel**

CEditView::OnReplaceAll

virtual void OnReplaceAll(LPCTSTR *lpszFind***, LPCTSTR** *lpszReplace***,**
   → **BOOL** *bCase* **);**

Parameters

lpszFind   The text to be found.

lpszReplace   The text to replace the search text.

bCase   Specifies whether search is case sensitive. If **TRUE**, the search is case sensitive. If **FALSE**, the search is not case sensitive.

Remarks

CEditView calls **OnReplaceAll** when the user selects the Replace All button in the standard Replace dialog box. **OnReplaceAll** searches the text in the buffer for the text specified by *lpszFind*, with case sensitivity specified by *bCase*. The search starts at the beginning of the current selection. Each time the search text is found, this function replaces that occurrence of the text with the text specified by *lpszReplace*. The search is accomplished through a call to **FindText**. In the default implementation, **OnTextNotFound** is called if the text is not found.

If the current selection does not match *lpszFind*, the selection is updated to the first occurrence of the text specified by *lpszFind* and a replace is not performed. This allows the user to confirm that this is what they want to do when the selection does not match the text to be replaced.

Override **OnReplaceAll** to change the way a **CEditView**-derived object replaces text.

See Also: **CEditView::OnFindNext, CEditView::OnTextNotFound, CEditView::FindText, CEditView::OnReplaceSel**

CEditView::OnReplaceSel

virtual void OnReplaceSel(LPCTSTR *lpszFind*, **BOOL** *bNext*, **BOOL** *bCase*,
➥ **LPCTSTR** *lpszReplace* **);**

Parameters

lpszFind   The text to be found.

bNext   Specifies the direction of the search. If **TRUE**, the search direction is toward the end of the buffer. If **FALSE**, the search direction is toward the beginning of the buffer.

bCase   Specifies whether the search is case sensitive. If **TRUE**, the search is case sensitive. If **FALSE**, the search is not case sensitive.

lpszReplace   The text to replace the found text.

Remarks

CEditView calls **OnReplaceSel** when the user selects the Replace button in the standard Replace dialog box.

After replacing the selection, this function searches the text in the buffer for the next occurrence of the text specified by *lpszFind*, in the direction specified by *bNext*, with case sensitivity specified by *bCase*. The search is accomplished through a call to **FindText**. If the text is not found, **OnTextNotFound** is called.

Override **OnReplaceSel** to change the way a **CEditView**-derived object replaces the selected text.

See Also: **CEditView::OnFindNext, CEditView::OnTextNotFound, CEditView::FindText, CEditView::OnReplaceAll**

CEditView::OnTextNotFound

virtual void OnTextNotFound(LPCTSTR *lpszFind* **);**

Parameters

lpszFind   The text to be found.

Remarks

Override this function to change the default implementation, which calls the Windows function **MessageBeep**.

See Also: **CEditView::FindText, CEditView::OnFindNext, CEditView::OnReplaceAll, CEditView::OnReplaceSel**

CEditView::PrintInsideRect

UINT PrintInsideRect(CDC **pDC*, **RECT&** *rectLayout*, **UINT** *nIndexStart*,
↪ **UINT** *nIndexStop* **);**

Return Value

The index of the next character to be printed (that is, the character following the last character rendered).

Parameters

pDC   Pointer to the printer device context.

rectLayout   Reference to a **CRect** object or **RECT** structure specifying the rectangle in which the text is to be rendered.

nIndexStart   Index within the buffer of the first character to be rendered.

nIndexStop   Index within the buffer of the character following the last character to be rendered.

Remarks

Call **PrintInsideRect** to print text in the rectangle specified by *rectLayout*.

If the **CEditView** control does not have the style **ES_AUTOHSCROLL**, text is wrapped within the rendering rectangle. If the control does have the style **ES_AUTOHSCROLL**, the text is clipped at the right edge of the rectangle.

The **rect.bottom** element of the *rectLayout* object is changed so that the rectangle's dimensions define the part of the original rectangle that is occupied by the text.

See Also: CEditView::SetPrinterFont, CEditView::GetPrinterFont

---

CEditView::SerializeRaw

void SerializeRaw(CArchive& *ar* **);**

Parameters

ar   Reference to the **CArchive** object that stores the serialized text.

Remarks

Call **SerializeRaw** to have a **CArchive** object read or write the text in the **CEditView** object to a text file. **SerializeRaw** differs from **CEditView**'s internal implementation of **Serialize** in that it reads and writes only the text, without preceding object-description data.

See Also: CArchive, CObject::Serialize

CEditView::SetPrinterFont

void SetPrinterFont(CFont* *pFont* **);**

Parameters

> *pFont*   A pointer to an object of type **CFont**. If **NULL**, the font used for printing is based on the display font.

Remarks

> Call **SetPrinterFont** to set the printer font to the font specified by *pFont*.
>
> If you want your view to always use a particular font for printing, include a call to **SetPrinterFont** in your class's **OnPreparePrinting** function. This virtual function is called before printing occurs, so the font change takes place before the view's contents are printed.
>
> **See Also:**   **CWnd::SetFont, CFont, CView::OnPreparePrinting**

CEditView::SetTabStops

void SetTabStops(int *nTabStops* **);**

Parameters

> *nTabStops*   Width of each tab stop, in dialog units.

Remarks

> Call this function to set the tab stops used for display and printing. Only a single tab-stop width is supported. (**CEdit** objects support multiple tab widths.) Widths are in dialog units, which equal one-fourth of the average character width (based on uppercase and lowercase alphabetic characters only) of the font used at the time of printing or displaying. You should not use **CEdit::SetTabStops** because **CEditView** must cache the tab-stop value.
>
> This function modifies only the tabs of the object for which it is called. To change the tab stops for each **CEditView** object in your application, call each object's **SetTabStops** function.
>
> **See Also:**   **CWnd::SetFont, CEditView::SetPrinterFont**

CEditView::UnlockBuffer

void UnlockBuffer( ) const;

Remarks

> Call this member function to unlock the buffer. Call **UnlockBuffer** after you have finished using the pointer returned by **LockBuffer**.
>
> **See Also:**   **CEditView::LockBuffer, CEditView::GetBufferLength**

Data Members
CEditView::dwStyleDefault

Remarks

Pass this static member as the *dwStyle* parameter of the **Create** function to obtain the default style for the **CEditView** object. **dwStyleDefault** is a public member of type **DWORD**.

CEvent

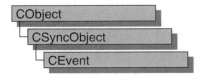

An object of class **CEvent** represents an "event"—a synchronization object that allows one thread to notify another that an event has occurred. Events are useful when a thread needs to know when to perform its task. For example, a thread that copies data to a data archive would need to be notified when new data is available. By using a **CEvent** object to notify the copy thread when new data is available, the thread can perform its task as soon as possible.

CEvent objects have two types: manual and automatic. A manual **CEvent** object stays in the state set by **SetEvent** or **ResetEvent** until the other function is called. An automatic **CEvent** object automatically returns to a nonsignaled (unavailable) state after at least one thread is released.

To use a **CEvent** object, construct the **CEvent** object when it is needed. Specify the name of the event you wish to wait on, and that your application should initially own it. You can then access the event when the constructor returns. Call **SetEvent** to signal (make available) the event object and then call **Unlock** when you are done accessing the controlled resource.

An alternative method for using **CEvent** objects is to add a variable of type **CEvent** as a data member to the class you wish to control. During construction of the controlled object, call the constructor of the **CEvent** data member specifying if the event is initially signaled, the type of event object you want, the name of the event (if it will be used across process boundaries), and desired security attributes.

To access a resource controlled by a **CEvent** object in this manner, first create a variable of either type **CSingleLock** or type **CMultiLock** in your resource's access member function. Then call the lock object's **Lock** member function (for example, **CMultiLock::Lock**). At this point, your thread will either gain access to the resource, wait for the resource to be released and gain access, or wait for the resource to be released and time out, failing to gain access to the resource. In any case, your resource has been accessed in a thread-safe manner. To release the resource, call **SetEvent** to signal the event object, and then use the lock object's **Unlock** member function (for example, **CMultiLock::Unlock**), or allow the lock object to fall out of scope.

For more information on using **CEvent** objects, see the article "Multithreading: How to Use the Synchronization Classes" in *Visual C++ Programmer's Guide* online.

#include <afxmt.h>

CEvent Class Members

Construction

CEvent	Constructs a **CEvent** object.

Methods

SetEvent	Sets the event to available (signaled) and releases any waiting threads.
PulseEvent	Sets the event to available (signaled), releases waiting threads, and sets the event to unavailable (nonsignaled).
ResetEvent	Sets the event to unavailable (nonsignaled).
Unlock	Releases the event object.

Member Functions

CEvent::CEvent

CEvent(BOOL *bInitiallyOwn* **= FALSE, BOOL** *bManualReset* **= FALSE,**
↳ **LPCTSTR** *lpszName* **= NULL,**
↳ **LPSECURITY_ATTRIBUTES** *lpsaAttribute* **= NULL);**

Parameters

bInitiallyOwn   If **TRUE**, the thread for the **CMultilock** or **CSingleLock** object is enabled. Otherwise, all threads wanting to access the resource must wait.

bManualReset   If **TRUE**, specifies that the event object is a manual event, otherwise the event object is an automatic event.

lpszName   Name of the **CEvent** object. Must be supplied if the object will be used across process boundaries. If the name matches an existing event, the constructor builds a new **CEvent** object which references the event of that name. If the name matches an existing synchronization object that is not an event, the construction will fail. If **NULL**, the name will be null.

lpsaAttribute   Security attributes for the event object. For a full description of this structure, see **SECURITY_ATTRIBUTES** in the *Win32 SDK Programmer's Reference*.

Remarks

Constructs a named or unnamed **CEvent** object. To access or release a **CEvent** object, create a **CMultiLock** or **CSingleLock** object and call its **Lock** and **Unlock** member functions.

To change the state of a **CEvent** object to signaled (threads do not have to wait), call **SetEvent** or **PulseEvent**. To set the state of a **CEvent** object to nonsignaled (threads must wait), call **ResetEvent**.

CEvent::PulseEvent

BOOL PulseEvent( );

Return Value

Nonzero if the function was successful; otherwise 0.

Remarks

Sets the state of the event to signaled (available), releases any waiting threads, and resets it to nonsignaled (unavailable) automatically. If the event is manual, all waiting threads are released, the event is set to nonsignaled, and **PulseEvent** returns. If the event is automatic, a single thread is released, the event is set to nonsignaled, and **PulseEvent** returns.

If no threads are waiting, or no threads can be released immediately, **PulseEvent** sets the state of the event to nonsignaled and returns.

CEvent::ResetEvent

BOOL ResetEvent( );

Return Value

Nonzero if the function was successful; otherwise 0.

Remarks

Sets the state of the event to nonsignaled until explicitly set to signaled by the **SetEvent** member function. This causes all threads wishing to access this event to wait.

This member function is not used by automatic events.

CEvent::SetEvent

BOOL SetEvent( );

Return Value

Nonzero if the function was successful, otherwise 0.

Remarks

Sets the state of the event to signaled, releasing any waiting threads. If the event is manual, the event will remain signaled until **ResetEvent** is called. More than one thread can be released in this case. If the event is automatic, the event will remain signaled until a single thread is released. The system will then set the state of the event to nonsignaled. If no threads are waiting, the state remains signaled until one thread is released.

CEvent::Unlock

virtual BOOL Unlock( );

Return Value

Nonzero if the thread owned the event object and the event is an automatic event; otherwise 0.

Remarks

Releases the event object. This member function is called by threads that currently own an automatic event to release it after they are done, if their lock object is to be reused. If the lock object is not to be reused, this function will be called by the lock object's destructor.

CException

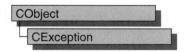

CException is the base class for all exceptions in the Microsoft Foundation Class Library. The derived classes and their descriptions are listed below:

CMemoryException	Out-of-memory exception
CNotSupportedException	Request for an unsupported operation
CArchiveException	Archive-specific exception
CFileException	File-specific exception
CResourceException	Windows resource not found or not createable
COleException	OLE exception
CDBException	Database exception (that is, exception conditions arising for MFC database classes based on Open Database Connectivity)
COleDispatchException	OLE dispatch (automation) exception
CUserException	Exception that indicates that a resource could not be found
CDaoException	Data access object exception (that is, exception conditions arising for DAO classes)
CInternetException	Internet exception (that is, exception conditions arising for Internet classes)

These exceptions are intended to be used with the **THROW**, **THROW_LAST**, **TRY**, **CATCH**, **AND_CATCH**, and **END_CATCH** macros. For more information on exceptions, see "Exception Processing," or see the article "Exceptions" in *Visual C++ Programmer's Guide* online.

To catch a specific exception, use the appropriate derived class. To catch all types of exceptions, use **CException**, and then use **CObject::IsKindOf** to differentiate among **CException**-derived classes. Note that **CObject::IsKindOf** works only for classes declared with the **IMPLEMENT_DYNAMIC** macro, in order to take advantage of dynamic type checking. Any **CException**-derived class that you create should use the **IMPLEMENT_DYNAMIC** macro, too.

You can report details about exceptions to the user by calling **GetErrorMessage** or **ReportError**, two member functions that work with any of **CException**'s derived classes.

If an exception is caught by one of the macros, the **CException** object is deleted automatically; do not delete it yourself. If an exception is caught by using a **catch** keyword, it is not automatically deleted. See the article "Exceptions" in *Visual C++ Programmer's Guide* online for more information about when to delete an exception object.

CException is an abstract base class. You cannot create **CException** objects; you must create objects of derived classes. If you need to create your own **CException** type, use one of the derived classes listed above as a model. Make sure that your derived class also uses **IMPLEMENT_DYNAMIC**.

#include <afx.h>

See Also: Exception Processing

CException Class Members

Operations

CException	Constructs a **CException** object.
Delete	Deletes a **CException** object.
GetErrorMessage	Retrieves the message describing an exception.
ReportError	Reports an error message in a message box to the user.

Member Functions

CException::CException

CException(BOOL b_AutoDelete);

Parameters

bAutoDelete   Specify **TRUE** if the memory for the **CException** object has been allocated on the heap. This will cause the **CException** object to be deleted when the **Delete** member function is called to delete the exception. Specify **FALSE** if the **CException** object is on the stack or is a global object. In this case, the **CException** object will not be deleted when the **Delete** member function is called.

Remarks

This member function constructs a **CException** object. You should not directly create a **CException** object using **new**. Use this constructor when you derive a class from **Cexception**.

CException::Delete

void CException::Delete( );

Remarks

This function checks to see if the **CException** object was created on the heap, and if so, it calls the **delete** operator on the object. When deleting a **CException** object, use the **Delete** member function to delete the exception. Do not use the **delete** operator directly, because the **CException** object may be a global object or have been created on the stack.

You can specify whether the object should be deleted when the object is constructed. For more information, see **CException::CException**.

You only need to call **Delete** if you are using the C++ **try-catch** mechanism. If you are using the MFC macros **TRY** and **CATCH**, then these macros will automatically call this function.

CException::GetErrorMessage

virtual BOOL GetErrorMessage(LPTSTR *lpszError*, **UINT** *nMaxError*,
↳ **PUINT** *pnHelpContext* = **NULL**);

Return Value

Nonzero if the function is successful; otherwise 0 if no error message text is available.

Parameters

lpszError   A pointer to a buffer that will receive an error message.

nMaxError   The maximum number of characters the buffer can hold, including the **NULL** terminator.

pnHelpContext   The address of a **UINT** that will receive the help context ID. If **NULL**, no ID will be returned.

Remarks

Call this member function to provide text about an error that has occurred. For example, call **GetErrorMessage** to retrieve a string describing the error which caused MFC to throw a **CFileException** when writing to a **CFile** object.

Note   **GetErrorMessage** will not copy more than *nMaxError -1* characters to the buffer, and it will always add a trailing null to end the string. If the buffer is too small, the error message may be truncated.

Example

Here is an example of the use of **CException::GetErrorMessage**.

```
CFile fileInput;
CFileException ex;

// try to open a file for reading.
// The file will certainly not
// exist because there are too many explicit
// directories in the name.
```

```
                    // if the call to Open() fails, ex will be
                    // initialized with exception
                    // information.  the call to ex.GetErrorMessage()
                    // will retrieve an appropriate message describing
                    // the error, and we'll add our own text
                    // to make sure the user is perfectly sure what
                    // went wrong.

                    if (!fileInput.Open("\\Too\\Many\\Bad\\Dirs.DAT", CFile::modeRead, &ex))
                    {
                        TCHAR szCause[255];
                        CString strFormatted;

                        ex.GetErrorMessage(szCause, 255);

                        // (in real life, it's probably more
                        // appropriate to read this from
                        //  a string resource so it would be easy to
                        // localize)

                        strFormatted = _T("The data file could not be opened because
                        ↪ of this error: ");
                        strFormatted += szCause;

                        AfxMessageBox(strFormatted);
                    }
                    else
                    {
                        // the file was opened, so do whatever work
                        // with fileInput
                        // we were planning...
                        // :

                        fileInput.Close();
                    }
```

See Also: **CException::ReportError**

CException::ReportError

virtual int ReportError(UINT *nType* **= MB_OK, UINT** *nMessageID* **= 0);**

Return Value

An **AfxMessageBox** value; otherwise 0 if there is not enough memory to display the message box. See **AfxMessageBox** for the possible return values.

Parameters

nType   Specifies the style of the message box. Apply any combination of the message-box styles to the box. If you don't specify this parameter, the default is **MB_OK**.

nMessageID Specifies the resource ID (string table entry) of a message to display if the exception object does not have an error message. If 0, the message "No error message is available" is displayed.

Remarks

Call this member function to report error text in a message box to the user.

Example

Here is an example of the use of **CException::ReportError**.

```
CFile fileInput;
CFileException ex;

// try to open a file for reading.
// The file will certainly not
// exist because there are too many explicit
// directories in the name.

// if the call to Open() fails, ex will be
// initialized with exception
// information.  the call to ex.ReportError() will
// display an appropriate
// error message to the user, such as
// "\Too\Many\Bad\Dirs.DAT contains an
// invalid path."  The error message text will be
// appropriate for the
// file name and error condition.

if (!fileInput.Open("\\Too\\Many\\Bad\\Dirs.DAT", CFile::modeRead, &ex))
{
    ex.ReportError();
}
else
{
    // the file was opened, so do whatever work
    // with fileInput we were planning...
    // :

    fileInput.Close();
}
```

See Also: **AfxMessageBox**, **CException::GetErrorMessage**

CFieldExchange

CFieldExchange does not have a base class.

The **CFieldExchange** class supports the record field exchange (RFX) and bulk record field exchange (Bulk RFX) routines used by the database classes. Use this class if you are writing data exchange routines for custom data types or when you are implementing bulk row fetching; otherwise, you will not directly use this class. RFX and Bulk RFX exchanges data between the field data members of your recordset object and the corresponding fields of the current record on the data source.

Note If you are working with the Data Access Objects (DAO) classes rather than the Open Database Connectivity (ODBC) classes, use class **CDaoFieldExchange** instead. For more information, see the articles "Database Topics (General)" and "DAO and MFC" in *Visual C++ Programmer's Guide* online.

A **CFieldExchange** object provides the context information needed for record field exchange or bulk record field exchange to take place. **CFieldExchange** objects support a number of operations, including binding parameters and field data members and setting various flags on the fields of the current record. RFX and Bulk RFX operations are performed on recordset-class data members of types defined by the **enum FieldType** in **CFieldExchange**. Possible **FieldType** values are:

- **CFieldExchange::outputColumn** for field data members.
- **CFieldExchange::inputParam** or **CFieldExchange::param** for input parameter data members.
- **CFieldExchange::outputParam** for output parameter data members.
- **CFieldExchange::inoutParam** for input/output parameter data members.

Most of the class's member functions and data members are provided for writing your own custom RFX routines. You will use **SetFieldType** frequently. For more information, see the articles "Record Field Exchange (RFX)" and "Recordset (ODBC)" in *Visual C++ Programmer's Guide* online. For information about bulk row fetching, see the article "Recordset:Fetching Records in Bulk (ODBC)" in *Visual C++ Programmer's Guide* online. For details about the RFX and Bulk RFX global functions, see "Record Field Exchange Functions" in the "MFC Macros and Globals" section in this manual.

#include <afxdb.h>

See Also: CRecordset

CFieldExchange Class Members

Operations

IsFieldType	Returns nonzero if the current operation is appropriate for the type of field being updated.
SetFieldType	Specifies the type of recordset data member— column or parameter— represented by all following calls to RFX functions until the next call to **SetFieldType**.

Member Functions

CFieldExchange::IsFieldType

BOOL IsFieldType(UINT* *pnField* **);**

Return Value

Nonzero if the current operation can be performed on the current field or parameter type.

Parameters

pnField The sequential number of the field or parameter data member is returned in this parameter. This number corresponds to the data member's order in the **CRecordset::DoFieldExchange** or **CRecordset::DoBulkFieldExchange** function.

Remarks

If you write your own RFX function, call **IsFieldType** at the beginning of your function to determine whether the current operation can be performed on a particular field or parameter data member type (a **CFieldExchange::outputColumn**, **CFieldExchange::inputParam**, **CFieldExchange::param**, **CFieldExchange::outputParam**, or **CFieldExchange::inoutParam**). Follow the model of the existing RFX functions.

CFieldExchange::SetFieldType

void SetFieldType(UINT *nFieldType* **);**

Parameters

nFieldType A value of the **enum FieldType**, declared in **CFieldExchange**, which can be one of the following:

- **CFieldExchange::outputColumn**
- **CFieldExchange::inputParam**

- **CFieldExchange::param**
- **CFieldExchange::outputParam**
- **CFieldExchange::inoutParam**

Remarks

You need a call to **SetFieldType** in your recordset class's **DoFieldExchange** or **DoBulkFieldExchange** override. For field data members, you must call **SetFieldType** with a parameter of **CFieldExchange::outputColumn**, followed by calls to the RFX or Bulk RFX functions. If you have not implemented bulk row fetching, then ClassWizard places this **SetFieldType** call for you in the field map section of **DoFieldExchange**.

If you parameterize your recordset class, you must call **SetFieldType** again, outside any field map section, followed by RFX calls for all the parameter data members. Each type of parameter data member must have its own **SetFieldType** call. The following table distinguishes the different values you can pass to **SetFieldType** to represent the parameter data members of your class:

SetFieldType parameter value	Type of parameter data member
CFieldExchange::inputParam	Input parameter. A value that is passed into the recordset's query or stored procedure.
CFieldExchange::param	Same as **CFieldExchange::inputParam**.
CFieldExchange::outputParam	Output parameter. A return value of the recordset's stored procedure.
CFieldExchange::inoutParam	Input/output parameter. A value that is passed into and returned from the recordset's stored procedure.

In general, each group of RFX function calls associated with field data members or parameter data members must be preceded by a call to **SetFieldType**. The *nFieldType* parameter of each **SetFieldType** call identifies the type of the data members represented by the RFX function calls that follow the **SetFieldType** call.

For more information about handling output and input/output parameters, see the **CRecordset** member function **FlushResultSet**. For more information about the RFX and Bulk RFX functions, see the topic "Record Field Exchange Functions." For related information about bulk row fetching, see the article "Recordset: Fetching Records in Bulk (ODBC)" in *Visual C++ Programmer's Guide* online.

Example

This example shows several calls to RFX functions with accompanying calls to **SetFieldType**. Note that **SetFieldType** is called through the *pFX* pointer to a **CFieldExchange** object.

```
void CSections::DoFieldExchange( CFieldExchange* pFX )
{
   //{{AFX_FIELD_MAP(CSections)
   pFX->SetFieldType( CFieldExchange::outputColumn );
   RFX_Text( pFX, "CourseID", m_strCourseID );
   RFX_Text( pFX, "InstructorID", m_strInstructorID );
   RFX_Text( pFX, "RoomNo", m_strRoomNo );
   RFX_Text( pFX, "Schedule", m_strSchedule );
   //}}AFX_FIELD_MAP

   // output parameter
   pFX->SetFieldType( CFieldExchange::outputParam );
   RFX_Long( pFX, "Instructor_Count", m_nCountParam );

   // input parameter
   pFX->SetFieldType( CFieldExchange::inputParam );
   RFX_Text( pFX, "Department_Name", m_strNameParam );
}
```

See Also: CRecordset::DoFieldExchange, **CRecordset::DoBulkFieldExchange**, **CRecordset::FlushResultSet**, "Record Field Exchange Functions"

CFile

CFile is the base class for Microsoft Foundation file classes. It directly provides unbuffered, binary disk input/output services, and it indirectly supports text files and memory files through its derived classes. **CFile** works in conjunction with the **CArchive** class to support serialization of Microsoft Foundation Class objects.

The hierarchical relationship between this class and its derived classes allows your program to operate on all file objects through the polymorphic **CFile** interface. A memory file, for example, behaves like a disk file.

Use **CFile** and its derived classes for general-purpose disk I/O. Use **ofstream** or other Microsoft iostream classes for formatted text sent to a disk file.

Normally, a disk file is opened automatically on **CFile** construction and closed on destruction. Static member functions permit you to interrogate a file's status without opening the file.

For more information on using **CFile**, see the article "Files in MFC" in *Visual C++ Programmer's Guide* online and "File Handling" in the *Run-Time Library Reference*.

#include <afx.h>

See Also: **CStdioFile**, **CMemFile**

CFile Class Members

Data Members

m_hFile	Usually contains the operating-system file handle.

Construction

CFile	Constructs a **CFile** object from a path or file handle.
Abort	Closes a file ignoring all warnings and errors.
Duplicate	Constructs a duplicate object based on this file.
Open	Safely opens a file with an error-testing option.
Close	Closes a file and deletes the object.

Input/Output

Read	Reads (unbuffered) data from a file at the current file position.
ReadHuge	Can read more than 64K of (unbuffered) data from a file at the current file position. Obsolete in 32-bit programming. See **Read**.

Input/Output *(continued)*

Write	Writes (unbuffered) data in a file to the current file position.
WriteHuge	Can write more than 64K of (unbuffered) data in a file to the current file position. Obsolete in 32-bit programming. See **Write**.
Flush	Flushes any data yet to be written.

Position

Seek	Positions the current file pointer.
SeekToBegin	Positions the current file pointer at the beginning of the file.
SeekToEnd	Positions the current file pointer at the end of the file.
GetLength	Retrieves the length of the file.
SetLength	Changes the length of the file.

Locking

LockRange	Locks a range of bytes in a file.
UnlockRange	Unlocks a range of bytes in a file.

Status

GetPosition	Retrieves the current file pointer.
GetStatus	Retrieves the status of this open file.
GetFileName	Retrieves the filename of the selected file.
GetFileTitle	Retrieves the title of the selected file.
GetFilePath	Retrieves the full file path of the selected file.
SetFilePath	Sets the full file path of the selected file.

Static

Rename	Renames the specified file (static function).
Remove	Deletes the specified file (static function).
GetStatus	Retrieves the status of the specified file (static, virtual function).
SetStatus	Sets the status of the specified file (static, virtual function).

Member Functions

CFile::Abort

virtual void Abort( );

Remarks

Closes the file associated with this object and makes the file unavailable for reading or writing. If you have not closed the file before destroying the object, the destructor closes it for you.

When handling exceptions, **CFile::Abort** differs from **CFile::Close** in two important ways. First, the **Abort** function will not throw an exception on failures because failures are ignored by **Abort**. Second, **Abort** will not **ASSERT** if the file has not been opened or was closed previously.

If you used **new** to allocate the **CFile** object on the heap, then you must delete it after closing the file. **Abort** sets **m_hFile** to **CFile::hFileNull**.

Example

```
//example for CFile::Abort
CStdioFile fileTest;
char* pFileName = "test.dat";
TRY
{
    // do stuff that may throw exceptions
    fileTest.Open( pFileName, CFile::modeWrite );
}
CATCH_ALL( e )
{
    fileTest.Abort(); // close file safely and quietly
    THROW_LAST();
}
END_CATCH_ALL
```

See Also: **CFile::Close**, **CFile::Open**

CFile::CFile

CFile( );
CFile(int *hFile* **);**
CFile(LPCTSTR *lpszFileName*, **UINT** *nOpenFlags* **);**
  throw(CFileException);

Parameters

hFile　The handle of a file that is already open.

lpszFileName　A string that is the path to the desired file. The path can be relative or absolute.

nOpenFlags　Sharing and access mode. Specifies the action to take when opening the file. You can combine options listed below by using the bitwise-OR (|) operator. One access permission and one share option are required; the **modeCreate** and **modeNoInherit** modes are optional. The values are as follows:

- **CFile::modeCreate**　Directs the constructor to create a new file. If the file exists already, it is truncated to 0 length.

- **CFile::modeNoTruncate**　Combine this value with **modeCreate**. If the file being created already exists, it is not truncated to 0 length. Thus the file is guaranteed to open, either as a newly created file or as an existing file. This might be useful, for example, when opening a settings file that may or may not exist already. This option applies to **CStdioFile** as well.

- **CFile::modeRead**   Opens the file for reading only.

- **CFile::modeReadWrite**   Opens the file for reading and writing.

- **CFile::modeWrite**   Opens the file for writing only.

- **CFile::modeNoInherit**   Prevents the file from being inherited by child processes.

- **CFile::shareDenyNone**   Opens the file without denying other processes read or write access to the file. **Create** fails if the file has been opened in compatibility mode by any other process.

- **CFile::shareDenyRead**   Opens the file and denies other processes read access to the file. **Create** fails if the file has been opened in compatibility mode or for read access by any other process.

- **CFile::shareDenyWrite**   Opens the file and denies other processes write access to the file. **Create** fails if the file has been opened in compatibility mode or for write access by any other process.

- **CFile::shareExclusive**   Opens the file with exclusive mode, denying other processes both read and write access to the file. Construction fails if the file has been opened in any other mode for read or write access, even by the current process.

- **CFile::shareCompat**   This flag is not available in 32 bit MFC. This flag maps to **CFile::shareExclusive** when used in **CFile::Open**.

- **CFile::typeText**   Sets text mode with special processing for carriage return–linefeed pairs (used in derived classes only).

- **CFile::typeBinary**   Sets binary mode (used in derived classes only).

Remarks

The default constructor does not open a file but rather sets **m_hFile** to **CFile::hFileNull**. Because this constructor does not throw an exception, it does not make sense to use **TRY/CATCH** logic. Use the **Open** member function, then test directly for exception conditions. For a discussion of exception-processing strategy, see the article "Exceptions" in *Visual C++ Programmer's Guide* online.

The constructor with one argument creates a **CFile** object that corresponds to an existing operating-system file identified by *hFile*. No check is made on the access mode or file type. When the **CFile** object is destroyed, the operating-system file will not be closed. You must close the file yourself.

The constructor with two arguments creates a **CFile** object and opens the corresponding operating-system file with the given path. This constructor combines the functions of the first constructor and the **Open** member function. It throws an exception if there is an error while opening the file. Generally, this means that the error is unrecoverable and that the user should be alerted.

Example

```
//example for CFile::CFile
char* pFileName = "test.dat";
TRY
{
    CFile f( pFileName, CFile::modeCreate | CFile::modeWrite );
}
CATCH( CFileException, e )
{
    #ifdef _DEBUG
        afxDump << "File could not be opened " << e->m_cause << "\n";
    #endif
}
END_CATCH
```

CFile::Close

virtual void Close( );
    throw(CFileException);

Remarks

Closes the file associated with this object and makes the file unavailable for reading or writing. If you have not closed the file before destroying the object, the destructor closes it for you.

If you used **new** to allocate the **CFile** object on the heap, then you must delete it after closing the file. **Close** sets **m_hFile** to **CFile::hFileNull**.

See Also: CFile::Open

CFile::Duplicate

virtual CFile* Duplicate( ) const;
    throw(CFileException);

Return Value

A pointer to a duplicate **CFile** object.

Remarks

Constructs a duplicate **CFile** object for a given file. This is equivalent to the C run-time function **_dup**.

CFile::Flush

virtual void Flush( );
    throw(CFileException);

Remarks

Forces any data remaining in the file buffer to be written to the file.

The use of **Flush** does not guarantee flushing of **CArchive** buffers. If you are using an archive, call **CArchive::Flush** first.

CFile::GetFileName

virtual CString GetFileName( ) const;

Return Value

The name of the file.

Remarks

Call this member function to retrieve the name of a specified file. For example, when you call **GetFileName** to generate a message to the user about the file `c:\windows\write\myfile.wri`, the filename, `myfile.wri`, is returned.

To return the entire path of the file, including the name, call **GetFilePath**. To return the title of the file (`myfile`), call **GetFileTitle**.

See Also: **CFile::GetFilePath**, **CFile::GetFileTitle**

CFile::GetFilePath

virtual CString GetFilePath( ) const;

Return Value

The full path of the specified file.

Remarks

Call this member function to retrieve the full path of a specified file. For example, when you call **GetFilePath** to generate a message to the user about the file `c:\windows\write\myfile.wri`, the file path, `c:\windows\write\myfile.wri`, is returned.

To return just the name of the file (`myfile.wri`), call **GetFileName**. To return the title of the file (`myfile`), call **GetFileTitle**.

See Also: **CFile::SetFilePath**, **CFile::GetFileTitle**, **CFile::GetFileName**

CFile::GetFileTitle

virtual CString GetFileTitle( ) const;

Return Value

The title of the specified file.

Remarks

Call this member function to retrieve the file title for a specified file. For example, when you call **GetFileTitle** to generate a message to the user about the file `c:\windows\write\myfile.wri`, the file title (`myfile`) is returned.

Note In Windows 95, the file title typically does not include the extention. For a explanation of this, see **GetFileTitle** in the Win32 documentation.

To return the entire path of the file, including the name, call **GetFilePath**. To return just the name of the file (`myfile.wri`), call **GetFileName**.

See Also: **CFile::GetFileName, CFile::GetFilePath, GetFileTitle**

CFile::GetLength

virtual DWORD GetLength( ) const;
  throw(CFileException);

Return Value

The length of the file.

Remarks

Obtains the current logical length of the file in bytes, not the amount.

See Also: **CFile::SetLength**

CFile::GetPosition

virtual DWORD GetPosition( ) const;
  throw(CFileException);

Return Value

The file pointer as a 32-bit doubleword.

Remarks

Obtains the current value of the file pointer, which can be used in subsequent calls to **Seek**.

Example

```
//example for CFile::GetPosition
extern CFile cfile;
DWORD dwPosition = cfile.GetPosition();
```

CFile::GetStatus

BOOL GetStatus(CFileStatus& *rStatus* **) const;**
static BOOL PASCAL GetStatus(LPCTSTR *lpszFileName***, CFileStatus&** *rStatus* **);**

Return Value

TRUE if the status information for the specified file is successfully obtained; otherwise, **FALSE**.

Parameters

rStatus   A reference to a user-supplied **CFileStatus** structure that will receive the status information. The **CFileStatus** structure has the following fields:

- **CTime m_ctime**   The date and time the file was created.

- **CTime m_mtime**   The date and time the file was last modified.

- **CTime m_atime**   The date and time the file was last accessed for reading.

- **LONG m_size**   The logical size of the file in bytes, as reported by the DIR command.

- **BYTE m_attribute**   The attribute byte of the file.

- **char m_szFullName[_MAX_PATH]**   The absolute filename in the Windows character set.

lpszFileName   A string in the Windows character set that is the path to the desired file. The path can be relative or absolute, but cannot contain a network name.

Remarks

The virtual version of **GetStatus** retrieves the status of the open file associated with this **CFile** object. It does not insert a value into the **m_szFullName** structure member.

The static version gets the status of the named file and copies the filename to **m_szFullName**. This function obtains the file status from the directory entry without actually opening the file. It is useful for testing the existence and access rights of a file.

The **m_attribute** is the file attribute. The Microsoft Foundation classes provide an **enum** type attribute so that you can specify attributes symbolically:

```
enum Attribute {
    normal =    0x00,
    readOnly =  0x01,
    hidden =    0x02,
    system =    0x04,
    volume =    0x08,
    directory = 0x10,
    archive =   0x20
    };
```

Example

```
//example for CFile::GetStatus
CFileStatus status;
extern CFile cfile;
if( cfile.GetStatus( status ) )     // virtual member function
    {
        #ifdef _DEBUG
            afxDump << "File size = " << status.m_size << "\n";
        #endif
    }
char* pFileName = "test.dat";
if( CFile::GetStatus( pFileName, status ) )   // static function
    {
        #ifdef _DEBUG
            afxDump << "Full file name = " << status.m_szFullName << "\n";
        #endif
    }
```

See Also: CFile::SetStatus, CTime

CFile::LockRange

virtual void LockRange(DWORD *dwPos*, **DWORD** *dwCount* **);**
   throw(CFileException);

Parameters

dwPos   The byte offset of the start of the byte range to lock.

dwCount   The number of bytes in the range to lock.

Remarks

Locks a range of bytes in an open file, throwing an exception if the file is already locked. Locking bytes in a file prevents access to those bytes by other processes. You can lock more than one region of a file, but no overlapping regions are allowed.

When you unlock the region, using the **UnlockRange** member function, the byte range must correspond exactly to the region that was previously locked. The **LockRange** function does not merge adjacent regions; if two locked regions are adjacent, you must unlock each region separately.

Note   This function is not available for the **CMemFile**-derived class.

Example

```
//example for CFile::LockRange
extern DWORD dwPos;
extern DWORD dwCount;
extern CFile cfile;
cfile.LockRange( dwPos, dwCount );
```

See Also: CFile::UnlockRange

CFile::Open

virtual BOOL Open(LPCTSTR *lpszFileName*, **UINT** *nOpenFlags*,
↵ **CFileException*** *pError* = **NULL**);

Return Value

Nonzero if the open was successful; otherwise 0. The *pError* parameter is meaningful only if 0 is returned.

Parameters

lpszFileName   A string that is the path to the desired file. The path can be relative or absolute but cannot contain a network name.

nOpenFlags   A **UINT** that defines the file's sharing and access mode. It specifies the action to take when opening the file. You can combine options by using the bitwise-OR (|) operator. One access permission and one share option are required; the **modeCreate** and **modeNoInherit** modes are optional. See the **CFile** constructor for a list of mode options.

pError   A pointer to an existing file-exception object that will receive the status of a failed operation.

Remarks

Open is designed for use with the default **CFile** constructor. The two functions form a "safe" method for opening a file where a failure is a normal, expected condition.

While the **CFile** constructor will throw an exception in an error condition, **Open** will return **FALSE** for error conditions. **Open** can still initialize a **CFileException** object to describe the error, however. If you don't supply the *pError* parameter, or if you pass **NULL** for *pError*, **Open** will return **FALSE** and not throw a **CFileException**. If you pass a pointer to an existing **CFileException**, and **Open** encounters an error, the function will fill it with information describing that error. In neither case will **Open** throw an exception.

The following table describes the possible results of **Open**.

pError	Error encountered?	Return value	CFileException content
NULL	No	**TRUE**	n/a
ptr to **CFileException**	No	**TRUE**	unchanged
NULL	Yes	**FALSE**	n/a
ptr to **CFileException**	Yes	**FALSE**	initialized to describe error

Example

```
//example for CFile::Open
CFile f;
CFileException e;
char* pFileName = "test.dat";
if( !f.Open( pFileName, CFile::modeCreate | CFile::modeWrite, &e ) )
```

685

```
    {
#ifdef _DEBUG
    afxDump << "File could not be opened " << e.m_cause << "\n";
#endif
    }
```

See Also: **CFile::CFile**, **CFile::Close**

CFile::Read

virtual UINT Read(void* *lpBuf*, **UINT** *nCount* **);**
    throw(CFileException);

Return Value

The number of bytes transferred to the buffer. Note that for all **CFile** classes, the return value may be less than *nCount* if the end of file was reached.

Parameters

lpBuf   Pointer to the user-supplied buffer that is to receive the data read from the file.

nCount   The maximum number of bytes to be read from the file. For text-mode files, carriage return–linefeed pairs are counted as single characters.

Remarks

Reads data into a buffer from the file associated with the **CFile** object.

Example

```
//example for CFile::Read
extern CFile cfile;
char pbuf[100];
UINT nBytesRead = cfile.Read( pbuf, 100 );
```

CFile::ReadHuge

DWORD ReadHuge(void* *lpBuffer*, **DWORD** *dwCount* **);**
    throw(CFileException);

Return Value

The number of bytes transferred to the buffer. Note that for all **CFile** objects, the return value can be less than *dwCount* if the end of file was reached.

Parameters

lpBuf   Pointer to the user-supplied buffer that is to receive the data read from the file.

dwCount   The maximum number of bytes to be read from the file. For text-mode files, carriage return–linefeed pairs are counted as single characters.

Remarks

Reads data into a buffer from the file associated with the **CFile** object.

This function differs from **Read** in that more than 64K–1 bytes of data can be read by **ReadHuge**. This function can be used by any object derived from **CFile**.

Note **ReadHuge** is provided only for backward compatibility. **ReadHuge** and **Read** have the same semantics under Win32.

See Also: **CFile::Write**, **CFile::WriteHuge**, **CFile::Read**

CFile::Remove

static void PASCAL Remove(LPCTSTR *lpszFileName* **);**
  throw(CFileException);

Parameters
lpszFileName   A string that is the path to the desired file. The path can be relative or absolute but cannot contain a network name.

Remarks
This static function deletes the file specified by the path. It will not remove a directory.

The **Remove** member function throws an exception if the connected file is open or if the file cannot be removed. This is equivalent to the DEL command.

Example
```
//example for CFile::Remove
char* pFileName = "test.dat";
TRY
{
   CFile::Remove( pFileName );
}
CATCH( CFileException, e )
{
   #ifdef _DEBUG
      afxDump << "File " << pFileName << " cannot be removed\n";
   #endif
}
END_CATCH
```

CFile::Rename

static void PASCAL Rename(LPCTSTR *lpszOldName*, **LPCTSTR** *lpszNewName* **);**
  throw(CFileException);

Parameters
lpszOldName   The old path.

lpszNewName   The new path.

Remarks

This static function renames the specified file. Directories cannot be renamed. This is equivalent to the REN command.

Example

```
//example for CFile::Rename
extern char* pOldName;
extern char* pNewName;
TRY
{
    CFile::Rename( pOldName, pNewName );
}
CATCH( CFileException, e )
{
    #ifdef _DEBUG
        afxDump << "File " << pOldName << " not found, cause = "
            << e->m_cause << "\n";
    #endif
}
END_CATCH
```

CFile::Seek

virtual LONG Seek(LONG *lOff*, **UINT** *nFrom* **);**
  throw(CFileException);

Return Value

If the requested position is legal, **Seek** returns the new byte offset from the beginning of the file. Otherwise, the return value is undefined and a **CFileException** object is thrown.

Parameters

lOff   Number of bytes to move the pointer.

nFrom   Pointer movement mode. Must be one of the following values:

- **CFile::begin**   Move the file pointer *lOff* bytes forward from the beginning of the file.

- **CFile::current**   Move the file pointer *lOff* bytes from the current position in the file.

- **CFile::end**   Move the file pointer *lOff* bytes from the end of the file. Note that *lOff* must be negative to seek into the existing file; positive values will seek past the end of the file.

Remarks

Repositions the pointer in a previously opened file. The **Seek** function permits random access to a file's contents by moving the pointer a specified amount, absolutely or relatively. No data is actually read during the seek.

When a file is opened, the file pointer is positioned at offset 0, the beginning of the file.

Example

```
//example for CFile::Seek
extern CFile cfile;
LONG lOffset = 1000, lActual;
lActual = cfile.Seek( lOffset, CFile::begin );
```

CFile::SeekToBegin

void SeekToBegin( );
   throw(CFileException);

Remarks

Sets the value of the file pointer to the beginning of the file. `SeekToBegin()` is equivalent to `Seek( 0L, CFile::begin )`.

Example

```
//example for CFile::SeekToBegin
extern CFile cfile;
cfile.SeekToBegin();
```

CFile::SeekToEnd

DWORD SeekToEnd( );
   throw(CFileException);

Return Value

The length of the file in bytes.

Remarks

Sets the value of the file pointer to the logical end of the file. `SeekToEnd()` is equivalent to `CFile::Seek( 0L, CFile::end )`.

Example

```
//example for CFile::SeekToEnd
extern CFile cfile;
DWORD dwActual = cfile.SeekToEnd();
```

See Also: CFile::GetLength, CFile::Seek, CFile::SeekToBegin

CFile::SetFilePath

virtual void SetFilePath(LPCTSTR *lpszNewName* **);**

Parameters

lpszNewName   Pointer to a string specifying the new path.

Remarks

Call this function to specify the path of the file; for example, if the path of a file is not available when a **CFile** object is constructed, call **SetFilePath** to provide it.

Note **SetFilePath** does not open the file or create the file; it simply associates the **CFile** object with a path name, which can then be used.

See Also: **CFile::GetFilePath**, **CFile::CFile**

CFile::SetLength

virtual void SetLength(DWORD *dwNewLen* **);**
    throw(CFileException);

Parameters

dwNewLen   Desired length of the file in bytes. This value can be larger or smaller than the current length of the file. The file will be extended or truncated as appropriate.

Remarks

Call this function to change the length of the file.

Note With **CMemFile**, this function could throw a **CMemoryException** object.

Example

```
//example for CFile::SetLength
extern CFile cfile;
DWORD dwNewLength = 10000;
cfile.SetLength( dwNewLength );
```

CFile::SetStatus

static void SetStatus(LPCTSTR *lpszFileName*, **const CFileStatus&** *status* **);**
    throw(CFileException);

Parameters

lpszFileName   A string that is the path to the desired file. The path can be relative or absolute but cannot contain a network name.

status   The buffer containing the new status information. Call the **GetStatus** member function to prefill the **CFileStatus** structure with current values, then make changes as required. If a value is 0, then the corresponding status item is not updated. See the **GetStatus** member function for a description of the **CFileStatus** structure.

Remarks

Sets the status of the file associated with this file location.

To set the time, modify the **m_mtime** field of *status*.

Please note that when you make a call to **SetStatus** in an attempt to change only the attributes of the file, and the **m_mtime** member of the file status structure is nonzero, the attributes may also be affected (changing the time stamp may have side effects on the attributes). If you want to only change the attributes of the file, first set the **m_mtime** member of the file status structure to zero and then make a call to **SetStatus**.

Example

```
//example for CFile::SetStatus
char* pFileName = "test.dat";
extern BYTE newAttribute;
CFileStatus status;
CFile::GetStatus( pFileName, status );
status.m_attribute = newAttribute;
CFile::SetStatus( pFileName, status );
```

See Also: CFile::GetStatus

CFile::UnlockRange

virtual void UnlockRange(DWORD *dwPos*, **DWORD** *dwCount* **);**
    throw(CFileException);

Parameters

dwPos   The byte offset of the start of the byte range to unlock.

dwCount   The number of bytes in the range to unlock.

Remarks

Unlocks a range of bytes in an open file. See the description of the **LockRange** member function for details.

Note   This function is not available for the **CMemFile**-derived class.

Example

```
//example for CFile::UnlockRange
extern DWORD dwPos;
extern DWORD dwCount;
extern CFile cfile;
cfile.UnlockRange( dwPos, dwCount );
```

See Also: CFile::LockRange

CFile::Write

virtual void Write(const void* *lpBuf***, UINT** *nCount* **);**
   throw(CFileException);

Parameters

lpBuf A pointer to the user-supplied buffer that contains the data to be written to the file.

nCount The number of bytes to be transferred from the buffer. For text-mode files, carriage return–linefeed pairs are counted as single characters.

Remarks

Writes data from a buffer to the file associated with the **CFile** object.

Write throws an exception in response to several conditions, including the disk-full condition.

Example

```
//example for CFile::Write
extern CFile cfile;
char pbuf[100];
cfile.Write( pbuf, 100 );
```

See Also: **CFile::Read, CStdioFile::WriteString**

CFile::WriteHuge

void WriteHuge(const void* *lpBuf***, DWORD** *dwCount* **);**
   throw(CFileException);

Parameters

lpBuf A pointer to the user-supplied buffer that contains the data to be written to the file.

dwCount The number of bytes to be transferred from the buffer. For text-mode files, carriage return–linefeed pairs are counted as single characters.

Remarks

Writes data from a buffer to the file associated with the **CFile** object. **WriteHuge** throws an exception in response to several conditions, including the disk-full condition.

This function differs from **Write** in that more than 64K–1 bytes of data can be written by **WriteHuge**. This function can be used by any object derived from **CFile**.

Note **WriteHuge** is provided only for backward compatibility. **WriteHuge** and **Write** have the same semantics under Win32.

See Also: **CFile::Read, CFile::ReadHuge, CFile::Write, CStdioFile::WriteString**

Data Members
CFile::m_hFile

Remarks

Contains the operating-system file handle for an open file. **m_hFile** is a public variable of type **UINT**. It contains **CFile::hFileNull** (an operating-system-independent empty file indicator) if the handle has not been assigned.

Use of **m_hFile** is not recommended because the member's meaning depends on the derived class. **m_hFile** is made a public member for convenience in supporting nonpolymorphic use of the class.

CFileDialog

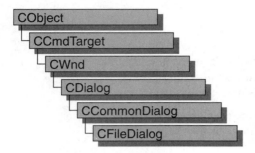

CObject
CCmdTarget
CWnd
CDialog
CCommonDialog
CFileDialog

The **CFileDialog** class encapsulates the Windows common file dialog box. Common file dialog boxes provide an easy way to implement File Open and File Save As dialog boxes (as well as other file-selection dialog boxes) in a manner consistent with Windows standards.

You can use **CFileDialog** "as is" with the constructor provided, or you can derive your own dialog class from **CFileDialog** and write a constructor to suit your needs. In either case, these dialog boxes will behave like standard Microsoft Foundation class dialog boxes because they are derived from the **CCommonDialog** class.

To use a **CFileDialog** object, first create the object using the **CFileDialog** constructor. After the dialog box has been constructed, you can set or modify any values in the **m_ofn** structure to initialize the values or states of the dialog box's controls. The **m_ofn** structure is of type **OPENFILENAME**. For more information, see the **OPENFILENAME** structure in the Win32 SDK documentation.

After initializing the dialog box's controls, call the **DoModal** member function to display the dialog box and allow the user to enter the path and file. **DoModal** returns whether the user selected the OK (**IDOK**) or the Cancel (**IDCANCEL**) button.

If **DoModal** returns **IDOK**, you can use one of **CFileDialog**'s public member functions to retrieve the information input by the user.

CFileDialog includes several protected members that enable you to do custom handling of share violations, filename validation, and list-box change notification. These protected members are callback functions that most applications do not need to use, since default handling is done automatically. Message-map entries for these functions are not necessary because they are standard virtual functions.

You can use the Windows **CommDlgExtendedError** function to determine whether an error occurred during initialization of the dialog box and to learn more about the error.

The destruction of **CFileDialog** objects is handled automatically. It is not necessary to call **CDialog::EndDialog**.

To allow the user to select multiple files, set the **OFN_ALLOWMULTISELECT** flag before calling **DoModal**. You need to supply your own filename buffer to accommodate the returned list of multiple filenames. Do this by replacing **m_ofn.lpstrFile** with a pointer to a buffer you have allocated, after constructing the **CFileDialog**, but before calling **DoModal**. Additionally, you must set **m_ofn.nMaxFile** with the number of characters in the buffer pointed to by **m_ofn.lpstrFile**.

CFileDialog relies on the COMMDLG.DLL file that ships with Windows versions 3.1 and later.

If you derive a new class from **CFileDialog**, you can use a message map to handle any messages. To extend the default message handling, derive a class from **CWnd**, add a message map to the new class, and provide member functions for the new messages. You do not need to provide a hook function to customize the dialog box.

To customize the dialog box, derive a class from **CFileDialog**, provide a custom dialog template, and add a message map to process the notification messages from the extended controls. Any unprocessed messages should be passed to the base class.

Customizing the hook function is not required.

For more information on using **CFileDialog**, see "Common Dialog Classes" in *Visual C++ Programmer's Guide* online.

#include <afxdlgs.h>

CFileDialog Class Members

Data Members

m_ofn	The Windows **OPENFILENAME** structure. Provides access to basic file dialog box parameters.

Construction

CFileDialog	Constructs a **CFileDialog** object.

Operations

DoModal	Displays the dialog box and allows the user to make a selection.
GetPathName	Returns the full path of the selected file.
GetFileName	Returns the filename of the selected file.
GetFileExt	Returns the file extension of the selected file.
GetFileTitle	Returns the title of the selected file.
GetNextPathName	Returns the full path of the next selected file.
GetReadOnlyPref	Returns the read-only status of the selected file.
GetStartPosition	Returns the position of the first element of the filename list.

Overridables

OnShareViolation	Called when a share violation occurs.
OnFileNameOK	Called to validate the filename entered in the dialog box.
OnLBSelChangedNotify	Called when the list box selection changes.
OnInitDone	Called to handle the **WM_NOTIFY CDN_INITDONE** message.
OnFileNameChange	Called to handle the **WM_NOTIFY CDN_SELCHANGE** message.
OnFolderChange	Called to handle the **WM_NOTIFY CDN_FOLDERCHANGE** message.
OnTypeChange	Called to handle the **WM_NOTIFY CDN_TYPECHANGE** message.

Member Functions

CFileDialog::CFileDialog

CFileDialog(BOOL *bOpenFileDialog***, LPCTSTR** *lpszDefExt* = **NULL,**
 ↳ **LPCTSTR** *lpszFileName* = **NULL, DWORD** *dwFlags* =
 ↳ **OFN_HIDEREADONLY | OFN_OVERWRITEPROMPT,**
 ↳ **LPCTSTR** *lpszFilter* = **NULL, CWnd*** *pParentWnd* = **NULL);**

Parameters

bOpenFileDialog   Set to **TRUE** to construct a File Open dialog box or **FALSE** to construct a File Save As dialog box.

lpszDefExt   The default filename extension. If the user does not include an extension in the Filename edit box, the extension specified by *lpszDefExt* is automatically appended to the filename. If this parameter is **NULL**, no file extension is appended.

lpszFileName   The initial filename that appears in the filename edit box. If **NULL**, no filename initially appears.

dwFlags   A combination of one or more flags that allow you to customize the dialog box. For a description of these flags, see the **OPENFILENAME** structure in the Win32 SDK documentation. If you modify the **m_ofn.Flags** structure member, use a bitwise-OR operator in your changes to keep the default behavior intact.

lpszFilter   A series of string pairs that specify filters you can apply to the file. If you specify file filters, only selected files will appear in the Files list box. See the Remarks section for more information on how to work with file filters.

pParentWnd   A pointer to the file dialog-box object's parent or owner window.

Remarks

Call this function to construct a standard Windows file dialog box-object. Either a File Open or File Save As dialog box is constructed, depending on the value of *bOpenFileDialog*.

To allow the user to select multiple files, set the **OFN_ALLOWMULTISELECT** flag before calling **DoModal**. You need to supply your own filename buffer to accommodate the returned list of multiple filenames. Do this by replacing **m_ofn.lpstrFile** with a pointer to a buffer you have allocated, after constructing the **CFileDialog**, but before calling **DoModal**. Additionally, you must set **m_ofn.nMaxFile** with the number of characters in the buffer pointed to by **m_ofn.lpstrFile**.

For example, Microsoft Excel permits users to open files with extensions .XLC (chart) or .XLS (worksheet), among others. The filter for Excel could be written as:

```
static char BASED_CODE szFilter[] = "Chart Files (*.xlc)|*.xlc|Worksheet Files
(*.xls)|*.xls|Data Files (*.xlc;*.xls)|*.xlc; *.xls|All Files (*.*)|*.*||";
```

See Also: **CFileDialog::DoModal**, **::GetOpenFileName**, **::GetSaveFileName**, **OPENFILENAME**

CFileDialog::DoModal

virtual int DoModal( );

Return Value

IDOK or **IDCANCEL** if the function is successful; otherwise 0. **IDOK** and **IDCANCEL** are constants that indicate whether the user selected the OK or Cancel button.

If **IDCANCEL** is returned, you can call the Windows **CommDlgExtendedError** function to determine whether an error occurred.

Remarks

Call this function to display the Windows common file dialog box and allow the user to browse files and directories and enter a filename.

If you want to initialize the various file dialog-box options by setting members of the **m_ofn** structure, you should do this before calling **DoModal**, but after the dialog object is constructed.

When the user clicks the dialog box's OK or Cancel buttons, or selects the Close option from the dialog box's control menu, control is returned to your application. You can then call other member functions to retrieve the settings or information the user inputs into the dialog box.

DoModal is a virtual function overridden from class **Cdialog**.

See Also: **CDialog::DoModal**, **CFileDialog::CFileDialog**

CFileDialog::GetFileExt

CString GetFileExt( ) const;

Return Value

The extension of the filename.

Remarks

Call this function to retrieve the extension of the filename entered into the dialog box. For example, if the name of the file entered is DATA.TXT, **GetFileExt** returns "TXT".

If **m_ofn.Flags** has the **OFN_ALLOWMULTISELECT** flag set, this string contains a sequence of null-terminated strings, with the first string being the directory path of the file group selected, followed by the names of all files selected by the user. To retrieve file pathnames, use the **GetStartPosition** and **GetNextPathName** member functions.

See Also: **CFileDialog::GetPathName, CFileDialog::GetFileName, CFileDialog::GetFileTitle**

CFileDialog::GetFileName

CString GetFileName( ) const;

Return Value

The name of the file.

Remarks

Call this function to retrieve the name of the filename entered in the dialog box. The name of the file includes both the prefix and the extension. For example, **GetFileName** will return "TEXT.DAT" for the file C:\FILES\TEXT.DAT.

If **m_ofn.Flags** has the **OFN_ALLOWMULTISELECT** flag set, you should call **GetStartPosition** and **GetNextPathName** to retrieve a file pathname.

See Also: **CFileDialog::GetPathName, CFileDialog::GetStartPosition, CFileDialog::GetFileTitle**

CFileDialog::GetFileTitle

CString GetFileTitle( ) const;

Return Value

The title of the file.

Remarks

Call this function to retrieve the title of the file entered in the dialog box. The title of the file includes only its prefix, without the path or the extension. For example, **GetFileTitle** will return "TEXT" for the file C:\FILES\TEXT.DAT.

If **m_ofn.Flags** has the **OFN_ALLOWMULTISELECT** flag set, this string contains a sequence of null-teminated strings, with the first string being the directory path of the file group selected, followed by the names of all files selected by the user. For this reason, use the **GetStartPosition** and **GetNextPathName** member functions to retrieve the next file name in the list.

See Also: **CFileDialog::GetPathName, CFileDialog::GetFileName, CFileDialog::GetFileExt, ::GetFileTitle**

CFileDialog::GetNextPathName

CString GetNextPathName(POSITION& *pos* **) const;**

Parameters

pos   A reference to a **POSITION** value returned by a previous **GetNextPathName** or **GetStartPosition** function call. **NULL** if the end of the list has been reached.

Return Value

The full path of the file.

Remarks

Call this function to retrieve the next filename from the group selected in the dialog box. The path of the filename includes the file's title plus the entire directory path. For example, **GetNextPathName** will return "C:\FILES\TEXT.DAT" for the file C:\FILES\TEXT.DAT. You can use **GetNextPathName** in a forward iteration loop if you establish the initial position with a call to **GetStartPosition**.

If the selection consists of only one file, that file name will be returned.

See Also: **CFileDialog::GetFileName, CFileDialog::GetStartPosition**

CFileDialog::GetPathName

CString GetPathName( ) const;

Return Value

The full path of the file.

Remarks

Call this function to retrieve the full path of the file entered in the dialog box. The path of the filename includes the file's title plus the entire directory path. For example, **GetPathName** will return "C:\FILES\TEXT.DAT" for the file C:\FILES\TEXT.DAT.

If **m_ofn.Flags** has the **OFN_ALLOWMULTISELECT** flag set, this string contains a sequence of null-terminated strings, with the first string being the directory path of the file group selected, followed by the names of all files selected by the user. For this reason, use the **GetStartPosition** and **GetNextPathName** member functions to retrieve the next file name in the list.

See Also: **CFileDialog::GetFileName**, **CFileDialog::GetFileExt**, **CFileDialog::GetFileTitle**

CFileDialog::GetReadOnlyPref

BOOL GetReadOnlyPref( ) const;

Return Value

Non-zero if the Read Only check box in the dialog box is selected; otherwise 0.

Remarks

Call this function to determine whether the Read Only check box has been selected in the Windows standard File Open and File Save As dialog boxes. The Read Only check box can be hidden by setting the **OFN_HIDEREADONLY** style in the **CFileDialog** constructor.

See Also: **CFileDialog::CFileDialog**, **CFileDialog::GetPathName**, **CFileDialog::GetFileExt**

CFileDialog::GetStartPosition

POSITION GetStartPosition( ) const;

Return Value

A **POSITION** value that can be used for iteration; **NULL** if the list is empty.

Remarks

Call this member function to retrieve the position of the first file pathname in the list, if **m_ofn.Flags** has the **OFN_ALLOWMULTISELECT** flag set.

See Also: **CFileDialog::GetFileName**, **CFileDialog::GetNextPathName**

CFileDialog::OnFileNameChange

virtual void OnFileNameChange( );

Remarks

Override this function to handle the **WM_NOTIFY CDN_SELCHANGE** message. The notification message is sent when the user selects a new file or folder in the file list of the Open or Save As dialog box.

Notification is sent only if the dialog box was created with the OFN_EXPLORER style. For more information about the notification, see **CDN_SELCHANGE**. For information about the OFN_EXPLORER style, see the **OPENFILENAME** structure and "Open and Save As Dialog Boxes."

See Also: **CFileDialog::OnFolderChange**

CFileDialog::OnFileNameOK

virtual BOOL OnFileNameOK( );

Return Value

1 if the filename is not a valid filename; otherwise 0.

Remarks

Override this function only if you want to provide custom validation of filenames that are entered into a common file dialog box. This function allows you to reject a filename for any application-specific reason. Normally, you do not need to use this function because the framework provides default validation of filenames and displays a message box if an invalid filename is entered.

If 1 is returned, the dialog box will remain displayed for the user to enter another filename. The dialog procedure dismisses the dialog if the return is 0. Other nonzero return values are currently reserved and should not be used.

See Also: OPENFILENAME

CFileDialog::OnFolderChange

virtual void OnFolderChange( );

Remarks

Override this function to handle the **WM_NOTIFY CDN_FOLDERCHANGE** message. The notification message is sent when a new folder is opened in the Open or Save As dialog box.

Notification is sent only if the dialog box was created with the OFN_EXPLORER style. For more information about the notification, see **CDN_FOLDERCHANGE**. For information about the OFN_EXPLORER style, see the **OPENFILENAME** structure and "Open and Save As Dialog Boxes."

See Also: CFileDialog::OnFileChange

CFileDialog::OnInitDone

virtual void OnInitDone( );

Remarks

Override this function to handle the **WM_NOTIFY CDN_INITDONE** message. The notification message is sent when the system has finished arranging controls in the Open or Save As dialog box to make room for the controls of the child dialog box.

Notification is sent only if the dialog box was created with the OFN_EXPLORER style. For more information about the notification, see **CDN_INITDONE**. For information about the OFN_EXPLORER style, see the **OPENFILENAME** structure and "Open and Save As Dialog Boxes."

CFileDialog::OnLBSelChangedNotify

virtual void OnLBSelChangedNotify(UINT *nIDBox*, **UINT** *iCurSel*, **UINT** *nCode***);**

Parameters

nIDBox   The ID of the list box or combo box in which the selection occurred.

iCurSel   The index of the current selection.

nCode   The control notification code. This parameter must have one of the following values:

- **CD_LBSELCHANGE**   Specifies *iCurSel* is the selected item in a single-selection list box.

- **CD_LBSELSUB**   Specifies that *iCurSel* is no longer selected in a multiselection list box.

- **CD_LBSELADD**   Specifies that *iCurSel* is selected in a multiselection list box.

- **CD_LBSELNOITEMS**   Specifies that no selection exists in a multiselection list box.

For more information, see "About Common Dialog Boxes" in the Win32 SDK documentation.

Remarks

This function is called whenever the current selection in a list box is about to change. Override this function to provide custom handling of selection changes in the list box. For example, you can use this function to display the access rights or date-last-modified of each file the user selects.

CFileDialog::OnShareViolation

virtual UINT OnShareViolation(LPCTSTR *lpszPathName* **);**

Return Value

One of the following values:

- **OFN_SHAREFALLTHROUGH**   The filename is returned from the dialog box.

- **OFN_SHARENOWARN**   No further action needs to be taken.

- **OFN_SHAREWARN**   The user receives the standard warning message for this error.

Parameters

lpszPathName   The path of the file on which the share violation occurred.

Remarks

Override this function to provide custom handling of share violations. Normally, you do not need to use this function because the framework provides default checking of share violations and displays a message box if a share violation occurs.

If you want to disable share violation checking, use the bitwise OR operator to combine the flag **OFN_SHAREAWARE** with **m_ofn.Flags**.

See Also: **CFileDialog::OnFileNameOK**

CFileDialog::OnTypeChange

virtual void OnInitDone( );

Remarks

Override this function to handle the **WM_NOTIFY CDN_TYPECHANGE** message. The notification message is sent when the user selects a new file type from the list of file types in the Open or Save As dialog box.

Notification is sent only if the dialog box was created with the OFN_EXPLORER style. For more information about the notification, see **CDN_TYPECHANGE**. For information about the OFN_EXPLORER style, see the **OPENFILENAME** structure and "Open and Save As Dialog Boxes."

See Also: **CFileDialog::OnFileChange**

Data Members

CFileDialog::m_ofn

Remarks

m_ofn is a structure of type **OPENFILENAME**. Use this structure to initialize the appearance of a File Open or File Save As dialog box after it is constructed but before it is displayed with the **DoModal** member function. For example, you can set the **lpstrTitle** member of **m_ofn** to the caption you want the dialog box to have.

For more information, see the **OPENFILENAME** structure in the Win32 SDK documentation.

CFileException

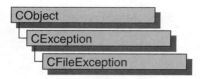

A **CFileException** object represents a file-related exception condition. The **CFileException** class includes public data members that hold the portable cause code and the operating-system-specific error number. The class also provides static member functions for throwing file exceptions and for returning cause codes for both operating-system errors and C run-time errors.

CFileException objects are constructed and thrown in **CFile** member functions and in member functions of derived classes. You can access these objects within the scope of a **CATCH** expression. For portability, use only the cause code to get the reason for an exception. For more information about exceptions, see the article "Exceptions" in *Visual C++ Programmer's Guide* online.

#include <afx.h>

See Also: "Exception Processing"

CFileException Class Members

Data Members

m_cause	Contains portable code corresponding to the exception cause.
m_lOsError	Contains the related operating-system error number.
m_strFileName	Contains the name of the file for this exception.

Construction

CFileException	Constructs a **CFileException** object.

Code Conversion

OsErrorToException	Returns a cause code corresponding to an operating system error code.
ErrnoToException	Returns cause code corresponding to a run-time error number.

Helper Functions

ThrowOsError	Throws a file exception based on an operating-system error number.
ThrowErrno	Throws a file exception based on a run-time error number.

Member Functions
CFileException::CFileException

CFileException(int *cause* **= CFileException::none, LONG** *lOsError* **= –1);**

Parameters

cause An enumerated type variable that indicates the reason for the exception. See **CFileException::m_cause** for a list of the possible values.

lOsError An operating-system-specific reason for the exception, if available. The *lOsError* parameter provides more information than *cause* does.

Remarks

Constructs a **CFileException** object that stores the cause code and the operating-system code in the object.

Do not use this constructor directly, but rather call the global function **AfxThrowFileException**.

Note The variable *lOsError* applies only to **CFile** and **CStdioFile** objects. The **CMemFile** class does not handle this error code.

See Also: **AfxThrowFileException**

CFileException::ErrnoToException

static int PASCAL ErrnoToException(int *nErrno* **);**

Return Value

Enumerated value that corresponds to a given run-time library error value.

Parameters

nErrno An integer error code as defined in the run-time include file ERRNO.H.

Remarks

Converts a given run-time library error value to a **CFileException** enumerated error value. See **CFileException::m_cause** for a list of the possible enumerated values.

Example

```
//example for CFileException::ErrnoToException
#include <errno.h>
ASSERT( CFileException::ErrnoToException( EACCES ) ==
                CFileException::accessDenied );
```

See Also: **CFileException::OsErrorToException**

CFileException::OsErrorToException

static int PASCAL OsErrorToException(LONG *lOsError* **);**

Return Value

Enumerated value that corresponds to a given operating-system error value.

Parameters

lOsError   An operating-system-specific error code.

Remarks

Returns an enumerator that corresponds to a given *lOsError* value. If the error code is unknown, then the function returns **CFileException::generic**.

Example

```
//example for CFileException::OsErrorToException
ASSERT( CFileException::OsErrorToException( 5 ) ==
                CFileException::accessDenied );
```

See Also: **CFileException::ErrnoToException**

CFileException::ThrowErrno

static void PASCAL ThrowErrno(int *nErrno* **);**

Parameters

nErrno   An integer error code as defined in the run-time include file ERRNO.H.

Remarks

Constructs a **CFileException** object corresponding to a given *nErrno* value, then throws the exception.

Example

```
//example for CFileException::ThrowErrno
#include <errno.h>
CFileException::ThrowErrno( EACCES );  // "access denied"
```

See Also: **CFileException::ThrowOsError**

CFileException::ThrowOsError

static void PASCAL ThrowOsError(LONG *lOsError*,
  ↪ **LPCTSTR** *lpszFileName* = NULL **);**

Parameters

lOsError   An operating-system-specific error code.

lpszFileName   A pointer to the string containing the name of the file that caused the exception, if available.

Remarks

Throws a **CFileException** corresponding to a given *lOsError* value. If the error code is unknown, then the function throws an exception coded as **CFileException::generic**.

Example

```
//example for CFileException::ThrowOsError
CFileException::ThrowOsError( 5 );  // "access denied"
```

See Also: **CFileException::ThrowErrno**

Data Members
CFileException::m_cause

Remarks

Contains values defined by a **CFileException** enumerated type. This data member is a public variable of type **int**. The enumerators and their meanings are as follows:

- **CFileException::none** No error occurred.
- **CFileException::generic** An unspecified error occurred.
- **CFileException::fileNotFound** The file could not be located.
- **CFileException::badPath** All or part of the path is invalid.
- **CFileException::tooManyOpenFiles** The permitted number of open files was exceeded.
- **CFileException::accessDenied** The file could not be accessed.
- **CFileException::invalidFile** There was an attempt to use an invalid file handle.
- **CFileException::removeCurrentDir** The current working directory cannot be removed.
- **CFileException::directoryFull** There are no more directory entries.
- **CFileException::badSeek** There was an error trying to set the file pointer.
- **CFileException::hardIO** There was a hardware error.
- **CFileException::sharingViolation** SHARE.EXE was not loaded, or a shared region was locked.
- **CFileException::lockViolation** There was an attempt to lock a region that was already locked.
- **CFileException::diskFull** The disk is full.
- **CFileException::endOfFile** The end of file was reached.

Note These **CFileException** cause enumerators are distinct from the **CArchiveException** cause enumerators.

Example

```
//example for CFileException::m_cause
extern char* pFileName;
TRY
{
   CFile f( pFileName, CFile::modeCreate | CFile::modeWrite );
}
CATCH( CFileException, e )
{
   if( e->m_cause == CFileException::fileNotFound )
      printf( "ERROR: File not found\n");
}
END_CATCH
```

CFileException::m_lOsError

Remarks

Contains the operating-system error code for this exception. See your operating-system technical manual for a listing of error codes. This data member is a public variable of type **LONG**.

CFileException::m_strFileName

CString m_strFileName;

Remarks

Contains the name of the file for this exception condition.

CFileFind

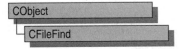

The MFC class **CFileFind** performs local file searches and is the base class for **CGopherFileFind** and **CFtpFileFind**, which perform Internet file searches. **CFileFind** includes member functions that begin a search, locate a file, and return the title, name, or path of the file. For Internet searches, the member function **GetFileURL** returns the file's URL.

CFileFind is the base class for two other MFC classes designed to search particular server types: **CGopherFileFind** works specifically with gopher servers, and **CFtpFileFind** works specifically with FTP servers. Together, these three classes provide a seamless mechanism for the client to find files, regardless of the server protocol, the file type, or location, on either a local machine or a remote server.

The following code will enumerate all the files in the current directory, printing the name of each file:

```
CFileFind finder;
BOOL bWorking = finder.FindFile("*.*");
while (bWorking)
{
    bWorking = finder.FindNextFile();
    cout << (LPCTSTR) finder.GetFileName() << endl;
}
```

To keep the example simple, this code uses the standard C++ library **cout** class. The **cout** line could be replaced with a call to **CListBox::AddString**, for example, in a program with a graphical user interface.

For more information about how to use **CFileFind** and the other WinInet classes, see the article "Internet Programming with WinInet" in *Visual C++ Programmer's Guide* online.

#include <afx.h>

See Also: **CFtpFileFind**, **CGopherFileFind**, **CInternetFile**, **CGopherFile**, **CHttpFile**

CFileFind Class Members

Construction

CFileFind	Constructs a **CFileFind** object.

Attributes

GetLength	Gets the length of the found file, in bytes.
GetFileName	Gets the name, including the extension, of the found file
GetFilePath	Gets the whole path of the found file.
GetFileTitle	Gets the title of the found file. The title does not include the extension.
GetFileURL	Gets the URL, including the file path, of the found file.
GetRoot	Gets the root directory of the found file.
GetCreationTime	Gets the time the file was created.
GetLastAccessTime	Gets the time that the file was last accessed.
GetLastWriteTime	Gets the time the file was last changed and saved.
MatchesMask	Indicates the desired file attributes of the file to be found.
IsDots	Determines if the name of the found file has the name "." or "..", indicating that is actually a directory.
IsReadOnly	Determines if the found file is read-only.
IsDirectory	Determines if the found file is a directory.
IsCompressed	Determines if the found file is compressed.
IsSystem	Determines if the found file is a system file.
IsHidden	Determines if the found file is hidden.
IsTemporary	Determines if the found file is temporary.
IsNormal	Determines if the found file is normal (in other words, has no other attributes).
IsArchived	Determines if the found file is archived.

Operations

Close	Closes the search request.
FindFile	Searches a directory for a specified file name.
FindNextFile	Continues a file search from a previous call to **FindFile**.

Member Functions

CFileFind::CFileFind

CFileFind( );

Remarks

This member function is called when a **CFileFind** object is constructed.

See Also: **CGopherFileFind**, **CFtpFileFind**

CFileFind::Close

void Close( );

Remarks

Call this member function to end the search, reset the context, and release all resources. After calling **Close**, you do not have to create a new **CFileFind** instance before calling **FindFile** to begin a new search.

CFileFind::FindFile

virtual BOOL FindFile(LPCTSTR *pstrName* **= NULL, DWORD** *dwUnused* **= 0);**

Return Value

Nonzero if successful; otherwise 0. To get extended error information, call the Win32 function **GetLastError**.

Parameters

pstrName   A pointer to a string containing the name of the file to find. If you pass **NULL** for *pstrName*, **FindFile** does a wildcard (*.*) search.

dwUnused   Reserved to make **FindFile** polymorphic with derived classes. Must be 0.

Remarks

Call this member function to open a file search.

After calling **FindFile** to begin the file search, call **FindNextFile** to retrieve subsequent files. You must call **FindNextFile** at least once before calling any of the following attribute member functions:

- **GetCreationTime**
- **GetFileName**
- **GetFileTitle**
- **GetFilePath**
- **GetFileURL**
- **GetLastAccessTime**
- **GetLastWriteTime**
- **GetLength**
- **GetRoot**

See Also: CFileFind::FindNextFile

CFileFind::FindNextFile

virtual BOOL FindNextFile( );

Return Value

Nonzero if successful; otherwise 0. To get extended error information, call the Win32 function **GetLastError**.

Remarks

Call this member function to continue a file search from a previous call to **FindFile**. You must call **FindNextFile** at least once before calling any of the following attribute member functions:

- **GetCreationTime**
- **GetFileName**
- **GetFileTitle**
- **GetFilePath**
- **GetFileURL**
- **GetLastAccessTime**
- **GetLastWriteTime**
- **GetLength**
- **GetRoot**

FindNextFile wraps the Win32 function **FindNextFile**.

CFileFind::GetCreationTime

virtual BOOL GetCreationTime(FILETIME* *pFileTime* **) const;**
virtual BOOL GetCreationTime(CTime& *refTime* **) const;**

Return Value

Nonzero if successful; 0 if unsuccessful. **GetCreationTime** returns 0 only if **FindNextFile** has never been called on this **CFileFind** object.

Parameters

pFileTime   A pointer to a **FILETIME** structure containing the time the file was created.

refTime   A reference to a **CTime** object.

Remarks

Call this member function to get the time the specified file was created.

You must call **FindNextFile** at least once before calling **GetCreationTime**.

Note Not all file systems use the same semantics to implement the time stamp returned by this function. This function may return the same value returned by other time stamp functions if the underlying file system or server does not support keeping the time attribute. See the **Win32_FIND_DATA** structure for information about time formats. On some operation systems, the returned time is in the time zone local to the machine were the file is located. See the Win32 **FileTimeToLocalFileTime** API for more information.

CFileFind::GetFileName

virtual CString GetFileName( ) const;

Return Value

The name of the most-recently-found file.

Remarks

Call this member function to get the name of the found file. You must call **FindNextFile** at least once before calling GetFileName.

GetFileName is one of three **CFileFind** member functions that return some form of the file name. The following list describes the three and how they vary:

- **GetFileName** returns the file name, including the extension. For example, calling **GetFileName** to generate a user message about the file c:\myhtml\myfile.txt returns the file name myfile.txt.

- **GetFilePath** returns the entire path for the file. For example, calling **GetFilePath** to generate a user message about the file c:\myhtml\myfile.txt returns the file path c:\myhtml\myfile.txt.

- **GetFileTitle** returns the file name, excluding the file extension. For example, calling **GetFileTitle** to generate a user message about the file c:\myhtml\myfile.txt returns the file title myfile.

See Also: **CFileFind::FindFile**

CFileFind::GetFilePath

virtual CString GetFilePath( ) const;

Return Value

The path of the specified file.

Remarks

Call this member function to get the full path of the specified file. You must call **FindNextFile** at least once before calling **GetFilePath**.

GetFilePath is one of three **CFileFind** member functions that return some form of the file name. The following list describes the three and how they vary:

- **GetFileName** returns the file name, including the extension. For example, calling **GetFileName** to generate a user message about the file `c:\myhtml\myfile.txt` returns the file name `myfile.txt`.

- **GetFilePath** returns the entire path for the file. For example, calling **GetFilePath** to generate a user message about the file `c:\myhtml\myfile.txt` returns the file path `c:\myhtml\myfile.txt`.

- **GetFileTitle** returns the file name, excluding the file extension. For example, calling **GetFileTitle** to generate a user message about the file `c:\myhtml\myfile.txt` returns the file title `myfile`.

See Also: CFileFind::FindFile

CFileFind::GetFileTitle

virtual CString GetFileTitle( ) const;

Return Value

The title of the file.

Remarks

Call this member function to get the title of the found file. You must call **FindNextFile** at least once before calling **GetFileTitle**.

GetFileTitle is one of three **CFileFind** member functions that return some form of the file name. The following list describes the three and how they vary:

- **GetFileName** returns the file name, including the extension. For example, calling **GetFileName** to generate a user message about the file `c:\myhtml\myfile.txt` returns the file name `myfile.txt`.

- **GetFilePath** returns the entire path for the file. For example, calling **GetFilePath** to generate a user message about the file `c:\myhtml\myfile.txt` returns the file path `c:\myhtml\myfile.txt`.

- **GetFileTitle** returns the file name, excluding the file extension. For example, calling **GetFileTitle** to generate a user message about the file `c:\myhtml\myfile.txt` returns the file title `myfile`.

See Also: CFileFind::FindFile

CFileFind::GetFileURL

virtual CString GetFileURL( ) const;

Return Value

The complete URL.

Remarks

Call this member function to retrieve the specified URL. You must call **FindNextFile** at least once before calling **GetFileURL**.

GetFileURL is similar to the member function **GetFilePath**, except that it returns the URL in the form `file://path`. For example, calling **GetFileURL** to get the complete URL for `myfile.txt` returns the URL `file://c:\myhtml\myfile.txt`.

See Also: **CFileFind::FindFile**

CFileFind::GetLastAccessTime

virtual BOOL GetLastAccessTime(CTime& *refTime* **) const;**
virtual BOOL GetLastAccessTime(FILETIME* *pFileTime* **) const;**

Return Value

Nonzero if successful; 0 if unsuccessful. **GetLastAccessTime** returns 0 only if **FindNextFile** has never been called on this **CFileFind** object.

Parameters

pFileTime   A pointer to a **FILETIME** structure containing the time the file was last accessed.

refTime   A reference to a **CTime** object.

Remarks

Call this member function to get the time that the specified file was last accessed.

You must call **FindNextFile** at least once before calling **GetLastAccessTime**.

Note Not all file systems use the same semantics to implement the time stamp returned by this function. This function may return the same value returned by other time stamp functions if the underlying file system or server does not support keeping the time attribute. See the **Win32_FIND_DATA** structure for information about time formats. On some operation systems, the returned time is in the time zone local to the machine were the file is located. See the Win32 **FileTimeToLocalFileTime** API for more information.

CFileFind::GetLastWriteTime

virtual BOOL GetLastWriteTime(FILETIME* *pFileTime* **) const;**
virtual BOOL GetLastWriteTime(CTime& *refTime* **) const;**

Return Value

Nonzero if successful; 0 if unsuccessful. **GetLastWriteTime** returns 0 only if **FindNextFile** has never been called on this **CFileFind** object.

Parameters

pFileTime   A pointer to a **FILETIME** structure containing the time the file was last written to.

refTime   A reference to a **CTime** object.

Remarks

Call this member function to get the last time the file was changed.

You must call **FindNextFile** at least once before calling **GetLastWriteTime**.

Note Not all file systems use the same semantics to implement the time stamp returned by this function. This function may return the same value returned by other time stamp functions if the underlying file system or server does not support keeping the time attribute. See the **Win32_Find_Data** structure for information about time formats. On some operation systems, the returned time is in the time zone local to the machine were the file is located. See the Win32 **FileTimeToLocalFileTime** API for more information.

CFileFind::GetLength

DWORD GetLength( ) const;

Return Value

The length of the found file, in bytes.

Remarks

Call this member function to get the length of the found file, in bytes. You must call **FindNextFile** at least once before calling **GetLength**.

GetLength uses the **nFileSizeLow** member of the Win32 structure, **WIN32_FIND_DATA**, to get and return the low-order **DWORD** value of the file size, in bytes. If the file may be more than four gigabytes in size, use the **GetLength64** member.

CFileFind::GetRoot

virtual CString GetRoot( ) const;

Return Value

The root of the active search.

Remarks

Call this member function to get the root of the found file. You must call **FindNextFile** at least once before calling **GetRoot**.

This member function returns the drive specifier and path name used to start a search. For example, calling **FindFile** with `*.dat` results in **GetRoot** returning an empty string. Passing a path, such as `c:\windows\system\*.dll`, to **FindFile** results **GetRoot** returning `c:\windows\system\`.

CFileFind::IsArchived

BOOL IsArchived( ) const;

Return Value

Nonzero if successful; otherwise 0.

Remarks

Call this member function to determine if the found file is archived. Applications mark an archive file, which is to be backed up or removed, with FILE_ATTRIBUTE_ARCHIVE, a file attribute identified in the **WIN32_FIND_DATA** structure.

See the member function **MatchesMask** for a complete list of file attributes.

CFileFind::IsCompressed

BOOL IsCompressed( ) const;

Return Value

Nonzero if successful; otherwise 0.

Remarks

Call this member function to determine if the found file is compressed. A compressed file is marked with FILE_ATTRIBUTE_COMPRESSED, a file attribute identified in the **WIN32_FIND_DATA** structure. For a file, this attribute indicates that all of the data in the file is compressed. For a directory, this attribute indicates that compression is the default for newly created files and subdirectories.

See the member function **MatchesMask** for a complete list of file attributes.

CFileFind::IsDirectory

BOOL IsDirectory( ) const;

Return Value

Nonzero if successful; otherwise 0.

Remarks

Call this member function to determine if the found file is a directory. A file that is a directory is marked with FILE_ATTRIBUTE_DIRECTORY a file attribute identified in the **WIN32_FIND_DATA** structure.

See the member function **MatchesMask** for a complete list of file attributes.

CFileFind::IsDots

virtual BOOL IsDots( ) const;

Return Value

Nonzero if the found file has the name ".." or "..", which indicates that the found file is actually a directory. Otherwise 0.

Remarks

Call this member function to test for the current directory and parent directory markers while iterating through files.

See Also: CFileFind::IsDirectory

CFileFind::IsHidden

BOOL IsHidden( ) const;

Return Value

Nonzero if successful; otherwise 0.

Remarks

Call this member function to determine if the found file is hidden. Hidden files, which are marked with FILE_ATTRIBUTE_HIDDEN, a file attribute identified in the **WIN32_FIND_DATA** structure. A hidden file is not included in an ordinary directory listing.

See the member function **MatchesMask** for a complete list of file attributes.

CFileFind::IsNormal

BOOL IsNormal( ) const;

Return Value

Nonzero if successful; otherwise 0.

Remarks

Call this member function to determine if the found file is a normal file. Files marked with FILE_ATTRIBUTE_NORMAL, a file attribute identified in the **WIN32_FIND_DATA** structure. A normal file has no other attributes set. All other file attributes override this attribute.

See the member function **MatchesMask** for a complete list of file attributes.

CFileFind::IsReadOnly

BOOL IsReadOnly( ) const;

Return Value

Nonzero if successful; otherwise 0.

Remarks

Call this member function to determine if the found file is read-only. A read-only file is marked with FILE_ATTRIBUTE_, a file attribute identified in the **WIN32_FIND_DATA** structure. Applications can read such a file, but they cannot write to it or delete it.

See the member function **MatchesMask** for a complete list of file attributes.

CFileFind::IsSystem

BOOL IsSystem( ) const;

Return Value

Nonzero if successful; otherwise 0.

Remarks

Call this member function to determine if the found file is a system file. A system file is marked with FILE_ATTRIBUTE_SYSTEM, , a file attribute identified in the **WIN32_FIND_DATA** structure. A system file is part of, or is used exclusively by, the operating system.

See the member function **MatchesMask** for a complete list of file attributes.

CFileFind::IsTemporary

BOOL IsTemporary( ) const;

Return Value

Nonzero if successful; otherwise 0.

Remarks

Call this member function to determine if the found file is a temporary file. A temporary file is marked with FILE_ATTRIBUTE_TEMPORARY, a file attribute identified in the **WIN32_FIND_DATA** structure. A temporary file is used for temporary storage. Applications should write to the file only if absolutely necessary. Most of the file's data remains in memory without being flushed to the media because the file will soon be deleted.

See the member function **MatchesMask** for a complete list of file attributes.

CFileFind::MatchesMask

virtual BOOL MatchesMask(DWORD *dwMask* **) const;**

Return Value

Nonzero if successful; otherwise 0. To get extended error information, call the Win32 function **GetLastError**.

Parameters

dwMask   Specifies one or more file attributes, identified in the **WIN32_FIND_DATA** structure, for the found file. To search for multiple attributes, use the bitwise OR (|) operator. Any combination of the following attributes is acceptable:

- FILE_ATTRIBUTE_ARCHIVE   The file is an archive file. Applications use this attribute to mark files for backup or removal.

- FILE_ATTRIBUTE_COMPRESSED   The file or directory is compressed. For a file, this means that all of the data in the file is compressed. For a directory, this means that compression is the default for newly created files and subdirectories.

- FILE_ATTRIBUTE_DIRECTORY   The file is a directory.

- FILE_ATTRIBUTE_NORMAL   The file has no other attributes set. This attribute is valid only if used alone. All other file attributes override this attribute.

- FILE_ATTRIBUTE_HIDDEN   The file is hidden. It is not to be included in an ordinary directory listing.

- FILE_ATTRIBUTE_READONLY   The file is read only. Applications can read the file but cannot write to it or delete it.

- FILE_ATTRIBUTE_SYSTEM   The file is part of or is used exclusively by the operating system.

- FILE_ATTRIBUTE_TEMPORARY   The file is being used for temporary storage. Applications should write to the file only if absolutely necessary. Most of the file's data remains in memory without being flushed to the media because the file will soon be deleted.

Remarks

Call this member function to test the file attributes on the found file.

See Also: **CFileFind::IsDots**, **CFileFind::IsReadOnly**, **CFileFind::IsDirectory**, **CFileFind::IsCompressed**, **CFileFind::IsSystem**, **CFileFind::IsHidden**, **CFileFind::IsTemporary**, **CFileFind::IsNormal**, **CFileFind::IsArchived**

CFindReplaceDialog

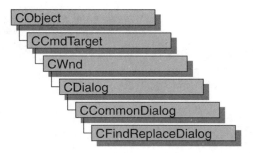

The **CFindReplaceDialog** class allows you to implement standard string Find/Replace dialog boxes in your application. Unlike the other Windows common dialog boxes, **CFindReplaceDialog** objects are modeless, allowing users to interact with other windows while they are on screen. There are two kinds of **CFindReplaceDialog** objects: Find dialog boxes and Find/Replace dialog boxes. Although the dialog boxes allow the user to input search and search/replace strings, they do not perform any of the searching or replacing functions. You must add these to the application.

To construct a **CFindReplaceDialog** object, use the provided constructor (which has no arguments). Since this is a modeless dialog box, allocate the object on the heap using the **new** operator, rather than on the stack.

Once a **CFindReplaceDialog** object has been constructed, you must call the **Create** member function to create and display the dialog box.

Use the **m_fr** structure to initialize the dialog box before calling **Create**. The **m_fr** structure is of type **FINDREPLACE**. For more information on this structure, see the Win32 SDK documentation.

In order for the parent window to be notified of find/replace requests, you must use the Windows **RegisterWindowMessage** function and use the **ON_REGISTERED_MESSAGE** message-map macro in your frame window that handles this registered message. You can call any of the member functions listed in the "Operations" section of the **CFindReplaceDialog** Class Members table from the frame window's callback function.

You can determine whether the user has decided to terminate the dialog box with the **IsTerminating** member function.

CFindReplaceDialog relies on the COMMDLG.DLL file that ships with Windows versions 3.1 and later.

To customize the dialog box, derive a class from **CFindReplaceDialog**, provide a custom dialog template, and add a message map to process the notification messages from the extended controls. Any unprocessed messages should be passed to the base class.

Customizing the hook function is not required.

For more information on using **CFindReplaceDialog**, see "Common Dialog Classes" in *Visual C++ Programmer's Guide* online.

#include <afxdlgs.h>

CFindReplaceDialog Class Members

Data Members

m_fr	A structure used to customize a **CFindReplaceDialog** object.

Construction

CFindReplaceDialog	Call this function to construct a **CFindReplaceDialog** object.
Create	Creates and displays a **CFindReplaceDialog** dialog box.

Operations

FindNext	Call this function to determine whether the user wants to find the next occurrence of the find string.
GetNotifier	Call this function to retrieve the **FINDREPLACE** structure in your registered message handler.
GetFindString	Call this function to retrieve the current find string.
GetReplaceString	Call this function to retrieve the current replace string.
IsTerminating	Call this function to determine whether the dialog box is terminating.
MatchCase	Call this function to determine whether the user wants to match the case of the find string exactly.
MatchWholeWord	Call this function to determine whether the user wants to match entire words only.
ReplaceAll	Call this function to determine whether the user wants all occurrences of the string to be replaced.
ReplaceCurrent	Call this function to determine whether the user wants the current word to be replaced.
SearchDown	Call this function to determine whether the user wants the search to proceed in a downward direction.

Member Functions
CFindReplaceDialog::CFindReplaceDialog

CFindReplaceDialog( );

Remarks

Constructs a **CFindReplaceDialog** object. **CFindReplaceDialog** objects are constructed on the heap with the **new** operator. For more information on the construction of **CFindReplaceDialog** objects, see the **CFindReplaceDialog** overview. Use the **Create** member function to display the dialog box.

See Also: **CFindReplaceDialog::Create**

CFindReplaceDialog::Create

BOOL Create(BOOL *bFindDialogOnly*, **LPCTSTR** *lpszFindWhat*,
↪ **LPCTSTR** *lpszReplaceWith* = **NULL**, **DWORD** *dwFlags* = **FR_DOWN**,
↪ **CWnd*** *pParentWnd* = **NULL**);

Return Value

Nonzero if the dialog box object was successfully created; otherwise 0.

Parameters

bFindDialogOnly   Set this parameter to **TRUE** to display the standard Windows Find dialog box. Set it to **FALSE** to display the Windows Find/Replace dialog box.

lpszFindWhat   Specifies the string for which to search.

lpszReplaceWith   Specifies the default string with which to replace found strings.

dwFlags   One or more flags you can use to customize the settings of the dialog box, combined using the bitwise OR operator. The default value is **FR_DOWN**, which specifies that the search is to proceed in a downward direction. See the **FINDREPLACE** structure in the Win32 SDK documentation for more information on these flags.

pParentWnd   A pointer to the dialog box's parent or owner window. This is the window that will receive the special message indicating that a find/replace action is requested. If **NULL**, the application's main window is used.

Remarks

Creates and displays either a Find or Find/Replace dialog box object, depending on the value of *bFindDialogOnly*.

In order for the parent window to be notified of find/replace requests, you must use the Windows **RegisterWindowMessage** function whose return value is a message number unique to the application's instance. Your frame window should have a message map entry that declares the callback function (**OnFindReplace** in the example that follows) that handles this registered message. The following code fragment is an example of how to do this for a frame window class named CMyFrameWnd:

```
class CMyFrameWnd : public CFrameWnd
{
protected:
    afx_msg LONG OnFindReplace(WPARAM wParam, LPARAM lParam);

    DECLARE_MESSAGE_MAP()
};
static UINT WM_FINDREPLACE = ::RegisterWindowMessage(FINDMSGSTRING);

BEGIN_MESSAGE_MAP( CMyFrameWnd, CFrameWnd )
    //Normal message map entries here.
    ON_REGISTERED_MESSAGE( WM_FINDREPLACE, OnFindReplace )
END_MESSAGE_MAP
```

Within your **OnFindReplace** function, you interpret the intentions of the user and create the code for the find/replace operations.

See Also: **CFindReplaceDialog::CFindReplaceDialog**

CFindReplaceDialog::FindNext

BOOL FindNext( ) const;

Return Value

Nonzero if the user wants to find the next occurrence of the search string; otherwise 0.

Remarks

Call this function from your callback function to determine whether the user wants to find the next occurrence of the search string.

See Also: **CFindReplaceDialog::GetFindString**, **CFindReplaceDialog::SearchDown**

CFindReplaceDialog::GetFindString

CString GetFindString( ) const;

Return Value

The default string to find.

Remarks

Call this function from your callback function to retrieve the default string to find.

See Also: **CFindReplaceDialog::FindNext**, **CFindReplaceDialog::GetReplaceString**

CFindReplaceDialog::GetNotifier

static CFindReplaceDialog* PASCAL GetNotifier(LPARAM *lParam*);

Return Value

A pointer to the current dialog box.

Parameters

lParam   The **lparam** value passed to the frame window's **OnFindReplace** member function.

Remarks

Call this function to retrieve a pointer to the current Find Replace dialog box. It should be used within your callback function to access the current dialog box, call its member functions, and access the **m_fr** structure.

CFindReplaceDialog::GetReplaceString

CString GetReplaceString( ) const;

Return Value

The default string with which to replace found strings.

Remarks

Call this function to retrieve the current replace string.

See Also: CFindReplaceDialog::GetFindString

CFindReplaceDialog::IsTerminating

BOOL IsTerminating( ) const;

Return Value

Nonzero if the user has decided to terminate the dialog box; otherwise 0.

Remarks

Call this function within your callback function to determine whether the user has decided to terminate the dialog box. If this function returns nonzero, you should call the **DestroyWindow** member function of the current dialog box and set any dialog box pointer variable to **NULL**. Optionally, you can also store the find/replace text last entered and use it to initialize the next find/replace dialog box.

CFindReplaceDialog::MatchCase

BOOL MatchCase( ) const;

Return Value

Nonzero if the user wants to find occurrences of the search string that exactly match the case of the search string; otherwise 0.

Remarks

Call this function to determine whether the user wants to match the case of the find string exactly.

See Also: **CFindReplaceDialog::MatchWholeWord**

CFindReplaceDialog::MatchWholeWord

BOOL MatchWholeWord( ) const;

Return Value

Nonzero if the user wants to match only the entire words of the search string; otherwise 0.

Remarks

Call this function to determine whether the user wants to match entire words only.

See Also: **CFindReplaceDialog::MatchCase**

CFindReplaceDialog::ReplaceAll

BOOL ReplaceAll( ) const;

Return Value

Nonzero if the user has requested that all strings matching the replace string be replaced; otherwise 0.

Remarks

Call this function to determine whether the user wants all occurrences of the string to be replaced.

See Also: **CFindReplaceDialog::ReplaceCurrent**

CFindReplaceDialog::ReplaceCurrent

BOOL ReplaceCurrent( ) const;

Return Value

Nonzero if the user has requested that the currently selected string be replaced with the replace string; otherwise 0.

Remarks

Call this function to determine whether the user wants the current word to be replaced.

See Also: **CFindReplaceDialog::ReplaceAll**

CFindReplaceDialog::SearchDown

BOOL SearchDown( ) const;

Return Value

Nonzero if the user wants the search to proceed in a downward direction; 0 if the user wants the search to proceed in an upward direction.

Remarks

Call this function to determine whether the user wants the search to proceed in a downward direction.

Data Members
CFindReplaceDialog::m_fr

Remarks

m_fr is a structure of type **FINDREPLACE**. Its members store the characteristics of the dialog-box object. After constructing a **CFindReplaceDialog** object, you can use **m_fr** to modify various values in the dialog box.

For more information on this structure, see the **FINDREPLACE** structure in the Win32 SDK documentation.

CFont

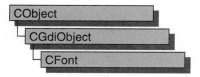

The **CFont** class encapsulates a Windows graphics device interface (GDI) font and provides member functions for manipulating the font. To use a **CFont** object, construct a **CFont** object and attach a Windows font to it with **CreateFont**, **CreateFontIndirect**, **CreatePointFont**, or **CreatePointFontIndirect**, and then use the object's member functions to manipulate the font.

The **CreatePointFont** and **CreatePointFontIndirect** functions are often easier to use than **CreateFont** or **CreateFontIndirect** since they do the conversion for the height of the font from a point size to logical units automatically.

For more information on **CFont**, see "Graphic Objects" in *Visual C++ Programmer's Guide* online.

#include <afxwin.h>

CFont Class Members

Construction

CFont	Constructs a **CFont** object.

Initialization

CreateFontIndirect	Initializes a **CFont** object with the characteristics given in a **LOGFONT** structure.
CreateFont	Initializes a **CFont** with the specified characteristics.
CreatePointFont	Initializes a **CFont** with the specified height, measured in tenths of a point, and typeface.
CreatePointFontIndirect	Same as **CreateFontIndirect** except that the font height is measured in tenths of a point rather than logical units.

Operations

FromHandle	Returns a pointer to a **CFont** object when given a Windows **HFONT**.

operator HFONT	Returns the Windows GDI font handle attached to the **CFont** object.
GetLogFont	Fills a **LOGFONT** with information about the logical font attached to the **CFont** object.

Member Functions

CFont::CFont

CFont( );

Remarks

Constructs a **CFont** object. The resulting object must be initialized with **CreateFont**, **CreateFontIndirect**, **CreatePointFont**, or **CreatePointFontIndirect** before it can be used.

See Also: **CFont::CreateFontIndirect**, **CFont::CreateFont**, **CFont::CreatePointFont**, **CFont::CreatePointFontIndirect**, **::EnumFonts**

CFont::CreateFont

BOOL CreateFont(int *nHeight*, **int** *nWidth*, **int** *nEscapement*, **int** *nOrientation*,
  ↳ **int** *nWeight*, **BYTE** *bItalic*, **BYTE** *bUnderline*, **BYTE** *cStrikeOut*,
  ↳ **BYTE** *nCharSet*, **BYTE** *nOutPrecision*, **BYTE** *nClipPrecision*,
  ↳ **BYTE** *nQuality*, **BYTE** *nPitchAndFamily*, **LPCTSTR** *lpszFacename*);

Return Value

Nonzero if successful; otherwise 0.

Parameters

nHeight   Specifies the desired height (in logical units) of the font. The font height can be specified in the following ways:

- Greater than 0, in which case the height is transformed into device units and matched against the cell height of the available fonts.

- Equal to 0, in which case a reasonable default size is used.

- Less than 0, in which case the height is transformed into device units and the absolute value is matched against the character height of the available fonts.

The absolute value of *nHeight* must not exceed 16,384 device units after it is converted. For all height comparisons, the font mapper looks for the largest font that does not exceed the requested size or the smallest font if all the fonts exceed the requested size.

nWidth   Specifies the average width (in logical units) of characters in the font. If *nWidth* is 0, the aspect ratio of the device will be matched against the digitization aspect ratio of the available fonts to find the closest match, which is determined by the absolute value of the difference.

nEscapement   Specifies the angle (in 0.1-degree units) between the escapement vector and the x-axis of the display surface. The escapement vector is the line through the origins of the first and last characters on a line. The angle is measured counterclockwise from the x-axis.

nOrientation   Specifies the angle (in 0.1-degree units) between the baseline of a character and the x-axis. The angle is measured counterclockwise from the x-axis for coordinate systems in which the y-direction is down and clockwise from the x-axis for coordinate systems in which the y-direction is up.

nWeight   Specifies the font weight (in inked pixels per 1000). Although *nWeight* can be any integer value from 0 to 1000, the common constants and values are as follows:

Constant	Value
FW_DONTCARE	0
FW_THIN	100
FW_EXTRALIGHT	200
FW_ULTRALIGHT	200
FW_LIGHT	300
FW_NORMAL	400
FW_REGULAR	400
FW_MEDIUM	500
FW_SEMIBOLD	600
FW_DEMIBOLD	600
FW_BOLD	700
FW_EXTRABOLD	800
FW_ULTRABOLD	800
FW_BLACK	900
FW_HEAVY	900

These values are approximate; the actual appearance depends on the typeface. Some fonts have only **FW_NORMAL**, **FW_REGULAR**, and **FW_BOLD** weights. If **FW_DONTCARE** is specified, a default weight is used.

bItalic   Specifies whether the font is italic.

bUnderline   Specifies whether the font is underlined.

cStrikeOut   Specifies whether characters in the font are struck out. Specifies a strikeout font if set to a nonzero value.

nCharSet   Specifies the font's character set. The following constants and values are predefined:

Constant	Value
ANSI_CHARSET	0
DEFAULT_CHARSET	1
SYMBOL_CHARSET	2
SHIFTJIS_CHARSET	128
OEM_CHARSET	255

The OEM character set is system-dependent.

Fonts with other character sets may exist in the system. An application that uses a font with an unknown character set must not attempt to translate or interpret strings that are to be rendered with that font. Instead, the strings should be passed directly to the output device driver.

The font mapper does not use the **DEFAULT_CHARSET** value. An application can use this value to allow the name and size of a font to fully describe the logical font. If a font with the specified name does not exist, a font from any character set can be substituted for the specified font. To avoid unexpected results, applications should use the **DEFAULT_CHARSET** value sparingly.

nOutPrecision   Specifies the desired output precision. The output precision defines how closely the output must match the requested font's height, width, character orientation, escapement, and pitch. It can be any one of the following values:

OUT_CHARACTER_PRECIS	OUT_STRING_PRECIS
OUT_DEFAULT_PRECIS	OUT_STROKE_PRECIS
OUT_DEVICE_PRECIS	OUT_TT_PRECIS
OUT_RASTER_PRECIS	

Applications can use the **OUT_DEVICE_PRECIS**, **OUT_RASTER_PRECIS**, and **OUT_TT_PRECIS** values to control how the font mapper chooses a font when the system contains more than one font with a given name. For example, if a system contains a font named Symbol in raster and TrueType form, specifying **OUT_TT_PRECIS** forces the font mapper to choose the TrueType version. (Specifying **OUT_TT_PRECIS** forces the font mapper to choose a TrueType font whenever the specified font name matches a device or raster font, even when there is no TrueType font of the same name.)

nClipPrecision   Specifies the desired clipping precision. The clipping precision defines how to clip characters that are partially outside the clipping region. It can be any one of the following values:

CLIP_CHARACTER_PRECIS	CLIP_MASK
CLIP_DEFAULT_PRECIS	CLIP_STROKE_PRECIS
CLIP_ENCAPSULATE	CLIP_TT_ALWAYS
CLIP_LH_ANGLES	

To use an embedded read-only font, an application must specify **CLIP_ENCAPSULATE**.

To achieve consistent rotation of device, TrueType, and vector fonts, an application can use the OR operator to combine the **CLIP_LH_ANGLES** value with any of the other *nClipPrecision* values. If the **CLIP_LH_ANGLES** bit is set, the rotation for all fonts depends on whether the orientation of the coordinate system is left-handed or right-handed. (For more information about the orientation of coordinate systems, see the description of the *nOrientation* parameter.) If **CLIP_LH_ANGLES** is not set, device fonts always rotate counterclockwise, but the rotation of other fonts is dependent on the orientation of the coordinate system.

nQuality   Specifies the font's output quality, which defines how carefully the GDI must attempt to match the logical-font attributes to those of an actual physical font. It can be one of the following values:

- **DEFAULT_QUALITY**   Appearance of the font does not matter.

- **DRAFT_QUALITY**   Appearance of the font is less important than when **PROOF_QUALITY** is used. For GDI raster fonts, scaling is enabled. Bold, italic, underline, and strikeout fonts are synthesized if necessary.

- **PROOF_QUALITY**   Character quality of the font is more important than exact matching of the logical-font attributes. For GDI raster fonts, scaling is disabled and the font closest in size is chosen. Bold, italic, underline, and strikeout fonts are synthesized if necessary.

nPitchAndFamily   Specifies the pitch and family of the font. The two low-order bits specify the pitch of the font and can be any one of the following values:

DEFAULT_PITCH   **VARIABLE_PITCH**   **FIXED_PITCH**

Applications can add **TMPF_TRUETYPE** to the *nPitchAndFamily* parameter to choose a TrueType font. The four high-order bits of the parameter specify the font family and can be any one of the following values:

- **FF_DECORATIVE**   Novelty fonts: Old English, for example.

- **FF_DONTCARE**   Don't care or don't know.

- **FF_MODERN**   Fonts with constant stroke width (fixed-pitch), with or without serifs. Fixed-pitch fonts are usually modern faces. Pica, Elite, and Courier New are examples.

- **FF_ROMAN**   Fonts with variable stroke width (proportionally spaced) and with serifs. Times New Roman and Century Schoolbook are examples.

- **FF_SCRIPT**   Fonts designed to look like handwriting. Script and Cursive are examples.

- **FF_SWISS**   Fonts with variable stroke width (proportionally spaced) and without serifs. MS Sans Serif is an example.

An application can specify a value for *nPitchAndFamily* by using the Boolean OR operator to join a pitch constant with a family constant.

Font families describe the look of a font in a general way. They are intended for specifying fonts when the exact typeface desired is not available.

lpszFacename   A **CString** or pointer to a null-terminated string that specifies the typeface name of the font. The length of this string must not exceed 30 characters. The Windows **EnumFontFamilies** function can be used to enumerate all currently available fonts. If *lpszFacename* is **NULL**, the GDI uses a device-independent typeface.

Remarks

Initializes a **CFont** object with the specified characteristics. The font can subsequently be selected as the font for any device context.

The **CreateFont** function does not create a new Windows GDI font. It merely selects the closest match from the fonts available in the GDI's pool of physical fonts.

Applications can use the default settings for most of these parameters when creating a logical font. The parameters that should always be given specific values are *nHeight* and *lpszFacename*. If *nHeight* and *lpszFacename* are not set by the application, the logical font that is created is device-dependent.

When you finish with the **CFont** object created by the **CreateFont** function, first select the font out of the device context, then delete the **CFont** object.

See Also: **CFont::CreateFontIndirect**, **CFont::CreatePointFont**, **::CreateFont**, **::EnumFontFamilies**, **::EnumFonts**

CFont::CreateFontIndirect

BOOL CreateFontIndirect(const LOGFONT* *lpLogFont* **);**

Return Value

Nonzero if successful; otherwise 0.

Parameters

lpLogFont   Points to a **LOGFONT** structure that defines the characteristics of the logical font.

Remarks

Initializes a **CFont** object with the characteristics given in a **LOGFONT** structure pointed to by *lpLogFont*. The font can subsequently be selected as the current font for any device.

This font has the characteristics specified in the **LOGFONT** structure. When the font is selected by using the **CDC::SelectObject** member function, the GDI's font mapper attempts to match the logical font with an existing physical font. If it fails to find an exact match for the logical font, it provides an alternative whose characteristics match as many of the requested characteristics as possible.

When you finish with the **CFont** object created by the **CreateFontIndirect** function, first select the font out of the device context, then delete the **CFont** object.

See Also: **CFont::CreateFont**, **CFont::CreatePointFontIndirect**, **CDC::SelectObject**, **CGdiObject::DeleteObject**, **::CreateFontIndirect**

CFont::CreatePointFont

BOOL CreatePointFont(int *nPointSize*, **LPCTSTR** *lpszFaceName*, **CDC*** *pDC* = **NULL**);

Return Value

Nonzero if successful, otherwise 0.

Parameters

nPointSize   Requested font height in tenths of a point. (For instance, pass 120 to request a 12-point font.)

lpszFaceName   A **CString** or pointer to a null-terminated string that specifies the typeface name of the font. The length of this string must not exceed 30 characters. The Windows **EnumFontFamilies** function can be used to enumerate all currently available fonts. If *lpszFaceName* is **NULL**, the GDI uses a device-independent typeface.

pDC   Pointer to the **CDC** object to be used to convert the height in *nPointSize* to logical units. If **NULL**, a screen device context is used for the conversion.

Remarks

This function provides a simple way to create a font of a specified typeface and point size. It automatically converts the height in *nPointSize* to logical units using the **CDC** object pointed to by *pDC*.

When you finish with the **CFont** object created by the **CreatePointFont** function, first select the font out of the device context, then delete the **CFont** object.

See Also: **CFont::CreatePointFontIndirect**, **CFont::CreateFont**

CFont::CreatePointFontIndirect

BOOL CreatePointFontIndirect(const LOGFONT* *lpLogFont*, **CDC*** *pDC* = **NULL**);

Return Value

Nonzero if successful, otherwise 0.

Parameters

lpLogFont   Points to a **LOGFONT** structure that defines the characteristics of the logical font. The **lfHeight** member of the **LOGFONT** structure is measured in tenths of a point rather than logical units. (For instance, set **lfHeight** to 120 to request a 12-point font.)

pDC   Pointer to the **CDC** object to be used to convert the height in **lfHeight** to logical units. If **NULL**, a screen device context is used for the conversion.

Remarks

This function is the same as **CreateFontIndirect** except that the **lfHeight** member of the **LOGFONT** is interpreted in tenths of a point rather than device units. This function automatically converts the height in **lfHeight** to logical units using the **CDC** object pointed to by *pDC* before passing the **LOGFONT** structure on to Windows.

When you finish with the **CFont** object created by the **CreatePointFontIndirect** function, first select the font out of the device context, then delete the **CFont** object.

See Also: **CFont::CreatePointFont, CFont::CreateFontIndirect**

CFont::FromHandle

static CFont* PASCAL FromHandle(HFONT *hFont* **);**

Return Value

A pointer to a **CFont** object if successful; otherwise **NULL**.

Parameters

hFont   An **HFONT** handle to a Windows font.

Remarks

Returns a pointer to a **CFont** object when given an **HFONT** handle to a Windows GDI font object. If a **CFont** object is not already attached to the handle, a temporary **CFont** object is created and attached. This temporary **CFont** object is valid only until the next time the application has idle time in its event loop, at which time all temporary graphic objects are deleted. Another way of saying this is that the temporary object is valid only during the processing of one window message.

CFont::GetLogFont

int GetLogFont(LOGFONT * *pLogFont* **);**

Return Value

Nonzero if the function succeeds, otherwise 0.

Parameters

pLogFont   Pointer to the **LOGFONT** structure to receive the font information.

Remarks

Call this function to retrieve a copy of the **LOGFONT** structure for **Cfont**.

See Also: **LOGFONT, ::GetObject**

CFont::operator HFONT

operator HFONT( ) const;

Return Value

The handle of the Windows GDI font object attached to **CFont** if successful; otherwise **NULL**.

Remarks

Use this operator to get the Windows GDI handle of the font attached to the **CFont** object.

Since this operator is automatically used for conversions from **CFont** to **Fonts and Text**, you can pass **CFont** objects to functions that expect **HFONT**s.

For more information about using graphic objects, see "Graphic Objects" in the Win32 SDK documentation.

CFontDialog

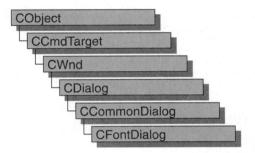

The **CFontDialog** class allows you to incorporate a font-selection dialog box into your application. A **CFontDialog** object is a dialog box with a list of fonts that are currently installed in the system. The user can select a particular font from the list, and this selection is then reported back to the application.

To construct a **CFontDialog** object, use the provided constructor or derive a new subclass and use your own custom constructor.

Once a **CFontDialog** object has been constructed, you can use the **m_cf** structure to initialize the values or states of controls in the dialog box. The **m_cf** structure is of type **CHOOSEFONT**. For more information on this structure, see the Win32 SDK documentation.

After initializing the dialog object's controls, call the **DoModal** member function to display the dialog box and allow the user to select a font. **DoModal** returns whether the user selected the OK (**IDOK**) or Cancel (**IDCANCEL**) button.

If **DoModal** returns **IDOK**, you can use one of **CFontDialog**'s member functions to retrieve the information input by the user.

You can use the Windows **CommDlgExtendedError** function to determine whether an error occurred during initialization of the dialog box and to learn more about the error. For more information on this function, see the Win32 SDK documentation.

CFontDialog relies on the COMMDLG.DLL file that ships with Windows versions 3.1 and later.

To customize the dialog box, derive a class from **CFontDialog**, provide a custom dialog template, and add a message-map to process the notification messages from the extended controls. Any unprocessed messages should be passed to the base class.

Customizing the hook function is not required.

For more information on using **CFontDialog**, see "Common Dialog Classes" in *Visual C++ Programmer's Guide* online.

#include <afxdlgs.h>

CFontDialog Class Members

Data Members

m_cf	A structure used to customize a **CFontDialog** object.

Construction

CFontDialog	Constructs a **CFontDialog** object.

Operations

DoModal	Displays the dialog and allows the user to make a selection.
GetCurrentFont	Retrieves the name of the currently selected font.
GetFaceName	Returns the face name of the selected font.
GetStyleName	Returns the style name of the selected font.
GetSize	Returns the point size of the selected font.
GetColor	Returns the color of the selected font.
GetWeight	Returns the weight of the selected font.
IsStrikeOut	Determines whether the font is displayed with strikeout.
IsUnderline	Determines whether the font is underlined.
IsBold	Determines whether the font is bold.
IsItalic	Determines whether the font is italic.

Member Functions

CFontDialog::CFontDialog

CFontDialog(LPLOGFONT *lplfInitial* = **NULL,**
  ↪ **DWORD** *dwFlags* = **CF_EFFECTS I CF_SCREENFONTS,**
  ↪ **CDC*** *pdcPrinter* = **NULL, CWnd*** *pParentWnd* = **NULL);**

Parameters

lplfInitial A pointer to a **LOGFONT** data structure that allows you to set some of the font's characteristics.

dwFlags Specifies one or more choose-font flags. One or more preset values can be combined using the bitwise OR operator. If you modify the **m_cf.Flags** structure member, be sure to use a bitwise OR operator in your changes to keep the default behavior intact. For details on each of these flags, see the description of the **CHOOSEFONT** structure in the Win32 SDK documentation.

pdcPrinter A pointer to a printer-device context. If supplied, this parameter points to a printer-device context for the printer on which the fonts are to be selected.

pParentWnd   A pointer to the font dialog box's parent or owner window.

Remarks

Constructs a **CFontDialog** object. Note that the constructor automatically fills in the members of the **CHOOSEFONT** structure. You should only change these if you want a font dialog different than the default.

See Also: **CFontDialog::DoModal**

CFontDialog::DoModal

virtual int DoModal( );

Return Value

IDOK or **IDCANCEL** if the function is successful; otherwise 0. **IDOK** and **IDCANCEL** are constants that indicate whether the user selected the OK or Cancel button.

If **IDCANCEL** is returned, you can call the Windows **CommDlgExtendedError** function to determine whether an error occurred.

Remarks

Call this function to display the Windows common font dialog box and allow the user to choose a font.

If you want to initialize the various font dialog controls by setting members of the **m_cf** structure, you should do this before calling **DoModal**, but after the dialog object is constructed.

If **DoModal** returns **IDOK**, you can call other member functions to retrieve the settings or information input by the user into the dialog box.

See Also: **CDialog::DoModal**, **CFontDialog::CFontDialog**

CFontDialog::GetColor

COLORREF GetColor( ) const;

Return Value

The color of the selected font.

Remarks

Call this function to retrieve the selected font color.

See Also: **CFontDialog::GetCurrentFont**

CFontDialog::GetCurrentFont

void GetCurrentFont(LPLOGFONT *lplf* **);**

Parameters

lplf A pointer to a **LOGFONT** structure.

Remarks

Call this function to assign the characteristics of the currently selected font to the members of a **LOGFONT** structure. Other **CFontDialog** member functions are provided to access individual characteristics of the current font.

If this function is called during a call to **DoModal**, it returns the current selection at the time (what the user sees or has changed in the dialog). If this function is called after a call to **DoModal** (only if **DoModal** returns **IDOK**), it returns what the user actually selected.

See Also: **CFontDialog::GetFaceName**, **CFontDialog::GetStyleName**

CFontDialog::GetFaceName

CString GetFaceName( ) const;

Return Value

The face name of the font selected in the **CFontDialog** dialog box.

Remarks

Call this function to retrieve the face name of the selected font.

See Also: **CFontDialog::GetCurrentFont**, **CFontDialog::GetStyleName**

CFontDialog::GetSize

int GetSize( ) const;

Return Value

The font's size, in tenths of a point.

Remarks

Call this function to retrieve the size of the selected font.

See Also: **CFontDialog::GetWeight**, **CFontDialog::GetCurrentFont**

CFontDialog::GetStyleName

CString GetStyleName( ) const;

Return Value

The style name of the font.

Remarks

Call this function to retrieve the style name of the selected font.

See Also: **CFontDialog::GetFaceName, CFontDialog::GetCurrentFont**

CFontDialog::GetWeight

int GetWeight( ) const;

Return Value

The weight of the selected font.

Remarks

Call this function to retrieve the weight of the selected font. For more information on the weight of a font, see **CFont::CreateFont**.

See Also: **CFontDialog::GetCurrentFont, CFontDialog::IsBold**

CFontDialog::IsBold

BOOL IsBold( ) const;

Return Value

Nonzero if the selected font has the Bold characteristic enabled; otherwise 0.

Remarks

Call this function to determine if the selected font is bold.

See Also: **CFontDialog::GetCurrentFont**

CFontDialog::IsItalic

BOOL IsItalic( ) const;

Return Value

Nonzero if the selected font has the Italic characteristic enabled; otherwise 0.

Remarks

Call this function to determine if the selected font is italic.

See Also: **CFontDialog::GetCurrentFont**

CFontDialog::IsStrikeOut

BOOL IsStrikeOut( ) const;

Return Value

Nonzero if the selected font has the Strikeout characteristic enabled; otherwise 0.

Remarks

Call this function to determine if the selected font is displayed with strikeout.

See Also: **CFontDialog::GetCurrentFont**

CFontDialog::IsUnderline

BOOL IsUnderline( ) const;

Return Value

Nonzero if the selected font has the Underline characteristic enabled; otherwise 0.

Remarks

Call this function to determine if the selected font is underlined.

See Also: **CFontDialog::GetCurrentFont**

Data Members
CFontDialog::m_cf

Remarks

A structure whose members store the characteristics of the dialog object. After constructing a **CFontDialog** object, you can use **m_cf** to modify various aspects of the dialog box before calling the **DoModal** member function. For more information on this structure, see **CHOOSEFONT** in the Win32 SDK documentation.

CFontHolder

CFontHolder does not have a base class.

The **CFontHolder** class, which encapsulates the functionality of a Windows font object and the **IFont** interface, is used to implement the stock Font property.

Use this class to implement custom font properties for your control. For information on creating such properties, see the article "ActiveX Controls: Using Fonts in an ActiveX Control" in *Visual C++ Programmer's Guide* online.

#include <afxctl.h>

See Also: CPropExchange

CFontHolder Class Members

Data Members

m_pFont	A pointer to the **CFontHolder** object's **IFont** interface.

Construction/Destruction

CFontHolder	Constructs a **CFontHolder** object.

Operations

GetFontDispatch	Returns the font's **IDispatch** interface.
GetDisplayString	Retrieves the string displayed in a container's property browser.
GetFontHandle	Returns a handle to a Windows font.
InitializeFont	Initializes a **CFontHolder** object.
ReleaseFont	Disconnects the **CFontHolder** object from the **IFont** and **IFontNotification** interfaces.
Select	Selects a font resource into a device context.
SetFont	Connects the **CFontHolder** object to an **IFont** interface.

Member Functions

CFontHolder::CFontHolder

CFontHolder(LPPROPERTYNOTIFYSINK *pNotify* **);**

Parameters

pNotify   Pointer to the font's **IPropertyNotifySink** interface.

Remarks

Constructs a **CFontHolder** object. You must call **InitializeFont** to initialize the resulting object before using it.

See Also: **CFontHolder::InitializeFont**

CFontHolder::GetDisplayString

BOOL GetDisplayString(CString& *strValue* **);**

Return Value

Nonzero if the string is successfully retrieved; otherwise 0.

Parameters

strValue Reference to the **CString** that is to hold the display string.

Remarks

Retrieves a string that can be displayed in a container's property browser.

CFontHolder::GetFontDispatch

LPFONTDISP GetFontDispatch( );

Return Value

A pointer to the **CFontHolder** object's **IFontDisp** interface. Note that the function that calls **GetFontDispatch** must call **IUnknown::Release** on this interface pointer when done with it.

Remarks

Call this function to retrieve a pointer to the font's dispatch interface. Call **InitializeFont** before calling **GetFontDispatch**.

See Also: **CFontHolder::InitializeFont**

CFontHolder::GetFontHandle

HFONT GetFontHandle( );
HFONT GetFontHandle(long *cyLogical,* **long** *cyHimetric* **);**

Return Value

A handle to the Font object; otherwise **NULL**.

Parameters

cyLogical Height, in logical units, of the rectangle in which the control is drawn.

cyHimetric Height, in **MM_HIMETRIC** units, of the control.

Remarks

Call this function to get a handle to a Windows font.

The ratio of *cyLogical* and *cyHimetric* is used to calculate the proper display size, in logical units, for the font's point size expressed in **MM_HIMETRIC** units:

Display size = (*cyLogical* / *cyHimetric*) X font size

The version with no parameters returns a handle to a font sized correctly for the screen.

CFontHolder::InitializeFont

void InitializeFont(const FONTDESC FAR* *pFontDesc* **= NULL,**
⮡ LPDISPATCH *pFontDispAmbient* **= NULL);**

Parameters

pFontDesc   Pointer to a font description structure (**FONTDESC**) that specifies the font's characteristics.

pFontDispAmbient   Pointer to the container's ambient Font property.

Remarks

Initializes a **CFontHolder** object.

If *pFontDispAmbient* is not **NULL**, the **CFontHolder** object is connected to a clone of the **IFont** interface used by the container's ambient Font property.

If *pFontDispAmbient* is **NULL**, a new Font object is created either from the font description pointed to by *pFontDesc* or, if *pFontDesc* is **NULL**, from a default description.

Call this function after constructing a **CFontHolder** object.

See Also: **CFontHolder::CFontHolder**

CFontHolder::ReleaseFont

void ReleaseFont( );

Remarks

This function disconnects the **CFontHolder** object from its **IFont** interface.

See Also: **CFontHolder::SetFont**

CFontHolder::Select

CFont* Select(CDC* *pDC*, **long** *cyLogical*, **long** *cyHimetric* **);**

Return Value

A pointer to the font that is being replaced.

Parameters

pDC   Device context into which the font is selected.

cyLogical   Height, in logical units, of the rectangle in which the control is drawn.

cyHimetric   Height, in **MM_HIMETRIC** units, of the control.

Remarks

Call this function to select your control's font into the specified device context.

See **GetFontHandle** for a discussion of the *cyLogical* and *cyHimetric* parameters.

CFontHolder::SetFont

void SetFont(LPFONT *pNewFont* **);**

Parameters

pNewFont   Pointer to the new **IFont** interface.

Remarks

Releases any existing font and connects the **CFontHolder** object to an **IFont** interface.

See Also: CFontHolder::ReleaseFont

Data Members
CFontHolder::m_pFont

Remarks

A pointer to the **CFontHolder** object's **IFont** interface.

See Also: CFontHolder::SetFont

CFormView

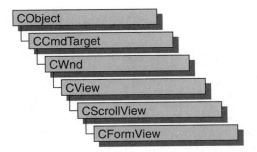

The **CFormView** class is the base class used for views containing controls. These controls are laid out based on a dialog-template resource. Use **CFormView** if you want form-based documents in your application. These views support scrolling, as needed, using the **CScrollView** functionality.

Creating a view based on **CFormView** is similar to creating a dialog box.

To use **CFormView**, take the following steps:

1. Design a dialog template.

   Use the dialog editor to design the dialog box. Then, in the Styles and More Styles property pages, set the following properties:

   - In the Style box, select Child (**WS_CHILD** on).
   - In the Border box, select None (**WS_BORDER** off).
   - Clear the Visible check box (**WS_VISIBLE** off).
   - Clear the Titlebar check box (**WS_CAPTION** off).

   These steps are necessary because a form view is not a true dialog box. For more information about creating a dialog-box resource, see "Dialog Editor" in *Developer Studio User's Guide* online.

2. Create a view class.

   With your dialog template open, run ClassWizard and choose **CFormView** as the class type when you are filling in the Add Class dialog box. ClassWizard creates a **CFormView**-derived class and connects it to the dialog template you just designed. This connection is established in the constructor for your class; ClassWizard generates a call to the base-class constructor, **CFormView::CFormView**, and passes the resource ID of your dialog template. For example:

```
CMyFormView::CMyFormView()
    : CFormView( CMyFormView::IDD )
{
  //{{AFX_DATA_INIT( CMyFormView )
  // NOTE: the ClassWizard will add member
  // initialization here
  //}}AFX_DATA_INIT

  // Other construction code, such as data initialization
}
```

Note If you choose not to use ClassWizard, you must define the appropriate ID you supply to the **CFormView** constructor (that is, `CMyFormView::IDD` is not predefined). ClassWizard declares `IDD` as an **enum** value in the class it creates for you.

If you want to define member variables in your view class that correspond to the controls in your form view, use the Edit Variables button in the ClassWizard dialog box. This allows you to use the dialog data exchange (DDX) mechanism. If you want to define message handlers for control-notification messages, use the Add Function button in the ClassWizard dialog box. For more information see "Using ClassWizard" in the *Visual C++ Programmer's Guide* online.

3. Override the **OnUpdate** member function.

The **OnUpdate** member function is defined by **CView** and is called to update the form view's appearance. Override this function to update the member variables in your view class with the appropriate values from the current document. Then, if you are using DDX, use the **UpdateData** member function (defined by **CWnd**) with an argument of **FALSE** to update the controls in your form view.

The **OnInitialUpdate** member function (also defined by **CView**) is called to perform one-time initialization of the view. **CFormView** overrides this function to use DDX to set the initial values of the controls you have mapped using ClassWizard. Override **OnInitialUpdate** if you want to perform custom initialization.

4. Implement a member function to move data from your view to your document.

This member function is typically a message handler for a control-notification message or for a menu command. If you are using DDX, call the **UpdateData** member function to update the member variables in your view class. Then move their values to the document associated with the form view.

5. Override the **OnPrint** member function (optional).

The **OnPrint** member function is defined by **CView** and prints the view. By default, printing and print preview are not supported by the **CFormView** class. To add printing support, override the **OnPrint** function in your derived class.

See the MFC General sample VIEWEX for more information about how to add printing capabilities to a view derived from **CFormView**.

6. Associate your view class with a document class and a frame-window class using a document template.

Unlike ordinary views, form views do not require you to override the **OnDraw** member function defined by **CView**. This is because controls are able to paint themselves. Only if you want to customize the display of your form view (for example, to provide a background for your view) should you override **OnDraw**. If you do so, be careful that your updating does not conflict with the updating done by the controls.

If your view contains controls that are derived from (or instances of) **CSliderCtrl** or **CSpinButtonCtrl** and you have message handlers for **WM_HSCROLL** and **WM_VSCROLL**, you should write code that calls the proper routines. The code example below calls **CWnd::OnHScroll** if a **WM_HSCROLL** message is sent by either a spin button or slider control.

```
void CMyFormView::OnHScroll( UINT nSBCode, UINT nPos, CScrollBar* pScrollBar )
{
    if ( pScrollBar->IsKindOf( RUNTIME_CLASS( CScrollBar ) ))
    {
        CFormView::OnHScroll( nSBCode, nPos, pScrollBar );
    }
    else if ( pScrollBar->IsKindOf( RUNTIME_CLASS( CSliderCtrl ) ))
    {
        CWnd::OnHScroll( nSBCode, nPos, pScrollBar );
    }
    else if ( pScrollBar->IsKindOf( RUNTIME_CLASS( CSpinButtonCtrl ) ))
    {
        CWnd::OnHScroll( nSBCode, nPos, pScrollBar );
    }
}
```

If the view becomes smaller than the dialog template, scroll bars appear automatically. Views derived from **CFormView** support only the **MM_TEXT** mapping mode.

If you are not using DDX, use the **CWnd** dialog functions to move data between the member variables in your view class and the controls in your form view.

For more information about DDX, see "Defining Member Variables for DDX" in the *Visual C++ Programmer's Guide* online. For more information on **CFormView**, see "Derived View Classes" and "Document/View Architecture Topics" also in the *Visual C++ Programmer's Guide* online.

#include <afxext.h>

See Also: **CDialog, CScrollView, CView::OnUpdate, CView::OnInitialUpdate, CView::OnPrint, CWnd::UpdateData, CScrollView::ResizeParentToFit**

CFormView Class Members

CFormView	Constructs a **CFormView** object.

Member Functions

CFormView::CFormView

CFormView(LPCTSTR *lpszTemplateName* **);**
CFormView(UINT *nIDTemplate* **);**

Parameters

lpszTemplateName   Contains a null-terminated string that is the name of a dialog-template resource.

nIDTemplate   Contains the ID number of a dialog-template resource.

Remarks

When you create an object of a type derived from **CFormView**, invoke one of the constructors to create the view object and identify the dialog resource on which the view is based. You can identify the resource either by name (pass a string as the argument to the constructor) or by its ID (pass an unsigned integer as the argument).

The form-view window and child controls are not created until **CWnd::Create** is called. **CWnd::Create** is called by the framework as part of the document and view creation process, which is driven by the document template.

Note   Your derived class *must* supply its own constructor. In the constructor, invoke the constructor, **CFormView::CFormView**, with the resource name or ID as an argument as shown in the preceding class overview.

See Also: **CWnd::Create**

CFrameWnd

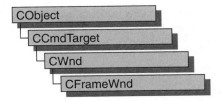

The **CFrameWnd** class provides the functionality of a Windows single document interface (SDI) overlapped or pop-up frame window, along with members for managing the window.

To create a useful frame window for your application, derive a class from **CFrameWnd**. Add member variables to the derived class to store data specific to your application. Implement message-handler member functions and a message map in the derived class to specify what happens when messages are directed to the window.

There are three ways to construct a frame window:

- Directly construct it using **Create**.
- Directly construct it using **LoadFrame**.
- Indirectly construct it using a document template.

Before you call either **Create** or **LoadFrame**, you must construct the frame-window object on the heap using the C++ **new** operator. Before calling **Create**, you can also register a window class with the **AfxRegisterWndClass** global function to set the icon and class styles for the frame.

Use the **Create** member function to pass the frame's creation parameters as immediate arguments.

LoadFrame requires fewer arguments than **Create**, and instead retrieves most of its default values from resources, including the frame's caption, icon, accelerator table, and menu. To be accessible by **LoadFrame**, all these resources must have the same resource ID (for example, **IDR_MAINFRAME**).

When a **CFrameWnd** object contains views and documents, they are created indirectly by the framework instead of directly by the programmer. The **CDocTemplate** object orchestrates the creation of the frame, the creation of the containing views, and the connection of the views to the appropriate document. The parameters of the **CDocTemplate** constructor specify the **CRuntimeClass** of the three classes involved (document, frame, and view). A **CRuntimeClass** object is used by the framework to dynamically create new frames when specified by the user (for example, by using the File New command or the multiple document interface (MDI) Window New command).

A frame-window class derived from **CFrameWnd** must be declared with **DECLARE_DYNCREATE** in order for the above **RUNTIME_CLASS** mechanism to work correctly.

A **CFrameWnd** contains default implementations to perform the following functions of a main window in a typical application for Windows:

- A **CFrameWnd** frame window keeps track of a currently active view that is independent of the Windows active window or the current input focus. When the frame is reactivated, the active view is notified by calling **CView::OnActivateView**.

- Command messages and many common frame-notification messages, including those handled by the **OnSetFocus**, **OnHScroll**, and **OnVScroll** functions of **CWnd**, are delegated by a **CFrameWnd** frame window to the currently active view.

- The currently active view (or currently active MDI child frame window in the case of an MDI frame) can determine the caption of the frame window. This feature can be disabled by turning off the **FWS_ADDTOTITLE** style bit of the frame window.

- A **CFrameWnd** frame window manages the positioning of the control bars, views, and other child windows inside the frame window's client area. A frame window also does idle-time updating of toolbar and other control-bar buttons. A **CFrameWnd** frame window also has default implementations of commands for toggling on and off the toolbar and status bar.

- A **CFrameWnd** frame window manages the main menu bar. When a pop-up menu is displayed, the frame window uses the **UPDATE_COMMAND_UI** mechanism to determine which menu items should be enabled, disabled, or checked. When the user selects a menu item, the frame window updates the status bar with the message string for that command.

- A **CFrameWnd** frame window has an optional accelerator table that automatically translates keyboard accelerators.

- A **CFrameWnd** frame window has an optional help ID set with **LoadFrame** that is used for context-sensitive help. A frame window is the main orchestrator of semimodal states such as context-sensitive help (SHIFT+F1) and print-preview modes.

- A **CFrameWnd** frame window will open a file dragged from the File Manager and dropped on the frame window. If a file extension is registered and associated with the application, the frame window responds to the dynamic data exchange (DDE) open request that occurs when the user opens a data file in the File Manager or when the **ShellExecute** Windows function is called.

- If the frame window is the main application window (that is, **CWinThread::m_pMainWnd**), when the user closes the application, the frame window prompts the user to save any modified documents (for **OnClose** and **OnQueryEndSession**).

- If the frame window is the main application window, the frame window is the context for running WinHelp. Closing the frame window will shut down WINHELP.EXE if it was launched for help for this application.

Do not use the C++ **delete** operator to destroy a frame window. Use **CWnd::DestroyWindow** instead. The **CFrameWnd** implementation of **PostNcDestroy** will delete the C++ object when the window is destroyed. When the user closes the frame window, the default **OnClose** handler will call **DestroyWindow**.

For more information on **CFrameWnd**, see "Frame Window Topics" in *Visual C++ Programmer's Guide* online.

#include <afxwin.h>

See Also: **CWnd, CMDIFrameWnd, CMDIChildWnd, CView, CDocTemplate, CRuntimeClass**

CFrameWnd Class Members

Data Members

m_bAutoMenuEnable	Controls automatic enable and disable functionality for menu items.
rectDefault	Pass this static **CRect** as a parameter when creating a **CFrameWnd** object to allow Windows to choose the window's initial size and position.

Construction

CFrameWnd	Constructs a **CFrameWnd** object.

Initialization

Create	Call to create and initialize the Windows frame window associated with the **CFrameWnd** object.
LoadFrame	Call to dynamically create a frame window from resource information.
LoadAccelTable	Call to load an accelerator table.
LoadBarState	Call to restore control bar settings.
SaveBarState	Call to save control bar settings.
ShowControlBar	Call to show the control bar.
SetDockState	Call to dock the frame window in the main window.
GetDockState	Retrieves the dock state of a frame window.

Operations

ActivateFrame	Makes the frame visible and available to the user.
InitialUpdateFrame	Causes the **OnInitialUpdate** member function belonging to all views in the frame window to be called.
GetActiveFrame	Returns the active **CFrameWnd** object.
SetActiveView	Sets the active **CView** object.
GetActiveView	Returns the active **CView** object.
CreateView	Creates a view within a frame that is not derived from **CView**.
GetActiveDocument	Returns the active **CDocument** object.
GetControlBar	Retrieves the control bar.
GetMessageString	Retrieves message corresponding to a command ID.
IsTracking	Determines if splitter bar is currently being moved.
SetMessageText	Sets the text of a standard status bar.
EnableDocking	Allows a control bar to be docked.
DockControlBar	Docks a control bar.
FloatControlBar	Floats a control bar.
BeginModalState	Sets the frame window to modal.
EndModalState	Ends the frame window's modal state. Enables all of the windows disabled by **BeginModalState**.
InModalState	Returns a value indicating whether or not a frame window is in a modal state.
ShowOwnedWindows	Shows all windows that are descendants of the **CFrameWnd** object.
RecalcLayout	Repositions the control bars of the **CFrameWnd** object.

Overridables

OnCreateClient	Creates a client window for the frame.
OnSetPreviewMode	Sets the application's main frame window into and out of print-preview mode.
GetMessageBar	Returns a pointer to the status bar belonging to the frame window.
NegotiateBorderSpace	Negotiates border space in the frame window.

Command Handlers

OnContextHelp	Handles SHIFT+F1 Help for in-place items.

Member Functions

CFrameWnd::ActivateFrame

virtual void ActivateFrame(int *nCmdShow* **= − 1);**

Parameters

>*nCmdShow*   Specifies the parameter to pass to **CWnd::ShowWindow**. By default, the frame is shown and correctly restored.

Remarks

>Call this member function to activate and restore the frame window so that it is visible and available to the user. This member function is usually called after a non-user interface event such as a DDE, OLE, or other event that may show the frame window or its contents to the user.

>The default implementation activates the frame and brings it to the top of the Z-order and, if necessary, carries out the same steps for the application's main frame window.

>Override this member function to change how a frame is activated. For example, you can force MDI child windows to be maximized. Add the appropriate functionality, then call the base class version with an explicit *nCmdShow*.

CFrameWnd::BeginModalState

>**virtual void BeginModalState( );**

Remarks

>Call this member function to make a frame window modal.

CFrameWnd::CFrameWnd

>**CFrameWnd( );**

Remarks

>Constructs a **CFrameWnd** object, but does not create the visible frame window. Call **Create** to create the visible window.

>**See Also:**   **CFrameWnd::Create**, **CFrameWnd::LoadFrame**

CFrameWnd::Create

>**BOOL Create(LPCTSTR** *lpszClassName*, **LPCTSTR** *lpszWindowName*,
> ↪ **DWORD** *dwStyle* = **WS_OVERLAPPEDWINDOW,**
> ↪ **const RECT&** *rect* = **rectDefault, CWnd*** *pParentWnd* = **NULL,**
> ↪ **LPCTSTR** *lpszMenuName* = **NULL, DWORD** *dwExStyle* = **0,**
> ↪ **CCreateContext*** *pContext* = **NULL);**

Return Value

>Nonzero if initialization is successful; otherwise 0.

Parameters

lpszClassName Points to a null-terminated character string that names the Windows class. The class name can be any name registered with the **AfxRegisterWndClass** global function or the **RegisterClass** Windows function. If **NULL**, uses the predefined default **CFrameWnd** attributes.

lpszWindowName Points to a null-terminated character string that represents the window name. Used as text for the title bar.

dwStyle Specifies the window style attributes. Include the **FWS_ADDTOTITLE** style if you want the title bar to automatically display the name of the document represented in the window.

rect Specifies the size and position of the window. The **rectDefault** value allows Windows to specify the size and position of the new window.

pParentWnd Specifies the parent window of this frame window. This parameter should be **NULL** for top-level frame windows.

lpszMenuName Identifies the name of the menu resource to be used with the window. Use **MAKEINTRESOURCE** if the menu has an integer ID instead of a string. This parameter can be **NULL**.

dwExStyle Specifies the window extended style attributes.

pContext Specifies a pointer to a **CCreateContext** structure. This parameter can be **NULL**.

Remarks

Construct a **CFrameWnd** object in two steps. First invoke the constructor, which constructs the **CFrameWnd** object, then call **Create**, which creates the Windows frame window and attaches it to the **CFrameWnd** object. **Create** initializes the window's class name and window name and registers default values for its style, parent, and associated menu.

Use **LoadFrame** rather than **Create** to load the frame window from a resource instead of specifying its arguments.

See Also: **CFrameWnd::CFrameWnd, CFrameWnd::LoadFrame, CCreateContext, CWnd::Create, CWnd::PreCreateWindow**

CFrameWnd::CreateView

CWnd* CreateView(CCreateContext* *pContext*,
  ↪ **UINT** *nID* = **AFX_IDW_PANE_FIRST**);

Return Value

Pointer to a **CWnd** object if successful; otherwise **NULL**.

Parameters

    pContext   Specifies the type of view and document.

    nID   The ID number of a view.

Remarks

Call **CreateView** to create a view within a frame. Use this member function to create "views" that are not **CView**-derived within a frame. After calling **CreateView**, you must manually set the view to active and set it to be visible; these tasks are not automatically performed by **CreateView**.

Note   The MFC Advanced Concepts sample COLLECT uses **CreateView** to get correct 3D effects in Windows 95.

CFrameWnd::DockControlBar

void DockControlBar(CControlBar * *pBar*, **UINT** *nDockBarID* = **0,**
   ↳ **LPCRECT** *lpRect* = **NULL);**

Parameters

    pBar   Points to the control bar to be docked.

    nDockBarID   Determines which sides of the frame window to consider for docking. It can be 0, or one or more of the following:

- **AFX_IDW_DOCKBAR_TOP**   Dock to the top side of the frame window.

- **AFX_IDW_DOCKBAR_BOTTOM**   Dock to the bottom side of the frame window.

- **AFX_IDW_DOCKBAR_LEFT**   Dock to the left side of the frame window.

- **AFX_IDW_DOCKBAR_RIGHT**   Dock to the right side of the frame window.

If 0, the control bar can be docked to any side enabled for docking in the destination frame window.

    lpRect   Determines, in screen coordinates, where the control bar will be docked in the nonclient area of the destination frame window.

Remarks

Causes a control bar to be docked to the frame window. The control bar will be docked to one of the sides of the frame window specified in the calls to both **CControlBar::EnableDocking** and **CFrameWnd::EnableDocking**. The side chosen is determined by *nDockBarID*.

See Also: **CFrameWnd::FloatControlBar**

CFrameWnd::EnableDocking

void EnableDocking(DWORD *dwDockStyle* **);**

Parameters

dwDockStyle   Specifies which sides of the frame window can serve as docking sites for control bars. It can be one or more of the following:

- **CBRS_ALIGN_TOP**   Allows docking at the top of the client area.
- **CBRS_ALIGN_BOTTOM**   Allows docking at the bottom of the client area.
- **CBRS_ALIGN_LEFT**   Allows docking on the left side of the client area.
- **CBRS_ALIGN_RIGHT**   Allows docking on the right side of the client area.
- **CBRS_ALIGN_ANY**   Allows docking on any side of the client area.

Remarks

Call this function to enable dockable control bars in a frame window. By default, control bars will be docked to a side of the frame window in the following order: top, bottom, left, right.

See Also: **CControlBar::EnableDocking**, **CFrameWnd::DockControlBar**, **CFrameWnd::FloatControlBar**

CFrameWnd::EndModalState

virtual void EndModalState( );

Remarks

Call this member function to change a frame window from modal to modeless. **EndModalState** enables all of the windows disabled by **BeginModalState**.

CFrameWnd::FloatControlBar

CFrameWnd* FloatControlBar(CControlBar * *pBar*, **CPoint** *point*,
 ↪ **DWORD** *dwStyle* = **CBRS_ALIGN_TOP**);

Return Value

Pointer to the current frame window.

Parameters

pBar   Points to the control bar to be floated.

point   The location, in screen coordinates, where the top left corner of the control bar will be placed.

dwStyle   Specifies whether to align the control bar horizontally or vertically within its new frame window. It can be any one of the following:

- **CBRS_ALIGN_TOP**   Orients the control bar vertically.

- **CBRS_ALIGN_BOTTOM**   Orients the control bar vertically.

- **CBRS_ALIGN_LEFT**   Orients the control bar horizontally.

- **CBRS_ALIGN_RIGHT**   Orients the control bar horizontally.

If styles are passed specifying both horizontal and vertical orientation, the toolbar will be oriented horizontally.

Remarks

Call this function to cause a control bar to not be docked to the frame window. Typically, this is done at application startup when the program is restoring settings from the previous execution.

This function is called by the framework when the user causes a drop operation by releasing the left mouse button while dragging the control bar over a location that is not available for docking.

See Also: **CFrameWnd::DockControlBar**

CFrameWnd::GetActiveDocument

virtual CDocument* GetActiveDocument( );

Return Value

A pointer to the current **CDocument**. If there is no current document, returns **NULL**.

Remarks

Call this member function to obtain a pointer to the current **CDocument** attached to the current active view.

See Also: **CFrameWnd::GetActiveView**

CFrameWnd::GetActiveFrame

virtual CFrameWnd* GetActiveFrame( );

Return Value

A pointer to the active MDI child window. If the application is an SDI application, or the MDI frame window has no active document, the implicit **this** pointer will be returned.

Remarks

Call this member function to obtain a pointer to the active multiple document interface (MDI) child window of an MDI frame window.

If there is no active MDI child or the application is a single document interface (SDI), the implicit **this** pointer is returned.

See Also: **CFrameWnd::GetActiveView**, **CFrameWnd::GetActiveDocument**, **CMDIFrameWnd**

CFrameWnd::GetActiveView

CView* GetActiveView( ) const;

Return Value

A pointer to the current **CView**. If there is no current view, returns **NULL**.

Remarks

Call this member function to obtain a pointer to the active view (if any) attached to a frame window (**CFrameWnd**).

This function returns **NULL** when called for an MDI main frame window (**CMDIFrameWnd**). In an MDI application, the MDI main frame window does not have a view associated with it. Instead, each individual child window (**CMDIChildWnd**) has one or more associated views. The active view in an MDI application can be obtained by first finding the active MDI child window and then finding the active view for that child window. The active MDI child window can be found by calling the function **MDIGetActive** or **GetActiveFrame** as demonstrated in the following:

```
CMDIFrameWnd *pFrame =
        (CMDIFrameWnd*)AfxGetApp()->m_pMainWnd;

// Get the active MDI child window.
CMDIChildWnd *pChild =
        (CMDIChildWnd *) pFrame->GetActiveFrame();

// or CMDIChildWnd *pChild = pFrame->MDIGetActive();

// Get the active view attached to the active MDI child
// window.
CMyView *pView = (CMyView *) pChild->GetActiveView();
```

See Also: **CFrameWnd::SetActiveView**, **CFrameWnd::GetActiveDocument**

CFrameWnd::GetControlBar

CControlBar* GetControlBar(UINT *nID*);

Return Value

A pointer to the control bar that is associated with the ID.

Parameters

nID   The ID number of a control bar.

Remarks

Call **GetControlBar** to gain access to the control bar that is associated with the ID. **GetControlBar** will return the control bar even if it is floating and thus is not currently a child window of the frame.

CFrameWnd::GetDockState

void GetDockState(CDockState& *state* **) const;**

Parameters

state   Contains the current state of the frame window's control bars upon return.

Remarks

Call this member function to store state information about the frame window's control bars in a **CDockState** object. You can then write the contents of **CDockState** to storage using **CDockState::SaveState** or **Serialize**. If you later want to restore the control bars to a previous state, load the state with **CDockState::LoadState** or **Serialize**, then call **SetDockState** to apply the previous state to the frame window's control bars.

See Also: **CFrameWnd::SetDockState, CDockState, CDockState::SaveState, CObject::Serialize**

CFrameWnd::GetMessageBar

virtual CWnd* GetMessageBar( );

Return Value

Pointer to the status-bar window.

Remarks

Call this member function to get a pointer to the status bar.

CFrameWnd::GetMessageString

virtual void GetMessageString(UINT *nID***, CString&** *rMessage* **) const;**

Parameters

nID   Resource ID of the desired message.

rMessage   **CString** object into which to place the message.

Remarks

Override this function to provide custom strings for command IDs. The default implementation simply loads the string specified by *nID* from the resource file. This function is called by the framework when the message string in the status bar needs updating.

See Also: **CFrameWnd::SetMessageText**

CFrameWnd::InitialUpdateFrame

void InitialUpdateFrame(CDocument* *pDoc***, BOOL** *bMakeVisible* **);**

Parameters

pDoc   Points to the document to which the frame window is associated. Can be **NULL**.

bMakeVisible   If **TRUE**, indicates that the frame should become visible and active. If **FALSE**, no descendants are made visible.

Remarks

Call **IntitialUpdateFrame** after creating a new frame with **Create**. This causes all views in that frame window to receive their **OnInitialUpdate** calls.

Also, if there was not previously an active view, the primary view of the frame window is made active. The primary view is a view with a child ID of **AFX_IDW_PANE_FIRST**. Finally, the frame window is made visible if *bMakeVisible* is nonzero. If *bMakeVisible* is 0, the current focus and visible state of the frame window will remain unchanged. It is not necessary to call this function when using the framework's implementation of File New and File Open.

See Also: **CView::OnInitialUpdate**, **CFrameWnd::SetActiveView**, **CDocTemplate::CreateNewFrame**

CFrameWnd::InModalState

BOOL InModalState( ) const;

Return Value

Nonzero if yes; otherwise 0.

Remarks

Call this member function to check if a frame window is modal or modeless.

CFrameWnd::IsTracking

BOOL IsTracking( ) const;

Return Value

Nonzero if a splitter operation is in progress; otherwise 0.

Remarks

    Call this member function to determine if the splitter bar in the window is currently being moved.

CFrameWnd::LoadAccelTable

    BOOL LoadAccelTable(LPCTSTR *lpszResourceName* **);**

Return Value

    Nonzero if the accelerator table was successfully loaded; otherwise 0.

Parameters

    lpszResourceName   Identifies the name of the accelerator resource. Use **MAKEINTRESOURCE** if the resource is identified with an integer ID.

Remarks

    Call to load the specified accelerator table. Only one table can be loaded at a time.

    Accelerator tables loaded from resources are freed automatically when the application terminates.

    If you call **LoadFrame** to create the frame window, the framework loads an accelerator table along with the menu and icon resources, and a subsequent call to this member function is then unnecessary.

    See Also: **CFrameWnd::LoadFrame**, **::LoadAccelerators**

CFrameWnd::LoadBarState

    void LoadBarState(LPCTSTR *lpszProfileName* **);**

Parameters

    lpszProfileName   Name of a section in the initialization file or a key in the Windows registry where state information is stored.

Remarks

    Call this function to restore the settings of each control bar owned by the frame window. This information is written to the initialization file using **SaveBarState**. Information restored includes visibility, horizontal/vertical orientation, docking state, and control-bar position.

    See Also: **CFrameWnd::SaveBarState**, **CWinApp::SetRegistryKey**, **CWinApp::m_pszProfileName**

CFrameWnd::LoadFrame

virtual BOOL LoadFrame(UINT *nIDResource*,
  ↳ **DWORD** *dwDefaultStyle* **= WS_OVERLAPPEDWINDOW | FWS_ADDTOTITLE,**
  ↳ **CWnd*** *pParentWnd* **= NULL, CCreateContext*** *pContext* **= NULL);**

Parameters

nIDResource   The ID of shared resources associated with the frame window.

dwDefaultStyle   The frame's style. Include the **FWS_ADDTOTITLE** style if you want the title bar to automatically display the name of the document represented in the window.

pParentWnd   A pointer to the frame's parent.

pContext   A pointer to a **CCreateContext** structure. This parameter can be **NULL**.

Remarks

Construct a **CFrameWnd** object in two steps. First invoke the constructor, which constructs the **CFrameWnd** object, then call **LoadFrame**, which loads the Windows frame window and associated resources and attaches the frame window to the **CFrameWnd** object. The *nIDResource* parameter specifies the menu, the accelerator table, the icon, and the string resource of the title for the frame window.

Use the **Create** member function rather than **LoadFrame** when you want to specify all of the frame window's creation parameters.

The framework calls **LoadFrame** when it creates a frame window using a document template object.

The framework uses the *pContext* argument to specify the objects to be connected to the frame window, including any contained view objects. You can set the *pContext* argument to **NULL** when you call **LoadFrame**.

See Also: **CDocTemplate, CFrameWnd::Create, CFrameWnd::CFrameWnd, CWnd::PreCreateWindow**

CFrameWnd::NegotiateBorderSpace

virtual BOOL NegotiateBorderSpace(UINT *nBorderCmd*, **LPRECT** *lpRectBorder* **);**

Return Value

Nonzero if successful; otherwise 0.

Parameters

nBorderCmd   Contains one of the following values from the **enum BorderCmd**:

- **borderGet** = 1
- **borderRequest** = 2
- **borderSet** = 3

lpRectBorder   Pointer to a **RECT** structure or a **CRect** object that specifies the coordinates of the border.

Remarks

Call this member function to negotiate border space in a frame window during OLE inplace activation. This member function is the **CFrameWnd** implementation of OLE border space negotiation.

See Also: IOleInPlaceUIWindow

CFrameWnd::OnContextHelp

afx_msg void OnContextHelp( );

Remarks

To enable context-sensitive help, you must add an

```
ON_COMMAND( ID_CONTEXT_HELP, OnContextHelp )
```

statement to your **CFrameWnd** class message map and also add an accelerator-table entry, typically SHIFT+F1, to enable this member function.

If your application is an OLE Container, **OnContextHelp** puts all in-place items contained within the frame window object into Help mode. The cursor changes to an arrow and a question mark, and the user can then move the mouse pointer and press the left mouse button to select a dialog box, window, menu, or command button. This member function calls the Windows function **WinHelp** with the Help context of the object under the cursor.

See Also: CWinApp::OnHelp, CWinApp::WinHelp

CFrameWnd::OnCreateClient

virtual BOOL OnCreateClient(LPCREATESTRUCT *lpcs*, CCreateContext* *pContext*);

Return Value

Nonzero if successful; otherwise 0.

Parameters

lpcs   A pointer to a Windows **CREATESTRUCT** structure.

pContext   A pointer to a **CCreateContext** structure.

Remarks

Called by the framework during the execution of **OnCreate**. Never call this function.

The default implementation of this function creates a **CView** object from the information provided in *pContext*, if possible.

Override this function to override values passed in the **CCreateContext** object or to change the way controls in the main client area of the frame window are created. The **CCreateContext** members you can override are described in the **CCreateContext** class.

Note Do not replace values passed in the **CREATESTRUCT** structure. They are for informational use only. If you want to override the initial window rectangle, for example, override the **CWnd** member function **PreCreateWindow**.

CFrameWnd::OnSetPreviewMode

virtual void OnSetPreviewMode(BOOL *bPreview*, **CPrintPreviewState*** *pModeStuff* **);**

Parameters

bPreview Specifies whether or not to place the application in print-preview mode. Set to **TRUE** to place in print preview, **FALSE** to cancel preview mode.

pModeStuff A pointer to a **CPrintPreviewState** structure.

Remarks

Call this member function to set the application's main frame window into and out of print-preview mode.

The default implementation disables all standard toolbars and hides the main menu and the main client window. This turns MDI frame windows into temporary SDI frame windows.

Override this member function to customize the hiding and showing of control bars and other frame window parts during print preview. Call the base class implementation from within the overridden version.

CFrameWnd::RecalcLayout

virtual void RecalcLayout(BOOL *bNotify* = **TRUE** **);**

Parameters

bNotify Determines whether the active in-place item for the frame window receives notification of the layout change. If **TRUE**, the item is notified; otherwise **FALSE**.

Remarks

Called by the framework when the standard control bars are toggled on or off or when the frame window is resized. The default implementation of this member function calls the **CWnd** member function **RepositionBars** to reposition all the control bars in the frame as well as in the main client window (usually a **CView** or **MDICLIENT**).

Override this member function to control the appearance and behavior of control bars after the layout of the frame window has changed. For example, call it when you turn control bars on or off or add another control bar.

See Also: **CWnd::RepositionBars**

CFrameWnd::SaveBarState

void SaveBarState(LPCTSTR *lpszProfileName* **) const;**

Parameters

lpszProfileName   Name of a section in the initialization file or a key in the Windows registry where state information is stored.

Remarks

Call this function to store information about each control bar owned by the frame window. This information can be read from the initialization file using **LoadBarState**. Information stored includes visibility, horizontal/vertical orientation, docking state, and control bar position.

See Also: **CFrameWnd::LoadBarState, CWinApp::SetRegistryKey, CWinApp::m_pszProfileName**

CFrameWnd::SetActiveView

void SetActiveView(CView* *pViewNew***, BOOL** *bNotify* = **TRUE);**

Parameters

pViewNew   Specifies a pointer to a **CView** object, or **NULL** for no active view.

bNotify   Specifies whether the view is to be notified of activation. If **TRUE**, **OnActivateView** is called for the new view; if **FALSE**, it is not.

Remarks

Call this member function to set the active view. The framework will call this function automatically as the user changes the focus to a view within the frame window. You can explicitly call **SetActiveView** to change the focus to the specified view.

See Also: **CFrameWnd::GetActiveView, CView::OnActivateView, CFrameWnd::GetActiveDocument**

CFrameWnd::SetDockState

void SetDockState(const CDockState& *state* **);**

Parameters

state   Apply the stored state to the frame window's control bars.

Remarks

Call this member function to apply state information stored in a **CDockState** object to the frame window's control bars. To restore a previous state of the control bars, you can load the stored state with **CDockState::LoadState** or **Serialize**, then use **SetDockState** to apply it to the frame window's control bars. The previous state is stored in the **CDockState** object with **GetDockState**

See Also: **CFrameWnd::GetDockState**, **CDockState**, **CDockState::LoadState**, **CObject::Serialize**

CFrameWnd::SetMessageText

void SetMessageText(LPCTSTR *lpszText* **);**
void SetMessageText(UINT *nID* **);**

Parameters

lpszText   Points to the string to be placed on the status bar.

nID   String resource ID of the string to be placed on the status bar.

Remarks

Call this function to place a string in the status-bar pane that has an ID of 0. This is typically the leftmost, and longest, pane of the status bar.

See Also: **CStatusBar**

CFrameWnd::ShowControlBar

void ShowControlBar(CControlBar* *pBar***, BOOL** *bShow***, BOOL** *bDelay* **);**

Parameters

pBar   Pointer to the control bar to be shown or hidden.

bShow   If **TRUE**, specifies that the control bar is to be shown. If **FALSE**, specifies that the control bar is to be hidden.

bDelay   If **TRUE**, delay showing the control bar. If **FALSE**, show the control bar immediately.

Remarks

Call this member function to show or hide the control bar.

CFrameWnd::ShowOwnedWindows

void ShowOwnedWindows(BOOL *bShow* **);**

Parameters

bShow   Specifies whether the owned windows are to be shown or hidden.

Remarks

Call this member function to show all windows that are descendants of the **CFrameWnd** object.

Data Members

CFrameWnd::m_bAutoMenuEnable

Remarks

When this data member is enabled (which is the default), menu items that do not have **ON_UPDATE_COMMAND_UI** or **ON_COMMAND** handlers will be automatically disabled when the user pulls down a menu.

Menu items that have an **ON_COMMAND** handler but no **ON_UPDATE_COMMAND_UI** handler will be automatically enabled.

When this data member is set, menu items are automatically enabled in the same way that toolbar buttons are enabled.

This data member simplifies the implementation of optional commands based on the current selection and reduces the need for an application to write **ON_UPDATE_COMMAND_UI** handlers for enabling and disabling menu items.

See Also: CCmdUI, CCmdTarget

CFrameWnd::rectDefault

Remarks

Pass this static **CRect** as a parameter when creating a window to allow Windows to choose the window's initial size and position.

CFtpConnection

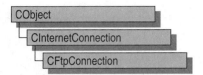

The MFC class **CFtpConnection** both manages your FTP connection to an Internet server and allows direct manipulation of directories and files on that server. FTP is one of the three Internet services recognized by the MFC WinInet classes.

To communicate with an FTP Internet server, you must first create an instance of **CInternetSession**, and then create a **CFtpConnection** object. You never create a **CFtpConnection** object directly; rather, call **CInternetSession::GetFtpConnection**, which creates the **CFtpConnection** object and returns a pointer to it.

To learn more about how **CFtpConnection** works with the other MFC Internet classes, see the article "Internet Programming with WinInet" in *Visual C++ Programmer's Guide* online. For more information about communicating with the the other two supported services, HTTP and gopher, see the classes **CHttpConnection** and **CGopherConnection**.

#include <afxinet.h>

See Also: **CInternetConnection**, **CInternetSession**

CFtpConnection Class Members

Construction

CFtpConnection	Constructs a **CFtpConnection** object.

Operations

SetCurrentDirectory	Sets the current FTP directory.
GetCurrentDirectory	Gets the current directory for this connection.
GetCurrentDirectoryAsURL	Gets the current directory for this connection as a URL.
RemoveDirectory	Removes the specified directory from the server.
CreateDirectory	Creates a directory on the server.
Rename	Renames a file on the server.
Remove	Removes a file from the server.
PutFile	Places a file on the server.
GetFile	Gets a file from the connected server
OpenFile	Opens a file on the connected server.
Close	Closes the connection to the server.

See Also: **CInternetConnection**

Member Functions
CFtpConnection::CFtpConnection

CFtpConnection( );

Remarks

This member function is called to construct a **CFtpConnection** object. You never create a **CFtpConnection** object directly. Instead, call **CInternetSession::GetFtpConnection**, which creates the **CFptConnection** object.

See Also: **CInternetSession::GetFtpConnection**, **CFtpFileFind**, **CGopherConnection**, **CHttpConnection**, **CInternetConnection**

CFtpConnection::Close

virtual void Close( );

Remarks

Call this member function to close the connection to the server. The connection will be closed by the **CFtpConnection** object's destructor, but you should close the connection explicitly to avoid a diagnostic message.

See Also: **CFtpFileFind**, **CGopherConnection**, **CHttpConnection**, **CInternetConnection**

CFtpConnection::CreateDirectory

BOOL CreateDirectory(LPCTSTR *pstrDirName* **);**

Return Value

Nonzero if successful; otherwise 0. If the call fails, the Windows function **GetLastError** may be called to determine the cause of the error.

Parameters

pstrDirName   A pointer to a string containing the name of the directory to create.

Remarks

Call this member function to create a directory on the connected server.

Use **GetCurrentDirectory** to determine the current working directory for this connection to the server. Do not assume that the remote system has connected you to the root directory.

The *pstrDirName* parameter can be either a partially or a fully qualified filename relative to the current directory. A backslash (\) or forward slash (/) can be used as the directory separator for either name. **CreateDirectory** translates the directory name separators to the appropriate characters before they are used.

See Also: CInternetConnection

CFtpConnection::GetCurrentDirectory

BOOL GetCurrentDirectory(CString& *strDirName* **) const;**
BOOL GetCurrentDirectory(LPTSTR *pstrDirName*, **LPDWORD** *lpdwLen* **) const;**

Return Value

Nonzero if successful; otherwise 0. If the call fails, the Win32 function **GetLastError** may be called to determine the cause of the error.

Parameters

strDirName   A reference to a string that will receive the name of the directory.

pstrDirName   A pointer to a string that will receive the name of the directory.

lpdwLen   A pointer to a DWORD that contains the following information:

On entry	The size of the buffer referenced by *pstrDirName*.
On return	The number of characters stored to *pstrDirName*. If the member function fails and ERROR_INSUFFICIENT_BUFFER is returned, then *lpdwLen* contains the number of bytes that the application must allocate in order to receive the string.

Remarks

Call this member function to get the name of the current directory. To get the directory name as a URL instead, call **GetCurrentDirectoryAsURL**.

The parameters *pstrDirName* or *strDirName* can be either partially qualified filenames relative to the current directory or fully qualified. A backslash (\) or forward slash (/) can be used as the directory separator for either name. **GetCurrentDirectory** translates the directory name separators to the appropriate characters before they are used.

See Also: CFtpConnection::GetCurrentDirectoryAsURL, CInternetConnection

CFtpConnection::GetCurrentDirectoryAsURL

BOOL GetCurrentDirectoryAsURL(CString& *strDirName* **) const;**
BOOL GetCurrentDirectoryAsURL(LPTSTR *pstrDirName*,
  ↳ **LPDWORD** *lpdwLen* **) const;**

Return Value

Nonzero if successful; otherwise 0. If the call fails, the Win32 function **GetLastError** may be called to determine the cause of the error.

Parameters

strDirName   A reference to a string that will receive the name of the directory.

pstrDirName   A pointer to a string that will receive the name of the directory.

lpdwLen   A pointer to a DWORD that contains the following information:

On entry	The size of the buffer referenced by *pstrDirName*.
On return	The number of characters stored to *pstrDirName*. If the member function fails and ERROR_INSUFFICIENT_BUFFER is returned, then *lpdwLen* contains the number of bytes that the application must allocate in order to receive the string.

Remarks

Call this member function to get the current directory's name as a URL. **GetCurrentDirectoryAsURL** behaves the same as **GetCurrentDirectory**

The parameter *strDirName* can be either partially qualified filenames relative to the current directory or fully qualified. A backslash (\) or forward slash (/) can be used as the directory separator for either name. **GetCurrentDirectoryAsURL** translates the directory name separators to the appropriate characters before they are used.

See Also: **CFtpConnection::GetCurrentDirectory**, **CInternetConnection**

CFtpConnection::GetFile

BOOL GetFile(LPCTSTR *pstrRemoteFile***, LPCTSTR** *pstrLocalFile***,**
  ↪ **BOOL** *bFailIfExists* = **TRUE,**
  ↪ **DWORD** *dwAttributes* = **FILE_ATTRIBUTE_NORMAL,**
  ↪ **DWORD** *dwFlags* = **FTP_TRANSFER_TYPE_BINARY,**
  ↪ **DWORD** *dwContext* = **1);**

Return Value

Nonzero if successful; otherwise 0. If the call fails, the Win32 function **GetLastError** may be called to determine the cause of the error.

Parameters

pstrRemoteFile   A pointer to a null-terminated string containing the name of a file to retrieve from the FTP server.

pstrLocalFile   A pointer to a null-terminated string containing the name of the file to create on the local system.

bFailIfExists   Indicates whether the file name may already be used by an existing file. If the local file name already exists, and this parameter is **TRUE**, **GetFile** fails. Otherwise, **GetFile** will erase the existing copy of the file.

dwAttributes   Indicates the attributes of the file. This can be any combination of the following FILE_ATTRIBUTE_* flags.

- FILE_ATTRIBUTE_ARCHIVE   The file is an archive file. Applications use this attribute to mark files for backup or removal.

- FILE_ATTRIBUTE_COMPRESSED   The file or directory is compressed. For a file, compression means that all of the data in the file is compressed. For a directory, compression is the default for newly created files and subdirectories.

- FILE_ATTRIBUTE_DIRECTORY   The file is a directory.

- FILE_ATTRIBUTE_NORMAL   The file has no other attributes set. This attribute is valid only if used alone. All other file attributes override FILE_ATTRIBUTE_NORMAL:

- FILE_ATTRIBUTE_HIDDEN   The file is hidden. It is not to be included in an ordinary directory listing.

- FILE_ATTRIBUTE_READONLY   The file is read only. Applications can read the file but cannot write to it or delete it.

- FILE_ATTRIBUTE_SYSTEM   The file is part of or is used exclusively by the operating system.

- FILE_ATTRIBUTE_TEMPORARY   The file is being used for temporary storage. Applications should write to the file only if absolutely necessary. Most of the file's data remains in memory without being flushed to the media because the file will soon be deleted.

dwFlags   Specifies the conditions under which the transfer occurs. This can be any of the following FTP_TRANSFER_TYPE_* constants:

- FTP_TRANSFER_TYPE_ASCII   Transfers the file using FTP's ASCII (Type A) transfer method. Converts control and formatting information to local equivalents.

- FTP_TRANSFER_TYPE_BINARY   The file transfers data using FTP Image (Type I) transfer method. The file transfers data exactly as it exists, with no changes. This is the default transfer method.

dwContext   The context identifier for the file retrieval. See **Remarks** for more information about *dwContext*.

Remarks

Call this member function to get a file from an FTP server and store it on the local machine.

GetFile is a high-level routine that handles all of the overhead associated with reading a file from an FTP server and storing it locally. Applications that only retrieve file data, or that require close control over the file transfer, should use **OpenFile** and **CInternetFile::Read** instead.

If *dwFlags* is FILE_TRANSFER_TYPE_ASCII, translation of file data also converts control and formatting characters to Windows equivalents. The default transfer is binary mode, where the file is downloaded in the same format as it is stored on the server.

Both *pstrRemoteFile* and *pstrLocalFile* can be either partially qualified filenames relative to the current directory or fully qualified. A backslash (\) or forward slash (/) can be used as the directory separator for either name. **GetFile** translates the directory name separators to the appropriate characters before they are used.

Override the *dwContext* default to set the context identifier to a value of your choosing. The context identifier is associated with this specific operation of the **CFtpConnection** object created by its **CInternetSession** object. The value is returned to **CInternetSession::OnStatusCallback** to provide status on the operation with which it is identified. See the article "Internet First Steps: WinInet" for more information about the context identifier.

See Also: CInternetConnection

CFtpConnection::OpenFile

CInternetFile* OpenFile(LPCTSTR *pstrFileName***,**
  ↳ **DWORD** *dwAccess* **= GENERIC_READ,**
  ↳ **DWORD** *dwFlags* **= FTP_TRANSFER_TYPE_BINARY,**
  ↳ **DWORD** *dwContext* **= 1);**

Return Value

A pointer to a **CInternetFile** object.

Parameters

pstrFileName   A pointer to a string containing the name of the file to be opened.

dwAccess   Determines how the file will be accessed. Can be either GENERIC_READ or GENERIC_WRITE, but not both.

dwFlags   Specifies the conditions under which subsequent transfers occur. This can be any of the following FTP_TRANSFER_* constants:

- FTP_TRANSFER_TYPE_ASCII   The file transfers using FTP ASCII (Type A) transfer method. Converts control and formatting information to local equivalents.

- FTP_TRANSFER_TYPE_BINARY   The file transfers data using FTP's Image (Type I) transfer method. The file transfers data exactly as it exists, with no changes. This is the default transfer method.

dwContext   The context identifier for opening the file. See **Remarks** for more information about *dwContext*.

Remarks

Call this member function to open a file located on an FTP server for reading or writing. **OpenFile** should be used in the following situations:

- An application has data that needs to be sent and created as a file on the FTP server, but that data is not in a local file. Once **OpenFile** opens a file, the application uses **CInternetFile::Write** to send the FTP file data to the server.

- An application must retrieve a file from the server and place it into application-controlled memory, instead of writing it to disk. The application uses **CInternetFile::Read** after using **OpenFile** to open the file.

- An application needs a fine level of control over a file transfer. For example, the application may want to display a progress control indicate the progress of the file transfer status while downloading a file.

After calling **OpenFile** and until calling **Close**, the application can only call **CInternetFile::Read**, **CInternetFile::Write**, **Close**, or **CFtpFileFind::FindFile**. Calls to other FTP functions for the same FTP session will fail and set the error code to FTP_ETRANSFER_IN_PROGRESS.

The *pstrFileName* parameter can be either a partially qualified filename relative to the current directory or fully qualified. A backslash (\) or forward slash (/) can be used as the directory separator for either name. **OpenFile** translates the directory name separators to the appropriate characters before using it.

Override the *dwContext* default to set the context identifier to a value of your choosing. The context identifier is associated with this specific operation of the **CFtpConnection** object created by its **CInternetSession** object. The value is returned to **CInternetSession::OnStatusCallback** to provide status on the operation with which it is identified. See the article "Internet First Steps: WinInet" for more information about the context identifier.

See Also: **CInternetConnection**, **CFtpConnection::GetFile**, **CGopherConnection::OpenFile**, **CInternetFile::Write**, **CInternetFile::Read**

CFtpConnection::PutFile

> **BOOL PutFile(LPCTSTR** *pstrLocalFile***, LPCTSTR** *pstrRemoteFile***,**
>   ↪ **DWORD** *dwFlags* = **FTP_TRANSFER_TYPE_BINARY,**
>   ↪ **DWORD** *dwContext* = **1);**

Return Value

Nonzero if successful; otherwise 0. If the call fails, the Win32 function **GetLastError** may be called to determine the cause of the error.

Parameters

pstrLocalFile　A pointer to a string containing the name of the file to send from the local system.

pstrRemoteFile　A pointer to a string containing the name of the file to create on the FTP server.

dwFlags　Specifies the conditions under which the transfer of the file occurs. Can be any of the FTP_TRANSFER_* constants described in **OpenFile**.

dwContext　The context identifier for placing the file. See **Remarks** for more information about *dwContext*.

Remarks

Call this member function to store a file on an FTP server.

PutFile is a high-level routine that handles all of the operations associated with storing a file on an FTP server. Applications that only send data, or that require closer control over the file transfer, should use **OpenFile** and **CInternetFile::Write**.

Override the *dwContext* default to set the context identifier to a value of your choosing. The context identifier is associated with this specific operation of the **CFtpConnection** object created by its **CInternetSession** object. The value is returned to **CInternetSession::OnStatusCallback** to provide status on the operation with which it is identified. See the article "Internet First Steps: WinInet" in *Visual C++ Programmer's Guide* online for more information about the context identifier.

See Also:　CInternetConnection

CFtpConnection::Remove

BOOL Remove(LPCTSTR *pstrFileName* **);**

Return Value

Nonzero if successful; otherwise 0. If the call fails, the Win32 function **GetLastError** may be called to determine the cause of the error.

Parameters

pstrFileName　A pointer to a string containing the file name to remove.

Remarks

Call this member function to delete the specified file from the connected server.

The *pstrFileName* parameter can be either a partially qualified filename relative to the current directory or fully qualified. A backslash (\) or forward slash (/) can be used as the directory separator for either name. The **Remove** function translates the directory name separators to the appropriate characters before they are used.

See Also:　CInternetConnection

CFtpConnection::RemoveDirectory

BOOL RemoveDirectory(LPCTSTR *pstrDirName* **);**

Return Value

Nonzero if successful; otherwise 0. If the call fails, the Win32 function **GetLastError** may be called to determine the cause of the error.

Parameters

pstrDirName   A pointer to a string containing the directory to be removed.

Remarks

Call this member function to remove the specified directory from the connected server.

Use **GetCurrentDirectory** to determine the server's current working directory. Do not assume that the remote system has connected you to the root directory.

The *pstrDirName* parameter can be either a partially or fully qualified filename relative to the current directory. A backslash (\) or forward slash (/) can be used as the directory separator for either name. **RemoveDirectory** translates the directory name separators to the appropriate characters before they are used.

See Also: CInternetConnection

CFtpConnection::Rename

BOOL Rename(LPCTSTR *pstrExisting*, **LPCTSTR** *pstrNew* **);**

Return Value

Nonzero if successful; otherwise 0. If the call fails, the Win32 function **GetLastError** may be called to determine the cause of the error.

Parameters

pstrExisting   A pointer to a string containing the current name of the file to be renamed.

pstrNew   A pointer to a string containing the file's new name.

Remarks

Call this member function to rename the specified file on the connected server.

The *pstrExisting* and *pstrNew* parameters can be either a partially qualified filename relative to the current directory or fully qualified. A backslash (\) or forward slash (/) can be used as the directory separator for either name. **Rename** translates the directory name separators to the appropriate characters before they are used.

See Also: CInternetConnection

CFtpConnection::SetCurrentDirectory

BOOL SetCurrentDirectory(LPCTSTR *pstrDirName* **);**

Return Value

Nonzero if successful; otherwise 0. If the call fails, the Win32 function **GetLastError** may be called to determine the cause of the error.

Parameters

pstrDirName   A pointer to a string containing the name of the directory.

Remarks

Call this member function to change to a different directory on the FTP server.

The *pstrDirName* parameter can be either a partially or fully qualified filename relative to the current directory. A backslash (\) or forward slash (/) can be used as the directory separator for either name. **SetCurrentDirectory** translates the directory name separators to the appropriate characters before they are used.

Use **GetCurrentDirectory** to determine an FTP server's current working directory. Do not assume that the remote system has connected you to the root directory.

See Also: CInternetConnection

CFtpFileFind

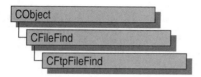

Class **CFtpFileFind** aids in Internet file searches of FTP servers. **CFtpFileFind** includes member functions that begin a search, locate a file, and return the URL or other descriptive information about the file.

Other MFC classes designed for Internet and local file searched include **CGopherFileFind** and **CFileFind**. Together with **CFtpFileFind**, these classes provide a seamless mechanism for the client to find specific files, regardless of the server protocol or file type (either a local machine or a remote server). Note that there is no MFC class for searching on HTTP servers because HTTP does not support the direct file manipulation required for searches.

For more information about how to use **CFtpFileFind** and the other WinInet classes, see the article "Internet Programming with WinInet" in *Visual C++ Programmer's Guide* online.

#include <afxinet.h>

See Also: CGopherFileFind, CInternetFile, CGopherFile, CHttpFile

---

CFtpFileFind Class Members

Construction

CFtpFileFind	Constructs a **CFtpFileFind** object.

Operations

FindFile	Finds a file on a FTP server.
FindNextFile	Continues a file search from a previous call to **FindFile**.
GetFileURL	Gets the URL, including path, of the found file.

See Also: CFtpFileFind, CGopherFileFind, CInternetFile, CGopherFile, CHttpFile

Member Functions
CFtpFileFind::CFtpFileFind

CFtpFileFind(CFtpConnection* *pConnection*, **DWORD** *dwContext* = **1**);

Parameters

pConnection   A pointer to a **CFtpConnection** object. You can obtain an FTP connection by calling **CInternetSession::GetFtpConnection**.

dwContext   The context identifier for the **CFtpFileFind** object. See **Remarks** for more information about this parameter.

Remarks

This member function is called to construct a **CFtpFileFind** object.

The default value for *dwContext* is sent by MFC to the **CFtpFileFind** object from the **CInternetSession** object that created the **CFtpFileFind** object. You can override the default to set the context identifier to a value of your choosing. The context identifier is returned to **CInternetSession::OnStatusCallback** to provide status on the object with which it is identified. See the article "Internet First Steps: WinInet" in the *Visual C++ Programmer's Guide* online for more information about the context identifier.

See Also: **CGopherFileFind**, **CFileFind**

CFtpFileFind::FindFile

virtual BOOL FindFile(LPCTSTR *pstrName* = **NULL**,
   ↳ **DWORD** *dwFlags* = **INTERNET_FLAG_RELOAD**);

Return Value

Nonzero if successful; otherwise 0. To get extended error information, call the Win32 function **GetLastError**.

Parameters

pstrName   A pointer to a string containing the name of the file to find. If **NULL**, the call will perform a wildcard search (*).

dwFlags   The flags describing how to handle this session. These flags can be combined with the bitwise OR operator (|) and are as follows:

- INTERNET_FLAG_RELOAD   Get the data from the wire even if it is locally cached. This is the default flag.

- INTERNET_FLAG_DONT_CACHE   Do not cache the data, either locally or in any gateways.

- INTERNET_FLAG_RAW_DATA   Override the default to return the raw data (**WIN32_FIND_DATA** structures for FTP).

- INTERNET_FLAG_SECURE   Secures transactions on the wire with Secure Sockets Layer or PCT. This flag is applicable to HTTP requests only.

- INTERNET_FLAG_EXISTING_CONNECT   If possible, reuse the existing connections to the server for new **FindFile** requests instead of creating a new session for each request.

Remarks

Call this member function to find an FTP file.

After calling **FindFile** to retrieve the first FTP file, you can call **FindNextFile** to retrieve subsequent FTP files.

See Also: CFtpFileFind::FindNextFile, CFileFind

CFtpFileFind::FindNextFile

virtual BOOL FindNextFile( );

Return Value

Nonzero if successful; otherwise 0. To get extended error information, call the Win32 function **GetLastError**.

Remarks

Call this member function to continue a file search begun with a call to the **FindFile** member function. You must call this function at least once before calling any attribute function.

FindNextFile wraps the Win32 function **FindNextFile**.

See Also: CFileFind

CFtpFileFind::GetFileURL

CString GetFileURL( ) const;

Return Value

The file and path of the Universal Resource Locator (URL) .

Remarks

Call this member function to get the URL of the specified file.

GetFileURL is similar to the member function **CFileFind::GetFilePath**, except that it returns the URL in the form `ftp://moose/dir/file.txt`.

See Also: CFtpFileFind::FindFile, CFileFind

CGdiObject

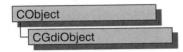

The **CGdiObject** class provides a base class for various kinds of Windows graphics device interface (GDI) objects such as bitmaps, regions, brushes, pens, palettes, and fonts. You never create a **CGdiObject** directly. Rather, you create an object from one of its derived classes, such as **CPen** or **CBrush**.

For more information on **CGdiObject**, see "Graphic Objects" in *Visual C++ Programmer's Guide* online.

#include <afxwin.h>

See Also: **CBitmap**, **CBrush**, **CFont**, **CPalette**, **CPen**, **CRgn**

CGdiObject Class Members

Data Members

m_hObject	A **HANDLE** containing the **HBITMAP**, **HPALETTE**, **HRGN**, **HBRUSH**, **HPEN**, or **HFONT** attached to this object.

Construction

CGdiObject	Constructs a **CGdiObject** object.

Operations

GetSafeHandle	Returns **m_hObject** unless **this** is **NULL**, in which case **NULL** is returned.
FromHandle	Returns a pointer to a **CGdiObject** object given a handle to a Windows GDI object.
Attach	Attaches a Windows GDI object to a **CGdiObject** object.
Detach	Detaches a Windows GDI object from a **CGdiObject** object and returns a handle to the Windows GDI object.
DeleteObject	Deletes the Windows GDI object attached to the **CGdiObject** object from memory by freeing all system storage associated with the object.
DeleteTempMap	Deletes any temporary **CGdiObject** objects created by **FromHandle**.
GetObject	Fills a buffer with data that describes the Windows GDI object attached to the **CGdiObject** object.
CreateStockObject	Retrieves a handle to one of the Windows predefined stock pens, brushes, or fonts.

(continued)

Member Functions

CGdiObject::Attach

BOOL Attach(HGDIOBJ *hObject* **);**

Return Value

Nonzero if attachment is successful; otherwise 0.

Parameters

hObject   A **HANDLE** to a Windows GDI object (for example, **HPEN** or **HBRUSH**).

Remarks

Attaches a Windows GDI object to a **CGdiObject** object.

See Also: CGdiObject::Detach

CGdiObject::CGdiObject

CGdiObject( );

Remarks

Constructs a **CGdiObject** object. You never create a **CGdiObject** directly. Rather, you create an object from one of its derived classes, such as **CPen** or **CBrush**.

See Also: CPen, CBrush, CFont, CBitmap, CRgn, CPalette

CGdiObject::CreateStockObject

BOOL CreateStockObject(int *nIndex* **);**

Return Value

Nonzero if the function is successful; otherwise 0.

Parameters

nIndex   A constant specifying the type of stock object desired. It can be one of the following values:

- **BLACK_BRUSH**   Black brush.

- **DKGRAY_BRUSH**   Dark gray brush.

- **GRAY_BRUSH**   Gray brush.

- **HOLLOW_BRUSH** Hollow brush.

- **LTGRAY_BRUSH** Light gray brush.

- **NULL_BRUSH** Null brush.

- **WHITE_BRUSH** White brush.

- **BLACK_PEN** Black pen.

- **NULL_PEN** Null pen.

- **WHITE_PEN** White pen.

- **ANSI_FIXED_FONT** ANSI fixed system font.

- **ANSI_VAR_FONT** ANSI variable system font.

- **DEVICE_DEFAULT_FONT** Device-dependent font.

- **OEM_FIXED_FONT** OEM-dependent fixed font.

- **SYSTEM_FONT** The system font. By default, Windows uses the system font to draw menus, dialog-box controls, and other text. In Windows versions 3.0 and later, the system font is proportional width; earlier versions of Windows use a fixed-width system font.

- **SYSTEM_FIXED_FONT** The fixed-width system font used in Windows prior to version 3.0. This object is available for compatibility with earlier versions of Windows.

- **DEFAULT_PALETTE** Default color palette. This palette consists of the 20 static colors in the system palette.

Remarks

Retrieves a handle to one of the predefined stock Windows GDI pens, brushes, or fonts, and attaches the GDI object to the **CGdiObject** object. Call this function with one of the derived classes that corresponds to the Windows GDI object type, such as **CPen** for a stock pen.

See Also: **CPen::CPen, CBrush::CBrush, CFont::CFont, CPalette::CPalette**

CGdiObject::DeleteObject

BOOL DeleteObject( );

Return Value

Nonzero if the GDI object was successfully deleted; otherwise 0.

Remarks

Deletes the attached Windows GDI object from memory by freeing all system storage associated with the Windows GDI object. The storage associated with the

CGdiObject object is not affected by this call. An application should not call **DeleteObject** on a **CGdiObject** object that is currently selected into a device context.

When a pattern brush is deleted, the bitmap associated with the brush is not deleted. The bitmap must be deleted independently.

See Also: **CGdiObject::Detach**

CGdiObject::DeleteTempMap

static void PASCAL DeleteTempMap( );

Remarks

Called automatically by the **CWinApp** idle-time handler, **DeleteTempMap** deletes any temporary **CGdiObject** objects created by **FromHandle**. **DeleteTempMap** detaches the Windows GDI object attached to a temporary **CGdiObject** object before deleting the **CGdiObject** object.

See Also: **CGdiObject::Detach**, **CGdiObject::FromHandle**

CGdiObject::Detach

HGDIOBJ Detach( );

Return Value

A **HANDLE** to the Windows GDI object detached; otherwise **NULL** if no GDI object is attached.

Remarks

Detaches a Windows GDI object from a **CGdiObject** object and returns a handle to the Windows GDI object.

See Also: **CGdiObject::Attach**

CGdiObject::FromHandle

static CGdiObject* PASCAL FromHandle(HGDIOBJ *hObject*);

Return Value

A pointer to a **CGdiObject** that may be temporary or permanent.

Parameters

hObject A **HANDLE** to a Windows GDI object.

Remarks

Returns a pointer to a **CGdiObject** object given a handle to a Windows GDI object. If a **CGdiObject** object is not already attached to the Windows GDI object, a temporary **CGdiObject** object is created and attached.

This temporary **CGdiObject** object is only valid until the next time the application has idle time in its event loop, at which time all temporary graphic objects are deleted. Another way of saying this is that the temporary object is only valid during the processing of one window message.

See Also: **CGdiObject::DeleteTempMap**

CGdiObject::GetObject

int GetObject(int *nCount*, **LPVOID** *lpObject*) **const;**

Return Value

The number of bytes retrieved; otherwise 0 if an error occurs.

Parameters

nCount   Specifies the number of bytes to copy into the *lpObject* buffer.

lpObject   Points to a user-supplied buffer that is to receive the information.

Remarks

Fills a buffer with data that defines a specified object. The function retrieves a data structure whose type depends on the type of graphic object, as shown by the following list:

Object	Buffer type
CPen	**LOGPEN**
CBrush	**LOGBRUSH**
CFont	**LOGFONT**
CBitmap	**BITMAP**
CPalette	**WORD**
CRgn	Not supported

If the object is a **CBitmap** object, **GetObject** returns only the width, height, and color format information of the bitmap. The actual bits can be retrieved by using **CBitmap::GetBitmapBits**.

If the object is a **CPalette** object, **GetObject** retrieves a **WORD** that specifies the number of entries in the palette. The function does not retrieve the **LOGPALETTE** structure that defines the palette. An application can get information on palette entries by calling **CPalette::GetPaletteEntries**.

See Also: **CBitmap::GetBitmapBits**, **CPalette::GetPaletteEntries**

CGdiObject::GetObjectType

UINT GetObjectType( ) const;

Return Value

The type of the object, if successful; otherwise 0. The value can be one of the following:

- **OBJ_BITMAP** Bitmap
- **OBJ_BRUSH** Brush
- **OBJ_FONT** Font
- **OBJ_PAL** Palette
- **OBJ_PEN** Pen
- **OBJ_EXTPEN** Extended pen
- **OBJ_REGION** Region
- **OBJ_DC** Device context
- **OBJ_MEMDC** Memory device context
- **OBJ_METAFILE** Metafile
- **OBJ_METADC** Metafile device context
- **OBJ_ENHMETAFILE** Enhanced metafile
- **OBJ_ENHMETADC** Enhanced-metafile device context

Remarks

Retrieves the type of the GDI object.

See Also: **CGdiObject::GetObject, CDC::SelectObject**

CGdiObject::GetSafeHandle

HGDIOBJ GetSafeHandle( ) const;

Return Value

A **HANDLE** to the attached Windows GDI object; otherwise **NULL** if no object is attached.

Remarks

Returns **m_hObject** unless **this** is **NULL**, in which case **NULL** is returned. This is part of the general handle interface paradigm and is useful when **NULL** is a valid or special value for a handle.

CGdiObject::UnrealizeObject

BOOL UnrealizeObject( );

Return Value

Nonzero if successful; otherwise 0.

Remarks

Resets the origin of a brush or resets a logical palette. While **UnrealizeObject** is a member function of the **CGdiObject** class, it should be invoked only on **CBrush** or **CPalette** objects.

For **CBrush** objects, **UnrealizeObject** directs the system to reset the origin of the given brush the next time it is selected into a device context. If the object is a **CPalette** object, **UnrealizeObject** directs the system to realize the palette as though it had not previously been realized. The next time the application calls the **CDC::RealizePalette** function for the specified palette, the system completely remaps the logical palette to the system palette.

The **UnrealizeObject** function should not be used with stock objects. The **UnrealizeObject** function must be called whenever a new brush origin is set (by means of the **CDC::SetBrushOrg** function). The **UnrealizeObject** function must not be called for the currently selected brush or currently selected palette of any display context.

See Also: **CDC::RealizePalette**, **CDC::SetBrushOrg**

Data Members
CGdiObject::m_hObject

Remarks

A **HANDLE** containing the **HBITMAP**, **HRGN**, **HBRUSH**, **HPEN**, **HPALETTE**, or **HFONT** attached to this object.

CGopherConnection

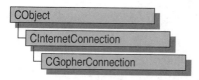

The MFC class **CGopherConnection** manages your connection to a gopher Internet server. The gopher service is one of three Internet services recognized by the MFC WinInet classes.

The class **CGopherConnection** contains a constructor and three additional member functions that manage the gopher service: **OpenFile**, **CreateLocator**, and **GetAttribute**.

To communicate with a gopher Internet server, you must first create an instance of **CInternetSession**, and then call **CInternetSession::GetGopherConnection**, which creates the **CGopherConnection** object and returns a pointer to it. You never create a **CGopherConnection** object directly.

To learn more about how **CGopherConnection** works with the other MFC Internet classes, see the article "Internet Programming with WinInet" in *Visual C++ Programmer's Guide* online. For more information about using the the the other two supported Internet services, FTP and HTTP see the classes **CHttpConnection** and **CFtpConnection**.

#include <afxinet.h>

See Also: **CFtpConnection**, **CHttpConnection**, **CInternetConnection**, **CGopherLocator**, **CGopherFile**, **CInternetSession**

CGopherConnection Class Members

Construction

CGopherConnection	Constructs a **CGopherConnection** object.

Operations

OpenFile	Opens a gopher file.
CreateLocator	Creates a **CGopherLocator** object to find files on a gopher server.
GetAttribute	Retrieves attribute information about the gopher object.

See Also: **CFtpConnection**, **CHttpConnection**, **CInternetConnection**, **CGopherFileFind**

Member Functions
CGopherConnection::CGopherConnection

CGopherConnection( );

Remarks

This member function is called to construct a **CGopherConnection** object. You never create a **CGopherConnection** directly. Rather, call **CInternetSession::GetGopherConnection**, which creates a **CGopherConnection** object and returns a pointer to it.

See Also: **CFtpConnection**, **CHttpConnection**, **CInternetConnection**

CGopherConnection::CreateLocator

CGopherLocator CreateLocator(LPCTSTR *pstrDisplayString*,
  ↳ **LPCTSTR** *pstrSelectorString*, **DWORD** *dwGopherType* **);**
static CGopherLocator CreateLocator(LPCTSTR *pstrLocator* **);**
static CGopherLocator CreateLocator(LPCTSTR *pstrServerName*,
  ↳ **LPCTSTR** *pstrDisplayString*, **LPCTSTR** *pstrSelectorString*,
  ↳ **DWORD** *dwGopherType*, **INTERNET_PORT** *nPort* =
  ↳ **INTERNET_INVALID_PORT_NUMBER** **);**

Return Value

A **CGopherLocator** object.

Parameters

pstrDisplayString   A pointer to a string containing the name of the gopher document or directory to be retrieved. If the *pstrDisplayString* parameter is **NULL**, the default directory for the gopher server is returned.

pstrSelectorString   A pointer to the selector string to be sent to the gopher server in order to retrieve an item. *pstrSelectorString* can be **NULL**.

dwGopherType   This specifies whether *pstrSelectorString* refers to a directory or document, and whether the request is gopher or gopher+. See the attributes for the structure **GOPHER_FIND_DATA** in the *ActiveX SDK*.

pstrLocator   A pointer to a string identifying the file to open. Generally, this string is returned from a call to **CGopherFileFind::GetLocator**.

pstrServerName   A pointer to a string containing the gopher server name.

nPort   The number identifying the Internet port for this connection.

Remarks

Call this member function to create a gopher locator to find or identify a file on a gopher server. The static version of the member function requires you to specify a server, while the non-static version uses the server name from the connection object.

In order to retrieve information from a gopher server, an application must first get a gopher locator. The application must then treat the locator as an opaque token (that is, the application can use the locator but not directly manipulate or compare it). Normally, the application uses the locator for calls to the **CGopherFileFind::FindFile** member function to retrieve a specific piece of information.

See Also: **CFtpConnection, CHttpConnection, CInternetConnection, CGopherLocator, CGopherFileFind**

CGopherConnection::GetAttribute

BOOL GetAttribute(LPGOPHER_ATTRIBUTE_TYPE& *lpType*,
↪ **CString** *strRequestedAttributes*, **CGopherLocator&** *refLocator* **);**

Return Value

Nonzero if successful; otherwise 0. If the call fails, the Win32 function **GetLastError** may be called to determine the cause of the error.

Parameters

lpType   A pointer to a **GOPHER_ATTRIBUTE_TYPE** structure. See the *ActiveX SDK* for more information about this structure.

strRequestedAttributes   A space-delimited string specifying the names of the requested attributes.

refLocator   A reference to a **CGopherLocator** object.

Remarks

Call this member function to retrieve specific attribute information about an item from the gopher server.

See Also: **CFtpConnection, CHttpConnection, CInternetConnection, CGopherLocator**

CGopherConnection::OpenFile

CGopherFile* OpenFile(CGopherLocator& *refLocator*, **DWORD** *dwFlags* **= 0,**
↪ **LPCTSTR** *pstrView* **= NULL, DWORD** *dwContext* **= 1);**

Return Value

A pointer to the **CGopherFile** object to be opened.

Parameters

    refLocator   A reference to a **CGopherLocator** object.

    dwFlags   Any combination of INTERNET_FLAG_* flags. See **CInternetSession::OpenUrl** for further information on INTERNET_FLAG_* flags.

    pstrView   A pointer to a file-view string. If several views of the file exist at the server, this parameter specifies which file view to open. If *pstrView* is **NULL**, the default file view is used.

    dwContext   The context ID for the file being opened. See **Remarks** for more information about *dwContext*.

Remarks

    Call this member function to open a file on a gopher server.

    Override the *dwContext* default to set the context identifier to a value of your choosing. The context identifier is associated with this specific operation of the **CGopherConnection** object created by its **CInternetSession** object. The value is returned to **CInternetSession::OnStatusCallback** to provide status on the operation with which it is identified. See the article "Internet First Steps: WinInet" in *Visual C++ Programmer's Guide* online for more information about the context identifier.

    See Also: **CFtpConnection**, **CHttpConnection**, **CInternetConnection**, **CGopherFile**, **CGopherLocator**, **CInternetSession**

CGopherFile

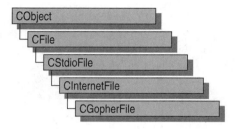

The MFC class **CGopherFile** provides the functionality to find and read files on a gopher server.

The gopher service does not allow users to write data to a gopher file because this service functions mainly as a menu-driven interface for finding information. The **CGopherFile** member functions **Write**, **WriteString**, and **Flush** are not implemented for **CGopherFile**. Calling these functions on a **CGopherFile** object, returns a **CNotSupportedException**.

To learn more about how **CGopherFile** works with the other MFC Internet classes, see the article "Internet Programming with WinInet" in *Visual C++ Programmer's Guide* online.

#include <afxinet.h>

See Also: CInternetFile, CGopherLocator, CGopherFileFind, CGopherConnection

CGopherFile Class Members

Construction

CGopherFile	Constructs a **CGopherFile** object.

Operations

Close	Closes the connection to a gopher server.

See Also: CInternetFile, CGopherLocator, CGopherFileFind, CGopherConnection

Member Functions
CGopherFile::CGopherFile

CGopherFile(HINTERNET *hFile*, **CGopherLocator&** *refLocator*,
↪ **CGopherConnection*** *pConnection*);

Parameters

hFile   A handle to an **HINTERNET** file.

refLocator   A reference to a **CGopherLocator** object.

pConnection   A pointer to a **CGopherConnection** object.

Remarks

This member function is called to construct a **CGopherFile** object.

You need a **CGopherFile** object to read from a file during a gopher Internet session.

You never create a **CGopherFile** object directly. Instead, call **CGopherConnection::OpenFile** to open a file on a gopher server.

See Also: **CInternetFile**, **CGopherLocator**, **CGopherFileFind**, **CGopherConnection**

CGopherFile::Close

virtual void Close( );

Remarks

Call this member function to close the gopher file.

See Also: **CInternetFile**, **CGopherLocator**, **CGopherFileFind**, **CGopherConnection**

CGopherFileFind

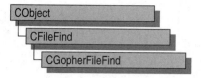

Class **CGopherFileFind** aids in Internet file searches of gopher servers. **CGopherFileFind** includes member functions that begin a search, locate a file, and return a file's URL.

Other MFC classes designed for Internet and local file searched include **CFtpFileFind** and **CFileFind**. Together with **CGopherFileFind**, these classes provide a seamless mechanism for the user to find specific files, regardless of the server protocol, file type, or location (either a local machine or a remote server.) Note that there is no MFC class for searching on HTTP servers because HTTP does not support the direct file manipulation required by searches.

Note   **CGopherFileFind** does not support the following member functions of its base class **CFileFind**:

- **GetRoot**
- **GetFileName**
- **GetFilePath**
- **GetFileTitle**
- **GetFileURL**

In addition, when used with **CGopherFileFind**, the **CFileFind** member function **IsDots** is always **FALSE**.

For more information about how to use **CGopherFileFind** and the other WinInet classes, see the article "Internet Programming with WinInet" in *Visual C++ Programmer's Guide* online.

#include <afxinet.h>

See Also: **CFtpFileFind**, **CFileFind**, **CInternetFile**, **CGopherFile**, **CHttpFile**

CGopherFileFind Class Members

Construction

CGopherFileFind	Constructs a **CGopherFileFind** object.

Attributes

FindFile	Finds a file on a gopher server.
FindNextFile	Continues a file search from a previous call to **FindFile**.
GetLocator	Get a **CGopherLocator** object.
GetScreenName	Gets the name of a gopher screen.
GetLength	Gets the length of the found file, in bytes.

See Also: **CFtpFileFind**, **CFileFind**, **CInternetFile**, **CGopherFile**, **CHttpFile**

Member Functions
CGopherFileFind::CGopherFileFind

CGopherFileFind(CGopherConnection* *pConnection***, DWORD** *dwContext* **= 1);**

Parameters

pConnection A pointer to a **CGopherConnection** object.

dwContext The context identifier for the operation. See **Remarks** for more information about *dwContext*.

Remarks

This member function is called to construct a **CGopherFileFind** object.

The default value for *dwContext* is sent by MFC to the **CGopherFileFind** object from the **CInternetSession** object that created the **CGopherFileFind** object. When you construct a **CGopherFileFind** object, you can override the default to set the context identifier to a value of your choosing. The context identifier is returned to **CInternetSession::OnStatusCallback** to provide status on the object with which it is identified. See the article "Internet First Steps: WinInet" in *Visual C++ Programmer's Guide* online for more information about the context identifier.

See Also: **CFtpFileFind**, **CFileFind**

CGopherFileFind::FindFile

virtual BOOL FindFile(CGopherLocator& *refLocator***, LPCTSTR** *pstrString***,**
  ↳ **DWORD** *dwFlags* **= INTERNET_FLAG_RELOAD);**
virtual BOOL FindFile(LPCTSTR *pstrString***,**
  ↳ **DWORD** *dwFlags* **= INTERNET_FLAG_RELOAD);**

Return Value

Nonzero if successful; otherwise 0. If the call fails, the Win32 function **GetLastError** may be called to determine the cause of the error.

Parameters

refLocator   A reference to a **CGopherLocator** object.

pstrString   A pointer to a string containing the file name.

dwFlags   The flags describing how to handle this session. The valid flags are:

- INTERNET_FLAG_RELOAD   Get the data from the remote server even if it is locally cached.

- INTERNET_FLAG_DONT_CACHE   Do not cache the data, either locally or in any gateways.

- INTERNET_FLAG_SECURE   Request secure transactions on the wire with Secure Sockets Layer or PCT. This flag is applicable to HTTP requests only.

- INTERNET_FLAG_USE_EXISTING   If possible, reuse the existing connections to the server for new **FindFile** requests, instead of creating a new session for each request.

Remarks

Call this member function to find a gopher file.

After calling **FindFile** to retrieve the first gopher object, you can call **FindNextFile** to retrieve subsequent gopher files.

See Also: **CFileFind::FindFile**

CGopherFileFind::FindNextFile

virtual BOOL FindNextFile( );

Return Value

Nonzero if successful; otherwise 0. To get extended error information, call the Win32 function **GetLastError**.

Remarks

Call this member function to continue a file search begun with a call to **CGopherFileFind::FindFile**.

See Also: **CFileFind::FindNextFile**

CGopherFileFind::GetLength

virtual DWORD GetLength( ) const;

Return Value

The length, in bytes, of the found file.

Remarks

Call this member function to get the length, in bytes, of the found file.

GetLength uses the **nFileSizeLow** member, of the Win32 structure **WIN32_FIND_DATA** to get the low-order **DWORD** value of the file size in bytes. If the file may be more than four gigabytes in size, use the **GetLength64** member.

See Also: **CFileFind**

CGopherFileFind::GetLocator

CGopherLocator GetLocator( ) const;

Return Value

A **CGopherLocator** object.

Remarks

Call this member function to get the **CGopherLocator** object that **FindFile** uses to find the gopher file.

See Also: **CGopherConnection::CreateLocator**

CGopherFileFind::GetScreenName

CString GetScreenName( ) const;

Return Value

The name of the gopher screen.

Remarks

Call this member function to get the name of the gopher screen.

CGopherLocator

The class **CGopherLocator** gets a gopher "locator" from a gopher server, determines the locator's type, and makes the locator available to **CGopherFileFind**.

An application must get a gopher server's locator before it can retrieve information from that server. Once it has the locator, it must treat the locator as an opaque token.

Each gopher locator has attributes that determine the type of file or server found. See **GetLocatorType** for a list of types of gopher locators.

An application normally uses the locator for calls to **CGopherFileFind::FindFile** to retrieve a specific piece of information.

To learn more about how **CGopherLocator** works with the other MFC Internet classes, see the article "Internet Programming with WinInet" in *Visual C++ Programmer's Guide* online.

#include <afxinet.h>

See Also: CGopherFileFind

CGopherLocator Class Members

Construction

CGopherLocator	Constructs a **CGopherLocator** object.

Attributes

GetLocatorType	Parses a gopher locator and determines its attributes.

Operators

operator LPCTSTR	Directly accesses characters stored in a **CGopherLocator** object as a C-style string.

Member Functions

CGopherLocator::CGopherLocator

CGopherLocator(const CGopherLocator& *ref* **);**

Parameters

ref A reference to a constant **CGopherLocator** object.

Remarks

This member function is called to create a **CGopherLocator** object. You never create a **CGopherLocator** object directly. Instead, call **CGopherConnection::CreateLocator** to create and return a pointer to the **CGopherLocator** object.

See Also: **CGopherFileFind**, **CGopherConnection**

CGopherLocator::GetLocatorType

BOOL GetLocatorType(DWORD& *dwRef* **) const;**

Return Value

Nonzero if successful; otherwise 0. If the call fails, the Win32 function **GetLastError** may be called to determine the cause of the error.

Parameters

dwRef A reference to a **DWORD** that will receive the locator type. See **Remarks** for a table of locator types.

Remarks

Call this member function to get the locator type. The possible types are as follows:

Value	Meaning
GOPHER_TYPE_TEXT_FILE	An ASCII text file.
GOPHER_TYPE_DIRECTORY	A directory of additional Gopher items.
GOPHER_TYPE_CSO	A CSO phone book server.
GOPHER_TYPE_ERROR	Indicates an error condition.
GOPHER_TYPE_MAC_BINHEX	A Macintosh file in BINHEX format.
GOPHER_TYPE_DOS_ARCHIVE	A DOS archive file.
GOPHER_TYPE_UNIX_UUENCODED	A UUENCODED file.
GOPHER_TYPE_INDEX_SERVER	An index server.
GOPHER_TYPE_TELNET	A Telnet Server.
GOPHER_TYPE_BINARY	A binary file.

(continued)

(continued)

Value	Meaning
GOPHER_TYPE_REDUNDANT	A duplicated server. The information contained within is a duplicate of the primary server. The primary server is the last directory entry that did not have a GOPHER_TYPE_REDUNDANT type.
GOPHER_TYPE_TN3270	A TN3270 server.
GOPHER_TYPE_GIF	A GIF graphics file.
GOPHER_TYPE_IMAGE	An image file.
GOPHER_TYPE_BITMAP	A bitmap file.
GOPHER_TYPE_MOVIE	A movie file.
GOPHER_TYPE_SOUND	A sound file.
GOPHER_TYPE_HTML	An HTML document.
GOPHER_TYPE_PDF	A PDF file.
GOPHER_TYPE_CALENDAR	A calendar file.
GOPHER_TYPE_INLINE	An inline file.
GOPHER_TYPE_UNKNOWN	The item type is unknown.
GOPHER_TYPE_ASK	An Ask+ item.
GOPHER_TYPE_GOPHER_PLUS	A Gopher+ item.

See Also: **CGopherFileFind**, **CGopherConnection**

Operators

CGopherLocator::operator LPCTSTR

operator LPCTSTR ( ) const;

Return Value

A character pointer to the string's data.

Remarks

This useful casting operator provides an efficient method to access the null-terminated C string contained in a **CGopherLocator** object. No characters are copied; only a pointer is returned.

CHeaderCtrl

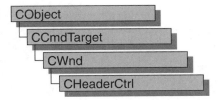

A "header control" is a window usually positioned above columns of text or numbers. It contains a title for each column, and it can be divided into parts. The user can drag the dividers that separate the parts to set the width of each column.

The **CHeaderCtrl** class provides the functionality of the Windows common header control. This control (and therefore the **CHeaderCtrl** class) is available only to programs running under Windows 95 and Windows NT version 3.51 and later.

For more information on using **CHeaderCtrl**, see Technical Note 60 online.

#include <afxcmn.h>

See Also: **CTabCtrl**, **CListCtrl**

CHeaderCtrl Class Members

Construction

CHeaderCtrl	Constructs a **CHeaderCtrl** object.
Create	Creates a header control and attaches it to a **CHeaderCtrl** object.

Attributes

GetItemCount	Retrieves a count of the items in a header control.
GetItem	Retrieves information about an item in a header control.
SetItem	Sets the attributes of the specified item in a header control.

Operations

InsertItem	Inserts a new item into a header control.
DeleteItem	Deletes an item from a header control.
Layout	Retrieves the size and position of a header control within a given rectangle.

Overridables

DrawItem	Draws the specified item of a header control.

Member Functions
CHeaderCtrl::CHeaderCtrl

CHeaderCtrl( );

Remarks

Creates a **CHeaderCtrl** object.

See Also: **CHeaderCtrl::Create**

CHeaderCtrl::Create

BOOL Create(DWORD *dwStyle*, **const RECT&** *rect*,
↪ **CWnd*** *pParentWnd*, **UINT** *nID* **);**

Return Value

Nonzero if initialization was successful; otherwise zero.

Parameters

dwStyle   Specifies the header control's style. Apply any combination of header control styles needed to the control.

rect   Specifies the header control's size and position. It can be either a **CRect** object or a **RECT** structure.

pParentWnd   Specifies the header control's parent window, usually a **CDialog**. It must not be **NULL**.

nID   Specifies the header control's ID.

Remarks

You construct a **CHeaderCtrl** object in two steps. First call the constructor, then call **Create**, which creates the header control and attaches it to the **CHeaderCtrl** object.

The following styles can be applied to a header control (see "About Header Control Styles" for more information):

- **HDS_BUTTONS**   Header items behave like buttons.
- **HDS_HORZ**   The header control is horizontal.
- **HDS_VERT**   The header control is vertical (this style is not currently implemented).
- **HDS_HIDDEN**   The header control is not visible in details mode.

In addition, you can use the following common control styles to determine how the header control positions and resizes itself (see "Common Control Styles" for more information):

- **CCS_BOTTOM** Causes the control to position itself at the bottom of the parent window's client area and sets the width to be the same as the parent window's width.

- **CCS_NODIVIDER** Prevents a two-pixel highlight from being drawn at the top of the control.

- **CCS_NOHILITE** Prevents a one-pixel highlight from being drawn at the top of the control.

- **CCS_NOMOVEY** Causes the control to resize and move itself horizontally, but not vertically, in response to a **WM_SIZE** message. If the **CCS_NORESIZE** style is used, this style does not apply. Header controls have this style by default.

- **CCS_NOPARENTALIGN** Prevents the control from automatically moving to the top or bottom of the parent window. Instead, the control keeps its position within the parent window despite changes to the size of the parent window. If the **CCS_TOP** or **CCS_BOTTOM** style is also used, the height is adjusted to the default, but the position and width remain unchanged.

- **CCS_NORESIZE** Prevents the control from using the default width and height when setting its initial size or a new size. Instead, the control uses the width and height specified in the request for creation or sizing.

- **CCS_TOP** Causes the control to position itself at the top of the parent window's client area and sets the width to be the same as the parent window's width.

You can also apply the following window styles to a header control (see "Window Styles" for more information):

- **WS_CHILD** Creates a child window. Cannot be used with the **WS_POPUP** style.

- **WS_VISIBLE** Creates a window that is initially visible.

- **WS_DISABLED** Creates a window that is initially disabled.

- **WS_GROUP** Specifies the first control of a group of controls in which the user can move from one control to the next with the arrow keys. All controls defined with the **WS_GROUP** style after the first control belong to the same group. The next control with the **WS_GROUP** style ends the style group and starts the next group (that is, one group ends where the next begins).

- **WS_TABSTOP** Specifies one of any number of controls through which the user can move by using the TAB key. The TAB key moves the user to the next control specified by the **WS_TABSTOP** style.

See Also: **CHeaderCtrl::CHeaderCtrl**

CHeaderCtrl::DeleteItem

BOOL DeleteItem(int *nPos* **);**

Return Value

Nonzero if successful; otherwise 0.

Parameters

nPos Specifies the zero-based index of the item to delete.

Remarks

Deletes an item from a header control.

See Also: CHeaderCtrl::InsertItem

CHeaderCtrl::DrawItem

void DrawItem(LPDRAWITEMSTRUCT *lpDrawItemStruct* **);**

Parameters

lpDrawItemStruct A pointer to a **DRAWITEMSTRUCT** structure describing the item to be painted.

Remarks

Called by the framework when a visual aspect of an owner-draw header control changes. The **itemAction** member of the **DRAWITEMSTRUCT** structure defines the drawing action that is to be performed.

By default, this member function does nothing. Override this member function to implement drawing for an owner-draw **CHeaderCtrl** object.

The application should restore all graphics device interface (GDI) objects selected for the display context supplied in *lpDrawItemStruct* before this member function terminates.

See Also: CWnd::OnDrawItem

CHeaderCtrl::GetItem

BOOL GetItem(int *nPos*, **HD_ITEM*** *pHeaderItem* **) const;**

Return Value

Nonzero if successful; otherwise 0.

Parameters

nPos Specifies the zero-based index of the item to retrieve.

pHeaderItem Pointer to an **HD_ITEM** structure that receives the new item. This structure is used with the **InsertItem** and **SetItem** member functions. You should set the flags in the mask element before calling to request the other elements get filled in. If **mask** is zero, no data will be returned.

Remarks

Retrieves information about a header control item.

The **HD_ITEM** structure is defined as follows:

```
typedef struct _HD_ITEM
{
    UINT    mask;
    int     cxy;            // width of item
    LPSTR   pszText;        // address of item string
    HBITMAP hbm;            // handle of item bitmap
    int     cchTextMax;     // length of item string, in characters
    int     fmt;
    LPARAM  lParam;         // application-defined item data
} HD_ITEM;
```

mask Mask flags that indicate which of the other structure members contain valid data. Can be a combination of these flags:

- **HDI_BITMAP** The **hbm** member is valid.

- **HDI_FORMAT** The **fmt** member is valid.

- **HDI_LPARAM** The **lParam** member is valid.

- **HDI_TEXT** The **pszText** and **cchTextMax** members are valid.

- **HDI_WIDTH** The **cxy** member is valid and specifies the width of the item. The **cxy** member, if it has a value, is used for the item's width, even if you do not use the **HDI_WIDTH** masks.

Note The **cxy** member can also return a height of an item if **HDI_HEIGHT** is specified in a mask. However, the header control currently cannot have vertical orientation, so **cxy** always returns a width.

fmt Format flags. Can be a combination of the following values:

- **HDF_CENTER** Center contents of item.

- **HDF_LEFT** Left justify contents of item.

- **HDF_RIGHT** Right justify contents of item.

- **HDF_BITMAP** The item displays a bitmap.

- **HDF_OWNERDRAW** The owner window of the header control draws the item.

- **HDF_STRING** The item displays a string.

See Also: CHeaderCtrl::SetItem

CHeaderCtrl::GetItemCount

int GetItemCount( ) const;

Return Value

Number of header control items if successful; otherwise −1.

Remarks

Retrieves a count of the items in a header control.

See Also: **CHeaderCtrl::GetItem**, **CHeaderCtrl::SetItem**

CHeaderCtrl::InsertItem

int InsertItem(int *nPos*, **HD_ITEM*** *phdi* **);**

Return Value

Index of the new item if successful; otherwise −1.

Parameters

nPos   The zero-based index of the item to be inserted. If the value is zero, the item is inserted at the beginning of the header control. If the value is greater than the maximum value, the item is inserted at the end of the header control.

phdi   Pointer to an **HD_ITEM** structure that contains information about the item to be inserted. For more information on this structure, see **CHeaderCtrl::GetItem**.

Remarks

Inserts a new item into a header control at the specified index.

See Also: **CHeaderCtrl::DeleteItem**, **CHeaderCtrl::GetItem**

CHeaderCtrl::Layout

BOOL Layout(HD_LAYOUT* *pHeaderLayout* **);**

Return Value

Nonzero if successful; otherwise 0.

Parameters

pHeaderLayout   Pointer to an **HD_LAYOUT** structure, which contains information used to set the size and position of a header control.

Remarks

Retrieves the size and position of a header control within a given rectangle. This function is used to determine the appropriate dimensions for a new header control that is to occupy the given rectangle.

The **HD_LAYOUT** structure is defined as follows:

```
typedef struct _HD_LAYOUT {  // hdl
    RECT FAR* prc;           // see below
    WINDOWPOS FAR* pwpos; // see below
} HD_LAYOUT;
```

prc Pointer to a **RECT** structure that contains the coordinates of the rectangle in which a header control is to be drawn.

pwpos Pointer to a **WINDOWPOS** structure that receives information about the appropriate size and position of the header control.

CHeaderCtrl::SetItem

BOOL SetItem(int *nPos*, **HD_ITEM*** *pHeaderItem* **);**

Return Value

Nonzero if successful; otherwise 0.

Parameters

nPos The zero-based index of the item to be manipulated.

pHeaderItem Pointer to an **HD_ITEM** structure that contains information about the new item. For more information on this structure, see **CHeaderCtrl::GetItem**.

Remarks

Sets the attributes of the specified item in a header control.

See Also: **CHeaderCtrl::GetItem**, **CHeaderCtrl::GetItemCount**

CHotKeyCtrl

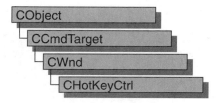

A "hot key control" is a window that enables the user to create a hot key. A "hot key" is a key combination that the user can press to perform an action quickly. (For example, a user can create a hot key that activates a given window and brings it to the top of the Z order.) The hot key control displays the user's choices and ensures that the user selects a valid key combination.

The **CHotKeyCtrl** class provides the functionality of the Windows common hot key control. This control (and therefore the **CHotKeyCtrl** class) is available only to programs running under Windows 95 and Windows NT version 3.51 and later.

When the user has chosen a key combination, the application can retrieve the specified key combination from the control and use the **WM_SETHOTKEY** message to set up the hot key in the system. Whenever the user presses the hot key thereafter, from any part of the system, the window specified in the **WM_SETHOTKEY** message receives a **WM_SYSCOMMAND** message specifying **SC_HOTKEY**. This message activates the window that receives it. The hot key remains valid until the application that called **WM_SETHOTKEY** exits.

This mechanism is different from the hot key support that depends on the **WM_HOTKEY** message and the Windows **RegisterHotKey** and **UnregisterHotKey** functions.

For more information on using **CHotKeyCtrl**, see Technical Note 60 online.

#include <afxcmn.h>

CHotKeyCtrl Class Members

Construction

CHotKeyCtrl	Constructs a **CHotKeyCtrl** object.
Create	Creates a hot key control and attaches it to a **CHotKeyCtrl** object.

Attributes

SetHotKey	Sets the hot key combination for a hot key control.
GetHotKey	Retrieves the virtual-key code and modifier flags of a hot key from a hot key control.

Operations

SetRules	Defines the invalid combinations and the default modifier combination for a hot key control.

Member Functions

CHotKeyCtrl::CHotKeyCtrl

> **CHotKeyCtrl( );**

Remarks

Constructs a **CHotKeyCtrl** object.

See Also: CHotKeyCtrl::Create

CHotKeyCtrl::Create

> **BOOL Create(DWORD** *dwStyle***, const RECT&** *rect***,**
> ↳ **CWnd*** *pParentWnd***, UINT** *nID* **);**

Return Value

Nonzero, if initialization was successful; otherwise 0.

Parameters

dwStyle   Specifies the hot key control's style. Apply any combination of control styles.

rect   Specifies the hot key control's size and position. It can be either a **CRect** object or a **RECT** structure.

pParentWnd   Specifies the hot key control's parent window, usually a **CDialog**. It must not be **NULL**.

nID   Specifies the hot key control's ID.

Remarks

You construct a **CHotKeyCtrl** object in two steps. First call the constructor, then call **Create**, which creates the hot key control and attaches it to the **CHotKeyCtrl** object.

See Also: CHotKeyCtrl::CHotKeyCtrl

CHotKeyCtrl::GetHotKey

DWORD GetHotKey( ) const;
void GetHotKey(WORD &*wVirtualKeyCode***, WORD &***wModifiers* **) const;**

Return Value

In the first usage above, a **DWORD** containing the virtual-key code and modifier flags. The low-order byte is the virtual-key code, and the high-order byte is the modifier flags. The 16-bit value can be used as the parameter in the **SetHotKey** member function.

Parameters

wVirtualKeyCode   Virtual-key code of the hot key.

wModifiers   Modifier flags indicating the keys that, when used in combination with *wVirtualKeyCode*, define a hot key combination.

Remarks

Call this function to retrieve the virtual-key code and modifier flags of a hot key from a hot key control.

The modifier flags can be a combination of the following values:

- **HOTKEYF_ALT**   ALT key
- **HOTKEYF_CONTROL**   CTRL key
- **HOTKEYF_EXT**   Extended key
- **HOTKEYF_SHIFT**   SHIFT key

See Also: CHotKeyCtrl::SetHotKey

CHotKeyCtrl::SetHotKey

void SetHotKey(WORD *wVirtualKeyCode***, WORD** *wModifiers* **);**

Parameters

wVirtualKeyCode   Virtual-key code of the hot key.

wModifiers   Modifier flags indicating the keys that, when used in combination with *wVirtualKeyCode*, define a hot key combination. For more information on the modifier flags, see **GetHotKey**.

Remarks

Call this function to set the hot key combination for a hot key control.

See Also: CHotKeyCtrl::GetHotKey

CHotKeyCtrl::SetRules

void SetRules(WORD *wInvalidComb***, WORD** *wModifiers* **);**

Parameters

wInvalidComb   Array of flags that specifies invalid key combinations. It can be a combination of the following values:

- **HKCOMB_A**   ALT

- **HKCOMB_C**   CTRL

- **HKCOMB_CA**   CTRL+ALT

- **HKCOMB_NONE**   Unmodified keys

- **HKCOMB_S**   SHIFT

- **HKCOMB_SA**   SHIFT+ALT

- **HKCOMB_SC**   SHIFT+CTRL

- **HKCOMB_SCA**   SHIFT+CTRL+ALT

wModifiers   Array of flags that specifies the key combination to use when the user enters an invalid combination. For more information on the modifier flags, see **GetHotKey**.

Remarks

Call this function to define the invalid combinations and the default modifier combination for a hot key control. When a user enters an invalid key combination, as defined by flags specified in *wInvalidComb*, the system uses the OR operator to combine the keys entered by the user with the flags specified in *wModifiers*. The resulting key combination is converted into a string and then displayed in the hot key control.

See Also: CHotKeyCtrl::GetHotKey, CHotKeyCtrl::SetHotKey

CHtmlStream

CHtmlStream does not have a base class.

CHtmlStream is a class that manages in-memory HTML. HTML memory files are useful for temporarily storing raw bytes or serialized objects prior to their transmission. Although it is not derived from **CFile**, **CHtmlStream** behaves like the **CFile**–derived class **CMemFile**, except **CHtmlStream** is used to store data in a temporary buffer prior to sending it out, and the data stored in a **CHtmlStream** memory file cannot be read.

CHtmlStream objects usually are created automatically and handed to you by **CHttpServer::ConstructStream**; however, you can override **CHttpServer::ConstructStream** and provide your own special functionality.

CHtmlStream objects can automatically allocate their own memory or you can attach your own memory block to the **CHtmlStream** object by calling **Attach**. In either case, memory for growing the memory file automatically is allocated in *nGrowBytes*-sized increments if *nGrowBytes* is not zero. Set *nGrowBytes* with a parameter to the constructor.

The memory will automatically be deleted upon destruction of the **CHtmlStream** object if the memory was originally allocated by the **CHtmlStream** object; otherwise, you are responsible for deallocating the memory you attached to the object.

CHtmlStream uses the run-time library functions **malloc**, **realloc**, and **free** to allocate, reallocate, and deallocate memory; and the intrinsic **memcpy** to block copy memory when growing the buffer. To change this behavior or the behavior when **CHtmlStream** grows a file, derive your own class from **CHtmlStream** and override the appropriate functions.

#include <afxisapi.h>

See Also: **CHttpServer**, **CHttpFilter**

CHtmlStream Class Members

Data Members

m_nStreamSize	Contains the size of the stream.

Construction

CHtmlStream	Constructs a **CHtmlStream** object.

Operations

Attach	Attaches a block of memory to **CHtmlStream**.
GetStreamSize	Gets the size of the **CHtmlStream**.
Close	Closes the stream and frees the buffer.
InitStream	Initializes a stream associated with a **CHtmlStream** object.

Overridables

Abort	Ends a stream and ignores all warnings and errors.
Reset	empties a **CHtmlStream** object.
Alloc	allocates memory in a **CHtmlStream** object.
Realloc	reallocates memory in a **CHtmlStream** object.
Memcpy	Copies memory to grow a **CHtmlStream** object.
Free	frees memory in a **CHtmlStream** object.
Detach	closes the **CHtmlStream**.
GrowStream	Grows a **CHtmlStream** object.
Write	Writes data from the buffer to the current stream.

Operators

operator <<	Writes data into a stream.

Member Functions

CHtmlStream::Abort

virtual void Abort( );

Remarks

Called by the framework to end the stream and make the **CHtmlStream** unavailable for writing.

Use **Abort** to clean up the stream after a catastrophic error. Use **Reset** to erase the content of the stream if you plan to write to it again.

Override this member function to implement custom cleanup.

See Also: **CHtmlStream::Reset, CHtmlStream::Close**

CHtmlStream::Alloc

virtual BYTE* Alloc(DWORD *nBytes*);

Return Value

A pointer to the memory block that was allocated, or **NULL** if the allocation failed.

Parameters

nBytes   Number of bytes of memory to be allocated.

Remarks

Called by the framework to allocate memory. Override this function to implement custom memory allocation. If you override this function, override **Free**, too.

The default implementation uses the run-time library function **malloc** to allocate memory.

See Also: **CHtmlStream::Realloc**

CHtmlStream::Attach

> **void Attach(BYTE*** *lpBuffer*, **UINT** *nBufferSize*, **UINT** *nGrowBytes* = **0**);

Parameters

lpBuffer   Pointer to the buffer to be attached to **CHtmlStream**.

nBufferSize   An integer that specifies the size of the buffer in bytes.

nGrowBytes   The memory allocation increment in bytes.

Remarks

Call this function to attach a block of memory to **CHtmlStream**. This causes **CHtmlStream** to use the block of memory as the memory file.

If *nGrowBytes* is 0, **CHtmlStream** will set the file length to *nBufferSize*. This means that the data in the memory block before it was attached to **CHtmlStream** will be used as the file data. Memory files created in this manner cannot be grown.

Because the file cannot be grown, be careful not to cause **CHtmlStream** to attempt to grow the file. Don't use **operator <<** to add data.

See Also: **CHtmlStream::Detach**

CHtmlStream::CHtmlStream

> **CHtmlStream(UINT** *nGrowBytes* = **4096**);
> **CHtmlStream(BYTE*** *lpBuffer*, **UINT** *nBufferSize*, **UINT** *nGrowBytes* = **0**);

Parameters

nGrowBytes   The memory allocation increment in bytes.

lpBuffer   Pointer to a buffer that receives information of the size *nBufferSize*.

nBufferSize   An integer that specifies the size of the file buffer, in bytes.

Remarks

This member function is called by the framework during the construction of a **CHtmlStream** object.

Normally, a **CHtmlStream** object is created automatically and handed to you by **CHttpServer::ConstructStream**. You can change the behavior of the **CHtmlStream** object associated with a **CHttpServerContext** object by overriding **CHttpServer::ConstructStream**. For example, you might want to set *nGrowBytes* to a specific value. Use caution if you set *nGrowBytes*, because it will affect the performance of your code. The *nGrowBytes* parameter tells MFC how rapidly to increase the memory block associated with the stream. If the value is large, your code will be faster, but it will waste memory. If the value is small, your code will use less memory, but it will waste time by allocating memory more frequently.

See Also: **CHtmlStream::InitStream**, **CHtmlStream::Attach**, **CHtmlStream::Alloc**

CHtmlStream::Close

virtual void Close( );

Remarks

Called by the framework to close the HTML stream and free the buffer.

Override this member function to perform an action before the HTML stream is closed.

See Also: **CHtmlStream::Abort**, **CHtmlStream::Reset**

CHtmlStream::Detach

BYTE* Detach( );

Return Value

A pointer to the memory block that contains the contents of the HTML stream.

Remarks

Call this function to get a pointer to the memory block being used by **CHtmlStream**.

Calling this function also closes the **CHtmlStream**. You can reattach the memory block to **CHtmlStream** by calling **Attach**. If you want to reattach the file and use the data in it, you should call **GetStreamSize** to get the length of the file before calling **Detach**. Note that if you attach a memory block to **CHtmlStream** so that you can use its data (*nGrowBytes* == 0), then you will not be able to grow the memory.

See Also: **CHtmlStream::Attach**

CHtmlStream::Free

virtual void Free(BYTE* *lpMem* **);**

Parameters

lpMem   Pointer to the memory to be deallocated.

Remarks

Called by the framework to free memory. Override this function to implement custom memory deallocation. If you override this function, you will probably want to override **Alloc** and **Realloc** as well.

See Also: CHtmlStream::Alloc, CHtmlStream::Realloc

CHtmlStream::GetStreamSize

DWORD GetStreamSize( ) const;

Return Value

The length of the file.

Remarks

Call this member function to obtain the size of the HTML stream in bytes.

See Also: CHtmlStream::m_nStreamSize, CHtmlStream::GrowStream

---

CHtmlStream::GrowStream

virtual void GrowStream(DWORD *dwNewLen* **);**

Parameters

dwNewLen   New size of the memory file.

Remarks

Called by the framework to expand memory. You can override it if you want to change how **CHtmlStream** expands its memory. The default implementation calls **Realloc** to increase an existing block (or **Alloc** to create a memory block), allocating memory in multiples of the *nGrowBytes* value specified in the constructor or **Attach** call.

See Also: CHtmlStream::m_nStreamSize, CHtmlStream::GetStreamSize

CHtmlStream::InitStream

virtual void InitStream( );

Remarks

Called by the framework to initialize a **CHtmlStream**. Override **InitStream** to implement per-instance initialization. For example, override this function to specify HTML headers that you always need.

See Also: **CHtmlStream::CHtmlStream**

CHtmlStream::Memcpy

virtual BYTE* Memcpy(BYTE* *lpMemTarget*, **const BYTE*** *lpMemSource*, **UINT** *nBytes* **);**

Return Value

A copy of *lpMemTarget*.

Parameters

lpMemTarget   Pointer to the memory block into which the source memory will be copied.

lpMemSource   Pointer to the source memory block.

nBytes   Number of bytes to be copied.

Remarks

Called by the framework to transfer data to and from the stream. Override this function if you want to change the way that **CHtmlStream** does these memory copies.

CHtmlStream::Realloc

virtual BYTE* Realloc(BYTE* *lpMem*, **DWORD** *nBytes* **);**

Return Value

A pointer to the memory block that was reallocated (and possibly moved), or **NULL** if the reallocation failed.

Parameters

lpMem   A pointer to the memory block to be reallocated.

nBytes   New size for the memory block.

Remarks

Called by the framework to reallocate memory. Override this function to implement custom memory reallocation. If you override this function, you'll probably want to override **Alloc** and **Free** as well.

See Also: **CHtmlStream::Free**, **CHtmlStream::Alloc**

CHtmlStream::Reset

virtual void Reset( );

Remarks

Called by the framework to empty a previously initialized **CHtmlStream** object. Override this member function to require a special action before emptying a **CHtmlStream** object.

See Also: **CHtmlStream::Close**, **CHtmlStream::Abort**

CHtmlStream::Write

virtual void Write(const void* *lpBuf*, **UINT** *nCount* **);**

Parameters

lpBuf A pointer to the user-supplied buffer that contains the data to be written to the stream.

nCount The number of bytes to be transferred from the buffer.

Remarks

Called by the framework to write data from a buffer to the stream associated with the **CHtmlStream** object.

See Also: **CHtmlStream::operator <<**

Operators
CHtmlStream::operator <<

CHtmlStream& operator<<(LPCTSTR *psz* **);**
CHtmlStream& operator<<(short int *w* **);**
CHtmlStream& operator<<(long int *dw* **);**
CHtmlStream& operator<<(const CHtmlStream& *stream* **);**
CHtmlStream& operator<<(double *d* **);**
CHtmlStream& operator<<(float *f* **);**
CHtmlStream& operator<<(const CByteArray& *array* **);**
CHtmlStream& operator<<(const CLongBinary& *blob* **);**

Remarks

The **CHtmlStream** insertion (<<) operator writes the specified string or integer to the HTML stream. The string version of the operator writes the string without modification. The integer override versions of the operator format the value as decimal text before writing it.

You can use the **CHtmlStream&** override of this function to append the content of one HTML stream to another.

See Also: **CHtmlStream::Write**

Data Members

CHtmlStream::m_nStreamSize

Remarks

Contains the size for an HTML stream. **m_nStreamSize** is a protected variable of type **UINT**. Only reference this variable if you want to override functions like **Alloc** and **Free** and **GrowStream**.

See Also: **CHtmlStream::GetStreamSize**, **CHtmlStream::GrowStream**

CHttpConnection

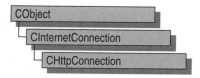

The MFC class **CHttpConnection** manages your connection to an HTTP server. HTTP is one of three Internet server protocols implemented by the MFC WinInet classes.

The class **CHttpConnection** contains a constructor and one member function, **OpenRequest**, that manages connections to a server with an HTTP protocol.

To communicate with an HTTP server, you must first create an instance of **CInternetSession**, and then create a **CHttpConnection** object. You never create a **CHttpConnection** object directly; rather, call **CInternetSession::GetHttpConnection**, which creates the **CHttpConnection** object and returns a pointer to it.

To learn more about how **CHttpConnection** works with the other MFC Internet classes, see the article "Internet Programming with WinInet" in *Visual C++ Programmer's Guide* online. For more information about connecting to servers using the other two supported Internet protocols, gopher and FTP, see the classes **CGopherConnection** and **CFtpConnection**.

#include <afxinet.h>

See Also: **CInternetConnection**, **CHttpFile**

CHttpConnection Class Members

Construction

CHttpConnection	Creates a **CHttpConnection** object.

Operations

OpenRequest	Opens an HTTP request.

See Also: **CFtpConnection**, **CGopherConnection**, **CInternetConnection**, **CHttpFile**

Member Functions
CHttpConnection::CHttpConnection

CHttpConnection( );

Remarks

This member function is called to construct a **CHttpConnection** object. You never create a **CHttpConnection** directly. Rather, you create an object by calling **CInternetSession::GetHttpConnection**.

See Also: **CInternetSession::GetHttpConnection**, **CFtpConnection**, **CGopherConnection**, **CInternetConnection**

CHttpConnection::OpenRequest

CHttpFile* OpenRequest(LPCTSTR *pstrVerb***, LPCTSTR** *pstrObjectName***,**
    ↳ **LPCTSTR** *pstrReferer* = **NULL, DWORD** *dwContext* = **1,**
    ↳ **LPCTSTR*** *pstrAcceptTypes* = **NULL, LPCTSTR** *pstrVersion* = **NULL,**
    ↳ **DWORD** *dwFlags* = **INTERNET_FLAG_EXISTING_CONNECT);**
CHttpFile* OpenRequest(int *nVerb***, LPCTSTR** *pstrObjectName***,**
    ↳ **LPCTSTR** *pstrReferer* = **NULL, DWORD** *dwContext* = **1,**
    ↳ **LPCTSTR*** *pstrAcceptTypes* = **NULL, LPCTSTR** *pstrVersion* = **NULL,**
    ↳ **DWORD** *dwFlags* = **INTERNET_FLAG_EXISTING_CONNECT);**

Return Value

A pointer to the **CHttpFile** object requested.

Parameters

pstrVerb A pointer to a string containing the verb to use in the request. If **NULL**, "GET" is used.

pstrObjectName A pointer to a string containing the target object of the specified verb. This is generally a filename, an executable module, or a search specifier.

pstrReferer A pointer to a string that specifies the address (URL) of the document from which the URL in the request (*pstrObjectName*) was obtained. If **NULL**, no HTTP header is specified.

dwContext The context identifier for the **OpenRequest** operation. See **Remarks** for more information about *dwContext*.

pstrAcceptTypes A pointer to a null-terminated string indicating content types accepted by the client. If the string is **NULL**, the servers interpret that the client only accepts documents of type "text/*" (that is, only text documents and not pictures or other binary files). The content type is equivalent to the CGI variable CONTENT_TYPE, which identifies the type of data for queries that have attached information, such as HTTP POST and PUT.

pstrVersion A pointer to a string defining the HTTP version. If **NULL**, "HTTP/1.0" is used.

dwFlags Any combination of the INTERNET_ FLAG_* flags. See the **Remarks** for a description of possible *dwFlags* values.

nVerb A number associated with the HTTP request type. Can be one of the following:

HTTP request type	*nVerb* value
HTTP_VERB_POST	0
HTTP_VERB_GET	1
HTTP_VERB_HEAD	2
HTTP_VERB_PUT	3
HTTP_VERB_LINK	4
HTTP_VERB_DELETE	5
HTTP_VERB_UNLINK	6

Remarks

Call this member function to open an HTTP connection.

dwFlags can be one of the following:

Internet flag	Description
INTERNET_FLAG_RELOAD	Forces a download of the requested file, object, or directory listing from the origin server, not from the cache.
INTERNET_FLAG_DONT_CACHE	Does not add the returned entity to the cache.
INTERNET_FLAG_MAKE_PERSISTENT	Adds the returned entity to the cache as a persistent entity. This means that standard cache cleanup, consistency checking, or garbage collection cannot remove this item from the cache.
INTERNET_FLAG_SECURE	Uses secure transaction semantics. This translates to using SSL/PCT and is only meaningful in HTTP requests
INTERNET_FLAG_NO_AUTO_REDIRECT	Used only with HTTP, specifies that redirections should not be automatically handled in **CHttpFile::SendRequest**.

Override the *dwContext* default to set the context identifier to a value of your choosing. The context identifier is associated with this specific operation of the **CHttpConnection** object created by its **CInternetSession** object. The value is returned to **CInternetSession::OnStatusCallback** to provide status on the operation with which it is identified. See the article "Internet First Steps: WinInet" online for more information about the context identifier.

See Also: **CHttpFile**, **CInternetSession**, **CFtpConnection**, **CGopherConnection**, **CInternetConnection**

CHttpFile

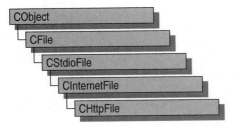

The class **CHttpFile** provides the functionality to request and read files on an HTTP server.

If your Internet session reads data from an HTTP server, you must create an instance of **CHttpFile**.

To learn more about how **CHttpFile** works with the other MFC Internet classes, see the article "Internet Programming with WinInet" in *Visual C++ Programmer's Guide* online.

#include <afxinet.h>

See Also: **CInternetFile**, **CGopherFile**, **CHttpConnection**

CHttpFile Class Members

Construction

CHttpFile	Creates a **CHttpFile** object.

Attributes

AddRequestHeaders	Adds headers to the request sent to an HTTP server.
SendRequest	Sends a request to an HTTP server.
QueryInfo	Returns the response or request headers from the HTTP server.
QueryInfoStatusCode	Retrieves the status code associated with an HTTP request and places it in the supplied *dwStatusCode* parameter.
GetVerb	Gets the verb that was used in a request to an HTTP server.
GetObject	Gets the target object of the verb in a request to an HTTP server.
GetFileURL	Gets the URL for the specified file.
Close	Closes the **CHttpFile** and frees its resources.

See Also: **CInternetFile**, **CGopherFile**, **CHttpConnection**

Member Functions
CHttpFile::AddRequestHeaders

BOOL AddRequestHeaders(LPCTSTR *pstrHeaders***, DWORD** *dwFlags* **=**
↪ **HTTP_ADDREQ_FLAG_ADD_IF_NEW, int** *dwHeadersLen* **= -1);**
BOOL AddRequestHeaders(CString& *str***, DWORD** *dwFlags* **=**
↪ **HTTP_ADDREQ_FLAG_ADD_IF_NEW);**

Return Value

Nonzero if successful; otherwise 0. If the call fails, the Win32 function **GetLastError**
may be called to determine the cause of the error.

Parameters

pstrHeaders   A pointer to a string containing the header or headers to append to the
request. Each header must be terminated by a CR/LF pair.

dwFlags   Modifies the semantics of the new headers. Can be one of the following:

- **HTTP_ADDREQ_FLAG_COALESCE**   Merges headers of the same name,
  using the flag to add the first header found to the subsequent header. For
  example, "Accept: text/*" followed by "Accept: audio/*" results in the
  formation of the single header "Accept: text/*, audio/*". It is up to the calling
  application to ensure a cohesive scheme with respect to data received by
  requests sent with coalesced or separate headers.

- **HTTP_ADDREQ_FLAG_REPLACE**   Performs a remove and add to replace
  the current header. The header name will be used to remove the current header,
  and the full value will be used to add the new header. If the header-value is
  empty and the header is found, it is removed. If not empty, the header-value is
  replaced.

- **HTTP_ADDREQ_FLAG_ADD_IF_NEW**   Only adds the header if it does
  not already exist. If one exists, an error is returned.

- **HTTP_ADDREQ_FLAG_ADD**   Used with REPLACE. Adds the header if it
  doesn't exist.

dwHeadersLen   The length, in characters, of *pstrHeaders*. If this is −1L, then
pstrHeaders is assumed to be zero-terminated and the length is computed.

str   A reference to a **CString** object containing the request header or headers to be
added.

Remarks

Call this member function to add one or more HTTP request headers to the HTTP
request handle.

AddRequestHeaders appends additional, free-format headers to the HTTP request handle. It is intended for use by sophisticated clients who need detailed control over the exact request sent to the HTTP server.

Note The application can pass multiple headers in *pstrHeaders* or *str* for an **AddRequestHeaders** call using **HTTP_ADDREQ_FLAG_ADD** or **HTTP_ADDREQ_FLAG_ADD_IF_NEW**. If the application tries to remove or replace a header using **HTTP_ADDREQ_FLAG_REMOVE** or **HTTP_ADDREQ_FLAG_REPLACE**, only one header can be supplied in *lpszHeaders*.

See Also: CInternetFile

CHttpFile::CHttpFile

CHttpFile(HINTERNET *hFile*, **HINTERNET** *hSession*, **LPCTSTR** *pstrObject*,
  ➥ **LPCTSTR** *pstrServer*, **LPCTSTR** *pstrVerb*, **DWORD** *dwContext*);
CHttpFile(HINTERNET *hFile*, **LPCTSTR** *pstrVerb*, **LPCTSTR** *pstrObject*,
  ➥ **CHttpConnection*** *pConnection*);

Parameters

hFile   A handle to an Internet file.

hSession   A handle to an Internet session.

pstrObject   A pointer to a string containing the **CHttpFile** object.

pstrServer   A pointer to a string containing the name of the server.

pstrVerb   A pointer to a string containing the method to be used when sending the request. Can be **POST**, **HEAD**, or **GET**.

dwContext   The context identifier for the **CHttpFile** object. See **Remarks** for more information about this parameter.

pConnection   A pointer to a **CHttpConnection** object.

Remarks

This member function is called to construct a **CHttpFile** object.

You never construct a **CHttpFile** object directly; rather call **CInternetSession::OpenURL** or **CHttpConnection::OpenRequest** instead.

The default value for *dwContext* is sent by MFC to the **CHttpFile** object from the **CInternetSession** object that created the **CHttpFile** object. When you call **CInternetSession::OpenURL** or **CHttpConnection** to construct a **CHttpFile** object, you can override the default to set the context identifier to a value of your choosing. The context identifier is returned to **CInternetSession::OnStatusCallback** to provide status on the object with which it is identified. See the article "Internet First Steps: WinInet" online for more information about the context identifier.

See Also: CInternetFile

CHttpFile::Close

virtual void Close( );

Remarks

Closes a **CHttpFile** and frees its resources. Use this member function only after a successful call to **SendRequest** or on a **CHttpFile** object successfully created by **OpenURL**.

See Also: **CInternetFile**

CHttpFile::GetFileURL

virtual CString GetFileURL( ) const;

Return Value

A **CString** object containing a URL referencing the resource associated with this file.

Remarks

Call this member function to get the name of the HTTP file as a URL. Use this member function only after a successful call to **SendRequest** or on a **CHttpFile** object successfully created by **OpenURL**.

See Also: **CInternetFile**

CHttpFile::GetObject

CString GetObject( ) const;

Return Value

A **CString** object containing the name of the object.

Remarks

Call this member function to get the name of the object associated with this **CHttpFile**. Use this member function only after a successful call to **SendRequest** or on a **CHttpFile** object successfully created by **OpenURL**.

See Also: **CInternetFile**

CHttpFile::GetVerb

CString GetVerb( ) const;

Return Value

A **CString** object containing the name of the HTTP verb (or method).

Remarks

Call this member function to get the HTTP verb (or method) associated with this **CHttpFile**. Use this member function only after a successful call to **SendRequest** or on a **CHttpFile** object successfully created by **OpenURL**.

See Also: **CInternetFile**

CHttpFile::QueryInfo

BOOL QueryInfo(DWORD *dwInfoLevel*, **LPVOID** *lpvBuffer*,
↪ **LPDWORD** *lpdwBufferLength*, **LPDWORD** *lpdwIndex* = **NULL**) **const**;
BOOL QueryInfo(DWORD *dwInfoLevel*, **CString&** *str*,
↪ **LPDWORD** *dwIndex* = **NULL**) **const**;
BOOL QueryInfo(DWORD *dwInfoLevel*, **SYSTEMTIME*** *pSysTime*,
↪ **LPDWORD** *dwIndex* = **NULL**) **const**;

Return Value

Nonzero if successful; otherwise 0. If the call fails, the Win32 function **GetLastError** may be called to determine the cause of the error.

Parameters

dwInfoLevel   A combination of the attribute to query and the following flags that specify the type of information requested:

- **HTTP_QUERY_CUSTOM**   Finds the header name and returns this value in *lpvBuffer* on output. **HTTP_QUERY_CUSTOM** throws an assertion if the header isn't found.

- **HTTP_QUERY_FLAG_REQUEST_HEADERS**   Typically, the application queries the response headers, but an application can also query request headers by using this flag.

- **HTTP_QUERY_FLAG_SYSTEMTIME**   For those headers whose value is a date/time string, such as "Last-Modified-Time," this flag returns the header value as a standard Win32 **SYSTEMTIME** structure that does not require the application to parse the data. If you use this flag, you may want to use the **SYSTEMTIME** override of the function.

- **HTTP_QUERY_FLAG_NUMBER**   For those headers whose value is a number, such as the status code, this flag returns the data as a 32-bit number.

lpvBuffer   A pointer to the buffer that receives the information.

lpdwBufferLength   On entry, this points to a value containing the length of the data buffer, in number of characters or bytes. See the **Remarks** section for more detailed information about this parameter.

lpdwIndex　A pointer to a zero-based header index. Can be **NULL**. Use this flag to enumerate multiple headers with the same name. On input, *lpdwIndex* indicates the index of the specified header to return. On output, *lpdwIndex* indicates the index of the next header. If the next index cannot be found, **ERROR_HTTP_HEADER_NOT_FOUND** is returned. See the **Remarks** section for a table of the possible values.

str　A reference to the **CString** object receiving the returned information.

dwIndex　An index value. See *lpdwIndex*.

pSysTime　A pointer to a Win32 **SYSTEMTIME** structure.

Remarks

Call this member function to return response or request headers from an HTTP request. Use this member function only after a successful call to **SendRequest** or on a **CHttpFile** object successfully created by **OpenURL**.

You can retrieve the following types of data from **QueryInfo**:

- strings (default)
- **SYSTEMTIME** (for "Data:" "Expires:" etc, headers)
- **DWORD** (for **STATUS_CODE**, **CONTENT_LENGTH**, etc.)

When a string is written to the buffer, and the member function succeeds, *lpdwBufferLength* contains the length of the string in characters minus 1 for the terminating **NULL** character.

The possible *lpdwIndex* or *dwIndex* values include:

- **HTTP_QUERY_MIME_VERSION**
- **HTTP_QUERY_CONTENT_TYPE**
- **HTTP_QUERY_CONTENT_TRANSFER_ENCODING**
- **HTTP_QUERY_CONTENT_ID**
- **HTTP_QUERY_CONTENT_DESCRIPTION**
- **HTTP_QUERY_CONTENT_LENGTH**
- **HTTP_QUERY_ALLOWED_METHODS**
- **HTTP_QUERY_PUBLIC_METHODS**
- **HTTP_QUERY_DATE**
- **HTTP_QUERY_EXPIRES**
- **HTTP_QUERY_LAST_MODIFIED**
- **HTTP_QUERY_MESSAGE_ID**
- **HTTP_QUERY_URI**

- **HTTP_QUERY_DERIVED_FROM**
- **HTTP_QUERY_LANGUAGE**
- **HTTP_QUERY_COST**
- **HTTP_QUERY_WWW_LINK**
- **HTTP_QUERY_PRAGMA**
- **HTTP_QUERY_VERSION**
- **HTTP_QUERY_STATUS_CODE**
- **HTTP_QUERY_STATUS_TEXT**
- **HTTP_QUERY_RAW_HEADERS**
- **HTTP_QUERY_RAW_HEADERS_CRLF**

See Also: **CInternetFile**, **CHttpConnection::OpenRequest**, **CFtpConnection**, **CGopherConnection**, **CInternetConnection**

CHttpFile::QueryInfoStatusCode

BOOL QueryInfoStatusCode(DWORD& *dwStatusCode* **) const;**

Return Value

Nonzero if successful; otherwise 0. If the call fails, the Win32 function **GetLastError** may be called to determine the cause of the error.

Parameters

dwStatusCode   A reference to a status code. Status codes indicate the success or failure of the requested event. See **Remarks** for a selection of status code descriptions.

Remarks

Call this member function to get the status code associated with an HTTP request and place it in the supplied *dwStatusCode* parameter. Use this member function only after a successful call to **SendRequest** or on a **CHttpFile** object successfully created by **OpenURL**.

HTTP status codes fall into groups indicating the success or failure of the request. The following tables outline the status code groups and the most common HTTP status codes.

Group	Meaning
200-299	Success
300-399	Information
400-499	Request error
500-599	Server error

Common HTTP Status Codes:

Status code	Meaning
200	URL located, transmission follows
400	Unintelligble request
404	Requested URL not found
405	Server does not support requested method
500	Unknown server error
503	Server capacity reached

See Also: CInternetFile

CHttpFile::SendRequest

BOOL SendRequest(LPCTSTR *pstrHeaders* **= NULL, DWORD** *dwHeadersLen* **= 0,**
↪ **LPVOID** *lpOptional* **= NULL, DWORD** *dwOptionalLen* **= 0);**
throw (CInternetException)
BOOL SendRequest(CString& *strHeaders*, **LPVOID** *lpOptional* **= NULL,**
↪ **DWORD** *dwOptionalLen* **= 0);**
throw (CInternetException)

Return Value

Nonzero if successful; otherwise 0. If the call fails, determine the cause of the failure by examining the thrown **CInternetException** object.

Parameters

pstrHeaders   A pointer to a string containing the name of the headers to send.

dwHeadersLen   The length of the headers identified by *pstrHeaders*.

lpOptional   Any optional data to send immediately after the request headers. This is generally used for **POST** and **PUT** operations. This can be **NULL** if there is no optional data to send.

dwOptionalLen   The length of *lpOptional*.

strHeaders   A string containing the name of the headers for the request being sent.

Remarks

Call this member function to send a request to an HTTP server.

See Also: CInternetFile

CHttpFilter

CHttpFilter does not have a base class.

CHttpFilter creates and manages, with **CHttpFilterContext**, a Hypertext Transfer Protocol (HTTP) filter object. An HTTP filter is a replaceable dynamic link library (DLL) that the server calls on every HTTP request. When the filter is loaded, it tells the server what sort of notifications it is interested in. After that, whenever the selected events occur, the filter is called and given the opportunity to process that event.

ISAPI (Internet Server API) filters are powerful enough to allow for the following applications:

1. Custom authentication schemes

2. Compression

3. Encryption

4. Logging

5. Traffic analysis or other request analysis

Multiple filters can be installed. The notification order is based on the priority specified by the filter and then the load order in the registry for any ties. Consult your filter's documentation to see exactly how to install your filter.

Note Once a filter begins processing a request, it will receive the data regardless of whether the request is for a file, a CGI (Common Gateway Interface) application or an ISAPI application.

The filter applications sit between the network connection to the client and the HTTP server. Depending on the options that the filter application chooses, it can act on several server actions, including reading raw data from the client, processing the headers, communications over a secure port (PCT—Personal Communications Technology, SSL— Secure Sockets Layer, and others), or several other stages in the processing of the HTTP request.

To set the filter notifications that your filter will use, see **GetFilterVersion**.

For more information on Internet filters, see "ISAPI Extensions: Filters" in *Visual C++ Programmer's Guide* online. For information about creating an Internet filter with ISAPI Extension Wizard, see "Steps to Create a Typical ISAPI Filter" in *Visual C++ Programmer's Guide* online.

#include <afxisapi.h>

See Also: **CHttpFilterContext**, **CHttpServer**, **CHttpServerContext**

CHttpFilter Class Members

Construction

CHttpFilter	Constructs a **CHttpFilter** object.

Attributes

GetFilterVersion	Gets the version of the filter after the **CHttpFilter** object is constructed.

Overridables

OnReadRawData	Allows the application to see the raw data. The data returned will contain both headers and data.
OnPreprocHeaders	Notifies the client that the server has preprocessed the client headers.
OnAuthentication	Authenticates the client.
OnUrlMap	Notifies a client when a server is mapping a logical URL to a physical path.
OnSendRawData	Sends raw data from the server to the client.
OnLog	Logs information to a server file.
OnEndOfNetSession	Notifies the client that the session is ending.

Operation

HttpFilterProc	Returns a message indicating how an event that passed through the filter was processed. Called each time an event occurs.

See Also: **CHttpFilterContext**

Member Functions
CHttpFilter::CHttpFilter

CHttpFilter( );

Remarks

This member function is called by the framework during the construction of a **CHttpFilter** object.

CHttpFilter::GetFilterVersion

virtual BOOL GetFilterVersion(PHTTP_FILTER_VERSION *pVer* **);**

Return Value

Nonzero if the filter was properly loaded. If the filter returns 0, then the filter application will be unloaded and it will not receive any notifications.

Parameters

pVer A pointer to the **HTTP_FILTER_VERSION** structure containing the server's version information and fields for the filter to indicate version number and notifications. The filter application also includes space to register a small description of itself. The following two flags are set in the structure by the default implementation:

- *dwFlags* The priority notification flag, **SF_NOTIFY_ORDER_DEFAULT**, is set by default. See **Remarks** for a list of the notification flags and their descriptions.

- *dwFilterVersion* **HTTP_FILTER_REVISION** is set by default. This flag indicates the version of the specification used by the server.

Remarks

This member function is called by the internet server to get the filter version indicated by *pVer*. It is called only once, after the **CHttpFilter** object is constructed.

Use *dwFlags* to specify the notifications in the *pVer* member that interest your server. Here is a list of the valid flags for *dwFlags*:

SF_NOTIFY_ORDER_DEFAULT Loads the filter at the default priority. This value is recommended because other priority notifications can have a strong impact on performance and scalability.

SF_NOTIFY_ORDER_LOW Loads the filter at low priority.

SF_NOTIFY_ORDER_MEDIUM Loads the filter at medium priority.

SF_NOTIFY_ORDER_HIGH Loads the filter at high priority.

SF_NOTIFY_SECURE_PORT Notifies the application that it is passing data through a secure port.

SF_NOTIFY_NONSECURE_PORT Notifies the application that it is passing data through a nonsecure port.

Note If you set neither **SF_NOTIFY_NONSECURE_PORT** nor **SF_NOTIFY_SECURE_PORT**, the server defaults to both, which allows processing data through any port.

SF_NOTIFY_READ_RAW_DATA Allows the application to see the raw data. The data returned to the client will contain both headers and data.

SF_NOTIFY_PREPROC_HEADERS The server has pre-processed the headers.

SF_NOTIFY_AUTHENTICATION   The server is authenticating the client.

SF_NOTIFY_URL_MAP   The server is mapping a logical URL to a physical path.

SF_NOTIFY_SEND_RAW_DATA   The server is sending raw data back to the client.

SF_NOTIFY_LOG   The server is writing information to the server log.

SF_NOTIFY_END_OF_NET_SESSION   The session with the client is ending.

See Also: HTTP_FILTER_VERSION, CHttpFilter::HttpFilterProc

CHttpFilter::HttpFilterProc

virtual DWORD HttpFilterProc(PHTTP_FILTER_CONTEXT *pfc*,
↪ **DWORD** *NotificationType*, **LPVOID** *pvNotification*);

Return Value

Indicates how the application handled the event. Indicated by a *dwFlags* value; see **GetFilterVersion Remarks** for a list of these values.

Parameters

pfc   A pointer to an **HTTP_FILTER_CONTEXT** structure. The **HTTP_FILTER_CONTEXT** structure pointed to by this parameter contains context information. The *pfc* structure member can be used by the filter to associate any context information with the HTTP request. The **SF_NOTIFY_END_OF_NET_SESSION** notification can be used to release any such context information.

NotificationType   Indicates the type of event being processed. Valid types are listed in **GetFilterVersion**.

pvNotification   A notification-specific structure.

Notification Type	*pvNotification* points to	MFC Calls
SF_NOTIFY_READ_RAW_DATA	**HTTP_FILTER_RAW_DATA**	**OnReadRawData**
SF_NOTIFY_SEND_RAW_DATA	**HTTP_FILTER_RAW_DATA**	**OnSendRawData**
SF_NOTIFY_PREPROC_HEADERS	**HTTP_FILTER_PREPROC_HEADERS**	**OnPreprocHeaders**
SF_NOTIFY_AUTHENTICATION	**HTTP_FILTER_AUTHENT**	**OnAuthentication**
SF_NOTIFY_URL_MAP	**HTTP_FILTER_URL_MAP**	**OnUrlMap**
SF_NOTIFY_LOG	**HTTP_FILTER_LOG**	**OnLog**

Remarks

This member function is called by the framework to process data every time it passes through the filter. **HttpFilterProc** will call the appropriate **CHttpFilter** member functions, depending on the notification types given. For example, **HttpFilterProc** will call **OnPreprocHeaders** if the notification type is **SF_NOTIFY_PREPROC_HEADERS**.

HttpFilterProc is where the core work of the ISAPI filter applications is done. The various structures pointed to by *pvNotification* (listed in the table above) contain data and function pointers specific to these operations. See the structure details for more information about how data is processed by **HttpFilterProc**.

You can override the individual handlers (listed in the third column, above) to change the way data in their associated structures is processed.

See Also: HTTP_FILTER_CONTEXT, HTTP_FILTER_AUTHENT, HTTP_FILTER_PREPROC_HEADERS, HTTP_FILTER_RAW_DATA, HTTP_FILTER_URL_MAP, HTTP_FILTER_LOG

CHttpFilter::OnAuthentication

virtual DWORD OnAuthentication(CHttpFilterContext* *pfc*, ↳ **PHTTP_FILTER_AUTHENT** *pAuthent* **);**

Return Value

One of the following notification types:

SF_STATUS_REQ_FINISHED The filter has handled the HTTP request. The server should disconnect the session.

SF_STATUS_REQ_FINISHED_KEEP_CONN Same as **SF_STATUS_REQ_FINISHED** except the server should keep the TCP session open if the option was negotiated.

SF_STATUS_REQ_NEXT_NOTIFICATION The next filter in the notification chain should be called.

SF_STATUS_REQ_HANDLED_NOTIFICATION This filter handled the notification. No other handlers should be called for this particular notification.

SF_STATUS_REQ_ERROR An error occurred. The server should use the Win32 API **SetLastError** to indicate the error to the client.

SF_STATUS_REQ_READ_NEXT The filter is an opaque stream filter; Negotiate the session parameters. Only valid for raw read notification.

If unsuccessful, the notification type **SF_STATUS_REQ_ERROR** should be returned. In this case, the server should use the Windows function **SetLastError** and indicate the error to the client.

Parameters

pfc A **CHttpFilterContext** object, which contains context information. The **CHttpFilterContext** object can be used by the filter to associate any context information with the HTTP request.

pAuthent A pointer to an **HTTP_FILTER_AUTHENT** structure.

Remarks

This member function is called by the framework to authenticate the client.

Override this member function to implement your own authentication. The default implementation does nothing.

See Also: **CHttpFilter::HttpFilterProc**, **HTTP_FILTER_AUTHENT**, **CHttpFilterContext**

CHttpFilter::OnEndOfNetSession

virtual DWORD OnEndOfNetSession(CHttpFilterContext* *pfc* **);**

Return Value

One of the following notification types:

SF_STATUS_REQ_FINISHED   The filter has handled the HTTP request. The server should disconnect the session.

SF_STATUS_REQ_FINISHED_KEEP_CONN   Same as **SF_STATUS_REQ_FINISHED** except the server should keep the TCP session open if the option was negotiated.

SF_STATUS_REQ_NEXT_NOTIFICATION   The next filter in the notification chain should be called.

SF_STATUS_REQ_HANDLED_NOTIFICATION   This filter handled the notification. No other handlers should be called for this particular notification.

SF_STATUS_REQ_ERROR   An error occurred. The server should use the Win32 API **SetLastError** to indicate the error to the client.

SF_STATUS_REQ_READ_NEXT   The filter is an opaque stream filter; Negotiate the session parameters. Only valid for raw read notification.

If unsuccessful, the notification type **SF_STATUS_REQ_ERROR** should be returned. In this case, the server should use the Windows function **SetLastError** and indicate the error to the client.

Parameters

pfc   A **CHttpFilterContext** object, which contains context information and can be used by the filter to associate any context information with the HTTP request.

Remarks

This member function is called by the framework to notify the filter that the session is ending.

Override this member function to provide your own end of session implementation. The default implementation does nothing.

See Also: **CHttpFilter::HttpFilterProc**, **CHttpFilterContext**

CHttpFilter::OnLog

virtual DWORD OnLog(CHttpFilterContext* *pfc*,
↳ **PHTTP_FILTER_LOG** *pLog*);

Return Value

One of the following notification types:

SF_STATUS_REQ_FINISHED   The filter has handled the HTTP request. The server should disconnect the session.

SF_STATUS_REQ_FINISHED_KEEP_CONN   Same as **SF_STATUS_REQ_FINISHED** except the server should keep the TCP session open if the option was negotiated.

SF_STATUS_REQ_NEXT_NOTIFICATION   The next filter in the notification chain should be called.

SF_STATUS_REQ_HANDLED_NOTIFICATION   This filter handled the notification. No other handlers should be called for this particular notification.

SF_STATUS_REQ_ERROR   An error occurred. The server should use the Win32 API **SetLastError** to indicate the error to the client.

SF_STATUS_REQ_READ_NEXT   The filter is an opaque stream filter; Negotiate the session parameters. Only valid for raw read notification.

If unsuccessful, the notification type **SF_STATUS_REQ_ERROR** should be returned. In this case, the server should use the Windows function **SetLastError** and indicate the error to the client.

Parameters

pfc   A **CHttpFilterContext** object, which contains context information, and can be used by the filter to associate any context information with the HTTP request.

pLog   A pointer to an **HTTP_FILTER_LOG** structure.

Remarks

This member function is called by the framework to inform the filter when the server is writing information to the server log.

Override this member function to provide your own method for logging information to the server file. The default implementation does nothing.

See Also: CHttpFilter::HttpFilterProc, HTTP_FILTER_LOG, CHttpFilterContext

CHttpFilter::OnPreprocHeaders

virtual DWORD OnPreprocHeaders(CHttpFilterContext* *pfc*,
↪ **PHTTP_FILTER_PREPROC_HEADERS** *pHeaders* **);**

Return Value

One of the following notification types:

SF_STATUS_REQ_FINISHED The filter has handled the HTTP request. The
server should disconnect the session.

SF_STATUS_REQ_FINISHED_KEEP_CONN Same as
SF_STATUS_REQ_FINISHED except the server should keep the TCP session
open if the option was negotiated.

SF_STATUS_REQ_NEXT_NOTIFICATION The next filter in the notification
chain should be called.

SF_STATUS_REQ_HANDLED_NOTIFICATION This filter handled the
notification. No other handlers should be called for this particular notification.

SF_STATUS_REQ_ERROR An error occurred. The server should use the Win32
API **SetLastError** to indicate the error to the client.

SF_STATUS_REQ_READ_NEXT The filter is an opaque stream filter; Negotiate
the session parameters. Only valid for raw read notification.

If unsuccessful, the notification type **SF_STATUS_REQ_ERROR** should be
returned. In this case, the server should use the Windows function **SetLastError** and
indicate the error to the client.

Parameters

pfc A **CHttpFilterContext** object, which contains context information. The
CHttpFilterContext object can be used by the filter to associate any context
information with the HTTP request.

pHeaders A pointer to a **HTTP_FILTER_PREPROC_HEADERS** structure.

Remarks

This member function is called by the framework to notify the client that the server
has preprocessed the client headers.

Override this member function to provide your own method for processing client
headers. The default does nothing.

See Also: CHttpFilter::HttpFilterProc,
HTTP_FILTER_PREPROC_HEADERS, CHttpFilterContext

CHttpFilter::OnReadRawData

virtual DWORD OnReadRawData(CHttpFilterContext* *pfc***,**
↪ PHTTP_FILTER_RAW_DATA *pRawData* **);**

Return Value

One of the following notification types:

SF_STATUS_REQ_FINISHED   The filter has handled the HTTP request. The
server should disconnect the session.

SF_STATUS_REQ_FINISHED_KEEP_CONN   Same as
SF_STATUS_REQ_FINISHED except the server should keep the TCP session
open if the option was negotiated.

SF_STATUS_REQ_NEXT_NOTIFICATION   The next filter in the notification
chain should be called.

SF_STATUS_REQ_HANDLED_NOTIFICATION   This filter handled the
notification. No other handlers should be called for this particular notification.

SF_STATUS_REQ_ERROR   An error occurred. The server should use the Win32
API **SetLastError** to indicate the error to the client.

SF_STATUS_REQ_READ_NEXT   The filter is an opaque stream filter; Negotiate
the session parameters. Only valid for raw read notification.

If unsuccessful, the notification type **SF_STATUS_REQ_ERROR** should be
returned. In this case, the server should use the Windows function **SetLastError** and
indicate the error to the client.

Parameters

pfc   A **CHttpFilterContext** object, which contains context information. The
CHttpFilterContext object can be used by the filter to associate any context
information with the HTTP request.

pRawData   A pointer to an **HTTP_FILTER_RAW_DATA** structure.

Remarks

This member function is called by the framework to allow the application to see the
raw data. The data returned will contain both headers and data.

Override this member function to process raw data differently.The default
implementation does nothing.

See Also: CHttpFilter::HttpFilterProc, HTTP_FILTER_RAW_DATA,
CHttpFilterContext, CHttpFilter::OnSendRawData

CHttpFilter::OnSendRawData

virtual DWORD OnSendRawData(CHttpFilterContext* *pfc***,**
↳ **PHTTP_FILTER_RAW_DATA** *pRawData* **);**

Return Value

If successful, the notification type **SF_STATUS_REQ_NEXT_NOTIFICATION**. Call the next filter in the notification chain.

If unsuccessful, the notification type **SF_STATUS_REQ_ERROR** should be returned. In this case, the server should use the Windows function **SetLastError** and indicate the error to the client.

Parameters

pfc　A **CHttpFilterContext** object, which contains context information. The **CHttpFilterContext** object can be used by the filter to associate any context information with the HTTP request. The **SF_NOTIFY_END_OF_NET_SESSION** notification can be used to release any such context information.

pRawData　A pointer to an **HTTP_FILTER_RAW_DATA** structure.

Remarks

This member function is called by the framework to notify the client that the server is sending raw data back to the client.

Override this member function only to change the default notification handler used by **HttpFilterProc** and process raw data differently.

See Also:　CHttpFilter::HttpFilterProc, HTTP_FILTER_RAW_DATA, CHttpFilterContext, CHttpFilter::OnReadRawData

---

CHttpFilter::OnUrlMap

virtual DWORD OnUrlMap(CHttpFilterContext* *pfc***,**
↳ **PHTTP_FILTER_URL_MAP** *pUrlMap* **);**

Return Value

One of the following notification types:

SF_STATUS_REQ_FINISHED　The filter has handled the HTTP request. The server should disconnect the session.

SF_STATUS_REQ_FINISHED_KEEP_CONN　Same as **SF_STATUS_REQ_FINISHED** except the server should keep the TCP session open if the option was negotiated.

SF_STATUS_REQ_NEXT_NOTIFICATION　The next filter in the notification chain should be called.

SF_STATUS_REQ_HANDLED_NOTIFICATION This filter handled the notification. No other handlers should be called for this particular notification.

SF_STATUS_REQ_ERROR An error occurred. The server should use the Win32 API **SetLastError** to indicate the error to the client.

SF_STATUS_REQ_READ_NEXT The filter is an opaque stream filter; Negotiate the session parameters. Only valid for raw read notification.

If unsuccessful, the notification type **SF_STATUS_REQ_ERROR** should be returned. In this case, the server should use the Windows function **SetLastError** and indicate the error to the client.

Parameters

pfc A **CHttpFilterContext** object, which contains context information. The **CHttpFilterContext** object can be used by the filter to associate any context information with the HTTP request.

pUrlMap A pointer to an **HTTP_FILTER_URL_MAP** structure.

Remarks

This member function is called by the framework when the server is mapping a logical URL to a physical path.

Override this member function handle URL mapping differently. The default implementation does nothing.

See Also: **CHttpFilter::HttpFilterProc**, **HTTP_FILTER_URL_MAP**, **CHttpFilterContext**

CHttpFilterContext

CHttpFilterContext does not have a base class.

CHttpFilterContext provides the tools that a **CHttpFilter** object needs to process data that passes through the filter. When the filter receives a request, a **CHttpFilter** object is created and initialized, and a **CHttpFilterContext** object is created. As the filter processes requests, it uses **CHttpFilterContext** member functions to perform tasks.

A **CHttpFilterContext** object exists separately from a **CHttpFilter** object in order to allow multi-threading. Only one **CHttpFilter** object exists in a module, but a filter might be required to process multiple client requests simultaneously.

CHttpFilter will create a **CHttpFilterContext** for each request to handle these multiple requests. A **CHttpFilter** uses multiple **CHttpFilterContext** objects to run in separate threads. This design allows simultaneous, multiple calls to the **CHttpFilter** object by different client connections.

When an extension DLL (ISA) is called, the member function **ServerSupportFunction** prompts the server to provide the general ISA information to the client.

If the filter must communicate something—for example, an error—back to the client immediately, call **WriteClient**.

#include <afxisapi.h>

See Also: CHttpServer, **CHttpFilter**, **HTTP_FILTER_CONTEXT**

CHttpFilterContext Class Members

Data Members

m_pFC	A pointer to an **HTTP_FILTER_CONTEXT** structure.

Construction

CHttpFilterContext	Constructs a **CHttpFilterContext** object.

Attributes

GetServerVariable	Copies information relating to an HTTP connection, or to the server itself, into a buffer supplied by the caller.
AddResponseHeaders	Adds a header to the HTTP response.
WriteClient	Writes raw data to the client immediately.
AllocMem	Allocates memory in a buffer.
ServerSupportFunction	Provides general ISA information to the client.

See Also: HTTP_FILTER_CONTEXT

Member Functions

CHttpFilterContext::AddResponseHeaders

BOOL AddResponseHeaders(LPTSTR *lpszHeaders***, DWORD** *dwReserved* **=0);**

Return Value

Nonzero if successful, otherwise 0.

Parameters

lpszHeaders   A pointer to a string containing headers to add.

dwReserved   Reserved for future use. Must be 0.

Remarks

Call this member function to add a header to an HTTP response. The header string is contained in *lpszHeaders*. See the **HSE_REQ_SEND_RESPONSE_HEADER** value described in the **CHttpServerContext::ServerSupportFunction** topic for information about how a **CHttpServer** object delivers information about an HTTP server response header.

CHttpFilterContext::AllocMem

LPVOID AllocMem(DWORD *cbSize***, DWORD** *dwReserved* **);**

Return Value

A pointer to a buffer.

Parameters

cbSize   Specifies the size of the memory buffer to allocate, in bytes.

dwReserved   Reserved for future use.

Remarks

Call this member function to allocate memory that is automatically freed when the communication with the client is terminated.

When an HTTP filter is registered, usually it will register for the end-of-net-session event. This event is a good time to recycle any buffers used by that client request. For performance reasons, most filters will probably keep a pool of filter buffers and only allocate or free a buffer when the pool becomes empty or too large to save on the overhead of the memory management. Calling **AllocMem** can have a negative impact on performance, but with careful use, it can be a valuable tool.

Memory blocks allocated with **AllocMem** cannot be managed with the normal C run-time or Windows API memory management functions.

CHttpFilterContext::CHttpFilterContext

CHttpFilterContext(PHTTP_FILTER_CONTEXT *pfc* **);**

Parameters

pfc   A pointer to a **HTTP_FILTER_CONTEXT** structure.

Remarks

This member function is called by the framework during the construction of a **CHttpFilterContext** object.

See Also: HTTP_FILTER_CONTEXT

CHttpFilterContext::GetServerVariable

BOOL GetServerVariable(LPTSTR *lpszVariableName*, **LPVOID** *lpvBuffer*, **LPDWORD** *lpdwSize* **);**

Return Value

Nonzero if successful, otherwise 0. The Win32 API call **GetLastError** can be used to determine why the call failed. Possible error values include:

Value	Meaning
ERROR_INVALID_PARAMETER	Bad connection handle.
ERROR_INVALID_INDEX	Bad or unsupported variable identifier.
ERROR_INSUFFICIENT_BUFFER	Buffer too small; the required size is returned in *lpdwSize*.
ERROR_MORE_DATA	Buffer too small, only part of data returned. The total size of the data is not returned.
ERROR_NO_DATA	The data requested is not available.

Parameters

lpszVariableName   Null-terminated string indicating which variable is being requested. See the Remarks section below for a selection of possible names. All variable names are as defined in the CGI specification located at **http://hoohoo.ncsa.uiuc.edu/cgi/env.html**.

lpvBuffer   Pointer to buffer to receive the requested information.

lpdwSize   Pointer to DWORD indicating the number of bytes available in the buffer. On successful completion the DWORD contains the number of bytes transferred into the buffer (including the null-terminating byte).

Remarks

This member function is called by the framework to copy information relating to an HTTP connection, or to the server itself, into a buffer supplied by the caller. Possible *lpszVariableNames* include:

Value	Meaning
ALL_HTTP	All HTTP headers that were not already parsed into one of the above variables. These variables are of the form HTTP_<header field name>.
AUTH_PASS	This will retrieve the password corresponding to **REMOTE_USER** as supplied by the client. It will be a null-terminated string.
AUTH_TYPE	Contains the type of authentication used. For example, if Basic authentication is used, the string will be "Basic". For Windows NT Challenge-response, it will be "NTLM". Other authentication schemes will have other strings. Because new authentication types can be added to Internet Server, it is not possible to list all possible strings. If the string is empty then no authentication is used.
CONTENT_LENGTH	The number of bytes which the script can expect to receive from the client.
CONTENT_TYPE	The content type of the information supplied in the body of a POST request.
GATEWAY_INTERFACE	The revision of the CGI specification to which this server complies. The current version is CGI/1.1.

HTTP_ACCEPT	Special case HTTP header. Values of the Accept: fields are concatenated, separated by ", ". For example, if the following lines are part of the HTTP header:
	
	`accept: */*; q=0.1`
	`accept: text/html`
	`accept: image/jpeg`
	
	then the **HTTP_ACCEPT** variable will have a value of:
	
	`*/*; q=0.1, text/html, image/jpeg`

PATH_INFO	Additional path information, as given by the client. This comprises the trailing part of the URL after the script name but before the query string (if any).
PATH_TRANSLATED	This is the value of **PATH_INFO**, but with any virtual path name expanded into a directory specification.
QUERY_STRING	The information which follows the **?** in the URL which referenced this script.
REMOTE_ADDR	The IP address of the client.
REMOTE_HOST	The hostname of the client.
REMOTE_USER	This contains the username supplied by the client and authenticated by the server.
REQUEST_METHOD	The HTTP request method.
SCRIPT_NAME	The name of the script program being executed.

(continued)

(continued)

Value	Meaning
SERVER_NAME	The server's hostname (or IP address) as it should appear in self-referencing URLs.
SERVER_PORT	The TCP/IP port on which the request was received.
SERVER_PROTOCOL	The name and version of the information retrieval protocol relating to this request. Normally HTTP/1.0.
SERVER_SOFTWARE	The name and version of the web server under which the CGI program is running.

CHttpFilterContext::ServerSupportFunction

BOOL ServerSupportFunction(enum SF_REQ_TYPE *sfReq***, PVOID** *pvData***,**
↳ LPDWORD *lpdwSize***, LPDDWORD** *lpdwDataType* **)**

Return Value

Nonzero if successful, otherwise 0.

Parameters

sfReq   Server request type. See the Remarks section for a list of of the possible values.

pvData   A pointer to a zero-terminated string. Its value is specific to the *sfReq* extension. When used with **SF_REQ_SEND_RESPONSE_HEADER**, it is an optional, null-terminated status string (for example, "401 Access Denied") or **NULL** for the default response of "200 OK". When used with **SF_REQ_ADD_HEADERS_ON_DENIAL**, it is a null-terminated string pointing to one or more header lines with terminating "\r\n".

lpdwSize   Null-terminated string. Its value is specific to the extension. When used with **SF_REQ_SEND_RESPONSE_HEADER**, it is a null-terminated string pointing to optional data to be appended and set with the header. If **NULL**, the header will be terminated with an empty line. When used with **SF_REQ_ADD_HEADERS_ON_DENIAL**, it is the size in bytes for the next read.

lpdwDataType   A null-terminated string pointing to optional headers or data to be appended and sent with the header. If **NULL**, the header will be terminated by a "\r\n" pair.

Remarks

Call this member function to extend the ISA APIs.

The HTTP Server Extension value represented by *sfReq,* can be one of the following:

SF_REQ_SEND_RESPONSE_HEADER   Sends a complete HTTP server response header including the status, server version, message time, and MIME

(Multipurpose Internet Mail Extension) version. Server extensions should append other information at the end, such as Content-type, Content-length, and so forth, followed by an extra "\r\n".

SF_REQ_ADD_HEADERS_ON_DENIAL If the server denies the HTTP request, add the specified headers to the server error response. This allows an authentication filter to advertise its services without filtering every request. Generally the headers will be WWW-Authenticate headers with custom authentication schemes, but no restriction is placed on what headers may be specified.

SF_REQ_SET_NEXT_READ_SIZE Only used by raw data filters that return **SF_STATUS_READ_NEXT**.

CHttpFilterContext::WriteClient

> **BOOL WriteClient(LPVOID** *lpvBuffer*, **LPDWORD** *lpdwBytes*,
> ↳ **DWORD** *dwReserved* = **0**);

Return Value

Nonzero if successful, otherwise 0. If 0, use the Windows function **GetLastError** to determine the cause of the error.

Parameters

lpvBuffer A pointer to the buffer containing the data.

lpdwBytes A pointer to a DWORD containing the number of bytes to write from the buffer.

dwReserved Reserved for future use. Must be 0.

Remarks

Call this member function to send raw data back to the client immediately.

See Also: HTTP_FILTER_CONTEXT, CHttpServerContext::WriteClient

Data Members

CHttpFilterContext::m_pFC

Remarks

The **m_pFC** data member is a pointer to an **HTTP_FILTER_CONTEXT** structure. The pointer points at the same structure passed to **CHttpFilter::HttpFilterProc**.

See Also: HTTP_FILTER_CONTEXT

CHttpServer

CHttpServer does not have a base class.

The class **CHttpServer**, with **CHttpServerContext**, provides a means to extend the functionality of an ISAPI-compliant HTTP server. The class **CHttpServer** wraps the Internet Server API (ISAPI) functionality and can process all types of client requests, including both Common Gateway Interface (CGI) executables and extension DLLs. These extension DLLs are sometimes called Internet Server Applications; however, they are DLLs, rather than EXEs. For brevity's sake, we refer to an extension DLL as an ISA.

For more information on the difference between CGI and ISA, see "Internet Server API (ISAPI) Extensions" in *Visual C++ Programmer's Guide* online.

When an ISAPI HTTP server receives a request from a client browser, a **CHttpServer** object is created and initialized, and a **CHttpServerContext** object is created. Only one instance of **CHttpServer** may exist for each module; however, one **CHttpServerContext** object is created for each call to the server. A **CHttpServer** object uses multiple **CHttpServerContext** objects to run in separate threads. This design allows simultaneous, multiple calls to the **CHttpServer** object by different client connections. The **CHttpServer** object communicates with the client or server itself via the **CHttpServerContext** object.

When the server loads the ISA, it calls the ISA at the entry point **GetExtensionVersion** to get the version number of the specification on which the extension is based. For every client request, the **HttpExtensionProc** member function is called. The default (recommended) implementation of **HttpExtensionProc** will read client data and decide what action is to be taken. You can override this member function to customize the implementation.

Other **CHttpServer** member functions process the client request, format the responses, and correspond with the client.

When a client command is received by a **CHttpServer** object, the parse maps associate the command to its class member function and parameters. Only one parse map is created per **CHttpServer** object.

See **Internet Server API (ISAPI) Parse Maps** for general information on using the parse map macros. See **BEGIN_PARSE_MAP** and **END_PARSE_MAP** for information on how to create a parse map to handle client commands.

See the following macro descriptions for information about how the client commands are mapped to member functions and their arguments:

- **ON_PARSE_COMMAND**
- **ON_PARSE_COMMAND_PARAMS**
- **DEFAULT_PARSE_COMMAND**

For more information on using parse maps to handle client commands, see "ISAPI Extensions: Parse Maps" in *Visual C++ Programmer's Guide* online.

For information on debugging internet extension DLLs, see Technical Note 63 online.

#include <afxisapi.h>

See Also: **CHtmlStream**

CHttpServer Class Members

Constructor

CHttpServer	Constructs a **CHttpServer** object.

Overridables

CallFunction	Finds and executes the appropriate function associated with the command in the URL.
OnParseError	Constructs a description of the error to be returned to the client.
HttpExtensionProc	Uses the callback functions to read client data and decide what action to take.
GetExtensionVersion	Gets the version number that the DLL extension is based on.
ConstructStream	Constructs a **CHtmlStream** object.

Attributes

StartContent	Inserts opening HTML tags into a **CHtmlStream** object to be returned to the client. Override to change or omit the default tags.
EndContent	Inserts closing HTML tags into a **CHtmlStream** object to be returned to the client. Override to change or omit the default tags.
WriteTitle	Inserts the title between the appropriate HTML tags in the **CHtmlStream** object to be returned to the client. Override to provide a different title.
GetTitle	Gets the title of an HTML document to be sent to the client.
AddHeader	Adds headers to a response before it is sent to the server.
InitInstance	Initializes the **CHttpServer** object.

See Also: **CHtmlStream, CHttpServerContext**

Member Functions
CHttpServer::AddHeader

void AddHeader(CHttpServerContext* *pCtxt*, **LPCTSTR** *pszString*) **const;**

Parameters

pCtxt   A pointer to a **CHttpServerContext** object.

pszString   A pointer to a string.

Remarks

Call this member function to add a header to the response before the response is sent to the server. Use **AddHeader** to append your own headers to those the server supplies when it receives **CHttpServerContext::ServerSupportFunction HSE_REQ_SEND_RESPONSE_HEADERS**. The extra header provides the client with more information.

For example, call **AddHeader** to specify your own "content-type," then call it to specify an encoding, and then call it once more to insert the "content-length" header. After you have called **AddHeader** as many times as you need, use << to stream your output until you are done.

Note   Once you put data in the HTML stream in the server context, do not call **AddHeader** again. If you do, your HTML stream will not work properly.

Example

Here's an example of a function that creates an on-the-fly web-page:

```
void CHelloExtension::Default(CHttpServerContext* pCtxt)
{
    AddHeader(pCtxt, "Content-type = text/plain\r\n");
    (*pCtxt) << "Hello world!\r\n";
}
```

See Also: CHttpServerContext,
CHttpServerContext::ServerSupportFunction

CHttpServer::CallFunction

virtual int CallFunction(CHttpServerContext* *pCtxt*, **LPTSTR** *pszQuery*,
↪ **LPTSTR** *pszCommand* **);**

Return Value

A value of one of the following enum types:

Enum value	Description
callOK	The function call was successful.
callParamRequired	A required parameter was missing.
callBadParamCount	There were too many or too few parameters.
callBadCommand	The command name was not found.
callNoStackSpace	No stack space was available.
callNoStream	No **CHtmlStream** was available.
callMissingQuote	A parameter had a bad format.
callMissingParams	No parameters were available.
callBadParam	A parameter had a bad format (i.e., only one quote).

Parameters

pCtxt   Pointer to a **CHttpServerContext** object.

pszQuery   A pointer to a query. Specific to the type of command received from the client. See **Remarks** for more information.

pszCommand   Either a pointer to a query or NULL. Specific to the type of command received from the client. See **Remarks** for more information.

Remarks

Called by the framework to find and execute the appropriate function associated with the command in the URL.

Below is a breakdown between the types of methods received and the parameters:

Method type	*pszQuery*	*pszCommand*
GET	A pointer to the **EXTENSION_CONTROL_BLOCK** structure query string.	NULL
POST	A pointer to a query sent in the body of the command.	Pointer to the **EXTENSION_CONTROL_BLOCK** structure query string.

Note Fill-out forms authors are advised to use only the POST method because of browser inconsistencies, and because GET methods are limited to a 1024-byte buffer. When writing forms for ISAPI, either use only the POST method, or design the ISA so that only the default function handles the form.

For example, some browsers sending a form via GET with an action of:

```
TestLet.DLL?Command
```

will truncate `Command` and send:

```
TestLet.DLL?name=value
```

instead of the correct command:

```
TestLet.DLL?Command?name=value
```

By truncating `Command`, the browser removes the association to the ISA function needed to map the request. Unless the function `Command` is the default function, the form will not be handled correctly.

If you want to handle parsing of the **EXTENSION_CONTROL_BLOCK** structure function **lpszQueryString** yourself, override **CallFunction** and do not use the **PARSE_MAP** macros. See **Internet Server API (ISAPI) Parse Maps** for more information on using the parse map macros.

See Also: **CHttpServerContext**, **Internet Server API (ISAPI) Parse Maps**

CHttpServer::CHttpServer

CHttpServer(TCHAR *cDelimiter* **);**

Parameters

cDelimiter   A character identifying the token delimiter. By default, this delimiter is '&'.

Remarks

The run-time calls this function when constructing a **CHttpServer** object. Only one instance of **CHttpServer** may exist for each module. Once a **CHttpServer** object is created, it can be initialized with **InitInstance**.

After the ISA has been initiated by a client command and acted upon by the server, the client receives a response page that reflects the *cDelimiter* parameter in the URL. The *cDelimiter* parameter separates the command's arguments that are parsed by the parse map macros **ON_PARSE_COMMAND** and **ON_PARSE_COMMAND_PARAMS**.

Example of *cDelimiter*

If the client initiates an ISA to view a colorized JPEG image from the URL **http://www.jungle.org/**, the command sent to the server could look like this:

http://www.Jungle.org/scripts/Apes.dll?Colorize

where **Colorize** is the command initiating the **Colorize** function.

The URL that the server returns to the client would look like this:

http://www.jungle.org/scripts/Apes.dll?Colorize?Target=Picture&Format=JPEG

The *cDelimiter* default delimiter & appears in the client's URL between the two parameters *Picture* and *Format* of the function **Colorize**.

See **ON_PARSE_COMMAND** and **ON_PARSE_COMMAND_PARAMS** for more information about parsing commands.

CHttpServer::ConstructStream

virtual CHtmlStream* ConstructStream( );

Return Value

A pointer to a **CHtmlStream** object.

Remarks

This member function is called by the framework to construct a **CHtmlStream** object. Override this member function to create an instance of your own class to give it functionality other than the default.

See the constructor **CHtmlStream::CHtmlStream** for information about why you might override **ConstructStream** and provide special functionality for a **CHtmlStream** object.

CHttpServer::EndContent

virtual void EndContent(CHttpServerContext* *pCtxt*) const;

Parameters

pCtxt A pointer to a **CHttpServerContext** object. Cannot be **NULL**.

Remarks

This member function is called by the framework to insert the closing HTML tags "</Body>" and "</HTML>" into an HTML document to be returned to the client.

Override this member function to implement a behavior different from the default. For example, override if you are returning a stream type other than an HTML stream (like a JPEG image).

See Also: CHttpServer::StartContent

CHttpServer::GetExtensionVersion

virtual BOOL GetExtensionVersion(HSE_VERSION_INFO *pVer);

Return Value

Nonzero if successful; otherwise zero.

Parameters

pVer A pointer to the **HSE_VERSION_INFO** structure containing version information for the server and fields for the client to indicate version number, notifications, and priority desired. There is also a space for the filter application to register a small description of itself.

Remarks

This member function is called by the framework when it loads an ISA. **GetExtensionVersion** gets the version number of the specification the DLL extension is based on. It also provides a short text description for server administrators.

GetExtensionVersion is one of two necessary entry points for an ISA. The second necessary entry point is the function **HttpExtensionProc**. Both of these are provided by MFC, with default implementation. Call the default implementation to set the version, and then override to replace the default text string with your own short description.

See Also: **HSE_VERSION_INFO**, **CHttpServer::HttpExtensionProc**

CHttpServer::GetTitle

virtual LPCTSTR GetTitle( ) const;

Return Value

A pointer to a string containing the title.

Remarks

This member function is called by the framework to get the title of an HTML document to be sent to the client.

Override to supply your own title.

CHttpServer::HttpExtensionProc

virtual DWORD HttpExtensionProc(EXTENSION_CONTROL_BLOCK *_pECB_);

Return Value

One of the following HTTP Server Extension messages:

HSE_STATUS_SUCCESS   The ISA has finished processing and the server can disconnect and free up allocated resources.

HSE_STATUS_SUCCESS_AND_KEEP_CONN   The ISA has finished processing and the server should wait for the next HTTP request if the client supports persistent connections. The application should only return this if it was able to send the correct content-length header to the client. The server is not required to keep the session open.

HSE_STATUS_PENDING   The ISA has queued the request for processing and will notify the server when it has finished. See **HSE_REQ_DONE_WITH_SESSION** under **CHttpServerContext::ServerSupportFunction**.

HSE_STATUS_ERROR   The ISA has encountered an error while processing the request and the server can disconnect and free up allocated resources.

Parameters

    pECB   A pointer to an **EXTENSION_CONTROL_BLOCK** structure.

Remarks

This member function is called by the framework for each request for an ISA. **HttpExtensionProc** uses the callback functions to read client data and decide what action to take. Before returning to the server, a properly formatted response must be sent to the client via either the **CHttpServerContext::WriteClient** or the **CHttpServerContext::ServerSupportFunction** member function.

The default implementation of **HttpExtensionProc** is recommended; however you can override this member function to customize the implementation.

See Also: **CHttpServerContext::WriteClient**, **CHttpServerContext::ServerSupportFunction**

CHttpServer::InitInstance

    virtual BOOL InitInstance(CHttpServerContext* *pCtxt* **);**

Return Value

Nonzero if initialization is successful; otherwise 0.

Parameters

    pCtxt   A pointer to a **CHttpServerContext** object.

Remarks

This member function is called by the framework to initialize a **CHttpServer** object. InitInstance is called in **CHttpServer::HttpExtensionProc**, which is called by the framework for each request for an ISA.

Override this member function to provide **CHttpServer** custom initialization.

CHttpServer::OnParseError

    virtual BOOL OnParseError(CHttpServerContext* *pCtxt*, **int** *nCause* **);**

Return Value

Nonzero error is successfully parsed; otherwise 0.

Parameters

    pCtxt   A pointer to a **CHttpServerContext** object that contains an **EXTENSION_CONTROL_BLOCK** structure function **dwHttpStatusCode**. These status values are:

- **HTTP_STATUS_BAD_REQUEST**

- **HTTP_STATUS_AUTH_REQUIRED**

- **HTTP_STATUS_FORBIDDEN**

- **HTTP_STATUS_NOT_FOUND**

- **HTTP_STATUS_SERVER_ERROR**

- **HTTP_STATUS_NOT_IMPLEMENTED**

nCause The cause of the error. Can be one of the following values:

Enum type	Description
callOK	**OnParseError** handled the error.
callParamRequired	A required parameter was missing.
callBadParamCount	There were too many or too few parameters.
callBadCommand	The command name was not found.
callNoStackSpace	No stack space was available.
callNoStream	No **CHtmlStream** was available.
callMissingQuote	A parameter is missing a quote mark.
callMissingParams	No parameters were available.
callBadParam	A parameter had a bad format.

Remarks

Called by the framework to parse errors. Once the error is identified, the message associated with the cause of the error is returned to the client either in an HTML stream or in a **CHttpServerContext::WriteClient** message.

Override this member function to customize the error parsing.

CHttpServer::StartContent

virtual void StartContent(CHttpServerContext* *pCtxt* **) const;**

Parameters

pCtxt A pointer to a **CHttpServerContext** object.

Remarks

This member function is called by the framework to insert the starting HTML tags "`<Body>`" and "`<HTML>`" into an HTML document to be returned to the client.

Override this member function to implement a behavior different from the default. For example, override if you are returning a stream type other than an HTML stream (like a JPEG image).

See Also: CHttpServer::EndContent

CHttpServer::WriteTitle

virtual void WriteTitle(CHttpServerContext* *pCtxt* **) const;**

Parameters

    pCtxt A pointer to a **CHttpServerContext** object.

Remarks

This member function is called by the framework to write the title to insert between the appropriate HTML tags on the document to be transmitted back to the client.

The default implementation writes the title returned from **GetTitle** between the HTML tags "`<Title>`" and "`</Title>`". Override this member function to provide a different title.

See Also: **CHttpServer::GetTitle**

CHttpServerContext

CHttpServerContext does not have a base class.

CHttpServerContext provides the tools that a **CHttpServer** object needs to process data that a client has sent to the HTTP server. When a Microsoft Internet Information Server (MIIS) receives a request from a client browser, a **CHttpServer** object is created and initialized, and a **CHttpServerContext** object is created. As the server extension DLL processes requests, it uses **CHttpServerContext** member functions to perform tasks.

A **CHttpServerContext** object exists separately from a **CHttpServer** object in order to allow multithreading. Only one **CHttpServer** exists in a module, but a server might be required to process multiple client requests simultaneously.

CHttpServer creates a **CHttpServerContext** for each request to handle these multiple requests. A **CHttpServer** uses multiple **CHttpServerContext** objects to run in separate threads. This design allows simultaneous, multiple calls to the **CHttpServer** object by different client connections.

When an extension DLL (ISA) is called, the member function **ServerSupportFunction** provides the ISA with some general-purpose functions as well as functions that are specific to HTTP server implementation.

If the server extension must communicate something—for example, an error—back to the client immediately, call **WriteClient**. Otherwise, the server should output a message to the client to the **m_pStream** data member owned by the *pCtxt* parameter passed to it.

#include <afxisapi.h>

CHttpServerContext Class Members

Data Members

m_pECB	A pointer to an **EXTENSION_CONTROL_BLOCK** structure.
m_pStream	A pointer to a **CHtmlStream**.

Construction

CHttpServerContext	Constructs a **CHttpServerContext** object.

Operations

GetServerVariable	Copies information relating to an HTTP connection, or to the server itself, into a supplied buffer.
WriteClient	Sends information to the HTTP client immediately.

ReadClient	Reads information from the body of the Web client's HTTP request into the buffer supplied by the caller.
ServerSupportFunction	Provides **ISAs** with some general-purpose functions as well as functions that are specific to HTTP server implementation.

Operators

operator <<	Writes data into a stream.

See Also: CHttpServer

Member Functions
CHttpServerContext::CHttpServerContext

CHttpServerContext(EXTENSION_CONTROL_BLOCK* *pECB* **);**

Parameters

pECB   A pointer to an **EXTENSION_CONTROL_BLOCK** data structure.

Remarks

This member function is called by the framework during the construction of a **CHttpServerContext** object.

CHttpServerContext::GetServerVariable

BOOL GetServerVariable(LPTSTR *lpszVariableName***, LPVOID** *lpvBuffer***,**
↪ **LPDWORD** *lpdwSize* **);**

Return Value

Nonzero if successful, otherwise 0. If the call fails, the Windows function **GetLastError** may be called to determine the cause of the error. Possible error values include:

Value	Meaning
ERROR_INVALID_PARAMETER	Bad connection handle.
ERROR_INVALID_INDEX	Bad or unsupported variable identifier.
ERROR_INSUFFICIENT_BUFFER	Buffer too small, required size returned in **lpdwSize*.
ERROR_MORE_DATA	Buffer too small, only part of data returned. The total size of the data is not returned.
ERROR_NO_DATA	The data requested is not available.

Parameters

lpszVariableName Null terminated string indicating which variable is being requested. See the Remarks section for a list of current variables.

lpvBuffer Pointer to buffer to receive the requested information.

lpdwSize Pointer to **DWORD** indicating the number of bytes available in the buffer. On successful completion the **DWORD** contains the number of bytes transferred into the buffer (including the null-terminating byte).

Remarks

This function copies information relating to an HTTP connection, or to the server itself, into a buffer supplied by the caller.

Possible values for *lpszVariableNames* include:

Value	Meaning
AUTH_TYPE	Contains the type of authentication used. For example, if Basic authentication is used, the string will be "Basic." For Windows NT Challenge-response, it will be "NTLM." Other authentication schemes will have other strings. Because new authentication types can be added to Internet Server, it is not possible to list all possible strings. If the string is empty, then no authentication is used.
CONTENT_LENGTH	The number of bytes which the script can expect to receive from the client.
CONTENT_TYPE	The content type of the information supplied in the body of a POST request.
GATEWAY_INTERFACE	The revision of the CGI specification to which this server complies. The current version is CGI/1.1.
PATH_INFO	Additional path information, as given by the client. This comprises the trailing part of the URL after the extension DLL (script) name but before the query string (if any).
PATH_TRANSLATED	This is the value of **PATH_INFO**, but with any virtual path name expanded into a directory specification.
QUERY_STRING	The information which follows the ? in the URL which referenced this extension DLL.
REMOTE_ADDR	The IP address of the client.
REMOTE_HOST	The hostname of the client.
REMOTE_USER	This contains the username supplied by the client and authenticated by the server.
REQUEST_METHOD	The HTTP request method.
SCRIPT_NAME	The name of the extension DLL that is being executed.
SERVER_NAME	The server's hostname (or IP address) as it should appear in self-referencing URLs.
SERVER_PORT	The TCP/IP port on which the request was received.
SERVER_PROTOCOL	The name and version of the information retrieval protocol relating to this request. Normally HTTP/1.0.

(continued)

Value	Meaning
SERVER_SOFTWARE	The name and version of the web server under which the ISA or server extension DLL program is running.
AUTH_PASS	This will retrieve the password corresponding to **REMOTE_USER** as supplied by the client. It will be a null-terminated string.
ALL_HTTP	All HTTP headers that were not already parsed into one of the above variables. These variables are of the form HTTP_<header field name>.
HTTP_ACCEPT	Special case HTTP header. Values of the Accept: fields are concatenated, separated by ",". For example, if the following lines are part of the HTTP header:

```
accept: */*; q=0.1
accept: text/html
accept: image/jpeg
```

then the **HTTP_ACCEPT** variable will have a value of:

```
*/*; q=0.1, text/html, image/jpeg
```

CHttpServerContext::ReadClient

BOOL ReadClient(LPVOID *lpvBuffer***, LPDWORD** *lpdwSize* **);**

Return Value

Nonzero if successful, otherwise 0. If the socket used by the server to listen to the client is closed, it will return nonzero, but with zero bytes read.

If the call fails, the Windows function **GetLastError** may be called to determine the cause of the error.

Parameters

lpvBuffer   Pointer to the buffer area to receive the requested information.

lpdwSize   Pointer to **DWORD** indicating the number of bytes available in the buffer. On return **lpdwSize* will contain the number of bytes actually transferred into the buffer.

Remarks

Call this member function to read information from the body of the Web client's HTTP request into the buffer supplied by the caller. **ReadClient** might be used to read data from an HTML form that uses the POST method. If more than **lpdwSize* bytes are immediately available to be read, **ReadClient** will return after transferring that amount of data into the buffer. Otherwise it will block incoming data and wait for buffer space to become available.

See Also: CHttpServerContext::WriteClient

CHttpServerContext::ServerSupportFunction

BOOL ServerSupportFunction(DWORD *dwHSERRequest*, **LPVOID** *lpvBuffer*,
↪ **LPDWORD** *lpdwSize*, **LPDWORD** *lpdwDataType* **);**

Return Value

Nonzero if successful, otherwise 0.

Parameters

dwHSERRequest   An HTTP Server Extension value. See the Remarks section for a
list of the supported values.

lpvBuffer   When used with **HSE_REQ_SEND_RESPONSE_HEADER**, it points to
a null terminated optional status string (for example, "401 Access Denied"). If this
buffer is null, a default response of "200 OK" will be sent by this function. When
used with **HSE_REQ_DONE_WITH_SESSION**, it points to a **DWORD**
indicating the status code of the request.

lpdwSize   When used with **HSE_REQ_SEND_RESPONSE_HEADER**, it points to
the size of the buffer *lpdwDataType*.

lpdwDataType   When used with **HSE_REQ_SEND_RESPONSE_HEADER**, this is
a null-terminated string pointing to optional headers or data to be appended and
sent with the header. If this is **NULL**, the header will be terminated by a "\r\n" pair.

Note   General purpose functions should have a *dwHSERequest* value larger than
HSE_REQ_END_RESERVED. Values up to **HSE_REQ_END_RESERVED** are reserved for
mandatory ServerSupportFunctions and should not be used.

Remarks

Call this member function to provide the ISA with some general purpose functions as
well as functions that are specific to HTTP server implementation.

The HTTP Server Extension value represented by *dwHSERRequest* can be one of the
following:

HSE_REQ_SEND_URL_REDIRECT_RESP   Sends a 302(URL Redirect) message
to the client. No further processing is needed after the call. This operation is similar
to specifying "URI: <URL>" in a CGI script header. The variable *lpvBuffer* should
point to a null terminated URL string. Variable *lpdwSize* should have the size of
lpvBuffer. Variable *lpdwDataType* is ignored.

HSE_REQ_SEND_URL   Sends the data specified by the URL to the client as if the
client had requested that URL. The Null terminated URL pointed to by *lpvBuffer*
MUST be on the server and must not specify protocol information (i.e. it must
begin with a "/"). No further processing is required after this call. Variable
lpdwSize points to a **DWORD** holding the size of *lpvBuffer*. Variable
lpdwDataType is ignored.

HSE_REQ_SEND_RESPONSE_HEADER Sends a complete HTTP server response header including the status, server version, message time and MIME version. The **ISA** or server extension should append other HTTP headers at the end such as the Content-Type, Content-Length, and so forth, followed by an extra "\r\n".

HSE_REQ_DONE_WITH_SESSION If the ISA or server extension wants to hold onto the session because it has extended processing requirements, it needs to tell the server when the session is finished so the server can close it and free the related structures. Variables *lpvBuffer*, *lpdwSize*, and *lpdwDataType* are all ignored.

HSE_REQ_END_RESERVED Functions higher than this value are server specific and may not be available on all web servers that support ISAPI.

HSE_REQ_MAP_URL_TO_PATH The *lpvBuffer* parameter is a pointer to the buffer that contains the logical path on entry and the physical path on exit. The *lpdwSize* parameter is a pointer to the **DWORD** containing the size of the buffer passed in *lpvBuffer* on entry, and the number of bytes placed in the buffer on exit. The *lpdwDataType* parameter is ignored). A Microsoft-specific extension.

HSE_REQ_GET_SSPI_INFO The *lpvBuffer* is filled in with the context handle and **lpdwDataType* is filled in with the credential handle. A context handle specifies a pointer type or a type identifier. A credential handle specifies authentication and authorization.

Note The server does not ensure that the buffers are large enough before filling in the handles, and *lpdwSize* is not updated to reflect the amount of data copied into the *lpvBuffer* buffer. Since these are fixed size structures, it is assumed the pointers passed in are pointers to the structure and must be at least as large as the request structures.

See Also: **CHttpFilterContext::ServerSupportFunction**

CHttpServerContext::WriteClient

BOOL WriteClient(LPVOID *lpvBuffer*, **LPDWORD** *lpdwBytes*,
↪ **DWORD** *dwReserved* = **0**);

Return Value

Nonzero if successful, otherwise 0. If the call fails, the Windows function **GetLastError** may be called to determine the cause of the error.

Parameters

lpvBuffer Pointer to the buffer where the data is to be written.

lpdwBytes Pointer to a DWORD that holds the number of characters to write from the buffer referenced by *Buffer*.

dwReserved Reserved for future use.

Remarks

Call this member function to send information to the HTTP client immediately. For example, use **WriteClient** to send an error message.

See Also: **CHttpServerContext::ReadClient**

Operators
CHttpServerContext::operator <<

void operator<<(LPCTSTR *psz* **);**
void operator<<(long int *dw* **);**
void operator<<(short int *w* **);**
void operator<<(const CHtmlStream& *stream* **);**
void operator<<(double *d* **);**
void operator<<(float *f* **);**
CHttpServerContext& operator<<(const CLongBinary& *blob* **);**
CHttpServerContext& operator<<(const CByteArray& *array* **);**

Remarks

The **CHttpServerContext** insertion (**<<**) operator writes the specified string or integer to the HTML stream owned by the **CHttpServerContext** object. The string version of the operator writes the string without modification. The integer overrides format the value as decimal text before writing it.

The operator parameters correspond directly to the ITS_ types that you can use in the ISAPI parse map.

See Also: Internet Server API (ISAPI) Parse Maps

Data Members
CHttpServerContext::m_pECB

Remarks

A pointer to an **EXTENSION_CONTROL_BLOCK** structure. This structure contains information describing the connection between the client which issued this server extension command and the server. See the **EXTENSION_CONTROL_BLOCK** structure for a description of the individual members.

See Also: **EXTENSION_CONTROL_BLOCK**

CHttpServerContext::m_pStream

Remarks

The **m_pStream** data member is the pointer to the initialized **CHtmlStream**, which your server can use to communicate with the client. Most extensions will write data to this stream as they do their work. MFC will write all of the data in this stream to the client when your function returns. If your function takes a long time to execute, you can use the **WriteClient** function to send data to the client immediately, even before your function ends.

See Also: CHtmlStream

CImageList

An "image list" is a collection of same-sized images, each of which can be referred to by its zero-based index. Image lists are used to efficiently manage large sets of icons or bitmaps. All images in an image list are contained in a single, wide bitmap in screen device format. An image list may also include a monochrome bitmap that contains masks used to draw images transparently (icon style). The Microsoft Win32 application programming interface (API) provides image list functions that enable you to draw images, create and destroy image lists, add and remove images, replace images, merge images, and drag images.

The **CImageList** class provides the functionality of the Windows common image list control. This control (and therefore the **CImageList** class) is available only to programs running under Windows 95 and Windows NT version 3.51 and later.

For more information on using **CImageList**, see Technical Note 60 online.

#include <afxcmn.h>

See Also: CListCtrl, **CTabCtrl**

CImageList Class Members

Data Members

m_hImageList	A handle containing the image list attached to this object.

Construction

CImageList	Constructs a **CImageList** object.
Create	Initializes an image list and attaches it to a **CImageList** object.

Attributes

GetSafeHandle	Retrieves **m_hImageList**.
GetImageCount	Retrieves the number of images in an image list.
SetBkColor	Sets the background color for an image list.
GetBkColor	Retrieves the current background color for an image list.
GetImageInfo	Retrieves information about an image.

Operations

Attach	Attaches an image list to a **CImageList** object.
Detach	Detaches an image list object from a **CImageList** object and returns a handle to an image list.
DeleteImageList	Deletes an image list.
Add	Adds an image or images to an image list.
Remove	Removes an image from an image list.
Replace	Replaces an image in an image list with a new image.
ExtractIcon	Creates an icon based on an image and mask in an image list.
Draw	Draws the image that is being dragged during a drag-and-drop operation.
SetOverlayImage	Adds the zero-based index of an image to the list of images to be used as overlay masks.
SetDragCursorImage	Creates a new drag image.
GetDragImage	Gets the temporary image list that is used for dragging.
Read	Reads an image list from an archive.
Write	Writes an image list to an archive.
BeginDrag	Begins dragging an image.
DragEnter	Locks updates during a drag operation and displays the drag image at a specified position.
EndDrag	Ends a drag operation.
DragLeave	Unlocks the window and hides the drag image so that the window can be updated.
DragMove	Moves the image that is being dragged during a drag-and-drop operation.
DragShowNolock	Shows or hides the drag image during a drag operation, without locking the window.

Member Functions

CImageList::Add

> int **Add**(**CBitmap*** *pbmImage*, **CBitmap*** *pbmMask*);
> int **Add**(**CBitmap*** *pbmImage*, **COLORREF** *crMask*);
> int **Add**(**HICON** *hIcon*);

Return Value

Zero-based index of the first new image if successful; otherwise −1.

Parameters

pbmImage   Pointer to the bitmap containing the image or images. The number of images is inferred from the width of the bitmap.

pbmMask   Pointer to the bitmap containing the mask. If no mask is used with the image list, this parameter is ignored.

crMask   Color used to generate the mask. Each pixel of this color in the given bitmap is changed to black and the corresponding bit in the mask is set to one.

hIcon   Handle of the icon that contains the bitmap and mask for the new image.

Remarks

Call this function to add one or more images or an icon to an image list.

See Also: **CImageList::Remove**, **CImageList::Replace**, **COLORREF**

CImageList::Attach

BOOL Attach(HIMAGELIST *hImageList* **);**

Return Value

Nonzero if the attachment was successful; otherwise 0.

Parameters

hImageList   A handle to an image list object.

Remarks

Call this function to attach an image list to a **CImageList** object.

See Also: **CImageList::Detach**, **CImageList::GetSafeHandle**

CImageList::BeginDrag

BOOL BeginDrag(int *nImage*, **CPoint** *ptHotSpot* **);**

Return Value

Nonzero if successful; otherwise 0.

Parameters

nImage   Zero-based index of the image to drag.

ptHotSpot   Coordinates of the starting drag position (typically, the cursor position). The coordinates are relative to the upper left corner of the image.

Remarks

Call this function to begin dragging an image. This function creates a temporary image list that is used for dragging. The image combines the specified image and its mask with the current cursor. In response to subsequent **WM_MOUSEMOVE** messages, you can move the drag image by using the **DragMove** member function. To end the drag operation, you can use the **EndDrag** member function.

See Also: **CImageList::Draw**, **CImageList::EndDrag**, **CImageList::DragMove**

CImageList::CImageList

CImageList( );

Remarks

Constructs a **CImageList** object.

See Also: **CImageList::Create**

CImageList::Create

BOOL Create(int *cx*, **int** *cy*, **UINT** *nFlags*, **int** *nInitial*, **int** *nGrow*);
BOOL Create(UINT *nBitmapID*, **int** *cx*, **int** *nGrow*, **COLORREF** *crMask*);
BOOL Create(LPCTSTR *lpszBitmapID*, **int** *cx*, **int** *nGrow*, **COLORREF** *crMask*);
BOOL Create(CImageList& *imagelist1*, **int** *nImage1*, **CImageList&** *imagelist2*,
  ↪ **int** *nImage2*, **int** *dx*, **int** *dy*);

Return Value

Nonzero if successful; otherwise 0.

Parameters

cx   Dimensions of each image, in pixels.

cy   Dimensions of each image, in pixels.

nFlags   Specifies the type of image list to create. This parameter can be a
combination of the following values, but it can include only one of the
ILC_COLOR values.

Value	Meaning
ILC_COLOR	Use the default behavior if none of the other **ILC_COLOR*** flags is specified. Typically, the default is **ILC_COLOR4**; but for older display drivers, the default is **ILC_COLORDDB**.
ILC_COLOR4	Use a 4-bit (16 color) device-independent bitmap (DIB) section as the bitmap for the image list.
ILC_COLOR8	Use an 8-bit DIB section. The colors used for the color table are the same colors as the halftone palette.
ILC_COLOR16	Use a 16-bit (32/64k color) DIB section.
ILC_COLOR24	Use a 24-bit DIB section.
ILC_COLOR32	Use a 32-bit DIB section.
ILC_COLORDDB	Use a device-dependent bitmap.
ILC_MASK	Uses a mask. The image list contains two bitmaps, one of which is a monochrome bitmap used as a mask. If this value is not included, the image list contains only one bitmap.

nInitial   Number of images that the image list initially contains.

nGrow   Number of images by which the image list can grow when the system needs to resize the list to make room for new images. This parameter represents the number of new images the resized image list can contain.

nBitmapID   Resource IDs of the bitmap to be associated with the image list.

crMask   Color used to generate a mask. Each pixel of this color in the specified bitmap is changed to black, and the corresponding bit in the mask is set to one.

lpszBitmapID   A string containing the resource IDs of the images.

imagelist1   A pointer to a **CImageList** object.

nImage1   Number of images contained in *imagelist1*.

imagelist2   A pointer to a **CImageList** object.

nImage2   Number of images contained in *imagelist2*.

dx   Dimensions of each image, in pixels.

dy   Dimensions of each image, in pixels.

Remarks

You construct a **CImageList** in two steps. First call the constructor, then call **Create**, which creates the image list and attaches it to the **CImageList** object.

See Also: **CImageList::CImageList, COLORREF**

CImageList::DeleteImageList

BOOL DeleteImageList( );

Return Value

Nonzero if successful; otherwise 0.

Remarks

Call this function to delete an image list.

See Also: **CImageList::Detach**

CImageList::Detach

HIMAGELIST Detach( );

Return Value

A handle to an image list object.

Remarks

Call this function to detach an image list object from a **CImageList** object. This function returns a handle to the image list object.

See Also: **CImageList::Attach, CImageList::DeleteImageList**

CImageList::DragEnter

static BOOL DragEnter(CWnd* *pWndLock***, CPoint** *point* **);**

Return Value

Nonzero if successful; otherwise 0.

Parameters

pWndLock   Pointer to the window that owns the drag image.

point   Position at which to display the drag image. Coordinates are relative to the upper left corner of the window (not the client area).

Remarks

During a drag operation, locks updates to the window specified by *pWndLock* and displays the drag image at the position specified by *point*.

The coordinates are relative to the window's upper left corner, so you must compensate for the widths of window elements, such as the border, title bar, and menu bar, when specifying the coordinates.

If *pWndLock* is **NULL**, this function draws the image in the display context associated with the desktop window, and coordinates are relative to the upper left corner of the screen.

This function locks all other updates to the given window during the drag operation. If you need to do any drawing during a drag operation, such as highlighting the target of a drag-and-drop operation, you can temporarily hide the dragged image by using the **CImageList::DragLeave** function.

See Also: CImageList::BeginDrag, CImageList::EndDrag, CImageList::DragMove, CImageList::DragLeave

---

CImageList::DragLeave

static BOOL DragLeave(CWnd* *pWndLock* **);**

Return Value

Nonzero if successful; otherwise 0.

Parameters

pWndLock   Pointer to the window that owns the drag image.

Remarks

Unlocks the window specified by *pWndLock* and hides the drag image, allowing the window to be updated.

See Also: CImageList::BeginDrag, CImageList::EndDrag, CImageList::DragMove, CImageList::DragEnter

CImageList::DragMove

static BOOL DragMove(CPoint *pt* **);**

Return Value

Nonzero if successful; otherwise 0.

Parameters

pt   New drag position.

Remarks

Call this function to move the image that is being dragged during a drag-and-drop operation. This function is typically called in response to a **WM_MOUSEMOVE** message. To begin a drag operation, use the **BeginDrag** member function.

See Also: **CImageList::BeginDrag, CImageList::EndDrag, CImageList::Draw**

CImageList::DragShowNolock

static BOOL DragShowNolock(BOOL *bShow* **);**

Return Value

Nonzero if successful; otherwise 0.

Parameters

bShow   Specifies whether the drag image is to be shown.

Remarks

Shows or hides the drag image during a drag operation, without locking the window.

The **CImageList::DragEnter** function locks all updates to the window during a drag operation. This function, however, does not lock the window.

See Also: **CImageList::BeginDrag, CImageList::EndDrag, CImageList::DragEnter, CImageList::DragLeave, CImageList::Draw**

CImageList::Draw

BOOL Draw(CDC* *pdc*, **int** *nImage*, **POINT** *pt*, **UINT** *nStyle* **);**

Return Value

Nonzero if successful; otherwise 0.

Parameters

pdc   Pointer to the destination device context.

nImage   Zero-based index of the image to draw.

pt Location at which to draw within the specified device context.

nStyle Flag specifying the drawing style. It can be one or more of these values:

Value	Meaning
ILD_BLEND25, **ILD_FOCUS**	Draws the image, blending 25 percent with the system highlight color. This value has no effect if the image list does not contain a mask.
ILD_BLEND50, **ILD_SELECTED**, **ILD_BLEND**	Draws the image, blending 50 percent with the system highlight color. This value has no effect if the image list does not contain a mask.
ILD_MASK	Draws the mask.
ILD_NORMAL	Draws the image using the background color for the image list. If the background color is the **CLR_NONE** value, the image is drawn transparently using the mask.
ILD_TRANSPARENT	Draws the image transparently using the mask, regardless of the background color.

Remarks

Call this function to draw the image that is being dragged during a drag-and-drop operation.

See Also: **CImageList::BeginDrag**, **CImageList::EndDrag**, **CImageList::DragMove**

CImageList::EndDrag

static void EndDrag( );

Remarks

Call this function to end a drag operation. To begin a drag operation, use the **BeginDrag** member function.

See Also: **CImageList::BeginDrag**, **CImageList::Draw**, **CImageList::DragMove**

CImageList::ExtractIcon

HICON ExtractIcon(int *nImage* **);**

Return Value

Handle of the icon if successful; otherwise **NULL**.

Parameters

nImage Zero-based index of the image.

Remarks

Call this function to create an icon based on an image and its related mask in an image list.

See Also: **CImageList::Replace**

CImageList::GetBkColor

COLORREF GetBkColor( ) const;

Return Value

The RGB color value of the **CImageList** object background color.

Remarks

Call this function to retrieve the current background color for an image list.

See Also: **CImageList::SetBkColor, COLORREF**

CImageList::GetDragImage

static CImageList* GetDragImage(LPPOINT *lpPoint*, **LPPOINT** *lpPointHotSpot* **);**

Return Value

If successful, a pointer to the temporary image list that is used for dragging; otherwise, **NULL**.

Parameters

lpPoint   Address of a **POINT** structure that receives the current drag position.

lpPointHotSpot   Address of a **POINT** structure that receives the offset of the drag image relative to the drag position.

Remarks

Gets the temporary image list that is used for dragging.

See Also: **CImageList::SetDragCursorImage**

CImageList::GetImageCount

int GetImageCount( ) const;

Return Value

The number of images.

Remarks

Call this function to retrieve the number of images in an image list.

See Also: **CImageList::GetImageInfo**

CImageList::GetImageInfo

BOOL GetImageInfo(int *nImage*, **IMAGEINFO*** *pImageInfo* **) const;**

Return Value

Nonzero if successful; otherwise 0.

Parameters

nImage   Zero-based index of the image.

pImageInfo   Pointer to an **IMAGEINFO** structure that receives information about the image. The information in this structure can be used to directly manipulate the bitmaps for the image.

Remarks

Call this function to retrieve information about an image.

The **IMAGEINFO** structure contains information about an image in an image list:

```
typedef struct _IMAGEINFO {
    HBITMAP hbmImage;        // bitmap containing the images
    HBITMAP hbmMask;
    int     cPlanes;         // number of color planes in hbmImage
    int     cBitsPerPixel;   // bits per pixel in hbmImage
    RECT    rcImage;
} IMAGEINFO;
```

hbmMask   Handle of a monochrome bitmap containing the masks for the images. If the image list does not contain a mask, this member is **NULL**.

rcImage   Bounding rectangle of the image within the bitmap specified by **hbmImage**.

See Also: CImageList::GetImageCount

CImageList::GetSafeHandle

HIMAGELIST GetSafeHandle( ) const;

Return Value

A handle to the attached image list; otherwise **NULL** if no object is attached.

Remarks

Call this function to retrieve the **m_hImageList** data member.

See Also: CImageList::Attach, CImageList::Detach, CImageList::m_hImageList

CImageList::Read

> **BOOL Read(CArchive*** *pArchive* **);**

Return Value

Nonzero if successful; otherwise 0.

Parameters

pArchive   A pointer to a **CArchive** object from which the image list is to be read.

Remarks

Call this function to read an image list from an archive.

> **See Also: CImageList::Write**

CImageList::Remove

> **BOOL Remove(int** *nImage* **);**

Return Value

Nonzero if successful; otherwise 0.

Parameters

nImage   Zero-based index of the image to remove.

Remarks

Call this function to remove an image from an image list object.

> **See Also: CImageList::DeleteImageList**

CImageList::Replace

> **BOOL Replace(int** *nImage***, CBitmap*** *pbmImage***, CBitmap*** *pbmMask* **);**
> **int Replace(int** *nImage***, HICON** *hIcon* **);**

Return Value

The version returning **BOOL** returns nonzero if successful; otherwise 0.

The version returning **int** returns the zero-based index of the image if successful; otherwise −1.

Parameters

nImage   Zero-based index of the image to replace.

pbmImage   A pointer to the bitmap containing the image.

pbmMask   A pointer to the bitmap containing the mask. If no mask is used with the image list, this parameter is ignored.

hIcon   A handle to the icon that contains the bitmap and mask for the new image.

Remarks

Call this function to replace an image in an image list with a new image.

See Also: CImageList::Remove

CImageList::SetBkColor

COLORREF SetBkColor(COLORREF *cr* **);**

Return Value

The previous background color if successful; otherwise **CLR_NONE**.

Parameters

cr   Background color to set. It can be **CLR_NONE**. In that case, images are drawn transparently using the mask.

Remarks

Call this function to set the background color for an image list.

See Also: CImageList::GetBkColor, COLORREF

CImageList::SetDragCursorImage

BOOL SetDragCursorImage(int *nDrag*, **CPoint** *ptHotSpot* **);**

Return Value

Nonzero if successful; otherwise 0.

Parameters

nDrag   Index of the new image to be combined with the drag image.

ptHotSpot   Position of the hot spot within the new image.

Remarks

Creates a new drag image by combining the given image (typically a mouse cursor image) with the current drag image.

Because the dragging functions use the new image during a drag operation, you should use the Windows **ShowCursor** function to hide the actual mouse cursor after calling **CImageList::SetDragCursorImage**. Otherwise, the system may appear to have two mouse cursors for the duration of the drag operation.

See Also: CImageList::BeginDrag, CImageList::EndDrag, CImageList::GetDragImage

CImageList::SetOverlayImage

BOOL SetOverlayImage(int *nImage***, int** *nOverlay* **);**

Return Value

Nonzero if successful; otherwise 0.

Parameters

nImage   Zero-based index of the image to use as an overlay mask.

nOverlay   One-based index of the overlay mask.

Remarks

Call this function to add the zero-based index of an image to the list of images to be used as overlay masks. Up to four indices can be added to the list.

An overlay mask is an image drawn transparently over another image. Draw an overlay mask over an image by using the **CImageList::Draw** member function with the one-based index of the overlay mask specified by using the **INDEXTOOVERLAYMASK** macro

See Also: CImageList::Add

CImageList::Write

BOOL Write(CArchive* *pArchive* **);**

Return Value

Nonzero if successful; otherwise 0.

Parameters

pArchive   A pointer to a **CArchive** object in which the image list is to be stored.

Remarks

Call this function to write an image list object to an archive.

See Also: CImageList::Read

Data Members

CImageList::m_hImageList

HIMAGELIST m_hImageList;

Remarks

A handle of the image list attached to this object. The **m_hImageList** data member is a public variable of type **HIMAGELIST**.

See Also: CImageList::Attach, CImageList::Detach, CImageList::Attach

CInternetConnection

The MFC class **CInternetConnection** manages your connection to an Internet server. It is the base class for MFC classes **CFtpConnection**, **CHttpConnection**, and **CGopherConnection**. Each of these classes provides additional functionality for communicating with the respective FTP, HTTP, or gopher server.

To communicate directly with an Internet server, you must have a **CInternetSession** object and a **CInternetConnection** object.

To learn more about how the WinInet classes work, see the article "Internet Programming with WinInet" in *Visual C++ Programmer's Guide* online.

#include <afxinet.h>

CInternetConnection Class Members

Construction

CInternetConnection	Constructs a **CinternetConnection** object.

Operations

GetContext	Gets the context ID for this connection object.
GetSession	Gets a pointer to the **CInternetSession** object associated with the connection.
GetServerName	Gets the name of the server associated with the connection.

Operators

operator HINTERNET	A handle to an Internet session.

Member Functions
CInternetConnection::CInternetConnection

> **CInternetConnection(CInternetSession*** *pSession*, **LPCTSTR** *pstrServer*,
>   ↳ **INTERNET_PORT** *nPort* = **INTERNET_INVALID_PORT_NUMBER**,
>   ↳ **DWORD** *dwContext* = **1**);

Parameters

pSession　A pointer to a **CInternetSession** object.

pstrServer　A pointer to a string containing the server name.

nPort　The number that identifies the Internet port for this connection.

dwContext　The context identifier for the **CInternetConnection** object. See **Remarks** for more information about *dwContext*.

Remarks

This member function is called when a **CInternetConnection** object is created.

You never call **CInternetConnection** yourself; instead, call the **CInternetSession** member function for the type of connection you want to establish:

- **CInternetSession::GetFtpConnection**
- **CInternetSession::GetHttpConnection**
- **CInternetSession::GetGopherConnection**

The default value for *dwContext* is sent by MFC to the **CInternetConnection**-derived object from the **CInternetSession** object that created the **InternetConnection**-derived object. The default is set to 1; however, you can explicitly assign a specific context identifier in the **CInternetSession** constructor for the connection. The object and any work it does will be associated with that context ID. The context identifier is returned to **CInternetSession::OnStatusCallback** to provide status on the object with which it is identified. See the article "Internet First Steps: WinInet" online for more information about the context identifier.

See Also:　**CInternetSession, CGopherConnection, CFtpConnection, CHttpConnection**

CInternetConnection::GetContext

DWORD GetContext( ) const;

Return Value

The application-assigned context ID.

Remarks

Call this member function to get the context ID for this session. The context ID is originally specified in **CInternetSession** and propagates to **CInternetConnection** and **CInternetFile**-derived classes, unless specified differently in the call to a function that opens the connection. The context ID is associated with any operation of the given object and identifies the operation's status information returned by **CInternetSession::OnStatusCallback**.

For more information about how **GetContext** works with other WinInet classes to give the user status information, see the article "Internet First Steps: WinInet" online for more information about the context identifier.

See Also: CInternetSession::EnableStatusCallback

CInternetConnection::GetServerName

CString GetServerName( ) const;

Return Value

The name of the server this connection object is working with.

Remarks

Call this member function to get the name of the server associated with this Internet connection.

See Also: CInternetSession, CGopherConnection, CFtpConnection, CHttpConnection

CInternetConnection::GetSession

CInternetSession* GetSession( ) const;

Return Value

A pointer to a **CInternetSession** object associated with this Internet connection object.

Remarks

Call this member function to get a pointer to the **CInternetSession** object that's associated with this connection.

See Also: CInternetSession, CGopherConnection, CFtpConnection, CHttpConnection

Operators
CInternetConnection::operator HINTERNET

operator HINTERNET( ) const;

Remarks

Use this operator to get the API-level handle for the current Internet session.

See Also: CInternetSession, CGopherConnection, CFtpConnection, CHttpConnection

CInternetException

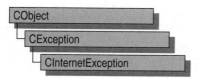

The **CInternetException** object represents an exception condition related to an
Internet operation. The **CInternetException** class includes two public data members:
one holds the error code associated with the exception, and the other holds the context
identifier of the Internet application associated with the error.

For more information about context identifiers for Internet applications, see the article
"Internet Programming with WinInet" in *Visual C++ Programmer's Guide* online.

#include <afxinet.h>

See Also: **CException**

CInternetException Class Members

Construction

CInternetException	Constructs a **CinternetException** object.

Data Members

m_dwError	The error that caused the exception.
m_dwContext	The context value associated with the operation that caused the exception.

See Also: **CException**

Member Functions
CInternetException::CInternetException

CInternetException(DWORD *dwError* **);**

Parameters

dwError   The error that caused the exception.

Remarks

This member function is called when a **CInternetException** object is created. To throw a CInternetException, call the MFC global function **AfxThrowInternetException**.

See Also: **CException**

Data Members

CInternetException::m_dwContext

Remarks

The context value associated with the related Internet operation. The context identifier is originally specified in **CInternetSession** and passed by MFC to **CInternetConnection**- and **CInternetFile**-derived classes. You can override this default and assign any *dwContext* parameter a value of your choosing. *dwContext* is associated with any operation of the given object. *dwContext* identifies the operation's status information returned by **CInternetSession::OnStatusCallback**.

See Also: **CException**

CInternetException::m_dwError

Remarks

The error that caused the exception. This error value may be a system error code, found in WINERROR.H, or an error value from WININET.H.

For a list of Win32 error codes, see "Error Codes" in the *Win32 SDK*. For a list of Internet-specific error codes, see the *ActiveX SDK* documentation.

See Also: **CException**

CInternetFile

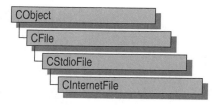

The MFC class **CInternetFile** provides a base class for the **CHttpFile** and **CGopherFile** file classes. **CInternetFile** and its derived classes allow access to files on remote systems that use Internet protocols. You never create a **CInternetFile** object directly. Instead, create an object of one of its derived classes by calling **CGopherConnection::OpenFile** or **CHttpConnection::OpenRequest**. You also can create a **CInternetFile** object by calling **CFtpConnection::OpenFile**.

The **CInternetFile** member functions **Open**, **LockRange**, **UnlockRange**, and **Duplicate** are not implemented for **CInternetFile**. If you call these functions on a **CInternetFile** object, you will get a **CNotSupportedException**.

To learn more about how **CInternetFile** works with the other MFC Internet classes, see the article "Internet Programming with WinInet" in *Visual C++ Programmer's Guide* online.

#include <afxinet.h>

See Also: **CInternetConnection**

CInternetFile Class Members

Construction

CInternetFile	Constructs a **CInternetFile** object.

Operations

SetWriteBufferSize	Sets the size of the buffer where data will be written.
SetReadBufferSize	Sets the size of the buffer where data will be read.

Overridables

Seek	Repositions the pointer in an open file.
Read	Reads the number of specified bytes.
Write	Writes the number of specified bytes.
Abort	Closes the file, ignoring all warnings and errors.

Overridables *(continued)*

Flush	Flushes the contents of the write buffer and makes sure the data in memory is written to the target machine.
Close	Closes a **CInternetFile** and frees its resources.
ReadString	Reads a stream of characters.
WriteString	Writes a null-terminated string to a file.

Data Members

m_hFile	A handle to a file.

Operators

operator HINTERNET	A casting operator for an Internet handle.

Member Functions

CInternetFile::Abort

virtual void Abort( );

Remarks

Closes the file associated with this object and makes the file unavailable for reading or writing. If you have not closed the file before destroying the object, the destructor closes it for you.

When handling exceptions, **Abort** differs from **Close** in two important ways. First, the **Abort** function does not throw an exception on failures because it ignores failures. Second, **Abort** does not **ASSERT** if the file has not been opened or was closed previously.

CInternetFile::CInternetFile

CInternetFile( );

Remarks

This member function is called when a **CInternetFile** object is created.

You never create a **CInternetFile** object directly. Instead, create an object of one of its derived classes by calling **CGopherConnection::OpenFile** or **CHttpConnection::OpenRequest**. You also can create a **CInternetFile** object by calling **CFtpConnection::OpenFile**.

See Also: **CInternetConnection**, **CHttpFile CGopherFile**

CInternetFile::Close

virtual void Close( );
    throw (CInternetException);

Remarks

Closes a **CInternetFile** and frees any of its resources. If the file was opened for writing, there is an implicit call to **Flush** to assure that all buffered data is written to the host. You should call **Close** when you are finished using a file.

CInternetFile::Flush

virtual void Flush( );
    throw (CInternetException);

Remarks

Call this member function to flush the contents of the write buffer. Use **Flush** to assure that all data in memory has actually been written to the target machine and to assure your transaction with the host machine has been completed. **Flush** is only effective on **CInternetFile** objects opened for writing.

CInternetFile::Read

virtual UINT Read(void* *lpBuf,* **UINT** *nCount* **);**
    throw CInternetException( );

Return Value

The number of bytes transferred to the buffer. The return value may be less than *nCount* if the end of file was reached.

Parameters

lpBuf A pointer to a memory address to which file data is read.

nCount The number of bytes to be written.

Remarks

Call this member function to read into the given memory, starting at *lpvBuf*, the specified number of bytes, *nCount*. The function returns the number of bytes actually read—a number that may be less than *nCount* if the file ends. If an error occurs while reading the file, the function throws a **CInternetException** object that describes the error. Note that reading past the end of the file is not considered an error and no exception will be thrown.

CInternetFile::ReadString

virtual BOOL ReadString(CString& *rString* **);**
    throw (CInternetException);
virtual LPTSTR ReadString(LPTSTR *pstr*, **UINT** *nMax* **);**
    throw (CInternetException);

Return Value

A pointer to the buffer containing the text data. **NULL** if end-of-file was reached without reading any data; or, if boolean, **FALSE** if end-of-file was reached without reading any data.

Parameters

pstr A pointer to a string which will receive the line being read.

nMax The maximum number of characters to be read.

rString A reference to the **CString** object that receives the read line.

Remarks

Call this member function to read a stream of characters until it finds a newline character. The function places the resulting line into the memory referenced by the *pstr* parameter. It stops reading characters when it reaches the maximum number of characters, specified by *nMax*. The buffer always receives a terminating null character.

If you call **ReadString** without first calling **SetReadBufferSize**, you will get a buffer of 4096 bytes.

CInternetFile::Seek

virtual LONG Seek(LONG *lOffset*, **UINT** *nFrom* **);**
    throw (CInternetException);

Return Value

The new byte offset from the beginning of the file if the requested position is legal; otherwise, the value is undefined and a **CInternetException** object is thrown.

Parameters

lOffset Offset in bytes to move the read/write pointer in the file.

nFrom Relative reference for the offset. Must be one of the following values:

- **CFile::begin** Move the file pointer *lOff* bytes forward from the beginning of the file.

- **CFile::current** Move the file pointer *lOff* bytes from the current position in the file.

- **CFile::end**   Move the file pointer *lOff* bytes from the end of the file. *lOff* must be negative to seek into the existing file; positive values will seek past the end of the file.

Remarks

Call this member function to reposition the pointer in a previously opened file. The **Seek** function permits random access to a file's contents by moving the pointer a specified amount, absolutely or relatively. No data is actually read during the seek.

At this time, a call to this member function is only supported for data associated with **CHttpFile** objects. It is not supported for FTP or gopher requests. If you call **Seek** for one of these unsupported services, it will pass back you to the Win32 error code **ERROR_INTERNET_INVALID_OPERATION**.

When a file is opened, the file pointer is at offset 0, the beginning of the file.

Note Using **Seek** may cause an implicit call to **Flush**.

CInternetFile::SetReadBufferSize

BOOL SetReadBufferSize(UINT *nReadSize* **);**

Return Value

Nonzero if successful; otherwise 0. If the call fails, the Win32 function **GetLastError** may be called to determine the cause of the error.

Parameters

nReadSize   The desired buffer size in bytes.

Remarks

Call this member function to set the size of the temporary read buffer used by a **CInternetFile**-derived object. The underlying WinInet APIs do not perform buffering, so choose a buffer size that allows your application to read data efficiently, regardless of the amount of data to be read. If each call to **Read** normally involves a large aount of data (for example, four or more kilobytes), you should not need a buffer. However, if you call **Read** to get small chunks of data, or if you use **ReadString** to read individual lines at a time, then a read buffer improves application performance.

By default, a **CInternetFile** object does not provide any buffering for reading. If you call this member function, you must be sure that the file has been opened for read access.

You can increase the buffer size at any time, but shrinking the buffer will have no effect. If you call **ReadString** without first calling **SetReadBufferSize**, you will get a buffer of 4096 bytes.

CInternetFile::SetWriteBufferSize

BOOL SetWriteBufferSize(UINT *nWriteSize* **);**

Return Value

Nonzero if successful; otherwise 0. If the call fails, the Win32 function **GetLastError** may be called to determine the cause of the error.

Parameters

nWriteSize   The size of the buffer in bytes.

Remarks

Call this member function to set the size of the temporary write buffer used by a **CInternetFile**-derived object. The underlying WinInet APIs don't perform buffering, so choose a buffer size that allows your application to write data efficiently regardless of the amount of data to be written. If each call to **Write** normally involves a large amount of data (for example, four or more kilobytes at a time), you should not need a buffer. However, if you call **Write** to write small chunks of data, a write buffer improves your application's performance.

By default, a **CInternetFile** object does not provide any buffering for writing. If you call this member function, you must be sure that the file has been opened for write access. You can change the size of the write buffer at any time, but doing so causes an implicit call to **Flush**.

CInternetFile::Write

virtual void Write(const void* *lpBuf*, **UINT** *nCount* **);**
    throw CInternetException( );

Parameters

lpvBuf   A pointer to the first byte to be written.

nCount   Specifies the number of bytes to be written.

Remarks

Call this member function to write into the given memory, *lpvBuf*, the specified number of bytes, *nCount*. If any error occurs while writing the data, the function throws a **CInternetException** describing the error.

CInternetFile::WriteString

virtual void WriteString(LPCTSTR *pstr* **);**
    throw CInternetException( );

Parameters

pstr   A pointer to a string containing the contents to be written.

Remarks

> This function writes a null-terminated string to the associated file.

Data Members
CInternetFile::m_hFile

> **HINTERNET m_hFile;**

Remarks

> A handle to the file associated with this object.

Operators
CInternetFile::operator HINTERNET

> **operator HINTERNET( ) const;**

Remarks

> Use this operator to get the Windows handle for the current Internet session.

CInternetSession

Use class **CInternetSession** to create and initialize a single or several simultaneous Internet sessions and, if necessary, to describe your connection to a proxy server. If your Internet connection must be maintained for the duration of an application, you can create a **CInternetSession** member of the class **CWinApp**.

Once you have established an Internet session, you can call **OpenURL**. **CInternetSession** then parses the URL for you by calling the global function **AfxParseURL**. Regardless of its protocol type, **CInternetSession** interprets the URL and manages it for you. It can handle requests for local files identified with the URL resource "file://". **OpenURL** will return a pointer to a **CStdioFile** object if the name you pass it is a local file.

If you open a URL on an Internet server using **OpenURL**, you can read information from the site. If you want to perform service-specific (for example, HTTP, FTP, or gopher) actions on files located on a server, you must establish the appropriate connection with that server. To open a particular kind of connection directly to a particular service, use one of the following member functions:

- **GetGopherConnection** to open a connection to a gopher service.
- **GetHttpConnection** to open a connection to an HTTP service.
- **GetFtpConnection** to open a connection to an FTP service.

QueryOption and **SetOption** allow you to set the query options of your session, such as time-out values, number of retries, and so on.

During an Internet session, a transaction such as a search or data download can take appreciable time. The user might want to continue working, or might want to have status information about the progress of the transaction. To handle this problem, **CInternetSession** provides for searches and data transfer to occur asynchronously, allowing the user to perform other tasks while waiting for the transfer to complete. If you want to provide the user with status information, or if you want to handle any operations asynchronously, three conditions must be set:

- In the constructor, *dwFlags* must include **INTERNET_FLAG_ASYNC**.
- In the constructor, *dwContext* must be set to 1.
- You must establish a call back function by calling **EnableStatusCallback**

Use the overridable member function **OnStatusCallback** to get status information on asynchronous retrieval. To use this overridable member function, you must derive your own class from **CInternetSession**.

For more information about asynchronous operations, see the article "Internet First Steps: WinInet" in *Visual C++ Programmer's Guide* online. For general information about using the MFC WinInet classes, see the article "Internet Programming with WinInet" in *Visual C++ Programmer's Guide* online.

Note **CInternetSession** will throw an **AfxThrowNotSupportedException** for unsupported service types. Only the following service types are currently supported: FTP, HTTP, gopher, and file.

#include <afxinet.h>

See Also: **CInternetConnection**, **CHttpConnection**, **CFtpConnection**, **CGopherConnection**

CInternetSession Class Members

Construction

CInternetSession	Constructs a **CInternetSession** object.

Attributes

QueryOption	Provides possible asserts for error checking.
SetOption	Sets options for the Internet session.
OpenURL	Parses and opens a URL.
GetFtpConnection	Opens an FTP session with a server. Logs on the user.
GetHttpConnection	Opens an HTTP server for an application that is trying to open a connection.
GetGopherConnection	Opens a gopher server for an application that is trying to open a connection.
EnableStatusCallback	Establishes a status callback routine. **EnableStatusCallback** is required for asynchronous operations.
ServiceTypeFromHandle	Gets the type of service from the Internet handle.

Operations

GetContext	Gets the context value for an Internet or application session.
Close	Closes the Internet connection when the Internet session is terminated.

Overridables

OnStatusCallback	Updates the status of an operation when status callback is enabled.

Operators

operator HINTERNET	A handle to the current Internet session.

Member Functions

CInternetSession::CInternetSession

CInternetSession(LPCTSTR *pstrAgent* **= NULL, DWORD** *dwContext* **= 1,**
↳ **DWORD** *dwAccessType* **= INTERNET_OPEN_TYPE_PRECONFIG,**
↳ **LPCTSTR** *pstrProxyName* **= NULL, LPCTSTR** *pstrProxyBypass* **= NULL,**
↳ **DWORD** *dwFlags* **= 0);**

Parameters

> *pstrAgent*   A pointer to a string that identifies the name of the application or entity calling the Internet functions (for example, "Microsoft Internet Browser"). If *pstrAgent* is **NULL** (the default), the framework calls the global function **AfxGetAppName**, which returns a null-terminated string containing an application's name. Some protocols use this string to identify your application to the server.

> *dwContext*   The context identifier for the operation. *dwContext* identifies the operation's status information returned by **CInternetSession::OnStatusCallback**. The default is set to 1; however, you can explicitly assign a specific context ID for the operation. The object and any work it does will be associated with that context ID. If *dwFlags* includes **INTERNET_FLAG_ASYNC**, then objects created by this object have asynchronous behavior as long as a status callback routine is registered. In order for a function to be completed synchronously, *dwContext* has to be set to zero for that call.

> *dwAccessType*   The type of access required. The following are valid values, exactly one of which may be supplied:

> - **INTERNET_OPEN_TYPE_PRECONFIG**   Preconfigured (in the registry). This access type is set as the default.

> - **INTERNET_OPEN_TYPE_DIRECT**   Direct to Internet.

> - **INTERNET_OPEN_TYPE_PROXY**   Through CERN proxy.

> *pstrProxyName*   The name of the preferred CERN proxy if *dwAccessType* is set as **INTERNET_OPEN_TYPE_PROXY**. The default is **NULL**.

> *pstrProxyBypass*   A pointer to a string containing an optional list of server addresses. These addresses may be bypassed when using proxy access. If a **NULL** value is supplied, the bypass list will be read from the registry. This parameter is meaningful only if *dwAccessType* is set to **INTERNET_OPEN_TYPE_PROXY**.

> *dwFlags*   Indicates various options such as caching and asynchronous behavior. The default is set to 0. The possible values include:

> - **INTERNET_FLAG_DONT_CACHE**   Do not cache the data, either locally or in any gateway servers.

- **INTERNET_FLAG_ASYNC** Future operations on this object may fail with **ERROR_IO_PENDING**. A status callback will be made with **INTERNET_STATUS_REQUEST_COMPLETE** when the operation finishes. This callback is on a thread other than the one for the original request. You must call **EnableStatusCallback** to establish a status callback routine, or the functions will be completed synchronously.

- **INTERNET_FLAG_OFFLINE** Download operations are satisfied through the persistent cache only. If the item does not exist in the cache, an appropriate error code is returned. This flag may be combined with the bitwise **OR** (|) operator.

Remarks

This member function is called when a **CInternetSession** object is created. **CInternetSession** is the first Internet function called by an application. It initializes internal data structures and prepares for future calls from the application.

If *dwFlags* includes **INTERNET_FLAG_ASYNC**, then all handles derived from this handle will have asynchronous behavior as long as a status callback routine is registered.

If no Internet connection can be opened, **CInternetSession** throws an **AfxThrowInternetException**.

See Also: CInternetSession::Close, CInternetSession::EnableStatusCallback, CInternetSession::GetContext

---

CInternetSession::Close

virtual void Close( );

Remarks

Call this member function when your application has finished using the **CInternetSession** object.

See Also: CInternetSession::CInternetSession

CInternetSession::EnableStatusCallback

BOOL EnableStatusCallback(BOOL *bEnable* **= TRUE);**
   throw (CInternetException);

Return Value

Nonzero if successful; otherwise 0. If the call fails, determine the cause of the failure by examining the thrown **CInternetException** object.

Parameters

bEnable Specifies whether callback is enabled or disabled. The default is **TRUE**.

Remarks

Call this member function to enable status callback. When handling status callback, you can provide status about the progress of the operation (such as resolving name, connecting to server, and so on) in the status bar of the application. Displaying operation status is especially desirable during a long-term operation.

You can set a callback routine for synchronous operations; however, you must establish a callback routine for asynchronous operations because the asynchronous API makes a callback with **INTERNET_STATUS_REQUEST_COMPLETE** to indicate that the request has completed.

A callback for an asynchronous operation will be on a thread other than the one for the original request. The call can fail with an **ERROR_IO_PENDING** error if the request is not complete when the status callback occurs. The callback may be callled in a thread context different from the thread which initiated the request.

Because callbacks occur during the request's processing, the application should spend as little time as possible in the callback to prevent degradation of data throughput to the network. For example, putting up a dialog box in a callback may be such a lengthy operation that the server terminates the request.

The status callback cannot be removed as long as any callbacks or any asynchronous functions are pending.

Note   To handle any operations asynchronously, three conditions must be set:

- In the constructor, *dwFlags* must include **INTERNET_FLAG_ASYNC**.
- In the constructor, *dwContext* must be set to 1.
- You must establish a call back function by calling **EnableStatusCallback**.

For more information about asynchronous operations, see the article "Internet First Steps: WinInet" in *Visual C++ Programmer's Guide* online.

See Also: **CInternetSession::CInternetSession**

CInternetSession::GetContext

DWORD GetContext( ) const;

Return Value

The application-defined context Identifier.

Remarks

Call this member function to get the context value for a particular application session. **OnStatusCallback** uses the context ID returned by **GetContext** to report the status of a particular application. For example, when a user activates an Internet request that involves returning status information, the status callback uses the context ID to report status on that particular request. If the user activates two separate Internet requests that both involve returning status information, **OnStatusCallback** uses the context identifiers to return status about their corresponding requests. Consequently, the context identifier is used for all status callback operations, and it is associated with the session until the session is ended.

For more information about asynchronous operations, see the article "Internet First Steps: WinInet" in *Visual C++ Programmer's Guide* online.

See Also: **CInternetConnection**, **CInternetSession::EnableStatusCallback**, **CInternetSession::OnStatusCallback**

CInternetSession::GetFtpConnection

CFtpConnection* GetFtpConnection(LPCTSTR *pstrServer*,
↳ **LPCTSTR** *pstrUserName* = **NULL, LPCTSTR** *pstrPassword* = **NULL,**
↳ **INTERNET_PORT** *nPort* = **INTERNET_INVALID_PORT_NUMBER,**
↳ **BOOL** *bPassive* = **FALSE**);
throw (CInternetException);

Return Value

A pointer to a **CFtpConnection** object. If the call fails, determine the cause of the failure by examining the thrown **CInternetException** object.

Parameters

pstrServer A pointer to a string containing the FTP server name.

pstrUserName Pointer to a null-terminated string that specifies the name of the user to log in. If **NULL**, the default is anonymous.

pstrPassword A pointer to a null-terminated string that specifies the password to use to log in. If both *pstrPassword* and *pstrUserName* are **NULL**, the default anonymous password is the user's email name. If *pstrPassword* is **NULL** (or an empty string) but *pstrUserName* is not **NULL**, a blank password is used. The following table describes the behavior for the four possible settings of *pstrUserName* and *pstrPassword*:

pstrUserName	*pstrPassword*	Username sent to FTP server	Password sent to FTP server
NULL or " "	**NULL** or " "	"anonymous"	User's email name
Non-**NULL** String	**NULL** or " "	*pstrUserName*	" "
NULL Non-**NULL** String	**ERROR**	**ERROR**	
Non-**NULL** String	Non-**NULL** String	*pstrUserName*	*pstrPassword*

nPort A number that identifies the TCP/IP port to use on the server.

bPassive Specifies passive or active mode for this FTP session. If set to **TRUE**, it sets the Win32 API *dwFlag* to **INTERNET_FLAG_PASSIVE**.

Remarks

Call this member function to establish an FTP connection and get a pointer to a **CFtpConnection** object.

GetFtpConnection connects to an FTP server, and creates and returns a pointer to a **CFTPConnection** object. It does not perform any specific operation on the server. If you intend to read or write to files, for example, you must perform those operations as separate steps. See the classes **CFtpConnection** and **CFtpFileFind** for information about searching for files, opening files, and reading or writing to files. See the article "Internet Programming with WinInet" in *Visual C++ Programmer's Guide* online for steps in performing common FTP connection tasks.

See Also: CFtpConnection CInternetSession::GetGopherConnection, CInternetSession::GetHttpConnection, CInternetSession::OpenURL

CInternetSession::GetGopherConnection

CGopherConnection* GetGopherConnection(LPCTSTR *pstrServer***,**
↳ **LPCTSTR** *pstrUserName* = **NULL, LPCTSTR** *pstrPassword* = **NULL,**
↳ **INTERNET_PORT** *nPort* = **INTERNET_INVALID_PORT_NUMBER);**
throw (CInternetException);

Return Value

A pointer to a **CGopherConnection** object. If the call fails, determine the cause of the failure by examining the thrown **CInternetException** object.

Parameters

pstrServer   A pointer to a string containing the gopher server name.

pstrUserName   A pointer to a string containing the user name.

pstrPassword   A pointer to a string containing the access password.

nPort   A number that identifies the TCP/IP port to use on the server.

Remarks

Call this member function to establish a new gopher connection and get a pointer to a **CGopherConnection** object.

GetGopherConnection connects to a gopher server, and creates and returns a pointer to a **CGopherConnection** object. It does not perform any specific operation on the server. If you intend to read or write data, for example, you must perform those operations as separate steps. See the classes **CGopherConnection**, **CGopherFile**, and **CGopherFileFind** for information about searching for files, opening files, and reading or writing to files. For information about browsing an FTP site, see the member function **OpenURL**. See the article "Internet Programming with WinInet" in *Visual C++ Programmer's Guide* online for steps in performing common gopher connection tasks.

See Also: **CGopherConnection**, **CInternetSession::GetFtpConnection**, **CInternetSession::GetHttpConnection**, **CInternetSession::OpenURL**

CInternetSession::GetHttpConnection

CHttpConnection* GetHttpConnection(LPCTSTR *pstrServer*,
  ↳ **INTERNET_PORT** *nPort* = **INTERNET_INVALID_PORT_NUMBER**,
  ↳ **LPCTSTR** *pstrUserName* = **NULL, LPCTSTR** *pstrPassword* = **NULL**);
throw (CInternetException);

Return Value

A pointer to a **CHttpConnection** object. If the call fails, determine the cause of the failure by examining the thrown **CInternetException** object.

Parameters

pstrServer A pointer to a string containing the HTTP server name.

nPort A number that identifies the TCP/IP port to use on the server.

pstrUserName A pointer to a string containing the user name.

pstrPassword A pointer to a string containing the access password.

Remarks

Call this member function to establish an HTTP connection and get a pointer to a **CHttpConnection** object.

GetHttpConnection connects to an HTTP server, and creates and returns a pointer to a **CHttpConnection** object. It does not perform any specific operation on the server. If you intend to query an HTTP header, for example, you must perform this operation as a separate step. See the classes **CHttpConnection** and **CHttpFile** for information about operations you can perform by using a connection to an HTTP server. For information about browsing an HTTP site, see the member function **OpenURL**. See the article "Internet Programming with WinInet" in *Visual C++ Programmer's Guide* online for steps in performing common HTTP connection tasks.

See Also: **CHttpConnection**, **CInternetSession::GetGopherConnection**, **CInternetSession::GetFtpConnection**, **CInternetSession::OpenURL**

CInternetSession::OnStatusCallback

virtual void OnStatusCallback(DWORD *dwContext*, **DWORD** *dwInternetStatus*,
  ↳ **LPVOID** *lpvStatusInformation*, **DWORD** *dwStatusInformationLength*);

Parameters

dwContext The context value supplied by the application.

dwInternetStatus A status code which indicates why the callback is being made.
  See **Remarks** for a table of possible values.

lpvStatusInformation   A pointer to a buffer containing information pertinent to this callback.

dwStatusInformationLength   The size of *lpvStatusInformation*.

Remarks

This member function is called by the framework to update the status when status callback is enabled and an operation is pending. You must first call **EnableStatusCallback** to take advantage of status callback.

The *dwInternetStatus* parameter indicates the operation being performed and determines what the contents of *lpvStatusInformation* will be. *dwStatusInformationLength* indicates the length of the data included in *lpvStatusInformation*. The following status values for *dwInternetStatus* are defined as follows:

Value	Meaning
INTERNET_STATUS_RESOLVING_NAME	Looking up the IP address of the name contained in *lpvStatusInformation*.
INTERNET_STATUS_NAME_RESOLVED	Successfully found the IP address of the name contained in *lpvStatusInformation*.
INTERNET_STATUS_CONNECTING_TO_SERVER	Connecting to the socket address (**SOCKADDR**) pointed to by *lpvStatusInformation*.
INTERNET_STATUS_CONNECTED_TO_SERVER	Successfully connected to the socket address (**SOCKADDR**) pointed to by *lpvStatusInformation*.
INTERNET_STATUS_SENDING_REQUEST	Sending the information request to the server. The *lpvStatusInformation* parameter is **NULL**.
INTERNET_STATUS_ REQUEST_SENT	Successfully sent the information request to the server. The *lpvStatusInformation* parameter is **NULL**.
INTERNET_STATUS_RECEIVING_RESPONSE	Waiting for the server to respond to a request. The *lpvStatusInformation* parameter is **NULL**.
INTERNET_STATUS_RESPONSE_RECEIVED	Successfully received a response from the server. The *lpvStatusInformation* parameter is **NULL**.
INTERNET_STATUS_CLOSING_CONNECTION	Closing the connection to the server. The *lpvStatusInformation* parameter is **NULL**.
INTERNET_STATUS_CONNECTION_CLOSED	Successfully closed the connection to the server. The *lpvStatusInformation* parameter is **NULL**.
INTERNET_STATUS_HANDLE_CREATED	Used by the Win32 API function **InternetConnect** to indicate that it has created the new handle. This lets the application call the Win32 function **InternetCloseHandle** from another thread if the connect is taking too long. See the *ActiveX SDK* for more information about these functions.
INTERNET_STATUS_HANDLE_CLOSING	Successfully terminated this handle value.

(continued)

(continued)

Value	Meaning
INTERNET_STATUS_REQUEST_COMPLETE	Successfully completed the asynchronous operation. See the **CInternetSession** constructor for details on **INTERNET_FLAG_ASYNC**. The *lpvStatusInformation* parameter will be **NULL** and *dwStatusInformationLength* will contain the final completion status of the asynchronous function. If this is **ERROR_INTERNET_EXTENDED_ERROR**, the application can retrieve the server error information by using the Win32 function **InternetGetLastResponseInfo**. See the *ActiveX SDK* for more information about this function.

In the case of **INTERNET_STATUS_REQUEST_COMPLETE**, *lpvStatusInformation* points at an **INTERNET_ASYNC_RESULT** structure, which is defined as:

- **DWORD** *dwResult*; The return code from the operation.
- **DWORD** *dwError*; If dwResult indicates that the operation failed, this member contains the error code. If the operation was successful, this member usually contains **ERROR_SUCCESS**.

Override this member function to require some action before a status callback routine is performed.

Note Status callbacks need thread-state protection. If you are using MFC in a shared library, add the following line to the beginning of your override:

```
AFX_MANAGE_STATE( AfxGetStaticModuleState( ) );
```

For more information about asynchronous operations, see the article "Internet First Steps: WinInet" in *Visual C++ Programmer's Guide* online.

See Also: **CInternetSession::EnableStatusCallback**, **CInternetSession::GetContext**

CInternetSession::OpenURL

CStdioFile* OpenURL(LPCTSTR *pstrURL*, **DWORD** *dwContext* = **1**,
    ↪ **DWORD** *dwFlags* = **INTERNET_FLAG_TRANSFER_ASCII**,
    ↪ **LPCTSTR** *pstrHeaders* = **NULL**, **DWORD** *dwHeadersLength* = **0**);
throw (CInternetException);

Return Value

Returns a file handle for FTP, GOPHER, HTTP, and FILE-type Internet services only. Returns **NULL** if parsing was unsuccessful.

The pointer that **OpenURL** returns depends on *pszURL*'s type of service. The table below illustrates the possible pointers **OpenURL** can return.

URL type	Returns
file://	**CStdioFile***
http://	**CHttpFile***
gopher://	**CGopherFile***
ftp://	**CInternetFile***

Parameters

pstrURL A pointer to the name of the URL to begin reading. Only URLs beginning with file:, ftp:, gopher:, or http: are supported. **ASSERTS** if *pszURL* is **NULL**.

dwContext An application-defined value passed with the returned handle in callback.

dwFlags The flags describing how to handle this connection. The valid flags, which can be combined with the bitwise **OR** operator (I), are:

- **INTERNET_FLAG_TRANSFER_ASCII** The default. Transfer any data as ASCII text.

- **INTERNET_FLAG_RELOAD** Get the data from the wire even if it is locally cached.

- **INTERNET_FLAG_DONT_CACHE** Do not cache the data, either locally or in any gateways.

- **INTERNET_FLAG_SECURE** This flag is applicable to HTTP requests only. It requests secure transactions on the wire with Secure Sockets Layer or PCT.

- **INTERNET_OPEN_FLAG_USE_EXISTING_CONNECT** If possible, reuse the existing connections to the server for new requests generated by **OpenUrl** instead of creating a new session for each connection request.

- **INTERNET_FLAG_PASSIVE** Used for an FTP site. Uses passive FTP semantics. Used with **CInternetConnection** of **OpenURL**.

pstrHeaders A pointer to a string containing the headers to be sent to the HTTP server.

dwHeadersLength The length, in characters, of the additional headers. If this is −1L and *pstrHeaders* is non-**NULL**, then *pstrHeaders* is assumed to be zero terminated and the length is calculated.

Remarks

Call this member function to send the specified request to the HTTP server and allow the client to specify additional RFC822, MIME, or HTTP headers to send along with the request.

OpenURL, which wraps the Win32 function **InternetOpenURL**, allows only downloading, retrieving, and reading the data from an Internet server. **OpenURL** allows no file manipulation on a remote location, so it requires no **CInternetConnection** object.

To use connection-specific (that is, protocol-specific) functions, such as writing to a file, you must open a session, then open a particular kind of connection, then use that connection to open a file in the desired mode. See **CInternetConnection** for more information about connection-specific functions.

See Also: **CInternetConnection**, **CGopherConnection**, **CInternetSession::GetFtpConnection**, **CInternetSession::GetHttpConnection**

CInternetSession::QueryOption

BOOL QueryOption(DWORD *dwOption*, **LPVOID** *lpBuffer*,
↪ **LPDWORD** *lpdwBufLen* **) const;**
BOOL QueryOption(DWORD *dwOption*, **DWORD&** *dwValue* **) const;**

Return Value

If the operation was successful, a value of **TRUE** is returned. If an error occurred, a value of **FALSE** is returned. If the call fails, the Win32 function **GetLastError** may be called to determine the cause of the error.

Parameters

dwOption   The Internet option to query. See **Remarks** for a table of the possible options.

lpBuffer   A buffer that receives the option setting.

lpdwBufLen   A pointer to a DWORD containing the length of *lpBuffer*. On return, this contains the length of the data placed into *lpBuffer*.

dwValue   Sent to **QueryOption** in place of *lpBuffer*.

Remarks

Provides five possible asserts for basic error-checking.

See **CInternetSession::SetOption** to select and set the specific option to query.

The following table defines values for the parameter *dwOption*:

Value	Meaning
INTERNET_OPTION_CALLBACK	The address of the callback function defined for this handle.
INTERNET_OPTION_CONNECT_TIMEOUT	The time-out value in milliseconds to use for Internet connection requests. If a connection request takes longer than this timeout, the request is canceled. The default timeout is infinite.
INTERNET_OPTION_CONNECT_RETRIES	The retry count to use for Internet connection requests. If a connection attempt still fails after the specified number of tries, the request is canceled. The default is five.

(continued)

Value	Meaning
INTERNET_OPTION_CONNECT_BACKOFF	The delay value in milliseconds to wait between connection retries.
INTERNET_OPTION_CONTROL_SEND_TIMEOUT	The timeout value in milliseconds to use for nondata (control) Internet send requests. If a nondata send request takes longer than this timeout, the request is canceled. The default time-out is infinite. Currently, this value only has meaning for FTP sessions.
INTERNET_OPTION_CONTROL_RECEIVE_TIMEOUT	The timeout value in milliseconds to use for nondata (control) Internet receive requests. If a nondata receive request takes longer than this timeout, the request is canceled. The default timeout is infinite. Currently, this value only has meaning for FTP sessions
INTERNET_OPTION_DATA_SEND_TIMEOUT	The timeout value in milliseconds to use for data Internet send requests. If a data send request takes longer than this timeout, the request is canceled. The default timeout is infinite.
INTERNET_OPTION_DATA_RECEIVE_TIMEOUT	The timeout value in milliseconds to use for data Internet receive requests. If a data receive request takes longer than this timeout, the request is canceled. The default timeout is infinite.
INTERNET_OPTION_HANDLE_TYPE	See below for a list of the possible Internet options.
INTERNET_OPTION_CONTEXT_VALUE	Returns the context value associated with this Internet handle.
INTERNET_OPTION_READ_BUFFER_SIZE	Returns the size of the read buffer (in othe words, used by **CFtpConnection::GetFile**).
INTERNET_OPTION_WRITE_BUFFER_SIZE	Returns the size of the write buffer (in othe words used by **CFtpConnection::PutFile**).
INTERNET_OPTION_ASYNC_ID	Returns the ID of the last async request made in this thread context.
INTERNET_OPTION_ASYNC_PRIORITY	Returns the priority of this download if it is an async download.
INTERNET_OPTION_PARENT_HANDLE	Returns the parent handle of this handle.
INTERNET_OPTION_KEEP_CONNECTION	Returns an indication whether this handle uses persistent connections.
INTERNET_OPTION_USERNAME	Returns the user name associated with a handle returned by the **InternetConnect** API.

(continued)

(continued)

Value	Meaning
INTERNET_OPTION_PASSWORD	Returns the password associated with the handle returned by **InternetConnect** API.
INTERNET_OPTION_REQUEST_FLAGS	Returns special status flags about the current download in progress. This option is available only for querying. The only flag currently returned is **INTERNET_REQFLAG_FROM_CACHE**. This flag is how the caller can discover whether a request is being satisfied from the cache.
INTERNET_OPTION_EXTENDED_ERROR	Returns the winsock error code that was mapped to the **ERROR_INTERNET_** error codes last returned in this thread context.

The possible settings for **INTERNET_OPTION_HANDLE_TYPE** include the following:

- **INTERNET_HANDLE_TYPE_INTERNET**
- **INTERNET_HANDLE_TYPE_CONNECT_FTP**
- **INTERNET_HANDLE_TYPE_CONNECT_GOPHER**
- **INTERNET_HANDLE_TYPE_CONNECT_HTTP**
- **INTERNET_HANDLE_TYPE_FTP_FIND**
- **INTERNET_HANDLE_TYPE_FTP_FIND_HTML**
- **INTERNET_HANDLE_TYPE_FTP_FILE**
- **INTERNET_HANDLE_TYPE_FTP_FILE_HTML**
- **INTERNET_HANDLE_TYPE_GOPHER_FIND**
- **INTERNET_HANDLE_TYPE_GOPHER_FIND_HTML**
- **INTERNET_HANDLE_TYPE_GOPHER_FILE**
- **INTERNET_HANDLE_TYPE_GOPHER_FILE_HTML**
- **INTERNET_HANDLE_TYPE_HTTP_REQUEST**

See Also: **CInternetSession::ServiceTypeFromHandle**, **CInternetSession::SetOption**

CInternetSession::ServiceTypeFromHandle

DWORD ServiceTypeFromHandle(HINTERNET *hQuery* **);**

Return Value

The Internet service type. See **Remarks** for a list of recognized service types.

Parameters

hQuery   A handle to an Internet query.

Remarks

Call this member function to get the type of service from the Internet handle. The following service types are recognized by MFC:

Service type	Return value
FTP	**INTERNET_SERVICE_FTP**
HTTP	**INTERNET_SERVICE_HTTP**
Gopher	**INTERNET_SERVICE_GOPHER**
File	**AFX_INET_SERVICE_FILE**

CInternetSession will throw an **AfxThrowNotSupportedException** for unsupported service types.

Note   The return value **AFX_INET_SERVICE_FILE** is used only by MFC and is not recognized by Win32. This feature allows the client to access local files in the same way he or she would access Internet services.

See Also: **CInternetSession::QueryOption,
CInternetSession::operator HINTERNET**

CInternetSession::SetOption

> **BOOL SetOption(DWORD** *dwOption*, **LPVOID** *lpBuffer*,
> ↪ **DWORD** *dwBufferLength*);
> **BOOL SetOption(DWORD** *dwOption*, **DWORD** *dwValue*);

Return Value

If the operation was successful, a value of **TRUE** is returned. If an error occurred, a value of **FALSE** is returned. If the call fails, the Win32 function **GetLastError** may be called to determine the cause of the error.

Parameters

dwOption   See **CInternetSession::QueryOption** for list of possible values.

lpBuffer   A buffer that contains the option setting.

dwBufferLength   The length of *lpBuffer* or the size of *dwValue*.

dwValue   A **DWORD** that contains the option setting.

Remarks

Call this member function to set options for the Internet session.

See Also: **CInternetSession::ServiceTypeFromHandle,
CInternetSession::QueryOption**

Operators
CInternetSession::operator HINTERNET

operator HINTERNET( ) const;

Remarks

Use this operator to get the Windows handle for the current Internet session.

See Also: **CInternetSession::ServiceTypeFromHandle**

CList

template< class *TYPE*, class *ARG_TYPE* >
 class CList : public CObject

Parameters

TYPE   Type of object stored in the list.

ARG_TYPE   Type used to reference objects stored in the list. Can be a reference.

Remarks

The **CList** class supports ordered lists of nonunique objects accessible sequentially or by value. **CList** lists behave like doubly-linked lists.

A variable of type **POSITION** is a key for the list. You can use a **POSITION** variable as an iterator to traverse a list sequentially and as a bookmark to hold a place. A position is not the same as an index, however.

Element insertion is very fast at the list head, at the tail, and at a known **POSITION**. A sequential search is necessary to look up an element by value or index. This search can be slow if the list is long.

If you need a dump of individual elements in the list, you must set the depth of the dump context to 1 or greater.

Certain member functions of this class call global helper functions that must be customized for most uses of the **CList** class. See "Collection Class Helpers" in the "Macros and Globals" section.

For more information on using **CList**, see the article "Collections" in *Visual C++ Programmer's Guide* online.

#include <afxtempl.h>

See Also: CMap, **CArray**

CList Class Members

Construction

CList	Constructs an empty ordered list.

Head/Tail Access

GetHead	Returns the head element of the list (cannot be empty).
GetTail	Returns the tail element of the list (cannot be empty).

Operations

RemoveHead	Removes the element from the head of the list.
RemoveTail	Removes the element from the tail of the list.
AddHead	Adds an element (or all the elements in another list) to the head of the list (makes a new head).
AddTail	Adds an element (or all the elements in another list) to the tail of the list (makes a new tail).
RemoveAll	Removes all the elements from this list.

Iteration

GetHeadPosition	Returns the position of the head element of the list.
GetTailPosition	Returns the position of the tail element of the list.
GetNext	Gets the next element for iterating.
GetPrev	Gets the previous element for iterating.

Retrieval/Modification

GetAt	Gets the element at a given position.
SetAt	Sets the element at a given position.
RemoveAt	Removes an element from this list, specified by position.

Insertion

InsertBefore	Inserts a new element before a given position.
InsertAfter	Inserts a new element after a given position.

Searching

Find	Gets the position of an element specified by pointer value.
FindIndex	Gets the position of an element specified by a zero-based index.

Status

GetCount	Returns the number of elements in this list.
IsEmpty	Tests for the empty list condition (no elements).

Member Functions
CList::AddHead

> **POSITION AddHead(** *ARG_TYPE newElement* **);**
> **void AddHead(CList*** *pNewList* **);**

Return Value

> The first version returns the **POSITION** value of the newly inserted element.

Parameters

> *ARG_TYPE*   Template parameter specifying the type of the list element (can be a reference).
>
> *newElement*   The new element.
>
> *pNewList*   A pointer to another **CList** list. The elements in *pNewList* will be added to this list.

Remarks

> Adds a new element or list of elements to the head of this list. The list can be empty before the operation.
>
> **See Also: CList::GetHead, CList::RemoveHead**

CList::AddTail

> **POSITION AddTail(** *ARG_TYPE newElement* **);**
> **void AddTail(CList*** *pNewList* **);**

Return Value

> The first version returns the **POSITION** value of the newly inserted element.

Parameters

> *ARG_TYPE*   Template parameter specifying the type of the list element (can be a reference).
>
> *newElement*   The element to be added to this list.
>
> *pNewList*   A pointer to another **CList** list. The elements in *pNewList* will be added to this list.

Remarks

> Adds a new element or list of elements to the tail of this list. The list can be empty before the operation.
>
> **See Also: CObList::GetTail, CObList::RemoveTail**

CList::CList

CList(int *nBlockSize* = **10**);

Parameters

nBlockSize   The memory-allocation granularity for extending the list.

Remarks

Constructs an empty ordered list. As the list grows, memory is allocated in units of *nBlockSize* entries.

CList::Find

POSITION Find(*ARG_TYPE searchValue*, **POSITION** *startAfter* = **NULL) const;**

Return Value

A **POSITION** value that can be used for iteration or object pointer retrieval; **NULL** if the object is not found.

Parameters

ARG_TYPE   Template parameter specifying the type of the list element (can be a reference).

searchValue   The value to be found in the list.

startAfter   The start position for the search.

Remarks

Searches the list sequentially to find the first element matching the specified *searchValue*. Note that the pointer values are compared, not the contents of the objects.

See Also: CList::GetNext, CList::GetPrev

CList::FindIndex

POSITION FindIndex(int *nIndex*) **const;**

Return Value

A **POSITION** value that can be used for iteration or object pointer retrieval; **NULL** if *nIndex* is negative or too large.

Parameters

nIndex   The zero-based index of the list element to be found.

Remarks

Uses the value of *nIndex* as an index into the list. It starts a sequential scan from the head of the list, stopping on the *n*th element.

See Also: **CObList::Find**, **CObList::GetNext**, **CObList::GetPrev**

CList::GetAt

TYPE& **GetAt(POSITION** *position* **);**
TYPE **GetAt(POSITION** *position* **) const;**

Return Value

See the return value description for **GetHead**.

Parameters

TYPE   Template parameter specifying the type of object in the list.

position   A **POSITION** value returned by a previous **GetHeadPosition** or **Find** member function call.

Remarks

A variable of type **POSITION** is a key for the list. It is not the same as an index, and you cannot operate on a **POSITION** value yourself. **GetAt** returns the element (or a reference to the element) associated with a given position.

You must ensure that your **POSITION** value represents a valid position in the list. If it is invalid, then the Debug version of the Microsoft Foundation Class Library asserts.

See Also: **CList::Find**, **CList::SetAt**, **CList::GetNext**, **CList::GetPrev**, **CList::GetHead**

CList::GetCount

int GetCount() const;

Return Value

An integer value containing the element count.

Remarks

Gets the number of elements in this list.

See Also: **CList::IsEmpty**

CList::GetHead

TYPE& **GetHead( );**
TYPE **GetHead( ) const;**

Return Value

If the list is **const**, **GetHead** returns a copy of the element at the head of the list.

This allows the function to be used only on the right side of an assignment statement and protects the list from modification.

If the list is not **const**, **GetHead** returns a reference to an element of the list. This allows the function to be used on either side of an assignment statement and thus allows the list entries to be modified.

Parameters

TYPE   Template parameter specifying the type of object in the list.

Remarks

Gets the head element (or a reference to the head element) of this list.

You must ensure that the list is not empty before calling **GetHead**. If the list is empty, then the Debug version of the Microsoft Foundation Class Library asserts. Use **IsEmpty** to verify that the list contains elements.

See Also: CList::GetTail, CList::GetTailPosition, CList::AddHead, CList::RemoveHead

CList::GetHeadPosition

POSITION GetHeadPosition( ) const;

Return Value

A **POSITION** value that can be used for iteration or object pointer retrieval; **NULL** if the list is empty.

Remarks

Gets the position of the head element of this list.

See Also: CList::GetTailPosition

CList::GetNext

TYPE& **GetNext(POSITION&** *rPosition* **);**
TYPE **GetNext(POSITION&** *rPosition* **) const;**

Return Value

If the list is **const**, **GetNext** returns a copy of the element at the head of the list. This allows the function to be used only on the right side of an assignment statement and protects the list from modification.

If the list is not **const**, **GetNext** returns a reference to an element of the list. This allows the function to be used on either side of an assignment statement and thus allows the list entries to be modified.

Parameters

TYPE   Template parameter specifying the type of the elements in the list.

rPosition   A reference to a **POSITION** value returned by a previous **GetNext**, **GetHeadPosition**, or other member function call.

Remarks

Gets the list element identified by *rPosition*, then sets *rPosition* to the **POSITION** value of the next entry in the list. You can use **GetNext** in a forward iteration loop if you establish the initial position with a call to **GetHeadPosition** or **Find**.

You must ensure that your **POSITION** value represents a valid position in the list. If it is invalid, then the Debug version of the Microsoft Foundation Class Library asserts.

If the retrieved element is the last in the list, then the new value of *rPosition* is set to **NULL**.

See Also: **CList::Find**, **CList::GetHeadPosition**, **CList::GetTailPosition**, **CList::GetPrev**, **CList::GetHead**

CList::GetPrev

TYPE& **GetPrev(POSITION&** *rPosition* **);**
TYPE **GetPrev(POSITION&** *rPosition* **) const;**

Return Value

If the list is **const**, **GetPrev** returns a copy of the element at the head of the list. This allows the function to be used only on the right side of an assignment statement and protects the list from modification.

If the list is not **const**, **GetPrev** returns a reference to an element of the list. This allows the function to be used on either side of an assignment statement and thus allows the list entries to be modified.

Parameters

TYPE   Template parameter specifying the type of the elements in the list.

rPosition   A reference to a **POSITION** value returned by a previous **GetPrev** or other member function call.

Remarks

Gets the list element identified by *rPosition*, then sets *rPosition* to the **POSITION** value of the previous entry in the list. You can use **GetPrev** in a reverse iteration loop if you establish the initial position with a call to **GetTailPosition** or **Find**.

You must ensure that your **POSITION** value represents a valid position in the list. If it is invalid, then the Debug version of the Microsoft Foundation Class Library asserts.

If the retrieved element is the first in the list, then the new value of *rPosition* is set to **NULL**.

See Also: **CList::Find**, **CList::GetTailPosition**, **CList::GetHeadPosition**, **CList::GetNext**, **CList::GetHead**

CList::GetTail

TYPE& **GetTail( );**
TYPE **GetTail() const;**

Return Value

See the return value description for **GetHead**.

Parameters

TYPE   Template parameter specifying the type of elements in the list.

Remarks

Gets the **CObject** pointer that represents the tail element of this list.

You must ensure that the list is not empty before calling **GetTail**. If the list is empty, then the Debug version of the Microsoft Foundation Class Library asserts. Use **IsEmpty** to verify that the list contains elements.

See Also: **CList::AddTail, CList::AddHead, CList::RemoveHead, CList::GetHead**

CList::GetTailPosition

POSITION GetTailPosition( ) const;

Return Value

A **POSITION** value that can be used for iteration or object pointer retrieval; **NULL** if the list is empty.

Remarks

Gets the position of the tail element of this list; **NULL** if the list is empty.

See Also: **CList::GetHeadPosition, CList::GetTail**

CList::InsertAfter

POSITION InsertAfter(POSITION *position*, *ARG_TYPE newElement* **);**

Return Value

A **POSITION** value that can be used for iteration or list element retrieval.

Parameters

position   A **POSITION** value returned by a previous **GetNext**, **GetPrev**, or **Find** member function call.

ARG_TYPE   Template parameter specifying the type of the list element.

newElement   The element to be added to this list.

Remarks

Adds an element to this list after the element at the specified position.

See Also: **CList::Find**, **CList::InsertBefore**

CList::InsertBefore

POSITION InsertBefore(POSITION *position***,** *ARG_TYPE newElement* **);**

Return Value

A **POSITION** value that can be used for iteration or list element retrieval; **NULL** if the list is empty.

Parameters

position   A **POSITION** value returned by a previous **GetNext**, **GetPrev**, or **Find** member function call.

ARG_TYPE   Template parameter specifying the type of the list element (can be a reference).

newElement   The element to be added to this list.

Remarks

Adds an element to this list before the element at the specified position.

See Also: **CList::Find**, **CList::InsertAfter**

CList::IsEmpty

BOOL IsEmpty( ) const;

Return Value

Nonzero if this list is empty; otherwise 0.

Remarks

Indicates whether this list contains no elements.

See Also: **CList::GetCount**

CList::RemoveAll

void RemoveAll( );

Remarks

Removes all the elements from this list and frees the associated memory. No error is generated if the list is already empty.

See Also: **CList::RemoveAt**

CList::RemoveAt

void RemoveAt(POSITION *position* **);**

Parameters

position The position of the element to be removed from the list.

Remarks

Removes the specified element from this list.

You must ensure that your **POSITION** value represents a valid position in the list. If it is invalid, then the Debug version of the Microsoft Foundation Class Library asserts.

See Also: CList::RemoveAll

CList::RemoveHead

TYPE **RemoveHead( );**

Return Value

The element previously at the head of the list.

Parameters

TYPE Template parameter specifying the type of elements in the list.

Remarks

Removes the element from the head of the list and returns a pointer to it.

You must ensure that the list is not empty before calling **RemoveHead**. If the list is empty, then the Debug version of the Microsoft Foundation Class Library asserts. Use **IsEmpty** to verify that the list contains elements.

See Also: CList::GetHead, CList::AddHead

CList::RemoveTail

TYPE **RemoveTail( );**

Return Value

The element that was at the tail of the list.

Parameters

TYPE Template parameter specifying the type of elements in the list.

Remarks

Removes the element from the tail of the list and returns a pointer to it.

You must ensure that the list is not empty before calling **RemoveTail**. If the list is empty, then the Debug version of the Microsoft Foundation Class Library asserts. Use **IsEmpty** to verify that the list contains elements.

See Also: **CList::GetTail**, **CList::AddTail**

CList::SetAt

void SetAt(POSITION *pos***,** *ARG_TYPE newElement* **);**

Parameters

pos   The **POSITION** of the element to be set.

ARG_TYPE   Template parameter specifying the type of the list element (can be a reference).

newElement   The element to be added to the list.

Remarks

A variable of type **POSITION** is a key for the list. It is not the same as an index, and you cannot operate on a **POSITION** value yourself. **SetAt** writes the element to the specified position in the list.

You must ensure that your **POSITION** value represents a valid position in the list. If it is invalid, then the Debug version of the Microsoft Foundation Class Library asserts.

See Also: **CList::Find**, **CList::GetAt**, **CList::GetNext**, **CList::GetPrev**

CListBox

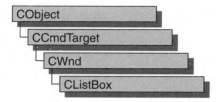

The **CListBox** class provides the functionality of a Windows list box. A list box displays a list of items, such as filenames, that the user can view and select.

In a single-selection list box, the user can select only one item. In a multiple-selection list box, a range of items can be selected. When the user selects an item, it is highlighted and the list box sends a notification message to the parent window.

You can create a list box either from a dialog template or directly in your code. To create it directly, construct the **CListBox** object, then call the **Create** member function to create the Windows list-box control and attach it to the **CListBox** object. To use a list box in a dialog template, declare a list-box variable in your dialog box class, then use **DDX_Control** in your dialog box class's **DoDataExchange** function to connect the member variable to the control. (ClassWizard does this for you automatically when you add a control variable to your dialog box class.)

Construction can be a one-step process in a class derived from **CListBox**. Write a constructor for the derived class and call **Create** from within the constructor.

If you want to handle Windows notification messages sent by a list box to its parent (usually a class derived from **CDialog**), add a message-map entry and message-handler member function to the parent class for each message.

Each message-map entry takes the following form:

ON_ Notification(*id*, *memberFxn*)

where *id* specifies the child window ID of the list-box control sending the notification and *memberFxn* is the name of the parent member function you have written to handle the notification.

The parent's function prototype is as follows:

afx_msg void *memberFxn*( );

Following is a list of potential message-map entries and a description of the cases in which they would be sent to the parent:

- **ON_LBN_DBLCLK**   The user double-clicks a string in a list box. Only a list box that has the **LBS_NOTIFY** style will send this notification message.

- **ON_LBN_ERRSPACE**   The list box cannot allocate enough memory to meet the request.
- **ON_LBN_KILLFOCUS**   The list box is losing the input focus.
- **ON_LBN_SELCANCEL**   The current list-box selection is canceled. This message is only sent when a list box has the **LBS_NOTIFY** style.
- **ON_LBN_SELCHANGE**   The selection in the list box is about to change. This notification is not sent if the selection is changed by the **CListBox::SetCurSel** member function. This notification applies only to a list box that has the **LBS_NOTIFY** style. The **LBN_SELCHANGE** notification message is sent for a multiple-selection list box whenever the user presses an arrow key, even if the selection does not change.
- **ON_LBN_SETFOCUS**   The list box is receiving the input focus.
- **ON_WM_CHARTOITEM**   An owner-draw list box that has no strings receives a **WM_CHAR** message.
- **ON_WM_VKEYTOITEM**   A list box with the **LBS_WANTKEYBOARDINPUT** style receives a **WM_KEYDOWN** message.

If you create a **CListBox** object within a dialog box (through a dialog resource), the **CListBox** object is automatically destroyed when the user closes the dialog box.

If you create a **CListBox** object within a window, you may need to destroy the **CListBox** object. If you create the **CListBox** object on the stack, it is destroyed automatically. If you create the **CListBox** object on the heap by using the **new** function, you must call **delete** on the object to destroy it when the user closes the parent window.

If you allocate any memory in the **CListBox** object, override the **CListBox** destructor to dispose of the allocation.

#include <afxwin.h>

See Also: **CWnd, CButton, CComboBox, CEdit, CScrollBar, CStatic**

CListBox Class Members

Construction

CListBox	Constructs a **CListBox** object.

Initialization

Create	Creates the Windows list box and attaches it to the **CListBox** object.
InitStorage	Preallocates blocks of memory for list box items and strings.

General Operations

GetCount	Returns the number of strings in a list box.
GetHorizontalExtent	Returns the width in pixels that a list box can be scrolled horizontally.
SetHorizontalExtent	Sets the width in pixels that a list box can be scrolled horizontally.
GetTopIndex	Returns the index of the first visible string in a list box.
SetTopIndex	Sets the zero-based index of the first visible string in a list box.
GetItemData	Returns the 32-bit value associated with the list-box item.
GetItemDataPtr	Returns a pointer to a list-box item.
SetItemData	Sets the 32-bit value associated with the list-box item.
SetItemDataPtr	Sets a pointer to the list-box item.
GetItemRect	Returns the bounding rectangle of the list-box item as it is currently displayed.
ItemFromPoint	Returns the index of the list-box item nearest a point.
SetItemHeight	Sets the height of items in a list box.
GetItemHeight	Determines the height of items in a list box.
GetSel	Returns the selection state of a list-box item.
GetText	Copies a list-box item into a buffer.
GetTextLen	Returns the length in bytes of a list-box item.
SetColumnWidth	Sets the column width of a multicolumn list box.
SetTabStops	Sets the tab-stop positions in a list box.
GetLocale	Retrieves the locale identifier for a list box.
SetLocale	Sets the locale identifier for a list box.

Single-Selection Operations

GetCurSel	Returns the zero-based index of the currently selected string in a list box.
SetCurSel	Selects a list-box string.

Multiple-Selection Operations

SetSel	Selects or deselects a list-box item in a multiple-selection list box.
GetCaretIndex	Determines the index of the item that has the focus rectangle in a multiple-selection list box.
SetCaretIndex	Sets the focus rectangle to the item at the specified index in a multiple-selection list box.
GetSelCount	Returns the number of strings currently selected in a multiple-selection list box.
GetSelItems	Returns the indices of the strings currently selected in a list box.
SelItemRange	Selects or deselects a range of strings in a multiple-selection list box.
SetAnchorIndex	Sets the anchor in a multiple-selection list box to begin an extended selection.
GetAnchorIndex	Retrieves the zero-based index of the current anchor item in a list box.

String Operations

AddString	Adds a string to a list box.
DeleteString	Deletes a string from a list box.
InsertString	Inserts a string at a specific location in a list box.
ResetContent	Clears all the entries from a list box.
Dir	Adds filenames from the current directory to a list box.
FindString	Searches for a string in a list box.
FindStringExact	Finds the first list-box string that matches a specified string.
SelectString	Searches for and selects a string in a single-selection list box.

Overridables

DrawItem	Called by the framework when a visual aspect of an owner-draw list box changes.
MeasureItem	Called by the framework when an owner-draw list box is created to determine list-box dimensions.
CompareItem	Called by the framework to determine the position of a new item in a sorted owner-draw list box.
DeleteItem	Called by the framework when the user deletes an item from an owner-draw list box.
VKeyToItem	Override to provide custom **WM_KEYDOWN** handling for list boxes with the **LBS_WANTKEYBOARDINPUT** style set.
CharToItem	Override to provide custom **WM_CHAR** handling for owner-draw list boxes which don't have strings.

Member Functions

CListBox::AddString

int AddString(LPCTSTR *lpszItem* **);**

Return Value

The zero-based index to the string in the list box. The return value is **LB_ERR** if an error occurs; the return value is **LB_ERRSPACE** if insufficient space is available to store the new string.

Parameters

lpszItem   Points to the null-terminated string that is to be added.

Remarks

Call this member function to add a string to a list box. If the list box was not created with the **LBS_SORT** style, the string is added to the end of the list. Otherwise, the string is inserted into the list, and the list is sorted. If the list box was created with the

LBS_SORT style but not the **LBS_HASSTRINGS** style, the framework sorts the list by one or more calls to the **CompareItem** member function.

Use **InsertString** to insert a string into a specific location within the list box.

See Also: **CListBox::InsertString, CListBox::CompareItem, LB_ADDSTRING**

CListBox::CharToItem

virtual int CharToItem(UINT *nKey***, UINT** *nIndex* **);**

Return Value

Returns −1 or −2 for no further action or a nonnegative number to specify an index of a list-box item on which to perform the default action for the keystroke. The default implementation returns −1.

Parameters

nKey   The ANSI code of the character the user typed.

nIndex   The current position of the list-box caret.

Remarks

This function is called by the framework when the list box's parent window receives a **WM_CHARTOITEM** message from the list box. The **WM_CHARTOITEM** message is sent by the list box when it receives a **WM_CHAR** message, but only if the list box meets all of these criteria:

- Is an owner-draw list box.
- Does not have the **LBS_HASSTRINGS** style set.
- Has at least one item.

You should never call this function yourself. Override this function to provide your own custom handling of keyboard messages.

In your override, you must return a value to tell the framework what action you performed. A return value of −1 or −2 indicates that you handled all aspects of selecting the item and requires no further action by the list box. Before returning −1 or −2, you could set the selection or move the caret or both. To set the selection, use **SetCurSel** or **SetSel**. To move the caret, use **SetCaretIndex**.

A return value of 0 or greater specifies the index of an item in the list box and indicates that the list box should perform the default action for the keystroke on the given item.

See Also: **CListBox::VKeyToItem, CListBox::SetCurSel, CListBox::SetSel, CListBox::SetCaretIndex, WM_CHARTOITEM**

CListBox::CListBox

CListBox( );

Remarks

You construct a **CListBox** object in two steps. First call the constructor **CListBox**, then call **Create**, which initializes the Windows list box and attaches it to the **CListBox**.

See Also: **CListBox::Create**

CListBox::CompareItem

virtual int CompareItem(LPCOMPAREITEMSTRUCT *lpCompareItemStruct* **);**

Return Value

Indicates the relative position of the two items described in the **COMPAREITEMSTRUCT** structure. It may be any of the following values:

Value	Meaning
−1	Item 1 sorts before item 2.
0	Item 1 and item 2 sort the same.
1	Item 1 sorts after item 2.

See **CWnd::OnCompareItem** for a description of the **COMPAREITEMSTRUCT** structure.

Parameters

lpCompareItemStruct   A long pointer to a **COMPAREITEMSTRUCT** structure.

Remarks

Called by the framework to determine the relative position of a new item in a sorted owner-draw list box. By default, this member function does nothing. If you create an owner-draw list box with the **LBS_SORT** style, you must override this member function to assist the framework in sorting new items added to the list box.

See Also: **WM_COMPAREITEM**, **CWnd::OnCompareItem**, **CListBox::DrawItem**, **CListBox::MeasureItem**, **CListBox::DeleteItem**

CListBox::Create

BOOL Create(DWORD *dwStyle*, **const RECT&** *rect*,
➥ **CWnd*** *pParentWnd*, **UINT** *nID* **);**

Return Value

Nonzero if successful; otherwise 0.

Parameters

dwStyle   Specifies the style of the list box. Apply any combination of list-box styles to the box.

rect   Specifies the list-box size and position. Can be either a **CRect** object or a **RECT** structure.

pParentWnd   Specifies the list box's parent window (usually a **CDialog** object). It must not be **NULL**.

nID   Specifies the list box's control ID.

Remarks

You construct a **CListBox** object in two steps. First call the constructor, then call **Create**, which initializes the Windows list box and attaches it to the **CListBox** object.

When **Create** executes, Windows sends the **WM_NCCREATE**, **WM_CREATE**, **WM_NCCALCSIZE**, and **WM_GETMINMAXINFO** messages to the list-box control.

These messages are handled by default by the **OnNcCreate**, **OnCreate**, **OnNcCalcSize**, and **OnGetMinMaxInfo** member functions in the **CWnd** base class. To extend the default message handling, derive a class from **CListBox**, add a message map to the new class, and override the preceding message-handler member functions. Override **OnCreate**, for example, to perform needed initialization for a new class.

Apply the following window styles to a list-box control.

- **WS_CHILD**   Always
- **WS_VISIBLE**   Usually
- **WS_DISABLED**   Rarely
- **WS_VSCROLL**   To add a vertical scroll bar
- **WS_HSCROLL**   To add a horizontal scroll bar
- **WS_GROUP**   To group controls
- **WS_TABSTOP**   To allow tabbing to this control

See Also: **CListBox::CListBox**

CListBox::DeleteItem

virtual void DeleteItem(LPDELETEITEMSTRUCT *lpDeleteItemStruct* **);**

Parameters

lpDeleteItemStruct   A long pointer to a Windows **DELETEITEMSTRUCT** structure that contains information about the deleted item.

Remarks

Called by the framework when the user deletes an item from an owner-draw **CListBox** object or destroys the list box. The default implementation of this function does nothing. Override this function to redraw an owner-draw list box as needed.

See **CWnd::OnDeleteItem** for a description of the **DELETEITEMSTRUCT** structure.

See Also: **CListBox::CompareItem**, **CWnd::OnDeleteItem**, **CListBox::DrawItem**, **CListBox::MeasureItem**, **::DeleteItem**

CListBox::DeleteString

int DeleteString(UINT *nIndex* **);**

Return Value

A count of the strings remaining in the list. The return value is **LB_ERR** if *nIndex* specifies an index greater than the number of items in the list.

Parameters

nIndex   Specifies the zero-based index of the string to be deleted.

Remarks

Deletes an item in a list box.

See Also: **LB_DELETESTRING**, **CListBox::AddString**, **CListBox::InsertString**

CListBox::Dir

int Dir(UINT *attr*, **LPCTSTR** *lpszWildCard* **);**

Return Value

The zero-based index of the last filename added to the list. The return value is **LB_ERR** if an error occurs; the return value is **LB_ERRSPACE** if insufficient space is available to store the new strings.

Parameters

attr   Can be any combination of the **enum** values described in **CFile::GetStatus**, or any combination of the following values:

Value	Meaning
0x0000	File can be read from or written to.
0x0001	File can be read from but not written to.
0x0002	File is hidden and does not appear in a directory listing.
0x0004	File is a system file.
0x0010	The name specified by *lpszWildCard* specifies a directory.
0x0020	File has been archived.
0x4000	Include all drives that match the name specified by *lpszWildCard*.
0x8000	Exclusive flag. If the exclusive flag is set, only files of the specified type are listed. Otherwise, files of the specified type are listed in addition to "normal" files.

lpszWildCard   Points to a file-specification string. The string can contain wildcards (for example, *.*).

Remarks

Adds a list of filenames and/or drives to a list box.

See Also: **CWnd::DlgDirList, LB_DIR, CFile::GetStatus**

CListBox::DrawItem

virtual void DrawItem(LPDRAWITEMSTRUCT *lpDrawItemStruct* **);**

Parameters

lpDrawItemStruct   A long pointer to a **DRAWITEMSTRUCT** structure that contains information about the type of drawing required.

Remarks

Called by the framework when a visual aspect of an owner-draw list box changes. The **itemAction** and **itemState** members of the **DRAWITEMSTRUCT** structure define the drawing action that is to be performed.

By default, this member function does nothing. Override this member function to implement drawing for an owner-draw **CListBox** object. The application should restore all graphics device interface (GDI) objects selected for the display context supplied in *lpDrawItemStruct* before this member function terminates.

See **CWnd::OnDrawItem** for a description of the **DRAWITEMSTRUCT** structure.

See Also: **CListBox::CompareItem, CWnd::OnDrawItem, WM_DRAWITEM, CListBox::MeasureItem, CListBox::DeleteItem**

CListBox::FindString

int FindString(int *nStartAfter***, LPCTSTR** *lpszItem* **) const;**

Return Value

The zero-based index of the matching item, or **LB_ERR** if the search was unsuccessful.

Parameters

nStartAfter   Contains the zero-based index of the item before the first item to be searched. When the search reaches the bottom of the list box, it continues from the top of the list box back to the item specified by *nStartAfter*. If *nStartAfter* is –1, the entire list box is searched from the beginning.

lpszItem   Points to the null-terminated string that contains the prefix to search for. The search is case independent, so this string may contain any combination of uppercase and lowercase letters.

Remarks

Finds the first string in a list box that contains the specified prefix without changing the list-box selection. Use the **SelectString** member function to both find and select a string.

See Also: **CListBox::SelectString, CListBox::AddString, CListBox::InsertString, LB_FINDSTRING**

CListBox::FindStringExact

int FindStringExact(int *nIndexStart***, LPCTSTR** *lpszFind* **) const;**

Return Value

The index of the matching item, or **LB_ERR** if the search was unsuccessful.

Parameters

nIndexStart   Specifies the zero-based index of the item before the first item to be searched. When the search reaches the bottom of the list box, it continues from the top of the list box back to the item specified by *nIndexStart*. If *nIndexStart* is –1, the entire list box is searched from the beginning.

lpszFind   Points to the null-terminated string to search for. This string can contain a complete filename, including the extension. The search is not case sensitive, so the string can contain any combination of uppercase and lowercase letters.

Remarks

An application calls the **FindStringExact** member function to find the first list-box string that matches the string specified in *lpszFind*. If the list box was created with an owner-draw style but without the **LBS_HASSTRINGS** style, the **FindStringExact** member function attempts to match the doubleword value against the value of *lpszFind*.

See Also: **CListBox::FindString, LB_FINDSTRING, LB_FINDSTRINGEXACT**

CListBox::GetAnchorIndex

int GetAnchorIndex( ) const;

Return Value

The index of the current anchor item, if successful; otherwise **LB_ERR**.

Remarks

Retrieves the zero-based index of the current anchor item in the list box. In a multiple-selection list box, the anchor item is the first or last item in a block of contiguous selected items.

See Also: **CListBox::SetAnchorIndex**

CListBox::GetCaretIndex

int GetCaretIndex( ) const;

Return Value

The zero-based index of the item that has the focus rectangle in a list box. If the list box is a single-selection list box, the return value is the index of the item that is selected, if any.

Remarks

An application calls the **GetCaretIndex** member function to determine the index of the item that has the focus rectangle in a multiple-selection list box. The item may or may not be selected.

See Also: CListBox::SetCaretIndex, LB_GETCARETINDEX

CListBox::GetCount

int GetCount( ) const;

Return Value

The number of items in the list box, or **LB_ERR** if an error occurs.

Remarks

Retrieves the number of items in a list box.

The returned count is one greater than the index value of the last item (the index is zero-based).

See Also: LB_GETCOUNT

CListBox::GetCurSel

int GetCurSel( ) const;

Return Value

The zero-based index of the currently selected item. It is **LB_ERR** if no item is currently selected or if the list box is a multiple-selection list box.

Remarks

Retrieves the zero-based index of the currently selected item, if any, in a single-selection list box.

GetCurSel should not be called for a multiple-selection list box.

See Also: LB_GETCURSEL, CListBox::SetCurSel

CListBox::GetHorizontalExtent

int GetHorizontalExtent( ) const;

Return Value

The scrollable width of the list box, in pixels.

Remarks

Retrieves from the list box the width in pixels by which it can be scrolled horizontally. This is applicable only if the list box has a horizontal scroll bar.

See Also: **CListBox::SetHorizontalExtent, LB_GETHORIZONTALEXTENT**

CListBox::GetItemData

DWORD GetItemData(int *nIndex*) const;

Return Value

The 32-bit value associated with the item, or **LB_ERR** if an error occurs.

Parameters

nIndex   Specifies the zero-based index of the item in the list box.

Remarks

Retrieves the application-supplied doubleword value associated with the specified list-box item.

The doubleword value was the *dwItemData* parameter of a **SetItemData** call.

See Also: **CListBox::AddString, CListBox::GetItemDataPtr, CListBox::SetItemDataPtr, CListBox::InsertString, CListBox::SetItemData, LB_GETITEMDATA**

CListBox::GetItemDataPtr

void* GetItemDataPtr(int *nIndex*) const;

Return Value

Retrieves a pointer, or −1 if an error occurs.

Parameters

nIndex   Specifies the zero-based index of the item in the list box.

Remarks

Retrieves the application-supplied 32-bit value associated with the specified list-box item as a pointer (**void***).

See Also: **CListBox::AddString, CListBox::GetItemData, CListBox::InsertString, CListBox::SetItemData, LB_GETITEMDATA**

CListBox::GetItemHeight

int GetItemHeight(int *nIndex* **) const;**

Return Value

The height, in pixels, of the items in the list box. If the list box has the **LBS_OWNERDRAWVARIABLE** style, the return value is the height of the item specified by *nIndex*. If an error occurs, the return value is **LB_ERR**.

Parameters

nIndex Specifies the zero-based index of the item in the list box. This parameter is used only if the list box has the **LBS_OWNERDRAWVARIABLE** style; otherwise, it should be set to 0.

Remarks

An application calls the **GetItemHeight** member function to determine the height of items in a list box.

See Also: **LB_GETITEMHEIGHT**, **CListBox::SetItemHeight**

CListBox::GetItemRect

int GetItemRect(int *nIndex*, **LPRECT** *lpRect* **) const;**

Return Value

LB_ERR if an error occurs.

Parameters

nIndex Specifies the zero-based index of the item.

lpRect Specifies a long pointer to a **RECT** tructure that receives the list-box client coordinates of the item.

Remarks

Retrieves the dimensions of the rectangle that bounds a list-box item as it is currently displayed in the list-box window.

See Also: **LB_GETITEMRECT**

CListBox::GetLocale

LCID GetLocale( ) const;

Return Value

The locale identifier (LCID) value for the strings in the list box.

Remarks

Retrieves the locale used by the list box. The locale is used, for example, to determine the sort order of the strings in a sorted list box.

See Also: **CListBox::SetLocale**, **::GetStringTypeW**, **::GetSystemDefaultLCID**, **::GetUserDefaultLCID**

CListBox::GetSel

int GetSel(int *nIndex* **) const;**

Return Value

A positive number if the specified item is selected; otherwise, it is 0. The return value is **LB_ERR** if an error occurs.

Parameters

nIndex   Specifies the zero-based index of the item.

Remarks

Retrieves the selection state of an item. This member function works with both single- and multiple-selection list boxes.

See Also: **LB_GETSEL**, **CListBox::SetSel**

CListBox::GetSelCount

int GetSelCount( ) const;

Return Value

The count of selected items in a list box. If the list box is a single-selection list box, the return value is **LB_ERR**.

Remarks

Retrieves the total number of selected items in a multiple-selection list box.

See Also: **CListBox::SetSel**, **LB_GETSELCOUNT**

CListBox::GetSelItems

int GetSelItems(int *nMaxItems*, **LPINT** *rgIndex* **) const;**

Return Value

The actual number of items placed in the buffer. If the list box is a single-selection list box, the return value is **LB_ERR**.

Parameters

nMaxItems   Specifies the maximum number of selected items whose item numbers are to be placed in the buffer.

rgIndex   Specifies a long pointer to a buffer large enough for the number of integers specified by *nMaxItems*.

Remarks

Fills a buffer with an array of integers that specifies the item numbers of selected items in a multiple-selection list box.

See Also: LB_GETSELITEMS

CListBox::GetText

> **int GetText(int** *nIndex*, **LPTSTR** *lpszBuffer*) **const;**
> **void GetText(int** *nIndex*, **CString&** *rString*) **const;**

Return Value

The length (in bytes) of the string, excluding the terminating null character. If *nIndex* does not specify a valid index, the return value is **LB_ERR**.

Parameters

nIndex Specifies the zero-based index of the string to be retrieved.

lpszBuffer Points to the buffer that receives the string. The buffer must have sufficient space for the string and a terminating null character. The size of the string can be determined ahead of time by calling the **GetTextLen** member function.

rString A reference to a **CString** object.

Remarks

Gets a string from a list box. The second form of this member function fills a **CString** object with the string text.

See Also: CListBox::GetTextLen, LB_GETTEXT

CListBox::GetTextLen

> **int GetTextLen(int** *nIndex*) **const;**

Return Value

The length of the string in bytes, excluding the terminating null character. If *nIndex* does not specify a valid index, the return value is **LB_ERR**.

Parameters

nIndex Specifies the zero-based index of the string.

Remarks

Gets the length of a string in a list-box item.

See Also: CListBox::GetText, LB_GETTEXTLEN

CListBox::GetTopIndex

int GetTopIndex( ) const;

Return Value

The zero-based index of the first visible item in a list box if successful, **CB_ERR** otherwise.

Remarks

Retrieves the zero-based index of the first visible item in a list box. Initially, item 0 is at the top of the list box, but if the list box is scrolled, another item may be at the top.

See Also: **CListBox::SetTopIndex, LB_GETTOPINDEX**

CListBox::InitStorage

int InitStorage(int *nItems*, **UINT** *nBytes* **);**

Return Value

If successful, the maximum number of items that the list box can store before a memory reallocation is needed, otherwise **LB_ERRSPACE**, meaning not enough memory is available.

Parameters

nItems   Specifies the number of items to add.

nBytes   Specifies the amount of memory, in bytes, to allocate for item strings.

Remarks

Allocates memory for storing list-box items. Call this function before adding a large number of items to a **CListBox**.

This function helps speed up the initialization of list boxes that have a large number of items (more than 100). It preallocates the specified amount of memory so that subsequent **AddString**, **InsertString**, and **Dir** functions take the shortest possible time. You can use estimates for the parameters. If you overestimate, some extra memory is allocated; if you underestimate, the normal allocation is used for items that exceed the preallocated amount.

Windows 95 only: The *nItems* parameter is limited to 16-bit values. This means list boxes cannot contain more than 32,767 items. Although the number of items is restricted, the total size of the items in a list box is limited only by available memory.

See Also: **CListBox::CListBox, CListBox::Create, CListBox::ResetContent, LB_INITSTORAGE**

CListBox::InsertString

> **int InsertString(int** *nIndex*, **LPCTSTR** *lpszItem* **);**

Return Value

The zero-based index of the position at which the string was inserted. The return value is **LB_ERR** if an error occurs; the return value is **LB_ERRSPACE** if insufficient space is available to store the new string.

Parameters

nIndex   Specifies the zero-based index of the position to insert the string. If this parameter is –1, the string is added to the end of the list.

lpszItem   Points to the null-terminated string that is to be inserted.

Remarks

Inserts a string into the list box. Unlike the **AddString** member function, **InsertString** does not cause a list with the **LBS_SORT** style to be sorted.

See Also: **CListBox::AddString, LB_INSERTSTRING**

CListBox::ItemFromPoint

> **UINT ItemFromPoint(CPoint** *pt*, **BOOL&** *bOutside* **) const;**

Return Value

The index of the nearest item to the point specified in *pt*.

Parameters

pt   Point for which to find the nearest item, specified relative to the upper-left corner of the client area of the list box.

bOutside   Reference to a **BOOL** variable which will be set to **TRUE** if *pt* is outside the client area of the list box, **FALSE** if *pt* is inside the client area of the list box.

Remarks

Call this function to determine the list-box item nearest the point specified in *pt*. You could use this function to determine which list-box item the mouse cursor moves over.

Note   Because the Win32 message **LB_ITEMFROMPOINT** works only with Windows 95, **ItemFromPoint**, which wraps the Win32 message also works only with Windows 95.

See Also: **CListBox::GetItemRect, LB_ITEMFROMPOINT**

CListBox::MeasureItem

> **virtual void MeasureItem(LPMEASUREITEMSTRUCT** *lpMeasureItemStruct* **);**

Parameters

lpMeasureItemStruct   A long pointer to a **MEASUREITEMSTRUCT** structure.

Remarks

Called by the framework when a list box with an owner-draw style is created.

By default, this member function does nothing. Override this member function and fill in the **MEASUREITEMSTRUCT** structure to inform Windows of the list-box dimensions. If the list box is created with the **LBS_OWNERDRAWVARIABLE** style, the framework calls this member function for each item in the list box. Otherwise, this member is called only once.

For further information about using the **LBS_OWNERDRAWFIXED** style in an owner-draw list box created with the **SubclassDlgItem** member function of **CWnd**, see the discussion in Technical Note 14 online.

See **CWnd::OnMeasureItem** for a description of the **MEASUREITEMSTRUCT** structure.

See Also: **CListBox::CompareItem**, **CWnd::OnMeasureItem**, **CListBox::DrawItem**, **CListBox::DeleteItem**

CListBox::ResetContent

void ResetContent( );

Remarks

Removes all items from a list box.

See Also: **LB_RESETCONTENT**

CListBox::SelectString

int SelectString(int *nStartAfter*, **LPCTSTR** *lpszItem* **);**

Return Value

The index of the selected item if the search was successful. If the search was unsuccessful, the return value is **LB_ERR** and the current selection is not changed.

Parameters

nStartAfter Contains the zero-based index of the item before the first item to be searched. When the search reaches the bottom of the list box, it continues from the top of the list box back to the item specified by *nStartAfter*. If *nStartAfter* is –1, the entire list box is searched from the beginning.

lpszItem Points to the null-terminated string that contains the prefix to search for. The search is case independent, so this string may contain any combination of uppercase and lowercase letters.

Remarks

Searches for a list-box item that matches the specified string, and if a matching item is found, it selects the item.

The list box is scrolled, if necessary, to bring the selected item into view.

This member function cannot be used with a list box that has the **LBS_MULTIPLESEL** style.

An item is selected only if its initial characters (from the starting point) match the characters in the string specified by *lpszItem*.

Use the **FindString** member function to find a string without selecting the item.

See Also: **CListBox::FindString, LB_SELECTSTRING**

CListBox::SelItemRange

    int SelItemRange(BOOL *bSelect***, int** *nFirstItem***, int** *nLastItem* **);**

Return Value

    LB_ERR if an error occurs.

Parameters

    bSelect   Specifies how to set the selection. If *bSelect* is **TRUE**, the string is selected and highlighted; if **FALSE**, the highlight is removed and the string is no longer selected.

    nFirstItem   Specifies the zero-based index of the first item to set.

    nLastItem   Specifies the zero-based index of the last item to set.

Remarks

    Selects multiple consecutive items in a multiple-selection list box.

    Use this member function only with multiple-selection list boxes. If you need to select only one item in a multiple-selection list box—that is, if *nFirstItem* is equal to *nLastItem*—call the **SetSel** member function instead.

    See Also: **LB_SELITEMRANGE, CListBox::GetSelItems**

CListBox::SetAnchorIndex

    void SetAnchorIndex(int *nIndex* **);**

Parameters

    nIndex   Specifies the zero-based index of the list-box item that will be the anchor.

Remarks

    Sets the anchor in a multiple-selection list box to begin an extended selection. In a multiple-selection list box, the anchor item is the first or last item in a block of contiguous selected items.

    See Also: **CListBox::GetAnchorIndex**

CListBox::SetCaretIndex

int SetCaretIndex(int *nIndex*, **BOOL** *bScroll* = **TRUE**);

Return Value

    LB_ERR if an error occurs.

Parameters

    nIndex   Specifies the zero-based index of the item to receive the focus rectangle in the list box.

    bScroll   If this value is 0, the item is scrolled until it is fully visible. If this value is not 0, the item is scrolled until it is at least partially visible.

Remarks

    An application calls the **SetCaretIndex** member function to set the focus rectangle to the item at the specified index in a multiple-selection list box. If the item is not visible, it is scrolled into view.

    See Also: **CListBox::GetCaretIndex, LB_SETCARETINDEX**

CListBox::SetColumnWidth

void SetColumnWidth(int *cxWidth*);

Parameters

    cxWidth   Specifies the width in pixels of all columns.

Remarks

    Sets the width in pixels of all columns in a multicolumn list box (created with the **LBS_MULTICOLUMN** style).

    See Also: **LB_SETCOLUMNWIDTH**

CListBox::SetCurSel

int SetCurSel(int *nSelect*);

Return Value

    LB_ERR if an error occurs.

Parameters

    nSelect   Specifies the zero-based index of the string to be selected. If *nSelect* is –1, the list box is set to have no selection.

Remarks

    Selects a string and scrolls it into view, if necessary. When the new string is selected, the list box removes the highlight from the previously selected string.

Use this member function only with single-selection list boxes. It cannot be used to set or remove a selection in a multiple-selection list box.

See Also: **LB_SETCURSEL**, **CListBox::GetCurSel**

CListBox::SetHorizontalExtent

void SetHorizontalExtent(int *cxExtent* **);**

Parameters

cxExtent   Specifies the number of pixels by which the list box can be scrolled horizontally.

Remarks

Sets the width, in pixels, by which a list box can be scrolled horizontally. If the size of the list box is smaller than this value, the horizontal scroll bar will horizontally scroll items in the list box. If the list box is as large or larger than this value, the horizontal scroll bar is hidden.

To respond to a call to **SetHorizontalExtent**, the list box must have been defined with the **WS_HSCROLL** style.

This member function is not useful for multicolumn list boxes. For multicolumn list boxes, call the **SetColumnWidth** member function.

See Also: **CListBox::GetHorizontalExtent**, **CListBox::SetColumnWidth**, **LB_SETHORIZONTALEXTENT**

CListBox::SetItemData

int SetItemData(int *nIndex*, **DWORD** *dwItemData* **);**

Return Value

LB_ERR if an error occurs.

Parameters

nIndex   Specifies the zero-based index of the item.

dwItemData   Specifies the value to be associated with the item.

Remarks

Sets a 32-bit value associated with the specified item in a list box.

See Also: **CListBox::SetItemDataPtr**, **CListBox::GetItemData**, **LB_SETITEMDATA**

CListBox::SetItemDataPtr

>   int **SetItemDataPtr**(int *nIndex*, **void*** *pData*);

Return Value
>   **LB_ERR** if an error occurs.

Parameters
>   *nIndex*   Specifies the zero-based index of the item.
>
>   *pData*   Specifies the pointer to be associated with the item.

Remarks
>   Sets the 32-bit value associated with the specified item in a list box to be the specified pointer (**void***). This pointer remains valid for the life of the list box, even though the item's relative position within the list box might change as items are added or removed. Hence, the item's index within the box can change, but the pointer remains reliable.

>   **See Also:**   **CListBox::SetItemData**, **CListBox::GetItemData**, **CListBox::GetItemDataPtr**, **LB_SETITEMDATA**

CListBox::SetItemHeight

>   int **SetItemHeight**(int *nIndex*, **UINT** *cyItemHeight*);

Return Value
>   **LB_ERR** if the index or height is invalid.

Parameters
>   *nIndex*   Specifies the zero-based index of the item in the list box. This parameter is used only if the list box has the **LBS_OWNERDRAWVARIABLE** style; otherwise, it should be set to 0.
>
>   *cyItemHeight*   Specifies the height, in pixels, of the item.

Remarks
>   An application calls the **SetItemHeight** member function to set the height of items in a list box. If the list box has the **LBS_OWNERDRAWVARIABLE** style, this function sets the height of the item specified by *nIndex*. Otherwise, this function sets the height of all items in the list box.

>   **See Also:**   **CListBox::GetItemHeight**, **LB_SETITEMHEIGHT**

CListBox::SetLocale

LCID SetLocale(LCID *nNewLocale* **);**

Return Value

The previous locale identifier (LCID) value for this list box.

Parameters

nNewLocale   The new locale identifier (LCID) value to set for the list box.

Remarks

Sets the locale identifier for this list box. If **SetLocale** is not called, the default locale is obtained from the system. This system default locale can be modified by using Control Panel's Regional (or International) application.

See Also: CListBox::GetLocale

CListBox::SetSel

int SetSel(int *nIndex*, **BOOL** *bSelect* = **TRUE**);

Return Value

LB_ERR if an error occurs.

Parameters

nIndex   Contains the zero-based index of the string to be set. If −1, the selection is added to or removed from all strings, depending on the value of *bSelect*.

bSelect   Specifies how to set the selection. If *bSelect* is **TRUE**, the string is selected and highlighted; if **FALSE**, the highlight is removed and the string is no longer selected. The specified string is selected and highlighted by default.

Remarks

Selects a string in a multiple-selection list box.

Use this member function only with multiple-selection list boxes.

See Also: CListBox::GetSel, LB_SETSEL

CListBox::SetTabStops

void SetTabStops( );
BOOL SetTabStops(const int& *cxEachStop* **);**
BOOL SetTabStops(int *nTabStops*, **LPINT** *rgTabStops* **);**

Return Value

Nonzero if all the tabs were set; otherwise 0.

Parameters

> *cxEachStop*   Tab stops are set at every *cxEachStop* dialog units. See *rgTabStops* for a description of a dialog unit.
>
> *nTabStops*   Specifies the number of tab stops to have in the list box.
>
> *rgTabStops*   Points to the first member of an array of integers containing the tab-stop positions in dialog units. A dialog unit is a horizontal or vertical distance. One horizontal dialog unit is equal to one-fourth of the current dialog base width unit, and one vertical dialog unit is equal to one-eighth of the current dialog base height unit. The dialog base units are computed based on the height and width of the current system font. The **GetDialogBaseUnits** Windows function returns the current dialog base units in pixels. The tab stops must be sorted in increasing order; back tabs are not allowed.

Remarks

> Sets the tab-stop positions in a list box.
>
> To set tab stops to the default size of 2 dialog units, call the parameterless version of this member function. To set tab stops to a size other than 2, call the version with the *cxEachStop* argument.
>
> To set tab stops to an array of sizes, use the version with the *rgTabStops* and *nTabStops* arguments. A tab stop will be set for each value in *rgTabStops*, up to the number specified by *nTabStops*.
>
> To respond to a call to the **SetTabStops** member function, the list box must have been created with the **LBS_USETABSTOPS** style.
>
> **See Also: LB_SETTABSTOPS, ::GetDialogBaseUnits**

CListBox::SetTopIndex

> **int SetTopIndex(int** *nIndex* **);**

Return Value

> Zero if successful, or **LB_ERR** if an error occurs.

Parameters

> *nIndex*   Specifies the zero-based index of the list-box item.

Remarks

> Ensures that a particular list-box item is visible.
>
> The system scrolls the list box until either the item specified by *nIndex* appears at the top of the list box or the maximum scroll range has been reached.
>
> **See Also: CListBox::GetTopIndex, LB_SETTOPINDEX**

CListBox::VKeyToItem

virtual int VKeyToItem(UINT *nKey***, UINT** *nIndex* **);**

Return Value

Returns −2 for no further action, −1 for default action, or a nonnegative number to specify an index of a list box item on which to perform the default action for the keystroke.

Parameters

nKey   The virtual-key code of the key the user pressed.

nIndex   The current position of the list-box caret.

Remarks

This function is called by the framework when the list box's parent window receives a **WM_VKEYTOITEM** message from the list box. The **WM_VKEYTOITEM** message is sent by the list box when it receives a **WM_KEYDOWN** message, but only if the list box meets both of the following:

- Has the **LBS_WANTKEYBOARDINPUT** style set.
- Has at least one item.

You should never call this function yourself. Override this function to provide your own custom handling of keyboard messages.

You must return a value to tell the framework what action your override performed. A return value of −2 indicates that the application handled all aspects of selecting the item and requires no further action by the list box. Before returning −2, you could set the selection or move the caret or both. To set the selection, use **SetCurSel** or **SetSel**. To move the caret, use **SetCaretIndex**.

A return value of −1 indicates that the list box should perform the default action in response to the keystroke.The default implementation returns −1.

A return value of 0 or greater specifies the index of an item in the list box and indicates that the list box should perform the default action for the keystroke on the given item.

See Also: **CListBox::CharToItem, CListBox::SetCurSel, CListBox::SetSel, CListBox::SetCaretIndex**

CListCtrl

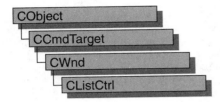

The **CListCtrl** class encapsulates the functionality of a "list view control," which displays a collection of items each consisting of an icon and a label. List views provide several ways of arranging items and displaying individual items. For example, additional information about each item can be displayed in colums to the right of the icon and label.

The **CListCtrl** class provides the functionality of the Windows common list view control. This control (and therefore the **CListCtrl** class) is available only to programs running under Windows 95 and Windows NT version 3.51 and later.

Views

List view controls can display their contents in four different ways, called "views." The current view is specified by the control's window style. Additional window styles specify the alignment of items and control-specific aspects of the list view control's functionality. Information about the four views follows.

View	Description
Icon view	Specified by the **LVS_ICON** window style.
	Each item appears as a full-sized icon with a label below it. The user can drag the items to any location in the list view window.
Small icon view	Specified by the **LVS_SMALLICON** window style.
	Each item appears as a small icon with the label to the right of it. The user can drag the items to any location.
List view	Specified by the **LVS_LIST** window style.
	Each item appears as a small icon with a label to the right of it. Items are arranged in columns and cannot be dragged to any arbitrary location by the user.
Report view	Specified by the **LVS_REPORT** window style.
	Each item appears on its own line with information arranged in columns. The leftmost column contains the small icon and label, and subsequent columns contain subitems as specified by the application. Unless the **LVS_NOCOLUMNHEADER** window style is also specified, each column has a header.

To change the view and alignment style after creating the control, use the Windows functions **GetWindowLong** and **SetWindowLong**.

You can control the way items are arranged in icon or small icon view by specifying a window style of **LVS_ALIGNTOP** (the default style) or **LVS_ALIGNLEFT**. You can change the alignment after a list view control is created. To isolate the window styles that specify the alignment of items, use the **LVS_ALIGNMASK** value.

Additional window styles control other options—for example, whether a user can edit labels in place, whether more than one item can be selected at a time, and so on.

Image Lists

The icons for list view items are contained in image lists, which you create and assign to the list view control. One image list contains the full-sized icons used in icon view, and a separate image list contains smaller versions of the same icons for use in other views. You can also specify a third image list that contains state images, which are displayed next to an item's icon to indicate an application-defined state.

You assign an image list to a list view control by using the **CListCtrl::SetImageList** function, specifying whether the image list contains large icons, small icons, or state images. You can retrieve the handle of an image list currently assigned to a list view control by using the **CListCtrl::GetImageList** function.

The large and small icon image lists typically contain icons for each type of list view item. You need not create both of these image lists if only one is used—for example, if a list view control is never in icon view. If you create both image lists, they must contain the same images in the same order because a single value is used to identify a list view item's icon in both image lists.

The large and small icon image lists can also contain overlay images, which are designed to be superimposed on item icons. A nonzero value in bits 8 through 11 of a list view item's state specifies the one-based index of an overlay image (zero indicates no overlay image). Because a 4-bit, one-based index is used, overlay images must be among the first 15 images in the image lists.

If a state image list is specified, a list view control reserves space to the left of each item's icon for a state image. An application can use state images, such as checked and cleared check boxes, to indicate application-defined item states. A nonzero value in bits 12 through 15 specifies the one-based index of a state image (zero indicates no state image). State images are typically not used in icon view.

By default, a list view control destroys the image lists assigned to it when it is destroyed. If a list view control has the **LVS_SHAREIMAGELISTS** window style, however, the application is responsible for destroying the image lists when they are no longer in use. You should specify this style if you assign the same image lists to multiple list view controls; otherwise, more than one control might try to destroy the same image list.

Items and Subitems

Each item in a list view control consists of an icon, a label, a current state, and an application-defined value. One or more subitems can also be associated with each item. A "subitem" is a string that, in report view, can be displayed in a column to the right of an item's icon and label. All items in a list view control have the same number of subitems. By using list view messages, you can add, modify, retrieve information about, and delete items. You can also find items with specific attributes.

The **LV_ITEM** structure defines a list view item or subitem. The **iItem** member is the zero-based index of the item. The **iSubItem** member is the one-based index of a subitem, or zero if the structure contains information about an item. Additional members specify the item's text, icon, state, and item data. "Item data" is an application-defined value associated with a list view item. For more information about the **LV_ITEM** structure, see **CListCtrl::GetItem**.

Callback Items

A "callback item" is a list view item for which the application—rather than the control—stores the text, icon, or both. Although a list view control can store these attributes for you, you may want to use callback items if your application already maintains some of this information. The callback mask specifies which item state bits are maintained by the application, and it applies to the whole control rather than to a specific item. The callback mask is zero by default, meaning that the control tracks all item states. If an application uses callback items or specifies a nonzero callback mask, it must be able to supply list view item attributes on demand.

You can define a callback item by specifying appropriate values for the **pszText** and **iImage** members of the **LV_ITEM** structure (see **CListCtrl::GetItem**). If the application maintains the item's or subitem's text, specify the **LPSTR_TEXTCALLBACK** value for the **pszText** member. If the application keeps track of the icon for the item, specify the **I_IMAGECALLBACK** value for the **iImage** member.

For more information on using **CListCtrl**, see Technical Note 60 online.

#include <afxcmn.h>

See Also: **CImageList**

CListCtrl Class Members

Construction

ListCtrl	Constructs a **CListCtrl** object.
Create	Creates a list control and attaches it to a **CListCtrl** object.

Attributes

GetBkColor	Retrieves the background color of a list view control.
SetBkColor	Sets the background color of the list view control.
GetImageList	Retrieves the handle of an image list used for drawing list view items.
SetImageList	Assigns an image list to a list view control.
GetItemCount	Retrieves the number of items in a list view control.
GetItem	Retrieves a list view item's attributes.
GetItemData	Retrieves the application-specific value associated with an item.
SetItem	Sets some or all of a list view item's attributes.
SetItemData	Sets the item's application-specific value.
GetCallbackMask	Retrieves the callback mask for a list view control.
SetCallbackMask	Sets the callback mask for a list view control.
GetNextItem	Searches for a list view item with specified properties and with specified relationship to a given item.
GetItemRect	Retrieves the bounding rectangle for an item.
SetItemPosition	Moves an item to a specified position in a list view control.
GetItemPosition	Retrieves the position of a list view item.
GetStringWidth	Determines the minimum column width necessary to display all of a given string.
GetEditControl	Retrieves the handle of the edit control used to edit an item's text.
GetColumn	Retrieves the attributes of a control's column.
SetColumn	Sets the attributes of a list view column.
GetColumnWidth	Retrieves the width of a column in report view or list view.
SetColumnWidth	Changes the width of a column in report view or list view.
GetViewRect	Retrieves the bounding rectangle of all items in the list view control.
GetTextColor	Retrieves the text color of a list view control.
SetTextColor	Sets the text color of a list view control.
GetTextBkColor	Retrieves the text background color of a list view control.
SetTextBkColor	Sets the background color of text in a list view control.
GetTopIndex	Retrieves the index of the topmost visible item.
GetCountPerPage	Calculates the number of items that can fit vertically in a list view control.
GetOrigin	Retrieves the current view origin for a list view control.
SetItemState	Changes the state of an item in a list view control.
GetItemState	Retrieves the state of a list view item.
GetItemText	Retrieves the text of a list view item or subitem.
SetItemText	Changes the text of a list view item or subitem.
SetItemCount	Prepares a list view control for adding a large number of items.
GetSelectedCount	Retrieves the number of selected items in the list view control.

Operations

InsertItem	Inserts a new item in a list view control.
DeleteItem	Deletes an item from the control.
DeleteAllItems	Deletes all items from the control.
FindItem	Searches for a list view item having specified characteristics.
SortItems	Sorts list view items using an application-defined comparison function.
HitTest	Determines which list view item is at a specified position.
EnsureVisible	Ensures that an item is visible.
Scroll	Scrolls the content of a list view control.
RedrawItems	Forces a list view control to repaint a range of items.
Update	Forces the control to repaint a specified item.
Arrange	Aligns items on a grid.
EditLabel	Begins in-place editing of an item's text.
InsertColumn	Inserts a new column in a list view control.
DeleteColumn	Deletes a column from the list view control.
CreateDragImage	Creates a drag image list for a specified item.

Overridables

DrawItem	Called when a visual aspect of an owner-draw control changes.

Member Functions

CListCtrl::Arrange

BOOL Arrange(UINT *nCode* **);**

Return Value

Nonzero if successful; otherwise zero.

Parameters

nCode   Specifies the alignment style for the items. It can be one of the following values:

- **LVA_ALIGNLEFT**   Aligns items along the left edge of the window.
- **LVA_ALIGNTOP**   Aligns items along the top edge of the window.
- **LVA_DEFAULT**   Aligns items according to the list view's current alignment styles (the default value).
- **LVA_SNAPTOGRID**   Snaps all icons to the nearest grid position.

Remarks

Call this function to reposition items in an icon view so that they align on a grid. The *nCode* parameter specifies the alignment style.

See Also: CListCtrl::EnsureVisible

CListCtrl::CListCtrl

CListCtrl( );

Remarks

Constructs a **CListCtrl** object.

See Also: CListCtrl::Create

CListCtrl::Create

BOOL Create(DWORD *dwStyle***, const RECT&** *rect***, CWnd*** *pParentWnd***, UINT** *nID* **);**

Return Value

Nonzero if successful; otherwise zero.

Parameters

dwStyle   Specifies the list control's style. Apply any combination of list control styles to the control. See the Remarks section for a list of possible styles.

rect   Specifies the list control's size and position. It can be either a **CRect** object or a **RECT** structure.

pParentWnd   Specifies the list control's parent window, usually a **CDialog**. It must not be **NULL**.

nID   Specifies the list control's ID.

Remarks

You construct a **CListCtrl** in two steps. First call the constructor, then call **Create**, which creates the list view control and attaches it to the **CListCtrl** object.

The *dwStyle* parameter can be a combination of the following values:

- **LVS_ALIGNLEFT**   Specifies that items are left-aligned in icon and small icon view.

- **LVS_ALIGNTOP**   Specifies that items are aligned with the top of the control in icon and small icon view.

- **LVS_AUTOARRANGE**   Specifies that icons are automatically kept arranged in icon view and small icon view.

- **LVS_EDITLABELS**   Allows item text to be edited in place. The parent window must process the **LVN_ENDLABELEDIT** notification message.

- **LVS_ICON** Specifies icon view.

- **LVS_LIST** Specifies list view.

- **LVS_NOCOLUMNHEADER** Specifies that a column header is not displayed in report view. By default, columns have headers in report view.

- **LVS_NOLABELWRAP** Displays item text on a single line in icon view. By default, item text can wrap in icon view.

- **LVS_NOSCROLL** Disables scrolling. All items must be within the client area.

- **LVS_NOSORTHEADER** Specifies that column headers do not work like buttons. This style is useful if clicking a column header in report view does not carry out an action, such as sorting.

- **LVS_OWNERDRAWFIXED** Enables the owner window to paint items in report view. The list view control sends a **WM_DRAWITEM** message to paint each item; it does not send separate messages for each subitem. The **itemData** member of the **DRAWITEMSTRUCT** structure contains the item data for the specified list view item.

- **LVS_REPORT** Specifies report view.

- **LVS_SHAREIMAGELISTS** Specifies that the control does not take ownership of the image lists assigned to it (that is, it does not destroy the image lists when it is destroyed). This style enables the same image lists to be used with multiple list view controls.

- **LVS_SHOWSELALWAYS** Always show the selection, if any, even if the control does not have the focus.

- **LVS_SINGLESEL** Allows only one item at a time to be selected. By default, multiple items can be selected.

- **LVS_SMALLICON** Specifies small icon view.

- **LVS_SORTASCENDING** Sorts items based on item text in ascending order.

- **LVS_SORTDESCENDING** Sorts items based on item text in descending order.

See Also: CListCtrl::CListCtrl

CListCtrl::CreateDragImage

CImageList* CreateDragImage(int *nItem*, LPPOINT *lpPoint*);

Return Value

A pointer to the drag image list if successful; otherwise **NULL**.

Parameters

nItem Index of the item whose drag image list is to be created.

lpPoint Address of a **POINT** structure that receives the initial location of the upper-left corner of the image, in view coordinates.

Remarks

Call this function to create a drag image list for the item specified by *nItem*. The **CImageList** object is permanent, and you must delete it when finished. For example:

```
CImageList* pImageList = MyListCtrl.CreateDragImage(nItem, &point);
    ...
    ...
    delete pImageList;
```

See Also: **CImageList**, **CListCtrl::GetImageList**, **CListCtrl::SetImageList**

CListCtrl::DeleteAllItems

BOOL DeleteAllItems( );

Return Value

Nonzero if successful; otherwise zero.

Remarks

Call this function to delete all items from the list view control.

See Also: **CListCtrl::InsertItem**, **CListCtrl::DeleteItem**

CListCtrl::DeleteColumn

BOOL DeleteColumn(int *nCol*);

Return Value

Nonzero if successful; otherwise zero.

Parameters

nCol   Index of the column to be deleted.

Remarks

Call this function to delete a column from the list view control.

See Also: **CListCtrl::InsertColumn**, **CListCtrl::DeleteAllItems**

CListCtrl::DeleteItem

BOOL DeleteItem(int *nItem*);

Return Value

Nonzero if successful; otherwise zero.

Parameters

nItem   Specifies the index of the item to be deleted.

Remarks

Call this function to delete an item from a list view control.

See Also: **CListCtrl::InsertItem, CListCtrl::DeleteAllItems**

CListCtrl::DrawItem

virtual void DrawItem(LPDRAWITEMSTRUCT *lpDrawItemStruct* **);**

Parameters

lpDrawItemStruct A long pointer to a **DRAWITEMSTRUCT** structure that contains information about the type of drawing required.

Remarks

Called by the framework when a visual aspect of an owner-draw list view control changes. The **itemAction** member of the **DRAWITEMSTRUCT** structure defines the drawing action that is to be performed.

By default, this member function does nothing. Override this member function to implement drawing for an owner-draw **CListCtrl** object.

The application should restore all graphics device interface (GDI) objects selected for the display context supplied in *lpDrawItemStruct* before this member function terminates.

See Also: **CWnd::OnDrawItem**

CListCtrl::EditLabel

CEdit* EditLabel(int *nItem* **);**

Return Value

If successful, a pointer to the **CEdit** object that is used to edit the item text; otherwise **NULL**.

Parameters

nItem Index of the list view item that is to be edited.

Remarks

A list view control that has the **LVS_EDITLABELS** window style enables a user to edit item labels in place. The user begins editing by clicking the label of an item that has the focus.

Use this function to begin in-place editing of the specified list view item's text.

See Also: **CListCtrl::GetEditControl**

CListCtrl::EnsureVisible

BOOL EnsureVisible(int *nItem*, **BOOL** *bPartialOK* **);**

Return Value

Nonzero if successful; otherwise zero.

Parameters

nItem   Index of the list view item that is to be visible.

bPartialOK   Specifies whether partial visibility is acceptable.

Remarks

Call this function to ensure that a list view item is at least partially visible. The list view control is scrolled if necessary. If the *bPartialOK* parameter is nonzero, no scrolling occurs if the item is partially visible.

See Also: CListCtrl::Scroll

CListCtrl::FindItem

int FindItem(LV_FINDINFO* *pFindInfo*, **int** *nStart* **= –1) const;**

Return Value

The index of the item if successful or –1 otherwise.

Parameters

pFindInfo   A pointer to a **LV_FINDINFO** structure containing information about the item to be searched for.

nStart   Index of the item to begin the search with, or –1 to start from the beginning. The item at *nStart* is excluded from the search if *nStart* is not equal to –1.

Remarks

Use this function to search for a list view item having specified characteristics.

The *pFindInfo* parameter points to an **LV_FINDINFO** structure, which contains information used to search for a list view item:

```
typedef struct _LV_FINDINFO {
    UINT flags;     //see below
    LPCSTR psz;     //see below
    LPARAM lParam; //see below
} LV_FINDINFO;
```

The members are as follows:

flags   Type of search to perform. It can be one or more of these values:

- **LVFI_PARAM**   Searches based on the **lParam** member. The **lParam** member of the matching item's **LV_ITEM** structure must match the **lParam** member of this structure. (For information on the **LV_ITEM** structure, see **CListCtrl::GetItem**.) If this value is specified, all other values are ignored.

- **LVFI_PARTIAL**   Matches if the item text begins with the string pointed to by the **psz** member. This value implies use of the **LVFI_STRING** value.

- **LVFI_STRING**   Searches based on item text. Unless additional values are specified, the item text of the matching item must exactly match the string pointed to by the **psz** member.

- **LVFI_WRAP**   Continues the search at the beginning if no match is found.

- **LVFI_NEARESTXY**   Finds the item nearest the specified position in the specified direction.

psz   Address of a null-terminated string to compare with item text if the **flags** member specifies the **LVFI_STRING** or **LVFI_PARTIAL** value.

lParam   Value to compare with the **lParam** member of a list view item's **LV_ITEM** structure if the **flags** member specifies the **LVFI_PARAM** value.

See Also: CListCtrl::SortItems

CListCtrl::GetBkColor

COLORREF GetBkColor( ) const;

Return Value

A 32-bit value used to specify an RGB color.

Remarks

Retrieves the background color of a list view control.

See Also: CListCtrl::SetBkColor COLORREF

CListCtrl::GetCallbackMask

UINT GetCallbackMask( ) const;

Return Value

The list view control's callback mask.

Remarks

Retrieves the callback mask for a list view control.

A "callback item" is a list view item for which the application—rather than the control—stores the text, icon, or both. Although a list view control can store these attributes for you, you may want to use callback items if your application already maintains some of this information. The callback mask specifies which item state bits are maintained by the application, and it applies to the whole control rather than to a specific item. The callback mask is zero by default, meaning that the control tracks all item states. If an application uses callback items or specifies a nonzero callback mask, it must be able to supply list view item attributes on demand.

See Also: **CListCtrl::SetCallbackMask**

CListCtrl::GetColumn

BOOL GetColumn(int *nCol*, **LV_COLUMN*** *pColumn* **) const;**

Return Value

Nonzero if successful; otherwise zero.

Parameters

nCol Index of the column whose attributes are to be retrieved.

pColumn Address of an **LV_COLUMN** structure that specifies the information to retrieve and receives information about the column. The **mask** member specifies which column attributes to retrieve. If the **mask** member specifies the **LVCF_TEXT** value, the **pszText** member must contain the address of the buffer that receives the item text and the **cchTextMax** member must specify the size of the buffer.

Remarks

Retrieves the attributes of a list view control's column.

The **LV_COLUMN** structure contains information about a column in report view:

```
typedef struct _LV_COLUMN {
    UINT mask;          // see below
    int fmt;            // see below
    int cx;             // width of the column, in pixels
    LPSTR pszText;      // see below
    int cchTextMax;     // see below
    int iSubItem;       // index of subitem associated with column
} LV_COLUMN;
```

The members are as follows:

mask Variable specifying which members contain valid information. It can be zero or one or more of these values (combine values with the bitwise-OR operator):

- **LVCF_FMT** The **fmt** member is valid.
- **LVCF_SUBITEM** The **iSubItem** member is valid.
- **LVCF_TEXT** The **pszText** member is valid.
- **LVCF_WIDTH** The **cx** member is valid.

fmt Alignment of the column. It can be one of these values: **LVCFMT_LEFT**, **LVCFMT_RIGHT**, or **LVCFMT_CENTER**.

pszText Address of a null-terminated string containing the column heading if the structure contains information about a column. If the structure is receiving information about a column, this member specifies the address of the buffer that receives the column heading.

cchTextMax   Size of the buffer pointed to by the **pszText** member. If the structure is not receiving information about a column, this member is ignored.

See Also: CListCtrl::SetColumn, CListCtrl::GetColumnWidth

CListCtrl::GetColumnWidth

int GetColumnWidth(int *nCol* **) const;**

Return Value

The width, in pixels, of the column specified by *nCol*.

Parameters

nCol   Specifies the index of the column whose width is to be retrieved.

Remarks

Retrieves the width of a column in report view or list view.

See Also: CListCtrl::SetColumnWidth, CListCtrl::GetColumn

CListCtrl::GetCountPerPage

int GetCountPerPage( ) const;

Return Value

The number of items that can fit vertically in the visible area of a list view control when in list view or report view.

Remarks

Calculates the number of items that can fit vertically in the visible area of a list view control when in list view or report view.

See Also: CListCtrl::GetTopIndex

CListCtrl::GetEditControl

CEdit* GetEditControl( ) const;

Return Value

If successful, a pointer to the **CEdit** object that is used to edit the item text; otherwise **NULL**.

Remarks

Retrieves the handle of the edit control used to edit a list view item's text.

See Also: **CListCtrl::EditLabel**

CListCtrl::GetImageList

CImageList* GetImageList(int *nImageList* **) const;**

Return Value

A pointer to the image list used for drawing list view items.

Parameters

nImageList   Value specifying which image list to retrieve. It can be one of these values:

- **LVSIL_NORMAL**   Image list with large icons.
- **LVSIL_SMALL**   Image list with small icons.
- **LVSIL_STATE**   Image list with state images.

Remarks

Retrieves the handle of an image list used for drawing list view items.

See Also: **CImageList**, **CListCtrl::SetImageList**

CListCtrl::GetItem

BOOL GetItem(LV_ITEM* *pItem* **) const;**

Return Value

Nonzero if successful; otherwise zero.

Parameters

pItem   Pointer to an **LV_ITEM** structure that receives the item's attributes.

Remarks

Retrieves some or all of a list view item's attributes.

The **LV_ITEM** structure specifies or receives the attributes of a list view item:

```
typedef struct _LV_ITEM {
    UINT    mask;           // see below
    int     iItem;          // see below
    int     iSubItem;       // see below
    UINT    state;          // see below
    UINT    stateMask;      // see below
    LPSTR   pszText;        // see below
    int     cchTextMax;     // see below
    int     iImage;         // see below
    LPARAM  lParam;         // 32-bit value to associate with item
} LV_ITEM;
```

Members are as follows:

mask Variable specifying which members contain valid data or which members are to be filled in. It can be one or more of these values:

- **LVIF_TEXT** The **pszText** member is valid.
- **LVIF_IMAGE** The **iImage** member is valid
- **LVIF_PARAM** The **lParam** member is valid.
- **LVIF_STATE** The **state** member is valid.

iItem Index of the item this structure refers to.

iSubItem A "subitem" is a string that, in report view, can be displayed in a column to the right of an item's icon and label. All items in a list view have the same number of subitems. This member is the one-based index of a subitem, or zero if the structure contains information about an item.

state and **stateMask** Current state of the item, and the valid states of the item. These members can be any valid combination of the following state flags:

- **LVIS_CUT** The item is marked for a cut and paste operation.
- **LVIS_DROPHILITED** The item is highlighted as a drag and drop target.
- **LVIS_FOCUSED** The item has the focus, so it is surrounded by a standard focus rectangle. Although more than one item may be selected, only one item can have the focus.
- **LVIS_SELECTED** The item is selected. The appearance of a selected item depends on whether it has the focus and on the system colors used for selection.
- **LVIS_OVERLAYMASK** The application stores the image list index of the current overlay image for each item.
- **LVIS_STATEIMAGEMASK** The application stores the image list index of the current state image for each item.

pszText Address of a null-terminated string containing the item text if the structure specifies item attributes. If this member is the **LPSTR_TEXTCALLBACK** value, the item is a callback item. If the structure is receiving item attributes, this member is the address of the buffer that receives the item text.

cchTextMax Size of the buffer pointed to by the **pszText** member if the structure is receiving item attributes. If the structure specifies item attributes, this member is ignored.

iImage Index of the list view item's icon in the large icon and small icon image lists. If this member is the **I_IMAGECALLBACK** value, the item is a callback item.

See Also: CListCtrl::SetItem

CListCtrl::GetItemCount

int GetItemCount( );

Return Value

The number of items in the list view control.

Remarks

Retrieves the number of items in a list view control.

See Also: **CListCtrl::SetItemCount, CListCtrl::GetSelectedCount**

CListCtrl::GetItemData

DWORD GetItemData(int *nItem* **) const;**

Return Value

A 32-bit application-specific value associated with the specified item.

Parameters

nItem Index of the list item whose data is to be retrieved.

Remarks

This function retrieves the 32-bit application-specific value associated with the item specified by *nItem*. This value is the **lParam** member of the **LV_ITEM** structure; for more information on this structure, see **GetItem**.

See Also: **CListCtrl::SetItemData**

CListCtrl::GetItemPosition

BOOL GetItemPosition(int *nItem***, LPPOINT** *lpPoint* **) const;**

Return Value

Nonzero if successful; otherwise zero.

Parameters

nItem The index of the item whose position is to be retrieved.

lpPoint Address of a **POINT** structure that receives the position of the item's upper-left corner, in view coordinates.

Remarks

Retrieves the position of a list view item.

See Also: **CListCtrl::SetItemPosition, CListCtrl::GetOrigin**

CListCtrl::GetItemRect

BOOL GetItemRect(int *nItem*, **LPRECT** *lpRect*, **UINT** *nCode* **) const;**

Return Value

Nonzero if successful; otherwise zero.

Parameters

nItem   The index of the item whose position is to be retrieved.

lpRect   Address of a **RECT** structure that receives the bounding rectangle.

nCode   Portion of the list view item for which to retrieve the bounding rectangle. It can be one of these values:

- **LVIR_BOUNDS**   Returns the bounding rectangle of the entire item, including the icon and label.

- **LVIR_ICON**   Returns the bounding rectangle of the icon or small icon.

- **LVIR_LABEL**   Returns the bounding rectangle of the item text.

Remarks

Retrieves the bounding rectangle for all or part of an item in the current view.

See Also: CListCtrl::GetItemPosition, CListCtrl::SetItemPosition, CListCtrl::GetOrigin

---

CListCtrl::GetItemState

UINT GetItemState(int *nItem*, **UINT** *nMask* **) const;**

Return Value

The state flags for the specified list view item.

Parameters

nItem   The index of the item whose state is to be retrieved.

nMask   Mask specifying which of the item's state flags to return.

Remarks

Retrieves the state of a list view item.

An item's state is specified by the **state** member of the **LV_ITEM** structure. When you specify or change an item's state, the **stateMask** member specifies which state bits you want to change. For more information on the **LV_ITEM** structure, see **CListCtrl::GetItem**.

See Also: CListCtrl::SetItemState, CListCtrl::GetItem

CListCtrl::GetItemText

int GetItemText(int *nItem*, **int** *nSubItem*, **LPTSTR** *lpszText*, **int** *nLen* **) const;**
CString GetItemText(int *nItem*, **int** *nSubItem* **) const;**

Return Value

The version returning **int** returns the length of the retrieved string.

The version returning a **CString** returns the item text.

Parameters

nItem   The index of the item whose text is to be retrieved.

nSubItem   Specifies the subitem whose text is to be retrieved.

lpszText   Pointer to a string that is to receive the item text.

nLen   Length of the buffer pointed to by *lpszText*.

Remarks

Retrieves the text of a list view item or subitem. If *nSubItem* is zero, this function retrieves the item label; if *nSubItem* is nonzero, it retrieves the text of the subitem. For more information on the subitem argument, see the discussion of the **LV_ITEM** structure in **CListCtrl::GetItem**.

See Also: CListCtrl::GetItem

CListCtrl::GetNextItem

int GetNextItem(int *nItem*, **int** *nFlags* **) const;**

Return Value

The index of the next item if successful, or –1 otherwise.

Parameters

nItem   Index of the item to begin the searching with, or –1 to find the first item that matches the specified flags. The specified item itself is excluded from the search.

nFlags   Geometric relation of the requested item to the specified item, and the state of the requested item. The geometric relation can be one of these values:

- **LVNI_ABOVE**   Searches for an item that is above the specified item.

- **LVNI_ALL**   Searches for a subsequent item by index (the default value).

- **LVNI_BELOW**   Searches for an item that is below the specified item.

- **LVNI_TOLEFT**   Searches for an item to the left of the specified item.

- **LVNI_TORIGHT**   Searches for an item to the right of the specified item.

The state can be zero, or it can be one or more of these values:

- **LVNI_DROPHILITED** The item has the **LVIS_DROPHILITED** state flag set.
- **LVNI_FOCUSED** The item has the **LVIS_FOCUSED** state flag set.
- **LVNI_SELECTED** The item has the **LVIS_SELECTED** state flag set.

If an item does not have all of the specified state flags set, the search continues with the next item.

Remarks

Searches for a list view item that has the specified properties and that bears the specified relationship to a given item.

See Also: **CListCtrl::GetItem**

CListCtrl::GetOrigin

BOOL GetOrigin(LPPOINT *lpPoint* **) const;**

Return Value

Nonzero if successful; otherwise zero.

Parameters

lpPoint Address of a **POINT** structure that receives the view origin.

Remarks

Retrieves the current view origin for a list view control.

See Also: **CListCtrl::GetItemPosition, CListCtrl::SetItemPosition**

CListCtrl::GetSelectedCount

UINT GetSelectedCount( ) const;

Return Value

The number of selected items in the list view control.

Remarks

Retrieves the number of selected items in the list view control.

See Also: **CListCtrl::SetItemCount, CListCtrl::GetItemCount**

CListCtrl::GetStringWidth

int GetStringWidth(LPCTSTR *lpsz* **) const;**

Return Value

The width, in pixels, of the string pointed to by *lpsz*.

Parameters

    lpsz   Address of a null-terminated string whose width is to be determined.

Remarks

    Determines the minimum column width necessary to display all of a given string.

    The returned width takes into account the control's current font and column margins, but not the width of a small icon.

    See Also: **CListCtrl::GetColumnWidth, CListCtrl::SetColumnWidth**

CListCtrl::GetTextBkColor

    COLORREF GetTextBkColor( ) const;

Return Value

    A 32-bit value used to specify an RGB color.

Remarks

    Retrieves the text background color of a list view control.

    See Also: **CListCtrl::SetTextBkColor, CListCtrl::GetTextColor COLORREF**

CListCtrl::GetTextColor

    COLORREF GetTextColor( ) const;

Return Value

    A 32-bit value used to specify an RGB color.

Remarks

    Retrieves the text color of a list view control.

    See Also: **CListCtrl::SetTextColor, CListCtrl::GetTextBkColor COLORREF**

CListCtrl::GetTopIndex

    int GetTopIndex( ) const;

Return Value

    The index of the topmost visible item.

Remarks

    Retrieves the index of the topmost visible item when in list view or report view.

    See Also: **CListCtrl::GetCountPerPage**

CListCtrl::GetViewRect

BOOL GetViewRect(LPRECT *lpRect* **) const;**

Return Value

Nonzero if successful; otherwise zero.

Parameters

lpRect   Address of a **RECT** structure.

Remarks

Retrieves the bounding rectangle of all items in the list view control. The list view must be in icon view or small icon view.

See Also: CListCtrl::GetTopIndex

CListCtrl::HitTest

int HitTest(LV_HITTESTINFO* *pHitTestInfo* **) const;**
int HitTest(CPoint *pt*, **UINT*** *pFlags* = **NULL) const;**

Return Value

The index of the item at the position specified by *pHitTestInfo*, if any, or –1 otherwise.

Parameters

pHitTestInfo   Address of a **LV_HITTESTINFO** structure that contains the position to hit test and that receives information about the results of the hit test.

pt   Point to be tested.

pFlags   Pointer to an integer that receives information about the results of the test. See the explanation of the **flags** member of the **LV_HITTESTINFO** structure under Remarks.

Remarks

Determines which list view item, if any, is at a specified position.

The **LV_HITTESTINFO** structure contains information about a hit test:

```
typedef struct _LV_HITTESTINFO {
    POINT pt;      // position to hit test, in client coordinates
    UINT flags;    // see below
    int iItem;     // receives the index of the matching item
} LV_HITTESTINFO;
```

Its members are as follows:

flags   Variable that receives information about the results of a hit test. It can be one or more of these values:

- **LVHT_ABOVE**   The position is above the client area of the control.
- **LVHT_BELOW**   The position is below the client area of the control.

- **LVHT_NOWHERE** The position is inside the list view control's client window but is not over a list item.
- **LVHT_ONITEMICON** The position is over a list view item's icon.
- **LVHT_ONITEMLABEL** The position is over a list view item's text.
- **LVHT_ONITEMSTATEICON** The position is over the state image of a list view item.
- **LVHT_TOLEFT** The position is to the left of the list view control's client area.
- **LVHT_TORIGHT** The position is to the right of the list view control's client area.

You can use the **LVHT_ABOVE**, **LVHT_BELOW**, **LVHT_TOLEFT**, and **LVHT_TORIGHT** values to determine whether to scroll the contents of a list view control. Two of these flags can be combined, for example, if the position is above and to the left of the client area.

You can test for the **LVHT_ONITEM** value to determine whether a given position is over a list view item. This value is a bitwise-OR operation on the **LVHT_ONITEMICON**, **LVHT_ONITEMLABEL**, and **LVHT_ONITEMSTATEICON** values.

See Also: **CListCtrl::SetItemPosition, CListCtrl::GetItemPosition**

CListCtrl::InsertColumn

int InsertColumn(int *nCol,* **const LV_COLUMN*** *pColumn* **);**
int InsertColumn(int *nCol,* **LPCTSTR** *lpszColumnHeading,*
 ↪ **int** *nFormat* **= LVCFMT_LEFT, int** *nWidth* **= –1, int** *nSubItem* **= –1);**

Return Value

The index of the new column if successful or –1 otherwise.

Parameters

nCol The index of the new column.

pColumn Address of an **LV_COLUMN** structure that contains the attributes of the new column.

lpszColumnHeading Address of a string containing the column's heading.

nFormat Integer specifying the alignment of the column. It can be one of these values: **LVCFMT_LEFT**, **LVCFMT_RIGHT**, or **LVCFMT_CENTER**.

nWidth Width of the column, in pixels. If this parameter is –1, the column width is not set.

nSubItem   Index of the subitem associated with the column. If this parameter is −1, no subitem is associatied with the column.

Remarks

Inserts a new column in a list view control.

The **LV_COLUMN** structure contains the attributes of a column in report view. It is also used to receive information about a column. For more information on the **LV_COLUMN** structure, see **CListCtrl::GetColumn**.

See Also: **CListCtrl::DeleteColumn**

CListCtrl::InsertItem

int InsertItem(const LV_ITEM* *pItem* **);**
int InsertItem(int *nItem,* **LPCTSTR** *lpszItem* **);**
int InsertItem(int *nItem,* **LPCTSTR** *lpszItem,* **int** *nImage* **);**
int InsertItem(UINT *nMask,* **int** *nItem,* **LPCTSTR** *lpszItem,* **UINT** *nState,*
↪ UINT *nStateMask,* **int** *nImage,* **LPARAM** *lParam* **);**

Return Value

The index of the new item if successful or −1 otherwise.

Parameters

pItem   Pointer to an **LV_ITEM** structure that specifies the item's attributes. For information on the **LV_ITEM** structure, see **CListCtrl::GetItem**.

nItem   Index of the item to be inserted.

lpszItem   Address of a string containing the item's label, or **LPSTR_TEXTCALLBACK** if the item is a callback item. For information on callback items, see **CListCtrl::GetCallbackMask**.

nImage   Index of the item's image, or **I_IMAGECALLBACK** if the item is a callback item. For information on callback items, see **CListCtrl::GetCallbackMask**.

nMask   Specifies which attributes are valid (see the Remarks).

nState   Specifies values for states to be changed (see the Remarks).

nStateMask   Specifies which states are valid (see the Remarks).

nImage   Index of the item's image within the image list.

lParam   A 32-bit application-specific value associated with the item.

Remarks

Inserts an item into the list view control.

The *nMask* parameter specifies which item attributes passed as parameters are valid. It can be one or more of the following values, combined with the bitwise OR operator:

- **LVIF_TEXT**   The *lpszItem* parameter is the address of a null-terminated string.
- **LVIF_STATE**   The *nStateMask* parameter specifies which item states are valid and the *nState* parameter contains the values for those states.
- **LVIF_IMAGE**   The *nImage* parameter specifies the index in the image list, established by **CListCtrl::SetImageList**, of the image to be displayed.

See Also: **CListCtrl::DeleteItem, CListCtrl::DeleteAllItems**

CListCtrl::RedrawItems

BOOL RedrawItems(int *nFirst***, int** *nLast* **);**

Return Value
Nonzero if successful; otherwise zero.

Parameters
nFirst   Index of the first item to be repainted.

nLast   Index of the last item to be repainted.

Remarks
Forces a list view control to repaint a range of items.

The specified items are not actually repainted until the list view window receives a **WM_PAINT** message. To repaint immediately, call the Windows **UpdateWindow** function after using this function.

See Also: **CListCtrl::DrawItem**

CListCtrl::Scroll

BOOL Scroll(CSize *size* **);**

Return Value
Nonzero if successful; otherwise zero.

Parameters
size   A **CSize** object specifying the amount of horizontal and vertical scrolling, in pixels. The **y** member of *size* is divided by the height, in pixels, of the list view control's line, and the control is scrolled by the resulting number of lines.

Remarks
Scrolls the content of a list view control.

See Also: **CListCtrl::EnsureVisible**

CListCtrl::SetBkColor

BOOL SetBkColor(COLORREF *cr* **);**

Return Value

Nonzero if successful; otherwise zero.

Parameters

cr   Background color to set, or the **CLR_NONE** value for no background color. List view controls with background colors redraw themselves significantly faster than those without background colors. For information, see **COLORREF** in the Win32 Programmer's Reference.

Remarks

Sets the background color of the list view control.

See Also: CListCtrl::GetBkColor

CListCtrl::SetCallbackMask

BOOL SetCallbackMask(UINT *nMask* **);**

Return Value

Nonzero if successful; otherwise zero.

Parameters

nMask   New value of the callback mask.

Remarks

Sets the callback mask for a list view control.

See Also: CListCtrl::GetCallbackMask

CListCtrl::SetColumn

BOOL SetColumn(int *nCol***, const LV_COLUMN*** *pColumn* **);**

Return Value

Nonzero if successful; otherwise zero.

Parameters

nCol   Index of the column whose attributes are to be set.

pColumn   Address of an **LV_COLUMN** structure that contains the new column attributes. The **mask** member specifies which column attributes to set. If the **mask** member specifies the **LVCF_TEXT** value, the **pszText** member is the address of a null-terminated string and the **cchTextMax** member is ignored. For more information on the **LV_COLUMN** structure, see **CListCtrl::GetColumn**.

Remarks

Sets the attributes of a list view column.

See Also: **CListCtrl::GetColumn**

CListCtrl::SetColumnWidth

BOOL SetColumnWidth(int *nCol***, int** *cx* **);**

Return Value

Nonzero if successful; otherwise zero.

Parameters

nCol   Index of the column whose width is to be set. In list view, this parameter must be −1.

cx   The new width of the column.

Remarks

Changes the width of a column in report view or list view.

See Also: **CListCtrl::GetColumnWidth**, **CListCtrl::GetStringWidth**

CListCtrl::SetImageList

CImageList* SetImageList(CImageList* *pImageList***, int** *nImageList* **);**

Return Value

A pointer to the previous image list.

Parameters

pImageList   Pointer to the image list to assign.

nImageList   Type of image list. It can be one of these values:

- **LVSIL_NORMAL**   Image list with large icons.
- **LVSIL_SMALL**   Image list with small icons.
- **LVSIL_STATE**   Image list with state images.

Remarks

Assigns an image list to a list view control.

See Also: **CImageList**, **CListCtrl::GetImageList**

CListCtrl::SetItem

BOOL SetItem(const LV_ITEM* *pItem* **);**
BOOL SetItem(int *nItem*, **int** *nSubItem*, **UINT** *nMask*, **LPCTSTR** *lpszItem*,
  ↳ **int** *nImage*, **UINT** *nState*, **UINT** *nStateMask*, **LPARAM** *lParam* **);**

Return Value

Nonzero if successful; otherwise zero.

Parameters

pItem   Address of an **LV_ITEM** structure that contains the new item attributes. The **iItem** and **iSubItem** members identify the item or subitem, and the **mask** member specifies which attributes to set. For more information on the **mask** member, see the Remarks. For more information on the **LV_ITEM** structure, see **CListCtrl::GetItem**.

nItem   Index of the item whose attributes are to be set.

nSubItem   Index of the subitem whose attributes are to be set.

nMask   Specifies which attributes are to be set (see the Remarks).

lpszItem   Address of a null-terminated string specifying the item's label.

nImage   Index of the item's image within the image list.

nState   Specifies values for states to be changed (see the Remarks).

nStateMask   Specifies which states are to be changed (see the Remarks).

lParam   A 32-bit application-specific value to be associated with the item.

Remarks

Sets some or all of a list view item's attributes.

The **iItem** and **iSubItem** members of the **LV_ITEM** structure and the *nItem* and *nSubItem* parameters identify the item and subitem whose attributes are to be set.

The **mask** member of the **LV_ITEM** structure and the *nMask* parameter specify which item attributes are to be set:

- **LVIF_TEXT**   The **pszText** member or the *lpszItem* parameter is the address of a null-terminated string; the **cchTextMax** member is ignored.
- **LVIF_STATE**   The **stateMask** member or *nStateMask* parameter specifies which item states to change and the **state** member or *nState* parameter contains the values for those states.

See Also: **CListCtrl::GetItem**

CListCtrl::SetItemCount

> **void SetItemCount(int** *nItems* **);**

Parameters

> *nItems*   Number of items that the control will ultimately contain.

Remarks

> Prepares a list view control for adding a large number of items.
>
> By calling this function before adding a large number of items, you enable a list view control to reallocate its internal data structures only once rather than every time you add an item.
>
> **See Also:**   **CListCtrl::GetItemCount, CListCtrl::GetSelectedCount**

CListCtrl::SetItemData

> **BOOL SetItemData(int** *nItem*, **DWORD** *dwData* **);**

Return Value

> Nonzero if successful; otherwise 0.

Parameters

> *nItem*   Index of the list item whose data is to be set.
>
> *dwData*   A 32-bit value to be associated with the item.

Remarks

> This function sets the 32-bit application-specific value associated with the item specified by *nItem*. This value is the **lParam** member of the **LV_ITEM** structure; for more information on this structure, see **GetItem**.
>
> **See Also:**   **CListCtrl::GetItemData**

CListCtrl::SetItemPosition

> **BOOL SetItemPosition(int** *nItem*, **POINT** *pt* **);**

Return Value

> Nonzero if successful; otherwise zero.

Parameters

> *nItem*   Index of the item whose position is to be set.
>
> *pt*   A **POINT** structure specifying the new position, in view coordinates, of the item's upper-left corner.

Remarks

Moves an item to a specified position in a list view control. The control must be in icon or small icon view.

If the list view control has the **LVS_AUTOARRANGE** style, the list view is arranged after the position of the item is set.

See Also: **CListCtrl::GetItemPosition**, **CListCtrl::GetOrigin**

CListCtrl::SetItemState

BOOL SetItemState(int *nItem*, **LV_ITEM*** *pItem* **);**
BOOL SetItemState(int *nItem*, **UINT** *nState*, **UINT** *nMask* **);**

Return Value

Nonzero if successful; otherwise zero.

Parameters

nItem   Index of the item whose state is to be set.

pItem   Address of an **LV_ITEM** structure. The **stateMask** member specifies which state bits to change, and the **state** member contains the new values for those bits. The other members are ignored. For more information on the **LV_ITEM** structure, see **CListCtrl::GetItem**.

nState   New values for the state bits.

nMask   Mask specifying which state bits to change.

Remarks

Changes the state of an item in a list view control.

An item's "state" is a value that specifies the item's availability, indicates user actions, or otherwise reflects the item's status. A list view control changes some state bits, such as when the user selects an item. An application might change other state bits to disable or hide the item, or to specify an overlay image or state image.

See Also: **CListCtrl::GetItemState**

CListCtrl::SetItemText

BOOL SetItemText(int *nItem*, **int** *nSubItem*, **LPTSTR** *lpszText* **);**

Return Value

Nonzero if successful; otherwise zero.

Parameters

nItem   Index of the item whose text is to be set.

nSubItem   Index of the subitem, or zero to set the item label.

lpszText   Pointer to a string that contains the new item text.

Remarks

Changes the text of a list view item or subitem.

See Also: CListCtrl::GetItemText

CListCtrl::SetTextBkColor

BOOL SetTextBkColor(COLORREF *cr* **);**

Return Value

Nonzero if successful; otherwise zero.

Parameters

cr   A **COLORREF** specifying the new text background color. For information, see **COLORREF** in the Win32 Programmer's Reference.

Remarks

Sets the background color of text in a list view control.

See Also: CListCtrl::GetTextBkColor

CListCtrl::SetTextColor

BOOL SetTextColor(COLORREF *cr* **);**

Return Value

Nonzero if successful; otherwise zero.

Parameters

cr   A **COLORREF** specifying the new text color. For information, see **COLORREF** in the Win32 Programmer's Reference.

Remarks

Sets the text color of a list view control.

See Also: CListCtrl::SetTextBkColor

CListCtrl::SortItems

BOOL SortItems(PFNLVCOMPARE *pfnCompare***, DWORD** *dwData* **);**

Return Value

Nonzero if successful; otherwise zero.

Parameters

pfnCompare   Address of the application-defined comparison function. The comparison function is called during the sort operation each time the relative order of two list items needs to be compared. The comparison function must be either a static member of a class or a stand alone function that is not a member of any class.

dwData   Application-defined value that is passed to the comparison function.

Remarks

Sorts list view items using an application-defined comparison function. The index of each item changes to reflect the new sequence.

The comparison function has the following form:

```
int CALLBACK CompareFunc(LPARAM lParam1, LPARAM lParam2,
    LPARAM lParamSort);
```

The comparison function must return a negative value if the first item should precede the second, a positive value if the first item should follow the second, or zero if the two items are equivalent.

The *lParam1* and *lParam2* parameters specify the item data for the two items being compared. The *lParamSort* parameter is the same as the *dwData* value.

See Also: CListCtrl::FindItem

CListCtrl::Update

BOOL Update(int *nItem* **);**

Return Value

Nonzero if successful; otherwise zero.

Parameters

nItem   Index of the item to be updated.

Remarks

Call this function to force the list view control to repaint the item specified by *nItem*. This function also arranges the list view control if it has the **LVS_AUTOARRANGE** style.

See Also: CListCtrl::DrawItem

CListView

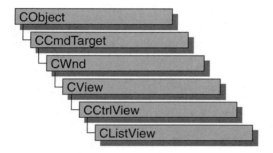

The **CListView** class simplifies use of the list control and of **CListCtrl**, the class that encapsulates list-control functionality, with MFC's document-view architecture. For more information on this architecture, see the overview for the **CView** class and the cross-references cited there.

#include <afxcview.h>

See Also: CCtrlView

CListView Class Members

Construction	
CListView	Constructs a **CListView** object.

Attributes	
GetListCtrl	Returns the list control associated with the view.

Member Functions
CListView::CListView

CListView( );

Remarks

Constructs a **CListView** object.

CListView::GetListCtrl

CListCtrl& GetListCtrl( ) const;

Return Value

A reference to the list control associated with the view.

Remarks

Call this member function to get a reference to the list control associated with the view.

See Also:　CListCtrl

CLongBinary

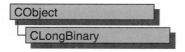

Class **CLongBinary** simplifies working with very large binary data objects (often called BLOBs, or "binary large objects") in a database. For example, a record field in an SQL table might contain a bitmap representing a picture. A **CLongBinary** object stores such an object and keeps track of its size.

Note In general, it is better practice now to use **CByteArray** in conjunction with the **DFX_Binary** function. You can still use **CLongBinary**, but in general **CByteArray** provides more functionality under Win32, since there is no longer the size limitation encountered with 16-bit **CByteArray**. This advice applies to programming with Data Access Objects (DAO) as well as Open Database Connectivity (ODBC).

To use a **CLongBinary** object, declare a field data member of type **CLongBinary** in your recordset class. This member will be an embedded member of the recordset class and will be constructed when the recordset is constructed. After the **CLongBinary** object is constructed, the record field exchange (RFX) mechanism loads the data object from a field in the current record on the data source and stores it back to the record when the record is updated. RFX queries the data source for the size of the binary large object, allocates storage for it (via the **CLongBinary** object's **m_hData** data member), and stores an **HGLOBAL** handle to the data in **m_hData**. RFX also stores the actual size of the data object in the **m_dwDataLength** data member. Work with the data in the object through **m_hData**, using the same techniques you would normally use to manipulate the data stored in a Windows **HGLOBAL** handle.

When you destroy your recordset, the embedded **CLongBinary** object is also destroyed, and its destructor deallocates the **HGLOBAL** data handle.

For more information about large objects and the use of **CLongBinary**, see the articles "Recordset (ODBC)" and "Recordset: Working with Large Data Items (ODBC)" in *Visual C++ Programmer's Guide* online.

#include <afxdb.h>

See Also: **CRecordset**

CLongBinary Class Members

Member Functions
CLongBinary::CLongBinary

CLongBinary( );

Remarks

Constructs a **CLongBinary** object.

Data Members
CLongBinary::m_dwDataLength

Remarks

Stores the actual size in bytes of the data stored in the **HGLOBAL** handle in **m_hData**. This size may be smaller than the size of the memory block allocated for the data. Call **::GlobalSize** to get the allocated size.

CLongBinary::m_hData

Remarks

Stores a Windows **HGLOBAL** handle to the actual binary large object data.

CMap

template< class *KEY*, **class** *ARG_KEY*, **class** *VALUE*,
↪ **class** *ARG_VALUE* >**class CMap : public CObject**

Parameters

KEY   Class of the object used as the key to the map.

ARG_KEY   Data type used for *KEY* arguments; usually a reference to *KEY*.

VALUE   Class of the object stored in the map.

ARG_VALUE   Data type used for *VALUE* arguments; usually a reference to *VALUE*.

Remarks

CMap is a dictionary collection class that maps unique keys to values. Once you have inserted a key-value pair (element) into the map, you can efficiently retrieve or delete the pair using the key to access it. You can also iterate over all the elements in the map.

A variable of type **POSITION** is used for alternate access to entries. You can use a **POSITION** to "remember" an entry and to iterate through the map. You might think that this iteration is sequential by key value; it is not. The sequence of retrieved elements is indeterminate.

Certain member functions of this class call global helper functions that must be customized for most uses of the **CMap** class. See "Collection Class Helpers" in the "Macros and Globals" section of the *MFC Reference*.

CMap incorporates the **IMPLEMENT_SERIAL** macro to support serialization and dumping of its elements. Each element is serialized in turn if a map is stored to an archive, either with the overloaded insertion (<<) operator or with the **Serialize** member function.

If you need a diagnostic dump of the individual elements in the map (the keys and the values), you must set the depth of the dump context to 1 or greater.

When a **CMap** object is deleted, or when its elements are removed, the keys and values both are removed.

Map class derivation is similar to list derivation. See the article "Collections" in *Visual C++ Programmer's Guide* online for an illustration of the derivation of a special-purpose list class.

#include <afxtempl.h>

CMap Class Members

Construction

CMap	Constructs a collection that maps keys to values.

Operations

Lookup	Looks up the value mapped to a given key.
SetAt	Inserts an element into the map; replaces an existing element if a matching key is found.
operator []	Inserts an element into the map—operator substitution for **SetAt**.
RemoveKey	Removes an element specified by a key.
RemoveAll	Removes all the elements from this map.
GetStartPosition	Returns the position of the first element.
GetNextAssoc	Gets the next element for iterating.
GetHashTableSize	Returns the size (number of elements) of the hash table.
InitHashTable	Initializes the hash table and specifies its size.

Status

GetCount	Returns the number of elements in this map.
IsEmpty	Tests for the empty-map condition (no elements).

Member Functions

CMap::CMap

CMap(int *nBlockSize* **= 10);**

Parameters

nBlockSize   Specifies the memory-allocation granularity for extending the map.

Remarks

Constructs an empty map. As the map grows, memory is allocated in units of *nBlockSize* entries.

CMap::GetCount

int GetCount( ) const;

Return Value

The number of elements.

Remarks

Call this member function to retrieve the number of elements in the map.

See Also: CMap::IsEmpty

CMap::GetHashTableSize

UINT GetHashTableSize( ) const;

Return Value

The number of elements in the hash table.

Remarks

Call this member function to determine the number of elements in the hash table for the map.

See Also: CMap::InitHashTable

CMap::GetNextAssoc

void GetNextAssoc(POSITION& *rNextPosition*, *KEY&* *rKey*,
↪ *VALUE&* *rValue* **) const;**

Parameters

rNextPosition   Specifies a reference to a **POSITION** value returned by a previous **GetNextAssoc** or **GetStartPosition** call.

KEY   Template parameter specifying the type of the map's key.

rKey   Specifies the returned key of the retrieved element.

VALUE   Template parameter specifying the type of the map's value.

rValue   Specifies the returned value of the retrieved element.

Remarks

Retrieves the map element at *rNextPosition*, then updates *rNextPosition* to refer to the next element in the map. This function is most useful for iterating through all the elements in the map. Note that the position sequence is not necessarily the same as the key value sequence.

If the retrieved element is the last in the map, then the new value of *rNextPosition* is set to **NULL**.

See Also: CMap::GetStartPosition

CMap::GetStartPosition

POSITION GetStartPosition( ) const;

Return Value

A **POSITION** value that indicates a starting position for iterating the map; or **NULL** if the map is empty.

Remarks

Starts a map iteration by returning a **POSITION** value that can be passed to a **GetNextAssoc** call. The iteration sequence is not predictable; therefore, the "first element in the map" has no special significance.

See Also: CMap::GetNextAssoc

CMap::InitHashTable

void InitHashTable(UINT *hashSize* **);**

Parameters

hashSize   Number of entries in the hash table.

Remarks

Initializes the hash table. For best performance, the hash table size should be a prime number. To minimize collisions the size should be roughly 20 percent larger than the largest anticipated data set.

See Also: CMap::GetHashTableSize

CMap::IsEmpty

BOOL IsEmpty( ) const;

Return Value

Nonzero if this map contains no elements; otherwise 0.

Remarks

Call this member function to determine whether the map is empty.

Example

See the example for **CMapStringToOB::RemoveAll**.

See Also: CMap::GetCount

CMap::Lookup

BOOL Lookup(*ARG_KEY key*, *VALUE& rValue* **) const;**

Return Value

Nonzero if the element was found; otherwise 0.

Parameters

ARG_KEY   Template parameter specifying the type of the *key* value.

key   Specifies the key that identifies the element to be looked up.

VALUE   Specifies the type of the value to be looked up.

rValue   Receives the looked-up value.

Remarks

Lookup uses a hashing algorithm to quickly find the map element with a key that exactly matches the given key.

See Also: CMap::operator []

CMap::RemoveAll

void RemoveAll( );

Remarks

Removes all the values from this map by calling the global helper function **DestructElements**.

The function works correctly if the map is already empty.

See Also: CMap::RemoveKey, **DestructElements**

CMap::RemoveKey

BOOL RemoveKey(*ARG_KEY key* **);**

Return Value

Nonzero if the entry was found and successfully removed; otherwise 0.

Parameters

ARG_KEY   Template parameter specifying the type of the key.

key   Key for the element to be removed.

Remarks

Looks up the map entry corresponding to the supplied key; then, if the key is found, removes the entry.

The **DestructElements** helper function is used to remove the entry.

See Also: **CMap::RemoveAll**

CMap::SetAt

void SetAt(*ARG_KEY key***,** *ARG_VALUE newValue* **);**

Parameters

ARG_KEY Template parameter specifying the type of the *key* parameter.

key Specifies the key of the new element.

ARG_VALUE Template parameter specifying the type of the *newValue* parameter.

newValue Specifies the value of the new element.

Remarks

The primary means to insert an element in a map. First, the key is looked up. If the key is found, then the corresponding value is changed; otherwise a new key-value pair is created.

See Also: **CMap::Lookup**, **CMap::operator []**

Operators
CMap::operator [ ]

*VALUE***& operator[](** *ARG_KEY key* **);**

Parameters

VALUE Template parameter specifying the type of the map value.

ARG_KEY Template parameter specifying the type of the key value.

key The key used to retrieve the value from the map.

Remarks

This operator is a convenient substitute for the **SetAt** member function. Thus it can be used only on the left side of an assignment statement (an l-value). If there is no map element with the specified key, then a new element is created.

There is no "right side" (r-value) equivalent to this operator because there is a possibility that a key may not be found in the map. Use the **Lookup** member function for element retrieval.

See Also: **CMap::SetAt**, **CMap::Lookup**

CMapPtrToPtr

The **CMapPtrToPtr** class supports maps of void pointers keyed by void pointers.

The member functions of **CMapPtrToPtr** are similar to the member functions of class **CMapStringToOb**. Because of this similarity, you can use the **CMapStringToOb** reference documentation for member function specifics. Wherever you see a **CObject** pointer as a function parameter or return value, substitute a pointer to **void**. Wherever you see a **CString** or a **const** pointer to **char** as a function parameter or return value, substitute a pointer to **void**.

```
BOOL CMapStringToOb::Lookup( const char* <key>,
                    CObject*& <rValue> ) const;
```

for example, translates to

```
BOOL CMapPtrToPtr::Lookup( void* <key>, void*& <rValue> ) const;
```

CMapPtrToPtr incorporates the **IMPLEMENT_DYNAMIC** macro to support run-time type access and dumping to a **CDumpContext** object. If you need a dump of individual map elements (pointer values), you must set the depth of the dump context to 1 or greater.

Pointer-to-pointer maps may not be serialized.

When a **CMapPtrToPtr** object is deleted, or when its elements are removed, only the pointers are removed, not the entities they reference.

For more information on **CMapPtrToPtr**, see the article "Collections" in *Visual C++ Programmer's Guide* online.

#include <afxcoll.h>

CMapPtrToPtr Class Members

Construction

CMapPtrToPtr	Constructs a collection that maps void pointers to void pointers.

Operations

Lookup	Looks up a void pointer based on the void pointer key. The pointer value, not the entity it points to, is used for the key comparison.

Operations *(continued)*

SetAt	Inserts an element into the map; replaces an existing element if a matching key is found.
operator [ ]	Inserts an element into the map—operator substitution for **SetAt**.
RemoveKey	Removes an element specified by a key.
RemoveAll	Removes all the elements from this map.
GetStartPosition	Returns the position of the first element.
GetNextAssoc	Gets the next element for iterating.

Status

GetCount	Returns the number of elements in this map.
IsEmpty	Tests for the empty-map condition (no elements).

CMapPtrToWord

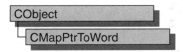

The **CMapPtrToWord** class supports maps of 16-bit words keyed by void pointers.

The member functions of **CMapPtrToWord** are similar to the member functions of class **CMapStringToOb**. Because of this similarity, you can use the **CMapStringToOb** reference documentation for member function specifics. Wherever you see a **CObject** pointer as a function parameter or return value, substitute **WORD**. Wherever you see a **CString** or a **const** pointer to **char** as a function parameter or return value, substitute a pointer to **void**.

```
BOOL CMapStringToOb::Lookup( const char* <key>,
                    CObject*& <rValue> ) const;
```

for example, translates to

```
BOOL CMapPtrToWord::Lookup( const void* <key>, WORD& <rValue> ) const;
```

CMapWordToPtr incorporates the **IMPLEMENT_DYNAMIC** macro to support run-time type access and dumping to a **CDumpContext** object. If you need a dump of individual map elements, you must set the depth of the dump context to 1 or greater.

Pointer-to-word maps may not be serialized.

When a **CMapPtrToWord** object is deleted, or when its elements are removed, the pointers and the words are removed. The entities referenced by the key pointers are not removed.

For more information on **CMapPtrToWord**, see the article "Collections" in *Visual C++ Programmer's Guide* online.

#include <afxcoll.h>

CMapPtrToWord Class Members

Construction

CMapPtrToWord	Constructs a collection that maps void pointers to 16-bit words.

Operations

Lookup	Returns a **WORD** using a void pointer as a key. The pointer value, not the entity it points to, is used for the key comparison.

Operations *(continued)*

SetAt	Inserts an element into the map; replaces an existing element if a matching key is found.
operator []	Inserts an element into the map—operator substitution for **SetAt**.
RemoveKey	Removes an element specified by a key.
RemoveAll	Removes all the elements from this map.
GetStartPosition	Returns the position of the first element.
GetNextAssoc	Gets the next element for iterating.

Status

GetCount	Returns the number of elements in this map.
IsEmpty	Tests for the empty-map condition (no elements).

CMapStringToOb

CMapStringToOb is a dictionary collection class that maps unique **CString** objects to **CObject** pointers. Once you have inserted a **CString**-**CObject*** pair (element) into the map, you can efficiently retrieve or delete the pair using a string or a **CString** value as a key. You can also iterate over all the elements in the map.

A variable of type **POSITION** is used for alternate entry access in all map variations. You can use a **POSITION** to "remember" an entry and to iterate through the map. You might think that this iteration is sequential by key value; it is not. The sequence of retrieved elements is indeterminate.

CMapStringToOb incorporates the **IMPLEMENT_SERIAL** macro to support serialization and dumping of its elements. Each element is serialized in turn if a map is stored to an archive, either with the overloaded insertion (**<<**) operator or with the **Serialize** member function.

If you need a diagnostic dump of the individual elements in the map (the **CString** value and the **CObject** contents), you must set the depth of the dump context to 1 or greater.

When a **CMapStringToOb** object is deleted, or when its elements are removed, the **CString** objects and the **CObject** pointers are removed. The objects referenced by the **CObject** pointers are not destroyed.

Map class derivation is similar to list derivation. See the article "Collections" in *Visual C++ Programmer's Guide* online for an illustration of the derivation of a special-purpose list class.

#include <afxcoll.h>

See Also: **CMapPtrToPtr**, **CMapPtrToWord**, **CMapStringToPtr**, **CMapStringToString**, **CMapWordToOb**, **CMapWordToPtr**

CMapStringToOb Class Members

Construction

CMapStringToOb	Constructs a collection that maps **CString** values to **CObject** pointers.

Operations

Lookup	Returns a **CObject** pointer based on a **CString** value.

Operations	*(continued)*
SetAt	Inserts an element into the map; replaces an existing element if a matching key is found.
operator []	Inserts an element into the map—operator substitution for **SetAt**.
RemoveKey	Removes an element specified by a key.
RemoveAll	Removes all the elements from this map.
GetStartPosition	Returns the position of the first element.
GetNextAssoc	Gets the next element for iterating.

Status	
GetCount	Returns the number of elements in this map.
IsEmpty	Tests for the empty-map condition (no elements).

Member Functions
CMapStringToOb::CMapStringToOb

CMapStringToOb(int *nBlockSize* **= 10);**

Parameters
nBlockSize   Specifies the memory-allocation granularity for extending the map.

Remarks
Constructs an empty **CString**-to-**CObject*** map. As the map grows, memory is allocated in units of *nBlockSize* entries.

Example
```
// example for CMapStringToOb::CMapStringToOb
CMapStringToOb map(20);  // Map on the stack with blocksize of 20

CMapStringToOb* pm = new CMapStringToOb;  // Map on the heap
                                          // with default blocksize
```

See **CObList::CObList** for a listing of the CAge class used in all collection examples.

CMapStringToOb::GetCount

int GetCount( ) const;

Return Value
The number of elements in this map.

Remarks
Call this member function to determine how many elements are in the map.

Example

See **CObList::CObList** for a listing of the CAge class used in all collection examples.

```
// example for CMapStringToOb::GetCount
CMapStringToOb map;

map.SetAt( "Bart", new CAge( 13 ) );
map.SetAt( "Homer", new CAge( 36 ) );
ASSERT( map.GetCount() == 2 );
```

See Also: **CMapStringToOb::IsEmpty**

CMapStringToOb::GetNextAssoc

void GetNextAssoc(POSITION& *rNextPosition*, **CString&** *rKey*,
↪ **CObject*&** *rValue* **) const;**

Parameters

rNextPosition   Specifies a reference to a **POSITION** value returned by a previous **GetNextAssoc** or **GetStartPosition** call.

rKey   Specifies the returned key of the retrieved element (a string).

rValue   Specifies the returned value of the retrieved element (a **CObject** pointer). See Remarks for more about this parameter.

Remarks

Retrieves the map element at *rNextPosition*, then updates *rNextPosition* to refer to the next element in the map. This function is most useful for iterating through all the elements in the map. Note that the position sequence is not necessarily the same as the key value sequence.

If the retrieved element is the last in the map, then the new value of *rNextPosition* is set to **NULL**.

For the *rValue* parameter, be sure to cast your object type to **CObject*&**, which is what the compiler requires, as shown in the following example:

```
CMyObject* ob;
map.GetNextAssoc(pos, key, (CObject*&)ob);
```

This is not true of **GetNextAssoc** for maps based on templates.

Example

See **CObList::CObList** for a listing of the CAge class used in all collection examples.

```
// example for CMapStringToOb::GetNextAssoc
// and CMapStringToOb::GetStartPosition
   CMapStringToOb map;
   POSITION pos;
   CString key;
   CAge* pa;
```

```
    map.SetAt( "Bart", new CAge( 13 ) );
    map.SetAt( "Lisa", new CAge( 11 ) );
    map.SetAt( "Homer", new CAge( 36 ) );
    map.SetAt( "Marge", new CAge( 35 ) );
    // Iterate through the entire map, dumping both name and age.
    for( pos = map.GetStartPosition(); pos != NULL; )
    {
    map.GetNextAssoc( pos, key, (CObject*&)pa );
#ifdef _DEBUG
        afxDump << key << " : " << pa << "\n";
#endif
    }
```

The results from this program are as follows:

```
Lisa : a CAge at $4724 11
Marge : a CAge at $47A8 35
Homer : a CAge at $4766 36
Bart : a CAge at $45D4 13
```

See Also: CMapStringToOb::GetStartPosition

CMapStringToOb::GetStartPosition

POSITION GetStartPosition( ) const;

Return Value

A **POSITION** value that indicates a starting position for iterating the map; or **NULL** if the map is empty.

Remarks

Starts a map iteration by returning a **POSITION** value that can be passed to a **GetNextAssoc** call. The iteration sequence is not predictable; therefore, the "first element in the map" has no special significance.

CMapStringToOb::IsEmpty

BOOL IsEmpty( ) const;

Return Value

Nonzero if this map contains no elements; otherwise 0.

Remarks

Call this member function to determine whether the map is empty.

Example

See the example for **RemoveAll**.

CMapStringToOb::Lookup

BOOL Lookup(LPCTSTR *key*, **CObject*&** *rValue*) **const;**

Return Value

Nonzero if the element was found; otherwise 0.

Parameters

key Specifies the string key that identifies the element to be looked up.

rValue Specifies the returned value from the looked-up element.

Remarks

Lookup uses a hashing algorithm to quickly find the map element with a key that matches exactly (**CString** value).

Example

See **CObList::CObList** for a listing of the CAge class used in all collection examples.

```
// example for CMapStringToOb::LookUp

CMapStringToOb map;
CAge* pa;

map.SetAt( "Bart", new CAge( 13 ) );
map.SetAt( "Lisa", new CAge( 11 ) );
map.SetAt( "Homer", new CAge( 36 ) );
map.SetAt( "Marge", new CAge( 35 ) );
ASSERT( map.Lookup( "Lisa", ( CObject*& ) pa ) ); // Is "Lisa" in the map?
ASSERT( *pa == CAge( 11 ) ); // Is she 11?
```

See Also: CMapStringToOb::operator []

CMapStringToOb::RemoveAll

void RemoveAll( );

Remarks

Removes all the elements from this map and destroys the **CString** key objects. The **CObject** objects referenced by each key are not destroyed. The **RemoveAll** function can cause memory leaks if you do not ensure that the referenced **CObject** objects are destroyed.

The function works correctly if the map is already empty.

Example

See **CObList::CObList** for a listing of the CAge class used in all collection examples.

```
// example for CMapStringToOb::RemoveAll
{
    CMapStringToOb map;
```

```
        CAge age1( 13 ); // Two objects on the stack
        CAge age2( 36 );
        map.SetAt( "Bart", &age1 );
        map.SetAt( "Homer", &age2 );
        ASSERT( map.GetCount() == 2 );
        map.RemoveAll(); // CObject pointers removed; objects not removed.
        ASSERT( map.GetCount() == 0 );
        ASSERT( map.IsEmpty() );
    } // The two CAge objects are deleted when they go out of scope.
```

See Also: CMapStringToOb::RemoveKey

CMapStringToOb::RemoveKey

BOOL RemoveKey(LPCTSTR *key*);

Return Value

Nonzero if the entry was found and successfully removed; otherwise 0.

Parameters

key   Specifies the string used for map lookup.

Remarks

Looks up the map entry corresponding to the supplied key; then, if the key is found, removes the entry. This can cause memory leaks if the **CObject** object is not deleted elsewhere.

Example

See **CObList::CObList** for a listing of the CAge class used in all collection examples.

```
// example for CMapStringToOb::RemoveKey
    CMapStringToOb map;

    map.SetAt( "Bart", new CAge( 13 ) );
    map.SetAt( "Lisa", new CAge( 11 ) );
    map.SetAt( "Homer", new CAge( 36 ) );
    map.SetAt( "Marge", new CAge( 35 ) );
    map.RemoveKey( "Lisa" ); // Memory leak: CAge object not
                             // deleted.
#ifdef _DEBUG
    afxDump.SetDepth( 1 );
    afxDump << "RemoveKey example: " << &map << "\n";
#endif
```

The results from this program are as follows:

```
RemoveKey example: A CMapStringToOb with 3 elements
    [Marge] = a CAge at $49A0 35
    [Homer] = a CAge at $495E 36
    [Bart] = a CAge at $4634 13
```

See Also: CMapStringToOb::RemoveAll

CMapStringToOb::SetAt

void SetAt(LPCTSTR *key*, **CObject*** *newValue* **);**
   throw(CMemoryException);

Parameters

key   Specifies the string that is the key of the new element.

newValue   Specifies the **CObject** pointer that is the value of the new element.

Remarks

The primary means to insert an element in a map. First, the key is looked up. If the key is found, then the corresponding value is changed; otherwise a new key-value element is created.

Example

See **CObList::CObList** for a listing of the CAge class used in all collection examples.

```
// example for CMapStringToOb::SetAt
CMapStringToOb map;
CAge* pa;

map.SetAt( "Bart", new CAge( 13 ) );
map.SetAt( "Lisa", new CAge( 11 ) ); // Map contains 2
                                     // elements.
#ifdef _DEBUG
afxDump.SetDepth( 1 );
afxDump << "before Lisa's birthday: " << &map << "\n";
#endif
if( map.Lookup( "Lisa", (CObject *&)pa ) )
{ // CAge 12 pointer replaces CAge 11 pointer.
    map.SetAt( "Lisa", new CAge( 12 ) );
    delete pa;  // Must delete CAge 11 to avoid memory leak.
}
#ifdef _DEBUG
afxDump << "after Lisa's birthday: " << &map << "\n";
#endif
```

The results from this program are as follows:

```
before Lisa's birthday: A CMapStringToOb with 2 elements
    [Lisa] = a CAge at $493C 11
    [Bart] = a CAge at $4654 13
after Lisa's birthday: A CMapStringToOb with 2 elements
    [Lisa] = a CAge at $49C0 12
    [Bart] = a CAge at $4654 13
```

See Also: **CMapStringToOb::Lookup, CMapStringToOb::operator []**

Operators
CMapStringToOb::operator [ ]

CObject*& operator [ ](LPCTSTR *key* **);**

Return Value

A reference to a pointer to a **CObject** object; or **NULL** if the map is empty or *key* is out of range.

Remarks

This operator is a convenient substitute for the **SetAt** member function. Thus it can be used only on the left side of an assignment statement (an l-value). If there is no map element with the specified key, then a new element is created.

There is no "right side" (r-value) equivalent to this operator because there is a possibility that a key may not be found in the map. Use the **Lookup** member function for element retrieval.

Example

See **CObList::CObList** for a listing of the CAge class used in all collection examples.

```
// example for CMapStringToOb::operator[]
   CMapStringToOb map;

   map["Bart"] = new CAge( 13 );
   map["Lisa"] = new CAge( 11 );
#ifdef _DEBUG
   afxDump.SetDepth( 1 );
   afxDump << "Operator [] example: " << &map << "\n";
#endif
```

The results from this program are as follows:

```
Operator [] example: A CMapStringToOb with 2 elements
   [Lisa] = a CAge at $4A02 11
   [Bart] = a CAge at $497E 13
```

See Also: CMapStringToOb::SetAt, CMapStringToOb::Lookup

CMapStringToPtr

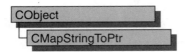

The **CMapStringToPtr** class supports maps of void pointers keyed by **CString** objects.

The member functions of **CMapStringToPtr** are similar to the member functions of class **CMapStringToOb**. Because of this similarity, you can use the **CMapStringToOb** reference documentation for member function specifics. Wherever you see a **CObject** pointer as a function parameter or return value, substitute a pointer to **void**.

```
BOOL CMapStringToOb::Lookup( const char* <key>,
                      CObject*& <rValue> ) const;
```

for example, translates to

```
BOOL CMapStringToPtr::Lookup( LPCTSTR <key>, void*& <rValue> )
                      const;
```

CMapStringToPtr incorporates the **IMPLEMENT_DYNAMIC** macro to support run-time type access and dumping to a **CDumpContext** object. If you need a dump of individual map elements, you must set the depth of the dump context to 1 or greater.

String-to-pointer maps may not be serialized.

When a **CMapStringToPtr** object is deleted, or when its elements are removed, the **CString** key objects and the words are removed.

#include <afxcoll.h>

CMapStringToPtr Class Members

Construction

CMapStringToPtr	Constructs a collection that maps **CString** objects to void pointers.

Operations

Lookup	Returns a void pointer based on a **CString** value.
SetAt	Inserts an element into the map; replaces an existing element if a matching key is found.
operator []	Inserts an element into the map—operator substitution for **SetAt**.
RemoveKey	Removes an element specified by a key.

Operations *(continued)*

RemoveAll	Removes all the elements from this map.
GetStartPosition	Returns the position of the first element.
GetNextAssoc	Gets the next element for iterating.

Status

GetCount	Returns the number of elements in this map.
IsEmpty	Tests for the empty-map condition (no elements).

CMapStringToString

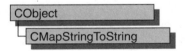

The **CMapStringToString** class supports maps of **CString** objects keyed by **CString** objects.

The member functions of **CMapStringToString** are similar to the member functions of class **CMapStringToOb**. Because of this similarity, you can use the **CMapStringToOb** reference documentation for member function specifics. Wherever you see a **CObject** pointer as a return value or "output" function parameter, substitute a pointer to **char**. Wherever you see a **CObject** pointer as an "input" function parameter, substitute a pointer to **char**.

```
BOOL CMapStringToOb::Lookup( const char* <key>,
                    CObject*& <rValue> ) const;
```

for example, translates to

```
BOOL CMapStringToString::Lookup( LPCTSTR <key>,
                    CString& <rValue> ) const;
```

CMapStringToString incorporates the **IMPLEMENT_SERIAL** macro to support serialization and dumping of its elements. Each element is serialized in turn if a map is stored to an archive, either with the overloaded insertion (<<) operator or with the **Serialize** member function.

If you need a dump of individual **CString-CString** elements, you must set the depth of the dump context to 1 or greater.

When a **CMapStringToString** object is deleted, or when its elements are removed, the **CString** objects are removed as appropriate.

For more information on **CMapStringToString**, see the article "Collections" in *Visual C++ Programmer's Guide*.

#include <afxcoll.h>

CMapStringToString Class Members

Construction

CMapStringToString	Constructs a collection that maps **CString** objects to **CString** objects.

Operations

Lookup	Returns a **CString** using a **CString** value as a key.
SetAt	Inserts an element into the map; replaces an existing element if a matching key is found.
operator []	Inserts an element into the map—operator substitution for **SetAt**.
RemoveKey	Removes an element specified by a key.
RemoveAll	Removes all the elements from this map.
GetStartPosition	Returns the position of the first element.
GetNextAssoc	Gets the next element for iterating.

Status

GetCount	Returns the number of elements in this map.
IsEmpty	Tests for the empty-map condition (no elements).

CMapWordToOb

The **CMapWordToOb** class supports maps of **CObject** pointers keyed by 16-bit words.

The member functions of **CMapWordToOb** are similar to the member functions of class **CMapStringToOb**. Because of this similarity, you can use the **CMapStringToOb** reference documentation for member function specifics. Wherever you see a **CString** or a **const** pointer to **char** as a function parameter or return value, substitute **WORD**.

```
BOOL CMapStringToOb::Lookup( const char* <key>,
                             CObject*& <rValue> ) const;
```

for example, translates to

```
BOOL CMapWordToOb::Lookup( WORD <key>, CObject*& <rValue> ) const;
```

CMapWordToOb incorporates the **IMPLEMENT_SERIAL** macro to support serialization and dumping of its elements. Each element is serialized in turn if a map is stored to an archive, either with the overloaded insertion (**<<**) operator or with the **Serialize** member function.

If you need a dump of individual **WORD-CObject** elements, you must set the depth of the dump context to 1 or greater.

When a **CMapWordToOb** object is deleted, or when its elements are removed, the **CObject** objects are deleted as appropriate.

For more information on **CMapWordToOb**, see the article "Collections" in *Visual C++ Programmer's Guide* online.

#include <afxcoll.h>

CMapWordToOb Class Members

Construction

CMapWordToOb	Constructs a collection that maps words to **CObject** pointers.

Operations

Lookup	Returns a **CObject** pointer using a word value as a key.
SetAt	Inserts an element into the map; replaces an existing element if a matching key is found.
operator []	Inserts an element into the map—operator substitution for **SetAt**.

Operations *(continued)*

RemoveKey	Removes an element specified by a key.
RemoveAll	Removes all the elements from this map.
GetStartPosition	Returns the position of the first element.
GetNextAssoc	Gets the next element for iterating.

Status

GetCount	Returns the number of elements in this map.
IsEmpty	Tests for the empty-map condition (no elements).

CMapWordToPtr

The **CMapWordToPtr** class supports maps of void pointers keyed by 16-bit words.

The member functions of **CMapWordToPtr** are similar to the member functions of class **CMapStringToOb**. Because of this similarity, you can use the **CMapStringToOb** reference documentation for member function specifics. Wherever you see a **CObject** pointer as a function parameter or return value, substitute a pointer to **void**. Wherever you see a **CString** or a **const** pointer to **char** as a function parameter or return value, substitute **WORD**.

```
BOOL CMapStringToOb::Lookup( const char* <key>,
                             CObject*& <rValue> ) const;
```

for example, translates to

```
BOOL CMapWordToPtr::Lookup( WORD <key>, void*& <rValue> ) const;
```

CMapWordToPtr incorporates the **IMPLEMENT_DYNAMIC** macro to support run-time type access and dumping to a **CDumpContext** object. If you need a dump of individual map elements, you must set the depth of the dump context to 1 or greater.

Word-to-pointer maps may not be serialized.

When a **CMapWordToPtr** object is deleted, or when its elements are removed, the words and the pointers are removed. The entities referenced by the pointers are not removed.

For more information on **CMapWordToPtr**, see the article "Collections" in *Visual C++ Programmer's Guide* online.

#include <afxcoll.h>

CMapWordToPtr Class Members

Construction

CMapWordToPtr	Constructs a collection that maps words to void pointers.

Operations

Lookup	Returns a void pointer using a word value as a key.
SetAt	Inserts an element into the map; replaces an existing element if a matching key is found.

Operations *(continued)*

operator []	Inserts an element into the map—operator substitution for **SetAt**.
RemoveKey	Removes an element specified by a key.
RemoveAll	Removes all the elements from this map.
GetStartPosition	Returns the position of the first element.
GetNextAssoc	Gets the next element for iterating.

Status

GetCount	Returns the number of elements in this map.
IsEmpty	Tests for the empty-map condition (no elements).

CMDIChildWnd

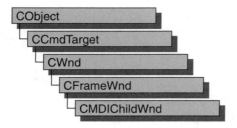

The **CMDIChildWnd** class provides the functionality of a Windows multiple document interface (MDI) child window, along with members for managing the window.

An MDI child window looks much like a typical frame window, except that the MDI child window appears inside an MDI frame window rather than on the desktop. An MDI child window does not have a menu bar of its own, but instead shares the menu of the MDI frame window. The framework automatically changes the MDI frame menu to represent the currently active MDI child window.

To create a useful MDI child window for your application, derive a class from **CMDIChildWnd**. Add member variables to the derived class to store data specific to your application. Implement message-handler member functions and a message map in the derived class to specify what happens when messages are directed to the window.

There are three ways to construct an MDI child window:

- Directly construct it using **Create**.
- Directly construct it using **LoadFrame**.
- Indirectly construct it through a document template.

Before you call **Create** or **LoadFrame**, you must construct the frame-window object on the heap using the C++ **new** operator. Before calling **Create** you can also register a window class with the **AfxRegisterWndClass** global function to set the icon and class styles for the frame.

Use the **Create** member function to pass the frame's creation parameters as immediate arguments.

LoadFrame requires fewer arguments than **Create**, and instead retrieves most of its default values from resources, including the frame's caption, icon, accelerator table, and menu. To be accessible by **LoadFrame**, all these resources must have the same resource ID (for example, **IDR_MAINFRAME**).

When a **CMDIChildWnd** object contains views and documents, they are created indirectly by the framework instead of directly by the programmer. The **CDocTemplate** object orchestrates the creation of the frame, the creation of the containing views, and the connection of the views to the appropriate document. The parameters of the **CDocTemplate** constructor specify the **CRuntimeClass** of the three classes involved (document, frame, and view). A **CRuntimeClass** object is used by the framework to dynamically create new frames when specified by the user (for example, by using the File New command or the MDI Window New command).

A frame-window class derived from **CMDIChildWnd** must be declared with **DECLARE_DYNCREATE** in order for the above **RUNTIME_CLASS** mechanism to work correctly.

The **CMDIChildWnd** class inherits much of its default implementation from **CFrameWnd**. For a detailed list of these features, please refer to the **CFrameWnd** class description. The **CMDIChildWnd** class has the following additional features:

- In conjunction with the **CMultiDocTemplate** class, multiple **CMDIChildWnd** objects from the same document template share the same menu, saving Windows system resources.

- The currently active MDI child window menu entirely replaces the MDI frame window's menu, and the caption of the currently active MDI child window is added to the MDI frame window's caption. For further examples of MDI child window functions that are implemented in conjunction with an MDI frame window, see the **CMDIFrameWnd** class description.

Do not use the C++ **delete** operator to destroy a frame window. Use **CWnd::DestroyWindow** instead. The **CFrameWnd** implementation of **PostNcDestroy** will delete the C++ object when the window is destroyed. When the user closes the frame window, the default **OnClose** handler will call **DestroyWindow**.

For more information on **CMDIChildWnd**, see "Frame Window Topics" in *Visual C++ Programmer's Guide* online.

#include <afxwin.h>

See Also: CWnd, CMDIFrameWnd

CMDIChildWnd Class Members

Construction

CMDIChildWnd	Constructs a **CMDIChildWnd** object.

Initialization

Create	Creates the Windows MDI child window associated with the **CMDIChildWnd** object.

Operations	
MDIDestroy	Destroys this MDI child window.
MDIActivate	Activates this MDI child window.
MDIMaximize	Maximizes this MDI child window.
MDIRestore	Restores this MDI child window from maximized or minimized size.
GetMDIFrame	Returns the parent MDI frame of the MDI client window.

Member Functions
CMDIChildWnd::CMDIChildWnd

CMDIChildWnd( );

Remarks

Call to construct a **CMDIChildWnd** object. Call **Create** to create the visible window.

See Also: **CMDIChildWnd::Create**

CMDIChildWnd::Create

BOOL Create(LPCTSTR *lpszClassName*, **LPCTSTR** *lpszWindowName*,
 ↳ **DWORD** *dwStyle* = **WS_CHILD | WS_VISIBLE | WS_OVERLAPPEDWINDOW**,
 ↳ **const RECT&** *rect* = **rectDefault, CMDIFrameWnd*** *pParentWnd* = **NULL**,
 ↳ **CCreateContext*** *pContext* = **NULL**);

Return Value

Nonzero if successful; otherwise 0.

Parameters

lpszClassName Points to a null-terminated character string that names the Windows class (a **WNDCLASS** structure). The class name can be any name registered with the **AfxRegisterWndClass** global function. Should be **NULL** for a standard **CMDIChildWnd**.

lpszWindowName Points to a null-terminated character string that represents the window name. Used as text for the title bar.

dwStyle Specifies the window style attributes. The **WS_CHILD** style is required.

rect Contains the size and position of the window. The **rectDefault** value allows Windows to specify the size and position of the new **CMDIChildWnd**.

pParentWnd Specifies the window's parent. If **NULL**, the main application window is used.

pContext Specifies a **CCreateContext** structure. This parameter can be **NULL**.

Remarks

Call this member function to create a Windows MDI child window and attach it to the **CMDIChildWnd** object.

The currently active MDI child frame window can determine the caption of the parent frame window. This feature is disabled by turning off the **FWS_ADDTOTITLE** style bit of the child frame window.

The framework calls this member function in response to a user command to create a child window, and the framework uses the *pContext* parameter to properly connect the child window to the application. When you call **Create**, *pContext* can be **NULL**.

See Also: **CMDIChildWnd::CMDIChildWnd, CWnd::PreCreateWindow**

CMDIChildWnd::GetMDIFrame

CMDIFrameWnd* GetMDIFrame( );

Return Value

A pointer to the MDI parent frame window.

Remarks

Call this function to return the MDI parent frame. The frame returned is two parents removed from the **CMDIChildWnd** and is the parent of the window of type **MDICLIENT** that manages the **CMDIChildWnd** object. Call the **GetParent** member function to return the **CMDIChildWnd** object's immediate **MDICLIENT** parent as a temporary **CWnd** pointer.

See Also: **CWnd::GetParent**

CMDIChildWnd::MDIActivate

void MDIActivate( );

Remarks

Call this member function to activate an MDI child window independently of the MDI frame window. When the frame becomes active, the child window that was last activated will be activated as well.

See Also: **CMDIFrameWnd::MDIGetActive, CWnd::OnNcActivate, CMDIFrameWnd::MDINext, WM_MDIACTIVATE**

CMDIChildWnd::MDIDestroy

void MDIDestroy( );

Remarks

Call this member function to destroy an MDI child window.

The member function removes the title of the child window from the frame window and deactivates the child window.

See Also: WM_MDIDESTROY, CMDIChildWnd::Create

CMDIChildWnd::MDIMaximize

void MDIMaximize( );

Remarks

Call this member function to maximize an MDI child window. When a child window is maximized, Windows resizes it to make its client area fill the client area of the frame window. Windows places the child window's Control menu in the frame's menu bar so that the user can restore or close the child window and adds the title of the child window to the frame-window title.

See Also: WM_MDIMAXIMIZE, CMDIChildWnd::MDIRestore

CMDIChildWnd::MDIRestore

void MDIRestore( );

Remarks

Call this member function to restore an MDI child window from maximized or minimized size.

See Also: CMDIChildWnd::MDIMaximize, WM_MDIRESTORE

CMDIFrameWnd

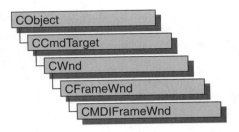

The **CMDIFrameWnd** class provides the functionality of a Windows multiple document interface (MDI) frame window, along with members for managing the window.

To create a useful MDI frame window for your application, derive a class from **CMDIFrameWnd**. Add member variables to the derived class to store data specific to your application. Implement message-handler member functions and a message map in the derived class to specify what happens when messages are directed to the window.

You can construct an MDI frame window by calling the **Create** or **LoadFrame** member function of **CFrameWnd**.

Before you call **Create** or **LoadFrame**, you must construct the frame window object on the heap using the C++ **new** operator. Before calling **Create** you can also register a window class with the **AfxRegisterWndClass** global function to set the icon and class styles for the frame.

Use the **Create** member function to pass the frame's creation parameters as immediate arguments.

LoadFrame requires fewer arguments than **Create**, and instead retrieves most of its default values from resources, including the frame's caption, icon, accelerator table, and menu. To be accessed by **LoadFrame**, all these resources must have the same resource ID (for example, **IDR_MAINFRAME**).

Though **MDIFrameWnd** is derived from **CFrameWnd**, a frame window class derived from **CMDIFrameWnd** need not be declared with **DECLARE_DYNCREATE**.

The **CMDIFrameWnd** class inherits much of its default implementation from **CFrameWnd**. For a detailed list of these features, refer to the **CFrameWnd** class description. The **CMDIFrameWnd** class has the following additional features:

- An MDI frame window manages the **MDICLIENT** window, repositioning it in conjunction with control bars. The MDI client window is the direct parent of MDI child frame windows. The **WS_HSCROLL** and **WS_VSCROLL** window styles specified on a **CMDIFrameWnd** apply to the MDI client window rather than the main frame window so the user can scroll the MDI client area (as in the Windows Program Manager, for example).

- An MDI frame window owns a default menu that is used as the menu bar when there is no active MDI child window. When there is an active MDI child, the MDI frame window's menu bar is automatically replaced by the MDI child window menu.

- An MDI frame window works in conjunction with the current MDI child window, if there is one. For instance, command messages are delegated to the currently active MDI child before the MDI frame window.

- An MDI frame window has default handlers for the following standard Window menu commands:

  - **ID_WINDOW_TILE_VERT**
  - **ID_WINDOW_TILE_HORZ**
  - **ID_WINDOW_CASCADE**
  - **ID_WINDOW_ARRANGE**

- An MDI frame window also has an implementation of **ID_WINDOW_NEW**, which creates a new frame and view on the current document. An application can override these default command implementations to customize MDI window handling.

Do not use the C++ **delete** operator to destroy a frame window. Use **CWnd::DestroyWindow** instead. The **CFrameWnd** implementation of **PostNcDestroy** will delete the C++ object when the window is destroyed. When the user closes the frame window, the default **OnClose** handler will call **DestroyWindow**.

For more information on **CMDIFrameWnd**, see "Frame Window Topics" in *Visual C++ Programmer's Guide* online.

#include <afxwin.h>

See Also: **CWnd, CMDIChildWnd**

CMDIFrameWnd Class Members

Construction

CMDIFrameWnd	Constructs a **CMDIFrameWnd**.

Operations

MDIActivate	Activates a different MDI child window.
MDIGetActive	Retrieves the currently active MDI child window, along with a flag indicating whether or not the child is maximized.

Operations *(continued)*

MDIIconArrange	Arranges all minimized document child windows.
MDIMaximize	Maximizes an MDI child window.
MDINext	Activates the child window immediately behind the currently active child window and places the currently active child window behind all other child windows.
MDIRestore	Restores an MDI child window from maximized or minimized size.
MDISetMenu	Replaces the menu of an MDI frame window, the Window pop-up menu, or both.
MDITile	Arranges all child windows in a tiled format.
MDICascade	Arranges all child windows in a cascaded format.

Overridables

CreateClient	Creates a Windows **MDICLIENT** window for this **CMDIFrameWnd**. Called by the **OnCreate** member function of **CWnd**.
GetWindowMenuPopup	Returns the Window pop-up menu.

Member Functions
CMDIFrameWnd::CMDIFrameWnd

CMDIFrameWnd( );

Remarks

Call this member function to construct a **CMDIFrameWnd** object. Call the **Create** or **LoadFrame** member function to create the visible MDI frame window.

See Also: **CFrameWnd::Create**, **CFrameWnd::LoadFrame**

CMDIFrameWnd::CreateClient

virtual BOOL CreateClient(LPCREATESTRUCT *lpCreateStruct*,
↪ **CMenu*** *pWindowMenu* **);**

Return Value

Nonzero if successful; otherwise 0.

Parameters

lpCreateStruct   A long pointer to a **CREATESTRUCT** structure.

pWindowMenu   A pointer to the Window pop-up menu.

Remarks

Creates the MDI client window that manages the **CMDIChildWnd** objects.

This member function should be called if you override the **OnCreate** member function directly.

See Also: **CMDIFrameWnd::CMDIFrameWnd**

CMDIFrameWnd::GetWindowMenuPopup

> **virtual HMENU GetWindowMenuPopup(HMENU** *hMenuBar* **);**

Return Value

The Window pop-up menu if one exists; otherwise **NULL**.

Parameters

hMenuBar   The current menu bar.

Remarks

Call this member function to obtain a handle to the current pop-up menu named "Window" (the pop-up menu with menu items for MDI window management).

The default implementation looks for a pop-up menu containing standard Window menu commands such as **ID_WINDOW_NEW** and **ID_WINDOW_TILE_HORZ**.

Override this member function if you have a Window menu that does not use the standard menu command IDs.

See Also: **CMDIFrameWnd::MDIGetActive**

CMDIFrameWnd::MDIActivate

> **void MDIActivate(CWnd*** *pWndActivate* **);**

Parameters

pWndActivate   Points to the MDI child window to be activated.

Remarks

Call this member function to activate a different MDI child window. This member function sends the **WM_MDIACTIVATE** message to both the child window being activated and the child window being deactivated.

This is the same message that is sent if the user changes the focus to an MDI child window by using the mouse or keyboard.

Note An MDI child window is activated independently of the MDI frame window. When the frame becomes active, the child window that was last activated is sent a **WM_NCACTIVATE** message to draw an active window frame and caption bar, but it does not receive another **WM_MDIACTIVATE** message.

See Also: **CMDIFrameWnd::MDIGetActive, CMDIFrameWnd::MDINext, WM_ACTIVATE, WM_NCACTIVATE**

CMDIFrameWnd::MDICascade

void MDICascade( );
void MDICascade(int *nType* **);**

Parameters

nType Specifies a cascade flag. Only the following flag can be specified: **MDITILE_SKIPDISABLED**, which prevents disabled MDI child windows from being cascaded.

Remarks

Call this member function to arrange all the MDI child windows in a cascade format.

The first version of **MDICascade**, with no parameters, cascades all MDI child windows, including disabled ones. The second version optionally does not cascade disabled MDI child windows if you specify **MDITILE_SKIPDISABLED** for the *nType* parameter.

See Also: **CMDIFrameWnd::MDIIconArrange, CMDIFrameWnd::MDITile, WM_MDICASCADE**

CMDIFrameWnd::MDIGetActive

CMDIChildWnd* MDIGetActive(BOOL* *pbMaximized* **= NULL) const;**

Return Value

A pointer to the active MDI child window.

Parameters

pbMaximized A pointer to a **BOOL** return value. Set to **TRUE** on return if the window is maximized; otherwise **FALSE**.

Remarks

Retrieves the current active MDI child window, along with a flag indicating whether the child window is maximized.

See Also: **CMDIFrameWnd::MDIActivate, WM_MDIGETACTIVE**

CMDIFrameWnd::MDIIconArrange

void MDIIconArrange( );

Remarks

Arranges all minimized document child windows. It does not affect child windows that are not minimized.

See Also: **CMDIFrameWnd::MDICascade**, **CMDIFrameWnd::MDITile**, **WM_MDIICONARRANGE**

CMDIFrameWnd::MDIMaximize

void MDIMaximize(CWnd* *pWnd* **);**

Parameters

pWnd   Points to the window to maximize.

Remarks

Call this member function to maximize the specified MDI child window. When a child window is maximized, Windows resizes it to make its client area fill the client window. Windows places the child window's Control menu in the frame's menu bar so the user can restore or close the child window. It also adds the title of the child window to the frame-window title.

If another MDI child window is activated when the currently active MDI child window is maximized, Windows restores the currently active child and maximizes the newly activated child window.

See Also: **WM_MDIMAXIMIZE**, **CMDIFrameWnd::MDIRestore**

CMDIFrameWnd::MDINext

void MDINext( );

Remarks

Activates the child window immediately behind the currently active child window and places the currently active child window behind all other child windows.

If the currently active MDI child window is maximized, the member function restores the currently active child and maximizes the newly activated child.

See Also: **CMDIFrameWnd::MDIActivate**, **CMDIFrameWnd::MDIGetActive**, **WM_MDINEXT**

CMDIFrameWnd::MDIRestore

void MDIRestore(CWnd* *pWnd* **);**

Parameters

pWnd   Points to the window to restore.

Remarks

Restores an MDI child window from maximized or minimized size.

See Also: **CMDIFrameWnd::MDIMaximize, WM_MDIRESTORE**

CMDIFrameWnd::MDISetMenu

CMenu* MDISetMenu(CMenu* *pFrameMenu***, CMenu*** *pWindowMenu* **);**

Return Value

A pointer to the frame-window menu replaced by this message. The pointer may be temporary and should not be stored for later use.

Parameters

pFrameMenu   Specifies the menu of the new frame-window menu. If **NULL**, the menu is not changed.

pWindowMenu   Specifies the menu of the new Window pop-up menu. If **NULL**, the menu is not changed.

Remarks

Call this member function to replace the menu of an MDI frame window, the Window pop-up menu, or both.

After calling **MDISetMenu**, an application must call the **DrawMenuBar** member function of **CWnd** to update the menu bar.

If this call replaces the Window pop-up menu, MDI child-window menu items are removed from the previous Window menu and added to the new Window pop-up menu.

If an MDI child window is maximized and this call replaces the MDI frame-window menu, the Control menu and restore controls are removed from the previous frame-window menu and added to the new menu.

Do not call this member function if you use the framework to manage your MDI child windows.

See Also: **CWnd::DrawMenuBar, WM_MDISETMENU**

CMDIFrameWnd::MDITile

void MDITile( );
void MDITile(int *nType* **);**

Parameters

nType   Specifies a tiling flag. This parameter can be any one of the following flags:

- **MDITILE_HORIZONTAL**   Tiles MDI child windows so that one window appears above another.

- **MDITILE_SKIPDISABLED**   Prevents disabled MDI child windows from being tiled.

- **MDITILE_VERTICAL**   Tiles MDI child windows so that one window appears beside another.

Remarks

Call this member function to arrange all child windows in a tiled format.

The first version of **MDITile**, without parameters, tiles the windows vertically under Windows versions 3.1 and later. The second version tiles windows vertically or horizontally, depending on the value of the *nType* parameter.

See Also: CMDIFrameWnd::MDICascade,
CMDIFrameWnd::MDIIconArrange, WM_MDITILE

CMemFile

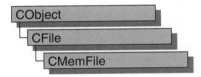

CMemFile is the **CFile**-derived class that supports memory files. These memory files behave like disk files except that the file is stored in RAM rather than on disk. A memory file is useful for fast temporary storage or for transferring raw bytes or serialized objects between independent processes.

CMemFile objects can automatically allocate their own memory or you can attach your own memory block to the **CMemFile** object by calling **Attach**. In either case, memory for growing the memory file automatically is allocated in *nGrowBytes*-sized increments if *nGrowBytes* is not zero.

The memory block will automatically be deleted upon destruction of the **CMemFile** object if the memory was originally allocated by the **CMemFile** object; otherwise, you are responsible for deallocating the memory you attached to the object.

You can access the memory block through the pointer supplied when you detach it from the **CMemFile** object by calling **Detach**.

The most common use of **CMemFile** is to create a **CMemFile** object and use it by calling **CFile** member functions. Note that creating a **CMemFile** automatically opens it: you do not call **CFile::Open**, which is only used for disk files. Because **CMemFile** doesn't use a disk file, the data member **CFile::m_hFile** is not used and has no meaning.

The **CFile** member functions **Duplicate**, **LockRange**, and **UnlockRange** are not implemented for **CMemFile**. If you call these functions on a **CMemFile** object, you will get a **CNotSupportedException**.

CMemFile uses the run-time library functions **malloc**, **realloc**, and **free** to allocate, reallocate, and deallocate memory; and the intrinsic **memcpy** to block copy memory when reading and writing. If you'd like to change this behavior or the behavior when **CMemFile** grows a file, derive your own class from **CMemFile** and override the appropriate functions.

For more information on **CMemFile**, see the articles "Files in MFC" and "Memory Management Topics (MFC)" in the *Visual C++ Programmer's Guide* online and see "File Handling" in the *Run-Time Library Reference*.

#include <afx.h>

CMemFile Class Members

Construction

CMemFile	Constructs a memory file object.

Operations

Attach	Attaches a block of memory to **CMemFile**.
Detach	Detaches the block of memory from **CMemFile** and returns a pointer to the block of memory detached.

Advanced Overridables

Alloc	Override to modify memory allocation behavior.
Free	Override to modify memory deallocation behavior.
Realloc	Override to modify memory reallocation behavior.
Memcpy	Override to modify memory copy behavior when reading and writing files.
GrowFile	Override to modify behavior when growing a file.

Member Functions

CMemFile::Alloc

BYTE * Alloc(DWORD *nBytes* **);**

Return Value

A pointer to the memory block that was allocated, or **NULL** if the allocation failed.

Parameters

nBytes   Number of bytes of memory to be allocated.

Remarks

This function is called by **CMemFile** member functions. Override this function to implement custom memory allocation. If you override this function, you'll probably want to override **Free** and **Realloc** as well.

The default implementation uses the run-time library function **malloc** to allocate memory.

See Also: **CMemFile::Free, CMemFile::Realloc, malloc**

CMemFile::Attach

void Attach(BYTE* *lpBuffer*, **UINT** *nBufferSize*, **UINT** *nGrowBytes* **= 0);**

Parameters

lpBuffer   Pointer to the buffer to be attached to **CMemFile**.

nBufferSize   An integer that specifies the size of the buffer in bytes.

nGrowBytes   The memory allocation increment in bytes.

Remarks

Call this function to attach a block of memory to **CMemFile**. This causes **CMemFile** to use the block of memory as the memory file.

If *nGrowBytes* is 0, **CMemFile** will set the file length to *nBufferSize*. This means that the data in the memory block before it was attached to **CMemFile** will be used as the file. Memory files created in this manner cannot be grown.

Since the file cannot be grown, be careful not to cause **CMemFile** to attempt to grow the file. For example, don't call the **CMemFile** overrides of **CFile:Write** to write past the end or don't call **CFile:SetLength** with a length longer than *nBufferSize*.

If *nGrowBytes* is greater than 0, **CMemFile** will ignore the contents of the memory block you've attached. You'll have to write the contents of the memory file from scratch using the **CMemFile** override of **CFile::Write**. If you attempt to write past the end of the file or grow the file by calling the **CMemFile** override of **CFile::SetLength**, **CMemFile** will grow the memory allocation in increments of *nGrowBytes*. Growing the memory allocation will fail if the memory block you pass to **Attach** wasn't allocated with a method compatible with **Alloc**. To be compatible with the default implementation of **Alloc**, you must allocate the memory with the run-time library function **malloc** or **calloc**.

See Also: **CMemFile::CMemFile, CMemFile::Detach, CMemFile::Alloc, CFile::Write, CFile::SetLength**

CMemFile::CMemFile

CMemFile(UINT *nGrowBytes* **= 1024);**
CMemFile(BYTE* *lpBuffer*, **UINT** *nBufferSize*, **UINT** *nGrowBytes* **= 0);**

Parameters

nGrowBytes   The memory allocation increment in bytes.

lpBuffer   Pointer to a buffer that receives information of the size *nBufferSize*.

nBufferSize   An integer that specifies the size of the file buffer, in bytes.

Remarks

The first overload opens an empty memory file. Note that the file is opened by the constructor and that you should not call **CFile::Open**.

The second overload acts the same as if you used the first constructor and immediately called **Attach** with the same parameters. See **Attach** for details.

Example

```
// example for CMemFile::CMemFile
CMemFile f; // Ready to use - no Open necessary.

BYTE * pBuf = (BYTE *)new char [1024];
CMemFile g( pBuf, 1024, 256 );
// same as CMemFile g; g.Attach( pBuf, 1024, 256 );
```

See Also: CMemFile::Attach

CMemFile::Detach

BYTE * Detach( );

Return Value

A pointer to the memory block that contains the contents of the memory file.

Remarks

Call this function to get a pointer to the memory block being used by **CMemFile**.

Calling this function also closes the **CMemFile**. You can reattach the memory block to **CMemFile** by calling **Attach**. If you want to reattach the file and use the data in it, you should call **CFile::GetLength** to get the length of the file before calling **Detach**. Note that if you attach a memory block to **CMemFile** so that you can use its data (*nGrowBytes* == 0), then you won't be able to grow the memory file.

See Also: CMemFile::Attach, CFile::GetLength

CMemFile::Free

void Free(BYTE * *lpMem*);

Parameters

lpMem   Pointer to the memory to be deallocated.

Remarks

This function is called by **CMemFile** member functions. Override this function to implement custom memory deallocation. If you override this function, you'll probably want to override **Alloc** and **Realloc** as well.

See Also: CMemFile::Alloc, CMemFile::Realloc

CMemFile::GrowFile

void GrowFile(DWORD *dwNewLen* **);**

Parameters

dwNewLen   New size of the memory file.

Remarks

This function is called by several of the **CMemFile** member functions. You can override it if you want to change how **CMemFile** grows its file. The default implementation calls **Realloc** to grow an existing block (or **Alloc** to create a memory block), allocating memory in multiples of the *nGrowBytes* value specified in the constructor or **Attach** call.

See Also: CMemFile::Alloc, CMemFile::Realloc, CMemFile::CMemFile, CMemFile::Attach

---

CMemFile::Memcpy

BYTE * Memcpy(BYTE* *lpMemTarget***, BYTE*** *lpMemSource***, UINT** *nBytes* **);**

Return Value

A copy of *lpMemTarget*.

Parameters

lpMemTarget   Pointer to the memory block into which the source memory will be copied.

lpMemSource   Pointer to the source memory block.

nBytes   Number of bytes to be copied.

Remarks

This function is called by the **CMemFile** overrides of **CFile::Read** and **CFile::Write** to transfer data to and from the memory file. Override this function if you want to change the way that **CMemFile** does these memory copies.

See Also: CFile::Read, CFile::Write

CMemFile::Realloc

BYTE * Realloc(BYTE* *lpMem***, DWORD** *nBytes* **);**

Return Value

A pointer to the memory block that was reallocated (and possibly moved), or **NULL** if the reallocation failed.

Parameters

> *lpMem*   A pointer to the memory block to be reallocated.
>
> *nBytes*   New size for the memory block.

Remarks

> This function is called by **CMemFile** member functions. Override this function to implement custom memory reallocation. If you override this function, you'll probably want to override **Alloc** and **Free** as well.
>
> **See Also:**   **CMemFile::Alloc, CMemFile::Free**

CMemoryException

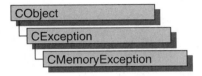

A **CMemoryException** object represents an out-of-memory exception condition. No further qualification is necessary or possible. Memory exceptions are thrown automatically by **new**. If you write your own memory functions, using **malloc**, for example, then you are responsible for throwing memory exceptions.

For more information on **CMemoryException**, see the article "Exceptions" in *Visual C++ Programmer's Guide* online.

#include <afx.h>

CMemoryException Class Members

Construction

CMemoryException	Constructs a **CMemoryException** object.

Member Functions
CMemoryException::CMemoryException

CMemoryException( );

Remarks

Constructs a **CMemoryException** object. Do not use this constructor directly, but rather call the global function **AfxThrowMemoryException**. This global function can succeed in an out-of-memory situation because it constructs the exception object in previously allocated memory. For more information about exception processing, see the article "Exceptions" in *Visual C++ Programmer's Guide* online.

See Also: Exception Processing

CMemoryState

CMemoryState does not have a base class.

CMemoryState provides a convenient way to detect memory leaks in your program. A "memory leak" occurs when memory for an object is allocated on the heap but not deallocated when it is no longer required. Such memory leaks can eventually lead to out-of-memory errors. There are several ways to allocate and deallocate memory in your program:

- Using the **malloc/free** family of functions from the run-time library.
- Using the Windows API memory management functions, **LocalAlloc/LocalFree** and **GlobalAlloc/GlobalFree**.
- Using the C++ **new** and **delete** operators.

The **CMemoryState** diagnostics only help detect memory leaks caused when memory allocated using the **new** operator is not deallocated using **delete**. The other two groups of memory-management functions are for non-C++ programs, and mixing them with **new** and **delete** in the same program is not recommended. An additional macro, **DEBUG_NEW**, is provided to replace the **new** operator when you need file and line-number tracking of memory allocations. **DEBUG_NEW** is used whenever you would normally use the **new** operator.

As with other diagnostics, the **CMemoryState** diagnostics are only available in debug versions of your program. A debug version must have the **_DEBUG** constant defined.

If you suspect your program has a memory leak, you can use the **Checkpoint**, **Difference**, and **DumpStatistics** functions to discover the difference between the memory state (objects allocated) at two different points in program execution. This information can be useful in determining whether a function is cleaning up all the objects it allocates.

If simply knowing where the imbalance in allocation and deallocation occurs does not provide enough information, you can use the **DumpAllObjectsSince** function to dump all objects allocated since the previous call to **Checkpoint**. This dump shows the order of allocation, the source file and line where the object was allocated (if you are using **DEBUG_NEW** for allocation), and the derivation of the object, its address, and its size. **DumpAllObjectsSince** also calls each object's **Dump** function to provide information about its current state.

For more information about how to use **CMemoryState** and other diagnostics, see "MFC Debugging Support" in *Visual C++ Programmer's Guide* online.

Note Declarations of objects of type **CMemoryState** and calls to member functions should be bracketed by `#if defined(_DEBUG)`/`#endif` directives. This causes memory diagnostics to be included only in debugging builds of your program.

CMemoryState Class Members

Member Functions

CMemoryState::Checkpoint

void Checkpoint( );

Remarks

Takes a snapshot summary of memory and stores it in this **CMemoryState** object. The **CMemoryState** member functions **Difference** and **DumpAllObjectsSince** use this snapshot data.

Example

See the example for the **CMemoryState** constructor.

CMemoryState::CMemoryState

CMemoryState( );

Remarks

Constructs an empty **CMemoryState** object that must be filled in by the **Checkpoint** or **Difference** member function.

Example

See **CObList::CObList** for a listing of the CAge class used in all collection examples.

```
// example for CMemoryState::CMemoryState
// Includes all CMemoryState functions
CMemoryState msOld, msNew, msDif;
msOld.Checkpoint();
CAge* page1 = new CAge( 21 );
CAge* page2 = new CAge( 22 );
```

```
msOld.DumpAllObjectsSince();
msNew.Checkpoint();
msDif.Difference( msOld, msNew );
msDif.DumpStatistics();
```

The results from this program are as follows:

```
Dumping objects ->
{2} a CObject at $190A
{1} a CObject at $18EA
Object dump complete.
0 bytes in 0 Free Blocks
8 bytes in 2 Object Blocks
0 bytes in 0 Non-Object Blocks
Largest number used: 8 bytes
Total allocations: 8 bytes
```

CMemoryState::Difference

BOOL Difference(const CMemoryState& *oldState*, **const CMemoryState&** *newState* **);**

Return Value

Nonzero if the two memory states are different; otherwise 0.

Parameters

oldState   The initial memory state as defined by a **CMemoryState** checkpoint.

newState   The new memory state as defined by a **CMemoryState** checkpoint.

Remarks

Compares two **CMemoryState** objects, then stores the difference into this **CMemoryState** object. **Checkpoint** must have been called for each of the two memory-state parameters.

Example

See the example for the **CMemoryState** constructor.

CMemoryState::DumpAllObjectsSince

void DumpAllObjectsSince( ) const;

Remarks

Calls the **Dump** function for all objects of a type derived from class **CObject** that were allocated (and are still allocated) since the last **Checkpoint** call for this **CMemoryState** object.

Calling **DumpAllObjectsSince** with an uninitialized **CMemoryState** object will dump out all objects currently in memory.

See the example for the **CMemoryState** constructor.

CMemoryState::DumpStatistics

void DumpStatistics( ) const;

Remarks

Prints a concise memory statistics report from a **CMemoryState** object that is filled by the **Difference** member function. The report, which is printed on the **afxDump** device, shows the following:

- Number of "object" blocks (blocks of memory allocated using **CObject::operator new**) still allocated on the heap.
- Number of nonobject blocks still allocated on the heap.
- The maximum memory used by the program at any one time (in bytes).
- The total memory currently used by the program (in bytes).

A sample report looks like this:

```
0 bytes in 0 Free Blocks
8 bytes in 2 Object Blocks
0 bytes in 0 Non-Object Blocks
Largest number used: 8 bytes
Total allocations: 8 bytes
```

- The first line describes the number of blocks whose deallocation was delayed if **afxMemDF** was set to **delayFreeMemDF**. For more information, see **afxMemDF**, in the "Macros and Globals" section.
- The second line describes how many object blocks still remain allocated on the heap.
- The third line describes how many nonobject blocks (arrays or structures allocated with new) were allocated on the heap and not deallocated.
- The fourth line gives the maximum memory used by your program at any one time.
- The last line lists the total amount of memory used by your program.

Example

See the example for the **CMemoryState** constructor.

CMenu

The **CMenu** class is an encapsulation of the Windows **HMENU**. It provides member functions for creating, tracking, updating, and destroying a menu.

Create a **CMenu** object on the stack frame as a local, then call **CMenu**'s member functions to manipulate the new menu as needed. Next, call **CWnd::SetMenu** to set the menu to a window, followed immediately by a call to the **CMenu** object's **Detach** member function. The **CWnd::SetMenu** member function sets the window's menu to the new menu, causes the window to be redrawn to reflect the menu change, and also passes ownership of the menu to the window. The call to **Detach** detaches the **HMENU** from the **CMenu** object, so that when the local **CMenu** variable passes out of scope, the **CMenu** object destructor does not attempt to destroy a menu it no longer owns. The menu itself is automatically destroyed when the window is destroyed.

You can use the **LoadMenuIndirect** member function to create a menu from a template in memory, but a menu created from a resource by a call to **LoadMenu** is more easily maintained, and the menu resource itself can be created and modified by the menu editor.

#include <afxwin.h>

See Also: **CObject**

CMenu Class Members

Data Members

m_hMenu	Specifies the handle to the Windows menu attached to the **CMenu** object.

Construction

CMenu	Constructs a **CMenu** object.

Initialization

Attach	Attaches a Windows menu handle to a **CMenu** object.
Detach	Detaches a Windows menu handle from a **CMenu** object and returns the handle.
FromHandle	Returns a pointer to a **CMenu** object given a Windows menu handle.

Initialization *(continued)*

GetSafeHmenu	Returns the **m_hMenu** wrapped by this **CMenu** object.
DeleteTempMap	Deletes any temporary **CMenu** objects created by the **FromHandle** member function.
CreateMenu	Creates an empty menu and attaches it to a **CMenu** object.
CreatePopupMenu	Creates an empty pop-up menu and attaches it to a **CMenu** object.
LoadMenu	Loads a menu resource from the executable file and attaches it to a **CMenu** object.
LoadMenuIndirect	Loads a menu from a menu template in memory and attaches it to a **CMenu** object.
DestroyMenu	Destroys the menu attached to a **CMenu** object and frees any memory that the menu occupied.

Menu Operations

DeleteMenu	Deletes a specified item from the menu. If the menu item has an associated pop-up menu, destroys the handle to the pop-up menu and frees the memory used by it.
TrackPopupMenu	Displays a floating pop-up menu at the specified location and tracks the selection of items on the pop-up menu.

Menu Item Operations

AppendMenu	Appends a new item to the end of this menu.
CheckMenuItem	Places a check mark next to or removes a check mark from a menu item in the pop-up menu.
CheckMenuRadioItem	Places a radio button next to a menu item and removes the radio button from all of the other menu items in the group.
EnableMenuItem	Enables, disables, or dims (grays) a menu item.
GetMenuItemCount	Determines the number of items in a pop-up or top-level menu.
GetMenuItemID	Obtains the menu-item identifier for a menu item located at the specified position.
GetMenuState	Returns the status of the specified menu item or the number of items in a pop-up menu.
GetMenuString	Retrieves the label of the specified menu item.
GetSubMenu	Retrieves a pointer to a pop-up menu.
InsertMenu	Inserts a new menu item at the specified position, moving other items down the menu.
ModifyMenu	Changes an existing menu item at the specified position.
RemoveMenu	Deletes a menu item with an associated pop-up menu from the specified menu.
SetMenuItemBitmaps	Associates the specified check-mark bitmaps with a menu item.
GetMenuContextHelpId	Retrieves the help context ID associated with the menu.
SetMenuContextHelpId	Sets the help context ID to be associated with the menu.

Overridables

DrawItem	Called by the framework when a visual aspect of an owner-drawn menu changes.
MeasureItem	Called by the framework to determine menu dimensions when an owner-drawn menu is created.

Member Functions

CMenu::AppendMenu

> **BOOL AppendMenu(UINT** *nFlags*, **UINT** *nIDNewItem* = **0,**
> ↪ **LPCTSTR** *lpszNewItem* = **NULL**);
> **BOOL AppendMenu(UINT** *nFlags*, **UINT** *nIDNewItem*, **const CBitmap*** *pBmp*);

Return Value

Nonzero if the function is successful; otherwise 0.

Parameters

nFlags   Specifies information about the state of the new menu item when it is added to the menu. It consists of one or more of the values listed in the Remarks section.

nIDNewItem   Specifies either the command ID of the new menu item or, if *nFlags* is set to **MF_POPUP**, the menu handle (**HMENU**) of a pop-up menu. The *nIDNewItem* parameter is ignored (not needed) if *nFlags* is set to **MF_SEPARATOR**.

lpszNewItem   Specifies the content of the new menu item. The *nFlags* parameter is used to interpret *lpszNewItem* in the following way:

nFlags	Interpretation of lpszNewItem
MF_OWNERDRAW	Contains an application-supplied 32-bit value that the application can use to maintain additional data associated with the menu item. This 32-bit value is available to the application when it processes **WM_MEASUREITEM** and **WM_DRAWITEM** messages. The value is stored in the **itemData** member of the structure supplied with those messages.
MF_STRING	Contains a pointer to a null-terminated string. This is the default interpretation.
MF_SEPARATOR	The *lpszNewItem* parameter is ignored (not needed).

pBmp   Points to a **CBitmap** object that will be used as the menu item.

Remarks

Appends a new item to the end of a menu. The application can specify the state of the menu item by setting values in *nFlags*. When *nIDNewItem* specifies a pop-up menu, it becomes part of the menu to which it is appended. If that menu is destroyed, the appended menu will also be destroyed. An appended menu should be detached from a **CMenu** object to avoid conflict. Note that **MF_STRING** and **MF_OWNERDRAW** are not valid for the bitmap version of **AppendMenu**.

The following list describes the flags that may be set in *nFlags*:

- **MF_CHECKED**   Acts as a toggle with **MF_UNCHECKED** to place the default check mark next to the item. When the application supplies check-mark bitmaps (see the **SetMenuItemBitmaps** member function), the "check mark on" bitmap is displayed.

- **MF_UNCHECKED**   Acts as a toggle with **MF_CHECKED** to remove a check mark next to the item. When the application supplies check-mark bitmaps (see the **SetMenuItemBitmaps** member function), the "check mark off" bitmap is displayed.

- **MF_DISABLED**   Disables the menu item so that it cannot be selected but does not dim it.

- **MF_ENABLED**   Enables the menu item so that it can be selected and restores it from its dimmed state.

- **MF_GRAYED**   Disables the menu item so that it cannot be selected and dims it.

- **MF_MENUBARBREAK**   Places the item on a new line in static menus or in a new column in pop-up menus. The new pop-up menu column will be separated from the old column by a vertical dividing line.

- **MF_MENUBREAK**   Places the item on a new line in static menus or in a new column in pop-up menus. No dividing line is placed between the columns.

- **MF_OWNERDRAW**   Specifies that the item is an owner-draw item. When the menu is displayed for the first time, the window that owns the menu receives a **WM_MEASUREITEM** message, which retrieves the height and width of the menu item. The **WM_DRAWITEM** message is the one sent whenever the owner must update the visual appearance of the menu item. This option is not valid for a top-level menu item.

- **MF_POPUP**   Specifies that the menu item has a pop-up menu associated with it. The ID parameter specifies a handle to a pop-up menu that is to be associated with the item. This is used for adding either a top-level pop-up menu or a hierarchical pop-up menu to a pop-up menu item.

- **MF_SEPARATOR**   Draws a horizontal dividing line. Can only be used in a pop-up menu. This line cannot be dimmed, disabled, or highlighted. Other parameters are ignored.

- **MF_STRING**   Specifies that the menu item is a character string.

Each of the following groups lists flags that are mutually exclusive and cannot be used together:

- **MF_DISABLED**, **MF_ENABLED**, and **MF_GRAYED**

- **MF_STRING**, **MF_OWNERDRAW**, **MF_SEPARATOR**, and the bitmap version

- **MF_MENUBARBREAK** and **MF_MENUBREAK**

- **MF_CHECKED** and **MF_UNCHECKED**

Whenever a menu that resides in a window is changed (whether or not the window is displayed), the application should call **CWnd::DrawMenuBar**.

See Also: CWnd::DrawMenuBar, CMenu::InsertMenu, CMenu::RemoveMenu, CMenu::SetMenuItemBitmaps, CMenu::Detach, ::AppendMenu

---

CMenu::Attach

BOOL Attach(HMENU *hMenu* **);**

Return Value

Nonzero if the operation was successful; otherwise 0.

Parameters

hMenu   Specifies a handle to a Windows menu.

Remarks

Attaches an existing Windows menu to a **CMenu** object. This function should not be called if a menu is already attached to the **CMenu** object. The menu handle is stored in the **m_hMenu** data member.

If the menu you want to manipulate is already associated with a window, you can use the **CWnd::GetMenu** function to get a handle to the menu.

Example

```
CMenu mnu;
HMENU hmnu = pWnd->GetMenu( );
mnu.Attach( hmnu );
// Now you can manipulate the window's menu as a CMenu
// object...
```

See Also: CMenu::Detach, CMenu::CMenu, CWnd::GetMenu

CMenu::CheckMenuItem

UINT CheckMenuItem(UINT *nIDCheckItem*, **UINT** *nCheck* **);**

Return Value

The previous state of the item: **MF_CHECKED** or **MF_UNCHECKED**, or 0xFFFFFFFF if the menu item did not exist.

Parameters

nIDCheckItem   Specifies the menu item to be checked, as determined by *nCheck*.

nCheck   Specifies how to check the menu item and how to determine the item's position in the menu. The *nCheck* parameter can be a combination of **MF_CHECKED** or **MF_UNCHECKED** with **MF_BYPOSITION** or **MF_BYCOMMAND** flags. These flags can be combined by using the bitwise OR operator. They have the following meanings:

- **MF_BYCOMMAND**   Specifies that the parameter gives the command ID of the existing menu item. This is the default.

- **MF_BYPOSITION**   Specifies that the parameter gives the position of the existing menu item. The first item is at position 0.

- **MF_CHECKED**   Acts as a toggle with **MF_UNCHECKED** to place the default check mark next to the item.

- **MF_UNCHECKED**   Acts as a toggle with **MF_CHECKED** to remove a check mark next to the item.

Remarks

Adds check marks to or removes check marks from menu items in the pop-up menu. The *nIDCheckItem* parameter specifies the item to be modified.

The *nIDCheckItem* parameter may identify a pop-up menu item as well as a menu item. No special steps are required to check a pop-up menu item. Top-level menu items cannot be checked. A pop-up menu item must be checked by position since it does not have a menu-item identifier associated with it.

See Also: CMenu::GetMenuState, **::CheckMenuItem**, **CMenu::CheckMenuRadioItem**

CMenu::CheckMenuRadioItem

BOOL CheckMenuRadioItem(UINT *nIDFirst*, **UINT** *nIDLast*, **UINT** *nIDItem*, **UINT** *nFlags* **);**

Return Value

Nonzero if successful; otherwise 0

Parameters

nIDFirst   Specifies (as an ID or offset, depending on the value of *nFlags*) the first menu item in the radio button group.

nIDLast   Specifies (as an ID or offset, depending on the value of *nFlags*) the last menu item in the radio button group.

nIDItem   Specifies (as an ID or offset, depending on the value of *nFlags*) the item in the group which will be checked with a radio button.

nFlags Specifies interpretation of *nIDFirst*, *nIDLast*, and *nIDItem* in the following way:

nFlags	Interpretation
MF_BYCOMMAND	Specifies that the parameter gives the command ID of the existing menu item. This is the default if neither **MF_BYCOMMAND** nor **MF_BYPOSITION** is set.
MF_BYPOSITION	Specifies that the parameter gives the position of the existing menu item. The first item is at position 0.

Remarks

Checks a specified menu item and makes it a radio item. At the same time, the function unchecks all other menu items in the associated group and clears the radio-item type flag for those items. The checked item is displayed using a radio button (or bullet) bitmap instead of a check mark bitmap.

See Also: **CMenu::CheckMenuItem, CMenu::GetMenuState, ::CheckMenuRadioItem**

CMenu::CMenu

CMenu( );

Remarks

The menu is not created until you call one of the create or load member functions of **CMenu:**

- **CreateMenu**
- **CreatePopupMenu**
- **LoadMenu**
- **LoadMenuIndirect**
- **Attach**

See Also: **CMenu::CreateMenu, CMenu::CreatePopupMenu, CMenu::LoadMenu, CMenu::LoadMenuIndirect, CMenu::Attach**

CMenu::CreateMenu

BOOL CreateMenu( );

Return Value

Nonzero if the menu was created successfully; otherwise 0.

Remarks

Creates a menu and attaches it to the **CMenu** object.

The menu is initially empty. Menu items can be added by using the **AppendMenu** or **InsertMenu** member function.

If the menu is assigned to a window, it is automatically destroyed when the window is destroyed.

Before exiting, an application must free system resources associated with a menu if the menu is not assigned to a window. An application frees a menu by calling the **DestroyMenu** member function.

See Also: **CMenu::CMenu, CMenu::DestroyMenu, CMenu::InsertMenu, CWnd::SetMenu, ::CreateMenu, CMenu::AppendMenu**

CMenu::CreatePopupMenu

BOOL CreatePopupMenu( );

Return Value

Nonzero if the pop-up menu was successfully created; otherwise 0.

Remarks

Creates a pop-up menu and attaches it to the **CMenu** object.

The menu is initially empty. Menu items can be added by using the **AppendMenu** or **InsertMenu** member function. The application can add the pop-up menu to an existing menu or pop-up menu. The **TrackPopupMenu** member function may be used to display this menu as a floating pop-up menu and to track selections on the pop-up menu.

If the menu is assigned to a window, it is automatically destroyed when the window is destroyed. If the menu is added to an existing menu, it is automatically destroyed when that menu is destroyed.

Before exiting, an application must free system resources associated with a pop-up menu if the menu is not assigned to a window. An application frees a menu by calling the **DestroyMenu** member function.

See Also: **CMenu::CreateMenu, CMenu::InsertMenu, CWnd::SetMenu, CMenu::TrackPopupMenu, ::CreatePopupMenu, CMenu::AppendMenu**

CMenu::DeleteMenu

BOOL DeleteMenu(UINT *nPosition***, UINT** *nFlags* **);**

Return Value

Nonzero if the function is successful; otherwise 0.

Parameters

nPosition Specifies the menu item that is to be deleted, as determined by *nFlags*.

nFlags Is used to interpret *nPosition* in the following way:

nFlags	Interpretation of nPosition
MF_BYCOMMAND	Specifies that the parameter gives the command ID of the existing menu item. This is the default if neither **MF_BYCOMMAND** nor **MF_BYPOSITION** is set.
MF_BYPOSITION	Specifies that the parameter gives the position of the existing menu item. The first item is at position 0.

Remarks

Deletes an item from the menu. If the menu item has an associated pop-up menu, **DeleteMenu** destroys the handle to the pop-up menu and frees the memory used by the pop-up menu.

Whenever a menu that resides in a window is changed (whether or not the window is displayed), the application must call **CWnd::DrawMenuBar**.

See Also: **CWnd::DrawMenuBar**, **::DeleteMenu**

CMenu::DeleteTempMap

static void PASCAL DeleteTempMap( );

Remarks

Called automatically by the **CWinApp** idle-time handler, **DeleteTempMap** deletes any temporary **CMenu** objects created by the **FromHandle** member function. **DeleteTempMap** detaches the Windows menu object attached to a temporary **CMenu** object before deleting the **CMenu** object.

CMenu::DestroyMenu

BOOL DestroyMenu( );

Return Value

Nonzero if the menu is destroyed; otherwise 0.

Remarks

Destroys the menu and any Windows resources that were used. The menu is detached from the **CMenu** object before it is destroyed. The Windows **DestroyMenu** function is automatically called in the **CMenu** destructor.

See Also: **::DestroyMenu**

CMenu::Detach

HMENU Detach( );

Return Value

The handle, of type **HMENU**, to a Windows menu, if successful; otherwise **NULL**.

Remarks

Detaches a Windows menu from a **CMenu** object and returns the handle. The **m_hMenu** data member is set to **NULL**.

See Also: CMenu::Attach

CMenu::DrawItem

virtual void DrawItem(LPDRAWITEMSTRUCT *lpDrawItemStruct* **);**

Parameters

lpDrawItemStruct A pointer to a **DRAWITEMSTRUCT** structure that contains information about the type of drawing required.

Remarks

Called by the framework when a visual aspect of an owner-drawn menu changes. The *itemAction* member of the **DRAWITEMSTRUCT** structure defines the drawing action that is to be performed. Override this member function to implement drawing for an owner-draw **CMenu** object. The application should restore all graphics device interface (GDI) objects selected for the display context supplied in *lpDrawItemStruct* before the termination of this member function.

See **CWnd::OnDrawItem** for a description of the **DRAWITEMSTRUCT** structure.

CMenu::EnableMenuItem

UINT EnableMenuItem(UINT *nIDEnableItem*, **UINT** *nEnable* **);**

Return Value

Previous state (**MF_DISABLED**, **MF_ENABLED**, or **MF_GRAYED**) or –1 if not valid.

Parameters

nIDEnableItem Specifies the menu item to be enabled, as determined by *nEnable*. This parameter can specify pop-up menu items as well as standard menu items.

nEnable Specifies the action to take. It can be a combination of **MF_DISABLED**, **MF_ENABLED**, or **MF_GRAYED**, with **MF_BYCOMMAND** or **MF_BYPOSITION**. These values can be combined by using the bitwise OR operator. These values have the following meanings:

- **MF_BYCOMMAND**   Specifies that the parameter gives the command ID of the existing menu item. This is the default.

- **MF_BYPOSITION**   Specifies that the parameter gives the position of the existing menu item. The first item is at position 0.

- **MF_DISABLED**   Disables the menu item so that it cannot be selected but does not dim it.

- **MF_ENABLED**   Enables the menu item so that it can be selected and restores it from its dimmed state.

- **MF_GRAYED**   Disables the menu item so that it cannot be selected and dims it.

Remarks

Enables, disables, or dims a menu item. The **CreateMenu**, **InsertMenu**, **ModifyMenu**, and **LoadMenuIndirect** member functions can also set the state (enabled, disabled, or dimmed) of a menu item.

Using the **MF_BYPOSITION** value requires an application to use the correct **CMenu**. If the **CMenu** of the menu bar is used, a top-level menu item (an item in the menu bar) is affected. To set the state of an item in a pop-up or nested pop-up menu by position, an application must specify the **CMenu** of the pop-up menu.

When an application specifies the **MF_BYCOMMAND** flag, Windows checks all pop-up menu items that are subordinate to the **CMenu**; therefore, unless duplicate menu items are present, using the **CMenu** of the menu bar is sufficient.

See Also: **CMenu::GetMenuState**, **::EnableMenuItem**

CMenu::FromHandle

static CMenu* PASCAL FromHandle(HMENU *hMenu* **);**

Return Value

A pointer to a **CMenu** that may be temporary or permanent.

Parameters

hMenu   A Windows handle to a menu.

Remarks

Returns a pointer to a **CMenu** object given a Windows handle to a menu. If a **CMenu** object is not already attached to the Windows menu object, a temporary **CMenu** object is created and attached.

This temporary **CMenu** object is only valid until the next time the application has idle time in its event loop, at which time all temporary objects are deleted.

CMenu::GetMenuContextHelpId

DWORD GetMenuContextHelpId( ) const;

Return Value

The context help ID currently associated with **CMenu** if it has one; zero otherwise.

Remarks

Call this function to retrieve the context help ID associated with **CMenu**.

See Also: **CMenu::SetMenuContextHelpID, ::GetMenuContextHelpId**

CMenu::GetMenuItemCount

UINT GetMenuItemCount( ) const;

Return Value

The number of items in the menu if the function is successful; otherwise −1.

Remarks

Determines the number of items in a pop-up or top-level menu.

See Also: **CWnd::GetMenu, CMenu::GetMenuItemID, CMenu::GetSubMenu, ::GetMenuItemCount**

CMenu::GetMenuItemID

UINT GetMenuItemID(int *nPos*) const;

Return Value

The item ID for the specified item in a pop-up menu if the function is successful. If the specified item is a pop-up menu (as opposed to an item within the pop-up menu), the return value is −1. If *nPos* corresponds to a **SEPARATOR** menu item, the return value is 0.

Parameters

nPos Specifies the position (zero-based) of the menu item whose ID is being retrieved.

Remarks

Obtains the menu-item identifier for a menu item located at the position defined by *nPos*.

See Also: **CWnd::GetMenu, CMenu::GetMenuItemCount, CMenu::GetSubMenu, ::GetMenuItemID**

CMenu::GetMenuState

UINT GetMenuState(UINT *nID*, **UINT** *nFlags* **) const;**

Return Value

The value 0xFFFFFFFF if the specified item does not exist. If *nId* identifies a pop-up menu, the high-order byte contains the number of items in the pop-up menu and the low-order byte contains the menu flags associated with the pop-up menu. Otherwise the return value is a mask (Boolean OR) of the values from the following list (this mask describes the status of the menu item that *nId* identifies):

- **MF_CHECKED**   Acts as a toggle with **MF_UNCHECKED** to place the default check mark next to the item. When the application supplies check-mark bitmaps (see the **SetMenuItemBitmaps** member function), the "check mark on" bitmap is displayed.

- **MF_DISABLED**   Disables the menu item so that it cannot be selected but does not dim it.

- **MF_ENABLED**   Enables the menu item so that it can be selected and restores it from its dimmed state. Note that the value of this constant is 0; an application should not test against 0 for failure when using this value.

- **MF_GRAYED**   Disables the menu item so that it cannot be selected and dims it.

- **MF_MENUBARBREAK**   Places the item on a new line in static menus or in a new column in pop-up menus. The new pop-up menu column will be separated from the old column by a vertical dividing line.

- **MF_MENUBREAK**   Places the item on a new line in static menus or in a new column in pop-up menus. No dividing line is placed between the columns.

- **MF_SEPARATOR**   Draws a horizontal dividing line. Can only be used in a pop-up menu. This line cannot be dimmed, disabled, or highlighted. Other parameters are ignored.

- **MF_UNCHECKED**   Acts as a toggle with **MF_CHECKED** to remove a check mark next to the item. When the application supplies check-mark bitmaps (see the **SetMenuItemBitmaps** member function), the "check mark off" bitmap is displayed. Note that the value of this constant is 0; an application should not test against 0 for failure when using this value.

Parameters

nID   Specifies the menu item ID, as determined by *nFlags*.

nFlags   Specifies the nature of *nID*. It can be one of the following values:

- **MF_BYCOMMAND**   Specifies that the parameter gives the command ID of the existing menu item. This is the default.

- **MF_BYPOSITION**   Specifies that the parameter gives the position of the existing menu item. The first item is at position 0.

Remarks

Returns the status of the specified menu item or the number of items in a pop-up menu.

See Also: **::GetMenuState**, **CMenu::CheckMenuItem**, **CMenu::EnableMenuItem**

CMenu::GetMenuString

int GetMenuString(UINT *nIDItem*, **LPTSTR** *lpString*, **int** *nMaxCount*,
↳ **UINT** *nFlags* **) const;**
int GetMenuString(UINT *nIDItem*, **CString&** *rString*, **UINT** *nFlags* **) const;**

Return Value

Specifies the actual number of bytes copied to the buffer, not including the null terminator.

Parameters

nIDItem Specifies the integer identifier of the menu item or the offset of the menu item in the menu, depending on the value of *nFlags*.

lpString Points to the buffer that is to receive the label.

rString A reference to a **CString** object that is to receive the copied menu string.

nMaxCount Specifies the maximum length (in bytes) of the label to be copied. If the label is longer than the maximum specified in *nMaxCount*, the extra characters are truncated.

nFlags Specifies the interpretation of the *nIDItem* parameter. It can be one of the following values:

nFlags	Interpretation of nIDItem
MF_BYCOMMAND	Specifies that the parameter gives the command ID of the existing menu item. This is the default if neither **MF_BYCOMMAND** nor **MF_BYPOSITION** is set.
MF_BYPOSITION	Specifies that the parameter gives the position of the existing menu item. The first item is at position 0.

Remarks

Copies the label of the specified menu item to the specified buffer.

The *nMaxCount* parameter should be one larger than the number of characters in the label to accommodate the null character that terminates a string.

See Also: **CMenu::GetMenuState**, **CMenu::ModifyMenu**, **::GetMenuString**

CMenu::GetSubMenu

CMenu* GetSubMenu(int *nPos* **) const;**

Return Value

A pointer to a **CMenu** object whose **m_hMenu** member contains a handle to the pop-up menu if a pop-up menu exists at the given position; otherwise **NULL**. If a **CMenu** object does not exist, then a temporary one is created. The **CMenu** pointer returned should not be stored.

Parameters

nPos   Specifies the position of the pop-up menu contained in the menu. Position values start at 0 for the first menu item. The pop-up menu's identifier cannot be used in this function.

Remarks

Retrieves the **CMenu** object of a pop-up menu.

See Also: CWnd::GetMenu, CMenu::GetMenuItemID, ::GetMenuString

---

CMenu::GetSafeHmenu

HMENU GetSafeHmenu( ) const;

Remarks

Returns the **HMENU** wrapped by this **CMenu** object, or a **NULL CMenu** pointer.

See Also: ::GetSubMenu

CMenu::InsertMenu

BOOL InsertMenu(UINT *nPosition,* **UINT** *nFlags,* **UINT** *nIDNewItem* **= 0,**
➥ **LPCTSTR** *lpszNewItem* **= NULL);**
BOOL InsertMenu(UINT *nPosition,* **UINT** *nFlags,* **UINT** *nIDNewItem,*
➥ **const CBitmap*** *pBmp* **);**

Return Value

Nonzero if the function is successful; otherwise 0.

Parameters

nPosition   Specifies the menu item before which the new menu item is to be inserted. The *nFlags* parameter can be used to interpret *nPosition* in the following ways:

nFlags	Interpretation of nPosition
MF_BYCOMMAND	Specifies that the parameter gives the command ID of the existing menu item. This is the default if neither **MF_BYCOMMAND** nor **MF_BYPOSITION** is set.

(continued)

nFlags	Interpretation of nPosition
MF_BYPOSITION	Specifies that the parameter gives the position of the existing menu item. The first item is at position 0. If *nPosition* is –1, the new menu item is appended to the end of the menu.

nFlags   Specifies how *nPosition* is interpreted and specifies information about the state of the new menu item when it is added to the menu. For a list of the flags that may be set, see the **AppendMenu** member function. To specify more than one value, use the bitwise OR operator to combine them with the **MF_BYCOMMAND** or **MF_BYPOSITION** flag.

nIDNewItem   Specifies either the command ID of the new menu item or, if *nFlags* is set to **MF_POPUP**, the menu handle (**HMENU**) of the pop-up menu. The *nIDNewItem* parameter is ignored (not needed) if *nFlags* is set to **MF_SEPARATOR**.

lpszNewItem   Specifies the content of the new menu item. *nFlags* can be used to interpret *lpszNewItem* in the following ways:

nFlags	Interpretation of lpszNewItem
MF_OWNERDRAW	Contains an application-supplied 32-bit value that the application can use to maintain additional data associated with the menu item. This 32-bit value is available to the application in the **itemData** member of the structure supplied by the **WM_MEASUREITEM** and **WM_DRAWITEM** messages. These messages are sent when the menu item is initially displayed or is changed.
MF_STRING	Contains a long pointer to a null-terminated string. This is the default interpretation.
MF_SEPARATOR	The *lpszNewItem* parameter is ignored (not needed).

pBmp   Points to a **CBitmap** object that will be used as the menu item.

Remarks

Inserts a new menu item at the position specified by *nPosition* and moves other items down the menu. The application can specify the state of the menu item by setting values in *nFlags*.

Whenever a menu that resides in a window is changed (whether or not the window is displayed), the application should call **CWnd::DrawMenuBar**.

When *nIDNewItem* specifies a pop-up menu, it becomes part of the menu in which it is inserted. If that menu is destroyed, the inserted menu will also be destroyed. An inserted menu should be detached from a **CMenu** object to avoid conflict.

If the active multiple document interface (MDI) child window is maximized and an application inserts a pop-up menu into the MDI application's menu by calling this function and specifying the **MF_BYPOSITION** flag, the menu is inserted one position farther left than expected. This happens because the Control menu of the active MDI child window is inserted into the first position of the MDI frame window's menu bar. To position the menu properly, the application must add 1 to the position value that would otherwise be used. An application can use the **WM_MDIGETACTIVE** message to determine whether the currently active child window is maximized.

See Also: **CMenu::AppendMenu, CWnd::DrawMenuBar, CMenu::SetMenuItemBitmaps, CMenu::Detach, ::InsertMenu**

CMenu::LoadMenu

BOOL LoadMenu(LPCTSTR *lpszResourceName* **);**
BOOL LoadMenu(UINT *nIDResource* **);**

Return Value

Nonzero if the menu resource was loaded successfully; otherwise 0.

Parameters

lpszResourceName   Points to a null-terminated string that contains the name of the menu resource to load.

nIDResource   Specifies the menu ID of the menu resource to load.

Remarks

Loads a menu resource from the application's executable file and attaches it to the **CMenu** object.

Before exiting, an application must free system resources associated with a menu if the menu is not assigned to a window. An application frees a menu by calling the **DestroyMenu** member function.

See Also: **CMenu::AppendMenu, CMenu::DestroyMenu, CMenu::LoadMenuIndirect, ::LoadMenu**

CMenu::LoadMenuIndirect

BOOL LoadMenuIndirect(const void* *lpMenuTemplate* **);**

Return Value

Nonzero if the menu resource was loaded successfully; otherwise 0.

Parameters

lpMenuTemplate   Points to a menu template (which is a single **MENUITEMTEMPLATEHEADER** structure and a collection of one or more **MENUITEMTEMPLATE** structures). For more information on these two structures, see the Win32 SDK documentation.

Remarks

Loads a resource from a menu template in memory and attaches it to the **CMenu** object. A menu template is a header followed by a collection of one or more **MENUITEMTEMPLATE** structures, each of which may contain one or more menu items and pop-up menus.

The version number should be 0.

The **mtOption** flags should include **MF_END** for the last item in a pop-up list and for the last item in the main list. See the **AppendMenu** member function for other flags. The **mtId** member must be omitted from the **MENUITEMTEMPLATE** structure when **MF_POPUP** is specified in **mtOption**.

The space allocated for the **MENUITEMTEMPLATE** structure must be large enough for **mtString** to contain the name of the menu item as a null-terminated string.

Before exiting, an application must free system resources associated with a menu if the menu is not assigned to a window. An application frees a menu by calling the **DestroyMenu** member function.

See Also: **CMenu::DestroyMenu, CMenu::LoadMenu, ::LoadMenuIndirect, CMenu::AppendMenu**

CMenu::MeasureItem

virtual void MeasureItem(LPMEASUREITEMSTRUCT *lpMeasureItemStruct* **);**

Parameters

lpMeasureItemStruct   A pointer to a **MEASUREITEMSTRUCT** structure.

Remarks

Called by the framework when a menu with the owner-draw style is created. By default, this member function does nothing. Override this member function and fill in the **MEASUREITEMSTRUCT** structure to inform Windows of the menu's dimensions.

See **CWnd::OnMeasureItem** for a description of the **MEASUREITEMSTRUCT** structure.

CMenu::ModifyMenu

BOOL ModifyMenu(UINT *nPosition*, **UINT** *nFlags*,
  ↳ **UINT** *nIDNewItem* = **0, LPCTSTR** *lpszNewItem* = **NULL);**
BOOL ModifyMenu(UINT *nPosition*, **UINT** *nFlags*, **UINT** *nIDNewItem*,
  ↳ **const CBitmap*** *pBmp* **);**

Return Value

Nonzero if the function is successful; otherwise 0.

Parameters

nPosition   Specifies the menu item to be changed. The *nFlags* parameter can be used to interpret *nPosition* in the following ways:

nFlags	Interpretation of nPosition
MF_BYCOMMAND	Specifies that the parameter gives the command ID of the existing menu item. This is the default if neither **MF_BYCOMMAND** nor **MF_BYPOSITION** is set.
MF_BYPOSITION	Specifies that the parameter gives the position of the existing menu item. The first item is at position 0.

nFlags   Specifies how *nPosition* is interpreted and gives information about the changes to be made to the menu item. For a list of flags that may be set, see the **AppendMenu** member function.

nIDNewItem   Specifies either the command ID of the modified menu item or, if *nFlags* is set to **MF_POPUP**, the menu handle (**HMENU**) of a pop-up menu. The *nIDNewItem* parameter is ignored (not needed) if *nFlags* is set to **MF_SEPARATOR**.

lpszNewItem   Specifies the content of the new menu item. The *nFlags* parameter can be used to interpret *lpszNewItem* in the following ways:

nFlags	Interpretation of lpszNewItem
MF_OWNERDRAW	Contains an application-supplied 32-bit value that the application can use to maintain additional data associated with the menu item. This 32-bit value is available to the application when it processes **MF_MEASUREITEM** and **MF_DRAWITEM**.
MF_STRING	Contains a long pointer to a null-terminated string or to a **CString**.
MF_SEPARATOR	The *lpszNewItem* parameter is ignored (not needed).

pBmp   Points to a **CBitmap** object that will be used as the menu item.

Remarks

Changes an existing menu item at the position specified by *nPosition*. The application specifies the new state of the menu item by setting values in *nFlags*. If this function replaces a pop-up menu associated with the menu item, it destroys the old pop-up menu and frees the memory used by the pop-up menu.

When *nIDNewItem* specifies a pop-up menu, it becomes part of the menu in which it is inserted. If that menu is destroyed, the inserted menu will also be destroyed. An inserted menu should be detached from a **CMenu** object to avoid conflict.

Whenever a menu that resides in a window is changed (whether or not the window is displayed), the application should call **CWnd::DrawMenuBar**. To change the attributes of existing menu items, it is much faster to use the **CheckMenuItem** and **EnableMenuItem** member functions.

See Also: CMenu::AppendMenu, CMenu::InsertMenu,
CMenu::CheckMenuItem, CWnd::DrawMenuBar, CMenu::EnableMenuItem,
CMenu::SetMenuItemBitmaps, CMenu::Detach, ::ModifyMenu

CMenu::RemoveMenu

BOOL RemoveMenu(UINT *nPosition*, **UINT** *nFlags* **);**

Return Value

Nonzero if the function is successful; otherwise 0.

Parameters

nPosition Specifies the menu item to be removed. The *nFlags* parameter can be used to interpret *nPosition* in the following ways:

nFlags	Interpretation of nPosition
MF_BYCOMMAND	Specifies that the parameter gives the command ID of the existing menu item. This is the default if neither **MF_BYCOMMAND** nor **MF_BYPOSITION** is set.
MF_BYPOSITION	Specifies that the parameter gives the position of the existing menu item. The first item is at position 0.

nFlags Specifies how *nPosition* is interpreted.

Remarks

Deletes a menu item with an associated pop-up menu from the menu. It does not destroy the handle for a pop-up menu, so the menu can be reused. Before calling this function, the application may call the **GetSubMenu** member function to retrieve the pop-up **CMenu** object for reuse.

Whenever a menu that resides in a window is changed (whether or not the window is displayed), the application must call **CWnd::DrawMenuBar**.

See Also: CWnd::DrawMenuBar, CMenu::GetSubMenu, ::RemoveMenu

CMenu::SetMenuContextHelpId

BOOL SetMenuContextHelpId(DWORD *dwContextHelpId* **);**

Return Value

Nonzero if successful; otherwise 0

Parameters

dwContextHelpId Context help ID to associate with **CMenu**.

Remarks

Call this function to associate a context help ID with **CMenu**. All items in the menu share this identifier¾ it is not possible to attach a help context identifier to the individual menu items.

See Also: **CMenu::GetMenuContextHelpID**, **::SetMenuContextHelpId**

CMenu::SetMenuItemBitmaps

BOOL SetMenuItemBitmaps(UINT *nPosition*, **UINT** *nFlags*,
↦ **const CBitmap*** *pBmpUnchecked*, **const CBitmap*** *pBmpChecked* **);**

Return Value

Nonzero if the function is successful; otherwise 0.

Parameters

nPosition Specifies the menu item to be changed. The *nFlags* parameter can be used to interpret *nPosition* in the following ways:

nFlags	Interpretation of nPosition
MF_BYCOMMAND	Specifies that the parameter gives the command ID of the existing menu item. This is the default if neither **MF_BYCOMMAND** nor **MF_BYPOSITION** is set.
MF_BYPOSITION	Specifies that the parameter gives the position of the existing menu item. The first item is at position 0.

nFlags Specifies how *nPosition* is interpreted.

pBmpUnchecked Specifies the bitmap to use for menu items that are not checked.

pBmpChecked Specifies the bitmap to use for menu items that are checked.

Remarks

Associates the specified bitmaps with a menu item. Whether the menu item is checked or unchecked, Windows displays the appropriate bitmap next to the menu item.

If either *pBmpUnchecked* or *pBmpChecked* is **NULL**, then Windows displays nothing next to the menu item for the corresponding attribute. If both parameters are **NULL**, Windows uses the default check mark when the item is checked and removes the check mark when the item is unchecked.

When the menu is destroyed, these bitmaps are not destroyed; the application must destroy them.

The Windows **GetMenuCheckMarkDimensions** function retrieves the dimensions of the default check mark used for menu items. The application uses these values to determine the appropriate size for the bitmaps supplied with this function. Get the size, create your bitmaps, then set them.

See Also: **::GetMenuCheckMarkDimensions**, **::SetMenuItemBitmaps**

CMenu::TrackPopupMenu

BOOL TrackPopupMenu(UINT *nFlags*, **int** *x*, **int** *y*,
↳ **CWnd*** *pWnd*, **LPCRECT** *lpRect* = **NULL**);

Return Value

Nonzero if the function is successful; otherwise 0.

Parameters

nFlags   Specifies a screen-position flag and a mouse-button flag. The screen-position flag can be one of the following:

- **TPM_CENTERALIGN**   Centers the pop-up menu horizontally relative to the coordinate specified by *x*.

- **TPM_LEFTALIGN**   Positions the pop-up menu so that its left side is aligned with the coordinate specified by *x*.

- **TPM_RIGHTALIGN**   Positions the pop-up menu so that its right side is aligned with the coordinate specified by *x*.

The mouse-button flag can be either of the following:

- **TPM_LEFTBUTTON**   Causes the pop-up menu to track the left mouse button.

- **TPM_RIGHTBUTTON**   Causes the pop-up menu to track the right mouse button.

x   Specifies the horizontal position in screen coordinates of the pop-up menu. Depending on the value of the *nFlags* parameter, the menu can be left-aligned, right-aligned, or centered relative to this position.

y   Specifies the vertical position in screen coordinates of the top of the menu on the screen.

pWnd   Identifies the window that owns the pop-up menu. This window receives all **WM_COMMAND** messages from the menu. In Windows versions 3.1 and later, the window does not receive **WM_COMMAND** messages until **TrackPopupMenu** returns. In Windows 3.0, the window receives **WM_COMMAND** messages before **TrackPopupMenu** returns.

lpRect   Points to a **RECT** structure or **CRect** object that contains the screen coordinates of a rectangle within which the user can click without dismissing the pop-up menu. If this parameter is **NULL**, the pop-up menu is dismissed if the user clicks outside the pop-up menu. This must be **NULL** for Windows 3.0.

For Windows 3.1 and later, you can use the following constants:

- **TPM_CENTERALIGN**
- **TPM_LEFTALIGN**

- **TPM_RIGHTALIGN**
- **TPM_RIGHTBUTTON**

Remarks

Displays a floating pop-up menu at the specified location and tracks the selection of items on the pop-up menu. A floating pop-up menu can appear anywhere on the screen.

See Also: **CMenu::CreatePopupMenu**, **CMenu::GetSubMenu**, **::TrackPopupMenu**

Data Members

CMenu::m_hMenu

Remarks

Specifies the **HMENU** handle of the Windows menu attached to the **CMenu** object.

CMetaFileDC

A Windows metafile contains a sequence of graphics device interface (GDI) commands that you can replay to create a desired image or text.

To implement a Windows metafile, first create a **CMetaFileDC** object. Invoke the **CMetaFileDC** constructor, then call the **Create** member function, which creates a Windows metafile device context and attaches it to the **CMetaFileDC** object.

Next send the **CMetaFileDC** object the sequence of **CDC** GDI commands that you intend for it to replay. Only those GDI commands that create output, such as **MoveTo** and **LineTo**, can be used.

After you have sent the desired commands to the metafile, call the **Close** member function, which closes the metafile device contexts and returns a metafile handle. Then dispose of the **CMetaFileDC** object.

CDC::PlayMetaFile can then use the metafile handle to play the metafile repeatedly. The metafile can also be manipulated by Windows functions such as **CopyMetaFile**, which copies a metafile to disk.

When the metafile is no longer needed, delete it from memory with the **DeleteMetaFile** Windows function.

You can also implement the **CMetaFileDC** object so that it can handle both output calls and attribute GDI calls such as **GetTextExtent**. Such a metafile is more flexible and can more easily reuse general GDI code, which often consists of a mix of output and attribute calls. The **CMetaFileDC** class inherits two device contexts, **m_hDC** and **m_hAttribDC**, from **CDC**. The **m_hDC** device context handles all **CDC** GDI output calls and the **m_hAttribDC** device context handles all **CDC** GDI attribute calls. Normally, these two device contexts refer to the same device. In the case of **CMetaFileDC**, the attribute DC is set to **NULL** by default.

Create a second device context that points to the screen, a printer, or device other than a metafile, then call the **SetAttribDC** member function to associate the new device context with **m_hAttribDC**. GDI calls for information will now be directed to the new **m_hAttribDC**. Output GDI calls will go to **m_hDC**, which represents the metafile.

For more information on **CMetaFileDC**, see "Device Contexts" in *Visual C++ Programmer's Guide* online.

#include <afxext.h>

CMetaFileDC Class Members

Construction	
CMetaFileDC	Constructs a **CMetaFileDC** object.

Initialization	
Create	Creates the Windows metafile device context and attaches it to the **CMetaFileDC** object.
CreateEnhanced	Creates a metafile device context for an enhanced-format metafile.

Operations	
Close	Closes the device context and creates a metafile handle.
CloseEnhanced	Closes an enhanced-metafile device context and creates an enhanced-metafile handle.

Member Functions
CMetaFileDC::Close

HMETAFILE Close( );

Return Value

A valid **HMETAFILE** if the function is successful; otherwise **NULL**.

Remarks

Closes the metafile device context and creates a Windows metafile handle that can be used to play the metafile by using the **CDC::PlayMetaFile** member function. The Windows metafile handle can also be used to manipulate the metafile with Windows functions such as **CopyMetaFile**.

Delete the metafile after use by calling the Windows **DeleteMetaFile** function.

See Also: **CDC::PlayMetaFile**, **::CloseMetaFile**, **::CopyMetaFile**, **::DeleteMetaFile**

CMetaFileDC::CloseEnhanced

HENHMETAFILE CloseEnhanced( );

Return Value

A handle of an enhanced metafile, if successful; otherwise **NULL**.

Remarks

Closes an enhanced-metafile device context and returns a handle that identifies an enhanced-format metafile. An application can use the enhanced-metafile handle returned by this function to perform the following tasks:

- Display a picture stored in an enhanced metafile
- Create copies of the enhanced metafile
- Enumerate, edit, or copy individual records in the enhanced metafile
- Retrieve an optional description of the metafile contents from the enhanced-metafile header
- Retrieve a copy of the enhanced-metafile header
- Retrieve a binary copy of the enhanced metafile
- Enumerate the colors in the optional palette
- Convert an enhanced-format metafile into a Windows-format metafile

When the application no longer needs the enhanced metafile handle, it should release the handle by calling the **::DeleteEnhMetaFile** function.

See Also: **CDC::PlayMetaFile**, **CMetaFileDC::CreateEnhanced**, **::DeleteEnhMetaFile**

CMetaFileDC::CMetaFileDC

CMetaFileDC( );

Remarks

Construct a **CMetaFileDC** object in two steps. First, call **CMetaFileDC**, then call **Create**, which creates the Windows metafile device context and attaches it to the **CMetaFileDC** object.

See Also: **CMetaFileDC::Create**

CMetaFileDC::Create

BOOL Create(LPCTSTR *lpszFilename* **= NULL);**

Return Value

Nonzero if the function is successful; otherwise 0.

Parameters

lpszFilename   Points to a null-terminated character string. Specifies the filename of the metafile to create. If *lpszFilename* is **NULL**, a new in-memory metafile is created.

Remarks

Construct a **CMetaFileDC** object in two steps. First, call the constructor **CMetaFileDC**, then call **Create**, which creates the Windows metafile device context and attaches it to the **CMetaFileDC** object.

See Also: **CMetaFileDC::CMetaFileDC**, **CDC::SetAttribDC**, **::CreateMetaFile**

CMetaFileDC::CreateEnhanced

BOOL CreateEnhanced(CDC* *pDCRef***, LPCTSTR** *lpszFileName***,**
↪ LPCRECT *lpBounds***, LPCTSTR** *lpszDescription* **);**

Return Value

A handle of the device context for the enhanced metafile, if successful; otherwise **NULL**.

Parameters

pDCRef   Identifies a reference device for the enhanced metafile.

lpszFileName   Points to a null-terminated character string. Specifies the filename for the enhanced metafile to be created. If this parameter is **NULL**, the enhanced metafile is memory based and its contents lost when the object is destroyed or when the **::DeleteEnhMetaFile** function is called.

lpBounds   Points to a **RECT** data structure or a **CRect** object that specifies the dimensions in **HIMETRIC** units (in .01-millimeter increments) of the picture to be stored in the enhanced metafile.

lpszDescription   Points to a zero-terminated string that specifies the name of the application that created the picture, as well as the picture's title.

Remarks

Creates a device context for an enhanced-format metafile. This DC can be used to store a device-independent picture.

Windows uses the reference device identified by the *pDCRef* parameter to record the resolution and units of the device on which a picture originally appeared. If the *pDCRef* parameter is **NULL**, it uses the current display device for reference.

The left and top members of the **RECT** data structure pointed to by the *lpBounds* parameter must be smaller than the right and bottom members, respectively. Points along the edges of the rectangle are included in the picture. If *lpBounds* is **NULL**, the graphics device interface (GDI) computes the dimensions of the smallest rectangle that can enclose the picture drawn by the application. The *lpBounds* parameter should be supplied where possible.

The string pointed to by the *lpszDescription* parameter must contain a null character between the application name and the picture name and must terminate with two null characters—for example, "XYZ Graphics Editor\0Bald Eagle\0\0," where \0 represents the null character. If *lpszDescription* is **NULL**, there is no corresponding entry in the enhanced-metafile header.

Applications use the DC created by this function to store a graphics picture in an enhanced metafile. The handle identifying this DC can be passed to any GDI function.

After an application stores a picture in an enhanced metafile, it can display the picture on any output device by calling the **CDC::PlayMetaFile** function. When displaying the picture, Windows uses the rectangle pointed to by the *lpBounds* parameter and the resolution data from the reference device to position and scale the picture. The device context returned by this function contains the same default attributes associated with any new DC.

Applications must use the **::GetWinMetaFileBits** function to convert an enhanced metafile to the older Windows metafile format.

The filename for the enhanced metafile should use the .EMF extension.

See Also: **CMetaFileDC::CloseEnhanced, CDC::PlayMetaFile, ::CloseEnhMetaFile, ::DeleteEnhMetaFile, ::GetEnhMetaFileDescription, ::GetEnhMetaFileHeader, ::GetWinMetaFileBits, ::PlayEnhMetaFile**

CMiniFrameWnd

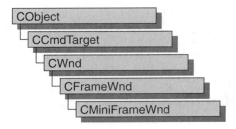

A **CMiniFrameWnd** object represents a half-height frame window typically seen around floating toolbars. These mini-frame windows behave like normal frame windows, except that they do not have minimize/maximize buttons or menus and you only have to single-click on the system menu to dismiss them.

To use a **CMiniFrameWnd** object, first define the object. Then call the **Create** member function to display the mini-frame window.

For more information on how to use **CMiniFrameWnd** objects, see the article "Toolbars: Docking and Floating" in *Visual C++ Programmer's Guide* online.

#include <afxwin.h>

See Also: CFrameWnd

CMiniFrameWnd Class Members

Construction

CMiniFrameWnd	Constructs a **CMiniFrameWnd** object.
Create	Creates a **CMiniFrameWnd** object after construction.

Member Functions
CMiniFrameWnd::CMiniFrameWnd

CMiniFrameWnd( );

Remarks

Constructs a **CMiniFrameWnd** object, but does not create the window. To create the window, call **CMiniFrameWnd::Create**.

See Also: CFrameWnd

CMiniFrameWnd::Create

BOOL Create(LPCTSTR *lpClassName,* **LPCTSTR** *lpWindowName,* **DWORD** *dwStyle,*
↪ **const RECT&** *rect,* **CWnd*** *pParentWnd* = **NULL, UINT** *nID* = **0);**

Return Value

Nonzero if successful; otherwise 0.

Parameters

lpClassName Points to a null-terminated character string that names the
Windows class. The class name can be any name registered with the global
AfxRegisterWndClass function. If **NULL**, the window class will be registered
for you by the framework.

lpWindowName Points to a null-terminated character string that contains the
window name.

dwStyle Specifies the window style attributes. These can include standard window
styles and one or more of the following special styles:

- **MFS_MOVEFRAME** Allows the mini-frame window to be moved by
  clicking on any edge of the window, not just the caption.

- **MFS_4THICKFRAME** Disables resizing of the mini-frame window.

- **MFS_SYNCACTIVE** Synchronizes the activation of the mini-frame window
  to the activation of its parent window.

- **MFS_THICKFRAME** Allows the mini-frame window to be sized as small as
  the contents of the client area allow.

  See **CWnd::Create** for a description of possible window style values. The typical
  combination used for mini-frame windows is
  WS_POPUP|WS_CAPTION|WS_SYSMENU.

rect A **RECT** structure specifying the desired dimensions of the window.

pParentWnd Points to the parent window. Use **NULL** for top-level windows.

nID If the mini-frame window is created as a child window, this is the identifier of
the child control; otherwise 0.

Remarks

Creates the Windows mini-frame window and attaches it to the **CMiniFrameWnd**
object. **Create** initializes the window's class name and window name and registers
default values for its style and parent.

See Also: **CFrameWnd::Create**, **CWnd::Create**, **CWnd::CreateEx**,
CFrameWnd

CMonikerFile

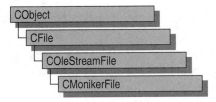

A **CMonikerFile** object represents a stream of data (**IStream**) named by an **IMoniker**.

A moniker contains information much like a pathname to a file. If you have a pointer to a moniker object's **IMoniker** interface, you can get access to the identified file without having any other specific information about where the file is actually located.

Derived from **COleStreamFile**, **CMonikerFile** takes a moniker or a string representation it can make into a moniker and binds to the stream for which the moniker is a name. You can then read and write to that stream. The real purpose of **CMonikerFile** is to provide simple access to **IStream**s named by **IMoniker**s so that you do not have to bind to a stream yourself, yet have **CFile** functionality to the stream.

CMonikerFile cannot be used to bind to anything other than a stream. If you want to bind to storage or an object, you must use the **IMoniker** interface directly.

For more information on streams and monikers, see **COleStreamFile** in the *MFC Class Library Reference* and **IStream** and **IMoniker** in the *OLE Programmer's Reference*.

#include <afxole.h>

See Also: **CAsyncMonikerFile**

CMonikerFile Class Members

Construction

CMonikerFile	Constructs a **CMonikerFile** object.

Operations

Close	Detaches and releases the stream and releases the moniker.
Detach	Detaches the **IMoniker** from this **CMonikerFile** object.
GetMoniker	Returns the current moniker.

Member Functions

CMonikerFile::Close

void Close( );

Remarks

Call this function to detach and release the stream and to release the moniker. Can be called on unopened or already closed streams.

See Also: CMonikerFile::Open

CMonikerFile::CMonikerFile

CMonikerFile( );

Remarks

Constructs a **CMonikerFile** object.

See Also: CAsyncMonikerFile, CMonikerFile::Open

CMonikerFile::CreateBindContext

virtual IBindCtx* CreateBindContext(CFileException* *pError*);

Return Value

A pointer to the bind context **IBindCtx** to bind with if successful; otherwise **NULL**. If the instance was opened with an **IBindHost** interface, the bind context is retrieved from the **IBindHost**. If there is no **IBindHost** interface or the interface fails to return a bind context, a bind context is created. For a description of the **IBindHost** interface, see the *ActiveX SDK*.

Parameters

pError   A pointer to a file exception. In the event of an error, it will be set to the cause.

Remarks

Call this function to create a default initialized bind context. A bind context is an object that stores information about a particular moniker binding operation. You can override this function to provide a custom bind context.

CMonikerFile::Detach

BOOL Detach(CFileException* *pError* **= NULL);**

Return Value

Nonzero if successful; otherwise 0.

Parameters

pError   A pointer to a file exception. In the event of an error, it will be set to the cause.

Remarks

Call this function to close the stream.

See Also: CMonikerFile::Close, CMonikerFile::Open

CMonikerFile::GetMoniker

IMoniker* GetMoniker( ) const;

Return Value

A pointer to the current moniker interface (**IMoniker**).

Remarks

Call this function to retrieve a pointer to the current moniker. Since **CMonikerFile** is not an interface, the pointer returned does not increment the reference count (through **AddRef**), and the moniker is released when the **CMonikerFile** object is released. If you want to hold onto the moniker or release it yourself, you must **AddRef** it.

CMonikerFile::Open

BOOL Open(LPCTSTR *lpszURL***, CFileException*** *pError* **= NULL);**
BOOL Open(IMoniker* *pMoniker***, CFileException*** *pError* **= NULL);**

Return Value

Nonzero if successful; otherwise 0.

Parameters

lpszURL   A URL or filename of the file to be opened.

pError   A pointer to a file exception. In the event of an error, it will be set to the cause.

pMoniker   A pointer to the moniker interface **IMoniker** to be used to obtain a stream.

Remarks

Call this member function to open a file or moniker object.

The *lpszURL* parameter cannot be used on a Macintosh. Only the *pMoniker* form of **Open** can be used on a Macintosh.

You can use a URL or a filename for the *lpszURL* parameter. For example:

```
CMyMonFile  mymonf;
mymonf.Open(_T("http://www.microsoft.com"));
```

—or—

```
CMyMonFile  mymonf;
mymonf.Open(_T("file:c:\mydata.dat"));
```

See Also: CMonikerFile::CMonikerFile, CAsyncMonikerFile::Open

CMultiDocTemplate

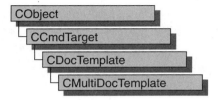

The **CMultiDocTemplate** class defines a document template that implements the multiple document interface (MDI). An MDI application uses the main frame window as a workspace in which the user can open zero or more document frame windows, each of which displays a document. For a more detailed description of the MDI, see *Windows Interface Guidelines for Software Design*.

A document template defines the relationships among three types of classes:

- A document class, which you derive from **CDocument**.
- A view class, which displays data from the document class listed above. You can derive this class from **CView**, **CScrollView**, **CFormView**, or **CEditView**. (You can also use **CEditView** directly.)
- A frame window class, which contains the view. For an MDI document template, you can derive this class from **CMDIChildWnd**, or, if you don't need to customize the behavior of the document frame windows, you can use **CMDIChildWnd** directly without deriving your own class.

An MDI application can support more than one type of document, and documents of different types can be open at the same time. Your application has one document template for each document type that it supports. For example, if your MDI application supports both spreadsheets and text documents, the application has two **CMultiDocTemplate** objects.

The application uses the document template(s) when the user creates a new document. If the application supports more than one type of document, then the framework gets the names of the supported document types from the document templates and displays them in a list in the File New dialog box. Once the user has selected a document type, the application creates a document class object, a frame window object, and a view object and attaches them to each other.

You do not need to call any member functions of **CMultiDocTemplate** except the constructor. The framework handles **CMultiDocTemplate** objects internally.

For more information on **CMultiDocTemplate**, see "Document Templates and the Document/View Creation Process" in *Visual C++ Programmer's Guide* online.

include# <afxwin.h>

See Also: **CDocTemplate**, **CSingleDocTemplate**, **CWinApp**

CMultiDocTemplate Class Members

Construction

CMultiDocTemplate	Constructs a **CMultiDocTemplate** object.

Member Functions

CMultiDocTemplate::CMultiDocTemplate

CMultiDocTemplate(**UINT** *nIDResource*, **CRuntimeClass*** *pDocClass*,
↪ **CRuntimeClass*** *pFrameClass*, **CRuntimeClass*** *pViewClass*);

Parameters

   nIDResource   Specifies the ID of the resources used with the document type.
   This may include menu, icon, accelerator table, and string resources.

   The string resource consists of up to seven substrings separated by the
   '\n' character (the '\n' character is needed as a place holder if a substring
   is not included; however, trailing '\n' characters are not necessary); these
   substrings describe the document type. For information on the substrings,
   see **CDocTemplate::GetDocString**. This string resource is found in the
   application's resource file. For example:

```
// MYCALC.RC
STRINGTABLE PRELOAD DISCARDABLE
BEGIN
   IDR_SHEETTYPE "\nSheet\nWorksheet\nWorksheets (*.myc)\n.myc\n
   ↪ MyCalcSheet\nMyCalc Worksheet"
END
```

   Note that the string begins with a '\n' character; this is because the first substring
   is not used for MDI applications and so is not included. You can edit this string
   using the string editor; the entire string appears as a single entry in the String
   Editor, not as seven separate entries.

   For more information about these resource types, see "Resource Editors" in the
   Developer Studio User's Guide online.

   pDocClass   Points to the **CRuntimeClass** object of the document class. This class is
   a **CDocument**-derived class you define to represent your documents.

   pFrameClass   Points to the **CRuntimeClass** object of the frame-window class. This
   class can be a **CMDIChildWnd**-derived class, or it can be **CMDIChildWnd** itself
   if you want default behavior for your document frame windows.

pViewClass   Points to the **CRuntimeClass** object of the view class. This class is a **CView**-derived class you define to display your documents.

Remarks

Constructs a **CMultiDocTemplate** object. Dynamically allocate one **CMultiDocTemplate** object for each document type that your application supports and pass each one to **CWinApp::AddDocTemplate** from the `InitInstance` member function of your application class.

Example

```
//example for CMultiDocTemplate
BOOL CMyApp::InitInstance()
{
    // ...
    // Establish all of the document types
    // supported by the application

    AddDocTemplate( new CMultiDocTemplate( IDR_SHEETTYPE,
                    RUNTIME_CLASS( CSheetDoc ),
                    RUNTIME_CLASS( CMDIChildWnd ),
                    RUNTIME_CLASS( CSheetView ) ) );

    AddDocTemplate( new CMultiDocTemplate( IDR_NOTETYPE,
                    RUNTIME_CLASS( CNoteDoc ),
                    RUNTIME_CLASS( CMDIChildWnd ),
                    RUNTIME_CLASS( CNoteView ) ) );
    // ...
}
```

See Also: **CDocTemplate::GetDocString, CWinApp::AddDocTemplate, CWinApp::InitInstance, CRuntimeClass**

CMultiLock

CMultiLock does not have a base class.

A object of class **CMultiLock** represents the access-control mechanism used in controlling access to resources in a multithreaded program. To use the synchronization classes **CSemaphore**, **CMutex**, **CCriticalSection**, and **CEvent**, you can create either a **CMultiLock** or **CSingleLock** object to wait on and release the synchronization object. Use **CMultiLock** when there are multiple objects that you could use at a particular time. Use **CSingleLock** when you only need to wait on one object at a time.

To use a **CMultiLock** object, first create an array of the synchronization objects that you wish to wait on. Next, call the **CMultiLock** object's constructor inside a member function in the controlled resource's class. Then call the **Lock** member function to determine if a resource is available (signaled). If one is, continue with the remainder of the member function. If no resource is available, either wait for a specified amount of time for a resource to be released, or return failure. After use of a resource is complete, either call the **Unlock** function if the **CMultiLock** object is to be used again, or allow the **CMultiLock** object to be destroyed.

CMultiLock objects are most useful when a thread has a large number of **CEvent** objects it can respond to. Create an array containing all the **CEvent** pointers, and call **Lock**. This will cause the thread to wait until one of the events is signaled.

For more information on how to use **CMultiLock** objects, see the article "Multithreading: How to Use the Synchronization Classes" in *Visual C++ Programmer's Guide* online.

#include <afxmt.h>

CMultiLock Class Members

Construction

CMultiLock	Constructs a **CMultiLock** object.

Methods

IsLocked	Determines if a specific synchronization object in the array is locked.
Lock	Waits on the array of synchronization objects.
Unlock	Releases any owned synchronization objects.

Member Functions
CMultiLock::CMultiLock

CMultiLock(CSyncObject* *ppObjects*[ ]**, DWORD** *dwCount*,
↳ **BOOL** *bInitialLock* = **FALSE**);

Parameters

ppObjects   Array of pointers to the synchronization objects to be waited on. Cannot be **NULL**.

dwCount   Number of objects in *ppObjects*. Must be greater than 0.

bInitialLock   Specifies whether to initially attempt to access any of the supplied objects.

Remarks

Constructs a **CMultiLock** object. This function is called after creating the array of synchronization objects to be waited on. It is usually called from within the thread that must wait for one of the synchronization objects to become available.

CMultiLock::IsLocked

BOOL IsLocked(DWORD *dwObject*);

Return Value

Nonzero if the specified object is locked; otherwise 0.

Parameters

dwObject   The index in the array of objects corresponding to the object whose state is being queried.

Remarks

Determines if the specified object is nonsignaled (unavailable).

CMultiLock::Lock

DWORD Lock(DWORD *dwTimeOut* = **INFINITE,**
↳ **BOOL** *bWaitForAll* = **TRUE, DWORD** *dwWakeMask* = **0**);

Return Value

If **Lock** fails, it returns −1. If successful, it returns one of the following values:

- Between **WAIT_OBJECT_0** and **WAIT_OBJECT_0** + (number of objects − 1)

If *bWaitForAll* is **TRUE**, all objects are signaled (available). If *bWaitForAll* is **FALSE**, the return value – **WAIT_OBJECT_0** is the index in the array of objects of the object that is signaled (available).

- **WAIT_OBJECT_0** + (number of objects)

  An event specified in *dwWakeMask* is available in the thread's input queue.

- Between **WAIT_ABANDONED_0** and **WAIT_ABANDONED_0** + (number of objects – 1)

  If *bWaitForAll* is **TRUE**, all objects are signaled, and at least one of the objects is an abandoned mutex object. If *bWaitForAll* is **FALSE**, the return value – **WAIT_ABANDONED_0** is the index in the array of objects of the abandoned mutex object that satisfied the wait.

- **WAIT_TIMEOUT**

  The timeout interval specified in *dwTimeOut* expired without the wait succeeding.

Parameters

dwTimeOut   Specifies the amount of time to wait for the synchronization object to be available (signaled). If **INFINITE**, **Lock** will wait until the object is signaled before returning.

bWaitForAll   Specifies whether all objects waited on must become signaled at the same time before returning. If **FALSE**, **Lock** will return when any one of the objects waited on is signaled.

dwWakeMask   Specifies other conditions that are allowed to abort the wait. For a full list of the available options for this parameter, see **MsgWaitForMultipleObjects** in the *Win32 Programmer's Reference*.

Remarks

Call this function to gain access to one or more of the resources controlled by the synchronization objects supplied to the **CMultiLock** constructor. If *bWaitForAll* is **TRUE**, **Lock** will return successfully as soon as all the synchronization objects become signaled simultaneously. If *bWaitForAll* is **FALSE**, **Lock** will return as soon as one or more of the synchronization objects becomes signaled.

If **Lock** is not able to return immediately, it will wait for no more than the number of milliseconds specified in the *dwTimeOut* parameter before returning. If *dwTimeOut* is **INFINITE**, **Lock** will not return until access to an object is gained or a condition specified in *dwWakeMask* was met. Otherwise, if **Lock** was able to acquire a synchronization object, it will return successfully; if not, it will return failure.

CMultiLock::Unlock

BOOL Unlock( );
BOOL Unlock(LONG *lCount*, **LPLONG** *lPrevCount* = **NULL**);

Return Value

Nonzero if the function was successful; otherwise 0.

Parameters

lCount   Number of reference counts to release. Must be greater than 0. If the specified amount would cause the object's count to exceed its maximum, the count is not changed and the function returns **FALSE**.

lPrevCount   Points to a variable to receive the previous count for the synchronization object. If **NULL**, the previous count is not returned.

Remarks

Releases the synchronization object owned by **CMultiLock**. This function is called by **CMultiLock**'s destructor.

The first form of **Unlock** tries to unlock the synchronization object managed by **CMultiLock**. The second form of **Unlock** tries to unlock the **CSemaphore** objects owned by **CMultiLock**. If **CMultiLock** does not own any locked **CSemaphore** object, the function returns **FALSE**; otherwise, it returns **TRUE**. *lCount* and *lpPrevCount* are exactly the same as the parameters of **CSingleLock::Unlock**. The second form of **Unlock** is rarely applicable to multilock situations.

CMutex

An object of class **CMutex** represents a "mutex"—a synchronization object that allows one thread mutually exclusive access to a resource. Mutexes are useful when only one thread at a time can be allowed to modify data or some other controlled resource. For example, adding nodes to a linked list is a process that should only be allowed by one thread at a time. By using a **CMutex** object to control the linked list, only one thread at a time can gain access to the list.

To use a **CMutex** object, construct the **CMutex** object when it is needed. Specify the name of the mutex you wish to wait on, and that your application should initially own it. You can then access the mutex when the constructor returns. Call **CSyncObject::Unlock** when you are done accessing the controlled resource.

An alternative method for using **CMutex** objects is to add a variable of type **CMutex** as a data member to the class you wish to control. During construction of the controlled object, call the constructor of the **CMutex** data member specifying if the mutex is initially owned, the name of the mutex (if it will be used across process boundaries), and desired security attributes.

To access resources controlled by **CMutex** objects in this manner, first create a variable of either type **CSingleLock** or type **CMultiLock** in your resource's access member function. Then call the lock object's **Lock** member function (for example, **CSingleLock::Lock**). At this point, your thread will either gain access to the resource, wait for the resource to be released and gain access, or wait for the resource to be released and time out, failing to gain access to the resource. In any case, your resource has been accessed in a thread-safe manner. To release the resource, use the lock object's **Unlock** member function (for example, **CSingleLock::Unlock**), or allow the lock object to fall out of scope.

For more information on using **CMutex** objects, see the article "Multithreading: How to Use the Synchronization Classes" in *Visual C++ Programmer's Guide* online.

#include <afxmt.h>

CMutex Class Members

CMutex   Constructs a **CMutex** object.

Member Functions
CMutex::CMutex

CMutex(BOOL *bInitiallyOwn* **= FALSE, LPCTSTR** *lpszName* **= NULL,**
↳ LPSECURITY_ATTRIBUTES *lpsaAttribute* **= NULL);**

Parameters

bInitiallyOwn   Specifies if the thread creating the **CMutex** object initially has access to the resource controlled by the mutex.

lpszName   Name of the **CMutex** object. If another mutex with the same name exists, *lpszName* must be supplied if the object will be used across process boundaries. If **NULL**, the mutex will be unnamed. If the name matches an existing mutex, the constructor builds a new **CMutex** object which references the mutex of that name. If the name matches an existing synchronization object that is not a mutex, the construction will fail.

lpsaAttribute   Security attributes for the mutex object. For a full description of this structure, see **SECURITY_ATTRIBUTES** in the *Win32 Programmer's Reference*.

Remarks

Constructs a named or unnamed **CMutex** object. To access or release a **CMutex** object, create a **CMultiLock** or **CSingleLock** object and call its **Lock** and **Unlock** member functions. If the **CMutex** object is being used stand-alone, call its **Unlock** member function to release it.

CNotSupportedException

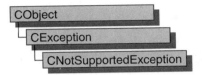

A **CNotSupportedException** object represents an exception that is the result of a request for an unsupported feature. No further qualification is necessary or possible.

For more information on using **CNotSupportedException**, see the article "Exceptions" in *Visual C++ Programmer's Guide* online.

#include <afx.h>

CNotSupportedException Class Members

Construction

CNotSupportedException	Constructs a **CNotSupportedException** object.

Member Functions
CNotSupportedException::CNotSupportedException

CNotSupportedException( );

Remarks

Constructs a **CNotSupportedException** object.

Do not use this constructor directly, but rather call the global function **AfxThrowNotSupportedException**. For more information about exception processing, see the article "Exceptions" in *Visual C++ Programmer's Guide* online.

See Also: **AfxThrowNotSupportedException**

CObArray

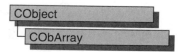

The **CObArray** class supports arrays of **CObject** pointers. These object arrays are similar to C arrays, but they can dynamically shrink and grow as necessary.

Array indexes always start at position 0. You can decide whether to fix the upper bound or allow the array to expand when you add elements past the current bound. Memory is allocated contiguously to the upper bound, even if some elements are null.

Under Win32, the size of a **CObArray** object is limited only to available memory.

As with a C array, the access time for a **CObArray** indexed element is constant and is independent of the array size.

CObArray incorporates the **IMPLEMENT_SERIAL** macro to support serialization and dumping of its elements. If an array of **CObject** pointers is stored to an archive, either with the overloaded insertion operator or with the **Serialize** member function, each **CObject** element is, in turn, serialized along with its array index.

If you need a dump of individual **CObject** elements in an array, you must set the depth of the **CDumpContext** object to 1 or greater.

When a **CObArray** object is deleted, or when its elements are removed, only the **CObject** pointers are removed, not the objects they reference.

Note Before using an array, use **SetSize** to establish its size and allocate memory for it. If you do not use **SetSize**, adding elements to your array causes it to be frequently reallocated and copied. Frequent reallocation and copying are inefficient and can fragment memory.

Array class derivation is similar to list derivation. For details on the derivation of a special-purpose list class, see the article "Collections" in *Visual C++ Programmer's Guide* online.

Note You must use the **IMPLEMENT_SERIAL** macro in the implementation of your derived class if you intend to serialize the array.

#include <afxcoll.h>

See Also: CStringArray, CPtrArray, CByteArray, CWordArray, CDWordArray

CObArray Class Members

Construction

CObArray	Constructs an empty array for **CObject** pointers.

Bounds

GetSize	Gets the number of elements in this array.
GetUpperBound	Returns the largest valid index.
SetSize	Sets the number of elements to be contained in this array.

Operations

FreeExtra	Frees all unused memory above the current upper bound.
RemoveAll	Removes all the elements from this array.

Element Access

GetAt	Returns the value at a given index.
SetAt	Sets the value for a given index; array not allowed to grow.
ElementAt	Returns a temporary reference to the element pointer within the array.
GetData	Allows access to elements in the array. Can be **NULL**.

Growing the Array

SetAtGrow	Sets the value for a given index; grows the array if necessary.
Add	Adds an element to the end of the array; grows the array if necessary.
Append	Appends another array to the array; grows the array if necessary.
Copy	Copies another array to the array; grows the array if necessary.

Insertion/Removal

InsertAt	Inserts an element (or all the elements in another array) at a specified index.
RemoveAt	Removes an element at a specific index.

Operators

operator []	Sets or gets the element at the specified index.

Member Functions
CObArray::Add

int Add(CObject* *newElement* **);**
   throw(CMemoryException);

Return Value

The index of the added element.

Parameters

newElement The **CObject** pointer to be added to this array.

Remarks

Adds a new element to the end of an array, growing the array by 1. If **SetSize** has been used with an *nGrowBy* value greater than 1, then extra memory may be allocated. However, the upper bound will increase by only 1.

The following table shows other member functions that are similar to **CObArray::Add**.

Class	Member Function
CByteArray	**int Add(BYTE** *newElement* **);** **throw(CMemoryException);**
CDWordArray	**int Add(DWORD** *newElement* **);** **throw(CMemoryException);**
CPtrArray	**int Add(void*** *newElement* **);** **throw(CMemoryException);**
CStringArray	**int Add(LPCTSTR** *newElement* **);** **throw(CMemoryException);**
CUIntArray	**int Add(UINT** *newElement* **);** **throw(CMemoryException);**
CWordArray	**int Add(WORD** *newElement* **);** **throw(CMemoryException);**

Example

See **CObList::CObList** for a listing of the CAge class used in all collection examples.

```
// example for CObArray::Add

   CObArray array;

   array.Add( new CAge( 21 ) ); // Element 0
   array.Add( new CAge( 40 ) ); // Element 1
#ifdef _DEBUG
   afxDump.SetDepth( 1 );
   afxDump << "Add example: " << &array << "\n";
#endif
```

The results from this program are as follows:

```
Add example: A CObArray with 2 elements
    [0] = a CAge at $442A 21
    [1] = a CAge at $4468 40
```

See Also: **CObArray::SetAt**, **CObArray::SetAtGrow**, **CObArray::InsertAt**, **CObArray::operator []**

CObArray::Append

int Append(const CObArray& *src* **);**

Return Value

The index of the first appended element.

Parameters

src   Source of the elements to be appended to the array.

Remarks

Call this member function to add the contents of another array to the end of the given array. The arrays must be of the same type.

If necessary, **Append** may allocate extra memory to accommodate the elements appended to the array.

The following table shows other member functions that are similar to **CObArray::Append**.

Class	Member Function
CByteArray	**int Append(const CByteArray&** *src* **);**
CDWordArray	**int Append(const CDWordArray&** *src* **);**
CPtrArray	**int Append(const CPtrArray&** *src* **);**
CStringArray	**int Append(const CStringArray&** *src* **);**
CUIntArray	**int Append(const CUIntArray&** *src* **);**
CWordArray	**int Append(const CWordArray&** *src* **);**

See Also: **CObArray::Copy**

CObArray::Copy

void Copy(const CObArray& *src* **);**

Parameters

src   Source of the elements to be copied to the array.

Remarks

Call this member function to overwrite the elements of the given array with the elements of another array of the same type.

Copy does not free memory; however, if necessary, **Copy** may allocate extra memory to accommodate the elements copied to the array.

The following table shows other member functions that are similar to **CObArray::Copy**.

Class	Member Function
CByteArray	**void Copy(const CByteArray&** *src* **);**
CDWordArray	**void Copy(const CDWordArray&** *src* **);**
CPtrArray	**void Copy(const CPtrArray&** *src* **);**
CStringArray	**void Copy(const CStringArray&** *src* **);**
CUIntArray	**void Copy(const CUIntArray&** *src* **);**
CWordArray	**void Copy(const CWordArray&** *src* **);**

See Also: **CObArray::Append**

CObArray::CObArray

CObArray( );

Remarks

Constructs an empty **CObject** pointer array. The array grows one element at a time.

The following table shows other constructors that are similar to **CObArray::CObArray**.

Class	Constructor
CByteArray	**CByteArray( );**
CDWordArray	**CDWordArray( );**
CPtrArray	**CPtrArray( );**
CStringArray	**CStringArray( );**
CUIntArray	**CUIntArray( );**
CWordArray	**CWordArray( );**

Example

```
CObArray array; //Array with default blocksize
CObArray* pArray = new CObArray; //Array on the heap with default blocksize
```

See Also: **CObList::CObList**

CObArray::ElementAt

CObject*& ElementAt(int *nIndex* **);**

Return Value

A reference to a **CObject** pointer.

Parameters

nIndex An integer index that is greater than or equal to 0 and less than or equal to the value returned by **GetUpperBound**.

Remarks

Returns a temporary reference to the element pointer within the array. It is used to implement the left-side assignment operator for arrays. Note that this is an advanced function that should be used only to implement special array operators.

The following table shows other member functions that are similar to **CObArray::ElementAt**.

Class	Member Function
CByteArray	**BYTE& ElementAt(int** *nIndex* **);**
CDWordArray	**DWORD& ElementAt(int** *nIndex* **);**
CPtrArray	**void*& ElementAt(int** *nIndex* **);**
CStringArray	**CString& ElementAt(int** *nIndex* **);**
CUIntArray	**UINT& ElementAt(int** *nIndex* **);**
CWordArray	**WORD& ElementAt(int** *nIndex* **);**

See Also: **CObArray::operator []**

CObArray::FreeExtra

void FreeExtra( );

Remarks

Frees any extra memory that was allocated while the array was grown. This function has no effect on the size or upper bound of the array.

The following table shows other member functions that are similar to **CObArray::FreeExtra**.

Class	Member Function
CByteArray	**void FreeExtra( );**
CDWordArray	**void FreeExtra( );**
CPtrArray	**void FreeExtra( );**
CStringArray	**void FreeExtra( );**
CUIntArray	**void FreeExtra( );**
CWordArray	**void FreeExtra( );**

CObArray::GetAt

CObject* GetAt(int *nIndex* **) const;**

Return Value

The **CObject** pointer element currently at this index.

Parameters

nIndex   An integer index that is greater than or equal to 0 and less than or equal to the value returned by **GetUpperBound**.

Remarks

Returns the array element at the specified index.

Note   Passing a negative value or a value greater than the value returned by **GetUpperBound** will result in a failed assertion.

The following table shows other member functions that are similar to **CObArray::GetAt**.

Class	Member Function
CByteArray	**BYTE GetAt(int** *nIndex* **) const;**
CDWordArray	**DWORD GetAt(int** *nIndex* **) const;**
CPtrArray	**void* GetAt(int** *nIndex* **) const;**
CStringArray	**CString GetAt(int** *nIndex* **) const;**
CUIntArray	**UINT GetAt(int** *nIndex* **) const;**
CWordArray	**WORD GetAt(int** *nIndex* **) const;**

Example

See **CObList::CObList** for a listing of the CAge class used in all collection examples.

```
// example for CObArray::GetAt

CObArray array;

array.Add( new CAge( 21 ) ); // Element 0
array.Add( new CAge( 40 ) ); // Element 1
ASSERT( *(CAge*) array.GetAt( 0 ) == CAge( 21 ) );
```

See Also: **CObArray::SetAt, CObArray::operator []**

CObArray::GetData

const CObject** GetData( ) const;
CObject** GetData( );

Return Value

A pointer to the array of **CObject** pointers.

Remarks

Use this member function to gain direct access to the elements in the array. If no elements are available, **GetData** returns a null value.

While direct access to the elements of an array can help you work more quickly, use caution when calling **GetData**; any errors you make directly affect the elements of your array.

The following table shows other member functions that are similar to **CObArray::GetData**.

Class	Member Function
CByteArray	**const BYTE* GetData( ) const;** **BYTE* GetData( );**
CDWordArray	**const DWORD* GetData( ) const;** **DWORD* GetData( );**
CPtrArray	**const void** GetData( ) const;** **void** GetData( );**
CStringArray	**const CString* GetData( ) const;** **CString* GetData( );**
CUIntArray	**const UINT* GetData( ) const;** **UINT* GetData( );**
CWordArray	**const WORD* GetData( ) const;** **WORD* GetData( );**

See Also: **CObArray::GetAt**, **CObArray::SetAt**, **CObArray::ElementAt**

CObArray::GetSize

int GetSize( ) const;

Remarks

Returns the size of the array. Since indexes are zero-based, the size is 1 greater than the largest index.

The following table shows other member functions that are similar to **CObArray::GetSize**.

Class	Member Function
CByteArray	**int GetSize( ) const;**
CDWordArray	**int GetSize( ) const;**
CPtrArray	**int GetSize( ) const;**
CStringArray	**int GetSize( ) const;**
CUIntArray	**int GetSize( ) const;**
CWordArray	**int GetSize( ) const;**

See Also: **CObArray::GetUpperBound**, **CObArray::SetSize**

CObArray::GetUpperBound

int GetUpperBound( ) const;

Return Value

The index of the upper bound (zero-based).

Remarks

Returns the current upper bound of this array. Because array indexes are zero-based, this function returns a value 1 less than **GetSize**.

The condition **GetUpperBound( ) = –1** indicates that the array contains no elements.

The following table shows other member functions that are similar to **CObArray::GetUpperBound**.

Class	Member Function
CByteArray	**int GetUpperBound( ) const;**
CDWordArray	**int GetUpperBound( ) const;**
CPtrArray	**int GetUpperBound( ) const;**
CStringArray	**int GetUpperBound( ) const;**
CUIntArray	**int GetUpperBound( ) const;**
CWordArray	**int GetUpperBound( ) const;**

Example

See **CObList::CObList** for a listing of the CAge class used in all collection examples.

```
// example for CObArray::GetUpperBound

CObArray array;

array.Add( new CAge( 21 ) ); // Element 0
array.Add( new CAge( 40 ) ); // Element 1
ASSERT( array.GetUpperBound() == 1 ); // Largest index
```

See Also: **CObArray::GetSize**, **CObArray::SetSize**

CObArray::InsertAt

void InsertAt(int *nIndex***, CObject*** *newElement***, int** *nCount* **= 1);**
    throw(CMemoryException);
void InsertAt(int *nStartIndex***, CObArray*** *pNewArray* **);**
    throw(CMemoryException);

Parameters

nIndex   An integer index that may be greater than the value returned by **GetUpperBound**.

newElement   The **CObject** pointer to be placed in this array. A *newElement* of value **NULL** is allowed.

nCount   The number of times this element should be inserted (defaults to 1).

nStartIndex   An integer index that may be greater than the value returned by **GetUpperBound**.

pNewArray   Another array that contains elements to be added to this array.

Remarks

The first version of **InsertAt** inserts one element (or multiple copies of an element) at a specified index in an array. In the process, it shifts up (by incrementing the index) the existing element at this index, and it shifts up all the elements above it.

The second version inserts all the elements from another **CObArray** collection, starting at the *nStartIndex* position.

The **SetAt** function, in contrast, replaces one specified array element and does not shift any elements.

The following table shows other member functions that are similar to **CObArray::InsertAt**.

Class	Member Function
CByteArray	**void InsertAt(int** *nIndex,* **BYTE** *newElement,* **int** *nCount* **= 1);** **throw(CMemoryException);**
	void InsertAt(int *nStartIndex,* **CByteArray*** *pNewArray* **);** **throw(CMemoryException);**
CDWordArray	**void InsertAt(int** *nIndex,* **DWORD** *newElement,* **int** *nCount* **= 1);** **throw(CMemoryException);**
	void InsertAt(int *nStartIndex,* **CDWordArray*** *pNewArray* **);** **throw(CMemoryException);**
CPtrArray	**void InsertAt(int** *nIndex,* **void*** *newElement,* **int** *nCount* **= 1);** **throw(CMemoryException);**
	void InsertAt(int *nStartIndex,* **CPtrArray*** *pNewArray* **);** **throw(CMemoryException);**
CStringArray	**void InsertAt(int** *nIndex,* **LPCTSTR** *newElement,* **int** *nCount* **= 1);** **throw(CMemoryException);**
	void InsertAt(int *nStartIndex,* **CStringArray*** *pNewArray* **);** **throw(CMemoryException);**
CUIntArray	**void InsertAt(int** *nIndex,* **UINT** *newElement,* **int** *nCount* **= 1);** **throw(CMemoryException);**
	void InsertAt(int *nStartIndex,* **CUIntArray*** *pNewArray* **);** **throw(CMemoryException);**
CWordArray	**void InsertAt(int** *nIndex,* **WORD** *newElement,* **int** *nCount* **= 1);** **throw(CMemoryException);**
	void InsertAt(int *nStartIndex,* **CWordArray*** *pNewArray* **);** **throw(CMemoryException);**

Example

See **CObList::CObList** for a listing of the CAge class used in all collection examples.

```
// example for CObArray::InsertAt

    CObArray array;

    array.Add( new CAge( 21 ) ); // Element 0
    array.Add( new CAge( 40 ) ); // Element 1 (will become 2).
    array.InsertAt( 1, new CAge( 30 ) );  // New element 1
#ifdef _DEBUG
    afxDump.SetDepth( 1 );
    afxDump << "InsertAt example: " << &array << "\n";
#endif
```

The results from this program are as follows:

```
InsertAt example: A CObArray with 3 elements
    [0] = a CAge at $45C8 21
    [1] = a CAge at $4646 30
    [2] = a CAge at $4606 40
```

See Also: **CObArray::SetAt**, **CObArray::RemoveAt**

CObArray::RemoveAll

void RemoveAll( );

Remarks

Removes all the pointers from this array but does not actually delete the **CObject** objects. If the array is already empty, the function still works.

The **RemoveAll** function frees all memory used for pointer storage.

The following table shows other member functions that are similar to **CObArray::RemoveAll**.

Class	Member Function
CByteArray	**void RemoveAll( );**
CDWordArray	**void RemoveAll( );**
CPtrArray	**void RemoveAll( );**
CStringArray	**void RemoveAll( );**
CUIntArray	**void RemoveAll( );**
CWordArray	**void RemoveAll( );**

Example

See **CObList::CObList** for a listing of the CAge class used in all collection examples.

```
// example for CObArray::RemoveAll
```

```
CObArray array;
CAge* pa1;
CAge* pa2;

array.Add( pa1 = new CAge( 21 ) ); // Element 0
array.Add( pa2 = new CAge( 40 ) ); // Element 1
ASSERT( array.GetSize() == 2 );
array.RemoveAll(); // Pointers removed but objects not deleted.
ASSERT( array.GetSize() == 0 );
delete pa1;
delete pa2;  // Cleans up memory.
```

CObArray::RemoveAt

void RemoveAt(int *nIndex***, int** *nCount* **= 1);**

Parameters

nIndex   An integer index that is greater than or equal to 0 and less than or equal to the value returned by **GetUpperBound**.

nCount   The number of elements to remove.

Remarks

Removes one or more elements starting at a specified index in an array. In the process, it shifts down all the elements above the removed element(s). It decrements the upper bound of the array but does not free memory.

If you try to remove more elements than are contained in the array above the removal point, then the Debug version of the library asserts.

The **RemoveAt** function removes the **CObject** pointer from the array, but it does not delete the object itself.

The following table shows other member functions that are similar to **CObArray::RemoveAt**.

Class	Member Function
CByteArray	**void RemoveAt(int** *nIndex***, int** *nCount* **= 1);**
CDWordArray	**void RemoveAt(int** *nIndex***, int** *nCount* **= 1);**
CPtrArray	**void RemoveAt(int** *nIndex***, int** *nCount* **= 1);**
CStringArray	**void RemoveAt(int** *nIndex***, int** *nCount* **= 1);**
CUIntArray	**void RemoveAt(int** *nIndex***, int** *nCount* **= 1);**
CWordArray	**void RemoveAt(int** *nIndex***, int** *nCount* **= 1);**

Example

See **CObList::CObList** for a listing of the CAge class used in all collection examples.

```
// example for CObArray::RemoveAt

    CObArray array;
    CObject* pa;

    array.Add( new CAge( 21 ) ); // Element 0
    array.Add( new CAge( 40 ) ); // Element 1
    if( ( pa = array.GetAt( 0 ) ) ) != NULL )
    {
        array.RemoveAt( 0 );   // Element 1 moves to 0.
        delete pa; // Delete the original element at 0.
    }
#ifdef _DEBUG
    afxDump.SetDepth( 1 );
    afxDump << "RemoveAt example: " << &array << "\n";
#endif
```

The results from this program are as follows:

```
RemoveAt example: A CObArray with 1 elements
    [0] = a CAge at $4606 40
```

See Also: **CObArray::SetAt, CObArray::SetAtGrow, CObArray::InsertAt**

CObArray::SetAt

void SetAt(int *nIndex***, CObject*** *newElement* **);**

Parameters

nIndex   An integer index that is greater than or equal to 0 and less than or equal to the value returned by **GetUpperBound**.

newElement   The object pointer to be inserted in this array. A **NULL** value is allowed.

Remarks

Sets the array element at the specified index. **SetAt** will not cause the array to grow. Use **SetAtGrow** if you want the array to grow automatically.

You must ensure that your index value represents a valid position in the array. If it is out of bounds, then the Debug version of the library asserts.

The following table shows other member functions that are similar to **CObArray::SetAt**.

Class	Member Function
CByteArray	**void SetAt(int** *nIndex*, **BYTE** *newElement* **);**
CDWordArray	**void SetAt(int** *nIndex*, **DWORD** *newElement* **);**

(continued)

Class	Member Function
CPtrArray	**void SetAt(int** *nIndex,* **void*** *newElement* **);**
CStringArray	**void SetAt(int** *nIndex,* **LPCTSTR** *newElement* **);**
CUIntArray	**void SetAt(int** *nIndex,* **UINT** *newElement* **);**
CWordArray	**void SetAt(int** *nIndex,* **WORD** *newElement* **);**

Example

See **CObList::CObList** for a listing of the CAge class used in all collection examples.

```
// example for CObArray::SetAt

    CObArray array;
    CObject* pa;

    array.Add( new CAge( 21 ) ); // Element 0
    array.Add( new CAge( 40 ) ); // Element 1
    if( ( pa = array.GetAt( 0 ) ) ) != NULL )
    {
        array.SetAt( 0, new CAge( 30 ) );  // Replace element 0.
        delete pa; // Delete the original element at 0.
    }
#ifdef _DEBUG
    afxDump.SetDepth( 1 );
    afxDump << "SetAt example: " << &array << "\n";
#endif
```

The results from this program are as follows:

```
SetAt example: A CObArray with 2 elements
    [0] = a CAge at $47E0 30
    [1] = a CAge at $47A0 40
```

See Also: **CObArray::GetAt**, **CObArray::SetAtGrow**, **CObArray::ElementAt**, **CObArray::operator []**

CObArray::SetAtGrow

> **void SetAtGrow(int** *nIndex,* **CObject*** *newElement* **);**
>   **throw(CMemoryException);**

Parameters

nIndex   An integer index that is greater than or equal to 0.

newElement   The object pointer to be added to this array. A **NULL** value is allowed.

Remarks

Sets the array element at the specified index. The array grows automatically if necessary (that is, the upper bound is adjusted to accommodate the new element).

The following table shows other member functions that are similar to
CObArray::SetAtGrow.

Class	Member Function
CByteArray	**void SetAtGrow(int** *nIndex*, **BYTE** *newElement* **);** **throw(CMemoryException);**
CDWordArray	**void SetAtGrow(int** *nIndex*, **DWORD** *newElement* **);** **throw(CMemoryException);**
CPtrArray	**void SetAtGrow(int** *nIndex*, **void*** *newElement* **);** **throw(CMemoryException);**
CStringArray	**void SetAtGrow(int** *nIndex*, **LPCTSTR** *newElement* **);** **throw(CMemoryException);**
CUIntArray	**void SetAtGrow(int** *nIndex*, **UINT** *newElement* **);** **throw(CMemoryException);**
CWordArray	**void SetAtGrow(int** *nIndex*, **WORD** *newElement* **);** **throw(CMemoryException);**

Example

See **CObList::CObList** for a listing of the CAge class used in all collection
examples.

```
// example for CObArray::SetAtGrow

    CObArray array;

    array.Add( new CAge( 21 ) ); // Element 0
    array.Add( new CAge( 40 ) ); // Element 1
    array.SetAtGrow( 3, new CAge( 65 ) ); // Element 2 deliberately
                                          // skipped.
#ifdef _DEBUG
    afxDump.SetDepth( 1 );
    afxDump << "SetAtGrow example: " << &array << "\n";
#endif
```

The results from this program are as follows:

```
SetAtGrow example: A CObArray with 4 elements
    [0] = a CAge at $47C0 21
    [1] = a CAge at $4800 40
    [2] = NULL
    [3] = a CAge at $4840 65
```

See Also: **CObArray::GetAt**, **CObArray::SetAt**, **CObArray::ElementAt**,
CObArray::operator []

CObArray::SetSize

void SetSize(int *nNewSize*, **int** *nGrowBy* **= –1);**
    throw(CMemoryException);

Parameters

nNewSize   The new array size (number of elements). Must be greater than or equal to 0.

nGrowBy   The minimum number of element slots to allocate if a size increase is necessary.

Remarks

Establishes the size of an empty or existing array; allocates memory if necessary. If the new size is smaller than the old size, then the array is truncated and all unused memory is released. For efficiency, call **SetSize** to set the size of the array before using it. This prevents the need to reallocate and copy the array each time an item is added.

The *nGrowBy* parameter affects internal memory allocation while the array is growing. Its use never affects the array size as reported by **GetSize** and **GetUpperBound**.

The following table shows other member functions that are similar to **CObArray::SetSize**.

Class	Member Function
CByteArray	**void SetSize(int** *nNewSize*, **int** *nGrowBy* **= –1);** **throw(CMemoryException);**
CDWordArray	**void SetSize(int** *nNewSize*, **int** *nGrowBy* **= –1);** **throw(CMemoryException);**
CPtrArray	**void SetSize(int** *nNewSize*, **int** *nGrowBy* **= –1);** **throw(CMemoryException);**
CStringArray	**void SetSize(int** *nNewSize*, **int** *nGrowBy* **= –1);** **throw(CMemoryException);**
CUIntArray	**void SetSize(int** *nNewSize*, **int** *nGrowBy* **= –1);** **throw(CMemoryException);**
CWordArray	**void SetSize(int** *nNewSize*, **int** *nGrowBy* **= –1);** **throw(CMemoryException);**

Operators
CObArray::operator [ ]

CObject*& operator [](int *nIndex* **);**
CObject* operator [](int *nIndex* **) const;**

Remarks

These subscript operators are a convenient substitute for the **SetAt** and **GetAt** functions.

The first operator, called for arrays that are not **const**, may be used on either the right (r-value) or the left (l-value) of an assignment statement. The second, called for **const** arrays, may be used only on the right.

The Debug version of the library asserts if the subscript (either on the left or right side of an assignment statement) is out of bounds.

The following table shows other operators that are similar to **CObArray::operator []**.

Class	Operator
CByteArray	**BYTE& operator [](int** *nIndex* **);** **BYTE operator [](int** *nIndex* **) const;**
CDWordArray	**DWORD& operator [](int** *nIndex* **);** **DWORD operator [](int** *nIndex* **) const;**
CPtrArray	**void*& operator [](int** *nIndex* **);** **void* operator [](int** *nIndex* **) const;**
CStringArray	**CString& operator [](int** *nIndex* **);** **CString operator [](int** *nIndex* **) const;**
CUIntArray	**UINT& operator [](int** *nIndex* **);** **UINT operator [](int** *nIndex* **) const;**
CWordArray	**WORD& operator [](int** *nIndex* **);** **WORD operator [](int** *nIndex* **) const;**

Example

See **CObList::CObList** for a listing of the CAge class used in all collection examples.

```
// example for CObArray::operator []

CObArray array;
CAge* pa;

array.Add( new CAge( 21 ) ); // Element 0
array.Add( new CAge( 40 ) ); // Element 1
pa = (CAge*)array[0]; // Get element 0
ASSERT( *pa == CAge( 21 ) ); // Get element 0
array[0] = new CAge( 30 );   // Replace element 0
delete pa;
ASSERT( *(CAge*) array[0] == CAge( 30 ) ); // Get new element 0
```

See Also: **CObArray::GetAt, CObArray::SetAt**

CObject

CObject is the principal base class for the Microsoft Foundation Class Library. It serves as the root not only for library classes such as **CFile** and **CObList**, but also for the classes that you write. **CObject** provides basic services, including

- Serialization support
- Run-time class information
- Object diagnostic output
- Compatibility with collection classes

Note that **CObject** does not support multiple inheritance. Your derived classes can have only one **CObject** base class, and that **CObject** must be leftmost in the hierarchy. It is permissible, however, to have structures and non-**CObject**-derived classes in right-hand multiple-inheritance branches.

You will realize major benefits from **CObject** derivation if you use some of the optional macros in your class implementation and declarations.

The first-level macros, **DECLARE_DYNAMIC** and **IMPLEMENT_DYNAMIC**, permit run-time access to the class name and its position in the hierarchy. This, in turn, allows meaningful diagnostic dumping.

The second-level macros, **DECLARE_SERIAL** and **IMPLEMENT_SERIAL**, include all the functionality of the first-level macros, and they enable an object to be "serialized" to and from an "archive."

For information about deriving Microsoft Foundation classes and C++ classes in general and using **CObject**, see "CObject Class Topics" and "Serialization (Object Persistence)" in *Visual C++ Programmer's Guide* online.

#include <afx.h>

CObject Class Members

Construction

CObject	Default constructor.
CObject	Copy constructor.
operator new	Special **new** operator.
operator delete	Special **delete** operator.
operator =	Assignment operator.

Diagnostics

AssertValid	Validates this object's integrity.
Dump	Produces a diagnostic dump of this object.

Serialization	
IsSerializable	Tests to see whether this object can be serialized.
Serialize	Loads or stores an object from/to an archive.

Miscellaneous	
GetRuntimeClass	Returns the **CRuntimeClass** structure corresponding to this object's class.
IsKindOf	Tests this object's relationship to a given class.

Member Functions

CObject::AssertValid

virtual void AssertValid( ) const;

AssertValid performs a validity check on this object by checking its internal state. In the Debug version of the library, **AssertValid** may assert and thus terminate the program with a message that lists the line number and filename where the assertion failed.

When you write your own class, you should override the **AssertValid** function to provide diagnostic services for yourself and other users of your class. The overridden **AssertValid** usually calls the **AssertValid** function of its base class before checking data members unique to the derived class.

Because **AssertValid** is a **const** function, you are not permitted to change the object state during the test. Your own derived class **AssertValid** functions should not throw exceptions but rather should assert whether they detect invalid object data.

The definition of "validity" depends on the object's class. As a rule, the function should perform a "shallow check." That is, if an object contains pointers to other objects, it should check to see whether the pointers are not null, but it should not perform validity testing on the objects referred to by the pointers.

See **CObList::CObList** for a listing of the CAge class used in all **CObject** examples.

```
// example for CObject::AssertValid
void CAge::AssertValid() const
{
   CObject::AssertValid();
   ASSERT( m_years > 0 );
   ASSERT( m_years < 105 );
}
```

CObject::CObject

CObject( );
CObject(constCObject& *objectSrc* **);**

Parameters

> *objectSrc*   A reference to another **Cobject**

Remarks

> These functions are the standard **CObject** constructors. The default version is
> automatically called by the constructor of your derived class.

> If your class is serializable (it incorporates the **IMPLEMENT_SERIAL** macro),
> then you must have a default constructor (a constructor with no arguments) in your
> class declaration. If you do not need a default constructor, declare a private or
> protected "empty" constructor. For more information, see "CObject Class Topics"
> in *Visual C++ Programmer's Guide* online.

> The standard C++ default class copy constructor does a member-by-member copy.
> The presence of the private **CObject** copy constructor guarantees a compiler error
> message if the copy constructor of your class is needed but not available. You must
> therefore provide a copy constructor if your class requires this capability.

CObject::Dump

virtual void Dump(CDumpContext& *dc* **) const;**

Parameters

> *dc*   The diagnostic dump context for dumping, usually **afxDump**.

Remarks

> Dumps the contents of your object to a **CDumpContext** object.

> When you write your own class, you should override the **Dump** function to provide
> diagnostic services for yourself and other users of your class. The overridden **Dump**
> usually calls the **Dump** function of its base class before printing data members unique
> to the derived class. **CObject::Dump** prints the class name if your class uses the
> **IMPLEMENT_DYNAMIC** or **IMPLEMENT_SERIAL** macro.

> **Note**   Your **Dump** function should not print a newline character at the end of its output.

> **Dump** calls make sense only in the Debug version of the Microsoft Foundation Class
> Library. You should bracket calls, function declarations, and function implementations
> with **#ifdef _DEBUG/#endif** statements for conditional compilation.

> Since **Dump** is a **const** function, you are not permitted to change the object state
> during the dump.

The **CDumpContext insertion (<<) operator** calls **Dump** when a **CObject** pointer is inserted.

Dump permits only "acyclic" dumping of objects. You can dump a list of objects, for example, but if one of the objects is the list itself, you will eventually overflow the stack.

Example

See **CObList::CObList** for a listing of the CAge class used in all **CObject** examples.

```
// example for CObject::Dump
void CAge::Dump( CDumpContext &dc ) const
  {
  CObject::Dump( dc );
  dc << "Age = " << m_years;
  }
```

CObject::GetRuntimeClass

virtual CRuntimeClass* GetRuntimeClass( ) const;

Return Value

A pointer to the **CRuntimeClass** structure corresponding to this object's class; never **NULL**.

Remarks

There is one **CRuntimeClass** structure for each **CObject**-derived class. The structure members are as follows:

- **LPCSTR m_lpszClassName**   A null-terminated string containing the ASCII class name.

- **int m_nObjectSize**   The size of the object, in bytes. If the object has data members that point to allocated memory, the size of that memory is not included.

- **UINT m_wSchema**   The schema number (−1 for nonserializable classes). See the **IMPLEMENT_SERIAL** macro for a description of schema number.

- **CObject* (PASCAL* m_pfnCreateObject)( )**   A function pointer to the default constructor that creates an object of your class (valid only if the class supports dynamic creation; otherwise, returns **NULL**).

- **CRuntimeClass* (PASCAL* m_pfn_GetBaseClass)( )**   If your application is dynamically linked to the AFXDLL version of MFC, a pointer to a function that returns the **CRuntimeClass** structure of the base class.

- **CRuntimeClass* m_pBaseClass**   If your application is statically linked to MFC, a pointer to the **CRuntimeClass** structure of the base class.

Feature Only in Professional and Enterprise Editions   Static linking to MFC is supported only in Visual C++ Professional and Enterprise Editions. For more information, see "Visual C++ Editions" online.

This function requires use of the **IMPLEMENT_DYNAMIC** or **IMPLEMENT_SERIAL** macro in the class implementation. You will get incorrect results otherwise.

Example

See **CObList::CObList** for a listing of the CAge class used in all **CObject** examples.

```
// example for CObject::GetRuntimeClass
CAge a(21);
CRuntimeClass* prt = a.GetRuntimeClass();
ASSERT( strcmp( prt->m_lpszClassName, "CAge" ) == 0 );
```

See Also: **CObject::IsKindOf, RUNTIME_CLASS**

CObject::IsKindOf

BOOL IsKindOf(const CRuntimeClass* *pClass* **) const;**

Return Value

Nonzero if the object corresponds to the class; otherwise 0.

Parameters

pClass   A pointer to a **CRuntimeClass** structure associated with your **CObject**-derived class.

Remarks

Tests *pClass* to see if (1) it is an object of the specified class or (2) it is an object of a class derived from the specified class. This function works only for classes declared with the **DECLARE_DYNAMIC** or **DECLARE_SERIAL** macro.

Do not use this function extensively because it defeats the C++ polymorphism feature. Use virtual functions instead.

Example

See **CObList::CObList** for a listing of the CAge class used in all **CObject** examples.

```
// example for CObject::IsKindOf
CAge a(21); // Must use IMPLEMENT_DYNAMIC or IMPLEMENT_SERIAL
ASSERT( a.IsKindOf( RUNTIME_CLASS( CAge ) ) );
ASSERT( a.IsKindOf( RUNTIME_CLASS( CObject ) ) );
```

See Also: **CObject::GetRuntimeClass, RUNTIME_CLASS, CObject Class: Accessing Run-Time Class Information**

CObject::IsSerializable

BOOL IsSerializable( ) const;

Return Value

Nonzero if this object can be serialized; otherwise 0.

Remarks

Tests whether this object is eligible for serialization. For a class to be serializable, its declaration must contain the **DECLARE_SERIAL** macro, and the implementation must contain the **IMPLEMENT_SERIAL** macro.

Note Do not override this function.

Example

See **CObList::CObList** for a listing of the CAge class used in all **CObject** examples.

```
// example for CObject::IsSerializable
CAge a(21);
ASSERT( a.IsSerializable() );
```

See Also: **CObject::Serialize**

CObject::Serialize

virtual void Serialize(CArchive& *ar* **);**
  throw(CMemoryException);
  throw(CArchiveException);
  throw(CFileException);

Parameters

ar   A **CArchive** object to serialize to or from.

Remarks

Reads or writes this object from or to an archive.

You must override **Serialize** for each class that you intend to serialize. The overridden **Serialize** must first call the **Serialize** function of its base class.

You must also use the **DECLARE_SERIAL** macro in your class declaration, and you must use the **IMPLEMENT_SERIAL** macro in the implementation.

Use **CArchive::IsLoading** or **CArchive::IsStoring** to determine whether the archive is loading or storing.

Serialize is called by **CArchive::ReadObject** and **CArchive::WriteObject**. These functions are associated with the **CArchive** insertion operator (**<<**) and extraction operator (**>>**).

For serialization examples, see the article "Serialization (Object Persistence)" in *Visual C++ Programmer's Guide* online.

Example

See **CObList::CObList** for a listing of the CAge class used in all **CObject** examples.

```
// example for CObject::Serialize
void CAge::Serialize( CArchive& ar )
 {
```

```
CObject::Serialize( ar );
    if( ar.IsStoring() )
    ar << m_years;
    else
    ar >> m_years;
}
```

Operators
CObject::operator =

> **void operator =(const CObject&** *src* **);**

Remarks

The standard C++ default class assignment behavior is a member-by-member copy. The presence of this private assignment operator guarantees a compiler error message if you assign without the overridden operator. You must therefore provide an assignment operator in your derived class if you intend to assign objects of your derived class.

CObject::operator delete

> **void operator delete(void*** *p* **);**

Remarks

For the Release version of the library, operator **delete** simply frees the memory allocated by operator **new**. In the Debug version, operator **delete** participates in an allocation-monitoring scheme designed to detect memory leaks. If you override operators **new** and **delete**, you forfeit the diagnostic capability.

See Also: **CObject::operator new**

CObject::operator new

> **void* operator new(size_t** *nSize* **);**
>   **throw(CMemoryException);**
> **void* operator new(size_t** *nSize*, **LPCSTR** *lpszFileName*, **int** *nLine* **);**
>   **throw(CMemoryException);**

Remarks

For the Release version of the library, operator **new** performs an optimal memory allocation in a manner similar to **malloc**. In the Debug version, operator **new** participates in an allocation-monitoring scheme designed to detect memory leaks.

If you use the code line

```
#define new DEBUG_NEW
```

before any of your implementations in a .CPP file, then the second version of **new** will be used, storing the filename and line number in the allocated block for later reporting. You do not have to worry about supplying the extra parameters; a macro takes care of that for you.

Even if you do not use **DEBUG_NEW** in Debug mode, you still get leak detection, but without the source-file line-number reporting described above.

Note If you override this operator, you must also override **delete**. Do not use the standard library **_new_handler** function.

See Also: **CObject::operator delete**

CObList

The **CObList** class supports ordered lists of nonunique **CObject** pointers accessible sequentially or by pointer value. **CObList** lists behave like doubly-linked lists.

A variable of type **POSITION** is a key for the list. You can use a **POSITION** variable both as an iterator to traverse a list sequentially and as a bookmark to hold a place. A position is not the same as an index, however.

Element insertion is very fast at the list head, at the tail, and at a known **POSITION**. A sequential search is necessary to look up an element by value or index. This search can be slow if the list is long.

CObList incorporates the **IMPLEMENT_SERIAL** macro to support serialization and dumping of its elements. If a list of **CObject** pointers is stored to an archive, either with an overloaded insertion operator or with the **Serialize** member function, each **CObject** element is serialized in turn.

If you need a dump of individual **CObject** elements in the list, you must set the depth of the dump context to 1 or greater.

When a **CObList** object is deleted, or when its elements are removed, only the **CObject** pointers are removed, not the objects they reference.

You can derive your own classes from **CObList**. Your new list class, designed to hold pointers to objects derived from **CObject**, adds new data members and new member functions. Note that the resulting list is not strictly type safe, because it allows insertion of any **CObject** pointer.

Note You must use the **IMPLEMENT_SERIAL** macro in the implementation of your derived class if you intend to serialize the list.

For more information on using **CObList**, see the article "Collections" in *Visual C++ Programmer's Guide* online.

#include <afxcoll.h>

See Also: **CStringList**, **CPtrList**

CObList Class Members

Construction

CObList	Constructs an empty list for **CObject** pointers.

Head/Tail Access

GetHead	Returns the head element of the list (cannot be empty).
GetTail	Returns the tail element of the list (cannot be empty).

Operations

RemoveHead	Removes the element from the head of the list.
RemoveTail	Removes the element from the tail of the list.
AddHead	Adds an element (or all the elements in another list) to the head of the list (makes a new head).
AddTail	Adds an element (or all the elements in another list) to the tail of the list (makes a new tail).
RemoveAll	Removes all the elements from this list.

Iteration

GetHeadPosition	Returns the position of the head element of the list.
GetTailPosition	Returns the position of the tail element of the list.
GetNext	Gets the next element for iterating.
GetPrev	Gets the previous element for iterating.

Retrieval/Modification

GetAt	Gets the element at a given position.
SetAt	Sets the element at a given position.
RemoveAt	Removes an element from this list, specified by position.

Insertion

InsertBefore	Inserts a new element before a given position.
InsertAfter	Inserts a new element after a given position.

Searching

Find	Gets the position of an element specified by pointer value.
FindIndex	Gets the position of an element specified by a zero-based index.

Status

GetCount	Returns the number of elements in this list.
IsEmpty	Tests for the empty list condition (no elements).

Member Functions
CObList::AddHead

POSITION AddHead(CObject* *newElement* **);**
    throw(CMemoryException);
void AddHead(CObList* *pNewList* **);**
    throw(CMemoryException);

Return Value
The first version returns the **POSITION** value of the newly inserted element.

Parameters
newElement   The **CObject** pointer to be added to this list.

pNewList   A pointer to another **CObList** list. The elements in *pNewList* will be added to this list.

Remarks
Adds a new element or list of elements to the head of this list. The list can be empty before the operation.

Example
```
    CObList list;
    list.AddHead( new CAge( 21 ) ); // 21 is now at head.
    list.AddHead( new CAge( 40 ) ); // 40 replaces 21 at head.
#ifdef _DEBUG
    afxDump.SetDepth( 1 );
    afxDump << "AddHead example: " << &list << "\n";
#endif
```

The results from this program are as follows:

```
AddHead example: A CObList with 2 elements
    a CAge at $44A8 40
    a CAge at $442A 21
```

See Also: **CObList::GetHead, CObList::RemoveHead**

CObList::AddTail

POSITION AddTail(CObject* *newElement* **);**
    throw(CMemoryException);
void AddTail(CObList* *pNewList* **);**
    throw(CMemoryException);

Return Value
The first version returns the **POSITION** value of the newly inserted element.

Parameters

newElement   The **CObject** pointer to be added to this list.

pNewList   A pointer to another **CObList** list. The elements in *pNewList* will be added to this list.

Remarks

Adds a new element or list of elements to the tail of this list. The list can be empty before the operation.

Example

```
        CObList list;
        list.AddTail( new CAge( 21 ) );
        list.AddTail( new CAge( 40 ) ); // List now contains (21, 40).
#ifdef _DEBUG
        afxDump.SetDepth( 1 );
        afxDump << "AddTail example: " << &list << "\n";
#endif
```

The results from this program are as follows:

```
AddTail example: A CObList with 2 elements
    a CAge at $444A 21
    a CAge at $4526 40
```

See Also: **CObList::GetTail**, **CObList::RemoveTail**

CObList::CObList

CObList(int *nBlockSize* **= 10);**

Parameters

nBlockSize   The memory-allocation granularity for extending the list.

Remarks

Constructs an empty **CObject** pointer list. As the list grows, memory is allocated in units of *nBlockSize* entries. If a memory allocation fails, a **CMemoryException** is thrown.

Example

Below is a listing of the **CObject**-derived class CAge used in all the collection examples:

```
// Simple CObject-derived class for CObList examples
class CAge : public CObject
{
    DECLARE_SERIAL( CAge )
private:
    int    m_years;
public:
    CAge() { m_years = 0; }
    CAge( int age ) { m_years = age; }
```

```
CAge( const CAge& a ) { m_years = a.m_years; } // Copy constructor
void Serialize( CArchive& ar);
void AssertValid() const;
const CAge& operator=( const CAge& a )
{
    m_years = a.m_years; return *this;
}
BOOL operator==(CAge a)
{
    return m_years == a.m_years;
}
#ifdef _DEBUG
  void Dump( CDumpContext& dc ) const
  {
      CObject::Dump( dc );
      dc << m_years;
  }
#endif
};
```

Below is an example of **CObList** constructor usage:

```
CObList list( 20 );  // List on the stack with blocksize = 20.

CObList* plist = new CObList; // List on the heap with default
                             // blocksize.
```

CObList::Find

POSITION Find(CObject* *searchValue*, **POSITION** *startAfter* = **NULL**) const;

Return Value

A **POSITION** value that can be used for iteration or object pointer retrieval; **NULL** if the object is not found.

Parameters

searchValue   The object pointer to be found in this list.

startAfter   The start position for the search.

Remarks

Searches the list sequentially to find the first **CObject** pointer matching the specified **CObject** pointer. Note that the pointer values are compared, not the contents of the objects.

Example

```
CObList list;
CAge* pa1;
CAge* pa2;
POSITION pos;
list.AddHead( pa1 = new CAge( 21 ) );
list.AddHead( pa2 = new CAge( 40 ) );    // List now contains (40, 21).
if( ( pos = list.Find( pa1 ) ) != NULL ) // Hunt for pa1
```

```
{                                              // starting at head by default.
    ASSERT( *(CAge*) list.GetAt( pos ) == CAge( 21 ) );
}
```

See Also: **CObList::GetNext, CObList::GetPrev**

CObList::FindIndex

POSITION FindIndex(int *nIndex* **) const;**

Return Value

A **POSITION** value that can be used for iteration or object pointer retrieval; **NULL** if *nIndex* is too large. (The framework generates an assertion if *nIndex* is negative.)

Parameters

nIndex   The zero-based index of the list element to be found.

Remarks

Uses the value of *nIndex* as an index into the list. It starts a sequential scan from the head of the list, stopping on the *n*th element.

Example

```
CObList list;
POSITION pos;

list.AddHead( new CAge( 21 ) );
list.AddHead( new CAge( 40 ) ); // List now contains (40, 21).
if( ( pos = list.FindIndex( 0 )) != NULL )
{
    ASSERT( *(CAge*) list.GetAt( pos ) == CAge( 40 ) );
}
```

See Also: **CObList::Find, CObList::GetNext, CObList::GetPrev**

CObList::GetAt

CObject*& GetAt(POSITION *position* **);**
CObject* GetAt(POSITION *position* **) const;**

Return Value

See the return value description for **GetHead**.

Parameters

position   A **POSITION** value returned by a previous **GetHeadPosition** or **Find** member function call.

Remarks

A variable of type **POSITION** is a key for the list. It is not the same as an index, and you cannot operate on a **POSITION** value yourself. **GetAt** retrieves the **CObject** pointer associated with a given position.

You must ensure that your **POSITION** value represents a valid position in the list. If it is invalid, then the Debug version of the Microsoft Foundation Class Library asserts.

Example

See the example for **FindIndex**.

See Also: **CObList::Find**, **CObList::SetAt**, **CObList::GetNext**, **CObList::GetPrev**, **CObList::GetHead**

CObList::GetCount

int GetCount( ) const;

Return Value

An integer value containing the element count.

Remarks

Gets the number of elements in this list.

Example

```
CObList list;

list.AddHead( new CAge( 21 ) );
list.AddHead( new CAge( 40 ) ); // List now contains (40, 21).
ASSERT( list.GetCount() == 2 );
```

See Also: **CObList::IsEmpty**

CObList::GetHead

CObject*& GetHead( );
CObject* GetHead( ) const;

Return Value

If the list is accessed through a pointer to a **const CObList**, then **GetHead** returns a **CObject** pointer. This allows the function to be used only on the right side of an assignment statement and thus protects the list from modification.

If the list is accessed directly or through a pointer to a **CObList**, then **GetHead** returns a reference to a **CObject** pointer. This allows the function to be used on either side of an assignment statement and thus allows the list entries to be modified.

Remarks

Gets the **CObject** pointer that represents the head element of this list.

You must ensure that the list is not empty before calling **GetHead**. If the list is empty, then the Debug version of the Microsoft Foundation Class Library asserts. Use **IsEmpty** to verify that the list contains elements.

Example

The following example illustrates the use of **GetHead** on the left side of an assignment statement.

```
const CObList* cplist;

CObList* plist = new CObList;
CAge* page1 = new CAge( 21 );
CAge* page2 = new CAge( 30 );
CAge* page3 = new CAge( 40 );
plist->AddHead( page1 );
plist->AddHead( page2 );   // List now contains (30, 21).
// The following statement REPLACES the head element.
plist->GetHead() = page3; // List now contains (40, 21).
ASSERT( *(CAge*) plist->GetHead() == CAge( 40 ) );
cplist = plist;   // cplist is a pointer to a const list.
cplist->GetHead() = page3; // Error: can't assign a pointer to a const list
ASSERT( *(CAge*) plist->GetHead() == CAge( 40 ) ); // OK

delete page1;
delete page2;
delete page3;
delete plist; // Cleans up memory.
```

See Also: **CObList::GetTail**, **CObList::GetTailPosition**, **CObList::AddHead**, **CObList::RemoveHead**

CObList::GetHeadPosition

POSITION GetHeadPosition( ) const;

Return Value

A **POSITION** value that can be used for iteration or object pointer retrieval; **NULL** if the list is empty.

Remarks

Gets the position of the head element of this list.

Example

```
CObList list;
POSITION pos;

list.AddHead( new CAge( 21 ) );
list.AddHead( new CAge( 40 ) ); // List now contains (40, 21).
if( ( pos = list.GetHeadPosition() ) != NULL )
{
    ASSERT( *(CAge*) list.GetAt( pos ) == CAge( 40 ) );
}
```

See Also: **CObList::GetTailPosition**

CObList::GetNext

CObject*& GetNext(POSITION& *rPosition* **);**
CObject* GetNext(POSITION& *rPosition* **) const;**

Return Value

See the return value description for **GetHead**.

Parameters

rPosition   A reference to a **POSITION** value returned by a previous **GetNext**,
GetHeadPosition, or other member function call.

Remarks

Gets the list element identified by *rPosition*, then sets *rPosition* to the **POSITION**
value of the next entry in the list. You can use **GetNext** in a forward iteration loop
if you establish the initial position with a call to **GetHeadPosition** or **Find**.

You must ensure that your **POSITION** value represents a valid position in the list.
If it is invalid, then the Debug version of the Microsoft Foundation Class Library
asserts.

If the retrieved element is the last in the list, then the new value of *rPosition* is set
to **NULL**.

It is possible to remove an element during an iteration. See the example for
RemoveAt.

Example

```
CObList list;
POSITION pos;
list.AddHead( new CAge( 21 ) );
list.AddHead( new CAge( 40 ) ); // List now contains (40, 21).
// Iterate through the list in head-to-tail order.
#ifdef _DEBUG
    for( pos = list.GetHeadPosition(); pos != NULL; )
    {
      afxDump << list.GetNext( pos ) << "\n";
    }
#endif
```

The results from this program are as follows:

```
a CAge at $479C 40
a CAge at $46C0 21
```

See Also: **CObList::Find, CObList::GetHeadPosition,**
CObList::GetTailPosition, CObList::GetPrev, CObList::GetHead

CObList::GetPrev

CObject*& GetPrev(POSITION& *rPosition* **);**
CObject* GetPrev(POSITION& *rPosition* **) const;**

Return Value

See the return value description for **GetHead**.

Parameters

rPosition   A reference to a **POSITION** value returned by a previous **GetPrev** or
other member function call.

Remarks

Gets the list element identified by *rPosition*, then sets *rPosition* to the **POSITION**
value of the previous entry in the list. You can use **GetPrev** in a reverse iteration loop
if you establish the initial position with a call to **GetTailPosition** or **Find**.

You must ensure that your **POSITION** value represents a valid position in the list.
If it is invalid, then the Debug version of the Microsoft Foundation Class Library
asserts.

If the retrieved element is the first in the list, then the new value of *rPosition* is set
to **NULL**.

Example

```
CObList list;
POSITION pos;

list.AddHead( new CAge(21) );
list.AddHead( new CAge(40) ); // List now contains (40, 21).
// Iterate through the list in tail-to-head order.
for( pos = list.GetTailPosition(); pos != NULL; )
    {
#ifdef _DEBUG
    afxDump << list.GetPrev( pos ) << "\n";
#endif
    }
```

The results from this program are as follows:

```
a CAge at $421C 21
a CAge at $421C 40
```

See Also: **CObList::Find, CObList::GetTailPosition,**
CObList::GetHeadPosition, CObList::GetNext, CObList::GetHead

CObList::GetTail

CObject*& GetTail( );
CObject* GetTail( ) const;

Return Value

See the return value description for **GetHead**.

Remarks

Gets the **CObject** pointer that represents the tail element of this list.

You must ensure that the list is not empty before calling **GetTail**. If the list is empty, then the Debug version of the Microsoft Foundation Class Library asserts. Use **IsEmpty** to verify that the list contains elements.

Example

```
CObList list;

list.AddHead( new CAge( 21 ) );
list.AddHead( new CAge( 40 ) ); // List now contains (40, 21).
ASSERT( *(CAge*) list.GetTail() == CAge( 21 ) );
```

See Also: **CObList::AddTail**, **CObList::AddHead**, **CObList::RemoveHead**, **CObList::GetHead**

CObList::GetTailPosition

POSITION GetTailPosition( ) const;

Return Value

A **POSITION** value that can be used for iteration or object pointer retrieval; **NULL** if the list is empty.

Remarks

Gets the position of the tail element of this list; **NULL** if the list is empty.

Example

```
CObList list;
POSITION pos;

list.AddHead( new CAge( 21 ) );
list.AddHead( new CAge( 40 ) ); // List now contains (40, 21).
if( ( pos = list.GetTailPosition() ) != NULL )
{
    ASSERT( *(CAge*) list.GetAt( pos ) == CAge( 21 ) );
}
```

See Also: **CObList::GetHeadPosition**, **CObList::GetTail**

CObList::InsertAfter

> **POSITION InsertAfter(POSITION** *position*, **CObject*** *newElement* **);**
> **throw (CMemoryException);**

Parameters

position　A **POSITION** value returned by a previous **GetNext**, **GetPrev**, or **Find** member function call.

newElement　The object pointer to be added to this list.

Remarks

Adds an element to this list after the element at the specified position.

Example

```
CObList list;
POSITION pos1, pos2;
list.AddHead( new CAge( 21 ) );
list.AddHead( new CAge( 40 ) ); // List now contains (40, 21).
if( ( pos1 = list.GetHeadPosition() ) != NULL )
{
    pos2 = list.InsertAfter( pos1, new CAge( 65 ) );
}
#ifdef _DEBUG
    afxDump.SetDepth( 1 );
    afxDump << "InsertAfter example: " << &list << "\n";
#endif
```

The results from this program are as follows:

```
InsertAfter example: A CObList with 3 elements
    a CAge at $4A44 40
    a CAge at $4A64 65
    a CAge at $4968 21
```

See Also:　**CObList::Find, CObList::InsertBefore**

CObList::InsertBefore

> **POSITION InsertBefore(POSITION** *position*, **CObject*** *newElement* **);**
> **throw (CMemoryException);**

Return Value

A **POSITION** value that can be used for iteration or object pointer retrieval; **NULL** if the list is empty.

Parameters

position　A **POSITION** value returned by a previous **GetNext**, **GetPrev**, or **Find** member function call.

newElement　The object pointer to be added to this list.

Remarks

Adds an element to this list before the element at the specified position.

Example

```
CObList list;
POSITION pos1, pos2;
list.AddHead( new CAge( 21 ) );
list.AddHead( new CAge( 40 ) ); // List now contains (40, 21).
if( ( pos1 = list.GetTailPosition() ) != NULL )
{
    pos2 = list.InsertBefore( pos1, new CAge( 65 ) );
}
#ifdef _DEBUG
    afxDump.SetDepth( 1 );
    afxDump << "InsertBefore example: " << &list << "\n";
#endif
```

The results from this program are as follows:

```
InsertBefore example: A CObList with 3 elements
    a CAge at $4AE2 40
    a CAge at $4B02 65
    a CAge at $49E6 21
```

See Also: **CObList::Find**, **CObList::InsertAfter**

CObList::IsEmpty

BOOL IsEmpty( ) const;

Return Value

Nonzero if this list is empty; otherwise 0.

Remarks

Indicates whether this list contains no elements.

Example

See the example for **RemoveAll**.

See Also: **CObList::GetCount**

CObList::RemoveAll

void RemoveAll( );

Remarks

Removes all the elements from this list and frees the associated **CObList** memory. No error is generated if the list is already empty.

When you remove elements from a **CObList**, you remove the object pointers from the list. It is your responsibility to delete the objects themselves.

Example

```
CObList list;
CAge* pa1;
CAge* pa2;
ASSERT( list.IsEmpty()); // Yes it is.
list.AddHead( pa1 = new CAge( 21 ) );
list.AddHead( pa2 = new CAge( 40 ) ); // List now contains (40, 21).
ASSERT( !list.IsEmpty()); // No it isn't.
list.RemoveAll(); // CAge's aren't destroyed.
ASSERT( list.IsEmpty()); // Yes it is.
delete pa1;      // Now delete the CAge objects.
delete pa2;
```

CObList::RemoveAt

void RemoveAt(POSITION *position* **);**

Parameters

position   The position of the element to be removed from the list.

Remarks

Removes the specified element from this list.

When you remove an element from a **CObList**, you remove the object pointer from the list. It is your responsibility to delete the objects themselves.

You must ensure that your **POSITION** value represents a valid position in the list. If it is invalid, then the Debug version of the Microsoft Foundation Class Library asserts.

Example

Be careful when removing an element during a list iteration. The following example shows a removal technique that guarantees a valid **POSITION** value for **GetNext**.

```
CObList list;
POSITION pos1, pos2;
CObject* pa;

list.AddHead( new CAge( 21 ) );
list.AddHead( new CAge( 40 ) );
list.AddHead( new CAge( 65 ) ); // List now contains (65 40, 21).
for( pos1 = list.GetHeadPosition(); ( pos2 = pos1 ) != NULL; )
{
   if( *(CAge*) list.GetNext( pos1 ) == CAge( 40 ) )
   {
      pa = list.GetAt( pos2 ); // Save the old pointer for
                               //deletion.
      list.RemoveAt( pos2 );
      delete pa; // Deletion avoids memory leak.
   }
}
#ifdef _DEBUG
```

```
    afxDump.SetDepth( 1 );
    afxDump << "RemoveAt example: " << &list << "\n";
#endif
```

The results from this program are as follows:

```
RemoveAt example: A CObList with 2 elements
    a CAge at $4C1E 65
    a CAge at $4B22 21
```

CObList::RemoveHead

CObject* RemoveHead( );

Return Value

The **CObject** pointer previously at the head of the list.

Remarks

Removes the element from the head of the list and returns a pointer to it.

You must ensure that the list is not empty before calling **RemoveHead**. If the list is empty, then the Debug version of the Microsoft Foundation Class Library asserts. Use **IsEmpty** to verify that the list contains elements.

Example

```
CObList list;
CAge* pa1;
CAge* pa2;

list.AddHead( pa1 = new CAge( 21 ) );
list.AddHead( pa2 = new CAge( 40 ) ); // List now contains (40, 21).
ASSERT( *(CAge*) list.RemoveHead() == CAge( 40 ) );  // Old head
ASSERT( *(CAge*) list.GetHead() == CAge( 21 ) );  // New head
delete pa1;
delete pa2;
```

See Also: **CObList::GetHead, CObList::AddHead**

CObList::RemoveTail

CObject* RemoveTail( );

Return Value

A pointer to the object that was at the tail of the list.

Remarks

Removes the element from the tail of the list and returns a pointer to it.

You must ensure that the list is not empty before calling **RemoveTail**. If the list is empty, then the Debug version of the Microsoft Foundation Class Library asserts. Use **IsEmpty** to verify that the list contains elements.

Example

```
CObList list;
CAge* pa1;
CAge* pa2;

list.AddHead( pa1 = new CAge( 21 ) );
list.AddHead( pa2 = new CAge( 40 ) ); // List now contains (40, 21).
ASSERT( *(CAge*) list.RemoveTail() == CAge( 21 ) );  // Old tail
ASSERT( *(CAge*) list.GetTail() == CAge( 40 ) );  // New tail
delete pa1;
delete pa2; // Clean up memory.
```

See Also: CObList::GetTail, CObList::AddTail

CObList::SetAt

void SetAt(POSITION *pos***, CObject*** *newElement* **);**

Parameters

pos The **POSITION** of the element to be set.

newElement The **CObject** pointer to be written to the list.

Remarks

A variable of type **POSITION** is a key for the list. It is not the same as an index, and you cannot operate on a **POSITION** value yourself. **SetAt** writes the **CObject** pointer to the specified position in the list.

You must ensure that your **POSITION** value represents a valid position in the list. If it is invalid, then the Debug version of the Microsoft Foundation Class Library asserts.

Example

```
CObList list;
CObject* pa;
POSITION pos;

list.AddHead( new CAge( 21 ) );
list.AddHead( new CAge( 40 ) ); // List now contains (40, 21).
if( ( pos = list.GetTailPosition()) != NULL )
{
    pa = list.GetAt( pos ); // Save the old pointer for
                            //deletion.
    list.SetAt( pos, new CAge( 65 ) );  // Replace the tail
                                        //element.
    delete pa;  // Deletion avoids memory leak.
}
#ifdef _DEBUG
   afxDump.SetDepth( 1 );
   afxDump << "SetAt example: " << &list << "\n";
#endif
```

The results from this program are as follows:

```
SetAt example: A CObList with 2 elements
    a CAge at $4D98 40
    a CAge at $4DB8 65
```

See Also: **CObList::Find, CObList::GetAt, CObList::GetNext, CObList::GetPrev**

COleBusyDialog

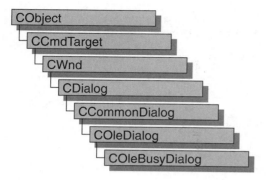

The **COleBusyDialog** class is used for the OLE Server Not Responding or Server Busy dialog boxes. Create an object of class **COleBusyDialog** when you want to call these dialog boxes. After a **COleBusyDialog** object has been constructed, you can use the **m_bz** structure to initialize the values or states of controls in the dialog box. The **m_bz** structure is of type **OLEUIBUSY**. For more information about using this dialog class, see the **DoModal** member function.

Note AppWizard-generated container code uses this class.

For more information, see the **OLEUIBUSY** structure in the *OLE 2.01 User Interface Library*.

For more information on OLE-specific dialog boxes, see the article "Dialog Boxes in OLE" in *Visual C++ Programmer's Guide* online.

#include <afxodlgs.h>

See Also: **COleDialog**

COleBusyDialog Class Members

Data Members

m_bz	Structure of type **OLEUIBUSY** that controls the behavior of the dialog box.

Construction

COleBusyDialog	Constructs a **COleBusyDialog** object.

Operations

DoModal	Displays the OLE Server Busy dialog box.
GetSelectionType	Determines the choice made in the dialog box.

Member Functions

COleBusyDialog::COleBusyDialog

COleBusyDialog(HTASK *htaskBusy***, BOOL** *bNotResponding* **= FALSE,**
↪ DWORD *dwFlags* **= 0, CWnd*** *pParentWnd* **= NULL);**

Parameters

htaskBusy   Handle to the server task that is busy.

bNotResponding   If **TRUE**, call the Not Responding dialog box instead of the Server Busy dialog box. The wording in the Not Responding dialog box is slightly different than the wording in the Server Busy dialog box, and the Cancel button is disabled.

dwFlags   Creation flag. Can contain zero or more of the following values combined with the bitwise-OR operator:

- **BZ_DISABLECANCELBUTTON**   Disable the Cancel button when calling the dialog box.

- **BZ_DISABLESWITCHTOBUTTON**   Disable the Switch To button when calling the dialog box.

- **BZ_DISABLERETRYBUTTON**   Disable the Retry button when calling the dialog box.

pParentWnd   Points to the parent or owner window object (of type **CWnd**) to which the dialog object belongs. If it is **NULL**, the parent window of the dialog object is set to the main application window.

Remarks

This function only constructs a **COleBusyDialog** object. To display the dialog box, call **DoModal**.

For more information, see the **OLEUIBUSY** structure in the *OLE 2.01 User Interface Library*.

See Also: **COleBusyDialog::DoModal**

COleBusyDialog::DoModal

virtual int DoModal( ) const;

Return Value

Completion status for the dialog box. One of the following values:

- **IDOK** if the dialog box was successfully displayed.

- **IDCANCEL** if the user canceled the dialog box.

- **IDABORT** if an error occurred. If **IDABORT** is returned, call the **COleDialog::GetLastError** member function to get more information about the type of error that occurred. For a listing of possible errors, see the **OleUIBusy** function in the *OLE 2.01 User Interface Library*.

Remarks

Call this function to display the OLE Server Busy or Server Not Responding dialog box.

If you want to initialize the various dialog box controls by setting members of the **m_bz** structure, you should do this before calling **DoModal**, but after the dialog object is constructed.

If **DoModal** returns **IDOK**, you can call other member functions to retrieve the settings or information that was input by the user into the dialog box.

See Also: **COleDialog::GetLastError**, **CDialog::DoModal**, **COleBusyDialog::GetSelectionType**, **COleBusyDialog::m_bz**

COleBusyDialog::GetSelectionType

UINT GetSelectionType( );

Return Value

Type of selection made.

Remarks

Call this function to get the selection type chosen by the user in the Server Busy dialog box.

The return type values are specified by the **Selection** enumeration type declared in the **COleBusyDialog** class.

```
enum Selection
{
    switchTo,
    retry,
    callUnblocked
};
```

Brief descriptions of these values follow:

- **COleBusyDialog::switchTo**   Switch To button was pressed.
- **COleBusyDialog::retry**   Retry button was pressed.
- **COleBusyDialog::callUnblocked**   Call to activate the server is now unblocked.

See Also: **COleBusyDialog::DoModal**

Data Members
COleBusyDialog::m_bz

Remarks

Structure of type **OLEUIBUSY** used to control the behavior of the Server Busy dialog box. Members of this structure can be modified directly or through member functions.

For more information, see the **OLEUIBUSY** structure in the *OLE 2.01 User Interface Library*.

See Also: **COleBusyDialog::COleBusyDialog**, **COleBusyDialog::DoModal**

COleChangeIconDialog

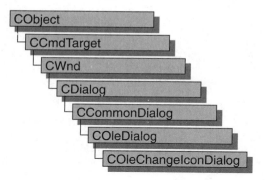

The **COleChangeIconDialog** class is used for the OLE Change Icon dialog box. Create an object of class **COleChangeIconDialog** when you want to call this dialog box. After a **COleChangeIconDialog** object has been constructed, you can use the **m_ci** structure to initialize the values or states of controls in the dialog box. The **m_ci** structure is of type **OLEUICHANGEICON**. For more information about using this dialog class, see the **DoModal** member function.

For more information, see the **OLEUICHANGEICON** structure in the *OLE 2.01 User Interface Library*.

For more information about OLE-specific dialog boxes, see the article "Dialog Boxes in OLE" in *Visual C++ Programmer's Guide* online.

#include <afxodlgs.h>

See Also: COleDialog

COleChangeIconDialog Class Members

Data Members

m_ci	A structure that controls the behavior of the dialog box.

Construction

COleChangeIconDialog	Constructs a **COleChangeIconDialog** object.

Operations and Attributes

DoModal	Displays the OLE 2 Change Icon dialog box.
DoChangeIcon	Performs the change specified in the dialog box.
GetIconicMetafile	Gets a handle to the metafile associated with the iconic form of this item.

Member Functions

COleChangeIconDialog::COleChangeIconDialog

> **COleChangeIconDialog** (**COleClientItem*** *pItem*, **DWORD** *dwFlags* =
> ↪ **CIF_SELECTCURRENT**, **CWnd*** *pParentWnd* = **NULL**);

Parameters

pItem Points to the item to be converted.

dwFlags Creation flag, which contains any number of the following values combined using the bitwise-or operator:

- **CIF_SELECTCURRENT** Specifies that the Current radio button will be selected initially when the dialog box is called. This is the default.

- **CIF_SELECTDEFAULT** Specifies that the Default radio button will be selected initially when the dialog box is called.

- **CIF_SELECTFROMFILE** Specifies that the From File radio button will be selected initially when the dialog box is called.

- **CIF_SHOWHELP** Specifies that the Help button will be displayed when the dialog box is called.

- **CIF_USEICONEXE** Specifies that the icon should be extracted from the executable specified in the **szIconExe** field of **m_ci** instead of retrieved from the type. This is useful for embedding or linking to non-OLE files.

pParentWnd Points to the parent or owner window object (of type **CWnd**) to which the dialog object belongs. If it is **NULL**, the parent window of the dialog box will be set to the main application window.

Remarks

This function constructs only a **COleChangeIconDialog** object. To display the dialog box, call the **DoModal** function.

For more information, see the **OLEUICHANGEICON** structure in the *OLE 2.01 User Interface Library*.

See Also: **COleClientItem**, **COleChangeIconDialog::DoModal**

COleChangeIconDialog::DoChangeIcon

> **BOOL DoChangeIcon**(**COleClientItem*** *pItem*);

Return Value

Nonzero if change is successful; otherwise 0.

Parameters

pItem Points to the item whose icon is changing.

Remarks

Call this function to change the icon representing the item to the one selected in the dialog box after **DoModal** returns **IDOK**.

See Also: **COleChangeIconDialog::DoModal**

COleChangeIconDialog::DoModal

virtual int DoModal( );

Return Value

Completion status for the dialog box. One of the following values:

- **IDOK** if the dialog box was successfully displayed.

- **IDCANCEL** if the user canceled the dialog box.

- **IDABORT** if an error occurred. If **IDABORT** is returned, call the **COleDialog::GetLastError** member function to get more information about the type of error that occurred. For a listing of possible errors, see the **OleUIChangeIcon** function in the *OLE 2.01 User Interface Library*.

Remarks

Call this function to display the OLE Change Icon dialog box.

If you want to initialize the various dialog box controls by setting members of the **m_ci** structure, you should do this before calling **DoModal**, but after the dialog object is constructed.

If **DoModal** returns **IDOK**, you can call other member functions to retrieve the settings or information that was input by the user into the dialog box.

See Also: **COleDialog::GetLastError, CDialog::DoModal, COleChangeIconDialog::m_ci, COleChangeIconDialog::DoChangeIcon, COleChangeIconDialog::GetIconicMetafile**

COleChangeIconDialog::GetIconicMetafile

HGLOBAL GetIconicMetafile( ) const;

Return Value

The handle to the metafile containing the iconic aspect of the new icon, if the dialog box was dismissed by choosing **OK**; otherwise, the icon as it was before the dialog was displayed.

Remarks

Call this function to get a handle to the metafile that contains the iconic aspect of the selected item.

See Also: **COleChangeIconDialog::DoModal**,
COleChangeIconDialog::COleChangeIconDialog,
COleChangeIconDialog::DoChangeIcon

Data Members
COleChangeIconDialog::m_ci

Remarks

Structure of type **OLEUICHANGEICON** used to control the behavior of the Change Icon dialog box. Members of this structure can be modified either directly or through member functions.

For more information, see the **OLEUICHANGEICON** structure in the *OLE 2.01 User Interface Library*.

See Also: **COleChangeIconDialog::COleChangeIconDialog**

COleChangeSourceDialog

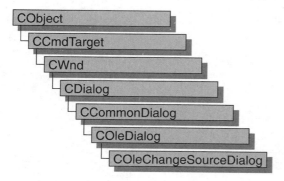

The **COleChangeSourceDialog** class is used for the OLE Change Source dialog box. Create an object of class **COleChangeSourceDialog** when you want to call this dialog box. After a **COleChangeSourceDialog** object has been constructed, you can use the **m_cs** structure to initialize the values or states of controls in the dialog box. The **m_cs** structure is of type **OLEUICHANGESOURCE**. For more information about using this dialog class, see the **DoModal** member function.

For more information, see the **OLEUICHANGESOURCE** structure in *OLE 2.01 User Interface Library*.

For more information about OLE-specific dialog boxes, see the article "Dialog Boxes in OLE" in *Visual C++ Programmer's Guide* online.

#include <afxodlgs.h>

See Also: COleDialog

COleChangeSourceDialog Class Members

Constructor

COleChangeSourceDialog	Constructs a **COleChangeSourceDialog** object.

Operations

DoModal	Displays the OLE Change Source dialog box.

Attributes

IsValidSource	Indicates if the source is valid.
GetFileName	Gets the filename from the source name.
GetDisplayName	Gets the complete source display name.

Attributes *(continued)*

GetItemName	Gets the item name from the source name.
GetFromPrefix	Gets the prefix of the previous source.
GetToPrefix	Gets the prefix of the new source

Data Member

m_cs	A structure that controls the behavior of the dialog box.

Member Functions
COleChangeSourceDialog::COleChangeSourceDialog

COleChangeSourceDialog(COleClientItem* *pItem*, **CWnd*** *pParentWnd* = **NULL**);

Parameters

    pItem Pointer to the linked **COleClientItem** whose source is to be updated.

    pParentWnd Points to the parent or owner window object (of type **CWnd**) to which the dialog object belongs. If it is **NULL**, the parent window of the dialog box will be set to the main application window.

Remarks

This function constructs a **COleChangeSourceDialog** object. To display the dialog box, call the **DoModal** function.

For more information, see the **OLEUICHANGESOURCE** structure and **OleUIChangeSource** function in *OLE 2.01 User Interface Library*.

COleChangeSourceDialog::DoModal

virtual int DoModal( );

Return Value

Completion status for the dialog box. One of the following values:

- **IDOK** if the dialog box was successfully displayed.

- **IDCANCEL** if the user canceled the dialog box.

- **IDABORT** if an error occurred. If **IDABORT** is returned, call the **COleDialog::GetLastError** member function to get more information about the type of error that occurred. For a listing of possible errors, see the **OleUIChangeSource** function in *OLE 2.01 User Interface Library*.

Remarks

Call this function to display the OLE Change Source dialog box.

If you want to initialize the various dialog box controls by setting members of the **m_cs** structure, you should do this before calling **DoModal**, but after the dialog object is constructed.

If **DoModal** returns **IDOK**, you can call member functions to retrieve user-entered settings or information from the dialog box. The following list names typical query functions:

- **GetFileName**
- **GetDisplayName**
- **GetItemName**

See Also: **COleChangeSourceDialog::COleChangeSourceDialog**

COleChangeSourceDialog::GetDisplayName

CString GetDisplayName( );

Return Value

The complete source display name (moniker) for the **COleClientItem** specified in the constructor.

Remarks

Call this function to retrieve the complete display name for the linked client item.

See Also: **COleChangeSourceDialog::GetFileName**, **COleChangeSourceDialog::GetItemName**

COleChangeSourceDialog::GetFileName

CString GetFileName( );

Return Value

The file moniker portion of the source display name for the **COleClientItem** specified in the constructor.

Remarks

Call this function to retrieve the file moniker portion of the display name for the linked client item. The file moniker together with the item moniker gives the complete display name.

See Also: **COleChangeSourceDialog::GetDisplayName**, **COleChangeSourceDialog::GetItemName**

COleChangeSourceDialog::GetFromPrefix

CString GetFromPrefix( );

Return Value

The previous prefix string of the source.

Remarks

Call this function to get the previous prefix string for the source. Call this function only after **DoModal** returns **IDOK**.

This value comes directly from the **lpszFrom** member of the **OLEUICHANGESOURCE** structure.

For more information, see the **OLEUICHANGESOURCE** structure in *OLE 2.01 User Interface Library*.

See Also: COleChangeSourceDialog::GetToPrefix

COleChangeSourceDialog::GetItemName

CString GetItemName( );

Return Value

The item moniker portion of the source display name for the **COleClientItem** specified in the constructor.

Remarks

Call this function to retrieve the item moniker portion of the display name for the linked client item. The file moniker together with the item moniker gives the complete display name.

See Also: COleChangeSourceDialog::GetFileName, COleChangeSourceDialog::GetDisplayName

---

COleChangeSourceDialog::GetToPrefix

CString GetToPrefix( );

Return Value

The new prefix string of the source.

Remarks

Call this function to get the new prefix string for the source. Call this function only after **DoModal** returns **IDOK**.

This value comes directly from the **lpszTo** member of the **OLEUICHANGESOURCE** structure.

For more information, see the **OLEUICHANGESOURCE** structure in *OLE 2.01 User Interface Library*.

See Also: **COleChangeSourceDialog::GetFromPrefix**

COleChangeSourceDialog::IsValidSource

BOOL IsValidSource( );

Return Value

Nonzero if the new source is valid, otherwise 0.

Remarks

Call this function to determine if the new source is valid. Call this function only after **DoModal** returns **IDOK**.

For more information, see the **OLEUICHANGESOURCE** structure in *OLE 2.01 User Interface Library*.

See Also: **COleChangeSourceDialog::DoModal**

Data Members
COleChangeSourceDialog::m_cs

Remarks

This data member is a structure of type **OLEUICHANGESOURCE**. **OLEUICHANGESOURCE** is used to control the behavior of the OLE Change Source dialog box. Members of this structure can be modified directly.

For more information, see the **OLEUICHANGESOURCE** structure in *OLE 2.01 User Interface Library*.

See Also: **COleChangeSourceDialog::COleChangeSourceDialog**

COleClientItem

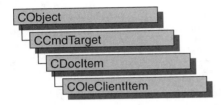

The **COleClientItem** class defines the container interface to OLE items. An OLE item represents data, created and maintained by a server application, which can be "seamlessly" incorporated into a document so that it appears to the user to be a single document. The result is a "compound document" made up of the OLE item and a containing document.

An OLE item can be either embedded or linked. If it is embedded, its data is stored as part of the compound document. If it is linked, its data is stored as part of a separate file created by the server application, and only a link to that file is stored in the compound document. All OLE items contain information specifying the server application that should be called to edit them.

COleClientItem defines several overridable functions that are called in response to requests from the server application; these overridables usually act as notifications. This allows the server application to inform the container of changes the user makes when editing the OLE item, or to retrieve information needed during editing.

COleClientItem can be used with either the **COleDocument**, **COleLinkingDoc**, or **COleServerDoc** class. To use **COleClientItem**, derive a class from it and implement the **OnChange** member function, which defines how the container responds to changes made to the item. To support in-place activation, override the **OnGetItemPosition** member function. This function provides information about the displayed position of the OLE item.

For more information about using the container interface, see the articles "Containers: Implementing a Container and Activation" in *Visual C++ Programmer's Guide* online.

Note The OLE documentation refers to embedded and linked items as "objects" and refers to types of items as "classes." This reference uses the term "item" to distinguish the OLE entity from the corresponding C++ object and the term "type" to distinguish the OLE category from the C++ class.

#include <afxole.h>

See Also: **COleServerItem**

COleClientItem Class Members

Construction

COleClientItem	Constructs a **COleClientItem** object.

Creation

CreateFromClipboard	Creates an embedded item from the Clipboard.
CreateFromData	Creates an embedded item from a data object.
CanCreateFromData	Indicates whether a container application can create an embedded object.
CreateFromFile	Creates an embedded item from a file.
CreateStaticFromClipboard	Creates a static item from the Clipboard.
CreateStaticFromData	Creates a static item from a data object.
CreateLinkFromClipboard	Creates a linked item from the Clipboard.
CreateLinkFromData	Creates a linked item from a data object.
CanCreateLinkFromData	Indicates whether a container application can create a linked object.
CreateLinkFromFile	Creates a linked item from a file.
CreateNewItem	Creates a new embedded item by launching the server application.
CreateCloneFrom	Creates a duplicate of an existing item.

Status

GetLastStatus	Returns the status of the last OLE operation.
GetType	Returns the type (embedded, linked, or static) of the OLE item.
GetExtent	Returns the bounds of the OLE item's rectangle.
GetCachedExtent	Returns the bounds of the OLE item's rectangle.
GetClassID	Gets the present item's class ID.
GetUserType	Gets a string describing the item's type.
GetIconicMetafile	Gets the metafile used for drawing the item's icon.
SetIconicMetafile	Caches the metafile used for drawing the item's icon.
GetDrawAspect	Gets the item's current view for rendering.
SetDrawAspect	Sets the item's current view for rendering.
GetItemState	Gets the item's current state.
GetActiveView	Gets the view on which the item is activated in place.
IsModified	Returns **TRUE** if the item has been modified since it was last saved.

Status *(continued)*

IsRunning	Returns **TRUE** if the item's server application is running.
IsInPlaceActive	Returns **TRUE** if the item is in-place active.
IsOpen	Returns **TRUE** if the item is currently open in the server application.

Data Access

GetDocument	Returns the **COleDocument** object that contains the present item.
AttachDataObject	Accesses the data in the OLE object.

Object Conversion

ConvertTo	Converts the item to another type.
ActivateAs	Activates the item as another type.
Reload	Reloads the item after a call to **ActivateAs**.

Clipboard Operations

CanPaste	Indicates whether the Clipboard contains an embeddable or static OLE item.
CanPasteLink	Indicates whether the Clipboard contains a linkable OLE item.
DoDragDrop	Performs a drag-and-drop operation.
CopyToClipboard	Copies the OLE item to the Clipboard.
GetClipboardData	Gets the data that would be placed on the Clipboard by calling the **CopyToClipboard** member function.

General Operations

Close	Closes a link to a server but does not destroy the OLE item.
Release	Releases the connection to an OLE linked item and closes it if it was open. Does not destroy the client item.
Delete	Deletes or closes the OLE item if it was a linked item.
Draw	Draws the OLE item.
Run	Runs the application associated with the item.
SetPrintDevice	Sets the print-target device for this client item.

Activation

Activate	Opens the OLE item for an operation and then executes the specified verb.
DoVerb	Executes the specified verb.
Deactivate	Deactivates the item.

(continued)

Activation *(continued)*

DeactivateUI	Restores the container application's user interface to its original state.
ReactivateAndUndo	Reactivates the item and undoes the last in-place editing operation.
SetItemRects	Sets the item's bounding rectangle.
GetInPlaceWindow	Returns a pointer to the item's in-place editing window.

Embedded Object Operations

SetHostNames	Sets the names the server displays when editing the OLE item.
SetExtent	Sets the bounding rectangle of the OLE item.

Linked Object Operations and Status

GetLinkUpdateOptions	Returns the update mode for a linked item (advanced feature).
SetLinkUpdateOptions	Sets the update mode for a linked item (advanced feature).
UpdateLink	Updates the presentation cache of an item.
IsLinkUpToDate	Returns **TRUE** if a linked item is up to date with its source document.

Overridables

OnChange	Called when the server changes the OLE item. Implementation required.
OnGetClipboardData	Called by the framework to get the data to be copied to the Clipboard.
OnInsertMenus	Called by the framework to create a composite menu.
OnSetMenu	Called by the framework to install and remove a composite menu.
OnRemoveMenus	Called by the framework to remove the container's menus from a composite menu.
OnUpdateFrameTitle	Called by the framework to update the frame window's title bar.
OnShowControlBars	Called by the framework to show and hide control bars.
OnGetItemPosition	Called by the framework to get the item's position relative to the view.
OnScrollBy	Called by the framework to scroll the item into view.
OnDeactivateUI	Called by the framework when the server has removed its in-place user interface.
OnDiscardUndoState	Called by the framework to discard the item's undo state information.
OnDeactivateAndUndo	Called by the framework to undo after activation.
OnShowItem	Called by the framework to display the OLE item.

Overridables *(continued)*

OnGetClipRect	Called by the framework to get the item's clipping-rectangle coordinates.
CanActivate	Called by the framework to determine whether in-place activation is allowed.
OnActivate	Called by the framework to notify the item that it is activated.
OnActivateUI	Called by the framework to notify the item that it is activated and should show its user interface.
OnGetWindowContext	Called by the framework when an item is activated in place.
OnDeactivate	Called by the framework when an item is deactivated.
OnChangeItemPosition	Called by the framework when an item's position changes.

Member Functions

COleClientItem::Activate

void Activate(LONG *nVerb*, **CView*** *pView*, **LPMSG** *lpMsg* = **NULL**);

Parameters

nVerb   Specifies the verb to execute. It can be one of the following:

Value	Meaning	Symbol
0	Primary verb	**OLEIVERB_PRIMARY**
1	Secondary verb	(None)
−1	Display item for editing	**OLEIVERB_SHOW**
−2	Edit item in separate window	**OLEIVERB_OPEN**
−3	Hide item	**OLEIVERB_HIDE**

The −1 value is typically an alias for another verb. If open editing is not supported, −2 has the same effect as −1. For additional values, see **IOleObject::DoVerb** in the OLE documentation.

pView   Pointer to the container view window that contains the OLE item; this is used by the server application for in-place activation. This parameter should be **NULL** if the container does not support in-place activation.

lpMsg   Pointer to the message that caused the item to be activated.

Remarks

Call this function to execute the specified verb instead of **DoVerb** so that you can do your own processing when an exception is thrown.

If the server application was written using the Microsoft Foundation Class Library, this function causes the **OnDoVerb** member function of the corresponding **COleServerItem** object to be executed.

If the primary verb is Edit and zero is specified in the *nVerb* parameter, the server application is launched to allow the OLE item to be edited. If the container application supports in-place activation, editing can be done in place. If the container does not support in-place activation (or if the Open verb is specified), the server is launched in a separate window and editing can be done there. Typically, when the user of the container application double-clicks the OLE item, the value for the primary verb in the *nVerb* parameter determines which action the user can take. However, if the server supports only one action, it takes that action, no matter which value is specified in the *nVerb* parameter.

For more information, see **IOleObject::DoVerb** in the OLE documentation.

See Also: **COleClientItem::DoVerb**, **COleServerItem::OnDoVerb**

COleClientItem::ActivateAs

BOOL ActivateAs(LPCTSTR *lpszUserType***, REFCLSID** *clsidOld***,**
↪ **REFCLSID** *clsidNew* **);**

Return Value

Nonzero if successful; otherwise 0.

Parameters

lpszUserType   Pointer to a string representing the target user type, such as "Word Document."

clsidOld   A reference to the item's current class ID. The class ID should represent the type of the actual object, as stored, unless it is a link. In that case, it should be the CLSID of the item to which the link refers. The **COleConvertDialog** automatically provides the correct class ID for the item.

clsidNew   A reference to the target class ID.

Remarks

Uses OLE's object conversion facilities to activate the item as though it were an item of the type specified by *clsidNew*. This is called automatically by **COleConvertDialog::DoConvert**. It is not usually called directly.

See Also: **COleConvertDialog**, **COleClientItem::ConvertTo**, **COleClientItem::Reload**

COleClientItem::AttachDataObject

void AttachDataObject(COleDataObject& *rDataObject* **) const;**

Parameters

rDataObject   Reference to a **COleDataObject** object that will be initialized to allow access to the data in the OLE item.

Remarks

Call this function to initialize a **COleDataObject** for accessing the data in the OLE item.

See Also: COleDataObject

COleClientItem::CanActivate

virtual BOOL CanActivate( );

Return Value

Nonzero if in-place activation is allowed; otherwise 0.

Remarks

Called by the framework when the user requests in-place activation of the OLE item; this function's return value determines whether in-place activation is allowed. The default implementation allows in-place activation if the container has a valid window. Override this function to implement special logic for accepting or refusing the activation request. For example, an activation request can be refused if the OLE item is too small or not currently visible.

For more information, see **IOleInPlaceSite::CanInPlaceActivate** in the OLE documentation.

COleClientItem::CanCreateFromData

static BOOL PASCAL CanCreateFromData(const COleDataObject* *pDataObject* **);**

Return Value

Nonzero if the container can create an embedded object from the **COleDataObject** object; otherwise 0.

Parameters

pDataObject   Pointer to the **COleDataObject** object from which the OLE item is to be created.

Remarks

Checks whether a container application can create an embedded object from the given **COleDataObject** object. The **COleDataObject** class is used in data transfers for retrieving data in various formats from the Clipboard, through drag and drop, or from an embedded OLE item.

Containers can use this function to decide to enable or disable their Edit Paste and Edit Paste Special commands.

For more information, see the article "Data Objects and Data Sources (OLE)" in *Visual C++ Programmer's Guide* online.

See Also: **COleDataObject**

COleClientItem::CanCreateLinkFromData

static BOOL PASCAL CanCreateLinkFromData(const COleDataObject* *pDataObject* **);**

Return Value

Nonzero if the container can create a linked object from the **COleDataObject** object.

Parameters

pDataObject   Pointer to the **COleDataObject** object from which the OLE item is to be created.

Remarks

Checks whether a container application can create a linked object from the given **COleDataObject** object. The **COleDataObject** class is used in data transfers for retrieving data in various formats from the Clipboard, through drag and drop, or from an embedded OLE item.

Containers can use this function to decide to enable or disable their Edit Paste Special and Edit Paste Link commands.

For more information, see the article "Data Objects and Data Sources (OLE)" in *Visual C++ Programmer's Guide* online.

See Also: **COleDataObject**

COleClientItem::CanPaste

static BOOL PASCAL CanPaste( );

Return Value

Nonzero if an embedded OLE item can be pasted from the Clipboard; otherwise 0.

Remarks

Call this function to see whether an embedded OLE item can be pasted from the Clipboard.

For more information, see **OleGetClipboard** and **OleQueryCreateFromData** in the OLE documentation.

See Also: **COleClientItem::CanPasteLink**,
COleClientItem::CreateFromClipboard,
COleClientItem::CreateStaticFromClipboard, **COleDocument**

COleClientItem::CanPasteLink

> static BOOL PASCAL CanPasteLink( );

Return Value

Nonzero if a linked OLE item can be pasted from the Clipboard; otherwise 0.

Remarks

Call this function to see whether a linked OLE item can be pasted from the Clipboard.

For more information, see **OleGetClipboard** and **OleQueryLinkFromData** in the OLE documentation.

See Also: **COleClientItem::CanPaste**,
COleClientItem::CreateLinkFromClipboard

COleClientItem::Close

> void Close(OLECLOSE *dwCloseOption* = OLECLOSE_SAVEIFDIRTY);

Parameters

dwCloseOption Flag specifying under what circumstances the OLE item is saved when it returns to the loaded state. It can have one of the following values:

- **OLECLOSE_SAVEIFDIRTY** Save the OLE item.
- **OLECLOSE_NOSAVE** Do not save the OLE item.
- **OLECLOSE_PROMPTSAVE** Prompt the user on whether to save the OLE item.

Remarks

Call this function to change the state of an OLE item from the running state to the loaded state, that is, loaded with its handler in memory but with the server not running. This function has no effect when the OLE item is not running.

For more information, see **IOleObject::Close** in the OLE documentation.

See Also: **COleClientItem::UpdateLink**

COleClientItem::COleClientItem

COleClientItem(COleDocument* *pContainerDoc* **= NULL);**

Parameters

pContainerDoc   Pointer to the container document that will contain this item. This can be any **COleDocument** derivative.

Remarks

Constructs a **COleClientItem** object and adds it to the container document's collection of document items, which constructs only the C++ object and does not perform any OLE initialization. If you pass a **NULL** pointer, no addition is made to the container document. You must explicitly call **COleDocument::AddItem**.

You must call one of the following creation member functions before you use the OLE item:

- **CreateFromClipboard**
- **CreateFromData**
- **CreateFromFile**
- **CreateStaticFromClipboard**
- **CreateStaticFromData**
- **CreateLinkFromClipboard**
- **CreateLinkFromData**
- **CreateLinkFromFile**
- **CreateNewItem**
- **CreateCloneFrom**

See Also: **COleDocument, COleDocument::AddItem**

COleClientItem::ConvertTo

BOOL ConvertTo(REFCLSID *clsidNew* **);**

Return Value

Nonzero if successful; otherwise 0.

Parameters

clsidNew   The class ID of the target type.

Remarks

Call this member function to convert the item to the type specified by *clsidNew*. This is called automatically by **COleConvertDialog**. It is not necessary to call it directly.

See Also: **COleClientItem::ActivateAs, COleConvertDialog**

COleClientItem::CopyToClipboard

void CopyToClipboard(BOOL *bIncludeLink* **= FALSE);**

Parameters

bIncludeLink   **TRUE** if link information should be copied to the Clipboard, allowing a linked item to be pasted; otherwise **FALSE**.

Remarks

Call this function to copy the OLE item to the Clipboard. Typically, you call this function when writing message handlers for the Copy or Cut commands from the Edit menu. You must implement item selection in your container application if you want to implement the Copy or Cut commands.

For more information, see **OleSetClipboard** in the OLE documentation.

COleClientItem::CreateCloneFrom

BOOL CreateCloneFrom(const COleClientItem* *pSrcItem* **);**

Return Value

Nonzero if successful; otherwise 0.

Parameters

pSrcItem   Pointer to the OLE item to be duplicated.

Remarks

Call this function to create a copy of the specified OLE item. The copy is identical to the source item. You can use this function to support undo operations.

See Also: COleClientItem::CreateNewItem

COleClientItem::CreateFromClipboard

BOOL CreateFromClipboard(OLERENDER *render* **= OLERENDER_DRAW,**
↪ CLIPFORMAT *cfFormat* **= 0, LPFORMATETC** *lpFormatEtc* **= NULL);**

Return Value

Nonzero if successful; otherwise 0.

Parameters

render   Flag specifying how the server will render the OLE item. For the possible values, see **OLERENDER** in the OLE documentation.

cfFormat   Specifies the Clipboard data format to be cached when creating the OLE item.

lpFormatEtc   Pointer to a **FORMATETC** structure used if *render* is
OLERENDER_FORMAT or **OLERENDER_DRAW**. Provide a value for this
parameter only if you want to specify additional format information beyond the
Clipboard format specified by *cfFormat*. If you omit this parameter, default values
are used for the other fields in the **FORMATETC** structure.

Remarks

Call this function to create an embedded item from the contents of the Clipboard. You
typically call this function from the message handler for the Paste command on the
Edit menu. (The Paste command is enabled by the framework if the **CanPaste**
member function returns nonzero.)

For more information, see **OLERENDER** and **FORMATETC** in the OLE
documentation.

See Also: **COleDataObject::AttachClipboard**,
COleClientItem::CreateFromData, **COleClientItem::CanPaste**

COleClientItem::CreateFromData

BOOL CreateFromData(COleDataObject* *pDataObject*,
↪ **OLERENDER** *render* = **OLERENDER_DRAW, CLIPFORMAT** *cfFormat* = **0,**
↪ **LPFORMATETC** *lpFormatEtc* = **NULL**);

Return Value

Nonzero if successful; otherwise 0.

Parameters

pDataObject   Pointer to the **COleDataObject** object from which the OLE item is to
be created.

render   Flag specifying how the server will render the OLE item. For the possible
values, see **OLERENDER** in the OLE documentation.

cfFormat   Specifies the Clipboard data format to be cached when creating the OLE
item.

lpFormatEtc   Pointer to a **FORMATETC** structure used if *render* is
OLERENDER_FORMAT or **OLERENDER_DRAW**. Provide a value for this
parameter only if you want to specify additional format information beyond the
Clipboard format specified by *cfFormat*. If you omit this parameter, default values
are used for the other fields in the **FORMATETC** structure.

Remarks

Call this function to create an embedded item from a **COleDataObject** object. Data
transfer operations, such as pasting from the Clipboard or drag-and-drop operations,
provide **COleDataObject** objects containing the information offered by a server
application. It is usually used in your override of **CView::OnDrop**.

For more information, see **OleCreateFromData**, **OLERENDER**, and **FORMATETC** in the OLE documentation.

See Also: **COleDataObject::AttachClipboard**, **COleClientItem::CreateFromClipboard**, **COleDataObject**

COleClientItem::CreateFromFile

BOOL CreateFromFile(LPCTSTR *lpszFileName*,
   ↪ **REFCLSID** *clsid* = **CLSID_NULL,**
   ↪ **OLERENDER** *render* = **OLERENDER_DRAW, CLIPFORMAT** *cfFormat* = **0,**
   ↪ **LPFORMATETC** *lpFormatEtc* = **NULL);**

Return Value

Nonzero if successful; otherwise 0.

Parameters

lpszFileName Pointer to the name of the file from which the OLE item is to be created.

clsid Reserved for future use.

render Flag specifying how the server will render the OLE item. For the possible values, see **OLERENDER** in the OLE documentation.

cfFormat Specifies the Clipboard data format to be cached when creating t he OLE item.

lpFormatEtc Pointer to a **FORMATETC** structure used if *render* is **OLERENDER_FORMAT** or **OLERENDER_DRAW**. Provide a value for this parameter only if you want to specify additional format information beyond the Clipboard format specified by *cfFormat*. If you omit this parameter, default values are used for the other fields in the **FORMATETC** structure.

Remarks

Call this function to create an embedded OLE item from a file. The framework calls this function from **COleInsertDialog::CreateItem** if the user chooses OK from the Insert Object dialog box when the Create from File button is selected.

For more information, see **OleCreateFromFile**, **OLERENDER**, and **FORMATETC** in the OLE documentation.

See Also: **COleInsertDialog::CreateItem**

COleClientItem::CreateLinkFromClipboard

BOOL CreateLinkFromClipboard(
  ↳ **OLERENDER** *render* = **OLERENDER_DRAW,**
  ↳ **CLIPFORMAT** *cfFormat* = **0, LPFORMATETC** *lpFormatEtc* = **NULL);**

Return Value

Nonzero if successful; otherwise 0.

Parameters

render   Flag specifying how the server will render the OLE item. For the possible values, see **OLERENDER** in the OLE documentation.

cfFormat   Specifies the Clipboard data format to be cached when creating the OLE item.

lpFormatEtc   Pointer to a **FORMATETC** structure used if *render* is **OLERENDER_FORMAT** or **OLERENDER_DRAW**. Provide a value for this parameter only if you want to specify additional format information beyond the Clipboard format specified by *cfFormat*. If you omit this parameter, default values are used for the other fields in the **FORMATETC** structure.

Remarks

Call this function to create a linked item from the contents of the Clipboard. You typically call this function from the message handler for the Paste Link command on the Edit menu. (The Paste Link command is enabled in the default implementation of **COleDocument** if the Clipboard contains an OLE item that can be linked to.)

For more information, see **OLERENDER** and **FORMATETC** in the OLE documentation.

See Also: **COleClientItem::CanPasteLink,**
COleClientItem::CreateLinkFromData, COleDataObject::AttachClipboard

---

COleClientItem::CreateLinkFromData

BOOL CreateLinkFromData(COleDataObject* *pDataObject***,**
  ↳ **OLERENDER** *render* = **OLERENDER_DRAW, CLIPFORMAT** *cfFormat* = **0,**
  ↳ **LPFORMATETC** *lpFormatEtc* = **NULL);**

Return Value

Nonzero if successful; otherwise 0.

Parameters

pDataObject   Pointer to the **COleDataObject** object from which the OLE item is to be created.

render   Flag specifying how the server will render the OLE item. For the possible values, see **OLERENDER** in the OLE documentation.

cfFormat Specifies the Clipboard data format to be cached when creating the OLE item.

lpFormatEtc Pointer to a **FORMATETC** structure used if *render* is **OLERENDER_FORMAT** or **OLERENDER_DRAW**. Provide a value for this parameter only if you want to specify additional format information beyond the Clipboard format specified by *cfFormat*. If you omit this parameter, default values are used for the other fields in the **FORMATETC** structure.

Remarks

Call this function to create a linked item from a **COleDataObject** object. Call this during a drop operation when the user indicates a link should be created. It can also be used to handle the Edit Paste command. It is called by the framework in **COleClientItem::CreateLinkFromClipboard** and in **COlePasteSpecialDialog::CreateItem** when the Link option has been selected.

For more information, see **OleCreateLinkFromData**, **OLERENDER**, and **FORMATETC** in the OLE documentation.

See Also: **COleDataObject::AttachClipboard**, **COleDataObject**, **COleClientItem::CreateLinkFromClipboard**

COleClientItem::CreateLinkFromFile

BOOL CreateLinkFromFile(LPCTSTR *lpszFileName***,**
↳ **OLERENDER** *render* **= OLERENDER_DRAW, CLIPFORMAT** *cfFormat* **= 0,**
↳ **LPFORMATETC** *lpFormatEtc* **= NULL);**

Return Value

Nonzero if successful; otherwise 0.

Parameters

lpszFileName Pointer to the name of the file from which the OLE item is to be created.

render Flag specifying how the server will render the OLE item. For the possible values, see **OLERENDER** in the OLE documentation.

cfFormat Specifies the Clipboard data format to be cached when creating the OLE item.

lpFormatEtc Pointer to a **FORMATETC** structure used if *render* is **OLERENDER_FORMAT** or **OLERENDER_DRAW**. Provide a value for this parameter only if you want to specify additional format information beyond the Clipboard format specified by *cfFormat*. If you omit this parameter, default values are used for the other fields in the **FORMATETC** structure.

Remarks

Call this function to create a linked OLE item from a file. The framework calls this function if the user chooses OK from the Insert Object dialog box when the Create from File button is selected and the Link check box is checked. It is called from **COleInsertDialog::CreateItem**.

For more information, see **OleCreateLinkToFile**, **OLERENDER**, and **FORMATETC** in the OLE documentation.

See Also: **COleInsertDialog::CreateItem**

COleClientItem::CreateNewItem

BOOL CreateNewItem(REFCLSID *clsid***,**
  ↪ **OLERENDER** *render* = **OLERENDER_DRAW,**
  ↪ **CLIPFORMAT** *cfFormat* = **0, LPFORMATETC** *lpFormatEtc* = **NULL);**

Return Value

Nonzero if successful; otherwise 0.

Parameters

clsid   ID that uniquely identifies the type of OLE item to create.

render   Flag specifying how the server will render the OLE item. For the possible values, see **OLERENDER** in the OLE documentation.

cfFormat   Specifies the Clipboard data format to be cached when creating the OLE item.

lpFormatEtc   Pointer to a **FORMATETC** structure used if *render* is **OLERENDER_FORMAT** or **OLERENDER_DRAW**. Provide a value for this parameter only if you want to specify additional format information beyond the Clipboard format specified by *cfFormat*. If you omit this parameter, default values are used for the other fields in the **FORMATETC** structure.

Remarks

Call this function to create an embedded item; this function launches the server application that allows the user to create the OLE item. The framework calls this function if the user chooses OK from the Insert Object dialog box when the Create New button is selected.

For more information, see **OleCreate**, **OLERENDER**, and **FORMATETC** in the OLE documentation.

See Also: **COleInsertDialog::CreateItem**

COleClientItem::CreateStaticFromClipboard

BOOL CreateStaticFromClipboard(
⤷ **OLERENDER** *render* = **OLERENDER_DRAW,**
⤷ **CLIPFORMAT** *cfFormat* = **0, LPFORMATETC** *lpFormatEtc* = **NULL);**

Return Value

Nonzero if successful; otherwise 0.

Parameters

render Flag specifying how the server will render the OLE item. For the possible values, see **OLERENDER** in the OLE documentation.

cfFormat Specifies the Clipboard data format to be cached when creating the OLE item.

lpFormatEtc Pointer to a **FORMATETC** structure used if *render* is **OLERENDER_FORMAT** or **OLERENDER_DRAW**. Provide a value for this parameter only if you want to specify additional format information beyond the Clipboard format specified by *cfFormat*. If you omit this parameter, default values are used for the other fields in the **FORMATETC** structure.

Remarks

Call this function to create a static item from the contents of the Clipboard. A static item contains the presentation data but not the native data; consequently it cannot be edited. You typically call this function if the **CreateFromClipboard** member function fails.

For more information, see **OLERENDER** and **FORMATETC** in the OLE documentation.

See Also: **COleDataObject::AttachClipboard, COleClientItem::CanPaste, COleClientItem::CreateStaticFromData**

COleClientItem::CreateStaticFromData

BOOL CreateStaticFromData(COleDataObject* *pDataObject***,**
⤷ **OLERENDER** *render* = **OLERENDER_DRAW,**
⤷ **CLIPFORMAT** *cfFormat* = **0, LPFORMATETC** *lpFormatEtc* = **NULL);**

Return Value

Nonzero if successful; otherwise 0.

Parameters

pDataObject Pointer to the **COleDataObject** object from which the OLE item is to be created.

> *render*   Flag specifying how the server will render the OLE item. For the possible values, see **OLERENDER** in the OLE documentation.
>
> *cfFormat*   Specifies the Clipboard data format to be cached when creating the OLE item.
>
> *lpFormatEtc*   Pointer to a **FORMATETC** structure used if *render* is **OLERENDER_FORMAT** or **OLERENDER_DRAW**. Provide a value for this parameter only if you want to specify additional format information beyond the Clipboard format specified by *cfFormat*. If you omit this parameter, default values are used for the other fields in the **FORMATETC** structure.

Remarks

Call this function to create a static item from a **COleDataObject** object. A static item contains the presentation data but not the native data; consequently, it cannot be edited. This is essentially the same as **CreateStaticFromClipboard** except that a static item can be created from an arbitrary **COleDataObject**, not just from the Clipboard.

Used in **COlePasteSpecialDialog::CreateItem** when Static is selected.

For more information, see **OleCreateStaticFromData**, **OLERENDER**, and **FORMATETC** in the OLE documentation.

See Also: **COleDataObject::AttachClipboard**, **COleDataObject**

COleClientItem::Deactivate

> **void Deactivate( );**

Remarks

Call this function to deactivate the OLE item and free any associated resources. You typically deactivate an in-place active OLE item when the user clicks the mouse on the client area outside the bounds of the item. Note that deactivating the OLE item will discard its undo state, making it impossible to call the **ReactivateAndUndo** member function.

If your application supports undo, do not call **Deactivate**; instead, call **DeactivateUI**.

For more information, see **IOleInPlaceObject::InPlaceDeactivate** in the OLE documentation.

See Also: **COleClientItem::ReactivateAndUndo**, **COleClientItem::DeactivateUI**

COleClientItem::DeactivateUI

void DeactivateUI( );

Remarks

Call this function when the user deactivates an item that was activated in place. This function restores the container application's user interface to its original state, hiding any menus and other controls that were created for in-place activation.

This function does not flush the undo state information for the item. That information is retained so that **ReactivateAndUndo** can later be used to execute an undo command in the server application, in case the container's undo command is chosen immediately after deactivating the item.

For more information, see **IOleInPlaceObject::InPlaceDeactivate** in the OLE documentation.

See Also: **COleClientItem::ReactivateAndUndo, COleClientItem::Activate**

COleClientItem::Delete

void Delete(BOOL *bAutoDelete* = **TRUE);**

Parameters

bAutoDelete Specifies whether the item is to be removed from the document.

Remarks

Call this function to delete the OLE item from the container document. This function calls the **Release** member function, which in turn deletes the C++ object for the item, permanently removing the OLE item from the document. If the OLE item is embedded, the native data for the item is deleted. It always closes a running server; therefore, if the item is an open link, this function closes it.

See Also: **COleClientItem::Release**

COleClientItem::DoDragDrop

DROPEFFECT DoDragDrop(LPCRECT *lpItemRect***, CPoint** *ptOffset***,**
  ↪ **BOOL** *bIncludeLink* = **FALSE,**
  ↪ **DWORD** *dwEffects* = **DROPEFFECT_COPY | DROPEFFECT_MOVE,**
  ↪ **LPCRECT** *lpRectStartDrag* = **NULL);**

Return Value

A **DROPEFFECT** value. If it is **DROPEFFECT_MOVE**, the original data should be removed.

Parameters

> *lpItemRect*   The item's rectangle on screen in client coordinates (pixels).
>
> *ptOffset*   The offset from *lpItemRect* where the mouse position was at the time of the drag.
>
> *bIncludeLink*   Set this to **TRUE** if the link data should be copied to the Clipboard. Set it to **FALSE** if your server application does not support links.
>
> *dwEffects*   Determines the effects that the drag source will allow in the drag operation.
>
> *lpRectStartDrag*   Pointer to the rectangle that defines where the drag actually starts. For more information, see the following Remarks section.

Remarks

> Call the **DoDragDrop** member function to perform a drag-and-drop operation. The drag-and-drop operation does not start immediately. It waits until the mouse cursor leaves the rectangle specified by *lpRectStartDrag* or until a specified number of milliseconds have passed. If *lpRectStartDrag* is **NULL**, the size of the rectangle is one pixel. The delay time is specified by the **DragDelay** value in the [Windows] section of WIN.INI. If this value is not in WIN.INI, the default value of 200 milliseconds is used.
>
> **See Also: COleDataSource::DoDragDrop, COleClientItem::CopyToClipboard**

COleClientItem::DoVerb

virtual BOOL DoVerb(LONG *nVerb*, **CView*** *pView*, **LPMSG** *lpMsg* = **NULL**);

Return Value

> Nonzero if the verb was successfully executed; otherwise 0.

Parameters

> *nVerb*   Specifies the verb to execute. It can include one of the following:

Value	Meaning	Symbol
0	Primary verb	**OLEIVERB_PRIMARY**
1	Secondary verb	(None)
−1	Display item for editing	**OLEIVERB_SHOW**
−2	Edit item in separate window	**OLEIVERB_OPEN**
−3	Hide item	**OLEIVERB_HIDE**

> The −1 value is typically an alias for another verb. If open editing is not supported, −2 has the same effect as −1. For additional values, see **IOleObject::DoVerb** in the OLE documentation.

This parameter should be **NULL** if the container application does not allow in-place activation.

lpMsg   Pointer to the message that caused the item to be activated.

Remarks

Call **DoVerb** to execute the specified verb. This function calls the **Activate** member function to execute the verb. It also catches exceptions and displays a message box to the user if one is thrown.

If the primary verb is Edit and zero is specified in the *nVerb* parameter, the server application is launched to allow the OLE item to be edited. If the container application supports in-place activation, editing can be done in place. If the container does not support in-place activation (or if the Open verb is specified), the server is launched in a separate window and editing can be done there. Typically, when the user of the container application double-clicks the OLE item, the value for the primary verb in the *nVerb* parameter determines which action the user can take. However, if the server supports only one action, it takes that action, no matter which value is specified in the *nVerb* parameter.

See Also: COleClientItem::Activate

COleClientItem::Draw

BOOL Draw(CDC* *pDC*, LPCRECT *lpBounds*,
↳ DVASPECT *nDrawAspect* = (DVASPECT)-1);

Return Value

Nonzero if successful; otherwise 0.

Parameters

pDC   Pointer to a **CDC** object used for drawing the OLE item.

lpBounds   Pointer to a **CRect** object or **RECT** structure that defines the bounding rectangle in which to draw the OLE item (in logical units determined by the device context).

nDrawAspect   Specifies the aspect of the OLE item, that is, how it should be displayed. If *nDrawAspect* is –1, the last aspect set by using **SetDrawAspect** is used. For more information about possible values for this flag, see **SetDrawAspect**.

Remarks

Call this function to draw the OLE item into the specified bounding rectangle using the specified device context. The function may use the metafile representation of the OLE item created by the **OnDraw** member function of **COleServerItem**.

Typically you use **Draw** for screen display, passing the screen device context as *pDC*. In this case, you need to specify only the first two parameters.

The *lpBounds* parameter identifies the rectangle in the target device context (relative to its current mapping mode). Rendering may involve scaling the picture and can be used by container applications to impose a view that scales between the displayed view and the final printed image.

For more information, see **IViewObject::Draw** in the OLE documentation.

See Also: **COleClientItem::SetExtent**, **COleServerItem::OnDraw**

COleClientItem::GetActiveView

CView* GetActiveView( ) const;

Return Value

A pointer to the view; otherwise **NULL** if the item is not in-place activated.

Remarks

Returns the view on which the item is in-place activated.

See Also: **COleClientItem::IsInPlaceActive**, **COleClientItem::GetDocument**

COleClientItem::GetCachedExtent

BOOL GetCachedExtent(LPSIZE *lpSize,*
   → **DVASPECT** *nDrawAspect* = **(DVASPECT)-1**);

Return Value

Nonzero if successful; 0 if the OLE item is blank.

Parameters

lpSize Pointer to a **SIZE** structure or a **CSize** object that will receive the size information.

nDrawAspect Specifies the aspect of the OLE item whose bounds are to be retrieved. For possible values, see **SetDrawAspect**.

Remarks

Call this function to retrieve the OLE item's size. This function provides the same information as **GetExtent**. However, you can call **GetCachedExtent** to get extent information during the processing of other OLE handlers, such as **OnChange**. The dimensions are in **MM_HIMETRIC** units.

This is possible because **GetCachedExtent** uses the **IViewObject2** interface rather than use the **IOleObject** interface to get the extent of this item. The **IViewObject2** COM object caches the extent information used in the previous call to **IViewObject::Draw**.

For more information, see **IViewObject2::GetExtent** in the OLE documentation.

See Also: **COleClientItem::GetExtent**, **COleClientItem::SetExtent**, **COleServerItem::OnGetExtent**

COleClientItem::GetClassID

void GetClassID(CLSID* *pClassID* **) const;**

Parameters

> *pClassID*   Pointer to an identifier of type **CLSID** to retrieve the class ID. For information on **CLSID**, see the OLE documentation.

Remarks

> Returns the class ID of the item into the memory pointed to by *pClassID*. The class ID is a 128-bit number that uniquely identifies the application that edits the item.
>
> For more information, see **IPersist::GetClassID** in the OLE documentation.

COleClientItem::GetClipboardData

void GetClipboardData(COleDataSource* *pDataSource*,
> ↳ **BOOL** *bIncludeLink* = **FALSE, LPPOINT** *lpOffset* = **NULL,**
> ↳ **LPSIZE** *lpSize* = **NULL**);

Parameters

> *pDataSource*   Pointer to a **COleDataSource** object that will receive the data contained in the OLE item.
>
> *bIncludeLink*   **TRUE** if link data should be included; otherwise **FALSE**.
>
> *lpOffset*   The offset of the mouse cursor from the origin of the object in pixels.
>
> *lpSize*   The size of the object in pixels.

Remarks

> Call this function to get a **COleDataSource** object containing all the data that would be placed on the Clipboard by a call to the **CopyToClipboard** member function.
>
> Override **GetClipboardData** only if you want to offer data formats in addition to those offered by **CopyToClipboard**. Place those formats in the **COleDataSource** object before or after calling **CopyToClipboard**, and then pass the **COleDataSource** object to the **COleDataSource::SetClipboard** function. For example, if you want the OLE item's position in its container document to accompany it on the Clipboard, you would define your own format for passing that information and place it in the **COleDataSource** before calling **CopyToClipboard**.
>
> **See Also:**   **COleDataSource, COleClientItem::CopyToClipboard, COleDataSource::SetClipboard**

COleClientItem::GetDocument

COleDocument* GetDocument( ) const;

Return Value

A pointer to the document that contains the OLE item. **NULL** if the item is not part of a document.

Remarks

Call this function to get a pointer to the document that contains the OLE item. This pointer allows access to the **COleDocument** object that you passed as an argument to the **COleClientItem** constructor.

See Also: **COleClientItem::COleClientItem, COleDocument, COleLinkingDoc**

COleClientItem::GetDrawAspect

DVASPECT GetDrawAspect( ) const;

Return Value

A value from the **DVASPECT** enumeration, whose values are listed in the reference for **SetDrawAspect**.

Remarks

Call the **GetDrawAspect** member function to determine the current "aspect," or view, of the item. The aspect specifies how the item is to be rendered.

See Also: **COleClientItem::SetDrawAspect, COleClientItem::Draw**

COleClientItem::GetExtent

BOOL GetExtent(LPSIZE *lpSize***, DVASPECT** *nDrawAspect* **= (DVASPECT)-1);**

Return Value

Nonzero if successful; 0 if the OLE item is blank.

Parameters

lpSize   Pointer to a **SIZE** structure or a **CSize** object that will receive the size information.

nDrawAspect   Specifies the aspect of the OLE item whose bounds are to be retrieved. For possible values, see **SetDrawAspect**.

Remarks

Call this function to retrieve the OLE item's size.

If the server application was written using the Microsoft Foundation Class Library, this function causes the **OnGetExtent** member function of the corresponding

COleServerItem object to be called. Note that the retrieved size may differ from the size last set by the **SetExtent** member function; the size specified by **SetExtent** is treated as a suggestion. The dimensions are in **MM_HIMETRIC** units.

Note Do not call **GetExtent** during the processing of an OLE handler, such as **OnChange**. Call **GetCachedExtent** instead.

For more information, see **IOleObject::GetExtent** in the OLE documentation.

See Also: **COleClientItem::SetExtent**, **COleClientItem::GetCachedExtent**, **COleServerItem::OnGetExtent**

COleClientItem::GetIconicMetafile

HGLOBAL GetIconicMetafile( );

Return Value

A handle to the metafile if successful; otherwise **NULL**.

Remarks

Retrieves the metafile used for drawing the item's icon. If there is no current icon, a default icon is returned. This is called automatically by the MFC/OLE dialogs and is usually not called directly.

This function also calls **SetIconicMetafile** to cache the metafile for later use.

See Also: **COleClientItem::SetIconicMetafile**

COleClientItem::GetInPlaceWindow

CWnd* GetInPlaceWindow( );

Return Value

A pointer to the item's in-place editing window; **NULL** if the item is not active or if its server is unavailable.

Remarks

Call the **GetInPlaceWindow** member function to get a pointer to the window in which the item has been opened for in-place editing. This function should be called only for items that are in-place active.

See Also: **COleClientItem::Activate**, **COleClientItem::Deactivate**, **COleClientItem::SetItemRects**

COleClientItem::GetItemState

UINT GetItemState( ) const;

Return Value

A **COleClientItem::ItemState** enumerated value, which can be one of the following: **emptyState**, **loadedState**, **openState**, **activeState**, **activeUIState**. For information about these states, see the article "Containers: Client-Item States" in *Visual C++ Programmer's Guide* online.

Remarks

Call this function to get the OLE item's current state. To be notified when the OLE item's state changes, use the **OnChange** member function.

For more information, see the article "Containers: Client-Item States" in *Visual C++ Programmer's Guide* online.

See Also: COleClientItem::OnChange

COleClientItem::GetLastStatus

SCODE GetLastStatus( ) const;

Return Value

An **SCODE** value.

Remarks

Returns the status code of the last OLE operation. For member functions that return a **BOOL** value of **FALSE**, or other member functions that return **NULL**, **GetLastStatus** returns more detailed failure information. Be aware that most OLE member functions throw exceptions for more serious errors. The specific information on the interpretation of the **SCODE** depends on the underlying OLE call that last returned an **SCODE** value.

For more information on **SCODE**, see "Structure of OLE Error Codes" in the OLE documentation.

COleClientItem::GetLinkUpdateOptions

OLEUPDATE GetLinkUpdateOptions( );

Return Value

One of the following values:

- **OLEUPDATE_ALWAYS** Update the linked item whenever possible. This option supports the Automatic link-update radio button in the Links dialog box.

- **OLEUPDATE_ONCALL**   Update the linked item only on request from the container application (when the **UpdateLink** member function is called). This option supports the Manual link-update radio button in the Links dialog box.

Remarks

Call this function to get the current value of the link-update option for the OLE item. This is an advanced operation.

This function is called automatically by the **COleLinksDialog** class.

For more information, see **IOleLink::GetUpdateOptions** in the OLE documentation.

See Also: **COleClientItem::SetLinkUpdateOptions**, **COleLinksDialog**

COleClientItem::GetType

OLE_OBJTYPE GetType( ) const;

Return Value

An unsigned integer with one of the following values:

- **OT_LINK**   The OLE item is a link.
- **OT_EMBEDDED**   The OLE item is embedded.
- **OT_STATIC**   The OLE item is static, that is, it contains only presentation data, not native data, and thus cannot be edited.

Remarks

Call this function to determine whether the OLE item is embedded or linked, or static.

See Also: **COleClientItem::GetUserType**

COleClientItem::GetUserType

void GetUserType(USERCLASSTYPE *nUserClassType*, **CString&** *rString*);

Parameters

nUserClassType   A value indicating the desired variant of the string describing the OLE item's type. This can have one of the following values:

- **USERCLASSTYPE_FULL**   The full type name displayed to the user.
- **USERCLASSTYPE_SHORT**   A short name (15 characters maximum) for use in pop-up menus and the Edit Links dialog box.
- **USERCLASSTYPE_APPNAME**   Name of the application servicing the class.

rString   A reference to a **CString** object to which the string describing the OLE item's type is to be returned.

Remarks

Call this function to get the user-visible string describing the OLE item's type, such as "Word document." This is often the entry in the system registration database.

If the full type name is requested but not available, the short name is used instead. If no entry for the type of OLE item is found in the registration database, or if there are no user types registered for the type of OLE item, then the user type currently stored in the OLE item is used. If that user type name is an empty string, "Unknown Object" is used.

For more information, see **IOleObject::GetUserType** in the OLE documentation.

See Also: COleClientItem::GetType

COleClientItem::IsInPlaceActive

BOOL IsInPlaceActive( ) const;

Return Value

Nonzero if the OLE item is in-place active; otherwise 0.

Remarks

Call this function to see whether the OLE item is in-place active. It is common to execute different logic depending on whether the item is being edited in place. The function checks whether the current item state is equal to either the **activeState** or the **activeUIState**.

See Also: COleClientItem::GetItemState

COleClientItem::IsLinkUpToDate

BOOL IsLinkUpToDate( ) const;

Return Value

Nonzero if the OLE item is up to date; otherwise 0.

Remarks

Call this function to see whether the OLE item is up to date. A linked item can be out of date if its source document has been updated. An embedded item that contains links within it can similarly become out of date. The function does a recursive check of the OLE item. Note that determining whether an OLE item is out of date can be as expensive as actually performing an update.

This is called automatically by the **COleLinksDialog** implementation.

For more information, see **IOleObject::IsUpToDate** in the OLE documentation.

COleClientItem::IsModified

BOOL IsModified( ) const;

Return Value

Nonzero if the OLE item is dirty; otherwise 0.

Remarks

Call this function to see whether the OLE item is dirty (modified since it was last saved).

For more information, see **IPersistStorage::IsDirty** in the OLE documentation.

COleClientItem::IsOpen

BOOL IsOpen( ) const;

Return Value

Nonzero if the OLE item is open; otherwise 0.

Remarks

Call this function to see whether the OLE item is open; that is, opened in an instance of the server application running in a separate window. It is used to determine when to draw the object with a hatching pattern. An open object should have a hatch pattern drawn on top of the object. You can use a **CRectTracker** object to accomplish this.

See Also: **COleClientItem::GetItemState, CRectTracker**

COleClientItem::IsRunning

BOOL IsRunning( ) const;

Return Value

Nonzero if the OLE item is running; otherwise 0.

Remarks

Call this function to see whether the OLE item is running; that is, whether the item is loaded and running in the server application.

For more information, see **OleIsRunning** in the OLE documentation.

COleClientItem::OnActivate

virtual void OnActivate( );

Called by the framework to notify the item that it has just been activated in place. Note that this function is called to indicate that the server is running, not to indicate that its user interface has been installed in the container application. At this point, the object does not have an active user interface (is not **activeUIState**). It has not installed its menus or toolbar. The **OnActivateUI** member function is called when that happens.

The default implementation calls the **OnChange** member function with **OLE_CHANGEDSTATE** as a parameter. Override this function to perform custom processing when an item becomes in-place active.

See Also: **COleClientItem::OnDeactivate**, **COleClientItem::OnDeactivateUI**, **COleClientItem::OnActivateUI**, **COleClientItem::CanActivate**

COleClientItem::OnActivateUI

virtual void OnActivateUI( );

The framework calls **OnActivateUI** when the object has entered the active UI state. The object has now installed its tool bar and menus.

The default implementation remembers the server's **HWND** for later **GetServerWindow** calls.

See Also: **COleClientItem::OnDeactivate**, **COleClientItem::OnDeactivateUI**, **COleClientItem::OnActivate**, **COleClientItem::CanActivate**

COleClientItem::OnChange

virtual void OnChange(OLE_NOTIFICATION *nCode*, **DWORD** *dwParam* **);**

nCode The reason the server changed this item. It can have one of the following values:

- **OLE_CHANGED** The OLE item's appearance has changed.
- **OLE_SAVED** The OLE item has been saved.
- **OLE_CLOSED** The OLE item has been closed.

- **OLE_CHANGED_STATE** The OLE item has changed from one state to another.

dwParam If *nCode* is **OLE_SAVED** or **OLE_CLOSED**, this parameter is not used. If *nCode* is **OLE_CHANGED**, this parameter specifies the aspect of the OLE item that has changed. For possible values, see the *dwParam* parameter of **COleClientItem::Draw**. If *nCode* is **OLE_CHANGED_STATE**, this parameter is a **COleClientItem::ItemState** enumerated value and describes the state being entered. It can have one of the following values: **emptyState**, **loadedState**, **openState**, **activeState**, or **activeUIState**.

Remarks

Called by the framework when the user modifies, saves, or closes the OLE item. (If the server application is written using the Microsoft Foundation Class Library, this function is called in response to the **Notify** member functions of **COleServerDoc** or **COleServerItem**.) The default implementation marks the container document as modified if *nCode* is **OLE_CHANGED** or **OLE_SAVED**.

For **OLE_CHANGED_STATE**, the current state returned from **GetItemState** will still be the old state, meaning the state that was current prior to this state change.

Override this function to respond to changes in the OLE item's state. Typically you update the item's appearance by invalidating the area in which the item is displayed. Call the base class implementation at the beginning of your override.

See Also: **COleClientItem::GetItemState**, **COleServerItem::NotifyChanged**, **COleServerDoc::NotifyChanged**, **COleServerDoc::NotifyClosed**, **COleServerDoc::NotifySaved**

COleClientItem::OnChangeItemPosition

virtual BOOL OnChangeItemPosition(const CRect& *rectPos* **);**

Return Value

Nonzero if the item's position is successfully changed; otherwise 0.

Parameters

rectPos Indicates the item's position relative to the container application's client area.

Remarks

Called by the framework to notify the container that the OLE item's extent has changed during in-place activation. The default implementation determines the new visible rectangle of the OLE item and calls **SetItemRects** with the new values. The default implementation calculates the visible rectangle for the item and passes that information to the server.

Override this function to apply special rules to the resize/move operation. If the application is written in MFC, this call results because the server called **COleServerDoc::RequestPositionChange**.

See Also: **COleServerDoc::RequestPositionChange**

COleClientItem::OnDeactivate

virtual void OnDeactivate( );

Remarks

Called by the framework when the OLE item transitions from the in-place active state (**activeState**) to the loaded state, meaning that it is deactivated after an in-place activation. Note that this function is called to indicate that the OLE item is closed, not that its user interface has been removed from the container application. When that happens, the **OnDeactivateUI** member function is called.

The default implementation calls the **OnChange** member function with **OLE_CHANGEDSTATE** as a parameter. Override this function to perform custom processing when an in-place active item is deactivated. For example, if you support the undo command in your container application, you can override this function to discard the undo state, indicating that the last operation performed on the OLE item cannot be undone once the item is deactivated.

See Also: **COleClientItem::OnGetWindowContext**, **COleClientItem::OnDeactivateUI**, **COleClientItem::OnActivateUI**, **COleClientItem::OnActivate**, **COleClientItem::CanActivate**, **CDocTemplate::SetContainerInfo**

COleClientItem::OnDeactivateAndUndo

virtual void OnDeactivateAndUndo( );

Remarks

Called by the framework when the user invokes the undo command after activating the OLE item in place. The default implementation calls **DeactivateUI** to deactivate the server's user interface. Override this function if you are implementing the undo command in your container application. In your override, call the base class version of the function and then undo the last command executed in your application.

For more information, see **IOleInPlaceSite::DeactivateAndUndo** in the OLE documentation.

See Also: **COleClientItem::DeactivateUI**

COleClientItem::OnDeactivateUI

virtual void OnDeactivateUI(BOOL *bUndoable* **);**

Parameters

bUndoable   Specifies whether the editing changes are undoable.

Remarks

Called when the user deactivates an item that was activated in place. This function restores the container application's user interface to its original state, hiding any menus and other controls that were created for in-place activation.

If *bUndoable* is **FALSE**, the container should disable the undo command, in effect discarding the undo state of the container, because it indicates that the last operation performed by the server is not undoable.

See Also: COleClientItem::OnActivateUI,
COleClientItem::OnDeactivateAndUndo, COleClientItem::OnDeactivate

---

COleClientItem::OnDiscardUndoState

virtual void OnDiscardUndoState( );

Remarks

Called by the framework when the user performs an action that discards the undo state while editing the OLE item. The default implementation does nothing. Override this function if you are implementing the undo command in your container application. In your override, discard the container application's undo state.

If the server was written with the Microsoft Foundation Class Library, the server can cause this function to be called by calling **COleServerDoc::DiscardUndoState**.

For more information, see **IOleInPlaceSite::DiscardUndoState** in the OLE documentation.

See Also: COleServerDoc::DiscardUndoState

COleClientItem::OnGetClipboardData

virtual COleDataSource* OnGetClipboardData(BOOL *bIncludeLink***,**
  ↳ LPPOINT *lpOffset***, LPSIZE** *lpSize* **);**

Return Value

A pointer to a **COleDataSource** object containing the Clipboard data.

Parameters

bIncludeLink   Set this to **TRUE** if link data should be copied to the Clipboard. Set this to **FALSE** if your server application does not support links.

lpOffset   Pointer to the offset of the mouse cursor from the origin of the object in pixels.

lpSize   Pointer to the size of the object in pixels.

Remarks

Called by the framework to get a **COleDataSource** object containing all the data that would be placed on the Clipboard by a call to either the **CopyToClipboard** or the **DoDragDrop** member function. The default implementation of this function calls **GetClipboardData**.

See Also: **COleDataSource, COleClientItem::CopyToClipboard, COleClientItem::GetClipboardData, COleDataSource::SetClipboard**

COleClientItem::OnGetClipRect

virtual void OnGetClipRect(CRect& *rClipRect* **);**

Parameters

rClipRect   Pointer to an object of class **CRect** that will hold the clipping-rectangle coordinates of the item.

Remarks

The framework calls the **OnGetClipRect** member function to get the clipping-rectangle coordinates of the item that is being edited in place. Coordinates are in pixels relative to the container application window's client area.

The default implementation simply returns the client rectangle of the view on which the item is in-place active.

See Also: **COleClientItem::OnActivate**

COleClientItem::OnGetItemPosition

virtual void OnGetItemPosition(CRect& *rPosition* **);**

Parameters

rPosition   Reference to the **CRect** object that will contain the item's position coordinates.

Remarks

The framework calls the **OnGetItemPosition** member function to get the coordinates of the item that is being edited in place. Coordinates are in pixels relative to the container application window's client area.

The default implementation of this function does nothing. Applications that support in-place editing require its implementation.

See Also: **COleClientItem::OnActivate, COleClientItem::OnActivateUI**

COleClientItem::OnGetWindowContext

virtual BOOL OnGetWindowContext(CFrameWnd** *ppMainFrame*,
↪ **CFrameWnd**** *ppDocFrame*,
↪ **LPOLEINPLACEFRAMEINFO** *lpFrameInfo* **);**

Return Value

Nonzero if successful; otherwise 0.

Parameters

ppMainFrame   Pointer to a pointer to the main frame window.

ppDocFrame   Pointer to a pointer to the document frame window.

lpFrameInfo   Pointer to an **OLEINPLACEFRAMEINFO** structure that will receive frame window information.

Remarks

Called by the framework when an item is activated in place. This function is used to retrieve information about the OLE item's parent window.

If the container is an MDI application, the default implementation returns a pointer to the **CMDIFrameWnd** object in *ppMainFrame* and a pointer to the active **CMDIChildWnd** object in *ppDocFrame*. If the container is an SDI application, the default implementation returns a pointer to the **CFrameWnd** object in *ppMainFrame* and returns **NULL** in *ppDocFrame*. The default implementation also fills in the members of *lpFrameInfo*.

Override this function only if the default implementation does not suit your application; for example, if your application has a user-interface paradigm that differs from SDI or MDI. This is an advanced overridable.

For more information, see **IOleInPlaceSite::GetWindowContext** and the **OLEINPLACEFRAMEINFO** structure in the OLE documentation.

COleClientItem::OnInsertMenus

virtual void OnInsertMenus(CMenu* *pMenuShared*,
↪ **LPOLEMENUGROUPWIDTHS** *lpMenuWidths* **);**

Parameters

pMenuShared   Points to an empty menu.

lpMenuWidths   Points to an array of six **LONG** values indicating how many menus are in each of the following menu groups: File, Edit, Container, Object, Window, Help. The container application is responsible for the File, Container, and Window menu groups, corresponding to elements 0, 2, and 4 of this array.

Remarks

Called by the framework during in-place activation to insert the container application's menus into an empty menu. This menu is then passed to the server, which inserts its own menus, creating a composite menu. This function can be called repeatedly to build several composite menus.

The default implementation inserts into *pMenuShared* the in-place container menus; that is, the File, Container, and Window menu groups. **CDocTemplate::SetContainerInfo** is used to set this menu resource. The default implementation also assigns the appropriate values to elements 0, 2, and 4 in *lpMenuWidths*, depending on the menu resource. Override this function if the default implementation is not appropriate for your application; for example, if your application does not use document templates for associating resources with document types. If you override this function, you should also override **OnSetMenu** and **OnRemoveMenus**. This is an advanced overridable.

For more information, see **IOleInPlaceFrame::InsertMenus** in the OLE documentation.

See Also: **COleClientItem::OnRemoveMenus, COleClientItem::OnSetMenu**

COleClientItem::OnRemoveMenus

virtual void OnRemoveMenus(CMenu* *pMenuShared* **);**

Parameters

pMenuShared   Points to the composite menu constructed by calls to the **OnInsertMenus** member function.

Remarks

Called by the framework to remove the container's menus from the specified composite menu when in-place activation ends.

The default implementation removes from *pMenuShared* the in-place container menus, that is, the File, Container, and Window menu groups. Override this function if the default implementation is not appropriate for your application; for example, if your application does not use document templates for associating resources with document types. If you override this function, you should probably override **OnInsertMenus** and **OnSetMenu** as well. This is an advanced overridable.

The submenus on *pMenuShared* may be shared by more than one composite menu if the server has repeatedly called **OnInsertMenus**. Therefore you should not delete any submenus in your override of **OnRemoveMenus**; you should only detach them.

For more information, see **IOleInPlaceFrame::RemoveMenus** in the OLE documentation.

See Also: **COleClientItem::OnInsertMenus, COleClientItem::OnSetMenu**

COleClientItem::OnScrollBy

virtual BOOL OnScrollBy(CSize *sizeExtent* **);**

Return Value

Nonzero if the item was scrolled; 0 if the item could not be scrolled.

Parameters

sizeExtent   Specifies the distances, in pixels, to scroll in the x and y directions.

Remarks

Called by the framework to scroll the OLE item in response to requests from the server. For example, if the OLE item is partially visible and the user moves outside the visible region while performing in-place editing, this function is called to keep the cursor visible. The default implementation does nothing. Override this function to scroll the item by the specified amount. Note that as a result of scrolling, the visible portion of the OLE item can change. Call **SetItemRects** to update the item's visible rectangle.

For more information, see **IOleInPlaceSite::Scroll** in the OLE documentation.

See Also: COleClientItem::SetItemRects

COleClientItem::OnSetMenu

virtual void OnSetMenu(CMenu* *pMenuShared,*
↪ HOLEMENU *holemenu,* **HWND** *hwndActiveObject* **);**

Parameters

pMenuShared   Pointer to the composite menu constructed by calls to the **OnInsertMenus** member function and the **::InsertMenu** function.

holemenu   Handle to the menu descriptor returned by the **::OleCreateMenuDescriptor** function, or **NULL** if the dispatching code is to be removed.

hwndActiveObject   Handle to the editing window for the OLE item. This is the window that will receive editing commands from OLE.

Remarks

Called by the framework two times when in-place activation begins and ends; the first time to install the composite menu and the second time (with *holemenu* equal to **NULL**) to remove it. The default implementation installs or removes the composite menu and then calls the **OleSetMenuDescriptor** function to install or remove the dispatching code. Override this function if the default implementation is not appropriate for your application. If you override this function, you should probably override **OnInsertMenus** and **OnRemoveMenus** as well. This is an advanced overridable.

For more information, see **OleCreateMenuDescriptor**, **OleSetMenuDescriptor**, and **IOleInPlaceFrame::SetMenu** in the OLE documentation.

See Also: **COleClientItem::OnInsertMenus**, **COleClientItem::OnRemoveMenus**

COleClientItem::OnShowControlBars

virtual BOOL OnShowControlBars(CFrameWnd* *pFrameWnd***, BOOL** *bShow* **);**

Return Value

Nonzero if the function call causes a change in the control bars' state; 0 if the call causes no change, or if *pFrameWnd* does not point to the container's frame window.

Parameters

pFrameWnd   Pointer to the container application's frame window. This can be either a main frame window or an MDI child window.

bShow   Specifies whether control bars are to be shown or hidden.

Remarks

Called by the framework to show and hide the container application's control bars. This function returns 0 if the control bars are already in the state specified by *bShow*. This would occur, for example, if the control bars are hidden and *bShow* is **FALSE**.

The default implementation removes the toolbar from the top-level frame window.

See Also: **COleClientItem::OnInsertMenus**, **COleClientItem::OnSetMenu**, **COleClientItem::OnRemoveMenus**, **COleClientItem::OnUpdateFrameTitle**

COleClientItem::OnShowItem

virtual void OnShowItem( );

Remarks

Called by the framework to display the OLE item, making it totally visible during editing. It is used when your container application supports links to embedded items (that is, if you have derived your document class from **COleLinkingDoc**). This function is called during in-place activation or when the OLE item is a link source and the user wants to edit it. The default implementation activates the first view on the container document. Override this function to scroll the document so that the OLE item is visible.

See Also: **COleLinkingDoc**

COleClientItem::OnUpdateFrameTitle

virtual BOOL OnUpdateFrameTitle( );

Return Value

Nonzero if this function successfully updated the frame title, otherwise zero.

Remarks

Called by the framework during in-place activation to update the frame window's title bar. The default implementation does not change the frame window title. Override this function if you want a different frame title for your application, for example "*server app - item* in *docname*" (as in, "Microsoft Excel - spreadsheet in REPORT.DOC"). This is an advanced overridable.

COleClientItem::ReactivateAndUndo

BOOL ReactivateAndUndo( );

Return Value

Nonzero if successful; otherwise 0.

Remarks

Call this function to reactivate the OLE item and undo the last operation performed by the user during in-place editing. If your container application supports the undo command, call this function if the user chooses the undo command immediately after deactivating the OLE item.

If the server application is written with the Microsoft Foundation Class Libraries, this function causes the server to call **COleServerDoc::OnReactivateAndUndo**.

For more information, see **IOleInPlaceObject::ReactivateAndUndo** in the OLE documentation.

See Also: COleServerDoc::OnReactivateAndUndo, COleClientItem::OnDeactivateAndUndo

COleClientItem::Release

virtual void Release(OLECLOSE *dwCloseOption* **= OLECLOSE_NOSAVE);**

Parameters

dwCloseOption Flag specifying under what circumstances the OLE item is saved when it returns to the loaded state. For a list of possible values, see **COleClientItem::Close**.

Remarks

Call this function to clean up resources used by the OLE item. **Release** is called by the **COleClientItem** destructor.

For more information, see **IUnknown::Release** in the OLE documentation.

See Also: **COleClientItem::Close**, **COleClientItem::Delete**

COleClientItem::Reload

BOOL Reload( );

Return Value

Nonzero if successful; otherwise 0.

Remarks

Closes and reloads the item. Call the **Reload** function after activating the item as an item of another type by a call to **ActivateAs**.

See Also: **COleClientItem::ActivateAs**

COleClientItem::Run

void Run( );

Remarks

Runs the application associated with this item.

Call the **Run** member function to launch the server application before activating the item. This is done automatically by **Activate** and **DoVerb**, so it is usually not necessary to call this function. Call this function if it is necessary to run the server in order to set an item attribute, such as **SetExtent**, before executing **DoVerb**.

See Also: **COleClientItem::IsRunning**

COleClientItem::SetDrawAspect

void SetDrawAspect(DVASPECT *nDrawAspect* **);**

Parameters

nDrawAspect   A value from the **DVASPECT** enumeration. This parameter can have one of the following values:

- **DVASPECT_CONTENT**   Item is represented in such a way that it can be displayed as an embedded object inside its container.

- **DVASPECT_THUMBNAIL**   Item is rendered in a "thumbnail" representation so that it can be displayed in a browsing tool.

- **DVASPECT_ICON**   Item is represented by an icon.
- **DVASPECT_DOCPRINT**   Item is represented as if it were printed using the Print command from the File menu.

Remarks

Call the **SetDrawAspect** member function to set the "aspect," or view, of the item. The aspect specifies how the item is to be rendered by **Draw** when the default value for that function's *nDrawAspect* argument is used.

This function is called automatically by the Change Icon (and other dialogs that call the Change Icon dialog directly) to enable the iconic display aspect when requested by the user.

See Also: **COleClientItem::GetDrawAspect, COleClientItem::Draw**

COleClientItem::SetExtent

void SetExtent(const CSize& *size*,
  ↳ **DVASPECT** *nDrawAspect* = **DVASPECT_CONTENT**);

Parameters

size   A **CSize** object that contains the size information.

nDrawAspect   Specifies the aspect of the OLE item whose bounds are to be set. For possible values, see **SetDrawAspect**.

Remarks

Call this function to specify how much space is available to the OLE item. If the server application was written using the Microsoft Foundation Class Library, this causes the **OnSetExtent** member function of the corresponding **COleServerItem** object to be called. The OLE item can then adjust its display accordingly. The dimensions must be in **MM_HIMETRIC** units. Call this function when the user resizes the OLE item or if you support some form of layout negotiation.

For more information, see **IOleObject::SetExtent** in the OLE documentation.

See Also: **COleClientItem::GetExtent, COleClientItem::GetCachedExtent, COleServerItem::OnSetExtent**

COleClientItem::SetHostNames

void SetHostNames(LPCTSTR *lpszHost*, **LPCTSTR** *lpszHostObj*);

Parameters

lpszHost   Pointer to the user-visible name of the container application.

lpszHostObj   Pointer to an identifying string of the container that contains the OLE item.

Remarks

Call this function to specify the name of the container application and the container's name for an embedded OLE item. If the server application was written using the Microsoft Foundation Class Library, this function calls the **OnSetHostNames** member function of the **COleServerDoc** document that contains the OLE item. This information is used in window titles when the OLE item is being edited. Each time a container document is loaded, the framework calls this function for all the OLE items in the document. **SetHostNames** is applicable only to embedded items. It is not necessary to call this function each time an embedded OLE item is activated for editing.

This is also called automatically with the application name and document name when an object is loaded or when a file is saved under a different name. Accordingly, it is not usually necessary to call this function directly.

For more information, see **IOleObject::SetHostNames** in the OLE documentation.

See Also: **COleServerDoc::OnSetHostNames**

COleClientItem::SetIconicMetafile

BOOL SetIconicMetafile(HGLOBAL *hMetaPict* **);**

Return Value

Nonzero if successful; otherwise 0.

Parameters

hMetaPict   A handle to the metafile used for drawing the item's icon.

Remarks

Caches the metafile used for drawing the item's icon. Use **GetIconicMetafile** to retrieve the metafile.

The *hMetaPict* parameter is copied into the item; therefore, *hMetaPict* must be freed by the caller.

See Also: **COleClientItem::GetIconicMetafile**

COleClientItem::SetItemRects

BOOL SetItemRects(LPCRECT *lpPosRect* **= NULL,**
   ↳ LPCRECT *lpClipRect* **= NULL);**

Return Value

Nonzero if successful; otherwise, 0.

Parameters

lprcPosRect   Pointer to the rectangle containing the bounds of the OLE item relative to its parent window, in client coordinates.

lprcClipRect   Pointer to the rectangle containing the bounds of the visible portion of the OLE item relative to its parent window, in client coordinates.

Remarks

Call this function to set the bounding rectangle or the visible rectangle of the OLE item. This function is called by the default implementation of the **OnChangeItemPosition** member function. You should call this function whenever the position or visible portion of the OLE item changes. Usually this means that you call it from your view's **OnSize** and **OnScrollBy** member functions.

For more information, see **IOleInPlaceObject::SetObjectRects** in the OLE documentation.

See Also: **COleClientItem::OnChangeItemPosition,
COleClientItem::OnGetItemPosition**

COleClientItem::SetLinkUpdateOptions

void SetLinkUpdateOptions(OLEUPDATE *dwUpdateOpt* **);**

Parameters

dwUpdateOpt   The value of the link-update option for this item. This value must be one of the following:

- **OLEUPDATE_ALWAYS**   Update the linked item whenever possible. This option supports the Automatic link-update radio button in the Links dialog box.

- **OLEUPDATE_ONCALL**   Update the linked item only on request from the container application (when the **UpdateLink** member function is called). This option supports the Manual link-update radio button in the Links dialog box.

Remarks

Call this function to set the link-update option for the presentation of the specified linked item. Typically, you should not change the update options chosen by the user in the Links dialog box.

For more information, see **IOleLink::SetUpdateOptions** in the OLE documentation.

See Also: **COleClientItem::GetLinkUpdateOptions, COleLinksDialog**

COleClientItem::SetPrintDevice

BOOL SetPrintDevice(const DVTARGETDEVICE* *ptd* **);**
BOOL SetPrintDevice(const PRINTDLG* *ppd* **);**

Return Value

Nonzero if the function was successful; otherwise 0.

Parameters

ptd   Pointer to a **DVTARGETDEVICE** data structure, which contains information about the new print-target device. Can be **NULL**.

ppd   Pointer to a **PRINTDLG** data structure, which contains information about the new print-target device. Can be **NULL**.

Remarks

Call this function to change the print-target device for this item. This function updates the print-target device for the item but does not refresh the presentation cache. To update the presentation cache for an item, call **UpdateLink**.

The arguments to this function contain information that the OLE system uses to identify the target device. The **PRINTDLG** structure contains information that Windows uses to initialize the common Print dialog box. After the user closes the dialog box, Windows returns information about the user's selections in this structure. The **m_pd** member of a **CPrintDialog** object is a **PRINTDLG** structure.

For more information about this structure, see **PRINTDLG** in the Win32 documentation.

For more information, see **DVTARGETDEVICE** in the OLE documentation.

See Also: **COleClientItem::UpdateLink, CPrintDialog**

COleClientItem::UpdateLink

BOOL UpdateLink( );

Return Value

Nonzero on success; otherwise 0.

Remarks

Call this function to update the presentation data of the OLE item immediately. For linked items, the function finds the link source to obtain a new presentation for the OLE item. This process may involve running one or more server applications, which could be time-consuming. For embedded items, the function operates recursively, checking whether the embedded item contains links that might be out of date and updating them. The user can also manually update individual links using the Links dialog box.

For more information, see **IOleLink::Update** in the OLE documentation.

See Also: **COleLinksDialog**

COleCmdUI

The **COleCmdUI** class implements a method for MFC to update the state of user-interface objects related to the **IOleCommandTarget**-driven features of your application. In an application that is not enabled for DocObjects, when the user views a menu in the application, MFC processes **UPDATE_COMMAND_UI** notifcations. Each notification is given a **CCmdUI** object that can be manipulated to reflect the state of a particular command. However, when your application is enabled for DocObjects, MFC processes **UPDATE_OLE_COMMAND_UI** notifications and assigns **COleCmdUI** objects.

COleCmdUI allows a DocObject to receive commands that originate in its container's user interface (such as FileNew, Open, Print, and so on), and allows a container to receive commands that originate in the DocObject's user interface. Although **IDispatch** could be used to dispatch the same commands, **IOleCommandTarget** provides a simpler way to query and execute because it relies on a standard set of commands, usually without arguments, and no type information is involved. **COleCmdUI** can be used to enable, update, and set other properties of DocObject user interface commands. When you want to invoke the command, call **COleServerDoc::OnExecOleCmd**.

For further information on DocObjects, see **CDocObjectServer** and **CDocObjectServerItem**. Also see "Internet First Steps: ActiveX Documents" and "ActiveX Documents" in *Visual C++ Programmer's Guide* online.

#include <afxdocobj.h>

COleCmdUI Class Members

Constructors

COleCmdUI	Constructs a **COleCmdUI** object.

Overridables

Enable	Sets or clears the enable command flag.
SetCheck	Sets the state of an on/off toggle command.
SetText	Returns a text name or status string for a command.

Member Functions
COleCmdUI::COleCmdUI

COleCmdUI(OLECMD* *rgCmds*, **ULONG** *cCmds*, **const GUID*** *pGroup* **);**

Parameters

>*rgCmds* A list of supported commands associated with the given GUID. The **OLECMD** structure associates commands with command flags.

>*cCmds* The count of commands in *rgCmds*.

>*pGroup* A pointer to a GUID that identifies a set of commands.

Remarks

>Constructs a **COleCmdUI** object associated with a particular user-interface command. The **COleCmdUI** object provides a programmatic interface for updating DocObject user-interface objects such as menu items or control-bar buttons. The user-interface objects can be enabled, disabled, checked, and/or cleared through the **COleCmdUI** object.

COleCmdUI::Enable

virtual void Enable(BOOL *bOn* = **TRUE);**

Parameters

>*bOn* Indicates whether the command associated with the **COleCmdUI** object should be enabled or disabled. Nonzero enables the command; 0 disables the command.

Remarks

>Call this function to set the command flag of the **COleCmdUI** object to **OLECOMDF_ENABLED**, which tells the interface the command is available and enabled, or to clear the command flag.

COleCmdUI::SetCheck

virtual void SetCheck(int *nCheck* = 1 **);**

Parameters

>*nCheck* A value determining the state to set an on/off toggle command. Values are:

Value	Description
1	Sets the command to on.
2	Sets the command to indeterminate; the state cannot be determined because the attribute of this command is in both on and off states in the relevant selection.
any other value	Sets the command to off.

Remarks

Call this function to set the state of an on/off toggle command.

See Also: COleCmdUI::SetText

COleCmdUI::SetText

virtual void SetText(LPCTSTR *lpszText* **);**

Parameters

lpszText   A pointer to the text to be used with the command.

Remarks

Call this function to return a text name or status string for a command.

See Also: COleCmdUI::SetCheck

COleControl

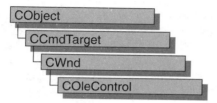

The **COleControl** class is a powerful base class for developing OLE controls. Derived from **CWnd**, this class inherits all the functionality of a Windows window object plus additional functionality specific to OLE, such as event firing and the ability to support methods and properties.

OLE controls can be inserted into OLE container applications and communicate with the container by using a two-way system of event firing and exposing methods and properties to the container. Note that standard OLE containers only support the basic functionality of an OLE control. They are unable to support extended features of an OLE control. Event firing occurs when events are sent to the container as a result of certain actions taking place in the control. In turn, the container communicates with the control by using an exposed set of methods and properties analogous to the member functions and data members of a C++ class. This approach allows the developer to control the appearance of the control and notify the container when certain actions occur.

Windowless Controls

OLE controls can be used in-place active without a window. Windowless controls have significant advantages:

- Windowless controls can be transparent and non-rectangular
- Windowless controls reduce instance size and creation time of the object

Controls do not need a window. Services that a window offers can easily be provided via a single shared window (usually the container's) and a bit of dispatching code. Having a window is mostly an unnecessary complication on the object.

When windowless activation is used, the container (which does have a window) is responsible for providing services that would otherwise have been provided by the control's own window. For example, if your control needs to query the keyboard focus, query the mouse capture, or obtain a device context, these operations are managed by the container. The **COleControl** windowless-operation member functions invoke these operations on the container.

When windowless activation is enabled, the container delegates input messages to the control's **IOleInPlaceObjectWindowless** interface (an extension of **IOleInPlaceObject** for windowless support). **COleControl**'s implementation of this interface will dispatch these messages through your control's message map, after adjusting the mouse coordinates appropriately. You can process these messages like ordinary window messages, by adding the corresponding entries to the message map.

In a windowless control, you should always use the **COleControl** member functions instead of the corresponding **CWnd** member functions or their related Windows API functions.

OLE control objects can also create a window only when they become active, but the amount of work needed for the inactive-active transition goes up and the speed of the transition goes down. There are cases when this is a problem: as an example, consider a grid of text boxes. When cursoring up and down through the column, each control must be in-place activated and then deactivated. The speed of the inactive/active transition will directly affect the scrolling speed.

For more information on developing an OLE control framework, see the articles "ActiveX Controls" and "Create a Program with the ActiveX ControlWizard" in *Visual C++ Programmer's Guide* online. For more information on adding functionality beyond the basic framework, see "Building an ActiveX Control" (the Circle tutorial) in *Visual C++ Tutorials* online. For information on optimizing OLE controls, including windowless and flicker-free controls, see "ActiveX Controls: Optimization" in *Visual C++ Programmer's Guide* online.

#include <afxctl.h>

See Also: **COlePropertyPage, CFontHolder, CPictureHolder**

COleControl Class Members

Construction/Destruction

COleControl	Creates a **COleControl** object.
RecreateControlWindow	Destroys and re-creates the control's window.

Initialization

InitializeIIDs	Informs the base class of the IIDs the control will use.
ResetStockProps	Initializes **COleControl** stock properties to their default values.
ResetVersion	Initializes the version number to a given value.
SetInitialSize	Sets the size of an OLE control when first displayed in a container.

Control Modification Functions

GetControlFlags	Retrieves the control flag settings.
IsModified	Determines if the control state has changed.
SetModifiedFlag	Changes the modified state of a control.

Persistence

ExchangeExtent	Serializes the control's width and height.
ExchangeStockProps	Serializes the control's stock properties.
ExchangeVersion	Serializes the control's version number.
IsConvertingVBX	Allows specialized loading of an OLE control.
SerializeExtent	Serializes or initializes the display space for the control.
SerializeStockProps	Serializes or initializes the **COleControl** stock properties.
SerializeVersion	Serializes or initializes the control's version information.
SetModifiedFlag	Changes the modified state of a control.
WillAmbientsBeValidDuringLoad	Determines whether ambient properties will be available the next time the control is loaded.

Update/Painting Functions

DoSuperclassPaint	Redraws an OLE control that has been subclassed from a Windows control.
InvalidateControl	Invalidates an area of the displayed control, causing it to be redrawn.
IsOptimizedDraw	Indicates whether the container supports optimized drawing for the current drawing operation.
SelectFontObject	Selects a custom Font property into a device context.
SelectStockFont	Selects the stock Font property into a device context.
TranslateColor	Converts an **OLE_COLOR** value to a **COLORREF** value.

Dispatch Exceptions

GetNotSupported	Prevents access to a control's property value by the user.
SetNotPermitted	Indicates that an edit request has failed.
SetNotSupported	Prevents modification to a control's property value by the user.
ThrowError	Signals that an error has occurred in an OLE control.

Ambient Property Functions

AmbientBackColor	Returns the value of the ambient BackColor property.
AmbientDisplayName	Returns the name of the control as specified by the container.
AmbientForeColor	Returns the value of the ambient ForeColor property.
AmbientFont	Returns the value of the ambient Font property.
AmbientLocaleID	Returns the container's locale ID.

Ambient Property Functions *(continued)*

AmbientScaleUnits	Returns the type of units used by the container.
AmbientShowGrabHandles	Determines if grab handles should be displayed.
AmbientShowHatching	Determines if hatching should be displayed.
AmbientTextAlign	Returns the type of text alignment specified by the container.
AmbientUIDead	Determines if the control should respond to user-interface actions.
AmbientUserMode	Determines the mode of the container.
GetAmbientProperty	Returns the value of the specified ambient property.

Event Firing Functions

FireClick	Fires the stock Click event.
FireDblClick	Fires the stock DblClick event.
FireError	Fires the stock Error event.
FireEvent	Fires a custom event.
FireKeyDown	Fires the stock KeyDown event.
FireKeyPress	Fires the stock KeyPress event.
FireKeyUp	Fires the stock KeyUp event.
FireMouseDown	Fires the stock MouseDown event.
FireMouseMove	Fires the stock MouseMove event.
FireMouseUp	Fires the stock MouseUp event.
FireReadyStateChange	Fires an event when the control's ready state changes.

Stock Methods/Properties

DoClick	Implementation of the stock DoClick method.
Refresh	Forces a repaint of a control's appearance.
GetAppearance	Returns the value of the stock Appearance property.
SetAppearance	Sets the value of the stock Appearance property.
GetBackColor	Returns the value of the stock BackColor property.
SetBackColor	Sets the value of the stock BackColor property.
GetBorderStyle	Returns the value of the stock BorderStyle property.
SetBorderStyle	Sets the value of the stock BorderStyle property.
GetEnabled	Returns the value of the stock Enabled property.
SetEnabled	Sets the value of the stock Enabled property.
GetForeColor	Returns the value of the stock ForeColor property.
SetForeColor	Sets the value of the stock ForeColor property.
GetFont	Returns the value of the stock Font property.
GetFontTextMetrics	Returns the metrics of a **CFontHolder** object.

(continued)

Stock Methods/Properties *(continued)*

GetStockTextMetrics	Returns the metrics of the stock Font property.
InternalGetFont	Returns a **CFontHolder** object for the stock Font property.
SetFont	Sets the value of the stock Font property.
SelectStockFont	Selects the control's stock Font property into a device context.
GetHwnd	Returns the value of the stock hWnd property.
GetText	Returns the value of the stock Text or Caption property.
InternalGetText	Retrieves the stock Caption or Text property.
SetText	Sets the value of the stock Text or Caption property.

OLE Control Sizing Functions

GetControlSize	Returns the position and size of the OLE control.
SetControlSize	Sets the position and size of the OLE control.
GetRectInContainer	Returns the control's rectangle relative to its container.
SetRectInContainer	Sets the control's rectangle relative to its container.

OLE Data Binding Functions

BoundPropertyChanged	Notifies the container that a bound property has been changed.
BoundPropertyRequestEdit	Requests permission to edit the property value.

Simple Frame Functions

EnableSimpleFrame	Enables simple frame support for a control.

OLE Control Site Functions

ControlInfoChanged	Call this function after the set of mnemonics handled by the control has changed.
GetClientSite	Queries an object for the pointer to its current client site within its container.
GetExtendedControl	Retrieves a pointer to an extended control object belonging to the container.
LockInPlaceActive	Determines if your control can be deactivated by the container.
TransformCoords	Transforms coordinate values between a container and the control.

Modal Dialog Functions

PreModalDialog	Notifies the container that a modal dialog box is about to be displayed.
PostModalDialog	Notifies the container that a modal dialog box has been closed.

Windowless Operations

ClipCaretRect	Adjusts a caret rectangle if it is overlapped by a control.
GetCapture	Determines whether a windowless, activated control object has the mouse capture.
GetClientRect	Retrieves the size of the control's client area.
GetDC	Provides a means for a windowless control to get a device context from its container.
GetFocus	Determines whether the control has the focus.
GetWindowlessDropTarget	Override to allow a windowless control to be the target of drag and drop operations.
InvalidateRgn	Invalidates the container window's client area within the given region. Can be used to redraw windowless controls in the region.
OnWindowlessMessage	Processes window messages (other than mouse and keyboard messages) for windowless controls.
ReleaseCapture	Releases mouse capture.
ReleaseDC	Releases the display device context of a container of a windowless control.
ScrollWindow	Allows a windowless control to scroll an area within its in-place active image on the display.
SetCapture	Causes the control's container window to take possession of the mouse capture on the control's behalf.
SetFocus	Causes the control's container window to take possession of the input focus on the control's behalf.

Inactive Pointer Handling Functions

ClientToParent	Translates a point relative to the control's origin to a point relative to its container's origin.
GetActivationPolicy	Alters the default activation behavior of a control that supports the **IPointerInactive** interface.
GetClientOffset	Retrieves the difference between the upper left corner of the control's rectangular area and the upper left corner of its client area.

(continued)

Inactive Pointer Handling Functions *(continued)*

OnInactiveMouseMove	Override to have the container for the inactive control under the mouse pointer dispatch **WM_MOUSEMOVE** messages to the control.
OnInactiveSetCursor	Override to have the container for the inactive control under the mouse pointer dispatch **WM_SETCURSOR** messages to the control.
ParentToClient	Translates a point relative to the container's origin to a point relative to the control's origin.

Asynchronous Control Functions

GetReadyState	Returns the control's readiness state.
InternalSetReadyState	Sets the control's readiness state and fires the ready-state-change event.
Load	Resets any previous asynchronous data and initiates a new load of the control's asynchronous property.

Overridables

DisplayError	Displays stock Error events to the control's user.
DoPropExchange	Serializes the properties of a **COleControl** object.
GetClassID	Retrieves the OLE class ID of the control.
GetMessageString	Provides status bar text for a menu item.
IsSubclassedControl	Called to determine if the control subclasses a Windows control.
OnClick	Called to fire the stock Click event.
OnDoVerb	Called after a control verb has been executed.
OnDraw	Called when a control is requested to redraw itself.
OnDrawMetafile	Called by the container when a control is requested to redraw itself using a metafile device context.
OnEdit	Called by the container to UI Activate an OLE control.
OnEnumVerbs	Called by the container to enumerate a control's verbs.
OnEventAdvise	Called when event handlers are connected or disconnected from a control.
OnKeyDownEvent	Called after the stock KeyDown event has been fired.
OnKeyPressEvent	Called after the stock KeyPress event has been fired.
OnKeyUpEvent	Called after the stock KeyUp event has been fired.
OnProperties	Called when the control's "Properties" verb has been invoked.
OnResetState	Resets a control's properties to the default values.

Change Notification Functions

OnAppearanceChanged	Called when the stock Appearance property is changed.
OnBackColorChanged	Called when the stock BackColor property is changed.
OnBorderStyleChanged	Called when the stock BorderStyle property is changed.
OnEnabledChanged	Called when the stock Enabled property is changed.
OnFontChanged	Called when the stock Font property is changed.
OnForeColorChanged	Called when the stock ForeColor property is changed.
OnTextChanged	Called when the stock Text or Caption property is changed.

OLE Interface Notification Functions

OnAmbientPropertyChange	Called when an ambient property is changed.
OnClose	Notifies the control that **IOleControl::Close** has been called.
OnFreezeEvents	Called when a control's events are frozen or unfrozen.
OnGetControlInfo	Provides mnemonic information to the container.
OnMnemonic	Called when a mnemonic key of the control has been pressed.
OnRenderData	Called by the framework to retrieve data in the specified format.
OnRenderFileData	Called by the framework to retrieve data from a file in the specified format.
OnRenderGlobalData	Called by the framework to retrieve data from global memory in the specified format.
OnSetClientSite	Notifies the control that **IOleControl::SetClientSite** has been called.
OnSetData	Replaces the control's data with another value.
OnSetExtent	Called after the control's extent has changed.
OnSetObjectRects	Called after the control's dimensions have been changed.

IViewObject Interface Notification Overridables

OnGetColorSet	Notifies the control that **IOleObject::GetColorSet** has been called.
OnGetNaturalExtent	Override to retrieve the control's display size closest to the proposed size and extent mode.
OnGetViewExtent	Override to retrieve the size of the control's display areas (can be used to enable two-pass drawing).
OnGetViewRect	Override to convert control's size into a rectangle starting at a specific position.

(continued)

IViewObject Interface Notification Overridables *(continued)*

OnGetViewStatus	Override to retrieve the control's view status.
OnQueryHitPoint	Override to query whether a control's display overlaps a given point.
OnQueryHitRect	Override to query whether a control's display overlaps any point in a given rectangle.

In-Place Activation Functions

OnGetInPlaceMenu	Requests the handle of the control's menu that will be merged with the container menu.
OnHideToolBars	Called by the container when the control is UI deactivated.
OnShowToolBars	Called when the control has been UI activated.

Property Browsing Functions

OnGetDisplayString	Called to obtain a string to represent a property value.
OnGetPredefinedStrings	Returns strings representing possible values for a property.
OnGetPredefinedValue	Returns the value corresponding to a predefined string.
OnMapPropertyToPage	Indicates which property page to use for editing a property.

Member Functions

COleControl::AmbientBackColor

OLE_COLOR AmbientBackColor( );

Return Value

The current value of the container's ambient BackColor property, if any. If the property is not supported, this function returns the system-defined Windows background color.

Remarks

The ambient BackColor property is available to all controls and is defined by the container. Note that the container is not required to support this property.

See Also: **COleControl::TranslateColor, COleControl::GetBackColor, COleControl::AmbientForeColor**

COleControl::AmbientDisplayName

CString AmbientDisplayName( );

Return Value

The name of the OLE control. The default is a zero-length string.

Remarks

The name the container has assigned to the control can be used in error messages displayed to the user. Note that the container is not required to support this property.

COleControl::AmbientFont

LPFONTDISP AmbientFont( );

Return Value

A pointer to the container's ambient Font dispatch interface. The default value is **NULL**. If the return is not equal to **NULL**, you are responsible for releasing the font by calling its **IUnknown::Release** member function.

Remarks

The ambient Font property is available to all controls and is defined by the container. Note that the container is not required to support this property.

See Also: COleControl::GetFont, COleControl::SetFont

COleControl::AmbientForeColor

OLE_COLOR AmbientForeColor( );

Return Value

The current value of the container's ambient ForeColor property, if any. If not supported, this function returns the system-defined Windows text color.

Remarks

The ambient ForeColor property is available to all controls and is defined by the container. Note that the container is not required to support this property.

See Also: COleControl::AmbientBackColor, COleControl::GetForeColor, COleControl::TranslateColor

COleControl::AmbientLocaleID

LCID AmbientLocaleID( );

Return Value

The value of the container's LocaleID property, if any. If this property is not supported, this function returns 0.

Remarks

The control can use the LocaleID to adapt its user interface for specific locales. Note that the container is not required to support this property.

COleControl::AmbientScaleUnits

CString AmbientScaleUnits( );

Return Value

A string containing the ambient ScaleUnits of the container. If this property is not supported, this function returns a zero-length string.

Remarks

The container's ambient ScaleUnits property can be used to display positions or dimensions, labeled with the chosen unit, such as twips or centimeters. Note that the container is not required to support this property.

See Also: COleControl::TransformCoords

COleControl::AmbientShowGrabHandles

BOOL AmbientShowGrabHandles( );

Return Value

Nonzero if grab handles should be displayed; otherwise 0. If this property is not supported, this function returns nonzero.

Remarks

Call this function to determine whether the container allows the control to display grab handles for itself when active. Note that the container is not required to support this property.

See Also: COleControl::AmbientShowHatching

COleControl::AmbientShowHatching

BOOL AmbientShowHatching( );

Return Value

Nonzero if the hatched pattern should be shown; otherwise 0. If this property is not supported, this function returns nonzero.

Remarks

Call this function to determine whether the container allows the control to display itself with a hatched pattern when UI active. Note that the container is not required to support this property.

See Also: **COleControl::AmbientShowGrabHandles**

COleControl::AmbientTextAlign

short AmbientTextAlign( );

Return Value

The status of the container's ambient TextAlign property. If this property is not supported, this function returns 0.

The following is a list of valid return values:

Return Value	Meaning
0	General alignment (numbers to the right, text to the left).
1	Left justify
2	Center
3	Right justify

Remarks

Call this function to determine the ambient text alignment preferred by the control container. This property is available to all embedded controls and is defined by the container. Note that the container is not required to support this property.

COleControl::AmbientUIDead

BOOL AmbientUIDead( );

Return Value

Nonzero if the control should respond to user-interface actions; otherwise 0. If this property is not supported, this function returns 0.

Remarks

Call this function to determine if the container wants the control to respond to user-interface actions. For example, a container might set this to **TRUE** in design mode.

See Also: COleControl::AmbientUserMode

COleControl::AmbientUserMode

BOOL AmbientUserMode( );

Return Value

Nonzero if the container is in user mode; otherwise 0 (in design mode). If this property is not supported, this function returns 0.

Remarks

Call this function to determine if the container is in design mode or user mode. For example, a container might set this to **FALSE** in design mode.

See Also: COleControl::AmbientUIDead

COleControl::BoundPropertyChanged

void BoundPropertyChanged(DISPID *dispid* **);**

Parameters

dispid The dispatch ID of a bound property of the control.

Remarks

Call this function to signal that the bound property value has changed. This must be called every time the value of the property changes, even in cases where the change was not made through the property Set method. Be particularly aware of bound properties that are mapped to member variables. Any time such a member variable changes, **BoundPropertyChanged** must be called.

See Also: COleControl::BoundPropertyRequestEdit

COleControl::BoundPropertyRequestEdit

BOOL BoundPropertyRequestEdit(DISPID *dispid* **);**

Return Value

Nonzero if the change is permitted; otherwise 0. The default value is nonzero.

Parameters

dispid The dispatch ID of a bound property of the control.

Remarks

Call this function to request permission from the **IPropertyNotifySink** interface to change a bound property value provided by the control. If permission is denied, the control must not let the value of the property change. This can be done by ignoring or failing the action that attempted to change the property value.

See Also: **COleControl::BoundPropertyChanged**

COleControl::ClientToParent

virtual void ClientToParent(LPCRECT *lprcBounds*, **LPPOINT** *pPoint* **) const;**

Parameters

lprcBounds   Pointer to the bounds of the OLE control within the container. Not the client area but the area of the entire control including borders and scroll bars.

pPoint   Pointer to the OLE client area point to be translated into the coordinates of the parent (container).

Remarks

Call this function to translate the coordinates of *pPoint* into parent coordinates. On input *pPoint* is relative to the origin of the client area of the OLE control (upper left corner of the client area of the control). On output *pPoint* is relative to the origin of the parent (upper left corner of the container).

See Also: **COleControl::ParentToClient, COleControl::GetClientOffset**

COleControl::ClipCaretRect

BOOL ClipCaretRect(LPRECT *lpRect* **);**

Return Value

Nonzero if successful; otherwise 0.

Parameters

lpRect   On input, a pointer to a **RECT** structure that contains the caret area to be adjusted. On output, the adjusted caret area, or **NULL** if the caret rectangle is completely covered.

Remarks

Call this function to adjust a caret rectangle if it is entirely or partially covered by overlapping, opaque objects. A caret is a flashing line, block, or bitmap that typically indicates where text or graphics will be inserted.

A windowless object cannot safely show a caret without first checking whether the caret is partially or totally hidden by overlapping objects. In order to make that possible, an object can use **ClipCaretRect** to get the caret adjusted (reduced) to ensure it fits in the clipping region.

Objects creating a caret should submit the caret rectangle to **ClipCaretRect** and use the adjusted rectangle for the caret. If the caret is entirely hidden, this method will return **FALSE** and the caret should not be shown at all in this case.

COleControl::COleControl

COleControl( );

Remarks

Constructs a **COleControl** object. This function is normally not called directly. Instead the OLE control is usually created by its class factory.

COleControl::ControlInfoChanged

void ControlInfoChanged( );

Remarks

Call this function when the set of mnemonics supported by the control has changed. Upon receiving this notification, the control's container obtains the new set of mnemonics by making a call to **IOleControl::GetControlInfo**. Note that the container is not required to respond to this notification.

COleControl::DisplayError

virtual void DisplayError(SCODE *scode*, **LPCTSTR** *lpszDescription*,
→ **LPCTSTR** *lpszSource*, **LPCTSTR** *lpszHelpFile*, **UINT** *nHelpID* **);**

Parameters

scode   The status code value to be reported. For a complete list of possible codes, see the article "ActiveX Controls: Advanced Topics" in *Visual C++ Programmer's Guide* online.

lpszDescription   The description of the error being reported.

lpszSource   The name of the module generating the error (typically, the name of the OLE control module).

lpszHelpFile   The name of the help file containing a description of the error.

nHelpID   The Help Context ID of the error being reported.

Remarks

Called by the framework after the stock Error event has been handled (unless the event handler has suppressed the display of the error). The default behavior displays a message box containing the description of the error, contained in *lpszDescription*.

Override this function to customize how errors are displayed.

See Also: COleControl::FireError

COleControl::DoClick

void DoClick( );

Remarks

Call this function to simulate a mouse click action on the control. The overridable **COleControl::OnClick** member function will be called, and a stock Click event will be fired, if supported by the control.

This function is supported by the **COleControl** base class as a stock method, called DoClick. For more information, see the article "ActiveX Controls: Methods" in *Visual C++ Programmer's Guide* online.

See Also: COleControl::OnClick

COleControl::DoPropExchange

virtual void DoPropExchange(CPropExchange* *pPX*);

Parameters

pPX   A pointer to a **CPropExchange** object. The framework supplies this object to establish the context of the property exchange, including its direction.

Remarks

Called by the framework when loading or storing a control from a persistent storage representation, such as a stream or property set. This function normally makes calls to the **PX_** family of functions to load or store specific user-defined properties of an OLE control.

If Control Wizard has been used to create the OLE control project, the overridden version of this function will serialize the stock properties supported by **COleControl** with a call to the base class function, **COleControl::DoPropExchange**. As you add user-defined properties to your OLE control you will need to modify this function to serialize your new properties. For more information on serialization, see the article "ActiveX Controls: Serializing" in *Visual C++ Programmer's Guide* online.

See Also: PX_Bool, PX_Short

COleControl::DoSuperclassPaint

void DoSuperclassPaint(CDC* *pDC*, **const CRect&** *rcBounds* **);**

Parameters

pDC   A pointer to the device context of the control container.

rcBounds   The area in which the control is to be drawn.

Remarks

Call this function to properly handle the painting of a nonactive OLE control. This function should only be used if the OLE control subclasses a Windows control and should be called in the OnDraw function of your control.

For more information on this function and subclassing a Windows control, see the article "ActiveX Controls: Subclassing a Windows Control" in *Visual C++ Programmer's Guide* online.

See Also: COleControl::OnDraw

COleControl::DrawContent

void DrawContent(CDC* *pDC*, **CRect&** *rc* **);**

Parameters

pDC   Pointer to the device context.

rc   Rectangular area to be drawn in.

Remarks

Called by the framework when the control's appearance needs to be updated. This function directly calls the overridable **OnDraw** function.

See Also: COleControl::OnDraw, **COleControl::DrawMetafile**,
COleControl::OnDrawMetafile

COleControl::DrawMetafile

void DrawMetafile(CDC* *pDC*, **CRect&** *rc*);

Parameters

pDC   Pointer to the metafile device context.

rc   Rectangular area to be drawn in.

Remarks

Called by the framework when the metafile device context is being used.

See Also: COleControl::OnDraw, COleControl::DrawContent,
COleControl::OnDrawMetafile

COleControl::EnableSimpleFrame

void EnableSimpleFrame( );

Remarks

Call this function to enable the simple frame characteristic for an OLE control. This characteristic allows a control to support visual containment of other controls, but not true OLE containment. An example would be a group box with several controls inside. These controls are not OLE contained, but they are in the same group box.

COleControl::ExchangeExtent

BOOL ExchangeExtent(CPropExchange* *pPX*);

Return Value

Nonzero if the function succeeded; 0 otherwise.

Parameters

pPX A pointer to a **CPropExchange** object. The framework supplies this object to establish the context of the property exchange, including its direction.

Remarks

Call this function to serialize or initialize the state of the control's extent (its dimensions in **HIMETRIC** units). This function is normally called by the default implementation of **COleControl::DoPropExchange**.

See Also: COleControl::DoPropExchange

COleControl::ExchangeStockProps

void ExchangeStockProps(CPropExchange* *pPX*);

Parameters

pPX A pointer to a **CPropExchange** object. The framework supplies this object to establish the context of the property exchange, including its direction.

Remarks

Call this function to serialize or initialize the state of the control's stock properties. This function is normally called by the default implementation of **COleControl::DoPropExchange**.

See Also: COleControl::DoPropExchange

COleControl::ExchangeVersion

BOOL ExchangeVersion(CPropExchange* *pPX*, **DWORD** *dwVersionDefault*,
↪ **BOOL** *bConvert* = **TRUE**);

Return Value

Nonzero of the function succeeded; 0 otherwise.

Parameters

pPX A pointer to a **CPropExchange** object. The framework supplies this object to
establish the context of the property exchange, including its direction.

dwVersionDefault The current version number of the control.

bConvert Indicates whether persistent data should be converted to the latest format
when saved, or maintained in the same format that was loaded.

Remarks

Call this function to serialize or initialize the state of a control's version information.
Typically, this will be the first function called by a control's override of
COleControl::DoPropExchange. When loading, this function reads the version
number of the persistent data, and sets the version attribute of the **CPropExchange**
object accordingly. When saving, this function writes the version number of the
persistent data.

For more information on persistence and versioning, see the article "ActiveX
Controls: Serializing" in *Visual C++ Programmer's Guide* online.

See Also: COleControl::DoPropExchange

COleControl::FireClick

void FireClick( );

Remarks

Called by the framework when the mouse is clicked over an active control. If this
event is defined as a custom event, you determine when the event is fired.

For automatic firing of a Click event to occur, the control's Event map must have a
stock Click event defined.

**See Also: COleControl::FireDblClick, COleControl::FireMouseDown,
COleControl::FireMouseUp**

COleControl::FireDblClick

void FireDblClick( );

Remarks

Called by the framework when the mouse is double-clicked over an active control. If this event is defined as a custom event, you determine when the event is fired.

For automatic firing of a DblClick event to occur, the control's Event map must have a stock DblClick event defined.

See Also: **COleControl::FireClick**, **COleControl::FireMouseDown**, **COleControl::FireMouseUp**

COleControl::FireError

void FireError(SCODE *scode*, **LPCTSTR** *lpszDescription*, **UINT** *nHelpID* **= 0);**

Parameters

scode   The status code value to be reported. For a complete list of possible codes, see the article "ActiveX Controls: Advanced Topics" in *Visual C++ Programmer's Guide* online.

lpszDescription   The description of the error being reported.

nHelpID   The Help ID of the error being reported.

Remarks

Call this function to fire the stock Error event. This event provides a way of signalling, at appropriate places in your code, that an error has occurred within your control. Unlike other stock events, such as Click or MouseMove, Error is never fired by the framework.

To report an error that occurs during a property get function, property set function, or automation method, call **COleControl::ThrowError**.

The implementation of an OLE control's Stock Error event uses an **SCODE** value. If your control uses this event, and is intended to be used in Visual Basic 4.0, you will receive errors because the **SCODE** value is not supported in Visual Basic.

To fix this, manually change the **SCODE** parameter in the control's .ODL file to a **long**. In addition, any custom event, method, or property that uses an **SCODE** parameter also causes the same problem.

See Also: **COleControl::DisplayError**

COleControl::FireEvent

void FireEvent(DISPID *dispid***, BYTE FAR*** *pbParams***, ...);**

Parameters

dispid   The dispatch ID of the event to be fired.

pbParams   A descriptor for the event's parameter types.

Remarks

Call this function, with any number of optional arguments, to fire a user-defined event from your control. Usually this function should not be called directly. Instead you will call the event-firing functions generated by ClassWizard in the event map section of your control's class declaration.

The *pbParams* argument is a space-separated list of **VTS_**. One or more of these values, separated by spaces (not commas), specifies the function's parameter list. Possible values are as follows:

Symbol	Parameter Type
VTS_COLOR	**OLE_COLOR**
VTS_FONT	**IFontDisp***
VTS_HANDLE	**HWND**
VTS_PICTURE	**IPictureDisp***
VTS_OPTEXCLUSIVE	**OLE_OPTEXCLUSIVE***
VTS_TRISTATE	**OLE_TRISTATE**
VTS_XPOS_HIMETRIC	**OLE_XPOS_HIMETRIC**
VTS_YPOS_HIMETRIC	**OLE_YPOS_HIMETRIC**
VTS_XPOS_PIXELS	**OLE_XPOS_PIXELS**
VTS_YPOS_PIXELS	**OLE_YPOS_PIXELS**
VTS_XSIZE_PIXELS	**OLE_XSIZE_PIXELS**
VTS_YSIZE_PIXELS	**OLE_XSIZE_PIXELS**
VTS_XSIZE_HIMETRIC	**OLE_XSIZE_HIMETRIC**
VTS_YSIZE_HIMETRIC	**OLE_XSIZE_HIMETRIC**

Note Additional variant constants have been defined for all variant types, with the exception of **VTS_FONT** and **VTS_PICTURE**, that provide a pointer to the variant data constant. These constants are named using the **VTS_P***constantname* convention. For example, **VTS_PCOLOR** is a pointer to a **VTS_COLOR** constant.

COleControl::FireKeyDown

void FireKeyDown(USHORT* *pnChar*, **short** *nShiftState* **);**

Parameters

pnChar   Pointer to the virtual-key code value of the pressed key.

nShiftState   Contains a combination of the following flags:

- **SHIFT_MASK**   The SHIFT key was pressed during the action.
- **CTRL_MASK**   The CTRL key was pressed during the action.
- **ALT_MASK**   The ALT key was pressed during the action.

Remarks

Called by the framework when a key is pressed while the control is UI active. If this event is defined as a custom event, you determine when the event is fired.

For automatic firing of a KeyDown event to occur, the control's Event map must have a stock KeyDown event defined.

See Also: COleControl::FireKeyUp, COleControl::FireKeyPress, COleControl::OnKeyPressEvent

---

COleControl::FireKeyPress

void FireKeyPress(USHORT* *pnChar* **);**

Parameters

pnChar   A pointer to the character value of the key pressed.

Remarks

Called by the framework when a key is pressed and released while the custom control is UI Active within the container. If this event is defined as a custom event, you determine when the event is fired.

The recipient of the event may modify *pnChar*, for example, convert all lowercase characters to uppercase. If you want to examine the modified character, override **OnKeyPressEvent**.

For automatic firing of a KeyPress event to occur, the control's Event map must have a stock KeyPress event defined.

See Also: COleControl::OnKeyPressEvent, COleControl::FireKeyDown, COleControl::FireKeyUp

COleControl::FireKeyUp

void FireKeyUp(USHORT* *pnChar*, **short** *nShiftState* **);**

Parameters

pnChar   Pointer to the virtual-key code value of the released key.

nShiftState   Contains a combination of the following flags:

- **SHIFT_MASK**   The SHIFT key was pressed during the action.

- **CTRL_MASK**   The CTRL key was pressed during the action.

- **ALT_MASK**   The ALT key was pressed during the action.

Remarks

Called by the framework when a key is released while the custom control is UI Active within the container. If this event is defined as a custom event, you determine when the event is fired.

For automatic firing of a KeyUp event to occur, the control's Event map must have a stock KeyUp event defined.

See Also: COleControl::FireKeyDown, COleControl::FireKeyPress, COleControl::OnKeyUpEvent

---

COleControl::FireMouseDown

void FireMouseDown(short *nButton*, **short** *nShiftState*, **OLE_XPOS_PIXELS** *x*,
↪ **OLE_YPOS_PIXEL** *y* **);**

Parameters

nButton   The numeric value of the mouse button pressed. It can contain one of the following values:

- **LEFT_BUTTON**   The left mouse button was pressed down.

- **MIDDLE_BUTTON**   The middle mouse button was pressed down.

- **RIGHT_BUTTON**   The right mouse button was pressed down.

nShiftState   Contains a combination of the following flags:

- **SHIFT_MASK**   The SHIFT key was pressed during the action.

- **CTRL_MASK**   The CTRL key was pressed during the action.

- **ALT_MASK**   The ALT key was pressed during the action.

x   The x-coordinate of the cursor when a mouse button was pressed down. The coordinate is relative to the upper-left corner of the control window.

y   The y-coordinate of the cursor when a mouse button was pressed down. The coordinate is relative to the upper-left corner of the control window.

Remarks

Called by the framework when a mouse button is pressed over an active custom control. If this event is defined as a custom event, you determine when the event is fired.

For automatic firing of a MouseDown event to occur, the control's Event map must have a stock MouseDown event defined.

See Also: **COleControl::FireMouseUp, COleControl::FireMouseMove, COleControl::FireClick**

COleControl::FireMouseMove

void FireMouseMove(short *nButton***, short** *nShiftState***, OLE_XPOS_PIXELS** *x***, ↳ OLE_YPOS_PIXELS** *y* **);**

Parameters

nButton   The numeric value of the mouse buttons pressed. Contains a combination of the following values:

- **LEFT_BUTTON**   The left mouse button was pressed down during the action.

- **MIDDLE_BUTTON**   The middle mouse button was pressed down during the action.

- **RIGHT_BUTTON**   The right mouse button was pressed down during the action.

nShiftState   Contains a combination of the following flags:

- **SHIFT_MASK**   The SHIFT key was pressed during the action.

- **CTRL_MASK**   The CTRL key was pressed during the action.

- **ALT_MASK**   The ALT key was pressed during the action.

x   The x-coordinate of the cursor. The coordinate is relative to the upper-left corner of the control window.

y   The y-coordinate of the cursor. The coordinate is relative to the upper-left corner of the control window.

Remarks

Called by the framework when the cursor is moved over an active custom control. If this event is defined as a custom event, you determine when the event is fired.

For automatic firing of a MouseMove event to occur, the control's Event map must have a stock MouseMove event defined.

COleControl::FireMouseUp

void FireMouseUp(short *nButton*, **short** *nShiftState*, **OLE_XPOS_PIXELS** *x*,
↪ **OLE_YPOS_PIXELS** *y*);

Parameters

nButton The numeric value of the mouse button released. It can have one of the following values:

- **LEFT_BUTTON** The left mouse button was released.
- **MIDDLE_BUTTON** The middle mouse button was released.
- **RIGHT_BUTTON** The right mouse button was released.

nShiftState Contains a combination of the following flags:

- **SHIFT_MASK** The SHIFT key was pressed during the action.
- **CTRL_MASK** The CTRL key was pressed during the action.
- **ALT_MASK** The ALT key was pressed during the action.

x The x-coordinate of the cursor when a mouse button was released. The coordinate is relative to the upper-left corner of the control window.

y The y-coordinate of a cursor when a mouse button was released. The coordinate is relative to the upper-left corner of the control window.

Remarks

Called by the framework when a mouse button is released over an active custom control. If this event is defined as a custom event, you determine when the event is fired.

For automatic firing of a MouseUp event to occur, the control's Event map must have a stock MouseUp event defined.

See Also: COleControl::FireMouseDown, COleControl::FireClick,
COleControl::FireDblClick

COleControl::FireReadyStateChange

void FireReadyStateChange( );

Remarks

Call this function to fire an event with the current value of the ready state of control. The ready state can be one of the following values:

READYSTATE_UNINITIALIZED Default initialization state

READYSTATE_LOADING Control is currently loading its properties

READYSTATE_LOADED Control has been initialized

READYSTATE_INTERACTIVE Control has enough data to be interactive but not all asynchronous data is yet loaded

READYSTATE_COMPLETE Control has all its data

Use **GetReadyState** to determine the control's current readiness.

InternalSetReadyState changes the ready state to the value supplied, then calls **FireReadyStateChange**.

See Also: **COleControl::GetReadyState**, **COleControl::InternalSetReadyState**

COleControl::GetActivationPolicy

virtual DWORD GetActivationPolicy( );

Return Value

A combination of flags from the **POINTERINACTIVE** enumeration. Possible flags are:

POINTERINACTIVE_ACTIVATEONENTRY The object should be in-place activated when the mouse enters it during a mouse move operation.

POINTERINACTIVE_DEACTIVATEONLEAVE The object should be deactivated when the mouse leaves the object during a mouse move operation.

POINTERINACTIVE_ACTIVATEONDRAG The object should be in-place activated when the mouse is dragged over it during a drag and drop operation.

Remarks

Override this function to alter the default activation behavior of a control that supports the **IPointerInactive** interface.

When the **IPointerInactive** interface is enabled, the container will delegate **WM_SETCURSOR** and **WM_MOUSEMOVE** messages to it. **COleControl**'s implementation of this interface will dispatch these messages through your control's message map, after adjusting the mouse coordinates appropriately.

Whenever the container receives a **WM_SETCURSOR** or **WM_MOUSEMOVE** message with the mouse pointer over an inactive object supporting **IPointerInactive**, it should call **GetActivationPolicy** on the interface and return flags from the **POINTERINACTIVE** enumeration.

You can process these messages just like ordinary window messages, by adding the corresponding entries to the message map. In your handlers, avoid using the **m_hWnd** member variable (or any member functions that uses it) without first checking that its value is non-**NULL**.

Any object intended to do more than set the mouse cursor and/or fire a mouse move event, such as give special visual feedback, should return the **POINTERINACTIVE_ACTIVATEONENTRY** flag and draw the feedback only when active. If the object returns this flag, the container should activate it in-place immediately and then forward it the same message that triggered the call to **GetActivationPolicy**.

If both the **POINTERINACTIVE_ACTIVATEONENTRY** and **POINTERINACTIVE_DEACTIVATEONLEAVE** flags are returned, then the object will only be activated when the mouse is over the object. If only the **POINTERINACTIVE_ACTIVATEONENTRY** flag is returned, then the object will only be activated once when the mouse first enters the object.

You may also want an inactive control to be the target of an OLE drag and drop operation. This requires activating the control at the moment the user drags an object over it, so that the control's window can be registered as a drop target. To cause activation to occur during a drag, return the **POINTERINACTIVE_ACTIVATEONDRAG** flag:

```
DWORD CMyCtrl::GetActivationPolicy()
{
    return POINTERINACTIVE_ACTIVATEONDRAG;
}
```

The information communicated by **GetActivationPolicy** should not be cached by a container. Instead, this method should be called every time the mouse enters an inactive object.

If an inactive object does not request to be in-place activated when the mouse enters it, its container should dispatch subsequent **WM_SETCURSOR** messages to this object by calling **OnInactiveSetCursor** as long as the mouse pointer stays over the object.

Enabling the **IPointerInactive** interface typically means that you want the control to be capable of processing mouse messages at all times. To get this behaviour in a container that doesn't support the **IPointerInactive** interface, you will need to have your control always activated when visible, which means the control should have the **OLEMISC_ACTIVATEWHENVISIBLE** flag among its miscellaneous flags. However, to prevent this flag from taking effect in a container that does support **IPointerInactive**, you can also specify the **OLEMISC_IGNOREACTIVATEWHENVISIBLE** flag:

```
static const DWORD BASED_CODE _dwMyOleMisc =
    OLEMISC_ACTIVATEWHENVISIBLE |
    OLEMISC_IGNOREACTIVATEWHENVISIBLE |
    OLEMISC_SETCLIENTSITEFIRST |
    OLEMISC_INSIDEOUT |
    OLEMISC_CANTLINKINSIDE |
    OLEMISC_RECOMPOSEONRESIZE;
```

See Also: **COleControl::OnInactiveSetCursor**, **COleControl::OnInactiveMouseMove**

COleControl::GetAmbientProperty

BOOL GetAmbientProperty(DISPID *dwDispid*, **VARTYPE** *vtProp*, **void*** *pvProp* **);**

Return Value

Nonzero if the ambient property is supported; otherwise 0.

Parameters

dwDispid   The dispatch ID of the desired ambient property.

vtProp   A variant type tag that specifies the type of the value to be returned in *pvProp*.

pvProp   A pointer to the address of the variable that will receive the property value or return value. The actual type of this pointer must match the type specified by *vtProp*.

vtProp	Type of pvProp
VT_BOOL	BOOL*
VT_BSTR	CString*
VT_I2	short*
VT_I4	long*
VT_R4	float*
VT_R8	double*
VT_CY	CY*
VT_COLOR	OLE_COLOR*
VT_DISPATCH	LPDISPATCH*
VT_FONT	LPFONTDISP*

Remarks

Call this function to get the value of an ambient property of the container. If you use **GetAmbientProperty** to retrieve the ambient DisplayName and ScaleUnits properties, set *vtProp* to **VT_BSTR** and *pvProp* to **CString***. If you are retrieving the ambient Font property, set *vtProp* to **VT_FONT** and *pvProp* to **LPFONTDISP***.

Note that functions have already been provided for common ambient properties, such as **AmbientBackColor** and **AmbientFont**.

See Also: **COleControl::AmbientForeColor**, **COleControl::AmbientScaleUnits**, **COleControl::AmbientShowGrabHandles**

COleControl::GetAppearance

short GetAppearance ( );

Return Value

The return value specifies the current appearance setting as a **short** (**VT_I2**) value, if successful. This value is zero if the control's appearance is flat and 1 if the control's appearance is 3D.

Remarks

This function implements the Get function of your control's stock Appearance property.

See Also: **COleControl::SetAppearance, COleControl::OnAppearanceChanged**

COleControl::GetBackColor

OLE_COLOR GetBackColor( );

Return Value

The return value specifies the current background color as a **OLE_COLOR** value, if successful. This value can be translated to a **COLORREF** value with a call to **TranslateColor**.

Remarks

This function implements the Get function of your control's stock BackColor property.

See Also: **COleControl::AmbientBackColor, COleControl::TranslateColor, COleControl::SetBackColor, COleControl::GetForeColor**

COleControl::GetBorderStyle

short GetBorderStyle( );

Return Value

1 if the control has a normal border; 0 if the control has no border.

Remarks

This function implements the Get function of your control's stock BorderStyle property.

See Also: **COleControl::SetBorderStyle, COleControl::OnBorderStyleChanged**

COleControl::GetCapture

CWnd* GetCapture( );

Return Value

If the control is activated and windowless, returns **this** if the control currently has the mouse capture (as determined by the control's container), or **NULL** if it does not have the capture.

Otherwise, returns the **CWnd** object that has the mouse capture (same as **CWnd::GetCapture**).

Remarks

Call this function to determine whether the **COleControl** object has the mouse capture. An activated windowless control receives the mouse capture when **SetCapture** is called.

See Also: **COleControl::SetCapture**, **COleControl::ReleaseCapture**

COleControl::GetClassID

virtual HRESULT GetClassID(LPCLSID *pclsid* **) = 0;**

Return Value

Nonzero if the call was not successful; otherwise 0.

Parameters

pclsid   Pointer to the location of the class ID.

Remarks

Called by the framework to retrieve the OLE class ID of the control. Usually implemented by the **IMPLEMENT_OLECREATE_EX** macro.

COleControl::GetClientOffset

virtual void GetClientOffset(long* *pdxOffset*, **long*** *pdyOffset* **) const;**

Parameters

pdxOffset   Pointer to the horizontal offset of the OLE control's client area.

pdyOffset   Pointer to the vertical offset of the OLE control's client area.

Remarks

The OLE control has a rectangular area within its container. The client area of the control is the control area excluding borders and scroll bars. The offset retrieved by **GetClientOffset** is the difference between the upper left corner of the control's rectangular area and the upper left corner of its client area. If your control has non-client elements other than the standard borders and scrollbars, override this member function to specify the offset.

See Also: COleControl::ParentToClient, COleControl::ClientToParent

---

COleControl::GetClientRect

virtual void GetClientRect(LPRECT *lpRect* **) const;**

Parameters

lpRect   Pointer to a **RECT** structure containing the dimensions of the windowless control's client area; that is, the control's size minus window borders, frames, scroll bars, and so on. The *lpRect* parameter indicates the size of the control's client rectangle, not its position.

Remarks

Call this function to retrieve the size of the control's client area.

COleControl::GetClientSite

LPOLECLIENTSITE GetClientSite( );

Return Value

A pointer to the control's current client site in its container.

Remarks

Call this function to query an object for the pointer to its current client site within its container.

The returned pointer points to an instance of **IOleClientSite**. The **IOleClientSite** interface, implemented by containers, is the object's view of its context: where it is anchored in the document, where it gets its storage, user interface, and other resources.

COleControl::GetControlFlags

virtual DWORD GetControlFlags( );

Return Value

An ORed combination of the flags in the ControlFlags enumeration:

```
enum ControlFlags {
    fastBeginPaint = 0x0001,
    clipPaintDC = 0x0002,
    pointerInactive = 0x0004,
```

```
    noFlickerActivate = 0x0008,
    windowlessActivate = 0x0010,
    canOptimizeDraw = 0x0020,
};
```

Remarks

`fastBeginPaint` If set, uses a begin-paint function tailored for OLE controls instead of the **BeginPaint** API (set by default).

`clipPaintDC` If not set, disables the call to **IntersectClipRect** made by **COleControl** and gains a small speed advantage. If you are using windowless activation, the flag has no effect.

`pointerInactive` If set, provides mouse interaction while your control is inactive by enabling **COleControl**'s implementation of the **IPointerInactive** interface, which is disabled by default.

`noFlickerActivate` If set, eliminates extra drawing operations and the accompanying visual flicker. Use when your control draws itself identically in the inactive and active states. If you are using windowless activation, the flag has no effect.

`windowlessActivate` If set, indicates your control uses windowless activation.

`canOptimizeDraw` If set, indicates that the control will perform optimized drawing, if the container supports it.

For more information about **GetControlFlags** and other optimizations of OLE controls, see "ActiveX Controls: Optimization."

See Also: **CDC::IntersectClipRect**, **COleControl::SetControlSize**

COleControl::GetControlSize

void GetControlSize(int* *pcx*, **int*** *pcy*);

Parameters

pcx Specifies the width of the control in pixels.

pcy Specifies the height of the control in pixels.

Remarks

Call this function to retrieve the size of the OLE control window.

Note that all coordinates for control windows are relative to the upper-left corner of the control.

See Also: **COleControl::GetRectInContainer**, **COleControl::SetControlSize**

COleControl::GetDC

CDC* GetDC(LPCRECT *lprcRect* **= NULL,**
    ↱ **DWORD** *dwFlags* **= OLEDC_PAINTBKGND);**

Return Value

Pointer to the display device context for the container **CWnd** client area if successful; otherwise, the return value is **NULL**. The display device context can be used in subsequent GDI functions to draw in the client area of the container's window.

Parameters

lprcRect   A pointer to the rectangle the windowless control wants to redraw, in client coordinates of the control. **NULL** means the full object's extent.

dwFlags   Drawing attributes of the device context. Choices are:

- **OLEDC_NODRAW** Indicates that the object won't use the device context to perform any drawing but merely to get information about the display device. The container should simply pass the window's DC without further processing.

- **OLEDC_PAINTBKGND** Requests that the container paint the background before returning the DC. An object should use this flag if it is requesting a DC for redrawing an area with transparent background.

- **OLEDC_OFFSCREEN** Informs the container that the object wishes to render into an off-screen bitmap that should then be copied to the screen. An object should use this flag when the drawing operation it is about to perform generates a lot of flicker. The container is free to honor this request or not. However, if this flag is not set, the container must hand back an on-screen DC. This allows objects to perform direct screen operations such as showing a selection (via an **XOR** operation).

Remarks

Call this function to provide a means for a windowless object to get a screen (or compatible) device context from its container. The **ReleaseDC** member function must be called to release the context after painting. When calling **GetDC**, objects pass the rectangle they wish to draw into in their own client coordinates. **GetDC** translates these to coordinates of the container client area. The object should not request a desired drawing rectangle larger than its own client area rectangle, the size of which can be retrieved with **GetClientRect**. This prevents objects from inadvertently drawing where they are not supposed to.

See Also: **COleControl::ReleaseDC**

COleControl::GetEnabled

BOOL GetEnabled( );

Return Value

Nonzero if the control is enabled; otherwise 0.

Remarks

This function implements the Get function of your control's stock Enabled property.

See Also: **COleControl::SetEnabled, COleControl::OnEnabledChanged**

COleControl::GetExtendedControl

LPDISPATCH GetExtendedControl( );

Return Value

A pointer to the container's extended control object. If there is no object available, the value is **NULL**.

This object may be manipulated through its **IDispatch** interface. You can also use **QueryInterface** to obtain other available interfaces provided by the object. However, the object is not required to support a specific set of interfaces. Note that relying on the specific features of a container's extended control object limits the portability of your control to other arbitrary containers.

Remarks

Call this function to obtain a pointer to an object maintained by the container that represents the control with an extended set of properties. The function that calls this function is responsible for releasing the pointer when finished with the object. Note that the container is not required to support this object.

COleControl::GetFocus

CWnd* GetFocus( );

Return Value

If the control is activated and windowless, returns **this** if the control currently has the keyboard focus (as determined by the control's container), or **NULL** if it does not have the focus.

Otherwise, returns the **CWnd** object that has the focus (same as **CWnd::GetFocus**).

Remarks

Call this function to determine whether the **COleControl** object has the focus. An activated windowless control receives the focus when **SetFocus** is called.

See Also: **COleControl::SetFocus**

COleControl::GetFont

LPFONTDISP GetFont( );

Return Value

A pointer to the font dispatch interface of the control's stock Font property.

Remarks

This function implements the Get function of the stock Font property. Note that the caller must release the object when finished. Within the implementation of the control, use **InternalGetFont** to access the control's stock Font object. For more information on using fonts in your control, see the article "ActiveX Controls: Using Fonts in an ActiveX Control" in *Visual C++ Programmer's Guide* online.

See Also: **COleControl::SetFont**, **COleControl::AmbientFont**, **COleControl::InternalGetFont**

COleControl::GetFontTextMetrics

void GetFontTextMetrics(LPTEXTMETRIC *lptm***, CFontHolder&** *fontHolder* **);**

Parameters

lptm   Pointer to a **TEXTMETRIC** structure.

fontHolder   Reference to a **CFontHolder** object.

Remarks

Call this function to measure the text metrics for any **CFontHolder** object owned by the control. Such a font can be selected with the **COleControl::SelectFontObject** function. **GetFontTextMetrics** will initialize the **TEXTMETRIC** structure pointed to by *lptm* with valid metrics information about *fontHolder*'s font if successful, or fill the structure with zeros if not successful. You should use this function instead of **::GetTextMetrics** when painting your control because controls, like any embedded OLE object, may be required to render themselves into a metafile.

The **TEXTMETRIC** structure for the default font is refreshed when the **SelectFontObject** function is called. You should call **GetFontTextMetrics** only after selecting the stock Font property to assure the information it provides is valid.

COleControl::GetForeColor

OLE_COLOR GetForeColor( );

Return Value

The return value specifies the current foreground color as a **OLE_COLOR** value, if successful. This value can be translated to a **COLORREF** value with a call to **TranslateColor**.

Remarks

This function implements the Get function of the stock ForeColor property.

See Also: COleControl::AmbientForeColor, COleControl::TranslateColor, COleControl::GetBackColor, COleControl::SetForeColor

COleControl::GetHwnd

OLE_HANDLE GetHwnd( );

Return Value

The OLE control's window handle, if any; otherwise **NULL**.

Remarks

This function implements the Get function of the stock hWnd property.

COleControl::GetMessageString

virtual void GetMessageString(UINT *nID*, CString& *rMessage*) const;

Parameters

nID   A menu item ID.

rMessage   A reference to a **CString** object through which a string will be returned.

Remarks

Called by the framework to obtain a short string that describes the purpose of the menu item identified by *nID*. This can be used to obtain a message for display in a status bar while the menu item is highlighted. The default implementation attempts to load a string resource identified by *nID*.

COleControl::GetNotSupported

void GetNotSupported( );

Remarks

Call this function in place of the Get function of any property where retrieval of the property by the control's user is not supported. One example would be a property that is write-only.

See Also: COleControl::SetNotSupported

COleControl::GetReadyState

long GetReadyState( );

Return Value

The readiness state of the control, one of the following values:

READYSTATE_UNINITIALIZED Default initialization state

READYSTATE_LOADING Control is currently loading its properties

READYSTATE_LOADED Control has been initialized

READYSTATE_INTERACTIVE Control has enough data to be interactive but not all asynchronous data is yet loaded

READYSTATE_COMPLETE Control has all its data

Remarks

Call this function to return the readiness state of the control.

Most simple controls never need to differentiate between **LOADED** and **INTERACTIVE**. However, controls that support data path properties may not be ready to be interactive until at least some data is received asynchronously. A control should attempt to become interactive as soon as possible.

See Also: **COleControl::FireReadyStateChange**, **COleControl::InternalSetReadyState**

COleControl::GetRectInContainer

BOOL GetRectInContainer(LPRECT *lpRect*);

Return Value

Nonzero if the control is in-place active; otherwise 0.

Parameters

lpRect A pointer to the rectangle structure into which the control's coordinates will be copied.

Remarks

Call this function to obtain the coordinates of the control's rectangle relative to the container, expressed in device units. The rectangle is only valid if the control is in-place active.

See Also: **COleControl::SetRectInContainer**, **COleControl::GetControlSize**

COleControl::GetStockTextMetrics

void GetStockTextMetrics(LPTEXTMETRIC *lptm* **);**

Parameters

lptm   A pointer to a **TEXTMETRIC** structure.

Remarks

Call this function to measure the text metrics for the control's stock Font property, which can be selected with the **SelectStockFont** function. The **GetStockTextMetrics** function will initialize the **TEXTMETRIC** structure pointed to by *lptm* with valid metrics information if successful, or fill the structure with zeros if not successful. Use this function instead of **::GetTextMetrics** when painting your control because controls, like any embedded OLE object, may be required to render themselves into a metafile.

The **TEXTMETRIC** structure for the default font is refreshed when the **SelectStockFont** function is called. You should call this function only after selecting the stock font to assure the information it provides is valid.

COleControl::GetText

BSTR GetText( );

Return Value

The current value of the control text string or a zero-length string if no string is present.

Note   For more information on the **BSTR** data type, see "Data Types" in the Macros and Globals section.

Remarks

This function implements the Get function of the stock Text or Caption property. Note that the caller of this function must call **SysFreeString** on the string returned in order to free the resource. Within the implementation of the control, use **InternalGetText** to access the control's stock Text or Caption property.

See Also: **COleControl::InternalGetText, COleControl::SetText**

COleControl::GetWindowlessDropTarget

virtual IDropTarget* GetWindowlessDropTarget( );

Return Value

Pointer to the object's **IDropTarget** interface. Since it does not have a window, a windowless object cannot register an **IDropTarget** interface. However, to participate in drag and drop, a windowless object can still implement the interface and return it in **GetWindowlessDropTarget**.

Remarks

Override **GetWindowlessDropTarget** when you want a windowless control to be the target of an OLE drag and drop operation. Normally, this would require that the control's window be registered as a drop target. But since the control has no window of its own, the container will use its own window as a drop target. The control simply needs to provide an implementation of the **IDropTarget** interface to which the container can delegate calls at the appropriate time. For example:

```
IDropTarget* CMyCtrl::GetWindowlessDropTarget()
{
    m_xDropTarget.AddRef();
    return &m_xDropTarget;
}
```

COleControl::InitializeIIDs

void InitializeIIDs(const IID* *piidPrimary*, **const IID*** *piidEvents* **);**

Parameters

piidPrimary　Pointer to the interface ID of the control's primary dispatch interface.

piidEvents　Pointer to the interface ID of the control's event interface.

Remarks

Call this function in the control's constructor to inform the base class of the interface IDs your control will be using.

COleControl::InternalGetFont

CFontHolder& InternalGetFont( );

Return Value

A reference to a **CFontHolder** object that contains the stock Font object.

Remarks

Call this function to access the stock Font property of your control

See Also: **COleControl::GetFont**, **COleControl::SetFont**

COleControl::InternalGetText

const CString& InternalGetText( );

Return Value

A reference to the control text string.

Remarks

Call this function to access the stock Text or Caption property of your control.

See Also: **COleControl::GetText**, **COleControl::SetText**

COleControl::InternalSetReadyState

void InternalSetReadyState(long *lNewReadyState* **);**

Parameters

lNewReadyState   The readiness state to set for the control, one of the following
values:

READYSTATE_UNINITIALIZED   Default initialization state

READYSTATE_LOADING   Control is currently loading its properties

READYSTATE_LOADED   Control has been initialized

READYSTATE_INTERACTIVE   Control has enough data to be interactive but not
all asynchronous data is yet loaded

READYSTATE_COMPLETE   Control has all its data

Remarks

Call this function to set the readiness state of the control.

Most simple controls never need to differentiate between **LOADED** and
INTERACTIVE. However, controls that support data path properties may not be
ready to be interactive until at least some data is received asynchronously. A control
should attempt to become interactive as soon as possible.

See Also: **COleControl::FireReadyStateChange**, **COleControl::GetReadyState**

COleControl::InvalidateControl

void InvalidateControl(LPCRECT *lpRect* **= NULL);**

Parameters

lpRect   A pointer to the region of the control to be invalidated.

Remarks

Call this function to force the control to redraw itself. If *lpRect* has a **NULL** value, the
entire control will be redrawn. If *lpRect* is not **NULL**, this indicates the portion of the
control's rectangle that is to be invalidated. In cases where the control has no window,
or is currently not active, the rectangle is ignored, and a call is made to the client site's
IAdviseSink::OnViewChange member function. Use this function instead of
CWnd::InvalidateRect or **::InvalidateRect**.

See Also: **COleControl::Refresh**

COleControl::InvalidateRgn

void InvalidateRgn(CRgn* *pRgn*, **BOOL** *bErase* = **TRUE**);

Parameters

pRgn   A pointer to a **CRgn** object that identifies the display region of the OLE object to invalidate, in client coordinates of the containing window. If this parameter is **NULL**, the extent is the entire object.

bErase   Specifies whether the background within the invalidated region is to be erased. If **TRUE**, the background is erased. If **FALSE**, the background remains unchanged.

Remarks

Call this function to invalidate the container window's client area within the given region. This can be used to redraw windowless controls within the container. The invalidated region, along with all other areas in the update region, is marked for painting when the next **WM_PAINT** message is sent.

If *bErase* is **TRUE** for any part of the update region, the background in the entire region, not just in the given part, is erased.

COleControl::IsConvertingVBX

BOOL IsConvertingVBX( );

Return Value

Nonzero if the control is being converted; otherwise 0.

Remarks

When converting a form that uses VBX controls to one that uses OLE controls, special loading code for the OLE controls may be required. For example, if you are loading an instance of your OLE control, you might have a call to **PX_Font** in your **DoPropExchange**:

```
PX_Font(pPx, "Font", m_MyFont, pDefaultFont);
```

However, VBX controls did not have a Font object; each font property was saved individually. In this case, you would use **IsConvertingVBX** to distinguish between these two cases:

```
if (IsConvertingVBX()==FALSE)
    PX_Font(pPX, "Font", m_MyFont, pDefaultFont);
else
{
    PX_String(pPX, "FontName", tempString, DefaultName);
    m_MyFont->put_Name(tempString);
    PX_Bool(pPX, "FontUnderline", tempBool, DefaultValue);
    m_MyFont->put_Underline(tempBool);
...
}
```

Another case would be if your VBX control saved proprietary binary data (in its **VBM_SAVEPROPERTY** message handler), and your OLE control saves its binary data in a different format. If you want your OLE control to be backward-compatible with the VBX control, you could read both the old and new formats using the **IsConvertingVBX** function by distinguishing whether the VBX control or the OLE control was being loaded.

In your control's **DoPropExchange** function, you can check for this condition and if true, execute load code specific to this conversion (such as the previous examples). If the control is not being converted, you can execute normal load code. This ability is only applicable to controls being converted from VBX counterparts.

See Also: **COleControl::DoPropExchange**

COleControl::IsModified

BOOL IsModified( );

Return Value

Nonzero if the control's state has been modified since it was last saved; otherwise 0.

Remarks

Call this function to determine if the control's state has been modified. The state of a control is modified when a property changes value.

See Also: **COleControl::SetModifiedFlag**

COleControl::IsOptimizedDraw

BOOL IsOptimizedDraw( );

Return Value

TRUE if the container supports optimized drawing for the current drawing operation; otherwise **FALSE**.

Remarks

Call this function to determine whether the container supports optimized drawing for the current drawing operation. If optimized drawing is supported, then the control need not select old objects (pens, brushes, fonts, etc.) into the device context when drawing is finished.

COleControl::IsSubclassedControl

virtual BOOL IsSubclassedControl( );

Return Value

Nonzero if the control is subclassed; otherwise 0.

Remarks

Called by the framework to determine if the control subclasses a Windows control. You must override this function and return **TRUE** if your OLE control subclasses a Windows control.

COleControl::Load

void Load(LPCTSTR *strNewPath*, **CDataPathProperty&** *prop* **);**

Parameters

strNewPath   A pointer to a string containing the path that references the absolute location of the asynchronous control property.

prop   A **CDataPathProperty** object implementing an asynchronous control property.

Remarks

Call this function to reset any previous data loaded asynchronously and to initiate a new loading of the control's asynchronous property.

See Also: CDataPathProperty

COleControl::LockInPlaceActive

BOOL LockInPlaceActive(BOOL *bLock* **);**

Return Value

Nonzero if the lock was successful; otherwise 0.

Parameters

bLock   **TRUE** if the in-place active state of the control is to be locked; **FALSE** if it is to be unlocked.

Remarks

Call this function to prevent the container from deactivating your control. Note that every locking of the control must be paired with an unlocking of the control when finished. You should only lock your control for short periods, such as while firing an event.

COleControl::OnAmbientPropertyChange

virtual void OnAmbientPropertyChange(DISPID *dispID* **);**

Parameters

dispID   The dispatch ID of the ambient property that changed, or
DISPID_UNKNOWN if multiple properties have changed.

Remarks

Called by the framework when an ambient property of the container has changed value.

See Also: **COleControl::GetAmbientProperty**

COleControl::OnAppearanceChanged

virtual void OnAppearanceChanged ( );

Remarks

Called by the framework when the stock Appearance property value has changed.

Override this function if you want notification after this property changes. The default implementation calls **InvalidateControl**.

See Also: **COleControl::GetAppearance, COleControl::SetAppearance,
COleControl::InvalidateControl**

COleControl::OnBackColorChanged

virtual void OnBackColorChanged( );

Remarks

Called by the framework when the stock BackColor property value has changed.

Override this function if you want notification after this property changes. The default implementation calls **InvalidateControl**.

See Also: **COleControl::GetBackColor, COleControl::InvalidateControl**

COleControl::OnBorderStyleChanged

virtual void OnBorderStyleChanged( );

Remarks

Called by the framework when the stock BorderStyle property value has changed. The default implementation calls **InvalidateControl**.

Override this function if you want notification after this property changes.

See Also: **COleControl::SetBorderStyle**, **COleControl::InvalidateControl**

COleControl::OnClick

virtual void OnClick(USHORT *iButton* **);**

Parameters

iButton   Index of a mouse button. Can have one of the following values:

- **LEFT_BUTTON**   The left mouse button was clicked.
- **MIDDLE_BUTTON**   The middle mouse button was clicked.
- **RIGHT_BUTTON**   The right mouse button was clicked.

Remarks

Called by the framework when a mouse button has been clicked or the DoClick stock method has been invoked. The default implementation calls **COleControl::FireClick**.

Override this member function to modify or extend the default handling.

See Also: **COleControl::DoClick**, **COleControl::FireClick**

COleControl::OnClose

virtual void OnClose(DWORD *dwSaveOption* **);**

Parameters

dwSaveOption   Flag that indicates whether the object should be saved before loading. Valid values are:

- **OLECLOSE_SAVEIFDIRTY**
- **OLECLOSE_NOSAVE**
- **OLECLOSE_PROMPTSAVE**

Remarks

Called by the framework when the container has called the control's **IOleControl::Close** function. By default, **OnClose** saves the control object if it has been modified and *dwSaveOption* is either **OLECLOSE_SAVEIFDIRTY** or **OLECLOSE_PROMPTSAVE**.

COleControl::OnDoVerb

virtual BOOL OnDoVerb(LONG *iVerb*, **LPMSG** *lpMsg*, **HWND** *hWndParent*,
↪ **LPCRECT** *lpRect* **);**

Return Value

Nonzero if call was successful; otherwise 0.

Parameters

iVerb   The index of the control verb to be invoked.

lpMsg   A pointer to the Windows message that caused the verb to be invoked.

hWndParent   The handle to the parent window of the control. If the execution of the verb creates a window (or windows), *hWndParent* should be used as the parent.

lpRect   A pointer to a **RECT** structure into which the coordinates of the control, relative to the container, will be copied.

Remarks

Called by the framework when the container calls the **IOleObject::DoVerb** member function. The default implementation uses the **ON_OLEVERB** and **ON_STDOLEVERB** message map entries to determine the proper function to invoke.

Override this function to change the default handling of verb.

See Also: **ON_OLEVERB, ON_STDOLEVERB, COleControl::OnEnumVerbs**

COleControl::OnDraw

virtual void OnDraw(CDC* *pDC*, **const CRect&** *rcBounds*, **const CRect&** *rcInvalid* **);**

Parameters

pDC   The device context in which the drawing occurs.

rcBounds   The rectangular area of the control, including the border.

rcInvalid   The rectangular area of the control that is invalid.

Remarks

Called by the framework to draw the OLE control in the specified bounding rectangle using the specified device context.

OnDraw is typically called for screen display, passing a screen device context as *pDC*. The *rcBounds* parameter identifies the rectangle in the target device context (relative to its current mapping mode). The *rcInvalid* parameter is the actual rectangle that is invalid. In some cases this will be a smaller area than *rcBounds*.

See Also: **COleControl::OnDrawMetafile, COleControl::DrawContent, COleControl::DrawMetafile**

COleControl::OnDrawMetafile

virtual void OnDrawMetafile(CDC* *pDC***, const CRect&** *rcBounds* **);**

Parameters

pDC   The device context in which the drawing occurs.

rcBounds   The rectangular area of the control, including the border.

Remarks

Called by the framework to draw the OLE control in the specified bounding rectangle using the specified metafile device context. The default implementation calls the **OnDraw** function.

See Also: **COleControl::OnDraw**, **COleControl::DrawContent**, **COleControl::DrawMetafile**

COleControl::OnEdit

virtual BOOL OnEdit(LPMSG *lpMsg***, HWND** *hWndParent***, LPCRECT** *lpRect* **);**

Return Value

Nonzero if the call is successful; otherwise 0.

Parameters

lpMsg   A pointer to the Windows message that invoked the verb.

hWndParent   A handle to the parent window of the control.

lpRect   A pointer to the rectangle used by the control in the container.

Remarks

Call this function to cause the control to be UI activated. This has the same effect as invoking the control's **OLEIVERB_UIACTIVATE** verb.

This function is typically used as the handler function for an **ON_OLEVERB** message map entry. This makes an "Edit" verb available on the control's "Object" menu. For example:

```
ON_OLEVERB(AFX_IDS_VERB_EDIT, OnEdit)
```

COleControl::OnEnabledChanged

virtual void OnEnabledChanged( );

Remarks

Called by the framework when the stock Enabled property value has changed.

Override this function if you want notification after this property changes. The default implementation calls **InvalidateControl**.

See Also: COleControl::SetEnabled, COleControl::GetEnabled

COleControl::OnEnumVerbs

virtual BOOL OnEnumVerbs(LPENUMOLEVERB FAR* *ppenumOleVerb* **);**

Return Value

Nonzero if verbs are available; otherwise 0.

Parameters

ppenumOleVerb   A pointer to the **IEnumOLEVERB** object that enumerates the control's verbs.

Remarks

Called by the framework when the container calls the **IOleObject::EnumVerbs** member function. The default implementation enumerates the **ON_OLEVERB** entries in the message map.

Override this function to change the default way of enumerating verbs.

See Also: ON_OLEVERB, ON_STDOLEVERB

COleControl::OnEventAdvise

virtual void OnEventAdvise(BOOL *bAdvise* **);**

Parameters

bAdvise   **TRUE** indicates that an event handler has been connected to the control. **FALSE** indicates that an event handler has been disconnected from the control.

Remarks

Called by the framework when an event handler is connected to or disconnected from an OLE control.

COleControl::OnFontChanged

virtual void OnFontChanged( );

Remarks

Called by the framework when the stock Font property value has changed. The default implementation calls **COleControl::InvalidateControl**. If the control is subclassing a Windows control, the default implementation also sends a **WM_SETFONT** message to the control's window.

Override this function if you want notification after this property changes.

See Also: **COleControl::GetFont, COleControl::InternalGetFont,
COleControl::InvalidateControl**

COleControl::OnForeColorChanged

virtual void OnForeColorChanged( );

Remarks

Called by the framework when the stock ForeColor property value has changed. The
default implementation calls **InvalidateControl**.

Override this function if you want notification after this property changes.

See Also: **COleControl::SetForeColor, COleControl::InvalidateControl**

COleControl::OnFreezeEvents

virtual void OnFreezeEvents(BOOL *bFreeze*);

Parameters

bFreeze   **TRUE** if the control's event handling is frozen; otherwise **FALSE**.

Remarks

Called by the framework after the container calls **IOleControl::FreezeEvents**. The
default implementation does nothing.

Override this function if you want additional behavior when event handling is frozen
or unfrozen.

COleControl::OnGetColorSet

**virtual BOOL OnGetColorSet(DVTARGETDEVICE FAR* *ptd*,
 ➡ HDC *hicTargetDev*, LPLOGPALETTE FAR* *ppColorSet*);**

Return Value

Nonzero if a valid color set is returned; otherwise 0.

Parameters

ptd   Points to the target device for which the picture should be rendered. If this value
is **NULL**, the picture should be rendered for a default target device, usually a
display device.

hicTargetDev   Specifies the information context on the target device indicated by *ptd*.
This parameter can be a device context, but is not one necessarily. If *ptd* is **NULL**,
hicTargetDev should also be **NULL**.

ppColorSet   A pointer to the location into which the set of colors that would be used
should be copied. If the function does not return the color set, **NULL** is returned.

Remarks

Called by the framework when the container calls the **IOleObject::GetColorSet** member function. The container calls this function to obtain all the colors needed to draw the OLE control. The container can use the color sets obtained in conjunction with the colors it needs to set the overall color palette. The default implementation returns **FALSE**.

Override this function to do any special processing of this request.

COleControl::OnGetControlInfo

virtual void OnGetControlInfo(LPCONTROLINFO *pControlInfo* **);**

Parameters

pControlInfo   Pointer to a **CONTROLINFO** structure to be filled in.

Remarks

Called by the framework when the control's container has requested information about the control. This information consists primarily of a description of the control's mnemonic keys. The default implementation fills *pControlInfo* with default information.

Override this function if your control needs to process mnemonic keys.

COleControl::OnGetDisplayString

virtual BOOL OnGetDisplayString(DISPID *dispid*, **CString&** *strValue* **);**

Return Value

Nonzero if a string has been returned in *strValue;* otherwise 0.

Parameters

dispid   The dispatch ID of a property of the control.

strValue   A reference to a **CString** object through which a string will be returned.

Remarks

Called by the framework to obtain a string that represents the current value of the property identified by *dispid*.

Override this function if your control has a property whose value cannot be directly converted to a string and you want the property's value to be displayed in a container-supplied property browser.

See Also: COleControl::OnMapPropertyToPage

COleControl::OnGetInPlaceMenu

> **virtual HMENU OnGetInPlaceMenu( );**

Return Value

The handle of the control's menu, or **NULL** if the control has none. The default implementation returns **NULL**.

Remarks

Called by the framework when the control is UI activated to obtain the menu to be merged into the container's existing menu.

For more information on merging OLE resources, see the article "Menus and Resources (OLE)" in *Visual C++ Programmer's Guide* online.

COleControl::OnGetNaturalExtent

> **virtual BOOL OnGetNaturalExtent(DWORD** *dwAspect*, **LONG** *lindex*,
> ↪ **DVTARGETDEVICE*** *ptd*, **HDC** *hicTargetDev*,
> ↪ **DVEXTENTINFO*** *pExtentInfo*, **LPSIZEL** *psizel*);

Return Value

Nonzero if it successfully returns or adjusts the size; otherwise 0.

Parameters

dwAspect   Specifies how the object is to be represented. Representations include content, an icon, a thumbnail, or a printed document. Valid values are taken from the enumeration **DVASPECT** or **DVASPECT2**.

lindex   The portion of the object that is of interest. Currently only −1 is valid.

ptd   Points to the **DVTARGETDEVICE** structure defining the target device for which the object's size should be returned.

hicTargetDev   Specifies the information context for the target device indicated by the *ptd* parameter from which the object can extract device metrics and test the device's capabilities. If *ptd* is **NULL**, the object should ignore the value in the *hicTargetDev* parameter.

pExtentInfo   Points to the **DVEXTENTINFO** structure that specifies sizing data. The **DVEXTENTINFO** structure is:

```
typedef struct  tagExtentInfo
    {
    UINT cb;
    DWORD dwExtentMode;
    SIZEL sizelProposed;
    }   DVEXTENTINFO;
```

The structure member dwExtentMode can take one of two values:

- **DVEXTENT_CONTENT** Inquire how big the control should be to exactly fit content (snap-to-size)

- **DVEXTENT_INTEGRAL** When resizing, pass proposed size to control

psizel Points to sizing data returned by control. The returned sizing data is set to −1 for any dimension that was not adjusted.

Remarks

Called by the framework in response to a container's **IViewObjectEx::GetNaturalExtent** request. Override this function to return the object's display size closest to the proposed size and extent mode in the **DVEXTENTINFO** structure. The default implementation returns **FALSE** and makes no adjustments to the size.

See Also: **COleControl::OnGetViewExtent**

COleControl::OnGetPredefinedStrings

virtual BOOL OnGetPredefinedStrings(DISPID *dispid*,
↳ **CStringArray*** *pStringArray*, **CDWordArray*** *pCookieArray* **);**

Return Value

Nonzero if elements have been added to *pStringArray* and *pCookieArray*.

Parameters

dispid The dispatch ID of a property of the control.

pStringArray A string array to be filled in with return values.

pCookieArray A **DWORD** array to be filled in with return values.

Remarks

Called by the framework to obtain a set of predefined strings representing the possible values for a property.

Override this function if your control has a property with a set of possible values that can be represented by strings. For each element added to *pStringArray*, you should add a corresponding "cookie" element to *pCookieArray*. These "cookie" values may later be passed by the framework to the **COleControl::OnGetPredefinedValue** function.

See Also: **COleControl::OnGetPredefinedValue**, **COleControl::OnGetDisplayString**

COleControl::OnGetPredefinedValue

> **virtual BOOL OnGetPredefinedValue(DISPID** *dispid*, **DWORD** *dwCookie*,
> ➙ **VARIANT FAR*** *lpvarOut* **);**

Return Value

Nonzero if a value has been returned in *lpvarOut*; otherwise 0.

Parameters

dispid   The dispatch ID of a property of the control.

dwCookie   A cookie value previously returned by an override of
COleControl::OnGetPredefinedStrings.

lpvarOut   Pointer to a **VARIANT** structure through which a property value will be
returned.

Remarks

Called by the framework to obtain the value corresponding to one of the predefined
strings previously returned by an override of
COleControl::OnGetPredefinedStrings.

See Also: **COleControl::OnGetPredefinedStrings**,
COleControl::OnGetDisplayString

COleControl::OnGetViewExtent

> **virtual BOOL OnGetViewExtent(DWORD** *dwDrawAspect*, **LONG** *lindex*,
> ➙ **DVTARGETDEVICE*** *ptd*, **LPSIZEL** *lpsizel* **);**

Return Value

Nonzero if extent information is successfully returned; otherwise 0.

Parameters

dwDrawAspect   **DWORD** describing which form, or aspect, of an object is to be
displayed. Valid values are taken from the enumeration **DVASPECT** or
DVASPECT2.

lindex   The portion of the object that is of interest. Currently only –1 is valid.

ptd   Points to the **DVTARGETDEVICE** structure defining the target device for
which the object's size should be returned.

lpsizel   Points to the location where the object's size is returned.

Remarks

Called by the framework in response to a container's **IViewObjectEx::GetExtent**
request. Override this function if your control uses two-pass drawing, and its opaque
and transparent parts have different dimensions.

See Also: **COleControl::OnGetViewRect**

COleControl::OnGetViewRect

virtual BOOL OnGetViewRect(DWORD *dwAspect*, **LPRECTL** *pRect* **);**

Return Value

Nonzero if the rectangle sized to the object is successfully returned; otherwise 0.

Parameters

dwAspect **DWORD** describing which form, or aspect, of an object is to be displayed. Valid values are taken from the enumeration **DVASPECT** or **DVASPECT2**:

- **DVASPECT_CONTENT** Bounding rectangle of the whole object. Top-left corner at the object's origin and size equal to the extent returned by **GetViewExtent**.

- **DVASPECT_OPAQUE** Objects with a rectangular opaque region return that rectangle. Others fail.

- **DVASPECT_TRANSPARENT** Rectangle covering all transparent or irregular parts.

pRect Points to the **RECTL** structure specifying the rectangle in which the object should be drawn. This parameter controls the positioning and stretching of the object.

Remarks

Called by the framework in response to a container's **IViewObjectEx::GetRect** request. The object's size is converted by **OnGetViewRect** into a rectangle starting at a specific position (the default is the upper left corner of the display). Override this function if your control uses two-pass drawing, and its opaque and transparent parts have different dimensions.

See Also: **COleControl::OnGetViewExtent**

COleControl::OnGetViewStatus

virtual DWORD OnGetViewStatus( );

Return Value

One of the values of the **VIEWSTATUS** enumeration if successful; otherwise 0. Possible values are any combination of the following:

VIEWSTATUS_OPAQUE Object is completely opaque. If this bit is not set, the object contains transparent parts. This bit applies only to content-related aspects and not to **DVASPECT_ICON** or **DVASPECT_DOCPRINT**.

VIEWSTATUS_SOLIDBKGND   Object has a solid background (consisting in a solid color, not a brush pattern). This bit is meaningful only if **VIEWSTATUS_OPAQUE** is set and applies only to content-related aspects and not to **DVASPECT_ICON** or **DVASPECT_DOCPRINT**.

VIEWSTATUS_DVASPECTOPAQUE   Object supports **DVASPECT_OPAQUE**. All **IViewObjectEx** methods that take a drawing aspect as a parameter can be called with this aspect.

VIEWSTATUS_DVASPECTTRANSPARENT   Object supports **DVASPECT_TRANSPARENT**. All **IViewObjectEx** methods that take a drawing aspect as a parameter can be called with this aspect.

Remarks

Called by the framework in response to a container's **IViewObjectEx::GetViewStatus** request. Override this function if your control uses two-pass drawing. The default implementation returns **VIEWSTATUS_OPAQUE**.

See Also: DVASPECT

COleControl::OnHideToolBars

virtual void OnHideToolBars( );

Remarks

Called by the framework when the control is UI deactivated. The implementation should hide all toolbars displayed by **OnShowToolbars**.

See Also: COleControl::OnShowToolbars

COleControl::OnInactiveMouseMove

virtual void OnInactiveMouseMove(LPCRECT *lprcBounds*, **long** *x*, **long** *y*,
➥ **DWORD** *dwKeyState* **);**

Parameters

lprcBounds   The object bounding rectangle, in client coordinates of the containing window. Tells the object its exact position and size on the screen when the **WM_MOUSEMOVE** message was received.

x   The x coordinate of the mouse location in client coordinates of the containing window.

y   The y coordinate of the mouse location in client coordinates of the containing window.

dwKeyState   Identifies the current state of the keyboard modifier keys on the keyboard. Valid values can be a combination of any of the flags **MK_CONTROL**, **MK_SHIFT**, **MK_ALT**, **MK_BUTTON**, **MK_LBUTTON**, **MK_MBUTTON**, and **MK_RBUTTON**.

Remarks

Called by the container for the inactive object under the mouse pointer on receipt of a **WM_MOUSEMOVE** message. Note that window client coordinates (pixels) are used to pass the mouse cursor position. This is made possible by also passing the bounding rectangle of the object in the same coordinate system.

See Also: **COleControl::GetActivationPolicy**, **COleControl::OnInactiveSetCursor**

COleControl::OnInactiveSetCursor

virtual BOOL OnInactiveSetCursor(LPCRECT *lprcBounds*, **long** *x*, **long** *y*, ↪ **DWORD** *dwMouseMsg*, **BOOL** *bSetAlways*);

Return Value

Nonzero if successful; otherwise 0.

Parameters

lprcBounds   The object bounding rectangle, in client coordinates of the containing window. Tells the object its exact position and size on the screen when the **WM_SETCURSOR** message was received.

x   The x coordinate of the mouse location in client coordinates of the containing window.

y   The y coordinate of the mouse location in client coordinates of the containing window.

dwMouseMsg   The identifier of the mouse message for which a **WM_SETCURSOR** occurred.

bSetAlways   Specifies whether or not the object must set the cursor. If **TRUE**, the object must set the cursor; if **FALSE**, the cursor is not obligated to set the cursor, and should return **S_FALSE** in that case.

Remarks

Called by the container for the inactive object under the mouse pointer on receipt of a **WM_SETCURSOR** message. Note that window client coordinates (pixels) are used to pass the mouse cursor position. This is made possible by also passing the bounding rectangle of the object in the same coordinate system.

See Also: **COleControl::GetActivationPolicy**, **COleControl::OnInactiveMouseMove**

COleControl::OnKeyDownEvent

virtual void OnKeyDownEvent(USHORT *nChar*, **USHORT** *nShiftState* **);**

Parameters

    nChar The virtual-key code value of the pressed key.

    nShiftState Contains a combination of the following flags:

- **SHIFT_MASK** The SHIFT key was pressed during the action.
- **CTRL_MASK** The CTRL key was pressed during the action.
- **ALT_MASK** The ALT key was pressed during the action.

Remarks

    Called by the framework after a stock KeyDown event has been processed.

    Override this function if your control needs access to the key information after the event has been fired.

    See Also: **COleControl::OnKeyUpEvent, COleControl::OnKeyPressEvent**

COleControl::OnKeyPressEvent

virtual void OnKeyPressEvent(USHORT *nChar* **);**

Parameters

    nChar Contains the virtual-key code value of the key pressed.

Remarks

    Called by the framework after the stock KeyPress event has been fired. Note that the *nChar* value may have been modified by the container.

    Override this function if you want notification after this event occurs.

    See Also: **COleControl::FireKeyPress**

COleControl::OnKeyUpEvent

virtual void OnKeyUpEvent(USHORT *nChar*, **USHORT** *nShiftState* **);**

Parameters

    nChar The virtual-key code value of the pressed key.

    nShiftState Contains a combination of the following flags:

- **SHIFT_MASK** The SHIFT key was pressed during the action.
- **CTRL_MASK** The CTRL key was pressed during the action.
- **ALT_MASK** The ALT key was pressed during the action.

Remarks

Called by the framework after a stock KeyDown event has been processed.

Override this function if your control needs access to the key information after the event has been fired.

See Also: **COleControl::OnKeyDownEvent**, **COleControl::OnKeyPressEvent**

COleControl::OnMapPropertyToPage

virtual BOOL OnMapPropertyToPage(DISPID *dispid*, **LPCLSID** *lpclsid*,
↳ **BOOL*** *pbPageOptional* **);**

Return Value

Nonzero if a class ID has been returned in *lpclsid*; otherwise 0.

Parameters

dispid   The dispatch ID of a property of the control.

lpclsid   Pointer to a **CLSID** structure through which a class ID will be returned.

pbPageOptional   Returns an indicator of whether use of the specified property page is optional.

Remarks

Called by the framework to obtain the class ID of a property page that implements editing of the specified property.

Override this function to provide a way to invoke your control's property pages from the container's property browser.

See Also: **COleControl::OnGetDisplayString**

COleControl::OnMnemonic

virtual void OnMnemonic(LPMSG *pMsg* **);**

Parameters

pMsg   Pointer to the Windows message generated by a mnemonic key press.

Remarks

Called by the framework when the container has detected that a mnemonic key of the OLE control has been pressed.

COleControl::OnProperties

virtual BOOL OnProperties(LPMSG *lpMsg*, **HWND** *hWndParent*, **LPCRECT** *lpRect*);

Return Value

Nonzero if the call is successful; otherwise 0.

Parameters

lpMsg   A pointer to the Windows message that invoked the verb.

hWndParent   A handle to the parent window of the control.

lpRect   A pointer to the rectangle used by the control in the container.

Remarks

Called by the framework when the control's properties verb has been invoked by the container. The default implementation displays a modal property dialog box.

COleControl::OnQueryHitPoint

virtual BOOL OnQueryHitPoint(DWORD *dwAspect*, **LPCRECT** *pRectBounds*,
➡ **POINT** *ptlLoc*, **LONG** *lCloseHint*, **DWORD*** *pHitResult*);

Return Value

Nonzero if a hit result is successfully returned; otherwise 0. A hit is an overlap with the OLE control display area.

Parameters

dwAspect   Specifies how the object is represented. Valid values are taken from the enumeration **DVASPECT** or **DVASPECT2**.

pRectBounds   Pointer to a **RECT** structure specifying the bounding rectangle of the OLE control client area.

ptlLoc   Pointer to the **POINT** structure specifying the point to be checked for a hit. The point is specified in OLE client area coordinates.

lCloseHint   The distance that defines "close" to the point checked for a hit.

pHitResult   Pointer to the result of the hit query. One of the following values:

- **HITRESULT_OUTSIDE**   *ptlLoc* is outside the OLE object and not close.
- **HITRESULT_TRANSPARENT**   *ptlLoc* is within the bounds of the OLE object, but not close to the image. For example, a point in the middle of a transparent circle could be **HITRESULT_TRANSPARENT**.
- **HITRESULT_CLOSE**   *ptlLoc* is inside or outside the OLE object but close enough to the object to be considered inside. Small, thin, or detailed objects may use this value. Even if a point is outside the bounding rectangle of an object it may still be close (this is needed for hitting small objects).
- **HITRESULT_HIT**   *ptlLoc* is within the image of the object.

Remarks

Called by the framework in response to a container's **IViewObjectEx::QueryHitPoint** request. Queries whether an object's display rectangle overlaps the given point (hits the point). **QueryHitPoint** can be overridden to test hits for non-rectangular objects.

See Also: **COleControl::OnQueryHitRect**

COleControl::OnQueryHitRect

virtual BOOL OnQueryHitRect(DWORD *dwAspect*, **LPCRECT** *pRectBounds*,
↳ **LPCRECT** *prcLoc*, **LONG** *lCloseHint*, **DWORD*** *pHitResult* **);**

Return Value

Nonzero if a hit result is successfully returned; otherwise 0.

Parameters

dwAspect Specifies how the object is to be represented. Valid values are taken from the enumeration **DVASPECT** or **DVASPECT2**.

pRectBounds Pointer to a **RECT** structure specifying the bounding rectangle of the OLE control client area.

prcLoc Pointer to the **RECT** structure specifying the rectangle to be checked for a hit (overlap with the object rectangle), relative to the upper left corner of the object.

lCloseHint Not used.

pHitResult Pointer to the result of the hit query. One of the following values:

- **HITRESULT_OUTSIDE** no point in the rectangle is hit by the OLE object.

- **HITRESULT_HIT** at least one point in the rectangle would be a hit on the object.

Remarks

Called by the framework in response to a container's **IViewObjectEx::QueryHitRect** request. Queries whether an object's display rectangle overlaps any point in the given rectangle (hits the rectangle). **QueryHitRect** can be overridden to test hits for non-rectangular objects.

See Also: **COleControl::OnQueryHitPoint**

COleControl::OnRenderData

virtual BOOL OnRenderData(LPFORMATETC *lpFormatEtc*,
↳ **LPSTGMEDIUM** *lpStgMedium* **);**

Return Value

Nonzero if successful; otherwise 0.

Parameters

lpFormatEtc Points to the **FORMATETC** structure specifying the format in which information is requested.

lpStgMedium Points to a **STGMEDIUM** structure in which the data is to be returned.

Remarks

Called by the framework to retrieve data in the specified format. The specified format is one previously placed in the control object using the **DelayRenderData** or **DelayRenderFileData** member functions for delayed rendering. The default implementation of this function calls **OnRenderFileData** or **OnRenderGlobalData**, respectively, if the supplied storage medium is either a file or memory. If the requested format is **CF_METAFILEPICT** or the persistent property set format, the default implementation renders the appropriate data and returns nonzero. Otherwise, it returns 0 and does nothing.

If *lpStgMedium->tymed* is **TYMED_NULL**, the **STGMEDIUM** should be allocated and filled as specified by *lpFormatEtc->tymed*. If not **TYMED_NULL**, the **STGMEDIUM** should be filled in place with the data.

Override this function to provide your data in the requested format and medium. Depending on your data, you may want to override one of the other versions of this function instead. If your data is small and fixed in size, override **OnRenderGlobalData**. If your data is in a file, or is of variable size, override **OnRenderFileData**.

For more information, see the **FORMATETC** and **STGMEDIUM** structures in the OLE documentation.

See Also: **COleControl::OnRenderFileData**, **COleControl::OnRenderGlobalData**

COleControl::OnRenderFileData

virtual BOOL OnRenderFileData(LPFORMATETC *lpFormatEtc*, **CFile*** *pFile* **);**

Return Value

Nonzero if successful; otherwise 0.

Parameters

lpFormatEtc Points to the **FORMATETC** structure specifying the format in which information is requested.

pFile Points to a **CFile** object in which the data is to be rendered.

Remarks

Called by the framework to retrieve data in the specified format when the storage medium is a file. The specified format is one previously placed in the control object using the **DelayRenderData** member function for delayed rendering. The default implementation of this function simply returns **FALSE**.

Override this function to provide your data in the requested format and medium. Depending on your data, you might want to override one of the other versions of this function instead. If you want to handle multiple storage mediums, override **OnRenderData**. If your data is in a file, or is of variable size, override **OnRenderFileData**.

For more information, see the **FORMATETC** structure in the OLE documentation.

See Also: **COleControl::OnRenderData**, **COleControl::OnRenderGlobalData**

COleControl::OnRenderGlobalData

virtual BOOL OnRenderGlobalData(LPFORMATETC *lpFormatEtc,*
↪ **HGLOBAL*** *phGlobal* **);**

Return Value

Nonzero if successful; otherwise 0.

Parameters

lpFormatEtc   Points to the **FORMATETC** structure specifying the format in which information is requested.

phGlobal   Points to a handle to global memory in which the data is to be returned. If no memory has been allocated, this parameter can be **NULL**.

Remarks

Called by the framework to retrieve data in the specified format when the specified storage medium is global memory. The specified format is one previously placed in the control object using the **DelayRenderData** member function for delayed rendering. The default implementation of this function simply returns **FALSE**.

If *phGlobal* is **NULL**, then a new **HGLOBAL** should be allocated and returned in *phGlobal*. Otherwise, the **HGLOBAL** specified by *phGlobal* should be filled with the data. The amount of data placed in the **HGLOBAL** must not exceed the current size of the memory block. Also, the block cannot be reallocated to a larger size.

Override this function to provide your data in the requested format and medium. Depending on your data, you may want to override one of the other versions of this function instead. If you want to handle multiple storage mediums, override **OnRenderData**. If your data is in a file, or is of variable size, override **OnRenderFileData**.

For more information, see the **FORMATETC** structure in the OLE documentation.

See Also: **COleControl::OnRenderFileData**, **COleControl::OnRenderData**

COleControl::OnResetState

virtual void OnResetState( );

Remarks

Called by the framework when the control's properties should be set to their default values. The default implementation calls **DoPropExchange**, passing a **CPropExchange** object that causes properties to be set to their default values.

The control writer can insert initialization code for the OLE control in this overridable. This function is called when **IPersistStream::Load** or **IPersistStorage::Load** fails, or **IPersistStreamInit::InitNew** or **IPersistStorage::InitNew** is called, without first calling either **IPersistStream::Load** or **IPersistStorage::Load**.

See Also: **COleControl::OnSetClientSite**

COleControl::OnSetClientSite

virtual void OnSetClientSite( );

Remarks

Called by the framework when the container has called the control's **IOleControl::SetClientSite** function. By default, **OnSetClientSite** checks whether data path properties are loaded and, if they are, calls `DoDataPathPropExchange`.

Override this function to do any special processing of this notification. In particular, overrides of this function should call the base class.

COleControl::OnSetData

virtual BOOL OnSetData(LPFORMATETC *lpFormatEtc*,
   → **LPSTGMEDIUM** *lpStgMedium*, **BOOL** *bRelease*);

Return Value

Nonzero if successful; otherwise 0.

Parameters

lpFormatEtc   Pointer to a **FORMATETC** structure specifying the format of the data.

lpStgMedium   Pointer to a **STGMEDIUM** structure in which the data resides.

bRelease   **TRUE** if the control should free the storage medium; **FALSE** if if the control should not free the storage medium.

Remarks

Called by the framework to replace the control's data with the specified data. If the data is in the persistent property set format, the default implementation modifies the control's state accordingly. Otherwise, the default implementation does nothing. If *bRelease* is **TRUE**, then a call to **ReleaseStgMedium** is made; otherwise not.

Override this function to replace the control's data with the specified data.

For more information, see the **FORMATETC** and **STGMEDIUM** structures in the OLE documentation.

See Also: **COleControl::DoPropExchange**

COleControl::OnSetExtent

virtual BOOL OnSetExtent(LPSIZEL *lpSizeL*);

Return Value
Nonzero if the size change was accepted; otherwise 0.

Parameters
lpSizeL   A pointer to the **SIZEL** structure that uses long integers to represent the width and height of the control, expressed in **HIMETRIC** units.

Remarks
Called by the framework when the control's extent needs to be changed, as a result of a call to **IOleObject::SetExtent**. The default implementation handles the resizing of the control's extent. If the control is in-place active, a call to the container's **OnPosRectChanged** is then made.

Override this function to alter the default resizing of your control.

COleControl::OnSetObjectRects

virtual BOOL OnSetObjectRects(LPCRECT *lpRectPos*, LPCRECT *lpRectClip*);

Return Value
Nonzero if the repositioning was accepted; otherwise 0.

Parameters
lpRectPos   A pointer to a **RECT** structure indicating the control's new position and size relative to the container.

lpRectClip   A pointer to a **RECT** structure indicating a rectangular area to which the control is to be clipped.

Remarks
Called by the framework to implement a call to **IOleInPlaceObject::SetObjectRects**. The default implementation automatically handles the repositioning and resizing of the control window and returns **TRUE**.

Override this function to alter the default behavior of this function.

COleControl::OnShowToolBars

virtual void OnShowToolBars( );

Remarks

Called by the framework when the control has been UI activated. The default implementation does nothing.

See Also: **COleControl::OnHideToolbars**

COleControl::OnTextChanged

virtual void OnTextChanged( );

Remarks

Called by the framework when the stock Caption or Text property value has changed. The default implementation calls **InvalidateControl**.

Override this function if you want notification after this property changes.

See Also: **COleControl::SetText**, **COleControl::InternalGetText**, **COleControl::InvalidateControl**

COleControl::OnWindowlessMessage

virtual BOOL OnWindowlessMessage(UINT *msg*, **WPARAM** *wParam*,
→ **LPARAM** *lParam*, **LRESULT*** *plResult* **);**

Return Value

Nonzero if successful; otherwise 0.

Parameters

msg   Message identifier as passed by Windows.

wParam   As passed by Windows. Specifies additional message-specific information. The contents of this parameter depend on the value of the *msg* parameter.

lParam   As passed by Windows. Specifies additional message-specific information. The contents of this parameter depend on the value of the *msg* parameter.

plResult   Windows result code. Specifies the result of the message processing and depends on the message sent.

Remarks

Called by the framework in response to a container's **IOleInPlaceObjectWindowless::OnWindowMessage** request. Processes window messages for windowless controls. **COleControl**'s **OnWindowlessMessage** should be used for window messages other than mouse messages and keyboard messages.

COleControl provides **SetCapture** and **SetFocus** specifically to get mouse capture and keyboard focus for windowless OLE objects.

Since windowless objects do not have a window, they need a mechanism to let the container dispatch messages to them. A windowless OLE object gets messages from its container, via the **OnWindowMessage** method on the **IOleInPlaceObjectWindowless** interface (an extension of **IOleInPlaceObject** for windowless support). **OnWindowMessage** does not take an **HWND** parameter.

See Also: COleControl::SetCapture, COleControl::SetFocus, COleControl::GetWindowlessDropTarget

COleControl::ParentToClient

virtual UINT ParentToClient(LPCRECT *lprcBounds*, **LPPOINT** *pPoint*,
➤ **BOOL** *bHitTest* = **FALSE**) **const;**

Return Value

If *bHitTest* is **FALSE**, returns **HTNOWHERE**. If *bHitTest* is **TRUE**, returns the location in which the parent (container) point landed in the client area of the OLE control and is one of the following mouse hit-test values:

- **HTBORDER**   In the border of a window that does not have a sizing border.
- **HTBOTTOM**   In the lower horizontal border of the window.
- **HTBOTTOMLEFT**   In the lower-left corner of the window border.
- **HTBOTTOMRIGHT**   In the lower-right corner of the window border.
- **HTCAPTION**   In a title-bar area.
- **HTCLIENT**   In a client area.
- **HTERROR**   On the screen background or on a dividing line between windows (same as **HTNOWHERE** except that the **DefWndProc** Windows function produces a system beep to indicate an error).
- **HTGROWBOX**   In a size box.
- **HTHSCROLL**   In the horizontal scroll bar.
- **HTLEFT**   In the left border of the window.
- **HTMAXBUTTON**   In a Maximize button.
- **HTMENU**   In a menu area.
- **HTMINBUTTON**   In a Minimize button.
- **HTNOWHERE**   On the screen background or on a dividing line between windows.
- **HTREDUCE**   In a Minimize button.
- **HTRIGHT**   In the right border of the window.

- **HTSIZE** In a size box (same as **HTGROWBOX**).
- **HTSYSMENU** In a Control menu or in a Close button in a child window.
- **HTTOP** In the upper horizontal border of the window.
- **HTTOPLEFT** In the upper-left corner of the window border.
- **HTTOPRIGHT** In the upper-right corner of the window border.
- **HTTRANSPARENT** In a window currently covered by another window.
- **HTVSCROLL** In the vertical scroll bar.
- **HTZOOM** In a Maximize button.

Parameters

lprcBounds Pointer to the bounds of the OLE control within the container. Not the client area but the area of the entire control including borders and scroll bars.

pPoint Pointer to the parent (container) point to be translated into the coordinates of the client area of the control.

bHitTest Specifies whether or not hit testing is to be done on the point.

Remarks

Call this function to translate the coordinates of *pPoint* into client coordinates. On input *pPoint* is relative to the origin of the parent (upper left corner of the container). On output *pPoint* is relative to the origin of the client area of the OLE control (upper left corner of the client area of the control).

See Also: **COleControl::ClientToParent, COleControl::GetClientOffset**

COleControl::PostModalDialog

void PostModalDialog( );

Remarks

Call this function after displaying any modal dialog box. You must call this function so that the container can enable any top-level windows disabled by **PreModalDialog**. This function should be paired with a call to **PreModalDialog**.

See Also: **COleControl::PreModalDialog**

COleControl::PreModalDialog

void PreModalDialog( );

Remarks

Call this function prior to displaying any modal dialog box. You must call this function so that the container can disable all its top-level windows. After the modal dialog box has been displayed, you must then call **PostModalDialog**.

See Also: COleControl::PostModalDialog

COleControl::RecreateControlWindow

void RecreateControlWindow( );

Remarks

Call this function to destroy and re-create the control's window. This may be necessary if you need to change the window's style bits.

COleControl::Refresh

void Refresh( );

Remarks

Call this function to force a repaint of the OLE control.

This function is supported by the **COleControl** base class as a stock method, called Refresh. This allows users of your OLE control to repaint the control at a specific time. For more information on this method, see the article "ActiveX Controls: Methods" in *Visual C++ Programmer's Guide* online.

See Also: COleControl::InvalidateControl

COleControl::ReleaseCapture

BOOL ReleaseCapture( );

Return Value

Nonzero if successful; otherwise 0.

Remarks

Call this function to release mouse capture. If the control currently has the mouse capture, the capture is released. Otherwise, this function has no effect.

See Also: COleControl::SetCapture, COleControl::GetCapture

COleControl::ReleaseDC

int ReleaseDC(CDC* *pDC*);

Return Value

Nonzero if successful; otherwise 0.

Parameters

pDC   Identifies the container device context to be released.

Remarks

Call this function to release the display device context of a container of a windowless control, freeing the device context for use by other applications. The application must call **ReleaseDC** for each call to **GetDC**.

See Also: **COleControl::GetDC**

COleControl::ResetStockProps

void ResetStockProps( );

Remarks

Call this function to initialize the state of the **COleControl** stock properties to their default values. The properties are: Appearance, BackColor, BorderStyle, Caption, Enabled, Font, ForeColor, hWnd, and Text. For a description of stock properties, see "ActiveX Controls: Adding Stock Properties."

You can improve a control's binary initialization performance by using **ResetStockProps** and **ResetVersion** to override **COleControl::OnResetState**. See the example below. For further information on optimizing initialization, see "ActiveX Controls: Optimization."

Example

```
void CMyCtrl::OnResetState()
{
   ResetVersion(MAKELONG(_wVerMinor, _wVerMajor));
   ResetStockProps();

   // initialize custom properties here
}
```

See Also: **COleControl::ResetVersion**, **COleControl::SerializeStockProps**

COleControl::ResetVersion

void ResetVersion(DWORD *dwVersionDefault* **);**

Parameters

dwVersionDefault The version number to be assigned to the control.

Remarks

Call this function to initialize the version number to specified value.

You can improve a control's binary initialization performance by using **ResetVersion** and **ResetStockProps** to override **COleControl::OnResetState**. See the example at **ResetStockProps**. For further information on optimizing initialization, see "ActiveX Controls: Optimization."

See Also: COleControl::ResetStockProps, COleControl::SerializeVersion

COleControl::ScrollWindow

void ScrollWindow(int *xAmount*, **int** *yAmount*, **LPCRECT** *lpRect* = **NULL**,
↳ **LPCRECT** *lpClipRect* = **NULL**);

Parameters

xAmount   Specifies the amount, in device units, of horizontal scrolling. This parameter must be a negative value to scroll to the left.

yAmount   Specifies the amount, in device units, of verticall scrolling. This parameter must be a negative value to scroll upward.

lpRect   Points to a **CRect** object or **RECT** structure that specifies the portion of the OLE object's client area to scroll, in client coordinates of the containing window. If *lpRect* is **NULL**, the entire OLE object's client area is scrolled.

lpClipRect   Points to a **CRect** object or **RECT** structure that specifies the rectangle to clip to. Only pixels inside the rectangle are scrolled. Bits outside the rectangle are not affected even if they are in the *lpRect* rectangle. If *lpClipRect* is **NULL**, no clipping is performed on the scroll rectangle.

Remarks

Call this function to allow a windowless OLE object to scroll an area within its in-place active image on the screen.

COleControl::SelectFontObject

CFont* SelectFontObject(CDC* *pDC*, **CFontHolder&** *fontHolder*);

Return Value

A pointer to the previously selected font. When the caller has finished all drawing operations that use *fontHolder*, it should reselect the previously selected font by passing it as a parameter to **CDC::SelectObject**.

Parameters

pDC   Pointer to a device context object.

fontHolder   Reference to the **CFontHolder** object representing the font to be selected.

Remarks

Call this function to select a font into a device context.

COleControl::SelectStockFont

CFont* SelectStockFont(CDC* *pDC* **);**

Return Value

A pointer to the previously selected **CFont** object. You should use **CDC::SelectObject** to select this font back into the device context when you are finished.

Parameters

pDC   The device context into which the font will be selected.

Remarks

Call this function to select the stock Font property into a device context.

See Also: **COleControl::GetFont, COleControl::SetFont**

COleControl::SerializeExtent

void SerializeExtent(CArchive& *ar* **);**

Parameters

ar   A **CArchive** object to serialize to or from.

Remarks

Call this function to serialize or initialize the state of the display space allotted to the control.

You can improve a control's binary persistence performance by using **SerializeExtent**, **SerializeStockProps**, and **SerializeVersion** to override **COleControl::Serialize**. See the example below. For further information on optimizing initialization, see "ActiveX Controls: Optimization" online.

Example

```
void CMyCtrl::Serialize(CArchive& ar)
{
    DWORD dwVersion =
        SerializeVersion(ar, MAKELONG(_wVerMinor, _wVerMajor));
    SerializeExtent(ar);
    SerializeStockProps(ar);

    if (ar.IsLoading())
    {
        // load custom properties here
    }
    else
    {
        // save custom properties here
    }
}
```

See Also: **COleControl::SerializeStockProps, COleControl::SerializeVersion**

COleControl::SerializeStockProps

void SerializeStockProps(CArchive& *ar* **);**

Parameters

ar   A **CArchive** object to serialize to or from.

Remarks

Call this function to serialize or initialize the state of the **COleControl** stock properties: Appearance, BackColor, BorderStyle, Caption, Enabled, Font, ForeColor, and Text. For a description of stock properties, see "ActiveX Controls: Adding Stock Properties" online.

You can improve a control's binary persistence performance by using **SerializeStockProps**, **SerializeExtent**, and **SerializeVersion** to override **COleControl::Serialize**. For an example, see the code at **SerializeExtent**. For further information on optimizing initialization, see "ActiveX Controls: Optimization" online.

See Also: **COleControl::SerializeExtent, COleControl::SerializeVersion, COleControl::ResetStockProps**

COleControl::SerializeVersion

DWORD SerializeVersion(CArchive& *ar*, **DWORD** *dwVersionDefault*, ↳ **BOOL** *bConvert* = **TRUE** **);**

Return Value

The version number of the control. If the specified archive is loading, **SerializeVersion** returns the version loaded from that archive. Otherwise, it returns the currently loaded version.

Parameters

ar   A **CArchive** object to serialize to or from.

dwVersionDefault   The current version number of the control.

bConvert   Indicates whether persistent data should be converted to the latest format when it is saved, or maintained in the same format it had when it was loaded.

Remarks

Call this function to serialize or initialize the state of a control's version information.

You can improve a control's binary persistence performance by using **SerializeVersion**, **SerializeExtent**, and **SerializeStockProps** to override **COleControl::Serialize**. For an example, see the code at **SerializeExtent**. For further information on optimizing initialization, see "ActiveX Controls: Optimization" online.

See Also: **COleControl::SerializeExtent, COleControl::SerializeStockProps, COleControl::ResetVersion**

COleControl::SetAppearance

void SetAppearance (short *sAppearance* **);**

Parameters

sAppearance   A **short** (**VT_I2**) value to be used for the appearance of your control. A value of zero sets the control's appearance to flat and a value of 1 sets the control's appearance to 3D.

Remarks

Call this function to set the stock Appearance property value of your control. For more about stock properties, see "ActiveX Controls: Properties" in *Visual C++ Programmer's Guide* online.

See Also: COleControl::GetAppearance, COleControl::OnAppearanceChanged

---

COleControl::SetBackColor

void SetBackColor(OLE_COLOR *dwBackColor* **);**

Parameters

dwBackColor   An **OLE_COLOR** value to be used for background drawing of your control.

Remarks

Call this function to set the stock BackColor property value of your control. For more information on using this property and other related properties, see "Adding a Custom Notification Property" in the Circle Sample Tutorial in *Visual C++ Tutorials* online and the article "ActiveX Controls: Properties" in *Visual C++ Programmer's Guide* online.

See Also: COleControl::SetForeColor, COleControl::GetBackColor, COleControl::OnBackColorChanged

---

COleControl::SetBorderStyle

void SetBorderStyle(short *sBorderStyle* **);**

Parameters

sBorderStyle   The new border style for the control; 0 indicates no border and 1 indicates a normal border.

Remarks

Call this function to set the stock BorderStyle property value of your control. The control window will then be re-created and **OnBorderStyleChanged** called.

See Also: COleControl::GetBorderStyle, COleControl::OnBorderStyleChanged

COleControl::SetCapture

CWnd* SetCapture( );

Return Value

A pointer to the **CWnd** window object that previously received mouse input.

Remarks

If the control is activated and windowless, this function causes the control's container window to take possession of the mouse capture, on the control's behalf.

Otherwise, this function causes the control itself to take possession of the mouse capture (same as **CWnd::SetCapture**).

See Also: **COleControl::GetCapture**, **COleControl::ReleaseCapture**

COleControl::SetControlSize

BOOL SetControlSize(int *cx,* **int** *cy* **);**

Return Value

Nonzero if the call was successful; otherwise 0.

Parameters

cx Specifies the new width of the control in pixels.

cy Specifies the new height of the control in pixels.

Remarks

Call this function to set the size of the OLE control window and notify the container that the control site is changing. This function should not be used in your control's constructor.

Note that all coordinates for control windows are relative to the upper-left corner of the control.

See Also: **COleControl::GetControlSize**, **COleControl::GetRectInContainer**

COleControl::SetEnabled

void SetEnabled(BOOL *bEnabled* **);**

Parameters

bEnabled **TRUE** if the control is to be enabled; otherwise **FALSE**.

Remarks

Call this function to set the stock Enabled property value of your control. After setting this property, **OnEnabledChange** is called.

See Also: **COleControl::GetEnabled**, **COleControl::OnEnabledChanged**

COleControl::SetFocus

CWnd* SetFocus( );

Return Value

A pointer to the **CWnd** window object that previously had the input focus, or **NULL** if there is no such window.

Remarks

If the control is activated and windowless, this function causes the control's container window to take possession of the input focus, on the control's behalf. The input focus directs keyboard input to the container's window, and the container dispatches all subsequent keyboard messages to the OLE object that calls **SetFocus**. Any window that previously had the input focus loses it.

If the control is not windowless, this function causes the control itself to take possession of the input focus (same as **CWnd::SetFocus**).

See Also: COleControl::GetFocus

COleControl::SetFont

void SetFont(LPFONTDISP *pFontDisp* **);**

Parameters

pFontDisp   A pointer to a Font dispatch interface.

Remarks

Call this function to set the stock Font property of your control.

**See Also: COleControl::GetFont, COleControl::InternalGetText,
COleControl::OnFontChanged**

COleControl::SetForeColor

void SetForeColor(OLE_COLOR *dwForeColor* **);**

Parameters

dwForeColor   An **OLE_COLOR** value to be used for foreground drawing of your control.

Remarks

Call this function to set the stock ForeColor property value of your control. For more information on using this property and other related properties, see "Adding a Custom Notification Property," in the Circle Sample Tutorial in *Visual C++ Tutorials* and the article "ActiveX Controls: Properties" in *Visual C++ Programmer's Guide* online.

See Also: **COleControl::SetBackColor, COleControl::GetForeColor, COleControl::OnForeColorChanged**

COleControl::SetInitialDataFormats

virtual void SetInitialDataFormats( );

Remarks

Called by the framework to initialize the list of data formats supported by the control.

The default implementation specifies two formats: **CF_METAFILEPICT** and the persistent property set.

COleControl::SetInitialSize

void SetInitialSize(int *cx*, **int** *cy* **);**

Parameters

cx The initial width of the OLE control in pixels.

cy The initial height of the OLE control in pixels.

Remarks

Call this function in your constructor to set the initial size of your control. The initial size is measured in device units, or pixels. It is recommended that this call be made in your control's constructor.

COleControl::SetModifiedFlag

void SetModifiedFlag(BOOL *bModified* = **TRUE);**

Parameters

bModified The new value for the control's modified flag. **TRUE** indicates that the control's state has been modified; **FALSE** indicates that the control's state has just been saved.

Remarks

Call this function whenever a change occurs that would affect your control's persistent state. For example, if the value of a persistent property changes, call this function with *bModified* **TRUE**.

See Also: **COleControl::IsModified**

COleControl::SetNotPermitted

void SetNotPermitted( );

Remarks

Call this function when **BoundPropertyRequestEdit** fails. This function throws an exception of type **COleDispScodeException** to indicate that the set operation was not permitted.

See Also: **COleControl::BoundPropertyRequestEdit**

COleControl::SetNotSupported

void SetNotSupported( );

Remarks

Call this function in place of the Set function of any property where modification of the property value by the control's user is not supported. One example would be a property that is read-only.

See Also: **COleControl::GetNotSupported**

COleControl::SetRectInContainer

BOOL SetRectInContainer(LPRECT *lpRect* **);**

Return Value

Nonzero if the call was successful; otherwise 0.

Parameters

lpRect　A pointer to a rectangle containing the control's new coordinates relative to the container.

Remarks

Call this function to set the coordinates of the control's rectangle relative to the container, expressed in device units. If the control is open, it is resized; otherwise the container's **OnPosRectChanged** function is called.

See Also: **COleControl::GetRectInContainer**, **COleControl::GetControlSize**

COleControl::SetText

void SetText(LPCTSTR *pszText* **);**

Parameters

pszText　A pointer to a character string.

Remarks

Call this function to set the value of your control's stock Caption or Text property.

Note that the stock Caption and Text properties are both mapped to the same value. This means that any changes made to either property will automatically change both properties. In general, a control should support either the stock Caption or Text property, but not both.

See Also: **COleControl::GetText**, **COleControl::InternalGetText**, **COleControl::OnTextChanged**

COleControl::ThrowError

void ThrowError(SCODE *sc***, UINT** *nDescriptionID***, UINT** *nHelpID* **= -1);**
void ThrowError(SCODE *sc***, LPCTSTR** *pszDescription* **= NULL, UINT** *nHelpID* **= 0);**

Parameters

sc   The status code value to be reported. For a complete list of possible codes, see the article "ActiveX Controls: Advanced Topics" in *Visual C++ Programmer's Guide* online.

nDescriptionID   The string resource ID of the exception to be reported.

nHelpID   The help ID of the topic to be reported on.

pszDescription   A string containing an explanation of the exception to be reported.

Remarks

Call this function to signal the occurrence of an error in your control. This function should only be called from within a Get or Set function for an OLE property, or the implementation of an OLE automation method. If you need to signal errors that occur at other times, you should fire the stock Error event.

See Also: **COleControl::FireError**, **COleControl::DisplayError**

COleControl::TransformCoords

void TransformCoords(POINTL FAR* *lpptlHimetric***,**
↪ POINTF FAR* *lpptfContainer***, DWORD** *flags* **);**

Parameters

lpptlHimetric   Pointer to a **POINTL** structure containing coordinates in **HIMETRIC** units.

lpptfContainer   Pointer to a **POINTF** structure containing coordinates in the container's unit size.

flags   A combination of the following values:

- **XFORMCOORDS_POSITION**   A position in the container.

- **XFORMCOORDS_SIZE**   A size in the container.

- **XFORMCOORDS_HIMETRICTOCONTAINER**   Transform **HIMETRIC** units to the container's units.

- **XFORMCOORDS_CONTAINERTOHIMETRIC**   Transform the container's units to **HIMETRIC** units.

Remarks

Call this function to transform coordinate values between **HIMETRIC** units and the container's native units.

The first two flags, **XFORMCOORDS_POSITION** and **XFORMCOORDS_SIZE**, indicate whether the coordinates should be treated as a position or a size. The remaining two flags indicate the direction of transformation.

See Also: **COleControl::AmbientScaleUnits**

COleControl::TranslateColor

> **COLORREF TranslateColor(OLE_COLOR** *clrColor*, **HPALETTE** *hpal* = **NULL**);

Return Value

An RGB (red, green, blue) 32-bit color value that defines the solid color closest to the *clrColor* value that the device can represent.

Parameters

clrColor   A **OLE_COLOR** data type. For more information, see the Windows **OleTranslateColor** function.

hpal   A handle to an optional palette; can be **NULL**.

Remarks

Call this function to convert a color value from the **OLE_COLOR** data type to the **COLORREF** data type. This function is useful to translate the stock ForeColor and BackColor properties to **COLORREF** types used by **CDC** member functions.

See Also: **COleControl::GetForeColor, COleControl::GetBackColor**

COleControl::WillAmbientsBeValidDuringLoad

> **BOOL WillAmbientsBeValidDuringLoad( );**

Return Value

Nonzero indicates that ambient properties will be valid; otherwise ambient properties will not be valid.

Remarks

Call this function to determine whether your control should use the values of ambient properties as default values, when it is subsequently loaded from its persistent state.

In some containers, your control may not have access to its ambient properties during the initial call to the override of **COleControl::DoPropExchange**. This is the case if the container calls **IPersistStreamInit::Load** or **IPersistStorage::Load** prior to calling **IOleObject::SetClientSite** (that is, if it does not honor the **OLEMISC_SETCLIENTSITEFIRST** status bit).

See Also: **COleControl::DoPropExchange**, **COleControl::GetAmbientProperty**

COleControlModule

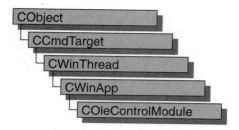

The **COleControlModule** class is the base class from which you derive an OLE control module object. This class provides member functions for initializing your control module. Each OLE control module that uses the Microsoft Foundation classes can only contain one object derived from **COleControlModule**. This object is constructed when other C++ global objects are constructed. Declare your derived **COleControlModule** object at the global level.

For more information on using the **COleControlModule** class, see the **CWinApp** class and the article "ActiveX Controls" in *Visual C++ Programmer's Guide* online.

#include <afxctl.h>

COleConvertDialog

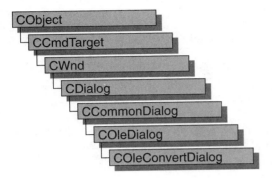

The **COleConvertDialog** class is used for the OLE Convert dialog box. Create an object of class **COleConvertDialog** when you want to call this dialog box. After a **COleConvertDialog** object has been constructed, you can use the **m_cv** structure to initialize the values or states of controls in the dialog box. The **m_cv** structure is of type **OLEUICONVERT**. For more information about using this dialog class, see the **DoModal** member function.

Note AppWizard-generated container code uses this class.

For more information, see the **OLEUICONVERT** structure in the OLE documentation.

For more information about OLE-specific dialog boxes, see the article "Dialog Boxes in OLE" in *Visual C++ Programmer's Guide* online.

#include <afxodlgs.h>

See Also: **COleDialog**

COleConvertDialog Class Members

Data Members

m_cv	A structure that controls the behavior of the dialog box.

Construction

COleConvertDialog	Constructs a **COleConvertDialog** object.

Operations and Attributes

DoModal	Displays the OLE Change Item dialog box.
DoConvert	Performs the conversion specified in the dialog box.

(continued)

Operations and Attributes *(continued)*	
GetSelectionType	Gets the type of selection chosen.
GetClassID	Gets the **CLSID** associated with the chosen item.
GetDrawAspect	Specifies whether to draw item as an icon.
GetIconicMetafile	Gets a handle to the metafile associated with the iconic form of this item.

Member Functions
COleConvertDialog::COleConvertDialog

COleConvertDialog (**COleClientItem*** *pItem*,
   ➥ **DWORD** *dwFlags* = **CF_SELECTCONVERTTO**,
   ➥ **CLSID FAR*** *pClassID* = **NULL**, **CWnd*** *pParentWnd* = **NULL**);

Parameters

   pItem Points to the item to be converted or activated.

   dwFlags Creation flag, which contains any number of the following values combined using the bitwise-or operator:

- **CF_SELECTCONVERTTO** Specifies that the Convert To radio button will be selected initially when the dialog box is called. This is the default.

- **CF_SELECTACTIVATEAS** Specifies that the Activate As radio button will be selected initially when the dialog box is called.

- **CF_SETCONVERTDEFAULT** Specifies that the class whose **CLSID** is specified by the **clsidConvertDefault** member of the **m_cv** structure will be used as the default selection in the class list box when the Convert To radio button is selected.

- **CF_SETACTIVATEDEFAULT** Specifies that the class whose **CLSID** is specified by the **clsidActivateDefault** member of the **m_cv** structure will be used as the default selection in the class list box when the Activate As radio button is selected.

- **CF_SHOWHELPBUTTON** Specifies that the Help button will be displayed when the dialog box is called.

   pClassID Points to the CLSID of the item to be converted or activated. If **NULL**, the **CLSID** associated with *pItem* will be used.

   pParentWnd Points to the parent or owner window object (of type **CWnd**) to which the dialog object belongs. If it is **NULL**, the parent window of the dialog box is set to the main application window.

Remarks

Constructs only a **COleConvertDialog** object. To display the dialog box, call the **DoModal** function.

For more information, see **CLSID Key** and the **OLEUICONVERT** structure.

See Also: **COleConvertDialog::DoModal, COleConvertDialog::m_cv**

COleConvertDialog::DoConvert

BOOL DoConvert(COleClientItem* *pItem* **);**

Return Value

Nonzero if successful; otherwise 0.

Parameters

pItem   Points to the item to be converted or activated. Cannot be **NULL**.

Remarks

Call this function, after returning successfully from **DoModal**, either to convert or to activate an object of type **COleClientItem**. The item is converted or activated according to the information selected by the user in the Convert dialog box.

See Also: **COleClientItem, COleConvertDialog::DoModal, COleConvertDialog::GetSelectionType, COleClientItem::ConvertTo, COleClientItem::ActivateAs**

COleConvertDialog::DoModal

virtual int DoModal( );

Return Value

Completion status for the dialog box. One of the following values:

- **IDOK** if the dialog box was successfully displayed.
- **IDCANCEL** if the user canceled the dialog box.
- **IDABORT** if an error occurred. If **IDABORT** is returned, call the **COleDialog::GetLastError** member function to get more information about the type of error that occurred. For a listing of possible errors, see the **OleUIConvert** function in the OLE documentation.

Remarks

Call this function to display the OLE Convert dialog box.

If you want to initialize the various dialog box controls by setting members of the **m_cv** structure, you should do this before calling **DoModal**, but after the dialog object is constructed.

If **DoModal** returns **IDOK**, you can call other member functions to retrieve the settings or information that was input by the user into the dialog box.

See Also: **COleDialog::GetLastError, CDialog::DoModal, COleConvertDialog::m_cv, COleConvertDialog::DoConvert, COleConvertDialog::GetSelectionType, COleConvertDialog::GetClassID, COleConvertDialog::GetDrawAspect, COleConvertDialog::GetIconicMetafile**

COleConvertDialog::GetClassID

const CLSID& GetClassID( ) const;

Return Value

The **CLSID** associated with the item that was selected in the Convert dialog box.

Remarks

Call this function to get the **CLSID** associated with the item the user selected in the Convert dialog box. Call this function only after **DoModal** returns **IDOK**.

For more information, see **CLSID Key** in the OLE documentation.

See Also: **COleConvertDialog::DoModal**

COleConvertDialog::GetDrawAspect

DVASPECT GetDrawAspect( ) const;

Return Value

The method needed to render the object.

- **DVASPECT_CONTENT**   Returned if the Display As Icon check box was not checked.
- **DVASPECT_ICON**   Returned if the Display As Icon check box was checked.

Remarks

Call this function to determine whether the user chose to display the selected item as an icon. Call this function only after **DoModal** returns **IDOK**.

For more information on drawing aspect, see the **FORMATETC** data structure in the OLE documentation.

See Also: **COleConvertDialog::DoModal, COleConvertDialog::COleConvertDialog**

COleConvertDialog::GetIconicMetafile

HGLOBAL GetIconPicture( ) const;

Return Value

The handle to the metafile containing the iconic aspect of the selected item, if the Display As Icon check box was checked when the dialog was dismissed by choosing **OK**; otherwise **NULL**.

Remarks

Call this function to get a handle to the metafile that contains the iconic aspect of the selected item.

See Also: **COleConvertDialog::DoModal, COleConvertDialog::COleConvertDialog, COleConvertDialog::GetDrawAspect**

COleConvertDialog::GetSelectionType

UINT GetSelectionType( ) const;

Return Value

Type of selection made.

Remarks

Call this function to determine the type of conversion selected in the Convert dialog box.

The return type values are specified by the **Selection** enumeration type declared in the **COleConvertDialog** class.

```
enum Selection
{
    noConversion,
    convertItem,
    activateAs
};
```

Brief descriptions of these values follow:

- **COleConvertDialog::noConversion** Returned if either the dialog box was canceled or the user selected no conversion. If **COleConvertDialog::DoModal** returned **IDOK**, it is possible that the user selected a different icon than the one previously selected.

- **COleConvertDialog::convertItem** Returned if the Convert To radio button was checked, the user selected a different item to convert to, and **DoModal** returned **IDOK**.

- **COleConvertDialog::activateAs** Returned if the Activate As radio button was checked, the user selected a different item to activate, and **DoModal** returned **IDOK**.

See Also: **COleConvertDialog::DoModal**,
COleConvertDialog::COleConvertDialog

Data Members
COleConvertDialog::m_cv

Remarks

Structure of type **OLEUICONVERT** used to control the behavior of the Convert dialog box. Members of this structure can be modified either directly or through member functions.

For more information, see the **OLEUICONVERT** structure in the OLE documentation.

See Also: **COleConvertDialog::COleConvertDialog**,
COleConvertDialog::DoModal

COleCurrency

COleCurrency does not have a base class.

A **COleCurrency** object encapsulates the **CURRENCY** data type of OLE automation. **CURRENCY** is implemented as an 8-byte, two's-complement integer value scaled by 10,000. This gives a fixed-point number with 15 digits to the left of the decimal point and 4 digits to the right. The **CURRENCY** data type is extremely useful for calculations involving money, or for any fixed-point calculation where accuracy is important. It is one of the possible types for the **VARIANT** data type of OLE automation.

COleCurrency also implements some basic arithmetic operations for this fixed-point type. The supported operations have been selected to control the rounding errors which occur during fixed-point calculations.

For more information, see the **CURRENCY** and **VARIANT** entries in the *Win32 SDK OLE Programmer's Reference*.

#include <afxdisp.h>

See Also: **COleVariant**

COleCurrency Class Members

Construction

COleCurrency	Constructs a **COleCurrency** object.

Attributes

GetStatus	Gets the status (validity) of this **COleCurrency** object.
SetStatus	Sets the status (validity) for this **COleCurrency** object.

Operations

SetCurrency	Sets the value of this **COleCurrency** object.
Format	Generates a formatted string representation of a **COleCurrency** object.
ParseCurrency	Reads a **CURRENCY** value from a string and sets the value of **COleCurrency**.

Operators

operator CURRENCY	Converts a **COleCurrency** value into a **CURRENCY**.
operator =	Copies a **COleCurrency** value.

(continued)

Operators *(continued)*

operator +, -	Adds, subtracts, and changes sign of **COleCurrency** values.
operator +=, -=	Adds and subtracts a **COleCurrency** value from this **COleCurrency** object.
operator *, /	Scales a **COleCurrency** value by an integer value.
operator *=, /=	Scales this **COleCurrency** value by an integer value.
operator ==, <, <=, etc.	Compares two **COleCurrency** values.

Data Members

m_cur	Contains the underlying **CURRENCY** for this **COleCurrency** object.
m_status	Contains the status of this **COleCurrency** object.

Archive/Dump

operator <<	Outputs a **COleCurrency** value to **CArchive** or **CDumpContext**.
operator >>	Inputs a **COleCurrency** object from **CArchive**.

Member Functions

COleCurrency::COleCurrency

COleCurrency( );
COleCurrency(CURRENCY *cySrc* **);**
COleCurrency(const COleCurrency& *curSrc* **);**
COleCurrency(const VARIANT& *varSrc* **);**
COleCurrency(long *nUnits*, **long** *nFractionalUnits* **);**

Parameters

cySrc   A **CURRENCY** value to be copied into the new **COleCurrency** object.

curSrc   An existing **COleCurrency** object to be copied into the new **COleCurrency** object.

varSrc   An existing **VARIANT** data structure (possibly a **COleVariant** object) to be converted to a currency value (**VT_CY**) and copied into the new **COleCurrency** object.

nUnits, nFractionalUnits   Indicate the units and fractional part (in 1/10,000's) of the value to be copied into the new **COleCurrency** object.

Remarks

All of these constructors create new **COleCurrency** objects initialized to the specified value. A brief description of each of these constructors follows. Unless otherwise noted, the status of the new **COleCurrency** item is set to valid.

- **COleCurrency( )**   Constructs a **COleCurrency** object initialized to 0 (zero).

- **COleCurrency(** *cySrc* **)**   Constructs a **COleCurrency** object from a **CURRENCY** value.

- **COleCurrency(** *curSrc* **)**   Constructs a **COleCurrency** object from an existing **COleCurrency** object. The new object has the same status as the source object.

- **COleCurrency(** *varSrc* **)**   Constructs a **COleCurrency** object. Attempts to convert a **VARIANT** structure or **COleVariant** object to a currency (**VT_CY**) value. If this conversion is successful, the converted value is copied into the new **COleCurrency** object. If it is not, the value of the **COleCurrency** object is set to zero (0) and its status to invalid.

- **COleCurrency(** *nUnits*, *nFractionalUnits* **)**   Constructs a **COleCurrency** object from the specified numerical components. If the absolute value of the fractional part is greater than 10,000, the appropriate adjustment is made to the units. Note that the units and fractional part are specified by signed long values.

For more information, see the **CURRENCY** and **VARIANT** entries in the *Win32 SDK OLE Programmer's Reference*.

Example

The following examples show the effects of the zero-parameter and two-parameter constructors:

```
COleCurrency curZero;              // value: 0.0000
COleCurrency curA(4, 500);         // value: 4.0500
COleCurrency curB(2, 11000);       // value: 3.1000
COleCurrency curC(2, -50);         // value: 1.9950
```

See Also: **COleCurrency::SetCurrency, COleCurrency::operator =, COleCurrency::GetStatus, COleCurrency::m_cur, COleCurrency::m_status**

COleCurrency::Format

CString Format(DWORD *dwFlags* **= 0, LCID** *lcid* **= LANG_USER_DEFAULT);**

Return Value

A **CString** that contains the formatted currency value.

Parameters

dwFlags   Indicates flags for locale settings, possibly the following flag:

- **LOCALE_NOUSEROVERRIDE**   Use the system default locale settings, rather than custom user settings.

lcid   Indicates locale ID to use for the conversion.

Remarks

Call this member function to create a formatted representation of the currency value. It formats the value using the national language specifications (locale IDs). A currency symbol is not included in the value returned. If the status of this **COleCurrency** object is null, the return value is an empty string. If the status is invalid, the return string is specified by the string resource **IDS_INVALID_CURRENCY**.

Example

```
COleCurrency curA;              // value: 0.0000
curA.SetCurrency(4, 500);       // value: 4.0500

// value returned: 4.05
curA.Format(0, MAKELCID(MAKELANGID(LANG_CHINESE,
    SUBLANG_CHINESE_SINGAPORE), SORT_DEFAULT));
// value returned: 4,05
curA.Format(0, MAKELCID(MAKELANGID(LANG_GERMAN,
    SUBLANG_GERMAN_AUSTRIAN), SORT_DEFAULT));
```

Note For a discussion of locale ID values, see the section "Supporting Multiple National Languages" in the *Win32 SDK OLE Programmer's Reference*.

See Also: **COleCurrency::ParseCurrency**, **COleCurrency::GetStatus**

COleCurrency::GetStatus

CurrencyStatus GetStatus( ) const;

Return Value

Returns the status of this **COleCurrency** value.

Remarks

Call this member function to get the status (validity) of a given **COleCurrency** object.

The return value is defined by the **CurrencyStatus** enumerated type which is defined within the **COleCurrency** class.

```
enum CurrencyStatus{
    valid = 0,
    invalid = 1,
    null = 2,
};
```

For a brief description of these status values, see the following list:

- **COleCurrency::valid** Indicates that this **COleCurrency** object is valid.

- **COleCurrency::invalid** Indicates that this **COleCurrency** object is invalid; that is, its value may be incorrect.

- **COleCurrency::null** Indicates that this **COleCurrency** object is null, that is, that no value has been supplied for this object. (This is "null" in the database sense of "having no value," as opposed to the C++ **NULL**.)

The status of a **COleCurrency** object is invalid in the following cases:

- If its value is set from a **VARIANT** or **COleVariant** value that could not be converted to a currency value.
- If this object has experienced an overflow or underflow during an arithmetic assignment operation, for example **+=** or ***=**.
- If an invalid value was assigned to this object.
- If the status of this object was explicitly set to invalid using **SetStatus**.

For more information on operations that may set the status to invalid, see the following member functions:

- **COleCurrency**
- **operator =**
- **operator +, -**
- **operator +=, -=**
- **operator *, /**
- **operator *=, /=**

See Also: **COleCurrency::SetStatus, COleCurrency::m_status**

COleCurrency::ParseCurrency

BOOL ParseCurrency(LPCTSTR *lpszCurrency*, **DWORD** *dwFlags* = **0,**
  ↪ **LCID** *lcid* = **LANG_USER_DEFAULT);**
  throw(CMemoryException);
  throw(COleException);

Return Value
Nonzero if the string was successfully converted to a currency value, otherwise 0.

Parameters
lpszCurrency   A pointer to the null-terminated string which is to be parsed.

dwFlags   Indicates flags for locale settings, possibly the following flag:

- **LOCALE_NOUSEROVERRIDE**   Use the system default locale settings, rather than custom user settings.

lcid   Indicates locale ID to use for the conversion.

Remarks
Call this member function to parse a string to read a currency value. It uses national language specifications (locale IDs) for the meaning of nonnumeric characters in the source string.

For a discussion of locale ID values, see the section "Supporting Multiple National Languages" in the *Win32 SDK OLE Programmer's Reference*.

If the string was successfully converted to a currency value, the value of this **COleCurrency** object is set to that value and its status to valid.

If the string could not be converted to a currency value or if there was a numerical overflow, the status of this **COleCurrency** object is invalid.

If the string conversion failed due to memory allocation errors, this function throws a **CMemoryException**. In any other error state, this function throws a **COleException**.

See Also: **COleCurrency::Format**, **COleCurrency::GetStatus**

COleCurrency::SetCurrency

void SetCurrency(long *nUnits***, long** *nFractionalUnits* **);**

Parameters

nUnits, nFractionalUnits Indicate the units and fractional part (in 1/10,000's) of the value to be copied into this **COleCurrency** object.

Remarks

Call this member function to set the units and fractional part of this **COleCurrency** object.

If the absolute value of the fractional part is greater than 10,000, the appropriate adjustment is made to the units, as shown in the third of the following examples.

Note that the units and fractional part are specified by signed long values. The fourth of the following examples shows what happens when the parameters have different signs.

Example

```
COleCurrency curA;              // value: 0.0000
curA.SetCurrency(4, 500);       // value: 4.0500
curA.SetCurrency(2, 11000);     // value: 3.1000
curA.SetCurrency(2, -50);       // value: 1.9950
```

See Also: **COleCurrency::COleCurrency**, **COleCurrency::operator =**, **COleCurrency::m_cur**

COleCurrency::SetStatus

void SetStatus(CurrencyStatus *nStatus* **);**

Parameters

nStatus The new status for this **COleCurrency** object.

Remarks

Call this member function to set the status (validity) of this **COleCurrency** object. The *nStatus* parameter value is defined by the **CurrencyStatus** enumerated type, which is defined within the **COleCurrency** class.

```
enum CurrencyStatus{
    valid = 0,
    invalid = 1,
    null = 2,
};
```

For a brief description of these status values, see the following list:

- **COleCurrency::valid** Indicates that this **COleCurrency** object is valid.

- **COleCurrency::invalid** Indicates that this **COleCurrency** object is invalid; that is, its value may be incorrect.

- **COleCurrency::null** Indicates that this **COleCurrency** object is null, that is, that no value has been supplied for this object. (This is "null" in the database sense of "having no value," as opposed to the C++ **NULL**.)

Caution This function is for advanced programming situations. This function does not alter the data in this object. It will most often be used to set the status to null or invalid. Note that the assignment operator (**operator =**) and **SetCurrency** do set the status to of the object based on the source value(s).

See Also: **COleCurrency::GetStatus, COleCurrency::operator =, COleCurrency::SetCurrency, COleCurrency::m_status**

Operators
COleCurrency::operator =

const COleCurrency& operator =(CURRENCY *cySrc* **);**
const COleCurrency& operator =(const COleCurrency& *curSrc* **);**
const COleCurrency& operator =(const VARIANT& *varSrc* **);**

Remarks

These overloaded assignment operators copy the source currency value into this **COleCurrency** object. A brief description of each operator follows:

- **operator =(** *cySrc* **)** The **CURRENCY** value is copied into the **COleCurrency** object and its status is set to valid.

- **operator =(** *curSrc* **)** The value and status of the operand, an existing **COleCurrency** object are copied into this **COleCurrency** object.

- **operator =(** *varSrc* **)**   If the conversion of the **VARIANT** value (or **COleVariant** object) to a currency (**VT_CY**) is successful, the converted value is copied into this **COleCurrency** object and its status is set to valid. If the conversion is not successful, the value of the **COleCurrency** object is set to 0 and its status to invalid.

For more information, see the **CURRENCY** and **VARIANT** entries in the *Win32 SDK OLE Programmer's Reference.*

See Also: **COleCurrency::COleCurrency, COleCurrency::SetCurrency, COleCurrency::GetStatus**

COleCurrency::operator +, -

COleCurrency operator +(const COleCurrency& *cur* **) const;**
COleCurrency operator -(const COleCurrency& *cur* **) const;**
COleCurrency operator -( ) const;

Remarks

These operators allow you to add and subtract two **COleCurrency** values to and from each other and to change the sign of a **COleCurrency** value.

If either of the operands is null, the status of the resulting **COleCurrency** value is null.

If the arithmetic operation overflows, the resulting **COleCurrency** value is invalid.

If the operands is invalid and the other is not null, the status of the resulting **COleCurrency** value is invalid.

For more information on the valid, invalid, and null status values, see the **m_status** member variable.

See Also: **OleCurrency::operator +=, -=, COleCurrency::GetStatus**

COleCurrency::operator +=, -=

const COleCurrency& operator +=(const COleCurrency& *cur* **);**
const COleCurrency& operator -=(const COleCurrency& *cur* **);**

Remarks

These operators allow you to add and subtract a **COleCurrency** value to and from this **COleCurrency** object.

If either of the operands is null, the status of this **COleCurrency** object is set to null.

If the arithmetic operation overflows, the status of this **COleCurrency** object is set to invalid.

If either of the operands is invalid and the other is not null, the status of this **COleCurrency** object is set to invalid.

For more information on the valid, invalid, and null status values, see the **m_status** member variable.

See Also: **COleCurrency::operator +, -, COleCurrency::GetStatus**

COleCurrency::operator *, /

COleCurrency operator *(long *nOperand* **) const;**
COleCurrency operator /(long *nOperand* **) const;**

Remarks

These operators allow you to scale a **COleCurrency** value by an integral value.

If the **COleCurrency** operand is null, the status of the resulting **COleCurrency** value is null.

If the arithmetic operation overflows or underflows, the status of the resulting **COleCurrency** value is invalid.

If the **COleCurrency** operand is invalid, the status of the resulting **COleCurrency** value is invalid.

For more information on the valid, invalid, and null status values, see the **m_status** member variable.

See Also: **COleCurrency::operator *=, /=, COleCurrency::GetStatus**

COleCurrency::operator *=, /=

const COleCurrency& operator *=(long *nOperand* **);**
const COleCurrency& operator /=(long *nOperand* **);**

Remarks

These operators allow you to scale this **COleCurrency** value by an integral value.

If the **COleCurrency** operand is null, the status of this **COleCurrency** object is set to null.

If the arithmetic operation overflows, the status of this **COleCurrency** object is set to invalid.

If the **COleCurrency** operand is invalid, the status of this **COleCurrency** object is set to invalid.

For more information on the valid, invalid, and null status values, see the **m_status** member variable.

See Also: **COleCurrency::operator *, /, COleCurrency::GetStatus**

COleCurrency::operator CURRENCY

operator CURRENCY( ) const;

Remarks

This operator returns a **CURRENCY** structure whose value is copied from this **COleCurrency** object.

For more information, see the **CURRENCY** entry in the *Win32 SDK OLE Programmer's Reference*.

See Also: **COleCurrency::m_cur, COleCurrency::SetCurrency**

COleCurrency Relational Operators

BOOL operator ==(const COleCurrency& *cur* **) const;**
BOOL operator !=(const COleCurrency& *cur* **) const;**
BOOL operator <(const COleCurrency& *cur* **) const;**
BOOL operator >(const COleCurrency& *cur* **) const;**
BOOL operator <=(const COleCurrency& *cur* **) const;**
BOOL operator >=(const COleCurrency& *cur* **) const;**

Remarks

These operators compare two currency values and return nonzero if the condition is true; otherwise 0.

Note The return value of the ordering operations (<, <=, >, >=) is undefined if the status of either operand is null or invalid. The equality operators (==, !=) consider the status of the operands.

Example

```
COleCurrency curOne(3, 5000);          // 3.5
COleCurrency curTwo(curOne);           // 3.5
BOOL b;
b = curOne == curTwo;                  // TRUE

curTwo.SetStatus(COleCurrency::invalid);
b = curOne == curTwo;                  // FALSE, different status
b = curOne != curTwo;                  // TRUE, different status
b = curOne < curTwo;                   // FALSE, same value
b = curOne > curTwo;                   // FALSE, same value
b = curOne <= curTwo;                  // TRUE, same value
b = curOne >= curTwo;                  // TRUE, same value
```

Note The last four lines of the preceding example will **ASSERT** in debug mode.

See Also: **COleCurrency::GetStatus**

COleCurrency::operator <<, >>

friend CDumpContext& operator <<(CDumpContext& *dc*, **COleCurrency** *curSrc*);
friend CArchive& operator <<(CArchive& *ar*, **COleCurrency** *curSrc*);
friend CArchive& operator >>(CArchive& *ar*, **COleCurrency&** *curSrc*);

Remarks

The **COleCurrency** insertion (<<) operator supports diagnostic dumping and storing to an archive. The extraction (>>) operator supports loading from an archive.

See Also: **CDumpContext, CArchive**

Data Members

COleCurrency::m_cur

Remarks

The underlying **CURRENCY** structure for this **COleCurrency** object.

Caution Changing the value in the **CURRENCY** structure accessed by the pointer returned by this function will change the value of this **COleCurrency** object. It does not change the status of this **COleCurrency** object.

For more information, see the **CURRENCY** entry in the *Win32 SDK OLE Programmer's Reference*.

See Also: **COleCurrency::COleCurrency, COleCurrency::operator CURRENCY, COleCurrency::SetCurrency**

COleCurrency::m_status

Remarks

The type of this data member is the enumerated type **CurrencyStatus**, which is defined within the **COleCurrency** class.

```
enum CurrencyStatus{
    valid = 0,
    invalid = 1,
    null = 2,
};
```

For a brief description of these status values, see the following list:

- **COleCurrency::valid**   Indicates that this **COleCurrency** object is valid.
- **COleCurrency::invalid**   Indicates that this **COleCurrency** object is invalid; that is, its value may be incorrect.
- **COleCurrency::null**   Indicates that this **COleCurrency** object is null, that is, that no value has been supplied for this object. (This is "null" in the database sense of "having no value," as opposed to the C++ **NULL**.)

The status of a **COleCurrency** object is invalid in the following cases:

- If its value is set from a **VARIANT** or **COleVariant** value that could not be converted to a currency value.
- If this object has experienced an overflow or underflow during an arithmetic assignment operation, for example **+=** or ***=**.
- If an invalid value was assigned to this object.
- If the status of this object was explicitly set to invalid using **SetStatus**.

For more information on operations that may set the status to invalid, see the following member functions:

- **COleCurrency**
- **operator =**
- **operator +, -**
- **operator +=, -=**
- **operator *, /**
- **operator *=, /=**

Caution   This data member is for advanced programming situations. You should use the inline member functions **GetStatus** and **SetStatus**. See **SetStatus** for further cautions regarding explicitly setting this data member.

See Also: **COleCurrency::GetStatus, COleCurrency::SetStatus**

COleDataObject

COleDataObject does not have a base class.

The **COleDataObject** class is used in data transfers for retrieving data in various formats from the Clipboard, through drag and drop, or from an embedded OLE item. These kinds of data transfers include a source and a destination. The data source is implemented as an object of the **COleDataSource** class. Whenever a destination application has data dropped in it or is asked to perform a paste operation from the Clipboard, an object of the **COleDataObject** class must be created.

This class enables you to determine whether the data exists in a specified format. You can also enumerate the available data formats or check whether a given format is available and then retrieve the data in the preferred format. Object retrieval can be accomplished in several different ways, including the use of a **CFile**, an **HGLOBAL**, or an **STGMEDIUM** structure.

For more information, see the **STGMEDIUM** structure in the *OLE 2 Programmer's Reference, Volume 1*.

For more information about using data objects in your application, see the article "Data Objects and Data Sources (OLE)" in *Visual C++ Programmer's Guide* online.

#include <afxole.h>

See Also: COleDataSource, COleClientItem, COleServerItem, COleDataSource::DoDragDrop, CView::OnDrop

COleDataObject Class Members

Construction

COleDataObject	Constructs a **COleDataObject** object.

Operations

AttachClipboard	Attaches the data object that is on the Clipboard.
IsDataAvailable	Checks whether data is available in a specified format.
GetData	Copies data from the attached OLE data object in a specified format.
GetFileData	Copies data from the attached OLE data object into a **CFile** pointer in the specified format.
GetGlobalData	Copies data from the attached OLE data object into an **HGLOBAL** in the specified format.
BeginEnumFormats	Prepares for one or more subsequent **GetNextFormat** calls.
GetNextFormat	Returns the next data format available.

(continued)

Operations *(continued)*

Attach	Attaches the specified OLE data object to the **COleDataObject**.
Release	Detaches and releases the associated **IDataObject** object.
Detach	Detaches the associated **IDataObject** object.

Member Functions

COleDataObject::Attach

void Attach(LPDATAOBJECT *lpDataObject*, **BOOL** *bAutoRelease* = **TRUE**);

Parameters

lpDataObject   Points to an OLE data object.

bAutoRelease   **TRUE** if the OLE data object should be released when the **COleDataObject** object is destroyed; otherwise **FALSE**.

Remarks

Call this function to associate the **COleDataObject** object with an OLE data object.

For more information, see **IDataObject** in the *OLE 2 Programmer's Reference, Volume 1*.

See Also: COleDataObject::AttachClipboard, COleDataObject::Detach, COleDataObject::Release

COleDataObject::AttachClipboard

BOOL AttachClipboard( );

Return Value

Nonzero if successful; otherwise 0.

Remarks

Call this function to attach the data object that is currently on the Clipboard to the **COleDataObject** object.

Note   Calling this function locks the Clipboard until this data object is released. The data object is released in the destructor for the **COleDataObject**. For more information, see **OpenClipboard** and **CloseClipboard** in the Win32 documention.

See Also: COleDataObject::Attach, COleDataObject::Detach, COleDataObject::Release

COleDataObject::BeginEnumFormats

void BeginEnumFormats( );

Remarks

Call this function to prepare for subsequent calls to **GetNextFormat** for retrieving a list of data formats from the item.

After a call to **BeginEnumFormats**, the position of the first format supported by this data object is stored. Successive calls to **GetNextFormat** will enumerate the list of available formats in the data object.

To check on the availability of data in a given format, use **COleDataObject::IsDataAvailable**.

For more information, see **IDataObject::EnumFormatEtc** in the *OLE 2 Programmer's Reference, Volume 1*.

See Also: **COleDataObject::GetNextFormat, COleDataObject::IsDataAvailable**

COleDataObject::COleDataObject

COleDataObject( );

Remarks

Constructs a **COleDataObject** object. A call to **COleDataObject::Attach** or **COleDataObject::AttachClipboard** must be made before calling other **COleDataObject** functions.

Note Since one of the parameters to the drag-and-drop handlers is a pointer to a **COleDataObject**, there is no need to call this constructor to support drag and drop.

See Also: **COleDataObject::Attach, COleDataObject::AttachClipboard, COleDataObject::Release**

COleDataObject::Detach

LPDATAOBJECT Detach( );

Return Value

A pointer to the OLE data object that was detached.

Remarks

Call this function to detach the **COleDataObject** object from its associated OLE data object without releasing the data object.

See Also: **COleDataObject::Attach, COleDataObject::Release**

COleDataObject::GetData

BOOL GetData(CLIPFORMAT *cfFormat*, **LPSTGMEDIUM** *lpStgMedium*,
↪ **LPFORMATETC** *lpFormatEtc* = **NULL**);

Return Value

Nonzero if successful; otherwise 0.

Parameters

cfFormat   The format in which data is to be returned. This parameter can be one of
the predefined Clipboard formats or the value returned by the native Windows
RegisterClipboardFormat function.

lpStgMedium   Points to a **STGMEDIUM** structure that will receive data.

lpFormatEtc   Points to a **FORMATETC** structure describing the format in which
data is to be returned. Provide a value for this parameter if you want to specify
additional format information beyond the Clipboard format specified by *cfFormat*.
If it is **NULL**, the default values are used for the other fields in the **FORMATETC**
structure.

Remarks

Call this function to retrieve data from the item in the specified format.

For more information, see **IDataObject::GetData**, **STGMEDIUM**, and
FORMATETC in the *OLE 2 Programmer's Reference*, *Volume 1*.

For more information, see **RegisterClipboardFormat** in the Win32 documentation.

See Also: **COleDataObject::GetFileData, COleDataObject::GetGlobalData,
COleDataObject::IsDataAvailable**

COleDataObject::GetFileData

CFile* GetFileData(CLIPFORMAT *cfFormat*, **LPFORMATETC** *lpFormatEtc* = **NULL**);

Return Value

Pointer to the new **CFile** or **CFile**-derived object containing the data if successful;
otherwise **NULL**.

Parameters

cfFormat   The format in which data is to be returned. This parameter can be one of
the predefined Clipboard formats or the value returned by the native Windows
RegisterClipboardFormat function.

lpFormatEtc   Points to a **FORMATETC** structure describing the format in which data
is to be returned. Provide a value for this parameter if you want to specify additional
format information beyond the Clipboard format specified by *cfFormat*. If it is **NULL**,
the default values are used for the other fields in the **FORMATETC** structure.

Remarks

Call this function to create a **CFile** or **CFile**-derived object and to retrieve data in the specified format into a **CFile** pointer. Depending on the medium the data is stored in, the actual type pointed to by the return value may be **CFile**, **CSharedFile**, or **COleStreamFile**.

Note The **CFile** object accessed by the return value of this function is owned by the caller. It is the responsibility of the caller to **delete** the **CFile** object, thereby closing the file.

For more information, see **FORMATETC** in the *OLE 2 Programmer's Reference, Volume 1*.

For more information, see **RegisterClipboardFormat** in the Win32 documentation.

See Also: COleDataObject::GetData, COleDataObject::GetGlobalData, COleDataObject::IsDataAvailable

---

COleDataObject::GetGlobalData

> **HGLOBAL GetGlobalData(CLIPFORMAT** *cfFormat,*
> ↪ **LPFORMATETC** *lpFormatEtc* = **NULL**);

Return Value

The handle of the global memory block containing the data if successful; otherwise **NULL**.

Parameters

cfFormat The format in which data is to be returned. This parameter can be one of the predefined Clipboard formats or the value returned by the native Windows **RegisterClipboardFormat** function.

lpFormatEtc Points to a **FORMATETC** structure describing the format in which data is to be returned. Provide a value for this parameter if you want to specify additional format information beyond the Clipboard format specified by *cfFormat*. If it is **NULL**, the default values are used for the other fields in the **FORMATETC** structure.

Remarks

Call this function to allocate a global memory block and to retrieve data in the specified format into an **HGLOBAL**.

For more information, see **FORMATETC** in the *OLE 2 Programmer's Reference, Volume 1*.

For more information, see **RegisterClipboardFormat** in the Win32 documentation.

See Also: COleDataObject::GetData, COleDataObject::GetFileData, COleDataObject::IsDataAvailable

COleDataObject::GetNextFormat

BOOL GetNextFormat(LPFORMATETC *lpFormatEtc* **);**

Return Value

Nonzero if another format is available; otherwise 0.

Parameters

lpFormatEtc   Points to the **FORMATETC** structure that receives the format
information when the function call returns.

Remarks

Call this function repeatedly to obtain all the formats available for retrieving data from
the item.

After a call to **COleDataObject::BeginEnumFormats**, the position of the first
format supported by this data object is stored. Successive calls to **GetNextFormat**
will enumerate the list of available formats in the data object. Use these functions to
list the available formats.

To check for the availability of a given format, call **COleDataObject::IsDataAvailable**.

For more information, see **IEnumXXXX::Next** in the *OLE 2 Programmer's
Reference, Volume 1*.

See Also: **COleDataObject::BeginEnumFormats, COleDataObject::GetData,
COleDataObject::GetFileData, COleDataObject::GetGlobalData**

COleDataObject::IsDataAvailable

BOOL IsDataAvailable(CLIPFORMAT *cfFormat*,
↳ **LPFORMATETC** *lpFormatEtc* = **NULL**);

Return Value

Nonzero if data is available in the specified format; otherwise 0.

Parameters

cfFormat   The Clipboard data format to be used in the structure pointed to by
lpFormatEtc. This parameter can be one of the predefined Clipboard formats or
the value returned by the native Windows **RegisterClipboardFormat** function.

lpFormatEtc   Points to a **FORMATETC** structure describing the format desired.
Provide a value for this parameter only if you want to specify additional format
information beyond the Clipboard format specified by *cfFormat*. If it is **NULL**,
the default values are used for the other fields in the **FORMATETC** structure.

Remarks

Call this function to determine if a particular format is available for retrieving data from the OLE item. This function is useful before calling **GetData**, **GetFileData**, or **GetGlobalData**.

For more information, see **IDataObject::QueryGetData** and **FORMATETC** in the *OLE 2 Programmer's Reference, Volume 1*.

For more information, see **RegisterClipboardFormat** in the Win32 documentation.

See Also: COleDataObject::BeginEnumFormats, COleDataObject::GetData, COleDataObject::GetFileData, COleDataObject::GetGlobalData, COleDataObject::GetNextFormat

COleDataObject::Release

void Release( );

Remarks

Call this function to release ownership of the **IDataObject** object that was previously associated with the **COleDataObject** object. The **IDataObject** was associated with the **COleDataObject** by calling **Attach** or **AttachClipboard** explicitly or by the framework. If the *bAutoRelease* parameter of **Attach** is **FALSE**, the **IDataObject** object will not be released. In this case, the caller is responsible for releasing the **IDataObject** by calling **IUnknown::Release**.

See Also: COleDataObject::Attach, COleDataObject::COleDataObject, COleDataObject::Detach

COleDataSource

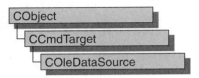

The **COleDataSource** class acts as a cache into which an application places the data that it will offer during data transfer operations, such as Clipboard or drag-and-drop operations.

You can create OLE data sources directly. Alternately, the **COleClientItem** and **COleServerItem** classes create OLE data sources in response to their **CopyToClipboard** and **DoDragDrop** member functions. See **COleServerItem::CopyToClipboard** for a brief description. Override the **OnGetClipboardData** member function of your client item or server item class to add additional Clipboard formats to the data in the OLE data source created for the **CopyToClipboard** or **DoDragDrop** member function.

Whenever you want to prepare data for a transfer, you should create an object of this class and fill it with your data using the most appropriate method for your data. The way it is inserted into a data source is directly affected by whether the data is supplied immediately (immediate rendering) or on demand (delayed rendering). For every Clipboard format in which you are providing data by passing the Clipboard format to be used (and an optional **FORMATETC** structure), call **DelayRenderData**.

For more information about data sources and data transfer, see the article "Data Objects and Data Sources (OLE)." In addition, the article "Clipboard Topics" in *Visual C++ Programmer's Guide* online describes the OLE Clipboard mechanism.

#include <afxole.h>

See Also: **COleDataObject**

COleDataSource Class Members

Construction

COleDataSource	Constructs a **COleDataSource** object.

Operations

CacheData	Offers data in a specified format using a **STGMEDIUM** structure.
CacheGlobalData	Offers data in a specified format using an **HGLOBAL**.
DoDragDrop	Performs drag-and-drop operations with a data source.
SetClipboard	Places a **COleDataSource** object on the Clipboard.

Operations *(continued)*

Empty	Empties the **COleDataSource** object of data.
FlushClipboard	Renders all data to the Clipboard.
GetClipboardOwner	Verifies that the data placed on the Clipboard is still there.
OnRenderData	Retrieves data as part of delayed rendering.
OnRenderFileData	Retrieves data into a **CFile** as part of delayed rendering.
OnRenderGlobalData	Retrieves data into an **HGLOBAL** as part of delayed rendering.
OnSetData	Called to replace the data in the **COleDataSource** object.
DelayRenderData	Offers data in a specified format using delayed rendering.
DelayRenderFileData	Offers data in a specified format in a **CFile** pointer.
DelaySetData	Called for every format that is supported in **OnSetData**.

Member Functions

COleDataSource::CacheData

void CacheData(CLIPFORMAT *cfFormat*, **LPSTGMEDIUM** *lpStgMedium*,
  ↪ **LPFORMATETC** *lpFormatEtc* = **NULL**);

Parameters

cfFormat The Clipboard format in which the data is to be offered. This parameter can be one of the predefined Clipboard formats or the value returned by the native Windows **RegisterClipboardFormat** function.

lpStgMedium Points to a **STGMEDIUM** structure containing the data in the format specified.

lpFormatEtc Points to a **FORMATETC** structure describing the format in which the data is to be offered. Provide a value for this parameter if you want to specify additional format information beyond the Clipboard format specified by *cfFormat*. If it is **NULL**, default values are used for the other fields in the **FORMATETC** structure.

Remarks

Call this function to specify a format in which data is offered during data transfer operations. You must supply the data, because this function provides it by using immediate rendering. The data is cached until needed.

Supply the data using a **STGMEDIUM** structure. You can also use the **CacheGlobalData** member function if the amount of data you are supplying is small enough to be transferred efficiently using an **HGLOBAL**.

After the call to **CacheData** the **ptd** member of *lpFormatEtc* and the contents of *lpStgMedium* are owned by the data object, not by the caller.

To use delayed rendering, call the **DelayRenderData** or **DelayRenderFileData** member function. For more information on delayed rendering as handled by MFC, see the article "Data Objects and Data Sources: Manipulation" in *Visual C++ Programmer's Guide* online.

For more information, see the **STGMEDIUM** and **FORMATETC** structures in the *OLE 2 Programmer's Reference, Volume 1*.

For more information, see **RegisterClipboardFormat** in the Win32 documentation.

See Also: **COleDataSource::CacheGlobalData**, **COleDataSource::DelayRenderData**, **COleDataSource::DelayRenderFileData**, **COleDataSource::SetClipboard**, **COleDataSource::DoDragDrop**

COleDataSource::CacheGlobalData

void CacheGlobalData(CLIPFORMAT *cfFormat***, HGLOBAL** *hGlobal***,**
  ↪ **LPFORMATETC** *lpFormatEtc* **= NULL);**

Parameters

cfFormat   The Clipboard format in which the data is to be offered. This parameter can be one of the predefined Clipboard formats or the value returned by the native Windows **RegisterClipboardFormat** function.

hGlobal   Handle to the global memory block containing the data in the format specified.

lpFormatEtc   Points to a **FORMATETC** structure describing the format in which the data is to be offered. Provide a value for this parameter if you want to specify additional format information beyond the Clipboard format specified by *cfFormat*. If it is **NULL**, default values are used for the other fields in the **FORMATETC** structure.

Remarks

Call this function to specify a format in which data is offered during data transfer operations. This function provides the data using immediate rendering, so you must supply the data when calling the function; the data is cached until needed. Use the **CacheData** member function if you are supplying a large amount of data or if you require a structured storage medium.

To use delayed rendering, call the **DelayRenderData** or **DelayRenderFileData** member function. For more information on delayed rendering as handled by MFC, see the article "Data Objects and Data Sources: Manipulation" in *Visual C++ Programmer's Guide* online.

For more information, see the **FORMATETC** structure in the *OLE 2 Programmer's Reference, Volume 1*.

For more information, see **RegisterClipboardFormat** in the Win32 documentation.

See Also: **COleDataSource::CacheData, COleDataSource::DelayRenderData, COleDataSource::DelayRenderFileData**

COleDataSource::COleDataSource

COleDataSource( );

Remarks

Constructs a **COleDataSource** object.

COleDataSource::DelayRenderData

void DelayRenderData(CLIPFORMAT *cfFormat***,**
↳ LPFORMATETC *lpFormatEtc* **= NULL);**

Parameters

cfFormat   The Clipboard format in which the data is to be offered. This parameter can be one of the predefined Clipboard formats or the value returned by the native Windows **RegisterClipboardFormat** function.

lpFormatEtc   Points to a **FORMATETC** structure describing the format in which the data is to be offered. Provide a value for this parameter if you want to specify additional format information beyond the Clipboard format specified by *cfFormat*. If it is **NULL**, default values are used for the other fields in the **FORMATETC** structure.

Remarks

Call this function to specify a format in which data is offered during data transfer operations. This function provides the data using delayed rendering, so the data is not supplied immediately. The **OnRenderData** or **OnRenderGlobalData** member function is called to request the data.

Use this function if you are not going to supply your data through a **CFile** object. If you are going to supply the data through a **CFile** object, call the **DelayRenderFileData** member function. For more information on delayed rendering as handled by MFC, see the article "Data Objects and Data Sources: Manipulation" in *Visual C++ Programmer's Guide* online.

To use immediate rendering, call the **CacheData** or **CacheGlobalData** member function.

For more information, see the **FORMATETC** structure in the *OLE 2 Programmer's Reference, Volume 1*.

For more information, see **RegisterClipboardFormat** in the Win32 documentation.

See Also: **COleDataSource::CacheData**, **COleDataSource::CacheGlobalData**, **COleDataSource::DelayRenderFileData**, **COleDataSource::OnRenderData**, **COleDataSource::OnRenderGlobalData**

COleDataSource::DelayRenderFileData

void DelayRenderFileData(CLIPFORMAT *cfFormat,*
  ↳ **LPFORMATETC** *lpFormatEtc* **= NULL);**

Parameters

cfFormat   The Clipboard format in which the data is to be offered. This parameter can be one of the predefined Clipboard formats or the value returned by the native Windows **RegisterClipboardFormat** function.

lpFormatEtc   Points to a **FORMATETC** structure describing the format in which the data is to be offered. Provide a value for this parameter if you want to specify additional format information beyond the Clipboard format specified by *cfFormat*. If it is **NULL**, default values are used for the other fields in the **FORMATETC** structure.

Remarks

Call this function to specify a format in which data is offered during data transfer operations. This function provides the data using delayed rendering, so the data is not supplied immediately. The **OnRenderFileData** member function is called to request the data.

Use this function if you are going to use a **CFile** object to supply the data. If you are not going to use a **CFile** object, call the **DelayRenderData** member function. For more information on delayed rendering as handled by MFC, see the article "Data Objects and Data Sources: Manipulation" in *Visual C++ Programmer's Guide* online.

To use immediate rendering, call the **CacheData** or **CacheGlobalData** member function.

For more information, see the **FORMATETC** structure in the *OLE 2 Programmer's Reference, Volume 1.*

For more information, see **RegisterClipboardFormat** in the Win32 documentation.

See Also: **COleDataSource::CacheData**, **COleDataSource::CacheGlobalData**, **COleDataSource::DelayRenderData**, **COleDataSource::OnRenderFileData**

COleDataSource::DelaySetData

void DelaySetData(CLIPFORMAT *cfFormat,*
↳ **LPFORMATETC** *lpFormatEtc* = **NULL) const;**

Parameters

cfFormat   The Clipboard format in which the data is to be placed. This parameter can be one of the predefined Clipboard formats or the value returned by the native Windows **RegisterClipboardFormat** function.

lpFormatEtc   Points to a **FORMATETC** structure describing the format in which the data is to be replaced. Provide a value for this parameter if you want to specify additional format information beyond the Clipboard format specified by *cfFormat.* If it is **NULL**, default values are used for the other fields in the **FORMATETC** structure.

Remarks

Call this function to support changing the contents of the data source. **OnSetData** will be called by the framework when this happens. This is only used when the framework returns the data source from **COleServerItem::GetDataSource**. If **DelaySetData** is not called, your **OnSetData** function will never be called. **DelaySetData** should be called for each Clipboard or **FORMATETC** format you support.

For more information, see the **FORMATETC** structure in the *OLE 2 Programmer's Reference, Volume 1.*

For more information, see **RegisterClipboardFormat** in the Win32 documentation.

See Also: **COleServerItem::GetDataSource, COleDataSource::OnSetData**

COleDataSource::DoDragDrop

DROPEFFECT DoDragDrop(DWORD *dwEffects* =
↳ **DROPEFFECT_COPY|DROPEFFECT_MOVE|DROPEFFECT_LINK,**
↳ **LPCRECT** *lpRectStartDrag* = **NULL, COleDropSource*** *pDropSource* = **NULL);**

Return Value

Drop effect generated by the drag-and-drop operation; otherwise **DROPEFFECT_NONE** if the operation never begins because the user released the mouse button before leaving the supplied rectangle.

Parameters

dwEffects   Drag-and-drop operations that are allowed on this data source. Can be one or more of the following:

- **DROPEFFECT_COPY**   A copy operation could be performed.

- **DROPEFFECT_MOVE**   A move operation could be performed.

- **DROPEFFECT_LINK**   A link from the dropped data to the original data could be established.

- **DROPEFFECT_SCROLL**   Indicates that a drag scroll operation could occur.

lpRectStartDrag   Pointer to the rectangle that defines where the drag actually starts. For more information, see the following Remarks section.

pDropSource   Points to a drop source. If **NULL** then a default implementation of **COleDropSource** will be used.

Remarks

Call the **DoDragDrop** member function to perform a drag-and-drop operation for this data source, typically in an **CWnd::OnLButtonDown** handler.

The drag-and-drop operation does not start immediately. It waits until the mouse cursor leaves the rectangle specified by *lpRectStartDrag* or until a specified number of milliseconds have passed. If *lpRectStartDrag* is **NULL**, the size of the rectangle is one pixel. The delay time is specified by the **DragDelay** value in the [Windows] section of WIN.INI. If this value is not in WIN.INI, the default value of 200 milliseconds is used.

For more information, see the article "Drag and Drop: Implementing a Drop Source" in *Visual C++ Programmer's Guide* online.

See Also: **COleDropSource::OnBeginDrag, COleDropSource**

COleDataSource::Empty

void Empty( );

Remarks

Call this function to empty the **COleDataSource** object of data. Both cached and delay render formats are emptied so they can be reused.

For more information, see **ReleaseStgMedium** in the *OLE 2 Programmer's Reference, Volume 1*.

COleDataSource::FlushClipboard

static void FlushClipboard( );

Remarks

Removes data from the Clipboard that was placed there by a previous call to **SetClipboard**. This function also causes any data still on the Clipboard to be immediately rendered. Call this function when it is necessary to delete the data object last placed on the Clipboard from memory.

Calling this function ensures that OLE will not require the original data source to perform Clipboard rendering.

See Also: **COleDataSource::GetClipboardOwner, COleDataSource::SetClipboard**

COleDataSource::GetClipboardOwner

static COleDataSource* GetClipboardOwner( );

Return Value

The data source currently on the Clipboard, or **NULL** if there is nothing on the Clipboard or if the Clipboard is not owned by the calling application.

Remarks

Determines whether the data on the Clipboard has changed since **SetClipboard** was last called and, if so, identifies the current owner.

See Also: **COleDataSource::FlushClipboard, COleDataSource::SetClipboard**

COleDataSource::OnRenderData

virtual BOOL OnRenderData(LPFORMATETC *lpFormatEtc*,
↳ **LPSTGMEDIUM** *lpStgMedium* **);**

Return Value

Nonzero if successful; otherwise 0.

Parameters

lpFormatEtc Points to the **FORMATETC** structure specifying the format in which information is requested.

lpStgMedium Points to a **STGMEDIUM** structure in which the data is to be returned.

Remarks

Called by the framework to retrieve data in the specified format. The specified format is one previously placed in the **COleDataSource** object using the **DelayRenderData** or **DelayRenderFileData** member function for delayed rendering. The default implementation of this function will call **OnRenderFileData** or **OnRenderGlobalData** if the supplied storage medium is either a file or memory, respectively. If neither of these formats are supplied, then the default implementation will return 0 and do nothing. For more information on delayed rendering as handled by MFC, see the article "Data Objects and Data Sources: Manipulation" in *Visual C++ Programmer's Guide* online.

If *lpStgMedium->tymed* is **TYMED_NULL**, the **STGMEDIUM** should be allocated and filled as specified by *lpFormatEtc->tymed*. If it is not **TYMED_NULL**, the **STGMEDIUM** should be filled in place with the data.

This is an advanced overridable. Override this function to supply your data in the requested format and medium. Depending on your data, you may want to override one of the other versions of this function instead. If your data is small and fixed in size, override **OnRenderGlobalData**. If your data is in a file, or is of variable size, override **OnRenderFileData**.

For more information, see the **STGMEDIUM** and **FORMATETC** structures, the **TYMED** enumeration type, and **IDataObject::GetData** in the *OLE 2 Programmer's Reference, Volume 1.*

See Also: **COleDataSource::DelayRenderData,
COleDataSource::DelayRenderFileData, COleDataSource::OnRenderFileData,
COleDataSource::OnRenderGlobalData, COleDataSource::OnSetData**

COleDataSource::OnRenderFileData

virtual BOOL OnRenderFileData(LPFORMATETC *lpFormatEtc***, CFile*** *pFile* **);**

Return Value
Nonzero if successful; otherwise 0.

Parameters
lpFormatEtc   Points to the **FORMATETC** structure specifying the format in which information is requested.

pFile   Points to a **CFile** object in which the data is to be rendered.

Remarks
Called by the framework to retrieve data in the specified format when the specified storage medium is a file. The specified format is one previously placed in the **COleDataSource** object using the **DelayRenderData** member function for delayed rendering. The default implementation of this function simply returns **FALSE**.

This is an advanced overridable. Override this function to supply your data in the requested format and medium. Depending on your data, you might want to override one of the other versions of this function instead. If you want to handle multiple storage media, override **OnRenderData**. If your data is in a file, or is of variable size, override **OnRenderFileData**. For more information on delayed rendering as handled by MFC, see the article "Data Objects and Data Sources: Manipulation" in *Visual C++ Programmer's Guide* online.

For more information, see the **FORMATETC** structure and **IDataObject::GetData** in the *OLE 2 Programmer's Reference, Volume 1.*

See Also: **COleDataSource::DelayRenderData,
COleDataSource::DelayRenderFileData, COleDataSource::OnRenderData,
COleDataSource::OnRenderGlobalData, COleDataSource::OnSetData, CFile**

COleDataSource::OnRenderGlobalData

virtual BOOL OnRenderGlobalData(LPFORMATETC *lpFormatEtc,*
↳ **HGLOBAL*** *phGlobal* **);**

Return Value

Nonzero if successful; otherwise 0.

Parameters

lpFormatEtc   Points to the **FORMATETC** structure specifying the format in which information is requested.

phGlobal   Points to a handle to global memory in which the data is to be returned. If one has not yet been allocated, this parameter can be **NULL**.

Remarks

Called by the framework to retrieve data in the specified format when the specified storage medium is global memory. The specified format is one previously placed in the **COleDataSource** object using the **DelayRenderData** member function for delayed rendering. The default implementation of this function simply returns **FALSE**.

If *phGlobal* is **NULL**, then a new **HGLOBAL** should be allocated and returned in *phGlobal*. Otherwise, the **HGLOBAL** specified by *phGlobal* should be filled with the data. The amount of data placed in the **HGLOBAL** must not exceed the current size of the memory block. Also, the block cannot be reallocated to a larger size.

This is an advanced overridable. Override this function to supply your data in the requested format and medium. Depending on your data, you may want to override one of the other versions of this function instead. If you want to handle multiple storage media, override **OnRenderData**. If your data is in a file, or is of variable size, override **OnRenderFileData**. For more information on delayed rendering as handled by MFC, see the article "Data Objects and Data Sources: Manipulation" in *Visual C++ Programmer's Guide* online.

For more information, see the **FORMATETC** structure and **IDataObject::GetData** in the *OLE 2 Programmer's Reference, Volume 1.*

**See Also: COleDataSource::DelayRenderData,
COleDataSource::DelayRenderFileData, COleDataSource::OnRenderData,
COleDataSource::OnRenderFileData, COleDataSource::OnSetData**

COleDataSource::OnSetData

virtual BOOL OnSetData(LPFORMATETC *lpFormatEtc*,
↳ **LPSTGMEDIUM** *lpStgMedium*, **BOOL** *bRelease*);

Return Value

Nonzero if successful; otherwise 0.

Parameters

lpFormatEtc Points to the **FORMATETC** structure specifying the format in which data is being replaced.

lpStgMedium Points to the **STGMEDIUM** structure containing the data that will replace the current contents of the **COleDataSource** object.

bRelease Indicates who has ownership of the storage medium after completing the function call. The caller decides who is responsible for releasing the resources allocated on behalf of the storage medium. The caller does this by setting *bRelease*. If *bRelease* is nonzero, the data source takes ownership, freeing the medium when it has finished using it. When *bRelease* is 0, the caller retains ownership and the data source can use the storage medium only for the duration of the call.

Remarks

Called by the framework to set or replace the data in the **COleDataSource** object in the specified format. The data source does not take ownership of the data until it has successfully obtained it. That is, it does not take ownership if **OnSetData** returns 0. If the data source takes ownership, it frees the storage medium by calling the **ReleaseStgMedium** function.

The default implementation does nothing. Override this function to replace the data in the specified format. This is an advanced overridable.

For more information, see the **STGMEDIUM** and **FORMATETC** structures and the **ReleaseStgMedium** and **IDataObject::GetData** functions in the *OLE 2 Programmer's Reference, Volume 1*.

See Also: **COleDataSource::DelaySetData, COleDataSource::OnRenderData, COleDataSource::OnRenderFileData, COleDataSource::OnRenderGlobalData, COleServerItem::OnSetData**

COleDataSource::SetClipboard

void SetClipboard( );

Remarks

Puts the data contained in the **COleDataSource** object on the Clipboard after calling one of the following functions: **CacheData, CacheGlobalData, DelayRenderData,** or **DelayRenderFileData**.

See Also: **COleDataSource::GetClipboardOwner, COleDataSource::FlushClipboard**

COleDateTime

COleDateTime does not have a base class.

A **COleDateTime** object encapsulates the **DATE** data type used in OLE automation. It is one of the possible types for the **VARIANT** data type of OLE automation. A **COleDateTime** value represents an absolute date and time value.

The **DATE** type is implemented as a floating-point value, measuring days from midnight, 30 December 1899. So, midnight, 31 December 1899 is represented by 1.0. Similarly, 6 AM, 1 January 1900 is represented by 2.25, and midnight, 29 December 1899 is –1.0. However, 6 AM, 29 December 1899 is –1.25.

Note   To interpret the time portion, take the absolute value of the fractional part of the number.

The **COleDateTime** class handles dates from 1 January 100–31 December 9999.

This type is also used to represent date-only or time-only values. By convention, the date 0 (30 December 1899) is used for time-only values. Similarly, the time 0:00 (midnight) is used for date-only values.

Basic arithmetic operations for the **COleDateTime** values use the companion class **COleDateTimeSpan**. **COleDateTimeSpan** values represent relative time, an interval. The relation between these classes is analogous to the one between **CTime** and **CTimeSpan**.

For more information on the **COleDateTime** and **COleDateTimeSpan** classes, see the article "Date and Time: Automation Support" in *Visual C++ Programmer's Guide* online.

#include <afxdisp.h>

See Also: **COleVariant**

COleDateTime Class Members

Construction

COleDateTime	Constructs a **COleDateTime** object.
GetCurrentTime	Creates a **COleDateTime** object that represents the current time (static member function).

Attributes

GetStatus	Gets the status (validity) of this **COleDateTime** object.
SetStatus	Sets the status (validity) of this **COleDateTime** object.
GetYear	Returns the year this **COleDateTime** object represents.

(continued)

Attributes *(continued)*

GetMonth	Returns the month this **COleDateTime** object represents (1–12).
GetDay	Returns the day this **COleDateTime** object represents (1–31).
GetHour	Returns the hour this **COleDateTime** object represents (0–23).
GetMinute	Returns the minute this **COleDateTime** object represents (0–59).
GetSecond	Returns the second this **COleDateTime** object represents (0–59).
GetDayOfWeek	Returns the day of the week this **COleDateTime** object represents (Sunday = 1).
GetDayOfYear	Returns the day of the year this **COleDateTime** object represents (Jan 1 = 1).

Operations

SetDateTime	Sets the value of this **COleDateTime** object to the specified date/time value.
SetDate	Sets the value of this **COleDateTime** object to the specified date-only value.
SetTime	Sets the value of this **COleDateTime** object to the specified time-only value.
Format	Generates a formatted string representation of a **COleDateTime** object.
ParseDateTime	Reads a date/time value from a string and sets the value of **COleDateTime**.

Operators

operator DATE	Converts a **COleDateTime** value into a **DATE**.
operator DATE*	Converts a **COleDateTime** value into a **DATE***.
operator =	Copies a **COleDateTime** value.
operator +, -	Add and subtract **COleDateTime** values.
operator +=, -=	Add and subtract a **COleDateTime** value from this **COleDateTime** object.
operator ==, <, <=, etc.	Compare two **COleDateTime** values.

Data Members

m_dt	Contains the underlying **DATE** for this **COleDateTime** object.
m_status	Contains the status of this **COleDateTime** object.

Archive/Dump

operator <<	Outputs a **COleDateTime** value to **CArchive** or **CDumpContext**.
operator >>	Inputs a **COleDateTime** object from **CArchive**.

Member Functions
COleDateTime::COleDateTime

COleDateTime( );
COleDateTime(const COleDateTime& *dateSrc* **);**
COleDateTime(const VARIANT& *varSrc* **);**
COleDateTime(DATE *dtSrc* **);**
COleDateTime(time_t *timeSrc* **);**
COleDateTime(const SYSTEMTIME& *systimeSrc* **);**
COleDateTime(const FILETIME& *filetimeSrc* **);**
COleDateTime(int *nYear***, int** *nMonth***, int** *nDay***, int** *nHour***, int** *nMin***, int** *nSec* **);**
COleDateTime(WORD *wDosDate***, WORD** *wDosTime* **);**

Parameters

dateSrc   An existing **COleDateTime** object to be copied into the new
COleDateTime object.

varSrc   An existing **VARIANT** data structure (possibly a **COleVariant** object) to be
converted to a date/time value (**VT_DATE**) and copied into the new
COleDateTime object.

dtSrc   A date/time (**DATE**) value to be copied into the new **COleDateTime** object.

timeSrc   A **time_t** value to be converted to a date/time value and copied into the new
COleDateTime object.

systimeSrc   A **SYSTEMTIME** structure to be converted to a date/time value and
copied into the new **COleDateTime** object.

filetimeSrc   A **FILETIME** structure to be converted to a date/time value and copied
into the new **COleDateTime** object.

nYear, nMonth, nDay, nHour, nMin, nSec   Indicate the date and time values to be
copied into the new **COleDateTime** object.

wDosDate, wDosTime   MS-DOS date and time values to be converted to a date/time
value and copied into the new **COleDateTime** object.

Remarks

All of these constructors create new **COleDateTime** objects initialized to the
specified value. The following table shows valid ranges for each date and time
component:

Date/Time Component	Valid Range
year	100–9999
month	0–12

(continued)

(continued)

Date/Time Component	Valid Range
day	0–31
hour	0–23
minute	0–59
second	0–59

Note that the actual upper bound for the day component varies based on the month and year components. For details, see the **SetDate** or **SetDateTime** member functions.

Following is a brief description of each constructor:

- **COleDateTime( )**   Constructs a **COleDateTime** object initialized to 0 (midnight, 30 December 1899).

- **COleDateTime(** *dateSrc* **)**   Constructs a **COleDateTime** object from an existing **COleDateTime** object.

- **COleDateTime(** *varSrc* **)**   Constructs a **COleDateTime** object. Attempts to convert a **VARIANT** structure or **COleVariant** object to a date/time (**VT_DATE**) value. If this conversion is successful, the converted value is copied into the new **COleDateTime** object. If it is not, the value of the **COleDateTime** object is set to 0 (midnight, 30 December 1899) and its status to invalid.

- **COleDateTime(** *dtSrc* **)**   Constructs a **COleDateTime** object from a **DATE** value.

- **COleDateTime(** *timeSrc* **)**   Constructs a **COleDateTime** object from a **time_t** value.

- **COleDateTime(** *systimeSrc* **)**   Constructs a **COleDateTime** object from a **SYSTEMTIME** value.

- **COleDateTime(** *filetimeSrc* **)**   Constructs a **COleDateTime** object from a **FILETIME** value.

- **COleDateTime(** *nYear*, *nMonth*, *nDay*, *nHour*, *nMin*, *nSec* **)**   Constructs a **COleDateTime** object from the specified numerical values.

- **COleDateTime(** *wDosDate*, *wDosTime* **)**   Constructs a **COleDateTime** object from the specified MS-DOS date and time values.

For more information, see the **VARIANT** entry in the *Win32 SDK OLE Programmer's Reference*.

For more information on the **time_t** data type, see the **time** function in the *Run-Time Library Reference*.

For more information, see the **SYSTEMTIME** and **FILETIME** structures in the Win32 SDK documentation.

For more information on MS-DOS date and time values, see **DosDateTimeToVariantTime** in the Win32 SDK documentation.

For more information about the bounds for **COleDateTime** values, see the article "Date and Time: Automation Support" in *Visual C++ Programmer's Guide* online.

See Also: **COleDateTime::SetDate, COleDateTime::SetDateTime, COleDateTime::SetTime, COleDateTime::GetStatus, COleDateTime::operator =, COleDateTime::m_dt, COleDateTime::m_status**

COleDateTime::Format

CString Format(DWORD *dwFlags* **= 0, LCID** *lcid* **= LANG_USER_DEFAULT);**
CString Format(LPCTSTR *lpszFormat* **) const;**
CString Format(UINT *nFormatID* **) const;**

Return Value

A **CString** that contains the formatted date/time value.

Parameters

dwFlags   Indicates flags for locale settings, possibly the following flag:

- **LOCALE_NOUSEROVERRIDE**   Use the system default locale settings, rather than custom user settings.

- **VAR_TIMEVALUEONLY**   Ignore the date portion during parsing.

- **VAR_DATEVALUEONLY**   Ignore the time portion during parsing.

lcid   Indicates locale ID to use for the conversion.

lpszFormat   A formatting string similar to the **printf** formatting string. Formatting codes, preceded by a percent (%) sign, are replaced by the corresponding **COleDateTime** component. Other characters in the formatting string are copied unchanged to the returned string. See the run-time function **strftime** for details. The value and meaning of the formatting codes for **Format** are listed below:

- **%D**   Total days in this **COleDateTime**

- **%H**   Hours in the current day

- **%M**   Minutes in the current hour

- **%S**   Seconds in the current minute

- **%%**   Percent sign

nFormatID   The resource ID for the format-control string.

Remarks

Call this member function to create a formatted representation of the date/time value. If the status of this **COleDateTime** object is null, the return value is an empty string. If the status is invalid, the return string is specified by the string resource **IDS_INVALID_DATETIME**.

A brief description of the three forms for this function follows:

Format(*dwFlags***,** *lcid* **)**   This form formats the value using the national language specifications (locale IDs) for date/time. Using the default parameters, this form will print a time only if the date portion of the date/time value is date 0 (30 December 1899). Similarly, with the default parameters, this form will print a date only if the time portion of the date/time value is time 0 (midnight). If the date/time value is 0 (30 December 1899, midnight), this form with the default parameters will print midnight.

Format(*lpszFormat* **)**   This form formats the value using the format string which contains special formatting codes that are preceded by a percent sign (%), as in **printf**. The formatting string is passed as a parameter to the function. For more information about the formatting codes, see **strftime, wcsftime** in the *Run-Time Library Reference*.

Format(*nFormatID* **)**   This form formats the value using the format string which contains special formatting codes that are preceded by a percent sign (%), as in **printf**. The formatting string is a resource. The ID of this string resource is passed as the parameter. For more information about the formatting codes, see **strftime, wcsftime** in the *Run-Time Library Reference*.

For a listing of locale ID values, see the section "Supporting Multiple National Languages" in the *Win32 SDK OLE Programmer's Reference*.

See Also: **COleDateTime::ParseDateTime**, **COleDateTime::GetStatus**

COleDateTime::GetCurrentTime

static COleDateTime PASCAL GetCurrentTime( );

Remarks

Call this static member function to return the current date/time value.

Example

```
COleDateTime dateTest;
    // dateTest value = midnight 30 December 1899

dateTest = COleDateTime::GetCurrentTime();
    // dateTest value = current date and time
```

COleDateTime::GetDay

int GetDay( ) const;

Return Value

The day of the month represented by the value of this **COleDateTime** object.

Remarks

Call this member function to get the day of the month represented by this date/time value.

Valid return values range between 1 and 31. If the status of this **COleDateTime** object is not valid, the return value is **AFX_OLE_DATETIME_ERROR**.

For information on other member functions that query the value of this **COleDateTime** object, see the following member functions:

- **GetMonth**
- **GetYear**
- **GetHour**
- **GetMinute**
- **GetSecond**
- **GetDayOfWeek**
- **GetDayOfYear**

See Also: **COleDateTime::COleDateTime, COleDateTime::SetDateTime, COleDateTime::operator =, COleDateTime::GetStatus**

COleDateTime::GetDayOfWeek

int GetDayOfWeek( ) const;

Return Value

The day of the week represented by the value of this **COleDateTime** object.

Remarks

Call this member function to get the day of the month represented by this date/time value.

Valid return values range between 1 and 7, where 1=Sunday, 2=Monday, and so on. If the status of this **COleDateTime** object is not valid, the return value is **AFX_OLE_DATETIME_ERROR**.

For information on other member functions that query the value of this **COleDateTime** object, see the following member functions:

- **GetDay**
- **GetMonth**
- **GetYear**
- **GetHour**
- **GetMinute**
- **GetSecond**
- **GetDayOfYear**

See Also: **COleDateTime::COleDateTime, COleDateTime::SetDateTime, COleDateTime::operator =, COleDateTime::GetStatus**

COleDateTime::GetDayOfYear

int GetDayOfYear( ) const;

Return Value

The day of the year represented by the value of this **COleDateTime** object.

Remarks

Call this member function to get the day of the year represented by this date/time value.

Valid return values range between 1 and 366, where January 1 = 1. If the status of this **COleDateTime** object is not valid, the return value is **AFX_OLE_DATETIME_ERROR**.

For information on other member functions that query the value of this **COleDateTime** object, see the following member functions:

- **GetDay**
- **GetMonth**
- **GetYear**
- **GetHour**
- **GetMinute**
- **GetSecond**
- **GetDayOfWeek**

See Also: **COleDateTime::COleDateTime, COleDateTime::SetDateTime, COleDateTime::operator =, COleDateTime::GetStatus**

COleDateTime::GetHour

int GetHour( ) const;

Return Value

The hour represented by the value of this **COleDateTime** object.

Remarks

Call this member function to get the hour represented by this date/time value.

Valid return values range between 0 and 23. If the status of this **COleDateTime** object is not valid, the return value is **AFX_OLE_DATETIME_ERROR**.

For information on other member functions that query the value of this
COleDateTime object, see the following member functions:

- **GetDay**
- **GetMonth**
- **GetYear**
- **GetMinute**
- **GetSecond**
- **GetDayOfWeek**
- **GetDayOfYear**

See Also: **COleDateTime::COleDateTime**, **COleDateTime::SetDateTime**,
COleDateTime::operator =, **COleDateTime::GetStatus**

COleDateTime::GetMinute

int GetMinute( ) const;

Return Value

The minute represented by the value of this **COleDateTime** object.

Remarks

Call this member function to get the minute represented by this date/time value.

Valid return values range between 0 and 59. If the status of this **COleDateTime** object
is not valid, the return value is **AFX_OLE_DATETIME_ERROR**.

For information on other member functions that query the value of this
COleDateTime object, see the following member functions:

- **GetDay**
- **GetMonth**
- **GetYear**
- **GetHour**
- **GetSecond**
- **GetDayOfWeek**
- **GetDayOfYear**

See Also: **COleDateTime::COleDateTime**, **COleDateTime::SetDateTime**,
COleDateTime::operator =, **COleDateTime::GetStatus**

COleDateTime::GetMonth

int GetMonth( ) const;

Return Value

The month represented by the value of this **COleDateTime** object.

Remarks

Call this member function to get the month represented by this date/time value.

Valid return values range between 1 and 12. If the status of this **COleDateTime** object is not valid, the return value is **AFX_OLE_DATETIME_ERROR**.

For information on other member functions that query the value of this **COleDateTime** object, see the following member functions:

- **GetDay**
- **GetYear**
- **GetHour**
- **GetMinute**
- **GetSecond**
- **GetDayOfWeek**
- **GetDayOfYear**

See Also: **COleDateTime::COleDateTime, COleDateTime::SetDateTime, COleDateTime::operator =, COleDateTime::GetStatus**

COleDateTime::GetSecond

int GetSecond( ) const;

Return Value

The second represented by the value of this **COleDateTime** object.

Remarks

Call this member function to get the second represented by this date/time value.

Valid return values range between 0 and 59. If the status of this **COleDateTime** object is not valid, the return value is **AFX_OLE_DATETIME_ERROR**.

Note The **COleDateTime** class does not support leap seconds.

For more information about the implementation for **COleDateTime**, see the article "Date and Time: Automation Support" in *Visual C++ Programmer's Guide* online.

For information on other member functions that query the value of this **COleDateTime** object, see the following member functions:

- **GetDay**
- **GetMonth**
- **GetYear**
- **GetHour**
- **GetMinute**
- **GetDayOfWeek**
- **GetDayOfYear**

See Also: **COleDateTime::COleDateTime, COleDateTime::SetDateTime, COleDateTime::operator =, COleDateTime::GetStatus**

COleDateTime::GetStatus

DateTimeStatus GetStatus( ) const;

Return Value

Returns the status of this **COleDateTime** value.

Remarks

Call this member function to get the status (validity) of a given **COleDateTime** object.

The return value is defined by the **DateTimeStatus** enumerated type, which is defined within the **COleDateTime** class.

```
enum DateTimeStatus{
    valid = 0,
    invalid = 1,
    null = 2,
};
```

For a brief description of these status values, see the following list:

- **COleDateTime::valid**   Indicates that this **COleDateTime** object is valid.
- **COleDateTime::invalid**   Indicates that this **COleDateTime** object is invalid; that is, its value may be incorrect.
- **COleDateTime::null**   Indicates that this **COleDateTime** object is null, that is, that no value has been supplied for this object. (This is "null" in the database sense of "having no value," as opposed to the C++ **NULL**.)

The status of a **COleDateTime** object is invalid in the following cases:

- If its value is set from a **VARIANT** or **COleVariant** value that could not be converted to a date/time value.
- If its value is set from a **time_t**, **SYSTEMTIME**, or **FILETIME** value that could not be converted to a valid date/time value.

- If its value is set by **SetDateTime** with invalid parameter values.
- If this object has experienced an overflow or underflow during an arithmetic assignment operation, namely, **+=** or **-=**.
- If an invalid value was assigned to this object.
- If the status of this object was explicitly set to invalid using **SetStatus**.

For more information about the operations that may set the status to invalid, see the following member functions:

- **COleDateTime**
- **SetDateTime**
- **operator +, -**
- **operator +=, -=**

For more information about the bounds for **COleDateTime** values, see the article "Date and Time: Automation Support" in *Visual C++ Programmer's Guide* online.

See Also: **COleDateTime::SetStatus**, **COleDateTime::m_status**

COleDateTime::GetYear

int GetYear( ) const;

Return Value

The year represented by the value of this **COleDateTime** object.

Remarks

Call this member function to get the year represented by this date/time value.

Valid return values range between 100 and 9999, which includes the century. If the status of this **COleDateTime** object is not valid, the return value is **AFX_OLE_DATETIME_ERROR**.

For information on other member functions that query the value of this **COleDateTime** object, see the following member functions:

- **GetDay**
- **GetMonth**
- **GetHour**
- **GetMinute**
- **GetSecond**
- **GetDayOfWeek**
- **GetDayOfYear**

For more information about the bounds for **COleDateTime** values, see the article "Date and Time: Automation Support" in *Visual C++ Programmer's Guide* online.

See Also: **COleDateTime::COleDateTime, COleDateTime::SetDateTime, COleDateTime::operator =, COleDateTime::GetStatus**

COleDateTime::ParseDateTime

BOOL ParseDateTime(LPCTSTR *lpszDate*, **DWORD** *dwFlags* **= 0,**
   ↳ **LCID** *lcid* **= LANG_USER_DEFAULT);**
throw(CMemoryException);
throw(COleException);

Return Value

Nonzero if the string was successfully converted to a date/time value, otherwise 0.

Parameters

lpszDate A pointer to the null-terminated string which is to be parsed. For details, see Remarks.

dwFlags Indicates flags for locale settings and parsing. One or more of the following flags:

- **LOCALE_NOUSEROVERRIDE** Use the system default locale settings, rather than custom user settings.

- **VAR_TIMEVALUEONLY** Ignore the date portion during parsing.

- **VAR_DATEVALUEONLY** Ignore the time portion during parsing.

lcid Indicates locale ID to use for the conversion.

Remarks

Call this member function to parse a string to read a date/time value. If the string was successfully converted to a date/time value, the value of this **COleDateTime** object is set to that value and its status to valid.

Note Year values must lie between 100 and 9999, inclusively.

The *lpszDate* parameter can take a variety of formats. For example, the following strings contain acceptable date/time formats:

```
"25 January 1996"
"8:30:00"
"20:30:00"
"January 25, 1996 8:30:00"
"8:30:00 Jan. 25, 1996"
"1/25/1996 8:30:00"   // always specify the full year,
                      // even in a 'short date' format
```

Note that the locale ID will also affect whether the string format is acceptable for conversion to a date/time value.

In the case of **VAR_DATEVALUEONLY**, the time value is set to time 0, or midnight. In the case of **VAR_TIMEVALUEONLY**, the date value is set to date 0, meaning 30 December 1899.

If the string could not be converted to a date/time value or if there was a numerical overflow, the status of this **COleDateTime** object is invalid.

If the string conversion failed due to memory allocation errors, this function throws a **CMemoryException**. In any other error state, this function throws a **COleException**.

For a listing of locale ID values, see the section "Supporting Multiple National Languages" in the *Win32 SDK OLE Programmer's Reference*.

For more information about the bounds and implementation for **COleDateTime** values, see the article "Date and Time: Automation Support" in *Visual C++ Programmer's Guide* online.

See Also: **COleDateTime::Format**, **COleDateTime::GetStatus**

COleDateTime::SetDate

int SetDate(int *nYear***, int** *nMonth***, int** *nDay* **);**

Return Value

Zero if the value of this **COleDateTime** object was set successfully; otherwise, 1. This return value is based on the **DateTimeStatus** enumerated type. For more information, see the **SetStatus** member function.

Parameters

nYear, nMonth, nDay Indicate the date components to be copied into this **COleDateTime** object.

Remarks

Call this member function to set the date and time of this **COleDateTime** object. The date is set to the specified values. The time is set to time 0, midnight.

See the following table for bounds for the parameter values:

Parameter	Bounds
nYear	100–9999
nMonth	1–12
nDay	1–31

The actual upper bound for *nDay* values varies based on the month and year. For months 1, 3, 5, 7, 8, 10, and 12, the upper bound is 31. For months 4, 6, 9, and 11, it is 30. For month 2, it is 28, or 29 in a leap year.

If the date value specified by the parameters is not valid, the status of this object is set to invalid and the value of this object is not changed.

Here are some examples of date values:

nYear	nMonth	nDay	Value
1995	4	15	15 April 1995
1789	7	14	17 July 1789
1925	2	30	Invalid
10000	1	1	Invalid

To set both date and time, see **COleDateTime::SetDateTime**.

For information on member functions that query the value of this **COleDateTime** object, see the following member functions:

- **GetDay**
- **GetMonth**
- **GetYear**
- **GetHour**
- **GetMinute**
- **GetSecond**
- **GetDayOfWeek**
- **GetDayOfYear**

For more information about the bounds for **COleDateTime** values, see the article "Date and Time: Automation Support" in *Visual C++ Programmer's Guide* online.

See Also: **COleDateTime::COleDateTime**, **COleDateTime::SetDateTime**, **COleDateTime::operator =**, **COleDateTime::GetStatus**, **COleDateTime::m_dt**

COleDateTime::SetDateTime

int **SetDateTime**(int *nYear*, int *nMonth*, int *nDay*, int *nHour*, int *nMin*, int *nSec*);

Return Value

Zero if the value of this **COleDateTime** object was set successfully; otherwise, 1. This return value is based on the **DateTimeStatus** enumerated type. For more information, see the **SetStatus** member function.

Parameters

nYear, *nMonth*, *nDay*, *nHour*, *nMin*, *nSec*   Indicate the date and time components to be copied into this **COleDateTime** object.

Remarks

Call this member function to set the date and time of this **COleDateTime** object.

See the following table for bounds for the parameter values:

Parameter	Bounds
nYear	100–9999
nMonth	1–12
nDay	1–31
nHour	0–23
nMin	0–59
nSec	0–59

The actual upper bound for *nDay* values varies based on the month and year. For months 1, 3, 5, 7, 8, 10, and 12, the upper bound is 31. For months 4, 6, 9, and 11, it is 30. For month 2, it is 28, or 29 in a leap year.

If the date or time value specified by the parameters is not valid, the status of this object is set to invalid and the value of this object is not changed.

Here are some examples of time values:

nHour	nMin	nSec	Value
1	3	3	01:03:03
23	45	0	23:45:00
25	30	0	Invalid
9	60	0	Invalid

Here are some examples of date values:

nYear	nMonth	nDay	Value
1995	4	15	15 April 1995
1789	7	14	17 July 1789
1925	2	30	Invalid
10000	1	1	Invalid

To set the date only, see **COleDateTime::SetDate**. To set the time only, see **COleDateTime::SetTime**.

For information on member functions that query the value of this **COleDateTime** object, see the following member functions:

- **GetDay**
- **GetMonth**
- **GetYear**
- **GetHour**
- **GetMinute**
- **GetSecond**
- **GetDayOfWeek**
- **GetDayOfYear**

For more information about the bounds for **COleDateTime** values, see the article "Date and Time: Automation Support" in *Visual C++ Programmer's Guide* online.

See Also: **COleDateTime::COleDateTime**, **COleDateTime::SetDate**, **COleDateTime::SetTime**, **COleDateTime::operator =**, **COleDateTime::GetStatus**, **COleDateTime::m_dt**

COleDateTime::SetStatus

void SetStatus(DateTimeStatus *nStatus* **);**

Parameters

nStatus   The new status value for this **COleDateTime** object.

Remarks

Call this member function to set the status of this **COleDateTime** object. The *nStatus* parameter value is defined by the **DateTimeStatus** enumerated type, which is defined within the **COleDateTime** class.

```
enum DateTimeStatus{
    valid = 0,
    invalid = 1,
    null = 2,
};
```

For a brief description of these status values, see the following list:

- **COleDateTime::valid**   Indicates that this **COleDateTime** object is valid.

- **COleDateTime::invalid**   Indicates that this **COleDateTime** object is invalid; that is, its value may be incorrect.

- **COleDateTime::null**   Indicates that this **COleDateTime** object is null, that is, that no value has been supplied for this object. (This is "null" in the database sense of "having no value," as opposed to the C++ **NULL**.)

Caution   This function is for advanced programming situations. This function does not alter the data in this object. It will most often be used to set the status to **null** or **invalid**. Note that the assignment operator (**operator =**) and **SetDateTime** do set the status of the object based on the source value(s).

See Also: **COleDateTime::GetStatus**, **COleDateTime::operator =**, **COleDateTime::SetDateTime**, **COleDateTime::m_dt**

COleDateTime::SetTime

int SetTime(int *nHour*, **int** *nMin*, **int** *nSec* **);**

Return Value

Zero if the value of this **COleDateTime** object was set successfully; otherwise, 1. This return value is based on the **DateTimeStatus** enumerated type. For more information, see the **SetStatus** member function.

Parameters

nHour, nMin, nSec   Indicate the time components to be copied into this **COleDateTime** object.

Remarks

Call this member function to set the date and time of this **COleDateTime** object. The time is set to the specified values. The date is set to date 0, meaning 30 December 1899.

See the following table for bounds for the parameter values:

Parameter	Bounds
nHour	0–23
nMin	0–59
nSec	0–59

If the time value specified by the parameters is not valid, the status of this object is set to invalid and the value of this object is not changed.

Here are some examples of time values:

nHour	nMin	nSec	Value
1	3	3	01:03:03
23	45	0	23:45:00
25	30	0	Invalid
9	60	0	Invalid

To set both date and time, see **COleDateTime::SetDateTime**.

For information on member functions that query the value of this **COleDateTime** object, see the following member functions:

- **GetDay**
- **GetMonth**
- **GetYear**
- **GetHour**
- **GetMinute**

- **GetSecond**
- **GetDayOfWeek**
- **GetDayOfYear**

For more information about the bounds for **COleDateTime** values, see the article "Date and Time: Automation Support" in *Visual C++ Programmer's Guide* online.

See Also: **COleDateTime::COleDateTime, COleDateTime::SetDateTime, COleDateTime::operator =, COleDateTime::GetStatus, COleDateTime::m_dt**

Operators
COleDateTime::operator =

const COleDateTime& operator =(const COleDateTime& *dateSrc*);
const COleDateTime& operator =(const VARIANT& *varSrc*);
const COleDateTime& operator =(DATE *dtSrc*);
const COleDateTime& operator =(const time_t& *timeSrc*);
const COleDateTime& operator =(const SYSTEMTIME& *systimeSrc*);
const COleDateTime& operator =(const FILETIME& *filetimeSrc*);

Remarks

These overloaded assignment operators copy the source date/time value into this **COleDateTime** object. A brief description of each these overloaded assignment operators follows:

- **operator =(** *dateSrc* **)**   The value and status of the operand are copied into this **COleDateTime** object.

- **operator =(** *varSrc* **)**   If the conversion of the **VARIANT** value (or **COleVariant** object) to a date/time (**VT_DATE**) is successful, the converted value is copied into this **COleDateTime** object and its status is set to valid. If the conversion is not successful, the value of this object is set to zero (30 December 1899, midnight) and its status to invalid.

- **operator =(** *dtSrc* **)**   The **DATE** value is copied into this **COleDateTime** object and its status is set to valid.

- **operator =(** *timeSrc* **)**   The **time_t** value is converted and copied into this **COleDateTime** object. If the conversion is successful, the status of this object is set to valid; if unsuccessful, it is set to invalid.

- **operator =(** *systimeSrc* **)**   The **SYSTEMTIME** value is converted and copied into this **COleDateTime** object. If the conversion is successful, the status of this object is set to valid; if unsuccessful, it is set to invalid.

- **operator =**(*filetimeSrc*)   The **FILETIME** value is converted and copied into this **COleDateTime** object. If the conversion is successful, the status of this object is set to valid; if unsuccessful, it is set to invalid.

For more information, see the **VARIANT** entry in the *Win32 SDK OLE Programmer's Reference*.

For more information on the **time_t** data type, see the **time** function in the *Run-Time Library Reference*.

For more information, see the **SYSTEMTIME** and **FILETIME** structures in the Win32 SDK documentation.

For more information about the bounds for **COleDateTime** values, see the article "Date and Time: Automation Support" in *Visual C++ Programmer's Guide* online.

See Also: **COleDateTime::COleDateTime, COleDateTime::SetDateTime, COleDateTime::GetStatus**

COleDateTime::operator +, -

COleDateTime operator +(const COleDateTimeSpan& *dateSpan* **) const;**
COleDateTime operator -(const COleDateTimeSpan& *dateSpan* **) const;**
COleDateTimeSpan operator -(const COleDateTime& *date* **) const;**

Remarks

COleDateTime objects represent absolute times. **COleDateTimeSpan** objects represent relative times. The first two operators allow you to add and subtract a **COleDateTimeSpan** value from a **COleDateTime** value. The third operator allows you to subtract one **COleDateTime** value from another to yield a **COleDateTimeSpan** value.

If either of the operands is null, the status of the resulting **COleDateTime** value is null.

If the resulting **COleDateTime** value falls outside the bounds of acceptable values, the status of that **COleDateTime** value is invalid.

If either of the operands is invalid and the other is not null, the status of the resulting **COleDateTime** value is invalid.

For more information on the valid, invalid, and null status values, see the **m_status** member variable.

For more information about the bounds for **COleDateTime** values, see the article "Date and Time: Automation Support" in *Visual C++ Programmer's Guide* online.

See Also: **COleDateTime::operator +=, -=, COleDateTime::GetStatus, COleDateTimeSpan**

COleDateTime::operator +=, -=

const COleDateTime& operator +=(const COleDateTimeSpan *dateSpan* **);**
const COleDateTime& operator -=(const COleDateTimeSpan *dateSpan* **);**

Remarks

These operators allow you to add and subtract a **COleDateTimeSpan** value to and from this **COleDateTime**.

If either of the operands is null, the status of the resulting **COleDateTime** value is null.

If the resulting **COleDateTime** value falls outside the bounds of acceptable values, the status of this **COleDateTime** value is set to invalid.

If either of the operands is invalid and other is not null, the status of the resulting **COleDateTime** value is invalid.

For more information on the valid, invalid, and null status values, see the **m_status** member variable.

For more information about the bounds for **COleDateTime** values, see the article "Date and Time: Automation Support" in *Visual C++ Programmer's Guide* online.

See Also: **COleDateTime::operator +, -, COleDateTime::GetStatus**

COleDateTime::operator DATE

operator DATE( ) const;

Remarks

This operator returns a **DATE** object whose value is copied from this **COleDateTime** object.

For more information about the implementation of the **DATE** object, see the article "Date and Time: Automation Support" in *Visual C++ Programmer's Guide* online.

See Also: **COleDateTime::m_dt**

COleDateTime Relational Operators

BOOL operator ==(const COleDateTime& *date* **) const;**
BOOL operator !=(const COleDateTime& *date* **) const;**
BOOL operator <(const COleDateTime& *date* **) const;**
BOOL operator >(const COleDateTime& *date* **) const;**
BOOL operator <=(const COleDateTime& *date* **) const;**
BOOL operator >=(const COleDateTime& *date* **) const;**

Remarks

These operators compare two date/time values and return nonzero if the condition is true; otherwise 0.

Note   The return value of the ordering operations (<, <=, >, >=) is undefined if the status of either operand is null or invalid. The equality operators (==, !=) consider the status of the operands.

Example

```
COleDateTime dateOne(95, 3, 15, 12, 0, 0);   // 15 March 1995 12 noon
COleDateTime dateTwo(dateOne);               // 15 March 1995 12 noon
BOOL b;
b = dateOne == dateTwo;                       // TRUE

dateTwo.SetStatus(COleDateTime::invalid);
b = dateOne == dateTwo;                       // FALSE, different status
b = dateOne != dateTwo;                       // TRUE, different status
b = dateOne < dateTwo;                        // FALSE, same value
b = dateOne > dateTwo;                        // FALSE, same value
b = dateOne <= dateTwo;                       // TRUE, same value
b = dateOne >= dateTwo;                       // TRUE, same value
```

Note   The last four lines of the preceding example will **ASSERT** in debug mode.

See Also: **COleDateTime::GetStatus**

COleDateTime::operator <<, >>

friend CDumpContext& AFXAPI operator <<(CDumpContext& *dc*,
   ↳ **COleDateTime** *timeSrc* **);**
friend CArchive& AFXAPI operator <<(CArchive& *ar*, **COleDateTime** *dateSrc* **);**
friend CArchive& AFXAPI operator >>(CArchive& *ar*, **COleDateTime&** *dateSrc* **);**

Remarks

The **COleDateTime** insertion (<<) operator supports diagnostic dumping and storing to an archive. The extraction (>>) operator supports loading from an archive.

See Also: **CDumpContext, CArchive**

Data Members
COleDateTime::m_dt

Remarks

The underlying **DATE** structure for this **COleDateTime** object.

Caution Changing the value in the **DATE** object accessed by the pointer returned by this function will change the value of this **COleDateTime** object. It does not change the status of this **COleDateTime** object.

For more information about the implementation of the **DATE** object, see the article "Date and Time: Automation Support" in *Visual C++ Programmer's Guide* online.

See Also: **COleDateTime::COleDateTime**, **COleDateTime::SetDateTime**, **COleDateTime::SetDate**, **COleDateTime::SetTime**, **COleDateTime::operator DATE**

COleDateTime::m_status

Remarks

The type of this data member is the enumerated type **DateTimeStatus**, which is defined within the **COleDateTime** class.

```
enum DateTimeStatus{
    valid = 0,
    invalid = 1,
    null = 2,
};
```

For a brief description of these status values, see the following list:

- **COleDateTime::valid** Indicates that this **COleDateTime** object is valid.

- **COleDateTime::invalid** Indicates that this **COleDateTime** object is invalid; that is, its value may be incorrect.

- **COleDateTime::null** Indicates that this **COleDateTime** object is null, that is, that no value has been supplied for this object. (This is "null" in the database sense of "having no value," as opposed to the C++ **NULL**.)

The status of a **COleDateTime** object is invalid in the following cases:

- If its value is set from a **VARIANT** or **COleVariant** value that could not be converted to a date/time value.

- If its value is set from a **time_t**, **SYSTEMTIME**, or **FILETIME** value that could not be converted to a valid date/time value.

- If its value is set by **SetDateTime** with invalid parameter values.

- If this object has experienced an overflow or underflow during an arithmetic assignment operation, namely, += or -=.

- If an invalid value was assigned to this object.

- If the status of this object was explicitly set to invalid using **SetStatus**.

For more information about the operations that may set the status to invalid, see the following member functions:

- **COleDateTime**
- **SetDateTime**
- **operator +, -**
- **operator +=, -=**

Caution This data member is for advanced programming situations. You should use the inline member functions **GetStatus** and **SetStatus**. See **SetStatus** for further cautions regarding explicitly setting this data member.

For more information about the bounds for **COleDateTime** values, see the article "Date and Time: Automation Support" in *Visual C++ Programmer's Guide* online.

See Also: **COleDateTime::GetStatus, COleDateTime::SetStatus**

Index

F

J

K

L

M

Q

S

T

Contributors to *MFC Reference*

Nancy Avinger, Writer

Walden Barcus, Writer

David Adam Edelstein, Art Director

Roger Haight, Editor

Lisa Hedley, Writer

Dan Jinguji, Writer

Nancy Rager, Writer

Robert Reynolds, Illustrator

Arlene Roth, Copy Editor

Kathleen Thompson, Writer

Qian Wen, Writer

Rod Wilkinson, Editor

WASSER*Studios*, Production

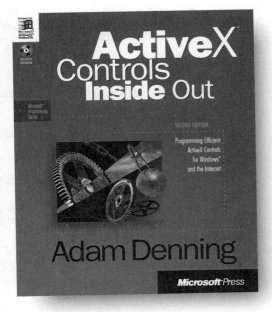

Blueprint for
excellence

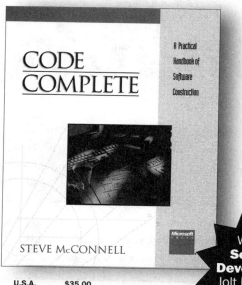

CODE COMPLETE

A Practical Handbook of Software Construction

STEVE McCONNELL

U.S.A.	$35.00
U.K.	£29.95
Canada	$44.95
ISBN 1-55615-484-4	

Winner—
Software Development
Jolt Excellence
Award, 1994!

This classic from Steve McConnell is a practical guide to the art and science of constructing software. Examples are provided in C, Pascal, Basic, Fortran, and Ada, but the focus is on successful programming techniques. CODE COMPLETE provides a larger perspective on the role of construction in the software development process that will inform and stimulate your thinking about your own projects—enabling you to take strategic action rather than fight the same battles again and again.

Get all of the *Best Practices* books.

"The definitive book on software construction. This is a book that belongs on every software developer's bookshelf."

—Warren Keuffel,
Software Development

"I cannot adequately express how good this book really is...a work of brilliance."

—Jeff Duntemann,
PC Techniques

"If you are or aspire to be a professional programmer, this may be the wisest $35 investment you'll ever make."

—*IEEE Micro*

Microsoft Press® products are available worldwide wherever quality computer books are sold. For more information, contact your book retailer, computer reseller, or local Microsoft Sales Office.

To locate your nearest source for Microsoft Press products, reach us at www.microsoft.com/mspress/, or call 1-800-MSPRESS in the U.S. (in Canada: 1-800-667-1115 or 416-293-8464).

To order Microsoft Press products, call 1-800-MSPRESS in the U.S. (in Canada: 1-800-667-1115 or 416-293-8464).

Prices and availability dates are subject to change.

Rapid Development
Steve McConnell
U.S.A. **$35.00** ($46.95 Canada; £32.49 U.K.)
ISBN 1-55615-900-5

"Very few books I have encountered in the last few years have given me as much pleasure to read as this one."
—*Ray Duncan*

Writing Solid Code
Steve Maguire
U.S.A. **$24.95** ($32.95 Canada; £21.95 U.K.)
ISBN 1-55615-551-4

"Every working programmer should own this book."
—*IEEE Spectrum*

Debugging the Development Process
Steve Maguire
U.S.A. **$24.95** ($32.95 Canada; £21.95 U.K.)
ISBN 1-55615-650-2

"A milestone in the game of hitting milestones."
—*ACM Computing Reviews*

Dynamics of Software Development
Jim McCarthy
U.S.A. **$24.95** ($33.95 Canada; £22.99 U.K.)
ISBN 1-55615-823-8

"I recommend it without reservation to every developer."
—Jesse Berst, editorial director, *Windows Watcher Newsletter*

Microsoft Press

Register Today!

Return this
Microsoft® Visual C++®
MFC Library Reference Part 1
registration card for
a Microsoft Press® catalog

U.S. and Canada addresses only. Fill in information below and mail postage-free. Please mail only the bottom half of this page.

Microsoft® *Press*
Quality Computer Books

For a free catalog of
Microsoft Press® products, call
1-800-MSPRESS

BUSINESS REPLY MAIL
FIRST-CLASS MAIL   PERMIT NO. 53   BOTHELL, WA

POSTAGE WILL BE PAID BY ADDRESSEE

MICROSOFT PRESS REGISTRATION
MICROSOFT® VISUAL C++®
MFC LIBRARY REFERENCE PART 1
PO BOX 3019
BOTHELL WA   98041-9946